Provided as an

education service

by AstraZeneca

This copy of *Harrison's Manual of Medicine* is
provided by AstraZeneca LP. The opinions and
information contained herein are those of the
authors and do not necessarily represent the
views of AstraZeneca.

HARRISON'S
MANUAL OF
MEDICINE

EDITORS

Eugene Braunwald, MD, MA(HON), MD(HON), ScD(HON)
Distinguished Hersey Professor of Medicine,
Faculty Dean for Academic Programs at
Brigham and Women's Hospital and
Massachusetts General Hospital, Harvard Medical School;
Vice President for Academic Programs,
Partners HealthCare Systems, Boston

Anthony S. Fauci, MD, ScD(HON)
Chief, Laboratory of Immunoregulation; Director,
National Institute of Allergy and Infectious Diseases,
National Institutes of Health, Bethesda

Dennis L. Kasper, MD, MA(HON)
William Ellery Channing Professor of Medicine,
Professor of Microbiology and Molecular Genetics,
Executive Dean for Academic Programs,
Harvard Medical School;
Director, Channing Laboratory,
Department of Medicine,
Brigham and Women's Hospital, Boston

Stephen L. Hauser, MD
Betty Anker Fife Professor and Chairman,
Department of Neurology, University of
California–San Francisco,
San Francisco

Dan L. Longo, MD, FACP
Scientific Director, National Institute on Aging,
National Institutes of Health,
Bethesda and Baltimore

J. Larry Jameson, MD, PhD
Irving S. Cutter Professor and Chairman,
Department of Medicine,
Northwestern University Medical School;
Physician-in-Chief, Northwestern
Memorial Hospital, Chicago

HARRISON'S
MANUAL OF MEDICINE

EDITORS

Eugene Braunwald, MD

Anthony S. Fauci, MD

Dennis L. Kasper, MD

Stephen L. Hauser, MD

Dan L. Longo, MD

J. Larry Jameson, MD, PhD

McGraw-Hill
Medical Publishing Division

New York   Chicago   San Francisco   Lisbon   London
Madrid   Mexico City   Milan   New Delhi   San Juan
Seoul   Singapore   Sydney   Toronto

McGraw-Hill

A Division of The **McGraw·Hill** *Companies*

Harrison's
PRINCIPLES OF INTERNAL MEDICINE
Fifteenth Edition
MANUAL OF MEDICINE

Copyright © 2002, 1998, 1995, 1991, 1988 by *The McGraw-Hill Companies*. All rights reserved. Printed in the United States of America. Except as permitted under the United States Copyright Act of 1976, no part of this publication may be reproduced or distributed in any form or by any means, or stored in a data bse or retrieval system, without the prior written consent of the author.

1 2 3 4 5 6 7 8 9 0   DOCDOC   0 9 8 7 6 5 4 3 2

ISBN 0-07-140853-3   NON RETURNABLE

This book was set in Times New Roman by Progressive Information Technologies. The editors were Martin J. Wonsiewicz and Mariapaz Ramos Englis; the production supervisor was Catherine H. Saggese; the designer was Marsha Cohen. The index was prepared by Irving Conde Tullar.
R. R. Donnelley & Sons, Inc., was printer and binder.

Library of Congress Cataloging-in-Publication Data

Harrison's manual of medicine / Eugene Braunwald . . . [et al.].
  p. ; cm.
 A distillation of clinical material from Harrison's principles of internal medicine.
 Includes bibliographical references and Index.
 ISBN 0-07-137377-2
   1. Internal medicine—Handbooks, manuals, etc. I. Title: Manual of medicine. II. Harrison, Tinsley Randolph, date III. Braunwald, Eugene, date-IV. Harrison's principles of internal medicine.
   [DNLM: 1. Clinical Medicine—Handbooks. 2. Internal Medicine—Handbooks. WB 39
H323 2002]
RC55 .H37 2002
616—dc21   2001031711

ABBREVIATED CONTENTS

CONTENTS

SECTION 1
IMPORTANT SIGNS AND SYMPTOMS

SECTION 2
MEDICAL EMERGENCIES

SECTION 9
RESPIRATORY DISEASES

SECTION 10
RENAL DISEASES

SECTION 11
GASTROINTESTINAL DISEASES

CONTRIBUTORS

Numbers in brackets refer to chapters in the *Manual*.

EUGENE BRAUNWALD, MD, MA(HON), MD(HON), SCD(HON)
Distinguished Hersey Professor of Medicine
Faculty Dean for Academic Programs at Brigham and Women's Hospital
and Massachusetts General Hospital, Harvard Medical School
Vice-President for Academic Programs
Partners HealthCare Systems
Boston [2, 14–17, 25, 26, 29, 30, 32, 112–130, 132–143, 145–147, 202]

SHARON B. BRODIE, MD, MPH
Instructor in Medicine, Division of Infectious Diseases
Department of Medicine, Beth Israel Deaconess Medical Center
Boston [6, 31, 77, 78, 81, 82, 84, 87–91, 97, 99–101, 105, 106, 108, 109, 131]

ANNE RENTOUMIS CAPPOLA, MD, SCM
Assistant Professor in Medicine
Division of Endocrinology, Diabetes, and Metabolism
University of Maryland School of Medicine
Baltimore [19, 40, 41, 47, 53–56, 169–179, 203]

GLENN M. CHERTOW, MD, MPH
Director of Clinical Services
Divisions of Nephrology
Moffitt-Long Hospitals and UCSF-Mt. Zion Medical Center
Assistant Professor of Medicine in Residence
University of California–San Francisco School of Medicine
San Francisco [25, 26, 137, 140, 142, 143, 145–147]

ROBERT L. DERESIEWICZ, MD
Assistant Professor of Medicine
Harvard Medical School
Boston [46, 77, 83, 89, 93, 96, 97, 99, 108, 110, 111, 144]

JOHN W. ENGSTROM, MD
Associate Professor and Vice-Chairman
Department of Neurology
University of California–San Francisco
San Francisco [4, 5, 183, 188, 189, 193]

ANTHONY S. FAUCI, MD, SCD(HON)
Chief, Laboratory of Immunoregulation
Director, National Institute of Allergy and Infectious Diseases
National Institutes of Health
Bethesda [7, 44, 45, 51, 52, 86, 157–159]

HOWARD L. FIELDS, MD, PHD
Professor of Neurology and Physiology
University of California–San Francisco
San Francisco [1]

STEPHEN L. HAUSER, MD
Betty Anker Fife Professor and Chairman
Department of Neurology
University of California–San Francisco
San Francisco [8, 9, 11–13, 33–38, 49, 76, 180–182, 184–187, 190–192, 194–197]

JONATHAN C. HORTON, MD, PHD
Associate Professor of Ophthalmology, Neurology, and Physiology
University of California–San Francisco
San Francisco [10, 48]

J. LARRY JAMESON, MD, PHD
Irving S. Cutter Professor and Chairman
Department of Medicine
Northwestern University Medical School
Physician-in-Chief
Northwestern Memorial Hospital
Chicago [19, 39–41, 47, 53–56, 169–179, 203]

DENNIS L. KASPER, MD, MA(HON)
William Ellery Channing Professor of Medicine
Professor of Microbiology and Molecular Genetics
Executive Dean for Academic Programs
Harvard Medical School
Director, Channing Laboratory
Department of Medicine
Brigham and Women's Hospital
Boston [81, 95, 98, 101, 105, 107]

CAROL LANGFORD, MD
National Institute of Allergy and Infectious Diseases
National Institutes of Health
Bethesda [7, 51, 52, 159–168]

LEONARD LILLY, MD
Associate Professor of Medicine
Harvard Medical School of Medicine
Chief, Brigham and Women's/Faulkner Cardiology
Boston [2, 17, 29, 30, 32, 112–125]

DAN L. LONGO, MD, FACP
Scientific Director, National Institute on Aging
National Institutes of Health
Bethesda and Baltimore [3, 18, 20–22, 27, 28, 43, 57–75, 148–150]

LAWRENCE C. MADOFF, MD
Assistant Professor of Medicine
Harvard Medical School
Associate Physician
Channing Laboratory and Division of Infectious Diseases
Brigham and Women's Hospital
Boston [6, 31, 78, 82, 84, 87, 88, 90, 94, 102–104, 106, 109, 131]

LORI A. PANTHER, MD
Instructor in Medicine, Division of Infectious Diseases
Department of Medicine, Beth Israel Deaconess Medical Center
Boston [42, 46, 50, 79, 80, 83, 85, 92–96, 98, 102–104, 107, 110, 111, 144]

ANN N. PONCELET, MD
Assistant Clinical Professor of Neurology
University of California–San Francisco
San Francisco [181]

MICHAEL SNELLER, MD
National Institute of Allergy and Infectious Diseases
National Institutes of Health
Bethesda [44, 45, 86, 157, 158]

SOPHIA VINOGRADOV, MD
Assistant Professor of Psychiatry
Department of Psychiatry
University of California–San Francisco
San Francisco [198–201]

J. WOODROW WEISS, MD
Associate Professor of Medicine
Harvard Medical School, Chief, Pulmonary and Critical Care Division
Beth Israel Deaconess Medical Center
Boston [14–16, 127–130, 132–136]

PREFACE

It would certainly be ideal to have a copy of the 15th edition of *Harrison's Principles of Internal Medicine (HPIM)* available at all times. This is particularly true for students and residents who are constantly on the move from outpatient clinics to inpatient wards to emergency rooms and other specialized facilities. However, the sheer weight and size of the book make this quite impractical. It is for this reason that the Editors have condensed the clinical portions of *HPIM* into this pocket-sized *Manual of Medicine* that contains key features of the diagnosis and treatment of the major diseases that are likely to be encountered on a medical service. We have developed this handbook with the able assistance of selected contributors.

HPIM is updated every 3 to 4 years and the total amount of information continues to grow. It has been a challenge to distill the broad field of internal medicine with each new edition in which we provide a solid base of classic and established principles while providing important updates in pathogenesis, treatment, and prevention of a broad range of diseases. In the *Manual of Medicine*, we try to distill this body of knowledge even further so that summaries of this important information can be available to the student and resident within the easy reach of a coat pocket.

The purpose of the *Manual of Medicine* is to provide on-the-spot summaries in preparation for a more in-depth analysis of the clinical problem. Therefore, it is important to point out that this book is not considered to be a replacement for a full textbook of medicine. Rather, it is an extension of the fifteenth edition of *HPIM*. The amount and depth of material are not adequate to stand on their own; however, it is an excellent introduction to or reminder of some aspects of clinical medicine. It has been written with easy reference to the full text of *HPIM* and it is recommended that the full textbook be consulted as soon as time permits. Thus, we consider *HPIM* and the *Manual of Medicine* as a combination that is complementary, but not interchangeable.

The Editors wish to acknowledge contributors to past editions of the Companion Handbook whose work formed the basis for many of the chapters herein: Kurt Isselbacher, MD; Joseph B. Martin, MD, PhD; Jean Wilson, MD; Robert Dobbins, MD; Lawrence Friedman, MD; Daryl R. Gress, MD; Lee Kaplan, MD; Walter J. Koroshetz, MD; Daniel H. Lowenstein, MD; Norman Nishioka, MD; Thomas A. Rando, MD, PhD; and Kenneth L. Tyler, MD.

THE EDITORS

1

PAIN AND ITS MANAGEMENT

Pain is the most common symptom of disease. Management depends on determining its cause and alleviating triggering and potentiating factors.

Organization of Pain Pathways

(See HPIM-15, Fig. 12-1.) Pain-producing (nociceptive) sensory stimuli in skin and viscera activate peripheral nerve endings of primary afferent neurons, which synapse on second-order neurons in cord or medulla. These second-order neurons form crossed ascending pathways that reach the thalamus and are projected to somatosensory cortex. Parallel ascending neurons connect with brainstem nuclei and ventrocaudal and medial thalamic nuclei. These parallel pathways project to the limbic system and underlie the emotional aspect of pain. Pain transmission is regulated at the dorsal horn level by descending bulbospinal pathways that contain serotonin, norepinephrine, and several neuropeptides.

Agents that modify pain perception may act to reduce tissue inflammation (glucocorticoids, NSAIDs, prostaglandin synthesis inhibitors), to interfere with pain transmission (narcotics), or to enhance descending modulation (narcotics and antidepressants). Anticonvulsants (gabapentin, carbamazepine) may be effective for aberrant pain sensations arising from peripheral nerve injury.

Evaluation

Pain may be of somatic (skin, joints, muscles), visceral, or neuropathic (injury to nerves, spinal cord pathways, or thalamus) origin. Characteristics of each are summarized in Table 1-1.

Sensory symptoms and signs in neuropathic pain are described by the following definitions: *neuralgia*: pain in the distribution of a single nerve, as in

Table 1-1

Characteristics of Somatic and Neuropathic Pain

Somatic pain
  Nociceptive stimulus usually evident
  Usually well localized
  Similar to other somatic pains in pt's experience
  Relieved by anti-inflammatory or narcotic analgesics
Visceral pain
  Most commonly activated by inflammation
  Pain poorly localized and usually referred
  Associated with diffuse discomfort, e.g., nausea, bloating
  Relieved by narcotic analgesics
Neuropathic pain
  No obvious nociceptive stimulus
  Associated evidence of nerve damage, e.g., sensory impairment, weakness
  Unusual, dissimilar from somatic pain, often shooting or electrical quality
  Only partially relieved by narcotic analgesics, may respond to antidepressants
    or anticonvulsants

Table 1-2

Drugs for Relief of Pain

NONNARCOTIC ANALGESICS: USUAL DOSES AND INTERVALS

Generic Name	Dose, mg
Acetylsalicylic acid	650 PO
Acetaminophen	650 PO
Ibuprofen	400 PO
Naproxen	250–500 PO
Fenoprofen	200 PO
Indomethacin	25–50 PO
Ketorolac	15–60 IM
Rofecoxib	12.5–25 PO
Celecoxib	100–200 PO

NARCOTIC ANALGESICS: USUAL DOSES AND INTERVALS

Generic Name	Parenteral Dose, mg
Codeine	30–60q4h
Oxycodone	—
Morphine	10q4h
Morphine sustained release	
Hydromorphone	1–2q4h
Levorphanol	2q6–8h
Methadone	10q6–8h
Meperidine	75–100q3–4h
Butorphanol	—
Fentanyl	2.5–10q72h
Tramadol	—

ANTICONVULSANTS AND ANTIARRHYTHMICS

Generic Name	PO Dose, mg
Phenytoin	300
Carbamazepine	200–300
Clonazepam	1
Mexiletine	150–300
Gabapentin	600–1200

ANTIDEPRESSANTS

Generic Name	Uptake Blockade		Sedative Potency
	5-HT	NE	
Doxepin	++	+	High
Amitriptyline	++++	++	High
Imipramine	++++	++	Moderate
Nortriptyline	+++	++	Moderate
Desipramine	+++	++++	Low
Venlafaxine	+++	++	Low

NOTE: 5-HT, serotonin; NE, norepinephrine.

Interval	Comments
q4h	Enteric-coated preparations available
q4h	Side effects uncommon
q4–6h	Available without prescription
q12h	Delayed effects may be due to long half-life
q4–6h	Contraindicated in renal disease
q8h	Gastrointestinal side effects common
q4–6h	Available for parenteral use (IM)
q24h	FDA approved for pain management
q12–24h	Useful for arthritis

PO Dose, mg	Comments
30–60q4h	Nausea common
5–10q4–6h	Usually available with acetaminophen or aspirin
60q4h	
30–200 bid to tid	Oral slow-release preparation
2–4q4h	Shorter acting than morphine sulfate
4q6–8h	Longer acting than morphine sulfate; absorbed well PO
20q6–8h	Delayed sedation due to long half-life
300q4h	Poorly absorbed PO; normeperidine a toxic metabolite
1–2q4h	Intranasal spray
—	Transdermal patch
50–100q4–6h	Mixed opioid/adrenergic action

Interval
daily/qhs
q6h
q6h
q6–12h
q8h

Anticholinergic Potency	Orthostatic Hypotension	Cardiac Arrhythmia	Average Dose, mg/day	Range, mg/day
Moderate	Moderate	Less	200	75–400
Highest	Moderate	Yes	150	25–300
Moderate	High	Yes	200	75–400
Moderate	Low	Yes	100	40–150
Low	Low	Yes	150	50–300
None	None	No	150	75–400

trigeminal neuralgia; *dysesthesia*: spontaneous, unpleasant, abnormal sensations; *hyperalgesia* and *hyperesthesia*: exaggerated responses to nociceptive or touch stimulus, respectively; *allodynia*: perception of light mechanical stimuli as painful, as when vibration evokes painful sensation. Reduced pain perception is called *hypalgesia* or, when absent, *analgesia*. *Causalgia* is continuous severe burning pain with indistinct boundaries and accompanying sympathetic nervous system dysfunction (sweating; vascular, skin, and hair changes—sympathetic dystrophy) that occurs after injury to a peripheral nerve.

 TREATMENT

Acute Somatic Pain   If moderate, it can usually be treated effectively with nonnarcotic analgesic agents (Table 1-2). For subacute musculoskeletal pain and arthritis, selective Cox-2 inhibitors such as rofecoxib or celecoxib are useful, especially if the pt is at risk for upper gastrointestinal ulceration or bleeding. Narcotic analgesics are usually required for relief of severe pain; the dose should be titrated to produce effective analgesia.

Neuropathic Pain   Often chronic; management is particularly difficult. Most pts are treated optimally with a combination of the anticonvulsant gabapentin and an antidepressant such as nortriptyline.

Chronic Pain

The problem is often difficult to diagnose, and pts may appear emotionally distraught. Psychological evaluation and behaviorally based treatment paradigms are frequently helpful, particularly in a multidisciplinary pain management center.

Several factors can cause, perpetuate, or exacerbate chronic pain: (1) painful disease for which there is no cure (e.g., arthritis, cancer, migraine headaches, diabetic neuropathy); (2) neural factors initiated by a bodily disease that persist after the disease has resolved (e.g., damaged sensory or sympathetic nerves); (3) psychological conditions.

Pay special attention to the medical history and to depression. Major depression is common, treatable, and potentially fatal (suicide).

 TREATMENT

After evaluation, an explicit treatment plan should be developed, including specific and realistic goals for therapy, e.g., getting a good night's sleep, being able to go shopping, or returning to work. A multidisciplinary approach that utilizes medications, counseling, physical therapy, nerve blocks, and even surgery may be required to improve the pt's quality of life. Some pts may require referral to a pain clinic; for others, pharmacologic management alone can provide significant help. The tricyclic antidepressants are useful in management of chronic pain from many causes, including headache, diabetic neuropathy, postherpetic neuralgia, atypical facial pain, and chronic low back pain. Anticonvulsants benefit pts with chronic neuropathic pain and little or no evidence of sympathetic dysfunction (e.g., diabetic neuropathy, trigeminal neuralgia).

For a more detailed discussion, see Fields HL, Martin JB: Pain: Pathophysiology and Management, Chap. 12, p. 55, in HPIM-15.

2

CHEST PAIN

There is little correlation between the severity of chest pain and the seriousness of its cause.

POTENTIALLY SERIOUS CAUSES

The differential diagnosis of chest pain is shown in Fig. 2-1. It is useful to characterize the chest pain as (1) new, acute, and ongoing; (2) recurrent, episodic; and (3) persistent, sometimes for days (Table 2-1).

MYOCARDIAL ISCHEMIA *Angina Pectoris* (Chap. 122)   Substernal pressure, squeezing, constriction, with radiation typically to left arm; usually on exertion, especially after meals or with emotional arousal. Characteristically relieved by rest and nitroglycerin.

Acute Myocardial Infarction (Chap. 121)   Similar to angina but usually more severe, of longer duration (≥ 30 min), and not immediately relieved by rest or nitroglycerin. S_3 and S_4 common.

PULMONARY EMBOLISM (Chap. 132)   May be substernal or lateral, pleuritic in nature, and associated with hemoptysis, tachycardia, and hypoxemia.

AORTIC DISSECTION (Chap. 125)   Very severe, in center of chest, a "ripping" quality, radiates to back, not affected by changes in position. May be associated with weak or absent peripheral pulses.

MEDIASTINAL EMPHYSEMA   Sharp, intense, localized to substernal region; often associated with audible crepitus.

ACUTE PERICARDITIS (Chap. 120)   Usually steady, crushing, substernal; often has pleuritic component aggravated by cough, deep inspiration, supine position, and relieved by sitting upright; one-, two-, or three-component pericardial friction rub often audible.

PLEURISY   Due to inflammation; less commonly tumor and pneumothorax. Usually unilateral, knifelike, superficial, aggravated by cough and respiration.

LESS SERIOUS CAUSES

COSTOCHONDRAL PAIN   In anterior chest, usually sharply localized, may be brief and darting or a persistent dull ache. Can be reproduced by pressure on costochondral and/or chondrosternal junctions. In Tietze's syndrome (costochondritis), joints are swollen, red, and tender.

CHEST WALL PAIN   Due to strain of muscles or ligaments from excessive exercise or rib fracture from trauma; accompanied by local tenderness.

ESOPHAGEAL PAIN   Deep thoracic discomfort; may be accompanied by dysphagia and regurgitation.

EMOTIONAL DISORDERS   Prolonged ache or dartlike, brief, flashing pain; associated with fatigue, emotional strain.

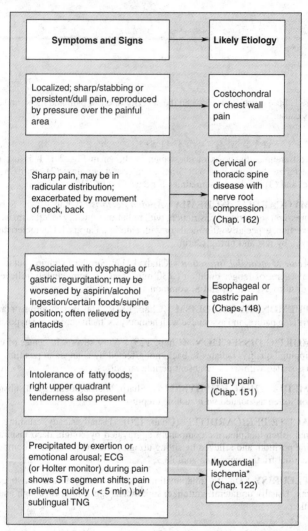

FIGURE 2-1   Differential diagnosis of recurrent chest pain. *If myocardial ischemia suspected, also consider aortic valve disease (Chap. 118) and hypertrophic obstructive cardiomyopathy (Chap. 119) if systolic murmur present.

OTHER CAUSES

(1) Cervical disk; (2) osteoarthritis of cervical or thoracic spine; (3) abdominal disorders: peptic ulcer, hiatus hernia, pancreatitis, biliary colic; (4) tracheo-bronchitis, pneumonia; (5) diseases of the breast (inflammation, tumor); (6) intercostal neuritis (herpes zoster).

Table 2-1

Some Causes of Chest Discomfort and the Types of Discomfort Associated with Them

Cause	New, Acute, Often Ongoing	Recurrent Episodic	Persistent, Even for Days
Cardiac			
Coronary artery disease	+	+	−
Aortic stenosis	−	+	−
Hypertrophic cardiomyopathy	−	+	−
Pericarditis	+	+	+
Vascular			
Aortic dissection	+	−	−
Pulmonary embolism	+	+	−
Pulmonary hypertension	+	+	−
Pulmonary			
Pleuritis or pneumonia	+	+	+
Tracheobronchitis	+	+	+
Pneumothorax	+	−	+
Mediastinitis or mediastinal emphysema	+	−	+
Gastrointestinal			
Esophageal reflux or spasm	+	+	+
Peptic ulcer disease	+	+	−
Biliary disease	+	+	−
Pancreatitis		+	+
Musculoskeletal			
Cervical disk disease	−	+	+
Arthritis of the shoulder, spine	−	+	+
Costochondritis	+	+	+
Intercostal muscle cramps	+	+	+
Subacromial bursitis	+	+	+
Other			
Disorders of the breast	−	+	+
Herpes zoster	+	−	+
Emotional	+	+	+

_____ *Approach to the Patient* _____

A meticulous history of the behavior of pain, what precipitates it and what relieves it, aids diagnosis of recurrent chest pain. Figure 2-2 presents clues to diagnosis and workup of acute, life-threatening chest pain.

For a more detailed discussion, see Lee TH: Chest Discomfort and Palpitations, Chap. 13, p. 60, in HPIM-15.

	Acute myocardial infarction (Chap. 121)	Aortic dissection (Chap. 125)	Acute pericarditis (Chap. 120)	Pulmonary embolism (Chap. 132)	Acute pneumothorax (Chap. 134)	Rupture of esophagus
Description of pain	Oppressive, constrictive, or squeezing; may radiate to arm(s), neck, back	"Tearing" or "ripping"; may travel from anterior chest to mid-back	Crushing, sharp, pleuritic; relieved by sitting forward	Pleuritic, sharp; possibly accompanied by cough/hemoptysis	Very sharp, pleuritic	Intense substernal and epigastric; accompanied by vomiting ± hematemesis
Background history	Less severe, similar pain on exertion; + coronary risk factors (Chap. 122)	Hypertension or Marfan syndrome (Chap. 159)	Recent upper respiratory tract infection, or other conditions which predispose to pericarditis (Chap. 120)	Recent surgery or other immobilization	Recent chest trauma, or history of chronic obstructive lung disease	Recent recurrent vomiting/retching
Key Physical findings	Diaphoresis, pallor; S4 common; S3 less common	Weak, asymmetric peripheral pulses; possible diastolic murmur or aortic insufficiency (Chap. 118)	Pericardial friction rub (usually 3 components, best heard by sitting patient forward)	Tachypnea; possible pleural friction rub	Tachypnea; breath sounds & hyperresonance over affected lung field	Subcutaneous emphysema; audible crepitus adjacent to the sternum
Consider						
Confirmatory tests	• Serial ECGs • Serial cardiac enzymes (esp. CK, LDH)	• CXR – widened mediastinal silhouette • MRI, CT, or transesophageal echogram: intimal flap visualized • Aortic angiogram: definitive diagnosis	• ECG: diffuse ST elevation and PR segment depression • Echogram: pericardial effusion often visualized	• Arterial blood gas: hypoxemia & respiratory alkalosis • Lung scan: V/Q mismatch • Pulmonary angiogram: arterial luminal filling defects	• CXR: radiolucency within pleural space; poss. collapse of adjacent lung segment; if tension pneumothorax, mediastinum is shifted to opp. side	• CXR: pneumo-mediastinum • Esophageal endoscopy is diagnostic

FIGURE 2-2 Differential diagnosis of acute chest pain.

3	

ABDOMINAL PAIN

Numerous causes, ranging from acute, life-threatening emergencies to chronic functional disease and disorders of several organ systems, can generate abdominal pain. Evaluation of acute pain requires rapid assessment of likely causes and early initiation of appropriate therapy. A more detailed and time-consuming approach to diagnosis may be followed in less acute situations. Table 3-1 lists the common causes of abdominal pain.

Approach to the Patient

History

Historic features are of critical diagnostic importance. Physical examination may be unrevealing or misleading and laboratory and radiologic exams delayed or unhelpful.

Characteristic Features of Abdominal Pain

Duration and Pattern These provide clues to nature and severity, although acute abdominal crisis may occasionally present insidiously or on a background of chronic pain.

Type and location provide a rough guide to nature of disease. *Visceral pain* (due to distention of a hollow viscus) localizes poorly and is often perceived in the midline. Intestinal pain tends to be crampy; when originating proximal to the ileocecal valve, it usually localizes above and around the umbilicus. Pain of colonic origin is perceived in the hypogastrium and lower quadrants. Pain from biliary or ureteral obstruction often causes pts to writhe in discomfort. *Somatic pain* (due to peritoneal inflammation) is usually sharper and more precisely localized to the diseased region (e.g., acute appendicitis; capsular distention of liver, kidney, or spleen), exacerbated by movement, causing pts to remain still. Pattern of radiation may be helpful: right shoulder (hepatobiliary origin), left shoulder (splenic), midback (pancreatic), flank (proximal urinary tract), groin (genital or distal urinary tract).

Factors That Precipitate or Relieve Pain Ask about its relationship to eating (e.g., upper GI, biliary, pancreatic, ischemic bowel disease), defecation (colorectal), urination (genitourinary or colorectal), respiratory (pleuropulmonary, hepatobiliary), position (pancreatic, gastroesophageal reflux, musculoskeletal), menstrual cycle/menarche (tuboovarian, endometrial, including endometriosis), exertion (coronary/intestinal ischemia, musculoskeletal), medication/specific foods (motility disorders, food intolerance, gastroesophageal reflux, porphyria, adrenal insufficiency, ketoacidosis, toxins), and stress (motility disorders, nonulcer dyspepsia, irritable bowel syndrome).

Associated Symptoms Look for fevers/chills (infection, inflammatory disease, infarction), weight loss (tumor, inflammatory diseases, malabsorption, ischemia), nausea/vomiting (obstruction, infection, inflammatory disease, metabolic disease), dysphagia/odynophagia (esophageal), early satiety (gastric), hematemesis (esophageal, gastric, duodenal), constipation (colorectal, perianal, genitourinary), jaundice (hepatobiliary, hemolytic), diarrhea (inflammatory disease, infection, malabsorption, secretory tumors, ischemia, genitourinary), dysuria/hematuria/vaginal or penile discharge (genitourinary), hematochezia (colorectal or, rarely, urinary), skin/joint/eye disorders (inflammatory disease, bacterial or viral infection).

Predisposing Factors Inquire about family history (inflammatory disease, tumors, pancreatitis), hypertension and atherosclerotic disease (ischemia), dia-

Table 3-1

Common Etiologies of Abdominal Pain

Mucosal or muscle inflammation in hollow viscera: Peptic disease (ulcers, erosions, inflammation), hemorrhagic gastritis, gastroesophageal reflux, appendicitis, diverticulitis, cholecystitis, cholangitis, inflammatory bowel diseases (Crohn's, ulcerative colitis), infectious gastroenteritis, mesenteric lymphadenitis, colitis, cystitis, or pyelonephritis

Visceral spasm or distention: Intestinal obstruction (adhesions, tumor, intussusception), appendiceal obstruction with appendicitis, strangulation of hernia, irritable bowel syndrome (muscle hypertrophy and spasm), acute biliary obstruction, pancreatic ductal obstruction (chronic pancreatitis, stone), ureteral obstruction (kidney stone, blood clot), fallopian tubes (tubal pregnancy)

Vascular disorders: Mesenteric thromboembolic disease (arterial or venous), arterial dissection or rupture (e.g., aortic aneurysm), occlusion from external pressure or torsion (e.g., volvulus, hernia, tumor, adhesions, intussusception), hemoglobinopathy (esp. sickle cell disease)

Distention or inflammation of visceral surfaces: Hepatic capsule (hepatitis, hemorrhage, tumor, Budd-Chiari syndrome, Fitz-Hugh–Curtis syndrome), renal capsule (tumor, infection, infarction, venous occlusion), splenic capsule (hemorrhage, abscess, infarction), pancreas (pancreatitis, pseudocyst, abscess, tumor), ovary (hemorrhage into cyst, ectopic pregnancy, abscess)

Peritoneal inflammation: Bacterial infection (perforated viscus, pelvic inflammatory disease, infected ascites), intestinal infarction, chemical irritation, pancreatitis, perforated viscus (esp. stomach and duodenum, mittelschmerz), reactive inflammation (neighboring abscess, incl. diverticulitis, pleuropulmonary infection or inflammation), serositis (collagen-vascular diseases, familial Mediterranean fever)

Abdominal wall disorders: Trauma, hernias, muscle inflammation or infection, hematoma (trauma, anticoagulant therapy), traction from mesentery (e.g., adhesions)

Toxins: Lead poisoning, black widow spider bite

Metabolic disorders: Uremia, ketoacidosis (diabetic, alcoholic), Addisonian crisis, porphyria, angioedema (C1 esterase deficiency), narcotic withdrawal

Neurologic disorders: Herpes zoster, tabes dorsalis, causalgia, compression or inflammation of spinal roots, (e.g., arthritis, herniated disk, tumor, abscess), psychogenic

Referred pain: From heart, lungs, esophagus, genitalia (e.g., cardiac ischemia, pneumonia, pneumothorax, pulmonary embolism, esophagitis, esophageal spasm, esophageal rupture)

---

betes mellitus (motility disorders, ketoacidosis), connective tissue disease (motility disorders, serositis), depression (motility disorders, tumors), smoking (ischemia), recent smoking cessation (inflammatory disease), ethanol use (motility disorders, hepatobiliary, pancreatic, gastritis, peptic ulcer disease).

Physical Examination

Evaluate abdomen for prior trauma or surgery, current trauma; abdominal distention, fluid, or air; direct, rebound, and referred tenderness; liver and spleen size; masses, bruits, altered bowel sounds, hernias, arterial masses. Rectal examination for presence and location of tenderness, masses, blood (gross or occult). Pelvic examination in women is essential. *General examination*: evaluate for evidence of hemodynamic instability, acid-base disturbances, nutritional deficiency, coagulopathy, arterial occlusive disease, stigmata of liver disease, cardiac dysfunction, lymphadenopathy, and skin lesions.

Routine Laboratory and Radiologic Studies

Choices depend on clinical setting (esp. severity of pain, rapidity of onset): may include CBC, serum electrolytes, coagulation parameters, serum glucose, and biochemical tests of liver, kidney, and pancreatic function; CXR to determine the presence of diseases involving heart, lung, mediastinum, and pleura; ECG is helpful to exclude referred pain from cardiac disease; plain abdominal radiographs to evaluate bowel displacement, intestinal distention, fluid and gas pattern, free peritoneal air, liver size, and abdominal calcifications (e.g., gallstones, renal stones, chronic pancreatitis).

Special Studies

These include abdominal ultrasonography (to visualize biliary ducts, gallbladder, liver, pancreas, and kidneys); CT to identify masses, abscesses, evidence of inflammation (bowel wall thickening, mesenteric "stranding," lymphadenopathy), aortic aneurysm; barium contrast radiographs (barium swallow, upper GI series, small-bowel follow-through, barium enema; upper GI endoscopy, sigmoidoscopy, or colonoscopy; cholangiography (endoscopic, percutaneous, or via MRI), angiography (direct or via CT or MRI), and radionuclide scanning. In selected cases, percutaneous biopsy, laparoscopy, and exploratory laparotomy may be required.

ACUTE, CATASTROPHIC ABDOMINAL PAIN

Intense abdominal pain of acute onset or pain associated with syncope, hypotension, or toxic appearance necessitates rapid yet orderly evaluation. Consider obstruction, perforation, or rupture of hollow viscus, dissection or rupture of major blood vessels (esp. aortic aneurysm), ulceration, abdominal sepsis, ketoacidosis, and adrenal crisis.

BRIEF HISTORY AND PHYSICAL EXAMINATION   These should focus on presence of fever or hypothermia, hyperventilation, cyanosis, direct or rebound abdominal tenderness, pulsating abdominal mass, abdominal bruits, ascites, rectal blood, rectal or pelvic tenderness, and evidence of coagulopathy. Useful laboratory studies include hematocrit (may be normal with acute hemorrhage or misleadingly high with dehydration), WBC, arterial blood gases, serum electrolytes, BUN, creatinine, glucose, lipase or amylase, and UA. Radiologic studies should include supine and upright abdominal films (left lateral decubitus view if upright unobtainable) to evaluate bowel caliber and presence of free peritoneal air, cross-table lateral film to assess aortic diameter; CT (when available) to detect evidence of bowel perforation, inflammation, solid organ infarction, retroperitoneal bleeding, abscess, or tumor. Abdominal paracentesis (or peritoneal lavage in cases of trauma) can detect evidence of bleeding or spontaneous peritonitis. Abdominal ultrasound (when available) reveals evidence of abscess, cholecystitis, biliary obstruction, or hematoma and is used to determine aortic diameter.

 TREATMENT

Intravenous fluids, correction of life-threatening acid-base disturbances, and assessment of need for emergent surgery are the first priority; careful follow-up with frequent reexamination (when possible, by the same examiner) is essential. The use of narcotic analgesia is controversial. Traditionally, narcotic analgesics were withheld pending establishment of diagnosis and therapeutic plan, since masking of diagnostic signs may delay needed intervention. However, evidence that narcotics actually mask a diagnosis is sparse.

For a more detailed discussion, see Silen W: Abdominal Pain, Chap. 14, p. 67, in HPIM-15.

4

HEADACHE AND FACIAL PAIN

Causes of headache are summarized in Table 4-1. First step—distinguish serious from benign etiologies. Symptoms that raise the suspicion for a serious cause are listed in Table 4-2; serious causes are summarized in Table 4-3. Intensity of head pain rarely has diagnostic value. Headache location can suggest involvement of local structures (temporal pain in giant cell arteritis, facial pain in sinusitis). Ruptured aneurysm (instant onset), cluster headache (peak over 3–5 min), and migraine (onset over minutes to hours) differ in time to peak intensity. Therapeutic trials of medication do not provide diagnostic information due to high frequency of placebo responders (~30%). Provocation by environmental factors suggests a benign cause.

MIGRAINE

Frequency of symptoms associated with migraine is listed in Table 4-4.

CLASSIC MIGRAINE Onset usually in childhood, adolescence, or early adulthood; however, initial attack may occur at any age. Family history often positive. More frequent in women. Classic triad: premonitory visual (scotoma or scintillations) sensory or motor symptoms, unilateral throbbing headache, nausea and vomiting. Photo- and phonophobia common. Focal neurologic disturbances without headache or vomiting (migraine equivalents) may also occur. An attack lasting 2–6 h is typical, as is relief after sleep. Attacks may be triggered by wine, cheese, chocolate, contraceptives, stress, exercise, or travel.

COMMON MIGRAINE Unilateral or bilateral headache with nausea, but no focal neurologic symptoms. Moderate-to-severe head pain, pulsating quality, unilateral, worse with activity; associated with photophobia, phonophobia, multiple attacks. More common in women. Onset more gradual than in classic migraine; duration 4–72 h.

 TREATMENT

Three approaches to migraine treatment: nonpharmacologic (Table 4-5), drug treatment of acute attacks (Table 4-6), and prophylaxis (Table 4-7). Drug

Table 4-1

The Classification of Headache

1. Migraine
     Migraine without aura
     Migraine with aura
     Ophthalmoplegic migraine
     Retinal migraine
     Childhood periodic syndromes that may be precursors to or
       associated with migraine
     Migrainous disorder not fulfilling above criteria
2. Tension-type headache
     Episodic tension-type headache
     Chronic tension-type headache
3. Cluster headache and chronic paroxysmal hemicrania
     Cluster headache
     Chronic paroxysmal hemicrania
4. Miscellaneous headaches not associated with structural lesion
     Idiopathic stabbing headache
     External compression headache
     Cold stimulus headache
     Benign cough headache
     Benign exertional headache
     Headache associated with sexual activity
5. Headache associated with head trauma
     Acute posttraumatic headache
     Chronic posttraumatic headache
6. Headache associated with vascular disorders
     Acute ischemic cerebrovascular disorder
     Intracranial hematoma
     Subarachnoid hemorrhage
     Unruptured vascular malformation
     Arteritis
     Carotid or vertebral artery pain
     Venous thrombosis
     Arterial hypertension
     Other vascular disorder
7. Headache associated with nonvascular intracranial disorder
     High CSF pressure
     Low CSF pressure
     Intracranial infection
     Sarcoidosis and other noninfectious inflammatory diseases
     Related to intrathecal injections
     Intracranial neoplasm
     Associated with other intracranial disorder
8. Headache associated with substances or their withdrawal
     Headache induced by acute substance use or exposure
     Headache induced by chronic substance use or exposure
     Headache from substance withdrawal (acute use)
     Headache from substance withdrawal (chronic use)
9. Headache associated with noncephalic infection
     Viral infection
     Bacterial infection
     Other infection

(continued)

Table 4-1 *(Continued)*

The Classification of Headache

10. Headache associated with metabolic disorder
    Hypoxia
    Hypercapnia
    Mixed hypoxia and hypercapnia
    Hypoglycemia
    Dialysis
    Other metabolic abnormality
11. Headache or facial pain associated with disorder of facial or
    cranial structures
    Cranial bone
    Eyes
    Ears
    Nose and sinuses
    Teeth, jaws, and related structures
    Temporomandibular joint disease
12. Cranial neuralgias, nerve trunk pain, and deafferentation pain
    Persistent (in contrast to ticlike) pain of cranial nerve origin
    Trigeminal neuralgia
    Glossopharyngeal neuralgia
    Nervus intermedius neuralgia
    Superior laryngeal neuralgia
    Occipital neuralgia
    Central causes of head and facial pain other than tic douloureux
13. Headache not classifiable

SOURCE: Modified from Raskin and Peroutka: HPIM, 15/e, p. 71.

treatment necessary for most migraine patients, but avoidance or management
of environmental triggers is sufficient for some. General principles of pharmacologic treatment: (1) response rates vary from 60–90%; (2) initial drug
choice is empirical—influenced by patient age, coexisting illnesses, and side
effect profile; (3) efficacy of prophylactic treatment may take several months
to assess with each drug; (4) when an acute attack requires additional medication 60 min after the first dose, then the initial drug dose should be increased
for subsequent attacks. Mild-to-moderate acute migraine attacks often respond
to over-the-counter (OTC) NSAIDs when taken early in the attack. Triptans
are widely used also, but recurrence of head pain after the first dose (40–
78%) is a major limitation. There is less frequent headache recurrence when
using ergots, but more frequent side effects. For prophylaxis, amitriptyline is

Table 4-2

Headache Symptoms That Suggest a Serious Underlying Disorder

"Worst" headache ever
First severe headache
Subacute worsening over days or weeks
Abnormal neurologic examination
Fever or unexplained systemic signs
Vomiting precedes headache
Induced by bending, lifting, cough
Disturbs sleep or present immediately upon awakening
Known systemic illness
Onset after age 55

Table 4-3

Serious Causes of Headache

Cause	Symptoms
Meningitis	Nuchal rigidity, headache, papilledema; pain with eye movements. May not be febrile. LP is diagnostic.
Intracranial hemorrhage	Nuchal rigidity; may not have clouded consciousness or seizures. Evaluation by CT; if negative, LP.
Brain tumor	High suspicion when new headache accompanies known systemic malignancy. Nonspecific headache initial symptom in 30%; may awaken pt from sleep. Consider prolactin-secreting adenoma if associated with galactorrhea. Vomiting preceding headache suggests posterior fossa tumor.
Temporal arteritis	Older patients (>50 years); headache, jaw claudication, proximal limb aching, visual obscuration, fever or weight loss. Scalp tenderness common. ESR usually elevated; temporal artery biopsy for diagnosis. Untreated—blindness in 50%. Glucocorticoids (prednisone 80 mg/d initial dose).
Pseudotumor cerebri	Headache, papilledema, no focal neurologic signs; occurs in young, obese women; elevated opening pressure on LP; MRI—no mass lesion. Rx: prevent blindness; acetazolamide (125–250 mg PO tid), repeated LPs, optic nerve fenestration.
Glaucoma	Severe eye pain; eye is usually red and pupil may be dilated. May have nausea, vomiting.

a good first choice for young people with difficulty falling asleep; verapamil is often a first choice for prophylaxis in the elderly.

CLUSTER HEADACHE   Characterized by episodes of recurrent, nocturnal, unilateral, retroorbital searing pain. Typically, a young male (90%) awakens 2–4 h after sleep onset with severe pain, unilateral lacrimation, and nasal and conjunctival congestion. Visual complaints, nausea, or vomiting are rare. Pain lasts 30–120 min but tends to recur at the same time of night or several times each 24 h over 4–8 weeks (a cluster). Diurnal periodicity (recurrent pain during the same hour each day of the cluster) occurs in 85%. A pain-free period of months or years may be followed by another cluster of headaches. Alcohol provokes attacks in 70%. Prophylaxis with lithium (600–900 mg qd) or prednisone (60 mg for 7 d followed by a rapid taper). Ergotamine, 1 mg suppository 1–2 h before expected attack, may prevent daily episode. High-flow oxygen (9 L/min) or sumatriptan (6 mg SC) is useful for the acute attack.

TENSION HEADACHE   Common in all age groups. Pain is holocephalic, described as pressure or a tight band. May persist for hours or days. Often related to stress; responds to relaxation and simple OTC analgesics (i.e., aspirin, acetaminophen, ibuprofen). Amitriptyline may be helpful for prophylaxis (Table 4-8). Distinction from common migraine may be difficult.

Table 4-4

Symptoms Accompanying Severe Migraine Attacks in a Group of 500 Patients

Symptom	Patients Affected, %
Nausea	87
Photophobia	82
Lightheadedness	72
Scalp tenderness	65
Vomiting	56
Visual disturbances	36
Photopsia	26
Fortification spectra	10
Paresthesia	33
Vertigo	33
Alteration of consciousness	18
Syncope	10
Seizure	4
Confusional state	4
Diarrhea	16

SOURCE: From NH Raskin: *Headache*, 2d ed. New York; Churchill Livingstone, 1988.

OTHER HEADACHES

Post-Concussion Headache   Common following motor vehicle collisions, other head trauma; severe injury or loss of consciousness often not present. Symptoms of headache, dizziness, vertigo, impaired memory, poor concentration, irritability; typically remits after several weeks to months. Neurologic examination and neuroimaging studies normal. Not a functional disorder; cause unknown.

Lumbar Puncture Headache   Typical onset 24–48 h after LP; follows 10–30% of LPs. Positional: onset when pt sits or stands, relief by lying flat. Most cases remit spontaneously in ≤1 week. Intravenous caffeine (500 mg IV, repeat

Table 4-5

Nonpharmacologic Approaches to Migraine

Identify and then avoid trigger factors such as:
    Alcohol (e.g., red wine)
    Foods (e.g., chocolate, certain cheeses, monosodium glutamate, nitrate-containing foods)
    Hunger (avoid missing meals)
    Irregular sleep patterns (both lack of sleep and excessive sleep)
    Organic odors
    Sustained exertion
    Acute changes in stress levels
    Miscellaneous (glare, flashing lights)
Attempt to manage environmental shifts
    Time zone shifts
    High altitude
    Barometric pressure changes
    Weather changes
Assess menstrual cycle relationship

Table 4-6

Drugs Effective in Acute Treatment of Migraine

Drug	Trade Name	Dosage
NSAIDS (SEE ALSO TABLE 4-8)		
Acetaminophen, aspirin, caffeine	Excedrin Migraine	Two tablets or caplets q6h (max 8 per day)
5-HT, AGONISTS		
Oral		
Ergotamine	Ergomar	One 2-mg sublingual tablet at onset and q1/2h (max 3 per day, 5 per week)
Ergotamine 1 mg, caffeine 100 mg	Ercaf, Wigraine	One or two tablets at onset, then one tablet q1/2h (max 6 per day, 10 per week)
Rizatriptan	Maxalt Maxalt-MLT	5- to 10-mg tablet at onset; may repeat after 2 h (max 30 mg/d)
Sumatriptan	Imitrex	50- to 100-mg tablet at onset; may repeat after 2 h (max 200 mg/d)
Nasal		
Dihydroergotamine	Migranal Nasal Spray	Prior to nasal spray, the pump must be primed 4 times; one spray (0.5 mg) per nostril is administered followed, in 15 min, by a second spray per nostril
Sumatriptan	Imitrex Nasal Spray	5- to 20-mg spray as 4 sprays of 5 mg per nostril or a single 20-mg spray (may repeat once after 2 h, not to exceed a dose of 40 mg/d)
Parenteral		
Dihydroergotamine	DHE-15	1 mg IV, IM, or SC at onset and q1h (max 3 mg/d, 6 mg per week)
Sumatriptan	Imitrex Injection	6 mg SC at onset (may repeat once after 1 h for max of two doses in 24 h)
DOPAMINE ANTAGONISTS		
Oral		
Metoclopramide	Reglan,[a] generic[a]	5–10 mg/d
Prochlorperazine	Compazine,[a] generic[a]	1–2.5 mg/d
Parenteral		
Chlorpromazine	Generic[a]	0.1 mg/kg IV at 2 mg/min; max 35 mg/d
Metoclopramide	Reglan,[a] generic	10 mg IV
Prochlorperazine	Compazine,[a] generic[a]	10 mg IV

(continued)

Table 4-6 *(Continued)*

Drugs Effective in Acute Treatment of Migraine

Drug	Trade Name	Dosage
OTHER		
Oral		
Acetaminophen, 325 mg, *plus* dichloralphena-zone, 100 mg, *plus* isometheptene, 65 mg	Midrin, Duradrin, generic	Two capsules at onset followed by 1 capsule q1h (max 5 capsules)

[a] Not specifically indicated by the U.S. Food and Drug Administration for migraine.
NOTE: 5-HT, 5-hydroxytryptamine.

in 1 h if dose ineffective) successful in 85%; epidural blood patch effective immediately in refractory cases.

    Cough Headache   Transient severe head pain with coughing, bending, lifting, sneezing, or stooping; lasts from seconds to several minutes; men > women. Usually benign, but posterior fossa mass lesion in ~25%. Consider brain MRI.

Table 4-7

Drugs Effective in the Prophylactic Treatment of Migraine

Drug	Trade Name	Dosage
β-Adrenergic agents		
Propranolol	Inderal Inderal LA	80–320 mg qd
Timolol	Blocadren	20–60 mg qd
Anticonvulsants		
Sodium valproate	Depakote	250 mg bid (max 1000 mg/d)
Tricyclic antidepressants		
Amitriptyline	Elavil,[a] generic	10–50 mg qhs
Nortriptyline	Pamelor,[a] generic	25–75 mg qhs
Monoamine oxidase inhibitors		
Phenelzine	Nardil[a]	15 mg tid
Isocarboxazid	Marplan[a]	10 mg qid
Serotonergic drugs		
Methysergide	Sansert	4–8 mg qd
Cyproheptadine	Periactin[a]	4–16 mg qd
Other		
Verapamil	Calan[a] Isoptin[a]	40–240 mg qd

[a] Not specifically indicated for migraine by the U.S. Food and Drug Administration.

Table 4-8

Drugs Effective in the Treatment of Tension-Type Headache

Drug	Trade Name	Dosage
NONSTEROIDAL ANTI-INFLAMMATORY AGENTS		
Acetaminophen	Tylenol, generic	650 mg PO q4–6h
Aspirin	Generic	650 mg PO q4–6h
Diclofenac	Cataflam, generic	50–100 mg q4–6h (max 200 mg/d)
Ibuprofen	Advil, Motrin, Nuprin, Generic	400 mg PO q3–4h
Naprosyn sodium	Aleve, Anaprox, generic	220–550 mg bid
COMBINATION ANALGESICS		
Acetaminophen, 325 mg, *plus* butalbital, 50 mg	Phrenelin, generic	1–2 tablets; max 6 per day
Acetaminophen, 650 mg, *plus* butalbital, 50 mg	Phrenelin Forte	1 tablet; max 6 per day
Acetaminophen, 325 mg, *plus* butalbital, 50 mg, *plus* caffeine, 40 mg	Fioricet: Esgic, generic	1–2 tablets; max 6 per day
Acetaminophen, 500 mg, *plus* butalbital, 50 mg, *plus* caffeine, 40 mg	Esgicplus	1–2 tablets; max 6 per day
Aspirin, 325 mg, *plus* butalbital, 50 mg, *plus* caffeine, 40 mg	Fiorinal	1–2 tablets; max 6 per day
Aspirin, 650 mg, *plus* butalbital, 50 mg	Axotal	1 tablet q4h; max 6 per day
PROPHYLACTIC MEDICATIONS		
Amitriptyline	Elavil, generic	10–50 mg at bedtime
Doxepin	Sinequan, generic	10–75 mg at bedtime
Nortriptyline	Pamelor, generic	25–75 mg at bedtime

FACIAL PAIN

Most common cause of facial pain is dental; triggered by hot, cold, or sweet foods. Exposure to cold repeatedly induces dental pain.

Trigeminal Neuralgia   Paroxysmal, fleeting, electric shock-like episodes of pain; maxillary distribution of trigeminal nerve more often affected than mandibular. Most cases idiopathic; patients under age 50 at risk for structural cause (multiple sclerosis, vascular anomaly, tumor). Treatment: carbamazepine (400–1600 mg/d) usually effective; phenytoin, baclofen, and valproic acid are other options.

Postherpetic Neuralgia   Pain following skin rash of herpes zoster; may be associated with sensory loss. Pain usually resolves over weeks.

Occipital Neuralgia   Entrapment of greater occipital nerve at exit from skull; unilateral, lancinating occipital pain. Percussion over exit point of greater occipital nerve may elicit symptoms. Treatment: block-injection of steroid and local anesthetic.

For a more detailed discussion, see Raskin NH, Peroutka SJ: Headache, Including Migraine and Cluster Headache, Chap. 15, p. 70, in HPIM- 15.

5

BACK AND NECK PAIN

LOW BACK PAIN

FIVE TYPES OF LOW BACK PAIN (LBP)

- *Local pain*—caused by activation of local, pain-sensitive nerve endings near affected part of the spine (i.e., tears, stretching).
- *Pain referred to the back*—abdominal or pelvic origin; back pain unaffected by spine movement.
- *Pain of spine origin*—restricted to the back or referred to lower limbs. Diseases of upper lumbar spine refer pain to upper lumbar region, groin, or anterior thighs. Diseases of lower lumbar spine refer pain to buttocks or posterior thighs.
- *Radicular pain*—radiates from spine to leg in specific nerve root territory. Coughing, sneezing, lifting heavy objects, or straining may elicit pain.
- *Pain associated with muscle spasm*—diverse origin; accompanied by taut paraspinal muscles.

EXAMINATION   Include abdomen, pelvis, and rectum to search for visceral sources of pain. Inspection may reveal scoliosis or muscle spasm. Palpation may elicit pain over a diseased spine segment. Pain from hip may be confused with spine pain. Manual internal/external rotation of leg at hip (knee and hip in flexion) may reproduce the pain. Straight-leg raising (SLR) sign—elicited by passive flexion of leg on abdomen with knee extended; pt in sitting or supine position; maneuver stretches L5/S1 nerve roots and sciatic nerve passing posterior to the hip; SLR is positive if maneuver reproduces the pain. Crossed SLR sign—positive when SLR on one leg reproduces symptoms in opposite leg or buttocks; nerve/nerve root lesion is on the painful side. Reverse SLR sign—passive extension of leg on trunk with the knee extended and pt prone or standing; maneuver stretches L2-L4 nerve roots and femoral nerve passing anterior to the hip. Neurologic exam—search for focal atrophy, weakness, reflex loss, diminished sensation in a dermatomal distribution. Findings with radiculopathy are summarized in Table 5-1.

LABORATORY STUDIES   "Routine" laboratory studies and lumbar spine x-rays—rarely needed for acute LBP but indicated when risk factors for

Table 5-1

Lumbosacral Radiculopathy—Neurologic Findings

Lubosacral Nerve Roots	Reflex	Sensory	Motor	Pain Distribution
L2[a]	—	Upper anterior thigh	Psoas[b] (hip flexion)	Anterior thigh
L3[a]	—	Lower anterior thigh	Psoas[b] (hip flexion)	Anterior thigh, knee
		Anterior knee	Quadriceps (knee extension)	
			Thigh adduction	
L4[a]	Quadriceps (knee)	Medial calf	Quadriceps[b] (knee extension)	Knee, medial calf
			Thigh adduction	
			Tibialis anterior (foot dorsiflexion)	
L5[c]	—	Dorsal surface—foot	Peronei[b] (foot eversion)	Lateral calf, dorsal foot, posterolateral thigh, buttocks
		Lateral calf	Tibialis anterior (foot dorsiflexion)	
			Gluteus medius (hip abduction)	
			Toe dorsiflexors	
S1[a]	Gastrocnemius/soleus (ankle)	Plantar surface—foot	Gastrocnemius/soleus[b] (foot plantar flexion)	Bottom foot, posterior calf, posterior thigh, buttocks
		Lateral aspect—foot	Abductor hallucis (toe flexors)	
			Gluteus maximus (hip extension)	

[a] Reverse straight-leg raising sign present—see "Examination."
[b] These muscles receive the majority of innervation from the root in the same horizontal row.
[c] Straight-leg raising sign present—see "Examination."

serious underlying disease are present (Table 5-2). MRI and CT-myelography are tests of choice for anatomic definition of spine disease.

ETIOLOGY   *Lumbar Disk Disease*   Common cause of low back and leg pain; usually at L4-L5 or L5-S1 levels. Dermatomal sensory loss, reduction or loss of deep tendon reflexes, or myotomal pattern of weakness more informative than pain pattern for localization. Usually unilateral; bilateral with large central disk herniations compressing multiple nerve roots—may cause cauda equina syndrome. Five possible indications for lumbar disk surgery: (1) progressive motor weakness from nerve root injury, (2) progressive motor impairment by EMG, (3) abnormal bowel or bladder function, (4) incapacitating nerve root pain despite conservative treatment, and (5) recurrent incapacitating pain despite conservative treatment. The latter two criteria are controversial.

Spinal Stenosis   A narrowed spinal canal producing back and bilateral leg pain induced by walking or standing and relieved by sitting. Unlike vascular claudication, symptoms are provoked by standing without walking. Unlike lumbar disk disease, symptoms are relieved by sitting. Focal neurologic deficits common; severe neurologic deficits (paralysis, incontinence) rare. Stenosis results from acquired (75%), congenital, or mixed acquired/congenital factors. Symptomatic treatment adequate for mild disease; surgery indicated when pain interferes with activities of daily living or focal neurologic signs present. Surgery successful in 65–80%; 25% develop recurrent stenosis within 5 years.

Trauma   *Low back strain* or *sprain* used to describe minor, self-limited injuries associated with LBP. *Vertebral fractures* from trauma result in wedging or compression of vertebral bodies; burst fractures involving anterior and posterior spine elements can occur. Neurologic impairment common with vertebral fractures; early treatment produces better outcome. Most common cause of *nontraumatic fracture* is osteoporosis; others are osteomalacia, hyperparathyroidism, hyperthyroidism, multiple myeloma, or metastatic carcinoma; glucocorticoid use may predispose vertebral body to fracture. Clinical context, exam findings, and spine x-rays establish diagnosis.

Table 5-2

Risk Factors for Possible Serious Causes of Acute LBP

HISTORY

Pain worse at rest or at night	Age >50 years
Prior history of cancer	Intravenous drug use
History of chronic infection (esp. pulmonary, urinary tract, or skin)	Glucocorticoid use
History of trauma	Rapidly progressive neurologic deficit

EXAMINATION

Unexplained fever
Unexplained weight loss
Straight-leg raising sign
Percussion tenderness—low spine or costovertebral angle
Abdominal, rectal, or pelvic mass
Rapidly progresive focal neurologic deficit (e.g., sensory loss, leg weakness, asymmetric or absent leg reflexes, abnormal bladder function)

Spondylolisthesis   Slippage of anterior spine forward, leaving posterior elements behind; L4-L5 > L5-S1 levels; can produce LBP or radiculopathy/cauda equina syndrome.

Osteoarthritis   Back pain induced by spine movement. Increases with age; radiologic findings do not correlate with severity of pain. Facet syndrome—radicular symptoms and signs, nerve root compression by unilateral facet hypertrophy. Foraminotomy and facetectomy—long-term pain relief in 80–90%. Loss of intervertebral disk height reduces vertical dimensions of intervertebral foramen; descending pedicle can compress the exiting nerve root.

Vertebral Metastases   Back pain most common neurologic symptom in patients with systemic cancer. Metastatic carcinoma, multiple myeloma, and lymphomas frequently involve spine. LBP may be presenting symptom of cancer; pain typically unrelieved by rest. MRI or CT-myelography demonstrate vertebral body metastasis; disk space is spared.

Vertebral Osteomyelitis   LBP unrelieved by rest; focal spine tenderness, elevated ESR. Primary source of infection (lung, urinary tract, or skin) found in 40%; *Staphylococcus* species most common. Destruction of the vertebral bodies and disk space common. Lumbar spinal epidural abscess presents as back pain and fever; exam may be normal or show radicular findings or cauda equina syndrome; abscess extent best defined by MRI.

Lumbar Arachnoiditis   May follow inflammatory response to local tissue injury within subarachnoid space; fibrosis results in clumping of nerve roots, best seen by MRI; treatment is unsatisfactory.

Immune Disorders   Ankylosing spondylitis, rheumatoid arthritis, Reiter's syndrome, psoriatic arthritis, and chronic inflammatory bowel disease. Ankylosing spondylitis—typically male <40 years with nocturnal back pain; pain unrelieved by rest but improves with exercise.

Osteoporosis   Loss of bone substance resulting from hyperparathyroidism, chronic steroid use, immobilization, or other medical disorders. Sole manifestation may be LBP exacerbated by movement.

Visceral Diseases (Table 5-3)   Pelvis refers pain to sacral region, lower abdomen to lumbar region, upper abdomen to lower thoracic or upper lumbar

Table 5-3

Visceral Causes of Low Back Pain

Stomach (posterior wall)—Gallbladder—gallstones
Pancreas—tumor, cyst, pancreatitis
Retroperitoneal—hemorrhage, tumor, pyelonephritis
Vascular—abdominal aortic aneurysm, renal artery, and vein thrombosis
Colon—colitis, diverticulitis, neoplasm
Uterosacral ligaments—endometriosis, carcinoma
Uterine malposition
Menstrual pain
Neoplastic infiltration of nerves
Radiation neurosis of tumors/nerves
Prostate—carcinoma, prostatitis
Kidney—renal stones, inflammatory disease, neoplasm, infection

region. Local signs are absent; normal movements of the spine are painless. Up to 20% of patients with contained rupture of abdominal aortic aneurysm have isolated LBP.

Other   Chronic LBP with no clear cause; psychiatric disorders, substance abuse may be associated.

℞ TREATMENT

Acute Low Back Pain (ABP)   Pain of <3 months' duration; full recovery occurs in 85%. Management controversial; few well-controlled clinical trials exist. Algorithms presented in Figs. 5-1 and 5-2. Entry begins with adults having < 3 months' activity intolerance due to ABP or back-related leg symptoms. Medical history and physical exam used to search for "risk factors" (Table 5-2); if absent, initial treatment is symptomatic and no diagnostic tests necessary (Fig. 5-1). Spine infections, fractures, tumors, or rapidly progressive neurologic deficits require urgent diagnostic evaluation. Patients with no risk factors and no improvement over 4 weeks are subdivided by the presence/ absence of leg symptoms (Fig. 5-2) and managed accordingly.

Clinical trials do not show benefit from bed rest >2 days. Possible benefits of early activity—cardiovascular conditioning, disk and cartilage nutrition, bone and muscle strength, increased endorphin levels. Studies of traction fail to show benefit. Proof lacking to support acupuncture, ultrasound, diathermy, transcutaneous electrical nerve stimulation, massage, biofeedback, or electrical stimulation. Self-application of ice or heat or use of shoe insoles is optional given low cost and risk; benefit of exercises or posture modification uncertain. Spinal manipulation may lessen pain and improve function; treatment >1 month or in radiculopathy is of unknown value and carries risk. Temporary suspension of activities known to increase mechanical stress on the spine (heavy lifting, straining at stool, prolonged sitting/bending/twisting) may relieve symptoms. Value of education ("back school") in long-term prevention is unclear.

Pharmacologic treatment of ABP includes NSAIDs, acetaminophen, muscle relaxants, and opioids. NSAIDs and acetaminophen are superior to placebo. Muscle relaxants provide short-term benefit (4–7 days), but drowsiness limits use. Opioids are not superior to NSAIDs or acetaminophen in the treatment of ABP. Epidural anesthetics, steroids, opioids, or tricyclic antidepressants are not indicated as initial treatment.

Chronic Low Back Pain (CLBP)   Pain lasting >3 months; differential diagnosis includes most conditions described above. Management is complex and not amenable to a simple algorithmic approach. Treatment based upon identification of underlying cause; when specific cause not found, conservative management necessary. Pharmacologic and comfort measures similar to those described for ABP. Exercise ("work hardening") regimens effective in returning some pts to work, diminishing pain, and improving walking distances.

CLBP causes can be clarified by neuroimaging and neurophysiologic (nerve conduction velocity/EMG) studies; diagnosis of radiculopathy secure when results concordant with findings on neurologic examination. Surgical intervention based upon neuroimaging alone not recommended: 25% of asymptomatic young adults have a herniated lumbar disk by CT or MRI.

NECK AND SHOULDER PAIN

ETIOLOGY   *Trauma to the Cervical Spine*   *Whiplash injury* is due to trauma (usually automobile accidents) causing cervical musculoligamental sprain or strain due to hyperflexion or hyperextension. This diagnosis should

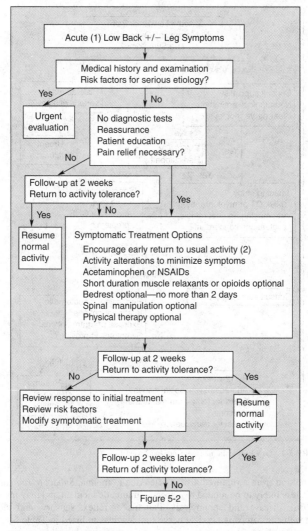

FIGURE 5-1 Low back pain management: first 4 weeks. (1) Adults ≤18 years old, symptoms <3mos. (2) Excluding heavy manual labor.

not be applied to pts with fractures, disk herniation, head injury, or altered consciousness. One study found that 18% of pts with whiplash injury had persistent injury-related symptoms 2 years after the car accident.

Cervical Disk Disease Herniation of a lower cervical disk is a common cause of neck, shoulder, arm, or hand pain. Neck pain (worse with movement), stiffness, and limited range of neck motion are common. With nerve root compression, pain may radiate into a shoulder or arm. Extension and lateral rotation of the neck narrows the intervertebral foramen and may reproduce radicular symptoms (Spurling's sign). In young individuals, acute cervical nerve root

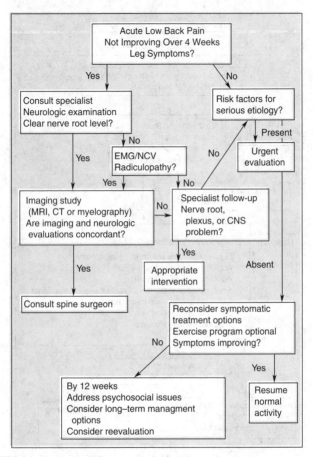

FIGURE 5-2 Low back pain management: 4–12 weeks.

compression from a ruptured disk is often due to trauma. *Subacute radiculopathy* is less likely to be related to a specific traumatic incident and may involve both disk disease and spondylosis. Patterns of reflex, sensory, and motor changes that accompany cervical nerve root lesions are listed in Table 5-4.

Cervical Spondylosis Osteoarthritis of the cervical spine may produce neck pain that radiates into the back of the head, shoulders, or arms; can also be source of headaches in the posterior occipital region. A combined radiculopathy and myelopathy may occur. An electrical sensation elicited by neck flexion and radiating down the spine from the neck (Lhermitte's symptom) usually indicates cervical or upper thoracic spinal cord involvement. MRI or CT-myelography can define the anatomic abnormalities, and EMG and nerve conduction studies can quantify the severity and localize the levels of nerve root injury.

Other Causes of Neck Pain Includes *rheumatoid arthritis* of the cervical apophyseal joints, ankylosing spondylitis, *herpes zoster* (shingles), *neoplasms* metastatic to the cervical spine, *infections* (osteomyelitis and epidural abscess),

Table 5-4

Cervical Radiculopathy—Neurologic Features

Cervical Nerve Roots	Examination Findings			
	Reflex	Motor	Sensory	Pain Distribution
C5	Biceps	Supraspinatus[a] (initial arm abduction) Infraspinatus[a] (arm external rotation) Deltoid[a] (arm abduction) Biceps (arm flexion)	Over lateral deltoid	Lateral arm, medial scapula
C6	Biceps	Biceps (arm flexion) Pronator teres (internal forearm rotation)	Thumb, index fingers Radial hand/forearm	Lateral forearm, thumb, index finger
C7	Triceps	Triceps[a] (arm extension) Wrist extensors[a] Extensor digitorum[a] (finger extension)	Middle fingers Dorsum forearm	Posterior arm, dorsal forearm, lateral hand
C8	Finger flexors	Abductor pollicis brevis (abduction D1) First dorsal interosseous (abduction D2) Abductor digiti minimi (abduction D5)	Little finger Medial hand and forearm	4th and 5th fingers, medial forearm
T1	Finger flexors	Abductor pollicis brevis (abduction D1) First dorsal interosseous (abduction D2) Abductor digiti minimi (abduction D5)	Axilla and medial arm	Medial arm, axilla

[a] These muscles receive the majority of innervation from this root.

and *metabolic bone diseases*. Neck pain may also be referred from the heart in the setting of coronary artery ischemia (cervical angina syndrome).

Thoracic Outlet   The thoracic outlet is an anatomic region containing the first rib, the subclavian artery and vein, the brachial plexus, the clavicle, and the lung apex. Injury to these structures may result in posture- or task-related pain around the shoulder and supraclavicular region. *True neurogenic thoracic outlet syndrome* results from compression of the lower trunk of the brachial plexus by an anomalous band of tissue; treatment consists of surgical division of the band. *Arterial thoracic outlet syndrome* results from compression of the subclavian artery by a cervical rib; treatment is with thrombolyis or anticoagulation, and surgical excision of the cervical rib. *Disputed thoracic outlet syndrome* includes a large number of patients with chronic arm and shoulder pain of unclear cause; surgery is controversial, and treatment often unsuccessful.

Brachial Plexus and Nerves   Pain from injury to the brachial plexus or arm peripheral nerves can mimic pain of cervical spine origin. *Neoplastic infiltration* or *postradiation fibrosis* can produce this syndrome. *Acute brachial neuritis* consists of acute onset of severe shoulder or scapular pain followed over days by weakness of proximal arm and shoulder girdle muscles innervated by the upper brachial plexus; onset often preceded by an infection or immunization. Complete recovery occurs in 75% of pts after 2 years and in 89% after 3 years.

Shoulder   If signs of radiculopathy are absent, differential diagnosis includes mechanical shoulder pain (tendonitis, bursitis, rotator cuff tear, dislocation, adhesive capsulitis, and cuff impingement under the acromion) and referred pain (subdiaphragmatic irritation, angina, Pancoast tumor). Mechanical pain is often worse at night, associated with shoulder tenderness, and aggravated by abduction, internal rotation, or extension of the arm.

 TREATMENT

Symptomatic treatment of neck pain includes analgesic medications and/or a soft cervical collar. Indications for cervical disk and lumbar disk surgery are similar; however, with cervical disease an aggressive approach is indicated if spinal cord injury is threatened. Surgery of *cervical herniated disks* consists of an anterior approach with diskectomy followed by anterior interbody fusion; a simple posterior partial laminectomy with diskectomy is an acceptable alternative. The cumulative risk of subsequent radiculopathy or myelopathy at cervical segments adjacent to the fusion is 3% per year and 26% per decade. *Nonprogressive cervical radiculopathy* (associated with a focal neurologic deficit) due to a herniated cervical disk may be treated conservatively with a high rate of success. *Cervical spondylosis* with bony, compressive cervical radiculopathy is generally treated with surgical decompression to interrupt the progression of neurologic signs; *spondylotic myelopathy* is managed with anterior decompression and fusion or laminectomy.

For more detailed discussion, see Engstrom JW: Back and Neck Pain, Chap. 16, p. 79, in HPIM-15.

6

FEVER, HYPERTHERMIA, CHILLS, AND RASH

Fever and Hyperthermia

Fever is an abnormal elevation of body temperature due to a change in the hypothalamic thermoregulatory center. Although "normal" temperature is said to be 37°C, the maximal normal temperature ranges from 37.2°C (98.9°F) at 6 A.M. to 37.7°C (99.9°F) at 4 P.M. Rectal temperatures are generally 0.4°C (0.7°F) higher than oral readings. Fever is caused by a resetting of the hypothalamic "set point" by prostaglandins (especially PGE_2), a process mediated by cytokines. Fever may result from infection, immune phenomena, vascular inflammation or thrombosis, infarction or trauma, granulomatous diseases (e.g., sarcoid), inflammatory bowel disease, neoplasms (especially Hodgkin's disease, lymphoma, leukemia, renal cell carcinoma, and hepatoma), or acute metabolic disorders (e.g., thyroid crisis, Addisonian crisis).

Hyperthermia is an uncontrolled increase in body temperature that exceeds the body's ability to lose heat without an elevation of the hypothalamic set point. Hyperthermia without fever may result from failure to dissipate body heat adequately (e.g., in a hot environment) or from drugs (e.g., neuroleptic malignant syndrome caused by phenothiazines and other neuroleptics, malignant hyperthermia caused by inhalation anesthetics or succinylcholine in genetically susceptible individuals).

CLINICAL MANIFESTATIONS   In addition to an elevated body temperature, patients with fever may develop generalized symptoms such as myalgias, arthralgias, anorexia, and somnolence. Chills—a sensation of cold—occur with most fevers. Rigors—profound chills—are associated with piloerection, chattering of the teeth, and severe shivering. Sweats accompany the activation of heat-loss mechanisms. Alterations in mental status, including delirium and convulsions, are most common among the very young, the very old, and the debilitated. Rash may occur with fever and may indicate a localized skin eruption or a systemic disease. The distinctive appearance of an eruption in association with a clinical syndrome may facilitate prompt diagnosis and treatment.

DIAGNOSIS   Few signs and symptoms in medicine suggest as many diagnostic possibilities as fever; thus a careful clinical evaluation is necessary. A detailed history must be obtained, including present illness and medical, social, travel, and family history. A meticulous physical exam must be performed and repeated on a regular basis. When rash accompanies fever, special attention should be given to the onset, configuration, arrangement, and distribution of the lesions. (For a more detailed description of systemic illnesses with fever and rash, see Table 18-1 in HPIM-15.) The lab workup must be individualized in light of the clinical circumstances. It should always include a CBC with differential and examination of any abnormal fluid collection (joint, pleural fluid). Other tests to consider include ESR determination, UA, LFTs, and cultures of blood, urine, sputum, or stool. Radiologic tests may include plain radiography, MRI and CT scanning (for detection of abscesses), and radionuclide scanning (esp. tagged WBC scanning). If no diagnosis can be made on the basis of less invasive tests, tissue must be obtained for biopsy, particularly from any abnormal organ; bone marrow biopsy may be useful, esp. for pts with anemia.

Table 6-1

Categories of FUO[a]

Feature	Category of FUO			
	Nosocomial	Neutropenic	HIV-Associated	Classic
Patient's situation	Hospitalized, acute care, no infection when admitted	Neutrophil count either <500/μL or expected to reach that level in 1–2 d	Confirmed HIV-positive	All others with fevers for ≥3 weeks
Duration of illness while under investigation	3 d[b]	3 d[b]	3 d[b] (or 4 weeks as outpatient)	3 d[b] or three outpatient visits
Examples of cause	Septic thrombophlebitis, sinusitis, *Clostridium difficile* colitis, drug fever	Perianal infection, aspergillosis, candidemia	MAI[c] infection, tuberculosis, non-Hodgkin's lymphoma, drug fever	Infections, malignancy, inflammatory diseases, drug fever

[a] All require temperatures of ≥38.3°C (101°F) on several occasions.
[b] Includes at least 2 days' incubation of microbiology cultures.
[c] *M. avium/M. intracellulare.*

SOURCE: J Gelfand: HPIM-15, p. 805 [modified from DT Durack, AC Street in JS Remington, MN Swartz (eds): Current Clinical Topics in Infectious Diseases. Cambridge, MA, Blackwell, 1991].

Fever of Unknown Origin (FUO)

Classic FUO is diagnosed when fever of >38.3°C (101°F) develops on several occasions over the course of >3 weeks and when 1 week of study in the hospital or three outpatient visits fail to result in a diagnosis. Most cases of FUO are due to infection, neoplasm, or collagen-vascular disease. Other causes include drugs, granulomatous diseases, inflammatory bowel disease, pulmonary embolism, factitious fever, erythema multiforme, familial Mediterranean fever, Behçet's syndrome, and Fabry's disease. FUO prolonged beyond 6 months is much less commonly due to infection and more often due to unusual or undetermined causes. When no cause can be identified, the prognosis is usually favorable. Treatment for classic FUO consists of continued observation and examination with avoidance of empirical therapy. Other specialized categories of FUO have been established for certain populations of pts (Table 6-1), with variations in diagnosis and treatment.

R̲x̲ TREATMENT

The first decision to make is whether an elevation in body temperature reflects fever or hyperthermia. The objectives in treating fever are to reduce the elevated hypothalamic set point and to facilitate heat loss. There is no evidence that fever itself facilitates recovery from infection. Low-grade or mild fevers do not necessarily require treatment except in pregnant women, children with febrile seizures, or pts with impaired cardiac, pulmonary, or cerebral function. High fever (>41°C) should be managed with antipyretics and with physical cooling with a cooling blanket or sponge bath. Acetaminophen (0.65 g) given every 3 h around the clock (rather than intermittently, which aggravates symptoms of sweats and chills) is effective for the management of most fever and is preferred because it does not (1) mask signs of inflammation that might indicate a cause of the fever, (2) impair platelet function, or (3) cause Reye's syndrome in children. NSAIDs and aspirin have anti-inflammatory as well as antipyretic effects. NSAIDs may be particularly useful in the management of fever due to malignancy.

By definition, hyperthermia does not respond to attempts to reset the already-normal hypothalamic set point (e.g., with acetaminophen) but does respond to physical cooling with measures such as sponging, fans, cooling blankets, and even ice baths. These measures should be instituted immediately in hyperthermia, and IV fluids should be administered. If insufficient cooling is achieved with these methods, gastric or peritoneal lavage with iced saline can be initiated; in extreme circumstances, hemodialysis or cardiopulmonary bypass with cooling of the blood can be undertaken. Malignant hyperthermia, neuroleptic malignant syndrome, drug-induced hyperthermia, and perhaps hyperthermia due to thyrotoxicosis respond to dantrolene (1–2.5 mg/kg IV q6h). Procainamide should be administered to pts with malignant hyperthermia because of the high risk of ventricular fibrillation in this syndrome.

For a more detailed discussion, see Dinarello CA, Gelfand JA: Fever and Hyperthermia, Chap. 17, p. 91; Kaye ET, Kaye KM: Fever and Rash, Chap. 18, p. 95; and Gelfand JA: Fever of Unknown Origin, Chap. 125, p. 804, in HPIM-15.

7

PAIN OR SWELLING OF JOINTS

Musculoskeletal complaints are extremely common in outpatient medical practice and are among the leading causes of disability and absenteeism from work. Pain in the joints must be evaluated in a uniform, thorough, and logical fashion to ensure the best chance of accurate diagnosis and to plan appropriate follow-up testing and therapy. Joint pain and swelling may be manifestations of disorders affecting primarily the musculoskeletal system or may reflect systemic disease.

Goals for the Initial Assessment of a Musculoskeletal Complaint   (See Fig. 7-1)

1. *Articular versus nonarticular.* Is the pain located in a joint or in a periarticular structure such as soft tissue or muscle?
2. *Inflammatory versus noninflammatory.* Inflammatory disease is suggested by local signs of inflammation (erythema, warmth, swelling), systemic features (morning stiffness, fatigue, fever, weight loss), or laboratory evidence of inflammation (thrombocytosis, elevated ESR or C-reactive protein).
3. *Acute (6 weeks or less) versus chronic.*
4. *Localized versus systemic.*

Historic Features

* Age, sex, race, and family history.
* Duration of symptoms: acute versus chronic.
* Number and distribution of involved structures: monarticular (one joint), oligoarticular (2–3 joints), polyarticular (>3 joints); symmetry.
* Other articular features: morning stiffness, effect of movement, features that improve/worsen Sx, migratory pain, Sx intermittent/continuous.
* Extraarticular Sx: e.g., fever, rash, weight loss, visual change, dyspnea, diarrhea, dysuria, numbness, weakness.
* Recent events: e.g., trauma, drug administration, travel, other illnesses.

Physical Examination

Complete examination is essential: particular attention to skin, mucous membranes, nails (may reveal characteristic pitting in psoriasis), eyes. Careful and thorough examination of involved and uninvolved joints and periarticular structures; this should proceed in an organized fashion from head to foot or from extremities inward toward axial skeleton; special attention should be paid to identifying the presence or absence of:

* Warmth and/or erythema
* Swelling
* Synovial thickening
* Subluxation, dislocation, joint deformity
* Joint instability
* Limitations to active and passive range of motion
* Crepitus
* Periarticular changes
* Muscular changes including weakness, atrophy

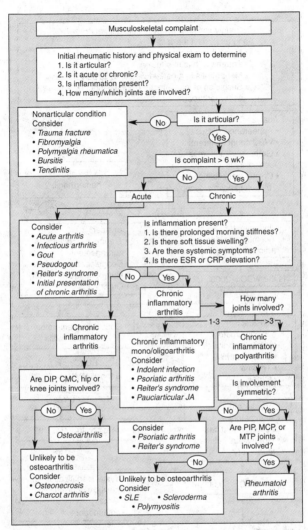

FIGURE 7-1 Algorithm for the diagnosis of musculoskeletal complaints. An approach to formulating a differential diagnosis (shown in italics). (ESR, erythrocyte sedimentation rate; CRP, C-reactive protein, DIP, distal interphalangeal; CMC, carpometacarpal; PIP, proximal interphalangeal; MCP, metacarpophalangeal; MTP, metatarsophalangeal; PMR, polymyalgia rheumatica; SLE, systemic lupus erythematosus; JA, juvenile arthritis.)

Laboratory Investigations

Additional evaluation usually indicated for monarticular, traumatic, inflammatory, or chronic conditions or for conditions accompanied by neurologic changes or systemic manifestations.

- For all evaluations: include CBC, ESR, or C-reactive protein.
- Should be performed where there are suggestive clinical features: rheumatoid factor, ANA, ANCA, antistreptolysin O titer, Lyme antibodies.

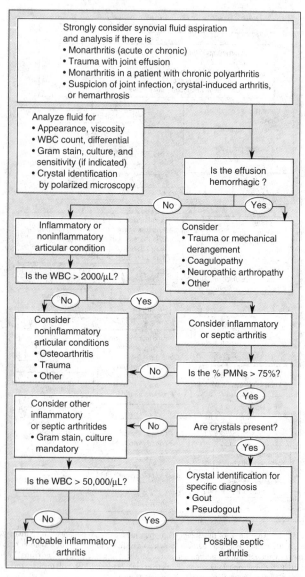

FIGURE 7-2 Algorithmic approach to the use and interpretation of synovial fluid aspiration and analysis.

- Where systemic disease is present or suspected: renal/hepatic function tests, UA.
- Uric acid—useful only when gout diagnosed and therapy contemplated.
- CPK, aldolase—consider with muscle pain, weakness.
- Synovial fluid aspiration and analysis: always indicated for acute monarthritis or when infectious or crystal-induced arthropathy is suspected. Should

be examined for (1) appearance, viscosity; (2) cell count and differential (suspect septic joint if WBC count $> 50,000/\mu L$); (3) crystals using polarizing microscope; (4) Gram's stain, cultures (Fig. 7-2).

Diagnostic Imaging

Plain radiographs should be considered for

- Trauma
- Suspected chronic infection
- Progressive disability
- Monarticular involvement
- Baseline assessment of a chronic process
- When therapeutic alterations are considered

Additional imaging procedures, including ultrasound, radionuclide scintigraphy, CT, and MRI, may be helpful in selected clinical settings.

Special Considerations in the Elderly Patient

The evaluation of joint and musculoskeletal disorders in the elderly pt presents a special challenge given the frequently insidious onset and chronicity of disease in this age group, the confounding effect of other medical conditions, and the increased variability of many diagnostic tests in the geriatric population. Although virtually all musculoskeletal conditions may afflict the elderly, certain disorders are especially frequent. Special attention should be paid to identifying the potential rheumatic consequences of intercurrent medical conditions and therapies when evaluating the geriatric pt with musculoskeletal complaints.

For a more detailed discussion, see Cush JJ, Lipsky PE: Approach to Articular and Musculoskeletal Disorders, Chap. 320, p. 1994, in HPIM-15.

SYNCOPE AND FAINTNESS

Syncope is defined as transient loss of consciousness due to reduced cerebral blood flow. Syncope is associated with postural collapse and spontaneous recovery. It may occur suddenly, without warning, or may be preceded by presyncopal symptoms such as lightheadedness, weakness, nausea, dimming vision, ringing in ears, or sweating. *Faintness* refers to prodromal symptoms that precede the loss of consciousness in syncope. The syncopal pt appears pale, has a faint, rapid, or irregular pulse, and breathing may be almost imperceptible; transient (5–10 s) myoclonic or clonic movements may occur. Recovery of consciousness is prompt if the pt is maintained in a horizontal position and cerebral perfusion is restored.

Features Distinguishing Syncope from Seizure

The differential diagnosis is often between syncope and a generalized, convulsive seizure. Syncope is more likely if the event was provoked by acute pain or anxiety or occurred immediately after arising from a lying or sitting position. Seizures are typically not related to posture. Pts with syncope often describe a stereotyped transition from consciousness to unconsciousness that develops over a few seconds. Seizures occur either very abruptly without a transition or are preceded by premonitory symptoms such as an epigastric rising sensation, perception of odd odors, or racing thoughts. Pallor is seen during syncope; cyanosis is usually seen during a seizure. The duration of unconsciousness is usually very brief (i.e., seconds) in syncope and more prolonged (i.e., >5 min) in a seizure. Injury from falling and incontinence are common in seizure, rare in syncope. Headache and drowsiness, which with mental confusion are the usual sequelae of a seizure, do not follow a syncopal attack.

Etiology

Transiently decreased cerebral blood flow is usually due to one of three general mechanisms: disorders of vascular tone or blood volume, cardiovascular disorders including cardiac arrhythmias, or cerebrovascular disease (Table 8-1). Disorders of vascular tone or blood volume, including vasovagal syncope and postural hypotension, are responsible for more than one-half of syncopal episodes in general practice. Not infrequently the cause of syncope is multifactorial.

Approach to the Patient

The cause of syncope may be apparent only at the time of the event, leaving few, if any, clues when the pt is seen by the physician. It is important to first consider causes that represent serious underlying etiologies; among these are massive internal hemorrhage or myocardial infarction, which may be painless, and cardiac arrhythmias. In elderly persons, a sudden faint without obvious cause should arouse the suspicion of complete heart block or a tachyarrhythmia, even if all findings are negative when the pt is seen. Loss of consciousness in particular situations, such as during venipuncture or micturition, suggests an abnormality of vascular tone. The position of the pt at the time of the syncopal episode is very important; syncope in the supine position is unlikely to be vasovagal and suggests an arrhythmia or a seizure. Medications must be considered, including nonprescription drugs or health store supplements, with particular attention to recent changes. An algorithmic approach to syncope is presented in Fig. 8-1.

R⃟ TREATMENT

Therapy is determined by the underlying cause. Pts with vasovagal syncope should be instructed to avoid situations or stimuli that provoke attacks. Episodes associated with intravascular volume depletion may be prevented by salt and fluid preloading. β-Adrenergic antagonists are the most widely used agents; the vagolytic drugs disopyramide and transdermal scopolamine are often useful. Other possible drugs include the serotonin reuptake inhibitor paroxetine, theophylline, and ephedrine. Permanent cardiac pacing is effective for pts whose episodes are frequent or associated with prolonged asystole. Pts with orthostatic hypotension should be instructed to rise slowly from the bed or chair and to move legs prior to rising to facilitate venous return from the extremities. Medications that aggravate the problem should be discontinued when possible. Other useful treatments may include elevation of the head of the bed, elastic stockings, antigravity or g suits, salt loading, and pharmacologic agents such as sympathomimetic amines, monomine oxidase inhibitors, and beta blockers.

Table 8-1
_____

Causes of Syncope
_____

 I. Disorders of vascular tone or blood volume
    A. Vasovagal (vasodepressor, neurocardiogenic)
    B. Postural (orthostatic) hypotension
       1. Drug-induced (especially antihypertensive or vasodilator drugs)
       2. Peripheral neuropathy (diabetic, alcoholic, nutritional, amyloid)
       3. Idiopathic postural hypotension
       4. Multisystem atrophies
       5. Physical deconditioning
       6. Sympathectomy
       7. Acute dysautonomia (Guillain-Barré syndrome variant)
       8. Decreased blood volume (adrenal insufficiency, acute blood loss, etc.)
    C. Carotid sinus hypersensitivity
    D. Situational
       1. Cough
       2. Micturition
       3. Defecation
       4. Valsalva
       5. Deglutition
    E. Glossopharyngeal neuralgia
 II. Cardiovascular disorders
    A. Cardiac arrhythmias
       1. Bradyarrhythmias
          a. Sinus bradycardia, sinoatrial block, sinus arrest, sick-sinus syndrome
          b. Atrioventricular block
       2. Tachyarrhythmias
          a. Supraventricular tachycardia with structural cardiac disease
          b. Atrial fibrillation associated with the Wolff-Parkinson-White syndrome
          c. Atrial flutter with 1:1 atrioventricular conduction
          d. Ventricular tachycardia
    B. Other cardiopulmonary etiologies
       1. Pulmonary embolism
       2. Pulmonary hypertension
       3. Atrial myxoma
       4. Myocardial disease (massive myocardial infarction)
       5. Left ventricular myocardial restriction or constriction
       6. Pericardial constriction or tamponade
       7. Aortic outflow tract obstruction
       8. Aortic valvular stenosis
       9. Hypertrophic obstructive cardiomyopathy
III. Cerebrovascular disease
    A. Vertebrobasilar insufficiency
    B. Basilar artery migraine
IV. Other disorders that may resemble syncope
    A. Metabolic
       1. Hypoxia
       2. Anemia
       3. Diminished carbon dioxide due to hyperventilation
       4. Hypoglycemia
    B. Psychogenic
       1. Anxiety attacks
       2. Hysterical fainting
    C. Seizures
_____

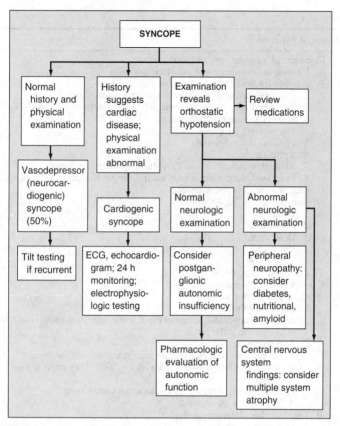

FIGURE 8-1 Approach to the patient with syncope.

For a more detailed discussion, see Daroff RB, Carlson MD: Faintness, Syncope, Dizziness, and Vertigo, Chap. 21, p. 111, in HPIM-15.

DIZZINESS AND VERTIGO

Patients use the term *dizziness* to describe a variety of head sensations or gait unsteadiness. With a careful history, symptoms can be placed into more specific neurologic categories, of which faintness and vertigo are the most important.

FAINTNESS Faintness is usually described as light-headedness followed by visual blurring and postural swaying. It is a symptom of insufficient blood, oxygen, or, rarely, glucose supply to the brain. It can occur prior to a syncopal event of any etiology (Chap. 8) and with hyperventilation or hypoglycemia. Lightheadedness can also occur as an aura before a seizure. Chronic light-headedness is a common somatic complaint in patients with depression.

VERTIGO Vertigo is an illusion of movement, most commonly a sensation of spinning. It is usually due to a disturbance in the vestibular system; abnormalities in the visual or somatosensory systems may also contribute to vertigo. *Physiologic vertigo* results from unfamiliar head movement (seasickness) or a mismatch between visual-proprioceptive-vestibular system inputs (height vertigo, visual vertigo). True vertigo almost never occurs in the presyncopal state.

Pathologic Vertigo

Frequently accompanied by nausea, postural unsteadiness, and gait ataxia, vertigo is provoked or worsened by head movement. May be caused by a peripheral (labyrinth or eighth nerve) or central CNS lesion. Distinguishing between peripheral and central causes is the essential first step in diagnosis (Table 9-1).

PERIPHERAL VERTIGO Usually severe, accompanied by nausea and emesis. Tinnitus, a feeling of ear fullness, or hearing loss may occur. The pt

Table 9-1

Differentiation of Peripheral and Central Vertigo

Sign or Symptom	Peripheral (Labyrinth)	Central (Brainstem or Cerebellum)
Direction of associated nystagmus	Unidirectional; fast phase opposite lesion[a]	Bidirectional or unidirectional
Purely horizontal nystagmus without torsional component	Uncommon	Common
Vertical or purely torsional nystagmus	Never present	May be present
Visual fixation	Inhibits nystagmus and vertigo	No inhibition
Severity of vertigo	Marked	Often mild
Direction of spin	Toward fast phase	Variable
Direction of fall	Toward slow phase	Variable
Duration of symptoms	Finite (minutes, days, weeks) but recurrent	May be chronic
Tinnitus and/or deafness	Often present	Usually absent
Associated central abnormalities	None	Extremely common
Common causes	Infection (labyrinthitis), Ménière's, neuronitis, ischemia, trauma, toxin	Vascular, demyelinating, neoplasm

[a] In Ménière's disease, the direction of the fast phase is variable.

may be pale and diaphoretic. A characteristic jerk nystagmus is almost always present. The nystagmus does not change direction with a change in direction of gaze, it is horizontal with a torsional component and has its fast phase to side of normal ear. It is inhibited by visual fixation. The pt senses spinning motion in direction of slow phase and falls or mispoints to that side. No other neurologic abnormalities are present.

Acute unilateral labyrinthine dysfunction may be caused by infection, trauma, or ischemia. Often no specific etiology is uncovered, and the nonspecific term *acute labyrinthitis* (or *vestibular neuronitis*) is used to describe the event. The attacks are brief and leave the patient for some days with a mild positional vertigo; recurrent episodes may occur. *Acute bilateral labyrinthine dysfunction* is usually due to drugs (aminoglycoside antibiotics) or alcohol. *Recurrent labyrinthine dysfunction* with signs of cochlear disease is usually due to *Ménière's disease* (recurrent vertigo accompanied by tinnitus and deafness). Positional vertigo is usually precipitated by a recumbant head position. *Benign paroxysmal positional vertigo* (BPPV) of the posterior semicircular canal is particularly common; the pattern of nystagmus is distinctive (Table 9-2). BPPV may follow trauma but is usually idiopathic; it generally abates spontaneously after weeks or months. *Schwannomas* of the eighth cranial nerve (acoustic neuroma) usually present as auditory symptoms of hearing loss and tinnitus, sometimes accompanied by facial weakness and sensory loss due to involvement of cranial nerves VII and V. *Psychogenic vertigo* should be suspected in pts with chronic incapacitating vertigo who also have agoraphobia, a normal neurologic exam, and no nystagmus.

CENTRAL VERTIGO   Identified by associated abnormal brainstem or cerebellar signs such as dysarthria, diplopia, paresthesia, headache, weakness, limb ataxia. The nystagmus can take almost any form, i.e., vertical or multidirectional, but is never purely horizontal without a torsional component. Central nystagmus is not inhibited by fixation. Central vertigo may be chronic, mild, and is often unaccompanied by tinnitus or hearing loss. It is usually a sign of brainstem dysfunction and may be due to demyelinating, vascular, or neoplastic disease. Rarely, it occurs as a manifestation of temporal lobe epilepsy.

——————————— *Approach to the Patient* ———————————

The "dizzy" patient usually requires provocative tests to reproduce the symptoms. Valsalva maneuver, hyperventilation, or postural changes may reproduce faintness. Rapid rotation in a swivel chair is a simple provocative test to repro-

Table 9-2

Benign Paroxysmal Positional Vertigo (BPPV) and Central Positional Vertigo

Features	BPPV	Central
Latency[a]	3–40 s	None: immediate vertigo and nystagmus
Fatigability[b]	Yes	No
Habituation[c]	Yes	No
Intensity of vertigo	Severe	Mild
Reproducibility[d]	Variable	Good

[a] Time between attaining head position and onset of symptoms.
[b] Disappearance of symptoms with maintenance of offending position.
[c] Lessening of symptoms with repeated trials.
[d] Likelihood of symptom production during any examination session.

Table 9-3

Treatment of Vertigo	
Agent	Dose[a]
Antihistamines	
Meclizine	25–50 mg 3 times/day
Dimenhydrinate	50 mg 1–2 times/day
Promethazine[b]	25–50 mg/d
Anticholinergic[c]	
Scopolamine transdermal patch	1.5 mg over 3 days
Sympathomimetic	
Ephedrine	25 mg/d
Benzodiazepine	
Diazepam	2.5 mg 1–3 times/day
Combination preparation	
Ephedrine and promethazine	25 mg/d of each
Exercise therapy	
Repositioning maneuvers[d]	
Vestibular rehabilitation[e]	
Other	
Diuretics or low-salt (1 g/d) diet[f]	
Inner ear surgery[g]	

[a] Usual starting dose in adults; maintenance dose can be increased by a factor of 2–3.
[b] Also has strong antiemetic effect.
[c] For motion sickness only.
[d] For benign paroxysmal positional vertigo.
[e] For vertigo other than Ménière's and positional.
[f] For Ménière's disease.
[g] For refractory cases of Ménière's disease.

duce vertigo. Benign positional vertigo is identified by positioning the turned head of a recumbent patient in extension over the edge of the bed to elicit vertigo and the characteristic nystagmus. If a vestibular nerve or central cause for the vertigo is suspected (e.g., signs of peripheral vertigo are absent or other neurologic abnormalities are present), then prompt evaluation for central pathology is indicated, including an MRI scan of the posterior fossa and possibly electronystagmography, evoked potential tests, or vertebrobasilar angiography.

 TREATMENT

Treatment of acute vertigo consists of bed rest and vestibular suppressant drugs (Table 9-3). If the vertigo persists more than a few days, most authorities advise ambulation in an attempt to induce central compensatory mechanisms. BPPV may respond to specific repositioning exercises such as the Epley procedure (*www.charite.de/ch/neuro/vertigo.html*). Ménière's disease may respond to a low-salt diet (1 g/d) or to a diuretic.

For a more detailed discussion, see Daroff RB, Carlson MD: Faintness, Syncope, Dizziness, and Vertigo, Chap. 21, p. 111, in HPIM-15.

10

ACUTE VISUAL LOSS AND DOUBLE VISION

Clinical Assessment

Accurate measurement of visual acuity in each eye (with glasses) is of primary importance. Additional assessments include testing of pupils, eye movements, ocular alignment, and visual fields. Slit-lamp examination can exclude corneal infection, trauma, glaucoma, uveitis, and cataract. Ophthalmoscopic exam to inspect the optic disc and retina often requires pupillary dilation using 1% topicamide and 2.5% phenylephrine; the risk of provoking an attack of narrow-angle glaucoma is remote.

Visual field mapping by finger confrontation permits localization of lesions in the visual pathway (Fig. 10-1); formal testing using a perimeter may be necessary. The goal is to determine whether the lesion is anterior, at, or posterior to the optic chiasm. A scotoma confined to one eye is caused by an anterior lesion affecting the optic nerve or globe; the swinging flashlight test may reveal an afferent pupil defect. History and ocular exam are usually sufficient for diagnosis. If a bitemporal hemianopia is present, the lesion is located at the optic chiasm (e.g., pituitary adenoma, meningioma). Homonymous visual field loss signals a retrochiasmal lesion, affecting the optic tract, lateral geniculate body, optic radiations, or visual cortex (e.g., stroke, tumor, abscess). Neuroimaging is recommended for any pt with a bitemporal or homonymous hemianopia.

Transient or Sudden Visual Loss

Amaurosis fugax or *transient monocular blindness* usually occurs from a retinal embolus or severe ipsilateral carotid stenosis. Prolonged occlusion of the central retinal artery results in the classic fundus appearance of a milky, infarcted retina with a cherry-red fovea. Any pt with compromise of the retinal circulation should be evaluated promptly for stroke factors (e.g., carotid atheromata, heart disease, atrial fibrillation). *Vertebrobasilar insufficiency* or emboli can be confused with amaurosis fugax, because many pts mistakenly ascribe symptoms to their left or right eye, when in fact they are occurring in the left or right hemifield of both eyes. Interruption of blood flow to the visual cortex causes sudden graying of vision, occasionally with flashing lights or other symptoms that mimic *migraine*. The history may be the only guide to the correct diagnosis. Pts should be questioned about the precise pattern and duration of visual loss and about other neurologic symptoms such as diplopia, vertigo, numbness, or weakness, which may help decide between compromise of the anterior or posterior cerebral circulation.

Malignant hypertension can cause visual loss from exudates, hemorrhages, cotton-wool spots (focal nerve fiber layer infarcts), and optic disc edema. In central or branch retinal vein occlusion, the fundus exam reveals engorged, dusky veins with extensive retinal bleeding. In age-related macular degeneration, characterized by extensive drusen and scarring of the pigment epithelium, leakage of blood or fluid from subretinal neovascular membranes can produce sudden central visual loss. Flashing lights and floaters may indicate a fresh vitreous detachment. Separation of the vitreous from the retina is a frequent involutional event in the elderly. It is not harmful unless it creates sufficient traction to produce a retinal detachment. Vitreous hemorrhage may occur in diabetic patients from retinal neovascularization.

Papilledema refers to bilateral optic disc edema from raised intracranial pressure. Transient visual obscurations are common, but visual acuity is not

OPTIC NERVE OR RETINA

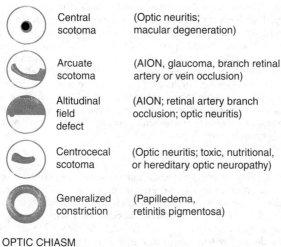

Central scotoma — (Optic neuritis; macular degeneration)

Arcuate scotoma — (AION, glaucoma, branch retinal artery or vein occlusion)

Altitudinal field defect — (AION; retinal artery branch occlusion; optic neuritis)

Centrocecal scotoma — (Optic neuritis; toxic, nutritional, or hereditary optic neuropathy)

Generalized constriction — (Papilledema, retinitis pigmentosa)

OPTIC CHIASM

Left   Right

Bitemporal hemianopia — (Optic chiasm compression by pituitary tumor, meningioma)

RETRO-CHIASMAL PATHWAY

Right homonymous hemianopia — (Lesion of left optic tract, lateral geniculate body, optic radiations, or visual cortex)

Superior right quadrantopia ("Pie in the Sky") — (Lesion of left optic radiations in temporal lobe)

Macular sparing — (Bilateral visual cortex lesions)

FIGURE 10-1   Deficits in visual fields caused by lesions affecting visual pathways.

affected unless the papilledema is severe, long-standing, or accompanied by macular exudates or hemorrhage. Neuroimaging should be obtained to exclude an intracranial mass. If negative, an LP is required to confirm elevation of the intracranial pressure. *Pseudotumor cerebri* (idiopathic intracranial hypertension) is a diagnosis of exclusion. Most pts are young, female, and obese; some are found to have occult cerebral venous sinus thrombosis. Treatment is with weight loss, acetazolamide, and repeated LPs; some pts require lumboperitoneal shunting or optic nerve sheath fenestration. *Optic neuritis* is a common cause of monocular optic disc swelling and visual loss, although it rarely affects both eyes. If the site of inflammation is retrobulbar, the fundus will appear normal on initial exam. The typical pt is female, aged 15–45, with pain provoked by eye movements. Glucocorticoids, consisting of intravenous methylprednisolone followed by oral prednisone (Table 187-3), may hasten recovery in severely affected patients. If an MR scan shows multiple demyelinating plaques, treatment for multiple sclerosis should be considered. *Anterior ischemic optic neuropathy* (AION) is an infarction of the optic nerve head due to inadequate perfusion via the posterior ciliary arteries. Pts have sudden visual loss, often upon awakening, and painless swelling of the optic disc. It is important to differentiate between nonarteritic (idiopathic) AION and arteritic AION. The latter is caused by *temporal arteritis* and requires immediate glucocorticoid therapy. The ESR should be checked in any elderly pt with acute optic disc swelling or symptoms suggestive of polymyalgia rheumatica.

Diplopia

If the pt has diplopia while being examined, motility testing will usually reveal a deficiency in ocular excursions. However, if the degree of angular separation between the double images is small, the limitation of eye movements may be subtle and difficult to detect. In this situation, the cover test is useful. While the pt is fixating upon a distant target, one eye is covered while observing the other eye for a movement of redress as it takes up fixation. If none is seen, the procedure is repeated upon the fellow eye. With genuine diplopia, this test should reveal ocular malalignment, especially if the head is turned or tilted in the position that gives rise to the worst symptoms.

The most frequent causes of diplopia are summarized in Table 10-1. The physical findings in isolated ocular motor nerve palsies are:

- CN III: Ptosis and deviation of the eye down and outwards, causing vertical and horizontal diplopia. Pupil dilation suggests direct compression of the

Table 10-1

Common Causes of Diplopia

Brainstem stroke (skew deviation, nuclear or fascicular palsy)
Microvascular infarction (III, IV, VI nerve palsy)
Tumor (brainstem, cavernous sinus, superior orbital fissure, orbit)
Multiple sclerosis (internuclear ophthalmoplegia, ocular motor nerve palsy)
Aneurysm (III nerve)
Raised intracranial pressure (VI nerve)
Postviral inflammation
Meningitis (bacterial, fungal, granulomatosis, neoplastic)
Carotid-cavernous fistula or thrombosis
Herpes zoster
Tolosa-Hunt syndrome
Wernicke-Korsakoff syndrome
Botulism
Myasthenia gravis
Guillain-Barré or Fisher syndrome
Graves' disease
Orbital pseudotumor
Orbital myositis
Trauma
Orbital cellulitis

third nerve; if present, the possibility of an aneurysm of the posterior communicating artery must be considered urgently.
- CN IV: Vertical diplopia with cyclotorsion; the affected eye is slightly elevated, and limitation of depression is seen when the eye is held in adduction. The pt may assume a head tilt to the opposite side (e.g., left head tilt in right fourth nerve paresis).
- CN VI: Horizontal diplopia with crossed eyes; the affected eye cannot abduct.

Isolated ocular motor nerve palsies often occur in pts with hypertension or diabetes. They usually resolve spontaneously over several months. The apparent occurrence of multiple ocular motor nerve palsies, or diffuse ophthalmoplegia, raises the possibility of myasthenia gravis. In this disease, the pupils are always normal. Systemic weakness may be absent. Diplopia that cannot be explained by a single ocular motor nerve palsy may also be caused by carcinomatous or fungal meningitis, Graves' disease, Guillain-Barré syndrome, Fisher's syndrome, or Tolosa-Hunt syndrome.

For a more detailed discussion, see Horton JC: Disorders of the Eye, Chap. 28, p. 164, in HPIM-15.

11

PARALYSIS AND MOVEMENT DISORDERS

PARALYSIS OR WEAKNESS

GENERAL CONSIDERATIONS The loss of power or control of voluntary muscle is usually described by pts as "weakness" or as some difficulty that can be interpreted as "loss of dexterity." The diagnostic approach to such a problem begins by determining which part of the nervous system is involved. It is important to distinguish weakness arising from disorders of upper motor neurons (i.e., motor neurons in the cerebral cortex and their axons that descend through the subcortical white matter, internal capsule, brainstem, and spinal cord) from that arising from disorders of the motor unit (i.e., the lower motor neurons in the ventral horn of the spinal cord and their axons in the spinal roots and peripheral nerves, the neuromuscular junction, and the skeletal muscle). In general:

- *Upper motor neuron dysfunction*: increased muscle tone (spasticity), brisk deep tendon reflexes, and Babinski's sign.
- *Lower motor neuron dysfunction*: reduced muscle tone, diminished reflexes, and muscle atrophy.

Table 11-1 presents patterns of weakness and signs associated with weakness arising from lesions of different parts of the nervous system. Table 11-2 lists common causes of weakness by the primary site of pathology.

Table 11-1

Clinical Differentiation of Weakness Arising from Different Areas of the Nervous System

Location of Lesion	Pattern of Weakness	Associated Signs
UPPER MOTOR NEURON		
Cerebral cortex	Hemiparesis (face and arm predominantly, or leg predominantly)	Hemisensory loss, seizures, homonymous hemianopia or quadrantopia, aphasia, apraxias, gaze preference
Internal capsule	Hemiparesis (face, arm, leg may be equally affected)	Hemisensory deficit; homonymous hemianopia or quadrantopia
Brainstem	Hemiparesis (arm and leg; face may not be involved at all)	Vertigo, nausea and vomiting, ataxia and dysarthria, eye movement abnormalities, cranial nerve dysfunction, altered level of consciousness, Horner's syndrome
Spinal cord	Quadriparesis if midcervical or above Paraparesis if low cervical or thoracic	Sensory level; bowel and bladder dysfunction
	Hemiparesis below level of lesion (Brown-Séquard)	Contralateral pain/temperature loss below level of lesion
MOTOR UNIT		
Spinal motor neuron	Diffuse weakness, may involve control of speech and swallowing	Muscle fasciculations and atrophy; no sensory loss
Spinal root	Radicular pattern of weakness	Dermatomal sensory loss; radicular pain common with compressive lesions
Peripheral nerve		
Polyneuropathy	Distal weakness, usually feet more than hands; usually symmetric	Distal sensory loss, usually feet more than hands
Mononeuropathy	Weakness in distribution of single nerve	Sensory loss in distribution of single nerve
Neuromuscular junction	Fatigable weakness, usually with ocular involvement producing diplopia and ptosis	No sensory loss; no reflex changes
Muscle	Proximal weakness	No sensory loss; diminished reflexes only when severe; may have muscle tenderness

Table 11-2

Common Causes of Weakness

UPPER MOTOR NEURON

Cortex: ischemia; hemorrhage; intrinsic mass lesion (primary or metastatic cancer, abscess); extrinsic mass lesion (subdural hematoma); degenerative (amyotrophic lateral sclerosis)

Subcortical white matter/internal capsule: ischemia; hemorrhage; intrinsic mass lesion (primary or metastatic cancer, abscess); immunologic (multiple sclerosis); infectious (progressive multifocal leukoencephalopathy)

Brainstem: ischemia; immunologic (multiple sclerosis)

Spinal cord: extrinsic compression (cervical spondylosis, metastatic cancer, epidural abscess); immunologic (multiple sclerosis, transverse myelitis); infectious (AIDS-associated myelopathy, HTLV-1–associated myelopathy, tabes dorsalis); nutritional deficiency (subacute combined degeneration)

MOTOR UNIT

Spinal motor neuron: degenerative (amyotrophic lateral sclerosis); infectious (poliomyelitis)

Spinal root: compressive (degenerative disc disease); immunologic (Guillain-Barré syndrome); infectious (AIDS-associated polyradiculopathy, Lyme disease)

Peripheral nerve: metabolic (diabetes mellitus, uremia, porphyria); toxic (ethanol, heavy metals, many drugs, diphtheria); nutritional (B_{12} deficiency); inflammatory (polyarteritis nodosa); hereditary (Charcot-Marie-Tooth); immunologic (paraneoplastic, paraproteinemia); infectious (AIDS-associated polyneuropathies and mononeuritis multiplex); compressive (entrapment)

Neuromuscular junction: immunologic (myasthenia gravis); toxic (botulism, aminoglycosides)

Muscle: inflammatory (polymyositis, inclusion body myositis); degenerative (muscular dystrophy); toxic (glucocorticoids, ethanol, AZT); infectious (trichinosis); metabolic (hypothyroid, periodic paralyses); congenital (central core disease)

EVALUATION   The history should focus on the tempo of development of weakness, presence of sensory and other neurologic symptoms, medication history, predisposing medical conditions, and family history. The physical exam aids in localization of the abnormality by criteria such as described above and in Table 11-1. An algorithm for the initial workup of a patient with weakness is shown in Fig. 11-1.

MOVEMENT DISORDERS

Movement disorders are often divided into akinetic rigid forms, in which there is muscle rigidity and slowness of movement, and hyperkinetic forms, in which there are involuntary movements. In either case, preservation of strength is the rule. Most movement disorders arise from dysfunction of the circuitry in the basal ganglia and can occur by virtually any pathogenic mechanism; common causes are degenerative diseases (hereditary and idiopathic), drug-induced, organ system failure, CNS infection, and ischemia. Clinical features of the various movement disorders are summarized below.

BRADYKINESIA   Inability to initiate changes in activity or perform ordinary volitional movements rapidly and easily. There is a slowness of move-

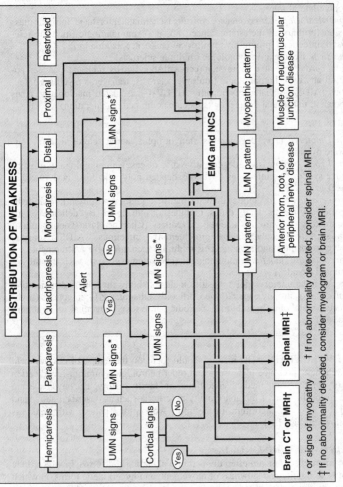

FIGURE 11-1 An algorithm for the initial work-up of a patient with weakness. CT, computed tomography; EMG, electromyography; LMN, lower motor neuron; MRI, magnetic resonance imaging; NCS, nerve conduction studies; UMN, upper motor neuron.

ment and a paucity of automatic motions such as eye blinking and arm swinging while walking. Usually due to Parkinson's disease.

TREMOR Rhythmic oscillation of a part of the body about a fixed point, usually involving the distal limbs and less commonly the head, tongue, and jaw. May be divided according to amplitude and relationship to posture. Most common—a coarse tremor at rest, 4–5 beats/s, usually due to Parkinson's disease; a fine postural tremor of 8–10 beats/s, which may be an exaggeration of normal physiologic tremor or indicative of familial essential tremor. The latter often responds to propranolol or primidone.

ASTERIXIS Brief, arrhythmic interruptions of sustained voluntary muscle contraction, usually observed as a brief lapse of posture of wrists in dorsiflexion with arms outstretched. This "liver flap" may be seen in any encephalopathy related to drug intoxication, organ system failure, or CNS infection. Therapy is correction of underlying disorder.

MYOCLONUS Brief, arrhythmic muscle contractions, or twitches. Like asterixis, usually indicative of a diffuse encephalopathy. Following cardiac arrest, diffuse cerebral hypoxia may produce multifocal myoclonus. Clonazepam, valproate, or baclofen may be effective.

DYSTONIA Involuntary, sustained posture or slowly changing involuntary postures. Postures attained are often bizarre, with forceful extensions and twisting about individual joints. Dystonias may be generalized or focal (e.g., spasmodic torticollis, blepharospasm). Symptoms may respond to high doses of anticholinergics, benzodiazepines, baclofen, and anticonvulsants. Local injection of botulinum toxin is effective in certain focal dystonias.

CHOREOATHETOSIS A combination of chorea (rapid, jerky movements) and athetosis (slow writhing movements). The two usually exist together though one may be more prominent. Choreic movements are the predominant involuntary movements in rheumatic (Sydenham's) chorea and Huntington's disease. Athetosis is prominent in some forms of cerebral palsy. Chronic neuroleptic use may lead to tardive dyskinesia, in which choreoathetotic movements are usually restricted to the buccal, lingual, and mandibular areas. Benzodiazepines, reserpine, and low-dose neuroleptics may suppress choreoathetotic movements but are often ineffective.

TICS Stereotypical, purposeless movements such as eye blinks, sniffling, and clearing of the throat. Gilles de la Tourette syndrome is a rare but severe multiple tic disorder that may involve motor tics (especially twitches of the face, neck, and shoulders), vocal tics (grunts, words), and "behavioral tics" (coprolalia, echolalia). The cause is unknown. Treatment with haloperidol usually reduces the frequency and severity of the tics.

For a more detailed discussion, see Olney RK, Aminoff MJ: **Weakness, Myalgias, Disorders of Movement, and Imbalance, Chap. 22, p. 118, in HPIM-15.**

12

APHASIAS AND RELATED DISORDERS

Aphasias are disturbances in the comprehension or production of spoken or written language. Aphasias may be classified based on their clinical manifestations, the anatomic location of the underlying lesion, their etiology, and associated clinical symptoms (Table 12-1).

Global Aphasia

ETIOLOGY   Occlusion of internal carotid artery (ICA) or middle cerebral artery (MCA) supplying dominant hemisphere (less commonly hemorrhage, trauma, or tumor), resulting in a large lesion of frontal, parietal, and superior temporal lobes.

CLINICAL MANIFESTATIONS   All aspects of speech and language are impaired. Patient cannot read, write, or repeat and has poor auditory comprehension. Speech output is minimal and nonfluent. Usually hemiplegia, hemisensory loss, and homonymous hemianopia are present.

Table 12-1

Clinical Features of Aphasias and Related Conditions

	Comprehension	Repetition of Spoken Language	Naming	Fluency
Wernicke's	Impaired	Impaired	Impaired	Preserved or increased
Broca's	Preserved (except grammar)	Impaired	Impaired	Decreased
Global	Impaired	Impaired	Impaired	Decreased
Conduction	Preserved	Impaired	Impaired	Preserved
Nonfluent (motor) transcortical	Preserved	Preserved	Impaired	Impaired
Fluent (sensory) transcortical	Impaired	Preserved	Impaired	Preserved
Isolation	Impaired	Echolalia	Impaired	No purposeful speech
Anomic	Preserved	Preserved	Impaired	Preserved except for word-finding pauses
Pure word deafness	Impaired only for spoken language	Impaired	Preserved	Preserved
Pure alexia	Impaired only for reading	Preserved	Preserved	Preserved

SOURCE: M-M Mesulam: HPIM-15, p. 141.

Broca's Aphasia (Motor or Nonfluent Aphasia)

ETIOLOGY Core lesion involves dominant inferior frontal convolution (Broca's area), although cortical and subcortical areas along superior sylvian fissure and insula are often involved. Commonly caused by vascular lesions involving the superior division of the MCA; less commonly due to tumor, abscess, metastasis, subdural hematoma, encephalitis.

CLINICAL MANIFESTATIONS Speech output is sparse, slow, effortful, dysmelodic, poorly articulated, and telegraphic. Most patients have severe writing impairment. Comprehension of written and spoken language is relatively preserved. Patient is often aware of and visibly frustrated by deficit. With large lesions, a dense hemiparesis may occur, and the eyes may deviate toward side of lesion. More commonly, lesser degrees of contralateral face and arm weakness are present. Sensory loss is rarely found, and visual fields are intact. Buccolingual apraxia is common, with difficulty imitating movements with tongue and lips or performing these movements on command. An apraxia involving the ipsilateral hand may occur due to involvement of fibers in the corpus callosum.

Wernicke's Aphasia (Sensory or Fluent Aphasia)

ETIOLOGY Embolic occlusion of inferior division of dominant MCA (less commonly hemorrhage, tumor, encephalitis, or abscess) involving posterior perisylvian region.

CLINICAL MANIFESTATIONS Although speech sounds grammatical, melodic, and effortless ("fluent"), it is often virtually incomprehensible due to errors in word usage, structure, and tense and the presence of neologisms and paraphasia. Comprehension of written and spoken material is severely impaired, as are reading, writing, and repetition. The patient usually seems unaware of the deficit. Associated clinical symptoms can include parietal lobe sensory deficits and homonymous hemianopia. Motor disturbances are rare.

Conduction Aphasia

Comprehension of speech and writing is largely intact, and speech output is fluent, although paraphasia is common. Repetition is severely affected. Most cases are due to lesions involving supramarginal gyrus of dominant parietal lobe, dominant superior temporal lobe, or arcuate fasciculus. Lesions are typically due to an embolus to either the ascending parietal or posterior temporal branch of the dominant MCA. Associated symptoms include contralateral hemisensory loss and hemianopia.

Pure Word Deafness

Almost total lack of auditory comprehension with inability to repeat or write to dictation and relatively preserved spoken language and spontaneous writing. Comprehension of visual or written material is superior to that of auditory information. The lesion(s) are typically in or near the primary auditory cortex (Heschl's gyrus) in the superior temporal gyrus. Causes are infarction, hemorrhage, or tumor.

Pure Word Blindness

Inability to read and often to name colors with preserved speech fluency, language comprehension, repetition, and writing to dictation (alexia without agraphia). Lesion usually involves left occipitostriate cortex and visual association areas as well as fibers in splenium of corpus callosum connecting right and left visual association areas. Most patients have an associated right homonymous hemianopia, hemisensory deficit, and memory disturbance due to vascular lesions involving the left posterior cerebral artery (PCA) territory. Rarely, tumor or hemorrhage may be the cause.

Isolation of Speech Area

Hypotension, ischemia, or hypoxia may result in borderzone infarctions between the anterior cerebral–MCA–PCA territories that spare the sylvian region of the MCA. Pts are severely brain damaged and have parrot-like repetition of spoken words (echolalia) with little or no spontaneous speech or comprehension.

Laboratory Studies in Aphasia

CT scan or MRI usually identifies the location and nature of the causative lesion. Angiography helps in accurate definition of specific vascular syndromes.

 TREATMENT

Speech therapy may be helpful in treatment of certain types of aphasia.

For a more detailed discussion, see Mesulam M-M: Aphasias and Other Focal Cerebral Disorders, Chap. 25, p. 140, in HPIM-15.

13

SLEEP DISORDERS

Disorders of sleep are among the most common problems seen by clinicians. More than one-half of adults experience at least occasional insomnia, and 15–20% have a chronic sleep disturbance.

Approach to the Patient

Patients may complain of: (1) difficulty in initiating and maintaining sleep (insomnia); (2) excessive daytime sleepiness, fatigue, or tiredness; (3) behavioral phenomena occurring during sleep [sleepwalking, rapid eye movement (REM) behavioral disorder, periodic leg movements of sleep, etc.]; or (4) circadian rhythm disorders associated with jet lag, shift work, and delayed sleep phase syndrome. A careful history of sleep habits and reports from the sleep partner (e.g., heavy snoring, falling asleep while driving) are a cornerstone of diagnosis. Completion of a day-by-day sleep-work-drug log for at least 2 weeks is often helpful. Work and sleep times (including daytime naps and nocturnal awakenings) as well as drug and alcohol use, including caffeine and hypnotics, should be noted each day. Objective sleep laboratory recording is necessary to evaluate sleep apnea, narcolepsy, REM behavior disorder, periodic leg movements, and other suspected disorders.

Insomnia

Insomnia, or the complaint of inadequate sleep, may be subdivided into difficulty falling asleep (*sleep-onset insomnia*), frequent or sustained awakenings (*sleep-offset insomnia*), or persistent sleepiness despite sleep of adequate duration (*nonrestorative sleep*). An insomnia complaint lasting one to several nights is termed *transient insomnia* and is typically due to situational stress or a change in sleep schedule or environment (e.g., jet lag). *Short-term insomnia* lasts from a few days up to 3 weeks; it is often associated with more protracted stress such as recovery from surgery or short-term illness. *Long-term (chronic) insomnia* lasts for months or years and, in contrast to short-term insomnia, requires a thorough evaluation for underlying causes. Chronic insomnia is often a waxing and waning disorder, with spontaneous or stressor-induced exacerbations.

EXTRINSIC INSOMNIA *Transient situational insomnia* can occur after a change in the sleeping environment (e.g., in an unfamiliar hotel or hospital bed) or before or after a significant life event or anxiety-provoking situation. Treatment is symptomatic, with intermittent use of hypnotics and resolution of the underlying stress. *Inadequate sleep hygiene* is characterized by a behavior pattern prior to sleep and/or a bedroom environment that is not conducive to sleep. In preference to hypnotic medications, the pt should attempt to avoid stressful activities before bed, reserve the bedroom environment for sleeping, and maintain regular rising times.

PSYCHOPHYSIOLOGIC INSOMNIA Pts with this behavioral disorder are preoccupied with a perceived inability to sleep adequately at night. Rigorous attention should be paid to sleep hygiene and correction of counterproductive, arousing behaviors before bedtime. Behavioral therapies are the treatment of choice.

DRUGS AND MEDICATIONS Caffeine is probably the most common pharmacologic cause of insomnia. Alcohol and nicotine can also interfere with sleep, despite the fact that many pts use these agents to relax and promote sleep. A number of prescribed medications, including antidepressants, sympathomimetics, and glucocorticoids, can produce insomnia. In addition, severe rebound insomnia can result from the acute withdrawal of hypnotics, especially following use of high doses of benzodiazepines with a short half-life. For this reason, hypnotic doses should be low to moderate, the total duration of hypnotic therapy should be limited to 2–3 weeks, and prolonged drug tapering is encouraged.

MOVEMENT DISORDERS Patients with *restless legs syndrome* complain of creeping dysesthesia deep within the calves or feet associated with an irresistible urge to move the affected limbs; symptoms are typically worse at night. Treatment is with dopaminergic drugs (L-dopa or dopamine agonists). *Periodic limb movement disorder* consists of stereotyped extensions of the great toe and dorsiflexion of the foot recurring every 20–40 s during non-rapid eye movement sleep. This common condition is present in 1% of the general population; treatment options include dopaminergic medications or benzodiazepines.

OTHER NEUROLOGIC DISORDERS A variety of neurologic disorders produce sleep disruption through both indirect, nonspecific mechanisms (e.g., neck or back pain) or by impairment of central neural structures involved in the generation and control of sleep itself. Common disorders to consider include *dementia* from any cause, *epilepsy*, *Parkinson's disease*, and *migraine*.

PSYCHIATRIC DISORDERS   Approximately 80% of pts with mental disorders complain of impaired sleep. The underlying diagnosis may be depression, mania, an anxiety disorder, or schizophrenia.

MEDICAL DISORDERS   In *asthma*, daily variation in airway resistance results in marked increases in asthmatic symptoms at night, especially during sleep. Treatment of asthma with theophylline-based compounds, adrenergic agonists, or glucocorticoids can independently disrupt sleep. Inhaled glucocorticoids that do not disrupt sleep may provide a useful alternative to oral drugs. *Cardiac ischemia* is also associated with sleep disruption; the ischemia itself may result from increases in sympathetic tone as a result of sleep apnea. Pts may present with complaints of nightmares or vivid dreams. *Paroxysmal nocturnal dyspnea* can also occur from cardiac ischemia that causes pulmonary congestion exacerbated by the recumbent posture. *Chronic obstructive pulmonary disease, hyperthyroidism, menopause*, and *gastroesophageal reflux* are other causes.

 TREATMENT

Insomnia treatment is usually effective. Cognitive therapy emphasizes understanding the nature of normal sleep, the circadian rhythm, the use of light therapy, and visual imagery to block unwanted thought intrusions. Behavioral modification involves bedtime restriction, set schedules, and careful sleep environment practices. Some pts benefit from low-dose sedating tricyclics (e.g., 10 mg amitriptyline) or the judicious use of benzodiazepine or its congeners. A judicious use would be either short-term (1 week) or limited use not to exceed 3 days/week.

Hypersomnias (Disorders of Excessive Daytime Sleepiness)

Differentiation of sleepiness from subjective complaints of fatigue may be difficult. Quantification of daytime sleepiness can be performed in a sleep laboratory using a multiple sleep latency test (MSLT), the repeated daytime measurement of sleep latency under standardized conditions. Common causes are summarized in Table 13-1.

SLEEP APNEA SYNDROME   Respiratory dysfunction during sleep is a common cause of excessive daytime sleepiness and/or disturbed nocturnal sleep, affecting an estimated 2 to 5 million individuals in the U.S. Episodes may be due to occlusion of the airway (obstructive sleep apnea), absence of respiratory effort (central sleep apnea), or a combination of these factors (mixed sleep apnea). Obstruction is exacerbated by obesity, supine posture, sedatives (especially alcohol), nasal obstruction, and hypothyroidism. Sleep apnea is particularly prevalent in overweight men and in the elderly, and is often undiagnosed. Treatment consists of correction of the above factors, positive airway pressure devices, oral appliances, and sometimes surgery.

NARCOLEPSY (Table 13-2)   Narcolepsy is a disorder of excessive daytime sleepiness and intrusion of REM-related sleep phenomena into wakefulness (cataplexy, hypnagogic hallucinations, and sleep paralysis). Cataplexy, the abrupt loss of muscle tone in arms, legs, or face, is precipitated by emotional stimuli such as laughter or sadness. The excessive daytime sleepiness usually appears in adolescence, and the other phenomena, variably, later in life. The

Table 13-1

Evaluation of the Patient with the Complaint of Excessive Daytime Somnolence

Findings on History and Physical Examination	Diagnostic Evaluation	Diagnosis	Therapy
Obesity, snoring, hypertension	Polysomnography with respiratory monitoring	Obstructive sleep apnea	Continuous positive airway pressure; ENT surgery (e.g., uvulopalatopharyngoplasty); dental appliance; pharmacologic therapy (e.g., protriptyline); weight loss
Cataplexy, hypnogogic hallucinations, sleep paralysis, family history	Polysomnography with multiple sleep latency test	Narcolepsy-cataplexy syndrome	Stimulants (e.g., methylphenidate, pemoline); REM-suppressant antidepressants (e.g., protriptyline); genetic counseling
Restless legs syndrome, disturbed sleep, predisposing medical condition (e.g., anemia or renal failure)	Polysomnography with bilateral anterior tibialis EMG	Periodic limb movements of sleep	Treatment of predisposing condition, if possible; dopamine agonists (e.g., levodopa-carbidopa); benzodiazepines (e.g., clonazepam)
Disturbed sleep, predisposing medical conditions (e.g., asthma) and/or predisposing medical therapies (e.g., theophylline)	Sleep-wake diary	Insomnias (see text)	Treatment of predisposing condition and/or change in therapy, if possible; behavioral therapy; short-acting benzodiazepine receptor agonist (e.g., zolpidem)

NOTE: ENT, ears, nose, throat; REM, rapid eye movement; EMG, electromyogram.

Table 13-2

Prevalence of Symptoms in Narcolepsy

Symptom	Prevalence, %
Excessive daytime somnolence	100
Disturbed sleep	87
Cataplexy	76
Hypnagogic hallucinations	68
Sleep paralysis	64
Memory problems	50

SOURCE: Modified from TA Roth, L Merlotti in SA Burton et al (eds), *Narcolepsy 3rd International Symposium: Selected Symposium Proceedings*, Chicago, Matrix Communications, 1989.

prevalence is 1 in 4000. Hypothalamic neurons containing the neuropeptide orexin (hypocretin) regulate the sleep/wake cycle and have been implicated in narcolepsy. Sleep studies confirm a pathologically short daytime sleep latency and a rapid transition to REM sleep.

 TREATMENT

Somnolence is treated with stimulants such as methylphenidate (10 mg bid–20 mg qid); pemoline, dextroamphetamine, and methamphetamine are alternatives. Modafinil, a novel wake-promoting agent, was recently approved for the treatment of excessive daytime sleepiness in narcolepsy; the usual dose is 200–400 mg/d given as a single dose. Adequate nocturnal sleep time and the use of short naps are other useful measures. Cataplexy, hypnagogic hallucinations, and sleep paralysis respond to the tricyclics protriptyline (10–40 mg/d) and clomipramine (25–50 mg/d) and to the selective serotonin uptake inhibitor fluoxetine (10–20 mg/d).

Disorders of Circadian Rhythmicity

Insomnia or hypersomnia may occur in disorders of sleep timing rather than sleep generation. Such conditions may be (1) organic—due to a defect in the hypothalamic circadian pacemaker, or (2) environmental—due to a disruption of entraining stimuli (light/dark cycle). Common examples of the latter include jet-lag syndrome and shift work. *Delayed sleep phase syndrome* is characterized by late sleep onset and awakening with otherwise normal sleep architecture. These patients usually respond to a rescheduling regimen in which bedtimes are successively delayed by 3 h/day until the desired early bedtime is achieved (chronotherapy). *Advanced sleep phase syndrome* moves sleep onset to the early evening hours with early morning awakening. Bright-light phototherapy in the morning hours or melatonin therapy during the evening hours may benefit pts with these disorders as well as those with jet lag and shift-work disorders.

For a more detailed discussion, see Czeisler CA, Winkleman JW, Richardson GS: Sleep Disorders, Chap. 27, p. 155, in HPIM-15.

14

DYSPNEA

Definition

An abnormally uncomfortable awareness of breathing; intensity can be quantified by establishing the amount of physical exertion necessary to produce the sensation, but the pt's general physical condition should be considered.

Causes

HEART DISEASE   Dyspnea is due to ↑ pulmonary capillary pressure, left atrial hypertension, and sometimes fatigue of respiratory muscles. Vital capacity and lung compliance are ↓ and airway resistance ↑. Begins as exertional breathlessness → orthopnea → paroxysmal nocturnal dyspnea and dyspnea at rest. Diagnosis depends on recognition of heart disease, e.g., Hx of MI, presence of S_3, S_4, murmurs, cardiomegaly, jugular vein distention, hepatomegaly, and peripheral edema (Chap. 116). Objective quantification of ventricular function (echocardiography, radionuclide ventriculography) is often helpful.

OBSTRUCTIVE DISEASE OF THE AIRWAYS   May occur with obstruction anywhere from extrathoracic airways to lung periphery. Acute dyspnea with difficulty *inhaling* suggests *upper* airway obstruction. Physical exam may reveal inspiratory stridor and retraction of supraclavicular fossae. Acute intermittent dyspnea with expiratory wheezing suggests reversible intrathoracic obstruction due to asthma. Chronic, slowly progressive exertional dyspnea characterizes emphysema and CHF. Chronic cough with expectoration is typical of chronic bronchitis and bronchiectasis.

DIFFUSE PARENCHYMAL LUNG DISEASES   Many parenchymal lung diseases, ranging from sarcoidosis to the pneumoconioses, may cause dyspnea. Dyspnea is usually related to exertion early in the course of the illness. Physical exam typically reveals tachypnea and late inspiratory rales.

PULMONARY EMBOLISM   (See Chap. 132)   Dyspnea is the most common symptom of pulmonary embolus. Repeated discrete episodes of dyspnea may occur with recurrent pulmonary emboli, but others describe slowly progressive dyspnea without abrupt worsening; tachypnea is frequent. Finding of deep venous thrombosis usually absent in chronic pulmonary embolism

DISEASE OF THE CHEST WALL OR RESPIRATORY MUSCLES Severe kyphoscoliosis may produce chronic dyspnea, often with chronic cor pulmonale. The spinal deformity must be severe before respiratory function is compromised. Pts with bilateral diaphragmatic paralysis appear normal while standing, but complain of severe orthopnea and display paradoxical abnormal respiratory movement when supine.

—————————— *Approach to the Patient* ——————————

Elicit a description of the amount of physical exertion necessary to produce the sensation and whether it varies under different conditions.

- If acute upper airway obstruction is suspected, lateral neck films or a fiberoptic exam of upper airway may be helpful. Pt should be accompanied by a physician adept in all aspects of airway management during the evaluation. With chronic upper airway obstruction the respiratory flow-volume curve may show inspiratory cutoff of flow, suggesting variable extrathoracic obstruction.

Table 14-1

Differentiation between Cardiac and Pulmonary Dyspnea

1. *Careful history*: Dyspnea of lung disease usually more gradual in onset than that of heart disease; nocturnal exacerbations common with each.
2. *Examination*: Usually obvious evidence of cardiac or pulmonary disease. Findings may be absent at rest when symptoms are present only with exertion.
3. *Pulmonary function tests*: Pulmonary disease rarely causes dyspnea unless tests of obstructive disease (FEV_1, FEV_1/FVC) or restrictive disease (total lung capacity) are reduced (<80% predicted).
4. *Ventricular performance*: LV ejection fraction at rest and/or during exercise usually depressed in cardiac dyspnea.

* Dyspnea due to emphysema is reflected in a reduction in expiratory flow rates (FEV_1), and often by a reduction in the diffusing capacity for carbon monoxide (DL_{CO}).
* Pts with intermittent dyspnea due to asthma may have normal pulmonary function if tested when asymptomatic. In severe acute asthma the intensity of dyspnea may fail to reflect the degree of compromise evident on pulmonary function testing.
* Cardiac dyspnea usually begins as breathlessness on strenuous exertion with gradual (months-to-years) progression to dyspnea at rest.
* Pts with dyspnea due to both cardiac and pulmonary diseases may report orthopnea. Paroxysmal nocturnal dyspnea occurring after awakening from sleep is characteristic of CHF.
* Dyspnea of chronic obstructive lung disease tends to develop more gradually than that of heart disease.
* PFTs should be performed when etiology is not clear. When the diagnosis remains obscure a pulmonary stress test is often useful.
* Management depends on elucidating etiology.

Differentiation between cardiac and pulmonary dyspnea is summarized in Table 14-1.

For a more detailed discussion, see Ingram RH Jr., Braunwald E: Dyspnea and Pulmonary Edema, Chap. 32, p. 199, HPIM-15.

15

COUGH AND HEMOPTYSIS

COUGH
Produced by inflammatory, mechanical, chemical, and thermal stimulation of cough receptors.

ETIOLOGY

* *Inflammatory*—edema and hyperemia of airways and alveoli due to laryngitis, tracheitis, bronchitis, bronchiolitis, pneumonitis, lung abscess.
* *Mechanical*—inhalation of particulates (dust) or compression of airways (pulmonary neoplasms, foreign bodies, granulomas, bronchospasm).
* *Chemical*—inhalation of irritant fumes, including cigarette smoke.
* *Thermal*—inhalation of cold or very hot air.

_____ *Approach to the Patient* _____

Diagnosis (Fig. 15-1)   *History* should consider: (1) duration—acute or chronic; (2) presence of fever or wheezing; (3) sputum quantity and character; (4) temporal or seasonal pattern; (5) risk factors for underlying disease; and (6) past medical history. Short duration with associated fever suggests acute viral or bacterial infection. Persistent cough after viral illness suggests postinflammatory cough. Postnasal drip is a common cause of chronic cough. Nocturnal cough may indicate chronic sinus drainage or esophageal reflux. Change in sputum character, color, or volume in a smoker with "smoker's cough" necessitates investigation. Seasonal cough may indicate "cough asthma." Environmental exposures may suggest occupational asthma or interstitial lung disease. Past history of recurrent pneumonias may indicate bronchiectasis, particularly if associated with purulent or copious sputum production. A change in the character of chronic cigarette cough raises suspicion of bronchogenic carcinoma.

Physical exam should assess upper and lower airways and lung parenchyma. Stridor suggests upper airway obstruction; wheezing suggests bronchospasm as the cause of cough. Midinspiratory crackles indicate airways disease (e.g., chronic bronchitis); fine end-inspiratory crackles occur in interstitial fibrosis and heart failure. *CXR* may show neoplasm, infection, interstitial disease, or the hilar adenopathy of sarcoidosis. PFTs may reveal obstruction or restriction. *Sputum exam* can indicate malignancy or infection.

COMPLICATIONS   (1) Syncope, due to transient decrease in venous return; (2) rupture of anemphysematous bleb with pneumothorax; (3) rib fractures—may occur in otherwise normal individuals.

℞ TREATMENT

When possible, therapy of cough is that of underlying disease. If no cause can be found, a trial of an inhaled β agonist (e.g., albuterol) or an inhaled steroid (e.g., triamcinelone) can be attempted. Inhaled steroids may take 7–10 days to be effective when used for an irritative cough. When symptoms from an irritative cough are severe (syncope, sleep disruption, rib fracture) the cough may be suppressed with a narcotic antitussive agent such as codeine, 15–30 mg up to qid, or a nonnarcotic such as dextromethorphan (15 mg qid). Cough productive of significant volumes of sputum should generally not be suppressed. Sputum clearance can be facilitated with adequate hydration, expectorants, and mechanical devices. Iodinated glycerol (30 mg qid) may be useful in asthma or chronic bronchitis.

HEMOPTYSIS

Includes both streaked sputum and coughing up of gross blood.

ETIOLOGY   (Table 15-1)   Bronchitis and bronchiectasis are most common causes. Neoplasm may be cause, particularly in smokers and when he-

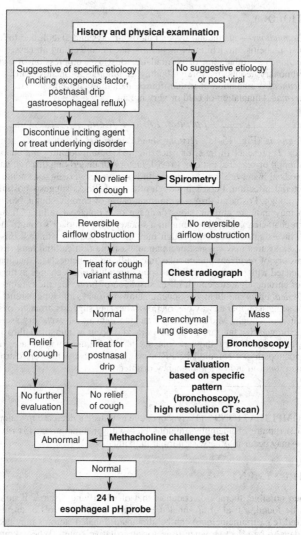

FIGURE 15-1 An algorithm for the evaluation of chronic cough.

moptysis is persistent. Hemoptysis rare in metastatic neoplasm to lung. Pulmonary thromboembolism, infection, CHF are other causes. Diffuse hemoptysis may occur with vasculitis involving the lung. Five to 15% of cases with hemoptysis remain undiagnosed.

Approach to the Patient

Diagnosis (Fig. 15-2) Essential to determine that blood is coming from respiratory tract. Often frothy, may be preceded by a desire to cough. History may suggest diagnosis: chronic hemoptysis in otherwise asymptomatic young woman suggests bronchial adenoma; recurrent hemoptysis in pts with chronic

Table 15-1

Causes of Hemoptysis

Inflammatory
   Bronchitis
   Bronchiectasis
   Tuberculosis
   Lung abscess
   Pneumonia, particularly *Klebsiella*
   Septic pulmonary embolism
Neoplastic
   Lung cancer: squamous cell, adenocarcinoma, oat cell
   Bronchial adenoma
Other
   Pulmonary thromboembolism
   Left ventricular failure
   Mitral stenosis
   Traumatic, including foreign body and lung contusion
   Primary pulmonary hypertension; AV malformation; Eisenmenger's syn-
      drome; pulmonary vasculitis, including Wegener's granulomatosis and
      Goodpasture's syndrome; idiopathic pulmonary hemosiderosis; and amyloid
   Hemorrhagic diathesis, including anticoagulant therapy

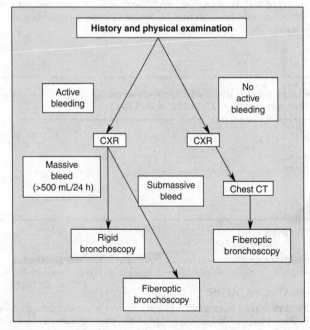

FIGURE 15-2   Diagnostic approach to hemoptysis.

copious sputum production suggests bronchiectasis; hemoptysis, weight loss, and anorexia in a smoker suggest carcinoma; hemoptysis with acute pleuritic pain suggests infarction.

Physical exam may also suggest diagnosis: pleural friction rub raises possibility of pulmonary embolism or some other pleural-based lesion (lung abscess, coccidioidomycosis cavity, vasculitis); diastolic rumble suggests mitral stenosis; localized wheeze suggests bronchogenic carcinoma. Initial evaluation includes CXR. A normal CXR does not exclude tumor or bronchiectasis as a source of bleeding. The CXR may show an air-fluid level suggesting an abscess or atelectasis distal to an obstructing carcinoma.

Most pts should then have chest CT scan followed by bronchoscopy. While rigid bronchoscopy is particularly helpful when bleeding is massive or from proximal airway lesion and when endotracheal intubation is contemplated, most pts should be assessed by fiberoptic bronchoscopy.

 TREATMENT

In addition to treatment of the underlying condition, mainstays of treatment are bed rest and cough suppression with an opiate (codeine, 15–30 mg, or hydrocodone, 5 mg q4–6h). Pts with massive hemoptysis (>600 mL/d) and pts with respiratory compromise due to aspiration of blood should be intensively monitored with suction and intubation equipment close by so that selective intubation to isolate the bleeding lung can be accomplished. In massive hemoptysis, choice of medical or surgical therapy relates often to the anatomic site of hemorrhage and the pt's baseline pulmonary function. Localized peripheral bleeding sites may be tamponaded by bronchoscopic placement of a balloon catheter in a lobar or segmental airway. Central bleeding sites may be managed with laser coagulation. Pts with severely compromised pulmonary function may be candidates for bronchial artery catherization and embolization.

For a more detailed discussion, see Weinberger SE, Braunwald E: Cough and Hemoptysis, Chap. 33, p. 203, in HPIM-15.

16

CYANOSIS

The circulating quantity of reduced hemoglobin is elevated [>50 g/L (>5 g/dL)] resulting in bluish discoloration of the skin and/or mucous membranes.

CENTRAL CYANOSIS

Results from arterial desaturation. Usually evident when arterial saturation is ≤85%. Particularly in dark-skinned individuals, cyanosis may not be detected until saturation is 75%.

1. *Impaired pulmonary function*: Poorly ventilated alveoli or impaired oxygen diffusion; most frequent in pneumonia, pulmonary edema, and chronic obstructive pulmonary disease (COPD); in COPD with cyanosis, polycythemia is often present.

2. *Anatomic vascular shunting*: Shunting of desaturated venous blood into the arterial circulation may result from congenital heart disease or pulmonary AV fistula.

3. *Decreased inspired O_2*: Cyanosis may develop in ascents to altitudes >2400 m (>8000 ft).

4. *Abnormal hemoglobins*: Methemoglobinemia, sulfhemoglobinemia, and mutant hemoglobins with low oxygen affinity (see HPIM-15, Chap. 106).

PERIPHERAL CYANOSIS

Occurs with normal arterial O_2 saturation with increased extraction of O_2 from capillary blood caused by decreased localized blood flow. Vasoconstriction due to cold exposure, decreased cardiac output (in shock, Chap. 30), and peripheral vascular disease (Chap. 126) with arterial obstruction or vasospasm (Table 16-1). Local (e.g., thrombophlebitis) or central (e.g., constrictive pericarditis) venous hypertension intensifies cyanosis.

--------- *Approach to the Patient* ---------

- Inquire about duration (cyanosis since birth suggests congenital heart disease) and exposures (drugs or chemicals that result in abnormal hemoglobins).
- Differentiate central from peripheral cyanosis by examining nailbeds, lips, and mucous membranes. Peripheral cyanosis may resolve with gentle warming of extremities.

Table 16-1

Causes of Cyanosis

I. Central cyanosis
  A. Decreased arterial oxygen saturation
    1. Decreased atmospheric pressure—high altitude
    2. Impaired pulmonary function
      a. Alveolar hypoventilation
      b. Uneven relationships between pulmonary ventilation and perfusion (perfusion of hypoventilated alveoli)
      c. Impaired oxygen diffusion
    3. Anatomic shunts
      a. Certain types of congenital heart disease
      b. Pulmonary arteriovenous fistulas
      c. Multiple small intrapulmonary shunts
    4. Hemoglobin with low affinity for oxygen
  B. Hemoglobin abnormalities
    1. Methemoglobinemia—hereditary, acquired
    2. Sulfhemoglobinemia—acquired
    3. Carboxyhemoglobinemia (not true cyanosis)
II. Peripheral cyanosis
  A. Reduced cardiac output
  B. Cold exposure
  C. Redistribution of blood flow from extremities
  D. Arterial obstruction
  E. Venous obstruction

- Check for clubbing of fingers and toes; clubbing is the selective enlargement of the distal segments of fingers and toes. Clubbing may be hereditary, idiopathic, or acquired and is associated with a variety of disorders. Combination of clubbing and cyanosis is frequent in congenital heart disease and occasionally with pulmonary disease (lung abscess, pulmonary AV shunts but *not* with uncomplicated obstructive lung disease).
- Examine chest for evidence of pulmonary disease, pulmonary edema, or murmurs associated with congenital heart disease.
- If cyanosis is localized to an extremity, evaluate for peripheral vascular obstruction.
- Obtain arterial blood gas to measure systemic O_2 saturation. Repeat while pt inhales 100% O_2; if saturation fails to increase to >95%, intravascular shunting of blood bypassing the lungs is likely (e.g., right-to-left intracardiac shunts).
- Evaluate abnormal hemoglobins by hemoglobin electrophoresis and measurement of methemoglobin level.

For a more detailed discussion, see Braunwald E: Hypoxia and Cyanosis, Chap. 36, p. 214, in HPIM-15.

17

EDEMA

Definition

Soft tissue swelling due to abnormal expansion of interstitial fluid volume. Edema fluid is a plasma transudate that accumulates when movement of fluid from vascular to interstitial space is favored. Since detectable generalized edema in the adult reflects a gain of ≥ 3 L, renal retention of salt and water is necessary for edema to occur. Distribution of edema can be an important guide to cause.

LOCALIZED EDEMA Limited to a particular organ or vascular bed; easily distinguished from generalized edema. Unilateral extremity edema is usually due to venous or lymphatic obstruction (e.g., deep venous thrombosis, tumor obstruction, primary lymphedema). Stasis edema of a paralyzed lower extremity may also occur. Allergic reactions ("angioedema") and superior vena caval obstruction are causes of localized facial edema. Bilateral lower extremity edema may have localized causes: e.g., inferior vena caval obstruction, compression due to ascites, abdominal mass. Ascites (fluid in peritoneal cavity) and hydrothorax (in pleural space) may also present as isolated localized edema, due to inflammation or neoplasm.

GENERALIZED EDEMA (See Fig. 17-1) Soft tissue swelling of most or all regions of the body. Bilateral lower extremity swelling, more pronounced

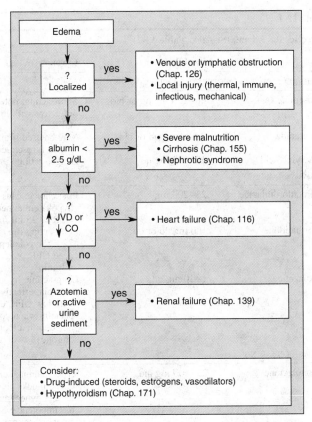

FIGURE 17-1 Diagnostic approach to edema. JVD, jugular venous distention; CO, cardiac output.

after standing for several hours, and pulmonary edema are usually cardiac in origin. Periorbital edema noted on awakening often results from renal disease and impaired Na excretion. Ascites and edema of lower extremities and scrotum are frequent in cirrhosis or CHF. In *CHF*, diminished cardiac output and effective arterial blood volume result in both decreased renal perfusion and increased venous pressure with resultant renal Na retention due to renal vasoconstriction, intrarenal blood flow redistribution, and secondary hyperaldosteronism.

In *cirrhosis*, arteriovenous shunts lower effective renal perfusion, resulting in Na retention. Ascites accumulates when increased intrahepatic vascular resistance produces portal hypertension. Reduced serum albumin and increased abdominal pressure promote lower extremity edema.

In *nephrotic syndrome*, massive renal loss of albumin lowers plasma oncotic pressure, promoting fluid transudation into interstitium; lowering of effective blood volume stimulates renal Na retention.

In acute or chronic *renal failure*, edema occurs if Na intake exceeds kidney's ability to excrete Na secondary to marked reductions in glomerular filtration. Severe *hypoalbuminemia* [<25 g/L (2.5 g/dL)] of any cause (e.g., nephrosis,

Table 17-1

Diuretics for Edema (See also Table 17-2)

Drug	Usual Dose	Comments
LOOP (MAY BE ADMINISTERED PO OR IV)		
Furosemide	40–120 mg qd or bid	Short-acting; potent; effective with low GFR
Bumetanide	0.5–2 mg qd or bid	May be used if allergic to furosemide
Ethacrynic acid	50–200 mg qd	Longer-acting
DISTAL, K-LOSING		
Hydrochlorothiazide	25–200 mg	First choice; causes hypokalemia; need GFR > 25 mL/min
Chlorthalidone	100 mg qd or qod	Long-acting (up to 72 h); hypokalemia; need GFR > 25 mL/min
Metolazone	1–10 mg qd	Long-acting; hypokalemia; effective with low GFR, especially when combined with a loop diuretic
DISTAL, K-SPARING		
Spironolactone	25–100 mg qid	Hyperkalemia; acidosis; blocks aldosterone; gynecomastia, impotence, amenorrhea; onset takes 2–3 days; avoid use in renal failure or in combination with ACE inhibitors or potassium supplements
Amiloride	5–10 mg qd or bid	Hyperkalemia; once daily; less potent than spironolactone
Triamterene	100 mg bid	Hyperkalemia; less potent than spironolactone; renal stones

nutritional deficiency states, chronic liver disease) may lower plasma oncotic pressure sufficiently to cause edema.

Less common causes of generalized edema: *idiopathic edema*, a syndrome of recurrent rapid weight gain and edema in women of reproductive age; *hypothyroidism*, in which myxedema is typically located in the pretibial region; *drugs* such as steroids, estrogens, and vasodilators; *pregnancy; refeeding* after starvation.

Table 17-2

Complications of Diuretics

Common	Uncommon
Volume depletion	Interstitial nephritis (thiazides,
Prerenal azotemia	furosemide)
Potassium depletion	Pancreatitis (thiazides)
Hyponatremia (thiazides)	Loss of hearing (loop diuretics)
Metabolic alkalosis	Anemia, leukopenia, thrombocyto-
Hypercholesterolemia	penia (thiazides)
Hyperglycemia (thiazides)	
Hyperkalemia (K-sparing)	
Hypomagnesemia	
Hyperuricemia	
Hypercalcemia (thiazides)	
GI complaints	
Rash (thiazides)	

 TREATMENT

Primary management is to identify and treat the underlying cause of edema (Fig. 17-1).

Dietary Na restriction (<500 mg/d) may prevent further edema formation. Bed rest enhances response to salt restriction in CHF and cirrhosis. Supportive stockings and elevation of edematous lower extremities will help mobilize interstitial fluid. If severe hyponatremia (<132 mmol/L) is present, water intake should also be reduced (<1500 mL/d). Diuretics (Table 17-1) are indicated for marked peripheral edema, pulmonary edema, CHF, inadequate dietary salt restriction. Complications are listed in Table 17-2. Weight loss by diuretics should be limited to 1–1.5 kg/d. Metolazone may be added to loop diuretics for enhanced effect. Note that intestinal edema may impair absorption of oral diuretics and reduce effectiveness. When desired weight is achieved, diuretic doses should be reduced.

In *CHF* (Chap. 116), avoid overdiuresis because it may bring a fall in cardiac output and prerenal azotemia. Avoid diuretic-induced hypokalemia, which predisposes to digitalis toxicity.

In *cirrhosis*, spironolactone is the diuretic of choice but may produce acidosis and hyperkalemia. Thiazides or small doses of loop diuretics may also be added. However, renal failure may result from volume depletion. Overdiuresis may result in hyponatremia and alkalosis, which may worsen hepatic encephalopathy (Chap. 155).

In *nephrotic syndrome*, albumin infusion should be limited to very severe cases (pts with associated hypotension), since rapid renal excretion prevents any sustained rise in serum albumin.

For a more detailed discussion, see Braunwald E: Edema, Chap. 37, p. 217, in HPIM-15.

18

NAUSEA, VOMITING, AND INDIGESTION

NAUSEA AND VOMITING

Nausea refers to the imminent desire to vomit and often precedes or accompanies vomiting. *Vomiting* refers to the forceful expulsion of gastric contents through the mouth. *Retching* refers to labored rhythmic respiratory activity that precedes emesis. *Regurgitation* refers to the gentle expulsion of gastric contents in the absence of nausea and abdominal diaphragmatic muscular contraction. *Rumination* refers to the regurgitation, rechewing, and reswallowing of food from the stomach.

Pathophysiology

Gastric contents are propelled into the esophagus when there is relaxation of the gastric fundus and gastroesophageal sphincter followed by a rapid increase in intraabdominal pressure produced by contraction of the abdominal and diaphragmatic musculature. Increased intrathoracic pressure results in further movement of the material to the mouth. Reflex elevation of the soft palate and closure of the glottis protects the nasopharynx and trachea and completes the act of vomiting. Vomiting is controlled by two brainstem areas, the vomiting center and chemoreceptor trigger zone. Activation of the chemoreceptor trigger zone results in impulses to the vomiting center, which controls the physical act of vomiting.

Etiology

Nausea and vomiting are manifestations of a large number of disorders (Table 18-1).

Evaluation

The history, including a careful drug history, and the timing and character of the vomitus can be helpful. For example, vomiting that occurs predominantly in the morning is often seen in pregnancy, uremia, and alcoholic gastritis; feculent emesis implies distal intestinal obstruction or gastrocolic fistula; projectile vomiting suggests increased intracranial pressure; vomiting during or shortly after a meal may be due to psychogenic causes or peptic ulcer disease. Associated symptoms also may be helpful: vertigo and tinnitus in Ménière's disease, relief of abdominal pain with vomiting in peptic ulcer, and early satiety in gastroparesis. Plain radiographs can suggest diagnoses such as intestinal obstruction. The upper GI series assesses motility of the proximal GI tract as well as the mucosa. Other studies may be indicated such as gastric emptying scans (diabetic gastroparesis) and CT scan of the brain.

Complications

Rupture of the esophagus (Boerhaave's syndrome), hematemesis from a mucosal tear (Mallory-Weiss syndrome), dehydration, malnutrition, dental caries, metabolic alkalosis, hypokalemia, and aspiration pneumonitis.

 TREATMENT

This should be directed toward correcting the specific cause. The effectiveness of antiemetic medications depends on etiology of symptoms, pt responsive-

Table 18-1

Causes of Nausea and Vomiting

Intraperitoneal	Extraperitoneal	Medications/Metabolic Disorders
Obstructing disorders	Cardiopulmonary disease	Drugs
Pyloric obstruction	Cardiomyopathy	Cancer chemotherapy
Small bowel obstruction	Myocardial infarction	Antibiotics
Colonic obstruction	Labyrinthine disease	Cardiac antiarrhythmics
Superior mesenteric artery syndrome	Motion sickness	Digoxin
Enteric infections	Labyrinthitis	Oral hypoglycemics
Viral	Malignancy	Oral contraceptives
Bacterial	Intracerebral disorders	Endocrine/metabolic disease
Inflammatory diseases	Malignancy	Pregnancy
Cholecystitis	Hemorrhage	Uremia
Pancreatitis	Abscess	Ketoacidosis
Appendicitis	Hydrocephalus	Thyroid and parathyroid disease
Hepatitis	Psychiatric illness	Adrenal insufficiency
Impaired motor function	Anorexia and bulimia nervosa	Toxins
Gastroparesis	Depression	Liver failure
Intestinal pseudoobstruction	Psychogenic vomiting	Ethanol
Functional dyspepsia	Postoperative vomiting	
Gastroesophageal reflux	Cyclic vomiting syndrome	
Biliary colic		
Abdominal irradiation		

ness, and side effects. Antihistamines such as dimenhydrinate and promethazine hydrochloride are effective for nausea due to inner ear dysfunction. Anticholinergics such as scopolamine are effective for nausea associated with motion sickness. Haloperidol and phenothiazine derivatives such as prochlorperazine are often effective in controlling mild nausea and vomiting, but sedation, hypotension, and parkinsonian symptoms are common side effects. Selective dopamine antagonists such as metoclopramide may be superior to the phenothiazines in treating severe nausea and vomiting and are particularly useful in treatment of gastroparesis. Intravenous metoclopramide may be effective as prophylaxis against nausea when given prior to chemotherapy. Cisapride, the preferred drug for gastroparesis, exerts peripheral antiemetic effects but is devoid of the CNS effects of metoclopramide. Ondansetron, a serotonin receptor blocker, and glucocorticoids are used for treating nausea and vomiting associated with cancer chemotherapy. Erythromycin is effective in some pts with gastroparesis.

INDIGESTION

Indigestion is a nonspecific term that encompasses a variety of upper abdominal complaints including heartburn, regurgitation, and dyspepsia (upper abdominal discomfort or pain). These symptoms are overwhelmingly due to gastroesophageal reflux disease (GERD).

Pathophysiology

GERD occurs as a consequence of acid reflux into the esophagus from the stomach, gastric motor dysfunction, or visceral afferent hypersensitivity. A wide variety of situations promote GERD: increased gastric contents (from a large meal, gastric stasis, or acid hypersecretion), physical factors (lying down, bending over), increased pressure on the stomach (tight clothes, obesity, ascites, pregnancy), loss (usually intermittent) of lower esophageal sphincter tone (diseases such as scleroderma, smoking, anticholinergics, calcium antagonists). Hiatal hernia also promotes acid flow into the esophagus.

Natural History

Heartburn is reported once monthly by 40% of Americans and daily by 7%. Functional dyspepsia is defined as >3 months of dyspepsia without an organic cause. Functional dyspepsia is the cause of symptoms in 60% of patients with dyspeptic symptoms. However, peptic ulcer disease from either *Helicobacter pylori* infection or ingestion of NSAIDs is present 15% of cases.

In most cases, the esophagus is not damaged, but 5% of patients develop esophageal ulcers and some form strictures. 8–20% develop glandular epithelial cell metaplasia, termed Barrett's esophagus, which can progress to adenocarcinoma.

Extraesophageal manifestations include asthma, laryngitis, chronic cough, aspiration pneumonitis, chronic bronchitis, sleep apnea, dental caries, halitosis, hiccups.

Evaluation

The presence of dysphagia, odynophagia, unexplained weight loss, recurrent vomiting leading to dehydration, occult or gross bleeding, or a palpable mass or adenopathy are "alarm" signals that demand directed radiographic, endoscopic, and surgical evaluation. Patients without alarm features are generally treated empirically. Individuals >45 years can be tested for the presence of *H. pylori*. Pts positive for the infection are treated to eradicate the organism. Pts who fail to respond to *H. pylori* treatment, those >45 years old, and those with alarm factors generally undergo upper GI endoscopy.

 TREATMENT

Weight reduction; elevation of the head of the bed; and avoidance of large meals, smoking, caffeine, alcohol, chocolate, fatty food, citrus juices, and NSAIDs may prevent GERD. Antacids are widely used. Clinical trials suggest that proton pump inhibitors (omeprazole) are more effective than histamine receptor blockers (ranitidine) in patients with or without esophageal erosions. *H. pylori* eradication regimens are discussed in Chap. 148. Cisapride can stimulate gastric emptying. Omeprazole plus cisapride is a rational combination.

Surgical techniques (Nissan fundoplication, Belsey procedure) can be used in the rare patients who are refractory to medical management. Clinical trials have not documented the superiority of one over another.

For a more detailed discussion, see Hasler WL: Nausea, Vomiting, and Indigestion, Chap. 41, p. 236, in HPIM-15.

19

WEIGHT LOSS

Significant unintentional weight loss in a previously healthy individual is often a harbinger of underlying systemic disease. The routine medical history should always include inquiry about changes in weight. Rapid fluctuations of weight over days suggest loss or gain of fluid, whereas long-term changes usually involve loss of tissue mass. Loss of 5% of body weight over 6-12 months should prompt further evaluation.

Etiology

A list of possible causes of weight loss is extensive (Table 19-1). In older persons the most common causes of weight loss are depression, cancer, and benign gastrointestinal disease. In younger individuals diabetes mellitus, hyperthyroidism, anorexia nervosa, and infection, especially with HIV, should be considered.

Clinical Features

Before extensive evaluation is undertaken, it is important to confirm that weight loss has occurred. In the absence of documentation, changes in belt notch size or the fit of clothing may help to determine loss of weight.

The *history* should include questions about fever, pain, shortness of breath or cough, palpitations, and evidence of neurologic disease. A history of GI

Table 19-1

Causes of Weight Loss

Cancer

Endocrine and metabolic causes
   Hyperthyroidism
   Diabetes mellitus
   Pheochromocytoma
   Adrenal insufficiency

Gastrointestinal disorders
   Malabsorption
   Obstruction
   Pernicious anemia

Cardiac disorders
   Chronic ischemia
   Chronic congestive heart failure

Respiratory disorders
   Emphysema
   Chronic obstructive pulmonary
    disease

Renal insufficiency

Rheumatologic disease

Infections
   HIV
   Tuberculosis
   Parasitic infection
   Subacute bacterial endocarditis

Medications
   Antibiotics
   Nonsteroidal anti-inflammatory drugs
   Serotonin reuptake inhibitors
   Metformin
   Levodopa
   ACE inhibitors
   Other drugs

Disorders of the mouth and teeth

Age-related factors
   Physiologic changes
   Decreased taste and smell
   Functional disabilities

Neurologic causes
   Stroke
   Parkinson's disease
   Neuromuscular disorders
   Dementia

Social causes
   Isolation
   Economic hardship

Psychiatric and behavioral causes
   Depression
   Anxiety
   Bereavement
   Alcoholism
   Eating disorders
   Increased activity or exercise

Idiopathic

---

symptoms should be obtained, including difficulty eating, dysphagia, anorexia, nausea, and change in bowel habits. Use of cigarettes, alcohol, and all medications should be reviewed, and patients should be questioned about previous illness or surgery as well as diseases in family members. Risk factors for HIV should be assessed. Signs of depression, evidence of dementia, and social factors, including financial issues that might affect food intake, should be considered.

Physical examination should begin with weight determination and documentation of vital signs. The skin should be examined for pallor, jaundice, turgor, surgical scars, and stigmata of systemic disease. Evaluation for oral thrush, dental disease, thyroid gland enlargement, and adenopathy and for respiratory, cardiac, or abdominal abnormalities should be performed. All men should have a rectal examination, including the prostate; all women should have a pelvic examination; and both should have testing of the stool for occult blood. Neurologic examination should include mental status assessment and screening for depression.

Initial *laboratory evaluation* is shown in Table 19-2, with appropriate treatment based on the underlying cause of the weight loss. If an etiology of weight

Table 19-2

Screening Tests for Evaluation of Involuntary Weight Loss

Initial testing	Additional testing
CBC	HIV test
Electrolytes, calcium, glucose	Upper and/or lower gastrointes-
Renal and liver function tests	tinal endoscopy
Urinalysis	Abdominal CT scan or MRI
TSH	Chest CT scan
Chest x-ray	
Recommended cancer screening	

loss is not found, careful clinical follow-up, rather than persistent undirected testing, is reasonable.

For a more detailed discussion, see Reife CM: Weight Loss, Chap. 43, p. 250, in HPIM-15.

20

DYSPHAGIA

DYSPHAGIA

Dysphagia is difficulty moving food or liquid through the mouth, pharynx, and esophagus. The pt senses swallowed material sticking along the path. Odynophagia is pain on swallowing. *Globus pharyngeus* is the sensation of a lump lodged in the throat, but swallowing is unaffected.

 PATHOPHYSIOLOGY Dysphagia is caused by two main mechanisms: mechanical obstruction or motor dysfunction. Mechanical causes of dysphagia can be luminal (e.g., large food bolus, foreign body), intrinsic to the esophagus (e.g., inflammation, webs and rings, strictures, tumors), or extrinsic to the esophagus (e.g., cervical spondylitis, enlarged thyroid or mediastinal mass, vascular compression). The motor function abnormalities that cause dysphagia may be related to defects in initiating the swallowing reflex (e.g., tongue paralysis, lack of saliva, lesions affecting sensory components of cranial nerves X and XI), disorders of the pharyngeal and esophageal striated muscle (e.g., muscle disorders such as polymyositis and dermatomyositis, neurologic lesions such as myasthenia gravis, polio, or amyotrophic lateral sclerosis), and disorders of the esophageal smooth muscle (e.g., achalasia, scleroderma, myotonic dystrophy).

_____ *Approach to the Patient* _____

History can provide a presumptive diagnosis in about 80% of pts. Difficulty only with solids implies mechanical dysphagia. Difficulty with both solids and liquids may occur late in the course of mechanical dysphagia but is an early sign of motor dysphagia. Pts can sometimes pinpoint the site of food sticking. Weight loss out of proportion to the degree of dysphagia may be a sign of underlying malignancy. Hoarseness may be related to involvement of the larynx in the primary disease process (e.g., neuromuscular disorders), neoplastic disruption of the recurrent laryngeal nerve, or laryngitis from gastroesophageal reflux.

Physical exam may reveal signs of skeletal muscle, neurologic, or oropharyngeal diseases. Neck exam can reveal masses impinging on the esophagus. Skin changes might suggest the systemic nature of the underlying disease (e.g., scleroderma).

Dysphagia is nearly always a symptom of organic disease rather than a functional complaint. If oropharyngeal dysphagia is suspected, videofluoroscopy of swallowing may be diagnostic. Mechanical dysphagia can be evaluated by barium swallow and esophagogastroscopy with endoscopic biopsy. Barium swallow and esophageal motility studies can show the presence of motor dysphagia.

OROPHARYNGEAL DYSPHAGIA Pt has difficulty initiating the swallow; food sticks at the level of the suprasternal notch; nasopharyngeal regurgitation and aspiration may be present.

Causes include: for solids only, carcinoma, aberrant vessel, congenital web (Plummer-Vinson syndrome), cervical osteophyte; for solids and liquids, cricopharyngeal bar (e.g., hypertensive or hypotensive upper esophageal sphincter), Zenker's diverticulum (outpouching in the posterior midline at the intersection of the pharynx and the cricopharyngeus muscle), myasthenia gravis, glucocorticoid myopathy, hyperthyroidism, hypothyroidism, myotonic dystrophy, amyotrophic lateral sclerosis, multiple sclerosis, Parkinson's disease, stroke, and bulbar and pseudobulbar palsy.

ESOPHAGEAL DYSPHAGIA Food sticks in the mid or lower sternal area; can be associated with regurgitation, aspiration, odynophagia. Causes include: for solids only, lower esophageal ring (Schatzki's ring, symptoms are usually intermittent), peptic stricture (heartburn accompanies this), carcinoma, lye stricture; for solids and liquids, diffuse esophageal spasm (occurs with chest pain and is intermittent), scleroderma (progressive and occurs with heartburn), achalasia (progressive and occurs without heartburn).

NONCARDIAC CHEST PAIN

Thirty percent of pts presenting with chest pain have esophageal source rather than angina. History and physical exam often cannot distinguish cardiac from noncardiac pain. Exclude cardiac disease first. Causes include: gastroesophageal reflux disease, esophageal motility disorders, peptic ulcer disease, gallstones, psychiatric disease (anxiety, panic attacks, depression).

Evaluation Consider a trial of antireflux therapy (omeprazole); if no response, 24-h ambulatory luminal pH monitoring; if negative, esophageal manometry may show motor disorder. Trial of imipramine, 50 mg PO qhs, may be worthwhile. Consider psychiatric evaluation in selected cases.

ESOPHAGEAL MOTILITY DISORDERS

Pts may have a spectrum of manometric findings ranging from nonspecific abnormalities to defined clinical entities.

ACHALASIA   Motor obstruction caused by hypertensive lower esophageal sphincter (LES), incomplete relaxation of LES, or loss of peristalsis in smooth-muscle portion of esophagus. Causes include: primary (idiopathic) or secondary due to Chagas' disease, lymphoma, carcinoma, chronic idiopathic intestinal pseudoobstruction, ischemia, neurotropic viruses, drugs, toxins, radiation therapy, postvagotomy.

Evaluation   Chest x-ray shows absence of gastric air bubble. Barium swallow shows dilated esophagus with distal beaklike narrowing and air-fluid level. Endoscopy is done to rule out cancer, particularly in people >50 years. Manometry shows normal or elevated LES pressure, decreased LES relaxation, absent peristalsis.

 TREATMENT

Pneumatic balloon dilatation is effective in 85%, 3–5% risk of perforation or bleeding. Injection of botulinum toxin at endoscopy to relax LES is safe and effective but effects last only about 12 months. Myotomy of LES (Heller procedure) is effective, but 10–30% of pts develop gastroesophageal reflux. Calcium antagonists (nifedipine 10–20 mg or isosorbide dinitrate 5–10 mg SL ac) may avert need for dilatation or surgery.

SPASTIC DISORDERS   Diffuse esophageal spasm involves multiple spontaneous and swallow-induced contractions of the esophageal body that are of simultaneous onset, long duration, and recurrent. Causes include: primary (idiopathic) or secondary due to gastroesophageal reflux disease, emotional stress, diabetes, alcoholism, neuropathy, radiation therapy, ischemia, or collagen vascular disease.

An important variant is *nutcracker esophagus*: high-amplitude (>180 mmHg) peristaltic contractions; particularly associated with chest pain or dysphagia, but correlation between symptoms and manometry is inconsistent. Condition may resolve over time or evolve into diffuse spasm; associated with increased frequency of depression, anxiety, and somatization.

Evaluation   Barium swallow shows corkscrew esophagus, pseudodiverticula, and diffuse spasm. Manometry shows spasm with multiple simultaneous esophageal contractions of high amplitude and long duration. In nutcracker esophagus, the contractions are peristaltic and of high amplitude. If heart disease has been ruled out, edrophonium, ergonovine, or bethanechol can be used to provoke spasm.

 TREATMENT

Anticholinergics are usually of limited value; nitrates (isosorbide dinitrate, 5–10 mg PO ac) and calcium antagonists (diltiazem, 60–90 mg PO tid) are more effective. Those refractory to medical management may benefit from balloon dilatation. Rare pts require surgical intervention; longitudinal myotomy of esophageal circular muscle. Treatment of concomitant depression or other psychological disturbance may help.

SCLERODERMA   Atrophy of the esophageal smooth muscle and fibrosis can make the esophagus aperistaltic and lead to an incompetent LES with attendant reflux esophagitis and stricture. Treatment of gastroesophageal reflux disease is discussed in Chap. 18.

ESOPHAGEAL INFLAMMATION

VIRAL ESOPHAGITIS   Herpesviruses I and II, varicella-zoster virus, and CMV can all cause esophagitis; particularly common in immunocompromised pts (e.g., AIDS). Odynophagia, dysphagia, fever, and bleeding are symptoms and signs. Diagnosis is made by endoscopy with biopsy, brush cytology, and culture.

 TREATMENT

Disease is usually self-limited in the immunocompetent person; viscous lidocaine can relieve pain; in prolonged cases and in immunocompromised hosts, herpes and varicella esophagitis are treated with acyclovir, 5–10 mg/kg IV q8h for 10–14 d, then 200–400 mg PO 5 times a day. CMV is treated with ganciclovir 5 mg/kg IV q12h until healing occurs, which may take weeks to months. In nonresponders, foscarnet, 60 mg/kg IV q12h for 21 d, may be effective.

CANDIDA ESOPHAGITIS   In immunocompromised hosts, malignancy, diabetes, hypoparathyroidism, hemoglobinopathy, SLE, corrosive esophageal injury, candidal esophageal infection may present with odynophagia, dysphagia, and oral thrush (50%). Diagnosis is made on endoscopy by identifying yellow-white plaques or nodules on friable red mucosa. Characteristic hyphae are seen on KOH stain. In patients with AIDS, the development of symptoms may prompt an empirical therapeutic trial.

 TREATMENT

Oral nystatin (100,000 U/mL) 5 mL q6h or clotrimazole 10-mg tablet sucked q6h is effective. In immunocompromised host, fluconazole, 100–200 mg PO daily for 1–3 weeks is treatment of choice; alternatives include itraconazole, 200 mg PO bid, or ketoconazole, 200–400 mg PO daily; long-term maintenance therapy is often required. Poorly responsive pts may respond to higher doses of fluconazole (400 mg/d) or to amphotericin 10–15 mg IV q6h for a total dose of 300–500 mg.

PILL-RELATED ESOPHAGITIS   Doxycycline, tetracycline, aspirin, NSAIDs, KCl, quinidine, ferrous sulfate, clindamycin, alprenolol, and alendronate can induce local inflammation in the esophagus. Predisposing factors include recumbency after swallowing pills with small sips of water, anatomic factors impinging on the esophagus and slowing transit.

 TREATMENT

Withdraw offending drug, use antacids, and dilate any resulting stricture.

OTHER CAUSES OF ESOPHAGITIS IN AIDS   *Mycobacteria, Cryptosporidium, Pneumocystis carinii*, idiopathic esophageal ulcers, giant ulcers (possible cytopathic effect of HIV) can occur. Ulcers may respond to systemic glucocorticoids.

For a more detailed discussion, see Goyal RK: Dysphagia, Chap. 40, p. 233; and Diseases of the Esophagus, Chap. 284, p. 1642, in HPIM-15.

21

DIARRHEA, CONSTIPATION, AND MALABSORPTION

NORMAL GASTROINTESTINAL FUNCTION

ABSORPTION OF FLUID AND ELECTROLYTES   Fluid delivery to the GI tract is 8–10 L/d, including 2 L/d ingested; most is absorbed in small bowel. Colonic absorption is normally 0.05–2 L/d, with capacity for 6 L/d if required. Intestinal water absorption passively follows active transport of Na^+, Cl^-, glucose, and bile salts. Additional transport mechanisms include Cl^-/HCO_3^- exchange, Na^+/H^+ exchange, H^+, K^+, Cl^-, and HCO_3^- secretion, Na^+-glucose cotransport, and active Na^+ transport across the basolateral membrane by Na^+, K^+-ATPase.

NUTRIENT ABSORPTION   (1) Proximal small intestine: iron, calcium, folate, fats (after hydrolysis of triglycerides to fatty acids by pancreatic lipase and colipase), proteins (after hydrolysis by pancreatic and intestinal peptidases), carbohydrates (after hydrolysis by amylases and disaccharidases); triglycerides absorbed as micelles after solubilization by bile salts; amino acids and dipeptides absorbed via specific carriers; sugars absorbed by active transport. (2) Distal small intestine: vitamin B_{12}, bile salts, water. (3) Colon: water, electrolytes.

INTESTINAL MOTILITY   Allows propulsion of intestinal contents from stomach to anus and separation of components to facilitate nutrient absorption. Propulsion is controlled by neural, myogenic, and hormonal mechanisms; mediated by migrating motor complex, an organized wave of neuromuscular activity that originates in the distal stomach during fasting and migrates slowly down the small intestine. Colonic motility is mediated by local peristalsis to propel feces. Defecation is effected by relaxation of internal anal sphincter in response to rectal distention, with voluntary control by contraction of external anal sphincter.

DIARRHEA

PHYSIOLOGY   Formally defined as fecal output >200 g/d on low-fiber (western) diet; also frequently used to connote loose or watery stools. Mediated by one or more of the following mechanisms:

Osmotic Diarrhea   Nonabsorbed solutes increase intraluminal oncotic pressure, causing outpouring of water; usually ceases with fasting; stool osmolal gap >40 (see below). Causes include disaccharidase (e.g., lactase) deficiencies, pancreatic insufficiency, bacterial overgrowth, lactulose or sorbitol ingestion, polyvalent laxative abuse, celiac or tropical sprue, and short bowel syndrome. Lactase deficiency can be either primary (more prevalent in blacks and Asians, usually presenting in early adulthood) or secondary (from viral, bacterial, or protozoal gastroenteritis, celiac or tropical sprue, or kwashiorkor).

Secretory Diarrhea   Active ion secretion causes obligatory water loss; diarrhea is usually watery, often profuse, unaffected by fasting; stool Na^+ and K^+ are elevated with osmolal gap <40. Causes include viral infections (e.g., rotavirus, Norwalk virus), bacterial infections (e.g., cholera, enterotoxigenic *Escherichia coli, Staphylococcus aureus*), protozoa (e.g., *Giardia, Isospora, Cryptosporidium*), AIDS-associated disorders (including mycobacterial and HIV-induced), medications (e.g., theophylline, colchicine, prostaglandins, diuretics), Zollinger-Ellison syndrome (excess gastrin production), vasoactive intestinal peptide (VIP)-producing tumors, carcinoid tumors (histamine and serotonin), medullary thyroid carcinoma (prostaglandins and calcitonin), systemic mastocytosis, basophilic leukemia, distal colonic villous adenomas (direct secretion of potassium-rich fluid), collagenous and microscopic colitis, and cholerrheic diarrhea (from ileal malabsorption of bile salts).

Exudative   Inflammation, necrosis, and sloughing of colonic mucosa; may include component of secretory diarrhea due to prostaglandin release by inflammatory cells; stools usually contain PMNs as well as occult or gross blood. Causes include bacterial infections [e.g., *Campylobacter, Salmonella, Shigella, Yersinia*, invasive or enterotoxigenic *E. coli, Vibrio parahemolyticus, Clostridium difficile* colitis (frequently antibiotic-induced)], colonic parasites (e.g., *Entamoeba histolytica*), Crohn's disease, ulcerative proctocolitis, idiopathic inflammatory bowel disease, radiation enterocolitis, cancer chemotherapeutic agents, and intestinal ischemia.

Altered Intestinal Motility   Alteration of coordinated control of intestinal propulsion; diarrhea often intermittent or alternating with constipation. Causes include diabetes mellitus, adrenal insufficiency, hyperthyroidism, collagen-vascular diseases, parasitic infestations, gastrin and VIP hypersecretory states, amyloidosis, laxatives (esp. magnesium-containing agents), antibiotics (esp. erythromycin), cholinergic agents, primary neurologic dysfunction (e.g., Parkinson's disease, traumatic neuropathy), fecal impaction, diverticular disease, and irritable bowel syndrome. Blood in intestinal lumen is cathartic, and major upper GI bleeding leads to diarrhea from increased motility.

Decreased Absorptive Surface   Usually arises from surgical manipulation (e.g., extensive bowel resection or rearrangement) that leaves inadequate absorptive surface for fat and carbohydrate digestion and fluid and electrolyte absorption; occurs spontaneously from enteroenteric fistulas (esp. gastrocolic).

EVALUATION   *History*   Diarrhea must be distinguished from fecal incontinence, change in stool caliber, rectal bleeding, and small, frequent, but otherwise normal stools. Careful medication history is essential. Alternating diarrhea and constipation suggests fixed colonic obstruction (e.g., from carcinoma) or irritable bowel syndrome. A sudden, acute course, often with nausea, vomiting, and fever, is typical of viral and bacterial infections, diverticulitis, ischemia, radiation enterocolitis, or drug-induced diarrhea and may be the initial presentation of inflammatory bowel disease. >90% of acute diarrheal illnesses are infectious in etiology. A longer (>4 weeks), more insidious course suggests malabsorption, inflammatory bowel disease, metabolic or endocrine disturbance, pancreatic insufficiency, laxative abuse, ischemia, neoplasm (hypersecretory state or partial obstruction), or irritable bowel syndrome. Parasitic and certain forms of bacterial enteritis can also produce chronic symptoms. Particularly foul-smelling or oily stool suggests fat malabsorption. Fecal impaction may cause apparent diarrhea because only liquids pass partial obstruction. Several infectious causes of diarrhea are associated with an immunocompromised state (Table 21-1).

Physical Examination   Signs of dehydration are often prominent in severe, acute diarrhea. Fever and abdominal tenderness suggest infection or inflammatory disease but are often absent in viral enteritis. Evidence of malnutrition suggests chronic course. Certain signs are frequently associated with specific deficiency states secondary to malabsorption (e.g., cheilosis with riboflavin or iron deficiency, glossitis with B_{12}, folate deficiency).

Stool Examination   Culture for bacterial pathogens, examination for leukocytes, measurement of *C. difficile* toxin, and examination for ova and parasites are important components of evaluation of pts with severe, protracted, or bloody diarrhea. Presence of blood (fecal occult blood test) or leukocytes (Wright's stain) suggests inflammation (e.g., ulcerative colitis, Crohn's disease, infection, or ischemia). Gram's stain of stool can be diagnostic of *Staphylococcus, Campylobacter*, or *Candida* infection. Steatorrhea (determined with Sudan III stain of stool sample or 72-h quantitative fecal fat analysis) suggests malabsorption or pancreatic insufficiency. Measurement of Na^+ and K^+ levels in fecal water helps to distinguish osmotic from other types of diarrhea; osmotic diarrhea is implied by stool osmolal gap >40, where stool osmolal gap = $osmol_{serum} - [2 \times (Na^+ + K^+)_{stool}]$.

Laboratory Studies   CBC may indicate anemia (acute or chronic blood loss or malabsorption of iron, folate, or B_{12}), leukocytosis (inflammation), eosinophilia (parasitic, neoplastic, and inflammatory bowel diseases). Serum levels of calcium, albumin, iron, cholesterol, folate, B_{12}, vitamin D, and carotene; serum iron-binding capacity; and prothrombin time can provide evidence of intestinal malabsorption or maldigestion.

Other Studies   D-Xylose absorption test is a convenient screen for small-bowel absorptive function. Small-bowel biopsy is especially useful for evaluating intestinal malabsorption. Specialized studies include Schilling test (B_{12} malabsorption), lactose H_2 breath test (carbohydrate malabsorption), [14C]xylose and lactulose H_2 breath tests (bacterial overgrowth), glycocholic breath test (ileal malabsorption), triolein breath test (fat malabsorption), and bentiromide and secretin tests (pancreatic insufficiency). Sigmoidoscopy or colonoscopy with biopsy is useful in the diagnosis of colitis (esp. pseudomembranous, ischemic,

Table 21-1

Infectious Causes of Diarrhea in Patients with AIDS

NONOPPORTUNISTIC PATHOGENS	OPPORTUNISTIC PATHOGENS
Shigella	Protozoa
Salmonella	*Cryptosporidium*
Campylobacter	*Isospora belli*
Entamoeba histolytica	Microsporidia
Chlamydia	*Blastocystis hominis*
Neisseria gonorrhoeae	Viruses
Treponema pallidum and other	Cytomegalovirus
spirochetes	Herpes simplex
Giardia lamblia	Adenovirus
	HIV
	Bacteria
	Mycobacterium avium complex

microscopic); it may not allow distinction between infectious and noninfectious (esp. idiopathic ulcerative) colitis. Barium contrast x-ray studies may suggest malabsorption (thickened bowel folds), inflammatory bowel disease (ileitis or colitis), tuberculosis (ileocecal inflammation), neoplasm, intestinal fistula, or motility disorders.

 TREATMENT

An approach to the management of acute diarrheal illnesses is shown in Fig. 21-1. Symptomatic therapy includes vigorous rehydration (IV or with oral glucose-electrolyte solutions), electrolyte replacement, binders of osmotically active substances (e.g., kaolin-pectin), and opiates to decrease bowel motility (e.g., loperamide, diphenoxylate); opiates may be contraindicated in infectious or inflammatory causes of diarrhea. An approach to the management of chronic diarrhea is shown in Fig. 21-2.

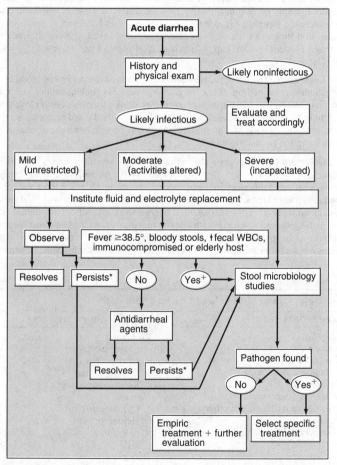

FIGURE 21-1 Algorithm for the management of acute diarrhea. Before evaluation, consider empiric Rx with (*) metronidazole and with (+) quinolone.

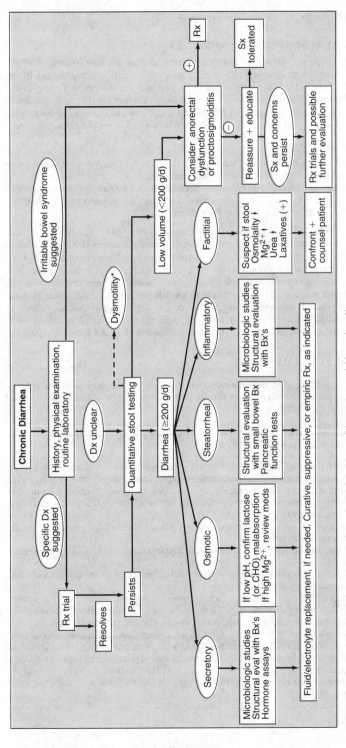

FIGURE 21-2 Algorithm for the management of chronic diarrhea. *Dysmotility presents variable stool profile.

MALABSORPTION SYNDROMES

Intestinal malabsorption of ingested nutrients may produce osmotic diarrhea, steatorrhea, or specific deficiencies (e.g., iron; folate; B_{12}; vitamins A, D, E, and K). Table 21-2 lists common causes of intestinal malabsorption. Protein-losing enteropathy may result from several causes of malabsorption; it is associated with hypoalbuminemia and can be detected by measuring stool α_1-antitrypsin or radiolabeled albumin levels. Therapy is directed at the underlying disease.

CONSTIPATION

Defined as decrease in frequency of stools to <1 per week or difficulty in defecation; may result in abdominal pain, distention, and fecal impaction, with consequent obstruction or, rarely, perforation. A frequent and often subjective complaint. Contributory factors may include inactivity, low-roughage diet, and inadequate allotment of time for defecation.

SPECIFIC CAUSES Altered colonic motility due to neurologic dysfunction (diabetes mellitus, spinal cord injury, multiple sclerosis, Chagas disease, Hirschsprung's disease, chronic idiopathic intestinal pseudoobstruction, idiopathic megacolon), scleroderma, drugs (esp. anticholinergic agents, opiates, aluminum- or calcium-based antacids, calcium channel blockers, iron supplements, sucralfate), hypothyroidism, Cushing's syndrome, hypokalemia, hypercalcemia, dehydration, mechanical causes (colorectal tumors, diverticulitis, volvulus, hernias, intussusception), and anorectal pain (from fissures, hemorrhoids, abscesses, or proctitis) leading to retention, constipation, and fecal impaction.

 TREATMENT

In absence of identifiable cause, constipation may improve with reassurance, exercise, increased dietary fiber, bulking agents (e.g., psyllium), and increased

Table 21-2

Common Causes of Malabsorption

Maldigestion: Chronic pancreatitis, cystic fibrosis, pancreatic carcinoma
Bile salt deficiency: Cirrhosis, cholestasis, bacterial overgrowth (blind loop syndromes, intestinal diverticula, hypomotility disorders), impaired ileal reabsorption (resection, Crohn's disease), bile salt binders (cholestyramine, calcium carbonate, neomycin)
Inadequate absorptive surface: Massive intestinal resection, gastrocolic fistula, jejunoileal bypass
Lymphatic obstruction: Lymphoma, Whipple's disease, intestinal lymphangiectasia
Vascular disease: Constrictive pericarditis, right-sided heart failure, mesenteric arterial or venous insufficiency
Mucosal disease: Infection (esp. *Giardia*, Whipple's disease, tropical sprue), inflammatory diseases (esp. Crohn's disease), radiation enteritis, eosinophilic enteritis, ulcerative jejunitis, mastocytosis, tropical sprue, infiltrative disorders (amyloidosis, scleroderma, lymphoma, collagenous sprue, microscopic colitis), biochemical abnormalities (gluten-sensitive enteropathy, disaccharidase deficiency, hypogammaglobulinemia, abetalipoproteinemia, amino acid transport deficiencies), endocrine disorders (diabetes mellitus, hypoparathyroidism, adrenal insufficiency, hyperthyroidism, Zollinger-Ellison syndrome, carcinoid syndrome)

fluid intake. Specific therapies include removal of bowel obstruction (fecolith, tumor), discontinuance of nonessential hypomotility agents (esp. aluminum- or calcium-containing antacids, opiates). For symptomatic relief, magnesium- containing agents or other cathartics are occasionally needed. With severe hypo- or dysmotility or in presence of opiates, osmotically active agents (e.g., oral lactulose, intestinal polyethylene glycol–containing lavage solutions) and oral or rectal emollient laxatives (e.g., docusate salts) and mineral oil are most effective.

For a more detailed discussion, see Ahlquist DA, Camilleri M: Diarrhea and Constipation, Chap. 42, p. 241; and Binder H: Disorders of Absorption, Chap. 286, p. 1665, in HPIM-15.

22

GASTROINTESTINAL BLEEDING

PRESENTATION

1. *Hematemesis*: Vomiting of blood or altered blood ("coffee grounds") indicates bleeding proximal to ligament of Treitz.

2. *Melena*: Altered (black) blood per rectum (>100 mL blood required for one melenic stool) usually indicates bleeding proximal to ligament of Treitz but may be as distal as ascending colon; pseudomelena may be caused by ingestion of iron, bismuth, licorice, beets, blueberries, charcoal.

3. *Hematochezia*: Bright red or maroon rectal bleeding usually implies bleeding beyond ligament of Treitz but may be due to rapid upper GI bleeding (>1000 mL).

4. *Positive fecal occult blood test with or without iron deficiency.*

5. *Symptoms of blood loss*: e.g., light-headedness or shortness of breath.

HEMODYNAMIC CHANGES   Orthostatic drop in bp >10 mmHg usually indicates >20% reduction in blood volume (± syncope, light-headedness, nausea, sweating, thirst).

SHOCK   bp <100 mmHg systolic usually indicates <30% reduction in blood volume (± pallor, cool skin).

LABORATORY CHANGES   Hematocrit may not reflect extent of blood loss because of delayed equilibration with extravascular fluid. Mild leukocytosis and thrombocytosis. Elevated BUN is common in upper GI bleeding.

ADVERSE PROGNOSTIC SIGNS   Age >60, associated illnesses, co-agulopathy, immunosuppression, presentation with shock, rebleeding, onset of bleeding in hospital, variceal bleeding, endoscopic stigmata of recent bleeding, [e.g., "visible vessel" in ulcer base (see below)].

UPPER GI BLEEDING

CAUSES *Common* Peptic ulcer, gastropathy (alcohol, aspirin, NSAIDs, stress), esophagitis, Mallory-Weiss tear (mucosal tear at gastroesophageal junction due to retching), gastroesophageal varices.

Less Common Swallowed blood (nosebleed); esophageal, gastric, or intestinal neoplasm; anticoagulant and fibrinolytic therapy; hypertrophic gastropathy (Ménétrier's disease); aortic aneurysm; aortoenteric fistula (from aortic graft); AV malformation; telangiectases (Osler-Rendu-Weber syndrome); Dieulafoy lesion (ectatic submucosal vessel); vasculitis; connective tissue disease (pseudoxanthoma elasticum, Ehlers-Danlos syndrome); blood dyscrasias; neurofibroma; amyloidosis; hemobilia (biliary origin).

EVALUATION After hemodynamic resuscitation (see below and Fig. 22-1).

* History and physical examination: Drugs (increased risk of upper and lower GI tract bleeding with aspirin and NSAIDs), prior ulcer, bleeding history, family history, features of cirrhosis or vasculitis, etc. Hyperactive bowel sounds favor upper GI source.
* Nasogastric aspirate for gross blood, if source (upper versus lower) not clear from history; may be falsely negative in up to 16% of pts if bleeding has ceased or duodenum is the source. Testing aspirate for occult blood is meaningless.
* Upper endoscopy: Accuracy >90%; allows visualization of bleeding site and possibility of therapeutic intervention; mandatory for suspected varices, aortoenteric fistulas; permits identification of "visible vessel" (protruding artery in ulcer crater), which connotes high (~50%) risk of rebleeding.
* Upper GI barium radiography: Accuracy ~80% in identifying a lesion, though does not confirm source of bleeding; acceptable alternative to endoscopy in resolved or chronic low-grade bleeding.
* Selective mesenteric arteriography: When brisk bleeding precludes identification at endoscopy.
* Radioisotope scanning (e.g., ^{99}Tc tagged to red blood cells or albumin); used primarily as screening test to confirm bleeding is rapid enough for arteriography to be of value or when bleeding is intermittent and of unclear origin.

LOWER GI BLEEDING

CAUSES Anal lesions (hemorrhoids, fissures), rectal trauma, proctitis, colitis (ulcerative colitis, Crohn's disease, infectious colitis, ischemic colitis, radiation), colonic polyps, colonic carcinoma, angiodysplasia (vascular ectasia), diverticulosis, intussusception, solitary ulcer, blood dyscrasias, vasculitis, connective tissue disease, neurofibroma, amyloidosis, anticoagulation.

EVALUATION See below and Fig. 22-2.

* History and physical examination.
* In the presence of hemodynamic changes, perform upper endoscopy followed by colonoscopy. In the absence of hemodynamic changes, perform anoscopy and either flexible sigmoidoscopy or colonoscopy: Exclude hemorrhoids, fissure, ulcer, proctitis, neoplasm.
* Colonoscopy: Often test of choice, but may be impossible if bleeding is massive.
* Barium enema: No role in active bleeding.

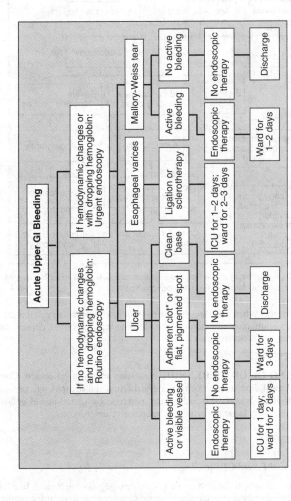

FIGURE 22-1 Suggested algorithm for patients with acute UGIB. Recommendations on level of care and time of discharge assume patient is stabilized without further bleeding or other concomitant medical problems. Upper GI endoscopy is the major diagnostic and therapeutic tool. *Some authors suggest endoscopic therapy for adherent clots.

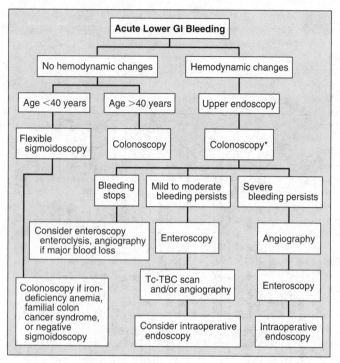

FIGURE 22-2   Suggested algorithm for patients with acute LGIB. *If massive bleeding does not allow time for colonic lavage, proceed to angiography.

- Arteriography: When bleeding is severe (requires bleeding rate >0.5 mL/min; may require prestudy radioisotope bleeding scan as above); defines site of bleeding or abnormal vasculature.

Surgical exploration (last resort).

BLEEDING OF OBSCURE ORIGIN   Often small-bowel source. Consider small-bowel enteroclysis x-ray (careful barium radiography via peroral intubation of small bowel), Meckel's scan, enteroscopy (small-bowel endoscopy), or exploratory laparotomy with intraoperative enteroscopy.

[Rx] **TREATMENT**

Upper and Lower GI Bleeding

- Venous access with large bore IV (14–18 gauge); central venous line for major bleed and pts with cardiac disease; monitor vital signs, urine output, Hct (fall may lag). Gastric lavage of unproven benefit but clears stomach before endoscopy. Iced saline may lyse clots; room-temperature tap water may be preferable. Intubation may be required to protect airway.
- Type and cross match blood (6 units for major bleed).
- Surgical standby when bleeding is massive.
- Support blood pressure with isotonic fluids (normal saline); albumin and fresh frozen plasma in cirrhotics. Packed red blood cells when available

(whole blood if massive bleeding); maintain Hct >25–30. Fresh frozen plasma and vitamin K (10 mg SC or IV) in cirrhotics with coagulopathy.
- IV calcium (e.g., up to 10–20 mL 10% calcium gluconate IV over 10–15 min) if serum calcium falls (due to transfusion of citrated blood). Empirical drug therapy (antacids, H$_2$ receptor blockers, omeprazole) of unproven benefit.
- Specific measures: Varices: IV vasopressin (0.4–0.9 U/min) with nitroglycerin IV, SL, or transdermally to maintain systolic bp >90 mmHg, Blakemore-Sengstaken tube tamponade, endoscopic sclerosis, or band ligation; propranolol or nadolol in doses sufficient to cause beta blockade reduces risk of recurrent or initial variceal bleeding (do not use in acute bleed) (Chap. 156); ulcer with visible vessel or active bleeding: endoscopic bipolar, heater-probe, or laser coagulation or injection of epinephrine; gastritis: embolization or vasopressin infusion of left gastric artery; GI telangiectases: ethinylestradiol/norethisterone (0.05/1.0 mg PO qd) may prevent recurrent bleeding, particularly in pts with chronic renal failure; diverticulosis: mesenteric arteriography with intraarterial vasopressin; angiodysplasia: colonoscopic bipolar or laser coagulation, may regress with replacement of stenotic aortic valve.
- Indications for emergency surgery: Uncontrolled or prolonged bleeding, severe rebleeding, aortoenteric fistula. For intractable variceal bleeding, consider transjugular intrahepatic portosystemic shunt (TIPS).

For a more detailed discussion, see Laine L: Gastrointestinal Bleeding, Chap. 44, p. 252, in HPIM-15.

23

JAUNDICE AND EVALUATION OF LIVER FUNCTION

JAUNDICE
DEFINITION   Yellow skin pigmentation caused by elevation in serum bilirubin level (also termed *icterus*); often more easily discernible in sclerae. Scleral icterus become clinically evident at a serum bilirubin level of ≥51 μmol/L (≥3 mg/dL); yellow skin discoloration also occurs with elevated serum carotene levels but without pigmentation of the sclerae.

BILIRUBIN METABOLISM   Bilirubin is the major breakdown product of hemoglobin released from senescent erythrocytes. Initially it is bound to albumin, transported into the liver, conjugated to a water-soluble form (glucuronide) by glucuronosyl transferase, excreted into the bile, and converted to urobilinogen in the colon. Urobilinogen is mostly excreted in the stool; a small portion is reabsorbed and excreted by the kidney. Bilirubin can be filtered by the kidney only in its conjugated form (measured as the "direct" fraction); thus increased *direct* serum bilirubin level is associated with bilirubinuria. Increased bilirubin production and excretion (even without hyperbilirubinemia, as in hemolysis) produce elevated urinary urobilinogen levels.

ETIOLOGY   Hyperbilirubinemia occurs as a result of (1) overproduction; (2) impaired uptake, conjugation, or excretion of bilirubin; (3) regurgitation of unconjugated or conjugated bilirubin from damaged hepatocytes or bile ducts (Table 23-1).

EVALUATION   The initial steps in evaluating the pt with jaundice are to determine whether (1) hyperbilirubinemia is conjugated or unconjugated, and (2) other biochemical liver tests are abnormal (Fig. 23-1). Essential clinical examination includes history (especially duration of jaundice, pruritus, associated pain, fever, weight loss, risk factors for parenterally transmitted diseases, medications, ethanol use, travel history, surgery, pregnancy), physical examination (hepatomegaly, tenderness over liver, palpable gallbladder, splenomegaly, gynecomastia, testicular atrophy), blood liver tests (see below), and complete blood count.

Gilbert's Syndrome   Impaired conjugation of bilirubin due to reduced bilirubin UDP glucoronosyltransferase activity. Results in mild unconjugated hyperbilirubinemia almost always <103 μmol/L (<6 mg/dL). Affects 3–7% of the population; males/females 2–7:1.

HEPATOMEGALY

DEFINITION   Generally a span of >12 cm in the right midclavicular line or a palpable left lobe in the epigastrium. It is important to exclude low-lying liver (e.g., with chronic obstructive pulmonary disease and lung hyperinflation)

Table 23-1

Causes of Hyperbilirubinemia

PREDOMINANTLY UNCONJUGATED (INDIRECT-REACTING) BILIRUBIN

Overproduction of bilirubin pigments: Intravascular hemolysis, hematoma resorption, ineffective erythropoiesis (bone marrow)

Decreased hepatic uptake: Sepsis, prolonged fasting, right-sided heart failure, drugs (e.g., rifampin, probenecid)

Decreased conjugation: Severe hepatocellular disease (e.g., hepatitis, cirrhosis), sepsis, drugs (e.g., chloramphenicol, pregnanediol), neonatal jaundice, inherited glucuronosyl transferase deficiency (Gilbert's syndrome, Crigler-Najjar syndromes type II or I)

PREDOMINANTLY CONJUGATED (DIRECT-REACTING) BILIRUBIN

Impaired hepatic excretion: Hepatocellular disease (e.g., drug-induced, viral, or ischemic hepatitis, cirrhosis), drug-induced cholestasis (e.g., oral contraceptives, methyltestosterone, chlorpromazine), sepsis, postoperative state, parenteral nutrition, biliary cirrhosis (primary or secondary), inherited disorders (Dubin-Johnson syndrome, Rotor syndrome, cholestasis of pregnancy, benign familial recurrent cholestasis)

Biliary obstruction: Biliary cirrhosis (primary or secondary), sclerosing cholangitis, intraluminal mechanical obstruction (e.g., stone, tumor, parasites, stricture, cyst), biliary compression (e.g., pancreatic tumor, portal lymphadenopathy, pancreatitis)

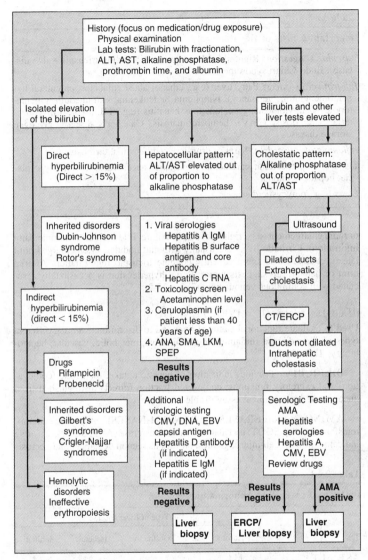

FIGURE 23-1   Evaluation of the patient with jaundice. ERCP, endoscopic retrograde cholangiopancreatography; CT, computed tomography; ALT, alanine aminotransferase; AST, aspartate aminotransferase; SMA, smooth muscle antibody; AMA, antimitochondrial antibody; LKM; liver-kidney microsomal antibody; SPEP, serum protein electrophoresis; CMV, cytomegalovirus; EBV, Epstein-Barr virus.

and other RUQ masses (e.g., enlarged gallbladder or bowel or kidney tumor). Independent assessment of size best obtained from ultrasound (US) or CT examination. Contour and texture are important: Focal enlargement or rocklike consistency suggests tumor; tenderness suggests inflammation (e.g., hepatitis)

Table 23-2

Important Causes of Hepatomegaly

Vascular congestion: Right-sided heart failure (including tricuspid valve disease), Budd-Chiari syndrome

Infiltrative disorders: Fatty liver (e.g., ethanol abuse, diabetes, parenteral hyperalimentation, pregnancy), lymphoma or leukemia, extramedullary hematopoiesis, amyloidosis, granulomatous hepatitis (e.g., TB, atypical mycobacteria, sarcoidosis, CMV), hemochromatosis, Gaucher's disease, glycogen storage diseases

Inflammatory disorders: Viral or drug-induced hepatitis, cirrhosis

Tumors: Hepatocellular carcinoma, metastatic cancer, focal nodular hyperplasia, hepatic adenoma

Cysts (e.g., polycystic disease)

---

or rapid enlargement (e.g., right-sided heart failure, Budd-Chiari syndrome, fatty infiltration). Cirrhotic livers are usually firm and nodular, often enlarged until late in course. Pulsations frequently connote tricuspid regurgitation. Arterial bruit or hepatic rub suggests tumor. Portal hypertension is occasionally associated with continuous venous hum (Table 23-2).

BLOOD TESTS OF LIVER FUNCTION

Used to evaluate functional status of liver and to discriminate among different types of liver disease (inflammatory, infiltrative, metabolic, vascular, hepatobiliary; Table 23-3).

BILIRUBIN   Provides indication of hepatic uptake, metabolic (conjugation) and excretory functions; conjugated fraction (direct) distinguished from unconjugated by chemical assay (Table 23-1).

AMINOTRANSFERASES (TRANSAMINASES)   Aspartate aminotransferase (AST; SGOT) and alanine aminotransferase (ALT; SGPT); sensitive indicators of liver cell injury; greatest elevations seen in hepatocellular necrosis

Table 23-3

Patterns of Liver Test Abnormalities

	Type of Liver Disease			
Test	Hepatocellular	Obstructive	Ischemic	Infiltrative
AST, ALT [a]	↑↑↑	↑	↑–↑↑↑	N–↑
Alkaline phosphatase	↑–↑↑	↑↑↑	↑–↑↑	↑–↑↑↑
5′-Nucleotidase	↑–↑↑	↑↑↑	↑	↑–↑↑↑
Bilirubin	↑–↑↑↑	↑–↑↑↑	N–↑	N
Prothrombin time	↑–↑↑↑	N[b]	N–↑↑	N
Albumin	N–↓↓↓	N[c]	N–↓	N

[a] In *acute complete obstruction*, serum transaminases may rise rapidly and dramatically but return to near normal levels after 1–3 days even in the presence of continued obstruction.
[b] May increase with prolonged biliary obstruction and secondary biliary cirrhosis.
[c] May decrease with prolonged biliary obstruction and secondary biliary cirrhosis.
NOTE: N, normal; ↑, elevated; ↓, decreased.

(e.g., viral hepatitis, toxic or ischemic liver injury, acute hepatic vein obstruction), occasionally with sudden, complete biliary obstruction (e.g., from gallstone); milder abnormalities in cholestatic, cirrhotic, and infiltrative disease; poor correlation between degree of liver cell damage and level of aminotransferases; ALT more specific measure of liver injury, since AST also found in striated muscle and other organs; ethanol-induced liver injury usually produces modest increases with more prominent elevation of AST than ALT.

ALKALINE PHOSPHATASE   Sensitive indicator of cholestasis, biliary obstruction (enzyme increases more quickly than serum bilirubin), and liver infiltration; mild elevations in other forms of liver disease; limited specificity because of wide tissue distribution; elevations also seen in childhood, pregnancy, and bone diseases; tissue-specific isoenzymes can be distinguished by differences in heat stability (liver enzyme activity stable under conditions that destroy bone enzyme activity).

5′-NUCLEOTIDASE (5′-NT)   Pattern of elevation in hepatobiliary disease similar to alkaline phosphatase; has greater specificity for liver disorders; used to determine whether liver is source of elevation in serum alkaline phosphatase, esp. in children, pregnant women, pts with possible concomitant bone disease.

γ-GLUTAMYLTRANSPEPTIDASE (GGT)   Correlates with serum alkaline phosphatase activity. Elevation is less specific for cholestasis than alkaline phosphatase or 5′-NT.

PROTHROMBIN TIME (PT)   (See also Chap. 60)   Measure of clotting factor activity; prolongation results from clotting-factor deficiency or inactivity; all clotting factors except factor VIII are synthesized in the liver, and deficiency can occur rapidly from widespread liver disease as in hepatitis, toxic injury, or cirrhosis; single best acute measure of hepatic synthetic function; helpful in Dx and prognosis of acute liver disease. Clotting factors II, VII, IX, X function only in the presence of the fat-soluble vitamin K; PT prolongation from fat malabsorption distinguished from hepatic disease by rapid and complete response to vitamin K replacement.

ALBUMIN   Decreased serum levels result from decreased hepatic synthesis (chronic liver disease or prolonged malnutrition) or excessive losses in urine or stool; insensitive indicator of acute hepatic dysfunction, since serum half-life is 2 to 3 weeks; in pts with chronic liver disease, degree of hypoalbuminemia correlates with severity of liver dysfunction.

GLOBULIN   Mild polyclonal hyperglobulinemia often seen in chronic liver diseases; marked elevation frequently seen in *autoimmune* chronic active hepatitis.

AMMONIA   Elevated blood levels result from deficiency of hepatic detoxification pathways and portal-systemic shunting, as in fulminant hepatitis, hepatotoxin exposure, and severe portal hypertension (e.g., from cirrhosis); elevation of blood ammonia does not correlate well with hepatic function or the presence or degree of acute encephalopathy.

HEPATOBILIARY IMAGING PROCEDURES

ULTRASONOGRAPHY   Rapid, noninvasive examination of abdominal structures; no radiation exposure; relatively low cost, equipment portable; images and interpretation strongly dependent on expertise of examiner; particularly valuable for detecting biliary duct dilatation and gallbladder stones (>95%);

much less sensitive for intraductal stones (~60%); most sensitive means of detecting ascites; moderately sensitive for detecting hepatic masses but excellent for discriminating solid from cystic structures; useful in directing percutaneous needle biopsies of suspicious lesions; Doppler US useful to determine patency and flow in portal, hepatic veins and portal-systemic shunts; imaging improved by presence of ascites but severely hindered by bowel gas; endoscopic US less affected by bowel gas and is sensitive for determination of depth of tumor invasion through bowel wall.

CT   Particularly useful for detecting, differentiating, and directing percutaneous needle biopsy of abdominal masses, cysts, and lymphadenopathy; imaging enhanced by intestinal or intravenous contrast dye and unaffected by intestinal gas; somewhat less sensitive than US for detecting stones in gallbladder but more sensitive for choledocholithiasis; may be useful in distinguishing certain forms of diffuse hepatic disease (e.g., fatty infiltration, iron overload).

MRI   Most sensitive detection of hepatic masses and cysts; allows easy differentiation of hemangiomas from other hepatic tumors; most accurate noninvasive means of assessing hepatic and portal vein patency, vascular invasion by tumor; useful for monitoring iron, copper deposition in liver (e.g., in hemochromatosis, Wilson's disease).

RADIONUCLIDE SCANNING   Using various radiolabeled compounds, different scanning methods allow sensitive assessment of biliary excretion (HIDA, PIPIDA, DISIDA scans), parenchymal changes (technetium sulfur colloid liver/spleen scan), and selected inflammatory and neoplastic processes (gallium scan); HIDA and related scans particularly useful for assessing biliary patency and excluding acute cholecystitis in situations where US is not diagnostic; CT, MRI, and colloid scans have similar sensitivity for detecting liver tumors and metastases; CT and combination of colloidal liver and lung scans sensitive for detecting right subphrenic (suprahepatic) abscesses.

CHOLANGIOGRAPHY   Most sensitive means of detecting biliary ductal calculi, biliary tumors, sclerosing cholangitis, choledochal cysts, fistulas, and bile duct leaks; may be performed via endoscopic (transampullary) or percutaneous (transhepatic) route; allows sampling of bile and ductal epithelium for cytologic analysis and culture; allows placement of biliary drainage catheter, and stricture dilatation; endoscopic route (ERCP) permits manometric evaluation of sphincter of Oddi, sphincterotomy, and stone extraction.

ANGIOGRAPHY   Most accurate means of determining portal pressures and assessing patency and direction of flow in portal and hepatic veins; highly sensitive for detecting small vascular lesions and hepatic tumors (esp. primary hepatocellular carcinoma); "gold standard" for differentiating hemangiomas from solid tumors; most accurate means of studying vascular anatomy in preparation for complicated hepatobiliary surgery (e.g., portal-systemic shunting, biliary reconstruction) and determining resectability of hepatobiliary and pancreatic tumors. Similar anatomic information (but not intravascular pressures) can often be obtained noninvasively by CT- and MR-based techniques.

PERCUTANEOUS LIVER BIOPSY   Most accurate in disorders causing diffuse changes throughout the liver; subject to sampling error in focal infiltrative disorders such as metastasis; should not be the initial procedure in the Dx of cholestasis.

For a more detailed discussion, see Pratt DS, Kaplan MM: Jaundice, Chap. 45, p. 255; and Pratt DS, Kaplan MM: Evaluation of Liver Function, Chap. 293, p. 1711, in HPIM-15.

24

ASCITES

Definition

Accumulation of fluid within the peritoneal cavity. Small amounts may be asymptomatic; increasing amounts cause abdominal distention and discomfort, anorexia, nausea, early satiety, heartburn, flank pain, and respiratory distress.

Detection

PHYSICAL EXAMINATION   Bulging flanks, fluid wave, shifting dullness, "puddle sign" (dullness over dependent abdomen with pt on hands and knees). May be associated with penile or scrotal edema, umbilical or inguinal herniation, pleural effusion. Evaluation should include rectal and pelvic examination, assessment of liver and spleen. Palmar erythema and spider angiomata seen in cirrhosis. Periumbilical nodule (*Sister Mary Joseph's nodule*) suggests metastatic disease from a pelvic or GI tumor.

ULTRASONOGRAPHY/CT   Very sensitive; able to distinguish fluid from cystic masses.

Evaluation

Diagnostic paracentesis (50–100 mL) essential; use 22-gauge needle in linea alba 2 cm below umbilicus or with "Z-track" insertion in LLQ or RLQ. Routine evaluation includes inspection, protein, albumin, glucose, cell count and differential, culture, cytology; in selected cases check amylase, LDH, triglycerides, culture for TB. Rarely, laparoscopy or even exploratory laparotomy may be required. Ascites due to CHF (e.g., pericardial constriction) may require evaluation by right-sided heart catheterization.

DIFFERENTIAL DIAGNOSIS   More than 90% of cases due to cirrhosis, neoplasm, CHF, tuberculosis.

1.   *Diseases of peritoneum*: Infections (bacterial, tuberculous, fungal, parasitic), neoplasms, connective tissue disease, miscellaneous (Whipple's disease, familial Mediterranean fever, endometriosis, starch peritonitis, etc.).
2.   *Diseases not involving peritoneum*: Cirrhosis, CHF, Budd-Chiari syndrome, hepatic venocclusive disease, hypoalbuminemia (nephrotic syndrome, protein-losing enteropathy, malnutrition), miscellaneous (myxedema, ovarian diseases, pancreatic disease, chylous ascites).

PATHOPHYSIOLOGIC CLASSIFICATION USING SERUM-ASCITES ALBUMIN GRADIENT   Difference in albumin concentrations between serum and ascites as a reflection of imbalances in hydrostatic pressures: *Low gradient* (serum-ascites albumin gradient <1.1): 2° bacterial peritonitis, neoplasm, pancreatitis, vasculitis, nephrotic syndrome. *High gradient* (serum-ascites albumin gradient >1.1 suggesting increased hydrostatic pressure): cirrhosis, CHF, Budd-Chiari syndrome.

REPRESENTATIVE FLUID CHARACTERISTICS (See Table 24-1)

CIRRHOTIC ASCITES

PATHOGENESIS Contributing factors: (1) portal hypertension, (2) hypoalbuminemia, (3) increased hepatic lymph formation, (4) renal sodium retention—secondary to hyperaldosteronism, increased sympathetic nervous activity (renin-angiotensin production). Initiating event may be peripheral arterial vasodilation triggered by endotoxin and cytokines and mediated by nitric oxide; results in decreased "effective" plasma volume and activation of compensatory mechanisms to retain renal Na and preserve intravascular volume. In severe ascites, plasma atrial natriuretic factor levels are high but insufficient to cause natriuresis.

℞ TREATMENT

Maximum mobilization ~700 mL/d (peripheral edema may be mobilized faster).

1. Rigid salt restriction (400 mg Na/d).
2. Fluid restriction of 1–1.5 L only if hyponatremia.
3. Diuretics if no response after 1 week or if urine Na concentration <25 meq/L; spironolactone (mild, potassium-sparing, aldosterone-antagonist) 100 mg/d PO increased by 100 mg q4–5d to maximum of 600 mg/d; furosemide 40–80 mg/d PO or IV may be added if necessary (greater risk of hepatorenal syndrome, encephalopathy), can increase by 40 mg/d to maximum of 240 mg/d until effect achieved or complication occurs. If still no diuresis, add hydrochlorothiazide 50–100 mg PO qd.
4. Monitor weight, urinary Na and K, serum electrolytes, and creatinine.
5. Repeated large-volume paracentesis (5 L) with IV infusions of albumin (10 g/L ascites removed) is preferable for initial management of massive ascites because of fewer side effects than diuretics.
6. In refractory cases, consider transjugular intrahepatic portosystemic shunt (TIPS), though 20–30% risk of encephalopathy and high rate of shunt stenosis and occlusion. Peritoneovenous (LeVeen, Denver) shunt (high complication rate—occlusion, infection, DIC) and side-to-side portacaval shunt (high mortality rate in end-stage cirrhotic pt) have fallen out of favor. Consider liver transplantation in appropriate candidates (Chap. 155).

Complications

SPONTANEOUS BACTERIAL PERITONITIS Suspect in cirrhotic pt with ascites and fever, abdominal pain, worsening ascites, ileus, hypotension, worsening jaundice, or encephalopathy; low ascitic protein concentration (low opsonic activity) is predisposing factor. Diagnosis suggested by ascitic fluid PMN cell count >250/μL and symptoms or PMN count >500/μL; confirmed by positive culture (usually Enterobacteriaceae, group D streptococci, *Streptococcus pneumoniae*, *S. viridans*). Initial treatment: Cefotaxime 2 g IV q8h; efficacy demonstrated by marked decrease in ascitic PMN count after 48 h; treat 5–10 days or until ascitic PMN count is normal. Risk of recurrence can be

Table 24-1

Representative Fluid Characteristics

Cause	Appearance	Protein, g/dL	Serum-Ascites Albumin Gradient	Cell Count, per μL		Other
				RBC	WBC	
Cirrhosis	Straw-colored	<2.5	>1.1	Low	<250	—
Neoplasm	Straw-colored, hemorrhagic, mucinous, or chylous	>2.5	Variable	Often high	>1000 (>50% lymphs)	+ Cytology
2° Bacterial peritonitis	Turbid or purulent	>2.5	<1.1	Low	>10,000	+ Gram's stain, culture (often multiple organisms)
Spontaneous bacterial peritonitis	Turbid or purulent	<2.5	>1.1	Low	>250 polys	+ Gram's stain, culture
Tuberculous peritonitis	Clear, hemorrhagic, or chylous	>2.5	<1.1	Occ. high	>1000 (>70% lymphs)	+ AFB stain, culture
CHF	Straw-colored, rarely chylous	>2.5	>1.1	Low	<1000 (mesothelial)	—
Pancreatitis	Turbid, hemorrhagic, or chylous	>2.5	<1.1	Variable	Variable	Increased amylase

reduced with norfloxacin 400 mg PO qd, trimethoprim-sulfamethoxazole 1 double-strength PO bid 5 days a week, or possibly ciprofloxacin 750 mg PO once a week. Consider prophylactic therapy (before first episode of peritonitis) in pts with cirrhotic ascites and an ascitic albumin level <10 g/L (<1 g/dl).

HEPATORENAL SYNDROME Progressive renal failure characterized by azotemia, oliguria with urinary sodium concentration <10 mmol/L, hypotension, and lack of response to volume challenge. May be spontaneous or precipitated by bleeding, excessive diuresis, paracentesis, or drugs (aminoglycosides, NSAIDs, ACE inhibitors). Thought to result from altered renal hemodynamics, elevated serum thromboxane and endothelin levels, and decreased urinary prostaglandin levels. Prognosis poor. Treatment: Trial of plasma expansion; TIPS of doubtful benefit; liver transplantation in selected cases.

For a more detailed discussion, see Glickman RM: Abdominal Swelling and Ascites, Chap. 46, p. 260, and Podolsky DK: Cirrhosis and Its Complications, Chap. 299, p. 1754, in HPIM-15.

25

OVERT MANIFESTATIONS OF RENAL DISEASE

ABNORMALITIES OF RENAL FUNCTION

Azotemia is the retention of nitrogenous waste products excreted by the kidney. Increased levels of blood urea nitrogen (BUN) (>30 mg/dL) and creatinine (>1.5 mg/dL) are ordinarily indicative of impaired renal function. Renal function can be estimated by determining the clearance of creatinine (CL_{cr}) (normal >100 mL/min). CL_{cr} overestimates glomerular filtration rate (GFR), particularly at lower levels. Isotopic markers (e.g., iothalamate) provide more accurate estimates of GFR.

Manifestations of impaired renal function include: volume overload, hypertension, electrolyte abnormalities (e.g., hyperkalemia, hypocalcemia, hyperphosphatemia), metabolic acidosis, hormonal disturbances (e.g., insulin resistance, functional vitamin D deficiency, secondary hyperparathyroidism), and, when severe, "uremia" (one or more of the following: anorexia, lethargy, confusion, asterixis, pleuritis, pericarditis, enteritis, pruritus, sleep and taste disturbance, nitrogenous fetor).

ABNORMALITIES OF URINE VOLUME

OLIGURIA This refers to sparse urine output, usually defined as <400 mL/d. Oligoanuria refers to a more marked reduction in urine output, i.e., <100 mL/d. Anuria indicates the absence of urine output. Oliguria most often occurs in the setting of volume depletion and/or renal hypoperfusion, resulting in "prerenal azotemia" and acute renal failure (Chap. 138). Anuria can be caused by complete bilateral urinary tract obstruction, a vascular catastrophe (dissection or arterial occlusion), renal vein thrombosis, and hypovolemic, cardiogenic, or septic shock. Oliguria is never normal, since at least 400 mL of maximally concentrated urine must be produced to excrete the obligate daily osmolar load.

POLYURIA Polyuria is defined as a urine output >3 L/d. It is often accompanied by nocturia and urinary frequency and must be differentiated from other more common conditions associated with lower urinary tract pathology and urinary urgency or frequency (e.g., cystitis, prostatism). It is often accompanied by hypernatremia (Chap. 26). Polyuria (Table 25-1) can occur as a response to a solute load (e.g., hyperglycemia) or to an abnormality in antidiuretic hormone (ADH) action. Diabetes insipidus is termed *central* if due to the insufficient hypothalmic production of ADH and *nephrogenic* if the result of renal insensitivity to the action of ADH. Excess fluid intake can lead to polyuria, but primary polydipsia rarely results in changes in plasma osmolality unless urinary diluting capacity is impaired, as with chronic renal failure. Tubulointerstitial diseases and urinary tract obstruction can be associated with nephrogenic diabetes insipidus.

The approach to the pt with polyuria is shown in Fig. 25-1.

ABNORMALITIES OF URINE COMPOSITION

PROTEINURIA This is the hallmark of glomerular disease. Levels up to 150 mg/d are considered within normal limits. Typical measurements are semi-quantitative, using a moderately sensitive dipstick that estimates protein concentration; therefore, the degree of hydration may influence the dipstick protein determination. Most commercially available urine dipsticks detect albumin and do not detect smaller proteins, such as light chains, that require testing with sulfosalicylic acid. More sensitive assays can be used to detect microalbuminuria in diabetes mellitus. A urine albumin to creatinine ratio >30 mg/g defines the presence of micoalbuminuria.

Urinary protein excretion rates between 500 mg/d and 3 g/d are nonspecific and can be seen in a variety of renal diseases (including hypertensive nephrosclerosis, interstitial nephritis, vascular disease, and other primary renal diseases with little or no glomerular involvement). Lesser degrees of proteinuria (500 mg/d to 1.5 g/d) may be seen after vigorous exercise, changes in body position,

Table 25-1

Major Causes of Polyuria

Excessive fluid intake	Nephrogenic diabetes insipidus
Primary polydipsia	Lithium exposure
Iatrogenic (intravenous fluids)	Urinary tract obstruction
Therapeutic	Papillary necrosis
Diuretic agents	Reflux nephropathy
Osmotic diuresis	Interstitial nephritis
Hyperglycemia	Hypercalcemia
Azotemia	Central diabetes insipidus
Mannitol	Tumor
Radiocontrast	Postoperative
	Head trauma
	Basilar meningitis
	Neurosarcoidosis

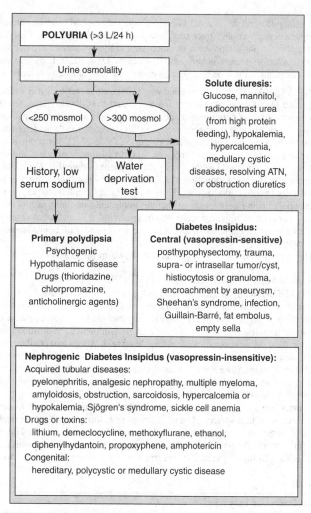

FIGURE 25-1   Approach to the patient with polyuria. (OSM, osmolality; ATN, acute tubular necrosis.)

fever, or congestive heart failure. Protein excretion rates >3 g/d are termed *nephrotic range proteinuria* and are accompanied by hypoalbuminemia, hyper-cholesterolemia, and edema in the nephrotic syndrome. Massive degrees of pro-teinuria (>10 g/d) can be seen with minimal change disease, primary focal segmental sclerosis, membranous nephropathy, collapsing glomerulopathy, and HIV-associated nephropathy and can be associated with a variety of extrarenal complications (Chap. 142).

Pharmacologic inhibition of ACE or blockade of angiotensin II receptors may reduce proteinuria in some pts, particularly those with diabetic nephropathy. Specific therapy for a variety of causes of nephrotic syndrome is discussed in Chap. 142.

HEMATURIA   Gross hematuria refers to the presence of frank blood in the urine and is more characteristic of lower urinary tract disease and/or bleeding diatheses than intrinsic renal disease (Table 25-2). Cyst rupture in polycystic kidney disease and flares of IgA nephropathy are exceptions. Microscopic hematuria ($>1-2$ RBC/high powered field) accompanied by proteinuria, hypertension, and an active urinary sediment (the "nephritic syndrome") is most likely related to an inflammatory glomerulonephritis (Chap. 142).

Free hemoglobin and myoglobin are detected by dipstick; a negative urinary sediment with strongly heme-positive dipstick are characteristic of either hemolysis or rhabdomyolysis, which can be differentiated by clinical history and laboratory testing. Red blood cell casts are not commonly seen but are highly specific for glomerulonephritis.

The approach to the pt with hematuria is shown in Fig. 25-2.

PYURIA   This may accompany hematuria in inflammatory glomerular diseases. Isolated pyuria is most commonly observed in association with an infection of the upper or lower urinary tract. Pyuria may also occur with allergic interstitial nephritis (often with a preponderance of eosinophils), transplant rejection, and noninfectious, nonallergic tubulointerstitial diseases. The finding of "sterile" pyuria (i.e., urinary white blood cells without bacteria) in the appropriate clinical setting should raise suspicion of renal tuberculosis.

Table 25-2

Major Causes of Hematuria

LOWER URINARY TRACT

Bacterial cystitis
Intestitial cystitis
Urethritis (infectious or inflammatory)
Passed or passing kidney stone
Transitional cell carcinoma of bladder or structures proximal to it
Squamous cell carcinoma of bladder (e.g., following schistosomiasis)

UPPER URINARY TRACT

Renal cell carcinoma
Age-related renal cysts
Other neoplasms (e.g., oncocytoma, hamartoma)
Acquired renal cystic disease
Congenital cystic disease, including autosomal dominant form
Glomerular diseases
Interstitial renal diseases
Nephrolithiasis
Pyelonephritis
Renal infarction

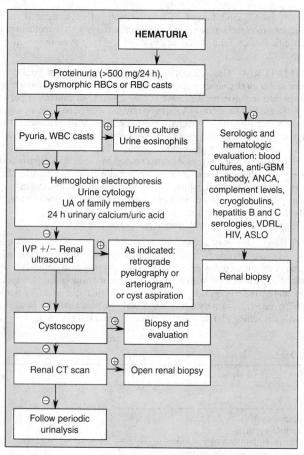

FIGURE 25-2 Approach to the patient with hematuria. (RBC, red blood cell; WBC, white blood cell; GBM, glomerular basement membrane; ANCA, antineutrophil cytoplasmic antibody; VDRL, venereal disease research laboratory; HIV, human immunodeficiency virus; ASLO, antistreptolysis O; UA, urinalysis; IVP, intravenous pyelography; CT, computed tomography.)

For a more detailed discussion, see Denker BM, Brenner BM: Azotemia and Urinary Abnormalities, Chap. 47, p. 262, in HPIM-15.

26

ELECTROLYTES/ACID-BASE BALANCE

SODIUM

In most cases, disturbances of sodium concentration [Na$^+$] result from abnormalities of water homeostasis. Disorders of Na$^+$ balance usually lead to hypo-

or hypervolemia. Attention to the dysregulation of volume (Na^+ balance) and osmolality (water balance) must be considered separately for each pt (see below).

HYPONATREMIA This is defined as a serum [Na^+] < 135 mmol/L and is among the most common electrolyte abnormalities encountered in hospitalized pts. Symptoms include confusion, lethargy, and disorientation; if severe (<120 mmol/L) and abrupt, seizures or coma may develop. Hyponatremia is often iatrogenic and almost always the result of an abnormality in the action of antidiuretic hormone (ADH), deemed either "appropriate" or "inappropriate," depending on the associated clinical conditions. The serum [Na^+] by itself does not yield diagnostic information regarding the total-body Na^+ content. Therefore, a useful way to categorize pts with hyponatremia is to place them into three groups, depending on the volume status (i.e., hypovolemic, euvolemic, and hypervolemic hyponatremia) (Fig. 26-1).

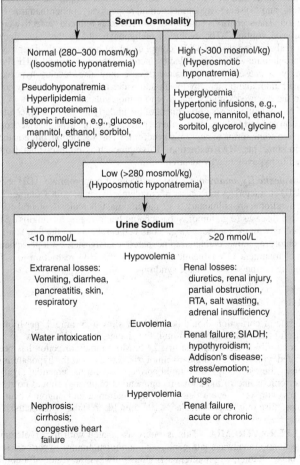

FIGURE 26-1 Evaluation of hyponatremia. RTA, renal tubular acidosis; SIADH, syndrome of inappropriate antidiuretic hormone secretion.

Hypovolemic Hyponatremia Mild to moderate degrees of hyponatremia ($[Na^+] = 125-135$ mmol/L) complicate GI fluid or blood loss for two reasons. First, there is activation of the three major "systems" responsive to reduced organ perfusion: the renin-angiotensin-aldosterone axis, the sympathetic nervous system, and ADH. This sets the stage for enhanced renal absorption of solutes and water. Second, replacement fluid before hospitalization or other intervention is usually hypotonic (e.g., water, fruit juices). The optimal treatment of hypovolemic hyponatremia is volume administration, either in the form of colloid or isotonic crystalloid (e.g., 0.9% NaCl or lactated Ringer's solution).

Hypervolemic Hyponatremia The edematous disorders (CHF, hepatic cirrhosis, and nephrotic syndrome) are often associated with mild to moderate degrees of hyponatremia ($[Na^+] = 125-135$ mmol/L); occasionally, pts with severe CHF or cirrhosis may present with serum $[Na^+] <120$ mmol/L. The pathophysiology is similar to that in hypovolemic hyponatremia, except that perfusion is decreased due to (1) reduced cardiac output, (2) arteriovenous shunting, and (3) severe hypoproteinemia, respectively, rather than true volume depletion. The scenario is sometimes referred to as reduced "effective circulating arterial volume." The evolution of hyponatremia is the same: increased water reabsorption due to ADH, complicated by hypotonic fluid replacement. This problem may be compounded by increased thirst in pts with CHF. Pts with a variety of causes of chronic renal disease may also develop hypervolemic hyponatremia, due principally to salt and water retention due to reduced GFR, and to the diseased kidneys' inability to osmoregulate.

Management consists of treatment of the underlying disorder (e.g., afterload reduction in heart failure, large-volume paracentesis in cirrhosis, glucocorticoid therapy in some forms of nephrotic syndrome), Na^+ restriction, diuretic therapy, and, in some pts, H_2O restriction. This approach is quite distinct from that applied to hypovolemic hyponatremia.

Euvolemic Hyponatremia The syndrome of inappropriate ADH secretion (SIADH) characterizes most cases of euvolemic hyponatremia. Common causes of the syndrome are pulmonary (e.g., pneumonia, tuberculosis, pleural effusion) and CNS diseases (e.g., tumor, subarachnoid hemorrhage, meningitis); SIADH also occurs with malignancies (e.g., small cell carcinoma of the lung) and drugs (e.g., chlorpropamide, carbamazepine, narcotic analgesics, cyclophosphamide). Optimal treatment of euvolemic hyponatremia is H_2O restriction to <1 L/d, depending on the severity of the syndrome.

℞ TREATMENT

The rate of correction should be relatively slow (0.5 mmol/L per h of Na^+). A useful "rule of thumb" is to limit the change in mmol/L of Na^+ to half of the total difference within the first 24 h. More rapid correction has been associated with central pontine myelinolysis, especially if the hyponatremia has been of long standing. More rapid correction (with the potential addition of hypertonic saline to the above-recommended regimens) should be reserved for pts with very severe degrees of hyponatremia and ongoing neurologic compromise (e.g., a pt with $Na^+ <105$ mmol/L in status epilepticus).

HYPERNATREMIA This is rarely associated with hypervolemia, and this association is always iatrogenic, e.g., administration of hypertonic sodium bicarbonate. Rather, hypernatremia is almost always the result of a combined water and volume deficit, with losses of H_2O in excess of Na^+. The most common causes are osmotic diuresis secondary to hyperglycemia, azotemia, or drugs (radiocontrast, mannitol, etc.) or central or nephrogenic diabetes insipidus (DI) (see "Polyuria," Chap. 25). The evaluation of hypernatremia is outlined in Fig. 26-2.

℞ TREATMENT

The approach to correction of hypernatremia is outlined in Fig. 26-2 and Table 26-1. As with hyponatremia, it is advisable to correct the water deficit slowly to avoid neurologic compromise. In addition to the water replacement formula provided, other forms of therapy may be helpful in selected cases of hypernatremia. Pts with central DI may respond well to the administration of intranasal desmopressin or to the use of chlorpropamide (if the risk of drug-induced hypoglycemia is not excessive). Pts with nephrogenic DI due to lithium may reduce their polyuria with amiloride (2.5–10 mg/d) or hydro-

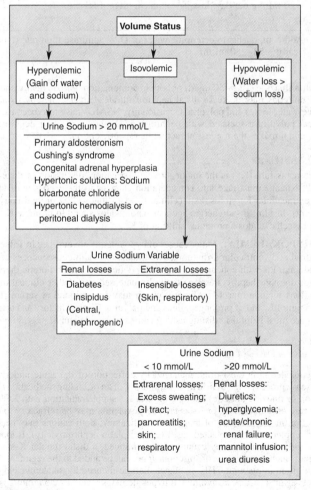

FIGURE 26-2   Evaluation of hypernatremia.

Table 26-1

Correction of Hypernatremia

WATER DEFICIT

1. Estimate total-body water (TBW): 50–60% body weight (kg) depending on body composition
2. Calculate free-water deficit: $[(Na^+ - 140)/140] \times TBW$
3. Administer deficit over 48–72 h

ONGOING WATER LOSSES

4. Calculate free-water clearance from urinary flow rate (V) and urine (U) Na^+ and K^+ concentrations $V - V \times (U_{Na} + U_K)/140$

INSENSIBLE LOSSES

5. ~10 mL/kg per day: less if ventilated, more if febrile

TOTAL

6. Add components to determine water of D_5W administration rate (typically ~50–250 mL/h)

---

chlorothiazide (12.5–50 mg/d) or both in combination. Paradoxically, the use of diuretics may decrease distal nephron filtrate delivery, thereby reducing free-water losses and polyuria. Occasionally, NSAIDs have also been used to treat polyuria associated with nephrogenic DI; however, their nephrotoxic potential makes them a less attractive therapeutic option.

POTASSIUM

Since potassium (K^+) is the major intracellular cation, discussion of disorders of K^+ balance must take into consideration changes in the exchange of intra- and extracellular K^+ stores (extracellular K^+ constitutes <2% of total-body K^+ content). Insulin, β_2-adrenergic agonists, and alkalosis tend to promote K^+ uptake by cells; acidosis promotes shifting of K^+.

HYPOKALEMIA Major causes of hypokalemia are outlined in Table 26-2. Atrial and ventricular arrhythmias are the major health consequences of hypokalemia. Pts with concurrent magnesium deficit (e.g., after diuretic therapy) and/or digoxin therapy are at particularly increased risk. Other clinical manifestations include muscle weakness, which may be profound at serum $[K+]$ <2.5 mmol/L, and, if prolonged, ileus and polyuria. Clinical history and urinary $[K^+]$ are most helpful in distinguishing causes of hypokalemia.

 TREATMENT

Hypokalemia is most often managed by correction of the acute underlying disease process (e.g., diarrhea) or withdrawal of an offending medication (e.g., loop or thiazide diuretic), along with oral K^+ supplementation with KCl, or, in rare cases, $KHCO_3$, or K-acetate. Hypokalemia may be refractory to correction in the presence of magnesium deficiency; both cations may need to be supplemented in selected cases (e.g., cisplatin nephrotoxicity). If loop or thiazide diuretic therapy cannot be discontinued, a distal tubular K-sparing agent, such as amiloride or spironolactone, can be added to the regimen. ACE inhibition in pts with CHF attenuates diuretic-induced hypokalemia and protects against cardiac arrhythmia. If hypokalemia is severe (<2.5 mmol/L) and/

Table 26-2

Causes of Hypokalemia

I. Decreased intake
  A. Starvation
  B. Clay ingestion
II. Redistribution into cells
  A. Acid-base
    1. Metabolic alkalosis
  B. Hormonal
    1. Insulin
    2. Beta$_2$-adrenergic agonists (endogenous or exogenous)
    3. Alpha-adrenergic antagonists
  C. Anabolic state
    1. Vitamin B$_{12}$ or folic acid (red blood cell production)
    2. Granulocyte-macrophage colony stimulating factor
    3. Total parenteral nutrition
  D. Other
    1. Pseudohypokalemia
    2. Hypothermia
    3. Hypokalemic periodic paralysis
III. Increased loss
  A. Nonrenal
    1. Gastrointestinal loss (diarrhea)
    2. Integumentary loss (sweat)
  B. Renal
    1. Increased distal flow; diuretics, osmotic diuresis, salt-wasting nephropathies
    2. Increased secretion of potassium
      a. Mineralocorticoid excess: primary hyperaldosteronism, secondary hyperaldosteronism (malignant hypertension, renin-secreting tumors, renal artery stenosis, hypovolemia), apparent mineralocorticoid excess (licorice, chewing tobacco, carbenoxolone), congenital adrenal hyperplasia, Cushing's syndrome, Bartter's syndrome
      b. Distal delivery of non-reabsorbed anions: vomiting, nasogastric suction, proximal (type 2) renal tubular acidosis, diabetic ketoacidosis, glue-sniffing (toluene abuse), penicillin derivatives
      c. Other: amphotericin B, Liddle's syndrome, hypomagnesemia

or if oral supplementation is not tolerated, intravenous KCl can be administered through a central vein at rates which must not exceed 20 mmol/h, with telemetry and skilled monitoring.

HYPERKALEMIA Causes are outlined in Table 26-3. In most cases, hyperkalemia is due to decreased K$^+$ excretion. Drugs can be implicated in many cases. Where the diagnosis is uncertain, calculation of the transtubular K gradient (TTKG) can be helpful. TTKG = $U_K P_{OSM}/P_K U_{OSM}$ (U, urine; P, plasma). TTKG < 10 suggests decreased K$^+$ excretion due to (1) hypoaldosteronism, or (2) renal resistance to the effects of mineralocorticoid. These can be differentiated by the administration of fludrocortisone (florinef) 0.2 mg, with the former increasing K$^+$ excretion (and decreasing TTKG).

The most important consequence of hyperkalemia is altered cardiac conduction, leading to bradycardic cardiac arrest in severe cases. Hypocalcemia

Table 26-3

Major Causes of Hyperkalemia

I. "Pseudo"-hyperkalemia
   A. Thrombocytosis, leukocytosis, in vitro hemolysis
II. Intra- to extracellular shift
   A. Acidosis
   B. Hyperosmolality; radiocontrast, hypertonic dextrose, mannitol
   C. Beta$_2$-adrenergic antagonists (noncardioselective agents)
   D. Digoxin or ouabain poisoning
   E. Hyperkalemic periodic paralysis
III. Inadequate excretion
   A. Distal K-sparing diuretic agents and analogues
      1. Amiloride, spironolactone, triamterene, trimethoprim
   B. Decreased distal delivery
      1. Congestive heart failure, volume depletion, NSAIDs, cyclosporine
   C. Renal tubular acidosis, type IV
      1. Tubulointerstitial diseases
         a. Reflux nephropathy, pyelonephritis, interstitial nephritis, heavy metal (e.g., Pb) nephropathy
      2. Diabetic glomerulosclerosis
   D. Advanced renal insufficiency with low GFR
   E. Decreased mineralocorticoid effects
      1. Addison's disease, congenital adrenal enzyme deficiency, other forms of adrenal insufficiency (e.g., adrenalitis), heparin, ACE inhibitors, AII antagonists

---

and acidosis accentuate the cardiac effects of hyperkalemia. Figure 26-3 shows serial ECG patterns of hyperkalemia. Stepwise treatment of hyperkalemia is summarized in Table 26-4.

ACID-BASE DISORDERS (See Fig. 26-4)

Regulation of normal pH (7.35–7.45) depends on both the lungs and kidneys. By the Henderson-Hasselbalch equation, pH is a function of the ratio of HCO_3 (regulated by the kidney) to P_{CO_2} (regulated by the lungs). The HCO_3/P_{CO_2} relationship is useful in classifying disorders of acid-base balance. Acidosis is due to gain of acid or loss of alkali; causes may be metabolic (fall in serum HCO_3) or respiratory (rise in P_{CO_2}). Alkalosis is due to loss of acid or addition of base and is either metabolic ($\uparrow$ serum HCO_3) or respiratory ($\downarrow P_{CO_2}$).

To limit the change in pH, metabolic disorders evoke an immediate compensatory response in ventilation; compensation to respiratory disorders by the kidneys takes days. Simple acid-base disorders consist of one primary disturbance and its compensatory response. In mixed disorders, a combination of primary disturbances is present. Mixed disorders should be suspected when the change in anion gap is significantly higher or lower than the change in serum HCO_3 (see below).

METABOLIC ACIDOSIS The low HCO_3^- results from the addition of acids (organic or inorganic) or loss of HCO_3^-. The causes of metabolic acidosis are categorized by the anion gap, which equals $Na^+ - (Cl^- + HCO_3^-)$ (Table 26-5). Increased anion gap acidosis (>12 mmol/L) is due to addition of acid (other than HCl) and unmeasured anions to the body. Causes include ketoacidosis (diabetes mellitus, starvation, alcohol), lactic acidosis, poisoning (salicylates, ethylene glycol, and ethanol) and renal failure.

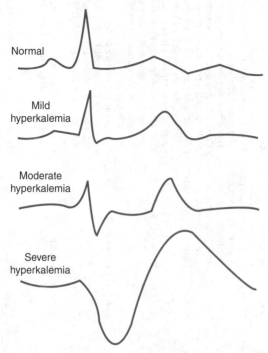

FIGURE 26-3 Diagrammatic ECGs at normal and high serum K. Peaked T waves (precordial leads) are followed by diminished R wave, wide QRS, prolonged P-R, loss of P wave, and ultimately a sine wave.

Diagnosis may be made by measuring BUN, creatinine, glucose, lactate, serum ketones, and serum osmolality and obtaining a toxic screen. Certain commonly prescribed drugs (e.g., metformin, antiretroviral agents) are occasionally associated with lactic acidosis.

Normal anion gap acidoses result from HCO_3^- loss from the GI tract or from the kidney, e.g., renal tubular acidosis, urinary obstruction, rapid volume expansion with saline-containing solutions, and administration of NH_4Cl, lysine HCl. Calculation of urinary anion gap may be helpful in evaluation of hyperchloremic metabolic acidosis. A negative anion gap suggests GI losses; a positive anion gap suggests altered urinary acidification.

Clinical features include hyperventilation, cardiovascular collapse, and nonspecific symptoms ranging from anorexia to coma.

℞ TREATMENT

Depends on cause and severity. Always correct the underlying disturbance. Administration of alkali is controversial. It may be reasonable to treat lactic acidosis with intravenous HCO_3^- at a rate sufficient to maintain a plasma HCO_3^- of 8–10 mmol/L and pH > 7.10. Lactic acidosis associated with cardiogenic shock may be worsened by bicarbonate administration.

Chronic acidosis should be treated when HCO_3^- < 18–20 mmol/L or symptoms of anorexia or fatigue are present. In pts with renal failure, there is some evidence that acidosis promotes protein catabolism and may worsen

Table 26-4

Management of Hyperkalemia

Treatment	Indication	Dose	Onset	Duration	Mechanism	Note
Calcium gluconate[a]	K$^+$ >6.5 mmol/L with advanced ECG changes	10 mL of 10% solution IV over 2–3 min	1–5 min	30 min	Lowers threshold potential. Antagonizes cardiac and neuromuscular toxicity of hyperkalemia.	Fastest action. Monitor ECG. Repeat in 5 min if abnormal ECG persists. Hazardous in presence of digitalis. Correct hyponatremia if present. Follow with other treatment for K$^+$.
Insulin + Glucose	Moderate hyperkalemia, peaked T waves only	10 U reg, IV + 50 mL, 50% IV	15–45 min	4–6 h	Moves K$^+$ into cells.	Glucose unnecessary if blood sugar elevated. Repeat insulin q 15 min with glucose infusion if needed.
NaHCO$_3$	Moderate hyperkalemia	90 mmol (2 ampules, IV push over 5 min)	Immediate	Short	Moves K$^+$ into cells.	Most effective when acidosis is present. Of more risk in CHF or hypernatremia. Beware of hypocalcemic tetany.
Kayexalate + Sorbitol	Moderate hyperkalemia	Oral: 30 g, with 50 mL 20% sorbitol; rectal: 50 g in 200 mL 20% sorbitol enema, retain 45 min	1 h	4–6 h	Removes K$^+$.	Each gram Kayexalate removes about 1 mmol K$^+$ and about 0.5 mmol K$^+$ when given rectally. Repeat every 4 h. Use with caution in CHF.
Furosemide	Moderate hyperkalemia, serum creatinine <265 mmol/L (<3 mg%)	20–40 mg IV push	15 min	4 h	Kaliuresis.	Most useful if inadequate K$^+$ excretion contributes to hyperkalemia.
Dialysis	Hyperkalemia with renal failure		Immediate after start-up	Variable	Removes K$^+$.	Hemodialysis most effective. Also improves acidosis.

[a] Calcium chloride may be preferable in presence of circulatory instability or impairment.

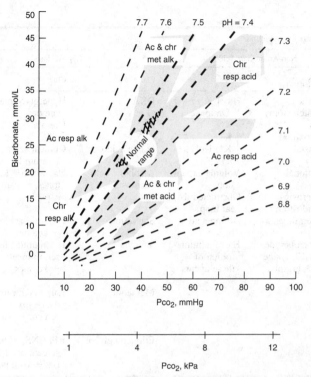

FIGURE 26-4 Nomogram, showing bands for uncomplicated respiratory or metabolic acid-base disturbances in intact subjects. Each "confidence" band represents the mean ±2 SD for the compensatory response of normal subjects or patients to a given primary disorder. Ac, acute; chr, chronic; resp, respiratory; met, metabolic; acid, acidosis; alk, alkalosis. (From Levinsky NG: HPIM-12, p. 290; modified from Arbus GS: Can Med Assoc J 109:291, 1973.)

bone disease. Na citrate may be more palatable than oral NaHCO$_3$, although the former should be avoided in pts with advanced renal insufficiency, as it augments aluminum absorption. Oral therapy with NaHCO$_3$ usually begins with 650 mg tid and is titrated upward to maintain desired serum [HCO$_3^-$]. Other therapies for lactic acidosis (e.g., dichloroacetate) remain unproven.

METABOLIC ALKALOSIS A primary increase in serum [HCO$_3^-$]. Most cases originate with volume concentration and loss of acid from the stomach or kidney. Less commonly, HCO$_3^-$ administered or derived from endogenous lactate is the cause and is perpetuated when renal HCO$_3^-$ reabsorption continues. In vomiting, Cl$^-$ loss reduces its availability for renal reabsorption with Na$^+$. Enhanced Na$^+$ avidity due to volume depletion then accelerates HCO$_3^-$ reabsorption and sustains the alkalosis. Urine Cl$^-$ is typically low (<10 mmol/L) (Table 26-6). Alkalosis may also be maintained by hyperaldosteronism, due to enhancement of H$^+$ secretion and HCO$_3^-$ reabsorption. Severe K$^+$ depletion also causes metabolic alkalosis by increasing HCO$_3^-$ reabsorption; urine Cl$^-$ >20 mmol/L.

Vomiting and nasogastric drainage cause HCl and volume loss, kaliuresis, and alkalosis. Diuretics are a common cause of alkalosis due to volume contraction, Cl$^-$ depletion, and hypokalemia. Pts with chronic pulmonary disease

Table 26-5

Metabolic Acidosis

Non-Anion Gap Acidosis		Anion Gap Acidosis	
Cause	Clue	Cause	Clue
Diarrhea Enterostomy	Hx; ↑ K^+ Drainage	DKA	Hyperglycemia, ketones
RTA		RF	Uremia, ↑ BUN, ↑ CR
Proximal	↓ K^+	Lactic acidosis	Clinical setting + ↑ serum lactate
Distal	↓ K^+; UpH > 5.5		
Dilutional	Volume expansion	Alcoholic keto-acidosis	Hx; weak + ketones; + osm gap
Ureterosig-moidostomy	Obstructed ileal loop		
Hyperalimentation	Amino acid infusion	Starvation	Hx; mild acidosis; + ketones
Acetazolamide, NH_4Cl, lysine HCl, arginine HCl	Hx of administration of these agents	Salicylates	Hx; tinnitus; high serum level; + ketones
		Methanol	Large AG; retinitis; + toxic screen; + osm gap
		Ethylene glycol	RF, CNS; + toxic screen; crystalluria; + osm gap

RTA, renal tubular acidosis; UpH, urinary pH; DKA, diabetic ketoacidosis; RF, renal failure; AG, anion gap; osm gap, osmolar gap

and high P_{CO_2} and serum HCO_3^- levels whose ventilation is acutely improved may develop alkalosis.

Excessive mineralocorticoid activity due to Cushing's syndrome (worse in ectopic ACTH or primary hyperaldosteronism) causes metabolic alkalosis not associated with volume or Cl^- depletion and not responsive to NaCl.

Table 26-6

Metabolic Alkalosis

Cl Responsive (Low U_α)	Cl Resistant (High U_α)
Gastrointestinal causes: Vomiting Nasogastric suction Chloride-wasting diarrhea Villous adenoma of colon Diuretic therapy Posthypercapnia Carbenicillin or penicillin	Adrenal disorders: Hyperaldosteronism Cushing's syndrome (1°, 2°, ectopic) Exogenous steroids: Gluco- or mineralocorticoid Licorice ingestion Carbenoxolone Bartter's syndrome Refeeding alkalosis Alkali ingestion

Severe K$^+$ depletion also causes metabolic alkalosis.

Diagnosis The [Cl$^-$] from a random urine sample is useful (Table 26-6) unless diuretics have been administered. Determining the fractional excretion of Cl$^-$, rather than the fractional excretion of Na$^+$, is the best way to identify an alkalosis responsive to volume expansion.

 TREATMENT

Correct the underlying cause. In cases of Cl$^-$ depletion, administer NaCl; and in hypokalemia, add KCl. Pts with adrenal hyperfunction require treatment of the underlying disorder. Severe alkalosis may require, in addition, treatment with acidifying agents such as NaCl, HCl, or acetazolamide. The initial amount of H$^+$ needed (in mmol) should be calculated from $0.5 \times$ (body wt in kg) $\times$ (serum HCO$_3^-$ $-$ 24).

RESPIRATORY ACIDOSIS Characterized by CO$_2$ retention due to ventilatory failure. Causes include sedatives, stroke, chronic pulmonary disease, airway obstruction, severe pulmonary edema, neuromuscular disorders, and cardiopulmonary arrest. Symptoms include confusion, asterixis, and obtundation.

 TREATMENT

The goal is to improve ventilation through pulmonary toilet and reversal of bronchospasm. Intubation may be required in severe acute cases. Acidosis due to hypercapnia is usually mild.

RESPIRATORY ALKALOSIS Excessive ventilation causes a primary reduction in CO$_2$ and ↑pH in pneumonia, pulmonary edema, interstitial lung disease, asthma. Pain and psychogenic causes are common; other etiologies include fever, hypoxemia, sepsis, delirium tremens, salicylates, hepatic failure, mechanical overventilation, and CNS lesions. Pregnancy is associated with a mild respiratory alkalosis. Severe respiratory alkalosis may cause seizures, tetany, cardiac arrhythmias, or loss of consciousness.

 TREATMENT

Should be directed at the underlying disorders. In psychogenic cases, sedation or a rebreathing bag may be required.

"MIXED" DISORDERS In many circumstances, more than a single acid-base disturbance exists. Examples include combined metabolic and respiratory acidosis with cardiogenic shock; metabolic alkalosis and acidosis in pts with vomiting and diabetic ketoacidosis; metabolic acidosis with respiratory alkalosis in pts with sepsis. The diagnosis may be clinically evident or suggested by relationships between the P$_{CO_2}$ and HCO$_3^-$ that are markedly different from those found in simple disorders.

In simple anion-gap acidosis, anion gap increases in proportion to fall in [HCO$_3^-$]. When increase in anion gap occurs despite a normal [HCO$_3^-$], simultaneous anion-gap acidosis and metabolic alkalosis are suggested. When fall in [HCO$_3^-$] due to metabolic acidosis is proportionately larger than increase in anion gap, mixed anion-gap and non-anion-gap metabolic acidosis is suggested.

For a more detailed discussion, see Singer GG, Brenner BM: Fluids and Electrolyte Disturbances, Chap. 49, p. 271; and DuBose TD Jr: Acidosis and Alkalosis, Chap. 50, p. 283, in HPIM-15.

27

ANEMIA AND POLYCYTHEMIA

ANEMIA

Anemia is defined as blood hemoglobin (Hb) concentration <140 g/L (<14 g/dL) or hematocrit (Hct) <42% in adult males; Hb <120 g/L (<12 g/dL) or Hct <37% in adult females.

Signs and symptoms of anemia are varied, depending on the level of anemia and the time course over which it developed. Acute anemia is nearly always due to blood loss or hemolysis. In acute blood loss, hypovolemia dominates the clinical picture; hypotension and decreased organ perfusion are the main issues. Symptoms associated with more chronic onset vary with the age of the pt and the adequacy of blood supply to critical organs. Moderate anemia is associated with fatigue, loss of stamina, breathlessness, and tachycardia. The pt's skin and mucous membranes may appear pale. If the palmar creases are lighter in color than the surrounding skin with the fingers extended, Hb level is often <80 g/L (8 g/dL). In pts with coronary artery disease, anginal episodes may appear or increase in frequency and severity. In pts with carotid artery disease, lightheadedness or dizziness may develop.

A physiologic approach to anemia diagnosis is based on the understanding that a decrease in circulating red blood cells (RBC) can be related to either inadequate production of RBCs or increased RBC destruction or loss. Within the category of inadequate production, erythropoiesis can be either ineffective, due to an erythrocyte maturation defect (which usually results in RBCs that are too small or too large), or hypoproliferative (which usually results in RBCs of normal size, but too few of them).

Basic evaluations include: (1) reticulocyte index (RI), (2) review of blood smear and RBC indices [particularly mean corpuscular volume (MCV)] (Fig. 27-1).

The RI is a measure of RBC production. The reticulocyte count is corrected for the Hct level and for early release of marrow reticulocytes into the circulation, which leads to an increase in the life span of the circulating reticulocyte beyond the usual 1 day. Thus, RI = (% reticulocytes × pt Hct/45%) × (1/shift correction factor). The shift correction factor varies with the Hct: 1.5 for Hct = 35%, 2 for Hct = 25%, 2.5 for Hct = 15%. RI < 2–2.5% implies inadequate RBC production for the particular level of anemia; RI > 2.5% implies excessive RBC destruction or loss.

If the anemia is associated with a low RI, RBC morphology helps distinguish a maturation disorder from hypoproliferative marrow states. Cytoplasmic maturation defects such as iron deficiency or Hb synthesis problems produce smaller RBCs, MCV <80; nuclear maturation defects such as B_{12} and folate deficiency

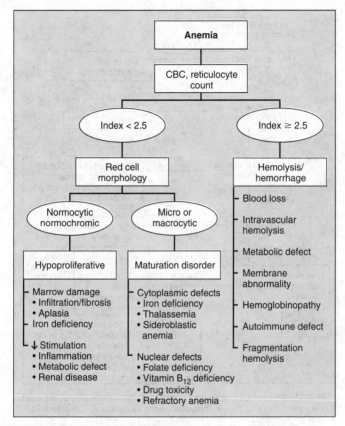

FIGURE 27-1   The physiologic classification of anemia. CBC, complete blood count.

and drug effects produce larger RBCs, MCV >100. In hypoproliferative marrow states, RBCs are generally normal in morphology but too few are produced. Bone marrow examination is often helpful in the evaluation of anemia but is done most frequently to diagnose hypoproliferative marrow states.

Other laboratory tests indicated to evaluate particular forms of anemia depend on the initial classification based on the pathophysiology of the defect. These are discussed in more detail in Chap. 58.

POLYCYTHEMIA (ERYTHROCYTOSIS)

This is an increase above the normal range of RBCs in the circulation. Concern that the Hb level may be abnormally high should be triggered at a level of 170 g/L (17 g/dL) in men and 150 g/L (15 g/dL) in women. Polycythemia is usually found incidentally at routine blood count. *Relative erythrocytosis*, due to plasma volume loss (e.g., severe dehydration, burns), does not represent a true increase in total RBC mass. *Absolute erythrocytosis* is a true increase in total RBC mass.

CAUSES   Polycythemia vera (a clonal myeloproliferative disorder), erythropoietin-producing neoplasms (e.g., renal cancer, cerebellar hemangioma), chronic hypoxemia (e.g., high altitude, pulmonary disease), carboxyhemoglobin excess (e.g., smokers), high-affinity hemoglobin variants, Cushing's syndrome,

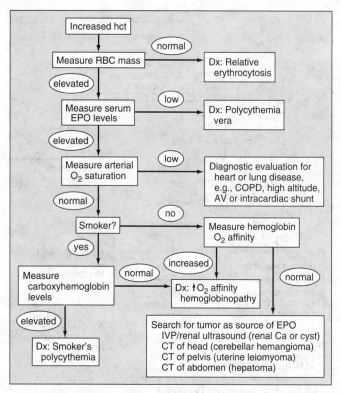

FIGURE 27-2   An approach to diagnosing patients with polycythemia. RBC, red blood cell; EPO, erythropoietin; COPD, chronic obstructive pulmonary disease; AV, atrioventricular; IVP, intravenous pyelogram; CT, computed tomography.

androgen excess. Polycythemia vera is distinguished from secondary polycythemia by the presence of splenomegaly, leukocytosis, thrombocytosis, and elevated vitamin B_{12} levels, and by decreased erythropoietin levels. An approach to evaluate polycythemic pts is shown in Fig. 27-2.

COMPLICATIONS   Hyperviscosity (with diminished O_2 delivery) with risk of ischemic organ injury and thrombosis (venous or arterial) are most common.

℞ TREATMENT

Phlebotomy recommended for Hct $\geq$ 55%, regardless of cause, to low-normal range.

For a more detailed discussion, see Adamson JW, Longo DL: Anemia and Polycythemia, Chap. 61, p. 348, in HPIM-15.

28

LYMPHADENOPATHY AND SPLENOMEGALY

LYMPHADENOPATHY

Exposure to antigen through a break in the skin or mucosa results in antigen being taken up by an antigen-presenting cell and carried via lymphatic channels to the nearest lymph node. Lymph channels course throughout the body except for the brain and the bones. Lymph enters the node through the afferent vessel and leaves through an efferent vessel. As antigen-presenting cells pass through lymph nodes, they present antigen to lymphocytes residing there. Lymphocytes in a node are constantly being replaced by antigen-naive lymphocytes from the blood. They are retained in the node via special homing receptors. B cells populate the lymphoid follicles in the cortex; T cells populate the paracortical regions. When a B cell encounters an antigen to which its surface immunoglobulin can bind, it stays in the follicle for a few days and forms a germinal center where the immunoglobulin gene is mutated in an effort to make an antibody with higher affinity for the antigen. The B cell then migrates to the medullary region, differentiates into a plasma cell, and secretes immunoglobulin into the efferent lymph.

When a T cell in the node encounters an antigen it recognizes, it proliferates and joins the efferent lymph. The efferent lymph laden with antibodies and T cells specific for the inciting antigen passes through several nodes on its way to the thoracic duct, which drains lymph from most of the body. From the thoracic duct, lymph enters the bloodstream at the left subclavian vein. Lymph from the head and neck and the right arm drain into the right subclavian vein. From the bloodstream, the antibody and T cells localize to the site of infection.

Lymphadenopathy may be caused by infections, immunologic diseases, malignancies, lipid storage diseases, or a number of disorders of uncertain etiology (e.g., sarcoidosis, Castleman's disease; Table 28-1). The two major mechanisms of lymphadenopathy are hyperplasia, in response to immunologic or infectious stimuli, and infiltration, by cancer cells or lipid- or glycoprotein-laden macrophages.

_____ *Approach to the Patient* _____

History   Age, occupation, animal exposures, sexual orientation, substance abuse history, medication history, and concomitant symptoms influence diagnostic workup. Adenopathy is more commonly malignant in origin in people over age 40. Farmers have an increased incidence of brucellosis and lymphoma. Male homosexuals may have AIDS-associated adenopathy. Alcohol and tobacco abuse increase risk of malignancy. Phenytoin may induce adenopathy. The concomitant presence of cervical adenopathy with sore throat or with fever, night sweats, and weight loss suggests particular diagnoses (mononucleosis in the former instance, Hodgkin's disease in the latter).

Physical Examination   Location of adenopathy, size, node texture, and the presence of tenderness are important in differential diagnosis. Generalized adenopathy (three or more anatomic regions) implies systemic infection or lymphoma. Subclavian or scalene adenopathy is always abnormal and should be biopsied. Nodes >4 cm should be biopsied immediately. Rock hard nodes fixed to surrounding soft tissue are usually a sign of metastatic carcinoma. Tender nodes are most often benign.

Table 28-1

Diseases Associated with Lymphadenopathy

1. Infectious diseases
   a. Viral—infectious mononucleosis syndromes (EBV, CMV), infectious hepatitis, herpes simplex, herpesvirus-6, varicella-zoster virus, rubella, measles, adenovirus, HIV, epidemic keratoconjunctivitis, vaccinia, herpesvirus-8
   b. Bacterial—streptococci, staphylococci, cat-scratch disease, brucellosis, tularemia, plague, chancroid, melioidosis, glanders, tuberculosis, atypical mycobacterial infection, primary and secondary syphilis, diphtheria, leprosy
   c. Fungal—histoplasmosis, coccidioidomycosis, paracoccidioidomycosis
   d. Chlamydial—lymphogranuloma venereum, trachoma
   e. Parasitic—toxoplasmosis, leishmaniasis, trypanosomiasis, filariasis
   f. Rickettsial—scrub typhus, rickettsialpox
2. Immunologic diseases
   a. Rheumatoid arthritis
   b. Juvenile rheumatoid arthritis
   c. Mixed connective tissue disease
   d. Systemic lupus erythematosus
   e. Dermatomyositis
   f. Sjögren's syndrome
   g. Serum sickness
   h. Drug hypersensitivity—diphenylhydantoin, hydralazine, allopurinol, primidone, gold, carbamazepine, etc.
   i. Angioimmunoblastic lymphadenopathy
   j. Primary biliary cirrhosis
   k. Graft-vs.-host disease
   l. Silicone-associated
3. Malignant diseases
   a. Hematologic—Hodgkin's disease, non-Hodgkin's lymphomas, acute or chronic lymphocytic leukemia, hairy cell leukemia, malignant histiocytosis, amyloidosis
   b. Metastatic—from numerous primary sites
4. Lipid storage diseases—Gaucher's, Niemann-Pick, Fabry, Tangier
5. Endocrine diseases—hyperthyroidism
6. Other disorders
   a. Castleman's disease (giant lymph node hyperplasia)
   b. Sarcoidosis
   c. Dermatopathic lymphadenitis
   d. Lymphomatoid granulomatosis
   e. Histiocytic necrotizing lymphadenitis (Kikuchi's disease)
   f. Sinus histiocytosis with massive lymphadenopathy (Rosai-Dorfman disease)
   g. Mucocutaneous lymph node syndrome (Kawasaki's disease)
   h. Histiocytosis X
   i. Familial mediterranean fever
   j. Severe hypertriglyceridemia
   k. Vascular transformation of sinuses
   l. Inflammatory pseudotumor of lymph node

NOTE: EBV, Epstein-Barr virus; CMV, cytomegalovirus.

Laboratory Tests Usually lab tests are not required in the setting of localized adenopathy. If generalized adenopathy is noted, an excisional node biopsy should be performed for diagnosis, rather than a panoply of laboratory tests.

 TREATMENT

Patients over age 40, those with scalene or supraclavicular adenopathy, those with lymph nodes >4 cm in diameter, and those with hard nontender nodes should undergo immediate excisional biopsy. In younger patients with smaller nodes that are rubbery in consistency or tender, a period of observation for 7–14 days is reasonable. Empirical antibiotics are not indicated. If the nodes shrink, no further evaluation is necessary. If they enlarge, excisional biopsy is indicated.

SPLENOMEGALY

Just as the lymph nodes are specialized to fight pathogens in the tissues, the spleen is the lymphoid organ specialized to fight bloodborne pathogens. It has no afferent lymphatics. The spleen has specialized areas like the lymph node for making antibodies (follicles) and amplifying antigen-specific T cells (periarteriolar lymphatic sheath, or PALS). In addition, it has a well-developed reticuloendothelial system for removing particles and antibody-coated bacteria. The flow of blood through the spleen permits it to filter pathogens from the blood and to maintain quality control over erythrocytes (RBCs)—those that are old and nondeformable are destroyed, and intracellular inclusions (sometimes including pathogens like babesia and malaria) are culled from the cells in a process called *pitting*. Under certain conditions, the spleen can generate hematopoietic cells in place of the marrow.

The normal spleen is about 12 cm in length and 7 cm in width and is not normally palpable. Dullness from the spleen can be percussed between the ninth and eleventh ribs with the pt lying on the right side. Palpation is best performed with the pt supine with knees flexed. The spleen may be felt as it descends when the pt inspires. Physical diagnosis is not sensitive. CT or ultrasound are superior tests.

Spleen enlargement occurs by three basic mechanisms: (1) hyperplasia or hypertrophy due to an increase in demand for splenic function (e.g., hereditary spherocytosis where demand for removal of defective RBCs is high or immune hyperplasia in response to systemic infection or immune diseases); (2) passive vascular congestion due to portal hypertension; and (3) infiltration with malignant cells, lipid- or glycoprotein-laden macrophages, or amyloid (Table 28-2). Massive enlargement, with spleen palpable >8 cm below the left costal margin, usually signifies a lymphoproliferative or myeloproliferative disorder.

Peripheral blood RBC count, WBC count, and platelet count may be normal, decreased, or increased depending on the underlying disorder. Decreases in one or more cell lineages could indicate hypersplenism, increased destruction. In cases with hypersplenism, the spleen is removed and the cytopenia is generally reversed. In the absence of hypersplenism, most causes of splenomegaly are diagnosed on the basis of signs and symptoms and laboratory abnormalities associated with the underlying disorder. Splenectomy is rarely performed for diagnostic purposes.

People who have had splenectomy are at increased risk of sepsis from a variety of organisms including the pneumococcus and *Haemophilus influenzae*.

Table 28-2

Diseases Associated with Splenomegaly Grouped by Pathogenic Mechanism

ENLARGEMENT DUE TO INCREASED DEMAND FOR SPLENIC FUNCTION

Reticuloendothelial system hyperplasia (for removal of defective erythrocytes)
    Spherocytosis
    Early sickle cell anemia
    Ovalocytosis
    Thalassemia major
    Hemoglobinopathies
    Paroxysmal nocturnal hemoglobinuria
    Nutritional anemias
Immune hyperplasia
    Response to infection (viral, bacterial, fungal, parasitic)
        Infectious mononucleosis
        AIDS
        Viral hepatitis
        Cytomegalovirus
        Subacute bacterial endocarditis
        Bacterial septicemia
        Congenital syphilis
        Splenic abscess
        Tuberculosis
        Histoplasmosis
        Malaria
        Leishmaniasis
        Trypanosomiasis
        Ehrlichiosis
    Disordered immunoregulation
        Rheumatoid arthritis (Felty's syndrome)
        Systemic lupus erythematosus
        Collagen vascular diseases
        Serum sickness
        Immune hemolytic anemias
        Immune thrombocytopenias
        Immune neutropenias
        Drug reactions
        Angioimmunoblastic lymphadenopathy
        Sarcoidosis
        Thyrotoxicosis (benign lymphoid hypertrophy)
        Interleukin-2 therapy
Extramedullary hematopoiesis
    Myelofibrosis
    Marrow damage by toxins, radiation, strontium
    Marrow infiltration by tumors, leukemias, Gaucher's disease

ENLARGEMENT DUE TO ABNORMAL SPLENIC OR PORTAL BLOOD FLOW

Cirrhosis
Hepatic vein obstruction
Portal vein obstruction, intrahepatic or extrahepatic
Cavernous transformation of the portal vein
Splenic vein obstruction

(continued)

Table 28-2 *(Continued)*

Diseases Associated with Splenomegaly Grouped by Pathogenic Mechanism

Splenic artery aneurysm
Hepatic schistosomiasis
Congestive heart failure
Hepatic echinococcosis
Portal hypertension (any cause including the above): "Banti's disease"

INFILTRATION OF THE SPLEEN

Intracellular or extracellular depositions
    Amyloidosis
    Gaucher's disease
    Niemann-Pick disease
    Tangier disease
    Hurler's syndrome and other mucopolysaccharidoses
    Hyperlipidemias
Benign and malignant cellular infiltrations
    Leukemias (acute, chronic, lymphoid, myeloid, monocytic)
    Lymphomas
    Hodgkin's disease
    Myeloproliferative syndromes (e.g., polycythemia vera)
    Angiosarcomas
    Metastatic tumors (melanoma is most common)
    Eosinophilic granuloma
    Histiocytosis X
    Hamartomas
    Hemangiomas, fibromas, lymphangiomas
    Splenic cysts

UNKNOWN ETIOLOGY

Idiopathic splenomegaly
Berylliosis
Iron-deficiency anemia

Vaccines for these agents should be given before splenectomy is performed. Splenectomy compromises the immune response to these T-independent antigens.

For a more detailed discussion, see Henry PH, Longo DL: Enlargement of the Lymph Nodes and Spleen, Chap. 63, p. 360, in HPIM-15.

29

CARDIOVASCULAR COLLAPSE AND SUDDEN DEATH

Unexpected cardiovascular collapse and death most often result from ventricular fibrillation in pts with underlying coronary artery disease, with or without acute MI. Other common causes are listed in Table 29-1. The arrhythmic causes may be provoked by electrolyte disorders (primarily hypokalemia), hypoxemia, acidosis, or massive sympathetic discharge, as may occur in CNS injury. Immediate institution of cardiopulmonary resuscitation (CPR) followed by advanced life support measures (see below) are mandatory. Ventricular fibrillation, or asystole, without institution of CPR within 4–6 min, usually causes death.

Management of Cardiac Arrest

Basic life support (BLS) commences immediately (Fig. 29-1):

1. Open mouth of patient and remove visible debris or dentures. If there is respiratory stridor, consider aspiration of a foreign body and perform Heimlich maneuver.
2. Tilt head backward, lift chin, and begin mouth-to-mouth respiration if rescue equipment is not available (pocket mask is preferable to prevent transmission of infection). The lungs should be inflated once for every 5 chest compressions when two persons are performing resuscitation or twice in rapid succession for every 15 chest compressions when one person performs both ventilation and chest compression.
3. If carotid pulse is absent, perform chest compressions (depressing sternum 3–5 cm) at rate of 80–100 per min. For one rescuer, 15 compressions are performed before returning to ventilating twice.

Table 29-1

Differential Diagnosis of Cardiovascular Collapse and Sudden Death

1. Ventricular fibrillation due to:
   Myocardial ischemia (severe coronary artery disease, acute MI)
   Congestive heart failure
   Dilated or hypertrophic cardiomyopathy
   Myocarditis
   Valvular disease [aortic stenosis, mitral valve prolapse (rare)]
   Preexcitation syndromes (Wolff-Parkinson-White)
   Prolonged QT syndromes (congenital, drug-induced)
2. Asystole or severe bradycardia
3. Sudden marked decrease in LV stroke volume from:
   Massive pulmonary embolism
   Cardiac tamponade
   Severe aortic stenosis
4. Sudden marked decrease in intravascular volume, e.g.:
   Ruptured aortic aneurysm
   Aortic dissection

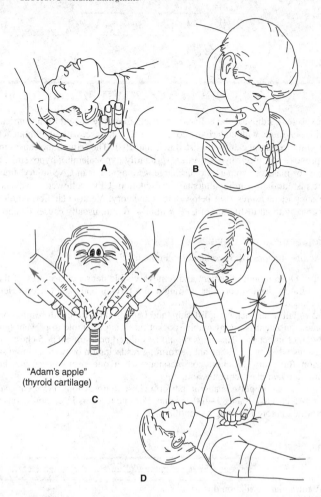

"Adam's apple"
(thyroid cartilage)

C

FIGURE 29-1 Major steps in cardiopulmonary resuscitation. *A*. Make certain the victim has an open airway. *B*. Start respiratory resuscitation immediately. *C*. Feel for the carotid pulse in the groove alongside the "Adam's apple" or thyroid cartilage. *D*. If pulse is absent, begin cardiac massage. Use 60 compressions/min with one lung inflation after each group of 5 chest compressions when two people are performing resuscitation or twice in rapid succession for every 15 compressions when one person performs both ventilation and compression. (*From J Henderson, Emergency Medical Guide, 4th ed, New York, McGraw-Hill, 1978.*)

As soon as resuscitation equipment is available, begin advanced life support (Fig. 29-2) with continued chest compressions and ventilation. Although performed as simultaneously as possible, defibrillation takes highest priority, followed by placement of intravenous access and intubation. 100% O_2 should be administered by endotracheal tube or, if rapid intubation cannot be accomplished, by bag-valve-mask device; respirations should not be interrupted for more than 30 s while attempting to intubate. Initial intravenous access should

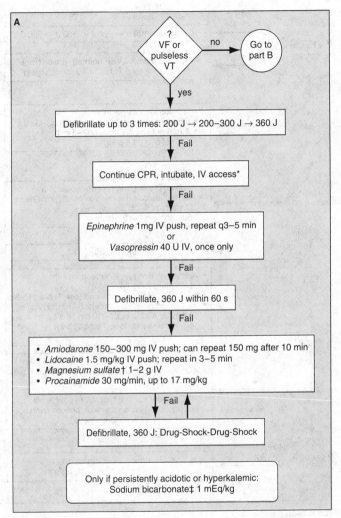

FIGURE 29-2A Advanced life support algorithm. *Antecubital route preferred; if infusions not effective, place central line. †If hypomagnesemic state or if rhythm is torsades de pointes. ‡Do not infuse sodium bicarbonate in same IV as calcium, epinephrine, or dopamine. LVEF, left ventricular ejection fraction; VF, ventricular fibrillation; VT, ventricular tachycardia; PEA, pulseless electrical activity (formerly termed electromechanical dissociation); SVT, supraventricular tachycardia. [*Modified from American Heart Association Circulation 102 (Suppl I): I-142–157, 2000.*]

be through the antecubital vein, but if drug administration is ineffective, a central line (internal jugular or subclavian) should be placed. Intravenous NaHCO₃ should be administered only if there is persistent severe acidosis (pH < 7.15) despite adequate ventilation. Calcium is *not* routinely administered but should be given to pts with known hypocalcemia, those who have received toxic doses

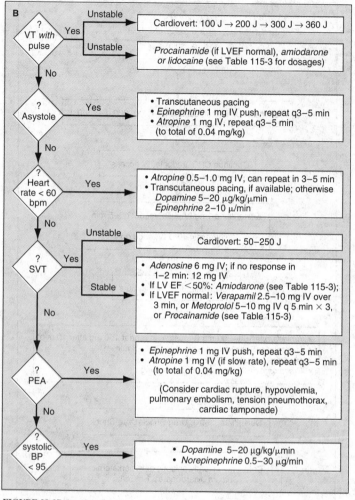

FIGURE 29-2B *(continued)*

of calcium channel antagonists, or if acute hyperkalemia is thought to be the triggering event for resistant ventricular fibrillation.

Follow-up

If cardiac arrest was due to ventricular fibrillation in initial hours of an acute MI, follow-up is standard post-MI care (Chap. 121). For other survivors of a ventricular fibrillation arrest, extensive evaluation, including evaluation of coronary anatomy, left ventricular function, and invasive electrophysiologic testing, is recommended. Long-term antiarrhythmic drug therapy, implantation of an automatic defibrillator, and/or cardiac surgery (coronary artery bypass graft, aneurysmectomy, or resection/ablation of arrhythmic foci) may be necessary.

For a more detailed discussion, see Myerburg RJ, Castellanos A: Cardio-vascular Collapse, Cardiac Arrest, and Sudden Death, Chap. 39, p. 228, in HPIM-15.

30

SHOCK

Definition

Condition of severe impairment of tissue perfusion. Rapid recognition and treatment are essential to prevent irreversible organ damage. Common causes are listed in Table 30-1.

Clinical Manifestations

Hypotension (systolic bp <90), tachycardia, tachypnea, pallor, restlessness, and altered sensorium; signs of intense peripheral vasoconstriction; weak pulses; cold clammy extremities [*note*: in distributive (e.g., septic) shock, vasodilatation predominates and extremities are warm]. Oliguria (<20 mL/h) and metabolic acidosis common.

Approach to the Patient

Tissue perfusion must be restored immediately (see below); also obtain history for underlying cause, including

- Known cardiac disease (coronary disease, CHF, pericarditis)
- Recent fever or infection (leading to sepsis)
- Drugs, i.e., excess diuretics or antihypertensives
- Predisposing conditions for pulmonary embolism (Chap. 132)
- Possible bleeding from any site, particularly GI tract.

Physical Examination

- Jugular veins are flat in oligemic or distributive shock; jugular venous distention (JVD) suggests cardiogenic shock; JVD in presence of paradoxical pulse (Chap. 112) may reflect cardiac tamponade (Chap. 120).
- Look for evidence of CHF (Chap. 116), murmurs of aortic stenosis, acute regurgitation (mitral or aortic), ventricular septal defect.
- Check for asymmetry of pulses (aortic dissection).
- Tenderness or rebound in abdomen may indicate peritonitis or pancreatitis; high-pitched bowel sounds suggest intestinal obstruction. Perform stool guaiac to rule out GI bleeding.
- Fever and chills usually accompany septic shock. Sepsis may not cause fever in elderly, uremic, or alcoholic patients.

Table 30-1

Common Forms of Shock

Oligemic shock
  Hemorrhage
  Volume depletion (e.g., vomiting, diarrhea, diuretic over-usage, ketoacidosis)
  Internal sequestration (ascites, pancreatitis, intestinal obstruction)
Cardiogenic shock
  Myopathic (acute MI, dilated cardiomyopathy)
  Mechanical (acute mitral regurgitation, ventricular septal defect, severe aortic
    stenosis)
  Arrhythmic
Extracardiac obstructive shock
  Pericardial tamponade
  Massive pulmonary embolism
  Tension pneumothorax
Distributive shock (profound decrease in systemic vascular tone)
  Sepsis
  Toxic overdoses
  Anaphylaxis
  Neurogenic (e.g., spinal cord injury)
  Endocrinologic (Addison's disease, myxedema)

- Skin lesion may suggest specific pathogens in septic shock: petechiae or
  purpura (*Neisseria meningitidis*), ecythyma gangrenosum (*Pseudomonas aeruginosa*), generalized erythroderma (toxic shock due to *Staphylococcus
  aureus* or *Streptococcus pyogenes*).

Laboratory

Obtain hematocrit, WBC, electrolytes. If actively bleeding, check platelet count,
PT, PTT, DIC screen. Arterial blood gas usually shows metabolic acidosis (in
septic shock, respiratory alkalosis precedes metabolic acidosis). If sepsis suspected, draw blood cultures, perform urinalysis, and obtain Gram stain and
cultures of sputum, urine, and other suspected sites.

Obtain ECG (myocardial ischemia or acute arrhythmia), chest x-ray (CHF,
tension pneumothorax, aortic dissection, pneumonia). Echocardiogram may be
helpful (cardiac tamponade, CHF). Central venous pressure or pulmonary capillary wedge (PCW) pressure measurements may be necessary to distinguish
between the different categories of shock (Table 30-2): Mean PCW < 6 mmHg
suggests oligemic or distributive shock; PCW > 20 mmHg suggests left ventricular failure. Cardiac output is decreased in pts with cardiogenic and oligemic
shock, and usually increased initially in septic shock.

 TREATMENT

Aimed at rapid improvement of tissue hypoperfusion and respiratory impairment:

1. Serial measurements of bp (intraarterial line preferred), heart rate,
continuous ECG monitor, urine output, pulse oximetry, blood studies: Hct,
electrolytes, creatinine, BUN, ABGs, calcium, phosphate, lactate, urine Na
concentration (<20 mmol/L suggests volume depletion). Continuous monitoring of CVP and/or pulmonary artery pressure, with serial PCW pressures.

Table 30-2

Hemodynamic Profiles in Shock States

Diagnosis	PCW Pressure	Cardiac Output (CO)	Systemic Vascular Resistance	Comments
Cardiogenic shock	↑	↓	↑	PCW is normal or ↓ in RV infarction
Extracardiac obstructive shock				
Cardiac tamponade	↑	↓	↑	Equalization of intracardiac diastolic pressures
Massive pulmonary embolus	Normal or ↓	↓	↑	Right-sided cardiac pressures may be elevated
Oligemic shock	↓	↓	↑	
Distributive shock	↓	↑	↓	CO may ↓ later if sepsis results in LV dysfunction or if intravascular volume is inadequate

2. Augment systolic bp to >100 mmHg: (a) place in reverse Trendelenburg position; (b) IV volume infusion (500–1000 mL bolus), unless cardiogenic shock suspected (begin with normal saline, then whole blood, dextran, or packed RBCs, if anemic); continue, volume replacement as needed to restore vascular volume; (c) vasoactive drugs are added after intravascular volume is optimized; administer vasopressors (Table 30-3) if systemic vascular resistance (SVR) is decreased (begin with norepinephrine or dopamine; for persistent hypotension add phenylephrine or vasopressin); (d) if CHF present, add inotropic agents (usually dobutamine) (Chap. 116; Table 116-2); aim to maintain cardiac index >2.2 (L/m^2)/min [>4.0 (L/m^2)/min in septic shock].

3. Administer 100% O_2; intubate with mechanical ventilation if P_{O_2} <70 mmHg.

4. If severe metabolic acidosis present (pH < 7.15), administer $NaHCO_3$ (44.6–89.2 mmol).

5. Identify and treat underlying cause of shock. Cardiogenic shock in acute MI is discussed in Chap. 121. Emergent coronary revascularization may be lifesaving if persistent ischemia is present.

Septic shock can rapidly result in the acute respiratory distress syndrome, acute renal failure, DIC, multiple organ failure, or death. Successful management relies on immediate hemodynamic and respiratory support and eliminating the infecting organism. A Gram stain of the primary site of infection, if known, helps to direct antimicrobial therapy. In overwhelming sepsis (e.g., pneumococcal bacteremia in a splenectomized patient), the organism may sometimes be identified on buffy coat smear of peripheral blood. If no source of infection is identified, initiate empirical antibiotic therapy after cultures of potentially infected tissues are obtained (e.g., blood urine, sputum, pleural effusion, CSF).

Table 30-3

Vasopressors Used in Shock States [a]

Drug	Dose, (μg/kg)/min	Notes
Dopamine	1–5	Facilitates diuresis
	5–10	Positive inotropic and chronotropic effects; may increase O_2 consumption as well as O_2 delivery; use may be limited by tachycardia
	10–20	Generalized vasoconstriction (decrease renal perfusion)
Norepinephrine	2–8	Potent vasoconstrictor; moderate inotropic effect; in septic shock is thought to increase tissue O_2 consumption as well as O_2 delivery; may be chosen over dopamine in sepsis due to less chronotropic effect; may be useful in cardiogenic shock with reduced SVR but should generally by reserved for refractory hypotension
Dobutamine	1–10	Primarily for cardiogenic shock (Chap. 121): positive inotrope; lacks vasoconstrictor activity; most useful when only mild hypotension present and avoidance of tachycardia desired
Phenylephrine	20–200	Potent vasoconstrictor without inotropic effect; may be useful in distributive (septive) shock
Vasopressin	0.01–0.04 U/min[b]	Occasionally used in refractory septic (distributive) shock; restores vascular tone in vasopressin-deficient states (e.g., sepsis)

[a] Isoproterenol not recommended in shock states because of potential hypotension and arrhythmogenic effects.
[b] Dose not based on weight.

It is essential to drain foci of septic material. Potentially infected intravenous or urinary catheters should be removed and cultured. Look for occult sites of infection, e.g., sinusitis, perianal abscess, dental abscess, infected decubitus ulcer. In suspected urosepsis, a renal or perinephric abscess can be evaluated by ultrasound, CT, or MRI.

Hemodynamic support must be provided as in other causes of shock to maintain tissue perfusion. Large volumes of intravascular fluid are often necessary and should be gauged by the PCW pressure (desired range 12–15 mmHg) or CVP (desired range 10–12 cmH$_2$O) and urinary output (aim for ≤30 mL/h). Maintain systolic bp ≤90 mmHg by repleting intravascular volume and, if necessary, by vasopressors (Table 30-3): dopamine 5–10 (μg/kg)/min, or norepinephrine 2–8 (μg/kg)/min. In refractory shock, vasopressin or phenylephrine may be added.

Consider the possible complication of adrenal insufficiency if patient has septic shock with fulminant *N. meningitidis* infection, refractory hypotension, recent glucocorticoid use, disseminated tuberculosis, or AIDS. Administer hydrocortisone 50 mg IV q6h while evaluating this possibility (Chap. 172).

For a more detailed discussion, see Maier RV: Shock, Chap. 38, 222; and Munford RS: Sepsis and Septic Shock, Chap. 124, p. 799, in HPIM-15.

31

SEPSIS AND SEPTIC SHOCK

Definitions

The systemic inflammatory response syndrome (SIRS), defined in the early 1990s by critical-care specialists, incorporates clinical criteria (fever or hypothermia, tachypnea, tachycardia, and abnormal WBC count) that may be manifestations of microbial infection or conditions of other etiologies. When the syndrome is caused by microbial infection, it is called *sepsis*. *Septic shock* refers to the overwhelming of host homeostatic mechanisms by sepsis, which results in hypotension and organ dysfunction. These and related terms are defined in Table 31-1.

Epidemiology/Etiology/Pathogenesis

There are 300,000–500,000 cases of sepsis annually in the U.S., and sepsis contributes to >100,000 deaths per year. Approximately two-thirds of cases occur in hospitalized pts. Moreover, ~20–40% of pts with severe sepsis and 40–70% of pts with septic shock have positive blood cultures: 35% of positive cultures yield gram-negative bacteria, ~40% yield gram-positive bacteria, and ~7% yield fungi. Risk factors for gram-negative rod bacteremia include diabetes, lymphoproliferative disease, cirrhosis, burns, invasive procedures or devices, and neutropenia. Risk factors for gram-positive bacteremia include the presence of intravascular catheters or mechanical devices, burns, and IV drug use. The incidence of sepsis appears to be increasing, probably because of an increase in the size of the population with risk factors. Sepsis results from complex host reactions to microbial signal molecules: lipopolysaccharide (LPS, also called endotoxin), peptidoglycan, and lipoteichoic acid of gram-positive bacteria as well as various extracellular enzymes and toxins. The host response is mediated by leukocytes, humoral factors (cytokines, prostaglandins, coagulation factors), and the vascular endothelium.

Clinical Manifestations

Signs of sepsis include the abrupt onset of fever, chills, tachycardia, tachypnea, altered mental status, and/or hypotension, particularly in a pt with localized infection. However, the septic response may develop gradually, and many or all of these signs may be absent. Hyperventilation, disorientation, and confusion are diagnostically useful early signs. Hypotension and DIC may develop. Cutaneous signs are frequent and include cyanosis and ischemic necrosis of peripheral tissue, cellulitis, pustules, bullae, and hemorrhagic lesions. Some skin lesions suggest specific pathogens: petechial or purpuric lesions suggest meningococcemia or Rocky Mountain spotted fever; a bullous lesion surrounded by edema with central hemorrhage and necrosis (ecthyma gangrenosum) suggests

Table 31-1

Definitions Used to Describe the Condition of Patients with Sepsis

Bacteremia	Presence of bacteria in the blood, as evidenced by positive blood cultures
Septicemia	Presence of microbes or their toxins in blood
Systemic inflammatory response syndrome (SIRS)	Two or more of the following conditions: (1) fever (oral temperature >38°C) or hypothermia (<36°C); (2) tachypnea (>24 breaths/min); (3) tachycardia (heart rate >90 beats/min); (4) leukocytosis (>12,000/μL), leukopenia (<4,000/μL), or >10% bands. May have an infectious or a noninfectious etiology
Sepsis	SIRS that has a proven or suspected microbial etiology
Severe sepsis (similar to "sepsis syndrome")	Sepsis with one or more signs of organ dysfunction (such as metabolic acidosis, acute encephalopathy, oliguria, hypoxemia, or DIC) or hypotension
Septic shock	Sepsis with hypotension (arterial blood pressure of <90 mmHg systolic or 40 mmHg less than pt's normal blood pressure) that is unresponsive to fluid resuscitation, along with organ dysfunction (see "severe sepsis")
Refractory septic shock	Septic shock that lasts for >1 h and does not respond to fluid or pressor administration
Multiple-organ dysfunction syndrome (MODS)	Dysfunction of more than one organ, requiring intervention to maintain homeostasis

SOURCE: Adapted from American College of Chest Physicians/Society of Critical Care Medicine Consensus Conference Committee by RS Munford: HPIM-15, p. 799.

Pseudomonas sepsis; generalized erythroderma in a septic pt suggests toxic shock syndrome; bullous lesions in a pt who has eaten raw oysters suggest *Vibrio vulnificus* sepsis; and the same lesions in a pt after a dog bite suggest *Capnocytophaga* sepsis. GI manifestations include nausea, vomiting, diarrhea, ileus, gastric ulceration with bleeding, and cholestatic jaundice.

Complications

ARDS ("shock lung"), mediated by pulmonary capillary microvascular injury, develops in ~50% of pts with severe sepsis or septic shock and causes diffuse pulmonary infiltrates and hypoxemia. Sepsis-induced hypotension usually results from a generalized maldistribution of blood flow and blood volume and from hypovolemia due to diffuse capillary leak. After fluid repletion, cardiac output typically increases and systemic vascular resistance falls. Oliguria, azotemia, proteinuria, and nonspecific renal casts are frequent. Renal failure is usually caused by acute tubular necrosis. Thrombocytopenia occurs in 10–30% of cases. Profound thrombocytopenia (<50,000 platelets/μL) usually reflects DIC. Dysfunction of multiple organs usually indicates widespread endovascular injury and is associated with high fatality rates.

Diagnosis

There is no reliable laboratory test for the early diagnosis of sepsis. Clinical manifestations (listed above) are variably present and nonspecific. Laboratory findings may include leukocytosis with a left shift, thrombocytopenia, hyperbilirubinemia, and proteinuria. Leukopenia may also develop. Active hemolysis may occur in clostridial bacteremia, malaria, drug reactions, or DIC. In DIC, there may be evidence of microangiopathic changes on peripheral smear. Early, hyperventilation-induced respiratory alkalosis may be followed by metabolic acidosis and hypoxemia. CXR may reveal ARDS or underlying pneumonia. Definitive diagnosis requires isolation of microorganisms from the blood or from a local site of infection. At least two blood samples should be obtained for culture from different venipuncture sites. If blood cultures are negative, the diagnosis depends on Gram's stain and culture of the primary site of infection or of secondarily infected cutaneous tissue. With overwhelming bacteremia, smears of peripheral-blood buffy coat may reveal microorganisms.

℞ TREATMENT

Sepsis is a medical emergency that requires immediate action to treat the local site of infection, to provide hemodynamic and respiratory support, and to eliminate the offending microorganism. Antibiotics should be given as soon as samples of blood and other sites have been obtained for culture. Empirical therapy should be based on information about the pt and about antimicrobial susceptibility patterns in the community and the hospital. Pending culture results, therapy including agents active against both gram-negative and -positive bacteria should be given. Suggested empirical regimens in different populations of pts are listed in Table 31-2. Removal or drainage of any focal site of infection is essential (indwelling IV or urinary catheters; paranasal sinuses; abdominal, perinephric, or pelvic collections). Hemodynamic support should restore oxygen delivery to tissue. IV fluid, typically 1–2 L of normal saline over 1–2 h, should be administered to restore effective intravascular volume. Monitoring of pulmonary capillary wedge pressure (target range, 12–16 mmHg) is essential in pts with refractory shock or underlying cardiac or renal disease. Dopamine [4–20 (μg/kg)/min] may be used to restore a mean arterial blood pressure of >60 mmHg and a cardiac index of ≥2.2 (L/min)/m². Higher doses may cause peripheral vasoconstriction with ischemia. Norepinephrine may be used when pts are refractory to dopamine, with dosing carefully titrated to maintain mean blood pressure at >60 mmHg (dose range, 2–20 μg/min). Ventilatory support is indicated for progressive hypoxemia, hypercapnia, neurologic deterioration, or respiratory muscle failure. Intubation can ensure adequate oxygenation, divert blood flow from the muscles of respiration, prevent aspiration of oropharyngeal contents, and reduce cardiac afterload. Glucocorticoid supplementation (hydrocortisone, 50 mg IV q6h) is indicated only in the rare instance of adrenal insufficiency, which should be suspected in cases of refractory hypotension, fulminant *Neisseria meningitidis* bacteremia, disseminated tuberculosis, prior glucocorticoid use, or AIDS.

Despite early diagnosis and prompt and aggressive management, ~20–35% of pts with severe sepsis and 40–60% of pts with septic shock die within 30 days. Prognosis is affected most by the severity of the pt's underlying disease and various physiologic parameters. Septic shock is also a strong predictor of short- and long-term mortality. Case-fatality rates are similar for both culture-positive and -negative severe sepsis. Prevention offers the best opportunity to reduce morbidity and mortality from sepsis. Preventive measures include minimizing the number of invasive procedures, limiting the use and duration of indwelling vascular and bladder catheters, reducing the incidence and duration of profound neutropenia, aggressively treating localized infection, and immunizing pts against specific pathogens.

Table 31-2

Initial Antimicrobial Therapy for Severe Sepsis with No Obvious Source in Adults with Normal Renal Function

Clinical Condition	Antimicrobial Regimens (Intravenous Therapy)
Immunocompetent adult	The many acceptable regimens include (1) ceftriaxone (1 g q12h) *or* ticarcillin-clavulanate (3.1 g q4–6h) *or* piperacillin-tazobactam (3.75 g q4–6h); (2) imipenem-cilastatin (0.5 g q6h) *or* meropenem (1 g q8h). Gentamicin or tobramycin (5 mg/kg q24h) may be *added* to either regimen. If the pt is allergic to β-lactam agents, use ciprofloxacin (400 mg q12h) *plus* clindamycin (600 mg q8h). If the institution has a high incidence of MRSA infections, *add* vancomycin (15 mg/kg q12h) to each of the above regimens.
Neutropenia[a] (<500 neutrophils/μL)	Regimens include (1) ceftazidime (2 g q8h) *or* ticarcillin-clavulanate (3.1 g q4h) *or* piperacillin-tazobactam (3.75 g q4h) *plus* tobramycin (5 mg/kg q24h); (2) imipenem-cilastatin (0.5 g q6h) *or* meropenem (1 g q8h) *or* ceftazidime *or* cefepime (2 g q12h). Vancomycin (15 mg/kg q12h) and ceftazidime should be used if the pt has an infected vascular catheter, if staphylococci are suspected, if the pt has received quinolone prophylaxy, if the pt has received intensive chemotherapy that produces mucosal damage, or if the institution has a high incidence of MRSA infections.
Splenectomy	Cefotaxime (2 g q6–8h) *or* ceftriaxone (2 g q12h) should be used. If the local prevalence of cephalosporin-resistant pneumococci is high, *add* vancomycin. If the pt is allergic to β-lactam drugs, vancomycin (15 mg/kg q12h) *plus* ciprofloxacin (400 mg q12h) *or* aztreonam (2 g q8h) should be used.
IV drug user	Nafcillin *or* oxacillin (2 g q4h) *plus* gentamicin (5 mg/kg q24h). If the local prevalence of MRSA is high or if the pt is allergic to β-lactam drugs, vancomycin (15 mg/kg q12h) with gentamicin should be used.
AIDS	Ceftazidime (2 g q8h), ticarcillin-clavulanate (3.1 g q4h), *or* piperacillin-tazobactam (3.75 g q4h) *plus* tobramycin (5 mg/kg q24h) should be used. If the pt is allergic to β-lactam drugs, ciprofloxacin (400 mg q12h) *plus* vancomycin (15 mg/kg q12h) *plus* tobramycin should be used.

[a] Adapted in part from WT Hughes et al: Clin Infect Dis 25:551, 1997, by Munford RS: HPIM-15, p. 802.

NOTE: MRSA, methicillin-resistant *Staphylococcus aureus.*

For a more detailed discussion, see Munford RS: Sepsis and Septic Shock, Chap. 124, p. 799, in HPIM-15.

32

ACUTE PULMONARY EDEMA

Life-threatening, acute development of alveolar lung edema is most often due to (1) elevation of hydrostatic pressure in the pulmonary capillaries (left heart failure, mitral stenosis) or (2) increased permeability of the pulmonary alveolar-capillary membrane. Specific precipitants (Table 32-1) result in cardiogenic pulmonary edema in pts with previously compensated CHF or without previous cardiac history.

Physical Findings

Patient appears severely ill, sitting bolt upright, tachypneic, dyspneic, with marked perspiration; cyanosis may be present. Bilateral pulmonary rales; third heart sound may be present. The sputum is frothy and blood-tinged.

Laboratory Data

In early stages, arterial blood gas measurements demonstrate reductions of both Pa_{O_2}; and Pa_{CO_2}; later, with progressive respiratory failure, hypercapnia develops with progressive acidemia. CXR shows pulmonary vascular redistribution, diffuse haziness in the lung fields with perihilar "butterfly" appearance.

℞ TREATMENT

Immediate, aggressive therapy is mandatory for survival. The following measures should be instituted nearly simultaneously:

1. Seat pt upright to reduce venous return.
2. Administer 100% O_2 by mask to achieve Pa_{O_2} >60 mmHg; In pts who will tolerate it, continuous positive airway pressure (10 cm H_2O pressure) by mask improves outcome.
3. Intravenous loop diuretic (furosemide 40–100 mg or bumetanide 1 mg); use lower dose if pt does not take diuretics chronically.
4. Morphine 2–5 mg IV (repetitively); assess frequently for hypotension or respiratory depression; naloxone should be available to reverse effects of morphine if necessary.
5. Afterload reduction [nitropaste 0.5–1 in. or IV sodium nitroprusside (20–300 μg/min) if systolic bp >100 mmHg]; arterial line should be placed for continuous bp monitoring.

Table 32-1

Precipitants of Acute Pulmonary Edema

Acute tachy- or bradyarrhythmia
Infection, fever
Acute MI
Severe hypertension
Acute mitral or aortic regurgitation
Increased circulating volume (Na ingestion, blood transfusion, pregnancy)
Increased metabolic demands (exercise, hyperthyroidism)
Pulmonary embolism
Noncompliance (sudden discontinuation) of chronic CHF medications

Table 32-2

Examples of Noncardiogenic Pulmonary Edema

Decreased plasma oncotic pressure
   Hypoalbuminemia
Excessive alveolar-capillary permeability
   Diffuse pulmonary infection
   Inhaled toxins (e.g., phosgene, smoke)
   Gram-negative sepsis or endotoxemia
   Aspiration pneumonia
   Thermal or radiation lung injury
   Disseminated intravascular coagulation
   Acute hemorrhagic pancreatitis
Lymphatic insufficiency
   After lung transplantation
   Lymphangitic carcinomatosis
Unknown mechanism
   High-altitude exposure
   Acute CNS disorders
   Narcotic overdose
   Following cardiopulmonary bypass

Additional therapy may be required if rapid improvement does not ensue:

1. Inotropic agents, such as dobutamine (Chap. 30), may be helpful in cardiogenic pulmonary edema with shock.
2. If rapid diuresis does not follow diuretic administration, intravascular volume can be reduced by phlebotomy (removal of ~250 mL through antecubital vein).
3. For persistent hypoxemia or hypercapnia, intubation may be required.
4. For refractory pulmonary edema associated with persistent cardiac ischemia, early coronary revascularization may be life-saving.

The precipitating cause of pulmonary edema with cardiogenic shock (Table 32-1) should be sought and treated, particularly acute arrhythmias or infection.

Several noncardiogenic conditions may result in pulmonary edema (Table 32-2) in the absence of left heart dysfunction; therapy is directed toward the primary condition.

For a more detailed discussion, see Ingram RH Jr, Braunwald E: Dyspnea and Pulmonary Edema, Chap. 32, p. 199, in HPIM-15.

33

CONFUSION, STUPOR, AND COMA

Disorders of consciousness are common in medical practice. Assessment should determine whether there is a change in level of consciousness (drowsy, stupor-

Table 33-1

Approach to the Differential Diagnosis of Coma

1. Diseases that cause no focal or lateralizing neurologic signs, usually with normal brainstem functions; CT scan and cellular content of the CSF are normal
   a. Intoxications: alcohol, sedative drugs, opiates, etc.
   b. Metabolic disturbances: anoxia, hyponatremia, hypernatremia, hypercalcemia, diabetic acidosis, nonketotic hyperosmolar hyperglycemia, hypoglycemia, uremia, hepatic coma, hypercarbia, addisonian crisis, hypo- and hyperthyroid states, profound nutritional deficiency
   c. Severe systemic infections: pneumonia, septicemia, typhoid fever, malaria, Waterhouse-Friderichsen syndrome
   d. Shock from any cause
   e. Postseizure states, status epilepticus, subclinical epilepsy
   f. Hypertensive encephalopathy, eclampsia
   g. Severe hyperthermia, hypothermia
   h. Concussion
   i. Acute hydrocephalus
2. Diseases that cause meningeal irritation with or without fever, and with an excess of WBCs or RBCs in the CSF, usually without focal or lateralizing cerebral or brainstem signs; CT or MRI shows no mass lesion
   a. Subarachnoid hemorrhage from ruptured aneurysm, arteriovenous malformation, occasionally trauma
   b. Acute bacterial meningitis
   c. Some forms of viral encephalitis
   d. Miscellaneous: Fat embolism, cholesterol embolism, carcinomatous and lymphamatous meningitis, etc.
3. Diseases that cause focal brainstem or lateralizing cerebral signs, with or without changes in the CSF; CT and MRI are abnormal
   a. Hemispheral hemorrhage (basal ganglionic, thalamic) or infarction (large middle cerebral artery territory) with secondary brainstem compression
   b. Brainstem infarction due to basilar artery thrombosis or embolism
   c. Brain abscess, subdural empyema
   d. Epidural and subdural hemorrhage, brain contusion
   e. Brain tumor with surrounding edema
   f. Cerebellar and pontine hemorrhage and infarction
   g. Widespread traumatic brain injury
   h. Metabolic coma (see above) with preexisting focal damage
   i. Miscellaneous: cortical vein thrombosis, herpes simplex viral encephalitis, multiple cerebral emboli due to bacterial endocarditis, acute hemorrhagic leukoencephalitis, acute disseminated (postinfectious) encephalomyelitis, thrombotic thrombocytopenic purpura, cerebral vasculitis, gliomatosus cerebri, pituitary apoplexy, intravascular lymphoma, etc.

ous, comatose) and/or content of consciousness (confusion, perseveration, hallucinations). *Confusion* is a lack of clarity in thinking with inattentiveness; *stupor*, a state in which vigorous stimuli are needed to elicit a response; *coma*, a condition of unresponsiveness. Patients in such states are usually seriously ill, and etiologic factors must be assessed (Table 33-1).

_____ *Approach to the Patient* _____

1. Support vital functions.
2. Administer glucose, thiamine, and naloxone if etiology is not clear.

3. Utilize history, examination, and laboratory and radiologic information to rapidly establish the cause of the disorder.
4. Provide the appropriate medical and surgical treatment.

History

The pt should be aroused, if possible, and questioned regarding use of insulin, narcotics, anticoagulants, other prescription drugs, suicidal intent, recent trauma, headache, epilepsy, significant medical problems, and preceding symptoms. Witnesses and family members should be interviewed, often by phone. History of sudden headache followed by loss of consciousness suggests intracranial hemorrhage; preceding vertigo, nausea, diplopia, ataxia, hemisensory disorder suggest basilar insufficiency; chest pain, palpitations, and faintness suggest cardiovascular cause.

Immediate Assessment

Vital signs should be evaluated, and appropriate support initiated. Blood should be drawn for glucose, Na, K, Ca, BUN, ammonia, alcohol, liver transaminase levels; also screen for presence of toxins. Fever, especially with petechial rash, should suggest meningitis. Fever with dry skin suggests heat shock or intoxication with anticholinergics. Hypothermia suggests myxedema, intoxication, sepsis, exposure, or hypoglycemia. Marked hypertension occurs with increased intracranial pressure (ICP) and hypertensive encephalopathy.

Neurologic Evaluation

Focus on establishing pt's best level of function and uncovering signs that enable a specific diagnosis. Although confused states may occur with unilateral cerebral lesions, stupor and coma are signs of bihemispheral dysfunction or damage to midbrain-tegmentum (reticular activating system).

RESPONSIVENESS Stimuli of increasing intensity are applied to body parts to gauge the degree of unresponsiveness and any asymmetry in sensory or motor function. Motor responses may be purposeful or reflexive. Spontaneous flexion of elbows with leg extension, termed *decortication*, accompanies severe damage to contralateral hemisphere above midbrain. Internal rotation of the arms with extension of elbows, wrists, and legs, termed *decerebration*, suggests damage to diencephalon or midbrain. These postural reflexes can occur in profound encephalopathic states.

PUPILS In comatose pts, equal, round, reactive pupils exclude midbrain damage as cause and suggest a metabolic abnormality. Pinpoint pupils occur in narcotic overdose (except meperidine, which causes midsize pupils). Small pupils also occur with hydrocephalus and thalamic or pontine damage. A unilateral, enlarged, often oval, poorly reactive pupil is caused by midbrain lesions or compression of third cranial nerve, as occurs in transtentorial herniation. Bilaterally dilated, unreactive pupils indicate severe bilateral midbrain damage, anticholinergic overdose, or ocular trauma.

EYE MOVEMENTS Spontaneous and reflex eye movements should be examined for limitations of movement, involuntary movements, and misalignment of ocular axes. Intermittent horizontal divergence is common in drowsiness. Slow, to-and-fro horizontal movements suggest bihemispheric dysfunction. An adducted eye at rest with impaired ability to turn eye laterally indicates an abducens (VI) nerve palsy, common in raised ICP or pontine damage. The eye with a dilated, unreactive pupil is often abducted at rest and cannot adduct fully due to third nerve dysfunction, as occurs with transtentorial herniation. Vertical separation of ocular axes (skew deviation) occurs in pontine or cerebellar lesions. Doll's head maneuver (oculocephalic reflex) and cold caloric–induced eye movements allow accurate diagnosis of gaze or cranial nerve palsies in pts who do not move their eyes purposefully. Doll's head maneuver is tested by observing eye movements in response to lateral rotation of head (significant neck injury is a contraindication); loose movement of eyes with the doll's head maneuver occurs in bihemispheric dysfunction. In comatose pts with intact brainstem function, raising head to 60° above the horizontal and irrigating external auditory canal with ice water causes tonic deviation of gaze to side of irrigated ear. In conscious pts, it causes nystagmus, vertigo, and emesis.

RESPIRATIONS   Respiratory pattern may suggest site of neurologic damage. Cheyne-Stokes (periodic) breathing occurs in bihemispheric dysfunction and is common in metabolic encephalopathies. Respiratory patterns composed of gasps or other irregular breathing patterns are indicative of lower brainstem damage; such pts usually require intubation and ventilatory assistance.

OTHER   Comatose pt's best motor and sensory function should be assessed by testing reflex responses to noxious stimuli; carefully note any asymmetric responses, which suggest a focal lesion. If possible, pts with disordered consciousness should have gait examined. Ataxia may be the prominent neurologic finding in a stuporous pt with a cerebellar mass.

Radiologic Examination

Lesions causing raised ICP commonly cause impaired consciousness. CT or MRI scan of the brain is often abnormal in coma but is not usually diagnostic in metabolic encephalopathy, meningitis, early infarction, early encephalitis, diffuse anoxic injury, or drug overdose. Postponing appropriate therapy in these pts while awaiting a CT or MRI scan may be deleterious. Pts with disordered consciousness due to high ICP can deteriorate rapidly; emergent CT study is necessary to confirm presence of mass effect and to guide surgical decompression. CT scan is normal in some pts with subarachnoid hemorrhage; the diagnosis then rests on clinical history combined with RBC in spinal fluid. Cerebral angiography or magnetic resonance angiography is frequently necessary to establish basilar artery insufficiency as cause of coma in pts with brainstem signs.

Brain Death

This results from total cessation of cerebral function and blood flow at a time when cardiopulmonary function continues but is dependent on ventilatory assistance. The pt is unresponsive to all forms of stimulation, brainstem reflexes are absent, and there is complete apnea. Demonstration of apnea requires that the P_{CO_2} be high enough to stimulate respiration, while P_{O_2} and bp are maintained. EEG is isoelectric at high gain. The absence of deep tendon reflexes is not required because the spinal cord may remain functional. Special care must be taken to exclude drug toxicity and hypothermia prior to making a diagnosis of brain death. Diagnosis should be made only if the state persists for some agreed upon period, usually 6–24 h.

For a more detailed discussion, see Ropper AH: Acute Confusional States and Coma, Chap. 24, p. 132, HPIM-15.

34

STROKE

A stroke is the sudden onset of a neurologic deficit from a vascular mechanism. 20% are primary hemorrhages, including subarachnoid and hypertensive lobar and deep cerebral hemorrhages. 80% are related to ischemia; ischemic brain tissue rapidly loses function but can remain viable with potential for recovery for hours. An ischemic deficit that rapidly resolves is termed a *transient ischemic* attack (TIA); 24 h is a useful boundary between TIA and stroke, although most TIAs last between 5 and 15 min. It is important to differentiate the clinical terms *TIA* and *stroke* from the underlying tissue processes of *ischemia* and *infarction*, as temporal correlation is imperfect. Stroke is the leading cause of adult neurologic disability, and much can be done to limit morbidity and mortality through prevention and acute intervention.

PATHOGENESIS Ischemic stroke is most often due to embolic occlusion of large cerebral vessels. Source of emboli may be the heart, aortic arch, or a more proximate arterial lesion. Primary involvement of intracerebral vessels with atherosclerosis is much less common than in coronary vessels. Small, deep ischemic lesions are most often related to intrinsic small-vessel disease (lacunar strokes), with hypertension and diabetes as main risk factors. Low-flow strokes are seen with severe proximal stenosis and inadequate collaterals challenged by significant hypotensive episodes. Hemorrhage most frequently results from rupture of aneurysms or small vessels within brain tissue.

CLINICAL PRESENTATION *Stroke* Abrupt and dramatic onset of focal neurologic symptoms; temporal pattern can suggest the underlying vascular mechanism. Vascular mechanisms causing TIA are the same as those causing ischemic stroke (Table 34-1). Symptoms reflect the vascular territory involved and provide clues to localization and identification of the vessel and pathology (Table 34-2). Transient monocular blindness (amaurosis fugax) is a particular form of TIA due to retinal ischemia; pts describe a shade descending over the visual field. Rapid resolution of TIA symptoms suggests resolution of the underlying ischemia, although small areas of tissue infarction are often found when symptoms persist more than 1–2 h. Variability in stroke recovery is influenced by collateral vessels, blood pressure, and specific site and mechanism of vessel occlusion. Reversible ischemia and salvage of tissue at risk have become real concepts with application of thrombolytic and neuroprotective agents.

Lacunar Syndromes Most common are (1) Pure motor hemiparesis of face, arm, and leg (internal capsule or pons; (2) pure sensory stroke (ventrolateral thalamus); (3) ataxic hemiparesis (pons); (4) dysarthria–clumsy hand (pons or genu of internal capsule); and (5) pure motor hemiparesis with motor (Broca's) aphasia (internal capsule and adjacent corona radiata).

Intracranial Hemorrhage Includes hypertensive and lobar hemorrhages (50%), ruptured saccular aneurysm (Chap. 35), and ruptured arteriovenous malformation (AVM). Vomiting occurs in most cases, and headache in about one-half. Signs and symptoms not usually confined to a single vascular territory. Hypertensive hemorrhage typically occurs in (1) the putamen, adjacent internal capsule, and central white matter; (2) thalamus; (3) pons; and (4) cerebellum. A neurologic deficit that evolves relentlessly over 5–30 min strongly suggests intracerebral bleeding. Ocular signs are important in localization: (1) putam-

Table 34-1

Causes of Stroke

Common Causes	Uncommon Causes
Thrombosis	Hypercoagulable disorders
Lacunar stroke (small vessel)	Protein C deficiency
Large vessel thrombosis	Protein S deficiency
Dehydration	Antithrombin III deficiency
Embolic occlusion	Antiphospholipid syndrome
Artery-to-artery	Factor V Leiden mutation[a]
Carotid bifurcation	Prothrombin G20210 mutation[a]
Aortic arch	Systemic malignancy
Arterial dissection	Sickle cell anemia
Cardioembolic	β-Thalassemia
Atrial fibrillation	Polycythemia vera
Mural thrombus	Systemic lupus erythematosus
Myocardial infarction	Homocysteinemia
Dilated cardiomyopathy	Thrombotic thrombocytopenic purpura
Valvular lesions	Disseminated intravascular coagulation
Mitral stenosis	Dysproteinemias
Mechanical valve	Nephrotic syndrome
Bacterial endocarditis	Inflammatory bowel disease
Paradoxical embolus	Oral contraceptives
Atrial septal defect	Venous sinus thrombosis[b]
Patent foramen ovale	Fibromuscular dysplasia
Atrial septal aneurysm	Vasculitis
Spontaneous echo contrast	Systemic vasculitis (PAN, Wegner's,
	Takayasu's, giant cell arteritis)
	Primary CNS vasculitis
	Meningitis (syphilis, tuberculosis,
	fungal, bacterial, zoster)
	Cardiogenic
	Mitral valve calcification
	Atrial myxoma
	Intracardiac tumor
	Marantic endocarditis
	Libman-Sacks endocarditis
	Subarachnoid hemorrhage vasospasm
	Drugs: cocaine, amphetamine
	Moyamoya disease
	Eclampsia

[a] Chiefly cause venous sinus thrombosis.
[b] May be associated with any hypercoagulable disorder.
NOTE: PAN, polyarteritis nodosa.

inal—eyes deviated to side opposite paralysis (toward lesion); (2) thalamic—eyes deviated downward, sometimes with unreactive pupils; (3) pontine—reflex lateral eye movements impaired and small (1–2 mm), reactive pupils; (4) cerebellar—eyes deviated to side opposite lesion (early on, in absence of paralysis).

RISK FACTORS   Atherosclerosis is a systemic disease affecting arteries throughout the body. Multiple factors including hypertension, diabetes, hyperlipidemia, and familial tendencies influence stroke and TIA risk. Cardioembolic risk factors include atrial fibrillation, MI, valvular heart disease, and cardio-

Table 34-2

Anatomic Localization of Cerebral Lesions in Stroke

Signs and Symptoms

CEREBRAL HEMISPHERE, LATERAL ASPECT (MIDDLE CEREBRAL A.)

Hemiparesis
Hemisensory deficit
Motor aphasia (Broca's)— hesitant speech with word-finding difficulty and preserved comprehension
Central aphasia (Wernicke's)—anomia, poor comprehension, jargon speech
Unilateral neglect, apraxias
Homonymous hemianopia or quadrantanopia
Gaze preference with eyes deviated to side of lesion

CEREBRAL HEMISPHERE, MEDIAL ASPECT (ANTERIOR CEREBRAL A.)

Paralysis of foot and leg with or without paresis of arm
Cortical sensory loss over leg
Grasp and sucking reflexes
Urinary incontinence
Gait apraxia

CEREBRAL HEMISPHERE, INFERIOR ASPECT (POSTERIOR CEREBRAL A.)

Homonymous hemianopia
Cortical blindness
Memory deficit
Dense sensory loss, spontaneous pain, dysesthesias, choreoathetosis

BRAINSTEM, MIDBRAIN (POSTERIOR CEREBRAL A.)

Third nerve palsy and contralateral hemiplegia
Paralysis/paresis of vertical eye movement
Convergence nystagmus, disorientation

BRAINSTEM, PONTOMEDULLARY JUNCTION (BASILAR A.)

Facial paralysis
Paresis of abduction of eye
Paresis of conjugate gaze
Hemifacial sensory deficit
Horner's syndrome
Diminished pain and thermal sense over half body (with or without face)
Ataxia

BRAINSTEM, LATERAL MEDULLA (VERTEBRAL A.)

Vertigo, nystagmus
Horner's syndrome (miosis, ptosis, decreased sweating)
Ataxia, falling toward side of lesion
Impaired pain and thermal sense over half body with or without face

myopathy. Prolonged hypertension and diabetes are also specific risk factors for lacunar stroke with small-vessel lipohyalinotic disease. Smoking is a potent risk factor for all vascular mechanisms of stroke. *Identification of modifiable risk factors and prophylactic interventions to lower risk is probably the best treatment for stroke overall.*

COMPLICATIONS Neurologic deficits can worsen after presentation because of several possible complications. Embolic stroke carries the risk of

Structures Involved

Contralateral parietal and frontal motor cortex
Contralateral somatosensory cortex
Motor speech area, dominant frontal lobe

Central, perisylvian speech area, dominant hemisphere
Nondominant parietal lobe
Optic radiation in inferior parietal or temporal lobe
Center for lateral gaze (frontal lobe)

Leg area with or without arm area of contralateral motor cortex
Foot and leg area of contralateral sensory cortex
Medial posterior frontal lobe
Sensorimotor area, paracentral lobule
Frontal cortices

Calcarine occipital cortex
Occipital lobes, bilaterally
Hippocampus, bilaterally or dominant
Thalamus plus subthalamus

Third nerve and cerebral peduncle (Weber's syndrome)
Supranuclear fibers to third nerve
Top of midbrain, periaqueductal

Seventh nerve, ipsilateral
Sixth nerve, ipsilateral
"Center" for lateral gaze, ipsilateral
Tract and nucleus of V, ipsilateral
Descending sympathetic pathways
Spinothalamic tract, contralateral
Middle cerebellar peduncle and cerebellum

Vestibular nucleus
Descending sympathetic fibers, ipsilateral
Cerebellar hemisphere or fibers
Contralateral spinothalamic tract

early recurrence. This can occur from cardiac sources and arterial stenoses and from acute arterial occlusions as distal stump emboli. Large, deep ischemic infarcts can develop hemorrhage into the affected tissue. Large cerebral or cerebellar infarcts can develop edema sufficient to lead to neurologic deterioration. While most intracerebral hemorrhages bleed only briefly, some may continue to expand with resultant mass effect. Seizures are uncommon in acute stroke but develop as a delayed complication in 5–10%.

LABORATORY EVALUATION   *CT*   Initial CT study without contrast is indicated to exclude hemorrhage or other mass lesions. Early signs of ischemic stroke can be recognized within the first few hours of large strokes, but small cortical infarcts can be difficult to assess by CT.

MRI   Compared with CT, increased sensitivity for small infarcts of cortex and brainstem.

MR Angiography   Special sequences that image blood flow can evaluate patency of intracranial vessels and extracranial carotid and vertebral vessels.

Noninvasive Carotid Tests   Most commonly used are "duplex" studies, combining ultrasound imaging of the vessel with Doppler evaluation of blood flow characteristics.

Cerebral Angiography   "Gold standard" for evaluation of vascular disease. Detects ulcerative lesions, severe stenosis, and mural thrombosis; can also visualize atherosclerotic disease or dissection in carotid siphon or intracranial vessels, demonstrate collateral circulation around the circle of Willis, and show embolic occlusion of cerebral branch vessels. Best method to demonstrate atherothrombotic disease of the basilar artery. It causes substantial morbidity (1–5%) and may precipitate a threatened stroke, and thus is used only when noninvasive studies fail to detect an arterial lesion that, if identified, would influence management.

Cardiac Evaluation   Indicated in suspected cardiogenic embolization; ECG, cardiac ultrasound with attention to right-to-left shunts, and 24-h Holter monitoring.

Blood Studies   Routine initial studies include CBC/platelets, electrolytes, ESR, PT, PTT, and serologic tests for syphilis. In cases where a hypercoagulable state is suspected, further studies of coagulation are indicated.

℞ TREATMENT   Table 34-3

Acute Ischemic Stroke   Careful evaluation and treatment are essential to minimize infarction and reduce recurrent stroke risk. Blood pressure should never be lowered precipitously (exacerbates the underlying ischemia), and only in the most extreme situations (systolic bp >220 mmHg) should gradual decreases be undertaken. Intravascular volume should be maintained with isotonic fluids as volume restriction is rarely helpful. Osmotic therapy with mannitol may be necessary to control edema in large infarcts, but isotonic volume must be replaced to avoid hypovolemia. In cerebellar infarction (or hemorrhage), rapid deterioration can occur from brainstem compression and hydrocephalus. These pts require neurosurgical evaluation and careful neurologic monitoring.

Thrombolysis   Ischemic deficits of <3 h duration, with no hemorrhage by CT criteria, may benefit from thrombolytic therapy with IV recombinant tissue plasminogen activator (Table 34-4). This therapy has been shown to improve neurologic outcome, but currently only a small percentage of stroke pts are seen early enough to receive treatment with this agent.

Anticoagulation   Indications for heparin are empirically based; objective clinical data are lacking. IV heparin is generally used when atherothrombotic vascular stenosis or occlusion is suspected, particularly in ischemic stroke with progression of symptoms ("stuttering stroke"), unstable TIA (crescendo or recent onset), or posterior circulation involvement. Heparin is usually administered as an infusion (without bolus) for 2–5 days with the PTT maintained at twice normal. The role of low-molecular-weight heparin remains to

Table 34-3

Clinical Management of Acute Stroke

New onset of neuro-logic deficit: Stroke or TIA?	Differential diagnosis of new focal deficit
	    Stroke or TIA
	    Seizure with postictal Todd's paresis
	    Tumor
	    Migraine
	    Metabolic encephalopathy
	        Fever/infection and old stroke
	        Hyperglycemia
	        Hypercalcemia
	        Hepatic encephalopathy

Initial assessment and management	ABCs, serum glucose
	Noncontrast head CT
	    Hemorrhage
	        Medical and surgical management
	    Tumor or other CNS process
	        Treat accordingly
	    Normal or hypodense area consistent with acute ischemic stroke
	        Consider thrombolysis, heparin, aspirin
	        Maintain blood pressure and hydrate
	        Admit patient to appropriate level of care depending on concomitant medical problems and airway

Subsequent hospital management	Establish cause of stroke and risk factors Plan for secondary prophylaxis (drugs, risk factor modifications) Obtain physical, occupational, and speech therapy consultation and social work as appropriate Establish nutrition Discharge planning should include prescriptions for risk factor reduction, including when to institute antihypertensive treatment, and antithrombotic medication prophylaxis

NOTE: ABCs, airway management, breathing, cardiac status.

be determined. Warfarin (INR=2–3) may be used long term for atherothrombotic disease when carotid surgery (see below) is not an option or for cardiac sources of embolism (anterior MI, atrial fibrillation, or valvular disease).

Antiplatelet agents   Aspirin (325 mg/d) has a small but definite benefit in acute stroke and can reduce risk of further TIA and stroke in symptomatic patients thus providing an alternative to anticoagulation. Other useful antiplatelet agents include clopidogrel (blocks the platelet ADP receptor) and dipyridamole (inhibits platelet uptake of adenosine). In general, antiplatelet agents reduce new stroke events by 25–30%.

Prevention of Embolic Stroke   In pts with atrial fibrillation, the choice between warfarin or aspirin prophylaxis is determined by age and risk factors (Table 34-5). Anticoagulation reduces the risk of embolism in acute MI; most clinicians recommend a 3-month course of therapy when there is anterior Q-wave infarction or other complications; warfarin is recommended long term if atrial fibrillation persists. For prosthetic heart valve pts, a combination of aspirin and warfarin (INR 3–4) is recommended. If an embolic source cannot be eliminated, anticoagulation is usually continued indefinitely. For patients

Table 34-4

Administration of Intravenous Recombinant Tissue Plasminogen Activator (rtPA) for Acute Ischemic Stroke[a]

Indication
   Clinical diagnosis of stroke
   Onset of symptoms to time of drug administration ≤3 h
   CT scan showing no hemorrhage or significant edema
   Age ≥18 years
   Consent by patient or surrogate

Contraindication
   Sustained bp > 185/110
   Platelets < 100,000; Hct < 25%; glucose < 50 or > 400
   Use of heparin within 48 h and prolonged PTT, or elevated INR
   Rapidly improving symptoms
   Prior stroke or head injury within 3 months; prior intracranial hemorrhage
   Major surgery in preceding 14 days
   Minor stroke symptoms
   Gastrointestinal bleeding in preceding 21 days
   Recent myocardial infarction
   Coma or stupor

Administration of rtPA
   Intravenous access with two peripheral IV lines (avoid arterial or central line placement)
   Review eligibility for rtPA
   Administer 0.9 mg/kg intravenously (maximum 90 mg) IV as 10% of total dose by bolus, followed by remainder of total dose over 1 h
   Continous cuff blood pressure monitoring
   No other antithrombotic treatment for 24 h
   For decline in neurologic status or uncontrolled blood pressure, stop infusion, give cryoprecipitate, and reimage brain emergently
   Avoid urethral catheterization for ≥2 h

[a] See Activase (tissue plasminogen activator) package insert for complete list of contraindications and dosing.
NOTE: INR, international normalized ratio.

Table 34-5

Consensus Recommendation for Antithrombotic Prophylaxis in Atrial Fibrillation

Age	Risk Factors[a]	Recommendation
Age ≤65	≥1	Warfarin INR 2–3
	0	Aspirin or no treatment
Age 65–75	≥1	Warfarin INR 2–3
	0	Warfarin INR 2–3 or aspirin
Age >75		Warfarin INR 2–3

[a] Risk factors include previous TIA or stroke, hypertension, heart failure, diabetes, clinical coronary artery disease, mitral stenosis, prosthetic heart valves, or thyrotoxicosis.
SOURCE: Modified from A Laupacis et al: Antithrombotic therapy for atrial fibrillation. Chest 114:5795, 1998

who "fail" one form of therapy, many neurologists recommend combining antiplatelet agents with anticoagulation. Secondary prophylaxis for ischemic stroke of unknown origin is controversial; some physicians prescribe anticoagulation for 3–6 months followed by antiplatelet treatment.

Surgical Therapy Carotid endarterectomy benefits many pts with *symptomatic* severe (>70%) *carotid stenosis*; the relative risk reduction is approximately 65%. However, if the perioperative stroke rate is >6% for any surgeon, the benefit is lost. Surgical results in pts with *asymptomatic carotid stenosis* are less robust, and medical therapy for reduction of atherosclerosis risk factors (including hypertension, hypercholesterolemia, diabetes, and smoking) and aspirin are generally recommended in this group.

Intracerebral Hemorrhage

Noncontrast head CT will confirm diagnosis. It is important to identify and correct any coagulopathy rapidly. Neurosurgical consultation should be sought for possible urgent evacuation of hematoma, especially in the case of cerebellar hemorrhage. Prophylactic anticonvulsant therapy is usually undertaken in supratentorial hemorrhage, especially when extending to the cortical surface. Treatment for edema and mass effect with mannitol may be necessary, and while glucocorticoids may be helpful in some cases, routine use leads to many complications.

For a more detailed discussion, see, Smith WS, Hauser SL, Easton JD, Martin JB: Cerebrovascular Diseases, Chap. 361, p. 2369 in HPIM-15.

35

SUBARACHNOID HEMORRHAGE

Most common cause of nontraumatic subarachnoid hemorrhage (SAH) is rupture of an intracerebral aneurysm; other etiologies include mycotic aneurysms in subacute bacterial endocarditis, bleeding dyscrasias, and rarely infections or tumors. Approximately 3–4% of the population harbor aneurysms; rupture risk for aneurysms ≥10mm in size is 0.5% per year.

CLINICAL PRESENTATION Sudden, severe headache, often with transient loss of consciousness at onset; vomiting is common. Bleeding may injure adjacent brain tissue and produce focal neurologic deficits. A progressive third nerve palsy with severe headache suggests posterior communicating artery aneurysm. In addition to dramatic presentations, aneurysms can undergo small ruptures with leaks of blood into the subarachnoid space (sentinel bleeds).

LABORATORY EVALUATION *CT* Noncontrast CT is the initial study of choice and usually demonstrates the hemorrhage. On occasion, LP is required for diagnosis of suspected SAH if CT is nondiagnostic.

Cerebral Angiography Necessary to define the anatomy, location, and type of vascular malformation, such as aneurysm or arteriovenous malformation; also assesses vasospasm. Usually performed as soon as possible after diagnosis of SAH is made.

ECG ST-segment changes, prolonged QRS complex, increased QT interval, and prominent or inverted T waves often present; some changes reflect SAH, others indicate associated myocardial ischemic injury.

Blood Studies Closely follow serum electrolytes and osmolality; hyponatremia frequently develops several days after SAH. Cerebral salt wasting is common, and supplemental sodium is used to overcome renal losses.

 TREATMENT

Standard management includes bed rest in a quiet darkened room, analgesics, and stool softeners. Anticonvulsants are begun at diagnosis and continued at least until the aneurysm is treated. Risk of early *rebleeding* is high (20–30% over 2 weeks), thus early treatment (within 1–3 days) is advocated to avoid rerupture and allow aggressive treatment of *vasospasm*. Neurosurgical clipping of the aneurysm neck is the most common treatment, although newer endovascular techniques are also possible. Severe *hydrocephalus* may require urgent placement of a ventricular catheter for external CSF drainage. Blood pressure is carefully monitored and regulated to assure adequate cerebral perfusion while avoiding excessive elevations. Symptomatic *vasospasm* may occur by day 4 and continue through day 14, leading to focal ischemia and possible stroke. Medical treatment, including nimodipine, may minimize the neurologic sequelae of vasospasm. Cerebral perfusion can be improved in vasospasm by increasing mean arterial pressure with vasopressor agents such as neosynephrine or dopamine. Intravascular volume can be expanded with crystalloid. Angioplasty of the cerebral vessels can be effective in cases of severe vasospasm when ischemic symptoms appear despite maximal medical therapy.

For a more detailed discussion, see Smith WS, Hauser SL, Easton JD: Cerebrovascular Diseases, Chap. 361, p. 2369 in HPIM-15.

36

INCREASED INTRACRANIAL PRESSURE AND HEAD TRAUMA

Increased Intracranial Pressure

A limited volume of extra tissue, blood, CSF, or edema fluid can be added to the intracranial contents without raising the intracranial pressure (ICP). Clinical deterioration or death may follow increases in ICP that shift intracranial contents, distort vital brainstem centers, or compromise cerebral perfusion. Cerebral perfusion pressure (CPP) = Blood pressure − ICP.

CLINICAL MANIFESTATIONS   Symptoms of high ICP include headache (especially a constant ache that is worse upon awakening), nausea, emesis, drowsiness, diplopia, and blurred vision. Papilledema and sixth nerve palsies are common. If not controlled, then cerebral hypoperfusion, pupillary dilation, coma, decerebrate posturing, abnormal respirations, systemic hypertension, and bradycardia may result.

A posterior fossa mass, which may initially cause ataxia, stiff neck, and nausea, is especially dangerous because it can compress vital brainstem structures and cause obstructive hydrocephalus. Masses that cause raised ICP also distort midbrain and diencephalic anatomy, leading to stupor and coma. Brain tissue is pushed away from the mass against fixed intracranial structures and into spaces not normally occupied. Herniation syndromes include (1) medial cortex displaced under the midline falx → anterior or posterior cerebral artery occlusion and stroke; (2) uncus displaced through the tentorium, compressing the third cranial nerve and pushing the cerebral peduncle against the tentorium → ipsilateral pupillary dilation, contralateral hemiparesis, and posterior cerebral artery occlusion; (3) cerebellar tonsils displaced into the foramen magnum, causing medullary compression → cardiorespiratory collapse; and (4) downward displacement of the diencephalon through the tentorium.

 TREATMENT

Elevated ICP may occur in a wide range of disorders including head trauma, intracerebral hemorrhage, subarachnoid hemorrhage with hydrocephalus, and fulminant hepatic failure. A number of different interventions may lower ICP, and ideally the selection of treatment will be based on the underlying mechanism responsible for the elevated ICP (Table 36-1). For example, in hydrocephalus from subarachnoid hemorrhage, the principal cause of elevated ICP is impaired CSF drainage; in this setting, ventricular drainage of CSF is likely to be sufficient. In head trauma and stroke, cytotoxic edema may be most responsible, and the use of osmotic diuretics such as mannitol becomes an appropriate early step. As noted above, elevated ICP may cause tissue ischemia. This can lead to reflex cerebral vasodilatation that further worsens ischemia; paradoxically, administration of vasopressor agents to increase mean arterial pressure may actually lower ICP by increasing perfusion. ICP monitoring can guide medical and surgical decisions in pts with cerebral edema due to stroke, head trauma, Reye's syndrome, and intracerebral hemorrhage. Hypertension should be treated carefully, if at all. Free H_2O should be restricted, and fever treated aggressively. Hyperventilation is best used for short periods of time until a more definitive treatment can be instituted. After stabilization and initiation of the above therapies, a CT scan (or MRI, if feasible) is performed to delineate the cause of the elevated ICP. Emergency surgical intervention is sometimes necessary to decompress the intracranial contents. Hydrocephalus, cerebellar stroke with edema, surgically accessible cerebral hemorrhage or tumor, and subdural or epidural hemorrhage often require life-saving neurosurgery.

Head Trauma

Head trauma can cause immediate loss of consciousness. If transient and unaccompanied by other serious brain pathology, it is called *concussion*. Prolonged alterations in consciousness may be due to parenchymal, subdural, or

Table 36-1

Stepwise Approach to Treatment of Elevated
Intracranial Pressure (ICP)[a]

Insert ICP monitor—General goals: maintain ICP < 20 mmHg and CPP > 70 mmHg

For ICP > 20–25 mmHg for >5 min:
1. Drain CSF via ventriculostomy (if in place)
2. Elevate head of the bed
3. Osmotherapy—mannitol 25–100 g q4h as needed (maintain serum osmolality <320 mOsm/L)
4. Glucocorticoids—dexamethasone 4 mg q6h for vasogenic edema from tumor, abscess (avoid glucocorticoids in head trauma, ischemic and hemorrhagic stroke)
5. Sedation (e.g., morphine, propofol, or midazolam); add neuromuscular paralysis if necessary (pt will require endotracheal intubation and mechanical ventilation at this point, if not before)
6. Hyperventilation—to Pa_{CO_2} 30–35 mmHg
7. Pressor therapy—phenylephrine, dopamine, or norepinephrine to maintain adequate MAP to ensure CPP > 70 mmHg, (maintain euvolemia to minimize deleterious systemic effects of pressors)
8. Consider second-tier therapies for refractory elevated ICP
   a. High-dose barbiturate therapy ("pentobarb coma")
   b. Aggressive hyperventilation to Pa_{CO_2} < 30 mmHg
   c. Hemicraniectomy

[a] Throughout ICP treatment algorithm, consider repeat head CT to identify mass lesions amenable to surgical evacuation.
NOTE: CPP, cerebral perfusion pressure; MAP, mean arterial pressure; Pa_{CO_2}, arterial partial pressure of carbon dioxide.

epidural hematoma or to diffuse shearing of axons in the white matter. Skull fracture should be suspected in pts with CSF rhinorrhea, hemotympanum, and periorbital or mastoid ecchymoses. Spinal cord trauma can cause transient loss of function or a permanent loss of motor, sensory, and autonomic function below the damaged spinal level.

Minor Concussive Injury The pt with minor head injury who is alert and attentive after a short period of unconsciousness (<1 min) may have headache, a brief amnestic period, difficulty with concentration, a single episode of emesis or mild vertigo; vasovagal syncope may also occur. After several hours of observation, pts with this category of injury can be accompanied home and observed by family or friends. Most pts do not have a skull fracture on x-ray or hemorrhage on CT. Constant headache is common in the days following trauma; persistent severe headache and repeated vomiting are usually benign if the neurologic exam remains normal, but in such situations radiologic studies should be obtained and hospitalization is justified.

Injury of Intermediate Severity Pts who are not comatose but who have persistent confusion, behavioral changes, subnormal alertness, extreme dizziness, or focal neurologic signs such as hemiparesis should be admitted to the hospital and soon thereafter have a CT scan. Usually a contusion or subdural hematoma is found. CT scan may be normal in comatose pts with axonal shearing lesions in cerebral white matter. Pts with intermediate head injury require medical observation to detect increasing drowsiness, respiratory dysfunction, and pupillary enlargement, as well as to ensure fluid restriction (unless there is diabetes insipidus). Abnormalities of attention, intellect, spontaneity, and memory tend to return to normal weeks or months after the injury.

Severe Injury Patients who are comatose from onset require immediate neurologic attention and often resuscitation. After intubation, with care taken to avoid deforming the cervical spine, the depth of coma, pupillary size and reactivity, limb movements, and Babinski responses are assessed. As soon as vital functions permit and cervical spine x-rays and a CT scan have been obtained, the pt should be transported to a critical care unit. The finding of an epidural or subdural hematoma or large intracerebral hemorrhage requires prompt decompressive surgery in otherwise salvageable pts. Subsequent treatment is probably best guided by direct measurement of ICP. All potentially exacerbating factors should be eliminated. Hypoxia, hyperthermia, hypercarbia, awkward head positions, and high mean airway pressures from mechanical ventilation all increase cerebral blood volume and ICP. Persistently raised ICP after institution of this therapy generally indicates a poor outcome.

For a more detailed discussion, see Ropper AH: Traumatic Injuries of the Head and Spine, Chap. 369, p. 2434, in HPIM-15, and Hemphill JC, Beal MF, and Gress DR: Critical Care Neurology, p. 2491, Chap. 376 in HPIM-15.

37

HYPOXIC-ISCHEMIC ENCEPHALOPATHY

Results from lack of delivery of oxygen to the brain because of hypotension or respiratory failure. Most common causes are MI, cardiac arrest, shock, asphyxiation, paralysis of respiration, and carbon monoxide or cyanide poisoning. In some circumstances, hypoxia may predominate. Carbon monoxide and cyanide poisoning are termed *histotoxic hypoxia* since they cause a direct impairment of the respiratory chain.

Clinical Manifestations

Mild degrees of pure hypoxia (e.g., high altitude) cause impaired judgment, inattentiveness, motor incoordination, and, at times, euphoria. However, with hypoxia-ischemia, such as occurs with circulatory arrest, consciousness is lost within seconds. If circulation is restored within 3–5 min, full recovery may occur, but with longer periods of hypoxia-ischemia some degree of permanent cerebral damage is the rule. Except in extreme cases, it may be difficult to judge the precise degree of hypoxia-ischemia, and some pts make a relatively full recovery even after 8–10 min of global ischemia. The distinction between pure hypoxia and hypoxia-ischemia is important, since a Pa_{O_2} as low as 2.7 kPa (20 mmHg) can be well tolerated if it develops gradually and normal blood pressure

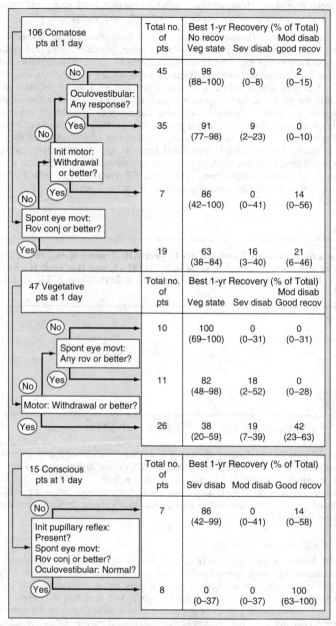

FIGURE 37-1 Clinical examination at day 1 provides useful prognostic information in hypoxic-ischemic encephalopathy. Numbers in parentheses represent 95% confidence intervals. Recov, recovery; veg, vegetative; sev, severe; mod, moderate; spont eye movt, spontaneous eye movement; rov conj, roving conjugate. (From DE Levy et al: Predicting outcome for hypoxic-ischemic coma. JAMA 253:1420, 1985.)

is maintained, but short periods of very low or absent cerebral circulation may result in permanent impairment.

Clinical examination at different time points after an insult (especially cardiac arrest) helps to assess prognosis (Fig. 37-1). The prognosis is better for pts with intact brainstem function, as indicated by normal pupillary light responses, intact oculocephalic (doll's eyes) reflexes, and oculovestibular (caloric) and corneal reflexes. Absence of these reflexes and the presence of persistently dilated pupils that do not react to light are grave prognostic signs. A uniformly dismal prognosis is conveyed by the absence of pupillary light reflex or absence of a motor response to pain on day 3 following the injury. Bilateral absence of the cortical somatosensory evoked response (Chap. 181) also conveys a poor prognosis. Long-term consequences include persistent coma or vegetative state, dementia, visual agnosis, parkinsonism, choreoathetosis, ataxia, myoclonus, seizures, and an amnestic state.

℞ TREATMENT

Initial treatment is directed at restoring normal cardiorespiratory function. This includes securing a clear airway, ensuring adequate oxygenation and ventilation, and restoring cerebral perfusion, whether by cardiopulmonary resuscitation, fluids, pressors, or cardiac pacing. Hypothermia and neuroprotective agents have not yet been shown to have clinical value. Severe carbon monoxide intoxication may be treated with hyperbaric oxygen. Anticonvulsants are not usually given prophylactically but may be used to control seizures. Posthypoxic myoclonus can be controlled with clonazepam (1.5–10 mg/d) or sodium valproate (300–1200 mg/d) in divided doses. Myoclonic status epilepticus after a hypoxic-ischemic insult portends a universally poor prognosis.

For a more detailed discussion, see Hemphill JC, Beal MF, Gress DR, Critical Care Neurology, Chap 376, p. 2491, in HPIM-15.

38

STATUS EPILEPTICUS

Defined as continuous seizures (>15–30 min) or repetitive, discrete seizures with impaired consciousness in the interictal period. Condition may occur with all kinds of seizures: grand mal (tonic-clonic) status, myoclonic status, petit mal status, and temporal lobe (complex partial) status. Generalized, tonic-clonic seizures are most common and are usually clinically obvious early in the course. After 30–45 min, the signs may become increasingly subtle and include mild clonic movements of the fingers or fine, rapid movements of the eyes. In some situations, EEG may be the only method of diagnosis. Generalized status may be life-threatening when accompanied by hyperpyrexia, acidosis (from prolonged muscle activity), or respiratory or cardiovascular compromise. Irreversible neuronal injury may occur when tonic-clonic seizures persist for more than 2 h.

Etiology

Principal causes of tonic-clonic status are antiepileptic drug withdrawal or noncompliance, alcohol-related, refractory epilepsy, CNS infection, drug toxicity, metabolic disturbances, CNS tumors, cerebrovascular disease, and head trauma.

℞ TREATMENT   (Fig. 38-1)

Generalized tonic-clonic status epilepticus is a medical emergency. Pts must be evaluated promptly and appropriate therapy instituted without delay. In parallel, it is essential to determine the cause of the seizures to prevent recurrence and treat any underlying abnormalities.

1. Assess carefully for evidence of respiratory or cardiovascular insufficiency. With careful monitoring and standard airway protection, pts usually do not require intubation (if intubation is necessary, use short-acting paraly-

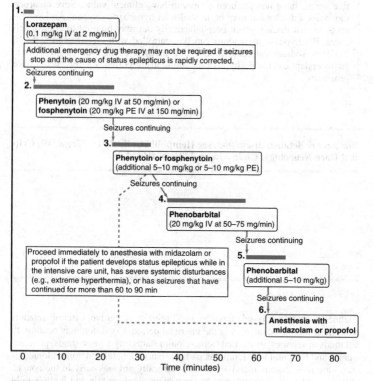

FIGURE 38-1   Pharmacologic treatment of generalized tonic-clonic status epilepticus in adults. IV, intravenous; PE, phenytoin equivalents. The horizontal bars indicate the approximate duration of drug infusions.

tics). Treat hyperthermia. Establish IV and administer 50 mL 50% dextrose in water, 100 mg thiamine, and 0.4 mg naloxone (Narcan).

2.   Perform a brief medical and neurologic examination; send samples for laboratory studies aimed at identifying metabolic abnormalities (CBC with differential, serum electrolytes including calcium, liver and renal function tests, toxicology if indicated).

3.   Administer lorazepam, 0.1 mg/kg (4–8 mg) at 2 mg/min.

4.   Immediately after lorazepam, administer phenytoin, 20 mg/kg (1000–1500 mg) IV slowly over 20 min (50 mg/min) or fosphenytoin, 20 mg/kg (150 mg/min). Monitor bp, ECG, and, if possible, EEG during infusion. Phenytoin can cause precipitous fall in bp if given too quickly, especially in elderly pts. (Do not administer phenytoin with 5% dextrose in water—phenytoin precipitates at low pH. This is not a problem with fosphenytoin.) If seizures are not controlled, a repeat bolus of phenytoin (5–10 mg/kg) or fosphenytoin (5–10 mg/kg) may be given.

5.   If seizures persist, administer phenobarbital 20 mg/kg (1000–1500 mg) slowly over 30 min. Endotracheal intubation will often be required by this stage. If seizures continue, give additional dose of phenobarbital (5–10 mg/kg).

6.   If seizures remain refractory after 60–90 min, consider placing pt in midazolam, propofol, or pentobarbital coma. Consultation with a neurologist and anesthesiologist is advised.

Prognosis

The mortality rate is 20% in tonic-clonic status, and the incidence of permanent neurologic sequelae is 10–30%.

For a more detailed discussion, see Lowenstein DH: Seizures and Epilepsy, Chap. 360, p. 2354, in HPIM-15.

39

POISONING AND DRUG OVERDOSE

Poisoning refers to the development of harmful effects following exposure to chemicals. *Overdosage* is exposure to excessive amounts of a substance normally intended for consumption and does not necessarily imply poisoning. Chemical exposures result in an estimated 5 million requests in the U.S. for medical advice or treatment each year, and about 5% of victims of chemical exposure require hospitalization. Suicide attempts account for most serious or fatal poisonings. Up to 30% of psychiatric admissions are prompted by attempted suicide via overdosage.

Carbon monoxide (CO) poisoning is the leading cause of death. Drug-related fatalities are most commonly due to analgesics, antidepressants, sedative-hypnotics, neuroleptics, stimulants and street drugs, cardiovascular drugs, anticonvulsants, antihistamines, and asthma therapies. Nonpharmaceutical agents implicated in fatal poisoning include alcohols and glycols, gases and fumes, chemicals, cleaning substances, pesticides, and automotive products. The diagnosis of poisoning or drug overdose must be considered in any pt who presents with coma, seizure, or acute renal, hepatic, or bone marrow failure.

DIAGNOSIS

The correct diagnosis can usually be reached by history, physical exam, and laboratory evaluation. Initial assessment of vital signs, cardiopulmonary status, and neurologic function determines the need for immediate supportive treatment. All available sources should be used to determine the exact nature of the ingestion or exposure. The Physicians Desk Reference, regional poison control centers, and local/hospital pharmacies may be useful for identification of ingredients and potential effects of toxins.

Examination of the eyes (for nystagmus, pupil size and reactivity), abdomen (for bowel activity and bladder size), and skin (for burns, bullae, color, warmth, moisture, pressure sores, and puncture marks) may narrow the diagnosis to a particular disorder. The pt should also be examined for evidence of trauma and underlying illnesses. When the history is unclear, all orifices should be examined for the presence of chemical burns and drug packets. The odor of breath or vomitus and the color of nails, skin, or urine may provide diagnostic clues.

Initial blood tests should include glucose, serum electrolytes, serum osmolality, BUN/Cr, LFTs, PT/PTT, and ABGs. An increased anion-gap metabolic acidosis is characteristic of advanced methanol, ethylene glycol, and salicylate intoxication but can occur with other agents and in any poisoning that results in hepatic, renal, or respiratory failure; seizures; or shock. An increased osmolal gap—the difference between the serum osmolality (measured by freezing point depression) and that calculated from the serum sodium, glucose, and BUN of >10 mmol/L—suggests the presence of a low-molecular- weight solute such as an alcohol, glycol, or ketone or an unmeasured electrolyte or sugar. Ketosis suggests acetone, isopropyl alcohol, or salicylate poisoning. Hypoglycemia may be due to poisoning with β-adrenergic blockers, ethanol, insulin, oral hypoglycemic agents, quinine, and salicylates, whereas hyperglycemia can occur in poisoning with acetone, β-adrenergic agonists, calcium channel-blockers, iron, theophylline, or Vacor.

Radiologic studies should include a chest x-ray to exclude aspiration or ARDS. Radiopaque densities may be visible on abdominal x-rays. Head CT or MRI is indicated in stuporous or comatose pts to exclude structural lesions or subarachnoid hemorrhage, and LP should be performed when CNS infection is suspected. The ECG can be useful to assist with the differential diagnosis and to guide treatment. Analysis of urine and blood (and occasionally of gastric contents and chemical samples) may be useful to confirm or rule out suspected poisoning. Although rapid screening tests for a limited number of drugs of abuse are available, comprehensive screening tests require 2 to 6 h for completion, and immediate management must be based on the history, physical exam, and routine ancillary tests. Quantitative analysis is useful for poisoning with acetaminophen, acetone, alcohol (including ethylene glycol), antiarrhythmics, anticonvulsants, barbiturates, digoxin, heavy metals, lithium, paraquat, salicylate, and theophylline, as well as for carboxyhemoglobin and methemoglobin. Results can often be available within an hour.

The response to antidotes may be useful for diagnostic purposes. Resolution of altered mental status and abnormal vital signs within minutes of intravenous administration of dextrose, naloxone, or flumazenil is virtually diagnostic of hypoglycemia, narcotic poisoning, and benzodiazepine intoxication, respectively. The prompt reversal of acute dystonic (extrapyramidal) reactions following an intravenous dose of benztropine or diphenhydramine confirms a drug etiology. Although physostigmine reversal of both central and peripheral manifestations of anticholinergic poisoning is diagnostic, it may cause arousal in patients with CNS depression of any etiology.

TREATMENT

Goals of therapy include support of vital signs, prevention of further absorption, enhancement of elimination, administration of specific antidotes, and prevention of reexposure. Fundamentals of poisoning management are listed in Table 39-1. Treatment is usually initiated before routine and toxicologic data are known. All symptomatic pts need large-bore IV access, supplemental O_2, cardiac monitoring, continuous observation, and, if mental status is altered, 100 mg thiamine (IM or IV), 1 ampule of 50% dextrose in water, and 4 mg of naloxone along with specific antidotes as indicated. Unconscious pts should be intubated. Activated charcoal may be given PO or via a large-bore

Table 39-1

Fundamentals of Poisoning Management

SUPPORTIVE CARE

Airway protection	Treatment of seizures
Oxygenation/ventilation	Correction of temperature abnormalities
Treatment of arrhythmias	Correction of metabolic derangements
Hemodynamic support	Prevention of secondary complications

PREVENTION OF FURTHER POISON ABSORPTION

GI decontamination	Decontamination of other sites
Syrup of ipecac–induced emesis	Eye decontamination
Gastric lavage	Skin decontamination
Activated charcoal	Body cavity evacuation
Whole-bowel irrigation	
Catharsis	
Dilution	
Endoscopic/surgical removal	

ENHANCEMENT OF POISON ELIMINATION

Multiple-dose activated charcoal	Extracorporal removal
Forced diuresis	Peritoneal dialysis
Alteration of urinary pH	Hemodialysis
Chelation	Hemoperfusion
Hyperbaric oxygenation	Hemofiltration
	Plasmapheresis
	Exchange transfusion

ADMINISTRATION OF ANTIDOTES

Neutralization by antibodies	Metabolic antagonism
Neutralization by chemical binding	Physiologic antagonism

PREVENTION OF REEXPOSURE

Adult education	Notification of regulatory agencies
Child-proofing	Psychiatric referral

SOURCE: Modified from CH Linden, MJ Burns: Table 396-4, p. 2598 in HPIM-15.

gastric tube; gastric lavage requires an orogastric tube. Severity of poisoning determines the management. Suicidal pts require constant observation by qualified personnel.

Supportive Care   Airway protection is mandatory. Gag reflex alone is not a reliable indicator of the need for intubation. Need for O_2, supplementation and ventilatory support can be assessed by measurement of ABGs. Drug-induced pulmonary edema is usually secondary to hypoxia, but myocardial depression may contribute. Measurement of pulmonary artery pressure may be necessary to establish etiology. Electrolyte imbalances should be corrected as soon as possible.

Supraventricular tachycardia (SVT) with hypertension and CNS excitation is almost always due to sympathetic, anticholinergic, or hallucinogenic stimulation or to drug withdrawal. Treatment is indicated if associated with hemodynamic instability, chest pain, or ischemia on ECG. Treatment with combined alpha and beta blockers or combinations of beta blocker and vasodilator is indicated in severe sympathetic hyperactivity. Physostigmine is useful for anticholinergic hyperactivity. SVT without hypertension usually responds to fluid administration.

Ventricular tachycardia (VT) can be caused by sympathetic stimulation, myocardial membrane destabilization, or metabolic derangements. Lidocaine and phenytoin are generally safe. Drugs that prolong the QT interval (quinidine, procainamide) should not be used in VT due to tricyclic antidepressant overdose. Magnesium sulfate and overdrive pacing (by isoproterenol or a pacemaker) may be useful for torsades de pointes. Arrhythmias may be resistant to therapy until underlying acid-base and electrolyte derangements, hypoxia, and hypothermia are corrected. It is acceptable to observe hemodynamically stable pts without pharmacologic intervention.

Seizures are best treated with γ-aminobutyric acid agonists such as benzodiazepines or barbiturates. Barbiturates should only be given after intubation. Seizures caused by isoniazid overdose may respond only to large doses of pyridoxine IV. Seizures from beta blockers or tricyclic antidepressants may require phenytoin and benzodiazepines.

Prevention of Poison Absorption   Whether or not to perform GI decontamination, and which procedure to use, depends on the time since ingestion; the existing and predicted toxicity of the ingestant; the availability, efficacy, and contraindications of the procedure; and the nature, severity, and risk of complications. The efficacy of activated charcoal, gastric lavage, and syrup of ipecac decreases with time, and there are insufficient data to support or exclude a beneficial effect when they are used >1 h after ingestion. Activated charcoal has comparable or greater efficacy, fewer contraindications and complications, and is less invasive than ipecac or gastric lavage and is the preferred method of GI decontamination in most situations.

Activated charcoal is prepared as a suspension in water, either alone or with a cathartic. It is given orally via a nippled bottle (for infants), or via a cup, straw, or small-bore nasogastric tube. The recommended dose is 1 g/kg body weight, using 8 mL of diluent per gram of charcoal if a premixed formulation is not available. Charcoal may inhibit absorption of other orally administered agents and is contraindicated in pts with corrosive ingestion.

When indicated, gastric lavage is performed using a 28F orogastric tube in children and a 40F orogastric tube in adults. Saline or tap water may be used in adults or children (use saline in infants). Place pt in Trendelenburg and left lateral decubitus position to minimize aspiration (occurs in 10% of pts). Lavage is contraindicated with corrosives and petroleum distillate hydrocarbons because of risk of aspiration-induced pneumonia and gastroesophageal perforation.

Whole-bowel irrigation may be useful with ingestions of foreign-bodies, drug packets, and slow-release medications. Golytely is given orally or by gastric tube up to a rate of 0.5 L/h. Cathartic salts (magnesium citrate) and saccharides (sorbitol, mannitol) promote evacuation of the rectum. Dilution of corrosive acids and alkali is accomplished by having pt drink 5 mL water/ kg. Endoscopy or surgical intervention may be required in large foreign-body ingestion, heavy metal ingestion, and when ingested drug packets leak or rupture.

Syrup of ipecac is administered orally in doses of 30 mL for adults, 15 mL for children, and 10 mL for infants. Vomiting should occur within 20 min. Ipecac is contraindicated with marginal airway patency, CNS depression, recent GI surgery, seizures, corrosive (lye) ingestion, petroleum hydrocarbon ingestion, and rapidly acting CNS poisons (camphor, cyanide, tricyclic anti-depressants, propoxyphene, strychnine). Ipecac is particularly useful in the field.

Skin and eyes are decontaminated by washing with copious amounts of water or saline.

Enhancement of Elimination   Activated charcoal in repeated doses of 1 g/kg q2–4h is useful for ingestions of drugs with enteral circulation such as carbamazepine, dapsone, diazepam, digoxin, glutethimide, meprobamate, methotrexate, phenobarbital, phenytoin, salicylate, theophylline, and valproic acid.

Forced alkaline diuresis enhances the elimination of chlorphenoxyacetic acid herbicides, chlorpropamide, diflunisal, fluoride, methotrexate, phenobarbital, sulfonamides, and salicylates. Sodium bicarbonate, 1–2 ampules per liter of 0.45% NaCl, is given at a rate sufficient to maintain urine pH $\geq$ 7.5 and urine output at 3–6 mL/kg per h. Acid diuresis is no longer recommended. Saline diuresis may enhance elimination of bromide, calcium, fluoride, lithium, meprobamate, potassium, and isoniazid; contraindications include CHF, renal failure, and cerebral edema.

Peritoneal dialysis or hemodialysis may be useful in severe poisoning due to barbiturates, bromide, chloral hydrate, ethanol, ethylene glycol, isopropyl alcohol, lithium, heavy metals, methanol, procainamide, and salicylate. Hemoperfusion may be indicated for chloramphenicol, disopyramide, and hypnotic sedative overdose. Exchange transfusion removes poisons affecting red blood cells.

SPECIFIC POISONS

ACETAMINOPHEN   A dose of $\geq$ 140 mg/kg of acetaminophen saturates metabolism to sulfate and glucuronide metabolites, resulting in increased metabolism of acetaminophen to mercapturic acid. Nonspecific toxic manifestations (and not predictive of hepatic toxicity) include nausea, vomiting, diaphoresis, and pallor 2–4 h after ingestion. Laboratory evidence of hepatotoxicity includes elevation of AST, ALT, and, in severe cases, PT and bilirubin, with ultimate hyperammonemia. A serum acetaminophen level drawn 4–24 h after ingestion is useful for purposes of predicting risk.

Initial therapy consists of activated charcoal, then N-acetylcysteine therapy, which is indicated up to 24 h after ingestion. Loading dose is 140 mg/kg PO, followed by 70 mg/kg PO q4h for 17 doses. Therapy should be started immediately and may be discontinued when serum level is below toxic range.

ALKALI AND ACID   Alkalis include industrial-strength bleach, drain cleaners (sodium hydroxide), surface cleaners (ammonia, phosphates), laundry and dishwashing detergents (phosphates, carbonates), disk batteries, denture cleaners (borates, phosphates, carbonates) and Clinitest tablets (sodium hydroxide). Common acids include toilet bowl cleaners (hydrofluoric, phosphoric, and sulfuric acids), soldering fluxes (hydrochloric acid), antirust compounds (hydrofluoric and oxalic acids), automobile battery fluid (sulfuric acid), and stone cleaners (hydrofluoric and nitric acids). Clinical signs include burns, pain, drooling, vomiting of blood or mucus, and ulceration. Lack of oral manifestations does not rule out esophageal involvement. The esophagus and stomach can perforate, and aspiration can cause fulminant tracheitis.

Endoscopy is safe within 48 h of ingestion to document site and severity of injury.

Immediate treatment consists of dilution with milk or water. Glucocorticoids should be given within 48 h to pts with alkali (not acid) burns of the esophagus and continued for at least 2 weeks. Antacids may be useful for stomach burns. Prophylactic broad-spectrum antibiotics are recommended.

ANTIARRHYTHMIC DRUGS Acute ingestion of $>2\times$ the usual daily dose is potentially toxic and causes symptoms within 1 h. Manifestations include nausea, vomiting, diarrhea, lethargy, confusion, ataxia, bradycardia, hypotension, and cardiovascular collapse. Anticholinergic effects are seen with disopyramide ingestion. Quinidine and class IB agents (lidocaine, mexiletine, phenytoin, tocainide) can cause agitation, dysphoria, and seizures. Ventricular fibrillation (including torsades de pointes) and QT prolongation are characteristic of class IA (disopyramide, procainamide, quinidine) and IC (encainide, moricizine, propafenone, flecainide) poisonings. Myocardial depression may precipitate pulmonary edema.

Activated charcoal is the treatment of choice for GI decontamination. Persistent hypotension and bradycardia may require monitoring of pulmonary artery pressure, cardiac pacing, intraaortic balloon pump counterpulsation, and cardiopulmonary bypass. Ventricular tachyarrhythmias are treated with lidocaine and bretylium. Sodium bicarbonate or lactate may be useful in class IA or IC overdoses. Torsades de pointes is treated with magnesium sulfate (4 g or 40 mL of 10% solution IV over 10–20 min) or overdrive pacing (with isoproterenol or pacemaker).

ANTICHOLINERGIC AGENTS Antimuscarinic agents inhibit acetylcholine in the CNS and parasympathetic postganglionic muscarinic neuroreceptors and include antihistamines (H_1-receptor blockers and over-the-counter hypnotics), belladonna alkaloids (atropine, glycopyrrolate, homatropine, yoscine, ipatropium, scopolamine), Parkinsonian drugs (benztropine, biperiden, trihexyphenidyl), mydriatics (cyclopentolate, tropicamide), phenothizaines, skeletal muscle relaxants (cyclobenzaprine, orphenadrine), smooth muscle relaxants (clinidinium, dicyclomine, isometheptene, oxybutynin), tricyclic antidepressants, and a variety of plants (stramonium, jimsonweed) and mushrooms. Manifestations begin 1 h to 3 d after ingestion; agitation, ataxia, confusion, delirium, hallucinations, and choreoathetosis can lead to lethargy, respiratory depression, and coma.

Treatment involves GI decontamination with activated charcoal, supportive measures, and in severe cases the acetylcholinesterase inhibitor physostigmine; 1 to 2 mg is given IV over 2 min, and the dose may be repeated for incomplete response or recurrent toxicity. Physostigmine is contraindicated in the presence of cardiac conduction defects or ventricular arrhythmias.

ANTICONVULSANTS These drugs include carbamazepine, lamotrigine, phenytoin and other hydantoins, topiramate, valproate, barbiturates, ethosuximide, methsuximide, felbamate, gabapentin, and benzodiazepines (see below). Anticonvulsants are well absorbed after oral administration and primarily cause CNS depression. Cerebellar and vestibular function are affected first, with cerebral depression occurring later. Ataxia, blurred vision, diplopia, dizziness, nystagmus, slurred speech, tremors, and nausea and vomiting are common initial manifestations. Coma with respiratory depression usually occurs at serum carbamazepine concentrations >20 $\mu g/mL$, serum phenytoin levels >60 $\mu g/mL$, and serum valproate levels of >180 μg/mL. Anticholinergic effects (see above) may be present in carbamazepine poisoning and tricyclic antidepressant-like cardiotoxicity (see below) can occur at drug levels >30 μg/mL. Hypotension and arrhythmias (e.g., bradycardia, conduction disturbances, ventricular tachyarrhythmias) can occur during the rapid infusion of phenytoin. Cardiovascular toxicity after oral phenytoin overdose, however, is essentially nonexistent. Extravasation of phenytoin can result in local tissue necrosis due to the high pH of this formulation. Intravenous phenytoin may also cause the "purple glove syndrome" (limb edema, discoloration, and pain). Multiple metabolic abnormalites, including anion-gap metabolic acidosis, hyperosmolality, hypocalcemia, hypoglycemia, hypophosphatemia, hypernatremia, and hyperammonemia (with or without other evidence of hepatotoxicity) can occur in valproate poisoning. Three or more days may be required for resolution of toxicity in severe carbamazepine, phenytoin, and valproate poisoning.

The diagnosis of carbamazepine, phenytoin, and valproate poisoning can be confirmed by measuring serum drug concentrations. Serial drug levels should be obtained until a peak is observed following acute overdose. Quantitative serum levels of other agents are not generally available. Most anticonvulsants can be detected by comprehensive urine screening tests.

Activated charcoal is the method of choice for GI decontamination. Multiple-dose charcoal therapy can enhance the elimination of carbamezpine, phenytoin, valproate, and perhaps other agents. Airway protection and support of respirations with endotracheal intubation and mechanical ventilation, if necessary, are the mainstays of treatment. Seizures should be treated with benzodiazepines or barbiturates. Physostigmine (see anticholinergic agent section) should be considered for anticholinergic poisoning due to carbamazepine. Occasionally, CNS depression due to valproate will respond to naloxone (2 mg IV). Hemodialysis and hemoperfusion should be reserved for patients with persistently high drug levels (e.g., carbamazepine $\geq$ 40 μg/mL and valproate $\geq$1000 μg/mL) who do not respond to supportive care.

ARSENIC Poisoning can occur from natural sources (contamination of deep-water wells); from occupational exposure (a byproduct of the smelting of ores and use in the microelectronic industry); commercial use of arsenic in wood preservatives, pesticides, herbicides, fungicides, and paints; and through foods and tobacco treated with arsenic-containing pesticides. Acute poisoning causes hemorrhagic gastroenteritis, fluid loss, and hypotension followed by delayed cardiomyopathy, delirium, coma, and seizures. Acute tubular necrosis and hemolysis may develop. Arsine gas causes severe hemolysis. Chronic exposure causes skin and nail changes (hyperkeratosis, hyperpigmentation, exfoliative dermatitis, and transverse white striae of the fingernails), sensory and motor polyneuritis that may lead to paralysis, and inflammation of the respiratory mucosa. Chronic exposure is associated with increased risk of skin cancer and possibly of systemic cancers and with vasospasm and peripheral vascular insufficiency.

Treatment of acute ingestion includes ipecac-induced vomiting, gastric lavage, activated charcoal with a cathartic, aggressive administration of IV fluids and electrolyte correction, and dimercaprol IM at an initial dose of 3–5 mg/kg every 4 h for 2 d, every 6 h on d 3, and every 12 h for 7 d. Succimer is an alternative agent if adverse reactions develop to dimercaprol. With renal failure doses should be adjusted carefully. Other than avoidance of additional exposure, specific therapy is not of proven benefit for chronic arsenic toxicity.

BARBITURATES Overdose may result in confusion, lethargy, coma, hypotension, hypothermia, pulmonary edema, and death.

Treatment consists of GI decontamination and repetitive charcoal administration for long-acting barbiturates. Renal excretion of phenobarbital is enhanced by alkalinization of urine to a pH of 8 and by saline diuresis. Hemoperfusion and hemodialysis can be used in severe poisoning with short-or
long-acting barbiturates.

BENZODIAZEPINES   Long-acting agents include chlordiazepoxide,
clonazepam, clorazepate, diazepam, flurazepam, prazepam, and quazepam;
short-acting drugs include alprazolam, flunitrazepam, lorazepam, and oxaze-
pam; and ultrashort-acting agents include estazolam, midazolam, temazepam,
and triazolam. Effects may begin within 30 min of overdosage and include
weakness, ataxia, drowsiness, coma, and respiratory depression. Pupils are constricted and do not respond to naloxone.

Treatment includes GI decontamination and support of vital signs. Flumazenil, a competitive benzodiazepine-receptor antagonist, can reverse CNS and
respiratory depression and is given IV in incremental doses of 0.2, 0.3, and 0.5
mg at 1-min intervals until the desired effect is achieved or a total dose of 3 to
5 mg is given; flumazenil must be used with caution in pts who have benzodiazepine dependency or have coingested stimulants and benzodiazepines.

BETA-ADRENERGIC BLOCKING AGENTS   Some beta blockers are
cardioselective (acebutolol, atenolol, betaxolol, bisoprolol, esmolol, metropro-
lol), some have sympathomimetic activity (acebutolol, cartelol, pindolol, timolol, possibly penbutolol), and some have quinidine-like effects (acebutolol,
metoprolol, pindolol, propranolol, sotalol, possibly betaxolol). Toxicity is usually manifest within 30 min of ingestion. Symptoms include nausea, vomiting,
diarrhea, bradycardia, hypotension, and CNS depression. Agents with intrinsic
sympathomimetic activity can cause hypertension and tachycardia. Bronchospasm and pulmonary edema may occur. Hyperkalemia, hypoglycemia, metabolic acidosis, all degrees of AV block, bundle branch block, QRS prolongation,
ventricular tachyarrhythmias, torsades de pointes, and asystole may occur.

Treatment includes GI decontamination, supportive measures, and administration of calcium (10% chloride or gluconate salt solution, IV 0.2 mL/kg, up
to 10 mL) and glucagon (5–10 mg IV, then infusion of 1–5 mg/L). Bradycardia
and hypotension sometimes respond to atropine, isoproterenol, and vasopressors. Cardiac pacing or an intraaortic balloon pump may be required. Bronchospasm is treated with inhaled β agonists.

CADMIUM   Foods can be contaminated with cadmium from sewage, polluted ground water, or mining effluents. Airborne cadmium can be released from
smelting or incineration of wastes containing plastics and batteries, and occupational exposure occurs in the metal-plating, pigment, battery, and plastics
industries. Acute inhalation can cause pleuritic chest pain, dyspnea, cyanosis,
fever, tachycardia, nausea, and pulmonary edema. Ingestion can cause severe
nausea, vomiting, salivation, abdominal cramps, and diarrhea. Chronic exposure
causes anosmia, microcytic hypochromic anemia, renal tubular dysfunction with
proteinuria, and osteomalacia with pseudofractures.

Treatment involves avoidance of further exposure and supportive therapy.
Chelation therapy is not useful, and dimercaprol may worsen nephrotoxicity
and is contraindicated. Succimer is useful in cadmium toxicity in animals and
may be useful for the disorder in humans.

CALCIUM CHANNEL BLOCKERS   These agents include amlodipine,
bepridil, diltiazem, felodipine, flunarizine, isradipine, lacidipine, nicardipine,
nifedipine, nimodipine, nisoldipine, nitrendipine, and verapamil. Toxicity usually develops within 30–60 min following ingestion of 5–10 X usual dose.

Manifestations include confusion, drowsiness, coma, seizure, hypotension, bradycardia, cyanosis, and pulmonary edema. ECG findings include all degrees of AV block, prolonged QRS and QT intervals, ischemia or infarction, and asystole. Metabolic acidosis and hyperglycemia may result.

Treatment consists of GI decontamination with activated charcoal, supportive care, calcium and glucagon (as above). Electrical pacing or intraaortic balloon pump may be required, and persistent hypotension may require vasopressors.

CARBON MONOXIDE CO binds to hemoglobin (forming carboxyhemoglobin) with an affinity 200 times that of O_2 and hence causes cellular anoxia. An elevated carboxyhemoglobin fraction confirms exposure but must be interpreted relative to the time elapsed from exposure. Once exposure is discontinued, CO is excreted via the lungs with a half-life of 4–6 h. The half-life decreases to 40–80 min with 100% O_2 therapy and to 15–30 min with hyperbaric O_2. Manifestations include shortness of breath, dyspnea, tachypnea, headache, nausea, vomiting, emotional lability, confusion, impaired judgment, and clumsiness. Pulmonary edema, aspiration pneumonia, arrhythmias, and hypotension may occur. The "cherry red" color of skin and mucous membranes is rare; cyanosis is usual.

Treatment consists of giving 100% O_2 via a tightly fitting mask until CO levels are <10% and all symptoms have resolved. Hyperbaric O_2 is recommended for comatose pts with CO levels $\geq$ 40%, for pts with CO levels $\geq$ 25% who also have seizures or intractable arrhythmias, and for pts with delayed onset of sequelae. Pts with loss of consciousness are at risk for neuropsychiatric sequelae 1 to 3 weeks later.

CARDIAC GLYCOSIDES, INCLUDING DIGOXIN Poisoning with digitalis occurs with therapeutic or suicidal use of digoxin and with plant (foxglove, oleander, squill) ingestion. Symptoms include vomiting, confusion, delirium, hallucinations, blurred vision, disturbed color perception (yellow vision), photophobia, all types of arrhythmias, and all degrees of AV block. The combination of SVT and AV block suggests digitalis toxicity. Hypokalemia is common with chronic intoxication, while hyperkalemia occurs with acute overdosage. Diagnosis is confirmed by measuring the serum digoxin level.

GI decontamination is done carefully to avoid vagal stimulation, repeated doses of activated charcoal are given, and hyperkalemia is treated with Kayexalate, insulin, and glucose. Atropine and electrical pacing may be required. In severe poisoning digoxin-specific Fab antibodies are given; dosage (in 40-mg vials) is calculated by dividing ingested dose of digoxin (mg) by 0.6 mg/vial. If dose and serum levels are unknown, give 5–10 vials to an adult.

CYANIDE Cyanide blocks electron transport, resulting in decreased oxidative metabolism and oxidative utilization, decreased ATP production, and lactic acidosis. Lethal dose is 200–300 mg of sodium cyanide and 500 mg of hydrocyanic acid. Early effects include headache, vertigo, excitement, anxiety, burning of mouth and throat, dyspnea, tachycardia, hypertension, nausea, vomiting, and diaphoresis. Breath may have a bitter almond odor. Later effects include coma, seizures, opisthotonos, trismus, paralysis, respiratory depression, arrhythmias, hypotension, and death.

Treatment should begin immediately based on history. Supportive measures, 100% O_2, and GI decontamination are begun concurrently with specific therapy. Amyl nitrite is inhaled for 30 s each min, and a new ampule is broken q3min. (Nitrite produces methemoglobinemia, which has a higher affinity for cyanide and promotes release from peripheral sites.) Sodium nitrite is then given as a 3% solution IV at a rate of 2.5–5.0 mL/min up to a total dose of 10–15 mL.

Then, 50 ml of 25% sodium thiosulfate is given IV over 1–2 min, producing sodium thiocyanate, which is excreted in urine. (Children should be given 0.33 mL/kg sodium nitrite and 1.65 mL/kg sodium thiosulfate.) If symptoms persist, repeat half the dose of sodium nitrite and sodium thiosulfate.

CYCLIC ANTIDEPRESSANTS These agents include amitriptyline, imipramine, nortriptyline, desipramine, chlomipramine, doxepin, protriptyline, trimipramine, amoxapine, bupropion, maprotiline, mirtazepine, and trazadone. Depending on the agent, they block reuptake of synaptic transmitters (norepinephrine, dopamine) and have central and peripheral anticholinergic activity. Manifestations include anticholinergic symptoms (fever, mydriasis, flushing of skin, urinary retention, decreased bowel motility). CNS manifestations include excitation, restlessness, myoclonus, hyperreflexia, disorientation, confusion, hallucinations, coma, and seizures. Cardiac effects include prolongation of the QRS complex, other AV blocks, and arrhythmias. QRS duration ≥ 0.10 ms is correlated with seizures and life-threatening cardiac arrhythmias. Serum levels ≥ 3300 nmol/L (≥1000 ng/mL) indicate serious poisoning.

Treatment with ipecac is contraindicated. Activated charcoal is the preferred method of GI decontamination and may require repeated treatments. Metabolic acidosis is treated with sodium bicarbonate; hypotension with volume expansion, norepinephrine, or high-dose dopamine; seizures with benzodiazepines and barbiturates; arrhythmias with sodium bicarbonate (0.5–1 mmol/kg), lidocaine, and bretyllium. β-Adrenergic blockers and class 1A antiarrhythmics should be avoided. The efficacy of phenytoin is not established. Physostigmine reverses anticholinergic signs and may be given in mild poisoning.

ETHYLENE GLYCOL Ethylene glycol is used as a solvent for paints, plastics, and pharmaceuticals and in the manufacture of explosives, fire extinguishers, foams, hydraulic fluids, windshield cleaners, radiator antifreeze, and de-icer preparations. As little as 120 mg or 0.1 mL/kg can be hazardous. Manifestations include nausea, vomiting, slurred speech, ataxia, nystagmus, lethargy, sweet breath odor, coma, seizures, cardiovascular collapse, and death. Hypocalcemia occurs in half of pts. Anion-gap metabolic acidosis, elevated serum osmolality, and oxalate crystalluria suggest the diagnosis. Renal failure may result from glycolic acid production.

GI lavage should be followed by activated charcoal, and airway protection should be initiated immediately. Calcium salts should be given IV at a rate of 1 mL/min for a total dose of 7–14 mL (10% solution diluted 10:1). Metabolic acidosis should be treated with sodium bicarbonate. Phenytoin and benzodiazepines are given for seizures. Ethanol and fomepizole bind to alcohol dehydrogenase with higher affinity than ethylene glycol and block the production of toxic metabolites. Ethanol is administered when ethylene glycol level is >3 mmol/L (>20 mg/dL) and acidosis is present; ethanol is given as follows: the loading dose is 10 mL/kg of 10% ethanol IV or 1 mL/kg of 95% ethanol PO; the maintenance dose is 1.5 (mL/kg)/h of 10% ethanol IV and 3 (mL/kg)/h of 10% ethanol during dialysis. A serum ethanol level of ≥20 mmol/L (≥100 mg/dL) is required to inhibit alcohol dehydrogenase, and levels must be monitored closely. Fomepizole is diluted in 100 mL of IV fluid and administered over 30 min in a loading dose of 15 mg/kg followed by 10 mg/kg every 12 h for four doses and 15 mg/kg thereafter until the ethylene glycol level falls below 1.5 mmol/L (10 mg/dL). Hemodialysis is indicated in cases not responding to above therapy, when serum levels are ≥ 8 mmol/L (≥50 mg/dL), and for renal failure. Give thiamine and pyridoxine supplements.

HALLUCINOGENS Mescaline, lysergic acid (LSD), and psilocybin cause disorders of mood, thought, and perception lasting 4–6 h. Psilocybin can cause fever, hypotension, and seizures. Symptoms include mydriasis, conjunctival injection, piloerection, hypertension, tachycardia, tachypnea, anorexia, tremors, and hyperreflexia.

Treatment is nonspecific: a calm environment, benzodiazepines for acute panic reactions, and haloperidol for psychotic reactions.

HYDROCARBONS Forms include aromatic hydrocarbons (xylene, toluene), halogenated hydrocarbons (carbon tetrachloride, trichlorethane), and petroleum distillate hydrocarbons (gasoline, lacquer thinner, mineral seal oil, kerosene, lighter fluid). All cause CNS excitation at low dose and depression at high doses. Other manifestations include nausea, vomiting, diarrhea, abdominal pain, renal tubular acidosis, bone marrow suppression, respiratory distress, rhabdomyolysis, psychosis and cerebral atrophy, and mucosal burns.

Prompt gastric lavage is required for aromatic hydrocarbons, but gastric lavage, ipecac, and activated charcoal are contraindicated for petroleum distillate hydrocarbons. Supportive care involves oxygen, respiratory support; monitoring of liver, renal, and myocardial function; and correction of metabolic abnormalities.

HYDROGEN SULFIDE Hydrogen sulfide is encountered in the petroleum and mining industries, tanning of leather, vulcanization of rubber, production of synthetic fabrics, refining of metal, production of heavy water for atomic reactors, and manufacture of glue and felt. The chemical is malodorous (rotten eggs) and irritative, producing rhinitis, conjunctivitis, and pharyngitis. Headache, vertigo, nausea, confusion, seizures, and coma may ensue. Respiratory depression causes hypoxia, cyanosis, and metabolic acidosis.

Treatment includes maintenance of airway, 100% O_2 and the use of amyl and sodium nitrite (as for cyanide poisoning) when pts do not respond to oxygen. Hyperbaric O_2 can be used in refractory cases.

IRON Ferrous iron injures mitochondria, causes lipid peroxidation, and results in renal, tubular, and hepatic necrosis and occasionally in myocardial and pulmonary injury. Ingestion of 20 mg/kg causes GI symptoms, and 60 mg/kg causes fever, hyperglycemia, leukocytosis, lethargy, hypotension, metabolic acidosis, seizures, coma, vascular collapse, jaundice, elevated liver enzymes, prolongation of PT, and hyperammonemia. X-ray may identify iron tablets in stomach. Serum iron levels greater than iron-binding capacity indicate serious toxicity. A positive urine deferoxamine provocative test (50 mg/kg IV or IM up to 1 g) produces a vin rosé color that indicates presence of ferrioxamine.

Gastric lavage and whole-bowel irrigation should be administered, followed by x-ray to check adequacy of decontamination. Charcoal is ineffective. Endoscopic removal of tablets may be necessary. Volume depletion should be corrected, and sodium bicarbonate is used to correct metabolic acidosis. Deferoxamine is infused at 10–15 (mg/kg)/h (up to 1–2 g) if iron exceeds binding capacity. If iron level is >180 μmol/L (>1000 μg/dL), larger doses of deferoxamine can be given, followed by exchange transfusion or plasmapheresis to remove deferoxamine complex.

ISONIAZID Acute overdose decreases synthesis of γ-aminobutyric acid and causes CNS stimulation. Symptoms begin within 30 min of ingestion and include nausea, vomiting, dizziness, slurred speech, coma, seizures, and metabolic acidosis.

Activated charcoal is the preferred method of GI decontamination. Pyridoxine (vitamin B_6) should be given slowly IV in weight equivalency to ingested dose of isoniazid. If dose is not known, give 5 g pyridoxine IV over 30 min as a 5–10% solution.

ISOPROPYL ALCOHOL   Isopropyl alcohol is present in rubbing alcohol, solvents, aftershave lotions, antifreeze, and window cleaners. Its metabolite, acetone, is found in cleaners, solvents, and nail polish removers. Manifestations begin promptly and include vomiting, abdominal pain, hematemesis, myopathy, headache, dizziness, confusion, coma, respiratory depression, hypothermia, and hypotension. Hypoglycemia, anion-gap (small) metabolic acidosis, elevated serum osmolality, false elevations of serum creatinine, and hemolytic anemia may be present.

Treatment consists of GI decontamination by gastric aspiration and supportive measures. Activated charcoal is not effective. Dialysis may be needed in severe cases.

LEAD   Exposure to lead occurs through paints, cans, plumbing fixtures, leaded gasolines, vegetables grown in lead-contaminated soils, improperly glazed ceramics, lead-containing glass, and industrial sources such as battery manufacturing, demolition of lead-contaminated buildings, and the ceramics industry. Manifestations in childhood include abdominal pain followed by lethargy, anorexia, anemia, ataxia, and slurred speech. Severe manifestations include convulsions, coma, generalized cerebral edema, and renal failure. Impairment of cognition is dose-dependent. In adults symptoms of chronic exposure include abdominal pain, headache, irritability, joint pain, fatigue, anemia, motor neuropathy, and deficits in memory. Encephalopathy is rare. A "lead line" may appear at the gingiva-tooth border. Chronic, low-level exposure can cause interstitial nephritis, tubular damage, hyperuricemia, and decreased glomerular filtration. Elevation of bone lead level is a risk for anemia and hypertension.

Treatment first involves prevention of further exposure and the use of chelating agents such as edetate calcium disodium, dimercaprol, penicillamine, and succimer. Chelation may not improve subclinical manifestations such as impaired cognition.

LITHIUM   Manifestations begin within 2–4 h of ingestion and include nausea, vomiting, diarrhea, weakness, fasciculations, twitching, ataxia, tremor, myoclonus, choreoathetosis, seizures, confusion, coma, and cardiovascular collapse. Laboratory abnormalities include leukocytosis, hyperglycemia, albuminuria, glycosuria, nephrogenic diabetes insipidus, ECG changes (AV block, prolonged QT), and ventricular arrhythmias.

Within 2–4 h of ingestion, gastric lavage and bowel irrigation should be performed. Charcoal is not effective. Endoscopy should be considered if concretions are suspected. Experimentally, Kayexalate has been shown to bind lithium, but its clinical efficacy is unproven. Serial serum lithium levels should be measured until trend is downward. Supportive care includes saline diuresis and alkalinization of the urine for levels > 2–3 mmol/L. Hemodialysis is indicated for acute or chronic intoxication with symptoms and/or a serum level >3mmol/L.

MERCURY   Mercury is used in thermometers, dental amalgams, and some batteries and is combined with other chemicals to form inorganic or organic mercury compounds. Fish can concentrate mercury at high levels, and occupational exposure continues in some chemical, metal-processing, electrical, and automotive manufacturing; building industries; and medical and dental services (e.g., ordinary dental amalgam). Inhalation of mercury vapor causes diffuse infiltrates or a pneumonitis, respiratory distress, pulmonary edema, fibrosis, and desquamation of the bronchiolar epithelium. Neurologic manifestations include tremors, emotional lability, and polyneuropathy. Chronic exposure to metallic mercury produces intention tremor and erethism (excitability, memory loss, insomnia, timidity, and sometimes delirium); acute high-dose ingestion of metallic mercury may lead to hematemesis and abdominal pain, acute renal failure, and cardiovascular collapse. Organic mercury compounds can cause a neurotoxicity characterized by paresthesia; impaired vision, hearing, taste, and smell; unsteadiness of gait; weakness; memory loss; and depression. Exposed mothers give birth to infants with mental retardation and multiple neurologic derangements.

Treatment acutely involves emesis or gastric lavage followed by the oral administration of polythiol resins to bind mercury in the GI tract. Chelating agents include dimercaprol, succimer, and penicillamine. Acute poisoning is treated with dimercaprol in divided doses IM, not exceeding 24 mg/kg per day; 5-day courses are usually separated by rest periods. N-acetyl penicillamine is also useful at a dose of 30 mg/kg per day in divided doses. Peritoneal dialysis, hemodialysis, and extracorporeal hemodialysis with succimer have been used for renal failure. Chronic inorganic mercury poisoning is best treated with acetyl penicillamine.

METHANOL   Methanol is a component of shellacs, varnishes, paint removers, Sterno, windshield-washer solutions, copy machine fluid, and denaturants for ethanol. It is metabolized to formic acid, which causes metabolic acidosis. Manifestations begin within 1–2 h of ingestion and include nausea, vomiting, abdominal pain, headache, vertigo, confusion, obtundation, and ethanol-like intoxication. Late manifestations are due to formic acid and include an anion-gap metabolic acidosis, coma, seizures, and death. Ophthalmic manifestations 15–19 h after ingestion include clouding, diminished acuity, dancing and flashing spots, dilated or fixed pupils, hyperemia of the disc, retinal edema, and blindness. An osmol gap is often present.

Gastric aspiration should be undertaken. Activated charcoal is not effective. Acidosis is corrected with sodium bicarbonate. Seizures respond to diazepam and phenytoin. Ethanol or fomepizole therapy (as described for ethylene glycol) is indicated in pts with visual symptoms or a methanol level >6 mmol/L (>20 mg/dL). Therapy with ethanol is continued until the methanol level falls <6 mmol/L. Hemodialysis is indicated when visual signs are present or when metabolic acidosis is unresponsive to sodium bicarbonate.

METHEMOGLOBINEMIA   Chemicals that oxidize ferrous hemoglobin (Fe^{2+}) to its ferric (Fe^{3+}) state include aniline, aminophenols, aminophenones, chlorates, dapsone, local anesthetics, nitrates, nitrites, nitroglycerine, naphthalene, nitrobenzene, nitrogen oxides, phenazopyridine, primiquine, and sulfonamides. Cyanosis occurs with methemoglobin levels >15%. When levels exceed 20–30%, symptoms include fatigue, headache, dizziness, tachycardia, and weakness. At levels >45%, dyspnea, bradycardia, hypoxia, acidosis, seizures, coma, and arrhythmias occur. Death usually occurs with levels >70%. Hemolytic anemia may lead to hyperkalemia and renal failure 1–3 days after exposure. Cyanosis in conjunction with a normal O_2 and decreased O_2 saturation (measured by oximeter) and "chocolate brown" blood suggest the diagnosis. The chocolate color does not redden with exposure to O_2 but fades when exposed to 10% potassium cyanide.

Ingested toxins should be removed by treatment with activated charcoal. Methylene blue is indicated for methemoglobin level >30 g/L or methemoglobinemia with hypoxia. Dosage is 1–2 mg/kg as a 1% solution over 5 min. Additional doses may be needed. Methylene blue is contraindicated in G6PD deficiency. Administration of 100% O_2 and packed red blood cell transfusion to a hemoglobin level of 150 g/L can enhance O_2 carrying capacity of the blood. Exchange transfusions may be indicated in G6PD-deficient pts.

MONOAMINE OXIDASE (MAO) INHIBITORS MAO inhibitors include furzolidone, isocarboxazid, nialamide, pargyline, phenelizine, procarbazine, and tranylcypromine. Manifestations are apparent within 6–12 h of ingestion and include CNS stimulation, fever, tachycardia, tachypnea, hypertension, nausea, vomiting, dilated pupils with nystagmus, and papilledema. Fasciculations, twitching, tremor, and rigidity may be present.

Activated charcoal is the preferred method of GI decontamination. Dantrolene (2.5 mg/kg PO or IV q6h) may be effective for hyperthermia. Control of hypertension may require nitroprusside, and tachycardia may require propranolol. Hypotension should be treated with fluids and cautious use of pressors. Seizures are treated with benzodiazepines and phenytoin. In severe cases hyperthermia may require external cooling, and neuromuscular paralysis may be necessary for agitation.

MUSCLE RELAXANTS Manifestations of poisoning by carisoprodol, chlorphenesin, chlorzoxazone, and methocarbamol include nausea, vomiting, dizziness, headache, nystagmus, hypotonia, and CNS depression. Cyclobenzaprine and orphenadrine cause agitation, hallucinations, seizures, stupor, coma, and hypotension. Orphenadrine can also cause ventricular tachyarrhythmias. Baclofen causes CNS depression, hypothermia, excitability, delirium, myoclonus, seizures, conduction abnormalities, arrhythmias, and hypotension.

Prompt GI decontamination, single-dose activated charcoal (repeated for baclofen overdose), and cathartics are indicated. Physostigmine (1–2 mg IV over 2–5 min) is useful for anticholinergic effects.

NEUROLEPTICS The phenothiazines chlorpromazine, fluphenazine, mesoridazine, perphenazine, prochlorperazine, promazine, promethazine, and thioridazine and pharmacologically similar agents such as haloperidol, loxapine, pimozide, and thiothixene are CNS depressants and can cause lethargy, obtundation, respiratory depression, and coma. Pupils are often constricted. Hypothermia, hypotension, SVT, AV block, arrhythmias (including torsades de pointes), prolongation of PR, QRS, and QT intervals, and T-wave abnormalities are seen. Malignant neuroleptic syndrome occurs rarely. Acute dystonic reaction symptoms include rigidity, opisthotonos, stiff neck, hyperreflexia, irritability, dystonia, fixed speech, torticollis, tremors, trismus, and oculogyric crisis.

Treatment of overdose includes GI decontamination with activated charcoal. Seizures should be treated with benzodiazepines; hypotension responds to volume expansion and α agonists. Sodium bicarbonate is given for metabolic acidosis. Avoid the use of procainamide, quinidine, or any agent that prolongs cardiac repolarization. Acute dystonic reactions respond to diphenhydramine (1–2 mg/kg IV) or benztropine (1–2 mg). Doses may be repeated in 20 min if necessary.

NONSTEROIDAL ANTI-INFLAMMATORY DRUGS (NSAIDS) All NSAIDs may cause gastroenteritis, drowsiness, headache, glycosuria, hematuria, and proteinuria. Ibuprofen toxicity is usually mild but can cause metabolic acidosis, coma, and seizures. Diflunisal produces, in addition, hyperventilation, tachycardia, and diaphoresis; fenoprofen is nephrotoxic. Seizures occur with mefenamic acid and phenylbutazone and rarely with ketoprofen and naproxen. Coma, respiratory depression, and cardiovascular collapse can occur with mefenamic acid and phenylbutazone.

Activated charcoal and cathartics are indicated. Charcoal treatment should be repeated with indomethacin, phenylbutazone, and piroxicam ingestions. Hemodialysis is not efficient because of protein binding but may be useful with severe toxicity.

ORGANOPHOSPHATE AND CARBAMATE INSECTICIDES   Organophosphates (chlorpyrifos, phosphorothioic acid, dichlorvos, fenthion, malathion, parathion, sarin, and numerous others) irreversibly inhibit acetylcholinesterase and cause accumulation of acetylcholine at muscarinic and nicotinic synapses. Carbamates (carbaryl, aldicarb, propoxur, and bendicarb) reversibly inhibit acetylcholinesterase; therapeutic carbonates include ambenonium, neostigmine, physostigmine, and pyridostigmine. Both types are absorbed through the skin, lungs, and GI tract and produce nausea, vomiting, abdominal cramps, urinary and fecal incontinence, increased bronchial secretions, coughing, sweating, salivation, lacrimation, and miosis; carbamates are shorter acting. Bradycardia, conduction blocks, hypotension, twitching, fasciculations, weakness, respiratory depression, seizures, confusion, and coma may result. A decrease in cholinesterase activity $\geq 50\%$ in plasma or red cells is diagnostic.

Treatment begins with washing exposed surfaces with soap and water and, in cases of ingestion, GI decontamination, then activated charcoal. Atropine, 0.5–2 mg is given IV q15 min until complete atropinization is achieved (dry mouth). Pralidoxime (2-PAM), 1–2 g IV over several minutes, can be repeated q8h until nicotinic symptoms resolve. Use of 2-PAM in carbamate poisoning is controversial. Seizures should be treated with benzodiazepines.

SALICYLATES   Poisoning with salicylates causes vomiting, tachycardia, hyperpnea, fever, tinnitus, lethargy, and confusion. Severe poisoning can result in seizures, coma, respiratory and cardiovascular failure, cerebral edema, and renal failure. Respiratory alkalosis is commonly coupled with metabolic acidosis (40–50%), but respiratory alkalosis (20%) and metabolic acidosis (20%) can occur separately. Lactic and other organic acids are responsible for the increased anion gap. PT may be prolonged. Salicylates in blood or urine can be detected by ferric chloride test. Levels >2.2 mmol/L (30 mg/dL) are associated with toxicity.

Treatment includes repeated administration of activated charcoal for up to 24 h. Forced alkaline diuresis (urine pH > 8.0) increases excretion and decreases serum half-life. Seizures can be controlled with diazepam or phenobarbital. Hemodialysis should be considered in pts who fail conventional therapy or have cerebral edema or hepatic or renal failure.

SEROTONIN SYNDROME   This syndrome is due to excessive CNS and peripheral serotonergic (5HT-1a and possibly 5HT-2) activity and results from the concomitant use of agents that promote the release of serotonin from presynaptic neurons (e.g., amphetamines, cocaine, codeine, methylenedioxy-methamphetamine, or MDMA (Ecstasy), reserpine, some MAO inhibitors), inhibit its reuptake (e.g., cyclic antidepressants, particularly the SSRIs, ergot derivatives, dextromethorphan, meperidine, pentacozine, sumatriptan and related agents, tramadol, some MAO inhibitors) or metabolism (e.g., cocaine, MAO inhibitors), or stimulate postsynaptic serotonin receptors (e.g., bromocryptine, bupropion, buspirone, levodopa, lithium, L-tryptophan, LSD, mescaline, trazodone). Less often, it results from the use or overdose of a single serotonergic agent or when one agent is taken soon after another has been discontinued (up to 2 weeks for some agents).

Manifestations include altered mental status (agitation, confusion, delirium, mutism, coma, and seizures), neuromuscular hyperactivity (restlessness, incoordination, hyperreflexia, myoclonus, rigidity, and tremors), and autonomic dysfunction (abdominal pain, diarrhea, diaphoresis, fever, elevated and fluctuating blood pressure, flushed skin, mydriasis, tearing, salivation, shivering, and tachycardia). Complications include hyperthermia, lactic acidosis, rhabdomyolysis, kidney and liver failure, ARDS, and DIC.

Gastrointestinal decontamination may be indicated for acute overdose. Supportive measures include hydration with intravenous fluids, airway protection and mechanical ventilation, benzodiazepines (and paralytics, if necessary) for neuromuscular hyperactivity, and mechanical cooling measures for hyperthermia. Cyproheptadine (Periactin), an antihistamine with 5HT-1a and 5HT-2 receptor blocking activity, and chlorpromazine (Thorazine), a nonspecific serotonin receptor antagonist, have been used with success. Cyproheptadine is given orally or by gastric tube in an initial dose of 4 to 8 mg and repeated as necessary every 2 to 4 h up to a maximum of 32 mg in 24 h. Chlorpromazine can be given parenterally (intramuscularly or by slow IV injection in doses of 50 to 100 mg).

SYMPATHOMIMETICS Amphetamines; bronchodilators such as albuterol and metaproterenol; decongestants such as ephedrine, pseudoephedrine, phenylephrine, and phenylpropanolamines; and cocaine can cause nausea, vomiting, diarrhea, abdominal cramps, irritability, confusion, delirium, euphoria, auditory and visual hallucinations, tremors, hyperreflexia, seizures, palpitations, tachycardia, hypertension, arrhythmias, and cardiovascular collapse. Sympathomimetic symptoms include dilated pupils, dry mouth, pallor, flushing of skin, and tachypnea. Severe manifestations include hyperpyrexia, seizures, rhabdomyolysis, hypertensive crisis, intracranial hemorrhage, cardiac arrhythmias, and cardiovascular collapse. Rhabdomyolysis and intracranial hemorrhage can occur.

Activated charcoal is preferred for GI decontamination. Seizures are treated with benzodiazepines; hypertension with a nonselective beta blocker or the α-adrenergic antagonist phentolamine (1 to 5 mg IV q5min); fever with salicylates; and agitation with sedatives and, if necessary, paralyzing agents. Lidocaine and propranolol are useful for cardiac arrhythmias.

THALLIUM Thallium is used as insecticide, in fireworks, in manufacturing, as an alloy, and in cardiac imaging, and epidemic poisoning has occurred with ingestion of grain contaminated with thallium. Acute manifestations include nausea and vomiting, abdominal pain, bloody diarrhea, and hematemesis. Subsequent manifestations include confusion, psychosis, choreoathetosis, organic brain syndrome, convulsions, coma, and sensory and motor neuropathy; autonomic nervous system effects include tachycardia, hypertension, and salivation. Optic neuritis, ophthalmoplegia, ptosis, strabismus, and cranial nerve palsies may occur. Late effects include diffuse hair loss, memory defects, ataxia, tremor, and foot drop.

Treatment includes GI decontamination by lavage or ipecac syrup and cathartics, forced diuresis with furosemide and KCl supplements, and either peritoneal dialysis, hemodialysis, or charcoal hemoperfusion.

THEOPHYLLINE Theophylline, caffeine, and other methylxanthines are phosphodiesterase inhibitors that reduce the degradation of cyclic AMP, thereby enhancing the actions of endogenous catecholamines. Vomiting, restlessness, irritability, agitation, tachypnea, tachycardia, and tremors are common. Coma and respiratory depression, generalized tonic-clonic and partial seizures, atrial arrhythmias, ventricular arrhythmias, and fibrillation can occur. Rhabdomyolysis with acute renal failure develops occasionally. Laboratory abnormalities include ketosis, metabolic acidosis, elevated amylase, hyperglycemia, and decreased potassium, calcium, and phosphorus.

Treatment requires prompt administration of activated charcoal every 2–4 h for 12–24 h after ingestion. Metoclopramide and ondansetron may be given to control vomiting. Tachyarrhythmias are treated with propranolol and standard antiarrhythmics; hypotension requires volume expansion. Seizures are treated with benzodiazepines and barbiturates; phenytoin is ineffective. Indications for hemodialysis and hemoperfusion with acute ingestion include a serum level >500 μmol/L (>100 mg/L) and with chronic ingestion a serum level >200–300 μmol/L (>40–60 mg/L). Dialysis is also indicated in pts with lower serum levels who have refractory seizures or arrhythmias.

For a more detailed discussion, see Linden CH, Burns MJ: Poisoning and Drug Overdosage, Chap. 396, p. 2595; and Hu H: Heavy Metal Poisoning, Chap. 395, p. 2590, in HPIM-15.

40

DIABETIC KETOACIDOSIS AND HYPEROSMOLAR COMA

Diabetic ketoacidosis (DKA) and nonketotic hyperosmolar state (NKHS) are acute complications of diabetes mellitus (DM). DKA is seen primarily in individuals with type 1 DM and NKHS in individuals with type 2 DM. Both disorders are associated with absolute or relative insulin deficiency, volume depletion, and altered mental status. The metabolic similarities and differences in DKA and NKHS are summarized in Table 40-1.

DIABETIC KETOACIDOSIS

ETIOLOGY   DKA results from insulin deficiency with a relative or absolute increase in glucagon and may be caused by inadequate insulin administration, infection (pneumonia, UTI, gastroenteritis, sepsis), infarction (cerebral, coronary, mesenteric, peripheral), surgery, or drugs (cocaine).

CLINICAL FEATURES   The initial symptoms of DKA include anorexia, nausea, vomiting, polyuria, and thirst. Abdominal pain, altered mental function, or frank coma may ensue. Classic signs of DKA include Kussmaul respirations and an acetone odor on the pt's breath. Volume depletion can lead to dry mucous membranes, tachycardia, and hypotension. Fever and abdominal tenderness may also be present. Laboratory evaluation reveals hyperglycemia, ketosis (β-hydroxybutyrate>acetoacetate), and metabolic acidosis (arterial pH 6.8–7.3) with an increased anion gap (Table 40-1). The fluid deficit is often 3–5L. Despite a total body potassium deficit, the serum potassium at presentation may be normal or mildly high as a result of acidosis. Leukocytosis, hypertriglyceridemia, and hyperlipoproteinemia are commonly found as well. Hyperamylasemia is usually of salivary origin but may suggest a diagnosis of pancreatitis. The measured serum sodium is reduced as a consequence of hyperglycemia (1.6 meq reduction for each 100=mg/dL rise in the serum glucose).

 TREATMENT

The management of DKA is outlined in Table 40-2.

Table 40-1

Laboratory Values in Diabetic Ketoacidosis (DKA) and Nonketotic Hyperosmolar States (NKHS) (Representative Ranges at Presentation)

	DKA	NKHS
Glucose,[a] mmol/L (mg/dL)	16.7–33.3 (300–600)	33.3–66.6 (600–1200)
Sodium, meq/L	125–135	135–145
Potassium,[a]	Normal to ↑[b]	Normal
Magnesium [a]	Normal [b]	Normal
Chloride[a]	Normal	Normal
Phosphate[a]	↓	Normal
Creatinine	Slightly ↑	Moderately ↑
Osmolality, mOsm/mL	300–320	330–380
Plasma ketones[a]	++++	+/−
Serum bicarbonate,[a] meq/L	<15 meq/L	Normal to slightly ↓
Arterial pH	6.8–7.3	>7.3
Arterial P_{CO_2}, mmHg	20–30	Normal
Anion gap[a] [Na − (Cl + HCO_3)], meq/L	↑	Normal to slightly ↑

[a] Large changes occur during treatment of DKA
[b] Although plasma levels may be normal or high at presentation, total-body stores are usually depleted.

NONKETOTIC HYPEROSMOLAR STATE

ETIOLOGY Insulin deficiency and inadequate fluid intake are the underlying causes of NKHS. Hyperglycemia induces an osmotic diuresis that leads to profound intravascular volume depletion. NKHS is often precipitated by a serious, concurrent illness such as myocardial infarction or sepsis, and compounded by conditions that impede access to water. Thiazide diuretics, glucocorticoids, and phenytoin have also been associated with the development of NKHS.

CLINICAL FEATURES Presenting symptoms include polyuria, thirst, and altered mental state, ranging from lethargy to coma. Notably absent are symptoms of nausea, vomiting, and abdominal pain and the Kussmaul respirations characteristic of DKA. The prototypical pt is a mildly diabetic, elderly individual with a several week history of polyuria, weight loss, and diminished oral intake. The laboratory features are summarized in Table 40-1. In contrast to DKA, acidosis and ketonemia are usually not found; however, a small anion gap may be due to lactic acidosis, and moderate ketonuria may occur from starvation. Though the measured serum sodium may be normal or slightly low, the corrected serum sodium is usually increased (add 1.6 meq to measured sodium for each 100=mg/dL rise in the serum glucose).

℞ TREATMENT

The precipitating problem should be sought and treated. Sufficient IV fluids (2–3 L of 0.9% normal saline over the first 1–3 h) must be given to support circulation and urine flow. The calculated free water deficit (usually 8–10 L) should be reversed over the next 1–2 days, using 0.45% saline initially then 5% dextrose in water. Potassium repletion is usually necessary. The plasma glucose may drop precipitously with hydration alone, though insulin therapy

Table 40-2

Management of Diabetic Ketoacidosis

1. Confirm diagnosis ($\uparrow$ plasma glucose, positive serum ketones, metabolic acidosis).
2. Admit to hospital; intensive-care setting may be necessary for frequent monitoring or if pH < 7.00 or unconscious.
3. Assess: Serum electrolytes (K^+, Na^+, Mg^{2+}, Cl^-, bicarbonate, phosphate)
   Acid-base status—pH, HCO_3^-, P_{CO_2}
   Renal function (creatinine, urine output)
4. Replace fluids: 2–3 L 0.9% saline over first 1–3 h (5–10 mL/kg per hour); subsequently, 0.45% saline at 150–300 mL/h; change to 5% glucose and 0.45% saline at 100–200 mL/h when plasma glucose reaches 14 mmol/L (250 mg/dL).
5. Administer regular insulin: 10–20 units IV or IM, then 5–10 units/h by continuous IV infusion; increase two- to ten-fold if no response by 2–4 h.
6. Assess patient: What precipitated the episode (noncompliance, infection, trauma, infarction, cocaine)? Initiate appropriate workup for precipitating event [cultures, chest x-ray, electrocardiogram (ECG)]
7. Measure capillary glucose every 1–2 h; measure electrolytes (especially K^+, bicarbonate, phosphate) and anion gap every 4 h for first 24 h.
8. Monitor blood pressure, pulse, respirations, mental status, fluid intake and output every 1–4 h.
9. Replace K^+: 10 meq/h when plasma K^+ < 5.5 meq/L, ECG normal, urine flow, and normal creatinine documented; administer 40–80 meq/h when plasma K^+ < 3.5 meq/L or if bicarbonate is given.
10. Continue above until patient is stable; glucose goal is 8.3–13.9 mmol/L (150–250 mg/dL), until acidosis is resolved. Insulin infusion may be decreased to 1–4 units/h.
11. Administer intermediate or long-acting insulin as soon as patient is eating. Allow for overlap in insulin infusion and subcutaneous insulin injection.

SOURCE: Adapted from M Sperling, in *Therapy for Diabetes Mellitus and Related Disorders*, 1998.

with an intravenous bolus of 5–10 units followed by a constant infusion rate (3–7 units/h) is usually required. Glucose should be added to intravenous fluid when the plasma glucose falls to 250 mg/dL. The insulin infusion should be continued until the patient has resumed eating and can be transferred to a subcutaneous insulin regimen. The mortality rate approaches 50%.

For a more detailed discussion, see Powers AC: Diabetes Mellitus, Chap 333, p. 2109; in HPIM-15.

41

HYPOGLYCEMIA

Glucose is an obligate metabolic fuel for the brain, making it particularly vulnerable to hypoglycemia. Counterregulatory responses to hypoglycemia include insulin suppression and the release of catecholamines, glucagon, growth hormone, and cortisol.

The laboratory diagnosis of hypoglycemia is usually defined as a plasma glucose level <2.5–2.8 mmol/L (<45–50 mg/dL), although the absolute glucose level at which symptoms occur varies among individuals. For this reason, *Whipple's triad* should be present: (1) symptoms consistent with hypoglycemia, (2) a low plasma glucose concentration, and (3) relief of symptoms after the plasma glucose level is raised.

Etiology

Hypoglycemia occurs most commonly as a result of treating patients with diabetes mellitus. However, a number of other disorders are also associated with hypoglycemia, and it is useful to divide these into those associated with fasting or the postprandial state.

1. Fasting:
    a. *Underproduction of glucose*: hormone deficiencies (hypopituitarism and adrenal insufficiency), inherited enzyme defects, hepatic failure, renal failure, hypothermia, and drugs (ethanol, beta blockers, and rarely salicylates).
    b. *Overutilization of glucose*: hyperinsulinism (exogenous insulin, sulfonylureas, insulin or insulin receptor antibodies, insulinoma, endotoxic shock, renal failure, and use of pentamidine, quinine, or disopyramide) and with appropriate insulin levels but increased levels of insulin-like growth factors such as IGF-II (mesenchymal or other extrapancreatic tumors and prolonged starvation).
2. Postprandial (reactive): after gastric surgery and in children with rare enzymatic defects.

Clinical Features

Symptoms of hypoglycemia can be divided into autonomic (adrenergic: palpitations, tremor, and anxiety; and cholinergic: sweating, hunger, and paresthesia) and neuroglycopenic (behavioral changes, confusion, fatigue, seizure, loss of consciousness, and, if hypoglycemia is severe and prolonged, death). Tachycardia, elevated systolic blood pressure, pallor, and diaphoresis may be present on physical examination.

Recurrent hypoglycemia shifts thresholds for the autonomic symptoms and counterregulatory responses to lower glucose levels, leading to hypoglycemic unawareness. Under these circumstances, the first manifestation of hypoglycemia is neuroglycopenia, placing patients at risk of being unable treat themselves.

Diagnosis

Diagnosis of the hypoglycemic mechanism is critical for choosing a treatment that prevents recurrent hypoglycemia (Fig. 41-1). Urgent treatment is often necessary in patients with suspected hypoglycemia. Nevertheless, blood should be drawn at the time of symptoms, whenever possible before the administration of glucose, to allow documentation of the glucose level. If the glucose level is low

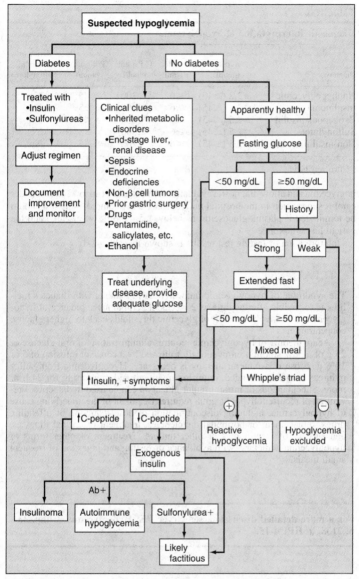

FIGURE 41-1 Diagnostic approach to a patient with suspected hypoglycemia based on a history of symptoms, a low plasma glucose concentration, or both.

and the cause of hypoglycemia is unknown, additional assays should be performed on blood obtained at the time of a low plasma glucose. These should include insulin, C-peptide, sulfonylurea levels, cortisol, and ethanol. In the absence of documented spontaneous hypoglycemia, overnight fasting or food deprivation during observation in the outpatient setting will sometimes elicit hy-

Table 41-1

Diagnostic interpretation of hypoglycemia

Diagnosis	Glucose, mmol/L (mg/dL)	Insulin, μU/mL	C-Peptide, pmol/L	Proinsulin, pmol/L	Urine or Plasma Sulfonylurea
Nonhypoglycemic	≥2.2 (≥40)	<6	<200	<5	No
Insulinoma	≤2.5 (≤45)	≥6	≥200	≥5	No
Exogenous insulin	≤2.5 (≤45)	≥6[a]	<200	<5	No
Sulfonylurea	≤2.5 (≤45)	≥6	≥200	≥5	Yes
Non-insulin mediated	≤2.5 (≤45)	<6	<200	<5	No

[a] Often very high.

poglycemia and allow diagnostic evaluation. An extended (up to 72 h) fast under careful supervision in the hospital may otherwise be required—the test should be terminated if plasma glucose drops below 2.5 mmol/L (45 mg/dL) and the patient has symptoms.

Interpretation of fasting test results is shown in Table 41-1.

R̽x TREATMENT

The syndrome of hypoglycemic unawareness in patients with diabetes mellitus is reversible after as little as 2 weeks of scrupulous avoidance of hypoglycemia. This involves a shift of glycemic thresholds back to higher glucose concentrations.

Acute therapy of hypoglycemia requires administration of oral glucose or 25 g of a 50% solution intravenously followed by a constant infusion of 5 or 10% dextrose if parenteral therapy is necessary. Hypoglycemia from sulfonylureas is often prolonged, requiring treatment and monitoring for 24 h or more. Subcutaneous or intramuscular glucagon can be used in diabetics. Prevention of recurrent hypoglycemia requires treatment of the underlying cause of hypoglycemia, including discontinuation or dose reduction of offending drugs, replacement of hormonal deficiencies, treatment of critical illnesses, and surgery of insulinomas or other tumors. Treatment of other forms of hypoglycemia is dietary, with avoidance of fasting and ingestion of frequent small meals.

For a more detailed discussion, see Cryer PE: Hypoglycemia, Chap. 334, p. 2138, in HPIM-15.

42

INFECTIOUS DISEASE EMERGENCIES

It is important to recognize potentially catastrophic infections that require emergent attention and empirical therapy. In many cases, appropriate therapy at presentation will decrease the likelihood of a fatal outcome in the acutely ill infected febrile patient.

General Considerations

A febrile patient who appears agitated or anxious should raise suspicion of impending decompensation. Information on symptom chronology, focal symptoms, travel, contact with animals (including insects), recent activities, and recent infections should be obtained, as should a vaccination history and a full review of systems. Comorbid conditions, such as lack of splenic function, alcoholism, liver disease, IV drug use, HIV infection, diabetes, presence of prosthetic material, malignancy, steroid use, and chemotherapy, may all predispose to increased severity of specific infections. Vital signs should be carefully measured, with the caveat that elderly, uremic, and cirrhotic individuals and patients taking steroids or NSAIDs may be afebrile despite serious underlying infection. A complete physical examination should be performed, with special attention to skin, soft tissue, and neurologic examination.

Sepsis without an Obvious Focus of Primary Infection

These pts have a brief prodrome of nonspecific Sx that progresses quickly to hemodynamic instability with hypotension, tachycardia, tachypnea, respiratory distress, or altered mental status. *Septic shock* is often due to gram-negative bacilli such as *Pseudomonas aeruginosa, Escherichia coli*, or *Aeromonas hydrophila* or to gram-positive organisms such as *Staphylococcus aureus* or group A streptococci. Treatment can usually be initiated empirically on the basis of the presentation (Table 42-1). *Sepsis in asplenic pts* is 600 times more common than sepsis in the general population, usually occurs within 2 years of loss of splenic function, and carries a mortality rate of 80%. Encapsulated bacteria, including *Streptococcus pneumoniae, Haemophilus influenzae*, and *Neisseria meningitidis*, are common etiologic agents; overwhelming infections with *E. coli, S. aureus*, group B streptococci, *P. aeruginosa, Capnocytophaga* spp., *Babesia* spp., and *Plasmodium* spp. have also been reported. *Babesiosis* manifests 1 to 4 weeks after the pt is bitten by the tick *Ixodes scapularis*, presenting with chills, fatigue, anorexia, nausea, myalgia, arthralgia, and headache; severe cases can include hemolysis and renal failure. Severe babesiosis is common in asplenic pts, those coinfected with *Borrelia burgdorferi* (the agent of Lyme disease) and/or *Ehrlichia* spp., and those infected with the European species *Babesia divergens*. In the appropriate epidemiologic circumstances, *tularemia* should be considered in the setting of wild rabbit, tick, or tabanid fly contact. Plague should be considered after contact with ground squirrels, prairie dogs, or chipmunks in the Southwest and Colorado.

Sepsis with Skin Manifestations

Maculopapular and petechial rashes may reflect early meningococcal or rickettsial disease. Exanthems are usually viral. *Meningococcemia* usually affects children 6 months to 5 years old although sporadic cases occur in students of school age and residents of army barracks. *N. meningitidis* sepsis (Waterhouse-Friderichsen syndrome) carries a mortality rate of 50–60%. This rapidly progressive form of disease is usually not associated with meningitis, but meningitis should be ruled out in any case of suspected meningococcemia. Initially, a blanching maculopapular rash appears on the trunk and extremities; then petechiae form on the ankles, wrists, mucosal surfaces, and pressure points. Rash, hypotension, and a normal or low WBC and ESR confer 90% mortality. Initiation of early treatment can be lifesaving (Table 42-1). *Rocky Mountain spotted*

Table 42-1

Common Infectious Disease Emergencies

Clinical Syndrome	Possible Etiologies	Treatment	Comments	Reference Chapter(s) in HPIM-15
Sepsis without a clear focus				
Gram-negative sepsis	*Pseudomonas* spp., gram-negative enteric bacilli	Piperacillin/tazobactam (3.75 g q4h) *or* Ceftazidime (2 g q8h) *plus* Tobramycin (5 mg/kg qd)	See Table 124-3 in HPIM-15.	124, 155
Gram-positive sepsis	*Staphylococcus* spp., *Streptococcus* spp.	Vancomycin (1 g q12h) *plus* Gentamicin (5 mg/kg qd)	If a β-lactam-sensitive strain is identified, antibiotics should be altered.	124, 139, 140
Overwhelming post-splenectomy sepsis	*Streptococcus pneumoniae, Haemophilus influenzae, Neisseria meningitidis*	Ceftriaxone (2 g q12h)[a]	If the isolate is penicillin-sensitive, penicillin is the drug of choice.	124
Babesiosis	*Babesia microti* (U.S.), *B. divergens* (Europe)	Clindamycin (600 mg tid) *plus* Quinine (650 mg tid)	Treatment with doxycycline (100 mg bid) for potential coinfection with *Borrelia burgdorferi* or *Ehrlichia* spp. may be prudent.	212, 214

(continued)

Table 42-1 (Continued)

Common Infectious Disease Emergencies

Clinical Syndrome	Possible Etiologies	Treatment	Comments	Reference Chapter(s) in HPIM-15
Sepsis with skin findings				
Petechiae				
Meningococcemia	*N. meningitidis*	Penicillin (4 million units q4h) *or* Ceftriaxone (2 g q12h)	If both meningococcemia and Rocky Mountain spotted fever are being considered, use chloramphenicol (50–75 mg/kg qd in four divided doses). *Do not add doxycycline to a regimen including a β-lactam agent.*	146, 177
Rocky Mountain spotted fever	*Rickettsia rickettsii*	Doxycycline (100 mg bid)		124, 146
Purpura fulminans	*S. pneumoniae, H. influenzae, N. meningitidis*	Ceftriaxone (2 g q12h)[a]	If the isolate is penicillin-sensitive, penicillin is the drug of choice.	
Erythroderma: toxic shock syndrome	Group A *Streptococcus, Staphylococcus aureus*	Penicillin (2 million units q4h) *or* Oxacillin (2 g q4h) *plus* Clindamycin (600 mg q8h)	Site of toxigenic bacteria should be debrided; if necessary, IV immunoglobulin can be used in severe cases.	139, 140

(continued)

Table 42-1 (*Continued*)

Common Infectious Disease Emergencies

Clinical Syndrome	Possible Etiologies	Treatment	Comments	Reference Chapter(s) in HPIM-15
Sepsis with soft tissue findings				
Necrotizing fasciitis	Group A *Streptococcus*, mixed aerobic/anaerobic flora	Penicillin (2 million units q4h) *plus* Clindamycin (600 mg q8h) *plus* Gentamicin (5 mg/kg qd)	Urgent surgical evaluation is critical.	128, 140
Clostridial myonecrosis	*Clostridium perfringens*	Penicillin (2 million units q4h) *plus* Clindamycin (600 mg q8h)	Urgent surgical evaluation is critical.	145
Neurologic infections				
Bacterial meningitis	*S. pneumoniae, N. meningitidis*	Ceftriaxone (2 g q12h)[a]	If the isolate is penicillin-sensitive, penicillin is the drug of choice. If the pt is >50 years old, add ampicillin for *Listeria* coverage.	372
Suppurative intracranial infections	*Staphylococcus* spp., *Streptococcus* spp., anaerobes, gram-negative bacilli	Oxacillin (2 g q4h)[b] *plus* Metronidazole (500 mg tid) *plus* Ceftriaxone (2 g q12h)	Urgent surgical evaluation is critical.	372

(*continued*)

178

Table 42-1 (Continued)

Common Infectious Disease Emergencies

Clinical Syndrome	Possible Etiologies	Treatment	Comments	Reference Chapter(s) in HPIM-15
Brain abscess	*Streptococcus* spp., anaerobes, *Staphylococcus* spp.	Penicillin (4 million units q4h) *or* Oxacillin (2 g q4h)[b] *plus* Metronidazole (500 mg tid)	Surgical evaluation is essential.	372
Cerebral malaria	*Plasmodium falciparum*	Quinine (650 mg tid for 3 d) *plus* Tetracycline (250 mg tid for 7 d)	Do not use glucocorticoids.	212, 214
Spinal epidural abscess	*Staphylococcus* spp.	Oxacillin (2 g q4h)[c]	Surgical evaluation is essential.	368
Focal infections Acute bacterial endocarditis	*S. aureus*, β-hemolytic streptococci, HACEK group,[d] *Neisseria* spp., *S. pneumoniae*	Ceftriaxone (2 g q12h) *plus* Vancomycin (1 g q12h)	Adjust treatment when culture data become available. Surgical evaluation is essential.	126

[a] If resistant pneumococci are prevalent, add vancomycin (1 g q12h).
[b] Vancomycin (1 g q12h) should replace oxacillin if methicillin-resistant strains are highly prevalent.
[c] In HIV-infected drug users with suspected spinal epidural abscess, empirical therapy must cover gram-negative rods and methicillin-resistant *S. aureus*.
[d] *Haemophilus aphrophilus, H. paraphrophilus, H. parainfluenzae, Actinobacillus actinomycetemcomitans, Cardiobacterium hominis, Eikenella corrodens,* and *Kingella kingae.*

SOURCE: TF Barlam, DL Kasper: HPIM-15, p. 104.

179

fever (RMSF) is caused by tick-transmitted *Rickettsia rickettsii* and occurs throughout the United States. RMSF begins with general symptoms of fever, malaise, myalgia, and nausea. In 50% of pts, blanching macules develop over the distal extremities after 72 h and progress centripetally. The lesions become hemorrhagic, and a septic picture with ARDS, encephalitis, and multiorgan failure can develop. The CSF contains 10–100 cells/μL with a monocytic predominance. Untreated infection has a mortality of 30%. *Purpura fulminans* is the cutaneous manifestation of DIC and most commonly results from overwhelming infection with *N. meningitidis, H. influenzae,* or *S. pneumoniae.* Skin lesions can rapidly progress from petechial to hemorrhagic, and rapidly progressive multiorgan failure may occur. *Ecthyma gangrenosum,* classically developing secondary to infection with *P. aeruginosa* or *A. hydrophila* in an immunocompromised pt, presents as hemorrhagic vesicles progressing to central necrosis, with a rim of erythema. In pts with underlying liver disease, *Vibrio vulnificus* infection from contaminated shellfish can progress rapidly to a septic picture with bullous or hemorrhagic skin lesions and a mortality rate of 50%. Asplenic pts with *Capnocytophaga canimorsus* infection from a dog bite can present with a diffuse exanthem or erythema multiforme before developing a septic picture. This infection has a 30% mortality. *Toxic shock syndrome* (TSS) has defined diagnostic criteria that include erythroderma, fever, confusion, hypotension, and multiorgan failure. TSS is due to toxin-producing *S. aureus* or *Streptococcus* spp., with higher mortality in streptococcal TSS.

Sepsis with a Soft Tissue/Muscle Primary Focus

Necrotizing fasciitis occurs in pts predisposed by diabetes, IV drug use, and peripheral vascular disease. It is most commonly due to group A *Streptococcus* or mixed aerobic/anaerobic organisms at a site of minor trauma. Fever and pain out of proportion to physical findings are common. Surgical intervention is mandatory. Necrotizing fasciitis due to *Clostridium perfringens* is associated with rapidly progressive hemolysis and a septic picture. *Clostridial myonecrosis* is characterized by massive necrotizing gangrene and a septic picture developing within hours of onset. The affected area has a bronzed appearance, and bullous lesions with serosanguineous drainage and a mousy odor may be noted. Myonecrosis due to *Clostridium septicum,* often spontaneous, occurs in pts with underlying malignancy and is associated with high mortality (highest among pts with involvement of the trunk).

Neurologic Infections with or without Septic Shock

Rapid recognition of the septic pt with central neurologic signs is crucial to improvement of the dismal prognosis of these entities. *Acute bacterial meningitis* is one of the most common infectious disease emergencies affecting the CNS. Most cases are caused by *S. pneumoniae* (30–50%) or *N. meningitidis* (10–35%); pts with immunosuppression or diabetes and the elderly are at increased risk for *Listeria monocytogenes* meningitis. The classic triad of fever, headache, and meningismus should be sought. Papilledema is uncommon on presentation. Palsies of cranial nerves IV, VI, and VII can be seen in 10–20% of cases. Mortality is associated with coma, a septic picture, a CSF protein level of >2.5 g/L, a peripheral WBC of <5000/μL, and hyponatremia. *Subdural empyema* arises from the paranasal sinuses in 60–70% of cases, and microaerophilic streptococci and staphylococci are usually the microbiologic causes. Focal signs are present in 75% of cases, and mortality is 6–20%. Unilateral or retroorbital headache associated with fever should raise suspicion of *septic cavernous sinus thrombosis,* an unusual complication of a facial or sphenoid sinus infection. Staphylococci and aerobic and anaerobic streptococci are the usual causes. Most pts have periorbital edema progressing to ptosis, proptosis, ophthalmoplegia, and papilledema. Mortality is 30%. Ethmoid or maxillary sinusitis is rarely complicated by *septic thrombosis of the superior sagittal sinus*, most commonly caused by *S. pneumoniae*, other streptococci, and staphylococci. A fulminant course presents as headache, nausea, and vomiting progressing to coma, nuchal rigidity, and brainstem signs, with death in >80% of cases. *Brain abscess* often presents as headache or focal neurologic signs in an afebrile pt. Abscesses can originate from a contiguous or hematogenous source, and those arising hematogenously have a greater chance of intraventricular rupture, which carries a high mortality rate. Prognosis is poor in pts with rapid deterioration, delayed diagnosis, intraventricular rupture, multiple abscesses, and an abnormal neurologic examination on presentation. High fever and deteriorating mental status after travel to endemic areas should raise the suspicion of *cerebral malaria* secondary to *Plasmodium falciparum* infection. Nuchal rigidity is rare, and mortality is 30% if diagnosis is delayed. *Spinal epidural abscess* presents with fever in 60% of cases and with back pain in 90% and is most commonly seen in pts with a history of diabetes, IV drug use, recent spinal trauma or surgery, and HIV infection. *S. aureus* is the most common etiology, although gram-negative rods or methicillin-resistant *S. aureus* can be present in HIV-infected IV drug users. Neurologic deficits develop late in the course of this infection. Urgent surgical intervention can minimize permanent neurologic sequelae.

Focal Syndromes with a Fulminant Course

Rapid death from sepsis can occur in TSS due to a toxin-producing infection of a joint, a wound, a postoperative site, the peritoneum, or sinuses. Sudden airway obstruction from an *oropharyngeal infection* can cause rapid deterioration and death (Chap. 50). Delayed diagnosis of and surgical intervention in *rhinocerebral mucormycosis* are associated with high mortality (Chap. 50). *Acute bacterial endocarditis* is usually due to *S. aureus, S. pneumoniae, L. monocytogenes, Haemophilus* spp., or group A, B, or G streptococci; mortality ranges from 10 to 40%. Pts present with fever of <2 weeks' duration, peripheral embolic stigmata are sometimes present, and a changing heart murmur or CHF may be noted. Mortality is associated with rapid valvular destruction, myocardial abscess, arterial emboli from friable valve vegetations, and metastatic infections. Rapid intervention is essential for a successful outcome.

Diagnostic Workup of the Acutely Ill Patient

Before antibiotic therapy is initiated, clinical assessment and procurement of diagnostic material should be accomplished as quickly as possible. Baseline blood exam should include blood cultures; CBC with differential; measurement of serum electrolytes, BUN, creatinine, and glucose; basic coagulation studies; and LFTs. Three sets of blood cultures should be obtained if endocarditis is suspected. Examination of the blood smear is useful in asplenic pts (to document Howell-Jolly bodies that indicate the absence of splenic function) and in cases of suspected malaria, babesiosis, and ehrlichiosis. Microscopic examination of a gram-stained buffy coat may reveal organisms in asplenic pts, given the high-grade bacteremia associated with sepsis in these pts. Pts with suspected meningitis should undergo LP before initiation of antibiotics; if brain imaging is needed before LP, antibiotics should be administered prior to imaging but after blood has been drawn for cultures. Imaging is indicated in pts with abnormal sensorium or focal neurologic signs. Appropriate radiographic examination and echocardiography are important, especially in cases that may merit emergent surgical intervention.

 TREATMENT

The most important task of the physician is to recognize the acute infectious emergency and proceed with appropriate urgency. Table 42-1 lists first-line treatments for the infections considered in this chapter. The acutely ill febrile pt requires close observation and, in most cases, admission to the ICU for aggressive supportive therapy. For infections such as necrotizing fasciitis, myonecrosis, subdural empyema, spinal epidural or brain abscess, mucormycosis, or acute endocarditis, rapid surgical intervention supersedes other diagnostic or therapeutic maneuvers.

For a more detailed discussion, see Barlam TF, Kasper DL: Approach to the Acutely Ill Infected Febrile Patient, Chap. 19, p. 102, in HPIM-15.

43

ONCOLOGIC EMERGENCIES

Emergencies in the cancer pt may be classified into three categories: effects from tumor expansion, metabolic or hormonal effects mediated by tumor products, and treatment complications.

STRUCTURAL/OBSTRUCTIVE ONCOLOGIC EMERGENCIES
The most common problems are: superior vena cava syndrome; pericardial effusion/tamponade, spinal cord compression; seizures (Chap. 182) and/or increased intracranial pressure; and intestinal, urinary, or biliary obstruction. The last three conditions are discussed in Chap. 102 in HPIM-15.

SUPERIOR VENA CAVA SYNDROME Obstruction of the superior vena cava reduces venous return from the head, neck, and upper extremities. About 85% of cases are due to lung cancer; lymphoma and thrombosis of central venous catheters are also causes. Pts often present with facial swelling, dyspnea, and cough. In severe cases, the mediastinal mass lesion may cause tracheal obstruction. Dilated neck veins and increased collateral veins on anterior chest wall are noted on physical exam. CXR documents widening of the superior mediastinum; 25% of pts have a right-sided pleural effusion.

 TREATMENT

Radiation therapy is the treatment of choice for non-small cell lung cancer; addition of chemotherapy to radiation therapy is effective in small cell lung cancer and lymphoma. Clotted central catheters producing this syndrome should be withdrawn, and anticoagulation therapy initiated.

PERICARDIAL EFFUSION/TAMPONADE Accumulation of fluid in the pericardium impairs filling of the heart and decreases cardiac output. Most commonly seen in pts with lung or breast cancers, leukemias, or lymphomas, pericardial tamponade may also develop as a late complication of mediastinal radiation therapy. Common symptoms are dyspnea, cough, chest pain, orthopnea, and weakness. Pleural effusion, sinus tachycardia, jugular venous distention, hepatomegaly, and cyanosis are frequent physical findings. Paradoxical pulse, decreased heart sounds, pulsus alternans, and friction rub are less common with malignant than nonmalignant pericardial disease. Echocardiography is diagnostic; pericardiocentesis may show serous or bloody exudate, and cytology usually shows malignant cells.

 TREATMENT

Drainage of fluid from the pericardial sac may be lifesaving until a definitive surgical procedure can be performed.

SPINAL CORD COMPRESSION Primary spinal cord tumors occur rarely, and cord compression is most commonly due to epidural metastases from vertebral bodies involved with tumor, especially from prostate, lung, breast, lymphoma, and myeloma primaries. Pts present with back pain, worse when recumbent, with local tenderness. Loss of bowel and bladder control may occur. On physical exam, pts have a loss of sensation below a horizontal line on the trunk, called a *sensory level*, that usually corresponds to one or two vertebrae below the site of compression. Weakness and spasticity of the legs and hyperactive reflexes with upgoing toes on Babinski testing are often noted. Spine radiographs may reveal erosion of the pedicles (winking owl sign), lytic or sclerotic vertebral body lesions, and vertebral collapse. Collapse alone is not a reliable indicator of tumor; it is a common manifestation of a more common disease, osteoporosis. MRI can visualize the cord throughout its length and define the extent of tumor involvement.

 TREATMENT

Radiation therapy plus dexamethasone, 4 mg IV or PO q4h, is successful in arresting and reversing symptoms in about 75% of pts who are diagnosed while still ambulatory. Only 10% of pts made paraplegic by the tumor recover the ability to ambulate.

EMERGENT PARANEOPLASTIC SYNDROMES

Most paraneoplastic syndromes have an insidious onset (Chap. 75). Hypercalcemia, syndrome of inappropriate antidiuretic hormone (SIADH), and adrenal insufficiency may present as emergencies.

HYPERCALCEMIA The most common paraneoplastic syndrome, it occurs in about 10% of cancer pts, particularly those with lung, breast, head and neck, and kidney cancer and myeloma. Bone resorption mediated by parathormone-related protein is the most common mechanism; IL-1, IL-6, tumor necrosis factor, and transforming growth factor-β may act locally in tumor-involved bone. Pts usually present with nonspecific symptoms: fatigue, anorexia, constipation, weakness. Hypoalbuminemia associated with malignancy may make symptoms worse for any given serum calcium level because less calcium will be protein bound and more will be free.

 TREATMENT

Saline hydration, antiresorptive agents (such as pamidronate, 60–90 mg IV over 4 h), and glucocorticoids usually lower calcium levels significantly within 1–3 days. Treatment of the underlying malignancy is also important.

SIADH   Induced by the action of arginine vasopressin produced by certain tumors (especially small cell cancer of the lung), SIADH is characterized by hyponatremia, inappropriately concentrated urine, and high urine sodium excretion in the absence of volume depletion. Most pts with SIADH are asymptomatic. When serum sodium falls to <115 meq/L, pts may experience anorexia, depression, lethargy, irritability, confusion, weakness, and personality changes.

 TREATMENT

Water restriction controls mild forms. Demeclocycline (900–1200 mg PO bid) inhibits the effects of vasopressin on the renal tubule. Treatment of the underlying malignancy is also important.

ADRENAL INSUFFICIENCY   The infiltration of the adrenals by tumor and their destruction by hemorrhage are the two most common causes. Symptoms such as nausea, vomiting, anorexia, and orthostatic hypotension may be attributed to progressive cancer or to treatment side effects. Certain treatments (e.g., ketoconazole, aminoglutethimide) may directly interfere with steroid synthesis in the adrenal.

 TREATMENT

In emergencies, a bolus of 100 mg IV hydrocortisone is followed by a continuous infusion of 10 mg/h. In nonemergent but stressful circumstances, 100–200 mg/d oral hydrocortisone is the beginning dose, tapered to maintenance of 15–37.5 mg/d. Fludrocortisone (0.1 mg/d) may be required in the presence of hyperkalemia.

TREATMENT COMPLICATIONS

Complications from treatment may occur acutely or emerge only many years after treatment. Toxicity may be related either to the agents used to treat the cancer or from the response of the cancer to the treatment (e.g., leaving a perforation in a hollow viscus or causing metabolic complications such as the tumor lysis syndrome). Several treatment complications present as emergencies. Fever and neutropenia and tumor lysis syndrome will be discussed here; others are discussed in Chap. 102 in HPIM-15.

FEVER AND NEUTROPENIA   Many cancer pts are treated with myelotoxic agents. When peripheral blood granulocyte counts are <1000/μL, the risk of infection is substantially increased (48 infections/100 pts). A neutropenic pt who develops a fever (>38°C) should undergo physical exam with special attention to skin lesions, mucous membranes, IV catheter sites, and perirectal area. Two sets of blood cultures from different sites should be drawn, and a CXR performed, and any additional tests should be guided by findings from the history and physical exam. Any fluid collections should be tapped, and urine and/or fluids should be examined under the microscope for evidence of infection.

 TREATMENT

After cultures are obtained, all pts should receive IV broad-spectrum antibiotics (e.g., ceftazidime 1 g q8h). If an obvious infectious site is found, the antibiotic regimen is designed to cover organisms that may cause the infection. Usually therapy should be started with an agent or agents that cover both gram-positive and -negative organisms. If the fever resolves, treatment should continue until neutropenia resolves. If the pt remains febrile and neutropenic after 7 days, amphotericin B should be added to the antibiotic regimen.

TUMOR LYSIS SYNDROME When rapidly growing tumors are treated with effective chemotherapy regimens, the rapid destruction of tumor cells can lead to the release of large amounts of nucleic acid breakdown products (chiefly uric acid), potassium, phosphate, and lactic acid. The phosphate elevations can lead to hypocalcemia. The increased uric acid, especially in the setting of acidosis, can precipitate in the renal tubules and lead to renal failure. The renal failure can exacerbate the hyperkalemia.

 TREATMENT

Prevention is the best approach. Maintain hydration with 3 L/d of saline, keep urine pH > 7.0 with bicarbonate administration, and start allopurinol 300 mg/m² per d 24 h before starting chemotherapy. Once chemotherapy is given, monitor serum electrolytes every 6 h. If serum potassium is > 6.0 meq/L and renal failure ensues, hemodialysis may be required. Maintain normal calcium levels.

For a more detailed discussion, see Finberg R: Infections in Patients with Cancer, Chap. 85, p. 547; and Gucalp R, Dutcher J: Oncologic Emergencies, Chap. 102, p. 642 in HPIM-15.

DROWNING AND NEAR-DROWNING

Pathophysiology

Approximately 90% of drowning victims aspirate fluid into lungs. Both freshwater and saltwater aspiration lead to severe hypoxemia due to ventilation/perfusion imbalance and significant pulmonary venous admixture, although mechanisms may differ between the two situations. In victims who do not as-pirate, hypoxemia results from apnea. Contaminated water may pose additional risks, including obstruction of small bronchioles by particulate matter and in-fection by pathogens in the water.

Other physiologic changes occurring in drowning and near-drowning vic-tims include changes in serum electrolytes and blood volume, although these are seen only rarely in persons successfully resuscitated. Hypotonicity may cause acute RBC lysis; however, this complication has been reported only rarely. Hypercarbia is less common than hypoxemia. Renal failure is uncom-mon, but when it does occur, it is secondary to hypoxemia, renal hypoperfusion, or, in extremely rare cases, significant hemoglobinuria.

R_x TREATMENT (See Fig. 44-1)

1. Remove victim from water as soon as possible and stabilize head and neck if trauma is suspected. The American Heart Association recom-mends that an abdominal thrust not be used routinely in victims of sub-mersion as this maneuver can lead to regurgitation and aspiration of gas-tric contents.
2. Restore airway patency, breathing, and circulation immediately. Recall that hypothermia is protective of CNS function, and victims should not be presumed to have failed resuscitation until they have also been re-warmed.
3. Protect airway with endotracheal intubation if the patient is unconscious or obtunded. Correct hypoxemia with supplemental oxygen and mechan-ical ventilation with PEEP or CPAP if needed.
4. Establish venous access as soon as possible.
5. Monitor core body temperature and rewarm if necessary.
6. Monitor cardiac rhythm.
7. If patient has cardiovascular instability, evaluate cardiac output and ef-fective circulatory volume by invasive monitoring.
8. Measure and monitor serum electrolytes, renal function, ABGs. Bicar-bonate administration for metabolic acidosis with a pH < 7.20 is contro-versial but may be indicated in severe cases.

Prognosis

Factors adversely affecting survival include prolonged submersion, delay in initiation of effective cardiopulmonary resuscitation, severe metabolic acidosis (pH < 7.1), asystole on arrival at a medical facility, fixed dilated pupils on presentation, and low Glasgow coma score (<5). No predictor is absolute, how-ever, and normal survivors have been reported despite presence of all these risk factors.

Accident Prevention

Effective means of preventing drowning and near-drowning include:

- Avoidance of the water or use of the buddy system by people at high risk (e.g., history of syncope or seizure)
- Early swimming instruction for children and enhanced pool safety
- Instruction of parents about drowning risks in the home
- Public safety education regarding risks associated with water-related recre-ational activities and the increased risk of alcohol use in the vicinity of the water.

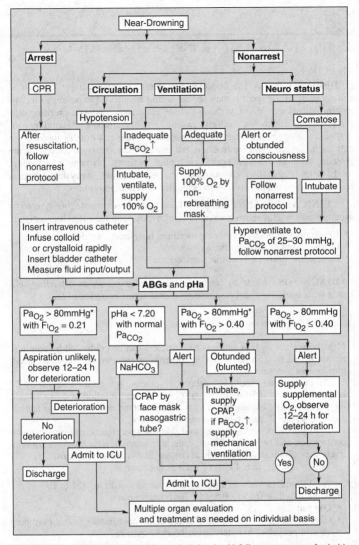

FIGURE 44-1 Treatment of a near-drowned victim should follow a sequence of priorities. *Guidelines only; assumes victim had normal arterial blood gas values (ABGs) before near-drowning. Abbreviations/definitions: CPAP, continuous positive airway pressure; CPR, cardiopulmonary resuscitation; $F_{I_{O_2}}$, fraction of inspired oxygen; intubate, endotracheal intubation; ICU, intensive care unit; $NaHCO_3$, bicarbonate; Pa_{O_2}/Pa_{CO_2}, arterial oxygen/carbon dioxide tension; pHa, arterial pH. (Modified from SA Graves and AJ Layon; in TC Kravis et al (eds): *Emergency Medicine: A Comprehensive Review*, 3d ed. New York, Raven, 1993.)

For a more detailed discussion, see Modell JH: Drowning and Near-Drowning, Chap. 392, p. 2581, in HPIM-15.

45

ANAPHYLAXIS AND TRANSFUSION REACTIONS

ANAPHYLAXIS

DEFINITION   A life-threatening systemic hypersensitivity reaction to contact with an allergen; it may appear within minutes of exposure to the offending substance. Manifestations include respiratory distress; pruritus; urticaria; mucous membrane swelling; gastrointestinal disturbances including nausea, vomiting, pain, and diarrhea; and vascular collapse. Virtually any allergen may incite an anaphylactic reaction, but among the more common agents are proteins such as antisera, hormones, pollen extracts, Hymenoptera venom, foods; drugs (especially antibiotics); and diagnostic agents. Atopy does not seem to predispose to anaphylaxis from penicillin or venom exposures.

CLINICAL PRESENTATION   Time to onset is variable, but symptoms usually occur within seconds to minutes of exposure to the offending antigen:

* Respiratory: mucous membrane swelling, hoarseness, stridor, wheezing
* Cardiovascular: tachycardia, hypotension
* Cutaneous: pruritus, urticaria, angioedema

DIAGNOSIS   Made by obtaining history of exposure to offending substance with subsequent development of characteristic complex of Sx.

 TREATMENT

Mild symptoms such as pruritus and urticaria can be controlled by administration of 0.2 to 0.5 mL of 1:1000 epinephrine solution SC, repeated at 20-min intervals as necessary.

An IV infusion should be initiated. Hypotension should be treated by IV administration of 2.5 mL of 1:10,000 epinephrine solution at 5- to 10-min intervals, volume expanders, e.g., as normal saline, and vasopressor agents, e.g., dopamine, if intractable hypotension occurs.

Epinephrine provides both α- and β-adrenergic effects, resulting in vasoconstriction and bronchial smooth-muscle relaxation. Beta blockers are relatively contraindicated in persons at risk for anaphylactic reactions.

The following should also be used as necessary:

* Antihistamines such as diphenhydramine 50 to 100 mg IM or IV
* Aminophylline 0.25 to 0.5 g IV for bronchospasm
* Oxygen
* Glucocorticoids—IV; not useful for acute manifestations but may help control persistent hypotension or bronchospasm

PREVENTION   Avoidance of offending antigen, where possible; skin testing and desensitization to materials such as penicillin and Hymenoptera venom, if necessary. Individuals should wear an informational bracelet and have immediate access to an unexpired epinephrine kit.

TRANSFUSION REACTIONS

Transfusion reactions may be classified as immune or nonimmune.

Immunologically Mediated Reactions

Reaction may be directed against red or white blood cells, platelets, or IgA; in addition, other, less well-characterized reactions may occur.

1. *Acute hemolytic transfusion reactions*: Usually due to ABO incompatibility, although alloantibodies directed against other antigens may result in intravascular hemolysis; very rapid and massive hemolysis occurs. Sx may include restlessness, anxiety, flushing, chest or back pain, tachypnea, tachycardia, nausea, shock, renal failure, coagulation disorders (including DIC).

2. *Delayed hemolytic transfusion reactions*: Occur in pts previously sensitized to RBC alloantigens who have a negative alloantibody screen due to low antibody levels. When the pt is transfused an anamnestic alloantibody response occurs, leading to extravascular hemolysis of the transfused RBCs.

3. *Allergic reactions*: Characterized by a pruritic rash, edema, headache, and dizziness. Related to plasma proteins found in transfused components.

4. *Anaphylactic reactions*: Severe reactions characterized by hypotension, difficulty breathing, bronchospasm, respiratory arrest, shock. Patients with IgA deficiency are at particular risk for severe reaction due to sensitization to IgA.

5. *Transfusion-related acute lung injury*: Rare reaction that results from transfusion of donor plasma that contains high titer anti-HLA antibodies that bind to corresponding antigens on recipient leukocytes. Recipient develops respiratory compromise and signs of noncardiogenic pulmonary edema. Treatment is supportive; most pts recover without sequelae.

6. *Graft-versus-host disease* (GVH): Rare complication of transfusion mediated by donor T lymphocytes that recognize host HLA antigens as foreign and mount an immune response. Can occur when blood components that contain viable T lymphocytes are transfused into immunodeficient recipients or into immunocompetent recipients who share HLA antigens with the donor. Clinically, characterized by pancytopenia, cutaneous eruption, diarrhea, and liver function abnormalities. Transfusion GVH is notoriously resistant to treatment with immunosuppressive medications and is usually fatal. Transfusion-related GVH can be prevented by irradiation of cellular components before transfusion into pts at risk.

LABORATORY INVESTIGATION OF IMMUNE-MEDIATED REACTIONS

- Careful check on identity of donor and recipient; samples of recipient blood to blood bank for analysis and further cross-matching
- Documentation of hemolysis—plasma and urine hemoglobin, haptoglobin, hematocrit, bilirubin
- Check renal status—urinalysis, BUN, creatinine
- Check coagulation status—platelet count, PT, PTT

℞ TREATMENT

- Avoid further transfusion unless absolutely necessary
- Management of shock and renal failure in intravascular hemolysis; osmotic diuresis and volume expansion may be indicated in certain cases; if renal failure ensues, adjust drug doses and closely monitor fluid/electrolyte status
- Factor replacement if needed to control coagulation abnormalities; platelet infusion if thrombocytopenia severe

Nonimmune Reactions

1. *Circulatory overload*: Especially in infants and pts with renal or cardiac insufficiency. Effects of massive transfusion include hyperkalemia, ammonia and citrate toxicity, dilutional coagulopathy, thrombocytopenia.

2. *Transmission of infection*: Hepatitis, syphilis, CMV, malaria, babesiosis, toxoplasmosis, brucellosis, and HIV can all be transmitted by transfused blood.

3. *Iron overload*: With repeated transfusions; may require chelation therapy.

For a more detailed discussion, see Austen KF: Allergies, Anaphylaxis, and Systemic Mastocytosis , Chap. 310, p. 1913; and Dzieczkowski JS, Anderson KC: Transfusion Biology and Therapy, Chap. 114, p. 733, in HPIM-15.

46

BITES, VENOMS, STINGS, AND MARINE POISONINGS

MAMMALIAN BITES

Between 1 and 2 million mammalian animal-bite wounds are sustained in the U.S. each year; the vast majority are inflicted by pet dogs and cats. A significant number result in infection, which may be life-threatening. The microbiology of bite-wound infections generally reflects the oropharyngeal flora of the biting animal, although organisms from the soil, the skin of the animal or victim, or the animal's feces may also be involved.

DOG BITES Dogs account for ~80% of bite wounds, and 15–20% of dog-bite wounds become infected. Infection typically manifests 8–24 h after the bite, with pain, cellulitis, and a purulent, sometimes foul-smelling discharge. Fever, lymphadenopathy, and lymphangitis may occur. If the dog's tooth penetrates synovium or bone, septic arthritis or osteomyelitis may develop. While infection usually remains localized, systemic spread (e.g., bacteremia, endocarditis, brain abscess) can take place. Dissemination is most likely in pts with poor lymphatic drainage of the affected area or with systemic immunocompromise.

The microbiology of dog-bite wound infections is usually mixed and includes staphylococci, α-hemolytic streptococci, *Pasteurella multocida*, *Eikenella corrodens*, and *Capnocytophaga canimorsus* (formerly designated DF-2). Anaerobes (*Actinomyces*, *Fusobacterium*, *Prevotella*, and *Porphyromonas* spp.) are often present as well. Infection with *C. canimorsus* can be fulminant, presenting as sepsis syndrome, DIC, and renal failure, particularly in pts who are splenectomized, have hepatic dysfunction, or are otherwise immunosuppressed. This fastidious, thin gram-negative rod is occasionally seen within PMNs on Wright-stained smears of peripheral blood from septic pts. In addition to bacterial infections, dog bites may transmit rabies (Chap. 107) and may lead to tetanus intoxication (Chap. 95).

CAT BITES More than half of cat bites and scratches result in infection due to deep tissue penetration of narrow, sharp feline incisors. Accordingly, cat bites are more likely than dog bites to cause septic arthritis or osteomyelitis, sequelae that are particularly likely following bites over joints (especially those involving the hand). The microflora of cat-bite infections is usually mixed, reflecting the feline oral flora, although *P. multocida* is the most important pathogen. Infection with *P. multocida* can cause rapidly advancing, painful inflammation that may manifest only a few hours after the bite as well as purulent or serosanguineous discharge. A mixed bacterial flora is often present, and dissemination may occur. Like dog bites, cat bites may transmit rabies or may lead to tetanus intoxication. Cat bites and scratches may also transmit *Bartonella henselae*, the agent of cat-scratch disease, as well as tularemia (Chap. 94).

OTHER ANIMAL BITES   Bite infections from other species reflect the oral flora of the biting animal. Bites from nonhuman primates contain bacteria similar to those found in human bites. Bites from Old World monkeys (*Macaca* spp.) may transmit herpes B virus (*Herpesvirus simiae*), which can cause CNS infection with high mortality.

Bites from small rodents and the animals that prey on them may transmit *rat-bite fever*, caused by *Streptobacillus moniliformis* (in the U.S.) or *Spirillum minor* (in Asia). Infection with *S. moniliformis* manifests as fever, chills, myalgias, headache, and migratory arthralgias, which are followed by a maculopapular rash 3–10 days after the bite (most often after the bite has healed). Complications can include metastatic abscesses, endocarditis, meningitis, or pneumonia. Diagnosis can be made by culture on enriched media and serologic testing. Infection with *S. minor* causes local inflammation, pain, and regional lymphadenopathy 1–4 weeks after the bite, with evolution into a systemic illness. Diagnosis can be made by detection of spirochetes on microscopic examination.

HUMAN BITES   Human bites are categorized as occlusional injuries, which are inflicted by actual biting, or clenched-fist injuries, which may result when the fist of one individual strikes the teeth of another. Human-bite wounds become infected more frequently than bite wounds from other animals. Clenched-fist injuries are particularly prone to serious infection due to spread and sequestration of oral flora along deep tissue planes as the fingers are extended after the bite. The flora of human-bite wounds is diverse, including viridans streptococci, *Staphylococcus aureus*, *E. corrodens*, and *Haemophilus influenzae*. Anaerobic species are isolated from 50% of human-bite wounds and include *Fusobacterium nucleatum* as well as *Prevotella*, *Porphyromonas*, and *Peptostreptococcus* spp.

 TREATMENT

Initial Assessment

Elicit a careful history including the type of animal responsible, whether or not the attack was provoked, and the time elapsed since the injury. Contact public health authorities if rabies is a consideration. Consider domestic abuse if confronted with suspicious human-bite wounds. Obtain details regarding possible antibiotic allergies, systemic immunosuppression, and immunization history. Assess the type of wound (e.g., puncture, laceration, crush injury, scratch); its depth; and the possibility of injury to joints, tendons, nerves, or bone. In addition to conducting a general physical examination, carefully examine the bite site for evidence of infection, including redness, exudate, foul odor, lymphangitis, or lymphadenopathy. Because of their potentially debilitating consequences, hand injuries warrant consultation with a hand surgeon. Obtain radiographs if bony injury or retained tooth fragments are suspected. Stain (Gram's) and culture drainage and/or tissue specimens from all infected wounds; include specimens for anaerobic culture. For bites of animals other than dogs or cats, staining (Gram's) and culture from an uninfected-appearing wound may be of use, since the flora causing infections of these bites is less predictable. A WBC count and blood cultures should be performed if systemic infection is suspected.

Table 46-1

Management of Wound Infections Following Animal Bites

Biting Species	Commonly Isolated Pathogens	Preferred Antibiotic(s)[a]
Dog	*Staphylococcus aureus, Streptococcus* spp., *Pasteurella* spp., anaerobes, *Capnocytophaga canimorsus*	Amoxicillin/clavulanic acid (250–500 mg PO tid); or ampicillin/sulbactam (1.5–3.0 g IV q6h)
Cat	*Pasteurella multocida, S. aureus, Streptococcus* spp., anaerobes	Amoxicillin/clavulanic acid or ampicillin/sulbactam, as for dog bite
Human; occlusional bite	Viridans streptococci, *S. aureus, Haemophilus influenzae,* anaerobes	Amoxicillin/clavulanic acid or ampicillin/sulbactam, as for dog bite
Human; clenched-fist injury	As for occlusional bite plus *Eikenella corrodens*	Ampicillin/sulbactam, as for dog bite, or imipenem
Monkey	As for human bite	As for human bite
Snake	*Pseudomonas aeruginosa, Proteus* spp., *Bacteroides fragilis, Clostridium* spp.	Ceftriaxone (1–2 g IV q12–24h); or ampicillin/ sulbactam, as for dog bite
Rodent	*Streptobacillus moniliformis, Leptospira* spp., *P. multocida*	Penicillin VK (500 mg PO bid)

[a] Antibiotic choices should be based on culture data, when available. Duration of therapy must be guided by response, but normally a minimum course of 10 to 14 days is required for established soft tissue infection. Osteomyelitis and septic arthritis require longer treatment. These suggestions for empirical therapy need to be tailored to individual circumstances and local conditions. IV regimens should be used for hospitalized pts. When the pt is to be discharged after initial management, a single IV dose of antibiotic may be given and followed by oral therapy.

Wound Management

Wound closure is controversial in bite injuries. After thorough cleansing, facial wounds are usually sutured for cosmetic reasons and because the abundant facial blood supply and absence of dependent edema lessen the risk of infection there. For wounds elsewhere, many authorities do not attempt primary closure, preferring instead to irrigate copiously, debride devitalized tissue, remove foreign bodies, and approximate the margins. Delayed primary closure may be undertaken after the risk of infection has passed. Puncture wounds due to cat bites should not be sutured because of their high risk of infection.

Antibiotic Therapy

Presumptive or Prophylactic Therapy All human and nonhuman primate bites and most cat bites (especially those on the hand) merit prophylactic

Alternative Agent(s) for Penicillin-Allergic Patients	Recommendations for Prophylaxis in Pts with Recent Uninfected Wounds[b]	Other Considerations
Clindamycin (150–300 mg PO qid) plus either TMP-SMZ (1 double-strength tablet bid) or ciprofloxacin (500 mg PO bid)	Sometimes[c]	Consider rabies prophylaxis.
Clindamycin plus either TMP-SMZ or a fluoroquinolone	Usually	Consider rabies prophylaxis; carefully evaluate for joint/bone penetration.
Erythromycin, fluoroquinolone	Always	—
Cefoxitin[d] (1.5 g IV q6h)	Always	Examine for tendon/nerve/joint involvement.
As for human bite	Always	For macaques, consider B virus prophylaxis with acyclovir.
Clindamycin plus either TMP-SMZ or a fluoroquinolone	Sometimes, especially for venomous snakebite	Use antivenin for venomous snakebite.
Doxycycline (100 mg PO qd)	Sometimes[c]	—

[b] Prophylactic antibiotics are usually given for 3 to 5 d.
[c] Prophylactic antibiotics are suggested for severe or extensive wounds, facial wounds, or crush injuries; when bone or joint may be involved; or when comorbidity exists.
[d] Cefoxitin may be hazardous to pts with immediate-type hypersensitivity to penicillin.
NOTE: TMP-SMZ, trimethoprim-sulfamethoxazole.
SOURCE: LC Madoff: HPIM-15, p. 819.

antibiotic therapy because of high infection rates (Table 46-1). Antibiotic therapy for other bite injuries <8 h old is controversial, although one meta-analysis of prophylaxis of dog-bite wounds showed a 50% reduction in the rate of infection. Factors favoring empirical therapy include the presence of severe and/or extensive wounds; bites involving joints, hands, or genitals; host immunocompromise, including that due to liver disease or splenectomy; and impaired lymphatic drainage of the bite site. When given, prophylaxis should continue for 3–5 days.

Therapy for Infected Bite Wounds Antibiotics should certainly be used for all established bite-wound infections and should target likely pathogens (Table 46-1). Initial treatment is usually continued for 10–14 days. Elevation and immobilization of the site of injury are important adjunctive measures. Therapeutic response must be carefully monitored. If treatment fails, alternative diagnoses (such as osteomyelitis or septic arthritis) should be considered, surgical evaluation performed for possible drainage or debridement, and a longer (several-week) course of antibiotic therapy planned.

C. canimorsus sepsis requires a 2-week course of IV penicillin G (2 × 10^6 U q4h); cephalosporins and quinolones are alternative agents. Serious *P. multocida* infection should also be treated with IV penicillin G; alternative agents with which there is less clinical experience include second- or third-generation cephalosporins and ciprofloxacin.

A tetanus booster immunization should be given for pts previously immunized but not boosted within 5 years. Pts not previously immunized should undergo primary immunization and should also receive tetanus immune globulin. Rabies prophylaxis includes administration of rabies immune globulin (infiltrated both around the wound site and intramuscularly) as well as rabies vaccine and should be given in consultation with local and regional public health authorities.

VENOMOUS SNAKEBITES

ETIOLOGY AND EPIDEMIOLOGY   Venomous snakebites are rare in most developed countries (Table 46-2). Worldwide, 30,000 to 40,000 people die from these injuries each year. Poisonous snakes indigenous to the U.S. include the rattlesnake, the copperhead, the coral snake, and the water moccasin. Eastern and western diamondback rattlesnakes (*Crotalus adamanteus* and *C. atrox*, respectively) are responsible for most deaths from snakebite in the U.S. Snake venoms are complex mixtures of enzymes and other substances that can

Table 46-2

Venomous Snakes of the World

Family	Subfamily	Representative Species	Remarks
Viperidae	Crotalinae	Rattlesnakes (*Crotalus* and *Sistrurus* spp.), water moccasins and copperheads (*Agkistrodon* spp.), lancehead vipers (*Bothrops* spp.)	New World and Asian pit vipers
	Viperinae	Russell's viper (*Vipera russelli*), saw-scaled viper (*Echis carinatus*), puff adder (*Bitis arietans*)	European, Asian, African vipers
Elapidae		Cobras (*Naja* spp.), mambas (*Dendroaspis* spp.), taipan (*Oxyuranus scutellatus*)	Temperate and tropical New and Old World; all venomous terrestrial snakes of Australia
Hydrophiidae		Pelagic sea snake (*Pelamis platurus*)	Pacific and Indian Oceans
Atractaspididae		Burrowing asps (*Atractaspis* spp.)	Africa, Middle East
Colubridae		Boomslang (*Dispholidus typus*), twig snake (*Thelotornis kirtlandii*)	Rear-fanged snakes with toxic salivary secretions

SOURCE: RL Norris et al: HPIM-14, p. 2545.

activate the coagulation cascade or induce proteolysis or neurotoxicity. Most snake venoms have multisystem effects in their victims. The overall mortality rate for venomous snakebite is <1% among U.S. victims who receive anti-venom.

 TREATMENT

Field Management

Prehospital measures should focus on delivering the victim to definitive care as soon as possible. The victim should be as inactive as is feasible in order to minimize systemic spread of the venom. After viperid bites, local suction to remove venom may be beneficial if applied within 3–5 min and should be continued for at least 30 min. A mechanical suction device should be used; mouth-to-wound suction should be avoided. If the victim is >60 min from medical care, a proximal lymphatic-occlusive constriction band may also limit the spread of venom if applied so as not to interfere with arterial flow within 30 min after the bite. A bitten extremity should be splinted, if possible, and kept at heart level. Incisions into the bite wound, cooling, giving alcoholic beverages to the victim, and electric shock should all be *avoided*.

Hospital Management

The victim should be closely monitored (vital signs, cardiac rhythm, O_2 saturation). The level of erythema and swelling should be marked and limb circumference measured every 15 min. IV access with a large-bore catheter should be established in an unaffected extremity. Shock should be treated initially with fluid resuscitation (normal saline or Ringer's lactate, up to 20–40 mL/kg of body weight). If hypotension persists, 5% albumin (10–20 mL/kg) should be tried next, followed by a dopamine infusion. Central hemodynamic monitoring may be helpful but must be instituted with great care if coagulopathy is present.

Blood for laboratory testing should be drawn as soon as possible, with a CBC, an assessment of renal and hepatic function, coagulation studies, and typing and cross-matching. Urine should be tested for blood or myoglobin. In severe cases, arterial blood gas studies, ECG, and CXR should also be done.

Attempts to locate an appropriate and specific antivenom should begin early in all cases of known venomous snakebite, regardless of symptoms. In the U.S., assistance in finding antivenom can be obtained 24 h a day from the University of Arizona Poison and Drug Information Center (520-626-6016).

Rapidly progressive and severe local findings or manifestations of systemic toxicity (signs and symptoms or laboratory abnormalities) are indications for the administration of IV antivenom. Most antivenoms are of equine origin and carry risks of anaphylactic, anaphylactoid, or delayed-hypersensitivity reactions; skin testing does not reliably predict the risk of allergic reaction. To limit acute reactions, pts should be premedicated with IV antihistamines (e.g., diphenhydramine, 1 mg/kg up to a maximum dose of 100 mg; plus cimetidine, 5–10 mg/kg up to a maximum dose of 300 mg) and given IV crystalloids to expand intravascular volume. Epinephrine should be immediately available. The antivenom should be administered slowly in dilute solution. Management of life-threatening envenomation in a victim apparently allergic to antivenom requires significant expertise but is often possible with intensive premedication (e.g., epinephrine, antihistamines, and steroids) and consultation from a poison specialist, an intensive care specialist, and/or an allergist.

The bite wound should be dressed with dry sterile gauze, splinted, and elevated only when antivenom is available. Tetanus immunization should be updated. Antibiotic prophylaxis is controversial, although many authorities recommend prophylactic therapy for the first few days (Table 46-1).

Whether or not antivenom is given, pts with signs of envenomation should be observed in the hospital for at least 24 h. Pts with apparently "dry" bites should be watched for at least 6–8 h. Symptoms from elapid or sea snake bites are commonly delayed for several hours, so victims should be observed in the hospital for 24 h.

MARINE ENVENOMATIONS

INVERTEBRATES   *Hydroids, fire coral, jellyfish, Portuguese man-of-war*, and *sea anemones* possess specialized stinging cells called nematocysts. The clinical consequences of envenomation by these species are similar but differ in severity. Pain (prickling, burning, and throbbing), pruritus, and paresthesia usually develop immediately. Neurologic, cardiovascular, respiratory, rheumatologic, GI, renal, and ocular symptoms have been described.

Rx TREATMENT

The skin should be decontaminated immediately with a forceful jet of vinegar (5% acetic acid) or rubbing alcohol (40–70% isopropanol) to inactivate nematocysts. Shaving the skin may also be helpful to remove nematocysts. After decontamination, topical anesthetics, antihistamines, or steroids may be helpful. Narcotics may be necessary for persistent pain. Muscle spasms may respond to IV 10% calcium gluconate (5–10 mL) or diazepam (2–5 mg titrated upwards as necessary).

VERTEBRATES   A number of marine vertebrates, including stingrays, scorpionfish, catfish, surgeonfish (doctorfish, tang), weeverfish, and horned venomous sharks, are capable of envenomating humans. Clinical manifestations include immediate and intense pain at the envenomation site; systemic symptoms, such as weakness, diaphoresis, nausea, vomiting, diarrhea, dysrhythmia, syncope, hypotension, muscle cramps, muscle fasciculations, and paralysis; and (in rare cases) death. A *stingray* injury is both an envenomation and a traumatic wound, with intense pain at the site lasting up to 48 h as well as systemic symptoms secondary to serotonin and enzymes contained in the venom. Stings from *stonefish, scorpionfish*, and *lionfish* cause similar local reactions and systemic responses, although the sting of a stonefish is the most life-threatening.

Rx TREATMENT

The management of most marine vertebrate stings is similar. Except for stonefish and serious scorpionfish envenomations (see below), no antivenom is available. The affected part should be immersed immediately in nonscalding hot water (113°F/45°C) for 30–90 min to inactivate venoms and relieve pain. Opiates or regional nerve block (with 1% lidocaine, 0.5% bupivacaine, and sodium bicarbonate mixed 5:5:1) may also help. After soaking and analgesia, the wound should be explored, debrided, and vigorously irrigated. Radiography of the envenomated area may help to locate foreign bodies. Wounds should be left to heal by secondary intention or by delayed primary closure. Tetanus immunization should be updated. Empirical antibiotics to cover *Staphylococcus* and *Streptococcus* spp. should be considered for serious wounds or envenomations in immunocompromised hosts. If the host is compromised or if infection develops, *Vibrio* spp. should also be targeted.

Sources of Antivenoms and Other Assistance

Antivenom for stonefish and severe scorpionfish envenomation is available in the U.S. through the pharmacies of Sharp Cabrillo Hospital Emergency Department, San Diego, CA (619-221-3429), and Community Hospital of Monterey Peninsula (CHOMP) Emergency Department, Monterey, CA (408-625-4900). CHOMP also has sea snake antivenom. If sea snake antivenom is unavailable, tiger snake (*N. scutatus*) antivenom should be used. Divers Alert Network may be a source of helpful information (24 h a day at 919-684-8111 or at *http://www.dan.ycg.org*).

MARINE POISONINGS

CIGUATERA Ciguatera poisoning is the most common nonbacterial food poisoning associated with fish in the U.S. Tropical and semitropical marine coral reef fish are usually the source; 75% of cases involve barracuda, snapper, jack, or grouper. Of the toxins (at least five) that may cause the ciguatera syndrome, not all affect the appearance or taste of the fish, and all are resistant to heat, cold, freeze-drying, and gastric acid. All oversized fish of any predacious reef species, moray eels, and the viscera of tropical marine fish should be suspected of harboring ciguatoxin and should not be eaten.

Most victims experience diarrhea, vomiting, and abdominal pain 3–6 h after ingestion of contaminated fish and develop systemic symptoms within 12 h. Symptoms are myriad and include paresthesia, pruritus, dysphagia, weakness, fasciculations, ataxia, blurred vision, seizures, maculopapular or vesicular rash, diaphoresis, and hemodynamic instability. A pathognomonic symptom—reversal of hot and cold perception—develops within 3–5 days and can last for months. Death is rare. Ciguatera poisoning is diagnosed on clinical grounds.

 TREATMENT

Therapy is supportive and based on symptoms. Symptoms are more severe in persons who have previously had ciguatera poisoning. Gastric lavage, ipecac-induced emesis, and PO administration of activated charcoal (100 g) in sorbitol are not of proven efficacy but may be considered if undertaken within 3 h of ingestion. Prochlorperazine (2.5–5 mg IV) can be given for control of emesis. Crystalloid or pressors are given for hypotension as indicated. IV atropine (0.5 mg, up to 2 mg) is given for clinically significant bradycardia. Cool showers, hydroxyzine (25 mg PO q6–8h), or amitriptyline (25 mg PO bid) may ameliorate pruritus, and amitriptyline or tocainide may relieve dysesthesias. IV-administered mannitol (1 g/kg per day over 45–60 min, days 1–5) may alleviate neurologic or cardiovascular symptoms via reversal of Schwann cell edema and may act as a "hydroxyl scavenger." During recovery, the pt should avoid ingestion of fish, shellfish, fish oils, fish or shellfish sauces, alcohol, nuts, and nut oils.

PARALYTIC SHELLFISH POISONING (PSP) PSP is induced by ingestion of contaminated feral or aquacultured filter-feeding organisms, including clams, oysters, scallops, mussels, chitons, limpets, starfish, and sand crabs. These species concentrate chemical toxins via feeding on planktonic dinoflagellates and protozoan organisms that "bloom" in nutrient-rich coastal temperate and semitropical waters. These toxins are water-soluble, are heat- and acid-stable, and are not destroyed by ordinary cooking. The best-known is saxitoxin, which blocks neuromuscular transmission via inhibition of sodium conduction.

Within minutes to hours after ingestion of contaminated shellfish, the victim experiences oral paresthesia progressing to the rest of the neck and the extremities and changing to numbness. Disequilibrium, weakness, hyperreflexia, sialorrhea, diarrhea, nausea, vomiting, headache, and incoherence may develop. Flaccid paralysis and respiratory insufficiency may follow 2–12 h after ingestion.

 TREATMENT

If medical attention is sought within the first few hours after ingestion, the pt should undergo gastric lavage and irrigation with 2 L of 2% sodium bicarbonate in 200-mL aliquots. Oral administration of activated charcoal (50–100 g) in sorbitol has not proved effective. Magnesium-containing cathartics may further suppress nerve conduction and should be avoided. The pt should be monitored for respiratory paralysis for at least 24 h.

DOMOIC ACID INTOXICATION   Ingestion of mussels contaminated with domoic acid, a potent heat-stable neuroexcitatory toxin, causes arousal, confusion, disorientation, and memory loss within 24 h (median time of onset, 5.5 h). Treatment is supportive, with a focus on anticonvulsive measures.

SCOMBROID   Scombroid poisoning is a histamine intoxication due to inadequately preserved or refrigerated fish. Scombroid (mackerel-like) fish include some types of tuna, mackerel, saury, needlefish, wahoo, skipjack, and bonito; since nonscombroid fish can also be implicated, the syndrome may more appropriately be called *pseudoallergic fish poisoning*. Victims present within 15–90 min of ingestion with flushing, pruritus or urticaria, bronchospasm, GI symptoms, tachycardia, and hypotension; symptoms generally resolve within 8–12 h and may be more severe in pts concurrently taking isoniazid. Treatment consists of antihistamine (H_1 or H_2) administration. Bronchodilators may be indicated for bronchospasm. Steroids are of no proven benefit.

PFIESTERIA   *Pfiesteria*, a dinoflagellate with a complex life cycle, releases a neurotoxin that causes fish to die within minutes and a fat-soluble toxin that causes epidermal delamination in fish. Casual exposure to waters infested with *Pfiesteria* can cause a syndrome defined by the CDC as either of two groups of signs or symptoms: (1) memory loss, confusion, or acute skin burning on contact with infested water; or (2) at least three of the following: headache, rash, eye irritation, upper respiratory irritation, muscle cramps, and GI symptoms. Polluted environments favor growth of *Pfiesteria*. Treatment consists of 1 teaspoon of milk of magnesia followed by 1 scoop of cholestyramine in 8 oz of water and 70% sorbitol solution, administered daily for 2 weeks.

ARTHROPOD BITES AND STINGS

SPIDER BITES   Only a small minority of all spider species defend themselves aggressively and have fangs capable of penetrating human skin. While most spider bites are painful but not otherwise harmful, envenomation by the brown or fiddle spiders (*Loxosceles* spp.), the widow spiders (*Latrodectus* spp.), and certain other spiders may be life-threatening. Identification of the offending spider should be attempted; specific treatments exist for bites of widow and brown recluse spiders.

Recluse Spider Bites and Necrotic Arachnidism   Severe necrosis of skin and subcutaneous tissue follows envenomation by *Loxosceles reclusa* (the brown recluse spider). Initially the bite is painless or stings. Over the next few hours, the site becomes painful, pruritic, indurated, and surrounded by zones of ischemia and erythema. Fever, chills, headache, and other nonspecific systemic symptoms may develop within 3 days of the bite. Lesions typically resolve without treatment in 2–3 days. In severe cases, erythema spreads; the lesion becomes hemorrhagic and necrotic, with an overlying bulla; and a black eschar develops, sloughs, and leaves a depressed scar. Deaths, although rare, are due to severe hemolysis and renal failure.

 TREATMENT

Initial management includes local cleansing, application of sterile dressings and cold compresses, elevation, and loose immobilization. Analgesics, antihistamines, antibiotics, and tetanus prophylaxis should be administered if indicated. Dapsone administration within 48–72 h (50–100 mg PO bid after G6PD deficiency has been ruled out) may halt progression of necrotic lesions. Local or systemic steroids have not proven efficacious. Immediate surgical excision of the wound is detrimental. Antivenom has not been approved for use in the U.S.

Widow Spider Bites Female widow spiders are notorious for their potent neurotoxin. The black widow (*Latrodectus mactans*) has been found in every U.S. state except Alaska. The initial bite goes unnoticed or is perceived as a sharp pinprick. Two small red marks, mild erythema, and edema develop at the fang entrance site. Some persons experience no other symptoms. In others, painful cramps spread from the bite site to large muscles of the extremities and trunk within 30–60 min. Extreme abdominal muscular rigidity and pain may mimic peritonitis, but the abdomen is not tender to palpation. Other features include salivation, diaphoresis, vomiting, hypertension, tachycardia, labored breathing, anxiety, headache, weakness, fasciculations, rhabdomyolysis, paresthesia, hyperreflexia, urinary retention, uterine contractions, and premature labor. Death from respiratory arrest, cerebral hemorrhage, or cardiac failure may occur.

 TREATMENT

Treatment consists of local cleansing, application of ice packs, and tetanus prophylaxis. Analgesics and antispasmodics (e.g., benzodiazepines and methocarbamol) may mitigate hypertension. If not, specific antihypertensives should be given. Equine antivenom is widely available; rapid IV administration of 1 or 2 vials relieves pain and can be life-saving. Given the risk of allergic reactions, however, the use of antivenom should be reserved for severe cases involving respiratory arrest, refractory hypertension, seizures, or pregnancy.

SCORPION STINGS Scorpions are crablike arachnids that can inject venom from a stinger on the tip of the tail; they sting human beings only when disturbed. Painful but relatively harmless scorpion stings must be distinguished from the potentially lethal envenomations produced by ~30 of the ~1000 known scorpion species, which annually cause >5000 deaths worldwide. In the U.S., only the bark scorpion (*Centruroides sculpturatus* or *C. exilicauda*) is potentially lethal. *C. sculpturatus* is yellow-brown and ~7 cm long. Envenomations are usually associated with little swelling, but pain, paresthesia, and hyperesthesia can be accentuated by tapping on the affected area. Dysfunction of cranial nerves and hyperexcitability of skeletal muscle develop within hours. Pts present with restlessness, blurred vision, abnormal eye movements, profuse salivation, lacrimation, rhinorrhea, slurred speech, diaphoresis, nausea, vomiting, and difficulty handling secretions. Complications include tachycardia, arrhythmias, hypertension, hyperthermia, rhabdomyolysis, and acidosis. Manifestations are maximal after ~5 h and may subside within a day or two.

 TREATMENT

Stings of nonlethal species require ice packs, analgesics, or antihistamines. Pressure dressings and cold packs can decrease the absorption of venom. For victims of envenomations who have cranial nerve or neuromuscular dysfunction, aggressive supportive care and judicious use of antivenom can reduce or eliminate mortality. Continuous IV midazolam infusion can decrease agitation and involuntary muscle movements; however, narcotics and sedatives should be avoided in the setting of neuromuscular dysfunction unless endotracheal intubation is planned. Hypertension, pulmonary edema, and bradyarrhythmias should be anticipated. An investigational caprine *C. sculpturatus* antivenom (available only in Arizona) carries a risk of anaphylaxis or serum sickness. The benefit of scorpion antivenom has not been established in controlled trials.

HYMENOPTERA AND FIRE ANT STINGS   *Hymenoptera Stings*
Stinging insects of the order Hymenoptera include apids (bees and bumblebees), vespids (wasps, hornets, and yellow jackets), and ants. About 50 deaths from hymenoptera stings occur annually in the U.S., nearly all from allergic reactions to venoms.

Bees can sting only once; vespids can sting many times in succession. The familiar honeybees (*Apis mellifera*) and bumblebees (*Bombus* and other genera) sting only when a colony is disturbed. The Africanized honeybees ("killer bees"), which have spread through South and Central America and the southeastern and western U.S., are extremely aggressive and respond to minimal intrusions in great numbers. Uncomplicated stings cause immediate pain, a wheal-and-flare reaction, and local edema that subside within hours. Multiple stings can lead to vomiting, diarrhea, generalized edema, dyspnea, hypotension, rhabdomyolysis, and renal failure. Victims have died after being stung by honeybees 300–500 times in succession.

Large (>10-cm) local reactions progressing over 1–2 days and resembling cellulitis are not uncommon and are caused by hypersensitivity. They are seldom accompanied by anaphylaxis. About 0.4–4% of the U.S. population exhibits immediate-type hypersensitivity to insect stings. Mild reactions manifest as nausea, abdominal cramps, urticaria, flushing, and angioedema. Serious reactions include upper airway edema, bronchospasm, hypotension, and shock and may be rapidly fatal. Onset usually comes within 10 min of the sting.

 TREATMENT

Stingers embedded in the skin should be scraped or brushed off but not removed with a forceps, which may squeeze more venom out. The site should be cleansed and ice packs applied to slow venom absorption. Elevation of the bite site and administration of analgesics, oral antihistamines, and topical calamine lotion may ease symptoms. Oral steroids are indicated for large local reactions. Pts with multiple stings should be monitored for 24 h. Anaphylaxis is treated with epinephrine hydrochloride (0.3–0.5 mL of a 1:1000 solution SC q20–30min as needed). For profound shock, epinephrine (2–5 mL of a 1:10,000 solution by slow IV push) is indicated. Parenteral antihistamines, fluid resuscitation, bronchodilators, oxygen, endotracheal intubation, and vasopressors may be required. Pts should be observed for 24 h until the risk of recurrence has passed. Pts with a history of allergy to insect stings should carry a sting kit and seek medical attention immediately after the kit is used. Those with a history of anaphylaxis should undergo desensitization.

Fire Ant Stings Stinging fire ants are an important medical problem in the southern U.S. Slight disturbances can provoke massive outpourings of ants from their tall mounds, resulting in as many as 10,000 stings. The initial wheal, burning, and itching resolve in ~30 min. A sterile pustule develops within a day, ulcerates over the next 2 days, and heals in 7–10 days. Stings are treated with ice packs, topical steroids, and oral antihistamines. Anaphylaxis occurs in 1–2% of cases and is managed with epinephrine and supportive measures. Immunotherapy appears to lower the rate of anaphylactic reactions.

TICK BITES AND TICK PARALYSIS

Hard ticks (Ixodidae) have become the most common carriers of vector-borne diseases in the U.S., and soft ticks are vectors of relapsing fever (Table 46-3). Ticks attach and feed painlessly on blood from their hosts; however, their secretions may produce local reactions.

Tick paralysis is an ascending flaccid paralysis that begins 5–6 days after the tick's attachment in the lower extremities and ascends symmetrically. Deep tendon reflexes are decreased or absent, but sensory examination is normal. LP is normal. Removal of the tick results in improvement within hours. Failure to remove the tick may lead to dysarthria, dysphagia, and ultimately respiratory paralysis and death. The tick is usually found on the scalp.

 TREATMENT

Ticks should be removed with a forceps close to the point of attachment and the skin disinfected. Retained mouth parts may cause ongoing inflammation or lead to secondary infection. Removal within 48 h of attachment usually prevents transmission of Lyme disease, babesiosis, and ehrlichiosis. Protective clothing and DEET application are protective measures against ticks.

Table 46-3

Diseases Transmitted by Ticks

Vector	Disease
Hard ticks	
Ixodes spp. (deer tick)	Lyme disease
	Babesiosis
	Human granulocytotropic ehrlichiosis
Dermacentor variabilis (dog tick)	Tularemia
D. andersoni (wood tick)	Rocky Mountain spotted fever
Amblyomma americanum (Lone Star tick)	Colorado tick fever
	Human monocytotropic ehrlichiosis
Soft ticks	
Ornithodoros spp.	Tick-borne relapsing fever

For a more detailed discussion, see Madoff LC: Infectious Complications of Bites and Burns, Chap. 127, p. 817; Norris RL, Auerbach PS: Disorders Caused by Reptile Bites and Marine Animal Exposures, Chap. 397, p. 2616; and Maguire JH, Spielman A: Ectoparasite Infestations, Arthropod Bites and Stings, Chap. 398, p. 2622, in HPIM-15.

47

HYPOTHERMIA AND FROSTBITE

HYPOTHERMIA

Hypothermia is defined as a core body temperature of ≤35°C, and is classified as mild (32–35°C), moderate (28–32°C), or severe (<28°C).

ETIOLOGY Most cases occur during the winter in cold climates, but hypothermia may occur in mild climates at any season and is usually multifactorial. Heat is generated in most tissues of the body and is lost by radiation, evaporation, respiration, conduction, and convection. Factors that impede heat generation and/or increase heat loss lead to hypothermia (Table 47-1).

CLINICAL FEATURES Acute cold exposure causes tachycardia, increased cardiac output, peripheral vasoconstriction, and increased peripheral vascular resistance. As body temperature drops below 32°C, cardiac conduction becomes impaired, the heart rate slows, and cardiac output decreases. Atrial fibrillation with slow ventricular response is common. Other ECG changes in-

Table 47-1

Risks Factors for Hypothermia

Age extremes	Endocrine-related
Elderly	Hypoglycemia
Neonates	Hypothyroidism
Outdoor exposure	Adrenal insufficiency
Occupational	Hypopituitarism
Sports-related	Neurologic-related
Inadequate clothing	Stroke
Drugs and intoxicants	Hypothalamic disorders
Ethanol	Parkinson's disease
Phenothiazines	Spinal cord injury
Barbiturates	Multisystem
Anesthetics	Malnutrition
Neuromuscular blockers	Sepsis
Others	Shock
	Hepatic or renal failure
	Burns and exfoliative dermato-
	logic disorders
	Immobility or debilitation

clude Osborn (J) waves. Additional manifestations of hypothermia include volume depletion, hypotension, increased blood viscosity (which can lead to thrombosis), coagulopathy, thrombocytopenia, DIC, acid-base disturbances, and bronchospasm. CNS abnormalities are diverse and can include ataxia, amnesia, hallucinations, delayed deep tendon reflexes, and (in severe hypothermia) an isoelectric EEG.

DIAGNOSIS Hypothermia is confirmed by measuring the core body temperature, preferably at two sites. Since oral thermometers are usually calibrated only as low as 34.4°C, the exact temperature of a patient whose initial reading is <35°C should be determined with a thermometer reading down to 15°C or, ideally, with a rectal thermocouple probe inserted to ≥15 cm.

 TREATMENT

Cardiac monitoring should be instituted, along with attempts to limit further heat loss. Mild hypothermia is managed by passive external rewarming and insulation. The pt should be placed in a warm environment and covered with blankets to allow endogenous heat production to restore normal body temperature. Moderate to severe hypothermia requires active rewarming, which may be external (by application of heat sources such as heating blankets or immersion in warm water at 44–45°C) or internal (by inspiration of heated, humidified oxygen; by administration of IV fluids warmed to 40–42°C; or by peritoneal or pleural lavage with dialysate or saline warmed to 40–45°C). The most efficient active internal rewarming techniques are extracorporeal rewarming by hemodialysis and cardiopulmonary bypass. External rewarming may cause a fall in blood pressure by relieving peripheral vasoconstriction. Volume should be repleted with warmed isotonic solutions; lactated Ringer's solution should be avoided because of impaired lactate metabolism in hypothermia. If sepsis is a possibility, empirical broad-spectrum antibiotics should be administered after sending blood cultures. Atrial arrhythmias usually require no specific treatment. Ventricular fibrillation is often refractory, and bretylium tosylate (10 mg/kg) is the drug of choice for its treatment. Only a single sequence of 3 defibrillation attempts (2 J/kg) should be attempted when the temperature is <30°C. Since it is sometimes difficult to distinguish profound hypothermia from death, cardiopulmonary resuscitation efforts and active internal rewarming should continue until the core temperature is >32°C or cardiovascular status has been stabilized.

FROSTBITE

Frostbite occurs when the tissue temperature drops below 0°C. Clinically, it is most practical to classify frostbite as superficial (without tissue loss) or deep (with tissue loss). Classically, frostbite is retrospectively graded like a burn (first- to fourth-degree) once the resultant pathology is demarcated over time.

CLINICAL FEATURES The initial presentation of frostbite can be deceptively benign. The symptoms always include a sensory deficit affecting light touch, pain, and temperature perception. Deep frostbitten tissue can appear waxy, mottled, yellow, or violaceous-white. Favorable presenting signs include some warmth or sensation with normal color.

 TREATMENT

A treatment protocol for frostbite is summarized in Table 47-2. Frozen tissue should be rapidly and completely thawed by immersion in circulating water at 37–40°C. Thawing should not be terminated prematurely due to pain from

Table 47-2

Treatment for Frostbite

Before Thawing	During Thawing	After Thawing
Remove from environment	Consider parenteral analgesia and ketorolac	Gently dry and protect part; elevate; pledgets between toes, if macerated
Prevent partial thawing and refreezing	Administer ibuprofen, 400 mg PO	If clear vesicles are intact, the fluid will reabsorb in days; if broken, debride and dress with antibiotic or sterile aloe vera ointment
Stabilize core temperature and treat hypothermia	Immerse part in 37°–40°C (thermometer-monitored) circulating water containing an antiseptic soap until distal flush (10–45 min)	Leave hemorrhagic vesicles intact to prevent infection
Protect frozen part—no friction or massage	Encourage patient to gently move part	Continue ibuprofen 400 mg PO (12 mg/kg per day) q8-12h
Address medical or surgical conditions	If pain is refractory, reduce water temperature to 33°–37°C	Consider tetanus and streptococcal prophylaxis; elevate part Hydrotherapy at 37°C

reperfusion; ibuprofen 400 mg [12 (mg/kg)/day] q8–12h should be given, and parenteral narcotics are often required. If cyanosis persists after rewarming, the tissue compartment pressures should be monitored carefully.

For a more detailed discussion, see Danzl DF: Hypothermia and Frostbite, Chap. 20, p. 107, in HPIM-15.

48

COMMON DISORDERS OF THE EYE

Clinical Assessment

The history and examination permit accurate diagnosis of most eye disorders, without resort to laboratory or imaging studies. The essential ocular exam includes assessment of the visual acuity, pupil reactions, eye movements, eye alignment, visual fields, and intraocular pressure. The lids, conjunctiva, cornea, anterior chamber, iris, and lens are examined with a slit lamp. The fundus is viewed with an ophthalmoscope.

Acute visual loss or double vision in a pt with quiet, uninflamed eyes often signifies a serious ocular or neurologic disorder and should be managed emergently (Chap. 10). Ironically, the occurrence of a red eye, even if painful, has less dire implications as long as the visual acuity is spared.

Specific Disorders

RED OR PAINFUL EYE The most common causes of a red or painful eye are listed in Table 48-1. Minor *trauma* may result in corneal abrasion, subconjunctival hemorrhage, or foreign body. The integrity of the corneal epithelium is assessed by placing a drop of fluorescein in the eye and looking with a slit lamp or a blue penlight. The conjunctival fornices should be searched carefully for foreign bodies. Topical anesthesia with a drop of 0.5% proparacaine may be necessary to perform an adequate examination.

 TREATMENT

> Chemical splashes and foreign bodies are treated by copious saline irrigation. Corneal abrasions may require application of a topical antibiotic, a mydriatic agent (1% cyclopentolate), and an eye patch for 24 h.

Table 48-1

Causes of a Red or Painful Eye

Blunt or penetrating trauma	Dacrocystitis
Chemical exposure	Episcleritis
Corneal abrasion	Scleritis
Foreign body	Anterior uveitis (iritis or
Contact lens (overuse or infection)	iridocyclitis)
Corneal exposure (5th, 7th nerve palsy,	Endophthalmitis
ectropion)	Acute angle-closure glaucoma
Subconjunctival hemorrhage	Medicamentosus
Blepharitis	Pinguecula
Conjunctivitis (infectious or allergic)	Pterygium
Corneal ulcer	Proptosis (retrobulbar mass, orbital
Herpes keratitis	cellulitis, Graves' ophthalmopa-
Herpes zoster ophthalmicus	thy, orbital pseudotumor, carotid-
Keratoconjunctivitis sicca (dry eye)	cavernous fistula)

Infection of the eyelids and conjunctiva (blepharoconjunctivitis) produces redness and irritation but should not cause visual loss or pain. Adenovirus is the most common cause of "pink eye." It produces a thin, watery discharge, whereas bacterial infection causes a more mucopurulent exudate. On slit-lamp exam one should confirm that the cornea is not affected, by observing that it remains clear and lustrous. Corneal infection (keratitis) is a more serious condition than blepharoconjunctivitis because it can cause scarring and permanent visual loss. A localized abscess or ulcer within the cornea produces visual loss, pain, anterior chamber inflammation, and hypopyon. A dendritic pattern of corneal fluorescein staining is characteristic of herpes keratitis.

 TREATMENT

Strict handwashing and broad-spectrum topical antibiotics for blepharoconjunctivitis (sulfacetamide 10%, polymixin-bacitracin-neomycin, or trimethoprim-polymixin). Trifluridine 1% 1 drop q2h, for herpetic keratitis.

Inflammation of the eye, without infection, can produce episcleritis, scleritis, or uveitis (iritis or iridocyclitis). Most cases are idiopathic, but some occur in conjunction with autoimmune disease. There is no discharge. A ciliary flush results from injection of deep conjunctival and episcleral vessels near the corneal limbus. The diagnosis of iritis hinges on the slit-lamp observation of inflammatory cells floating in the aqueous of the anterior chamber (cell and flare) or deposited on the corneal endothelium (keratic precipitates).

 TREATMENT

Mydriatic agents (1% cyclopentolate), NSAIDs, and topical steroids (note: prolonged treatment with ocular steroids causes cataract and glaucoma).

Acute angle-closure glaucoma is a rare but important cause of a red, painful eye. Because the anterior chamber is shallow, aqueous outflow via the canal of Schlemm becomes blocked by the peripheral iris. Intraocular pressure rises abruptly, causing ocular pain, injection, headache, nausea, and blurred vision. The key diagnostic step is measurement of the intraocular pressure during an attack.

 TREATMENT

The acute attack is broken by constricting the pupil with a drop of 4% pilocarpine and by lowering the intraocular pressure with topical 0.5% apraclonidine, 0.5% timolol, and a single oral dose of acetazolamide, 500 mg. Future attacks are prevented by performing an iridotomy with a laser.

CHRONIC VISUAL LOSS   The major causes of chronic visual loss are listed in Table 48-2. A *cataract* is a cloudy lens, due principally to aging. It is treated by surgical extraction and replacement with an artificial intraocular lens.

Glaucoma is an optic neuropathy that leads to progressive visual loss from death of retinal ganglion cells. It is associated with elevated intraocular pressure, but many pts have normal pressure. Angle closure accounts for only a few cases; most pts have open angles and no identifiable cause for their pressure elevation. The diagnosis is made by documenting arcuate (nerve fiber bundle) scotomas on visual field exam and by observing "cupping" of the optic disc.

Table 48-2

Causes of Chronic, Progressive Visual Loss

Cataract	Intraocular tumor
Glaucoma	Retinitis pigmentosa
Macular degeneration	Epiretinal membrane
Diabetic retinopathy	Macular hole
Optic nerve or optic chiasm tumor	

 TREATMENT

Topical adrenergic agonists (epinephrine, dipivefrin, apraclonidine, brimonidine), cholinergic agents (pilocarpine), beta blockers (betaxolol, carteolol, levobunolol, metipranolol, timolol), and prostaglandin analogues (latanaprost); oral carbonic anhydrase inhibitors (acetazolamide). Surgical filter to reduce pressure (trabeculectomy).

Macular degeneration occurs in both a "dry" and "wet" form. In the dry form, clumps of extracellular debris, called *drusen*, are deposited beneath the retinal pigment epithelium. As they accumulate, vision is slowly lost. In the wet form, neovascular vessels proliferate beneath the retinal pigment epithelium. Bleeding from these neovascular vessels can cause sudden, central visual loss in the elderly. Macular exam shows drusen and subretinal hemorrhage.

 TREATMENT

There is no treatment for dry macular degeneration. Wet macular degeneration can be treated with laser photocoagulation of the leaking vessels.

Diabetic retinopathy appears in most pts 10–15 years after onset of the disease. Background diabetic retinopathy consists of intraretinal hemorrhage, exudates, nerve fiber layer infarcts (cotton wool spots), and macular edema. Proliferative diabetic retinopathy is characterized by ingrowth of neovascular vessels on the retinal surface, causing blindness from vitreous hemorrhage and retinal detachment.

 TREATMENT

All diabetics should be examined regularly by an ophthalmologist for surveillance of diabetic retinopathy. Macular edema is treated by focal or grid laser application. Neovascularization is treated by panretinal laser photocoagulation.

Tumors of the optic nerve or chiasm are comparatively rare but often escape detection because they produce insidious visual loss and few physical findings, except for optic disc pallor. Pituitary tumor is the most common lesion. It causes bitemporal or monocular visual loss.

 TREATMENT

Large pituitary tumors producing chiasm compression are removed transphenoidally. In some cases, small tumors can be observed or controlled pharmacologically (e.g., bromocriptine for prolactinoma).

For a more detailed discussion, see Horton JC: Disorders of the Eye, Chap. 28, p 164, in HPIM-15.

49

HEARING DISORDERS

Hearing loss is one of the most common sensory disorders in humans. Nearly 10% of the adult population has some hearing loss, and up to 35% of individuals over the age of 65 have a hearing loss of sufficient magnitude to require a hearing aid.

Causes of Hearing Loss

Hearing loss can result from disorders of the auricle, external auditory canal, middle ear, inner ear, or central auditory pathways. *In general, lesions in the auricle, external auditory canal or middle ear cause conductive hearing losses, while lesions in the inner ear or eighth nerve cause sensorineural hearing losses.*

CONDUCTIVE HEARING LOSS May result from obstruction of the external auditory canal by cerumen, debris, and foreign bodies; swelling of the lining of the canal; atresia of the ear canal; neoplasms of the canal; perforations of the tympanic membrane; disruption of the ossicular chain, as occurs with necrosis of the long process of the incus in trauma or infection; otosclerosis; and fluid, scarring, or neoplasms in the middle ear.

Cholesteatoma, i.e., stratified squamous epithelium in the middle ear or mastoid, is a benign, slowly growing lesion that destroys bone and normal ear tissue. A chronically draining ear that fails to respond to appropriate antibiotic therapy should raise the suspicion of a cholesteatoma; surgery is required.

Conductive hearing loss with a normal ear canal and intact tympanic membrane suggests ossicular pathology. Fixation of the stapes from *otosclerosis* is a common cause of low-frequency conductive hearing loss; onset is between the late teens to the forties. In women, the hearing loss is often first noticeable during pregnancy. A hearing aid or a surgical stapedectomy can provide auditory rehabilitation.

Eustachian tube dysfunction is common in adults and may predispose to acute otitis media (AOM) or serous otitis media (SOM). Trauma, AOM, or chronic otitis media are the usual factors responsible for tympanic membrane perforation. While small perforations often heal spontaneously, larger defects usually require surgical tympanoplasty (>90% effective). Otoscopy is usually sufficient to diagnose AOM, SOM, chronic otitis media, cerumen impaction, tympanic membrane perforation, and eustachian tube dysfunction.

SENSORINEURAL HEARING LOSS Damage to the hair cells of the organ of Corti may be caused by intense noise, viral infections, ototoxic drugs (e.g., salicylates, quinine and its analogues, aminoglycoside antibiotics, diuretics such as furosemide and ethacrynic acid, and cancer chemotherapeutic agents such as cisplatin), fractures of the temporal bone, meningitis, cochlear otosclerosis (see above), Ménière's disease, and aging. Congenital malformations of the inner ear may cause hearing loss in some adults. Genetic predisposition alone or in concert with environmental influences may also be responsible.

Presbycusis (age-associated hearing loss) is the most common cause of sensorineural hearing loss in adults. In early stages, it is characterized by symmetric high frequency hearing loss; with progression, the hearing loss involves all frequencies. The hearing impairment is associated with significant loss in clarity. Hearing aids provide limited rehabilitation; cochlear implants are the treatment of choice for severe cases.

Ménière's disease is characterized by episodic vertigo, fluctuating sensorineural hearing loss, tinnitus, and aural fullness. It is caused by an increase in endolymphatic fluid pressure due to endolymphatic sac dysfunction. Low-frequency, unilateral sensorineural hearing impairment is usually present. MRI should be obtained to exclude retrocochlear pathology such as cerebellopontine angle tumors or demyelinating disorders. Therapy is directed toward the control of vertigo; a low-salt diet, diuretics, a short course of glucocorticoids, and intratympanic gentamicin may be useful. For unresponsive cases, labyrinthectomy and vestibular nerve section abolish rotatory vertigo. There is no effective therapy for hearing loss, tinnitus, or aural fullness.

Sensorineural hearing loss may also result from any neoplastic, vascular, demyelinating, infectious (including HIV), or degenerative disease or trauma affecting the central auditory pathways.

TINNITUS   Defined as the perception of a sound when there is no sound in the environment. It may have a buzzing, roaring, or ringing quality and may be pulsatile (synchronous with the heartbeat). Tinnitus is often associated with either a conductive or sensorineural hearing loss and may be the first symptom of a serious condition such as a vestibular schwannoma. Pulsatile tinnitus requires evaluation of the vascular system of the head to exclude vascular tumors such as glomus jugulare tumors, aneurysms, and stenotic arterial lesions; it may also occur with SOM.

———————————— *Approach to the Patient* ————————————

(See Figure 49-1) The history should define the duration of deafness, nature of onset (sudden vs. insidious), rate of progression (rapid vs. slow), and involvement of the ear (unilateral vs. bilateral). The presence or absence of tinnitus, vertigo, imbalance, aural fullness, otorrhea, headache, facial nerve dysfunction, and head and neck paresthesias should be ascertained. Information regarding head trauma, exposure to ototoxins, occupational or recreational noise exposure, and family history of hearing impairment may also be important. Sudden unilateral hearing loss may represent a viral infection of the inner ear or a vascular accident. Pts with unilateral hearing loss (sensory or conductive) usually complain of reduced hearing, poor sound localization, and difficulty hearing clearly with background noise. Gradual progression is common with otosclerosis, noise-induced hearing loss, vestibular schwannoma, or Ménière's disease. Small vestibular schwannomas typically present with asymmetric hearing impairment, tinnitus, imbalance (rarely vertigo); cranial neuropathy (trigeminal or facial nerve) may accompany larger tumors. Hearing loss with otorrhea is most likely due to chronic otitis media or cholesteatoma.

The exam should include the auricle, external ear canal, and tympanic membrane. The external ear canal of the elderly is often dry and fragile; it is preferable to clean cerumen with wall-mounted suction and cerumen loops and to

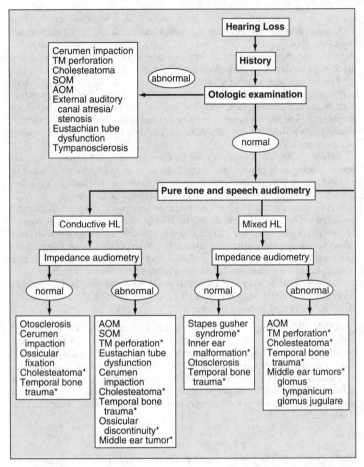

FIGURE 49-1 An algorithm for the approach to hearing loss. HL, hearing loss; SNHL, sensorineural hearing loss; TM, tympanic membrane; SOM, serous otitis media; AOM, acute otitis media; *, CT scan of temporal bone; †, MRI scan.

avoid irrigation. Careful inspection of the nose, nasopharynx, cranial nerves, and upper respiratory tract is indicated. Unilateral serous effusion in the adult should prompt a fiberoptic exam of the nasopharynx to exclude neoplasms.

The Weber and Rinne tuning fork tests help to differentiate conductive from sensorineural hearing losses. The *Rinne test* compares hearing by air and bone conduction. The tines of a vibrating tuning fork are held near the opening of the external auditory canal, and then the stem is placed on the mastoid process. Normally, and with sensorineural hearing loss, a tone is heard louder by air conduction than bone conduction; however, with conductive hearing losses the bone-conduction stimulus is perceived as louder. The *Weber test* uses the stem of a vibrating tuning fork placed on the head in the midline. With a unilateral conductive hearing loss, the tone is perceived in the affected ear; with a unilateral sensorineural hearing loss, the tone is perceived in the unaffected ear.

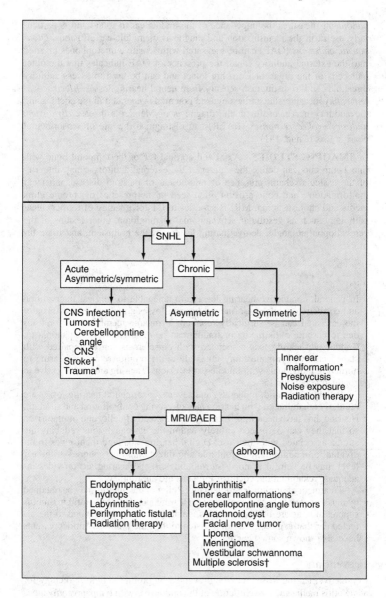

Laboratory Assessment of Hearing

AUDIOLOGIC ASSESSMENT   *Pure tone audiometry* assesses hearing acuity for pure tones. Responses are measured in decibels. Pure tone audiometry establishes the presence and severity of hearing impairment, unilateral vs. bilateral involvement, and the type of hearing loss. Speech recognition requires greater synchronous neural firing than is necessary for appreciation of pure tones; the clarity with which one hears is tested in *speech audiometry*. *Tym-*

panometry measures the impedance of the middle ear to sound and is particularly useful in the identification and diagnosis of middle-ear effusions. *Otoacoustic emissions* (OAE) can be measured with sensitive microphones inserted into the external auditory canal; the presence of OAE indicates that the outer hair cells of the organ of Corti are intact and can be used to assess auditory thresholds and to distinguish sensory from neural hearing losses. *Electrocochleography* measures the earliest evoked potentials generated in the cochlea and the auditory nerve; useful in the diagnosis of Ménière's disease. *Brainstem auditory evoked responses* (BAER) can distinguish the site of sensorineural hearing loss (Chap. 181).

IMAGING STUDIES Axial and coronal CT of the temporal bone with fine 1-mm cuts can define the caliber of the external auditory canal, integrity of the ossicular chain, presence of middle ear or mastoid disease, inner ear malformations, and bone erosion often seen in the presence of chronic otitis media and cholesteatoma. MRI is superior to CT for imaging of retrocochlear pathology such as vestibular schwannoma, meningioma, other lesions of the cerebellopontine angle, demyelinating lesions of the brainstem, and brain tumors.

 TREATMENT

In general, conductive hearing losses are amenable to surgical intervention and correction, while sensorineural hearing losses are permanent. Atresia of the ear canal can be surgically repaired. Tympanic membrane perforations due to chronic otitis media or trauma can be repaired with tympanoplasty. Conductive hearing loss associated with otosclerosis can be repaired with stapedectomy. Tympanostomy tubes allow the prompt return of hearing to normal in individuals with middle-ear effusions. Hearing aids are effective in conductive hearing losses.

Patients with mild, moderate, and severe sensorineural hearing losses are regularly rehabilitated with hearing aids of varying configuration and strength. Hearing aids have been improved to provide greater fidelity and miniaturized so that they can be placed entirely within the ear canal, thus reducing the stigma associated with their use. Digital hearing aids lend themselves to individual programming, and multiple and directional microphones at the ear level may be helpful in noisy surroundings. If the hearing aid provides inadequate rehabilitation, cochlear implants are appropriate.

Treatment of tinnitus is problematic. Relief of the tinnitus may be obtained by masking it with background music. Hearing aids are also helpful in tinnitus suppression, as are tinnitus maskers, devices that present a sound to the affected ear that is more pleasant to listen to than the tinnitus. Antidepressants have also shown some benefit.

Prevention

Conductive hearing losses may be prevented by prompt antibiotic therapy for acute otitis media and by ventilation of the middle ear with tympanostomy tubes in middle-ear effusions lasting ≥ 12 weeks. Loss of vestibular function and deafness due to aminoglycoside antibiotics can largely be prevented by careful monitoring of serum peak and trough levels. Ten million Americans have noise-induced hearing loss, and 20 million are exposed to hazardous noise in their employment. Noise-induced hearing loss can be prevented by avoidance of exposure to loud noise or by regular use of ear plugs or fluid-filled muffs to attenuate intense sound.

For a more detailed discussion, see Lalwani AK, Snow JB Jr., Disorders of Smell, Taste, and Hearing, Chap. 29, p. 178 in HPIM-15.

50

INFECTIONS OF THE UPPER RESPIRATORY TRACT

Most upper respiratory tract infections (URIs) can be treated on an outpatient basis. However, the potential complications of such infections that go untreated or are inadequately treated must be recognized.

NOSE AND FACE

Although the microbiologic etiologies of nasal mucosal infections are diverse, most acute infections at this site manifest as the *common cold* and are due to rhinovirus, coronavirus, parainfluenza virus, respiratory syncytial virus (RSV), influenza virus, or adenovirus. Treatment is symptom-based and is limited to antihistamines, decongestants, and ipratropium bromide nasal spray. Zinc gluconate lozenges may reduce the duration of symptoms.

Chronic infections of the nasal mucosa include congenital syphilis and infection with *Mycobacterium leprae*, both of which may present as chronic nasal congestion and saddle-nose deformity. *Rhinosporidium seeberi* causes obstructing nasal masses requiring surgery. *Blastomyces dermatitidis* can cause chronic ulcerations. *Mucormycosis*, a life-threatening infection in pts with neutropenia or diabetic ketoacidosis, presents as black crusts overlying necrotic tissue within the nasal cavity and may extend through to the palate or intracerebral compartment. Microbiologic diagnosis of chronic nasal infections from a tissue sample is usually indicated, and a serologic workup is done if congenital syphilis is suspected. Mucormycosis requires urgent surgical debridement, IV antifungal therapy, and correction of the underlying immunologic or metabolic predisposition.

PARANASAL SINUSES

ETIOLOGY AND PATHOGENESIS Obstruction of ostia in the anterior ethmoid and middle meatal complex by retained secretions, mucosal edema (often caused by an antecedent viral respiratory infection), or polyps promotes *sinusitis*. Barotrauma and ciliary transport defects also can predispose to infection. Nasal cannulation beyond 48 h is the chief risk factor for nosocomial sinusitis.

Acute bacterial sinusitis occurs in the setting of a viral URI. Only 0.5% of viral URIs are complicated by bacterial superinfection of the sinuses. Acute bacterial sinusitis in children and adults is caused most often by *Streptococcus pneumoniae* or *Haemophilus influenzae* (not type b); in children, *Moraxella catarrhalis* is also an important cause. *Staphylococcus aureus* and gram-negative organisms are most often involved in hospital-acquired sinusitis. Respiratory viruses are isolated alone or with bacteria in one-fifth of adult cases. In chronic sinusitis, *S. aureus* or *Pseudomonas aeruginosa* is often cultured from sinus fluid; however, it is unclear whether these organisms represent colonization or true infection. Pathogens of chronic sinusitis can also include anaerobes. Fungal sinusitis can be noninvasive due to *Aspergillus* spp. or invasive secondary to *Aspergillus* spp. or other fungi, including those causing mucormycosis.

CLINICAL MANIFESTATIONS   Sinus pain can be dental, retroorbital, supraorbital, or occipital. Facial pain or pressure, nasal congestion, and purulent nasal or postnasal drainage are frequent manifestations of acute bacterial sinusitis. Pain often worsens if the pt bends forward or lies supine. Fever is an insensitive indicator of sinusitis, although it is present in about half of pts with acute maxillary sinusitis. In acute infection, tenderness over the involved sinus may be elicited.

Chronic sinusitis features congestion and postnasal drip but rarely fever, and there is usually a paucity of physical signs. Serious complications include orbital cellulitis, frontal subperiosteal abscess (Pott's puffy tumor), and intracranial processes such as epidural abscess, subdural empyema, meningitis, cerebral abscess, and septic dural-vein (including cavernous sinus) thrombophlebitis.

DIAGNOSIS   Nasal cultures are not useful. Acute sinusitis is usually diagnosed on the basis of a history of prolonged cold symptoms. Plain radiographs of the sinuses may show opacification, air-fluid levels, or mucosal thickening of ≥4 mm, although CT is much more sensitive, especially for diagnosis of ethmoid and sphenoid disease. MRI or magnetic resonance angiography (MRA) is usually indicated in the evaluation of intracranial or vascular complications.

℞ TREATMENT

Reestablishment of ostial patency and bacterial eradication are the goals of therapy for acute bacterial sinusitis. Humidification, hydration, and use of vasoconstricting drugs (but not antihistamines) are indicated. Amoxicillin (500 mg tid) or trimethoprim-sulfamethoxazole (TMP-SMZ, 160/800 mg bid) may be effective for first-time cases; more expensive alternative agents include amoxicillin/clavulanate (40 mg/kg PO qd divided tid, up to 500 mg per dose) or a second-generation cephalosporin (e.g., cefuroxime axetil, 250 mg bid for pts >2 years old and 125 mg bid for pts <2 years old). Treatment should be administered for 1 to 2 weeks. Empirical therapy for nosocomial sinusitis should focus on *S. aureus* and gram-negative rods with nafcillin (2 g IV q4h) plus ceftriaxone (2 g IV qd) and should be tailored on the basis of sinus-fluid culture results. Therapy for chronic sinusitis is best guided by intraoperative culture results, with careful attention paid to adequate sinus drainage. Fungal sinusitis is best treated with surgical debridement and IV antifungal therapy.

Treatment of the complications of sinusitis (e.g., orbital cellulitis and orbital abscess, Pott's puffy tumor, and intracranial suppurative complications) includes adequate drainage if indicated and at least 2 weeks of antibiotic treatment based on the organisms recovered. Treatment for osteomyelitis (6 weeks of IV antibiotic therapy after adequate surgical debridement) is indicated for Pott's puffy tumor.

Outpatient and Home Care Considerations   Most persons with bacterial sinusitis may be treated as outpatients with oral antibiotics. Severe disease (i.e., sinusitis with complications or systemic toxicity) should be treated with IV antibiotics. Adjunctive surgery to widen ostia and drain thick secretions may be necessary in severe cases or when disease fails to respond to initial IV therapy.

EAR PINNA AND LOBULE

Auricular cellulitis presents as a tender swollen pinna and lobule, most commonly due to *S. aureus* or *Streptococcus* spp., and is treated with nafcillin (1–2 g IV q6h) or cefazolin (1 g IV q8h). *Perichondritis* is associated with tenderness of the pinna, spares the lobule, is usually due to *P. aeruginosa* or *S. aureus*, and should be treated with IV ticarcillin/clavulanate (3.1 g q4–6h) or IV nafcillin (plus oral ciprofloxacin) for at least 4 weeks. These infections must be distinguished from relapsing polychondritis.

EXTERNAL AND MIDDLE EAR

ETIOLOGY AND PATHOGENESIS A viral URI, which can cause edema of the eustachian tube mucosa, often precedes or accompanies episodes of *acute otitis media* (AOM). Mastoid air cells are connected with the middle-ear cavity and thus are involved in otitis media. The incidence of AOM declines with age; the prevalence in adults is only 0.25%. Recurrent episodes of AOM in adults should prompt an evaluation for an anatomic abnormality that impedes eustachian tube drainage, such as a nasopharyngeal or skull base neoplasm. *S. pneumoniae, H. influenzae* (usually nontypable), and *M. catarrhalis* are the most common bacterial pathogens in AOM. Early recurrences in children are likely to be reinfections with different organisms or with organisms resistant to previously administered antibiotics. *Serous otitis media* is characterized by culture-negative middle-ear effusion that typically causes conductive hearing loss.

Untreated acute or *recurrent otitis media* may lead to chronic otitis with otorrhea from tympanic membrane perforation. Chronic otitis most often yields *P. aeruginosa, S. aureus, Klebsiella* spp., and aerobic gram-negative rods. Anaerobes, often mixed with aerobes, are implicated in half of cases of chronic otitis media. Tympanic membrane perforation and cholesteatoma are associated with chronic infection.

Otitis externa (OE), or swimmer's ear, often follows water exposure and is thought to be due to alkalinization of the external canal and consequent bacterial overgrowth. OE is usually due to *P. aeruginosa, S. aureus,* or *Streptococcus* spp. In diabetic patients, *Pseudomonas* causes invasive ("malignant") OE, which may invade the adjacent skull base.

CLINICAL MANIFESTATIONS AOM causes pain in the affected ear, conductive hearing loss, fever, and a red, bulging, or perforated eardrum. Diagnostic tympanocentesis is indicated for pts who appear toxic or are immunosuppressed. Associated mastoiditis presents as pain, tenderness, and swelling behind the affected ear and, if a subperiosteal abscess is present, can cause inferolateral displacement of the pinna and the development of a red fluctuant mass behind it. Serous otitis media features a dull retracted membrane with fluid. Chronic suppurative otitis media causes painless conductive hearing loss and intermittent purulent ear drainage. OE causes severe pain, typically exacerbated by manipulation of the external ear. Malignant OE usually causes a "deep" pain in the affected ear that is associated with swelling of the external auditory canal and may be associated with a paralysis of cranial nerve VII, IX, X, or XI.

DIAGNOSIS In all suspected ear infections, direct examination of the external ear canal and tympanic membrane is required. In cases of suspected accompanying mastoiditis or bony necrosis from malignant OE, CT is helpful.

Ⓡ TREATMENT

The agents used to treat AOM include amoxicillin (500 mg PO tid or 875 mg PO bid); although 25–35% of *H. influenzae* and *M. catarrhalis* strains produce β-lactamase, empirical amoxicillin is still successful in routine cases. Amoxicillin/clavulanate (875/125 mg PO bid) and cefuroxime axetil (500 mg PO bid), each given for 10 days, are also commonly used. If penicillin-resistant pneumococci are not detected, TMP-SMZ (160/800 mg PO bid) or clarithromycin (500 mg PO bid) may be used, and levofloxacin (500 mg PO qd) may also be effective in adults. Drainage is indicated for unresolved or recurrent infection. Surgical drainage and placement of tympanostomy tubes have been the mainstay of treatment for chronic otitis media. Uncomplicated OE is treated with topical antibiotics such as polymyxin-neomycin (4 drops qid for 5 days). Complicated or refractory OE requires debridement of the canal. Irrigation is contraindicated. Malignant OE is treated with surgical debridement, antibacterial ear drops, control of coexisting metabolic abnormalities, and a 6- to 8-week course of IV antipseudomonal antibiotics: imipenem/cilastatin, 500 mg IV q6h; meropenem, 0.5–1 g IV q8h; ciprofloxacin, 500–750 mg PO bid; ceftazidime, 1–2 g IV q8–12h; or cefepime, 1–2 g IV q12h) plus an aminoglycoside. If the recovered *Pseudomonas* strain is sensitive to quinolones, treatment may be changed to ciprofloxacin (750 mg PO bid for 6 weeks) after an initial 2 weeks of IV combination therapy.

Outpatient and Home Care Considerations Most persons with AOM can be treated as outpatients with oral antibiotics. Severe disease (i.e., with systemic toxicity) should be treated with IV antibiotics; both therapeutic and diagnostic drainage should be undertaken by a surgeon.

ORAL CAVITY

Oral anaerobes, especially *Prevotella* spp., cause *gingivitis*. *Vincent's angina* (acute necrotizing ulcerative gingivitis, trench mouth) is characterized by halitosis and ulcerations of the gingiva. Treatment includes penicillin V (500 mg PO qid) plus metronidazole (500 mg PO q8h) or clindamycin alone (300 mg PO q6h). Streptococci and anaerobes are usually involved in *Ludwig's angina*, or cellulitis of the submandibular and sublingual spaces. Surgical debridement may be indicated and airway obstruction can occur. Therapy with IV antibiotics is indicated—e.g., ampicillin/sulbactam (3 g q6h) or penicillin (24 million units per day by continuous infusion or divided q4–6h) plus metronidazole (7.5 mg/kg q8h)—and should be followed by oral antibiotic treatment once improvement is documented, with a total course of 14 days. Fulminant gangrene of the facial tissues (*noma, cancrum oris*) commonly involves *Fusobacterium nucleatum*, classically occurs in malnourished children, and is treated with surgical debridement and IV penicillin (24 million units per day by continuous infusion or divided q4–6h). Cold sores—vesicular lesions affecting the lip, buccal mucosa, or tongue—are commonly due to *herpes simplex virus* (HSV). Primary HSV infection of the oral cavity can be severe; antiviral treatment decreases symptom severity and time to healing (acyclovir, 400 mg PO tid; famciclovir, 250 mg PO tid; or valacyclovir, 500–1000 mg PO bid, each for 7 to 10 days). Recurrent orolabial HSV infection in an immunocompetent pt does not require antiviral therapy; in immunocompromised pts antiviral therapy for 7–10 days is indicated. A burning tongue or sore throat in an immunocompromised person should raise suspicion of *thrush* due to *Candida* spp. (most commonly *C. albicans*), which should be treated with topical antifungals (clotrimazole troches or nystatin liquid) four times daily, fluconazole (200 mg PO the first day, then 100 mg PO qd for 14 days), or itraconazole (200 mg PO qd for 14 days).

PHARYNX

ETIOLOGY AND PATHOGENESIS   Most cases of *acute pharyngitis* are nonexudative and secondary to infection with respiratory viruses such as EBV, RSV, parainfluenza virus, influenza virus, and adenovirus; EBV- and adenovirus-associated pharyngitis can mimic streptococcal pharyngitis. Group A coxsackievirus causes herpangina. Exudative bacterial pharyngitis is most often caused by group A β-hemolytic streptococci, which are responsible for 15% of all cases of pharyngitis. Other bacterial causes of pharyngitis include group C and group G streptococci, *Neisseria gonorrhoeae*, *Corynebacterium diphtheriae*, *Mycoplasma pneumoniae*, *Chlamydia pneumoniae*, *Arcanobacterium haemolyticum*, and *Yersinia enterocolitica*.

CLINICAL MANIFESTATIONS   Acute pharyngitis features sore throat with erythema, exudate, and edema. Classic findings in streptococcal pharyngitis include fever, sore throat, cervical lymphadenopathy, and tonsillar exudate. Associated peritonsillar abscess (quinsy) causes fever, pain, dysphagia and odynophagia, palatal fullness, tonsillar asymmetry, trismus, and a "hot-potato" voice.

DIAGNOSIS   In exudative pharyngitis, the "rapid strep" test is specific for group A *Streptococcus*. However, since this test is not sufficiently sensitive, a throat swab should be inoculated for confirmatory culture if the rapid test is negative. Herpes simplex is confirmed by culture or immunofluorescence staining. Neisseriae must be isolated on selective medium.

 TREATMENT

Penicillin or erythromycin (500 mg qid for 10 days) treats streptococcal pharyngitis and helps prevent rheumatic fever but not poststreptococcal glomerulonephritis. Peritonsillar abscess requires incision and drainage. Resistance of streptococci to erythromycin has been reported. Data on prevention of rheumatic fever are available only for penicillin.

LARYNX

ETIOLOGY AND PATHOGENESIS   *Acute laryngitis* manifests with hoarseness; it is usually viral in etiology (due to rhinovirus, influenza virus, parainfluenza virus, coxsackievirus, adenovirus, or RSV) but may also be caused by group A *Streptococcus* or *M. catarrhalis*. Etiologies of *chronic laryngitis* include *Mycobacterium tuberculosis*, *Histoplasma capsulatum*, *B. dermatitidis*, and *Candida* spp. *Croup* (laryngotracheobronchitis) occurs as subglottic edema almost exclusively in children 2–3 years old, manifesting as a "seal's bark" cough. Croup is largely attributable to parainfluenza virus, influenza virus, RSV, and *M. pneumoniae*. *Epiglottitis* is a rapidly progressive cellulitis of the supraglottic area presenting with fever, dysphonia, and drooling. In children it may rapidly progress to airway obstruction; such airway emergencies are less common in adults. Organisms responsible for acute epiglottitis in adults include *H. influenzae*, *H. parainfluenzae*, *S. pneumoniae*, group A *Streptococcus*, and *S. aureus*. Use of the *H. influenzae* type b (Hib) vaccine has decreased epiglottitis due to this organism by >95% in children, but its incidence has not changed in adults.

DIAGNOSIS   Subglottic narrowing on lateral neck film ("hourglass sign") indicates croup. A "thumb sign" on lateral neck film indicates epiglottitis, but negative films do not reliably exclude the diagnosis. Direct fiberoptic examination should be performed only in the operating room, with preparations made for securing the airway via tracheostomy if needed.

 TREATMENT

Rapid antigen testing and throat culture for group A *Streptococcus* should be performed if this organism is suspected in laryngitis; if tests are positive, the pt should be treated with penicillin VK (250 mg qid for 10 days) or IM benzathine penicillin (a single injection of 1.2 million units). Other cases should be managed in light of symptoms. Laryngoscopy should be considered for any pt with hoarseness that lasts over 4 weeks.

Croup must be differentiated from epiglottitis. Children with severe symptoms should be hospitalized and monitored. Systemic antibiotics are not indicated. Nebulized racemic epinephrine gives temporary relief, and both systemic and nebulized steroids have been shown to decrease the rate of hospitalization in affected pts.

A child in whom epiglottitis is suspected should be treated as having an impending airway emergency. Epiglottitis must be managed in the ICU with intubation and administration of empirical antibiotics effective against *H. influenzae*, such as cefuroxime (1.5 g IV q8h), cefotaxime (2 g IV q8h), or ceftriaxone (2 g IV q24h) for 7–10 days. The pediatric doses of cefuroxime and cefotaxime are 50 mg/kg IV q8h; the pediatric dose of ceftriaxone is 50 mg/kg IV q24h. If the pt has unvaccinated household contacts <4 years old, they and all other members of the household should receive prophylaxis with rifampin (20 mg/kg PO qd, up to 600 mg for 4 days) to eliminate carriage.

DEEP NECK SPACES

ETIOLOGY AND PATHOGENESIS   Infection in the deep neck spaces may be fatal as a result of airway compromise, septic thrombophlebitis, or extension of infection into the mediastinum. Group A streptococci, *Peptostreptococcus* spp., *Prevotella* spp., *Porphyromonas* spp., and *Fusobacterium* spp. are the common isolates from these infections. The infections originate in dental abscesses, sites of oral infection, sites of oropharyngeal trauma, sinuses, and infected retropharyngeal lymph nodes that track into the submandibular, lateral pharyngeal, or retropharyngeal spaces.

CLINICAL MANIFESTATIONS   Pts with *lateral pharyngeal space infections* appear toxic, with fever, sore throat, odynophagia, trismus, and leukocytosis. On examination, medial pharyngeal wall displacement may be evident. Associated septic thrombosis of the internal jugular vein by *Fusobacterium necrophorum* causes a septic picture associated with mandibular angle tenderness and septic pulmonary emboli (Lemierre's syndrome). Carotid artery rupture occurs rarely. *Infection of the retropharyngeal space* can produce marked dysphagia and odynophagia, drooling, a "hot-potato" voice, and—in severe cases—dyspnea and inspiratory stridor. Examination may show nuchal rigidity or bulging of the posterior pharyngeal wall.

DIAGNOSIS   Diagnosis of deep neck space infection involves contrast CT and, for vascular involvement, MRI or MRA.

℞ TREATMENT

Treatment requires establishment of a stable airway, drainage of the abscess, and antibiotic therapy effective against streptococci, anaerobes, *S. aureus*, and *H. influenzae*. Antibiotic treatment consists of ampicillin/sulbactam alone (3.1 g IV q6h) or clindamycin (900 mg IV q8h) plus ceftriaxone (2 g IV q24h). Infections due to *F. necrophorum* are treated with penicillin G (24 million units per day by continuous infusion or divided q4–6h) or clindamycin (900 mg IV q8h). Antibiotic therapy is recommended for at least 4 weeks.

For a more detailed discussion, see Durand M, Joseph M: Infections of the Upper Respiratory Tract, Chap. 30, p. 187, in HPIM-15.

51

GENERAL EXAMINATION OF THE SKIN

As dermatologic evaluation relies heavily on the objective cutaneous appearance, physical examination is often performed prior to taking a complete history in pts presenting with a skin problem. A differential diagnosis can usually be generated on the basis of a thorough examination with precise descriptions of the skin lesion(s) and narrowed with pertinent facts from the history. Laboratory or diagnostic procedures are then used, when appropriate, to clarify the diagnosis.

PHYSICAL EXAMINATION

Examination of skin should take place in a well-illuminated room with pt completely disrobed. Helpful ancillary equipment includes a hand lens and a pocket flashlight to provide peripheral illumination of lesions. The examination often begins with an assessment of the entire skin viewed at a distance, which is then narrowed down to focus on the individual lesions.

DISTRIBUTION As illustrated in Fig. 51-1, the distribution of skin lesions can provide valuable clues to the identification of the disorder. Generalized (systemic diseases); sun-exposed (SLE, photoallergic, phototoxic, polymorphous light eruption, porphyria cutanea tarda); dermatomal (herpes zoster); extensor surfaces (elbows and knees in psoriasis); flexural surfaces (antecubital and popliteal fossae in atopic dermatitis).

ARRANGEMENT AND SHAPE Can describe individual or multiple lesions.

Linear [contact dermatitis such as poison ivy, lesions that appear at sites of local skin trauma (Koebner phenomenon)]; *annular*—"ring-shaped" lesion with an active border and central clearing (erythema chronicum migrans, erythema annulare centrificum, tinea corporis); *iris* or *target lesion*—two or three concentric circles of differing hue (erythema multiforme); *circinate*—circular lesion (urticaria, herald patch of pityriasis rosea); *nummular*—"coin-shaped" (nummular eczema); *guttate*—droplike (guttate psoriasis); *morbilliform*—"measles-like" with small confluent papules coalescing into unusual shapes (measles, drug eruption); *reticulated*—"netlike" (livedo reticularis); *herpetiform*— grouped vesicles, papules, or erosions (herpes simplex).

PRIMARY LESIONS Cutaneous changes caused directly by disease process.

Macule—a flat circumscribed lesion of a different color, allowing for differentiation from surrounding skin; *patch*—macule >2 cm in diameter; *papule*—elevated, circumscribed lesion of any color <1 cm in diameter, with the major portion of lesion projecting above surrounding skin; *nodule*—palpable lesion similar to a papule but >1 cm in diameter; *plaque*—an elevated, flat-topped lesion >1 cm in diameter; *vesicle*—sharply marginated elevated lesion <1 cm in diameter filled with clear fluid; *bulla*—vesicular lesion >1 cm in diameter; *pustule*—a well-marginated focal accumulation of inflammatory cells within skin; *wheal*—a transient elevated lesion due to accumulation of fluid in upper dermis; *cyst*—lesion consisting of liquid or semisolid material contained within limits of cyst wall (true cyst).

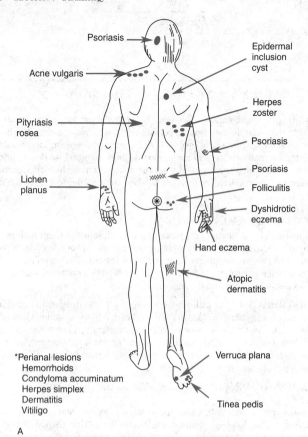

FIGURE 51-1A The distribution of some common dermatologic diseases and lesions.

SECONDARY LESIONS Changes in area of primary pathology often due to secondary events, e.g., scratching, secondary infection, bleeding.

Scale—a flaky accumulation of excess keratin that is partially adherent to skin; *crust*—a circumscribed collection of inflammatory cells and dried serum on skin surface; *excoriation*—linear, angular erosions caused by scratching; *erosion*—a circumscribed, usually depressed, moist lesion resulting from loss of overlying epidermis; *ulcer*—a deeper erosion involving epidermis plus underlying papillary dermis; may leave a scar on healing; *atrophy*: (1) epidermal—thinning of skin with loss of normal skin surface markings, (2) dermal—depression of skin surface due to loss of underlying collagen or dermal ground substance; *lichenification*—thickening of skin with accentuation of normal skin surface markings most commonly due to chronic rubbing; *scar*—collection of fibrous tissue replacing normal dermal constituents.

OTHER DESCRIPTIVE TERMS Color, e.g., violaceous, erythematous; physical characteristics, e.g., warm, tender; sharpness of edge, surface contour—flat-topped, pedunculated (on a stalk), verrucous (wartlike), umbilicated (containing a central depression).

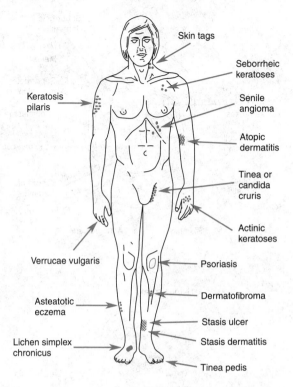

Skin tags

Seborrheic keratoses

Keratosis pilaris

Senile angioma

Atopic dermatitis

Tinea or candida cruris

Actinic keratoses

Verrucae vulgaris

Psoriasis

Asteatotic eczema

Dermatofibroma

Stasis ulcer

Lichen simplex chronicus

Stasis dermatitis

Tinea pedis

B

FIGURE 51-1B

HISTORY

A complete history should be obtained, with special attention being paid to the following points:

1. Evolution of the lesion—site of onset, manner in which eruption progressed or spread, duration, periods of resolution or improvement in chronic eruptions
2. Symptoms associated with the eruption—itching, burning, pain, numbness; what has relieved symptoms; time of day when symptoms are most severe
3. Current or recent medications—both prescription and over-the-counter
4. Associated systemic symptoms (e.g., malaise, fatigue, arthralgias)
5. Ongoing or previous illnesses
6. History of allergies
7. Presence of photosensitivity
8. Review of systems

ADDITIONAL DIAGNOSTIC PROCEDURES

POTASSIUM HYDROXIDE PREPARATION Useful for detection of dermatophyte or yeast. Scale is collected from advancing edge of a scaling lesion by gently scraping with side of a microscope slide. Nail lesions are best sampled by trimming back nail and scraping subungual debris. A drop of 10–15% potassium hydroxide is added to slide, and cover slip is applied. The slide

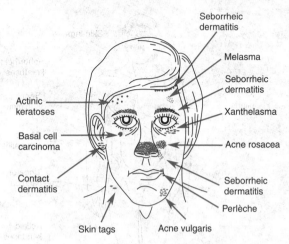

C

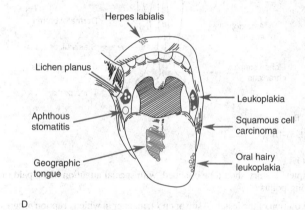

D

FIGURE 51-1C and 1D

may be gently heated and examined under microscope. Positive preparations show translucent, septate branching hyphae among keratinocytes.

TZANCK PREPARATION   Useful for determining presence of herpes viruses. Optimal lesion to sample is an early vesicle. Lesion is gently unroofed with no. 15 scalpel blade, and base of vesicle is gently scraped with belly of blade (keep blade perpendicular to skin surface to prevent laceration). Scrapings are transferred to slide and stained with Wright's or Giemsa stain. A positive preparation has multinucleate giant cells.

SKIN BIOPSY   Minor surgical procedure. Choice of site very important.

DIASCOPY   Assesses whether a lesion blanches with pressure. Done by pressing a magnifying lens or microscope slide on lesion and observing changes in vascularity. For example, hemangiomas will usually blanch; purpuric lesions will not.

WOOD'S LIGHT EXAMINATION   Useful for detecting bacterial or fungal infection or accentuating features of some skin lesions.

PATCH TESTS   To document cutaneous sensitivity to specific antigens.

For a more detailed discussion, see Lawley TJ, Yancey KB: Approach to the Patient with a Skin Disorder, Chap. 55, p. 305, in HPIM-15.

52

COMMON SKIN CONDITIONS

PAPULOSQUAMOUS DISORDERS
Disorders exhibiting papules and scale.

PSORIASIS   A chronic, recurrent disorder. Classic lesion is a well-marginated, erythematous plaque with silvery-white surface scale. Distribution includes extensor surfaces (i.e., knees, elbows, and buttocks); may also involve palms and scalp (particularly anterior scalp margin). Associated findings include psoriatic arthritis (Chap. 164) and nail changes (onycholysis, pitting or thickening of nail plate with accumulation of subungual debris).

 TREATMENT

Maintain cutaneous hydration; topical glucocorticoids; coal tar ointment; topical vitamin D analogue (calcipotriol); UV light (PUVA when UV used in combination with psoralens); methotrexate or cyclosporine for severe advanced disease.

PITYRIASIS ROSEA   A self-limited condition lasting 3–8 weeks. Initially, there is a single 2–6 cm annular salmon-colored patch (herald patch) with a peripheral rim of scale, followed in days to weeks by a generalized eruption involving the trunk and proximal extremities. Individual lesions are similar to but smaller than the herald patch and are arranged in symmetric fashion with long axis of each individual lesion along skin lines of cleavage. Appearance may be similar to that of secondary syphilis.

 TREATMENT

Disorder is self-limited, so treatment is directed at symptoms; oral antihistamines for pruritus; topical glucocorticoids; UV-B phototherapy in some cases.

LICHEN PLANUS   Disorder of unknown cause; can follow administration of certain drugs and in chronic graft-versus-host disease; lesions are pruritic, polygonal, flat-topped, and violaceous. Course is variable, but most pts have spontaneous remissions 6–24 months after onset of disease.

 TREATMENT

Topical glucocorticoids.

ECZEMATOUS DISORDERS

ECZEMA Eczema, or dermatitis, is a reaction pattern that presents with variable clinical and histologic findings; it is the final common expression for a number of disorders.

ATOPIC DERMATITIS One aspect of atopic triad of hayfever, asthma, and eczema. Usually an intermittent, chronic, severely pruritic, eczematous dermatitis with scaly erythematous patches, vesiculation, crusting, and fissuring. Lesions are most commonly on flexures, with prominent involvement of antecubital and popliteal fossae; generalized erythroderma in severe cases. Most pts with atopic dermatitis are chronic carriers of *Staphylococcus aureus* in anterior nares and on skin.

 TREATMENT

Avoidance of irritants; cutaneous hydration; topical glucocorticoids; treatment of infected lesions. Systemic glucocorticoids only for severe exacerbations unresponsive to topical conservative therapy.

ALLERGIC CONTACT DERMATITIS A delayed hypersensitivity reaction that occurs after cutaneous exposure to an antigenic substance. Lesions occur at site of contact and are vesicular, weeping, crusting; linear arrangement of vesicles is common. Most frequent allergens are resin from plants of the *Rhus* (or *Toxicodendron*) genus (poison ivy, oak, sumac), nickel, rubber, and cosmetics.

 TREATMENT

Avoidance of sensitizing agent; topical glucocorticoids; consideration of systemic glucocorticoids over 2–3 weeks for widespread disease or involvement of face or genitals.

IRRITANT CONTACT DERMATITIS Inflammation of the skin due to direct injury by an exogenous agent. The most frequent cause of hand eczema, where dermatitis is initiated or aggravated by chronic exposure to water and detergents. Features may include skin dryness, cracking, erythema, edema.

 TREATMENT

Avoidance of irritants; barriers (use of vinyl gloves); topical glucocorticoids; treatment of secondary bacterial or dermatophyte infection.

SEBORRHEIC DERMATITIS A chronic noninfectious process characterized by erythematous patches with greasy yellowish scale. Lesions are generally on scalp, eyebrows, nasolabial folds, axillae, central chest, and posterior auricular area.

TREATMENT

Nonfluorinated topical glucocorticoids; shampoos containing coal tar, salicylic acid, or selenium sulfide.

INFECTIONS AND INFESTATIONS

IMPETIGO A superficial infection of skin secondary to either *S. aureus* or group A β-hemolytic streptococci. The primary lesion is a superficial pustule that ruptures and forms a "honey-colored" crust. Tense bullae are associated with *S. aureus* infections (bullous impetigo). Lesions may occur anywhere but commonly involve the face.

 TREATMENT

Gentle debridement of adherent crusts with soaks and topical antibiotics; appropriate oral antibiotics depending on organism (Chap. 78).

ERYSIPELAS Superficial cellulitis, most commonly on face, characterized by a bright red, sharply demarcated, intensely painful, warm plaque. Because of superficial location of infection and associated edema, surface of plaque may exhibit a *peau d'orange* (orange peel) appearance. Most commonly due to infection with group A β-hemolytic streptococci, occurring at sites of trauma or other breaks in skin.

 TREATMENT

Appropriate antibiotics depending on organism (Chap. 78).

SCABIES A common infestation of children and adults due to the mite *Sarcoptes scabiei*. Often presents as pruritus, commonly worse at night. Typical lesions include burrows (short linear lesions often in web spaces of fingers) and small vesiculopapular lesions in intertriginous areas. Excoriations, often with bleeding, may be prominent.

 TREATMENT

Topical permethrin; topical lindane (penetrates skin and has potential for CNS toxicity; should not be used in pregnant women or infants). To prevent reinfestation, clothing should be washed in hot water and close contacts treated simultaneously.

HERPES SIMPLEX (See also Chap. 102) Recurrent eruption characterized by grouped vesicles on an erythematous base that progress to erosions; often secondarily infected with staphylococci or streptococci. Infections frequently involve mucocutaneous surfaces around the oral cavity, genitals, or anus. Can also cause severe visceral disease including esophagitis, pneumonitis, encephalitis, and disseminated herpes simplex virus infection. Tzanck preparation of an unroofed early vesicle reveals multinucleate giant cells.

 TREATMENT

Will differ based on disease manifestations and level of immune competence (Chap. 102); appropriate antibiotics for secondary infections, depending on organism.

HERPES ZOSTER (See also Chap. 102) Eruption of grouped vesicles on an erythematous base usually limited to a single dermatome ("shingles"); disseminated lesions can also occur, especially in immunocompromised pts. Tzanck preparation reveals multinucleate giant cells; indistinguishable from herpes simplex except by culture. Postherpetic neuralgia, lasting months to years, may occur, especially in elderly.

 TREATMENT

Will differ based on disease manifestations and level of immune competence (Chap. 102)

DERMATOPHYTE INFECTION Skin fungus, may involve any area of body; due to infection of stratum corneum, nail plate, or hair. Appearance may vary from mild scaliness to florid inflammatory dermatitis. Common sites of infection include the foot (tinea pedis), nails (tinea unguium), groin (tinea cruris), or scalp (tinea capitis). Classic lesion of tinea corporis ("ringworm") is an erythematous papulosquamous patch, often with central clearing and scale along peripheral advancing border. Hyphae are often seen on KOH preparation, although tinea capitis and tinea corporis may require culture or biopsy.

 TREATMENT

Depends on affected site and type of infection. Topical imidazoles, triazoles, and allylamines may be effective. Haloprogin, undecylenic acid, ciclopiroxolamine, and tolnaftate are also effective, but nystatin is not active against dermatophytes. Griseofulvin, 500 mg/d, if systemic therapy required. Itraconazole may be effective for nail infections.

CANDIDIASIS Fungal infection caused by a related group of yeasts. Manifestations may be localized to the skin or rarely systemic and life-threatening. Predisposing factors include diabetes mellitus, cellular immune deficiencies, and HIV (Chap. 86). Frequent sites include the oral cavity, chronically wet macerated areas, around nails, intertriginous areas. Diagnosed by clinical pattern and demonstration of yeast on KOH preparation or culture.

 TREATMENT

(See also Chap. 108) Removal of predisposing factors; topical nystatin or azoles; systemic therapy reserved for immunosuppressed patients, unresponsive chronic or recurrent disease; vulvovaginal candidiasis may respond to a single dose of fluconazole, 150 mg.

WARTS Cutaneous neoplasms caused by human papilloma viruses (HPVs). Typically dome-shaped lesions with irregular filamentous surface. Propensity for the face, arms, and legs; often spread by shaving. HPVs are also associated with genital or perianal lesions and play a role in the development of neoplasia of the uterine cervix and external genitalia in females (Chap. 83).

 TREATMENT

Cryotherapy with liquid nitrogen, keratinolytic agents (salicylic acid). For genital warts, application of podophyllin solution is effective but can be associated with marked local reactions.

ACNE

ACNE VULGARIS Usually a self-limited disorder of teenagers and young adults. Comedones (small cyst formed in hair follicle) are clinical hallmark; often accompanied by inflammatory lesions of papules, pustules, or nodules. May scar in severe cases.

 TREATMENT

Careful cleaning and removal of oils; oral tetracycline or erythromycin; topical antibacterials (e.g., benzoyl peroxide), topical retinoic acid. Systemic isotretinoin only for unresponsive severe nodulocystic acne (teratogenic—all females must be screened for pregnancy prior to drug initiation and maintain effective contraception during treatment course).

ACNE ROSACEA Inflammatory disorder affecting predominantly the central face, rarely affecting pts <30 years of age. Tendency toward exaggerated flushing, with eventual superimposition of papules, pustules, and telangiectases. May lead to rhinophyma and ocular problems.

 TREATMENT

Oral tetracycline, 250–1500 mg/d; topical metronidazole and topical non-fluorinated glucocorticoids may be useful.

VASCULAR DISORDERS

ERYTHEMA NODOSUM Septal panniculitis characterized by erythematous, warm, tender subcutaneous nodular lesions typically over anterior tibia. Lesions are usually flush with skin surface but are indurated and have appearance of an erythematous/violaceous bruise. Lesions usually resolve spontaneously in 3–6 weeks without scarring. Commonly seen in sarcoidosis, treatment with some drugs (esp. sulfonamides, oral contraceptives, and estrogens), and a wide range of infections including streptococcal and tubercular; may be idiopathic.

 TREATMENT

Identification and treatment/removal of underlying cause. NSAID for severe or recurrent lesions; systemic glucocorticoids are effective but dangerous if underlying infection is not appreciated.

ERYTHEMA MULTIFORME A reaction pattern of skin consisting of a variety of lesions but most commonly erythematous papules and bullae. "Target" or "iris" lesion is characteristic and consists of concentric circles of erythema and normal flesh-colored skin, often with a central vesicle or bulla. Distribution of lesions classically acral, esp. palms and soles. Three most common causes are drug reaction (particularly penicillins and sulfonamides) or concurrent herpetic or *Mycoplasma* infection. Can rarely affect mucosal surfaces and internal organs (erythema multiforme major or Stevens-Johnson syndrome).

 TREATMENT

Provocative agent should be sought and eliminated if drug-related. In mild cases limited to skin, only symptomatic treatment is needed (antihistamines, NSAID). For Stevens-Johnson, systemic glucocorticoids are controversial but often used; prevention of secondary infection and maintenance of nutrition and fluid/electrolyte balance are critical.

URTICARIA   A common disorder, either acute or chronic, characterized by evanescent (individual lesions lasting <24 h), pruritic, edematous, pink to erythematous plaques with a whitish halo around margin of individual lesions. Lesions range in size from papules to giant coalescent lesions (10–20 cm in diameter). Often due to drugs, systemic infection, or foods (esp. shellfish). Food additives such as tartrazine dye (FD & C yellow no. 5), benzoate, or salicylates have also been implicated. If individual lesions last >24 h, consider diagnosis of urticarial vasculitis.

 TREATMENT

See Chap. 157.

VASCULITIS   Palpable purpura (nonblanching, elevated lesions) is the cutaneous hallmark of vasculitis. Other lesions include petechiae (esp. early lesions), necrosis with ulceration, bullae, and urticarial lesions (urticarial vasculitis). Lesions usually most prominent on lower extremities. Associations include infections, collagen-vascular disease, primary systemic vasculitides, malignancy, hepatitis B, drugs (esp. thiazides), and inflammatory bowel disease. May occur as an idiopathic, predominantly cutaneous vasculitis.

 TREATMENT

Will differ based on cause. Pursue identification and treatment/elimination of an exogenous cause or underlying disease. If part of a systemic vasculitis, treat based on major organ-threatening features (Chap. 160). Immunosuppressive therapy should be avoided in idiopathic predominantly cutaneous vasculitis as disease frequently does not respond and rarely causes irreversible organ system dysfunction.

CUTANEOUS DRUG REACTIONS

Cutaneous reactions are among the most frequent medication toxicities. These can have a wide range of severity and manifestations including urticaria, photosensitivity, erythema multiforme, fixed drug reactions, erythema nodosum, vasculitis, lichenoid reactions, bullous drug reactions, and toxic epidermal necrolysis (TEN). Diagnosis is usually made by appearance and careful medication history.

 TREATMENT

Withdrawal of the medication. Treatment based on nature and severity of cutaneous pathology.

For a more detailed discussion, see Swerlick RA, Lawley TJ: Eczema, Psoriasis, Cutaneous Infections, Acne, and Other Common Skin Disorders, Chap. 56, p. 309; Stern RS, Chosidow OM, Wintroub BU: Cutaneous Drug Reactions, Chap. 59, p. 336; and Bologna JL, Braverman IM: Skin Manifestations of Internal Disease, Chap. 57, p. 315, in HPIM-15.

53

ASSESSMENT OF NUTRITIONAL STATUS

Stability of body weight requires that energy intake and expenditures are balanced over time. The major categories of energy output are resting energy expenditure (REE) and physical activity; minor sources include the energy cost of metabolizing food (thermic effect of food or specific dynamic action) and shivering thermogenesis. The average energy intake is about 2800 kcal/day for men and about 1800 kcal/d for women, though these estimates vary with body size and activity level. Dietary reference intakes (DRI) and recommended dietary allowances (RDA) have been defined for many nutrients, including 9 essential amino acids, 4 fat-soluble and 10 water-soluble vitamins, several minerals, fatty acids, choline, and water (Tables 73-1 and 73-2 in HPIM-15). The usual water requirements are 1.0–1.5 mL/kcal energy expenditure in adults, with adjustments for excessive losses. The RDA for protein is 0.6 g/kg body weight. Fat should comprise ≤ 30% of calories, and saturated fat should be <10% of calories. At least 55% of calories should be derived from carbohydrates.

Malnutrition

Malnutrition results from inadequate intake or abnormal gastrointestinal assimilation of dietary calories; excessive energy expenditure; or altered metabolism of energy supplies by an intrinsic disease process.

Both outpatients and inpatients should be considered at risk for malnutrition if they meet one or more of the following criteria:

- Unintentional loss of >10% of usual body weight in the preceding 3 months
- Body weight <90% of ideal for height (Table 53-1)
- Body mass index (BMI: weight/height^2 in kg/m^2) < 18.5

A body weight <90% of ideal for height represents *risk of malnutrition*, body weight <85% of ideal constitutes *malnutrition*, <70% of ideal represents *severe malnutrition*, and <60% of ideal is usually incompatible with survival. In underdeveloped countries, two forms of severe malnutrition can be seen: *marasmus*, which refers to generalized starvation with loss of body fat and protein, and *kwashiorkor*, which refers to selective protein malnutrition with edema and fatty liver. In more developed societies, features of combined *protein-calorie malnutrition* (PCM) are more commonly seen in the context of a variety of acute and chronic illnesses.

ETIOLOGY The major etiologies of malnutrition are starvation, stress from surgery or severe illness, and mixed mechanisms. Starvation results from decreased dietary intake (from poverty, chronic alcoholism, anorexia nervosa, fad diets, severe depression, neurodegenerative disorders, dementia, or strict vegetarianism; abdominal pain from intestinal ischemia or pancreatitis; or anorexia associated with AIDS, disseminated cancer, or renal failure) or decreased assimilation of the diet (from pancreatic insufficiency; short bowel syndrome; celiac disease; or esophageal, gastric, or intestinal obstruction). Contributors to physical stress include fever, acute trauma, major surgery, burns, acute sepsis, hyperthyroidism, and inflammation as occurs in pancreatitis, collagen vascular diseases, and chronic infectious diseases such as tuberculosis or AIDS oppor-

Table 53-1

Ideal Weight for Height

	Men				Women		
Height[a]	Weight[a]	Height	Weight	Height	Weight	Height	Weight
145	51.9	166	64.0	140	44.9	161	56.9
146	52.4	167	64.6	141	45.4	162	57.6
147	52.9	168	65.2	142	45.9	163	58.3
148	53.5	169	65.9	143	46.4	164	58.9
149	54.0	170	66.6	144	47.0	165	59.5
150	54.5	171	67.3	145	47.5	166	60.1
151	55.0	172	68.0	146	48.0	167	60.7
152	55.6	173	68.7	147	48.6	168	61.4
153	56.1	174	69.4	148	49.2	169	62.1
154	56.6	175	70.1	149	49.8		
155	57.2	176	70.8	150	50.4		
156	57.9	177	71.6	151	51.0		
157	58.6	178	72.4	152	51.5		
158	59.3	179	73.3	153	52.0		
159	59.9	180	74.2	154	52.5		
160	60.5	181	75.0	155	53.1		
161	61.1	182	75.8	156	53.7		
162	61.7	183	76.5	157	54.3		
163	62.3	184	77.3	158	54.9		
164	62.9	185	78.1	159	55.5		
165	63.5	186	78.9	160	56.2		

[a] Values are expressed in cm for height and kg for weight. To obtain height in inches, divide by 2.54. To obtain weight in pounds, multiply by 2.2.
SOURCE: Adapted from GL Blackburn et al.: Nutritional and metabolic assessment of the hospitalized patient. J Parenter Enteral Nutr 1:11, 1977.

tunistic infections. Mixed mechanisms occur in AIDS, disseminated cancer, COPD, chronic liver disease, Crohn's disease, ulcerative colitis, and renal failure.

CLINICAL FEATURES

- General: weight loss, temporal and proximal muscle wasting, decreased skin-fold thickness
- Skin, hair, nails: easily plucked hair, easy bruising, petechiae, and perifollicular hemorrhages (vit. C), "flaky paint" rash of lower extremities (zinc), hyperpigmentation of skin exposed areas (niacin, tryptophan); spooning of nails (iron)
- Eyes: conjunctival pallor (anemia), night blindness, dryness and Bitot spots (vit. A), ophthalmoplegia (thiamine)
- Mouth and mucous membranes: glossitis and/or cheilosis (riboflavin, niacin, vit. B12, pyridoxine, folate), diminished taste (zinc); inflamed and bleeding gums (vit. C)
- Neurologic: disorientation (niacin, phosphorus), confabulation, cerebellar gait, or past pointing (thiamine), peripheral neuropathy (thiamine, pyridoxine, vit. E), lost vibratory and position sense (vit. B_{12})

Laboratory findings include a low serum albumin, elevated PT, and decreased cell-mediated immunity manifest as anergy to skin testing. Specific vitamin deficiencies may also be present.

For a more detailed discussion, see Dwyer J: Nutritional Requirements and Dietary Assessment, Chap. 73, p. 451; Halsted CH: Malnutrition and Nutritional Assessment, Chap. 74, p. 455 ; and Russell RM: Vitamin and Trace Mineral Deficiency and Excess, Chap. 75, p. 461, in HPIM-15.

54

ENTERAL AND PARENTERAL NUTRITION

Nutritional support should be initiated in pts with malnutrition or in those at risk for malnutrition (e.g., conditions that preclude adequate oral feeding or pts in catabolic states, such as sepsis, burns, or trauma). An approach for deciding when to use various types of specialized nutrition support (SNS) is summarized in Fig. 54-1.

Enteral therapy refers to feeding via the gut, using oral supplements or infusion of formulas via various feeding tubes (nasogastric, nasojejunal, gastrostomy, jejunostomy, or combined gastrojejunostomy). *Parenteral* therapy refers to the infusion of nutrient solutions into the bloodstream via a peripherally inserted central catheter (PICC), a centrally inserted externalized catheter, or a centrally inserted tunneled catheter or subcutaneous port. Where feasible, enteral nutrition is the preferred route because it sustains the digestive, absorptive, and immunologic functions of the GI tract, at about one-tenth the cost of parenteral feeding. Parenteral nutrition is often indicated in severe pancreatitis, necrotizing enterocolitis, prolonged ileus, and distal bowel obstruction.

ENTERAL NUTRITION

The components of a standard enteral formula are shown in Table 54-1; however, modification of the enteral formula may be required based on various clinical indications and/or associated disease states (Table 54-2). After elevation of the head of the bed, continuous gastric infusion is initiated using a half-strength diet at a rate of 25–50 mL/h. This can be advanced to full strength as tolerated to meet the energy target. The major risks of enteral tube feeding are aspiration, diarrhea, electrolyte imbalance, warfarin resistance, sinusitis, and esophagitis.

PARENTERAL NUTRITION

The components of parenteral nutrition include adequate fluid (35 mL/kg body weight for adults, plus any abnormal loss); energy from glucose, protein, and lipid solutions; nutrients essential in severely ill pts, such as glutamine, nucleotides, and products of methionine metabolism; vitamins and minerals. The risks of parenteral therapy include mechanical complications from insertion of the infusion catheter, catheter sepsis, fluid overload, hyperglycemia, hypophosphatemia, hypokalemia, acid-base and electrolyte imbalance, cholestasis, metabolic bone disease, and micronutrient deficiencies.

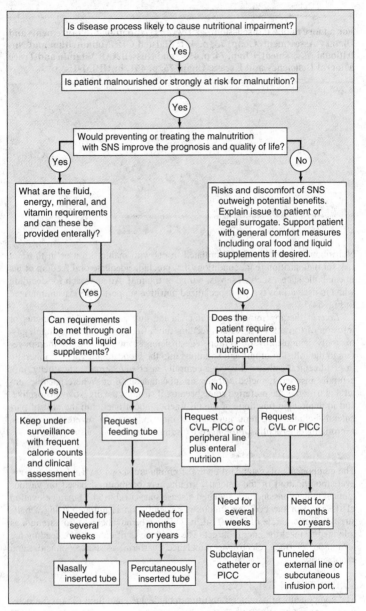

FIGURE 54-1

Table 54-1

Composition Characteristics

STANDARD ENTERAL FORMULA

1. Complete dietary products (+)[a]
   a. Caloric density 1 kcal/mL
   b. Protein ~14% cals, caseinates, soy, lactalbumin
   c. Fat ~30% cals, corn, soy, safflower oils
   d. CHO ~60% cals, hydrolysed corn starch, maltodextrin, sucrose
   e. Recommended daily intake of all minerals and vitamins in ≥1500 kcal/d
   f. Osmolality (mosmol/kg) ~300

[a] Cost: + inexpensive; + + moderately expensive; + + + very expensive.
NOTE: CHO, carbohydrate; MCT, medium-chain triglyceride; MUFA, monounsaturated fatty acid, $\omega 3$ or $\omega 6$ polyunsaturated fat with first double bond at carbon 3 (fish oils) or carbon 6 (vegetable oils).

The following parameters should be monitored in all patients receiving supplemental nutrition, whether enteral or parenteral:

- Fluid balance (weight, intake vs. output)
- Glucose, electrolytes, BUN (daily until stable, then 2× per week)
- Serum creatinine, albumin, phosphorus, calcium, magnesium, Hb/Hct, WBC (baseline, then 2× per week)
- INR (baseline, then weekly)
- Micronutrient tests as indicated

SPECIFIC MICRONUTRIENT DEFICIENCY
Appropriate therapies for micronutrient deficiencies are outlined in Table 54-3.

Table 54-2

Modified Enteral Formulas

1. Caloric density 1.5–2 kcal/mL (+)
2. a. High protein ~20% cals (+)
   b. Hydrolysed protein to small peptides (+ +)
   c. ↑ Glutamine, arginine, S-containing amino acids, nucleotides (+ + +)
   d. ↑ Branch-chain amino acids, ↓ aromatic amino acids (+ + +)
   e. ↓ Protein, ↓ K, Mg, and P diets (+ +)
   f. ↓ Protein, ↑ essential amino acids, ↓ minerals and vitamins (+ + +)
3. a. Low fat, partial MCT substitution (+)
   b. ↑ Fat >40% cals (+ +)
   c. ↑ Fat from MUFA (+ +)
   d. Fat ↑ in $\omega 3$ (fish oil) and ↓ $\omega 6$ (+ + +)
4. a. Fiber provided as soy polysaccharide (+)
   b. Fiber provided as blenderized fruits and vegetables (+ +)
5. ↑ Minerals (Zn) and vitamins (A and C) (+ +)

Table 54-3

Therapy for Common Vitamin and Mineral Deficiencies

Nutrient	Therapy
Vitamin A[a,b,c]	100,000 IU (30 mg) IM or 200,000 IU (60 mg) PO × 1 if ocular changes
	50,000 IU (15 mg) PO qd × 1 month if chronic malab- sorption
Vitamin C	200 mg PO qd
Vitamin E[a]	800–1200 mg PO qd
Vitamin K[a]	10 mg IV × 1, or 1–2 mg PO qd in chronic malabsorption
Thiamine[b]	100 mg IV qd × 7 days, followed by 10 mg PO qd
Niacin	100–200 mg PO tid for 5 days
Pyridoxine	50 mg PO qd, 100–200 mg PO qd if deficiency related to medication
Zinc[b,c]	60 mg PO bid

[a] Associated with fat malabsorption, along with vitamin D deficiency.
[b] Associated with chronic alcoholism; always replete thiamine before carbohydrates in alcoholics to avoid precipitation of acute thiamine deficiency.
[c] Associated with protein-calorie malnutrition.

For a more detailed discussion, see Russell RM: Vitamin and Trace Mineral Deficiency and Excess, Chap. 75, p. 461, and Howard L: Enteral and Parenteral Nutrition Therapy, Chap. 76, p. 470, HPIM-15.

55

EATING DISORDERS

Definitions

Anorexia nervosa is characterized by refusal to maintain normal body weight, resulting in a body weight < 85% of the expected weight for age and height. *Bulimia nervosa* is characterized by recurrent episodes of binge eating followed by abnormal compensatory behaviors, such as self-induced vomiting, laxative abuse, or excessive exercise. Weight is in the normal range or above.

Both anorexia nervosa and bulimia nervosa occur primarily among previously healthy young women who become overly concerned with body shape and weight. Binge eating and purging behavior may be present in both conditions, with the critical distinction between the two resting on the weight of the individual. The diagnostic criteria for each of these disorders are shown in Tables 55-1 and 55-2.

Clinical Features
ANOREXIA NERVOSA

- General: hypothermia
- Skin, hair, nails: alopecia, lanugo, acrocyanosis, edema

Table 55-1

Diagnostic Criteria for Anorexia Nervosa

1. Refusal to maintain body weight at or above a minimally normal weight for age and height (e.g., weight loss leading to maintenance of body weight <85% of that expected; or failure to make expected weight gain during period of growth, leading to body weight <85% of that expected).
2. Intense fear of gaining weight or becoming fat, even though underweight.
3. Disturbance in the way in which one's body weight or shape is experienced, undue influence of body weight or shape on self-evaluation, or denial of the seriousness of the current low body weight.
4. In postmenarchal females, amenorrhea, i.e., the absence of at least three consecutive menstrual cycles, (A woman is considered to have amenorrhea if her periods occur only following hormone, e.g., estrogen administration.)

Specify type:
  Restricting type: During the episode of anorexia nervosa, the person has not regularly engaged in binge-eating or purging behavior (i.e., self-induced vomiting or the misuse of laxatives, diuretics or enemas).
  Binge eating/purging type: During the episode of anorexia nervosa, the person has regularly engaged in binge-eating or purging behavior (i.e., self-induced vomiting or the misuse of laxatives, diuretics, or enemas).

SOURCE: From the *Diagnostic and Statistical Manual of Mental Disorders*, 4th ed, Washington, DC, American Psychiatric Association, 1994.

Table 55-2

Diagnostic Criteria for Bulimia Nervosa

1. Recurrent episodes of binge eating. An episode of binge eating is characterized by both of the following:
   a. Eating, in a discrete period of time (e.g., within any 2-h period), an amount of food that is definitely larger than most people would eat during a similar period of time and under similar circumtances.
   b. A sense of lack of control over eating during the episode (e.g., a feeling that one cannot stop eating or control what or how much one is eating).
2. Recurrent inappropriate compensatory behavior in order to prevent weight gain, such as self-induced vomiting, misuse of laxatives or diuretics, enemas, or other medications; fasting; or excessive exercise.
3. The binge eating and inappropriate compensatory behaviors both occur, on average, at least twice a week for 3 months.
4. Self-evaluation is unduly influenced by body shape and weight.
5. The disturbance does not occur exclusively during episodes of anorexia nervosa.

Specify type:
  Purging type: during the current episode of bulimia nervosa, the person has regularly engaged in self-induced vomiting or the misuse of laxatives, diuretics, or enemas.
  Nonpurging type: during the current episode of bulimia nervosa, the person has used other inappropriate compensatory behaviors such as fasting or excessive exercise but has not regularly engaged in self-induced vomiting or the misuse of laxatives, diuretics, or enemas.

SOURCE: From the *Diagnostic and Statistical Manual of Mental Disorders*, 4th ed, Washington, DC, American Psychiatric Association, 1994.

- Cardiovascular: bradycardia, hypotension
- Gastrointestinal: salivary gland enlargement, slow gastric emptying, constipation, elevated liver enzymes
- Hematopoietic: normochromic, normocytic anemia; leukopenia
- Fluid/electrolyte: increased BUN, increased creatinine, hyponatremia, hypokalemia
- Endocrine: low luteinizing hormone and follicle-stimulating hormone with secondary amenorrhea, hypoglycemia, normal thyroid-stimulating hormone with low normal thyroxine, increased plasma cortisol, osteopenia

BULIMIA NERVOSA

- Gastrointestinal: salivary gland enlargement, dental erosion
- Fluid/electrolyte: hypokalemia, hypochloremia, alkalosis (from vomiting) or acidosis (from laxative abuse)
- Other: loss of dental enamel, callus on dorsum of hand

℞ TREATMENT

Anorexia Nervosa   Weight restoration to 90% of predicted weight is the primary goal in the treatment of anorexia nervosa. The intensity of the initial treatment, including the need for hospitalization, is determined by the pt's current weight, the rapidity of recent weight loss, and the severity of medical and psychological complications (Fig. 55-1). Severe electrolyte imbalances

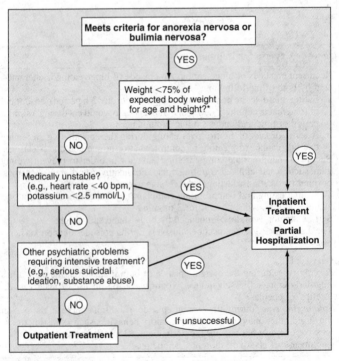

FIGURE 55-1

should be identified and corrected. Nutritional restoration can almost always be successfully accomplished by oral feeding. For severely underweight pts, sufficient calories should be provided initially in divided meals as food or liquid supplements to maintain weight and to permit stabilization of fluid and electrolyte balance (1500–1800 kcal/d intake). Calories can be gradually increased to achieve a weight gain of 1 to 2 kg per week (3000–4000 kcal/d intake). Meals must be supervised. Intake of vitamin D (400 IU/d) and calcium (1500 mg/d) should be sufficient to minimize bone loss. The assistance of psychiatrists or psychologists experienced in the treatment of anorexia nervosa is usually necessary. No psychotropic medications are of established value in the treatment of anorexia nervosa. Medical complications occasionally occur during refeeding; most patients transiently retain excess fluid, occasionally resulting in peripheral edema. Congestive heart failure and acute gastric dilatation have been described when refeeding is rapid. Transient modest elevations in serum levels of liver enzymes occasionally occur. Low levels of magnesium and phosphate should be replaced. Mortality is 5% per decade, either from chronic starvation or suicide.

Bulimia Nervosa Bulimia nervosa can usually be treated on an outpatient basis (Fig. 55-1). Cognitive behavioral therapy and fluoxetine (Prozac) are first-line therapies. The recommended treatment dose for fluoxetine (60 mg/d) is higher than that typically used to treat depression.

For a more detailed discussion, see Walsh TB: Eating Disorders, Chap. 78, p. 486, in HPIM-15.

56

OBESITY

Obesity is a state of excess adipose mass. It is a chronic disorder that is increasing in prevalence. Obesity should not be defined by body weight alone, as muscular individuals may be overweight by arbitrary standards without having increased adiposity. The most widely used method to gauge obesity is the *body mass index* (BMI), which is equal to weight/height^2 in kg/m^2. At a similar BMI, women have more body fat than men. A BMI between 20 and 25 kg/m^2 is considered an appropriate weight for most individuals. Overweight is defined as a BMI > 25–27 kg/m^2, and obesity is defined as a BMI > 30 kg/m^2.

Pathogenesis

Excess accumulation of body fat is the consequence of environmental and genetic factors; social factors and economic conditions also represent important influences. The susceptibility to obesity is polygenic in nature, and 30–50% of the variability in total fat stores is believed to be genetically determined. Rare genetic syndromes associated with obesity include the Prader-Willi syndrome,

Ahlstrom's syndrome, Laurence-Moon-Biedl syndrome, Cohen's syndrome, and Carpenter's syndrome. Animal models also exist in which a single-gene mutation causes obesity, but defects in the corresponding genes in humans appear to be very rare. These include mutations in leptin, the leptin receptor, the melanocortin 4 receptor, and the pro-opiomelanocortin locus, among others. Animal models of obesity make clear the central role of the adipocyte in the pathogenesis. In addition to storing fat, these cells secrete lipoprotein lipase, tumor necrosis factor, angiotensinogen, and leptin. Leptin is an important satiety signal that acts directly in the hypothalamus to reduce food intake.

Weight gain or loss in individuals is determined by the balance between energy (food) intake and energy expenditure. The strong correlation between energy expenditure and fat-free body mass indicates that heavier people must on average ingest more food to provide the excess energy for weight gain. Obese individuals tend to underreport food intake by 50% or more. Physiologic variables that promote weight gain in the absence of significant increase in food intake include low metabolic rate, enhanced oxidation of carbohydrate relative to lipid, and insulin resistance. Secondary causes of obesity include hypothalamic injury, hypothyroidism, Cushing's syndrome, hypogonadism, and certain drugs (Table 56-1). Insulin-secreting tumors can also cause overeating.

Associated Risks

Increased mortality from obesity is primarily due to cardiovascular disease, hypertension, gall bladder disease, diabetes mellitus, and certain forms of cancer. The incidence of non-insulin-dependent diabetes is increased in individuals with a BMI > 22 kg/m². Cardiovascular mortality is linked to increased risk of sudden death from arrhythmias and the complications of atherosclerosis that are due to an atherogenic lipid profile (increased LDL cholesterol, very low density lipoprotein, and triglyceride; decreased HDL cholesterol). Hypertension is also common and is related to hyperinsulinemia and insulin resistance. The incidence of endometrial cancer and postmenopausal breast cancer, prostate cancer, and colorectal cancer in both men and women is increased with obesity. Sleep apnea in severely obese individuals poses potentially serious health risks. Obesity is also associated with an increased incidence of symptomatic gallstones and osteoarthritis.

Regional fat distribution may also influence the risks associated with obesity. Central obesity (high ratio of the circumference of the waist to the circumference of the hips) is associated with high triglyceride levels, low HDL cholesterol levels, and insulin resistance.

Table 56-1

Drugs That Enhance Appetite and Predispose to Obesity

Phenothiazines (chlorpromazine > thioridazine ≥ trifluoperazine > mesoridazine > promazine ≥ mepazine ≥ perphenazine ≥ prochlorperazine > haloperidol ≥ loxapine)
Antidepressants (amitriptyline > imipramine = doxepine = phenelzine ≥ amoxapine = desipramine = trazodone = tranylcypromine)
Antiepileptics (valproate; carbamazepine)
Steroids (glucocorticoids; megestrol acetate)
Antihypertensives (terazosin)

SOURCE: Bray GA; HPIM-14, p. 457.

℞ TREATMENT

Obesity is a chronic medical condition that requires ongoing treatment and lifestyle modifications. Palliation is the aim as cure is unlikely. Treatment is important because of the associated health risks but is made difficult by a limited repertoire of effective therapeutic options. Weight regain after weight loss is common with all forms of nonsurgical therapy. The urgency and selection of treatment modalities should be based on the BMI and a risk assessment. Associated risk factors such as age > 40, family history of coronary artery disease or diabetes mellitus, or presence of an obesity-related condition such as hypertension or osteoarthritis make treatment more urgent.

Low to Moderate Risk   Behavior modification including group counseling, diet diaries, and changes in eating patterns should be initiated. Food-related behaviors should be monitored carefully (avoid cafeteria-style settings, eat small and frequent meals, eat breakfast). A deficit of 7500 kcal will produce a weight loss of approximately 1 kg. Therefore, eating 100 kcal/d less for a year should cause a 5-kg weight loss, and a deficit of 1000 kcal/d should cause a loss of approximately 1 kg per week. Physical activity should be increased. Exercise is not useful as a primary strategy to lose weight but helps to maintain weight loss and may reinforce efforts to reduce caloric intake.

High Risk   Appetite-suppressing drugs such as fenfluramine and phentermine may result in greater weight loss than behavior modification alone; unfortunately, these drugs are associated with development of pulmonary hypertension and valvular heart disease and are no longer FDA approved in combination. Sibutramine is a central reuptake inhibitor of both norepinephrine and serotonin with efficacy in short-term trials, though it increases pulse and bp in some pts. Orlistat is an inhibitor of intestinal lipase that causes modest weight loss due to drug-induced fat malabsorption. Surgery is also an option in morbid obesity, which is defined as either 45 kg or 100% above ideal body weight. Weight regain and other medical problems are minimal with either a Roux-en-Y gastric bypass procedure or vertically banded gastroplasty (Fig. 77-8 in HPIM-15).

For a more detailed discussion, see Flier JS: Obesity, Chap. 77, p. 479, in HPIM-15.

57

EXAMINATION OF BLOOD SMEARS AND BONE MARROW

BLOOD SMEARS
Erythrocyte (RBC) Morphology

- Normal: 7.5-μm diameter.
- *Reticulocytes* (Wright's stain)—large, grayish-blue, admixed with pink (polychromasia).
- *Anisocytosis*—variation in RBC size; large cells imply delay in erythroid precursor DNA synthesis caused by folate or B_{12} deficiency or drug effect; small cells imply a defect in hemoglobin synthesis caused by iron deficiency or abnormal hemoglobin genes.
- *Poikilocytosis*—abnormal RBC shapes; the following are examples:
  Acanthocytes (spur cells)—irregularly spiculated; abetalipoproteinemia, severe liver disease, rarely anorexia nervosa.
  Echinocytes (burr cells)—regularly shaped, uniformly distributed spiny projections; uremia, RBC volume loss.
  Elliptocytes—elliptical; hereditary elliptocytosis.
  Schistocytes (schizocytes)—fragmented cells of varying sizes and shapes; microangiopathic or macroangiopathic hemolytic anemia.
  Sickled cells—elongated, crescentic; sickle cell anemias.
  Spherocytes—small hyperchromic cells lacking normal central pallor; hereditary spherocytosis, extravascular hemolysis as in autoimmune hemolytic anemia, (G6PD) deficiency.
  Target cells—central and outer rim staining with intervening ring of pallor; liver disease, thalassemia, hemoglobin C and sickle C diseases.
  Teardrop cells—myelofibrosis, other infiltrative processes of marrow (e.g., carcinoma).
  Rouleaux formation—alignment of RBCs in stacks; may be artifactual or due to paraproteinemia (e.g., multiple myeloma, macroglobulinemia).

RBC Inclusions

- *Howell-Jolly bodies*—1-μm diameter basophilic cytoplasmic inclusion that represents a residual nuclear fragment, usually single; asplenic pts.
- *Basophilic stippling*—multiple, punctate basophilic cytoplasmic inclusions composed of precipitated mitochondria and ribosomes; lead poisoning, thalassemia, myelofibrosis.
- *Pappenheimer (iron) bodies*—iron-containing granules usually composed of mitochondria and ribosomes resemble basophilic stippling but also stain with Prussian blue; lead poisoning, other sideroblastic anemias.
- *Heinz bodies*—spherical inclusions of precipitated hemoglobin seen only with supravital stains, such as crystal violet; G6PD deficiency (after oxidant stress such as infection, certain drugs), unstable hemoglobin variants.
- *Parasites*—characteristic intracytoplasmic inclusions; malaria, babesiosis.

Leukocyte Inclusions and Nuclear Contour Abnormalities

- *Toxic granulations*—dark cytoplasmic granules; bacterial infection.
- *Döhle bodies*—1- to 2-μm blue, oval cytoplasmic inclusions; bacterial infection, Chédiak-Higashi anomaly.

- *Auer rods*—eosinophilic, rodlike cytoplasmic inclusions; acute myeloid leukemia (some cases).
- *Hypersegmentation*—neutrophil nuclei contain more than the usual 2–4 lobes; usually >5% have ≥5 lobes or a single cell with 7 lobes is adequate to make the diagnosis; folate or B_{12} deficiency, drug effects.
- *Hyposegmentation*—neutrophil nuclei contain fewer lobes than normal, either one or two: Pelger-Hüet anomaly, pseudo-Pelger-Hüet or acquired Pelger-Hüet anomaly in acute leukemia.

Platelet Abnormalities

Platelet clumping—an in vitro artifact—is often readily detectable on smear; can lead to falsely low platelet count by automated cell counters.

BONE MARROW

Aspiration assesses cell morphology. *Biopsy* assesses overall marrow architecture, including degree of cellularity. Biopsy should precede aspiration to avoid aspiration artifact in the specimen.

Indications

ASPIRATION Hypoproliferative or unexplained anemia, leukopenia, or thrombocytopenia, suspected leukemia or myeloma or marrow defect, evaluation of iron stores, workup of some cases of fever of unknown origin.

Special Tests Histochemical staining (leukemias), cytogenetic studies (leukemias, lymphomas), microbiology (bacterial, mycobacterial, fungal cultures), Prussian blue (iron) stain (assess iron stores, diagnosis of sideroblastic anemias).

BIOPSY Performed in addition to aspiration for pancytopenia (aplastic anemia), metastatic tumor, granulomatous infection (e.g., mycobacteria, brucellosis, histoplasmosis), myelofibrosis, lipid storage disease (e.g., Gaucher's, Niemann-Pick), any case with "dry tap" on aspiration; evaluation of marrow cellularity.

Special Tests Histochemical staining (e.g., acid phosphatase for metastatic prostate carcinoma), immunoperoxidase staining (e.g., immunoglobulin or cell surface marker detection in multiple myeloma, leukemia, or lymphoma, lysozyme detection in monocytic leukemia), reticulin staining (increased in myelofibrosis), microbiologic staining (e.g., acid-fast staining for mycobacteria).

Interpretation

CELLULARITY Decreases with age after age 65 years from about 50% to 25–30%.

ERYTHROID:GRANULOCYTIC (E:G) RATIO Normally about 1:2, the E:G ratio is decreased in acute and chronic infection, leukemoid reactions (e.g., chronic inflammation, metastatic tumor), acute and chronic myeloid leukemia, myelodysplastic disorders ("preleukemia"), and pure red cell aplasia; increased in agranulocytosis, anemias with erythroid hyperplasia (megaloblastic, iron-deficiency, thalassemia, hemorrhage, hemolysis, sideroblastic), and erythrocytosis (excessive RBC production); normal in aplastic anemia (though marrow hypocellular), myelofibrosis (marrow hypocellular), multiple myeloma, lymphoma, anemia of chronic disease.

For a more detailed discussion, see Adamson JW, Longo DL: Anemia and Polycythemia, Chap. 61, p. 348; and Holland SM, Gallin JI: Disorders of Granulocytes and Monocytes, Chap. 64, p. 366, in HPIM-15.

58

RED BLOOD CELL DISORDERS

Anemia is a common clinical problem in medicine. A physiologic approach to anemia diagnosis (outlined in Chap. 27) provides the most efficient path to diagnosis and management. Anemias arise either because RBC production is inadequate or RBC lifespan is shortened through loss from the circulation or destruction.

HYPOPROLIFERATIVE ANEMIAS

These are the most common anemias encountered in clinical practice. Usually the RBC morphology is normal and the reticulocyte index (RI) is low. Marrow damage, early iron deficiency, and decreased erythropoietin production or action may produce anemia of this type.

Marrow damage may be caused by infiltration of the marrow with tumor or fibrosis that crowds out normal erythroid precursors or by the absence of erythroid precursors (aplastic anemia) as a consequence of exposure to drugs, radiation, chemicals, viruses (e.g., hepatitis), or genetic factors, either hereditary (e.g., Fanconi's anemia) or acquired (e.g., paroxysmal nocturnal hemoglobinuria). Most cases of aplasia are idiopathic. The tumor or fibrosis that infiltrates the marrow may originate in the marrow (as in leukemia or myelofibrosis) or be secondary to processes originating outside the marrow (as in metastatic cancer or myelophthisis).

Early iron-deficiency anemia (or iron-deficient erythropoiesis) is associated with a decrease in serum ferritin levels (<15 μg/L), moderately elevated total iron-binding capacity (>380 μg/dL), serum iron level <50 μg/dL, and an iron saturation of $<30\%$ but $>10\%$ (Fig. 58-1). RBC morphology is generally normal until iron deficiency is severe (see below).

Decreased stimulation of erythropoiesis can be a consequence of inadequate erythropoietin production [e.g., renal disease destroying the renal tubular cells that produce it or hypometabolic states (endocrine deficiency or protein starvation) in which insufficient erythropoietin is produced] or of inadequate erythropoietin action. The anemia of chronic disease is a common entity. It is multifactorial in pathogenesis: inhibition of erythropoietin production, inhibition of iron reutilization (which blocks the response to erythropoietin), and inhibition of erythroid colony proliferation by inflammatory cytokines (e.g., tumor necrosis factor, interferon-γ). The laboratory tests shown in Table 58-1 may assist in the differential diagnosis of hypoproliferative anemias.

MATURATION DISORDERS

These result from a defect in either hemoglobin synthesis, leading to cytoplasmic maturation defects and small red cells, or DNA replication, leading to nu-

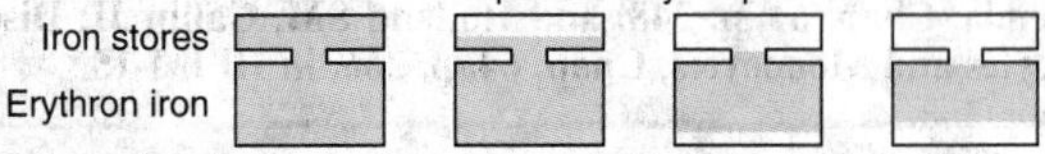

	Normal	Iron-store depletion	Iron-deficient erythropoiesis	Iron-deficiency anemia
Iron stores				
Erythron iron				
Marrow iron stores	1–3+	0–1+	0	0
Serum ferritin (μg/L)	50–200	<20	<15	<15
TIBC (μg/dL)	300–360	>360	>380	>400
SI (μg/dL)	50–150	NL	<50	<30
Saturation (%)	30–50	NL	<30	<10
Marrow sideroblasts (%)	40–60	NL	<10	<10
RBC protoporphyrin (μg/dL)	30–50	NL	>100	>200
RBC morphology	NL	NL	NL	Microcytic/ hypochromic

FIGURE 58-1 Laboratory studies in the evolution of iron deficiency. Measurements of marrow iron stores, serum ferritin, and TIBC are sensitive to early iron-store depletion. Iron-deficient erythropoiesis is recognized from additional abnormalities in the SI, percent saturation of transferrin, the pattern of marrow sideroblasts, and the red blood cell protoporphyrin level. Finally, patients with iron-deficiency anemia demonstrate all of these same abnormalities plus an anemia characterized by microcytic hypochromic morphology. (*From RS Hillman, CA Finchi: Red Cell Manual, 7th. ed, Philadelphia, Davis, 1996, with permission.*)

Table 58-1

Diagnosis of Hypoproliferative Anemias

Tests	Iron Deficiency	Inflammation	Renal Disease	Hypo- metabolic States
Anemia	Mild to severe	Mild	Mild to severe	Mild
MCV (fL)	70–90	80–90	90	90
Morphology	Normmicrocytic	Normocytic	Normocytic	Normocytic
SI	<30	<50	Normal	Normal
TIBC	>360	>300	Normal	Normal
Saturation (%)	<10	10–20	Normal	Normal
Serum ferri- tin (μg/L)	<15	30–200	115–150	Normal
Iron stores	0	2–4+	1–4+	Normal

NOTE: MCV, mean corpuscular volume.

clear maturation defects and large red cells. Defects in hemoglobin synthesis usually result from insufficient iron supply (iron deficiency), decreased globin production (thalassemia), or are idiopathic (sideroblastic anemia). Defects in DNA synthesis are usually due to nutritional problems (vitamin B_{12} and folate deficiency), toxic (methotrexate or other cancer chemotherapeutic agent) exposure, or intrinsic marrow maturation defects (refractory anemia, myelodysplasia).

Laboratory tests useful in the differential diagnosis of the microcytic anemias are shown in Table 58-2. Mean corpuscular volume (MCV) is generally 60 to 80 fL. Increased lactic dehydrogenase (LDH) and indirect bilirubin levels suggest an increase in RBC destruction and favor a cause other than iron deficiency. Iron status is best assessed by measuring serum iron, total iron-binding capacity, and ferritin levels. Macrocytic MCVs are >94 fL. Folate status is best assessed by measuring red blood cell folate levels. Vitamin B_{12} status is best assessed by measuring serum B_{12}, homocysteine, and methylmalonic acid levels. Homocysteine and methylmalonic acid levels are elevated in the setting of B_{12} deficiency.

ANEMIA DUE TO RBC DESTRUCTION OR ACUTE BLOOD LOSS

BLOOD LOSS   Trauma, GI hemorrhage (may be occult) are common causes; less common are genitourinary sources (menorrhagia, gross hematuria), internal bleeding such as intraperitoneal from spleen or organ rupture, retroperitoneal, iliopsoas hemorrhage (e.g., in hip fractures). Acute bleeding is associated with manifestations of hypovolemia, reticulocytosis, macrocytosis; chronic bleeding is associated with iron deficiency, hypochromia, microcytosis.

HEMOLYSIS   Causes are listed in Table 58-3.

1.   *Intracellular RBC abnormalities*—most are inherited enzyme defects [glucose-6-phosphate dehydrogenase (G6PD) deficiency >> pyruvate kinase deficiency], hemoglobinopathies, sickle cell anemia and variants, thalassemia, unstable hemoglobin variants.

G6PD deficiency leads to episodes of hemolysis precipitated by ingestion of drugs that induce oxidant stress on RBCs. These include antimalarials (chloroquine), sulfonamides, analgesics (phenacetin), and other miscellaneous drugs (Table 58-4).

Sickle cell anemia is characterized by a single amino acid change in β globin (valine for glutamic acid in the 6th residue) that produces a molecule of decreased solubility, especially in the absence of O_2. Although anemia and chronic hemolysis are present, the major disease manifestations relate to vasoocclusion

Table 58-2

Diagnosis of Microcytic Anemias

Tests	Iron Deficiency	Thalassemia	Sideroblastic Anemia
Smear	Micro/hypo	Micro/hypo with targeting	Variable
SI	Low	Normal to high	Normal to high
TIBC	High	Normal	Normal
Percent saturation	<10	30–80	30–80
Ferritin (μg/L)	<15	50–300	50–300
Hemoglobin pattern	Normal	Abnormal	Normal

Table 58-3

Classifications of Hemolytic Anemias

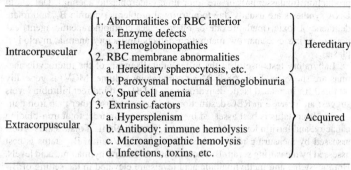

Table 58-4

Drugs Causing Hemolysis in Subjects Deficient in G6PD

Antimalarials: Primaquine, pamaquine, dapsone
Sulfonamides: Sulfamethoxazole
Nitrofurantoin
Analgesics: Acetanilid
Miscellaneous: Vitamin K (water-soluble form), doxorubicin, methylene blue,
  nalidixic acid, furazolidone, niridazole, phenazopyridine

Table 58-5

Clinical Manifestations of Sickle Cell Anemia

Constitutional
  Impaired growth and development
  Increased susceptibility to infection
Vasoocclusive
  Microinfarcts ⟶ Painful crisis
  Macroinfarcts ⟶ Organ damage
Anemia
  Severe hemolysis
  Aplastic crises ◄

SOURCE: See Chap. 107, p. 648 in HPIM-14.

from misshapen sickled RBCs. Infarcts in lung, bone, spleen, retina, brain, and
other organs lead to symptoms and dysfunction (Table 58-5).

    2. *Membrane abnormalities* (rare)—spur cell anemia (cirrhosis, anorexia
nervosa), paroxysmal nocturnal hemoglobinuria, hereditary spherocytosis (increased RBC osmotic fragility, spherocytes), hereditary elliptocytosis (causes
mild hemolytic anemia).

    3. *Immunohemolytic anemia* (positive Coombs' test, spherocytes). Two
types: (a) *warm antibody* (usually IgG)—idiopathic, lymphoma, chronic lymphocytic leukemia, SLE, drugs (e.g., methyldopa, penicillins, quinine, quini-

dine, isoniazid, sulfonamides); and (b) *cold antibody*—cold agglutinin disease (IgM) due to *Mycoplasma* infection, infectious mononucleosis, lymphoma, idiopathic; paroxysmal cold hemoglobinuria (IgG) due to syphilis, viral infections.

4.   *Mechanical trauma* (macro- and microangiopathic hemolytic anemias; schistocytes)—prosthetic heart valves, vasculitis, malignant hypertension, eclampsia, renal graft rejection, giant hemangioma, scleroderma, thrombotic thrombocytopenic purpura, hemolytic-uremic syndrome, DIC, march hemoglobinuria (e.g., marathon runners).

5.   *Direct toxic effect*—infections (e.g., malaria, *Clostridium welchii* toxin, toxoplasmosis).

6.   *Hypersplenism* (pancytopenia may be present).

LABORATORY ABNORMALITIES   Elevated reticulocyte index, polychromasia and nucleated RBCs on smear; also spherocytes, elliptocytes, schistocytes, target, spur, or sickle cells may be present depending on disorder; elevated unconjugated serum bilirubin and LDH, elevated plasma hemoglobin, low or absent haptoglobin; urine hemosiderin present in intravascular but not extravascular hemolysis, Coombs' test (immunohemolytic anemias), osmotic fragility test (hereditary spherocytosis), hemoglobin electrophoresis (sickle cell anemia, thalassemia), G6PD assay (best performed after resolution of hemolytic episode to prevent false-negative result).

 TREATMENT

General Approaches   The acuteness and severity of the anemia determine whether transfusion therapy with packed RBCs is indicated. Rapid occurrence of severe anemia (e.g., after acute GI hemorrhage resulting in Hct < 25%, following volume repletion) is an indication for transfusion. Hct should increase 3 to 4% [Hb by 10 g/L (1 g/dL)] with each unit of packed RBCs, assuming no ongoing losses. Chronic anemia (e.g., vitamin B_{12} deficiency), even when severe, may not require transfusion therapy if the pt is compensated and specific therapy (e.g., vitamin B_{12}) is instituted.

Specific Disorders

1.   *Iron deficiency*: find and treat cause of blood loss, oral iron (e.g., $FeSO_4$ 300 mg tid)
2.   *Folate deficiency*: common in malnourished, alcoholics; folic acid 1 mg PO qd (5 mg qd for pts with malabsorption)
3.   *Vitamin B_{12} deficiency*: can be managed either with parenteral vitamin B_{12} 100 μg IM qd for 7 d, then 100–1000 μg IM per month or 2 mg oral crystalline vitamin B_{12} per day
4.   *Anemia of chronic disease*: treat underlying disease; in uremia use recombinant human erythropoietin, 50–150 U/kg tiw; role of erythropoietin in other forms of anemia of chronic disease is less clear; response more likely if serum erythropoietin levels are low
5.   *Sickle cell anemia*: hydroxyurea (antisickling) 10–30 mg/kg/d PO, treat infections early, supplemental folic acid; painful crises treated with oxygen, analgesics, hydration, and hypertransfusion; consider allogeneic bone marrow transplantation in pts with increasing frequency of crises
6.   *Thalassemia*: transfusion to maintain Hb > 90 g/L (> 9 g/dL), folic acid, prevention of Fe overload with deferoximine chelation; consider splenectomy and allogeneic bone marrow transplantation
7.   *Aplastic anemia*: antithymocyte globulin ± cyclosporine, bone marrow transplantation in young pts with a matched donor
8.   *Autoimmune hemolysis*: glucocorticoids, sometimes immunosuppressive agents, danazol, plasmapheresis, rituximab
9.   *G6PD deficiency*: avoid agents known to precipitate hemolysis.

For a more detailed discussion, see Adamson JW et al: Chaps. 105–110, pp. 660–701, in HPIM-15.

59

LEUKOCYTOSIS AND LEUKOPENIA

LEUKOCYTOSIS
Approach

Review smear (? abnormal cells present) and obtain differential count. The normal values for concentration of blood leukocytes are shown in Table 59-1.

Neutrophilia

Absolute neutrophil count (polys and bands) >10,000/μL. The pathophysiology of neutrophilia involves increased production, increased marrow mobilization, or decreased margination (adherence to vessel walls).

CAUSES (1) *Exercise, stress*; (2) *infections*—esp. bacterial; smear shows increased numbers of immature neutrophils ("left shift"), toxic granulations, Döhle bodies; (3) *burns*; (4) *tissue necrosis* (e.g., myocardial, pulmonary, renal infarction); (5) *chronic inflammatory disorders* (e.g., gout, vasculitis); (6) *drugs* (e.g., glucocorticoids, epinephrine, lithium); (7) *cytokines* (e.g., G-CSF, GM-CSF); (8) *myeloproliferative disorders* (Chap. 63); (9) *metabolic* (e.g., ketoacidosis, uremia); (10) *other*—malignant neoplasms, acute hemorrhage or hemolysis, after splenectomy.

Leukemoid Reaction

Extreme elevation of leukocyte count (>50,000/μL) composed of mature and/ or immature neutrophils.

CAUSES (1) *Infection* (severe, chronic, e.g., tuberculosis), esp. in children; (2) *hemolysis* (severe); (3) *malignant neoplasms* (esp. carcinoma of the breast, lung, kidney); (4) *cytokines* (e.g., G-CSF, GM-CSF). May be distinguished from chronic myeloid leukemia (CML) by measurement of the leukocyte alkaline phosphatase (LAP) level: elevated in leukemoid reactions, depressed in CML.

Table 59-1

Normal Values for Leukocyte Concentration in Blood

Cell Type	Mean, cells/μL	95% Confidence Limits, cells/μL	Percent Total WBC
Neutrophil	3650	1830–7250	30–60%
Lymphocyte	2500	1500–4000	20–50%
Monocyte	430	200–950	2–10%
Eosinophil	150	0–700	0.3–5%
Basophil	30	0–150	0.6–1.8%

Leukoerythroblastic Reaction

Similar to leukemoid reaction with addition of nucleated RBCs and schistocytes on blood smear.

CAUSES (1) *Myelophthisis*—invasion of the bone marrow by tumor, fibrosis, granulomatous processes; smear shows "teardrop" RBCs; (2) *myelofibrosis*—same pathophysiology as myelophthisis, but the fibrosis is a primary marrow disorder; (3) *hemorrhage* or *hemolysis* (rarely, in severe cases).

Lymphocytosis

Absolute lymphocyte count >5000/μL.

CAUSES (1) *Infection*—infectious mononucleosis, hepatitis, CMV, rubella, pertussis, tuberculosis, brucellosis, syphilis; (2) *endocrine disorders*—thyrotoxicosis, adrenal insufficiency; (3) *neoplasms*—chronic lymphocytic leukemia (CLL), most common cause of lymphocyte count >10,000/μL.

Monocytosis

Absolute monocyte count >800/μL.

CAUSES (1) *Infection*—subacute bacterial endocarditis, tuberculosis, brucellosis, rickettsial diseases (e.g., Rocky Mountain spotted fever), malaria, leishmaniasis; (2) *granulomatous diseases*—sarcoidosis, Crohn's disease; (3) *collagen vascular diseases*—rheumatoid arthritis, SLE, polyarteritis nodosa, polymyositis, temporal arteritis; (4) *hematologic diseases*—leukemias, lymphoma, myeloproliferative and myelodysplastic syndromes, hemolytic anemia, chronic idiopathic neutropenia; (5) *malignant neoplasms*.

Eosinophilia

Absolute eosinophil count >500/μL.

CAUSES (1) *Drugs*, (2) *parasitic infections*, (3) *allergic diseases*, (4) *collagen vascular diseases*, (5) *malignant neoplasms*, (6) *hypereosinophilic syndromes*.

Basophilia

Absolute basophil count >100/μL.

CAUSES (1) *Allergic diseases*, (2) *myeloproliferative disorders* (esp. CML), (3) *chronic inflammatory disorders* (rarely).

LEUKOPENIA

Total leukocyte count <4300/μL.

Neutropenia

Absolute neutrophil count <2000/μL (increased risk of bacterial infection with count <1000/μL). The pathophysiology of neutropenia involves decreased production or increased peripheral destruction.

CAUSES (1) *Drugs*—cancer chemotherapeutic agents are most common cause, also phenytoin, carbamazepine, indomethacin, chloramphenicol, penicillins, sulfonamides, cephalosporins, propylthiouracil, phenothiazines, captopril, methyldopa, procainamide, chlorpropamide, thiazides, cimetidine, allopurinol, colchicine, ethanol, penicillamine, and immunosuppressive agents; (2) *infections*—viral (e.g., influenza, hepatitis, infectious mononucleosis, HIV), bacterial (e.g., typhoid fever, miliary tuberculosis, fulminant sepsis), malaria; (3)

nutritional—B_{12}, folate deficiencies; (4) *benign*—mild cyclic neutropenia common in blacks, no associated risk of infection; (5) *hematologic diseases*—cyclic neutropenia (q21d, with recurrent infections common), leukemia, myelodysplasis (preleukemia), aplastic anemia, bone marrow infiltration (uncommon cause), Chédiak-Higashi syndrome; (6) *hypersplenism*—e.g., Felty's syndrome, congestive splenomegaly, Gaucher's disease; (7) *autoimmune diseases*—idiopathic, SLE, lymphoma (may see positive antineutrophil antibodies).

 TREATMENT

Of the Febrile, Neutropenic Patient (See Chap. 42) In addition to usual sources of infection, consider paranasal sinuses, oral cavity (including teeth and gums), anorectal region; empirical therapy with broad-spectrum antibiotics (e.g., ceftazidime) is indicated after blood and other appropriate cultures are obtained. Prolonged febrile neutropenia (>7 d) leads to increased risk of disseminated fungal infections; requires addition of antifungal chemotherapy (e.g., amphotericin B). The duration of chemotherapy-induced neutropenia may be shortened by a few days by treatment with the cytokines GM-CSF or G-CSF.

Lymphopenia

Absolute lymphocyte count <1000/μL.

CAUSES (1) *Acute stressful illness*—e.g., myocardial infarction, pneumonia, sepsis; (2) *glucocorticoid therapy*; (3) *lymphoma* (esp. Hodgkin's disease); (4) *immunodeficiency syndromes*—ataxia telangiectasia and Wiskott-Aldrich and DiGeorge's syndromes; (5) *immunosuppressive therapy*—e.g., antilymphocyte globulin, cyclophosphamide; (6) *large-field radiation therapy* (esp. for lymphoma); (7) *intestinal lymphangiectasia* (increased lymphocyte loss); (8) *chronic illness*—e.g., CHF, uremia, SLE, disseminated malignancies; (9) *bone marrow failure/replacement*—e.g., aplastic anemia, miliary tuberculosis.

Monocytopenia

Absolute monocyte count <100/μL.

CAUSES (1) *Acute stressful illness*, (2) *glucocorticoid therapy*, (3) *aplastic anemia*, (4) *leukemia* (certain types, e.g., hairy cell leukemia), (5) *chemotherapeutic* and *immunosuppressive agents*.

Eosinopenia

Absolute eosinophil count <50/μL.

CAUSES (1) *Acute stressful illness*, (2) *glucocorticoid therapy*.

For a more detailed discussion, see Holland SM, Gallin JI: Disorders of Granulocytes and Monocytes, Chap. 64, p. 366; Young NS: Aplastic Anemia, Myelodysplasia, and Related Bone Marrow Failure Syndromes, Chap. 109, p. 692; Spivak JL: Polycythemia Vera and Other Myeloproliferative Diseases, Chap. 110, p. 701, in HPIM-15.

60

BLEEDING AND THROMBOTIC DISORDERS

BLEEDING DISORDER

Bleeding may result from abnormalities of (1) platelets, (2) blood vessel walls, or (3) coagulation. Platelet disorders characteristically produce petechial and purpuric skin lesions and bleeding from mucosal surfaces. Defective coagulation results in ecchymoses, hematomas, and mucosal and, in some disorders, recurrent joint bleeding (hemarthroses).

Platelet Disorders

THROMBOCYTOPENIA   Normal platelet count is 150,000–350,000/μL. Thrombocytopenia is defined as a platelet count <100,000/μL. Bleeding time, a measurement of platelet function, is abnormally increased if platelet count <100,000/μL; injury or surgery may provoke excess bleeding. Spontaneous bleeding is unusual unless count is <20,000/μL; platelet count <10,000/μL is often associated with serious hemorrhage. Bone marrow examination shows increased number of megakaryocytes in disorders associated with accelerated platelet destruction; decreased number in disorders of platelet production.

Causes   (1) Production defects such as marrow injury (e.g., drugs, irradiation), marrow failure (e.g., aplastic anemia), marrow invasion (e.g., carcinoma, leukemia, fibrosis); (2) sequestration due to splenomegaly; (3) accelerated destruction: causes include:

- *Drugs* such as chemotherapeutic agents, thiazides, ethanol, estrogens, sulfonamides, quinidine, quinine, methyldopa.
- *Heparin-induced thrombocytopenia* is seen in 5% of pts receiving >5 d of therapy and is due to in vivo platelet aggregation. Arterial and occasionally venous thromboses may result.
- *Autoimmune destruction* by an antibody mechanism; may be idiopathic or associated with SLE, lymphoma, HIV.
- *Idiopathic thrombocytopenic purpura* (ITP) has two forms: an acute, self-limited disorder of childhood requiring no specific therapy, and a chronic disorder of adults (esp. women 20–40 years). Chronic ITP may be due to autoantibodies to glycoprotein IIb-IIIa or glycoprotein Ib-IX complexes.
- *Disseminated intravascular coagulation* (DIC)—platelet consumption with coagulation factor depletion (prolonged PT, PTT) and stimulation of fibrinolysis (generation of fibrin split products, FSP). Blood smear shows microangiopathic hemolysis (schistocytes). Causes include infection (esp. meningococcal, pneumococcal, gram-negative bacteremias), extensive burns, trauma, or thrombosis; giant hemangioma, retained dead fetus, heat stroke, mismatched blood transfusion, metastatic carcinoma, acute promyelocytic leukemia.
- *Thrombotic thrombocytopenic purpura*—rare disorder characterized by microangiopathic hemolytic anemia, fever, thrombocytopenia, renal dysfunction (and/or hematuria), and neurologic dysfunction.
- Hemorrhage with extensive transfusion.

PSEUDOTHROMBOCYTOPENIA   Platelet clumping secondary to collection of blood in EDTA (0.3% of pts). Examination of blood smear establishes diagnosis.

THROMBOCYTOSIS Platelet count >350,000/μL. Either primary (thrombocythemia; Chap. 63) or secondary (reactive); latter secondary to severe hemorrhage, iron deficiency, surgery, after splenectomy (transient), malignant neoplasms (esp. Hodgkin's disease), chronic inflammatory diseases (e.g., inflammatory bowel disease), recovery from acute infection, vitamin B_{12} deficiency, drugs (e.g., vincristine, epinephrine). Rebound thrombocytosis may occur after marrow recovery from cytotoxic agents, alcohol. Primary thrombocytosis may be complicated by bleeding and/or thrombosis; secondary rarely causes hemostatic problems.

DISORDERS OF PLATELET FUNCTION Suggested by the finding of prolonged bleeding time with normal platelet count. Defect is in platelet adhesion, aggregation, or granule release. Causes include: (1) Drugs—aspirin, other NSAIDs, dipyridamole, heparin, penicillins, esp. carbenicillin, ticarcillin; (2) uremia; (3) cirrhosis; (4) dysproteinemias; (5) myeloproliferative and myelodysplastic disorders; (6) von Willebrand's disease (see below); (7) cardiopulmonary bypass.

Hemostatic Disorders due to Blood Vessel Wall Defects

Causes include: (1) aging; (2) drugs—e.g., glucocorticoids (chronic therapy), penicillins, sulfonamides; (3) vitamin C deficiency; (4) thrombotic thrombocytopenic purpura (TTP); (5) hemolytic uremic syndrome; (6) Henoch-Schönlein purpura; (7) paraproteinemias; (8) hereditary hemorrhagic telangiectasia (Osler-Rendu-Weber disease).

Disorders of Blood Coagulation

CONGENITAL DISORDERS

1. *Hemophilia A*—incidence 1:10,000; sex-linked recessive deficiency of factor VIII (low plasma factor VIII coagulant activity, but normal amount of factor VIII–related antigen—von Willebrand's factor). Laboratory features: elevated PTT, normal PT.

2. *Hemophilia B* (Christmas disease)—incidence 1:100,000, sex-linked recessive, due to factor IX deficiency. Clinical and laboratory features similar to hemophilia A.

3. *von Willebrand's disease*—most common inherited coagulation disorder (1:800–1000), usually autosomal dominant; primary defect is reduced synthesis or chemically abnormal factor VIII–related antigen produced by platelets and endothelium, resulting in abnormal platelet function.

ACQUIRED DISORDERS

1. *Vitamin K deficiency*—impairs production of factors II (prothrombin), VII, IX, and X; vitamin K is a cofactor in the carboxylation of glutamate residues on prothrombin complex proteins; major source of vitamin K is dietary (esp. green vegetables), with minor production by gut bacteria. Laboratory features: elevated PT and PTT.

2. *Liver disease*—results in deficiencies of all clotting factors except VIII. Laboratory features: elevated PT, normal or elevated PTT.

3. *Other disorders*—DIC, fibrinogen deficiency (liver disease, L-asparaginase therapy, rattlesnake bites), other factor deficiencies, circulating anticoagulants (lymphoma, SLE, idiopathic), massive transfusion (dilutional coagulopathy).

R̩ TREATMENT

Thrombocytopenia Caused by Drugs Includes discontinuation of possible offending agents; expect recovery in 7–10 d. Platelet transfusions may be needed if platelet count <10,000/μL.

Heparin-Induced Thrombocytopenia Includes prompt discontinuation of heparin. Warfarin and/or a fibrinolytic agent (see below) should be used for treatment of thromboses.

Chronic ITP Prednisone, initially 1–2 (mg/kg)/d, then slow taper, to keep the platelet count >60,000/μL. IV immunoglobulin to block phagocytic destruction may be useful. Splenectomy, danazol (androgen), or other agents (e.g., vincristine, cyclophosphamide, fludarabine) are indicated for pts requiring >5–10 mg prednisone daily.

DIC Control of underlying disease most important; platelets, fresh-frozen plasma (FFP) to correct clotting parameters. Heparin may be beneficial in pts with acute promyelocytic leukemia.

Thrombotic Thrombocytopenic Purpura Plasmapheresis and FFP infusions, possibly IV IgG; recovery in two-thirds of cases.

Disorders of Platelet Function Remove or reverse underlying cause. Dialysis and/or cryoprecipitate infusions (10 bags/24 h) may be helpful for platelet dysfunction associated with uremia.

Hemostatic Disorders Withdraw offending drugs, replace vitamin C, plasmapheresis and plasma infusion for TTP.

Hemophilia A Factor VIII replacement for bleeding or before surgical procedure; degree and duration of replacement depends on severity of bleeding. Give factor VIII to obtain a 15% (for mild bleeding) to 50% (for severe bleeding) factor VIII level. The duration should range from a single dose of factor VIII to therapy bid for up to 2 weeks.

Hemophilia B FFP or factor IX concentrates (Proplex, Konyne).

von Willebrand's Disease Cryoprecipitate (plasma product rich in factor VIII) or factor VIII concentrate (Humate-P, Koate HS); up to 10 bags bid for 48–72 h, depending on the severity of bleeding. Desmopressin (vasopressin analogue) may benefit some pts.

Vitamin K Deficiency Vitamin K 10 mg SC or slow IV.

Liver Disease Fresh-frozen plasma.

THROMBOTIC DISORDERS
Hypercoagulable State

Consider in pts with recurrent episodes of venous thrombosis (i.e., deep venous thrombosis, DVT; pulmonary embolism). Causes include: (1) Venous stasis (e.g., pregnancy, immobilization); (2) vasculitis; (3) myeloproliferative disorders; (4) oral contraceptives; (5) lupus anticoagulant—antibody to platelet phospholipid, stimulates coagulation; (6) heparin-induced thrombocytopenia; (7) deficiencies of endogenous anticoagulant factors—antithrombin III, protein C, protein S; (8) factor V Leiden—mutation in factor V (Arg → Glu at position 506) confers resistance to inactivation by protein C, accounts for 25% of cases of recurrent thrombosis; (9) prothrombin gene mutation—Glu → Arg at position 20210 results in increased prothrombin levels; accounts for about 6% of thromboses; (10) other—paroxysmal nocturnal hemoglobinuria, dysfibrinogenemias (abnormal fibrinogen).

R̩ TREATMENT

Correct underlying disorder whenever possible; long-term warfarin therapy is otherwise indicated.

Anticoagulant agents

1. *Heparin* (Table 60-1)—enhances activity of antithrombin III; parenteral agent of choice. Low-molecular-weight heparin is the preparation of choice (enoxaparin or dalteparin). It can be administered SC, monitoring of the PTT is unnecessary, and it is less likely to induce antibodies and thrombocytopenia. The usual dose is 100 U/kg SC bid. Unfractionated heparin should be given only if low-molecular-weight heparin is unavailable. In adults, the dose of unfractionated heparin is 25,000–40,000 U continuous IV infusion over 24 h following initial IV bolus of 5000 U; monitor by following PTT; should be maintained between 1.5 and 2 times upper normal limit. Prophylactic anticoagulation to lower risk of venous thrombosis recommended in some pts (e.g., postoperative, immobilized) (Table 60-1). Major complication of unfractionated heparin therapy is hemorrhage—manage by discontinuing heparin; for severe bleeding, administer protamine (1 mg/100 U heparin); results in rapid neutralization.

2. Warfarin (Coumadin)—vitamin K antagonist, decreases levels of factors II, VII, IX, X, and anticoagulant proteins C and S. Administered over 2–3 d; initial load of 5–10 mg PO qd followed by titration of daily dose to

Table 60-1

Anticoagulant Therapy with Low-Molecular-Weight and Unfractionated Heparin

Clinical Indication	Heparin Dose and Schedule	Target PTT[a]	LMWH Dose and Schedule[b]
Venous thrombosis pulmonary embolism			
Treatment	5000 U IV bolus; 1000–1500 U/h	2–2.5	100 U/kg SC bid
Prophylaxis	5000 U SC q8–12h	<1.5	100 U/kg SC bid
Acute myocardial infarction			
With thrombo-lytic therapy	5000 U IV bolus; 1000 U/h	1.5–2.5	100 U/kg SC bid
With mural thrombus	8000 U SC q8h + warfarin	1.5–2.0	100 U /kg SC bid
Unstable angina	5000 U IV bolus; 1000 U/h	1.5–2.5	100 U/kg SC bid
Prophylaxis			
General surgery	5000 U SC bid	<1.5	100 U/kg SC before and bid
Orthopedic surgery	10000 U SC bid	1.5	100 U/kg SC before and bid
Medical patients with CHF, MI	10000 U SC bid	1.5	100 U/kg SC bid

[a] Times normal control; assumes PTT has been standardized to heparin levels so that 1.5–2.5× normal equals 0.2–0.4 U/mL; if PTT is normal (27–35 S), start with 5000 U bolus 1300 U/h infusion monitoring PTT; if PTT at recheck is <50 S, rebolus with 5000 U and increase infusion by 100 U/h; if PTT at recheck is 50–60 s, increase infusion rate by 100 U/h; if PTT at recheck is 60–85 s, no change; if PTT at recheck is 85–100 s, decrease infusion rate 100 U/h; if PTT at recheck is 100–120 s, stop infusion for 30 min and decrease rate 100 U/h at restart; if PTT at recheck is >120 s, stop infusion for 60 min and decrease rate 200 U/h at restart.
[b] LMWH does not affect PTT and PTT is not used to adjust dosage.
NOTE: PTT, partial thromboplastin time; LMWH, low-molecular-weight heparin; CHF, congestive heart failure; MI, myocardial infarction.

keep PT 1.5–2 times control PT or 2–3 times if the International Normalized Ratio method is used. Complications include hemorrhage, warfarin-induced skin necrosis (rare, occurs in persons deficient in protein C), teratogenic effects. Warfarin effect reversed by administration of vitamin K; FFP infused if urgent reversal necessary. Numerous drugs potentiate or antagonize warfarin effect. Potentiating agents include chlorpromazine, chloral hydrate, sulfonamides, chloramphenicol, other broad-spectrum antibiotics, allopurinol, cimetidine, tricyclic antidepressants, disulfiram, laxatives, high-dose salicylates, thyroxine, clofibrate. Antagonizing agents include vitamin K, barbiturates, rifampin, cholestyramine, oral contraceptives, thiazides.

In-hospital anticoagulation usually initiated with heparin, with subsequent maintenance on warfarin after an overlap of 3 d.

Fibrinolytic Agents

Tissue plasminogen activator (tPA, alteplase), streptokinase, and urokinase; mediate clot lysis by activating plasmin, which degrades fibrin. Indications include treatment of DVT, with lower incidence of postphlebitic syndrome (chronic venous stasis, skin ulceration) than with heparin therapy; massive pulmonary embolism, arterial embolic occlusion of extremity, treatment of acute MI, unstable angina pectoris. Dosages for fibrinolytic agents: (1) *tPA*— for acute MI and massive PE (adult >65 kg), 10-mg IV bolus over 1–2 min, then 50 mg IV over 1 h and 40 mg IV over next 2 h (total dose = 100 mg). tPA is slightly more effective but more expensive than streptokinase for treatment of acute MI. (2) *Streptokinase*—for acute MI, 1.5 million IU IV over 60 min; or 20,000 IU as a bolus intracoronary (IC) infusion, followed by 2000 IU/min for 60 min IC. For pulmonary embolism or arterial or deep venous thrombosis, 250,000 IU over 30 min, then 100,000 IU/h for 24 h (pulmonary embolism) or 72 h (arterial or deep venous thrombosis). (3) *Urokinase*—for pulmonary embolism, 4400 IU/kg IV over 10 min, then 4400 (IU/kg)/h IV for 12 h.

Fibrinolytic therapy is usually followed by period of anticoagulant therapy with heparin. Fibrinolytic agents are contraindicated in pts with: (1) active internal bleeding; (2) recent (<2–3 months) cerebrovascular accident; (3) intracranial neoplasm, aneurysm, or recent head trauma.

Antiplatelet Agents

Aspirin (160–325 mg/d) with or without dipyridamole (50–100 mg qid) may be beneficial in lowering incidence of arterial thrombotic events (stroke, MI) in high-risk pts.

For a more detailed discussion, see Handin RI: Bleeding and Thrombosis, Chap. 62, p. 354; Disorders of the Platelet and Vessel Wall, Chap. 116, p. 745; Disorders of Coagulation and Thrombosis, Chap. 117, p. 751; and Anticoagulant, Fibrinolytic, and Antiplatelet Therapy, Chap. 118, p. 758, in HPIM-15.

61

TRANSFUSION AND PHERESIS THERAPY

TRANSFUSIONS
Whole Blood Transfusion

Indicated when acute blood loss is sufficient to produce hypovolemia, whole blood provides both oxygen-carrying capacity and volume expansion. In acute blood loss, hematocrit may not accurately reflect degree of blood loss for 48 h until fluid shifts occur.

Red Blood Cell Transfusion

Indicated for symptomatic anemia unresponsive to specific therapy or requiring urgent correction. Packed RBC transfusions may be indicated in pts who are symptomatic from cardiovascular or pulmonary disease when Hb is between 70 and 90 g/L (7 and 9 g/dL). Transfusion is usually necessary when Hb <70 g/L (<7 g/dL). One unit of packed RBCs raises the Hb by approximately 10 g/L (1 g/dL). If used instead of whole blood in the setting of acute hemorrhage, packed RBCs, fresh-frozen plasma (FFP), and platelets in an approximate ratio of 3:1:10 units are an adequate replacement for whole blood. Removal of leukocytes reduces risk of alloimmunization and transmission of CMV. Washing to remove donor plasma reduces risk of allergic reactions. Irradiation prevents graft-versus-host disease in immunocompromised recipients.

OTHER INDICATIONS   (1) *Hypertransfusion therapy* to block production of defective cells e.g., thalassemia, sickle cell anemia; (2) *exchange transfusion*—hemolytic disease of newborn, sickle cell crisis; (3) *transplant recipients*—decreases rejection of cadaveric kidney transplants.

COMPLICATIONS   (1) *Transfusion reaction*—immediate or delayed, seen in 1–4% of transfusions; IgA-deficient pts at particular risk for severe reaction; (2) *infection*—bacterial (rare); hepatitis C, 1 in 103,000 transfusions; HIV transmission, 1 in 490,000; (3) *circulatory overload*; (4) *iron overload*—each unit contains 200–250 mg iron; hemachromatosis may develop after 100 U of RBCs (less in children), in absence of blood loss; iron chelation therapy with deferoxamine indicated; (5) *graft-versus-host disease*; (6) alloimmunization.

Autologous Transfusion

Use of pt's own stored blood avoids hazards of donor blood; also useful in pts with multiple RBC antibodies. Pace of autologous donation may be accelerated using erythropoietin (50–150 U/kg SC three times a week) in the setting of normal iron stores.

Platelet Transfusion

Prophylactic transfusions usually reserved for platelet count <10,000/μL (<20,000/μL in acute leukemia). One unit elevates the count by about 10,000/μL if no platelet antibodies are present as a result of prior transfusions. Efficacy assessed by 1-h and 24-h posttransfusion platelet counts. HLA-matched single-donor platelets may be required in pts with platelet alloantibodies.

Transfusion of Plasma Components

FFP is a source of coagulation factors, fibrinogen, antithrombin, and proteins C and S. It is used to correct coagulation factor deficiencies, rapidly reverse warfarin effects, and treat thrombotic thrombocytopenic purpura (TTP). Cryoprecipitate is a source of fibrinogen, factor VIII, and von Willebrand factor; it may be used when recombinant factor VIII or factor VIII concentrates are not available.

THERAPEUTIC HEMAPHERESIS

Hemapheresis is removal of a cellular or plasma constituent of blood; specific procedure referred to by the blood fraction removed.

Leukapheresis

Removal of WBCs; most often used in acute leukemia, esp. acute myeloid leukemia (AML) in cases complicated by marked elevation (>100,000/μL) of the peripheral blast count, to lower risk of leukostasis (blast-mediated vasoocclusive events resulting in CNS or pulmonary infarction, hemorrhage). Leukapheresis is increasingly being used to harvest hematopoietic stem cells from the peripheral blood of cancer pts; such cells are then used to promote hematopoietic reconstitution after high-dose myeloablative therapy.

Plateletpheresis

Used in some pts with thrombocytosis associated with myeloproliferative disorders with bleeding and/or thrombotic complications. Other treatments are generally used first. Also used to enhance platelet yield from blood donors.

Plasmapheresis

INDICATIONS (1) *Hyperviscosity states*—e.g., Waldenström's macroglobulinemia; (2) *TTP*; (3) *immune-complex* and *autoantibody disorders*—e.g., Goodpasture's syndrome, rapidly progressive glomerulonephritis, myasthenia gravis; possibly Guillain-Barré, SLE, idiopathic thrombocytopenic purpura; (4) cold agglutinin disease, cryoglobulinemia.

For a more detailed discussion, see Dzieczkowski JS and Anderson KC: Transfusion Biology and Therapy, Chap. 114, p. 733, in HPIM-15.

62

CANCER CHEMOTHERAPY

BIOLOGY OF TUMOR GROWTH

Two essential features of cancer cells are uncontrolled growth and the ability to metastasize. The malignant phenotype of a cell is the end result of a series of genetic changes that remove safeguards restricting cell growth and induce new features that enable the cell to metastasize, including surface receptors for binding to basement membranes, enzymes to poke holes in anatomic barriers, cytokines to facilitate mobility, and angiogenic factors to develop a new vascular lifeline for nutrients and oxygen. These genetic changes usually involve increased or abnormal expression or activity of certain genes known as proto-oncogenes (often growth factors or their receptors, enzymes in growth pathways, or transcription factors), deletion or inactivation of tumor suppressor genes, and defects in DNA repair enzymes. These genetic changes may occur by point mutation, gene amplification, gene rearrangement, or epigenetic changes such as altered gene methylation.

Once cells are malignant, their growth kinetics are similar to those of normal cells but lack regulation. For unclear reasons, tumor growth kinetics follow a Gompertzian curve: as the tumor mass increases, the fraction of dividing cells declines. Thus, by the time a cancer is large enough to be detected clinically, its growth fraction is often small. Unfortunately, tumor growth usually does not stop altogether before the tumor reaches a lethal tumor burden. Cancer cells proceed through the same cell-cycle stages as normal cycling cells: G_1 (period of preparation for DNA synthesis), S (DNA synthesis), G_2 (tetraploid phase preceding mitosis in which integrity of DNA replication is assessed), and M (mitosis). Some noncycling cells may remain in a G_0, or resting, phase for long periods. Certain chemotherapeutic agents are specific for cells in certain phases of the cell cycle, a fact that is important in designing effective chemotherapeutic regimens.

DEVELOPMENT OF DRUG RESISTANCE

Drug resistance can be divided into de novo resistance or acquired resistance. De novo resistance refers to the tendency of many of the most common solid tumors to be unresponsive to chemotherapeutic agents. In acquired resistance, tumors initially responsive to chemotherapy develop resistance during treatment, usually because resistant clones appear within tumor cell populations. (Table 62-1).

Resistance can be specific to single drugs, because of defective transport of the drug, decreased activating enzymes, increased drug inactivation, increases in target enzyme levels, or alterations in target molecules. Multiple drug resistance occurs in cells overexpressing the P glycoprotein, a membrane glycoprotein responsible for enhanced efflux of drugs from cells, but there are other mechanisms as well.

CATEGORIES OF CHEMOTHERAPEUTIC AGENTS AND MAJOR TOXICITIES

A partial list of toxicities is shown in Table 62-2; some toxicities may apply only to certain members of a group of drugs.

COMPLICATIONS OF THERAPY

While the effects of cancer chemotherapeutic agents may be exerted primarily on the malignant cell population, virtually all currently employed regimens have profound effects on normal tissues as well. Every side effect of treatment must be balanced against potential benefits expected, and pts must always be fully apprised of the toxicities they may encounter. While the duration of certain adverse effects may be short-lived, others, such as sterility and the risk of secondary malignancy, have long-term implications; consideration of these effects is of importance in the use of regimens as adjuvant therapy. The combined toxicity of regimens involving radiotherapy and chemotherapy is greater than that seen with each modality alone. Teratogenesis is a special concern in treating women of childbearing years with radiation or chemotherapy. The most serious late toxicities are sterility (common; from alkylating agents), secondary acute

Table 62-1

Response of Tumors to Chemotherapy

CURABLE BY CHEMOTHERAPY

Acute lymphocytic leukemia	Non-Hodgkin's lymphoma
Acute myeloid leukemia	Diffuse large B cell
Ewing's sarcoma	Follicular mixed
Gestational trophoblastic carcinoma	Lymphoblastic
Hodgkin's disease	Burkitt's lymphoma/leukemia
Testicular carcinoma	Rhabdomyosarcoma
Wilms' tumor	

CHEMOTHERAPY HAS SIGNIFICANT ACTIVITY

Anal carcinoma	Head and neck cancer
Bladder carcinoma	Small cell lung cancer
Breast carcinoma	Multiple myeloma
Chronic lymphoid leukemia	Follicular lymphoma
Chronic myeloid leukemia	Ovarian cancer
Endometrial carcinoma	Hairy cell leukemia

CHEMOTHERAPY HAS MINOR ACTIVITY

Brain tumors	Melanoma
Cervical carcinoma	Pancreatic cancer
Colorectal carcinoma	Renal cell cancer
Prostate cancer	Soft tissue sarcoma
Hepatocellular carcinoma	Kaposi's sarcoma
Nonsmall cell lung cancer	Gastric cancer

ADJUVANT CHEMOTHERAPY IS EFFECTIVE

Breast carcinoma (axillary lymph node
  positive)
Colorectal carcinoma (Dukes B2 or C)
Osteogenic sarcoma
Ovarian carcinoma (stage III)
Testicular carcinoma

Table 62-2

List of Toxicities

Alkylating agents	Toxicity
(add alkyl groups to N-7 or O-6 of guanine)	
Busulfan	Nausea and vomiting, bone mar-
Chlorambucil	row depression, pulmonary fi-
Cyclophosphamide	brosis, sterility, hemorrhagic
Dacarbazine (DTIC)	cystitis, secondary malignan-
Mechlorethamine (nitrogen mustard)	cies, alopecia
Nitrosoureas	
L-Phenylalanine mustard	
Thiotepa	

(continued)

Table 62-2 *(Continued)*

List of Toxicities

Antimetabolites
  (inhibit DNA or RNA synthesis)
  Azathioprine
  Chlorodeoxyadenosine
  Cytarabine
  Fludarabine
  Fluorouracil
  Hydroxyurea
  Methotrexate
  6-Mercaptopurine
  Pentostatin
  6-Thioguanine

Nausea and vomiting, bone marrow depression, oral and GI ulceration, hepatic toxicity, alopecia, neurologic symptoms

Tubulin poisons
  (block tubule polymerization or
  depolymerization)
  Docetaxel
  Paclitaxel (Taxol)
  Vinblastine
  Vincristine

Nausea and vomiting, local pain upon extravasation, ileus, bone marrow depression, peripheral neuropathy, alopecia, SIADH, hypersensitivity rxn

Antibiotics
  (diverse antitumor mechanisms
  Bleomycin
  Dactinomycin (actinomycin D)
  Mithramycin
  Mitomycin

Nausea and vomiting, bone marrow depression, cardiotoxicity, lung fibrosis, hypocalcemia, alopecia, hypersensitivity rxn

Topoisomerase inhibitors
  (interfere with DNA unwinding)
  9-Aminocamptothecin
  Daunarubicin
  Doxorubicin
  Etoposide
  Idarubicin
  Mitoxantrone
  Teniposide

Nausea, vomiting, tissue necrosis upon extravasation, bone marrow depression, cardiotoxicity

Enzymes
  L-Asparaginase

Nausea and vomiting, fever, anaphylaxis, CNS changes, thrombosis, pancreatitis, renal and hepatic damage

Miscellaneous agents
  Interferon-α
  Carboplatin
  Cisplatin
  Flutamide
  Interleukin 2
  Leuprolide
  Procarbazine
  Tamoxifen

Nausea and vomiting, bone marrow depression, fever, chills, renal damage, antiestrogen effects, gynecomastia, impotence, hot flashes leukemia (rare; from alkylating agents and topoisomerase inhibitors), secondary solid tumors (0.5–1%/year risk for at least 25 years after treatment; from radiation therapy), premature atherosclerosis (3-fold increased risk of fatal MI; from radiation therapy), heart failure (rare; from anthracyclines), and pulmonary fibrosis (rare; from bleomycin).

For a more detailed discussion, see Sausville EA and Longo DL: Principles of Cancer Treatment, Chap. 84, p. 530, in HPIM-15.

63

MYELOID LEUKEMIAS, MYELODYSPLASIA, AND MYELOPROLIFERATIVE SYNDROMES

ACUTE MYELOID LEUKEMIA

Acute myeloid leukemia (AML) is a clonal malignancy of myeloid bone marrow precursors in which poorly differentiated cells accumulate in the bone marrow and circulation.

Signs and symptoms occur because of the absence of mature cells normally produced by the bone marrow including granulocytes (susceptibility to infection) and platelets (susceptibility to bleeding). In addition, if large numbers of immature malignant myeloblasts circulate, they may invade organs and rarely produce dysfunction. Distinct morphologic subtypes exist (Table 63-1) that have largely overlapping clinical features. Of note is the propensity of pts with acute promyelocytic leukemia (APL) (FAB M3) to develop bleeding and DIC, especially during induction chemotherapy, because of the release of procoagulants from their cytoplasmic granules.

INCIDENCE AND ETIOLOGY   About 7000 cases occur each year. AML accounts for about 80% of acute leukemias in adults. Etiology is unknown for the vast majority. Three environmental exposures increase the risk: chronic benzene exposure, radiation exposure, and prior treatment with alkylating agents and topoisomerase II inhibitors (e.g., doxorubicin and etoposide). Chronic myeloid leukemia, myelodysplasia, and myeloproliferative syndromes may all evolve into AML. Certain genetic abnormalities are associated with particular morphologic variants; t(15;17) with APL, inv(16) with eosinophilic leukemia; others occur in a number of types. Chromosome 11q23 abnormalities are often seen in leukemias developing after exposure to topoisomerase II inhibitors. The particular genetic abnormality has a strong influence on treatment outcome. Expression of MDR1 (multidrug resistance efflux pump) is common in older pts and adversely affects prognosis.

CLINICAL AND LABORATORY FEATURES   Initial symptoms of acute leukemia have usually been present for <3 months; a preleukemic syn-

Table 63-1

Acute Myeloid Leukemia (AML) Classification Systems

French-American-British (FAB) Classification[a]
M0: Minimally differentiated leukemia
M1: Myeloblastic leukemia without maturation
M2: Myeloblastic leukemia with maturation
M3: Hypergranular promyelocytic leukemia
M4Eo: Variant: Increase in abnormal marrow eosinophils
M4: Myelomonocytic leukemia
M5: Monocytic leukemia
M6: Erythroleukemia (DiGuglielmo's disease)
M7: Megakaryoblastic leukemia

World Health Organization Classification[b]
I. AML with recurrent cytogenetic translocations
   AML with t(8;21)(q22;q22); *AML1(CBFα)/ETO*
   Acute promyelocytic leukemia [AML with t(15;17)(q22;q12) and variants; *PML/RARα*]
   AML with abnormal bone marrow eosinophils [inv(16)(p13q22) or t(16;16)(p13;q22) *CBFβ/MYH1*]
   AML with 11q23 (*MLL*) abnormalities
II. AML with multilineage dysplasia
   With prior myelodysplastic syndrome
   Without prior myelodysplastic syndrome
III. AML and myelodysplastic syndrome, therapy-related
   Alkylating agent-related
   Epipodophyllotoxin-related
   Other types
IV. AML not otherwise categorized
   AML minimally differentiated
   AML without maturation
   AML with maturation
   Acute myelomonocytic leukemia
   Acute monocytic leukemia
   Acute erythroid leukemia
   Acute megakaryocytic leukemia
   Acute basophilic leukemia
   Acute panmyelosis with myelofibrosis

[a] JM Bennett et al: Ann Intern Med 103:620, 1985
[b] NL Harris et al: J Clin Oncol 17:3835, 1999

drome may be present in some 25% of pts with AML. Signs of anemia, pallor, fatigue, weakness, palpitations, and dyspnea on exertion are most common. WBC may be low, normal, or markedly elevated; circulating blast cells may or may not be present; with WBC >100 × 10⁹ blasts per liter, leukostasis in lungs and brain may occur. Minor pyogenic infections of the skin are common. Thrombocytopenia leads to spontaneous bleeding, epistaxis, petechiae, conjunctival hemorrhage, gingival bleeding, bruising, especially with platelet count <20 × 10⁹/L. Anorexia and weight loss are common; fever may be present.

Bacterial and fungal infection are common; risk is heightened with total neutrophil count <0.5 × 10⁹/L, breakdown of mucosal and cutaneous barriers aggravates susceptibility; infections may be clinically occult in presence of severe leukopenia, and prompt recognition requires a high degree of clinical suspicion.

Hepatosplenomegaly occurs in about one-third of pts; leukemic meningitis may present with headache, nausea, seizures, papilledema, cranial nerve palsies.

Metabolic abnormalities may include hyponatremia, hypokalemia, elevated serum lactate dehydrogenase (LDH), hyperuricemia, and (rarely) lactic acidosis. With very high blast cell count in the blood, spurious hyperkalemia and hypoglycemia may occur.

R TREATMENT

Leukemic cell mass at time of presentation may be 10^{11}–10^{12} cells; when total leukemic cell numbers fall below ~10^9, they are no longer detectable in blood or bone marrow and pt appears to be in complete remission (CR). Thus aggressive therapy must continue past the point when initial cell bulk is reduced if leukemia is to be eradicated. Typical phases of chemotherapy include remission induction and postremission therapy, with treatment lasting about 1 year.

Supportive care with transfusions of red cells and platelets (from CMV-seronegative donors, if pt is a candidate for bone marrow transplantation) is very important, as are aggressive prevention, diagnosis, and treatment of infections. Colony-stimulating factors offer little or no benefit; some recommend their use in older pts and those with active infections. Febrile neutropenia should be treated with broad-spectrum antibiotics (e.g., ceftazidime 1 g q8h); if febrile neutropenia persists beyond 7 days, amphotericin B should be added.

60–80% of pts will achieve initial remission when treated with cytarabine 100–200 mg/m^2/d by continuous infusion for 7 d and daunorubicin [45 mg/m^2/d] or idarubicin [12–13 mg/m^2/d] for 3 d. Addition of etoposide may improve CR duration. Half of treated pts enter CR with the first cycle of therapy and another 25% require two cycles. 10–30% of pts achieve 5-year disease-free survival and probable cure. Response to treatment after relapse is short, and prognosis for pts who have relapsed is poor. In APL, addition of trans-retinoic acid (tretinoin) to chemotherapy induces differentiation of the leukemic cells and may improve outcome. Arsenic trioxide also induces differentiation in APL cells.

Bone marrow transplantation from identical twin or HLA-identical sibling is effective treatment for AML. Typical protocol uses high-dose chemotherapy ± total-body irradiation to ablate host marrow, followed by infusion of marrow from donor. Risks are substantial (unless marrow is from identical twin). Complications include graft-versus-host disease, interstitial pneumonitis, opportunistic infections (especially CMV). Comparison between transplantation and high-dose cytarabine as postremission therapy has not produced a clear advantage for either approach. Up to 30% of otherwise end-stage pts with refractory leukemia achieve probable cure from transplantation; results are better when transplant is performed during remission. Results are best for children and young adults.

CHRONIC MYELOID LEUKEMIA (CML)

CML is a clonal malignancy usually characterized by splenomegaly and production of increased numbers of granulocytes; course is initially indolent but eventuates in leukemic phase (blast crisis) that has a poorer prognosis than de novo AML; rate of progression to blast crisis is variable; overall survival averages 4 years from diagnosis.

INCIDENCE AND ETIOLOGY   About 4000 cases occur each year. Over 90% of cases have a reciprocal translocation between chromosomes 9 and 22, creating the Philadelphia (Ph)chromosome and a fusion gene product called *bcr-abl* (*bcr* is from 9, *abl* from 22). The chromosome abnormality appears in all bone marrow–derived cells except T cells. The protein made by the chimeric gene is 210 kDa in chronic phase and 190 kDa in acute blast transformation. In some pts, the chronic phase is clinically silent and pts present with acute leukemia with the Ph chromosome.

CLINICAL AND LABORATORY FEATURES   Symptoms develop gradually; easy fatigability, malaise, anorexia, abdominal discomfort and early satiety from the large spleen, excessive sweating. Occasional pts are found incidentally based upon elevated leukocyte count. WBC count is usually >25 × 10^9/L with the increase accounted for by granulocytes and their precursors back to the myelocyte stage; bands and mature forms predominate. Basophils may account for 10–15% of the cells in the blood. Platelet count is normal or increased. Anemia is often present. Neutrophil alkaline phosphatase score is low. Marrow is hypercellular with granulocytic hyperplasia. Marrow blast cell count is normal or slightly elevated. Serum levels of vitamin B_{12}, B_{12}-binding proteins, and LDH are elevated in proportion to the WBC. With high blood counts, spurious hyperkalemia and hypoglycemia may be seen.

NATURAL HISTORY   Chronic phase lasts 2–4 years. Accelerated phase is marked by anemia disproportionate to the disease activity or treatment. Platelet counts fall. Additional cytogenetic abnormalities appear. Blast cell counts increase. Usually within 6–8 months, overt blast crisis develops in which maturation ceases and blasts predominate. The clinical picture is that of acute leukemia. Half of the cases become AML, one-third have morphologic features of acute lymphoid leukemia, 10% are erythroleukemia, and the rest are undifferentiated. Survival in blast crisis is often <4 months.

 TREATMENT

Chronic-phase disease may be treated with interferon-α (IFN) at 3 million units SC daily or tiw. The majority of pts obtain a hematologic response, and ~15% obtain cytogenetic remissions. Allopurinol, 300 mg/d, prevents urate nephropathy. The only curative therapy for the disease is HLA-matched allogeneic bone marrow transplantation. The optimal timing of transplantation is unclear, but transplantation in chronic phase is more effective than transplantation in accelerated phase or blast crisis. Transplantation appears most effective in pts treated within a year of diagnosis who have not received long-term IFN. Long-term disease-free survival may be obtained in 50–60% of transplanted pts. Infusion of donor lymphocytes can restore remission in relapsing pts. In pts without a matched donor, autologous transplantation may be helpful using peripheral blood stem cells. Treatment of pts in blast crisis is generally ineffective.

MYELODYSPLASTIC SYNDROMES (MDS)

These are clonal abnormalities of marrow cells characterized by varying degrees of cytopenias affecting one or more cell lines. These entities have been divided into five clinical syndromes (Table 63-2). Other terms that have been used to describe one or more of the entities include *preleukemia* and *oligoblastic leukemia*.

Table 63-2

French-American-British (FAB) Classification of Myelodysplastic Syndromes

| | FAB Types | | | | |
	RA	RARS	RAEB	CMML	RAEB-t
% Cases	28	24	23	16	9
% Blasts					
Marrow	<5	<5	5–20	1–20	20–30
Blood	<1	<1	<5	<5	>5
% Ringed Sideroblasts	<15	>15	<15	<15	<15
Monocytes	Rare	Rare	Rare	>1 × 10^9/L	Variable
Dyspoiesis	+	+	++	++	++
% Leukemic transformation	11	5	23	20	48
Median survival, months	37	49	9	22	6

ABBREVIATIONS: RA, refractory anemia; RARS, refractory anemia with ringed sideroblasts; RAEB, refractory anemia with excess blasts; CMML, chronic myelomonocytic leukemia; RAEB-t, refractory anemia with excess blasts in transformation.

INCIDENCE AND ETIOLOGY About 3000 cases occur each year, mainly in people >50 years old. Like AML, exposure to benzene, radiation, and chemotherapeutic agents may lead to MDS. Chromosome abnormalities occur in up to 80% of cases, including deletion of part or all of chromosomes 5, 7, and 9 (20 or 21 less commonly) and addition of part or all of chromosome 8.

CLINICAL AND LABORATORY FEATURES Symptoms depend on the affected lineages. 85% of pts are anemic, 50% have neutropenia, and about one-third have thrombocytopenia. The pathologic features of MDS are a cellular marrow with varying degrees of cytologic atypia including delayed nuclear maturation, abnormal cytoplasmic maturation, accumulation of ringed sideroblasts (iron-laden mitochondria surrounding the nucleus), uni- or bilobed megakaryocytes, micromegakaryocytes, and increased myeloblasts. Table 63-2 lists features used to identify distinct entities.

 TREATMENT

Allogeneic bone marrow transplantation is the only curative therapy and may cure 60% of those so treated. However, the majority of pts with MDS are too old to receive transplantation. Chemotherapy has not clearly altered the natural history of disease. Pts with low erythropoietin levels may respond to erythropoietin, and a minority of pts with neutropenia respond to granulocyte colony-stimulating factor. Supportive care is the cornerstone of treatment.

MYELOPROLIFERATIVE SYNDROMES

The three major myeloproliferative syndromes are polycythemia vera, idiopathic myelofibrosis, and essential thrombocytosis. All are clonal disorders of hematopoietic stem cells.

Polycythemia Vera

The most common myeloproliferative syndrome, this is characterized by an increase in RBC mass, massive splenomegaly, and clinical manifestations related to increased blood viscosity, including neurologic symptoms (vertigo, tinnitus, headache, visual disturbances) and thromboses (myocardial infarction, stroke, peripheral vascular disease; uncommonly, mesenteric and hepatic). It must be distinguished from other causes of increased RBC mass (Chap. 27). This is most readily done by assaying serum erythropoietin levels. Polycythemia vera is associated with very low erythropoietin levels; in other causes of erythrocytosis, erythropoietin levels are high. Pts are effectively managed with phlebotomy. Some pts require splenectomy to control symptoms, and those with severe pruritus may benefit from psoralens and UV light. 20% develop myelofibrosis, <5% acute leukemia.

Idiopathic Myelofibrosis

This rare entity is characterized by marrow fibrosis, myeloid metaplasia with extramedullary hematopoiesis, and splenomegaly. Evaluation of a blood smear reveals tear-drop shaped RBC, nucleated RBC, and some early granulocytic forms, including promyelocytes. However, many entities may lead to marrow fibrosis and extramedullary hematopoiesis, and the diagnosis of primary idiopathic myelofibrosis is made only when the many other potential causes are ruled out. The following diseases are in the differential diagnosis: CML, polycythemia vera, Hodgkin's disease, cancer metastatic to the marrow (especially from breast and prostate), infection (particularly granulomatous infections), and hairy cell leukemia. Supportive therapy is generally used; no specific therapy is known.

Essential Thrombocytosis

This is usually noted incidentally upon routine platelet count done in an asymptomatic person. Like myelofibrosis, many conditions can produce elevated platelet counts; thus, the diagnosis is one of exclusion. Platelet count must be >500,000/μL, and known causes of thrombocytosis must be ruled out including CML, iron deficiency, splenectomy, malignancy, infection, hemorrhage, polycythemia vera, myelodysplasia, and recovery from vitamin B_{12} deficiency. Although usually asymptomatic, pts should be treated if they develop migraine headache, transient ischemic attack, or other bleeding or thrombotic disease manifestations. Interferon-α is effective therapy, as are anagrelide and hydroxyurea. Treatment should not be given just because the absolute platelet count is high in the absence of other symptoms.

For a more detailed discussion, see Young NS: Aplastic Anemia, Myelodysplasia, and Related Bone Marrow Failure Syndromes, Chap. 109, p. 692; Spivak JL: Polycythemia Vera and Other Myeloproliferative Diseases, Chap. 110, p. 701; and Wetzler M, Byrd JC, Bloomfield CD: Acute and Chronic Myeloid Leukemia, Chap. 111, p. 706, in HPIM-15.

64

LYMPHOID MALIGNANCIES

DEFINITION Neoplasms of lymphocytes usually represent malignant counterparts of cells at discrete stages of normal lymphocyte differentiation. When bone marrow and peripheral blood involvement dominate the clinical picture, the disease is classified as a *lymphoid leukemia*. When lymph nodes and/or other extranodal sites of disease are the dominant site(s) of involvement, the tumor is called a *lymphoma*. The distinction between lymphoma and leukemia is sometimes blurred; for example, small lymphocytic lymphoma and chronic lymphoid leukemia are tumors of the same cell type and are distinguished arbitrarily on the basis of the absolute number of peripheral blood lymphocytes ($>5 \times 10^9$/L defines leukemia).

CLASSIFICATION Historically, lymphoid tumors have had separate pathologic classifications based on the clinical syndrome—lymphomas according to the Rappaport, Kiel, or Working Formulation systems, acute leukemias according to the French-American-British (FAB) system, Hodgkin's disease according to the Rye classification. Myelomas have generally not been subclassified by pathologic features of the neoplastic cells. Recently, the World Health Organization (WHO) has proposed a unifying classification system that brings together all lymphoid neoplasms into a single framework. Although the new system codifies and standardizes the definitions of disease entities based upon histology, genetic abnormalities, and cell surface immunophenotype, its organization is based upon cell of origin (B cell vs. T cell) and maturation stage (precursor vs. mature) of the tumor, features that are of limited value to the clinician. Table 64-1 lists the disease entities according to a more clinically useful schema based upon the clinical manifestations and natural history of the diseases.

INCIDENCE Lymphoid tumors are increasng in incidence. Nearly 90,000 cases were diagnosed in 2000 in the U.S.

ETIOLOGY The cause(s) for the vast majority of lymphoid neoplasms is unknown. Like other cancers, the malignant cells are monoclonal and often contain numerous genetic abnormalities. Some genetic alterations are characteristic of particular histologic entities: t(8;14) in Burkitt's lymphoma, t(14;18) in follicular lymphoma, t(11;14) in mantle cell lymphoma, t(2;5) in anaplastic large cell lymphoma, translocations or mutations involving *bcl*-6 on 3q27 in diffuse large cell lymphoma, and others. In most cases, translocations involve insertion of a distant chromosome segment into the antigen receptor genes (either immunoglobulin or T cell receptor) during the rearrangement of the gene segments that form the receptors.

Three viruses, Epstein-Barr virus, human herpesvirus-8 (HHV-8) (both herpes family viruses), and human T-lymphotropic virus type I (HTLV-I, a retrovirus), may cause some lymphoid tumors. EBV has been strongly associated with African Burkitt's lymphoma and the lymphomas that complicate immunodeficiencies (disease-related or iatrogenic). EBV has an uncertain relationship to mixed cellularity Hodgkin's disease and angiocentric lymphoma. HHV-8 causes a rare entity, body cavity lymphoma, mainly in patients with AIDS. HTLV-I is associated with adult T cell leukemia/lymphoma. Both the virus and the disease are endemic to southwestern Japan and the Caribbean.

Table 64-1

Clinical Schema of Lymphoid Neoplasms

Chronic lymphoid leukemias/lymphomas
  Chronic lymphocytic leukemia/small lymphocytic lymphoma (99% B cell, 1% T cell)
  Prolymphocytic leukemia (90% B cell, 10% T cell)
  Large granular lymphocyte leukemia [80% natural killer (NK) cell, 20% T cell]
  Hairy cell leukemia (99-100% B cell)
Indolent lymphoma
  Follicular center cell lymphoma, grades I and II (100% B cell)
  Lymphoplasmacytic lymphoma/Waldenström's macroglobulinemia (100% B cell)
  Marginal zone lymphoma (100% B cell)
    Extranodal [mucosa-associated lymphatic tissue (MALT) lymphoma]
    Nodal (monocytoid B cell lymphoma)
    Splenic marginal zone lymphoma
  Cutaneous T cell lymphoma (mycosis fungoides) (100% T cell)
Aggressive lymphoma
  Diffuse large cell lymphoma (85% B cell, 15% T cell), includes immuno-blastic
  Follicular center cell lymphoma, grade III (100% B cell)
  Mantle cell lymphoma (100% B cell)
  Primary mediastinal (thymic) large B cell lymphoma (100% B cell)
  Burkitt-like lymphoma (100% B cell)
  Peripheral T cell lymphoma (100% T cell)
  Angioimmunoblastic lymphoma (100% T cell)
  Angiocentric lymphoma (80% T cell, 20% NK cell)
  Intestinal T cell lymphoma (100% T cell)
  Anaplastic large cell lymphoma (70% T cell, 30% null cell)
Acute lymphoid leukemias/lymphomas
  Precursor lymphoblastic leukemia/lymphoma (80% T cell, 20% B cell)
  Burkitt's leukemia/lymphoma (100% B cell)
  Adult T cell leukemia/lymphoma (100% T cell)
Plasma cell disorders (100% B cell)
  Monoclonal gammopathy of uncertain significance
  Solitary plasmacytoma
  Extramedullary plasmacytoma
  Multiple myeloma
  Plasma cell leukemia
Hodgkin's disease (cell of origin mainly B cell)
  Lymphocyte predominant
  Nodular sclerosis
  Mixed cellularity
  Lymphocyte depleted

Gastric *Helicobacter pylori* infection is associated with gastric MALT lymphoma and perhaps gastric large cell lymphoma. Eradication of the infection produces durable remissions in about half of pts with gastric MALT lymphoma.

Inherited or acquired immunodeficiencies and autoimmune disorders predispose individuals to lymphoma. Lymphoma occurs with increased incidence in farmers and meat workers; Hodgkin's disease is increased in wood workers.

DIAGNOSIS AND STAGING   Excisional biopsy is the standard diagnostic procedure; adequate tissue must be obtained. Tissue undergoes three kinds of studies: (1) light microscopy to discern the pattern of growth and the morphologic features of the malignant cells, (2) flow cytometry for assessment of immunophenotype, and (3) genetic studies (cytogenetics, DNA extraction). Needle aspirates of nodal or extranodal masses are not adequate diagnostic procedures. Leukemia diagnosis and lymphoma staging include generous bilateral iliac crest bone marrow biopsies. Differential diagnosis of adenopathy is reviewed in Chap. 28.

Staging varies with the diagnosis. In Hodgkin's disease, defining the anatomic extent of disease is essential to define the optimal treatment approach. In acute leukemia, peripheral blood blast counts are most significant in assessing prognosis. In chronic leukemia, peripheral blood red blood cell and platelet counts are most significant in assessing prognosis. In indolent lymphoma, which is usually widespread at diagnosis, and in aggressive lymphoma, age, stage, lactate dehydrogenase (LDH) level, number of extranodal sites, and Karnofsky index predict outcome. In myeloma, serum levels of paraprotein, creatinine, and β_2-microglobulin levels predict survival.

CHRONIC LYMPHOID LEUKEMIAS/LYMPHOMAS

Most of these entities have a natural history measured in years (prolymphocytic leukemia is very rare and can be very aggressive). Chronic lymphocytic leukemia is the most common entity in this group and the most common leukemia in the western world.

CHRONIC LYMPHOCYTIC LEUKEMIA (CLL)   Usually presents as asymptomatic lymphocytosis in pts >60 years. The malignant cell is a CD5+ B cell that looks like a normal small lymphocyte. Trisomy 12 is the most common genetic abnormality. Prognosis is related to stage; stage is determined mainly by the degree to which the tumor cells crowd out normal hematopoietic elements from the marrow (Table 64-2). Cells may infiltrate nodes and spleen as well as marrow. Nodal involvement may be related to the expression of an adhesion molecule that allows the cells to remain in the node rather than recirculate. Pts often have hypogammaglobulinemia. Up to 20% have autoimmune

Table 64-2

Staging of B Cell CLL and Relation to Survival

Stage	Clinical Features	Median Survival, Years
RAI		
0	Lymphocytosis	12
I	Lymphocytosis + adenopathy	9
II	Lymphocytosis + splenomegaly	7
III	Anemia	1–2
IV	Thrombocytopenia	1–2
BINET		
A	No anemia/thrombocytopenia, <3 involved sites	>10
B	No anemia/thrombocytopenia, >3 involved sites	5
C	Anemia and/or thrombocytopenia	2

antibodies that may produce autoimmune hemolytic anemia, thrombocytopenia, or red cell aplasia. Death is from infection, marrow failure, or intercurrent illnesses. In 5%, the disease evolves to aggressive lymphoma (Richter's syndrome) that is refractory to treatment.

Subsets of CLL may exist based on whether the immunoglobulin expressed by the tumor cell contains mutations (more indolent course, good prognosis) or retains the germline sequence (more aggressive course, poor response to therapy). Methods to distinguish the two subsets clinically are not well defined; CD38+ tumors may have poorer prognosis.

 TREATMENT

Supportive care is generally given until anemia or thrombocytopenia develop. At that time, tests are indicated to assess the cause of the anemia or thrombocytopenia. Decreased red blood cell and/or platelet counts related to peripheral destruction may be treated with splenectomy or glucocorticoids without cytotoxic therapy in many cases. If marrow replacement is the mechanism, cytotoxic therapy is indicated. Fludarabine 25 mg/m^2/d IV $\times$ 5 days every 4 weeks induces responses in about 75% of pts, complete responses in half. Glucocorticoids increase the risk of infection without adding a substantial antitumor benefit. Monthly IV immunoglobulin significantly reduces risk of serious infection but is expensive. Alkylating agents are also active against the tumor. Therapeutic intent is palliative in most pts. Young pts may be candidates for high-dose therapy and autologous or allogeneic hematopoietic cell transplantation; long-term disease-free survival has been noted. Mini-transplant, in which the preparative regimen is immunosuppressive but not myeloablative, may be less toxic and as active or more active in disease treatment than high-dose therapy.

See Chap. 112 in HPIM-15 for discussion of the rarer entities.

INDOLENT LYMPHOMAS

These entities have a natural history measured in years. Median survival is about 10 years. Follicular center lymphoma is the most common indolent lymphoma, accounting for about one-third of all lymphoid malignancies.

FOLLICULAR CENTER LYMPHOMA Usually presents with painless peripheral lymphadenopathy, often involving several nodal regions. "B symptoms" (fever, sweats, weight loss) occur in 10%, less common than with Hodgkin's disease. In about 25%, nodes wax and wane before the pt seeks medical attention. Median age is 55 years. Disease is widespread at diagnosis in 85%. Liver and bone marrow are commonly involved extranodal sites.

The tumor has a follicular or nodular growth pattern reflecting the follicular center origin of the malignant cell. The t(14;18) is present in 85% of cases, resulting in the overexpression of *bcl*-2, a protein involved in prevention of programmed cell death. The normal follicular center B cell is undergoing active mutation of the immunoglobulin variable regions in an effort to generate antibody of higher affinity for the selecting antigen. Follicular center lymphoma cells also have a high rate of mutation that leads to the accumulation of genetic damage. Over time, follicular center lymphomas acquire sufficient genetic damage (e.g., mutated p53) to accelerate their growth and evolve into diffuse large cell lymphomas that are refractory to treatment. The majority of pts dying from follicular lymphoma have undergone histologic transformation.

TREATMENT

Only 15% of pts have localized disease, but the majority of these pts are curable with radiation therapy. Although many forms of treatment induce tumor regression in advanced-stage pts, it is not clear that treatment of any kind alters the natural history of disease. No therapy, single-agent alkylators, nucleoside analogues (fludarabine, cladribine), combination chemotherapy, radiation therapy, and biologic agents (interferon-α, monoclonal antibodies such as rituxan, anti-CD20) are all considered appropriate. Over 90% of pts are responsive to treatment; complete responses are seen in about half of pts treated aggressively. Younger pts are being treated experimentally with high-dose therapy and autologous hematopoietic stem cells or mini-transplant. It is not yet clear whether this is curative. There is some evidence that combination chemotherapy with or without interferon maintenance may prolong survival and delay or prevent histologic progression, especially in pts with poor prognostic features.

See Chap. 112 in HPIM-15 for discussion of the other indolent lymphomas.

AGGRESSIVE LYMPHOMAS

A large number of pathologic entities share an aggressive natural history; survival untreated is 6–8 months, and nearly all untreated pts are dead within 1 year. Pts may present with asymptomatic adenopathy or symptoms referable to involvement of practically any nodal or extranodal site: mediastinal involvement may produce superior vena cava syndrome or pericardial tamponade; retroperitoneal nodes may obstruct ureters, abdominal masses may produce pain, ascites, or GI obstruction or perforation; CNS involvement may produce confusion, cranial nerve signs, headache, seizures, and/or spinal cord compression; bone involvement may produce pain or pathologic fracture. About 45% of pts have B symptoms.

Diffuse large B cell lymphoma is the most common histologic diagnosis among the aggressive lymphomas, accounting for ~30% of all lymphomas. Aggressive lymphomas together account for ~55% of all lymphoid tumors. About 85% of aggressive lymphomas are of mature B cell origin; 15% are derived from peripheral (postthymic) T cells.

———————————— *Approach to the Patient* ————————————

Early diagnostic biospy is critical. Pt workup is directed by symptoms and known patterns of disease. Pts with Waldeyer's ring involvement should undergo careful evaluation of the GI tract. Pts with bone or bone marrow involvement should have a lumbar puncture to evaluate meningeal CNS involvement.

 TREATMENT

Localized aggressive lymphomas are usually treated with 4 cycles of CHOP (cyclophosphamide, doxorubicin, vincristine, prednisone) combination chemotherapy followed by involved-field radiation therapy. About 85% of these pts are cured. The specific therapy used for pts with more advanced disease is controversial. Treatment outcome with CHOP is influenced by tumor bulk (usually measured by LDH levels, stage, and number of extranodal sites) and physiologic reserve (usually measured by age and Karnofsky status). The influence of these factors on outcome is shown in Table 64-3. In

Table 64-3

The International Index and Prognosis in Diffuse Aggressive Non-Hodgkin's Lymphoma

Risk Group (Patients of All Ages)	Risk Factors[a]	Distribution of Cases, %	Complete Response Rate, %	5-Year Survival Rate, %
Low	0, 1	35	87	73
Low-intermediate	2	27	67	51
High-intermediate	3	22	55	43
High	4, 5	16	44	26

[a] Age (≤60 vs. >60); serum LDH (normal vs. >1 × normal); performance status (0 or 1 vs. 2–4); stage (I or II vs. III or IV); and extranodal involvement (≥1 site vs. >1 site)

SOURCE: Adapted from MA Shipp: Blood 83:1165, 1994.

most series, CHOP cures about one-third of pts. Some investigators have demonstrated cure rates about twice those achieved by CHOP using more aggressive combination chemotherapy regimens that do not require hematopoietic stem cell support. However, randomized trials have not shown significant outcome differences. Furthermore, the use of a sequential high-dose chemotherapy regimen in pts with high-intermediate- and high-risk disease has yielded long-term survival in about 75% of pts in some institutions. Other studies fail to confirm a role for high-dose therapy. The use of rituxan plus chemotherapy appears to improve response rates.

About 30–45% of pts not cured with initial standard combination chemotherapy may be salvaged with high-dose therapy and autologous hematopoietic stem cell transplantation.

Specialized approaches are required for lymphomas involving certain sites (e.g., CNS, stomach) or under certain complicating clinical circumstances (e.g., concurrent illness, AIDS). Lymphomas occurring in iatrogenically immunosuppressed people may regress when immunosuppressive medication is withheld. Lymphomas occurring postallogeneic marrow transplant may regress with infusions of donor leukocytes.

Pts with rapidly growing bulky aggressive lymphoma may experience tumor lysis syndrome when treated (Chap. 43); prophylactic measures (hydration, urine alkalinization, allopurinol) may be lifesaving.

ACUTE LYMPHOID LEUKEMIAS/LYMPHOMAS

ACUTE LYMPHOBLASTIC LEUKEMIA AND LYMPHOBLASTIC LYMPHOMA   These are more common in children than adults. The majority of cases have tumor cells that appear to be of thymic origin, and pts may have mediastinal masses. Pts usually present with recent onset of signs of marrow failure (pallor, fatigue, bleeding, fever, infection). Hepatosplenomegaly and adenopathy are common. Males may have testicular enlargement reflecting leukemic involvement. Meningeal involvement may be present at diagnosis or develop later. Elevated LDH, hyponatremia, and hypokalemia may be present, in addition to anemia, thrombocytopenia, and high peripheral blood blast counts. The leukemic cells are more often FAB L2 in type in adults than in children, where L1 predominates. Leukemia diagnosis requires at least 30% lymphoblasts in the marrow. Prognosis is adversely affected by high presenting white count, age >35 years, and the presence of t(9;22), t(1;19), and t(4;11) translocations.

TREATMENT

Successful treatment requires intensive induction phase, CNS prophylaxis, and maintenance chemotherapy that extends for about 2 years. Vincristine, L-asparaginase, cytarabine, daunorubicin, and prednisone are particularly effective agents. Intrathecal or high-dose systemic methotrexate is effective CNS prophylaxis. Long-term survival of 60–65% of pts may be achieved. The role and timing of bone marrow transplantation in primary therapy is debated, but up to 30% of relapsed pts may be cured with salvage transplantation.

BURKITT'S LYMPHOMA/LEUKEMIA This is also more common in children. It is associated with translocations involving the c-*myc* gene on chromosome 8 rearranging with immunoglobulin heavy or light chain genes. Pts often have disseminated disease with large abdominal masses, hepatomegaly, and adenopathy. If a leukemic picture predominates, it is classified as FAB L3.

 TREATMENT

Resection of large abdominal masses improves treatment outcome. Aggressive leukemia regimens that include vincristine, cyclophosphamide, 6-mercaptopurine, doxorubicin, and prednisone are active. Cure may be achieved in 50–60%. The need for maintenance therapy is unclear. Prophylaxis against tumor lysis syndrome is important (Chap. 43).

ADULT T CELL LEUKEMIA/LYMPHOMA (ATL) This is very rare, and only a small fraction of persons infected with HTLV-I go on to develop the disease. Some HTLV-I-infected pts develop spastic paraplegia from spinal cord involvement without developing cancer. The characteristic clinical syndrome of ATL includes high white count without severe anemia or thrombocytopenia, skin infiltration, hepatomegaly, pulmonary infiltrates, meningeal involvement, and opportunistic infections. The tumor cells are CD4+ T cells with cloven hoof- or flower-shaped nuclei. Hypercalcemia occurs in nearly all pts and is related to cytokines produced by the tumor cells.

 TREATMENT

Aggressive therapy is associated with serious toxicity related to the underlying immunodeficiency. Glucocorticoids relieve hypercalcemia. The tumor is responsive to therapy, but responses are generally short-lived. Zidovudine and interferon may be palliative in some pts.

PLASMA CELL DISORDERS

The hallmark of plasma cell disorders is the production of immunoglobulin molecules or fragments from abnormal plasma cells. The intact immunoglobulin molecule, or the heavy chain or light chain produced by the abnormal plasma cell clone, is detectable in the serum and/or urine and is called the M (for monoclonal) component. The amount of the M component in any given pt reflects the tumor burden in that pt. In some, the presence of a clonal light chain in the urine (Bence Jones protein) is the only tumor product that is detectable. M components may be seen in pts with other lymphoid tumors, nonlymphoid cancers, and noncancerous conditions such as cirrhosis, sarcoidosis, parasitic infestations, and autoimmune diseases.

MULTIPLE MYELOMA   A malignant proliferation of plasma cells in the bone marrow (notably not in lymph nodes). About 14,000 new cases are diagnosed each year. Disease manifestations result from tumor expansion, local and remote actions of tumor products, and the host response to the tumor. About 70% of pts have bone pain, usually involving the back and ribs, precipitated by movement. Bone lesions are multiple, lytic, and rarely accompanied by an osteoblastic response. Thus, bone scans are less useful than radiographs. The production of osteoclast-activating cytokines by tumor cells leads to substantial calcium mobilization, hypercalcemia, and symptoms related to it. Decreased synthesis and increased catabolism of normal immunoglobulins leads to hypogammaglobulinemia, and a poorly defined tumor product inhibits granulocyte migration. These changes create a susceptibility to bacterial infections, especially the pneumococcus, *Klebsiella pneumoniae*, and *Staphylococcus aureus* affecting the lung and *Escherichia coli* and other gram-negative pathogens affecting the urinary tract. Infections affect at least 75% of pts at some time in their course. Renal failure may affect 25% of pts; its pathogenesis is multifactorial—hypercalcemia, infection, toxic effects of light chains, urate nephropathy, dehydration. Neurologic symptoms may result from hyperviscosity, cryoglobulins, and rarely amyloid deposition in nerves. Anemia occurs in 80% related to myelophthisis and inhibition of erythropoiesis by tumor products. Clotting abnormalities may produce bleeding.

Diagnosis   Marrow plasmacytosis >10%, lytic bone lesions, and a serum and/or urine M component are the classic triad. Monoclonal gammopathy of uncertain significance (MGUS) is much more common than myeloma, affecting about 6% of people over age 70; in general, MGUS is associated with a level of M component <20 g/L, low serum β_2-microglobulin, <10% marrow plasma cells, and no bone lesions. Lifetime risk of progression of MGUS to myeloma is about 25%.

Staging   Disease stage influences survival (Table 64-4).

Rx | **TREATMENT**

About 10% of pts have very slowly progressive disease and do not require treatment until the paraprotein levels rise above 50 g/L or progressive bone disease occurs. Pts with solitary plasmacytoma and extramedullary plasmacytoma are usually cured with localized radiation therapy. Supportive care includes early treatment of infections; control of hypercalcemia with glucocorticoids, hydration, and natriuresis; chronic administration of bisphosphonates to antagonize skeletal destruction; and prophylaxis against urate nephropathy and dehydration. Therapy aimed at the tumor is usually palliative: melphalan 8 mg/m^2 orally for 4–7 days every 4–6 weeks plus prednisone. About 60% of pts have significant symptomatic improvement plus a 75% decline in the M component. Experimental approaches using sequential high-dose pulses of melphalan plus two successive autologous stem cell transplants have produced complete responses in about 50% of pts <65 years. Long-term follow-up is required to see whether survival is enhanced. Palliatively treated pts generally follow a chronic course for 2–5 years, followed by an acceleration characterized by organ infiltration with myeloma cells and marrow failure.

HODGKIN'S DISEASE   About 8000 new cases are diagnosed each year. Hodgkin's disease (HD) is a tumor of Reed-Sternberg cells, aneuploid cells that usually express CD30 and CD15 but may also express other B or T cell markers.

Table 64-4

Myeloma Staging System

Stage	Criteria	Estimated Tumor Burden, $\times 10^{12}$ cells/m^2

I	All the following:
	1. Hemoglobin >100 g/L (>10 g/dL)
	2. Serum calcium <3 mmol/L
	3. Normal bone x-ray or solitary lesion
	4. Low M-component production
	  a. IgG level <50 g/L (<5 g/dL)
	  b. IgA level <30 g/L (<3 g/dL)
	  c. Urine light chain <4 g/24 h)
		<0.6 (low)

II	Fitting neither I nor III	0.6–1.20 (intermediate)

III	One or more of the following:
	1. Hemoglobin <85 g/L (<8.5 g/dL)
	2. Serum calcium >3 mmol/L (<12 mg/dL)
	3. Advanced lytic bone lesions
	4. High M-component production
	  a. IgG level >70 g/L (>7 g/dL)
	  b. IgA level >50 g/L (>5 g/dL)
	  c. Urine light chains >12 g/24 h
		<1.20 (high)

SUBCLASSIFICATION BASED ON SERUM CREATININE LEVELS

Level	Stage	Median Survival Months
A < 177 μmol/L ($\leq$2 mg/dL)	IA	61
B > 177 μmol/L (>2 mg/dL)	IIA, B	55
	IIIA	30
	IIIB	15

STAGING BASED ON SERUM β_2-MICROGLOBULIN LEVELS

<0.004 g/L ($\leq$4 μg/mL)	I	43
>0.004 g/L (>4 μg/mL)	II	12

Most tumors are derived from B cells in that immunoglobulin genes are rearranged, but some tumors are of T cell phenotype. Most of the cells in an enlarged node are normal lymphoid, plasma cells, monocytes, and eosinophils. The etiology is unknown, but the incidence in both identical twins is 99-fold increased over the expected concordance, suggesting a genetic susceptibility. Distribution of histologic subtypes is 75% nodular sclerosis, 20% mixed cellularity, with lymphocyte predominant and lymphocyte depleted representing about 5%.

Clinical Manifestations   Usually presents with asymptomatic lymph node enlargement or with adenopathy associated with fever, night sweats, weight loss, and sometimes pruritus. Mediastinal adenopathy (common in nodular sclerosing HD) may produce cough. Spread of disease tends to be to contiguous lymph node groups. SVC obstruction or spinal cord compression may be presenting manifestation. Involvement of bone marrow and liver is rare.

Differential Diagnosis

- Infection—mononucleosis, viral syndromes, toxoplasma, histoplasma, primary tuberculosis

- Other malignancies—especially head and neck cancers
- Sarcoidosis—mediastinal and hilar adenopathy

Immunologic and Hematologic Abnormalities

- Defects in cell-mediated immunity (remains even after successful treatment of lymphoma); cutaneous anergy; diminished antibody production to capsular antigens of *Haemophilus* and pneumococcus
- Anemia; elevated ESR; leukemoid reaction; eosinophilia; lymphocytopenia; fibrosis and granulomas in marrow

Staging The Ann Arbor staging classification is shown in Table 64-5. It is important to determine extent of disease to guide choice of treatment; physical exam, CXR, thoracoabdominal CT, bone marrow biopsy; ultrasound examinations, lymphangiogram. Staging laparotomy should be used, especially to evaluate the spleen, if pt has early-stage disease on clinical grounds and radiation therapy is being contemplated.

 TREATMENT

About 85% of pts are curable. Therapy should be performed by experienced clinicians in centers with appropriate facilities. Pts with stages I and II disease documented by negative laparotomy are treated with subtotal nodal radiation therapy. Those with stage III or IV disease receive six cycles of combination chemotherapy, usually either ABVD or MOPP-ABV hybrid therapy or MOPP/ABVD alternating therapy. Pts with any stage disease accompanied by a large mediastinal mass (>1/3 the greatest chest diameter) should receive combined modality therapy with MOPP/ABVD or MOPP-ABV hybrid followed by mantle field radiation therapy (radiation plus ABVD is too toxic to the lung). About two-thirds of pts not cured by their initial radiation therapy treatment are rescued by salvage combination chemotherapy. About one half of pts not cured by their initial chemotherapy regimen may be rescued by high-dose therapy and autologous stem cell transplant.

With long-term follow-up, it has become clear that more pts are dying of late fatal toxicities related to radiation therapy (myocardial infarction, second cancers) than from HD. It may be possible to avoid radiation exposure by using combination chemotherapy in early-stage disease as well as in advanced-stage disease.

Table 64-5

Ann Arbor Staging System	
Stage I	Involvement in single lymph node region or single extralymphatic site
Stage II	Involvement of two or more lymph node regions on the same side of diaphragm
	Localized contiguous involvement of only one extralymphatic site and lymph node region (stage IIE)
Stage III	Involvement of lymph node regions on both sides of diaphragm; may include spleen
Stage IV	Disseminated involvement of one or more extralymphatic organs with or without lymph node involvement

For a more detailed discussion, see Armitage JO, Longo DL: Malignancies of Lymphoid Cells, Chap. 112, p. 715; and Longo DL: Plasma Cell Disorders, Chap. 113, p. 727, in HPIM-15.

65

SKIN CANCER

MALIGNANT MELANOMA

Most dangerous cutaneous malignancy; high metastatic potential; poor prognosis with metastatic spread.

INCIDENCE   Melanoma is diagnosed in 38,300 people annually in the U.S. and causes 7300 deaths.

PREDISPOSING FACTORS

Fair complexion, sun exposure, family history of melanoma, dysplastic nevus syndrome (autosomal dominant disorder with multiple nevi of distinctive appearance and cutaneous melanoma, may be associated with 9p deletion), and presence of a giant congenital nevus. Blacks have a low incidence.

PREVENTION   Sun avoidance lowers risk. Sunscreens are not proven effective.

TYPES

1. *Superficial spreading melanoma*: Most common; begins with initial radial growth phase before invasion.
2. *Lentigo maligna melanoma*: Very long radial growth phase before invasion, lentigo maligna (Hutchinson's melanotic freckle) is precursor lesion, most common in elderly and in sun-exposed areas (esp. face).
3. *Acral lentiginous*: Most common form in darkly pigmented pts; occurs on palms and soles, mucosal surfaces, in nail beds and mucocutaneous junctions; similar to lentigo maligna melanoma but with more aggressive biologic behavior.
4. *Nodular*: Generally poor prognosis because of invasive growth from onset.

CLINICAL APPEARANCE   Generally pigmented (rarely amelanotic); color of lesions varies, but red, white, and/or blue are common, in addition to brown and/or black. Suspicion should be raised by a pigmented skin lesion that is >6 mm in diameter, asymmetric, has an irregular surface or border, or has variation in color.

PROGNOSIS   Best with thin lesions without evidence of metastatic spread; with increasing thickness or evidence of spread, prognosis worsens. Stage I and II (primary tumor without spread) have 85% 5-year survival. Stage III (palpable regional nodes with tumor) has a 50% 5-year survival when only one node is involved and 15-20% when 4 or more are involved. Stage IV (disseminated disease) has <5% 5-year survival.

 TREATMENT

Early recognition and local excision for localized disease is best; 1- to 2-cm margins are as effective as 4- to 5-cm margins and do not usually require skin grafting. Elective lymph node dissection offers no advantage in overall survival compared with deferral of surgery until clinical recurrence. Pts with stage II disease may have improved disease-free survival with adjuvant interferon-α (IFN) 3 million units tiw for 12–18 months; no overall survival advantage has been shown. In one study, pts with stage III disease had improved survival with adjuvant IFN, 20 million units IV daily × 5 for 4 weeks, then 10 million units SC tiw for 11 months. This result was not confirmed in a second study. Metastatic disease may be treated with chemotherapy or immunotherapy. Dacarbazine (250 mg/m^2 IV daily × 5 q3w) plus tamoxifen (20 mg/m^2 PO daily) may induce partial responses in 1/3 of patients. IFN and interleukin 2 (IL-2) at maximum tolerated doses induce partial responses in 15% of pts. Rare long remissions occur with IL-2. No therapy for metastatic disease is curative.

BASAL CELL CARCINOMA (BCC)
Most common form of skin cancer; most frequently on sun-exposed skin, esp. face.

PREDISPOSING FACTORS Fair complexion, chronic UV exposure, exposure to inorganic arsenic (i.e., Fowler's solution or insecticides such as Paris green), or exposure to ionizing radiation.

PREVENTION Avoidance of sun exposure and use of sunscreens lower risk.

TYPES Five general types: *noduloulcerative* (most common), *superficial* (mimics eczema), *pigmented* (may be mistaken for melanoma), *morpheaform* (plaquelike lesion with telangiectasia—with keratotic is most aggressive), *keratotic* (basosquamous carcinoma).

CLINICAL APPEARANCE Classically a pearly, translucent, smooth papule with rolled edges and surface telangiectasia.

 TREATMENT

Local removal with electrodesiccation and curettage, excision, cryosurgery, or radiation therapy; metastases are rare but may spread locally. Exceedingly unusual for BCC to cause death.

SQUAMOUS CELL CARCINOMA (SCC)
Less common than basal cell but more likely to metastasize.

PREDISPOSING FACTORS Fair complexion, chronic UV exposure, previous burn or other scar (i.e., scar carcinoma), exposure to inorganic arsenic or ionizing radiation. Actinic keratosis is a premalignant lesion.

TYPES Most commonly occurs as an ulcerated nodule or a superficial ersion on the skin. Variants include:

1. *Bowen's disease*: Erythematous patch or plaque, often with scale; noninvasive; involvement limited to epidermis and epidermal appendages (i.e., SCC in situ).

2. *Scar carcinoma*: Suggested by sudden change in previously stable scar, esp. if ulceration or nodules appear.

3. *Verrucous carcinoma*: Most commonly on plantar aspect of foot; low-grade malignancy but may be mistaken for a common wart.

CLINICAL APPEARANCE   Hyperkeratotic papule or nodule or erosion; nodule may be ulcerated.

 TREATMENT

> Local excision and Moh's micrographic surgery are most common; radiation therapy in selected cases. Metastatic disease may be treated with radiation therapy or with combination biologic therapy; 13-*cis*-retinoic acid 1 mg/d PO plus IFN 3 million units/d SC.

PROGNOSIS   Favorable if secondary to UV exposure; less favorable if in sun-protected areas or associated with ionizing radiation.

SKIN CANCER PREVENTION
Most skin cancer is related to sun exposure. Encourage pts to avoid the sun and use sunscreen.

For a more detailed discussion, see Sober AJ et al: Melanoma and Other Skin Cancers, Chap. 86, p. 554, in HPIM-15.

HEAD AND NECK CANCER

Epithelial cancers may arise from the mucosal surfaces of the head and neck including the sinuses, oral cavity, nasopharynx, oropharynx, hypopharynx, and larynx. These tumors are usually squamous cell cancers. Thyroid cancer is discussed in Chap. 171.

Incidence and Epidemiology
About 40,000 cases are diagnosed each year. Oral cavity, oropharynx, and larynx are the most frequent sites of primary lesions in the U.S.; nasopharyngeal primaries are more common in the Far East and Mediterranean countries. Alcohol and tobacco (including smokeless) abuse are risk factors.

Pathology
Nasopharyngeal cancer in the Far East has a distinct histology, nonkeratinizing undifferentiated carcinoma with infiltrating lymphocytes called *lymphoepithe-*

lioma, and a distinct etiology, Epstein-Barr virus. Squamous cell head and neck cancer may develop from premalignant lesions (erythroplakia, leukoplakia), and the histologic grade affects prognosis. Pts who have survived head and neck cancer commonly develop a second cancer of the head and neck, lung, or esophagus, presumably reflecting the exposure of the upper aerodigestive mucosa to similar carcinogenic stimuli.

Genetic Alterations

Chromosomal deletions and mutations have been found in chromosomes 3p, 9p, 17p, 11q, and 13q; mutations in p53 have been reported. Cyclin D1 may be overexpressed.

Clinical Presentation

Most occur in people > 50 years. Symptoms vary with the primary site. Nasopharynx lesions do not usually cause symptoms until late in the course and then cause unilateral serous otitis media or nasal obstruction or epistaxis. Oral cavity cancers present as nonhealing ulcers, sometimes painful. Oropharyngeal lesions also present late with sore throat or otalgia. Hoarseness may be an early sign of laryngeal cancer. Rare pts present with painless, rock-hard cervical or supraclavicular lymph node enlargement. Staging is based upon size of primary tumor and involvement of lymph nodes. Distant metastases occur in < 10% of pts.

 TREATMENT

Three categories of disease are common: localized, locally or regionally advanced, and recurrent or metastatic. *Local disease* is treated with curative intent by surgery or radiation therapy. Radiation therapy is preferred for localized larynx cancer to preserve organ function; surgery is used more commonly for oral cavity lesions. *Locally advanced disease* is the most common presentation. Surgery followed by radiation therapy is standard; however, the disease is responsive to chemotherapy, and the use of three cycles of cisplatin (100 mg/m² IV day 1) plus 5-fluorouracil (1000 (mg/m²)/d by 96- to 120-h continuous infusion) before or delivery of the same regimen during radiation therapy is as effective as (or more effective than) surgery plus radiation therapy. Head and neck cancer pts are frequently malnourished and often have intercurrent illness. Concomitant chemotherapy and radiation therapy shows a survival advantage, but mucositis is worse. Pts with *recurrent* or *metastatic disease* are treated palliatively with cisplatin plus 5-fluorouracil or paclitaxel (200–250 mg/m² with G-CSF support). Treatment outcome varies somewhat with primary site; in general, pts with localized disease have about 75% 5-year survival, those with locally advanced disease have about 35% 5-year survival, and those with metastatic disease have about 15% 5-year survival.

Prevention

Pts with head and neck cancer who are rendered disease-free may benefit from chemopreventive therapy with *cis*-retinoic acid (3 months of 1.5 (mg/kg)/d followed by 9 months of 0.5 (mg/kg)/d PO). Trial results are mixed.

For a more detailed discussion, see Vokes EE: Head and Neck Cancer, Chap. 87, p. 559, in HPIM-15.

67

LUNG CANCER

Incidence

Lung cancer is diagnosed in about 90,000 men and 75,000 women in the U.S. each year, and 86% of pts die within 5 years. Lung cancer, the leading cause of cancer death, accounts for 32% of all cancer deaths in men and 25% in women. Peak incidence occurs between ages 55 and 65 years.

Histologic Classification

Four major types account for 88% of primary lung cancers: epidermoid (squamous), 29%; adenocarcinoma (including bronchioloalveolar), 32%; large cell, 9%; and small cell (or oat cell), 18%. Histology (small cell versus non-small cell types) is a major determinant of treatment approach. Small cell is usually widely disseminated at presentation, while non-small cell may be localized. Epidermoid and small cell typically present as central masses, while adenocarcinomas and large cell usually present as peripheral nodules or masses. Epidermoid and large cell cavitate in 20–30% of pts.

Etiology

The major cause of lung cancer is tobacco use, particularly cigarette smoking. Lung cancer cells may have ≥10 acquired genetic lesions, most commonly point mutations in *ras* oncogenes; amplification, rearrangement, or transcriptional activation of *myc* family oncogenes; overexpression of *bcl*-2, *Her*-2/*neu*, and telomerase; and deletions involving chromosomes 1p, 1q, 3p12-13, 3p14 (*FHIT* gene region), 3p21, 3p24-25, 3q, 5q, 9p (p16 and p15 cyclin-dependent kinase inhibitors), 11p13, 11p15, 13q14 (*rb*gene), 16q, and 17p13 (*p53* gene). Loss of 3p and 9p are the earliest events, detectable even in hyperplastic bronchial epithelium; *p53* abnormalities and *ras* point mutations are usually found only in invasive cancers.

Clinical Manifestations

Only 5–15% are detected while asymptomatic. Central endobronchial tumors cause cough, hemoptysis, wheeze, stridor, dyspnea, pneumonitis. Peripheral lesions cause pain, cough, dyspnea, symptoms of lung abscess resulting from cavitation. Metastatic spread of primary lung cancer may cause tracheal obstruction, dysphagia, hoarseness, Horner's syndrome. Other problems of regional spread include superior vena cava syndrome, pleural effusion, respiratory failure. Extrathoracic metastatic disease affects 50% of pts with epidermoid cancer, 80% with adenocarcinoma and large cell, and >95% with small cell. Clinical problems result from brain metastases, pathologic fractures, liver invasion, and spinal cord compression. Paraneoplastic syndromes may be a presenting finding of lung cancer or first sign of recurrence (Chap. 75). Systemic symptoms occur in 30% and include weight loss, anorexia, fever. Endocrine syndromes occur in 12% and include hypercalcemia (epidermoid), syndrome of inappropriate antidiuretic hormone secretion (small cell), gynecomastia (large cell). Skeletal connective tissue syndromes include clubbing in 30% (most often non-small cell) and hypertrophic pulmonary osteoarthropathy in 1–10% (most often adenocarcinomas), with clubbing, pain, and swelling.

Staging See Table 67-1.

Two parts to staging are: (1) determination of location (anatomic staging) and (2) assessment of pt's ability to withstand antitumor treatment (physiologic staging). Non-small cell tumors are staged by the TNM/International Staging System (ISS). The T (tumor), N (regional node involvement), and M (presence or absence of distant metastasis) factors are taken together to define different stage groups. Small cell tumors are staged by two-stage system: limited stage disease—confined to one hemithorax and regional lymph nodes; extensive disease—involvement beyond this. General staging procedures include careful ENT examination, CXR, and chest CT scanning. CT scans may suggest mediastinal lymph node involvement and pleural extension in non-small cell lung cancer, but definitive evaluation of mediastinal spread requires histologic examination. Routine radionuclide scans are not obtained in asymptomatic pts. If a mass lesion is on CXR and no obvious contraindications to curative surgical approach are noted, mediastinum should be investigated. Major contraindications to curative surgery include extrathoracic metastases, superior vena cava syndrome, vocal cord and phrenic nerve paralysis, malignant pleural effusions, metastases to contralateral lung, and histologic diagnosis of small cell cancer.

Table 67-1

International TNM Staging System for Lung Cancer

Stage	TNM Descriptors	5-Year Survival, %
I	T1–2, N0, M0	60–80
II	T1–2, N1, M0	25–50
IIIA	T3, N0–1, M0	25–40
	T1–3, N2, M0	10–30
IIIB	Any T4 or N3, M0	<5
IV	Any M1	<5

PRIMARY TUMOR (T)

T1	Tumor <3 cm diameter
T2	Tumor >3 cm diameter or has associated atelectasis-obstructive pneumonitis extending to the hilar region
T3	Tumor with direct extension into the chest wall (including superior sulcus tumors), diaphragm, mediastinal pleura, or pericardium
T4	Tumor invades the mediastinum (heart, great vessels, trachea, esophagus, vertebral body, or carina) or the presence of a malignant pleural effusion

REGIONAL LYMPH NODES (N)

N0	No node involvement
N1	Metastasis to lymph nodes in the peribronchial and/or ipsilateral hilar region
N2	Metastasis to ipsilateral mediastinal or subcarinal lymph nodes
N3	Metastasis to contralateral mediastinal or hilar nodes, or any scalene or supraclavicular nodes

DISTANT METASTASIS (M)

M0	No known distant metastasis
M1	Distant metastasis present with site specified (e.g., brain)

SOURCE: Modified from J Minna, Chap. 88, p. 562, HPIM-15.

℞ TREATMENT

See Table 67-2.

1.   Surgery in pts with localized disease and non-small cell cancer; however, majority initially thought to have curative resection ultimately succumb to metastatic disease.

2.   Solitary pulmonary nodule: factors suggesting resection include cigarette smoking, age $\geq$35, relatively large (>2 cm) lesion, lack of calcification, chest symptoms, and growth of lesion compared to old CXR.

3.   For unresectable stage II non-small cell lung cancer, combined thoracic radiation therapy and cisplatin-based chemotherapy reduces mortality by about 25% at 1 year.

4.   For unresectable non-small cell cancer, metastatic disease, or refusal of surgery: consider for radiation therapy; addition of cisplatin-based chemotherapy may reduce death risk by 13% at 2 years and improve quality of life.

5.   Small cell cancer: combination chemotherapy is standard mode of therapy; response after 6–12 weeks predicts median- and long-term survival.

6.   Addition of radiation therapy to chemotherapy in limited stage small cell lung cancer can increase 5-year survival from about 11% to 20%.

Table 67-2

Summary of Treatment Approach to Lung Cancer Patients

NON-SMALL CELL LUNG CANCER

Resectable (stages I, II, IIIa, and selected T3, N2 lesions)
  Surgery
  Radiation therapy for nonoperable pts
  Postoperative radiotherapy for N2 disease
Nonresectable (N2 and M1)
  Confined to chest: high-dose chest radiation therapy (RT) plus cisplatin-based
    chemotherapy (CT); consider neoadjuvant CT followed by surgery
  Extrathoracic: RT to symptomatic local sites; CT (for good-performance-
    status pts, with evaluable lesions)

SMALL CELL LUNG CANCER

Limited stage (good performance status)
  Concurrent CT + chest RT
Extensive stage (good performance status)
  Combination CT
Complete tumor responders (all stages)
  Prophylactic cranial RT
Poor-performance-status pts (all stages)
  Modified dose CT
  Palliative RT

ALL PATIENTS

RT for brain metastases, spinal cord compression, weight-bearing lytic bony
  lesions, symptomatic local lesions (nerve paralyses, obstructed airway, hemoptysis in non-small cell lung cancer and in small cell cancer not responding
  to chemotherapy)
Appropriate diagnosis and treatment of other medical problems
Supportive care during therapy
Encouragement to stop smoking

7. Prophylactic cranial irradiation improves survival of limited stage small cell lung cancer by another 5%.

8. Laser obliteration of tumor through bronchoscopy in presence of bronchial obstruction.

9. Radiation therapy for brain metastases, spinal cord compression, symptomatic masses, bone lesions.

10. Encourage cessation of smoking.

Prognosis

At time of diagnosis, only 20% of pts have localized disease. Overall 5-year survival is 30% for males and 50% for females with localized disease and 5% for pts with advanced disease.

For a more detailed discussion, see Minna JD: Neoplasms of the Lung, Chap. 88, p. 562, in HPIM-15.

68

BREAST CANCER

Incidence and Epidemiology

The most common tumor in women, 182,800 women in the U.S. are diagnosed and 40,000 die each year with breast cancer. Men also get breast cancer at a rate of 150:1. Breast cancer is hormone-dependent. Women with late menarche, early menopause, and first full-term pregnancy by age 18 have a significantly reduced risk. The average American woman has about a 1 in 9 lifetime risk of developing breast cancer. Dietary fat is controversial risk factor. Oral contraceptives have little, if any, effect on risk. Estrogen replacement therapy may slightly increase the risk, but the beneficial effects of estrogen on quality of life, bone mineral density, and decreased risk of cardiovascular mortality appear to far outweigh the risk. Women who received therapeutic radiation before age 30 are at increased risk. Breast cancer risk is increased when a sister and mother also had the disease.

Genetics

Perhaps 8–10% of breast cancer is familial. BRCA-1 mutations account for about 5%. BRCA-1 maps to chromosome 17q21 and appears to be involved in transcription-coupled DNA repair. Ashkenazi Jewish women have a 1% chance of having a common mutation (deletion of adenine and guanine at position 185). The BRCA-1 syndrome includes an increased risk of ovarian cancer in women and prostate cancer in men. BRCA-2 on chromosome 11 may account for 2–3% of breast cancer. Mutations are associated with an increased risk of breast cancer in men and women. Germline mutations in p53 (Li-Fraumeni syndrome) are very rare, but breast cancer, sarcomas, and other malignancies occur in such families. Sporadic breast cancers show many genetic alterations including overexpression of *HER-2/neu* in 25% of cases, p53 mutations in 40%, and loss of heterozygosity at other loci.

Diagnosis

Breast cancer is usually diagnosed by biopsy of a nodule detected by mammogram or by palpation. Women should be strongly encouraged to examine their breasts monthly. In premenopausal women, questionable or nonsuspicious (small) masses should be reexamined in 2–4 weeks (Fig. 68-1). A mass in a premenopausal woman that persists throughout her cycle and any mass in a postmenopausal woman should be aspirated. If the mass is a cyst filled with non-bloody fluid that goes away with aspiration, the pt is returned to routine screening. If the cyst aspiration leaves a residual mass or reveals bloody fluid, the pt should have a mammogram and excisional biopsy. If the mass is solid, the pt should undergo a mammogram and excisional biopsy. Screening mammograms performed every other year beginning at age 50 have been shown to save lives. The controversy regarding screening mammograms beginning at age 40 relates to the following facts: (1) the disease is much less common in the 40- to 49-year age group; screening is generally less successful for less common problems; (2) workup of mammographic abnormalities in the 40- to 49-year age group less commonly diagnoses cancer; and (3) about 35% of women who are screened annually during their forties have an abnormality at some point that requires a diagnostic procedure (usually a biopsy); yet very few evaluations

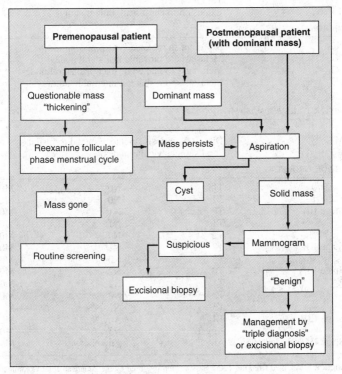

FIGURE 68-1   Approach to a palpable breast mass.

reveal cancer. However, many believe in the value of screening mammography beginning at age 40. After 13–15 years of follow-up, women who start screening at age 40 have a small survival benefit.

Staging

Therapy and prognosis are dictated by stage of disease (Table 68-1). Unless the breast mass is large or fixed to the chest wall, staging of the ipsilateral axilla is performed at the time of lumpectomy (see below). Within pts of a given stage, individual characteristics of the tumor may influence prognosis: expression of estrogen receptor improves prognosis, while overexpression of *HER-1/neu*, mutations in p53, high growth fraction, and aneuploidy worsen the prognosis. Breast cancer can spread almost anywhere but commonly goes to bone, lungs, liver, soft tissue, and brain.

Table 68-1

Staging of Breast Cancer

PRIMARY TUMOR (T)

T0	No evidence of primary tumor
Tis	Carcinoma in situ
T1	Tumor ≤2 cm
T2	Tumor >2 cm but ≤5 cm
T3	Tumor >5 cm
T4	Extension to chest wall, inflammation

REGIONAL LYMPH NODES (N)

N0	No tumor in regional lymph nodes
N1	Metastasis to movable ipsilateral nodes
N2	Metastasis to matted or fixed ipsilateral nodes
N3	Metastasis to ipsilateral internal mammary nodes

DISTANT METASTASIS (M)

M0	No distant metastasis
M1	Distant metastasis (includes spread to ipsilateral supraclavicular nodes)

STAGE GROUPING

Stage 0	TIS	N0	M0
Stage 1	T1	N0	M0
Stage IIA	T0	N1	M0
	T1	N1	M0
	T2	N0	M0
Stage IIB	T2	N1	M0
	T3	N0	M0
Stage IIIA	T0	N2	M0
	T1	N2	M0
	T2	N2	M0
	T3	N1, N2	M0
Stage IIIB	T4	Any N	M0
	Any T	N3	M0
Stage IV	Any T	Any N	M1

SOURCE: Modified from the TNM classification proposed by the American Joint Committee on Cancer, 1992.

Ⓡ TREATMENT

Five-year survival rate by stage is shown in Table 68-2. Treatment varies with stage of disease.

Ductal carcinoma in situ is noninvasive tumor present in the breast ducts. Treatment of choice is wide excision with breast radiation therapy. In one study, adjuvant tamoxifen further reduced the risk of recurrence.

Invasive breast cancer can be classified as operable, locally advanced, and metastatic. In operable breast cancer, outcome of primary therapy is the same with modified radical mastectomy or lumpectomy followed by breast radiation therapy. Axillary dissection may be replaced with sentinel node biopsy to evaluate node involvement. The sentinel node is identified by injecting a dye in the tumor site at surgery; the first node in which dye appears is the sentinel node. Women with tumors <1 cm and negative axillary nodes require no additional therapy beyond their primary lumpectomy and breast radiation. Adjuvant combination chemotherapy for 6 months appears to benefit pre-menopausal women with positive lymph nodes, pre- and postmenopausal women with negative lymph nodes but with large tumors or poor prognostic features, and postmenopausal women with positive lymph nodes whose tumors do not express estrogen receptors. Estrogen receptor–positive tumors >1 cm with or without involvement of lymph nodes are treated with tamoxifen; one study suggests chemotherapy plus tamoxifen may be superior. Various regimens have been used. In women with up to three positive nodes, CMF (cyclophosphamide, 100 mg/m^2; PO days 1–14 or 600 mg/m^2; IV days 1 and 8; methotrexate, 40 mg/m^2; IV days 1 and 8; 5-fluorouracil, 600 mg/m^2; IV days 1 and 8) or CAF (cyclophosphamide, 500 mg/m^2; IV days 1 and 8; doxorubicin, 50 mg/m^2; IV days 1 and 8; 5-fluorouracil, 500 mg/m^2; IV days 1 and 8) are commonly given for six cycles. Women with 4–10 positive nodes may benefit from doxorubicin, 75 mg/m^2; IV q21d × 4 followed by CMF (same doses as above given on day 1 only, *not* days 1 and 8; cycles repeated q21d × 6). Tamoxifen adjuvant therapy (20 mg/d for 5 years) is used for pre- or postmenopausal women with tumors expressing estrogen receptors whose nodes are positive or whose nodes are negative but with large tumors or poor prognostic features. Breast cancer will recur in about half of pts with localized disease.

Pts with locally advanced breast cancer benefit from neoadjuvant chemotherapy that includes an anthracycline (CAF) followed by surgery plus breast radiation therapy.

Treatment for metastatic disease depends upon estrogen receptor status and treatment philosophy. No therapy is known to cure pts with metastatic

Table 68-2

5-Year Survival Rate for Breast Cancer by Stage

Stage	5-Year Survival (Percent of Patients)
0	99
I	92
IIA	82
IIB	65
IIIA	47
IIIB	44
IV	14

SOURCE: Modified from data of the National Cancer Institute—Surveillance, Epidemiology, and End Results (SEER).

disease, but many pts receive high-dose therapy with autologous stem cell transplantation, some of whom have excellent survival. Randomized trials do not show that the use of high-dose therapy improves survival. Median survival is about 16 months with conventional treatment; tamoxifen for estrogen receptor–positive tumors, and combination chemotherapy for receptor-negative tumors. Pts progressing on adjuvant tamoxifen may benefit from a selective aromatase inhibitor such as letrozole or anastrazole. Bisphosphonates reduce skeletal complications and may promote antitumor effects of other therapy. Radiation therapy is useful for palliation of symptoms.

For a more detailed discussion, see Lippman ME: Breast Cancer, Chap. 89, p. 571, in HPIM-15.

69

TUMORS OF THE GASTROINTESTINAL TRACT

ESOPHAGEAL CARCINOMA

In 2000 in the U.S., 12,300 cases and 12,100 deaths; less frequent in women than men. Highest incidence in focal regions of China, Iran, Afghanistan, Siberia, Mongolia. In U.S., blacks more frequently affected than whites; usually presents sixth decade or later; 5-year survival <5% because most pts present with advanced disease.

PATHOLOGY 60% squamous cell carcinoma, most commonly in upper two-thirds; <40% adenocarcinoma, usually in distal third, arising in region of columnar metaplasia (Barrett's esophagus), glandular tissue, or as direct extension of proximal gastric adenocarcinoma; lymphoma and melanoma rare.

RISK FACTORS Major risk factors for squamous cell carcinoma: ethanol abuse, smoking (combination is synergistic); other risks: lye ingestion and esophageal stricture, radiation exposure, head and neck cancer, achalasia, smoked opiates, Plummer-Vinson syndrome, tylosis, chronic ingestion of extremely hot tea, deficiency of vitamin A, zinc, molybdenum. Barrett's esophagus is a risk for adenocarcinoma.

CLINICAL FEATURES Progressive dysphagia (first with solids, then liquids), rapid weight loss common, chest pain (from mediastinal spread), odynophagia, pulmonary aspiration (obstruction, tracheoesophageal fistula), hoarseness (laryngeal nerve palsy), hypercalcemia (parathyroid hormone–related peptide hypersecretion by squamous carcinomas); bleeding infrequent, occasionally severe; examination often unremarkable.

DIAGNOSIS Double-contrast barium swallow useful as initial test in dysphagia; flexible esophagogastroscopy most sensitive and specific test; pathologic confirmation by combining endoscopic biopsy and cytologic examination of mucosal brushings (neither alone sufficiently sensitive); CT and endoscopic ultrasonography valuable to assess local and nodal spread.

TREATMENT

Surgical resection feasible in only 40% of pts; associated with high complication rate (fistula, abscess, aspiration). *Squamous cell carcinoma*: Surgical resection after chemotherapy [5-fluorouracil (5-FU), cisplatin] plus radiation therapy prolongs survival and may provide improved cure rate. *Adenocarcinoma*: Curative resection rarely possible; fewer than one-fifth of pts with resectable tumors survive 5 years. Palliative measures include laser ablation, mechanical dilatation, radiotherapy, and a luminal prosthesis to bypass the tumor. Gastrostomy or jejunostomy are frequently required for nutritional support.

GASTRIC CARCINOMA

Highest incidence in Japan, China, Chile, Ireland; incidence decreasing worldwide, eightfold in U.S. over past 60 years; in 2000, 21,500 new cases and 13,000 deaths. Male:female = 2:1; peak incidence sixth and seventh decades; overall 5-year survival <15%.

RISK FACTORS Increased incidence in lower socioeconomic groups; environmental component is suggested by studies of migrants and their offspring. Several dietary factors correlated with increased incidence: nitrates, smoked foods, heavily salted foods; genetic component suggested by increased incidence in first-degree relatives of affected pts; other risk factors: atrophic gastritis, *Helicobacter pylori* infection, Billroth II gastrectomy, gastrojejunostomy, adenomatous gastric polyps, pernicious anemia, hyperplastic gastric polyps (latter two associated with atrophic gastritis), Ménétrier's disease, slight increased risk with blood group A.

PATHOLOGY Adenocarcinoma in 85%; usually focal (polypoid, ulcerative), two-thirds arising in antrum or lesser curvature, frequently ulcerative ("intestinal type"); less commonly diffuse infiltrative (linitis plastica) or superficial spreading (diffuse lesions more prevalent in younger pts; exhibit less geographic variation; have extremely poor prognosis); spreads primarily to local nodes, liver, peritoneum; systemic spread uncommon; lymphoma accounts for 15% (most frequent extranodal site in immunocompetent pts), either low-grade tumor of mucosa-associated lymphoid tissue (MALT) or aggressive diffuse large cell lymphoma; leiomyosarcoma is rare.

CLINICAL FEATURES Most commonly presents with progressive upper abdominal discomfort, frequently with weight loss, anorexia, nausea; acute or chronic GI bleeding (mucosal ulceration) common; dysphagia (location in cardia); vomiting (pyloric and widespread disease); early satiety; examination often unrevealing early in course; later, abdominal tenderness, pallor, and cachexia most common signs; palpable mass uncommon; metastatic spread may be manifest by hepatomegaly, ascites, left supraclavicular or scalene adenopathy, periumbilical, ovarian, or prerectal mass (Blummer's shelf), low-grade fever, skin abnormalities (nodules, dermatomyositis, acanthosis nigricans, or multiple seborrheic keratoses). Laboratory findings: iron-deficiency anemia in two-thirds of pts; fecal occult blood in 80%; rarely associated with pancytopenia and microangiopathic hemolytic anemia (from marrow infiltration), leukemoid reaction, migratory thrombophlebitis or acanthosis nigricans.

DIAGNOSIS Double-contrast barium swallow useful; gastroscopy most sensitive and specific test; pathologic confirmation by biopsy and cytologic examination of mucosal brushings; superficial biopsies less sensitive for lymphomas (frequently submucosal); important to differentiate benign from malignant gastric ulcers with multiple biopsies and follow-up examinations to demonstrate ulcer healing.

 TREATMENT

Adenocarcinoma: Gastrectomy offers only chance of cure; the rare tumors limited to mucosa are resectable for cure in 80%; deeper invasion, nodal metastases decrease 5-year survival to 20% of pts with resectable tumors in absence of obvious metastatic spread (Table 69-1); CT and endoscopic ultrasonography may aid in determining tumor resectability. Subtotal gastrectomy has similar efficacy to total gastrectomy for distal stomach lesions, but with less morbidity; no clear benefit for resection of spleen and a portion of the pancreas, or for radical lymph node removal. Adjuvant chemotherapy following primary surgery is of little benefit but when combined with radiation therapy, some improvement in survival has been observed. Palliative therapy for pain, obstruction, and bleeding includes surgery, endoscopic dilatation, radiation therapy, chemotherapy.

Lymphoma: Low-grade MALT lymphoma is caused by *H. pylori* infection, and eradication of the infection causes complete remissions in 50% of pts; rest are responsive to combination chemotherapy including cyclophosphamide, doxorubicin, vincristine, prednisone (CHOP). Diffuse large cell lymphoma may be treated with either combination chemotherapy alone or subtotal gastrectomy followed by chemotherapy; 50–60% 5-year survival.

Leiomyosarcoma: Surgical resection curative in most pts.

Table 69-1

Staging System for Gastric Carcinoma

Stage	TNM	Features	Number of Cases, %	5-Year Survival, %
			Data from American College of Surgeons	
0	TisN0M0	Node negative; limited to mucosa	1	90
IA	T1N0M0	Node negative; invasion of lamina propria or submucosa	7	59
IB	T2N0M0	Node negative; invasion of muscularis propria	10	44
II	T1N2M0 T2N1M0	Node positive; invasion beyond mucosa but within wall		
		or	17	29
	T3N0M0	Node negative; extension through wall		
IIIA	T2N2M0 T3N1-2M0	Node positive; invasion of muscularis propria or through wall	21	15
IIIB	T4N0-1M0	Node negative; adherence to surrounding tissue	14	9
IV	T4N2M0	Node positive; adherence to surrounding tissue		
		or	30	3
	T1-4N0-2M1	Distant metastases		

BENIGN GASTRIC TUMORS

Much less common than malignant gastric tumors; hyperplastic polyps most common, with adenomas, hamartomas, and leiomyomas rare; 30% of adenomas and occasional hyperplastic polyps are associated with gastric malignancy; polyposis syndromes include Peutz-Jeghers and familial polyposis (hamartomas and adenomas), Gardner's (adenomas), and Cronkhite-Canada (cystic polyps). See "Colonic Polyps," below.

CLINICAL FEATURES Usually asymptomatic; occasionally present with bleeding or vague epigastric discomfort.

 TREATMENT

Endoscopic or surgical excision.

SMALL BOWEL TUMORS

CLINICAL FEATURES Uncommon tumors (~5% of all GI neoplasms); usually present with bleeding, abdominal pain, weight loss, fever, or intestinal obstruction (intermittent or fixed); increased incidence of lymphomas in pts with gluten-sensitive enteropathy, Crohn's disease involving small bowel, AIDS, prior organ transplantation, autoimmune disorders.

PATHOLOGY Usually benign; most common are adenomas (usually duodenal), leiomyomas (intramural), and lipomas (usually ileal); 50% of malignant tumors are adenocarcinoma, usually in duodenum (at or near ampulla of Vater) or proximal jejunum, commonly coexisting with benign adenomas; primary intestinal lymphomas (non-Hodgkin's) account for 25% and occur as focal mass (western type), which is usually a T cell lymphoma associated with prior celiac disease, or diffuse infiltration (Mediterranean type), which is usually immuno-proliferative small-intestinal disease (IPSID; α-chain disease), or a B cell lymphoma, which can present as intestinal malabsorption; carcinoid tumors (usually asymptomatic) occasionally produce bleeding or intussusception (see below).

DIAGNOSIS Endoscopy and biopsy most useful for tumors of duodenum and proximal jejunum; otherwise barium x-ray examination best diagnostic test; direct small-bowel instillation of contrast (enteroclysis) occasionally reveals tumors not seen with routine small-bowel radiography; angiography (to detect plexus of tumor vessels) or laparotomy often required for diagnosis; CT useful to evaluate extent of tumor (esp. lymphomas).

 TREATMENT

Surgical excision; adjuvant chemotherapy appears helpful for focal lymphoma; IPSID appears to be curable with combination chemotherapy used in aggressive lymphoma plus oral antibiotics (e.g., tetracycline); no proven role for chemotherapy or radiation therapy for other small-bowel tumors.

COLONIC POLYPS

TUBULAR ADENOMAS Present in ~30% of adults; pedunculated or sessile; usually asymptomatic; ~5% cause occult blood in stool; may cause obstruction; overall risk of malignant degeneration correlates with size (<2% if <1.5 cm diam; >10% if >2.5 cm diam) and is higher in sessile polyps; 65% found in rectosigmoid colon; diagnosis by barium enema, sigmoidoscopy, or colonoscopy. *Treatment*: Full colonoscopy to detect synchronous lesions (present in 30%); endoscopic resection (surgery if polyp large or inaccessible by colonoscopy); follow-up surveillance by colonoscopy every 2–3 years.

VILLOUS ADENOMAS Generally larger than tubular adenomas at diagnosis; often sessile; high risk of malignancy (up to 30% when >2 cm); more prevalent in left colon; occasionally associated with potassium-rich secretory diarrhea. *Treatment*: As for tubular adenomas.

HYPERPLASTIC POLYPS Asymptomatic; usually incidental finding at colonoscopy; rarely >5 mm; no malignant potential. No treatment required.

HEREDITARY POLYPOSIS SYNDROMES See Table 69-2.

1. *Familial polyposis coli* (FPC): Diffuse pancolonic adenomatous polyposis (up to several thousand polyps); autosomal dominant inheritance associated with deletion in adenomatous polyposis coli (*APC*) gene on chromosome 5; colon carcinoma from malignant degeneration of polyp in 100% by age 40. *Treatment*: Prophylactic total colectomy or subtotal colectomy with ileoproctostomy before age 30; subtotal resection avoids ileostomy but necessitates frequent proctoscopic surveillance; periodic colonoscopic or annual radiologic

Table 69-2

Hereditable (Autosomal Dominant) Gastrointestinal Polyposis Syndromes

Syndrome	Distribution of Polyps	Histologic Type	Malignant Potential	Associated Lesions
Familial adenomatous polyposis	Large intestine	Adenoma	Common	None
Gardner's syndrome	Large and small intestine	Adenoma	Common	Osteomas, fibromas, lipomas, epidermoid cysts, ampullary cancers, congenital hypertrophy of retinal pigment epithelium
Turcot's syndrome	Large intestine	Adenoma	Common	Brain tumors
Nonpolyposis syndrome (Lynch syndrome)	Large intestine (often proximal)	Adenoma	Common	Endometrial and ovarian tumors
Peutz-Jeghers syndrome	Small and large intestines, stomach	Hamartoma	Rare	Mucocutaneous pigmentation; tumors of the ovary, breast, pancreas, endometrium
Juvenile polyposis	Large and small intestines, stomach	Hamartoma, rarely progressing to adenoma	Rare	Various congenital abnormalities

screening of siblings and offspring of pts with FPC until age 35; sulindac and other NSAIDs cause regression of polyps and inhibit their development.

2. *Gardner's syndrome*: Variant of FPC with associated soft tissue tumors (epidermoid cysts, osteomas, lipomas, fibromas, desmoids); higher incidence of gastroduodenal polyps, ampullary adenocarcinoma. *Treatment*: As for FPC; surveillance for small-bowel disease with fecal occult blood testing after colectomy.

3. *Turcot's syndrome*: Rare variant of FPC with associated malignant brain tumors. *Treatment*: As for FPC.

4. *Nonpolyposis syndrome*: Familial syndrome with up to 50% risk of colon carcinoma; peak incidence in fifth decade; associated with multiple primary cancers (esp. endometrial); autosomal dominant; due to defective DNA repair.

5. *Juvenile polyposis*: Multiple benign colonic and small-bowel hamartomas; intestinal bleeding common. Other symptoms: abdominal pain, diarrhea; occasional intussusception. Rarely recur after excision; low risk of colon cancer from malignant degeneration of interspersed adenomatous polyps. Prophylactic colectomy controversial.

6. *Peutz-Jeghers syndrome*: Numerous hamartomatous polyps of entire GI tract, though denser in small bowel than colon; GI bleeding common; somewhat increased risk for the development of cancer at GI and non-GI sites. Prophylactic surgery not recommended.

COLORECTAL CANCER

Second most common internal cancer in humans; accounts for 20% of cancer-related deaths in U.S., incidence increases dramatically above age 50, nearly equal in men and women. In 2000, 130,200 new cases, 56,300 deaths.

ETIOLOGY AND RISK FACTORS Most colon cancers arise from adenomatous polyps. Genetic steps from polyp to dysplasia to carcinoma in situ to invasive cancer have been defined, including: point mutation in K-*ras* proto-oncogene, hypomethylation of DNA leading to enhanced gene expression, allelic loss at the *APC* gene (a tumor suppressor), allelic loss at the *DCC* (deleted in colon cancer) gene on chromosome 18, and loss and mutation of p53 on chromosome 17. Hereditary nonpolyposis colon cancer arises from mutations in the DNA mismatch repair genes, *hMSH2* gene on chromosome 2 and *hMLH1* gene on chromosome 3. Mutations lead to colon and other cancers. Diagnosis requires three or more relatives with colon cancer, one of whom is a first-degree relative; one or more cases diagnosed before age 50; and involvement of at least two generations. Environmental factors also play a role: increased prevalence in developed countries, urban areas, advantaged socioeconomic groups; increased risk in pts with hypercholesterolemia, coronary artery disease; correlation of risk with low-fiber, high animal fat diets, although direct effect of diet remains unproven; decreased risk with long-term dietary calcium supplementation and, possibly, daily aspirin ingestion; risk increased in first-degree relatives of pts, families with increased prevalence of cancer, and pts with history of breast or gynecologic cancer, familial polyposis syndromes, >10-year history of ulcerative colitis or Crohn's colitis, >15-year history of ureterosigmoidostomy. Tumors in pts with strong family history of malignancy are frequently located in right colon and commonly present before age 50; high prevalence in pts with *Streptococcus bovis* bacteremia.

PATHOLOGY

Nearly always adenocarcinoma; 75% located distal to the splenic flexure (except in association with polyposis or hereditary cancer syndromes); may be polypoid, sessile, fungating, or constricting; subtype and degree of differentiation do not correlate with course. Degree of invasiveness at surgery (Dukes' classification) is single best predictor of prognosis (Table 69-3). Rectosigmoid tumors may spread to lungs early because of systemic paravertebral venous drainage of this area. Other predictors of poor prognosis: preoperative serum carcinoembryonic antigen (CEA) >5 ng/mL (>5 μg/L), poorly differentiated histology, bowel perforation, venous invasion, adherence to adjacent organs, aneuploidy, specific deletions in chromosomes 5, 17, 18, and mutation of *ras* proto-oncogene. 15% have defects in DNA repair.

CLINICAL FEATURES Left-sided colon cancers present most commonly with rectal bleeding, altered bowel habits (narrowing, constipation, intermittent diarrhea, tenesmus), and abdominal or back pain; cecal and ascending colon cancers more frequently present with symptoms of anemia, occult blood in stool, or weight loss; other complications: perforation, fistula, volvulus, inguinal hernia; laboratory findings: anemia in 50% of right-sided lesions.

DIAGNOSIS Early diagnosis aided by screening asymptomatic persons with fecal occult blood testing (see below); more than half of all colon cancers are within reach of a 60-cm flexible sigmoidoscope; air-contrast barium enema will diagnose approximately 85% of colon cancers not within reach of sigmoidoscope; colonoscopy most sensitive and specific, permits tumor biopsy and removal of synchronous polyps (thus preventing neoplastic conversion), but is more expensive.

℞ TREATMENT

Local disease: Surgical resection of colonic segment containing tumor; preoperative evaluation to assess prognosis and surgical approach includes full colonoscopy, chest films, biochemical liver tests, plasma CEA level, and possible abdominal CT. Resection of isolated hepatic metastases possible in selected cases. Adjuvant radiation therapy to pelvis (with or without concomitant 5-FU chemotherapy) decreases local recurrence rate of rectal carcinoma (no apparent effect on survival); radiation therapy without benefit on colon tumors; preoperative radiation therapy may improve resectability and local control in pts with rectal cancer. Total mesorectal excision may be more effective than conventional anteroposterior resection in rectal cancer. Adjuvant chemotherapy (5-FU and leucovorin) decreases recurrence rate and im-

Table 69-3

Staging of and Prognosis for Colorectal Cancer

Stage				Approximate 5-Year Survival, %
Dukes	TNM	Numerical	Pathologic Description	
A	T1N0M0	I	Cancer limited to mucosa and submucosa	>90
B$_1$	T2N0M0	I	Cancer extends into muscularis	85
B$_2$	T3N0M0	II	Cancer extends into or through serosa	70–80
C	TxN1M0	III	Cancer involves regional lymph nodes	35–65
D	TxNxM1	IV	Distant metastases (i.e., liver, lung, etc.)	5

proves survival of stage C tumors and perhaps stage B; periodic determination of serum CEA level useful to follow therapy and assess recurrence. *Follow-up after curative resection*: Yearly liver tests, CBC, follow-up radiologic or colonoscopic evaluation at 1 year—if normal, repeat every 3 years, with routine screening interim (see below); if polyps detected, repeat 1 year after resection. *Advanced tumor* (locally unresectable or metastatic): Systemic chemotherapy (5-FU and leucovorin plus irinotecan), intraarterial chemotherapy [floxuridine (FUDR)] and/or radiation therapy may palliate symptoms from hepatic metastases.

PREVENTION Early detection of colon carcinoma may be facilitated by routine screening of stool for occult blood (Hemoccult II, Colo-Test, etc.); however, sensitivity only ~50% for carcinoma; specificity for tumor or polyp ~25–40%. False positives: ingestion of red meat, iron, aspirin; upper GI bleeding. False negatives: vitamin C ingestion, intermittent bleeding. Annual digital exam and fecal occult blood testing recommended for pts over age 40, screening flexible sigmoidoscopy every 3 years after age 50, earlier in pts at increased risk (see above); careful evaluation of all pts with positive fecal occult blood tests (flexible sigmoidoscopy and air-contrast barium enema or colonoscopy alone) reveals polyps in 20–40% and carcinoma in ~5%; screening of asymptomatic persons allows earlier detection of colon cancer (i.e., earlier Dukes' stage) and achieves greater resectability rate; decreased overall mortality from colon carcinoma seen only after 13 years of follow-up. More intensive evaluation of first-degree relatives of pts with colon carcinoma frequently includes screening air-contrast barium enema or colonoscopy after age 40. NSAIDs and cyclooxygenase-2 inhibitors appear to prevent polyp development and induce regression in high-risk groups but have not been recommended for average-risk pts at this time.

Anal Cancer

Accounts for 1–2% of large-bowel cancer, 3400 cases and 500 deaths in 2000; associated with chronic irritation, e.g., from condyloma accuminata, perianal fissures/fistulae, chronic hemorrhoids, leukoplakia, trauma from anal intercourse. Women are more commonly affected than men. Homosexual men are at increased risk. Presents with bleeding, pain, and perianal mass. Radiation therapy plus chemotherapy (5-FU and mitomycin) leads to complete response in 80% when the primary lesion is <3 cm. Abdominoperineal resection with permanent colostomy is reserved for those with large lesions or whose disease recurs after chemoradiotherapy.

BENIGN LIVER TUMORS

Hepatocellular adenomas occur most commonly in women in the third or fourth decades who take birth control pills. Most are found incidentally but may cause pain; intratumoral hemorrhage may cause circulatory collapse. 10% may become malignant. Women with these adenomas should stop taking birth control pills. Large tumors near the liver surface may be resected. Focal nodular hyperplasia is also more common in women but seems not to be caused by birth control pills. Lesions are vascular on angiography and have septae and are usually asymptomatic.

HEPATOCELLULAR CARCINOMA

About 15,300 cases in the U.S. in 2000, but worldwide this may be the most common tumor. Male:female = 4:1; tumor usually develops in cirrhotic liver in persons in fifth or sixth decade. High incidence in Asia and Africa is related to etiologic relationship between this cancer and hepatitis B and C infections. Aflatoxin exposure contributes to etiology and leaves a molecular signature, a mutation in codon 249 of the gene for p53. Surgical resection or liver transplantation is therapeutic option but rarely successful. Screening populations at risk has given conflicting results. Hepatitis B vaccine prevents the disease. Interferon-α may prevent liver cancer in persons with chronic active hepatitis C disease and possibly in those with hepatitis B.

PANCREATIC CANCER

In 2000 in the U.S., about 28,300 new cases and 28,200 deaths. The incidence is decreasing somewhat, but nearly all diagnosed cases are fatal. The tumors are ductal adenocarcinomas and are not usually detected until the disease has spread. About 70% of tumors are in the pancreatic head, 20% in the body, and 10% in the tail. Mutations in K-*ras* have been found in 85% of tumors, and the p16 cyclin-dependent kinase inhibitor on chromosome 9 may also be implicated. Long-standing diabetes, chronic pancreatitis, and smoking increase the risk; coffee-drinking, alcoholism, and cholelithiasis do not. Pts present with pain and weight loss, the pain often relieved by bending forward. Jaundice commonly complicates tumors of the head, due to biliary obstruction. Curative surgical resections are feasible in about 10%. Gemcitabine may palliate symptoms in pts with advanced disease.

ENDOCRINE TUMORS OF THE GI TRACT AND PANCREAS

CARCINOID TUMOR   Carcinoid tumor accounts for 75% of GI endocrine tumors; incidence is about 15 cases per million population. 90% originate in Kulchitsky cells of the GI tract, most commonly the appendix, ileum, and rectum. Carcinoid tumors of the small bowel and bronchus have a more malignant course than tumors of other sites. About 5% of pts with carcinoid tumors develop symptoms of the carcinoid syndrome, the classic triad being cutaneous flushing, diarrhea, and valvular heart disease. For tumors of GI tract origin, symptoms imply metastases to liver.

Diagnosis can be made by detecting the site of tumor or documenting production of more than 15 mg/d of the serotonin metabolite, 5-hydroxyindole-acetic acid (5-HIAA) in the urine. Octreotide scintigraphy identifies sites of primary and metastatic tumor in about $\frac{2}{3}$ of cases.

Rx TREATMENT

Surgical resection where feasible. Symptoms may be controlled with histamine blockers and octreotide, 150–1500 mg/d in three doses. Hepatic artery embolization and chemotherapy (5-FU plus streptozotocin or doxorubicin) have been used for metastatic disease. Interferon-α at 3–10 million units subcutaneously three times a week may relieve symptoms. Prognosis ranges from 95% 5-year survival for localized disease to 20% 5-year survival for those with liver metastases. Median survival of pts with carcinoid syndrome is 2.5 years from the first episode of flushing.

PANCREATIC ISLET-CELL TUMORS

Gastrinoma, insulinoma, VIPoma, glucagonoma, and somatostatinoma account for the vast majority of pancreatic islet-cell tumors; their characteristics are shown in Table 69-4. The tumors are named for the dominant hormone they produce. They are generally slow-growing and produce symptoms related to hormone production. *Gastrinomas* and *peptic ulcer disease* comprise the Zollinger-Ellison syndrome. Gastrinomas are rare (4 cases per 10 million popula-

Table 69-4

Gastrointestinal Endocrine Tumor Syndromes

Syndrome	Cell Type	Percentage Malignant	Clinical Features	Major Products
Carcinoid syndrome	Enterochromaffin, enterochromaffin-like	~100	Flushing, diarrhea, wheezing, hypotension	Serotonin, histamine, miscellaneous peptides
Zollinger-Ellison, gastrinoma	Non-β islet cell, duodenal G cell	~70	Peptic ulcers, diarrhea	Gastrin
Insulinoma	Islet β cell	~10	Hypoglycemia	Insulin
VIPoma (Verner-Morrison, WDHA)	Islet D_1 cell	~60	Diarrhea, hypokalemia, hypochlorhydria	Vasoactive intestinal peptide
Glucagonoma	Islet A cell	>75	Mild diabetes mellitus, erythema necrolytica migrans, glossitis	Glucagon
Somatostatinoma	Islet D cell	~70	Diabetes mellitus, diarrhea, steatorrhea, gallstones	Somatostatin

tion), and in 25–50%, the tumor is a component of a MEN I syndrome (Chap. 176).

Insulinoma may present with Whipple's triad, fasting hypoglycemia, symptoms of hypoglycemia, and relief after intravenous glucose. Normal or elevated serum insulin levels in the presence of fasting hypoglycemia are diagnostic. Insulinomas may also be associated with MEN I.

Verner and Morrison described a syndrome of watery diarrhea, hypokalemia, achlorhydria, and renal failure associated with pancreatic islet tumors that produce vasoactive intestinal polypeptide (VIP). *VIPomas* are rare (1 case per 10 million) but often grow to a large size before producing symptoms.

Glucagonoma is associated with diabetes mellitus and necrolytic migratory erythema, a characteristic red, raised, scaly rash usually located on the face, abdomen, perineum, and distal extremities. Glucagon levels >1000 ng/L not suppressed by glucose are diagnostic.

The classic triad of *somatostatinoma* is diabetes mellitus, steatorrhea, and cholelithiasis.

Provocative tests may facilitate diagnosis of functional endocrine tumors: tolbutamide enhances somatostatin secretion by somatostatinomas; pentagastrin enhances calcitonin secretion from medullary thyroid (C cell) tumors; secretin enhances gastrin secretion from gastinomas. If imaging techniques fail to detect tumor masses, angiography or selective venous sampling for hormone determination may reveal the site of tumor. Metastases to nodes and liver should be sought by CT or MRI.

 TREATMENT

Tumor is surgically removed, if possible. Octreotide inhibits hormone secretion in the majority of cases. Interferon-α may reduce symptoms. Streptozotocin plus doxorubicin combination chemotherapy may produce responses in 60–90% of cases. Embolization of hepatic metastases may be palliative.

For a more detailed discussion, see Mayer RJ: Gastrointestinal Tract Cancer, Chap. 90, p. 578; Dienstag JL, Isselbacher KJ: Tumors of the Liver and Biliary Tract, Chap. 91, p. 588; Mayer RJ: Pancreatic Cancer, Chap. 92, p. 591; Jensen RT: Endocrine Tumors of the Gastrointestinal Tract and Pancreas, Chap. 93, p. 593, in HPIM-15.

70

GENITOURINARY TRACT CANCER

BLADDER CANCER
INCIDENCE AND EPIDEMIOLOGY Annual incidence in the U.S. is about 53,200 cases with 12,200 deaths. Median age is 65 years. Smoking ac-

counts for 50% of the risk. Exposure to polycyclic aromatic hydrocarbons increases the risk, especially in slow acetylators. Risk is increased in chimney sweeps, dry cleaners, and those involved in aluminum manufacturing. Chronic cyclophosphamide exposure increases risk 9-fold. *Schistosoma haematobium* infection also increases risk, especially of squamous histology.

ETIOLOGY Lesions involving chromosome 9q are an early event. Deletions in 17p (p53), 18q (the *DCC* locus), 13q (RB), 3p, and 5q are characteristic of invasive lesions. Overexpression of epidermal growth factor receptors and HER-2/neu receptors is common.

PATHOLOGY Over 90% of tumors are derived from transitional epithelium; 3% are squamous, 2% are adenocarcinomas, and <1% are neuroendocrine small cell tumors. Field effects are seen that place all sites lined by transitional epithelium at risk including the renal pelvis, ureter, bladder, and proximal 2/3 of the urethra. 90% of tumors are in the bladder, 8% in the renal pelvis, and 2% in the ureter or urethra. Histologic grade influences survival. Lesion recurrence is influenced by size, number, and growth pattern of the primary tumor.

CLINICAL PRESENTATION Hematuria is the initial sign in 80–90%; however, cystitis is a more common cause of hematuria (22% of all hematuria) than is bladder cancer (15%). Pts are initially staged and treated by endoscopy. Superficial tumors are removed at endoscopy; muscle invasion requires more extensive surgery.

 TREATMENT

Management is based on extent of disease: superficial, invasive, or metastatic. Frequency of presentation is 75% superficial, 20% invasive, and 5% metastatic. Superficial lesions are resected at endoscopy. Although complete resection is possible in 80%, 30–80% of cases recur; grade and stage progression occur in 30%. Intravesical instillation of bacille Calmette-Guérin (BCG) reduces the risk of recurrence by 40–45%. Recurrence is monitored every 3 months.

The standard management of muscle-invasive disease is radical cystectomy. 5-year survival is 70% for those without invasion of perivesicular fat or lymph nodes, 50% for those with invasion of fat but not lymph nodes, 35% for those with one node involved, and 10% for those with six or more involved nodes. Pts who cannot withstand radical surgery may have 30–35% 5-year survival with 5000 to 7000-cGy external beam radiation therapy. Bladder sparing may be possible in up to 45% of pts with two cycles of chemotherapy with CMV (methotrexate 30 mg/m² days 1 and 8, vinblastine 4 mg/m² days 1 and 8, cisplatin 100 mg/m² day 2, q21d) followed by 4000-cGy radiation therapy given concurrently with cisplatin.

Metastatic disease is treated with combination chemotherapy, either CMV (see above) or M-VAC (methotrexate 30 mg/m² days 1, 15, 22; vinblastine 3 mg/m² days 2, 15, 22; doxorubicin 30 mg/m² day 2; cisplatin 70 mg/m² day 2; q28d) or cisplatin plus paclitaxel or gemcitabine. About 70% of pts respond to treatment, and 20% have a complete response; 10–15% have long-term disease-free survival.

RENAL CANCER

INCIDENCE AND EPIDEMIOLOGY Annual incidence in U.S. is about 31,200 cases with 11,900 deaths. Cigarette smoking accounts for 20–30% of cases. Risk is increased in acquired renal cystic disease. There are two familial forms: a rare autosomal dominant syndrome and von Hippel-Lindau disease. About 35% of pts with von Hippel-Lindau disease develop renal cancer. Incidence is also increased in tuberous sclerosis and polycystic kidney disease.

ETIOLOGY Most cases are sporadic; however, the most frequent chromosomal abnormality (occurs in 60%) is deletion or rearrangement of 3p21-26. The von Hippel-Lindau gene has been mapped to that region and appears to have novel activities, regulation of speed of transcription and participation in turnover of damaged proteins. It is unclear how lesions in the gene lead to cancer.

PATHOLOGY Five variants are recognized: clear cell tumors (75%), chromophilic tumors (15%), chromophobic tumors (5%), oncocytic tumors (3%), and collecting duct tumors (2%). Clear cell tumors arise from cells of the proximal convoluted tubules. Chromophilic tumors tend to be bilateral and multifocal and often show trisomy 7 and/or trisomy 17. Chromophobic and eosinophilic tumors less frequently have chromosomal aberrations and follow a more indolent course.

CLINICAL PRESENTATION The classic triad of hematuria, flank pain, and flank mass is seen in only 10–20% of pts; hematuria (40%), flank pain (40%), palpable mass (33%), weight loss (33%) are the most common individual symptoms. Paraneoplastic syndromes of erythrocytosis (3%), hypercalcemia (5%), and nonmetastatic hepatic dysfunction (Stauffers' syndrome) (15%) may also occur. Workup should include IV pyelography, renal ultrasonography, CT of abdomen and pelvis, CXR, urinalysis, and urine cytology. Stage I is disease restricted to the kidney, stage II is disease contained within Gerota's fascia, stage III is locally invasive disease involving nodes and/or inferior vena cava, stage IV is invasion of adjacent organs or metastatic sites. Prognosis is related to stage: 66% 5-year survival for I, 64% for II, 42% for III, and 11% for IV.

 TREATMENT

Radical nephrectomy is standard for stages I, II, and most stage III pts. Surgery may also be indicated in the setting of metastatic disease for intractable local symptoms (bleeding, pain). About 10–15% of pts with advanced stage disease may benefit from interleukin 2 and/or interferon-α. Some remissions are durable. Chemotherapy is of little or no benefit.

TESTICULAR CANCER

INCIDENCE AND EPIDEMIOLOGY Annual incidence is about 6900 cases with 300 deaths. Peak age incidence is 20–40. Occurs 4–5 times more frequently in white than black men. Cryptorchid testes are at increased risk. Early orchiopexy may protect against testis cancer. Risk is also increased in testicular femininization syndromes, and Klinefelter's syndrome is associated with mediastinal germ cell tumor.

ETIOLOGY The cause is unknown. Disease is associated with a characteristic cytogenetic defect, isochromosome 12p.

PATHOLOGY Two main subtypes are noted; seminoma and nonseminoma. Each accounts for about ~50% of cases. Seminoma has a more indolent natural history and is highly sensitive to radiation therapy. Four subtypes of nonseminoma are defined; embryonal carcinoma, teratoma, choriocarcinoma, and endodermal sinus (yolk sac) tumor.

CLINICAL PRESENTATION Painless testicular mass is the classic initial sign. In the presence of pain, differential diagnosis includes epididymitis or orchitis; a brief trial of antibiotics may be undertaken. Staging evaluation includes measurement of serum tumor markers alphafetoprotein (AFP) and β-human chorionic gonadotropin (hCG), CXR, and CT scan of abdomen and pelvis. Lymph nodes are staged at resection of the primary tumor through an inguinal approach. Stage I disease is limited to the testis, epididymis, or spermatic cord; stage II involves retroperitoneal nodes; and stage III is disease outside the retroperitoneum. Among seminoma pts, 70% are stage I, 20% are stage II, and 10% are stage III. Among nonseminoma germ cell tumor pts, 33% are found in each stage. hCG may be elevated in either seminoma or nonseminoma, but AFP is elevated only in nonseminoma. 95% of pts are cured if treated appropriately.

℞ TREATMENT

For stages I and II seminoma, inguinal orchiectomy followed by retroperitoneal radiation therapy to 2500–3000 cGy is effective. For stages I and II nonseminoma germ cell tumors, inguinal orchiectomy followed by retroperitoneal lymph node dissection is effective. For pts of either histology with bulky nodes or stage III disease, chemotherapy is given. Cisplatin (20 mg/m² days 1–5), etoposide (100 mg/m² days 1–5), and bleomycin (30 U days 2, 9, 16) given every 21 d for four cycles is the standard therapy. If tumor markers return to zero, residual masses are resected. Most are necrotic debris or teratomas. Salvage therapy rescues about 25% of those not cured with primary therapy.

For more detailed discussion, see Scher HI, Motzer RJ: Bladder and Renal Cell Carcinomas, Chap. 94, p. 604; and Motzer RJ, Bosl GL: Testicular Cancer, Chap. 96, p. 616, in HPIM-15.

71

GYNECOLOGIC CANCER

OVARIAN CANCER

INCIDENCE AND EPIDEMIOLOGY Annually in the U.S., about 27,000 new cases are found and nearly 15,000 women die of ovarian cancer. Incidence begins to rise in the fifth decade, peaking in the eighth decade. Risk is increased in nulliparous women and reduced by pregnancy (risk decreased about 10% per pregnancy) and oral contraceptives. About 5% of cases are familial.

GENETICS Mutations in *BRCA-1* predispose women to both breast and ovarian cancer. Cytogenetic analysis of epithelial ovarian cancers that are not familial often reveals complex karyotypic abnormalities including structural lesions on chromosomes 1 and 11 and loss of heterozygosity for loci on chromosomes 3q, 6q, 11q, 13q, and 17. C-*myc*, H-*ras*, K-*ras*, and *HER2/neu* are often mutated or overexpressed.

CLINICAL PRESENTATION Most pts present with abdominal pain, bloating, urinary symptoms, and weight gain indicative of disease spread beyond the true pelvis. Localized ovarian cancer is usually asymptomatic and detected on routine pelvic examination as a palpable nontender adnexal mass. Most ovarian masses detected incidentally in ovulating women are ovarian cysts that resolve over one to three menstrual cycles. Adnexal masses in postmenopausal women are more often pathologic and should be surgically removed. CA-125 serum levels are ≥35 U/mL in 80–85% of women with ovarian cancer, but other conditions may also cause elevations. Screening is not effective outside of high-risk families.

PATHOLOGY Half of ovarian tumors are benign, one-third are malignant, and the rest are tumors of low malignant potential. These borderline lesions have cytologic features of malignancy but do not invade. Malignant epithelial tumors may be of five different types: serous (50%), mucinous (25%), endometrioid (15%), clear cell (5%), and Brenner tumors (1%, derived from urothelial or transitional epithelium). The remaining 4% of ovarian tumors are stromal or germ cell tumors, which are managed like testicular cancer in men (Chap. 70). Histologic grade is an important prognostic factor for the epithelial varieties.

STAGING Extent of disease is ascertained by a surgical procedure that permits visual and manual inspection of all peritoneal surfaces and the diaphragm. Total abdominal hysterectomy, bilateral salpingo-oopherectomy, partial omentectomy, pelvic and paraaortic lymph node sampling, and peritoneal washings should be performed. The staging system and its influence on survival is shown in Table 71-1.

℞ TREATMENT

Pts with stage I disease, no residual tumor after surgery, and well- or moderately differentiated tumors need no further treatment after surgery and have a 5-year survival >95%. For stage II pts totally resected and stage I pts with poor histologic grade, adjuvant therapy with single-agent cisplatin, or cisplatin plus paclitaxel produces 5-year survival of 80%. Advanced-stage pts should receive paclitaxel, 175 mg/m^2 by 3-h infusion, followed by carboplatin dosed to an area under the curve (AUC) of 7.5 every 3 or 4 weeks. Carboplatin dose is calculated by the Calvert formula: dose = target AUC × (glomerular filtration rate + 25). The complete response rate is about 55%, and median survival is 38 months.

ENDOMETRIAL CANCER

INCIDENCE AND EPIDEMIOLOGY The most common gynecologic cancer, 34,000 cases are diagnosed in the U.S. and 6000 pts die annually. It is primarily a disease of postmenopausal women. Obesity, altered menstrual cycles, infertility, late menopause, and postmenopausal bleeding are commonly encountered in women with endometrial cancer. Women taking tamoxifen to prevent breast cancer recurrence and those taking estrogen replacement therapy are at a modestly increased risk. Peak incidence is in the sixth and seventh decades.

CLINICAL PRESENTATION Abnormal vaginal discharge (90%), abnormal vaginal bleeding (80%), and leukorrhea (10%) are the most common symptoms.

Table 71-1

Staging and Survival in Gynecologic Malignancies

Stage	Ovarian	5-Year Survival, %	Endometrial	5-Year Survival, %	Cervix	5-Year Survival, %
0	—		—		Carcinoma in situ	100
I	Confined to ovary	90	Confined to corpus	89	Confined to uterus	85
II	Confined to pelvis	70	Involves corpus and cervix	80	Invades beyond uterus but not pelvic wall	60
III	Intraabdominal spread	15–20	Extends outside the uterus but not outside the true pelvis	30	Extends to pelvic wall and/or lower third of vagina, or hydronephrosis	33
IV	Spread outside abdomen	1–5	Extends outside the true pelvis or involves the bladder or rectum	9	Invades mucosa of bladder or rectum or extends beyond the true pelvis	7

PATHOLOGY   Endometrial cancers are adenocarcinomas in 75–80% of cases. The remaining cases include mucinous carcinoma; papillary serous carcinoma; and secretory, ciliate, and clear cell varieties. Prognosis depends on stage, histologic grade, and degree of myometrial invasion.

STAGING   Total abdominal hysterectomy and bilateral salpingo-oopherectomy comprise both the staging procedure and the treatment of choice. The staging scheme and its influence on prognosis are shown in Table 71-1.

℞ TREATMENT

In women with poor histologic grade, deep myometrial invasion, or extensive involvement of the lower uterine segment or cervix, intracavitary or external beam radiation therapy is given. If cervical invasion is deep, preoperative radiation therapy may improve the resectability of the tumor. Stage III disease is managed with surgery and radiation therapy. Stage IV disease is usually treated palliatively. Progestational agents such as hydroxyprogesterone or megastrol and the antiestrogen tamoxifen may produce responses in 20% of pts. Doxorubicin, 60 mg/m^2 IV day 1, and cisplatin, 50 mg/m^2 IV day 1, every 3 weeks for 8 cycles produces a 45% response rate.

CERVICAL CANCER

INCIDENCE AND EPIDEMIOLOGY   In the U.S. about 16,000 cases of invasive cervical cancer are diagnosed each year and 50,000 cases of carcinoma in situ are detected by Pap smear. Cervical cancer kills 4900 women a year, 85% of whom never had a Pap smear. It is a major cause of disease in underdeveloped countries and is more common in lower socioeconomic groups, women with early sexual activity, multiple sexual partners, and in smokers. Human papilloma virus (HPV) types 16 and 18 are the major types associated with cervical cancer. The virus attacks the G_1 checkpoint of the cell cycle; its E7 protein binds and inactivates Rb protein, and E6 induces the degradation of p53.

SCREENING   Women should begin screening when they begin sexual activity or at age 20. After two consecutive negative annual Pap smears, the test should be repeated every 3 years. Abnormal smears dictate the need for a cervical biopsy, usually under colposcopy, with the cervix painted with 3% acetic acid, which shows abnormal areas as white patches. If there is evidence of carcinoma in situ, a cone biopsy is performed, which is therapeutic.

CLINICAL PRESENTATION   Pts present with abnormal bleeding or postcoital spotting or menometrorrhagia or intermenstrual bleeding. Vaginal discharge, low back pain, and urinary symptoms may also be present.

STAGING   Staging is clinical and consists of a pelvic exam under anesthesia with cystoscopy and proctoscopy. CXR, IV pyelography, and abdominal CT are used to search for metastases. The staging system and its influence on prognosis are shown in Table 71-1.

℞ TREATMENT

Carcinoma in situ is cured with cone biopsy. Stage I disease may be treated with radical hysterectomy or radiation therapy. Stages II–IV disease are usually treated with radiation therapy, often with both brachytherapy and teletherapy, or combined modality therapy. Pelvic exenteration is used uncommonly to control the disease, especially in the setting of centrally recurrent or persistent disease. Women with locally advanced (stage IIB to IVA) disease usually receive concurrent chemotherapy and radiation therapy. The role of chemotherapy is to act as a radiosensitizer. Hydroxyurea, 5-fluorouracil (5-FU), and cisplatin have all shown promising results given concurrently with radiation therapy. Cisplatin 75 mg/m^2 IV over 4 h on day 1 and 5-FU 4 g given by 96-h infusion on days 1–5 of radiation therapy is a common regimen.

For a more detailed discussion, see Young RC: Gynecologic Malignancies, Chap. 97, p. 620, in HPIM-15.

72

PROSTATE HYPERPLASIA AND CARCINOMA

PROSTATE HYPERPLASIA

Enlargement of the prostate is nearly universal in aging men. Hyperplasia usually begins by age 45 years, occurs in the area of the prostate gland surrounding the urethra, and produces urinary outflow obstruction. Symptoms develop on average by age 65 in whites and 60 in blacks. Symptoms develop late because hypertrophy of the bladder detrusor compensates for ureteral compression. As obstruction progresses, urinary stream caliber and force diminish, hesitancy in stream initiation develops, and postvoid dribbling occurs. Dysuria and urgency are signs of bladder irritation (perhaps due to inflammation or tumor) and are usually not seen in prostate hyperplasia. As the postvoid residual increases, nocturia and overflow incontinence may develop. Common medications such as tranquilizing drugs and decongestants, infections, or alcohol may precipitate urinary retention. Because of the prevalence of hyperplasia, the relationship to neoplasia is unclear.

On digital rectal exam (DRE), a hyperplastic prostate is smooth, firm, and rubbery in consistency; the median groove may be lost. Prostate-specific antigen (PSA) levels may be elevated but are ≤10 ng/mL unless cancer is also present (see below).

 TREATMENT

Asymptomatic pts do not require treatment, and those with complications of urethral obstruction such as inability to urinate, renal failure, recurrent UTI, hematuria, or bladder stones clearly require surgical extirpation of the prostate, usually by transurethral resection (TURP). However, the approach to the remaining pts should be based on the degree of incapacity or discomfort from the disease and the likely side effects of any intervention. If the pt has only mild symptoms, watchful waiting is not harmful and permits an assessment of the rate of symptom progression. If therapy is desired by the pt, two medical approaches may be helpful: terazosin, an α_1-adrenergic blocker (1 mg at bedtime, titrated to symptoms up to 20 mg/d), relaxes the smooth muscle of the bladder neck and increases urine flow; finasteride (5 mg/d), an inhibitor of 5α-reductase, blocks the conversion of testosterone to dihydrotestosterone and causes an average decrease in prostate size of ~24%. TURP has the greatest success rate but also the greatest risk of complications. Transurethral microwave thermotherapy (TUMT) may be comparably effective to TURP. Direct comparison has not been made between medical and surgical management.

PROSTATE CARCINOMA

Prostate cancer was diagnosed in 180,400 men in 2000 in the U.S, comparable to the incidence of breast cancer. The early diagnosis of cancers in mildly symptomatic men found on screening to have elevated serum levels of PSA has complicated management. Like most other cancers, incidence is age-related. The disease is more common in blacks than whites. Symptoms are generally similar to and indistinguishable from those of prostate hyperplasia, but those with cancer more often have dysuria and back or hip pain. On histology, 95% are adenocarcinomas. Biologic behavior is affected by histologic grade (Gleason score).

In contrast to hyperplasia, prostate cancer generally originates in the periphery of the gland and may be detectable on DRE as one or more nodules on the posterior surface of the gland, hard in consistency and irregular in shape. An approach to diagnosis is shown in Fig. 72-1. Those with a negative DRE and PSA ≤4 ng/mL may be followed annually. Those with an abnormal DRE or a PSA >10 ng/mL should undergo transrectal ultrasound-guided biopsy (TRUS). Those with normal DRE and PSA of 4.1–10 ng/mL may be handled differently in different centers. Some would perform transrectal ultrasound and biopsy any abnormality or follow if no abnormality is found. Some would repeat

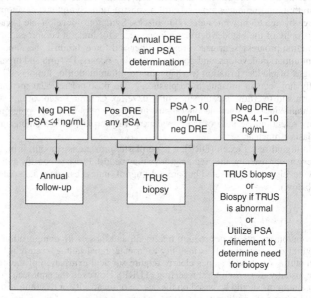

FIGURE 72-1 The use of the annual digital rectal examination (DRE) and measurement of prostate-specific antigen (PSA) as guides for deciding which men should have transrectal prostate biopsy under sonography (TRUS). There are at least three schools of thought about what to do if the DRE is negative and the PSA is equivocal (4.1 to 10 ng/mL).

the PSA in a year and biopsy if the increase over that period was >0.75 ng/mL. Other methods of using PSA to distinguish early cancer from hyperplasia include quantitating bound and free PSA and relating the PSA to the size of the prostate (PSA density). Perhaps $\frac{1}{3}$ of persons with prostate cancer do not have PSA elevations.

Lymphatic spread is assessed surgically; it is present in only 10% of those with Gleason grade 5 or lower and in 70% of those with grade 9 or 10. PSA level also correlates with spread; only 10% of those with PSA <10 ng/mL have lymphatic spread. Bone is the most common site of distant metastasis. Whitmore-Jewett staging includes A: tumor not palpable but detected at TURP; B: palpable tumor in one (B1) or both (B2) lobes; C: palpable tumor outside capsule; and D: metastatic disease.

Ⓡ TREATMENT

For pts with stages A through C disease, surgery (radical retropubic prostatectomy) and radiation therapy (conformal 3-dimensional fields) are said to have similar outcomes; however, most pts are treated surgically. Both modalities are associated with impotence. Surgery is more likely to lead to incontinence. Radiation therapy is more likely to produce proctitis, perhaps with bleeding or stricture. Addition of radiation therapy, chemotherapy, or hormonal therapy to surgical treatment of stage A through C disease does not appear to improve results. Patients usually must have a 5-year life expectancy to undergo radical prostatectomy. Stage A pts have survival identical to age-matched controls without cancer. Stage B and C pts have a 10-year survival of 82% and 42%, respectively.

Pts treated surgically for localized disease who develop rising PSA may undergo prostascint scanning (antibody to a prostate-specific membrane antigen). If no uptake is seen, the pt is observed. If uptake is seen in the prostate bed, local recurrence is implied and external beam radiation therapy is delivered to the site. (If the pt was initially treated with radiation therapy, this local recurrence may be treated with surgery.)

For pts with metastatic disease, androgen deprivation is the treatment of choice. Surgical castration is effective, but most pts prefer to take leuprolide, 7.5 mg depot form IM monthly (to inhibit pituitary gonadotrophin production), plus flutamide, 250 mg PO tid (an androgen receptor blocker). The value of added flutamide is debated. Alternative approaches include adrenalectomy, hypophysectomy, estrogen administration, and medical adrenalectomy with aminoglutethimide. The median survival of stage D pts is 33 months. Pts occasionally respond to withdrawal of hormonal therapy with tumor shrinkage. Rarely a second hormonal manipulation will work, but most pts who progress on hormonal therapy have androgen-independent tumors, often associated with genetic changes in the androgen receptor and new expression of bcl-2, which may contribute to chemotherapy resistance. Chemotherapy is used for palliation in prostate cancer. Chemotherapy-treated pts are more likely to have pain relief than those receiving supportive care alone. Bone pain from metastases may be palliated with strontium-89 or samarium-153. Bisphosphonates have not been adequately evaluated.

For a more detailed discussion, see Scher HI: Hyperplastic and Neoplastic Diseases of the Prostate, Chap. 95, p. 608, in HPIM-15.

73

CANCER OF UNKNOWN PRIMARY SITE

Cancer of unknown primary site (CUPS) is defined as follows: biopsy-proven malignancy; primary site unapparent after history, physical exam, CXR, abdominal and pelvic CT, CBC, chemistry survey, mammography (women), β-human chorionic gonadotropin (hCG) levels (men), α-fetoprotein (AFP) levels (men), and prostate-specific antigen (PSA) levels (men); and histologic evaluation not consistent with a primary tumor at the biopsy site. CUPS incidence is declining, probably because of better pathology diagnostic criteria; they account for about 3% of all cancers today, down from 10–15% 10 years ago. Most pts are over age 60. Cell lines derived from such tumors frequently have abnormalities in chromosome 1.

CLINICAL PRESENTATION   Pts may present with fatigue, weight loss, pain, bleeding, abdominal swelling, subcutaneous masses, and lymphadenopathy. Once metastatic malignancy is confirmed, diagnostic efforts should be confined to evaluating the presence of potentially curable tumors, such as lymphoma, Hodgkin's disease, germ cell tumor, ovarian cancer, head and neck cancer, and primitive neuroectodermal tumor, or tumors for which therapy may be of significant palliative value such as breast cancer or prostate cancer. In general, efforts to evaluate the presence of these tumor types depends more on the pathologist than on expensive clinical diagnostic testing. Localizing symptoms, a history of carcinogen exposure, or a history of fulguration of skin lesion may direct some clinical testing; however, the careful light microscopic, ultrastructural, immunologic, karyotypic, and molecular biologic examination of adequate volumes of tumor tissue is the most important feature of the diagnostic workup in the absence of suspicious findings on history and physical exam (Table 73-1).

HISTOLOGY   About 60% of CUPS tumors are adenocarcinomas, 10–20% are squamous cell carcinomas, and 20–30% are poorly differentiated neoplasms not further classified on light microscopy.

PROGNOSIS   Pts with squamous cell carcinoma have a median survival of 9 months; those with adenocarcinoma or unclassifiable tumors have a median survival of 4–6 months. Pts in whom a primary site is identified usually have a better prognosis. Limited sites of involvement and neuroendocrine histology are favorable prognostic factors. Pts without a primary diagnosis should be treated palliatively with radiation therapy to symptomatic lesions. All-purpose chemotherapy regimens rarely produce responses but always produce toxicity. Certain clinical features may permit individualized therapy.

Syndrome of Unrecognized Extragonadal Germ Cell Cancer

In pts <50 years with tumor involving midline structures, lung parenchyma, or lymph nodes and evidence of rapid tumor growth, germ cell tumor is a possible diagnosis. Serum tumor markers may or may not be elevated. Cisplatin, etoposide, and bleomycin (Chap. 70) chemotherapy may induce complete responses in ≥25%, and ~15% may be cured. A trial of such therapy should probably also be undertaken in pts whose tumors have abnormalities in chromosome 12.

Table 73-1

Possible Pathologic Evaluation of Biopsy Specimens from Patients with Metastatic Cancer of Unknown Primary Site

Evaluation/Findings	Suggested Primary Site or Neoplasm
HISTOLOGY (HEMATOXYLIN AND EOSIN STAINING)	
Psammoma bodies, papillary configuration	Ovary, thyroid
Signet ring cells	Stomach
IMMUNOHISTOLOGY	
Leukocyte common antigen (LCA, CD45)	Lymphoid neoplasm
Leu-M1	Hodgkin's disease
Epithelial membrane antigen	Carcinoma
Cytokeratin intermediate filaments	Carcinoma
CEA	Carcinoma
HMB45	Melanoma
Desmin	Sarcoma
Thyroglobulin	Thyroid carcinoma
Calcitonin	Medullary carcinoma of the thyroid
Myoglobin	Rhabdomyosarcoma
PSA/prostatic acid phosphatase	Prostate
AFP	Liver, stomach, germ cell
Placental alkaline phosphatase	Germ cell
B, T cell markers	Lymphoid neoplasm
S-100 protein	Neuroendocrine tumor, melanoma
Gross cystic fluid protein	Breast, sweat gland
Factor VIII	Kaposi's sarcoma, angiosarcoma
FLOW CYTOMETRY	
B, T cell markers	Lymphoid neoplasm
ULTRASTRUCTURE	
Actin-myosin filaments	Rhabdomyosarcoma
Secretory granules	Neuroendocrine tumors
Desmosomes	Carcinoma
Premelanosomes	Melanoma
CYTOGENETICS	
Isochromosome 12p; 12q(−)	Germ cell
t(11;22)	Ewing's sarcoma, primitive neuro-ectodermal tumor
t(8;14)	Lymphoid neoplasm
3p(−)	Small cell lung carcinoma; renal cell carcinoma, mesothelioma
t(X;18)	Synovial sarcoma
t(12;16)	Myxoid liposarcoma
t(12;22)	Clear cell sarcoma (melanoma of soft parts)

(continued)

Table 73-1 *(Continued)*

Possible Pathologic Evaluation of Biopsy Specimens from Patients with Metastatic Cancer of Unknown Primary Site

Evaluation/Findings	Suggested Primary Site or Neoplasm
t(2;13)	Alveolar rhabdomyosarcoma
1p(−)	Neuroblastoma
RECEPTOR ANALYSIS	
Estrogen/progesterone receptor	Breast
MOLECULAR BIOLOGIC STUDIES	
Immunoglobulin, *bcl*-2, T-cell receptor gene rearrangement	Lymphoid neoplasm

Peritoneal Carcinomatosis in Women

Women who present with pelvic mass or pain and an adenocarcinoma diffusely throughout the peritoneal cavity, but without a clear site of origin, have primary peritoneal papillary serous carcinoma. The presence of psammoma bodies in the tumor or elevated CA-125 levels may favor ovarian origin. Such pts should undergo debulking surgery followed by paclitaxel plus cisplatin combination chemotherapy (Chap. 71). About 20% of pts will respond, and 10% will survive at least 2 years.

Carcinoma in an Axillary Lymph Node in Women

Such women should receive adjuvant breast cancer therapy appropriate for their menopausal status even in the absence of a breast mass on physical examination or mammography and undetermined or negative estrogen and progesterone receptors on the tumor (Chap. 68). Unless the ipsilateral breast is radiated, up to 50% of these pts will later develop a breast mass. Although this is a rare clinical situation, long-term survival similar to women with stage II breast cancer is possible.

Osteoblastic Bone Metastases in Men

The probability of prostate cancer is high; a trial of empirical hormonal therapy (leuprolide and flutamide) is warranted (Chap. 72).

Cervical Lymph Node Metastases

Even if panendoscopy fails to reveal a head and neck primary, treatment of such pts with cisplatin and 5-fluorouracil chemotherapy may produce a response; some responses are long-lived (Chap. 66).

For a more detailed discussion, see Stone RM: Metastatic Cancer of Unknown Primary Site, Chap. 99, p. 628, in HPIM-15.

74

SARCOMAS OF BONE AND SOFT TISSUES

SOFT TISSUE SARCOMAS

INCIDENCE AND ETIOLOGY About 6400 cases are diagnosed each year in the U.S. 60% arise in extremities, lower:upper = 3:1; 30% on the the trunk, often the retroperitoneum; 10% in the head and neck region. Although malignant nerve sheath tumors may develop from neurofibromas, nearly all other sarcomas arise de novo and are not malignant transformations of benign tumors. Sarcomas occur with increased frequency in persons who have undergone radiation therapy (usually within the treatment port), who are immunosuppressed (congenital or acquired), or who have been exposed to chemical carcinogens such as polycyclic hydrocarbons, asbestos, and dioxin. Sarcomas may rarely develop within a scar from a prior operation, burn, injury, or foreign body implantation. Kaposi's sarcoma is associated with human herpes virus 8 infection. Individuals with germline mutations in the p53 gene (Li-Fraumeni syndrome) are at increased risk for these and other malignancies. Those who have survived congenital retinoblastoma (germline mutations in the *Rb* gene) are at risk of developing sarcomas.

PATHOLOGY AND CLINICAL FEATURES A common presentation is with an asymptomatic mass. Local symptoms may be related to pressure, traction, or entrapment of nerves. The tumor spreads hematogenously; lung is the most common site. About 20 different types of sarcomas are recognized, based upon the normal tissue from which they derive (e.g., fibrous tissue, skeletal muscle, smooth muscle, blood vessels, fat). Diagnosis is based upon an incisional biopsy placed so that it can be encompassed by a subsequent definitive surgical procedure. Imaging of the primary tumor is best with plain radiographs and MRI for extremity or head and neck lesions and by CT for truncal primaries.

STAGING The only routine staging test is the CXR. Other tests should be done only when indicated by signs and symptoms. Two staging systems exist: American Joint Commission on Cancer (AJCC) and Musculoskeletal Tumor Society. Both are predominantly based upon the histologic grade of the tumor. The AJCC system classifies grade 1 (well differentiated) tumors as stage I, grade 2 (intermediate differentiation) as stage II, and grade 3 (poorly differentiated) as stage III. Tumors are also classified on the basis of size: A, <5cm; B, ≥5cm. Pts with metastatic disease are stage IV. Prognosis is related to stage: 75% 5-year survival for stage I; 55% for stage II; 29% for stage III; <20% for stage IV.

 TREATMENT

Radical excision with documented histologic negative margins is the treatment of choice. Although some histologies behave differently (e.g., chondrosarcoma and GI leiomyosarcomas are refractory to chemotherapy), soft tissue sarcomas are generally lumped together for treatment. Adjuvant radiation therapy and/or chemotherapy improve local control and permit the use of a limb-sparing surgical procedure. Several doxorubicin-based combination chemotherapy programs are similar in efficacy and improve disease-free survival. Impact on overall survival is less consistent. Combination chemotherapy with doxorubicin and ifosfamide is used in the setting of metastatic disease and may cure 10–15% of pts.

BONE SARCOMAS

INCIDENCE AND ETIOLOGY Multiple myeloma is the most common neoplasm of bone (Chap 64). Osteosarcoma, chondrosarcoma, Ewing's sarcoma, and malignant fibrous histiocytoma are the major sarcomas involving bone. About 2500 new cases occur each year. Benign bone tumors such as enchondromas and osteochondromas may transform into chondrosarcoma, and fibrous dysplasia and Paget's disease of bone may transform into osteosarcoma or malignant fibrous histiocytoma.

Osteosarcoma

Osteosarcoma accounts for ~45% of bone sarcomas; 60% of osteosarcomas occur in children and adolescents. Males are affected 1.5–2 times more frequently than females. Osteosarcoma has a predilection for the metaphyses of long bones, epecially the distal femur and proximal tibia and humerus. Malignant fibrous histiocytoma is considered part of the spectrum of osteosarcoma. Pts present with pain and swelling of the affected area. Plain radiograph reveals a destructive lesion with a moth-eaten appearance, a spiculated periosteal reaction (sunburst appearance), and a cuff of periosteal new bone formation at the margin of the soft tissue mass (known as Codman's triangle). It spreads hematogenously to the lungs. The most important prognostic factor is response to chemotherapy. Preoperative chemotherapy with doxorubicin, ifosfamide, cisplatin, and high-dose methotrexate followed by limb-sparing surgery and postoperative chemotherapy is the standard treatment approach. The disease is radioresistant. Long-term survival of extremity primaries is 60–70%. Resection of pulmonary metastases may lead to long-term survival in pts with metastatic disease.

Chondrosarcoma

Chondrosarcoma accounts for ~25% of bone sarcomas; peak incidence is in the fourth to sixth decades of life. It has a predilection for flat bones, especially the shoulder and pelvis. The disease has an indolent natural history, presenting with pain and swelling. On radiography, lesions may appear lobular with mottled, punctate, or annular calcification. Chondrosarcomas are difficult to distinguish from benign cartilage tumors radiographically; clinical signs of progressive tumor growth and inflammation favor the malignant diagnosis. This neoplasm is resistant to chemotherapy. Surgery is the treatment of choice.

Ewing's Sarcoma

Ewing's sarcoma comprises 10–15% of sarcomas; peak incidence is in teenagers. It has a predilection for the diaphyses of long bones and for flat bones. Radiographs show a characteristic onion peel periosteal reaction with a soft tissue mass. The tumor consists of sheets of small, round, blue-staining cells that may be confused with lymphoma, small cell lung cancer, or embryonal rhabdomyosarcoma. The diagnosis is confirmed by detecting p30/32, the product of the *mic-2* gene on the cell surface. Ewing's sarcoma is a member of a family of tumors called *peripheral primitive neuroectodermal tumors* (PNETs), most of which occur in soft tissues. The characteristic chromosomal translocation associated with PNETs including Ewing's sarcoma is t(11;22), which creates a chimeric gene product with components from the *fli-1* gene on chromosome 11 and *ews* on 22. The disease commonly spreads to lungs, other bones, and bone marrow. Systemic chemotherapy with doxorubicin, ifosfamide, etoposide, and vincristine is effective treatment and usually employed before limbsparing surgery. Peripheral primary lesions (below the elbow and mid-calf) have a 5-year survival of 80%. Even with metastatic disease, 25–40% are curable with high-dose therapy and stem cell transplantation.

For a more detailed discussion, see Patel SR, Benjamin RS: Soft Tissue and Bone Sarcomas and Bone Metastases, Chap. 98, p. 625, in HPIM-15.

<table>
<tr><td>75</td></tr>
</table>

PARANEOPLASTIC ENDOCRINE SYNDROMES

Both benign and malignant tumors of nonendocrine tissue can secrete a variety of hormones, principally peptide hormones, and many tumors produce more than one hormone (Table 75-1). At the clinical level, ectopic hormone production is important for two reasons.

First, endocrine syndromes that result may either be the presenting manifestations of the neoplasm or occur late in the course. The endocrine manifestations in some instances are of greater significance than the tumor itself, as in

Table 75-1

Common Paraneoplastic Endocrine Syndromes

Syndrome	Proteins	Tumors Typically Associated with Syndrome
Hypercalcemia of malignancy	Parathyroid hormone-related peptide (PTHrP)	Non-small cell lung cancer
		Breast cancer
	Parathyroid hormone (PTH)	Renal cell carcinoma
		Head and neck cancer
		Bladder cancer
		Myeloma
Syndrome of inappropriate vasopressin secretion (SIADH)	Arginine vasopressin (AVP)	Small cell lung cancer
		Head and neck cancer
	Atrial natriuretic peptide	Non-small cell lung cancer
Cushing's syndrome	Adrenocorticotropic hormone (ACTH)	Small cell lung cancer
		Carcinoid tumors
	Corticotropin-releasing hormone (CRH)	
Acromegaly	Growth hormone–releasing hormone (GHRH)	Carcinoid
		Small cell lung cancer
		Pancreatic islet cell tumors
	Growth hormone (GH)	
Gynecomastia	Human chorionic gonadotropin (hCG)	Testicular cancer
		Lung cancer
		Carcinoid tumors of the lung and gastrointestinal tract
Non-islet cell tumor hypoglycemia	Insulin-like growth factor-2 (IGF-2)	Sarcomas

pts with benign or slowly growing malignancies that secrete corticotropin-releasing hormone and cause fulminant Cushing's syndrome. The frequency with which ectopic hormone production is recognized varies with the criteria used for diagnosis. The most common syndromes of clinical import are those of ACTH hypersecretion, hypercalcemia, and hypoglycemia. Indeed, ectopic ACTH secretion is responsible for 15–20% of pts with Cushing's syndrome, and ~50% of pts with persistent hypercalcemia have a malignancy rather than hyperparathyroidism. Because of the rapidity of development of hormone secretion in some rapidly growing tumors, diagnosis may require a high index of suspicion, and hormone levels may be elevated out of proportion to the manifestations.

Second, ectopic hormones serve as valuable peripheral markers for neoplasia. Because of the broad spectrum of ectopic hormone secretion, screening measurements of plasma hormone levels for diagnostic purposes are not cost-effective. However, in pts with malignancies that are known to secrete hormones, serial measurements of circulating hormone levels can serve as markers for completeness of tumor excision and for effectiveness of radiation therapy or chemotherapy. Likewise, tumor recurrence may be heralded by reappearance of elevated plasma hormone levels before mass effects of the tumor are evident. However, some tumors at recurrence do not secrete hormones, so that hormone measurements cannot be relied on as the sole evidence of tumor activity.

 TREATMENT

> Therapy of ectopic hormone-secreting tumors should be directed when possible toward removal of the tumor. When the tumor cannot be removed or is incurable, specific therapy can be directed toward inhibiting hormone secretion (octreotide for ectopic acromegaly or mitotane to inhibit adrenal steroidogenesis in the ectopic ACTH syndrome) or blocking the action of the hormone at the tissue level (demeclocycline for inappropriate vasopressin secretion).

Hypercalcemia

The most common paraneoplastic syndrome, hypercalcemia of malignancy accounts for 40% of all hypercalcemia. 80% of cancer pts with hypercalcemia have humoral hypercalcemia mediated by parathyroid hormone–related peptide; 20% have local osteolytic hypercalcemia mediated by cytokines such as interleukin-1 and tumor necrosis factor. Many tumor types may produce hypercalcemia (Table 75-1). Pts may have malaise, fatigue, confusion, anorexia, bone pain, polyuria, weakness, constipation, nausea, and vomiting. At high calcium levels, confusion, lethargy, coma, and death may ensue. Median survival of hypercalcemic cancer pts is 1–3 months. Treatment with saline hydration, furosemide diuresis, and pamidronate (60–90 mg IV) controls calcium levels within 7 days in 80% of cases.

Hyponatremia

Most commonly discovered in asymptomatic individuals as a result of serum electrolyte measurements, hyponatremia is usually due to tumor secretion of arginine vasopressin and is called syndrome of inappropriate antidiuretic hormone (SIADH). Atrial natriuretic hormone may also produce hyponatremia. SIADH occurs most commonly in small cell lung cancer (15%) and head and neck cancer (3%). A number of drugs may produce the syndrome. Symptoms of fatigue, poor attention span, nausea, weakness, anorexia, and headache may be controlled by restricting fluid intake to 500 mL/d or blocking the effects of the hormone with 600–1200 mg demeclocycline a day.

Ectopic ACTH Syndrome

When pro-opiomelanocortin mRNA in the tumor is processed into ACTH, excessive secretion of glucocorticoids and mineralocorticoids may ensue. Pts develop Cushing's syndrome with hypokalemic alkalosis, weakness, hypertension, and hyperglycemia. About half the cases occur in small cell lung cancer. ACTH production adversely affects prognosis. Ketoconazole (400–1200 mg/d) or metyrapone (1–4 g/d) may be used to inhibit adrenal steroid synthesis.

For a more detailed discussion, see Johnson BE: Paraneoplastic Syndromes, Chap. 100, p. 632, in HPIM-15.

76

NEUROLOGIC PARANEOPLASTIC SYNDROMES

Varied neurologic disorders occur in pts with systemic neoplasia (Table 76-1). Paraneoplastic syndromes are those related to a remotely located neoplasm; they often evolve over days to weeks and may precede detection of neoplasm by

Table 76-1

Effects of Malignancy on the Nervous System

Direct invasion
Metastatic invasion
  Parenchymatous
  Vascular neoplastic angioendotheliosis
  Meningeal (meningeal carcinomatosis)
Opportunistic infections
  Bacterial (e.g., listeriosis)
  Nonbacterial
    Typical and atypical viral (e.g., progressive multifocal
      leukoencephalopathy)
    Fungal (e.g., cryptococcosis)
Complications of antineoplastic therapy
  Complications of radiation therapy (e.g., radiation necrosis)
  Complications of chemotherapy (e.g., vincristine neuropathy)
Metabolic complications
  Nutritional deficiency
  Ectopic hormone production
Paraneoplastic syndromes

Table 76-2

Neurologic Paraneoplastic Syndromes

Syndrome	Features
BRAIN	
Limbic encephalitis	Onset: subacute
	Confusion; memory loss; temporal lobe seizures
Brainstem encephalitis	Vertigo
	Cerebellar: ataxia, nystagmus
	Ocular: diplopia, gaze palsies
Cerebellar degeneration	Cerebellar: ataxia, dysarthria
Opsoclonus/myoclonus	Involuntary eye movements: rapid, random directions
	Ataxia; encephalopathy
SPINAL CORD	
Necrotizing myelopathy	Weakness: paraplegia or quadriplegia
	Sensory loss: spinal level
	Urinary incontinence
PERIPHERAL NERVE	
Neuronopathies	
Sensory neuronopathy	Onset: subacute
	Sensory loss; diffuse, asymmetric, numbness/paresthesia, dysesthesia/pain
	Sensory ataxia: pseudoathetosis ± encephalomyelitis
Motor neuronopathy	Onset: subacute
	Weakness: arms > legs
	Usually asymmetric
Axonal neuropathies	
Sensorimotor neuropathy	Distal motor and sensory loss
	Most common paraneoplastic neuropathy, especially with >15% weight loss
	Axonal neuropathy
Mononeuritis multiplex	Weakness and/or sensory loss in the distribution of multiple nerves
	Onset: acute to subacute
Neuromyotonia (Isaacs)	Weakness: distal and proximal
	Stiffness; fasciculations
Amyloid neuropathy	Distal symmetric axonal loss: small > large
	Autonomic symptoms prominent
Autonomic neuropathies	
Enteric neuropathy	Gastroparesis; intestinal pseudo-obstruction; esophageal achalasia; dysphagia
Demyelinating neuropathies	
Anti-MAG	Sensory > motor
	Distal, symmetric; gait disorder; tremor; slowly progressive
	NCV: Long distal latencies, conduction block uncommon

Antibody Target	Neoplasm/Percentage
Hu	SCLC, testicular cancer, breast, colon, bladder, lymphoma
Hu	SCLC
Yo; Tr Glutamate receptors Ri (NOVA) Hu Neurofilament	Ovary, uterus, SCLC, Hodgkin's lymphoma Neuroblastoma, lung, breast
Not known	SCLC, lymphoma
Hu	SCLC (90% of cases), breast, ovary, prostate
Not known	Lymphoma
None	Many neoplasms
Not known	Cryoglobulinemia, leukemia, lymphoma
Voltage-gated potassium channels	Thymoma
Not known	Multiple myeloma
Hu	Thymoma, SCLC
Myelin-associated glycoprotein (MAG)	MGUS, IgM M-protein in 85%

(continued)

Table 76-2 *(Continued)*

Neurologic Paraneoplastic Syndromes

Syndrome	Features
Demyelinating neuropathies *(continued)*	
Multifocal motor neuropathy	Slowly progressive
	Motor; distal > proximal
	Asymmetric
	NCV: Motor conduction block
	Motor axon loss (late)
Anti-sulfatide	Slowly progressive
	Sensory > motor
	Distal, symmetric
	Demyelinating or axonal
POEMS	Sensorimotor neuropathy
	Symmetric
	Mixed demyelinating and axonal
CIDP	Chronic or relapsing
	Motor > sensory
	Distal and proximal weakness
	Usually symmetric
	NCV: Conduction block, slow sensory and motor conduction velocities
NEUROMUSCULAR JUNCTION	
LEMS	Weakness: proximal and distal
	Ocular: ptosis
	May improve with exercise
	Dry mouth
	Rapid repetitive stimulation: increment
Myasthenia gravis	Weakness
	Cranial: ocular, face, bulbar
	Respiratory, limbs, trunk
	Fatigue
	Slow repetitive stimulation: decrement
MUSCLE	
Necrotizing myopathy	Males > 40
	Rapid-onset weakness
	Necrosis on muscle biopsy
	May improve with treatment of cancer
Dermatomyositis	Females > 40
	Proximal muscle weakness
	Skin rash
Type II atrophy	Especially with weight loss > 15%
	Wasting > weakness
Myopathy with anti-decorin antibodies	> 50 years of age
	Proximal symmetric weakness
	Mildly elevated creatine kinase
Rippling muscle disease	Cramps induced by touching muscle
	Muscle waves induced by percussion
	Electrically silent

Antibody Target	Neoplasm/Percentage
G_{M1} ganglioside	MGUS, IgM M-protein in 20%
Sulfatide	MGUS, IgM M-protein in 90% with demyelinating neuropathy
Not known	Multiple myeloma, IgG or IgA M-protein in 90%
β-Tubulin in 20%	MGUS, IgM or IgG M-protein in 15%, lymphoma

Voltage-gated P/Q calcium channels	SCLC in 60% of cases, especially older and smoking history
Nicotinic acetylcholine receptor	Thymoma in 10%, especially >30 years

Not known	Lung, breast, alimentary tract
Not known	Ovarian, nasopharyngeal
Not known	Many neoplasms
Decorin	Waldenström's macroglobulinemia, IgM M-protein
Not known	Thymoma

(continued)

Table 76-2 *(Continued)*

Neurologic Paraneoplastic Syndromes

Syndrome	Features
Scleromyxedema	Skin papules
	Raynaud's phenomenon
	Proximal muscle weakness
	High creatine kinase
	Myopathic electromyography

NOTE: SCLC, small cell lung cancer; NCV, nerve conduction velocity; MGUS, monoclonal gammopathy of undetermined significance; POEMS, *p*olyneuropathy, *o*rganomegaly, *e*ndocrinopathy, *m*-protein, *s*kin changes; CIDP, chronic inflammatory demyelinating polyneuropathy; LEMS, Lambert-Eaton myasthenic syndrome.

months or even years. Recognition of a distinctive paraneoplastic syndrome should prompt a search for cancer, although these disorders also occur without cancer (idiopathic). Diagnosis is based upon the clinical pattern (Table 76-2), exclusion of other cancer-related disorders, confirmatory serum or CSF antibodies, or electrodiagnostic testing. Tumors most often associated are cancers of lung, stomach, breast, ovary, and colon, but neurologic disorders occur with 1 in 6 ovarian tumors and 1 in 7 lung tumors. One postulated mechanism is an autoimmune response directed against common antigenic determinants expressed by tumor and neural cells; demonstrated in Lambert-Eaton myasthenic syndrome (antibodies to presynaptic calcium channels and associated proteins) and myasthenia gravis (antibodies to postsynaptic acetylcholine receptors). Known autoantibodies are associated with a number of paraneoplastic syndromes (Table 101-3, p. 641, in HPIM-15). Treatment is difficult, usually unsuccessful. Resection of underlying tumor is usually ineffective, but isolated reports of improvement exist. Immunosuppression is generally without benefit, although plasma exchange or immunosuppression has been used successfully to treat Lambert-Eaton syndrome or myasthenia gravis.

Antibody Target	Neoplasm/Percentage
Not known	MGUS, IgG or IgA λ M-protein

For a more detailed discussion, see Al-lozi MT, Pestronk A: Paraneoplastic Neurologic Syndromes, Chap. 101, p. 636, in HPIM-15.

77

DIAGNOSIS

The laboratory diagnosis of infection requires the demonstration, either directly or indirectly, of viral, bacterial, mycotic, or parasitic agents of disease in tissues, fluids, or excreta of the host. The cornerstone for the diagnosis of parasitic infections (Table 77-1), as of many other infections, is a thorough history of the pt's illness, including occupation, recreation, and travel. The traditional detection methods of microscopy and/or culture are increasingly being complemented by more rapid and sensitive techniques, including serology, nucleic acid probing, and polymerase chain reaction (PCR).

DIRECT DETECTION

MICROSCOPY   *Wet Mounts*   The wet mount is the simplest method for microscopic evaluation, involving no fixation of the specimen prior to examination. In general, it is used for certain large and/or motile organisms that can be visualized without staining. Wet mounts of duodenal aspirates may show pathogenic protozoans (e.g., giardial trophozoites), while mounts of fresh stool may reveal protozoans or helminths (e.g., amebic cysts, *Strongyloides* larvae, ascarid or schistosome eggs). Mounts of fresh blood may reveal microfilariae (in brugian or bancroftian filariasis or loiasis) or spirochetes (in relapsing fever). Motile trichomonads may be found in cervical secretions. Wet mounts with dark-field illumination are used to detect *Treponema* in spirochetal genital lesions and to reveal *Borrelia* or *Leptospira* in blood. To detect fungal elements in skin scrapings or hair, 10% KOH preparations may be used. For certain wet-mount applications, staining is used to enhance detection or visualization of morphologic elements (e.g., India ink to visualize encapsulated cryptococci in CSF, lactophenol cotton blue for fungal speciation).

Gram's Stain   Gram's stain enhances detection of bacteria and PMNs and differentiates bacteria with thick peptidoglycan cell walls (gram-positive; purple) from those with alcohol- or acetone-labile outer membranes (gram-negative; pink). In a properly decolorized slide, the nuclei of PMNs appear pink. Purulent respiratory secretions have >25 PMNs and <10 epithelial cells per low-power field; the presence of >10 epithelial cells per low-power field reflects contamination of the specimen by saliva. A bacterial content of $>10^4$/mL in a specimen from a normally sterile site should be detectable by Gram's stain. Specimens may be concentrated by centrifugation to promote the detection of rare organisms.

Acid-Fast Stain   The acid-fast stains detect organisms, such as *Mycobacterium* spp., that are capable of retaining carbol fuchsin dye after acid/organic solvation (e.g., 3% HCl in 95% ethanol). The modified acid-fast stains detect weakly acid-fast organisms, such as *Nocardia* and *Cryptosporidium*, which retain the dye on treatment with dilute acid (e.g., 1% HCl) but not acid-alcohol. Acid-fast organisms appear pink or red against the blue background of the counterstain. Because mycobacteria may be sparse in clinical specimens, the more sensitive auramine-rhodamine combination fluorescent dye technique was developed.

Table 77-1

Diagnosis of Some Common Parasitic Infections

Parasite	Geographic Distribution	Parasite Stage
Blood flukes		
Schistosoma mansoni	Africa, Central and South America, West Indies	Ova, adults
S. haematobium	Africa	Ova, adults
S. japonicum	Far East	Ova, adults
Intestinal roundworms		
Strongyloides stercoralis (strongyloidiasis)	Moist tropics and subtropics	Larvae
Intestinal protozoans		
Entamoeba histolytica (amebiasis)	Worldwide, especially tropics	Troph, cyst
Giardia lamblia (giardiasis)	Worldwide	Troph, cyst
Isospora belli	Worldwide	Oocyst
Cryptosporidium	Worldwide	Oocyst
Blood and tissue protozoans		
Plasmodium spp. (malaria)	Subtropics and tropics	Asexual
Babesia microti (babesiosis)	U.S., especially New England	Asexual
Toxoplasma gondii (toxoplasmosis)	Worldwide	Cyst, troph

NOTE: WB, western blot; CT, computed tomography; CNS, central nervous system; EIA, enzyme immunoassay; ID, immunodiffusion by commercial kit; troph, trophozoite; IIF, indirect immunofluorescence; PCR, polymerase chain reaction. Serologic tests listed are available from the Centers for Disease Control and Prevention, Atlanta, GA.
SOURCE: Adapted from Davis CE: HPIM-15, p. 1186.

Table 77-2

Instructions for Collection and Transport of Specimens for Culture

Type of Culture (Synonyms)	Specimen	Minimum Volume
BLOOD		
Blood, routine (blood culture for aerobes, anaerobes, and yeasts)	Whole blood	10 mL in each of 2 bottles for adults and children; 5 mL, if possible, in each of 2 bottles for infants; less for neonates

[a] For samples from adults and children, two bottles (smaller for pediatric samples) should be used; one with dextrose phosphate, tryptic soy, or another appropriate broth and the other with thioglycollate or another broth containing reducing agents appropriate for isolation of obligate anaerobes. For special situations (e.g., suspected fungal infection, culture-negative endocarditis, or mycobacteremia), different blood collection systems may be used (Isolator systems; see table).

Diagnosis		
Body Fluid or Tissue	Serologic Tests	Other Tests/Comments
Feces	EIA, WB	Rectal snips, liver biopsy
Urine	WB	Liver, urine, or bladder biopsy
Feces	WB	Liver biopsy
Feces, sputum, duodenal fluid	EIA	Dissemination in immuno-deficiency
Feces, liver	EIA, ID, antigen detection	Ultrasound, liver CT, PCR
Feces	Antigen detection	String test
Feces	—	Acid-fast
Feces	Antigen detection	Acid-fast, biopsy, PCR
Blood	Limited use	PCR
Blood	IIF	PCR
CNS, eye, muscles, other	EIA, IIF	Reactivation in immuno-suppression

Other Stains for Light Microscopy Giemsa or Wright's stain of peripheral blood may reveal certain bacteria and intra- or extracellular parasites (e.g., *Borrelia recurrentis, Plasmodium, Babesia,* or *Trypanosoma*). Other commonly used stains include toluidine blue (for *Pneumocystis carinii*) and methenamine silver (for *P. carinii* and for fungal hyphae in tissue sections).

Container	Other Considerations
See below.[a]	See below.[b]

[b] *Collection:* An appropriate disinfecting technique should be used on both the bottle septum and the patient. Do not allow air bubbles to get into anaerobic broth bottles. *Special considerations:* There is no more important clinical microbiology test than the detection of blood-borne pathogens. The rapid identification of bacterial and fungal agents is a major determinant of pts' survival. Bacteria may be present in blood either continuously (as in endocarditis, overwhelming sepsis, and the early stages of salmonellosis and brucellosis) or intermittently

Table 77-2 *(Continued)*

Instructions for Collection and Transport of Specimens for Culture

Type of Culture (Synonyms)	Specimen	Minimum Volume
Blood for fungi/*Mycobacterium* spp.	Whole blood	10 mL in each of 2 bottles, as for routine blood cultures, or in Isolator tube requested from laboratory
Blood, Isolator (lysis centrifugation)	Whole blood	10 mL
RESPIRATORY TRACT		
Nose	Swab from nares	1 swab
Throat	Swab of posterior pharynx, ulcerations, or areas of suspected purulence	1 swab
Sputum	Fresh sputum (not saliva)	2 mL
Bronchial aspirates	Transtracheal aspirate, bronchoscopy specimen, or bronchial aspirate	1 mL of aspirate or brush in transport medium
STOOL		
Stool for routine culture; stool for *Salmonella*, *Shigella*, and *Campylobacter*	Rectal swab or (preferably) fresh, randomly collected stool	1 g of stool or 2 rectal swabs
Stool for *Yersinia*, *Escherichia coli* O157	Fresh, randomly collected stool	1 g

(as in most other bacterial infections, in which bacteria are shed into the blood on a sporadic basis). Most blood culture systems employ two separate bottles containing broth medium: one that is vented in the laboratory for the growth of facultative and aerobic organisms and a second that is maintained under anaerobic conditions. In cases of suspected continuous bacteremia/fungemia, two or three samples should be drawn before the start of therapy, with additional sets obtained if fastidious organisms are thought to be involved. For intermittent bacteremia, two or three samples should be obtained at least 1 h apart during the first 24 h.

Container	Other Considerations
Same as for routine blood culture	Specify "hold for extended incubation," since fungal agents may require 4 weeks or more to grow.
Isolator tubes	Use mainly for isolation of fungi, *Mycobacterium*, or other fastidious aerobes and for elimination of antibiotics from cultured blood in which organisms are concentrated by centrifugation.
Sterile culturette or similar transport system containing holding medium Sterile culturette or similar swab specimen collection system containing holding medium	Swabs made of calcium alginate may be used. See below.[c]
Commercially available sputum collection system or similar sterile container with screw cap	*Cause for rejection:* Care must be taken to ensure that the specimen is sputum and not saliva. Examination of Gram's stain, with number of epithelial cells and PMNs noted, can be an important part of the evaluation process. Induced sputum specimens should not be rejected.
Sterile aspirate or bronchoscopy tube, bronchoscopy brush in a separate sterile container	Special precautions may be required, depending on diagnostic considerations (e.g., *Pneumocystis*).
Plastic-coated cardboard cup or plastic cup with tight-fitting lid. Other leak-proof containers are also acceptable.	If *Vibrio* spp. are suspected, the laboratory must be notified, and appropriate collection/transport methods should be used.
Plastic-coated cardboard cup or plastic cup with tight-fitting lid.	*Limitations:* Procedure requires enrichment techniques.

[c] Normal microflora includes α-hemolytic streptococci, saprophytic *Neisseria* spp., diphtheroids, and *Staphylococcus* spp. Aerobic culture of the throat ("routine") includes screening for and identification of β-hemolytic *Streptococcus* spp. and other potentially pathogenic organisms. Although considered components of the normal microflora, organisms such as *Staphylococcus aureus, Haemophilus influenzae,* and *Streptococcus pneumoniae* will be identified by most laboratories, if requested. When *Neisseria gonorrhoeae* or *Corynebacterium diphtheriae* is suspected, a special culture request is recommended.

Table 77-2 *(Continued)*

Instructions for Collection and Transport of Specimens for Culture

Type of Culture (Synonyms)	Specimen	Minimum Volume
Stool for *Aeromonas* and *Plesiomonas*	Fresh, randomly collected stool	1 g

UROGENITAL TRACT

Urine	Clean-voided urine specimen or urine collected by catheter	0.5 mL
Urogenital secretions	Vaginal or urethral secretions, cervical swabs, uterine fluid, prostatic fluid, etc.	1 swab or 0.5 mL of fluid

BODY FLUIDS, ASPIRATES, AND TISSUES

CSF (LP)	Spinal fluid	1 mL for routine cultures; ≥5 mL for *Mycobacterium*
Body fluids	Aseptically aspirated body fluids	1 mL for routine cultures
Biopsy and aspirated materials	Tissue removed at surgery, bone, anticoagulated bone marrow, biopsy samples, or other specimens from normally sterile areas	1 mL of fluid or a 1-g piece of tissue
Wounds	Purulent material or abscess contents obtained from wound or abscess without contamination by normal microflora	2 swabs or 0.5 mL of aspirated pus

---

[d] (1) Clean-voided specimens, midvoid specimens, and Foley or indwelling catheter specimens that yield ≥50,000 organisms/mL and from which no more than three species are isolated should have organisms identified. (2) Straight-catheterized, bladder-tap, and similar urine specimens should undergo a complete workup (identification and susceptibility testing) for

Container	Other Considerations
Plastic-coated cardboard cup or plastic cup with tight-fitting lid	*Limitations:* Stool should not be cultured for these organisms unless also cultured for other enteric pathogens.
Sterile, leak-proof container with screw cap or special urine transfer tube	See below.[d]
Transwab containing Amies transport medium or similar system containing holding medium for *Neisseria gonorrhoeae;* modified Todd-Hewitt broth for group B *Streptococcus* surveillance cultures	Vaginal swab samples for "routine culture" should be discouraged whenever possible unless a particular pathogen is suspected. For detection of multiple organisms (e.g., group B *Streptococcus, Trichomonas, Chlamydia,* or *Candida* spp.), 1 swab per test should be obtained.
Sterile tube with tight-fitting cap	Do not refrigerate; transfer to laboratory as soon as possible.
Sterile tube with tight-fitting cap. Specimen may be left in syringe used for collection if the syringe is capped before transport.	For some body fluids (e.g., peritoneal lavage samples), increased volumes enhance detection of rare bacteria.
Sterile culturette-type swab or similar transport system containing holding medium. Sterile bottle or jar should be used for tissue specimens.	Accurate identification of specimen and source is critical. Enough tissue should be collected for both microbiologic and histopathologic evaluations.
Culturette swab or similar transport system or sterile tube with tight-fitting screw cap. For simultaneous anaerobic cultures, send specimen in anaerobic transport device or closed syringe.	*Collection:* Abscess contents or other fluids should be collected in a syringe (see above) when possible to provide an adequate sample volume and an anaerobic environment.

all potentially pathogenic organisms, regardless of colony count. (3) Certain clinical problems (e.g., acute dysuria in women) may warrant identification and susceptibility testing of isolates present at concentrations of <50,000 organisms/mL.

Table 77-2 *(Continued)*

Instructions for Collection and Transport of Specimens for Culture

Type of Culture (Synonyms)	Specimen	Minimum Volume
SPECIAL RECOMMENDATIONS		
Fungi	Specimen types listed above may be used. When urine or sputum is cultured for fungi, a first morning specimen is usually preferred.	1 mL or as specified above for individual listing of specimens. Large volumes may be useful for urinary fungi.
Mycobacterium (acid-fast bacilli)	Sputum, tissue, urine, body fluids	10 mL of fluid or small piece of tissue. Swabs should not be used.
Legionella	Pleural fluid, lung biopsy, bronchoalveolar lavage fluid, bronchial/transbronchial biopsy. Rapid transport to laboratory is critical.	1 mL of fluid; any size tissue sample, although a 0.5-g sample should be obtained when possible
Anaerobic organisms	Aspirated specimens from abscesses or body fluids	1 mL of aspirated fluid or 2 swabs
Viruses[f]	Respiratory secretions, wash aspirates from respiratory tract, nasal swabs, blood samples (including buffy coats), vaginal and rectal swabs, swab specimens from suspicious skin lesions, stool samples (in some cases)	1 mL of fluid, 1 swab, or 1 g of stool in each appropriate transport medium

[e] Aspirated specimens in capped syringes or other transport devices designed to limit oxygen exposure are suitable for the cultivation of obligate anaerobes. A variety of commercially available transport devices may be used. Contamination of specimens with normal microflora from the skin, rectum, vaginal vault, or another body site should be avoided. Collection containers for aerobic culture (such as dry swabs) and inappropriate specimens (such as refrigerated

Immunofluorescent Stains   Immunofluorescent stains can be used to detect viruses within cultured cells or tissue specimens (e.g., herpesviruses, rabies virus) or to reveal difficult-to-grow bacterial agents within clinical specimens (e.g., *Legionella pneumophila*). Direct immunofluorescent antibody (DFA)

Container	Other Considerations
Sterile, leak-proof container with tight-fitting cap	*Collection:* Specimen should be transported to microbiology laboratory within 1 h of collection. Contamination with normal flora from skin, rectum, vaginal tract, or other body surfaces should be avoided.
Sterile container with tight-fitting cap	Detection of *Mycobacterium* spp. is improved by use of concentration techniques. Smears and cultures of pleural, peritoneal, and pericardial fluids often have low yields. Multiple cultures from the same patient are encouraged. Culturing in liquid media shortens the time to detection.
—	—
An appropriate anaerobic transport device is required.ᵉ	Specimens cultured for obligate anaerobes should be cultured for facultative bacteria as well.
Fluid or stool samples in sterile containers or swab samples in viral culturette devices (kept on ice but not frozen) are generally suitable. Plasma samples and buffy coats in sterile collection tubes should be kept at 4 to 8°C. If specimens are to be shipped or kept for a long time, freezing at −80°C is usually adequate.	Most samples for culture are transported in holding medium containing antibiotics to prevent bacterial overgrowth and viral inactivation. Many specimens should be kept cool but not frozen, provided they are transported promptly to the laboratory. Procedures and transport media vary with the agent to be cultured and the duration of transport.

samples; expectorated sputum; stool; gastric aspirates; and vaginal, throat, nose, and rectal swabs) should be rejected as unsuitable.
ᶠ Laboratories generally use diverse methods to detect viral agents, and the specific requirements for each specimen should be checked before a sample is sent.
SOURCE: Appendix B, HPIM-15, p. A-11.

stains use antibodies directed at the agent of interest coupled to a fluorescent compound such as fluorescein, which directly labels the target. Indirect immunofluorescent antibody (IFA) stains use an unlabeled primary antibody to the target antigen followed by a labeled secondary antibody to the primary antibody. Since a single primary antibody molecule is bound by many secondary antibody molecules, the fluorescent signal is amplified with the indirect approach. In either case, the stained specimen is examined under UV light, and visible light is emitted.

MACROSCOPIC ANTIGEN DETECTION Latex agglutination assays and enzyme immunoassays (EIAs) are rapid and inexpensive methods for identifying bacteria, viruses, or extracellular bacterial toxins by means of their protein or polysaccharide antigens. These assays can be performed either directly on clinical specimens or after growth of organisms in the laboratory. Conditions that may be diagnosed by these means include cryptococcosis, histoplasmosis, salmonellosis, shigellosis, and infections due to *Clostridium difficile* toxins A and B.

DETECTION BY CULTURE
The success or failure of efforts to culture bacterial, mycotic, or viral pathogens depends critically on the nature of the sample provided, the means by which it is collected and transported, and the use of a laboratory processing algorithm suitable for the specific sample. Table 77-2 lists procedures for collection and transport of common clinical specimens. Physicians in doubt about the procedure appropriate for a particular situation should seek advice from the microbiology laboratory before obtaining the specimen.

DETECTION BY SEROLOGIC METHODS
Measurement of serum antibody to a specific agent provides indirect evidence of past or current infection. Serologic methods are used to detect many viral infections and have applications in other areas of microbiologic diagnosis as well. The value of antibody assays in parasitic diagnosis is limited by slow development and the inability to distinguish between past and present infection. However, the restricted geographic distribution of many parasites increases the diagnostic usefulness of these assays in travelers from industrialized countries. Detection systems include agglutination reactions, immunofluorescence, EIA, hemagglutination inhibition, and CF. Serologic methods may be used to establish the existence of immunity by documenting that antibody quantity exceeds the protective level (e.g., for rubella, rubeola, or varicella-zoster virus) or to detect current infection by demonstrating a rise in antibody titer between acute- and convalescent-phase samples collected 10–14 d apart (e.g., for arboviral infections, brucellosis, legionellosis, or ehrlichiosis).

DETECTION BY NUCLEIC ACID PROBES
Techniques to detect pathogen-specific DNA or RNA sequences in clinical specimens have become powerful tools for microbiologic diagnosis. All such techniques capitalize on the great specificity of Watson-Crick base pairing. Probes are available to detect a number of pathogens directly in clinical specimens (e.g., *L. pneumophila, Chlamydia trachomatis, Neisseria gonorrhoeae*, group A *Streptococcus, Gardnerella vaginalis, Trichomonas vaginalis, Mycoplasma hominis*, and *Giardia lamblia*). Other probes are available for confirmation of culture results (e.g., those for *Mycobacterium* and *Salmonella* spp.). The sensitivity and specificity of probe assays are comparable to those of culture or EIA. Nucleic acid amplification strategies have also entered the clinical arena. PCR is the best known of these and is far more sensitive than traditional detection methods. It is, however, susceptible to false-positives from even low levels of contaminaton. Amplification assays are currently available to detect *Mycobacterium tuberculosis, N. gonorrhoeae, M. hominis*, and *C. trachomatis*.

For a more detailed discussion, see Onderdonk AB: Laboratory Diagnosis of Infectious Diseases, Chap. 121, p. 775; and Davis CE: Laboratory Diagnosis of Parasitic Infections, Chap. 211, p. 1186, in HPIM-15.

78

ANTIMICROBIAL THERAPY

Antimicrobial agents represent one of the twentieth century's major contributions to human longevity and quality of life. They are among the most commonly prescribed drugs and may be lifesaving. Used inappropriately, however, they can drive up the cost of health care, cause drug interactions and other adverse events, and foster the emergence of resistant pathogens.

Adherence to several guiding principles will promote the most effective use of antimicrobial agents. (1) Whenever possible, material for diagnostic purposes (culture, stains, and special studies) should be obtained before the initiation of therapy so that the pathogen can be identified and its antimicrobial susceptibility determined. (2) Once the pathogen and its susceptibility are known, the antimicrobial therapy chosen should have the narrowest possible spectrum so that the emergence of resistance and the perturbation of the normal flora are minimized. (3) The choice of antimicrobial agent should be guided by the pharmacokinetic and adverse-reaction profile of active compounds, the site of infection, the immune status of the host, and evidence of efficacy from appropriate, well-designed clinical trials. (4) If other factors are equal, the least expensive regimen should be used.

ANTIBACTERIAL THERAPY
See Table 78-1.

ANTIVIRAL THERAPY
See Chaps. 102 through 107.

ANTIFUNGAL THERAPY
See Chaps. 108 and 109.

ANTIPARASITIC THERAPY
See Chaps. 110 and 111.

For a more detailed discussion, see Archer GL, Polk RE: Treatment and Prophylaxis of Bacterial Infections, Chap. 137, p. 867; Wright PW, Wallace RJ Jr: Antimycobacterial Agents, Chap. 168, p. 1017; Dolin R: Antiviral Chemotherapy, Excluding Antiretroviral Drugs, Chap. 181, p. 1092; Bennett JE: Diagnosis and Treatment of Fungal Infections, Chap. 200, p. 1168; and Moore TA: Therapy for Parasitic Infections, Chap. 212, p. 1192, in HPIM-15.

Table 78-1

Major Antibacterial Agents

Drug	Organisms	Dosage Range
PENICILLINS		
Penicillin G	*Streptococcus, Listeria, Neisseria meningitidis, Actinomyces, Clostridium* (but not *difficile*), *Treponema pallidum*	1,200,000 to 24,000,000 U/d IV divided q4h
Penicillin V	*Streptococcus*	0.25–0.5 g qid
Oxacillin	*Staphylococcus aureus* [but not methicillin-resistant strains (MRSA)], *Streptococcus*	1–2 g q4h IV
Dicloxacillin	As for oxacillin	125–500 mg qid
Ampicillin	*Streptococcus, Enterococcus, Listeria, N. meningitidis, Salmonella, Shigella, Proteus*	1–2 g q4h IV
Piperacillin	Most gram-negative bacilli (including *Pseudomonas aeruginosa*), anaerobes, *Streptococcus, Enterococcus faecalis*	3–4 g q4–6h
Ampicillin/ sulbactam	Most gram-negative bacilli (not *P. aeruginosa*), *Streptococcus, S. aureus* (not MRSA), anaerobes	1.5–3.0 g q6h IV
Piperacillin/ tazobactam	As for piperacillin but slightly more active against gram-negative and anaerobic organisms	3.375–4.5 g q6h
CEPHALOSPORINS		
Cefazolin	*Streptococcus, S. aureus* (not MRSA), *Escherichia coli, Klebsiella*	1–2 g q8h IV
Cefuroxime	*Streptococcus, S. aureus* (not MRSA), *Neisseria gonorrhoeae, N. meningitidis, Haemophilus influenzae, E. coli, Klebsiella, Salmonella, Shigella*	750 mg to 1.5 g q8h IV or IM, 125–250 mg bid PO (cefuroxime axetil)
Cefoxitin	As for cefuroxime (not *H. influenzae*) plus anaerobes	1 g q8h to 2 g q4h
Cefotetan	As for cefoxitin (but not as active against *Bacteroides* other than *B. fragilis*)	1–3 g q12h
Ceftizoxime	*Streptococcus, S. aureus* (not MRSA and not as active as cefazolin), gram-negative organisms except *Stenotrophomonas maltophilia* and *Legionella*; anaerobes controversial	1 g q12h to 4 g q8h
Ceftriaxone	As for ceftizoxime (but not active against *P. aeruginosa* or anaerobes)	1–2 g q24h (or q12h)
Ceftazidime	As for ceftizoxime except active against most strains of *P. aeruginosa* (but not against anaerobes)	1–2 g q8h

Routes of Administration	Dose Reduction for Renal Insufficiency	Major Toxicities
IV, IM	Moderate	Hypersensitivity (rash, fever, anaphylaxis 1:10,000)
PO	None	Same as penicillin G
IV, IM	None	Hypersensitivity (rash, fever), hepatitis
PO	None	Hypersensitivity (rash, fever)
IV, IM	Minor	Diarrhea, rash, urticarial rash (not allergy) in infectious mononucleosis
IV	Minor	Hypersensitivity (rash, fever)
IV, IM	Minor	Same as for ampicillin
IV	Minor	Same as piperacillin
IV, IM	Moderate	↑Alkaline phosphatase
IV, IM, PO	Moderate	Phlebitis, hypersensitivity (eosinophilia), ↑SGOT, ↑alkaline phosphatase
IV, IM	Moderate	Hypersensitivity, false ↑creatinine
IV, IM	Moderate	Bleeding (check PT before and during therapy; consider alternatives in cases of pre-existing coagulopathy), ↑LFTs
IV, IM	Moderate	Phlebitis, hypersensitivity (rash, eosinophilia), ↑SGOT
IV, IM	None	As for ceftizoxime; sludge in gallbladder on US with symptomatic cholelithiasis in 9%
IV, IM	Moderate	As for ceftizoxime

(continued)

Table 78-1 *(Continued)*

Major Antibacterial Agents

Drug	Organisms	Dosage Range
Cefepime	As for ceftazidime, except more active against *S. aureus* (not MRSA) and some resistant strains of *Enterobacter* and *Serratia*	1–2 g q12h
CARBAPENEMS		
Imipenem/cilastatin	Gram-positive cocci (but not *Enterococcus faecium* or MRSA), gram-negative organisms (but not *S. maltophilia*), anaerobes	500 mg to 1 g q6h
Meropenem	As for imipenem, except slightly more active against aerobic gram-negative organisms and slightly less active against staphylococci and streptococci	500 mg q8h
MONOBACTAMS		
Aztreonam	Only gram-negative aerobes	1 g q8h to 2 g q6h
AMINOGLYCOSIDES		
Gentamicin	Gram-negative aerobes; synergistic with penicillins against *Enterococcus*	3–5 (mg/kg)/d divided q8h
Tobramycin	Same as gentamicin but more active against *P. aeruginosa*	Same as gentamicin
Amikacin	Same as gentamicin but more active against gentamicin-resistant organisms	15 (mg/kg)/d divided q8–12h
TETRACYCLINES		
Doxycycline	*Francisella tularensis, Brucella, Vibrio vulnificus, Chlamydia, Mycoplasma pneumoniae, Rickettsia*	100 mg q12h
MACROLIDES		
Erythromycin	*Streptococcus, M. pneumoniae, Legionella*	250 mg to 1 g q6h
Clarithromycin	As for erythromycin but also active against *H. influenzae, Mycobacterium avium* complex	500 mg bid

Routes of Administration	Dose Reduction for Renal Insufficiency	Major Toxicities
IV	Moderate	As for ceftizoxime
IV, IM (requires dose reduction and lidocaine)	Moderate	Phlebitis, hypersensitivity, seizures (especially in pts with renal dysfunction), nausea, vomiting, diarrhea
IV	Moderate	Same as imipenem, but less likely to cause seizures
IV	Moderate	Phlebitis, hypersensitivity (but no cross-reaction with penicillins), ↑SGOT
IV, IM	Major	Nephrotoxicity, ototoxicity; peak and trough levels should be monitored
IV, IM	Major	Same as gentamicin
IV, IM	Major	Same as gentamicin
IV, PO	Minor	Nausea, erosive esophagitis; phototoxicity and tooth deposition less than with tetracycline
IV, PO	None	Nausea, vomiting, cramps, ↑SGOT, cholestatic jaundice (especially with estolate), phlebitis, transient deafness
PO	Minor	Adverse GI effects less prominent than with erythromycin

(continued)

Table 78-1 *(Continued)*

Major Antibacterial Agents

Drug	Organisms	Dosage Range
Azithromycin	As for erythromycin but more active against *M. avium* complex, *H. influenzae, Chlamydia* (FDA-approved for urethritis/cervicitis)	500 mg qd
QUINOLONES		
Ciprofloxacin	Gram-positive cocci (but not serious pneumococcal or enterococcal infections or MRSA), gram-negative organisms (but not *Burkholderia cepacia*), not active against anaerobes; only some staphylococcal strains known to be sensitive	500 or 750 mg bid PO; 200–400 mg q12h IV
Levofloxacin	As for ciprofloxacin, except more active against gram-positive organisms, esp. *Streptococcus pneumoniae*	250 or 500 mg PO qd; 250–500 mg IV qd
OTHER		
Vancomycin	Gram-positive organisms	1 g q12h IV; 125–500 mg q6h PO
Clindamycin	*Streptococcus, S. aureus* (not MRSA), anaerobes	600–900 mg q8h IV; 150–450 mg q6h PO
Metronidazole	Anaerobes	500 mg q6–8h
Quinupristin/ dalfopristin	Most gram-positive organisms, including vancomycin-resistant *E. faecium* and MRSA; not active against *E. faecalis*	7.5 mg/kg q12h
Trimethoprim-sulfamethoxazole	Gram-negative aerobes, including *Moraxella catarrhalis* and *H. influenzae, Salmonella, Shigella; Streptococcus* (if sensitive)	8 (mg/kg)/d TMP component divided q6h up to 15–20 (mg/kd)/d; for *Pneumocystis* pneumonia, 1–2 DS tabs PO bid

SOURCE: Adapted from GL Archer, RE Polk: Chap. 137, p. 867, in HPIM-15; and DN Gilbert et al: *Guide to Antimicrobial Therapy*. Hyde Park, VT, Antimicrobial Therapy, Inc., 2000.

Routes of Administration	Dose Reduction for Renal Insufficiency	Major Toxicities
PO	Minor	As with clarithromycin, adverse GI effects less prominent than with erythromycin
IV, PO	Minor	Adverse GI effects, including nausea, diarrhea, vomiting; not to be used for children or pregnant women because of effects on cartilage
PO, IV	Minor	Nausea, diarrhea, insomnia, headache
IV, PO (for *C. difficile* colitis only)	Major	Phlebitis, "red man" syndrome, ototoxicity, +/− nephrotoxicity; may be increased when given with aminoglycosides (trough levels should be <10 mg/mL)
IV, IM, PO	None	Diarrhea, *C. difficile* colitis, rash
IV, PO	None	Nausea, vomiting, metallic taste, headache, disulfiram-like reaction with alcohol; dose must be reduced in severe liver disease
IV	None	Phlebitis, rash, asymptomatic hyperbilirubinemia
IV, PO	Moderate	Rash, nausea, vomiting, diarrhea, neutropenia

79

IMMUNIZATION AND ADVICE TO TRAVELERS

IMMUNIZATION

Vaccination against infectious diseases is one of the most potent and effective tools of medicine. Through immunization, many once-prevalent infectious diseases (e.g., smallpox, polio, measles, *Haemophilus influenzae* infection) have been eliminated or drastically curtailed. However, complacency and socioeconomic barriers have impeded the attainment of universal and appropriate immunization. Adults in particular often fail to receive indicated immunizations, such as pneumococcal vaccination, influenza vaccination, and tetanus-diphtheria boosters.

Active immunization refers to administration of a vaccine or a toxoid in order to elicit long-lasting protection. Live vaccines are usually contraindicated for pts who are immunosuppressed, febrile, or pregnant. *Passive* immunization refers to the provision of temporary immunity by administration of exogenously produced immune substances such as antibodies.

VACCINES FOR ROUTINE USE

ADULTS   Recommendations for adult immunization are summarized in Table 79-1. Routine immunization against polio is not recommended for adults unless they are at particularly high risk of exposure (e.g., during travel to endemic regions) or are the guardians of a child with an immunodeficiency disorder. Rubella vaccine should be given to all women of childbearing age unless they have documented proof of immunization or have positive rubella antibody on laboratory testing. College students, particularly freshmen living in a dormitory, should be offered the option of immunization against meningococcal meningitis. A vaccine for Lyme disease is licensed for persons 15–70 years old. Its use is based on individual risk.

IMMUNOCOMPROMISED STATES   Immune responses may not be as vigorous in immunocompromised persons as in those with a normal immune system. Immunization of HIV-infected persons is summarized in Table 79-2. In other immunocompromised patients, including those receiving immunosuppressive therapy, passive immunization can be considered either as postexposure prophylaxis or as part of the treatment for established infection (Table 79-3).

POSTEXPOSURE IMMUNIZATION   Active or passive immunization prevents or attenuates disease after exposure to certain infections. Recommended regimens are compiled in Table 79-3.

ADVICE TO TRAVELERS

Immunizations for travel are generally divided into three categories: routine (Table 79-1), required (mandated for entry into certain areas—e.g., yellow fever and meningococcal meningitis), and recommended (desirable but not required—e.g., hepatitis A and B, typhoid, meningococcal meningitis, Japanese encephalitis, cholera, and rabies). Vaccines commonly given to travelers are listed in Table 79-4.

MALARIA   Prevention of malaria, a major cause of life-threatening illness in travelers, should stress avoidance of mosquitoes by staying indoors and use

Table 79-1

Adult Immunization Schedule

Vaccine	Timing of Immunization
Hepatitis A[a]	Two doses are recommended for individuals requiring long-term protection, with the second dose 6–12 months after the first.
Hepatitis B[a]	Three doses are given, with the second dose 1 month after the first and the third dose 5 months after the second.
Measles/mumps/rubella	One dose is given to adults born in 1957 or later *and not previously immunized*. A second dose may be required in some work or school settings.
Tetanus/diphtheria toxoids, adsorbed	A three-dose schedule applies for individuals who *have not received an initial immunization series in childhood*. The second dose is given 1 month after the first and the third dose 6 months after the second. Boosters are then given every 10 years.
Varicella	Two doses are given to individuals ≥13 years of age who have not had chickenpox. The second dose is given 1–2 months after the first.
Influenza	Vaccine is administered yearly to individuals ≥55 years of age; to younger people with chronic medical problems, such as heart disease and diabetes; and to those who work or live with high-risk persons.
Streptococcus pneumoniae (polysaccharide)	Vaccine is usually given once to individuals ≥65 years of age. A repeat dose may be given 5 years later for those at highest risk. Immunization is also recommended for younger people with chronic medical problems, such as heart disease, diabetes, renal failure, and sickle cell anemia, and for those who work or live with high-risk persons.

[a] For individuals at risk.
SOURCE: Modified from GT Keusch, KJ Bart: HPIM-15, p. 788, and from the National Coalition for Adult Immunization.

of DEET-containing mosquito repellents. Table 79-5 lists the currently recommended drugs of choice for prophylaxis of malaria, by destination.

DIARRHEA Traveler's diarrhea, which is usually caused by enterotoxigenic *Escherichia coli* but may also be caused by many other pathogens, can often be avoided by consuming only well-cooked hot foods, peeled or cooked fruits and vegetables, and bottled or boiled beverages. When diarrhea occurs without fever or bloody stool, it can be self-treated with a 3-day course of an oral quinolone. For diarrhea acquired in areas such as Thailand, where >70% of *Campylobacter* infections are quinolone-resistant, azithromycin is a better choice.

Table 79-2

Recommendations for Routine Immunization of HIV-Infected Persons in the United States

Vaccine	HIV Clinical Status		Comments
	Asymptomatic	Symptomatic	
DTaP/Td	Yes	Yes	No change in usual immunization schedule
OPV	No	No	Increased risk of vaccine virus proliferation and paralytic polio; IPV used for household contacts of HIV-infected pts
IPV	Yes	Yes	Antibody response potentially impaired in symptomatic persons
MMR	Yes	Yes	No change in usual immunization schedule; with high risk of exposure to measles, first dose given at 6–11 months of age, second dose at >12 months of age; with documented infection, measles immune globulin potentially administered (see Table 79-3)
Hib conjugate	Yes	Yes	No change in usual immunization schedule
HBV	Yes	Yes	Antibody response potentially impaired; higher-dose vaccine available, but no data address optimal dose; possibly wise to check antibody titer after immunization and give additional doses if titer is inadequate
Pneumococcus	Yes	Yes	Should be given to all ≥2 years old
Influenza	Yes	Yes	Antibody response potentially impaired in symptomatic pts
Varicella	No	No	Use in asymptomatic HIV-infected persons not studied

NOTE: DTaP, diphtheria/tetanus/acellular pertussis; Td, tetanus/diphtheria; OPV, oral poliovirus vaccine; IPV, inactivated poliovirus vaccine; MMR, measles/mumps/rubella; Hib, *H. influenzae* type b; HBV, hepatitis B virus.
SOURCE: GT Keusch, KJ Bart: HPIM-15, p. 790, and the Centers for Disease Control and Prevention.

Table 79-3

Recommended Postexposure Immunization with Immunoglobulin Preparations in the United States

Disease	Indicated	Comments
Measles	Yes	Standard human immune globulin is recommended for exposed infants and adults with normal immunocompetence (but with a contraindication to measles vaccine) and for immunocompromised pts (regardless of immunization status). Pts should be immunized 3–6 months after immunoglobulin administration. Recommended dose: 0.25–0.5 mL/kg (40–80 mg of IgG/kg) IM; 80 mg of IgG/kg for immunocompromised contacts; maximum, 15 mL.
Rubella	No	Efficacy is unreliable; therefore, standard human immune globulin is recommended for administration only to antibody-negative pregnant women in the first trimester who have a documented rubella exposure and who will not consider terminating the pregnancy. Recommended dose: 0.55 mL/kg (90 mg of IgG/kg) IM.
Tetanus	Yes	Human tetanus immune globulin (TIG) has replaced equine tetanus antitoxin because of the risk of serum sickness with equine serum. Recommended dose for postexposure prophylaxis: 250–500 units of TIG (10–20 mg of IgG/kg) IM. Recommended dose for treatment of tetanus: 3000–6000 units of TIG IM.
Rabies	Yes	Human rabies immune globulin (RIG) is preferred over equine rabies antiserum because of the risk of serum sickness. RIG or antiserum is recommended for nonimmunized individuals with animal bites in which rabies cannot be ruled out and with other exposures to known rabid animals. Recommended dose of RIG: 20 IU/kg (22 mg of IgG/kg). Recommended dose of antiserum: 40 IU/kg. Rabies vaccine is given as well at 0, 3, 7, 14, and 28 d.
Hepatitis A	Yes	Standard immune serum globulin is given in a single dose of 0.02–0.04 mL/kg or (for continuous exposure) in a dose of up to 0.06 mL/kg every 5 months. Postexposure treatment with hepatitis A immune globulin has not been studied.
Hepatitis B	Yes	Standard immune serum globulin is not reliably effective. Special human hepatitis B immune globulin is useful and is recommended for neonates born to an infected mother and after mucous-membrane or parenteral contact with infected persons or infected blood or serum. Recommended dose for neonates: 0.5 mL IM within 12 h of birth. Recommended dose for percutaneous or mucosal exposure: 0.06 mL/kg (10 mg of IgG/kg) IM.
Non-A, non-B hepatitis	Yes	Standard immune serum globulin may be valuable. Recommended dose: 0.12 mL/kg (10 mg of IgG/kg) IM, up to 10 mL.
Varicella-zoster	Yes	Exposed infants and children at high risk of seroconversion, including perinatally exposed newborns, should receive immune globulin, which is also indicated for exposed susceptible adults. Recommended dose: 125 U (1 vial)/10 kg IM (minimum, 125 U; maximum, 625 U).

SOURCE: Modified from GT Keusch, KJ Bart: HPIM-15, p. 791.

Table 79-4

Vaccines Commonly Used for Travel

Vaccine	Primary Series	Booster Interval
Cholera, parenteral	2 doses, ≥1 week apart, SC or IM	6 months
Cholera, live oral (CVD 103 - HgR)	1 dose	6 months
Hepatitis A (Havrix), 1440 enzyme immunoassay units/mL	2 doses, 6–12 months apart, IM	>10 years
Hepatitis A (VAQTA)[a]	2 doses, 6–12 months apart, IM	>10 years
Hepatitis A/B combined (Twinrix)	3 doses at 0, 1, and 6–12 months, IM	>10 years
Hepatitis B (Engerix B): accelerated schedule	3 doses at 0, 1, and 2 months *or* 0, 7, and 21 days, IM	12 months, once only
Hepatitis B (Engerix B or Recombivax): standard schedule	3 doses at 0, 1, and 6 months, IM	None required
Immune globulin (hepatitis A prevention)	1 dose IM	Intervals of 3–5 months, depending on initial dose
Japanese encephalitis (JEV, Biken)	3 doses, 1 week apart, SC	12–18 months (first booster), then 4 years
Lyme disease (PMC)	3 doses at 0, 1, and 12 months, IM	Optimum booster schedule not yet determined
Meningococcus, quadrivalent	1 dose SC	>3 years (optimum booster schedule not yet determined)
Rabies, human diploid cell vaccine (HDCV)	3 doses at 0, 7, and 21 or 28 d, ID	None required except with exposure
Rabies (HDCV), rabies vaccine absorbed (RVA), or purified chick embryo cell vaccine (PCEC)	3 doses at 0, 7, and 21 or 28 d, IM	None required except with exposure
Typhoid, heat-phenol-inactivated	2 doses, ≥4 weeks apart, SC	3 years
Typhoid Ty21a, oral live attenuated (Vivotif)	1 capsule every other day ×4 doses	5 years
Typhoid Vi capsular polysaccharide, injectable (Typhim Vi)	1 dose IM	2 years
Yellow fever	1 dose SC	10 years

[a] Two new vaccines have been marketed (AVAXIM and EPAXAL).
SOURCE: JS Keystone, PE Kozarsky: HPIM-15, p. 794.

Table 79-5

Malaria Chemosuppressive Regimens According to Geographic Area[a]

Geographic Area	Drug of Choice	Alternatives
Central America (north of Panama), Haiti, Dominican Republic, Iraq, Egypt, Turkey, northern Argentina, and Paraguay	Chloroquine	Mefloquine Doxycycline Atovaquone/ proguanil
South America including Panama (except northern Argentina and Paraguay); Asia (including Southeast Asia); Africa; and Oceania	Mefloquine	Doxycycline Atovaquone/ proguanil
Thai, Myanmar, and Cambodian borders	Doxycycline	Atovaquone/ proguanil Primaquine?

[a] See CDC's *Health Information for International Travel 1999–2000*.
NOTE: See also Chap. 214, HPIM-15.
SOURCE: JS Keystone, PE Kozarsky: HPIM-15, p. 795.

For a more detailed discussion, see Keusch GT, Bart KJ: Immunization Principles and Vaccine Use, Chap. 122, p. 780; and Keystone JS, Kozarsky PE: Health Advice for International Travel, Chap. 123, p. 793, in HPIM-15.

80

INFECTIVE ENDOCARDITIS

When classified according to temporal evolution, *acute endocarditis* is a hectically febrile illness associated with damage to cardiac structures, seeding of extracardiac sites, and progression to death within weeks if left untreated. *Subacute endocarditis* is an indolent illness associated with slow or no destruction of cardiac structures and rare metastatic infection; it is gradually progressive unless complicated by an embolic event or a ruptured mycotic aneurysm. Other bases for the classification of endocarditis include site of infection, microbiologic cause, or predisposing risk factors (such as injection drug use).

Etiology

A small number of bacterial species cause the majority of endocarditis cases (see Table 126-1, HPIM-15, p. 810). The causative microorganisms vary somewhat among the major clinical types of endocarditis, depending in part on which portal of entry into the bloodstream is used and where the infection is acquired (i.e., nosocomially or in the community). In native valve endocarditis, the viridans streptococci, staphylococci, and HACEK organisms (*Haemophilus* spp., *Actinobacillus actinomycetemcomitans, Cardiobacterium hominis, Eikenella corrodens, Kingella kingae*) enter through the skin and upper respiratory tract, *Streptococcus bovis* enters via the GI tract, enterococci tend to enter through the genitourinary tract, and nosocomially acquired *Staphylococcus aureus* usually enters via an infected IV catheter. Prosthetic valve endocarditis (PVE) arising within 2 months of valve replacement is due to a number of organisms associated with postoperative bacteremia. Coagulase-negative staphylococcal PVE arising within 12 months of valve replacement is usually nosocomially acquired. The microbiologic etiology of PVE arising >12 months after valve replacement is similar to that of native valve endocarditis. Transvenous pacemaker or implanted defibrillator-associated endocarditis is usually nosocomial and due to *S. aureus* or coagulase-negative staphylococci. Injection drug users (IDUs) with endocarditis usually have *S. aureus* (often methicillin-resistant) isolated, but a number of organisms can cause left-sided endocarditis in IDUs. Polymicrobial endocarditis occurs more often in IDUs than in pts who do not inject drugs. In the 5–15% of pts with "culture-negative" endocarditis, the negative cultures are attributable to prior antibiotic exposure in up to one-half of cases. The remainder of "culture-negative" cases are due to fastidious organisms, including the HACEK group, pyridoxal-requiring streptococci (*Abiotrophia* spp.), *Bartonella* spp., *Coxiella burnetii*, and *Brucella* spp.

Clinical Manifestations

The clinical syndrome of endocarditis is highly variable and spans a continuum between acute and subacute presentations. β-Hemolytic streptococci, *S. aureus*, pneumococci, *Staphylococcus lugdunensis*, and enterococci typically cause acute endocarditis. Viridans streptococci, coagulase-negative staphylococci, agents of "culture-negative" endocarditis, and occasionally enterococci and *S. aureus* typically cause subacute endocarditis.

The clinical features of endocarditis are nonspecific (Table 80-1), but these symptoms in a febrile pt with predisposing factors, bloodstream infection due to organisms that frequently cause endocarditis, unexplained arterial emboli, or progressive cardiac valvular incompetence should heighten the suspicion of endocarditis. Fever may be higher in acute than in subacute endocarditis and may be blunted or absent entirely in pts with cardiac or renal failure, in the severely debilitated, and in the elderly. Cardiac murmurs are ultimately detected in 85% of pts with acute endocarditis of a native valve. Congestive heart failure develops in 30–40% of pts as a result of valvular dysfunction, myocarditis, or intracardiac fistula formation. Extension of infection into the valve ring structure results in perivalvular abscesses, which in turn may extend to cause fistulae, pericarditis, or heart block. The classic peripheral manifestations are related to the duration of infection and, because of early diagnosis and treatment, have become less common. Back pain and myalgias are common presenting features that remit promptly with treatment. Renal dysfunction usually results from immune complex deposition and glomerulonephritis; embolic renal infarcts rarely cause renal insufficiency. Almost 50% of IDUs with endocarditis have infection limited to the tricuspid valve; these pts frequently present with pulmonary symptoms, such as cough and chest pain, and have nodular pulmonary infiltrates detectable on CXR.

Arterial emboli may be present in up to 50% of pts; vegetations that are >10 mm in diameter on echocardiogram and mitral vegetations are most likely to embolize. Emboli can travel to almost any organ or site. The risk of embolization is highest in the first week of antibiotic therapy, decreasing from 13 events/100,000 pt-days during the first week to 1.2 events/100,000 pt-days after the third week. Neurologic symptoms (most often due to embolic phenomena)

Table 80-1

Clinical and Laboratory Features of Infective Endocarditis

Feature	Frequency, %
Fever	80–90
Chills and sweats	40–75
Anorexia, weight loss, malaise	25–50
Myalgias, arthralgias	15–30
Back pain	7–15
Heart murmur	80–85
New/worsened regurgitant murmur	10–40
Arterial emboli	20–50
Splenomegaly	15–50
Clubbing	10–20
Neurologic manifestations	20–40
Peripheral manifestations (Osler's nodes, subungual hemorrhages, Janeway lesions, Roth's spots)	2–15
Petechiae	10–40
Laboratory manifestations	
Anemia	70–90
Leukocytosis	20–30
Microscopic hematuria	30–50
Elevated erythrocyte sedimentation rate	>90
Rheumatoid factor	50
Circulating immune complexes	65–100
Decreased serum complement	5–40

SOURCE: AW Karchmer: HPIM-15, p. 810.

occur in up to 40% of endocarditis pts; purulent meningitis, brain abscesses, ruptured mycotic aneurysm, seizures, and encephalopathy are also observed in some pts.

Diagnosis

The Duke Criteria constitute a highly sensitive and specific diagnostic schema developed on the basis of clinical, laboratory, and echocardiographic findings (Table 80-2). Documentation of two major criteria, of one minor criterion and three major criteria, or of five minor criteria allows a clinical diagnosis of definite endocarditis. Three blood cultures separated by at least 1 h but not by >24 h should be obtained. If the initial blood cultures are negative after 48–72 h, two or three additional sets, including a lysis-centrifugation culture, should be obtained and the laboratory alerted to pursue fastidious organisms by prolonging incubation time and performing special subcultures. Serology for *Brucella, Bartonella, Legionella,* and *C. burnetii* can be useful in identifying fastidious organisms.

Echocardiography should be strongly considered for pts with a clinical diagnosis of endocarditis and for pts in whom endocarditis is strongly suspected. Transesophageal echocardiography (TEE) is >90% sensitive for detection of vegetations, whereas transthoracic echocardiography (TTE) is only 65% sensitive. TTE is not adequate for evaluating prosthetic valves or intracardiac complications. In pts with a low (<5%) pretest probability of having endocarditis, a negative TTE is sufficient to exclude endocarditis. In pts with a 5–50% pretest probability of having endocarditis, initial evaluation with TEE is cost-effective.

Table 80-2

The Duke Criteria for the Clinical Diagnosis of Infective Endocarditis

MAJOR CRITERIA

Positive blood culture
 Typical microorganism for infective endocarditis from two separate blood
 cultures
  Viridans streptococci, *Streptococcus bovis*, HACEK group, *or*
  Community-acquired *Staphylococcus aureus* or enterococci in the absence
  of a primary focus, *or*
 Persistently positive blood culture, defined as recovery of a microorganism
 consistent with infective endocarditis from:
  Blood cultures drawn >12 h apart; *or*
  All of three or a majority of four or more separate blood cultures, with
  first and last drawn at least 1 h apart
Evidence of endocardial involvement
 Positive echocardiogram
  Oscillating intracardiac mass on valve or supporting structures or in the
  path of regurgitant jets or in implanted material, in the absence of an
  alternative anatomic explanation, *or*
  Abscess, *or*
  New partial dehiscence of prosthetic valve, *or*
 New valvular regurgitation (increase or change in preexisting murmur not
 sufficient)

MINOR CRITERIA

Predisposition: predisposing heart condition or injection drug use
Fever ≥38.0°C (≥100.4°F)
Vascular phenomena: major arterial emboli, septic pulmonary infarcts, mycotic
 aneurysm, intracranial hemorrhage, conjunctival hemorrhages, Janeway lesions
Immunologic phenomena: glomerulonephritis, Osler's nodes, Roth's spots,
 rheumatoid factor
Microbiologic evidence: positive blood culture but not meeting major criterion
 as noted previously[a] or serologic evidence of active infection with organism
 consistent with infective endocarditis
Echocardiogram: consistent with infective endocarditis but not meeting major
 criterion

---

[a] Excluding single positive cultures for coagulase-negative staphylococci and diphtheroids,
which are common culture contaminants, and organisms that do not cause endocarditis frequently, such as gram-negative bacilli.
SOURCE: Adapted (by AW Karchmer: HPIM-15, p. 812) from D Durack et al. Am J Med 96:
200, 1999, with permission from Excerpta Medica, Inc.

 TREATMENT

Empirical antibiotics should be reserved for pts with deteriorating hemodynamics. The regimens recommended for treatment of PVE (except for staphylococcal infections) are similar to those used to treat native valve infection
(Table 80-3). Effective treatment for some intracardiac and CNS complications of endocarditis requires valve replacement, although most of the clinical
indications for surgical treatment of endocarditis are not absolute (Table 80-
4). Surgery should not be delayed when valvular dysfunction, progressive
congestive heart failure, or uncontrolled or perivalvular infection is present.
Surgery should be delayed for 2–3 weeks after a nonhemorrhagic embolic

Table 80-3

Antibiotic Treatment for Infective Endocarditis Caused by Common Organisms[a]

Organism	Drug, Dose, Duration	Comments
Streptococci		
Penicillin-susceptible[b] streptococci, S. bovis	Penicillin G 2–3 million units IV q4h for 4 weeks	—
	Penicillin G 2–3 million units IV q4h *plus* gentamicin[c] 1 mg/kg IM or IV q8h, both for 2 weeks	Avoid penicillin plus gentamicin if risks of aminoglycoside toxicity are increased or case is complicated
	Ceftriaxone 2 g/d IV as single dose for 4 weeks	Can use ceftriaxone in pts with nonimmediate penicillin allergy
	Vancomycin[d] 15 mg/kg IV q12h for 4 weeks	Use vancomycin in pts with severe or immediate β-lactam allergy
Relatively penicillin-resistant[e] streptococci	Penicillin G 3 million units IV q4h for 4–6 weeks *plus* gentamicin[c] 1 mg/kg IV q8h for 2 weeks	Preferred for treatment of prosthetic valve endocarditis caused by penicillin-susceptible streptococci; continue penicillin for 6 weeks in this setting
Penicillin-resistant[f] streptococci, pyridoxal-requiring streptococci (*Abiotrophia* spp.)	Penicillin G 3–4 million units IV q4h *plus* gentamicin[c] 1 mg/kg IV q8h, both for 4–6 weeks	—
Enterococci[g]	Penicillin G 3–4 million units IV q4h *plus* gentamicin[c] 1 mg/kg IV q8h, both for 4–6 weeks	Can use streptomycin 7.5 mg/kg q12h in lieu of gentamicin if there is not high-level resistance to streptomycin
	Ampicillin 2 g IV q4h *plus* gentamicin[c] 1 mg/kg IV q8h, both for 4–6 weeks	Do not use cephalosporins or carbapenems for treatment of enterococcal endocarditis
	Vancomycin[d] 15 mg/kg IV q12h *plus* gentamicin[c] 1 mg/kg IV q8h, both for 4–6 weeks	Use vancomycin plus gentamicin for penicillin-allergic pts or desensitize to penicillin
Staphylococci		
Methicillin-susceptible, infecting native valves (no foreign devices)	Nafcillin or oxacillin 2 g IV q4h for 4–6 weeks *plus* (optional) gentamicin[c] 1 mg/kg IM or IV q8h for 3–5 days	May use penicillin 3–4 million units q6h if isolate is penicillin-susceptible (does not produce β-lactamase)
	Cefazolin 2 g IV q8h for 4–6 weeks *plus* (optional) gentamicin[c] 1 mg/kg IM or IV q8h for 3–5 days	Can use cefazolin regimen for pts with nonimmediate penicillin allergy
	Vancomycin[d] 15 mg/kg IV q12h for 4–6 weeks	Use vancomycin for pts with immediate (urticarial) or severe penicillin allergy

(continued)

Table 80-3 *(Continued)*

Antibiotic Treatment for Infective Endocarditis Caused by Common Organisms[a]

Organism	Drug, Dose, Duration	Comments
Methicillin-resistant, infecting native valves (no foreign devices)	Vancomycin[d] 15 mg/kg IV q12h for 4–6 weeks	No role for routine use of rifampin
Methicillin-susceptible, infecting prosthetic valves	Nafcillin or oxacillin 2 g IV q4h for 6–8 weeks *plus* gentamicin[c] 1 mg/kg IM or IV q8h for 2 weeks *plus* rifampin[h] 300 mg PO q8h for 6–8 weeks	Use gentamicin during initial 2 weeks; determine susceptibility to gentamicin before initiating rifampin (see text); if pt is highly allergic to penicillin, use regimen for methicillin-resistant staphylococci; if β-lactam allergy is of the minor, nonimmediate type, can substitute cefazolin for oxacillin/nafcillin
Methicillin-resistant, infecting prosthetic valves	Vancomycin[d] 15 mg/kg IV q12h for 6–8 weeks *plus* gentamicin[c] 1 mg/kg IM or IV q8h for 2 weeks *plus* rifampin[h] 300 mg PO q8h for 6–8 weeks	Use gentamicin during initial 2 weeks; determine gentamicin susceptibility before initiating rifampin
HACEK organisms	Ceftriaxone 2 g/d IV for 4 weeks Ampicillin 2 g IV q4h *plus* gentamicin[c] 1 mg/kg IM or IV q8h, both for 4 weeks	May use another third-generation cephalosporin at comparable dosage Determine ampicillin susceptibility; do not use ampicillin if β-lactamase is produced

[a] Doses are for adults with normal renal function. Doses of gentamicin, streptomycin, and vancomycin must be adjusted for reduced renal function. Ideal body weight is used to calculate doses per kilogram (men = 50 kg + 2.3 kg per inch over 5 feet; women = 45.5 kg + 2.3 kg per inch over 5 feet).

[b] MIC ≤ 0.1 μg/mL.

[c] Aminoglycosides should not be administered as single daily doses and should be introduced as part of the initial treatment. Target peak and trough serum concentrations of gentamicin 1 h after a 20- to 30-min infusion or IM injection are 3–5 μg/mL and ≤1 μg/mL, respectively; the target peak serum concentration of streptomycin (timing as with gentamicin) is 20–25 μg/mL.

[d] Desirable peak vancomycin level 1 h after completion of a 1-h infusion is 30–45 μg/mL.

[e] MIC > 0.1 μg/mL and <0.5 μg/mL.

[f] MIC ≥ 0.5 μg/mL.

[g] Antimicrobial susceptibility must be evaluated.

[h] Rifampin increases warfarin and dicumarol requirements for anticoagulation.

SOURCE: AW Karchmer: HPIM-15, p. 813.

Table 80-4

Indications for Cardiac Surgical Intervention in Patients with Endocarditis

Surgery required for optimal outcome
  Moderate to severe congestive heart failure due to valve dysfunction
  Partially dehisced unstable prosthetic valve
  Persistent bacteremia despite optimal antimicrobial therapy
  Lack of effective microbicidal therapy (e.g., fungal or *Brucella* endocarditis)
  S. aureus prosthetic valve endocarditis with an intracardiac complication
  Relapse of prosthetic valve endocarditis after optimal antimicrobial therapy
  Persistent unexplained fever ($\geq$10 days) in culture-negative prosthetic valve
    endocarditis
Surgery to be strongly considered for improved outcome[a]
  Perivalvular extension of infection
  Poorly responsive *S. aureus* endocarditis involving the aortic or mitral valve
  Large (>10-mm diameter) hypermobile vegetations with increased risk of
    embolism
  Persistent unexplained fever ($\geq$10 days) in culture-negative native valve en-
    docarditis
  Poorly responsive or relapsed endocarditis due to highly antibiotic-resistant
    enterococci or gram-negative bacilli

[a] Surgery must be carefully considered; findings are often combined with other indications to
prompt surgery.
SOURCE: AW Karchmer: HPIM-15, p. 815.

Table 80-5

Procedures for which Endocarditis Prophylaxis Is Advised in Patients at High or Moderate Risk for Endocarditis[a]

Dental procedures
  Extractions
  Periodontal procedures, cleaning causing gingival bleeding
  Implant placement, reimplantation of avulsed teeth
  Endodontic instrumentation (root canal) or surgery beyond the apex
  Subgingival placement of antibiotic fibers or strips
  Placement of orthodontic bands but not brackets
  Intraligamentary injections (anesthetic)
Respiratory procedures
  Operations involving the mucosa
  Bronchoscopy with rigid bronchoscope
Gastrointestinal procedures[b]
  Esophageal: Sclerotherapy of varices, stricture dilation
  Biliary tract: Endoscopic retrograde cholangiography with biliary obstruc-
    tion, biliary tract surgery
  Intestinal tract: Surgery involving the mucosa
Genitourinary procedures
  Urethral dilation, prostate or urethral surgery
  Cystoscopy

[a] Prophylaxis is optional for high-risk pts undergoing bronchoscopy or gastrointestinal endoscopy
with/without biopsy, vaginal delivery, vaginal hysterectomy, or transesophageal echocardiography.
[b] Prophylaxis is recommended for high-risk pts and optional for moderate-risk group (see Table 80-7).
SOURCE: Adapted (by AW Karchmer: HPIM-15, p. 816) from AS Dajani et al: Prevention of
bacterial endocarditis: Recommendations by the American Heart Association, from the Committee on Rheumatic Fever, Endocarditis, and Kawasaki Disease, Council on Cardiovascular
Diseases in the Young. JAMA 277:1794, 1997

Table 80-6

Cardiac Lesions for which Endocarditis Prophylaxis Is Advised

High Risk	Moderate Risk
Prosthetic heart valves	Congenital cardiac malformations (other
Prior bacterial endocarditis	than high-/low-risk lesions), ventricular
Complex cyanotic congenital heart	septal defect, bicuspid aortic valve
disease; other complex congenital	Acquired aortic and mitral valve dysfunc-
lesions after correction	tion
Patent ductus arteriosus	Hypertrophic cardiomyopathy (asymmetric
Coarctation of the aorta	septal hypertrophy)
Surgically constructed systemic-	Mitral valve prolapse with valvular regur-
pulmonary shunts	gitation and/or thickened leaflets

SOURCE: AW Karchmer: HPIM-15, p. 816.

Table 80-7

Antibiotic Regimens for Prophylaxis of Endocarditis in Adults at Moderate or High Risk[a]

I. Oral cavity, respiratory tract, or esophageal procedures[b]
  A. Standard regimen
    1. Amoxicillin 2.0 g PO 1 h before procedure
  B. Inability to take oral medication
    1. Ampicillin 2.0 g IV or IM within 30 min of procedure
  C. Penicillin allergy
    1. Clarithromycin 500 mg PO 1 h before procedure
    2. Cephalexin[c] or cefadroxil[c] 2.0 g PO 1 h before procedure
    3. Clindamycin 600 mg PO 1 h before procedure or IV 30 min before procedure
  D. Inability to take oral medication
    1. Cefazolin[c] 1.0 g IV or IM 30 min before procedure
II. Genitourinary and gastrointestinal tract[d] procedures
  A. High-risk pts
    1. Ampicillin 2.0 g IV or IM *plus* gentamicin 1.5 mg/kg (not to exceed 120 mg) IV or IM within 30 min of procedure; repeat ampicillin 1.0 g IV or IM or amoxicillin 1.0 g PO 6 h later
  B. High-risk, penicillin-allergic pts
    1. Vancomycin 1.0 g IV over 1-2 h *plus* gentamicin 1.5 mg/kg (not to exceed 120 mg) IV or IM within 30 min before procedure; no second dose recommended
  C. Moderate-risk pts
    1. Amoxicillin 2.0 g PO 1 h before procedure or ampicillin 2.0 g IV or IM within 30 min before procedure
  D. Moderate-risk, penicillin-allergic pts
    1. Vancomycin 1.0 g IV infused over 1-2 h and completed within 30 min of procedure

[a] Dosing for children: for amoxicillin, ampicillin, cephalexin, or cefadroxil, use 50 mg/kg PO; cefazolin, 25 mg/kg IV; clindamycin, 20 mg/kg PO, 25 mg/kg IV; clarithromycin, 15 mg/kg PO; gentamicin, 1.5 mg/kg IV or IM; and vancomycin, 20 mg/kg IV.
[b] For pts at high risk, administer a half-dose 6 h after the initial dose.
[c] Do not use cephalosporins in pts with immediate hypersensitivity (urticaria, angioedema, anaphylaxis) to penicillin.
[d] Excludes esophageal procedures.
SOURCE: Adapted (by AW Karchmer: HPIM-15, p. 816) from AS Dajani et al: Prevention of bacterial endocarditis: Recommendations by the American Heart Association, from the Committee on Rheumatic Fever, Endocarditis, and Kawasaki Disease, Council on Cardiovascular Diseases in the Young. JAMA 277:1794, 1997

stroke and for 4 weeks after a hemorrhagic embolic stroke. Splenic abscesses develop 3–5% of the time and should be drained or eliminated by splenectomy. Mycotic aneurysms develop in 2–15% of pts; half of these cases involve the cerebral arteries. Although some will resolve, these aneurysms should be watched closely for signs of enlargement or leakage indicating the need for excision.

Prophylaxis

The benefits of endocarditis prophylaxis are not established and in fact may be modest: only 50% of pts with native valve endocarditis know they have a valve lesion predisposing to endocarditis, most cases do not follow an identified procedure during which inoculation occurs, and 35% of cases are caused by organisms not targeted by prophylaxis. Nevertheless, the American Heart Association has identified procedures that may precipitate high-risk bacteremia (Table 80-5), cardiac lesions for which prophylaxis is advised (Table 80-6), and recommended regimens for prophylaxis (Table 80-7).

For a more detailed discussion, see Karchmer AW: Infective Endocarditis, Chap. 126, p. 809, in HPIM-15.

81

INTRAABDOMINAL INFECTIONS

PERITONITIS

PATHOGENESIS Intraperitoneal infections generally arise when a normal anatomic barrier is disrupted and the usually sterile peritoneal space becomes seeded with microorganisms. Peritonitis is either *primary* (without an apparent inciting event) or *secondary*. In adults, primary or spontaneous bacterial peritonitis (SBP) is most common among pts with cirrhosis of the liver due to alcoholism. Pts with preexisting ascites are predisposed to infection at this site. The pathogenic mechanism is presumed to be seeding of ascites when the diseased liver with altered portal circulation is unable to perform its usual filtration function. A single bacterial species usually causes SBP, and accompanying bacteremia is common. Secondary peritonitis develops when bacteria contaminate the peritoneum as a result of spillage from a ruptured viscus. Mixed aerobic and anaerobic bacteria are the rule in secondary peritonitis.

CLINICAL MANIFESTATIONS *SBP* Fever, the most common presenting symptom, is documented in 80% of cases of SBP. Abdominal pain, acute onset of symptoms, and peritoneal signs on physical examination are diagnostically helpful, but absence of these findings does not exclude this subtle diagnosis. Ascites virtually always predates infection.

Secondary Peritonitis Localized symptoms, if present, depend on the inciting event. In cases of perforated gastric ulcer, epigastric pain is evident. In appendicitis, initial symptoms may be vague and may include nausea or periumbilical discomfort gradually localizing to the RLQ. Symptoms of secondary peritonitis include abdominal pain that increases with motion, coughing, or sneezing. Pts often lie with knees drawn up to avoid stretching peritoneal nerve fibers. Findings on abdominal exam include voluntary and involuntary guarding, tenderness, and, at a later stage, rebound tenderness.

DIAGNOSIS To diagnose SBP, a primary intraabdominal source of infection must be excluded; abdominal CT with contrast may be helpful. A tap of the ascites is essential in every febrile cirrhotic pt to diagnose SBP. Peritoneal fluid should be placed in a blood culture bottle to increase yield. Blood should be cultured. For secondary peritonitis, diagnosis should focus on identifying the inciting event; a tap of peritoneal fluid is rarely needed.

℞ TREATMENT

Therapy for SBP should be directed at the organism recovered. Empirical therapy should include coverage for gram-negative aerobic bacilli and gram-positive cocci. Third-generation cephalosporins, carbapenems, or broad-spectrum penicillin/β-lactamase inhibitor combinations are reasonable initial options. After the infecting organism is identified, therapy should be narrowed to target that specific pathogen. If mixed flora (particularly anaerobes) are recovered in suspected SBP, the pt should be evaluated for secondary peritonitis. Treatment for secondary peritonitis includes antibiotics directed at aerobic gram-negative bacilli and at anaerobes as well as surgical intervention for the inciting process.

INTRAPERITONEAL ABSCESSES

PATHOGENESIS Intraperitoneal abscesses represent both a disease process and a host response. Anaerobic organisms, particularly *Bacteroides fragilis*, are critical in the development of these abscesses. The most important virulence factor of this organism is the capsular polysaccharide, which is responsible for the development of abscesses. Several host factors, including peritoneal macrophages, PMNs, and T cells, also appear to interact and stimulate abscess formation.

CLINICAL MANIFESTATIONS Intraabdominal abscesses can be either intraperitoneal or retroperitoneal and are not visceral in 74% of cases. Infections of the female genital tract and pancreatitis are common causative events. Fever is the most common presenting symptom. As in secondary peritonitis, localizing symptoms depend on the inciting process. In psoas abscess, back or abdominal pain is common and associated osteomyelitis is found frequently.

VISCERAL ABSCESSES *Liver Abscesses* The liver is the intraabdominal organ in which abscesses develop most often. Fever is the most common presenting symptom. Only 50% of pts have signs or symptoms that direct attention to the RUQ, including hepatomegaly, tenderness, or jaundice.

Splenic Abscesses These frequently are diagnosed only at autopsy. Generally, abscesses in the spleen arise from hematogenous spread. Bacterial endocarditis is the most common associated infection. Abdominal pain is reported in 50% of cases but is localized to the LUQ in only half of these instances. Fever is common; splenomegaly is documented in about 50% of cases.

Perinephric and Renal Abscesses These are not common and generally arise from an initial UTI, often in association with nephrolithiasis. The clinical presentation is nonspecific. Pts may have flank and abdominal pain; 50% have fever. Pain may be referred to the groin or leg.

DIAGNOSIS Scanning procedures generally are diagnostic; CT is most useful. Ultrasonography is particularly helpful for the RUQ, kidneys, and pelvis. Gallium- and indium-labeled WBCs localize in abscesses and may be useful in finding a collection. If one study is negative, a second study is sometimes revealing.

 TREATMENT

Treatment of intraabdominal infections involves establishment of an initial focus of infection, administration of antibiotics targeted at likely organisms, and performance of a drainage procedure if one or more definitive abscesses are found. Antibiotic treatment is adjunctive to drainage (percutaneous or surgical) and is usually directed at organisms involved in the inciting infection, which generally include aerobic gram-negative bacilli and anaerobes. Against gram-negative aerobic and facultative bacteria, aminoglycosides, third-generation cephalosporins, and the quinolones are the most widely tested agents, but they must be used in combination with another antibiotic active against anaerobes (e.g., metronidazole) when the latter organisms are likely to be involved in the process.

For a more detailed discussion, see Zaleznik DF, Kasper DL: Intraabdominal Infections and Abscesses, Chap. 130, p. 829, in HPIM-15; and Anaerobic Infections, Chap. 95, p. 441, in the Clinical Manual.

82

INFECTIOUS DIARRHEAS

Etiology and Pathogenesis

Infectious diarrhea may be caused by a wide variety of microorganisms and may be mediated by toxins and/or by direct invasion of the GI mucosa. It is useful to categorize diarrheal diseases according to whether the responsible pathogens cause inflammatory or noninflammatory intestinal changes. Infections with pathogens that induce acute inflammation (e.g., *Shigella* species, *Campylobacter jejuni*, and *Entamoeba histolytica*) tend to involve the lower GI tract; cause small, purulent, or bloody stools; and are accompanied by fever. Infections due to noninflammatory pathogens (e.g., enterotoxigenic *Escherichia coli, Giardia lamblia*) tend to involve the upper GI tract and cause more voluminous but nonbloody stools that do not contain PMNs.

Approach to the Patient

The history should include inquiries about fever, abdominal pain, nausea/vomiting, frequency and character of stools (whether watery or bloody; volume), food recently ingested (seafood; a possible common source, such as a picnic or restaurant), travel (exact location, duration, and nature of trip), sexual exposures, and general medical history (especially other illnesses and therapy with immunosuppressive drugs, antibiotics, or gastric-acid inhibitors). A complete physical exam should be performed, with particular attention to abdominal findings. Stool specimens should be examined grossly for consistency and the presence of blood and microscopically for the presence of PMNs. Stool should be cultured for *Salmonella, Shigella*, and *Campylobacter* if the diarrhea is inflammatory. The other diagnostic tests selected will depend on the clinical circumstances and may include an assay for *Clostridium difficile* cytotoxin (in the setting of recent use of antibiotics), an examination for ova and parasites (travel), and cultures for vibrios (seafood ingestion) and for *Yersinia* and enterohemorrhagic *E. coli.*

NONINFLAMMATORY DIARRHEA

ENTEROTOXIGENIC *E. COLI* ETEC causes most cases of traveler's diarrhea. The illness presents after 24–48 h of incubation as watery diarrhea, which is usually mild and is only occasionally accompanied by fever or vomiting. This diarrhea is usually self-limited (3–4 d in duration) and may be treated with oral fluid replacement (commercial or homemade solution consisting of 3.5 g of sodium chloride, 2.5 g of sodium bicarbonate, 1.5 g of potassium chloride, and 20 g of glucose per liter of water) or antimotility agents (e.g., loperamide, 4 mg at onset and 2 mg after each loose stool; up to 16 mg/d). Antibiotic therapy reduces the duration of illness to 24–36 h. Bismuth subsalicylate, which has both antimicrobial and anti-inflammatory properties, has only a minimal effect on the normal GI flora. It may be taken as 2 tablets (525 mg) every 30–60 min for up to 8 doses. TMP-SMZ (160/800 mg bid) or a quinolone such as levofloxacin (500 mg/d, for adults only) may also be used, each for a 3-d course.

CLOSTRIDIUM PERFRINGENS *C. perfringens* produces a preformed toxin in food that causes illness 8–14 h after ingestion of contaminated meat, poultry, or legumes. The illness is manifest by diarrhea and crampy abdominal pain and rarely lasts >24 h. It is treated by fluid replacement, if necessary, and does not require antibiotics.

STAPHYLOCOCCUS AUREUS Ingestion of *S. aureus* preformed enterotoxin causes a rapid onset (within 1–6 h) of vomiting and diarrhea. Staphylococcal food poisoning is associated epidemiologically with institutional outbreaks and high attack rates. The illness is of short duration (<12 h) and requires, at most, fluid replacement for treatment.

BACILLUS CEREUS *B. cereus* produces two clinical syndromes. An emetic form, caused by a staphylococcal type of enterotoxin, resembles staphylococcal food poisoning and is epidemiologically associated with contaminated fried rice. A diarrheal form, caused by an *E. coli* LT–like enterotoxin, presents commonly in conjunction with abdominal cramps. The diarrheal form has a longer incubation period (8–16 h) than the emetic form.

VIBRIO CHOLERAE Caused by toxin-producing *V. cholerae*, cholera occurs principally in the Ganges delta on the Indian subcontinent, in Southeast Asia, and in Africa. An ongoing epidemic in South and Central America began in 1991. The disease occurs sporadically in coastal Texas and Louisiana. Ingestion of water contaminated by human feces is the most common means of acquisition, although ingestion of contaminated food may play a role. Clinical signs developing after an incubation period of 12–48 h include profuse gray watery diarrhea, vomiting, and dehydration. Cholera is diagnosed by culture of stool on special medium. *Treatment* consists primarily of fluid replacement (IV or oral). Antibiotics are not necessary for cure, but tetracycline administration

(2 g as a single oral dose in adults) decreases the duration and volume of fluid loss and hastens the clearance of the organism. Ciprofloxacin (30 mg/kg as a single oral dose, not to exceed 1 g) may be used for strains resistant to tetracycline. Erythromycin (40 mg/kg daily, given tid for 3 d) is the preferred treatment for children.

ROTAVIRUS   The most important cause of severe dehydrating diarrhea in children <3 years of age worldwide, rotavirus infection presents as vomiting of <24 h duration, diarrhea, and low-grade fever. Rotaviruses may also be associated with mild diarrhea in adults (household contacts), elderly pts, and immunocompromised persons. Rotavirus infection occurs more commonly in colder months and is treated by fluid replacement.

NORWALK-LIKE VIRUSES   These food- and waterborne agents cause one-third of epidemics of nonbacterial diarrhea in developed countries. Disease occurs year-round, mainly affecting older children and adults. The illness is usually mild and does not require treatment.

G. LAMBLIA* AND *CRYPTOSPORIDIUM   See Chap. 110.

INFLAMMATORY DIARRHEA

CAMPYLOBACTER   *C. jejuni* is a leading cause of food-borne diarrhea in the U.S. and is also associated with exposure to infected (often asymptomatic) animals and with travel to developing countries. In the U.S., ingestion of contaminated poultry that has not been sufficiently cooked accounts for 50–70% of cases. After an incubation period of 2–4 d, the illness presents as fever, crampy abdominal pain, and diarrhea. It is generally self-limited but may persist for >1 week in up to 20% of pts. Similar disease may be caused by related species of *Campylobacter* (e.g., *C. coli, C. upsaliensis*). Diagnosis requires culture of the pathogen from stool on special medium at 42°C. *Treatment* consists of fluid and electrolyte repletion. In severe cases, erythromycin (250 mg PO qid for 5–7 d) may be used. *C. fetus* is an occasional agent of diarrhea that can cause septicemia in immunocompromised hosts.

SHIGELLA   Shigellosis is caused most often by *S. sonnei* in the U.S. and by *S. flexneri* and *S. dysenteriae* in the developing world. Person-to-person transmission is common, and 20–40% of household contacts develop disease. The prevalence is greatest among children and homosexual men. Although referred to as bacillary dysentery, shigellosis has clinical manifestations ranging from mild watery diarrhea to severe dysentery, often accompanied by fever, with onset after an incubation period of 1–7 d. Without treatment, fever persists for 3–4 d and diarrhea for 1–2 weeks. Hemolytic-uremic syndrome is a rare but serious complication of shigellosis. The diagnosis of shigellosis is based on the finding of fecal leukocytes and the culture of the organism from stool. *Treatment* includes fluid replacement and antibiotic administration. Resistance to ampicillin is now common among shigellae, and resistance to TMP-SMZ is increasing in frequency. Susceptible isolates may still be treated with one of these agents (ampicillin, 500 mg qid; TMP-SMZ, 160/800 mg bid for 5 d) or with ciprofloxacin (500 mg bid; for adults only for 3 d) or IV ceftriaxone (50 mg/kg qd for 5 d). Antimotility agents should be avoided in the dysenteric phase of the disease.

ENTEROHEMORRHAGIC *E. COLI*   Certain *E. coli* organisms, particularly serotype O157:H7, produce a Shiga-like toxin and cause a syndrome of bloody diarrhea. Outbreaks are frequently food-borne. Hemolytic-uremic syndrome is a rare but serious complication of infection with EHEC. The diagnosis may be made by identification of the organism in stool cultured on special medium.

CLOSTRIDIUM DIFFICILE Infection with the cytotoxin-producing anaerobe *C. difficile* is commonly associated with antibiotic use and classically causes pseudomembranous colitis. Clinical manifestations include fever, elevated WBC count, and diarrhea. The infection is diagnosed by the detection of cytotoxin in stool specimens. *Treatment* should include the discontinuation of any offending antibiotics and the administration of metronidazole (500 mg PO tid for 10–14 d). Vancomycin (125 mg PO qid) may be substituted in refractory cases but is generally avoided because of concerns about the development of vancomycin-resistant enterococci.

VIBRIO PARAHAEMOLYTICUS Present in coastal waters throughout the world, *V. parahaemolyticus* causes disease most frequently in association with the consumption of raw or under-cooked seafood. After an incubation period of 4 h to 4 d, it most commonly produces acute watery diarrhea accompanied by abdominal cramps, nausea, and vomiting and sometimes by fever and chills. The diagnosis is made by culture of the organism on special medium and must be suspected on the basis of exposure to seafood or the sea. *Treatment* of severe cases consists of fluid repletion and antibiotic administration (tetracycline, 500 mg qid).

E. HISTOLYTICA See Chap. 110.

SALMONELLA Salmonellae are acquired by consumption of contaminated food or drink, most commonly from eggs or poultry, and may cause clinical illness ranging from gastroenteritis to enteric fever. *S. typhimurium* and *S. enteritidis* cause most cases of human disease in the U.S. Pts at increased risk for salmonellosis include those with decreased stomach acidity (antacid use, achlorhydric disease) and those with decreased intestinal integrity (inflammatory bowel disease, history of GI surgery, antibiotic use). Gastroenteritis is the most common manifestation. After an incubation period of 6–48 h, diarrhea develops and may be accompanied by abdominal cramps, nausea, vomiting, and fever. Stools may show fecal leukocytes and are sometimes frankly dysenteric. Illness is usually mild and self-limited but may become severe in elderly pts or neonates as well as in immunocompromised pts (e.g., those with HIV infection or sickle cell disease). The diagnosis is based on culture of stool or blood.

Bacteremia/Enteric Fevers Up to 5% of pts with nontyphoidal *Salmonella* gastroenteritis have positive blood cultures, and 5–10% of these bacteremic persons develop localized infections. This illness is similar to typhoid fever (see below) but may be more acute and is not associated with classic manifestations of typhoid such as rose spots, leukopenia, and relative bradycardia. This syndrome, frequently associated with *S. choleraesuis* or *S. dublin*, is serious and carries a high mortality. Pts with HIV infection have a high risk of *Salmonella* (particularly *S. typhimurium*) bacteremia, which may be refractory to treatment.

Localization of Systemic Infection Bloodborne salmonellae, usually present following GI infection, can invade any tissue or organ. Salmonellae have a propensity for vascular sites. Arterial infection may occur in preexisting arteriosclerotic aortic aneurysms, especially in men over age 50. Osteomyelitis (associated with sickle cell disease), hepatobiliary infection, splenic abscess, cholecystitis, and UTI are all examples of localized *Salmonella* infection.

Typhoid Fever This form of enteric fever, caused by the exclusively human pathogen *S. typhi* (and less commonly by *S. paratyphi*), is linked epidemiologically to the ingestion of contaminated food, water, or milk and occurs most frequently in travelers. The risk of infection is increased by antibiotic use, malnutrition, and HIV infection. After an average incubation period of 3–21 d, clinical manifestations include prolonged fever and the nonspecific symptoms of chills, headache, malaise, anorexia, and (rarely) an altered sensorium. Findings on physical exam include rose spots (a salmon-colored maculopapular rash, primarily on the trunk and chest), relative bradycardia, and hepatosplenomegaly. Complications include intestinal perforation, GI bleeding, and localized infection (meningitis, hepatitis, hepatic and splenic abscesses, cholecystitis, nephritis, myocarditis, endocarditis, pneumonia, parotitis, orchitis). Chronic carriage develops in 1–5% and relapse in ~10% of treated immunocompetent pts. Diagnosis depends on isolation of the organism from blood (with a 90% positivity rate in the first week and a decline thereafter), stool (greater positivity by the third week in untreated pts), urine, bone marrow, and gastric or intestinal secretions. Serologic (Widal) testing is less reliable and not clinically useful.

 TREATMENT

Uncomplicated *Salmonella* gastroenteritis does not require antibiotic treatment, and such treatment may in fact increase rates of relapse and prolong carriage. However, treatment should be considered in neonates, pts >50 years old, transplant recipients, pts with prosthetic joints or vascular grafts, and persons with underlying immunosuppression (HIV disease, lymphoma, malignancy, sickle cell disease). The treatment of these pts includes a third-generation cephalosporin (e.g., ceftriaxone, 1–2 g/d) and/or ciprofloxacin (500 mg bid) for 2–3 d or until defervescence. For focal infections or bacteremia, the pt should be treated for 7–14 d or — if immunocompromised— even longer. Many strains of *Salmonella* are resistant to ampicillin, chloramphenicol, and TMP-SMZ. Typhoid fever may be treated with ceftriaxone (1–2 g/d IV) or ciprofloxacin (500 mg PO bid) for 10–14 d. Other agents effective against sensitive typhoid include amoxicillin (1–1.5 g PO qid) and TMP-SMZ (160/800 mg PO qid), each for 2 weeks. Glucocorticoids (dexamethasone, loading dose of 3 mg/kg followed by 1 mg/kg q6h for 24–48 h) may have an adjunctive role in severe typhoid.

For a more detailed discussion, see Butterton JR, Calderwood SB: Acute Infectious Diarrheal Diseases and Bacterial Food Poisoning, Chap. 131, p. 834; Kasper DL, Zaleznik DF: Gas Gangrene, Antibiotic-Associated Colitis, and Other Clostridial Infections, Chap. 145, p. 922; Lesser CF, Miller SI: Salmonellosis, Chap. 156, p. 970; Keusch GT: Shigellosis, Chap. 157, p. 975; Blaser MJ: Infections Due to *Campylobacter* and Related Species, Chap. 158, p. 978; Keusch GT, Deresiewicz RL, Waldor MK: Cholera and Other Vibrioses, Chap. 159, p. 980; and Greenberg HB: Viral Gastroenteritis, Chap. 192, p. 1135, in HPIM-15.

83

SEXUALLY TRANSMITTED DISEASES AND REPRODUCTIVE TRACT INFECTIONS

See Table 83-1 for a list of sexually transmitted pathogens and Table 83-2 for pathogens associated with clinical syndromes.

COMMON STD SYNDROMES
Most pts with STD syndromes are initially managed on the basis of presenting Sx.

Table 83-1

Sexually Transmitted and Sexually Transmissible Microorganisms

Bacteria	Viruses	Other[a]
TRANSMITTED IN ADULTS PREDOMINANTLY BY SEXUAL INTERCOURSE		
Neisseria gonorrhoeae	HIV (types 1 and 2)	*Trichomonas vaginalis*
Chlamydia trachomatis	Human T cell lympho-	*Phthirus pubis*
Treponema pallidum	tropic virus type I	
Haemophilus ducreyi	Herpes simplex virus	
Calymmatobacterium	type 2	
granulomatis	Human papillomavirus	
Ureaplasma urealyti-	(multiple genotypes)	
cum	Hepatitis B virus[b]	
	Molluscum conta-	
	giosum virus	
SEXUAL TRANSMISSION REPEATEDLY DESCRIBED BUT NOT WELL DEFINED OR NOT THE PREDOMINANT MODE		
Mycoplasma hominis	Cytomegalovirus	*Candida albicans*
Mycoplasma genital-	Human T cell lympho-	*Sarcoptes scabiei*
ium	tropic virus type II	
Gardnerella vaginalis	(?) Hepatitis C, D vi-	
and other vaginal	ruses	
bacteria	Herpes simplex virus	
Group B *Streptococcus*	type 1	
Mobiluncus spp.	(?) Epstein-Barr virus	
Helicobacter cinaedi	Kaposi's sarcoma–as-	
Helicobacter fennelliae	sociated herpesvirus[c]	
	Transfusion-transmit-	
	ted virus	
TRANSMITTED BY SEXUAL CONTACT INVOLVING ORAL-FECAL EXPOSURE; OF DECLINING IMPORTANCE IN HOMOSEXUAL MEN		
Shigella spp.	Hepatitis A virus	*Giardia lamblia*
Campylobacter spp.		*Entamoeba histolytica*

[a] Includes protozoa, ectoparasites, and fungi.
[b] Among U.S. patients for whom a risk factor can be ascertained, most hepatitis B virus infections are transmitted sexually or by injection drug use.
[c] Human herpesvirus type 8.
SOURCE: Holmes KK: HPIM-15, p.840.

Table 83-2

Major STD Syndromes and Sexually Transmitted (ST) Microbial Etiologies

Syndrome	ST Microbial Etiologies
AIDS	HIV types 1 and 2
Urethritis: males	*Neisseria gonorrhoeae, Chlamydia trachomatis, Ureaplasma urealyticum, Trichomonas vaginalis,* HSV
Epididymitis	*C. trachomatis, N. gonorrhoeae*
Lower genital tract infections: females	
Cystitis/urethritis	*C. trachomatis, N. gonorrhoeae,* HSV
Mucopurulent cervicitis	*C. trachomatis, N. gonorrhoeae*
Vulvitis	*Candida albicans,* HSV
Vulvovaginitis	*C. albicans, T. vaginalis*
Bacterial vaginosis (BV)	BV-associated bacteria[a]
Acute pelvic inflammatory disease	*N. gonorrhoeae, C. trachomatis,* BV-associated bacteria, group B streptococci
Infertility	*N. gonorrhoeae, C. trachomatis,* BV-associated bacteria
Ulcerative lesions of the genitalia	HSV-1, HSV-2, *Treponema pallidum, Haemophilus ducreyi, C. trachomatis* (LGV strains), *Calymmatobacterium granulomatis*
Complications of pregnancy/ puerperium	Several agents implicated
Intestinal infections	
Proctitis	*C. trachomatis, N. gonorrhoeae,* HSV, *T. pallidum*
Proctocolitis or enterocolitis	*Campylobacter* spp., *Shigella* spp., *Entamoeba histolytica,* other enteric pathogens
Enteritis	*Giardia lamblia*
Acute arthritis with urogenital infection or viremia	*N. gonorrhoeae* (e.g., DGI), *C. trachomatis* (e.g., Reiter's syndrome), HBV
Genital and anal warts	HPV (30 genital types)
Mononucleosis syndrome	CMV, HIV, EBV
Hepatitis	Hepatitis viruses, *T. pallidum,* CMV, EBV
Neoplasias	
Squamous cell dysplasias and cancers of the cervix, anus, vulva, vagina, or penis	HPV (especially types 16, 18, 31, 45)
Kaposi's sarcoma, body-cavity lymphomas	HHV-8
T cell leukemia	HTLV-I
Hepatocellular carcinoma	HBV
Tropical spastic paraparesis	HTLV-I
Scabies	*Sarcoptes scabiei*
Pubic lice	*Phthirus pubis*

[a] *Gardnerella vaginalis,* various anaerobic bacteria, and mycoplasmas.
NOTE: HSV, herpes simplex virus; LGV, lymphogranuloma venereum; DGI, disseminated gonococcal infection; HPV, human papillomavirus; CMV, cytomegalovirus; EBV, Epstein-Barr virus; HBV, hepatitis B virus; HTLV, human T cell lymphotropic virus; HHV-8, human herpesvirus type 8.
SOURCE: KK Holmes: HPIM-15, p. 841.

Urethritis in Men

CLINICAL PRESENTATION   Pts usually present with a purulent or mucopurulent urethral discharge that can be expressed by milking of the urethra.

ETIOLOGY   *Neisseria gonorrhoeae, Chlamydia trachomatis, Trichomonas vaginalis,* herpes simplex virus (HSV), *Mycoplasma genitalium,* and *Ureaplasma urealyticum* are among the pathogens that can cause urethritis in men.

DIAGNOSIS   If milking of the urethra yields no discharge, the centrifuged sediment of the first 20–30 mL of voided urine should be examined with Gram's stain. Urethritis is usually present if microscopy shows ≥5 PMNs/1000× field. Absence of gram-negative diplococci (presumably *N. gonorrhoeae*) warrants a preliminary diagnosis of nongonococcal urethritis (NGU). Culture or nucleic acid detection should be performed for *N. gonorrhoeae* and *C. trachomatis* (see "Gonococcal Infections" and "Chlamydial Infections," below).

 TREATMENT

See organism-specific sections below.

Epididymitis

CLINICAL PRESENTATION   Pts usually present with unilateral testicular pain of acute onset, intrascrotal swelling, tenderness, and fever.

ETIOLOGY   In sexually active men <35 years old, acute epididymitis is caused most frequently by *C. trachomatis* and less frequently by *N. gonorrhoeae* and is usually associated with overt or subclinical urethritis. Epididymitis in men who have practiced insertive rectal intercourse is often caused by Enterobacteriaceae.

DIAGNOSIS   Testicular torsion and tumor must be excluded. Gram's stain and culture or nucleic acid detection should be performed as for urethritis.

 TREATMENT

See organism-specific sections below.

Urethral Syndrome in Women

CLINICAL PRESENTATION   Pts present with symptomatic urethritis, primarily with dysuria and pyuria.

ETIOLOGY   *N. gonorrhoeae, C. trachomatis,* and HSV cause this syndrome.

DIAGNOSIS   *Escherichia coli* or other common uropathogens characteristically are present at counts of ≤10^2/mL in urine culture. Young age, more than one sexual partner, a new sexual partner, or coexisting mucopurulent cervicitis (MPC) suggests an STD etiology.

 TREATMENT

See organism-specific sections below.

Vaginitis

CLINICAL PRESENTATION   Unsolicited reporting of abnormal vaginal discharge suggests bacterial vaginosis or trichomoniasis.

ETIOLOGY   *T. vaginalis, Gardnerella vaginalis, Mycoplasma hominis*, and anaerobic bacteria can be associated with vaginitis.

DIAGNOSIS AND TREATMENT   See Table 83-3.

Mucopurulent Cervicitis

CLINICAL PRESENTATION   MPC is symptomatically silent, with yellow mucopurulent discharge from the cervical os.

ETIOLOGY   *N. gonorrhoeae* or *C. trachomatis* may be involved, but 50% of cases are idiopathic.

DIAGNOSIS   The diagnosis rests on the detection of yellow mucopurulent discharge from the cervical os or of ≥20 PMNs/1000× field on a Gram's stain of cervical mucus. Culture or nucleic acid detection should be performed as for urethritis.

 TREATMENT

See organism-specific sections below.

Ulcerative Genital Lesions

See "Ulcerative Genital Lesions," below.

Proctitis, Proctocolitis, Enterocolitis, and Enteritis

CLINICAL PRESENTATION   Proctitis or proctocolitis presents as pain and mucopurulent bloody discharge. Proctitis commonly produces tenesmus and constipation, whereas proctocolitis and enterocolitis more often cause true diarrhea.

ETIOLOGY   Sexually acquired proctitis is usually due to the typical STD pathogens. Proctocolitis, enterocolitis, and enteritis can result from ingestion of typical intestinal pathogens through oral-anal exposure during sexual contact.

DIAGNOSIS   Culture or nucleic acid detection should be used to identify the pathogen.

 TREATMENT

See sections on individual pathogens, below and elsewhere.

GONOCOCCAL INFECTIONS

ETIOLOGY   Gonorrhea, an infection of columnar and transitional epithelium, is caused by *N. gonorrhoeae*, a gram-negative diplococcus.

EPIDEMIOLOGY   The incidence of gonorrhea has decreased significantly in the U.S., although there are still ~315,000 newly reported cases each year. Gonorrhea predominantly affects young, nonwhite, unmarried, less educated members of urban populations. It is transmitted most efficiently from males to females, with a 40–60% rate of transmission to a woman after a single episode of unprotected vaginal intercourse with an infected man.

CLINICAL MANIFESTATIONS   *Males*   Urethritis develops 2–7 d after exposure, with symptoms of purulent urethral discharge (90–95%), dysuria, and meatal erythema; some gonococcal strains may cause less overt symptoms. Balanitis may develop in uncircumcised men. In the antibiotic era, complications due to *N. gonorrhoeae* (e.g., epididymitis, prostatitis, inguinal lymphadenitis) are rare.

Table 83-3

Diagnostic Features and Management of Vaginal Infection

Feature	Normal Vaginal Examination	Vulvovaginal Candidiasis
Etiology	Uninfected; lactobacilli predominant	*Candida albicans*
Typical symptoms	None	Vulvar itching and/or irritation
Discharge		
Amount	Variable; usually scant	Scant
Color[a]	Clear or white	White
Consistency	Nonhomogeneous, floccular	Clumped; adherent plaques
Inflammation of vulvar or vaginal epithelium	None	Erythema of vaginal epithelium, introitus; vulvar dermatitis common
pH of vaginal fluid[b]	Usually ≤4.5	Usually ≤4.5
Amine ("fishy") odor with 10% KOH	None	None
Microscopy[c]	Normal epithelial cells; lactobacilli predominant	Leukocytes, epithelial cells; mycelia or pseudomycelia in up to 80% of *C. albicans* culture-positive persons with typical symptoms
Usual treatment	None	Azole cream, tablet, or suppository—e.g., miconazole 100-mg vaginal suppository or clotrimazole 100-mg vaginal tablet, once daily for 7 days. Fluconazole, 150 mg orally (single dose)
Usual management of sexual partner	None	None; topical treatment if candidal dermatitis of penis is detected

[a] Color of discharge is best determined by examination against the white background of a swab.
[b] pH determination is not useful if blood is present.
[c] To detect fungal elements, vaginal fluid is digested with 10% KOH prior to microscopic examination; to examine for other features, fluid is mixed (1:1) with physiologic saline. Gram's stain is also excellent for detecting yeasts and pseudomycelia and for distinguishing normal

Females Gonococcal infection in the female involves (in descending order of frequency) the endocervix, urethra, anal canal, and pharynx. The incubation period is less well defined in women than in men; if symptoms develop, they usually do so within 10 d. Increased vaginal discharge and dysuria are the most common symptoms. Acute uncomplicated gonococcal cervicitis produces mucopurulent (yellow) endocervical discharge, causes easily induced cervical bleeding, and may coexist with *C. trachomatis* or the organisms causing vaginitis. Gonococcal urethritis and proctitis are common, but the urethra and the rectum are rarely the sole infected sites. Unilateral acute Bartholin's gland inflammation frequently is due to gonorrhea. The pt's report of dyspareunia, lower abdominal pain, or back pain makes it imperative to consider a diagnosis of

Trichomonal Vaginitis	Bacterial Vaginosis
Trichomonas vaginalis	Associated with *Gardnerella vaginalis*, various anaerobic bacteria, and mycoplasmas
Profuse purulent discharge; vulvar itching	Malodorous, slightly increased discharge
Profuse	Moderate
Yellow	White or gray
Homogeneous	Homogeneous, low viscosity; uniformly coats vaginal walls
Erythema of vaginal and vulvar epithelium; colpitis macularis	None
Usually ≥5.0	Usually >4.5
May be present	Present
Leukocytes; motile trichomonads seen in 80–90% of symptomatic patients, less often in the absence of symptoms	Clue cells; few leukocytes; no lactobacilli or only a few outnumbered by profuse mixed flora, nearly always including *G. vaginalis* plus anaerobic species on Gram's stain
Metronidazole, 2 g orally (single dose)	Metronidazole, 500 mg PO bid for 7 days
Metronidazole, 500 mg PO bid for 7 days	Clindamycin, 2% cream, one full applicator vaginally each night for 7 days
	Metronidazole gel, 0.75%, one full applicator vaginally twice daily for 5 days
	Metronidazole, 2 g PO (single dose)[d]
Examination for STD; treatment with metronidazole, 2 g PO (single dose)	Examination for STD; no treatment if normal

flora from the mixed flora seen in bacterial vaginosis, but it is less sensitive than the saline preparation for detection of *T. vaginalis*.
[d] Single-dose regimen is less effective than 7-day metronidazole regimen.
SOURCE: KK Holmes: HPIM-15, p. 843.

pelvic inflammatory disease (PID), which complicates ~20% of cases of gonococcal cervicitis.

Anorectal Gonorrhea Gonococcal anorectal infection can occur in females as well as males. Symptoms include anorectal pain or pruritus, tenesmus, purulent rectal discharge, and rectal bleeding. Rectal isolates of *N. gonorrhoeae* from homosexual men tend to be more resistant to antibiotics than other gonococcal isolates.

Pharyngeal Gonorrhea Fellatio is a more efficient means of contracting pharyngeal gonorrhea than cunnilingus. Symptoms are usually mild or lacking, although this syndrome almost always coexists with genital infection. Transmission from the pharynx to sexual contacts is rare. Pharyngeal infection may be more common in pregnancy because of altered sexual practices.

Ocular Gonorrhea in Adults Ocular gonococcal infection may result in a markedly swollen eyelid, chemosis, and profuse purulent discharge. Corneal ulceration and, in rare instances, perforation may occur. Prompt recognition and treatment are of paramount importance.

Disseminated Gonococcal Infection (DGI) Two-thirds of pts with DGI are women; symptoms of bacteremia often begin during menses. Strains causing DGI tend not to cause inflammation or (consequently) symptoms at genital or pharyngeal sites. Pts present either with manifestations of gonococcemia (fever, polyarthralgias, and the appearance—usually on the distal extremities—of 3–20 papular, petechial, pustular, hemorrhagic, or necrotic skin lesions) or with purulent oligoarthritis. Initial joint manifestations are characteristically limited to tenosynovitis involving several joints asymmetrically, most commonly the knees, wrists, ankles, and elbows. Septic arthritis may ensue, often without prior fever, polyarthralgia, or skin lesions; it usually causes pain and swelling of a single joint and is indistinguishable from septic arthritis caused by other pathogens. Up to 13% of pts with DGI have complement deficiencies.

DIAGNOSIS The presence of intracellular gram-negative diplococci on Gram's stain of urethral or endocervical exudate is grounds for a presumptive diagnosis of urethral gonorrhea. However, Gram's stain of the cervical os is not sensitive for the diagnosis of gonorrhea in women; rather, specimens of cervical exudate should be submitted for culture or nonculture assay. Material should be collected on a Dacron or rayon swab and cultured on Thayer-Martin selective medium in a humidified, CO_2-enriched atmosphere. Acceptable specimens may be obtained with swabs of the urethra, endocervix, anorectum, and pharynx. Endocervical culture is positive in 80–90% of cases of gonorrhea in women; the yield can be increased by concomitant rectal, urethral, and pharyngeal cultures. *N. gonorrhoeae* is recovered from <5% of skin lesions in DGI. Isolator blood cultures may enhance the yield in suspected cases. Gonococci are frequently recovered from early joint effusions and may be recovered from effusions with >80,000 WBCs/μL.

Nucleic acid probe tests are now widely used for the detection of *N. gonorrhoeae* in urogenital specimens. However, using nonculture methods as the sole means of detection precludes antibiotic susceptibility testing.

 TREATMENT

Table 83-4 summarizes current guidelines for the treatment of gonorrhea. Because of resistance to fluoroquinolones in several parts of Southeast Asia, these agents should not be used for gonorrhea acquired in that region. Third-generation cephalosporins remain the mainstay of therapy for uncomplicated genital, rectal, and pharyngeal gonorrhea, although symptomatic gonococcal pharyngitis is more difficult to eradicate than genital infection.

CHLAMYDIAL INFECTIONS
C. trachomatis Genital Infections

EPIDEMIOLOGY An estimated 4 million cases of *C. trachomatis* genital infection occur each year; thus these infections are the most common bacterial STDs in the U.S. *C. trachomatis* and *N. gonorrhoeae* often coinfect women with cervicitis and heterosexual men with urethritis.

CLINICAL MANIFESTATIONS *Nongonococcal and Postgonococcal Urethritis* These terms refer, respectively, to symptomatic urethritis in the absence of gonococcal infection and to nongonococcal urethritis developing in men 2–3 weeks after single-dose treatment for gonococcal urethritis. *C. tra-*

Table 83-4

Recommended Treatment for Gonococcal Infections: 1998 Guidelines of the Centers for Disease Control and Prevention

Diagnosis	Treatment of Choice
Uncomplicated gonococcal infection of the cervix, urethra, pharynx, or rectum[a]	
First-line regimens	Cefixime (400 mg PO, single dose) *or* Ceftriaxone (125 mg IM, single dose) *or* Ciprofloxacin (500 mg PO, single dose) *or* Ofloxacin (400 mg PO, single dose) *plus* A regimen effective against possible *Chlamydia* co-infection, such as: Azithromycin (1 g PO, single dose) *or* Doxycycline (100 mg PO bid for 7 days)
Alternative regimens	Spectinomycin (2 g IM, single dose) *or* Ceftizoxime (500 mg IM, single dose) *or* Cefotaxime (500 mg IM, single dose) *or* Cefotetan (1 g IM, single dose) *or* Cefoxitin (2 g IM, single dose) *plus* probenecid (1 g PO, single dose)
Epididymitis	See Chap. 132 in HPIM-15
Pelvic inflammatory disease	See Chap. 133 in HPIM-15
Gonococcal conjunctivitis in an adult	Ceftriaxone (1 g IM, single dose)[b]
Ophthalmia neonatorum[c]	Ceftriaxone (25–50 mg/kg IV or IM, single dose, not to exceed 125 mg)
Disseminated gonococcal infection[d]	
Initial therapy[e]	
Pts tolerant of β-lactam drugs	Ceftriaxone (1 g IM or IV q24h; *recommended*) *or* Cefotaxime (1 g IV q8h) *or* Ceftizoxime (1 g IV q8h)
Pts allergic to β-lactam drugs	Ciprofloxacin (500 mg IV q12h) *or* Ofloxacin (400 mg IV q12h) *or* Spectinomycin (2 g IM q12h)

(continued)

Table 83-4 *(Continued)*

Recommended Treatment for Gonococcal Infections: 1998 Guidelines of the Centers for Disease Control and Prevention

Diagnosis	Treatment of Choice
Continuation therapy	Cefixime (400 mg PO bid) *or* Ciprofloxacin (500 mg PO bid) *or* Ofloxacin (400 mg PO bid)
Meningitis or endocarditis	Ceftriaxone (1–2 g IV bid)[f]

[a] True failure of treatment with a recommended regimen is rare and should prompt an evaluation for reinfection or consideration of an alternative diagnosis. In cases of quinolone failure, the isolate should be tested for drug resistance if possible.

[b] Plus lavage of the infected eye with saline solution (once).

[c] Prophylactic regimens are discussed in Chap. 147, HPIM-15.

[d] Hospitalization is indicated if the diagnosis is uncertain, if the pt has frank arthritis with an effusion, or if the pt cannot be relied on to comply with treatment.

[e] All initial regimens should be continued for 24–48 h after clinical improvement begins, at which time therapy may be switched to one of the continuation regimens to complete a full week of antimicrobial treatment.

[f] Hospitalization is recommended to exclude suspected meningitis or endocarditis. Therapy should be continued for 10–14 d for meningitis and for at least 4 weeks for endocarditis.

SOURCE: Ram S, Rice PA: HPIM-15, p. 937.

chomatis accounts for 20–40% of cases of NGU among heterosexual men but is a less common cause among homosexual men.

Epididymitis *C. trachomatis* is the major cause of epididymitis in heterosexual men <35 years old in the U.S., accounting for 70% of cases. Men typically present with unilateral scrotal pain, fever, and epididymal tenderness or swelling. Testicular torsion should be excluded.

Reiter's Syndrome This syndrome consists of conjunctivitis, urethritis (in males) or cervicitis (in females), arthritis, and characteristic mucocutaneous lesions. *C. trachomatis* may be recovered from the urethra of up to 70% of men with nondiarrheal Reiter's syndrome and associated urethritis.

Proctitis Cases occur in persons of either sex who practice receptive anal intercourse. *C. trachomatis* strains of either the genital immunotypes or the lymphogranuloma venereum (LGV) immunotypes cause proctitis in homosexual men. Pts present with mild rectal pain, mucous discharge, tenesmus, and (occasionally) bleeding. Anoscopy in non-LGV cases reveals patchy mucosal friability and mucopurulent discharge; LGV strains produce more severe ulcerations that can be confused with HSV infection.

Mucopurulent Cervicitis MPC, an inflammation of the columnar epithelium and subepithelium of the endocervix, is the most common major STD syndrome among women and can be a harbinger of PID. *C. trachomatis* is its most common cause, although *N. gonorrhoeae* is often responsible. Although many females with *C. trachomatis* infection of the cervix have no signs or symptoms, a careful speculum examination reveals MPC in 30–50% of cases.

DIAGNOSIS The "gold standard" for diagnosis of *C. trachomatis* genital infections is the isolation of the organism by cell culture techniques, which are generally available only at larger medical centers and have a sensitivity of 60–80%. Since the organism is an intracellular pathogen, specimens for culture must include epithelial cells. Because of these limitations, nonculture methods have been developed. The direct immunofluorescent antibody (DFA) slide test is 70–85% sensitive. ELISA-based assays are 60–80% sensitive and 97–99% specific and are better suited for screening than DFA. PCR and ligase chain reaction are the most sensitive tests available and can be used with urine specimens rather than conventional swabs. Serologic tests are of limited usefulness.

 TREATMENT

For uncomplicated genital infection, doxycycline (100 mg bid PO) or tetracycline (500 mg qid PO) can be given for 7 d. For complicated infections (e.g., epididymitis, PID), a 14-d course is recommended. Azithromycin (1 g PO in a single dose) is effective in uncomplicated chlamydial infection and has appeal when follow-up care may not be possible. Ofloxacin (300 mg bid PO for 7 d) is also effective. These agents, however, are expensive. For pregnant pts, erythromycin base (500 mg qid PO for 10–14 d) is recommended. Sexual partners should be screened and treated, whether or not they are symptomatic.

Lymphogranuloma Venereum

See under "Ulcerative Genital Lesions," below.

PELVIC INFLAMMATORY DISEASE

ETIOLOGY The term *PID* usually refers to an ascending infection involving the endometrium and/or fallopian tubes. PID is generally caused by *N. gonorrhoeae, C. trachomatis,* and/or organisms that can be regarded as components of an altered vaginal microflora (anaerobes, *G. vaginalis,* Enterobacteriaceae, group B *Streptococcus, Mycoplasma* spp., and *Ureaplasma* spp.). First episodes of PID are more likely to be caused by the sexually transmitted pathogens. Tuberculous salpingitis is an unusual but well-described syndrome.

EPIDEMIOLOGY The annual incidence of PID in the U.S. has declined since the mid-1970s. Risk factors for the development of PID include a history of salpingitis and recent vaginal douching. The use of an IUD in nulliparous women and recent IUD insertion in any woman are also risk factors. Oral contraceptive use decreases the risk of PID. Tuberculous salpingitis is found more often in older women, with 50% of cases documented after menopause.

CLINICAL MANIFESTATIONS Symptoms usually develop in the first half of the menstrual cycle and evolve by stage of infection, which proceeds from cervicitis (mucopurulent vaginal discharge) to endometritis (midline abdominal pain and abnormal vaginal bleeding) to salpingitis (bilateral lower abdominal and pelvic pain) to peritonitis (nausea, vomiting, and increased abdominal tenderness). Abnormal uterine bleeding precedes or coincides with abdominal pain in 40% of women with PID; symptoms of urethritis (dysuria) occur in 20%. Symptoms of proctitis (anorectal pain, tenesmus, and rectal discharge or bleeding) are seen occasionally in pts with gonococcal or chlamydial infection. Spread of infection to the upper abdomen causes perihepatitis (Fitz-Hugh–Curtis syndrome) in 3–10% of cases, with right-sided or bilateral upper quadrant abdominal tenderness and occasionally a hepatic friction rub; this syndrome is usually a complication of chlamydial PID. Appendiceal serositis (periappendicitis) can occur. On speculum examination, MPC is found in the majority of pts with either gonococcal or chlamydial PID. On bimanual examination, cervical motion tenderness, uterine fundal tenderness, and abnormal adnexal tenderness are noted. Gonococcal PID presents more acutely than chlamydial PID. IUD-associated PID tends to be relatively indolent. HIV-infected women with PID are more likely than women without HIV infection to present with tuboovarian abscess requiring hospitalization and surgical drainage.

DIAGNOSIS Laparoscopy is the most specific method for diagnosis of PID but is generally impractical. In addition to a clinical exam consistent with the disease, findings favoring PID include fever, a palpable adnexal mass, an ESR of >15 mm/h, and >30 PMNs/high-power field on Gram's stain of cervical mucus. Aerobic and anaerobic culture of cervical mucus and/or culdocentesis fluid should be done, with culture and amplification assays for *N. gonorrhoeae* and *C. trachomatis*. Pregnancy testing should also be performed in women of childbearing age. Endometrial biopsy with the finding of tuberculous granulomas confirms the diagnosis of tuberculous salpingitis.

℞ **TREATMENT**

Two inpatient regimens have been used extensively: (1) doxycycline (100 mg IV q12h) plus cefotetan (2 g IV q12h) or cefoxitin (2 g IV q6h); and (2) clindamycin (900 mg IV q8h) plus gentamicin (1.5 mg/kg IV q8h after a loading dose of 2 mg/kg IV). Parenteral therapy should be continued until at least 48 h after the pt's condition improves, at which time doxycycline (100 mg PO bid) should be given to complete a 14-d course. For pts treated with regimen 2, clindamycin (450 mg qid) is an alternative oral agent; its enhanced anaerobic spectrum is particularly useful in cases with tuboovarian abscess. Suggested outpatient regimens include (1) ofloxacin (400 mg PO bid) plus metronidazole (500 mg PO bid) for 14 d, or (2) ceftriaxone (a single dose of 250 mg IM) followed by doxycycline (100 mg PO bid for 14 d). Sexual partners of pts with acute PID should be evaluated for STDs and treated promptly with a regimen effective against uncomplicated gonococcal and chlamydial infection.

ULCERATIVE GENITAL LESIONS
Syphilis

ETIOLOGY Syphilis is a chronic systemic infection caused by the spirochete *Treponema pallidum*.

EPIDEMIOLOGY Nearly all cases of syphilis follow sexual contact with infectious lesions; less common modes of transmission include nonsexual personal contact, in utero exposure, and blood transfusion. A rather steady increase since 1956 in the number of new cases of infectious syphilis in the U.S. has been punctuated by four cycles of 7–10 years, each with a rapid rise and fall in incidence. Since the most recent peak in 1990, the number of cases reported annually has again declined by >80%. During the early part of the AIDS epidemic, about half of all pts with early syphilis were homosexual and bisexual men. Because of changes in sexual practices due to the epidemic, this proportion has decreased. The most recent epidemic of syphilis predominantly involved African-American heterosexual men and women and occurred largely in urban areas. The incidence of congenital syphilis parallels that of infectious syphilis in women. Fifty percent of all named contacts of index cases are infected; thus "epidemiologic" treatment of all contacts is important for syphilis control.

CLINICAL MANIFESTATIONS Syphilis is characterized by episodes of active disease interrupted by periods of latency and conventionally is divided into stages.

Primary Syphilis The typical primary chancre usually begins as a single painless papule that rapidly becomes eroded, usually becomes indurated, and has a characteristic cartilaginous consistency. Atypical primary lesions are common. In heterosexual men, the chancre is most often located on the penis. In homosexual men it can be found in the anal canal or rectum, in the mouth, or on the external genitalia, while in women common sites are the cervix and labia. Consequently, primary syphilis is less often recognized in women and homosexual men than in heterosexual men. Regional lymphadenopathy usually appears within 1 week of the primary lesion. The nodes are firm, nonsuppurative, and painless. The chancre generally heals within 4–6 weeks, but lymphadenopathy may persist for months.

Secondary Syphilis   Manifestations of secondary syphilis vary widely but include skin lesions, lymphadenopathy, and constitutional symptoms. The skin rash begins as pale, pink or red macules that may go unnoticed; proceeds to papules; and may progress to lesions that resemble pustules. The palms and soles are frequently involved. In 10% of pts, papules enlarge to form moist, pink or gray-white, highly infectious lesions called *condylomata lata* in intertriginous areas. Mucous patches, which are superficial mucosal erosions, occur in 10–15% of cases. Constitutional symptoms may precede or accompany other manifestations. Syphilitic meningitis develops in only 1–2% of cases, but protein levels or WBC counts may be elevated in the CSF in ≥30%. Less common complications of secondary syphilis include hepatitis, nephropathy, GI involvement, arthritis, periostitis, and iridocyclitis.

Latent Syphilis   Positive serologic tests for syphilis in a pt with a normal CSF examination and no clinical manifestations of syphilis indicate a diagnosis of latent syphilis. *Early latent syphilis* refers to latency during the first year after infection, whereas *late latent syphilis* refers to latency that has persisted longer. Untreated latent syphilis progresses to clinically evident late syphilis in 30% of cases. Positive serologic tests rarely if ever revert to negative without treatment.

Late Syphilis (Tertiary Stage)

1. *Neurosyphilis:* The spectrum of symptomatic neurosyphilis includes meningeal syphilis (usually occurring within the first year), meningovascular syphilis (5–10 years after infection), general paresis (20 years), and tabes dorsalis (25–30 years). Symptoms of meningeal syphilis include headache, nausea, vomiting, neck stiffness, cranial nerve palsies, seizures, and changes in mental status. Meningovascular syphilis presents most commonly as a stroke syndrome in the middle cerebral artery distribution, often preceded by a subacute encephalitic syndrome (headaches, vertigo, insomnia, psychological abnormalities). General paresis (corresponding to the mnemonic "paresis") includes abnormalities of the *p*ersonality, *a*ffect, *r*eflexes (hyperactive), *e*ye (Argyll Robertson pupils), *s*ensorium, *i*ntellect, and *s*peech. Tabes dorsalis presents as symptoms and signs of demyelination of the posterior columns, dorsal roots, and dorsal root ganglia (e.g., ataxic wide-based gait; footslap; paresthesia; bladder disturbances; impotence; areflexia; and loss of position, deep pain, and temperature sensations). Trophic joint degeneration (Charcot's joints) results from loss of pain sensation. The small, irregular Argyll Robertson pupil, a feature of both general paresis and tabes dorsalis, reacts to accommodation but not to light.

2. *Cardiovascular syphilis:* Cardiovascular manifestations occur in ~10% of pts with untreated late latent disease and include aortitis, aortic regurgitation, saccular aneurysm (particularly in the ascending and transverse segments of the aortic arch), and coronary ostial stenosis. Symptoms appear 10–40 years after infection. Syphilitic aneurysms do not lead to dissection.

3. *Gummas:* Gummas are granulomatous inflammatory lesions that range from microscopic size to several centimeters in diameter. The most commonly involved sites are skin, bones, mouth, upper respiratory tract, larynx, liver, and stomach. The rapid healing of gummas after penicillin treatment may be diagnostically helpful.

DIAGNOSIS Syphilis is most often diagnosed serologically. Nontreponemal tests, including the VDRL and the RPR, are used for initial screening and serum antibody quantitation and usually become negative with treatment. Specific treponemal tests, including the FTA-ABS and MHA-TP, confirm syphilis (when positive), identify false-positive nontreponemal tests (when negative), and remain positive even after therapy. False-positive nontreponemal tests occur in a variety of conditions, but titers in these instances rarely exceed 1:8. Darkfield examination is used to evaluate suspicious moist cutaneous lesions. DFA is used for identification of the organism in fixed smears. PCR-based techniques are being developed. Evaluation for neurosyphilis by lumbar puncture (LP) is recommended for pts with neurologic signs, untreated syphilis of unknown or >1 year's duration, treatment failure, a serum VDRL or RPR titer of >1:32, or anticipated nonpenicillin therapy. In addition, LP should be considered for pts whose VDRL or RPR tests remain positive 1 year after treatment. Because standard agents for the treatment of early syphilis fail to reach treponemicidal levels in the CSF, some experts advise LP in secondary and early latent syphilis, especially for HIV-infected pts. The most common CSF findings are pleocytosis and an elevated protein level. The CSF VDRL is a highly specific but relatively insensitive diagnostic test. An unabsorbed FTA test on CSF is more sensitive but less specific. A *negative* unabsorbed FTA test on CSF rules out neurosyphilis. All pts with newly diagnosed syphilis should undergo HIV testing. Conversely, pts with newly diagnosed HIV infection should be tested for syphilis. There is no evidence that the sensitivity of serologic testing for syphilis differs in HIV-infected pts. Some authorities recommend CSF evaluation for all HIV-infected pts with syphilis. Serologic testing after treatment is important in all pts, particularly those also infected with HIV.

℞ TREATMENT (See Table 83-5)

Therapy for syphilis should be administered according to the stage of the disease, regardless of pregnancy status. The Jarisch-Herxheimer reaction to treatment for syphilis and certain other spirochetal infections consists of fever, chills, myalgias, headache, tachycardia, increased respiratory rate, increased circulating neutrophil count, and vasodilatation with mild hypotension. This reaction is self-limited and of undefined pathogenesis. It occurs in ~50% of pts treated for primary syphilis, 90% treated for secondary syphilis, and 25% treated for early latent syphilis. The onset usually comes within 2 h of the initiation of treatment, with resolution in 12–24 h. In neurosyphilis, the reaction is more delayed, peaking after about 12–14 h. The response of early syphilis to treatment should be determined by monitoring the quantitative VDRL or RPR titer 1, 3, 6, and 12 months after treatment (more frequently in HIV-infected pts). If the titer fails to fall by fourfold, if it rises, or if symptoms persist or recur, the pt should be re-treated and LP should be considered to rule out neurosyphilis. After treatment for neurosyphilis, CSF cell counts should be determined every 3–6 months for 3 years or until findings normalize.

Herpes Simplex Virus Infections

CLINICAL MANIFESTATIONS Fever, headache, malaise, and myalgias, along with the local symptoms of pain, itching, dysuria, vaginal and urethral discharge, and tender inguinal lymphadenopathy, characterize primary genital infection with HSV. Lesions include vesicles, pustules, or painful erythematous ulcers. More than 80% of women have cervical or urethral involvement in first-episode infection. Recurrence rates within 12 months are ~90%

Table 83-5

Recommendations for the Treatment of Syphilis[a]

Stage of Syphilis	Patients without Penicillin Allergy	Patients with Confirmed Penicillin Allergy
Primary, secondary, or early latent	Penicillin G benzathine (single dose of 2.4 million units IM, 1.2 million units in each buttock)	Tetracycline hydrochloride (500 mg PO qid) or doxycycline (100 mg PO bid) for 2 weeks
Late latent (or latent of uncertain duration), cardiovascular, or benign tertiary	Lumbar puncture CSF normal: Penicillin G benzathine (2.4 million units IM weekly for 3 weeks) CSF abnormal: Treat as neurosyphilis	Lumbar puncture CSF normal: Tetracycline hydrochloride (500 mg PO qid) or doxycycline (100 mg PO bid) for 4 weeks CSF abnormal: Treat as neurosyphilis
Neurosyphilis (asymptomatic or symptomatic)	Aqueous penicillin G (18–24 million units/d IV, given in divided doses every 4 h) for 10–14 d *or* Aqueous penicillin G procaine (2.4 million units/d IM) plus oral probenecid (500 mg qid), both for 10–14 d	Desensitization and treatment with penicillin if allergy is confirmed by skin testing
Syphilis in pregnancy	According to stage	Desensitization and treatment with penicillin if allergy is confirmed by skin testing

[a] See Chap. 172 in HPIM-15 for detailed discussion of syphilis therapy in HIV-infected individuals.
SOURCE: SA Lukehart: HPIM-15, p. 1051. These recommendations are modified from those issued by the Centers for Disease Control and Prevention in 1998.

for HSV-2 and ~55% for HSV-1. HSV-1 and HSV-2 can cause rectal and perianal infections.

DIAGNOSIS   The diagnosis can be made clinically with support from a positive Tzanck preparation showing multinucleated giant cells. The definitive diagnosis is made by isolation of the virus in tissue culture.

  TREATMENT   See Table 102-1

Chancroid

EPIDEMIOLOGY   Chancroid, genital ulceration and inguinal adenitis caused by *Haemophilus ducreyi*, occurs throughout the world and is a significant health problem in developing countries. Although less common in the U.S., its incidence has increased dramatically in recent years.

CLINICAL MANIFESTATIONS   After an incubation period of 7 d, a papule appears, develops into a pustule, and then ulcerates, resulting in a painful, sharply circumscribed genital ulcer with minimal inflammation that bleeds easily. Ulcers are occasionally multiple. About half of pts develop enlarged, tender inguinal lymph nodes that become fluctuant and may rupture.

DIAGNOSIS   An accurate diagnosis of chancroid relies on cultures of *H. ducreyi* from the lesion. Selective, nutritionally rich medium is necessary. Gram's stain may show a predominance of characteristic gram-negative coccobacilli.

 TREATMENT

Effective regimens include ceftriaxone, 250 mg IM as a single dose; azithromycin, 1g PO as a single dose; erythromycin, 500 mg PO qid for 7 d; and ciprofloxacin, 500 mg PO bid for 3 d.

Lymphogranuloma Venereum

ETIOLOGY   LGV is a sexually transmitted infection caused by the L serovars of *C. trachomatis.*

CLINICAL MANIFESTATIONS   A primary genital lesion is noted in fewer than one-third of heterosexual men with LGV and in only a few women with this infection. When present, this lesion is small and painless and usually heals in a few days without scarring. Primary anal or rectal infection can develop after receptive anal intercourse; in women, it may also arise via contiguous perineal spread of infected vaginal secretions. Lymphadenitis results from spread from the primary site to regional nodes. The inguinal syndrome is the most common presentation in heterosexual men and is characterized by painful inguinal adenopathy beginning 2–6 weeks after exposure. In two-thirds of cases, the adenopathy is unilateral. Lymph nodes become matted, fluctuant, and suppurative. The overlying skin becomes inflamed, and draining fistulas may develop. Constitutional symptoms are common. LGV proctitis may present as anorectal pain; mucopurulent, bloody rectal discharge; and tenesmus. Symptoms accompanying regional lymphadenopathy include fever, chills, headache, meningismus, anorexia, myalgias, and arthralgias. Systemic complications are infrequent but may include arthritis with sterile effusion, aseptic meningitis, meningoencephalitis, conjunctivitis, hepatitis, and erythema nodosum.

DIAGNOSIS   LGV strains can be isolated from lymph nodes or the rectum and rarely from the urethra or cervix. Serologic testing is more useful diagnostically for LGV than for other *C. trachomatis* infections.

 TREATMENT

Fluctuant buboes should be aspirated through normal-appearing skin. The recommended antibiotic is tetracycline (500 mg qid PO) for a minimum of 14 d.

Donovanosis (Granuloma Inguinale)

EPIDEMIOLOGY   Donovanosis, of which the bacterial agent is *Calymmatobacterium granulomatis*, is a rare cause of genital ulcers in the U.S.

CLINICAL MANIFESTATIONS   Most lesions appear within 4 weeks of sexual exposure. The disease begins as a papule that ulcerates and develops into a usually painless, clean, friable, granulomatous lesion. Labial swelling, phimosis, and paraphimosis are common. Oral lesions are unusual but have been described.

DIAGNOSIS   The diagnosis is best made by examination of impression smears prepared from specimens obtained by punch biopsy of granulation tissue from the periphery of a lesion. The specimen is subjected to Giemsa, Leishman's, or Wright's staining. Donovan bodies appear as rounded coccobacilli of

1 by 2 μm lying within cystic spaces in the cytoplasm of large mononuclear cells. A serologic test has been developed.

 TREATMENT

Commonly used antibiotics include tetracycline (500 mg PO q6h), doxycycline (100 mg PO q12h), TMP-SMZ (160/800 mg PO q12h), erythromycin (500 mg PO q6h), azithromycin (1 g PO weekly), and chloramphenicol (500 mg PO q6h). Treatment is usually continued until the lesion has healed completely (3–5 weeks).

HUMAN PAPILLOMAVIRUS (HPV) INFECTIONS

ETIOLOGY AND EPIDEMIOLOGY   HPVs are nonenveloped viruses of the Papovaviridae family that infect the epithelium of the skin or mucous membranes.

CLINICAL MANIFESTATIONS   The incubation period of HPV infection is usually 3–4 months, with a range of 1 month to 2 years. Anogenital warts (condylomata acuminata) are sexually transmitted, beige to brown, exophytic, hyperkeratotic papules that occur on skin and mucosal surfaces of external genitalia and perianal areas. Some of the >80 HPV types are strongly associated with cancer of the cervix, penis, anus, vagina, and vulva. HPV types 6 and 11 are most commonly associated with condylomata acuminata, whereas types 16, 18, and 31 are most frequently detected in dysplasias and carcinomas of the genital tract.

DIAGNOSIS   Most visible genital warts can be diagnosed clinically. Colposcopy is invaluable in assessing vaginal and cervical lesions. Papanicolaou smears from cervical specimens may reveal cytologic evidence of HPV. Histologic examination of biopsy specimens is useful for persistent or atypical lesions. PCR can be used to detect HPV nucleic acids and to identify specific virus types. Serologic techniques are not widely available.

 TREATMENT

Available modes of treatment are not completely effective, and some have significant side effects. Moreover, lesions may resolve spontaneously. Frequently used therapies include cryosurgery, application of caustic agents, electrodesiccation, surgical excision, and laser ablation. Topical 5-fluorouracil has also been used. Various interferon preparations have been employed with modest success; a topically applied interferon inducer, imiquimod, is also of benefit.

For a more detailed discussion, see Holmes KK: Sexually Transmitted Diseases: Overview and Clinical Approach, Chap. 132, p. 839; Holmes KK, Brunham RC: Pelvic Inflammatory Disease, Chap. 133, p. 848; Ram S, Rice PA: Gonococcal Infections, Chap. 147, p. 931; Murphy TF: *Haemophilus* Infections, Chap. 149, p. 939; Kasper DL, Barlam TF: Infections Due to the HACEK Group and Miscellaneous Gram-Negative Bacteria, Chap. 150, p. 942; Hart G: Donovanosis, Chap. 164, p. 1004; Lukehart SA: Syphilis, Chap. 172, p. 1044; Stamm WE: Chlamydial Infections, Chap. 179, p. 1075; Corey L: Herpes Simplex Viruses, Chap. 182, p. 1100; and Reichman RC: Human Papillomaviruses, Chap. 188, p. 1118, in HPIM-15.

84

INFECTIONS OF SKIN, SOFT TISSUES, JOINTS, AND BONES

SKIN AND SOFT TISSUE INFECTIONS

The etiologic agents of various types of skin and soft tissue infections are listed in Table 84-1. Antimicrobial agents used to treat several prominent infections are shown in Table 84-2.

Erysipelas

Erysipelas, or lymphangitis of the dermis, features a fiery red, intensely painful, demarcated swelling of the face or extremities. Classic erysipelas is due to *Streptococcus pyogenes* and may be treated with penicillin. If the condition's appearance is not sufficiently distinctive to exclude cellulitis, it is prudent to broaden coverage as described below for cellulitis.

Cellulitis

Cellulitis is an acute inflammatory condition of the skin caused either by indigenous flora colonizing the skin or by a wide variety of exogenous bacteria. These organisms can (1) be inoculated through small breaks in the skin (*S. pyogenes*) or via bites (*Pasteurella, Eikenella,* anaerobes); (2) originate in wounds, ulcers, or abscesses (*Staphylococcus aureus*); (3) be associated with sinusitis (*Haemophilus influenzae*); or (4) gain entry during immersion in water (*Aeromonas, Vibrio vulnificus*). Cellulitis is characterized by localized pain, erythema, swelling, and heat.

℞ TREATMENT

If an etiologic agent is suggested by the pt's history, treatment is directed at a specific pathogen or group of pathogens. Both blood and any abscess, open wound, or drainage should be cultured. In the absence of a specific etiology, treatment is directed at gram-positive pathogens. IV therapy with oxacillin (2 g q4–6h) or cefazolin (1–2 g q8h) is administered until signs of systemic toxicity have resolved and acute inflammation has improved substantially; oral treatment is then given to complete a 2-week course.

Impetigo

Impetigo begins as multiple pruritic erythematous lesions that evolve into yellow crusts. This infection may be caused by *S. pyogenes* (*impetigo contagiosa*) or *S. aureus* (*bullous impetigo*). It is important to recognize impetigo caused by *S. pyogenes* because of the risk of poststreptococcal glomerulonephritis. *Treatment* consists of dicloxacillin (500 mg PO qid), cephalexin (500 mg PO qid), or topical mupirocin ointment.

Necrotizing Fasciitis

This life-threatening infection of the fascia and soft tissues investing the muscles of the trunk or extremities may be caused by group A streptococci (often from apparent or inapparent infection via the skin), *Clostridium perfringens* (accompanying gas gangrene), or mixed aerobic and anaerobic bacteria (usually of GI origin). The infection presents acutely as pain, fever, and systemic toxicity, often with a paucity of cutaneous findings. Necrotizing fasciitis can extend to cuta-

Table 84-1

Skin and Soft Tissue Infections

Lesion, Clinical Syndrome	Infectious Agent
Vesicles	
Smallpox	Variola virus
Chickenpox	Varicella-zoster virus
Shingles (herpes zoster)	Varicella-zoster virus
Cold sores, herpetic whitlow, herpes gladiatorum	Herpes simplex virus
Hand-foot-and-mouth disease	Coxsackievirus A16
Orf	Parapoxvirus
Molluscum contagiosum	Pox-like virus
Rickettsialpox	*Rickettsia akari*
Bullae	
Staphylococcal scalded-skin syndrome	*Staphylococcus aureus*
Blistering distal dactylitis	*S. aureus* or *Streptococcus pyogenes*
Necrotizing fasciitis	*S. pyogenes, Clostridium* spp., mixed aerobes and anaerobes
Gas gangrene	*Clostridium* spp.
Halophilic vibrio	*Vibrio vulnificus*
Crusted lesions	
Bullous impetigo/ecthyma	*S. aureus*
Impetigo contagiosa	*S. pyogenes*
Ringworm	Superficial dermatophyte fungi
Sporotrichosis	*Sporothrix schenckii*
Histoplasmosis	*Histoplasma capsulatum*
Coccidioidomycosis	*Coccidioides immitis*
Blastomycosis	*Blastomyces dermatitidis*
Cutaneous leishmaniasis	*Leishmania* spp.
Cutaneous tuberculosis	*Mycobacterium tuberculosis*
Nocardiosis	*Nocardia asteroides*
Folliculitis	
Furunculosis	*S. aureus*
Hot-tub folliculitis	*Pseudomonas aeruginosa*
Swimmer's itch	*Schistosoma* spp.
Acne vulgaris	*Propionibacterium acnes*
Papular and nodular lesions	
Fish-tank or swimming-pool granuloma	*Mycobacterium marinum*
Creeping eruption (cutaneous larva migrans)	*Ancylostoma braziliense*
Dracunculiasis	*Dracunculus medinensis*
Cercarial dermatitis	*Schistosoma mansoni*
Verruca vulgaris	Human papillomaviruses 1, 2, 4
Condylomata acuminata (ano-genital warts)	Human papillomaviruses 6, 11, 16, 18
Onchocerciasis nodule	*Onchocerca volvulus*
Cutaneous myiasis	*Dermatobia hominis*
Verruca peruana	*Bartonella bacilliformis*
Cat-scratch disease	*Bartonella henselae*
Lepromatous leprosy	*Mycobacterium leprae*

(continued)

Table 84-1 *(Continued)*

Skin and Soft Tissue Infections

Lesion, Clinical Syndrome	Infectious Agent
Secondary syphilis (papulo-squamous, nodular, and condylomata lata lesions)	*Treponema pallidum*
Tertiary syphilis (nodular gummatous lesions)	*T. pallidum*
Ulcers with or without eschars	
Anthrax	*Bacillus anthracis*
Ulceroglandular tularemia	*Francisella tularensis*
Bubonic plague	*Yersinia pestis*
Buruli ulcer	*Mycobacterium ulcerans*
Leprosy	*M. leprae*
Cutaneous tuberculosis	*M. tuberculosis*
Chancroid	*Haemophilus ducreyi*
Primary syphilis	*T. pallidum*
Erysipelas	*S. pyogenes*
Cellulitis	*Staphylococcus* spp., *Streptococcus* spp., various other bacteria
Necrotizing fasciitis	
Streptococcal gangrene	*S. pyogenes*
Fournier's gangrene	Mixed aerobic and anaerobic bacteria
Myositis and myonecrosis	
Pyomyositis	*S. aureus*
Streptococcal necrotizing myositis	*S. pyogenes*
Gas gangrene	*Clostridium* spp.
Nonclostridial (crepitant) myositis	Mixed aerobic and anaerobic bacteria
Synergistic nonclostridial anaerobic myonecrosis	Mixed aerobic and anaerobic bacteria

SOURCE: DL Stevens: HPIM-15, p. 822.

neous structures, causing thrombosis, skin discoloration, crepitus, anesthesia, and bulla formation. As the infection extends rapidly along fascial planes and via veins and lymphatics, cutaneous and fascial necrosis and shock occur (e.g., streptococcal toxic shock syndrome). Early surgical exploration is critical to both diagnosis and therapy.

℞ TREATMENT

Antibiotic therapy is directed at the offending pathogen; for group A streptococci and clostridia, experimental data suggest that a combination of clindamycin (600–900 mg IV q8h) and penicillin G (4 million U, IV q4h) may be superior to penicillin alone. When polymicrobial infection is suspected, therapy consists of a three-drug combination of either ampicillin (2 g IV q4h) plus clindamycin (600–900 mg IV q6–8h) plus ciprofloxacin (400 mg IV q12h) or vancomycin (1 g IV q12h) plus metronidazole (500 mg IV q6h) plus ciprofloxacin. Hyperbaric oxygen therapy may be useful in clostridial disease.

Table 84-2

Treatment of Common Infections of the Skin

Diagnosis/Condition	Primary Treatment	Alternative Treatment
Animal bite (prophylaxis or early infection)[a] Animal bite[a] (established infection)	Amoxicillin/clavulanate, 875/125 mg PO bid Ampicillin/sulbactam, 1.5 g IV q6h	Doxycycline, 100 mg PO bid Clindamycin, 600–900 mg IV q8h, *plus* Ciprofloxacin, 400 mg IV q12h *or*
Bacillary angiomatosis Herpes simplex (primary genital)	Erythromycin, 500 mg PO qid Acyclovir, 400 mg PO tid for 10 days	Cefoxitin, 2 g IV q6h Doxycycline, 100 mg PO bid Famciclovir, 250 mg PO tid for 5–10 days *or* Valacyclovir, 1000 mg PO bid for 10 days
Herpes zoster (immunocompetent host >50 years of age)	Acyclovir, 800 mg PO 5 times daily for 7–10 days	Famciclovir, 500 mg PO tid for 7–10 days *or* Valacyclovir, 1000 mg PO tid for 7 days
Cellulitis (staphylococcal or streptococcal[b,c])	Nafcillin or oxacillin, 2 g IV q4–6h	Cefazolin, 1–2 g q8h, *plus* Ampicillin/sulbactam, 1.5–3.0 g IV q6h *or* Erythromycin, 0.5–1.0 g IV q6h
Necrotizing fasciitis (group A streptococcal[b])	Clindamycin, 600–900 mg IV q6–8h, *plus* Penicillin G, 4 million units IV q4h	Clindamycin, 600–900 mg IV q8h Clindamycin, 600–900 mg IV q6–8h, *plus* Cephalosporin (first- or second-generation)

(continued)

Table 84-2 (Continued)

Treatment of Common Infections of the Skin

Diagnosis/Condition	Primary Treatment	Alternative Treatment
Necrotizing fasciitis (mixed aerobes and an-aerobes)	Ampicillin, 2 g IV q4h, *plus* Clindamycin, 600–900 mg IV q6–8h, *plus* Ciprofloxacin, 400 mg IV q6–8h	Vancomycin, 1 g IV q6h, *plus* Metronidazole, 500 mg IV q6h, *plus* Ciprofloxacin, 400 mg IV q6–8h
	Clindamycin, 600–900 mg IV q6–8h, *plus* Penicillin G, 4 million units IV q4–6h	Clindamycin, 600–900 mg IV q6–8h, *plus* Cefoxitin, 2 g IV q6h
Gas gangrene		

[a] *Pasteurella multocida*, a species commonly associated with both dog and cat bites, is resistant to cephalexin, dicloxacillin, clindamycin, and erythromycin. *Eikenella corrodens*, a bacterium commonly associated with human bites, is resistant to clindamycin, penicillinase-resistant penicillins, and metronidazole but is sensitive to TMP-SMZ and fluoroquinolones.

[b] The frequency of erythromycin resistance in group A *Streptococcus* is currently about 5% in the United States but has reached 70–100% in some other countries. Most, but not all, erythromycin-resistant group A streptococci are susceptible to clindamycin. Approximately 90–95% of *Staphylococcus aureus* strains are sensitive to clindamycin.

[c] Severe hospital-acquired *S. aureus* infections or community-acquired *S. aureus* infections that are not responding to the β-lactam antibiotics recommended in this table may be caused by methicillin-resistant strains, requiring a switch to vancomycin.

SOURCE: Modified from DL Stevens: HPIM-15, p. 824.

Myositis/Myonecrosis

Myositis/myonecrosis can arise spontaneously (*S. aureus, S. pyogenes*) or after penetrating trauma (*Clostridium*). Streptococcal necrotizing myositis can accompany necrotizing fasciitis and can cause a systemic toxic shock syndrome.

BONE AND JOINT INFECTIONS
Infectious Arthritis

Acute bacterial arthritis is a common medical problem affecting individuals of all ages and requiring prompt recognition and treatment. While bacteria are the most common causes of infectious arthritis, various fungi and viruses also infect joints.

ETIOLOGY AND PATHOGENESIS Gonococcal infection is a common cause of septic arthritis (Chap. 83). Approximately 75% of nongonococcal pyoarthroses are due to gram-positive cocci. *S. aureus* is the most common pathogen; next most common are streptococci of groups A and G, viridans streptococci, pneumococci, and—in neonates—group B streptococci. Gram-negative bacilli account for 20% of infections, typically affecting pts with risk factors for gram-negative bacteremia. In general, infection occurs via hematogenous seeding of the synovium. Predisposing factors include infancy, immunosuppressive illness or therapy, diabetes mellitus, hemodialysis, alcoholism, IV drug use, and prior joint damage (including rheumatoid arthritis). Persons with HIV infection are at increased risk of septic arthritis due to pneumococci, salmonellae, and *H. influenzae*. Direct seeding of the joint may be attributable to trauma, arthroscopy, or surgery. An extraarticular focus of infection is identified in 25% of cases. Prosthetic joint infections are usually due to staphylococci (either coagulase-negative staphylococci or *S. aureus*) and occur in 1–4% of prosthetic joints over a 10-year period, with an increased rate in joints that have undergone revision. Other causes of acute infectious arthritis include rubella virus, hepatitis B virus, mumps virus, coxsackievirus, adenovirus, and parvovirus. *Borrelia burgdorferi* and *Treponema pallidum* may cause a more chronic, slowly progressive arthritis, as do *Mycobacterium tuberculosis* and fungal agents such as *Coccidioides, Sporothrix,* and *Histoplasma. Candida* and *Blastomyces* may cause acute or chronic arthritis.

CLINICAL MANIFESTATIONS Acute bacterial arthritis presents as a monarticular process in ~90% of pts, involving the large joints (most commonly the knee and hip; next most commonly the ankle, wrist, elbow, and shoulder and the sternoclavicular and sacroiliac joints). Fever may be lacking in persons who have rheumatoid arthritis or who are receiving immunosuppressive therapy. In the hip or shoulder, effusion may be difficult to detect, and pain may be minimal. Symptoms are similar to those of cellulitis, bursitis, and acute osteomyelitis, and these infections must be distinguished from septic arthritis by their greater range of motion and less-than-circumferential swelling. Infection due to gram-positive cocci usually presents as an acute onset of swelling, pain, warmth, and limitation of movement. Gram-negative infections tend to be more indolent, and pts typically present after 3 weeks of illness, frequently with coexistent osteomyelitis. Infections of prosthetic joints are even more indolent, with presenting symptoms so mild that diagnosis may be delayed by several months; there is always accompanying osteomyelitis.

DIAGNOSIS Analysis of aspirated synovial fluid is necessary for the diagnosis of bacterial joint infection. The fluid is usually turbid, with >25,000 WBCs/μL (typically >100,000/μL, with >90% neutrophils). Gram's staining identifies the pathogen in 75% of gram-positive and 30–50% of gram-negative infections. Cultures of joint fluid are usually positive. Blood should also be cultured. In gonococcal infection, Gram's staining rarely gives a positive result and synovial fluid culture is positive in only ~40% of cases. Culture of skin and mucosal lesions on special medium and PCR-based assays of synovial fluid will improve the diagnostic yield for gonococcal infection. Prosthetic joint infections are generally diagnosed by the finding of loosening of the implant or of osteomyelitis on radiographs; the diagnosis is confirmed by needle aspiration of the joint. The ESR and C-reactive protein levels are usually elevated.

℞ TREATMENT

Optimal management requires IV antibiotic administration, drainage (usually by repeated daily aspiration), and avoidance of weight bearing. Open surgical drainage should be considered when the hip, shoulder, or sternoclavicular joint is infected; when fluid loculations occur; when cultures are persistently positive; or when effusion persists for >7 d. Prosthetic joints should be removed and replaced after antibiotic therapy. The choice of antibiotics is based initially on Gram's stain and then on culture. An IV third-generation cephalosporin such as ceftriaxone (1–2 g q24h) provides adequate empirical coverage when Gram's stain is unrevealing. Staphylococcal infections are initially treated IV with oxacillin (2 g q4h) for 4 weeks or—if methicillin-resistant *S. aureus* is suspected—with vancomycin (1 g q12h). Streptococcal arthritis due to a penicillin-susceptible organism is treated with penicillin G (2 million U q4h) for 2 weeks. Gram-negative septic arthritis is treated with a second- or third-generation cephalosporin (e.g., cefuroxime, 1.5 g IV q8h; or ceftriaxone, 1–2 g IV q12–24h) or a quinolone (e.g., levofloxacin, 500 mg IV q24h) for 3–4 weeks. Infection due to *Pseudomonas aeruginosa* is treated for at least 3 weeks with a combination of an extended-spectrum penicillin such as mezlocillin (3 g IV q4h) or ceftazidime (1 g IV q8h) plus an aminoglycoside such as tobramycin (1.7 mg/kg IV q8h). If tolerated, this regimen is continued for an additional 2–3 weeks; alternatively, oral ciprofloxacin (750 mg bid) may be substituted for the aminoglycoside. Gonococcal arthritis is treated initially with ceftriaxone (1 g IV/IM q24h). After signs of local and systemic inflammation begin to resolve, therapy may be switched to an oral agent (cefixime, 400 mg bid; or ciprofloxacin, 500 mg bid) to complete a 7- to 10-d course. Amoxicillin (500 mg PO tid) may be used to complete therapy against penicillin-susceptible isolates.

Osteomyelitis

ETIOLOGY AND PATHOGENESIS   Osteomyelitis, an infection of bone, is caused most commonly by pyogenic bacteria and mycobacteria. Microorganisms enter the bone by hematogenous spread or directly via a wound or from an adjacent site of infection. The metaphyses of long bones in children (tibia, femur, humerus) and the vertebrae in adults are the most frequently involved sites. More than 95% of cases of hematogenous osteomyelitis are caused by a single organism, with *S. aureus* responsible for ~50% of the total number. Other common pathogens in adults include gram-negative bacillary organisms (*Pseudomonas, Serratia, Salmonella, Escherichia coli*). Tuberculosis, brucellosis, histoplasmosis, coccidioidomycosis, and blastomycosis are less frequent causes of osteomyelitis. Infections due to a contiguous focus of infection (e.g., diabetic foot ulcers) are often polymicrobial and are more likely to involve gram-negative and anaerobic bacteria. In addition, *S. aureus* is the principal cause of postoperative infections, and coagulase-negative staphylococci often cause prosthetic device–associated infections.

CLINICAL MANIFESTATIONS   Half of pts with osteomyelitis present with vague pain in the affected limb or the back (or in vertebral osteomyelitis, with pain due to nerve root irritation) of 1–3 months' duration with little or no fever. Children may experience an acute onset of fever, irritability, and lethargy, with local inflammation of <3 weeks' duration. Findings on physical exam may include point tenderness, muscle spasm, and draining sinus (especially with chronic osteomyelitis or an infected prosthetic joint).

DIAGNOSIS   Osteomyelitis is diagnosed by culture of appropriate specimens. If blood cultures are negative, pus obtained by needle aspiration from bone or bone biopsy should be cultured. Cultures from superficial sites are not reliable. Findings on plain films do not become positive for at least 10 d, and lytic lesions may not be visible for 2–6 weeks. Radionuclide bone scan may become positive within 2 d of infection. CT or MRI may become positive early and may aid in the localization of lesions and the demonstration of sequestra and soft tissue collections. The ESR is usually elevated but falls in response to therapy.

 TREATMENT

With prompt treatment, <5% of pts with acute hematogenous osteomyelitis develop chronic disease. Antibiotics should be given only after appropriate specimens have been obtained for culture. For acute hematogenous osteomyelitis, IV antibiotics active against the organisms identified should be given for 4–6 weeks. Surgical debridement should be considered if there is a poor response to therapy in the first 48 h or if there is undrained pus or septic arthritis. In vertebral osteomyelitis, surgery is also necessary in cases of spinal instability, new or progressive neurologic deficits, or large undrainable soft tissue abscesses. Chronic osteomyelitis requires complete drainage, debridement of sequestra, and removal of any prosthetic material as well as a 4- to 6-week course of antibiotics whose selection is based on culture of the bone. Skin flaps and bone grafts may facilitate healing. If the identity of the infecting organism(s) is known, antibiotic therapy should begin several days before surgery. Appropriate therapy for *S. aureus* or empirical therapy in the absence of a positive culture includes oxacillin (2 g IV q4h) or cefazolin (2 g IV q8h). Treatment of gram-negative osteomyelitis must be based on identification of the organism and determination of its susceptibility. Because *Pseudomonas* and *Enterobacter* show a propensity to develop resistance during therapy, osteomyelitis due to these organisms should be treated with a combination of an aminoglycoside (e.g., tobramycin for *Pseudomonas* infection and gentamicin for *Enterobacter* at doses of 1.7 mg/kg q8h) and a β-lactam antibiotic (e.g., mezlocillin, 3 g q4h). A quinolone (e.g., ciprofloxacin, 400 mg IV q12h; or levofloxacin, 500 mg IV q24h) may be substituted for the β-lactam antibiotic against *Pseudomonas* or used alone against *Enterobacter*. For other gram-negative bacillary infections of bone, treatment is based on susceptibility of the organism and ordinarily consists of a single agent, such as a cephalosporin (e.g., cefazolin, 2 g IV q8h; or ceftriaxone, 1 g IV q12h) or a fluoroquinolone (e.g., ciprofloxacin, 400 mg IV q12h). When sensitivity of the organism allows, oral ciprofloxacin (750 mg q12h) or levofloxacin (500 mg q24h) may be given after or instead of IV therapy.

For a more detailed discussion, see Maguire JH: Osteomyelitis, Chap. 129, p. 825; Stevens DL: Infections of the Skin, Muscle, and Soft Tissues, Chap.

128, p. 821; Wessels MR: Streptococcal and Enterococcal Infections, Chap. 140, p. 901; and Thaler SJ, Maguire JH: Infectious Arthritis, Chap. 323, p. 1998, in HPIM-15.

85

INFECTIONS IN THE IMMUNOCOMPROMISED HOST

The immunocompromised pt is at increased risk for infection with both common and opportunistic pathogens and may have a blunted clinical response that challenges diagnosis. Acquired disease, loss of physical barriers, or an inborn immune defect may lower a person's immunity. Table 85-1 summarizes infections associated with acquired or inborn defects in immune response.

In addition, infections are a common cause of death and an even more common cause of morbidity in pts with a wide variety of neoplasms (Table 85-2). Pts undergoing intensive chemotherapy for any form of cancer will have defects due not only to granulocytopenia but also to lymphocyte dysfunction. Neutropenic febrile pts should receive empirical antibiotic treatment to prevent death. Several general guidelines are useful in the initial treatment of neutropenic pts (Fig. 85-1). Prophylaxis for *Pneumocystis carinii* is mandatory for pts with acute lymphocytic leukemia and for all cancer pts receiving glucocorticoid-containing chemotherapy regimens.

Infections in pts during the first month after bone marrow transplantation (BMT) are similar to those in leukemia pts who are granulocytopenic as a result of chemotherapy. Prophylactic trimethoprim-sulfamethoxazole or ciprofloxacin decreases the incidence of gram-negative bacteremia in these pts. Cytomegalovirus (CMV) disease is the major concern in the second through fourth months after BMT. In addition, most pts should receive prophylaxis for *P. carinii* starting 1 month after engraftment and continuing for at least 1 year.

The organisms that cause infections in recipients of solid organ transplants are different from those that infect bone marrow transplant recipients because solid organ recipients do not go through a period of neutropenia. However, they are immunosuppressed for longer periods than bone marrow recipients (often permanently), and they are susceptible to infections with the same organisms as pts with chronically impaired T cell immunity. During the first month after transplantation, infections of wound or anastomotic sites prevail. CMV is most often a problem in the first 6 months as a consequence of the administration of agents that suppress cell-mediated immunity and of the acquisition or reactivation of viruses. Beyond 6 months after transplantation, infections characteristic of pts with defects in cell-mediated immunity may be a problem (Table 85-2).

Table 85-1

Infections Associated with Selected Defects in Immunity

Host Defect	Disease or Therapy Associated with Defect	Common Etiologic Agent of Infection
NONSPECIFIC IMMUNITY		
Impaired cough	Rib fracture, neuromuscular dysfunction	Bacteria causing pneumonia, aerobic and anaerobic oral flora
Loss of gastric acidity	Achlorhydria, histamine blockade	*Salmonella* spp., enteric pathogens
Loss of cutaneous integrity	Penetrating trauma, athlete's foot	*Staphylococcus* spp., *Streptococcus* spp.
	Burn	*Pseudomonas aeruginosa*
	IV catheter	*Staphylococcus* spp., *Streptococcus* spp., gram-negative rods, coagulase-negative staphylococci
Implantable device	Heart valve	*Streptococcus* spp., coagulase-negative staphylococci, *Staphylococcus aureus*
	Artificial joint	*Staphylococcus* spp. *Streptococcus* spp., gram-negative rods
Loss of normal bacterial flora	Antibiotic use	*Clostridium difficile*, *Candida* spp.
Impaired clearance		
Poor drainage	UTI	*Escherichia coli*
Abnormal secretions	Cystic fibrosis	Chronic pulmonary infection with *P. aeruginosa*
INFLAMMATORY RESPONSE		
Neutropenia	Hematologic malignancy, cytotoxic chemotherapy, aplastic anemia, HIV infection	Gram-negative enteric bacilli, *Pseudomonas* spp., *Staphylococcus* spp., *Candida* spp.
Chemotaxis	Chédiak-Higashi syndrome, Job's syndrome, protein-calorie malnutrition	*S. aureus*, *Streptococcus pyogenes*, *Haemophilus influenzae*, gram-negative bacilli
Phagocytosis (cellular)	SLE, chronic myelogenous leukemia, megaloblastic anemia	*Streptococcus pneumoniae*, *H. influenzae*
Splenectomy	—	*H. influenzae*, *S. pneumoniae*, other streptococci, *Capnocytophaga* spp., *Babesia microti*, *Salmonella* spp.
Microbicidal defect	Chronic granulomatous disease	Catalase-positive bacteria and fungi: staphylococci, *E. coli*, *Klebsiella* spp., *P. aeruginosa*, *Aspergillus* spp., *Nocardia* spp.

(continued)

Table 85-1 *(Continued)*

Infections Associated with Selected Defects in Immunity

Host Defect	Disease or Therapy Associated with Defect	Common Etiologic Agent of Infection
	Chédiak-Higashi syndrome	*S. aureus, S. pyogenes*
	Interferon γ receptor defect, interleukin 12 deficiency, interleukin 12 receptor defect	*Mycobacterium* spp., *Salmonella* spp.
COMPLEMENT SYSTEM		
C3	Congenital liver disease, SLE, nephrotic syndrome	*S. aureus, S. pneumoniae, Pseudomonas* spp., *Proteus* spp.
C5	Congenital	*Neisseria* spp., gram-negative rods
C6, C7, C8	Congenital, SLE	*Neisseria meningitidis, Neisseria gonorrhoeae*
Alternative pathway	Sickle cell disease	*S. pneumoniae, Salmonella* spp.
IMMUNE RESPONSE		
T lymphocyte deficiency/dysfunction	Thymic aplasia, thymic hypoplasia, Hodgkin's disease, sarcoidosis, lepromatous leprosy	*Listeria monocytogenes, Mycobacterium* spp., *Candida* spp., *Aspergillus* spp., *Cryptococcus neoformans*, herpes simplex virus, varicella-zoster virus
	AIDS	*Pneumocystis carinii*, cytomegalovirus, herpes simplex virus, *Mycobacterium avium-intracellulare, C. neoformans, Candida* spp.
	Mucocutaneous candidiasis	*Candida* spp.
	Purine nucleoside phosphorylase deficiency	Fungi, viruses
B cell deficiency/dysfunction	Bruton's X-linked agammaglobulinemia	*S. pneumoniae*, other streptococci
	Agammaglobulinemia, chronic lymphocytic leukemia, multiple myeloma, dysglobulinemia	*H. influenzae, N. meningitidis, S. aureus, Klebsiella pneumoniae, E. coli, Giardia lamblia, P. carinii*, enteroviruses
	Selective IgM deficiency	*S. pneumoniae, H. influenzae, E. coli*
	Selective IgA deficiency	*G. lamblia*, hepatitis virus, *S. pneumoniae, H. influenzae*
Mixed T and B cell deficiency/dysfunction	Common variable hypogammaglobulinemia	*P. carinii*, cytomegalovirus, *S. pneumoniae, H. influenzae*, various other bacteria
	Ataxia-telangiectasia	*S. pneumoniae, H. influenzae, S. aureus*, rubella virus, *G. lamblia*

(continued)

Table 85-1 *(Continued)*

Infections Associated with Selected Defects in Immunity

Host Defect	Disease or Therapy Associated with Defect	Common Etiologic Agent of Infection
	Severe combined immunodeficiency	*S. aureus, S. pneumoniae, H. influenzae, Candida albicans, P. carinii*, varicella-zoster virus, rubella virus, cytomegalovirus
	Wiskott-Aldrich syndrome	Agents of infections associated with T and B cell abnormalities
	X-linked hyper-IgM syndrome	*P. carinii*, cytomegalovirus, *Cryptosporidium parvum*

SOURCE: LC Madoff, DL Kasper: HPIM-15, p. 765 (as adapted from H Masur, A Fauci: HPIM-13, p. 497).

Table 85-2

Infections and Cancer

Cancer	Underlying Immune Abnormality	Organisms Causing Infection
Multiple myeloma	Hypogammaglobulinemia	*Streptococcus pneumoniae, Haemophilus influenzae, Neisseria meningitidis*
Chronic lymphocytic leukemia	Hypogammaglobulinemia	*S. pneumoniae, H. influenzae, N. meningitidis*
Acute myelocytic or lymphocytic leukemia	Granulocytopenia, skin and mucous-membrane lesions	Extracellular gram-positive and gram-negative bacteria, fungi
Hodgkin's disease	Abnormal T cell function	Intracellular pathogens (*Mycobacterium tuberculosis, Listeria, Salmonella, Cryptococcus, Mycobacterium avium*)
Non-Hodgkin's lymphoma and acute lymphocytic leukemia	Glucocorticoid chemotherapy, T and B cell dysfunction	*Pneumocystis carinii*
Colon and rectal tumors	Local abnormalities[a]	*Streptococcus bovis* (bacteremia)
Hairy cell leukemia	Abnormal T cell function	Intracellular pathogens (*M. tuberculosis, Listeria, Cryptococcus, M. avium*)

[a] The reason for this association is not well defined.
SOURCE: R Finberg: HPIM-15, p. 549.

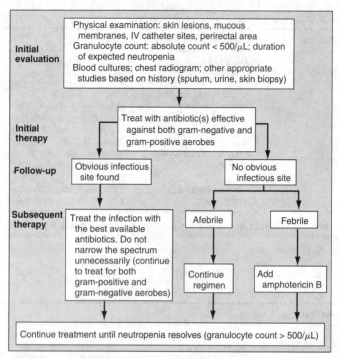

FIGURE 85-1 Diagnosis and treatment of febrile neutropenic pts: an algorithm. Several general guidelines are useful in the initial treatment of these pts: (1) It is necessary to use antibiotics active against both gram-negative and gram-positive bacteria in the initial regimen. (2) An aminoglycoside or an antibiotic without good activity against gram-positive organisms (e.g., cipro-floxacin) alone is not adequate in this setting. (3) The agents used should reflect both the epidemiology and the antibiotic resistance pattern of the hospital. For example, in hospitals where there is gentamicin resistance, amikacin-containing regimens should be considered; in hospitals with frequent *P. aeruginosa* infections, a regimen with the highest level of activity against this pathogen (such as tobramycin plus a semisynthetic penicillin) would be reasonable for initial therapy. (4) A single third-generation cephalosporin constitutes an appropriate initial regimen in many hospitals (if the pattern of resistance justifies its use). (5) Most standard regimens are designed for pts who have not previously received prophylactic antibiotics. The development of fever in a pt receiving antibiotics affects the choice of subsequent therapy (which should target resistant organisms and organisms known to cause infections in pts being treated with the antibiotics already administered). (6) Randomized trials have indicated that it is safe to use oral antibiotic regimens to treat "low-risk" pts with fever and neutropenia. Outpatients who are expected to remain neutropenic for <10 days and who have no concurrent medical problems (such as hypotension, pulmonary compromise, or abdominal pain) can be classified as low risk and treated with a broad-spectrum oral regimen. On the basis of large studies, it can be concluded that this therapy is safe and effective, at least when delivered in the inpatient setting. Outpatient treatment has been assessed in small studies, but data from large randomized trials demonstrating the safety of outpatient treatment of fever and neutropenia are not yet available. (*Adapted from R Finberg: HPIM-15, p. 552.*)

For a more detailed discussion, see Finberg R: Infections in Patients with Cancer, Chap. 85, p. 547; and Finberg R, Fingeroth J: Infections in Transplant Recipients, Chap. 136, p. 860, in HPIM-15.

86

HIV INFECTION AND AIDS

Definition

AIDS was originally defined empirically by the Centers for Disease Control and Prevention (CDC) as "the presence of a reliably diagnosed disease that is at least moderately indicative of an underlying defect in cell-mediated immunity." Following the recognition of the causative virus, HIV (formerly called HTLV-III/LAV), and the development of sensitive and specific tests for HIV infection, the definition of AIDS has undergone substantial revision. The current surveillance definition categorizes HIV-infected persons on the basis of clinical conditions associated with HIV infection and CD4+ T lymphocyte counts (Tables 309-1 and 309-2, p. 1852 and p. 1853, respectively, in HPIM-15). From a practical standpoint, the clinician should view HIV infection as a spectrum of disorders ranging from primary infection, with or without the acute HIV syndrome, to the asymptomatic infected state to advanced disease.

Etiology

AIDS is caused by infection with the human retroviruses HIV-1 or -2. HIV-1 is the most common cause worldwide; HIV-2 has about 40% sequence homology with HIV-1, is more closely related to simian immunodeficiency viruses, and has been identified predominantly in western Africa. HIV-2 infection has now, however, been reported in Europe, South America, Canada, and the United States. These viruses are passed through sexual contact; through contact with blood, blood products, or other bodily fluids (as in drug abusers who share contaminated intravenous needles); intrapartum or perinatally from mother to infant; or via breast milk. There is no evidence that the virus can be passed through casual or family contact or by insects such as mosquitoes. There is a definite, though small, occupational risk of infection for health care workers and laboratory personnel who work with HIV-infected specimens. The risk of transmission of HIV from an infected health care worker to his or her pts through invasive procedures is extremely low.

Epidemiology

By July 1, 1999, >702,745 cumulative cases of AIDS had been reported in the U.S.; ~60% of those had died. However, the death rate from AIDS has decreased substantially in the past 4 years primarily due to the increased use of potent antiretroviral drugs. It has been estimated that there are between 650,000 and 900,000 HIV-infected people in the U.S. Major risk groups continue to be men who have had sex with men and men and women injection drug users (IDUs); however, the number of cases that are transmitted heterosexually, particularly among women, is increasing rapidly (see Table 309-4; Figs. 309-12, p. 1861, and 309-13, p. 1862, in HPIM-15). These women also transmit the infection to their children. As the majority of IDU-associated cases are among inner-city minority populations, the burden of HIV infection and AIDS falls increasingly and disproportionately on minorities, especially in the cities of the Northeast and Southeast U.S. Cases of AIDS are still being found among individuals who have received contaminated blood products in the past, although the risk of acquiring new infection through this route is extremely small in the U.S. HIV infection/AIDS is a global pandemic, especially in developing countries. The current estimate of the number of cases of HIV infection worldwide is ~34 million, two-thirds of whom are in sub-Saharan Africa; 46% of cases are in women (Fig. 309-10, p. 1859, in HPIM-15).

Pathophysiology and Immunopathogenesis

The hallmark of HIV disease is a profound immunodeficiency resulting from a progressive quantitative and qualitative deficiency of the subset of T lymphocytes referred to as helper or inducer T cells. This subset of T cells is defined phenotypically by the expression on the cell surface of the CD4 molecule, which serves as the primary cellular receptor for HIV. A coreceptor must be present with CD4 for efficient entry of HIV-1 into target cells. The two major coreceptors for HIV-1 are CCR5 and CXCR4. Both of these receptors belong to the seven-transmembrane-domain G protein–coupled family of receptors. Although the CD4+ T lymphocyte and CD4+ monocyte lineage are the principal cellular targets of HIV, virtually any cell that expresses CD4 along with one of the coreceptors can potentially be infected by HIV.

PRIMARY INFECTION Following initial transmission, the virus infects CD4+ cells, probably T lymphocytes, monocytes, or bone marrow–derived dendritic cells. Both during this initial stage and later in infection, the lymphoid system is a major site for the establishment and propagation of HIV infection. Initially, lymph node architecture is preserved, but ultimately it is completely disrupted and the efficiency of the node in trapping virions declines, leading to equilibration of the viral burden between peripheral blood cells and lymph node cells.

Most pts undergo a viremic stage during primary infection, in some pts this is associated with the "acute retroviral syndrome," a mononucleosis-like illness. This phase is important in disseminating virus to lymphoid and other organs throughout the body, and it is ultimately contained partially by the development of an HIV-specific immune response and the trapping of virions in lymphoid tissue.

ESTABLISHMENT OF CHRONIC AND PERSISTENT INFECTION Despite the robust immune response that is mounted following primary infection, the virus, with very few exceptions, is not cleared from the body. Instead, a chronic infection develops that persists for a median time of 10 years before the patient becomes clinically ill. During this period of clinical latency, the number of CD4+ T cells gradually declines but few, if any, clinical findings are evident; however, active viral replication can almost always be detected by measurable plasma viremia and the demonstration of virus replication in lymphoid tissue. The level of steady-state viremia (referred to as the viral set point) at approximately 1 year postinfection has important prognostic implications for the progression of HIV disease; individuals with a low viral set point at 6 months to 1 year after infection progress to AIDS more slowly than those whose set point is very high at this time.

ADVANCED HIV DISEASE After some period of time (often years), CD4+ T cell counts will fall below some critical level (~200/μL) and pts become highly susceptible to opportunistic disease. However, control of plasma viremia by effective antiretroviral therapy, even in individuals with extremely low CD4+ T cell counts, has increased survival in these pts despite the fact that their CD4+ T cell counts may not increase significantly as a result of therapy.

Immune Abnormalities in HIV Disease

A broad range of immune abnormalities has been documented in HIV-infected pts. These include both quantitative and qualitative defects in lymphocyte, monocyte/macrophage, and natural killer (NK) cell function, as well as the development of autoimmune phenomena.

Immune Response to HIV Infection

Both humoral and cellular immune responses to HIV develop soon after primary infection (see summary in Table 309-8, and Fig. 309-21, p. 1875, in HPIM-15). Humoral responses include antibodies with HIV binding and neutralizing activity, as well as antibodies participating in antibody-dependent cellular cytotoxicity (ADCC). Cellular immune responses include the generation of HIV-specific CD4+ and CD8+ T lymphocytes, as well as NK cells and mononuclear cells mediating ADCC. CD8+ T lymphocytes may also suppress HIV replication in a noncytolytic, non-MHC restricted manner. This effect is mediated by soluble factors such as the β-chemokines RANTES, MIP-1α, and MIP-1β as well as other as-yet-unidentified factors secreted by CD8+ T lymphocytes.

Diagnosis of HIV Infection

Laboratory diagnosis of HIV infection depends on the demonstration of anti-HIV antibodies and/or the detection of HIV or one of its components.

The standard screening test for HIV infection is the detection of anti-HIV antibodies using an enzyme immunoassay (EIA). This test is highly sensitive (>99.5%) and is quite specific. Most commercial EIA kits are able to detect antibodies to both HIV-1 and -2. Western blot is the most commonly used confirmatory test and detects antibodies to HIV antigens of specific molecular weights. Antibodies to HIV begin to appear within 2 weeks of infection, and the period of time between initial infection and the development of detectable antibodies is rarely >3 months. The HIV p24 antigen can be measured using a capture assay, an EIA-type assay. Plasma p24 antigen levels rise during the first few weeks following infection, prior to the appearance of anti-HIV antibodies. A guideline for the use of these serologic tests in the diagnosis of HIV infection is depicted in Fig. 86-1.

HIV can be cultured directly from tissue, peripheral blood cells, or plasma, but this is most commonly done in a research setting. HIV genetic material can be detected using RT-PCR. This is a useful test in pts with a positive or indeterminate EIA and an indeterminate western blot or in pts in whom serologic testing may be unreliable (such as those with hypogammaglobulinemia).

Laboratory Monitoring of Patients with HIV Infection

Measurement of the CD4+ T cell count and level of plasma HIV RNA are important parts of the routine evaluation and monitoring of HIV-infected individuals. The CD4+ T cell count is a generally accepted indicator of the immunologic competence of the pt with HIV infection, and there is a close relationship between the CD4+ T cell count and the clinical manifestations of AIDS (Fig. 309-26, p. 1879, in HPIM-15). Pts with CD4+ T cell counts below <200/μL are at high risk of infection with *Pneumocystis carinii*, while pts with CD4+ T cell counts below <50/μL are at high risk for developing CMV disease and infection with *Mycobacterium avium-intracellulare*. While the CD4+ T cell count provides information on the current immunologic status of the pt, the HIV RNA level predicts what will happen to the CD4+ T cell count in the near future and hence predicts the clinical prognosis. Measurements of plasma HIV

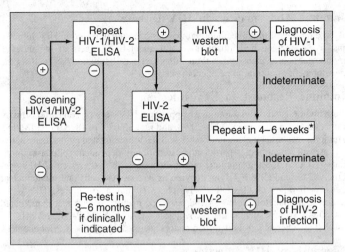

FIGURE 86-1   Algorithm for the use of serologic tests in the diagnosis of HIV-1 or HIV-2 infection. * Stable indeterminate western blot 4 to 6 weeks later makes HIV infection unlikely. However, it should be repeated twice at 3-month intervals to rule out HIV infection. Alternatively, one may test for HIV-1 p24 antigen on HIV RNA.

RNA levels should be made at the time of HIV diagnosis and every 3–4 months thereafter in the untreated pt. Measurement of plasma HIV RNA is also useful in making therapeutic decisions about antiretroviral therapy. A level of HIV RNA >20,000 copies/mL is felt by many experts to be an indication for initiation of antiretroviral therapy regardless of the CD4+ T cell count (see below). Following the initiation of therapy or any change in therapy, HIV RNA levels should be monitored approximately every 4 weeks until the effectiveness of the therapeutic regimen is determined by the development of a new steady-state level of HIV RNA. During therapy, levels of HIV RNA should be monitored every 3–4 months to evaluate the continuing effectiveness of therapy.

The sensitivity of an individual's HIV virus(es) to different antiretroviral agents can be tested by either genotypic or phenotypic assays. The clinical value of HIV resistance testing is still under investigation.

Clinical Manifestations of HIV Infection

A complete discussion is beyond the scope of this chapter. The major clinical features of the various stages of HIV infection are summarized below (see also Chap. 309, HPIM-15).

ACUTE HIV (RETROVIRAL) SYNDROME   Approximately 50 to 70% of infected individuals experience an acute syndrome following primary infection. Acute syndrome follows infection by 3 to 6 weeks. Characterized by fevers, rigors, arthralgias, myalgias, maculopapular rash, urticaria, abdominal cramps, diarrhea, and aseptic meningitis; lasts 1 to 2 weeks and resolves spontaneously as immune response to HIV develops. Most pts will then enter a phase of clinical latency, although an occasional pt will experience progressive immunologic and clinical deterioration.

ASYMPTOMATIC INFECTION   Length of time between infection and development of disease varies greatly, but the median is estimated to be 10 years. HIV disease with active viral replication usually progresses during this asymptomatic period, and CD4+ T cell counts fall. The rate of disease progression is directly correlated with plasma HIV RNA levels. Pts with high levels of HIV RNA progress to symptomatic disease faster than do those with low levels of HIV RNA.

SYMPTOMATIC DISEASE Symptoms of HIV disease can develop at any time during the course of HIV infection. In general, the spectrum of illness changes as the CD4+ T cell count declines. The more severe and life-threatening complications of HIV infection occur in patients with a CD4+ T cell count <200/µl. Approximately 80% of the deaths among AIDS pts are a direct result of infection other than HIV, with bacterial infections heading the list. Overall, the clinical spectrum of HIV disease is constantly changing as pts live longer and new and better approaches to treatment and prophylaxis of opportunistic infections are developed. The key element to treating symptomatic complications of HIV disease, whether primary or secondary, is achieving good control of HIV replication through the use of combination antiretroviral therapy and instituting primary and secondary prophylaxis as indicated. Major clinical syndromes seen in the symptomatic stage of HIV infection are summarized below.

* *Persistent generalized lymphadenopathy*: Palpable adenopathy at two or more extrainguinal sites that persists for >3 months without explanation other than HIV infection. Many pts will go on to disease progression.
* *Constitutional symptoms*: Fever persisting for more than 1 month, involuntary weight loss of more than 10% of baseline, diarrhea for longer than 1 month in absence of explainable cause.
* *Neurologic disease*: Most common is HIV encephalopathy (AIDS dementia complex); other neurologic complications include opportunistic infections, primary CNS lymphoma, CNS Kaposi's sarcoma, aseptic meningitis, myelopathy, peripheral neuropathy and myopathy.
* *Secondary infectious diseases*: P. carinii pneumonia is most common opportunistic infection, occurring in approximately ~80% of individuals during the course of their illness. Other common pathogens include CMV (chorioretinitis, colitis, pneumonitis, adrenalitis), *Candida albicans* (oral thrush, esophagitis), *M. avium-intracellulare* (localized or disseminated infection), *M. tuberculosis, Cryptococcus neoformans* (meningitis, disseminated disease), *Toxoplasma gondii* (encephalitis, intracerebral mass lesion), herpes simplex virus (severe mucocutaneous lesions, esophagitis), diarrhea due to *Cryptosporidium* spp. or *Isospora belli*, bacterial pathogens (especially in pediatric cases).
* *Secondary neoplasms*: Kaposi's sarcoma (cutaneous and visceral, more fulminant course than in non-HIV-infected pts), lymphoid neoplasms (especially B cell lymphomas of brain, marrow, GI tract).
* *Other diseases*: A variety of organ-specific syndromes can be seen in HIV-infected pts, either as primary manifestations of the HIV infection or as complications of treatment.

℞ **TREATMENT** (See Chap. 309, HPIM-15)
General principles of pt management include counseling, psychosocial support, and screening for infections and require comprehensive knowledge of the disease processes associated with HIV infection.

Antiretroviral Therapy (See Table 309-21 p. 1901, in HPIM-15)

The cornerstone of medical management of HIV infection is combination antiretroviral therapy, or HAART. Suppression of HIV replication is an important component in prolonging life as well as in improving the quality of life of pts with HIV infection. However, several important questions related to the treatment of HIV disease lack definitive answers. Among them are questions of when antiretroviral therapy should be started, what is the best HAART regimen, when should a given regimen be changed, and what drugs in a regimen should be changed when a change is made. The drugs that are currently licensed for the treatment of HIV infection are listed below. These drugs fall into two main categories: those that inhibit the viral reverse transcriptase enzyme and those that inhibit the viral protease enzyme. There are numerous drug-drug interactions that must be taken into consideration when using these medications (Table 309-22, p. 1994, in HPIM-15). One of the main problems that has been encountered with the widespread use of HAART regimens has been a syndrome of hyperlipidemia and fat distribution often referred to as *lipodystrophy syndrome* (Chap. 309, HPIM-15).

Nucleoside Analogues These should only be used in combination with other antiretroviral agents. The most common usage is together with another nucleoside analogue and a protease inhibitor (see below). *Zidovudine* (AZT, 3'-azido-2',3'-dideoxythymidine) is the prototype of these agents. The only indication for zidovudine monotherapy is the prophylaxis of maternal-fetal transmission of HIV when the mother herself does not require antiretroviral therapy based on the stage of her disease. Major toxicities are due to bone marrow suppression, especially anemia. Other toxicities include myopathy, cardiomyopathy, and lactic acidosis associated with hepatic steatosis. Standard dose is 200 mg 3 times daily.

Didanosine (ddI, 2',3'-dideoxyinosine) is the second drug to be approved for anti-HIV therapy. Major toxicities include painful sensory peripheral neuropathy and pancreatitis. Standard dose is 200 mg bid, for pts weighing >60 kg; 125 mg bid, for pts <60 kg.

Zalcitabine (ddC, 2',3'-dideoxycytidine) has toxicities similar to didanosine, although pancreatitis is not seen as frequently. Standard dose is 0.75 mg tid.

Stavudine (d4T, 2',3'-didehydro-3'-deoxythymidine) is antagonistic with zidovudine in vitro and possibly in vivo; hence, this combination should be avoided. The standard dose of stavudine is 40 mg bid, for pts weighing >60 kg; 30 mg bid, for pts <60 kg. Peripheral neuropathy is the predominant toxicity seen with this drug.

The combination of *lamivudine* (3TC, 2',3'-dideoxy-3'-thiacytidine), and zidovudine in vitro is the most potent nucleoside combination studied to date. The standard dose of lamivudine is 150 mg bid. Lamivudine is available either alone or in combination with zidovudine (Combivir). Although the main toxicities of lamivudine are peripheral neuropathy and pancreatitis, it is among the best tolerated of the nucleoside analogues.

Abacavir {(1S,*cis*)-4-[2-amino-6-(cyclopropylamino)-9H-purin-9-yl]-2-cyclopentene-1-methanol sulfate} is a synthetic analogue of the nucleoside guanosine. It is licensed to be used in combination with other antiretroviral drugs for the treatment of HIV infection. Hypersensitivity reactions have been reported in ~5% of pts treated with abacavir, and pts developing signs or symptoms such as fever, skin rash, fatigue, and GI symptoms should discontinue the drug and not restart it. Fatal hypersensitivity reactions have been reported with rechallange. Abacavir is available either alone or in a fixed-dose combination with zidovudine and lamivudine (Trizivir).

Nonnucleoside Reverse Transcriptase Inhibitors These agents interfere with the function of HIV-1 reverse transcriptase by binding to regions outside the active site and causing conformational changes in the enzyme that render it inactive. These agents are very potent; however, when they are used as monotherapy, they induce rapid emergence of drug-resistant mutants. Three members of this class, *nevirapine, delavirdine, and efavirenz* are currently available for clinical use. These drugs are licensed for use in combination with other antiretrovirals. The main toxicities of these drugs are maculopapular rash and elevations in hepatic enzymes levels. While it is possible to treat through the rash, it is important to be sure that one is not dealing with more severe eruptions (such as Stevens-Johnson syndrome), which are characterized by mucosal involvement, significant fever, or painful lesions with desquamation. Efavirenz therapy may be associated with CNS symptoms such as light-headedness, dizziness, or vivid dreams. These symptoms tend to abate after several weeks of therapy. The usual dose of delavirdine is 400 mg tid; for nevirapine it is 200 mg/d for 1 week, then 200 mg bid; for efavirenz it is 600 mg once a day at bedtime.

Protease Inhibitors   These drugs are potent and selective inhibitors of the HIV-1 protease enzyme and are active in the nanomolar range. Unfortunately, as in the case of the nonnucleoside reverse transcriptase inhibitors, this potency is accompanied by the rapid emergence of resistant isolates when these drugs are used as monotherapy. Thus, the protease inhibitors should be used only in combination with other antiretroviral drugs.

Saquinavir was the first protease inhibitor licensed; it is one of the better tolerated protease inhibitors. Initially marketed as a hard gel (Invirase) with poor bioavailability, the current soft-gel formulation (Fortavase) provides good plasma levels of drug. HIV resistance to protease inhibitors is quite complex, but it seems that strains of HIV resistant to saquinavir are generally not resistant to either ritonavir or indinavir (see below), suggesting that combination therapy with different protease inhibitors may be of value. This must be approached with caution, since saquinavir is metabolized by the cytochrome P450 system and ritonavir therapy results in inhibition of the P450 system. Thus, the use of both drugs together has the potential to result in unpredictable increases in saquinavir levels. The usual dose of saquinavir is 600 mg q8h (Invirase) or 1200 mg tid (Fortovase).

Ritonavir is the first protease inhibitor for which clinical efficacy was demonstrated. Strains of HIV resistant to ritonavir are also resistant to indinavir. The main side effects of ritonavir are nausea, abdominal pain, diarrhea, and circumoral paresthesia. These side effects can be reduced somewhat by initiating therapy at 300 mg bid and then rapidly escalating the dose over 5 to 7 days to the full dose of 600 mg bid. Ritonavir has a high affinity for certain isoforms of cytochrome P450, and thus it can produce large increases in the plasma levels of drugs that are metabolized by this enzyme. Among the agents affected in this manner are saquinavir, macrolide antibiotics, terfenadine, astemizole, warfarin, ondansetron, rifampin, most calcium channel blockers, glucocorticoids, sedative-hypnotics (alprazolam, diazepam, flurazepam, midazolam, and triazolam), and analgesics (fentanyl citrate, hydrocodone, oxycodone, methadone). Great care should be taken when prescribing additional drugs to pts receiving ritonavir. The use of low doses of ritonavir (100–200 mg bid) to provide pharmacodynamic boosting of other antiretroviral agents has become a fairly common strategy in HIV therapy.

Indinavir was the third protease inhibitor licensed. The usual dose is 800 mg q8h (1000 mg q8h with nevirapine or efavirenz; 400–600 mg q8h with delavirdine). HIV isolates that are resistant to indinavir show cross-resistance to ritonavir and varying degrees of cross-resistance to saquinavir. The main side effects of indinavir are nephrolithiasis and asymptomatic indirect hyperbilirubinemia. Indinavir is also metabolized by cytochrome P450, and coadministration of indinavir with any of the antihistamines, sedative-hypnotics, and analgesics listed above should be avoided. Levels of indinavir are decreased during concurrent therapy with rifampin and nevirapine and increased during concurrent therapy with ketoconazole and delavirdine. Dosages of indinavir should be appropriately modified in these situations. Rifampin should not be administered concurrently with indinavir or the other currently available protease inhibitors. Concurrent administration of indinavir with rifabutin results in a twofold increase in rifabutin levels; thus, the rifabutin dose should be decreased by one-half if given with indinavir.

Nelfinavir was approved in 1997, and *amprenavir* was approved in 1999 for the treatment of adult or pediatric HIV infection when antiretroviral therapy is warranted. At present, limited clinical data are available for these drugs. GI side effects are associated with both agents. The usual dose of nelfinavir is 750 mg tid; the dose of amprenavir is 1200 mg (8 large capsules) bid; 1200 mg tid if given with nevirapine or efavirenz

Lopinavir/ritonavir (Kaletra) is a coformulation of lopinavir, an inhibitor of HIV protease that is metabolized by cytochrome P450, and low-dose ritonavir, which inhibits cytochrome P450 and boosts lopinavir levels. Based on controlled and uncontrolled trials that demonstrated decreases in plasma HIV RNA and increases in CD4+ T cell counts, this drug was approved in 2000 for use in combination with other antiretroviral agents. The side effect profile is similar to that of ritonavir and nelfinavir. The usual adult dose is 400 mg (lopinavir)/100 mg (ritonavir) bid.

Choice of Antiretroviral Treatment Strategy

The large number of available antiretroviral agents coupled with a relative paucity of clinical end-point studies make the subject of antiretroviral therapy one of the more controversial in the management of HIV-infected pts.

The principles of therapy for HIV infection have been articulated by a panel sponsored by the U.S. Department of Health and Human Services and the Henry J. Kaiser Family Foundation (Table 86-1). Treatment decisions must take into account the fact that one is dealing with a chronic infection and that complete eradication of HIV infection is probably not possible with currently available HAART regimens. Thus, immediate treatment of HIV infection upon diagnosis may not be prudent, and therapeutic decisions must take into account the balance between risks and benefits. At present a reasonable course of action is to initiate antiretroviral therapy in anyone with the acute HIV syndrome; pts with symptomatic disease; pts with asymptomatic infection and CD4+ counts <500/µl or with >20,000 copies/mL of HIV RNA. In addition, one may wish to administer a 4-week course of therapy to uninfected individuals immediately following a high-risk exposure to HIV (see below).

When the decision to initiate therapy is made, the physician must decide which drugs to use in the initial regimen. The two options for initial therapy most commonly in use today are: two nucleoside analogues (one of which is usually lamivudine) combined with a protease inhibitor; or two nucleoside analogues and a nonnucleoside reverse transcriptase inhibitor. There are no clear data at present on which to base distinctions between these two approaches. Following the initiation of therapy, one should expect a 1-log (tenfold) reduction in plasma HIV RNA within 1–2 months and eventually a decline in plasma HIV RNA to <50 copies/mL. There should also be a rise in CD4+ T cell count of 100–150/µL. Many physicians feel that failure to achieve this endpoint is an indication for a change in therapy. Other reasons for changing therapy are listed in Table 86-2. When changing therapy because of treatment failure, it is important to attempt to provide a regimen with at least two new drugs. In the pt in whom a change is made for reasons of drug toxicity, a simple replacement of one drug is reasonable.

Treatment of Secondary Infections and Neoplasms

Specific for each infection and neoplasm (Chap. 309, in HPIM-15).

Prophylaxis against Secondary Infections (Table 309-11, p. 1881, in HPIM-15) Primary prophylaxis is clearly indicated for *P. carinii* pneumonia (especially when CD4+ T cell counts fall below to <200 cells/µL),

Table 86-1

Principles of Therapy of HIV Infection

1. Ongoing HIV replication leads to immune system damage and progression to AIDS.
2. Plasma HIV RNA levels indicate the magnitude of HIV replication and the rate of CD4+ T cell destruction. CD4+ T cell counts indicate the current level of competence of the immune system.
3. Rates of disease progression differ among individuals, and treatment decisions should be individualized based upon plasma HIV RNA levels and CD4+ T cell counts.
4. Maximal suppression of viral replication is a goal of therapy; the greater the suppression the less likely the appearance of drug-resistance quasi-species.
5. The most effective therapeutic strategies involve the simultaneous initiation of combinations of effective anti-HIV drugs with which the patient has not been previously treated and that are not cross-resistant with antiretroviral agents that patient has already received.
6. The antiretroviral drugs used in combination regimens should be used according to optimum schedules and dosages.
7. The number of available drugs is limited. Any decisions on antiretroviral therapy have a long-term impact on future options for the patient.
8. Women should receive optimal antiretroviral therapy regardless of pregnancy status.
9. The same principals apply to children and adults. The treatment of HIV-infected children involves unique pharmacologic, virologic, and immunologic considerations.
10. Compliance is an important part of ensuring maximal effect from a given regimen. The simpler the regimen, the easier it is for the patient to be compliant.

SOURCE: Modified from, *Principles of Therapy of HIV Infection*, USPHS and the Henry J. Kaiser Family Foundation.

Table 86-2

Indications for Changing Antiretroviral Therapy in Patients with HIV Infection[a]

Less than a 1-log drop in plasma HIV RNA by 4 weeks following the initiation of therapy
A reproducible significant increase (defined as 3-fold or greater) from the nadir of plasma HIV RNA level not attributable to intercurrent infection, vaccination, or test methodology
Persistently declining CD4+ T cell numbers
Clinical deterioration
Side effects

[a] Generally speaking, a change should involve the initiation of at least 2 drugs felt to be effective in the given patient. The exception to this is when change is being made to manage toxicity, in which case a single substitution is reasonable.
SOURCE: *Guidelines for the Use of Antiretroviral Agents in HIV-Infected Adults and Adolescents.*

M. avium complex infections, and *M. tuberculosis* infections in pts with a positive PPD or anergy if at high risk of TB. Vaccination with pneumococcal polysaccharide and *H. influenzae* type b vaccines is recommended. Secondary prophylaxis, when available, is indicated for virtually every infection experienced by HIV-infected pts.

HIV and the Health Care Worker

There is a small but definite risk to health care workers of acquiring HIV infection via needle stick exposures, large mucosal surface exposures, or exposure of open wounds to HIV-infected secretions or blood products. The risk of HIV transmission after a skin puncture by an object contaminated with blood from a person with documented HIV infection is ~0.3%, compared to 20–30% risk for hepatitis B infection from a similar incident. The role of antiretroviral agents in postexposure prophylaxis is still controversial. However, a U.S. Public Health Service working group has recommended that chemoprophylaxis be given as soon as possible after occupational exposure. While the precise regimen remains a subject of debate, the U.S. Public Health Service guidelines recommend (1) a combination of two nucleoside analogue reverse transcriptase inhibitors given for 4 weeks for routine exposures, or (2) a combination of two nucleoside analogue reverse transcriptase inhibitors plus a protease inhibitor given for 4 weeks for high-risk or otherwise complicated exposures. Most clinicians administer the latter regimen in all cases in which a decision to treat is made. Regardless of which regimen is used, treatment should be initiated as soon as possible after exposure.

Prevention of exposure is the best strategy and includes following universal precautions and proper handling of needles and other potentially contaminated objects.

Transmission of TB is another potential risk for all health care workers, including those dealing with HIV-infected pts. All workers should know their PPD status, which should be checked yearly.

Vaccines

Development of a safe and effective HIV vaccine is the object of active investigation at present. Extensive animal work is ongoing, and clinical trials of candidate vaccines have begun in humans.

Prevention

Education, counseling, and behavior modification remain the cornerstones of HIV prevention efforts. While abstinence is an absolute way to prevent sexual transmission, other strategies include "safe sex" practices such as use of condoms together with the spermatocide nonoxynol-9. Avoidance of shared needle use by IDUs is critical. If possible, breast feeding should be avoided by HIV-positive women, as the virus can be transmitted to infants via this route.

For a more detailed discussion, see Fauci AS, Lane HC: Human Immunodeficiency Virus (HIV) Disease: AIDS and Related Disorders, Chap. 309, p. 1852, in HPIM-15.

87

HOSPITAL-ACQUIRED INFECTIONS

Nosocomial infections are acquired during or as a result of hospitalization and generally manifest after 48 h of hospitalization.

Epidemiology

It is estimated that 5% of pts admitted to an acute-care hospital in the U.S. acquire a new infection; this estimate translates into about 2 million nosocomial infections per year, with an annual cost >$2 billion. The most common types of hospital-acquired infections are UTI, surgical wound infection, and pneumonia. Primary bacteremias, especially those associated with intravascular devices, have increased in frequency, as have infections in ICUs and those caused by antimicrobial-resistant pathogens.

Risk factors for the development of UTI include female sex, prolonged urinary catheterization, absence of systemic antibiotics, and inappropriate catheter care. Risk factors for surgical wound infection include presence of a drain, longer preoperative hospital stay, preoperative shaving of the field, longer duration of surgery, presence of an untreated remote infection, and higher-risk surgeon. An index for assessing the risk of wound infection has been developed, with risk factors including abdominal surgery, surgery lasting >2 h, contaminated or dirty-infected surgery (according to the classic classification system), and three or more diagnoses for one pt.

Risk factors for pneumonia include ICU stay, intubation, altered level of consciousness (esp. with a nasogastric tube in place), old age, chronic lung disease, prior surgery, and use of H_2 blockers or antacids. There are conflicting data on whether sucralfate (a medication that heals ulcers without altering gastric pH) decreases the risk of pneumonia in intubated pts. The major risk factors for the development of primary bacteremia are the presence of an indwelling intravascular device and hyperalimentation.

Clinical Manifestations and Diagnosis

DIFFERENTIAL DIAGNOSIS OF FEVER Other important infectious sources of new fever in a hospitalized pt include antibiotic-associated diarrhea usually caused by *Clostridium difficile*, decubitus ulcers, and sinusitis. Noninfectious sources of fever to consider include drugs (drug fever may occur with or without eosinophilia or rash), thrombophlebitis, pulmonary embolism, hematoma, pancreatitis, atelectasis, and acalculous cholecystitis.

WORKUP FOR NEW FEVER The workup of a hospitalized pt with new fever should include a thorough history directed at symptoms such as headache, cough, abdominal pain, diarrhea, flank pain, dysuria, urinary frequency, and leg pain. Features of the hospitalization, such as the presence of IV devices, use of a urinary catheter, performance of surgical procedures, and use of new medications, are all important items. The physical exam should pay particular attention to skin, lungs, abdomen (esp. the RUQ), costovertebral angles, surgical wounds, calves, and current or old IV sites. Laboratory tests for all febrile hospitalized pts should include CBC with differential, CXR, and blood and urine cultures. Other diagnostic tests to consider include LFTs; abdominal studies; routine aerobic cultures of sputum, stool, or other relevant body fluids; and testing of stool for *C. difficile* toxin in cases of diarrhea.

URINARY TRACT INFECTION Fever, dysuria, frequency, leukocytosis, and flank pain or costovertebral angle tenderness correlate well with bladder infection or pyelonephritis in pts who have had urinary catheters in place. In pts with fever alone, the finding of WBCs without epithelial cells in the urinary sediment or the detection of leukocyte esterase or nitrite on urinalysis is suggestive of UTI. A urine culture positive for a single organism in an asymptomatic hospitalized pt is not diagnostic of UTI.

SURGICAL WOUND INFECTION Erythema extending >2 cm beyond the margin of the wound, localized tenderness and induration, fluctuance, drainage of purulent material, and dehiscence of sutures are all findings suggestive of a wound infection. In pts with sternal wounds, ongoing fever or the development of rocking or instability of the sternum may indicate the need for surgical exploration of the wound.

PNEUMONIA In pts outside the ICU, pneumonia should be suspected in the setting of a new infiltrate on CXR, a new cough, fever, leukocytosis, and sputum production. In pts receiving intensive care, esp. those who are intubated, signs may be more subtle; purulent sputum and abnormal CXRs are common. A change in character or quantity of sputum in an intubated pt with fever, with or without accompanying CXR changes, is significant. Organisms of concern in nosocomial pneumonia are gram-negative aerobic bacilli—particularly *Pseudomonas aeruginosa, Klebsiella pneumoniae,* and *Enterobacter* spp.—and *Staphylococcus aureus.* Viruses such as respiratory syncytial virus and adenovirus are also important. Depending on the institution, pathogens such as methicillin-resistant *S. aureus, Stenotrophomonas maltophilia, Flavobacterium* spp., and even *Legionella* spp. may be of special concern.

BACTEREMIA AND INTRAVASCULAR DEVICE–RELATED INFECTION The only presenting symptom may be fever. The exit site of an existing or previous IV line should be evaluated for erythema, induration, tenderness, and/or purulent drainage. Organisms of particular concern include coagulase-negative staphylococci, *Candida* spp., *S. aureus,* and enterococci.

 TREATMENT

Therapy should be directed at the most likely cause of infection and, when possible, should be chosen on the basis of culture results. To reduce the rate of development of antibiotic-resistant infections, antibiotic courses should be kept as short as possible, with coverage as narrow as possible for the organism(s) involved. When an infection is known to be related to an intravascular device or when no other source of infection is apparent, the device should usually be removed and the catheter tip sent for quantitative culture. Whenever feasible, a new intravascular device should be inserted at a different site. Use of antiseptic- or antibiotic-impregnated devices should be considered.

Hospital Infection Control

Infection control departments determine the general and specific measures used to control infections. Cross-infection is particularly important, and hand washing is the single most important preventive measure in hospitals. Minimizing invasive procedures and vascular and bladder catheterizations to those that are absolutely necessary will also reduce rates of nosocomial infection. Standard precautions are designed for the care of all pts to reduce the risk of infection from both recognized and unrecognized sources. These precautions include the use of hand washing and gloves for all potential contacts with blood, body fluids, and mucous membranes. In some cases gowns, masks, and eye protection are also indicated. Three more specific sets of precautions are based on probable routes of transmission: droplet precautions (e.g., for untreated meningitis), airborne precautions (e.g., for suspected tuberculosis, with fulfillment of specific ventilation requirements), and contact precautions (e.g., for *C. difficile* diarrhea). Sets of precautions may be combined for diseases that have more than one route of transmission (e.g., varicella).

For a more detailed discussion, see Zaleznik DF: Hospital-Acquired and Intravascular Device–Related Infections, Chap. 135, p. 857; and Weinstein RA: Infection Control in the Hospital, Chap. 134, p. 853, in HPIM-15.

88

PNEUMOCOCCAL INFECTIONS

The pneumococcus (*Streptococcus pneumoniae*) is a gram-positive encapsulated coccus that colonizes the oropharynx and causes serious illness, including pneumonia, meningitis, and otitis media.

EPIDEMIOLOGY AND PATHOGENESIS

Pneumococci colonize the oropharynx of 5–10% of healthy adults and 20–40% of children. After colonization, protection is afforded by nonspecific immune mechanisms until type-specific antibody is produced. Otitis media, a common childhood illness, develops when inflamed mucosal surfaces impede clearance of the organisms from the inner ear. Pneumococci cause 40–50% of otitis media cases in which a causative agent is identified. Any perturbation in the normal defenses of the lower respiratory tract (e.g., depressed cough, alcohol intoxication, impaired ciliary activity, viral infection) may allow infection of the lungs with pneumococci. Impaired production of specific antibody by any mechanism (e.g., multiple myeloma, HIV infection) also predisposes to infection. Once a pneumococcal infection has been initiated, the absence of a spleen predisposes to fulminant disease. Certain populations, including Native Americans and Alaskans, appear to be unusually susceptible to invasive pneumococcal disease; this increased susceptibility probably has a genetic basis. Pneumococcal pneumonia occurs at an annual rate of 20 cases per 100,000 young adults and 280 cases per 100,000 individuals >70 years of age. Epidemic pneumococcal pneumonia may occur in crowded living conditions such as prisons or military barracks but does not generally occur in schools or workplaces. Of all cases of pneumococcal pneumonia, ~25% result in bacteremia. Bacteremia, with or without pneumonia, leads to pneumococcal infection at other sites, such as the joints, the meninges, or the cardiac valves.

PNEUMONIA

Pts frequently present with a preexisting respiratory illness that has worsened. Often the temperature rises to 38.9–39.4°C (102–103°F) and sputum production becomes prominent. The "classic" presentation with coryza, followed by the abrupt onset of a shaking chill and fever and cough productive of blood-tinged sputum, is not common. In the elderly the onset may be insidious. On physical exam, pts usually appear ill and anxious. Dullness to percussion is frequently found, and tubular breath sounds and fine crepitant rales may be heard. Without treatment, high fever and cough persist for 7–10 d, with subsequent defervescence. Most pts defervesce within 12–36 h of the initiation of therapy, but some take up to 4 d. The physical exam yields normal findings within 2–4 weeks, but the CXR may remain abnormal for 8–18 weeks. Pleural effusions, which are found in up to 50% of cases, are usually sterile, but empyema may occur in 2% of treated cases. Empyema can cause extensive pleural scarring if the fluid is not drained. Other complications include abdominal distention, herpes labialis, and abnormal LFTs or frank jaundice. Rarely, pts develop pericarditis, arthritis (esp. in children), endocarditis (see below), and paralytic ileus.

Gram's stain of sputum shows large numbers of PMNs and slightly elongated gram-positive cocci in pairs and chains. Culture is less sensitive than Gram's stain. Blood cultures are positive in ~25% of pts. The WBC count is usually >12,000/μL but may be low in overwhelming infection. In pts with asplenia or multiple myeloma and rarely in immunocompetent hosts, pneumococci may be seen in Wright's-stained buffy coat. CXR shows homogeneous density in an involved lobe or segment in one-fourth of cases, but abnormalities may be multilobar or atypical, especially with underlying pulmonary disease.

EXTRAPULMONARY INFECTION

MENINGITIS The pneumococcus is the leading cause of bacterial meningitis in adults (except during outbreaks due to the meningococcus). Because of the success of the *Haemophilus influenzae* vaccine, the pneumococcus is now the leading cause in children (except for neonates) as well. Pneumococcal meningitis may present as a primary disease; as a complication of pneumonia; by extension from otitis, mastoiditis, or sinusitis; or subsequent to a skull fracture with CSF leak. The CSF is a secondary site of infection in pneumococcal endocarditis. Pts present with sudden onset of fever, headache, and stiff neck, with progression to obtundation over 24–48 h in the absence of treatment. Physical exam reveals an acutely ill pt with nuchal rigidity. LP should be performed immediately except in cases with papilledema or focal neurologic findings. If LP is deferred for any reason, treatment should be started immediately. CSF findings include increased pressure, cloudiness, pleocytosis with a predominance of PMNs, increased protein level, and decreased glucose level. The Gram's stain is usually positive for bacteria. Although these methods have fallen out of favor, latex agglutination or counterimmunoelectrophoresis is positive in 80% of culture-positive cases and may be positive when culture is negative (e.g., in the presence of antibiotics). With appropriate therapy, 70% of pts recover.

ENDOCARDITIS Endocarditis is a rare complication of pneumococcal pneumonia. The clinical picture is one of acute bacterial endocarditis with fever, splenomegaly, loud murmurs, metastatic infections, and rapid destruction of previously normal heart valves (particularly the aortic valve), sometimes with the development of CHF. Blood cultures are uniformly positive in the absence of antibiotics.

PERITONITIS Pneumococcal peritonitis is a rare complication of transient pneumococcal bacteremia. Infection via the vagina and fallopian tubes may account for an increased incidence among adolescent girls and among women using intrauterine devices. The disease is also associated with cirrhosis, carcinoma of the liver, and nephrotic syndrome. Diagnosis is based on an elevated cell count and a positive culture of ascitic fluid. Blood cultures are often positive.

℞ TREATMENT

In the past, pneumococcal infection was uniformly susceptible to penicillin. During the past several years, however, resistance to penicillin as well as to many other antibiotics has emerged; by 1997 in the U.S., ~20% of isolates were intermediately susceptible to penicillin and 15% were resistant. Susceptibility testing should thus be routinely performed on all pneumococcal isolates, and empirical treatment should be guided by local patterns of susceptibility and the type of infection being treated. Susceptibility of a pneumococcal isolate varies with the site infected due to pharmacokinetic considerations.

Pneumonia Pts with pneumococcal pneumonia may be treated as outpatients if they are at low risk (as determined by PORT score, according to the criteria described by the Pneumonia Outcomes Research Team, HPIM-15, Chap. 255). However, if the physician is in doubt about the severity of illness, the social circumstances, or the likelihood of compliance with the prescribed antibiotic regimen, it may be best to hospitalize the pt, at least briefly.

For outpatient treatment, amoxicillin (500 mg PO q6h) is effective in all cases except those caused by the most highly penicillin-resistant isolates. One of the newer fluoroquinolones in an accepted dosage for pneumonia is likely to be highly effective (e.g., levofloxacin, 500 mg PO qd). Clindamycin (300 mg PO q8h) is active against >90% of strains that are susceptible or intermediately susceptible to penicillin. Doxycycline, azithromycin, or clarithromycin will be effective in 85–90% of cases. For inpatient therapy, an empirical regimen active against resistant pneumococci should be considered. This regimen can consist of cefotaxime (1–2 g IV q6–8h), ceftriaxone (1–2 g IV qd), or ampicillin (1–2 g IV q6h). A quinolone or azithromycin can be given parenterally or orally (with resistance at 10–15% and 1–2%, respectively). Vancomycin (1 g IV q12h) is uniformly effective against pneumococci and should be used as initial therapy if there is reason to suspect infection with a strain resistant to the drugs listed above. The optimal duration of therapy has not been established by controlled trial, but 3–5 days of observed therapy with IV antibiotics followed by oral antibiotics for a total duration of 5 afebrile days appears reasonable.

All pleural effusions should be aspirated for diagnosis and as a guide to therapy. Drainage by chest tube is indicated if pleural fluid has a pH of <7.1, contains frank pus, or contains bacteria visible on Gram's stain. Complete drainage should be confirmed by CT. Empyema complicates ~2% of pneumonia cases.

Meningitis Because this pneumococcal infection is the most life-threatening, empirical therapy should include vancomycin (1 g IV q12h) *and* a third-generation cephalosporin—either ceftriaxone (1–2 g IV q12h) or cefotaxime (2 g IV q6h)—pending the availability of susceptibility data. For isolates shown to be penicillin susceptible, treatment may continue with penicillin (4 million units IV q4h). For isolates with intermediate susceptibility to penicillin but susceptibility to the third-generation cephalosporins, vancomycin may be discontinued. The total duration of therapy is 10–14 days. The use of adjunctive glucocorticoids remains controversial. Pts with pneumococcal meningitis should be cared for initially in an ICU.

Endocarditis Treatment with vancomycin (1 g IV q12h) should be begun pending susceptibility information. Treatment may continue with a β-lactam antibiotic should the isolate prove susceptible. Pts with pneumococcal endocarditis should be cared for initially in an ICU. Surgical intervention may be mandated by valvular injury or myocardial abscess.

PREVENTION

The 23-valent pneumococcal vaccine (0.5 mL IM) should be given to all persons >65 years of age; those with cardiac, pulmonary, hepatic, or renal disease; those with diabetes, malignancy, asplenia, CSF leak, or HIV infection; and those >2 years of age with sickle cell disease. Revaccination is recommended after 5 years (esp. in persons over age 65 and in splenectomized pts).

A multivalent pneumococcal polysaccharide-protein conjugate vaccine was licensed in February 2000 for use in children.

For a more detailed discussion, see Musher DM: Pneumococcal Infections, Chap. 138, p. 882, in HPIM-15.

89

STAPHYLOCOCCAL INFECTIONS

The staphylococci are hardy and ubiquitous colonizers of human skin and mucous membranes. They cause a variety of syndromes, including superficial and deep pyogenic infections, systemic intoxications, and UTIs. Staphylococci are nonmotile, nonsporulating gram-positive cocci, 0.5–1.5 μm in diameter, that occur singly and in pairs, short chains, and irregular three-dimensional clusters. The more virulent staphylococci clot plasma ("coagulase-positive"), while the less virulent ones do not ("coagulase-negative"). Of coagulase-positive staphylococci, *S. aureus* is the only important human pathogen. Coagulase-negative staphylococci, especially *S. epidermidis*, adhere avidly to prosthetic materials and are increasingly important nosocomial pathogens. *S. saprophyticus*, another coagulase-negative species, is a common cause of UTIs.

STAPHYLOCOCCUS AUREUS
Epidemiology and Pathogenesis

Humans constitute the major reservoir of *S. aureus* in nature. The mucous membranes of the anterior nasopharynx are the principal site of carriage, with ~30% of healthy adults being colonized at any point in time.

S. aureus causes two types of syndromes: *intoxications* and *infections*. In intoxications, the manifestations of illness are attributable solely to the action of one or a few toxins. Infections involve bacterial colonization, invasion across epithelial or mucosal barriers, adherence, evasion of host defenses, and destruction of host tissues. Hosts at particular risk for staphylococcal infection include those with frequent or chronic disruptions in epithelial integrity, disordered leukocyte chemotaxis, phagocytes defective in oxidative killing, or indwelling foreign bodies. Pts with disorders of immunoglobulin or complement are also at increased risk of infection.

STAPHYLOCOCCAL INTOXICATIONS   *Toxic Shock Syndrome*

TSS is an acute, life-threatening intoxication characterized by fever, hypotension, rash, multiorgan dysfunction, and desquamation during the early convalescent period. Overt infection with *S. aureus* is not required; mere colonization with a toxigenic strain may suffice. TSS toxin 1 and staphylococcal enterotoxin B are responsible for virtually all cases. The reported incidence of TSS among menstruating women is 1 case per 100,000. About half of all cases are nonmenstrual and occur in individuals of both sexes. TSS is primarily a disease of the young but can affect all ages. Nonmenstrual TSS can ensue after superinfection of skin lesions of many types, including chemical or thermal burns, insect bites, varicella infections, and surgical wounds. Mortality is ~2.5% for menstrual TSS and ~6.4% for nonmenstrual TSS.

TSS is a clinically defined syndrome whose differential diagnosis is that of a severe febrile exanthem with hypotension. Other diagnoses to consider include streptococcal TSS, staphylococcal scalded skin syndrome, Kawasaki syndrome, Rocky Mountain spotted fever, leptospirosis, meningococcemia, gram-negative sepsis, exanthematous viral syndromes, and severe drug reactions. Staphylococcal and streptococcal TSS can be clinically indistinguishable. Recovery of *S. aureus* supports the diagnosis, as does demonstration of toxin production by the isolate and serologic susceptibility to the toxin.

 TREATMENT

Treatment of TSS involves drainage of the toxin production site, aggressive fluid resuscitation, and administration of antibiotics. Recent surgical wounds should be explored and irrigated. Pressors should be used for hypotension unresponsive to fluids. Electrolyte abnormalities must be corrected. Clindamycin (900 mg IV q8h) should be given either alone or with a β-lactam antibiotic [or vancomycin for pts perceived to be at risk for infection with methicillin-resistant *S. aureus* (MRSA)]. A 14-d course of therapy is reasonable, some of which may be oral. For severe illness or an undrainable focus of infection, immunoglobulin (a single dose of 400 mg/kg IV) should be given. The risk of recurrent menstrual illness can be assessed by testing for seroconversion to TSST-1: women who do not seroconvert after acute illness should refrain indefinitely from using tampons or barrier contraceptives.

Staphylococcal Scalded Skin Syndrome   SSSS encompasses a range of cutaneous diseases of varying severity caused by exfoliative toxin–producing strains of *S. aureus*. The most severe form is termed *Ritter's disease* in newborns and *toxic epidermal necrolysis* (TEN) in older subjects. TEN or Ritter's disease often begins with a nonspecific prodrome. The acute phase starts with an erythematous rash beginning in the periorbital and perioral areas and spreading to the trunk and limbs. The skin has a sandpaper texture and is often tender. Periorbital edema is common. In infants and children, fever and irritability or lethargy are common, but systemic toxicity is not. Within hours or days, wrinkling and sloughing of the epidermis begin; Nikolsky's sign is present. The denuded areas are red and glistening but not purulent. Exfoliation may continue in large sheets or in ragged snippets of tissue. Large flaccid bullae may develop. Significant fluid and electrolyte loss and secondary infection can occur at this stage. Within ~48 h, exfoliated areas dry and secondary desquamation begins. The entire illness resolves within ~10 d. Mortality (from hypovolemia or sepsis) is ~3% in children but up to 50% in adults.

TREATMENT

Treatment includes antistaphylococcal antibiotics, fluid and electrolyte management, and local care of denuded skin.

Staphylococcal Food Poisoning Staphylococcal food poisoning, caused by the ingestion of any of the enterotoxins produced by *S. aureus* in contaminated food before it is eaten, has a high attack rate and is most common during summer. This brief illness begins abruptly 2–6 h after ingestion of contaminated food, with nausea, vomiting, crampy abdominal pain, and diarrhea. The diarrhea is usually noninflammatory and is of lower volume than that in cholera or toxigenic *Escherichia coli* infection. Fever and rash are absent, and the pt is neurologically normal.

 TREATMENT

The majority of cases are self-limited and require no specific treatment.

STAPHYLOCOCCAL INFECTIONS *Skin and Soft Tissue Infections*
S. aureus is the most common etiologic agent of skin and soft tissue infections. Staphylococcal infections originating in hair follicles range in severity from trivial to life-threatening. *Folliculitis*, denoting infection of follicular ostia, presents as domed, yellow pustules with a narrow red margin. Infection is often self-limited, although healing may be hastened by topical antiseptics and more severe cases may benefit from topical or systemic antibiotics. A *furuncle* ("boil") reflects deep-seated necrotic infection of a hair follicle, most often located on the buttocks, face, or neck. Furuncles are painful and tender and are often accompanied by fever and constitutional symptoms. Surgical drainage and systemic antibiotics are frequently required. *Carbuncles* denote deep infection of a group of contiguous follicles. These painful necrotic lesions, commonly accompanied by high fever and malaise, occur most often on the back of the neck, shoulders, hips, and thighs, typically in middle-aged or elderly men. Surrounding and underlying connective tissue is intensely inflamed; bacteremia may be present. Surgical drainage and systemic antibiotics are indicated.

Cellulitis, a spreading infection of subcutaneous tissue, is occasionally caused by *S. aureus*. Although β-hemolytic streptococci are much more commonly responsible, secondary infection of surgical and traumatic wounds is more likely to be staphylococcal, and empirical treatment directed against both *S. aureus* and streptococci is reasonable.

Respiratory Tract Infections Staphylococcal pneumonia is a relatively uncommon but severe infection characterized clinically by chest pain, systemic toxicity, and dyspnea and pathologically by intense neutrophilic infiltration, necrosis, and abscess formation. It is typical in tracheally intubated hospitalized pts and after viral respiratory infection. The diagnosis is often readily established by Gram's staining of expectorated sputum. *Empyema* is a common sequela of staphylococcal pneumonia and increases the already considerable morbidity of this infection.

Hematogenous seeding of the lungs with *S. aureus* follows embolization from an intravascular nidus of infection. Common settings for septic pulmonary embolization are right-sided endocarditis, which is especially common among injection drug users, and septic thrombophlebitis, which is usually a complication of indwelling venous catheterization. CXR typically shows multiple nodular infiltrates.

Infections of the CNS   *S. aureus* is a major cause of *brain abscess*, especially as a result of embolization during left-sided endocarditis. Brain abscess can also develop by direct extension from frontoethmoid or sphenoid sinuses or from soft tissue.

S. aureus is the most common cause of *spinal epidural abscess*, most often in association with vertebral osteomyelitis or diskitis. While the diagnosis is suggested by fever, back pain, radicular pain, lower extremity weakness, bowel or bladder dysfunction, and leukocytosis, the presentation is often subtle (e.g., difficulty walking in the absence of objective findings). The principal danger is spinal cord necrosis, which must be recognized early if sequelae are to be averted. Spinal MRI detects an epidural collection, and needle aspiration or open drainage confirms the infectious etiology. Prompt surgical decompression is often required, although a trial of antibiotics alone may be considered if focal neurologic deficits are absent.

Endovascular Infections   *S. aureus* is the most common cause of acute bacterial *endocarditis* of both native and prosthetic valves. Staphylococcal endocarditis presents as an acute febrile illness, rarely of more than a few weeks' duration; complications include meningitis, brain or visceral abscess, peripheral embolization, valvular incompetence with heart failure, myocardial abscess, and purulent pericarditis. The diagnosis is suggested by a heart murmur and conjunctival hemorrhages, subungual petechiae, or purpuric lesions on the distal extremities. It is confirmed by multiple positive blood cultures and valvular vegetations on echocardiography. Evaluation for metastatic infection is often warranted. Staphylococcal endocarditis carries a mortality rate of ~40% and mandates prompt antimicrobial therapy. Indications for valve replacement are the same as for endocarditis caused by other organisms. Early consultation with a cardiothoracic surgeon is advisable; about half of pts require valve replacement—many urgently. Once removal of an infected valve is indicated, nothing is gained and much may be lost by delaying surgery. *S. aureus* infection of a prosthetic valve almost always requires surgery.

Right-sided endocarditis, most often a complication of injection drug use or venous catheterization, is frequently complicated in turn by septic pulmonary emboli but otherwise has a lower rate of serious complications than left-sided disease. Short-course parenteral therapy (2 weeks) may be curative, and the prognosis is relatively good. Surgery is rarely required.

S. aureus is the major cause of endovascular infections other than endocarditis. Vascular infection may follow hematogenous seeding of damaged vessels, resulting in development of a "mycotic aneurysm"; spread from a contiguous focus of infection, often resulting in an infected pseudoaneurysm; or contamination of an intravascular device, resulting in "septic phlebitis." Staphylococcal infection of an atherosclerotic artery, which may be aneurysmal to begin with, is potentially catastrophic. Such infections are associated with high-grade bacteremia, may result in rupture and massive hemorrhage, and are almost never curable without surgical resection and bypass of the infected vessel. Septic phlebitis is also associated with high-grade bacteremia and systemic toxicity but is less likely than arteritis to result in rupture. Persistent bacteremia suggests the need for surgical removal of infected thrombus or vein, but the technical difficulty of surgery may warrant an attempt at cure with antibiotics and anticoagulants alone.

Several criteria increase the probability that a pt has endocarditis as opposed to simple bacteremia: community-acquired (vs. nosocomial) infection, absence of an identifiable primary site of infection, and evidence of metastatic infection. Transesophageal echocardiography has demonstrated valvular abnormalities in up to one-fourth of bacteremic pts; this test should be performed in pts with persistent fever or bacteremia.

Musculoskeletal Infections   *S. aureus* is the most common cause of *acute osteomyelitis* in adults and one of the leading causes in children. Acute osteomyelitis results from either hematogenous seeding of bone, especially damaged bone, or direct extension from a contiguous focus of infection. The most common site of hematogenous staphylococcal osteomyelitis in adults is the vertebral bodies; in children, it is the highly vascular metaphyses of long bones. Acute osteomyelitis in adults usually presents with constitutional symptoms and pain over the affected area, often developing over weeks or months. The diagnosis may be subtle; leukocytosis and an elevated ESR or C-reactive protein level are laboratory clues. Bacteremia may or may not be demonstrable. Cure usually follows 4 weeks of parenteral antibiotics.

S. aureus is also a major cause of *chronic osteomyelitis*, which develops at sites of previous surgery, trauma, or devascularization.

A special form of osteomyelitis is that associated with prosthetic joints or orthopedic fixation devices. Pain, fever, swelling, and decreased range of motion are cardinal features of an infected prosthesis. A plain film may suggest loosening of the prosthesis, often as radiolucency at the interface between bone and cement. Cure with antibiotics alone is rare.

S. aureus is a prominent cause of *septic arthritis* in adults. Predisposing factors include injection drug use, rheumatoid arthritis, use of systemic or intraarticular steroids, penetrating trauma, and previous damage to joints. In addition to parenteral antibiotics, cure requires either repeated joint aspirations or open or arthroscopic debridement and drainage. Failure to drain joints adequately risks permanent loss of function.

S. aureus infections of muscle (*pyomyositis*) are relatively uncommon in the U.S. *Psoas abscess*, the major exception, is easily diagnosed by abdominal CT or MRI.

Diagnosis

S. aureus infection generally is readily diagnosed by isolation of the organism from purulent material or normally sterile body fluid. Gram's staining of purulent material from a staphylococcal abscess invariably reveals abundant neutrophils and intra- and extracellular gram-positive cocci—singly or in pairs, short chains, tetrads, or clusters. *S. aureus* grows readily on standard laboratory media. Rarely, if ever, should *S. aureus* growing from even a single blood culture be considered a contaminant. The diagnosis of staphylococcal intoxications (e.g., TSS) may be more difficult and may rely entirely on clinical data.

℞ TREATMENT

The essential elements of therapy for staphylococcal infections are drainage of purulent collections of pus, debridement of necrotic tissue, removal of foreign bodies, and administration of antibiotics. The importance of adequate drainage cannot be overemphasized. In skin and soft tissue infections, surgical drainage alone is occasionally curative. It is almost impossible to eradicate *S. aureus* infection in the presence of a foreign body.

Antimicrobial Resistance   Today, >90% of *S. aureus* strains are resistant to penicillin. In tertiary care institutions, MRSA isolates are increasingly prevalent and are resistant to the action of all β-lactam antibiotics and often to chloramphenicol, tetracyclines, and macrolides. In the last decade, community-acquired MRSA has been found in pts without apparent risk factors.

In 1996, the first vancomycin-intermediate *S. aureus* (VISA) strain, with decreased susceptibility to vancomycin, appeared. Vancomycin resistance is expressed in a heterogeneous manner, and VISA should be suspected in any pt for whom seemingly appropriate therapy with vancomycin is ineffective. Risk factors for VISA infection include a history of dialysis, multiple prior courses of antibiotic therapy, admission to the ICU, and prior infection with MRSA.

Selection of Antibiotics Nafcillin or oxacillin, β-lactamase-resistant penicillins, are the drugs of choice for parenteral treatment of serious staphylococcal infections. Penicillin remains the drug of choice for infections caused by susceptible organisms. Combinations of a penicillin plus a β-lactamase inhibitor are also effective but are best reserved for polymicrobial infections. Penicillin-allergic pts can usually be treated with a cephalosporin, although caution is essential if the adverse reaction to penicillin was anaphylaxis; first-generation agents (e.g., cefazolin) are preferred. For pts who are intolerant of all β-lactam agents, the best alternatives for parenteral administration are vancomycin and clindamycin. Dicloxacillin and cephalexin are recommended for oral administration for minor infections or for continuation therapy; clindamycin is an alternative for most strains. Routine use of quinolones is not recommended.

Vancomycin remains the drug of choice for treatment of infections caused by MRSA. Two new agents offer promise for treatment of MRSA infections, but further studies are needed before their routine use can be recommended: quinupristin/dalfopristin, a streptogramin combination, is bactericidal for *S. aureus*, and linezolid, an oxazolidone, is bacteriostatic but with only rare resistance. To date, all isolates of VISA have been susceptible to alternative agents.

There is usually no significant benefit to treating *S. aureus* infections with more than a single drug to which the organism is susceptible. An aminoglycoside/β-lactam combination hastens the sterilization of blood in endocarditis and is often used for the first 5–7 days of therapy for *S. aureus* bacteremia. Thereafter, the added toxicity of an aminoglycoside outweighs its benefit. Use of rifampin with a β-lactam antibiotic (or vancomycin) occasionally results in sterilization in otherwise refractory infections, particularly those involving foreign bodies or avascular tissue. Rifampin should never be administered as monotherapy because resistance emerges rapidly.

Route and Duration of Therapy To minimize seeding of secondary sites, bacteremic infections should be treated with high doses of antibiotics (e.g., 2 g of nafcillin IV q4h). For infections requiring high serum antibiotic levels for adequate tissue levels (e.g., endocarditis, osteomyelitis, infections of the CNS), parenteral therapy should be used for the duration. Oral agents may suffice for treatment of nonbacteremic infections in which high antibiotic levels are not requisite, such as skin, soft tissue, or upper respiratory tract infections.

Except for bacteremia and osteomyelitis, duration of therapy for *S. aureus* infections can be tailored to the severity of illness, the immunologic status of the host, and the response to therapy. Acute osteomyelitis in adults requires at least 4 weeks of parenteral therapy, with the actual duration depending on vascular supply at the site of infection and response to treatment. Chronic osteomyelitis is occasionally treated parenterally for 6–8 weeks and then orally for several months. Acute endocarditis and other endovascular infections should be treated with parenteral antibiotics for 4 weeks (6 weeks for prosthetic valves). Simple bacteremia requires shorter therapy, but a 2-week course of *parenteral* therapy is recommended *for all patients* with *S. aureus* bacteremia. A challenge in treating staphylococcal bacteremia is deciding whether to administer parenteral therapy for 2 or 4 weeks. A conservative approach supported by numerous studies dictates that *4 weeks* should be standard unless specific criteria are met (Fig. 89-1). For more information on antimicrobial therapy for *S. aureus* infections, please refer to Table 89-1.

Prevention and Control

Pts with exposed wounds and those with nasal colonization are important reservoirs of *S. aureus*, whose transmission can be reduced most effectively by meticulous hand washing before and after pt contact. More stringent infection control measures must be taken to prevent the nosocomial spread of resistant strains.

COAGULASE-NEGATIVE STAPHYLOCOCCI

Coagulase-negative staphylococci are a major cause of nosocomial infection and are the organisms most frequently isolated from the blood of hospitalized patients. Most such infections are indolent, are caused by strains resistant to multiple antibiotics, and are associated with a medical device of some kind, removal of which is usually required to effect cure.

CLINICAL SYNDROMES   Coagulase-negative staphylococci are the most common pathogens complicating the use of IV catheters, hemodialysis shunts and grafts, CSF shunts, peritoneal dialysis catheters, pacemaker wires and electrodes, prosthetic joints, vascular grafts, and prosthetic valves. Coagulase-negative staphylococcal infection of IV catheters may be accompanied by signs of inflammation at the site of insertion, and the degree of systemic toxicity (including fever) ranges from minimal to considerable. The diagnosis is established by culture of blood drawn from the catheter and by venipuncture. Infection of CSF shunts usually becomes evident within several weeks of implantation; malfunction of the shunt may be the only manifestation of infection. Infection of a prosthetic joint often becomes evident long after implantation.

Coagulase-negative staphylococci are a prominent cause of *bacteremia* in immunosuppressed pts. Those with neutropenia may have high-grade bacteremia resulting in significant systemic toxicity. A serious consequence of bacteremia is seeding of a secondary foreign body.

Coagulase-negative staphylococci are the foremost cause of *prosthetic valve endocarditis*, accounting for the majority of infections occurring within several months of implantation and for many late infections. They also cause <5% of cases of *native valve endocarditis*, usually affecting abnormal valves.

S. saprophyticus is a major cause of UTI, especially among sexually active young women. The syndrome, which is indistinguishable from that caused by other etiologic agents, is amenable to therapy with most drugs commonly used to treat UTIs.

DIAGNOSIS   Although coagulase-negative staphylococci are the most common cause of nosocomial bacteremia, they are also the most common contaminant of blood cultures. "True positives" are more likely when a clinical illness suggests infection, when an indwelling catheter or some other risk factor is involved, and when multiple cultures of blood drawn from separate sites yield organisms similar in phenotype and antimicrobial susceptibility pattern.

℞ TREATMENT

When coagulase-negative staphylococcal infection is related to a foreign body, removing the foreign body often constitutes adequate therapy. Most such infections require this measure, but cures of such infections with antibiotics alone have been reported. Infections of peritoneal dialysis catheters can be cured with antibiotics alone often enough that an attempt should be

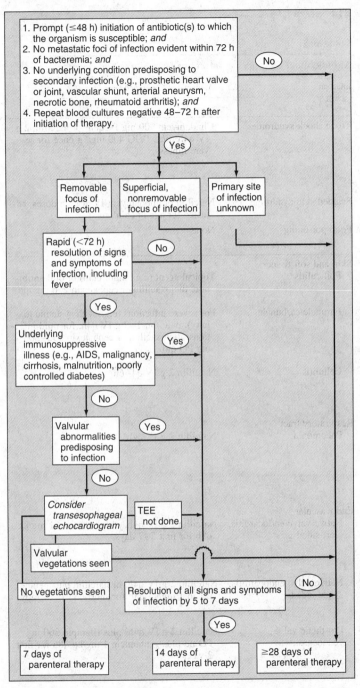

1. Prompt (≤48 h) initiation of antibiotic(s) to which the organism is susceptible; *and*
2. No metastatic foci of infection evident within 72 h of bacteremia; *and*
3. No underlying condition predisposing to secondary infection (e.g., prosthetic heart valve or joint, vascular shunt, arterial aneurysm, necrotic bone, rheumatoid arthritis); *and*
4. Repeat blood cultures negative 48–72 h after initiation of therapy.

No

Yes

Removable focus of infection

Superficial, nonremovable focus of infection

Primary site of infection unknown

Rapid (<72 h) resolution of signs and symptoms of infection, including fever

No

Yes

Underlying immunosuppressive illness (e.g., AIDS, malignancy, cirrhosis, malnutrition, poorly controlled diabetes)

Yes

No

Valvular abnormalities predisposing to infection

Yes

No

Consider transesophageal echocardiogram

TEE not done

Valvular vegetations seen

No vegetations seen

Resolution of all signs and symptoms of infection by 5 to 7 days

No

Yes

7 days of parenteral therapy

14 days of parenteral therapy

≥28 days of parenteral therapy

FIGURE 89-1 Factors to be considered in determining the duration of therapy for *S. aureus* bacteremia. (*Modified by Parsonnet and Deresiewicz from Fowler VG Jr et al: Outcome of Staphylococcus aureus bacteremia according to compliance with recommendations of infectious disease specialists: Experience with 244 patients. Clin Infect Dis 27:478, 1998.*)

413

Table 89-1

Antimicrobial Therapy for Infections Caused by *Staphylococcus aureus*

Infection	Antibiotic of Choice and Dose
INTOXICATIONS	
Toxic shock syndrome	Clindamycin 900 mg IV q8h[a] or nafcillin 2 g IV q4h[a] *plus* IVIG 400 mg/kg once for severe illness
Scalded skin syndrome	Nafcillin or clindamycin IV at high doses, adjusted for age in children
Food poisoning	None
INVASIVE INFECTIONS	
Skin and soft tissue Folliculitis	Topical agent (e.g., mupirocin) or oral antibiotic: dicloxacillin or cephalexin 250 mg qid
Furuncle/carbuncle	For severe infections (e.g., with systemic toxicity): nafcillin 1–2 g IV q4h; for mild infections: dicloxacillin or cephalexin 250–500 mg PO qid
Cellulitis	Nafcillin 2 g IV q4–6h
Respiratory tract Pneumonia	Nafcillin 2 g IV q4h[b]
Endovascular Native valve endocarditis, left-sided	Nafcillin 2 g IV q4h,[b] ± gentamicin 1 mg/kg q8h for first 5–7 days
Native valve endocarditis, right-sided	Nafcillin 2 g IV q4h; or nafcillin plus gentamicin 1 mg/kg q8h for short-course therapy
Prosthetic valve endocarditis	Nafcillin 2 g IV q4h[b] plus rifampin 300 mg PO tid plus gentamicin 1 mg/kg q8h for first 2 weeks

Alternative Agents	Duration of Therapy
Cefazolin 1 g IV q8h for penicillin-allergic patients (instead of nafcillin);[a] vancomycin 1 g IV q12h for suspected MRSA	Total of 14 days; conversion from IV to PO therapy after resolution of fever, hypotension, and GI symptoms; oral agents: dicloxacillin 500 mg qid, cephalexin 500 mg qid, clindamycin 300 mg qid
Cefazolin	Total of 10–14 days, parenteral followed by oral therapy
—	—
Clindamycin 150–300 mg PO tid, TMP-SMZ DS 1 tablet bid, tetracycline 250 mg qid	Until resolution of infection, often 5–7 days
Cefazolin 1 g IV q8h, clindamycin 600 mg IV q8h or 300 mg PO tid, vancomycin 1 g IV q12h (for severe penicillin allergy or suspected MRSA)	Until resolution of infection, often 7–10 days
Cefazolin 1 g IV q8h, clindamycin 600 mg IV q8h; vancomycin 1 g IV q12h for suspected infection with MRSA	Total of 10–14 days; conversion from IV to PO agent (as for TSS) after erythema and systemic symptoms have resolved
Cefazolin 1 g IV q8h[b] or cefuroxime 1.5 g IV q8h or clindamycin 900 mg IV q8h;[b] vancomycin 1 g IV q12h for suspected MRSA	Prolonged course of parenteral therapy, often 14–21 days, as dictated by severity of illness and response to therapy; longer course of therapy in pneumonia caused by hematogenous seeding of lung parenchyma
Cephalothin 2 g IV q4h or cefazolin 1 g IV q8h[b] (penicillin allergy) or vancomycin 1 g IV q12h (for MRSA or severe penicillin allergy), ± gentamicin	4 weeks of parenteral therapy
Cefazolin 1 g IV q8h or vancomycin 1 g IV q12h, plus gentamicin; ciprofloxacin 750 mg PO bid plus rifampin 300 mg PO bid	4 weeks of parenteral monotherapy or oral combination therapy; 2 weeks of combination parenteral therapy
Cephalothin 2 g IV q4h or cefazolin 1 g IV q8h,[b] or vancomycin 1 g IV q12h (as above) plus gentamicin, ± rifampin	6 weeks

(continued)

Table 89-1 *(Continued)*

Antimicrobial Therapy for Infections Caused by *Staphylococcus aureus*

Infection	Antibiotic of Choice and Dose
Endovascular *(cont.)*	
Simple bacteremia	Nafcillin 2 g IV q4h[b]
Complicated bacteremia	Nafcillin 2 g IV q4h[b]
Musculoskeletal	
Acute osteomyelitis	Nafcillin 2 g IV q4h
Chronic osteomyelitis	Nafcillin 2 g IV q4h, ± rifampin 300 mg PO bid
Septic arthritis, native joint	Nafcillin 2 g IV q4h
Septic arthritis, prosthetic joint	Nafcillin 2 g IV q4h; add rifampin 300 mg PO bid if retention of prosthesis is to be attempted

[a] Vancomycin 1 g IV q12h should be given in addition to the antibiotic listed as part of initial therapy when the risk of infection with MRSA is thought to be significant or in life-threatening illness; vancomycin should be discontinued when susceptibilities are known, as appropriate.

[b] Vancomycin may be substituted for the antibiotic shown when the risk of infection with MRSA is thought to be significant or in life-threatening illness; switch to alternative agent if possible when susceptibilities are known.

ABBREVIATIONS: IVIG, intravenous immunoglobulin; MRSA, methicillin-resistant *S. aureus*; TMP-SMZ, trimethoprim-sulfamethoxazole; DS, double-strength.

COMMENTS: A. Penicillin is the β-lactam antibiotic of choice for strains of *S. aureus* that are shown to be susceptible. Penicillin should not be used before results of sensitivity testing are known, however, because of the high prevalence of resistance.

made to do so. Coagulase-negative staphylococcal infections of central venous catheters are also amenable to medical therapy, although relapses are common. Persistent bacteremia during therapy is an absolute indication for removing a catheter, and bacteremia after a catheter's removal suggests seeding of a secondary site.

Most strains of coagulase-negative staphylococci isolated from pts in U.S. hospitals are resistant not only to penicillin but also to penicillinase-resistant penicillins and cephalosporins. Nosocomial isolates are usually resistant to other classes of antibiotics as well. Vancomycin, to which the vast majority of coagulase-negative staphylococci remain susceptible, is by necessity the drug of choice for *empirical* treatment of serious infections caused by these organisms. Strains proven to be susceptible to nafcillin (oxacillin) or penicillin should be treated with one of these agents or with a first-generation cephalosporin.

Synergistic antibiotic combinations are often useful. Rifampin plays a unique and important role by virtue of its potency against most staphylococci, its excellent penetration into tissues (including those that are poorly vascularized), and its high levels within human cells and biofilm. Unfortunately,

Alternative Agents	Duration of Therapy
Cefazolin 1 g IV q8h or vancomycin 1 g IV q12h (as above)	14 days of parenteral therapy; 7 days probably adequate under some circumstances
Cefazolin 1 g IV q8h or vancomycin 1 g IV q12h (as above)	4 weeks of parenteral therapy
Cefazolin 1 g IV q8h, clindamycin 900 mg IV q8h, or vancomycin 1 g IV q12h (for MRSA)	4 weeks of parenteral therapy
Cefazolin 1 g IV q8h, clindamycin 900 mg IV q8h, or vancomycin 1 g IV q12h (for MRSA), ± rifampin	6 to 8 weeks of parenteral therapy, often followed by several months of oral therapy (dicloxacillin or cephalexin 500 mg qid, clindamycin 300 mg qid, TMP-SMZ DS 1 tablet bid)
Cefazolin 1 g IV q8h or vancomycin 1 g IV q12h (for severe penicillin allergy or MRSA)	At least 3 weeks of parenteral therapy, as indicated by cultures and clinical course
Cefazolin 1 g IV q8h or vancomycin 1 g IV q12h (for severe penicillin allergy or MRSA)	4 weeks

B. Patients with a history of hypersensitivity reactions to penicillin *other than anaphylaxis* may generally be treated with cephalosporins. Patients with a history of anaphylaxis to penicillin should be treated with non-β-lactam agents until hypersensitivity testing can be performed.
C. Oxacillin may be substituted for nafcillin, at the same dosages, for all indications.
D. Additional agents with excellent antistaphylococcal activity in vitro are linezolid (available in peroral and parenteral formulations), quinupristin/dalfopristin (parenteral only), and new quinolones. Until additional experience is gained with these agents, however, they should be reserved for situations in which antibiotics with established efficacies cannot be used for reasons of tolerability or antimicrobial resistance.
SOURCE: Adapted from J Parsonnet, RL Deresiewicz: HPIM-15, p. 898–899.

rifampin must be used with other antibiotics because of frequent and rapid emergence of microbial resistance during monotherapy. The concomitant use of a β-lactam antibiotic to which the organism is susceptible plus rifampin (300 mg PO bid) plus an aminoglycoside (usually gentamicin) affords the best chance for eradication of infection of a medical device without its removal. Vancomycin is substituted for the β-lactam if so dictated by an organism's susceptibility pattern or a pt's drug allergy.

For a more detailed discussion, see Parsonnet J, Deresiewicz RL: Staphylococcal Infections, Chap. 139, p. 889, in HPIM-15.

90

STREPTOCOCCAL/ENTEROCOCCAL INFECTIONS AND DIPHTHERIA

STREPTOCOCCAL INFECTIONS
Group A *Streptococcus* (*S. pyogenes*)

Streptococci of group A commonly cause pharyngitis as well as skin and soft tissue infection; they less often cause pneumonia, puerperal sepsis, and the post-infectious complications of acute rheumatic fever (ARF) and acute glomerulo-nephritis (AGN). Streptococci possess many virulence factors, including anti-phagocytic M proteins and a hyaluronic acid capsule, as well as a variety of extracellular toxins and enzymes, including pyrogenic toxins, streptolysins, streptokinase, and DNases.

PHARYNGITIS Streptococcal pharyngitis is a common infection among children over age 3; streptococci account for 20–40% of all cases of exudative pharyngitis in children. This infection usually spreads from person to person via respiratory droplets, although other routes, including food-borne outbreaks, have been described. After an incubation period of 1–4 d, pts develop sore throat, fever, chills, and malaise and sometimes abdominal symptoms and vomiting. Both symptoms and signs are quite variable, ranging from mild with minimal findings to severe with markedly enlarged tonsils; a purulent exudate over the tonsils and posterior pharyngeal wall; and tender, enlarged cervical lymph nodes. The usual course of uncomplicated streptococcal pharyngitis lasts 3–5 d.

Scarlet fever, a group A streptococcal infection, usually takes the form of pharyngitis accompanied by a characteristic rash. In the past this infection was thought to occur in hosts who were not immune to one of the streptococcal pyrogenic exotoxins (A, B, or C). More recent studies suggest that the rash may be due to a hypersensitivity reaction requiring prior exposure to the toxin. The rash typically develops within 2 d of the sore throat; it begins on the neck, upper chest, and back and then spreads over the remainder of the body, sparing the palms and soles. This diffuse, blanching erythema with 1- to 2-mm punctate elevations has a "sandpaper" texture and is most intense along skin folds (Pastia's lines). Circumoral pallor and a "strawberry tongue" (enlarged papillae on a coated tongue, which later becomes denuded) frequently accompany the rash. The rash subsides after 6–9 d and is followed by desquamation of the palms and soles.

Suppurative complications of streptococcal pharyngitis, uncommon since the widespread use of antibiotics, include acute otitis media, sinusitis, cervical lymphadenitis, peritonsillar or retropharyngeal abscess, meningitis, pneumonia, bacteremia and endocarditis. The most feared complications are the late non-suppurative complications. ARF is a rare but serious disease that follows strep-tococcal pharyngitis. AGN (Chap. 142) may follow either pharyngitis or skin infection.

Diagnosis Clinical criteria alone are unreliable for the diagnosis of strep-tococcal pharyngitis. Throat culture remains the "gold standard." Rapid diag-nostic kits are useful if the result is positive; however, because of low sensitivity, a negative result must be confirmed with a throat culture. Serologic tests such as antistreptolysin O confirm past infection in pts with suspected ARF or AGN but are not useful for the diagnosis of pharyngitis.

℞ TREATMENT

Treatment is given mainly to prevent ARF and must be started within 9 d of onset (Table 90-1).

SKIN AND SOFT TISSUE INFECTION   *Impetigo (Pyoderma)*   Impetigo is a localized purulent skin infection that occurs predominantly in young children living in warm climates under conditions of poor hygiene. The usual sites of involvement are the face and lower extremities. Minor trauma may serve to inoculate the organisms into the skin. While it is usually due to group A streptococci, impetigo is occasionally caused by other streptococci or by *Staphylococcus aureus*. Papules become vesicular, with surrounding erythema, and form thick, honey-like crusts over 4–6 d. This infection is diagnosed by culture of the base of the lesion. Impetigo is not associated with ARF but frequently precedes AGN.

℞ TREATMENT

Agents active against both streptococci and *S. aureus* provide the most reliable therapy for impetigo. These drugs include dicloxacillin (500 mg PO qid), cephalexin (500 mg PO qid), and topical mupirocin ointment. If the infection is known to be due to group A streptococci, the regimens used for pharyngitis (Table 90-1) are cheaper and equally effective.

Cellulitis   Cellulitis, an infection of the skin and SC tissue, is caused by group A streptococci or *S. aureus*. The involved area is red, warm, and tender; fever and systemic symptoms often develop, and regional lymphadenopathy may be documented. Erysipelas is a form of cellulitis caused almost exclusively

Table 90-1

Treatment of Group A Streptococcal Infections

Infection	Treatment[a]
Pharyngitis	Benzathine penicillin G, 1.2 million U IM; or penicillin V, 250 mg PO qid × 10 d (Children <27 kg: Benzathine penicillin G, 600,000 U IM; or penicillin V, 125 mg PO qid × 10 d)
Impetigo	Same as pharyngitis
Erysipelas/cellulitis	Severe: Penicillin G, 1–2 million U IV q4h Mild to moderate: Procaine penicillin, 1.2 million U IM bid
Necrotizing fasciitis/myositis	Surgical debridement plus penicillin G, 2–4 million U IV q4h
Pneumonia/empyema	Penicillin G, 2–4 million U IV q4h, plus drainage of empyema

[a] Penicillin allergy: Erythromycin (10 mg/kg PO qid up to a maximum of 250 mg/dose) may be substituted for oral penicillin. Alternative agents for parenteral therapy include first-generation cephalosporins—if the penicillin allergy does not manifest as immediate hypersensitivity (anaphylaxis or urticaria) or as another potentially life-threatening reaction (e.g., severe rash and fever)—and vancomycin.
SOURCE: MR Wessels: HPIM-15, p. 903.

by group A streptococci and occasionally by group C or G organisms. It typically involves the face or lower extremities. There is an acute onset of pain and of a raised plateau of redness (formed by engorgement of lymphatic tissue) that is sharply demarcated from normal skin. Erysipelas may be associated with high fever and bacteremia.

 TREATMENT

Agents active against both streptococci and *S. aureus* provide the most reliable therapy for cellulitis. Therapy is initiated with oxacillin (2 g IV q4h) or cefazolin (2 g IV q8h); if the pt is allergic to penicillin or if methicillin-resistant *S. aureus* infection is suspected, vancomycin (1 g IV q12h) is used. If the infection is known to be due to group A streptococci, penicillin is preferred (Table 90-1).

Necrotizing Fasciitis   A rapidly life-threatening infection of the superficial or deep fascia, necrotizing fasciitis is caused by group A streptococci in 60% of cases. (Other cases, particularly those related to an abdominal or peritoneal process or surgery, are caused by bowel flora.) The onset of symptoms is acute and is marked by severe pain at the site of infection, malaise, fever, chills, and a toxic appearance. As the process evolves (often quite rapidly), skin changes become increasingly apparent, with dusky or mottled erythema; edema and anesthesia of the involved area may be noted. Surgical exploration is required both for confirmation of the diagnosis and for treatment. While antibiotic *therapy* (Table 90-1) is adjunctive, surgical debridement and resection are lifesaving.

PNEUMONIA AND EMPYEMA   Group A streptococci occasionally cause pneumonia, generally in previously healthy individuals. Pleuritic chest pain, fever, chills, and dyspnea are characteristic presenting symptoms, with either an abrupt or a gradual onset. Streptococcal pneumonia is accompanied by pleural effusion in 50% of cases, and the effusion is almost always infected. *Treatment* should include antibiotics and early drainage of the empyema (Table 90-1).

BACTEREMIA, PUERPERAL SEPSIS, AND STREPTOCOCCAL TOXIC SHOCK–LIKE SYNDROME   Bacteremia may complicate an identifiable local infection, particularly cellulitis, pneumonia, or necrotizing fasciitis. In the absence of a focus, evaluation for endocarditis, abscess, or osteomyelitis should be pursued. Occasionally, group A streptococci still cause endometritis and bacteremia complicating childbirth. Outbreaks of these infections have been associated with asymptomatic carriage of group A streptococci by delivery room personnel.

A toxic shock–like syndrome (see Table 140-3 in HPIM-15 for proposed case definition) has been described in association with group A streptococcal infections, especially necrotizing fasciitis, cellulitis, and myositis. This syndrome manifests as fever, hypotension, and multisystem organ failure and is associated with 30% mortality. In contrast to staphylococcal toxic shock syndrome, the streptococcal syndrome is usually characterized by the lack of a rash and by positive blood cultures.

 TREATMENT

Treatment of these infections requires aggressive supportive care, surgical debridement of involved local sites, and antibiotic administration. Data from experimental animals suggest that clindamycin (600 mg IV q6h) might be more effective than β-lactam antibiotics; however, there are currently no data on the treatment of humans with this regimen. Although clindamycin resistance in group A streptococci is uncommon, it has been documented. If clindamycin is used for initial treatment of a critically ill pt, penicillin (2–4 million U IV q4h) should be given as well until antibiotic susceptibility data are available for the isolate. The IV administration of immune globulin preparations has been used adjunctively in the treatment of streptococcal toxic shock syndrome, but no relevant controlled trials have been performed.

Groups C and G Streptococci

Streptococci of groups C and G cause infections similar to those caused by group A streptococci, including pharyngitis, bacteremia, pneumonia, cellulitis, soft tissue infection, septic arthritis, and endocarditis. Bacteremia involving these organisms tends to occur in elderly, debilitated, or chronically ill pts.

 TREATMENT

Appropriate therapy for adult infection consists of high-dose penicillin (18 million U/d) and aspiration or open debridement of infected joint spaces; for endocarditis or septic arthritis, gentamicin (1 mg/kg q8h) is added for synergy.

Group B *Streptococcus* (GBS)

NEONATAL INFECTIONS   GBS is the most frequent cause of neonatal sepsis and meningitis, with an incidence of 0.5–2 per 1000 births. (*Escherichia coli* is the second most frequent cause.) Early-onset infections become evident within 7 d of birth, with signs often present at birth. The infants involved most often present with respiratory distress, lethargy, and hypotension. Almost all are bacteremic, one-third to one-half have pneumonia or respiratory distress syndrome, and one-third have meningitis. Late-onset disease occurs between 1 week and 3 months after birth; generally presents as meningitis, occasionally with other focal infections or bacteremia; and is associated with a lower mortality rate than early-onset disease. Many meningitis survivors have neurologic sequelae. Infants with suspected neonatal sepsis should be treated with high-dose penicillin and gentamicin; penicillin may be given alone once GBS has been identified as the causative organism. Between 5 and 40% of women are identified by antenatal culture as carriers of GBS in the vagina or rectum. The CDC has suggested two strategies for the prevention of GBS infection in neonates. *(1) Prenatal screening–based approach:* Women are screened for colonization by swab culture of the lower vagina and rectum at 35–37 weeks of gestation. Intrapartum chemoprophylaxis should be *offered* to all carriers and is *recommended* for women with any risk factor (preterm delivery, rupture of membranes >24 h before delivery, prolonged labor, fever, chorioamnionitis, multiple gestation, or prior birth of an infant with GBS infection). *(2) Risk factor–based approach:* No screening is performed and intrapartum prophylaxis is recommended for all women with one or more of the risk factors just mentioned. The recommended regimen for prophylaxis is penicillin G (5 million U IV followed by 2.5 million U q4h until delivery), with clindamycin or erythromycin substituted in women who are allergic to penicillin.

ADULT INFECTIONS   Peripartum infections are the most common GBS infections in adults. The organism may cause puerperal sepsis, endometritis, or chorioamnionitis. Bacteremic cases may be complicated by meningitis or endocarditis. Other adult infections involve the elderly or those with other underlying conditions, such as diabetes mellitus or malignancy. These GBS infections include UTIs, diabetic skin ulcers, pneumonia, endocarditis, septic arthritis, intraabdominal abscesses, and osteomyelitis.

 TREATMENT

Appropriate treatment consists of penicillin G (12 million U/d IV). Meningitis and endocarditis should be treated with even higher doses (18–24 million U/ d IV in divided doses). Vancomycin (1 g IV q12h) may be substituted for penicillin in cases of allergy.

Group D *Streptococcus*

S. bovis is the main human pathogen among group D streptococci. Endocarditis due to *S. bovis* is associated with neoplasms and other lesions of the GI tract. In contrast to enterococci, *S. bovis* is highly susceptible to penicillin, which is the drug of choice for the infections it causes.

Viridans Streptococci

The viridans streptococci include multiple species of α-hemolytic streptococci. These organisms are part of the normal mouth flora and are the most frequent causative agents of bacterial endocarditis. Viridans streptococcal endocarditis may be treated with penicillin (12 million U/d). Occasional isolates characterized as nutritional variants (reclassified as *Abiotrophia*) require vitamin B_6 for growth; against these isolates, gentamicin (1 mg/kg q8h) should be added for optimal coverage. The organisms of the *S. milleri* or *S. intermedius* group (*S. intermedius, S. anginosus,* and *S. constellatus*) are usually considered viridans streptococci but may be β-hemolytic and often cause suppurative infections such as intraabdominal or brain abscesses. These organisms are sensitive to penicillin, which is the drug of choice for treatment of the infections they cause. Viridans streptococcal bacteremia occurs with relatively high frequency among neutropenic pts with cancer and may cause a sepsis syndrome with high fever and shock. Risk factors include profound neutropenia, antibiotic prophylaxis with TMP-SMZ or fluoroquinolones, mucositis, and antacid/histamine antagonist therapy. In this setting, viridans streptococci are more commonly resistant to penicillin, and the infections they cause should be treated empirically with vancomycin (1 g IV q12h) pending susceptibility testing.

ENTEROCOCCAL INFECTIONS

Previously classified as group D streptococci, enterococci are now recognized as a separate genus. Enterococcal infections tend to occur in pts who are elderly or debilitated or whose mucosal or skin barriers have been disrupted. Enterococci also cause superinfections in antibiotic-treated pts. Enterococcal infections most commonly involve the urinary tract, particularly in pts with anatomic abnormalities and in those who have undergone instrumentation. Enterococci account for 10–20% of cases of bacterial endocarditis. The presentation of enterococcal endocarditis is usually subacute but may also be acute with valvular destruction. Enterococci are frequently isolated from the biliary tract and may cause infections related to biliary surgery. Moreover, these organisms are often recovered in mixed infections from intraabdominal abscesses, surgical wounds, and diabetic foot ulcers.

℞ TREATMENT

While it is not always necessary to direct antimicrobial therapy at enterococci in mixed infections, these organisms should be covered by treatment when they are predominant or when they are present in blood cultures. Ampicillin (2 g IV q4h) is usually sufficient for the treatment of uncomplicated UTI. However, other types of enterococcal infection require penicillin or ampicillin and the addition of an aminoglycoside, usually gentamicin (1 mg/kg IV q8h with normal renal function), for synergy. Vancomycin (1 g q12h) may be substituted for penicillin in penicillin-allergic pts. Because of the increasing incidence of antibiotic resistance in enterococci (especially *E. faecium*), susceptibility testing should be performed for all isolates causing serious infections. Strains with high-level gentamicin resistance may be susceptible to other aminoglycosides or may respond to ampicillin alone. Infections due to enterococci that are resistant to penicillins on the basis of β-lactamase production may be treated with vancomycin, ampicillin/sulbactam, amoxicillin/clavulanate, or imipenem in combination with an aminoglycoside. Moderately resistant enterococci (MIC of penicillin and ampicillin, 16–64 μg/mL) may be susceptible to high-dose penicillin or ampicillin in combination with gentamicin, but strains with MICs of $\geq$200 μg/mL require treatment with vancomycin and gentamicin. Vancomycin-resistant enterococci, first reported in the late 1980s, have become common pathogens in many hospitals. For isolates resistant to both vancomycin and β-lactam antibiotics, there are no established therapies. Regimens that have been tried with some success include combinations such as ciprofloxacin/rifampin/gentamicin or ampicillin/vancomycin as well as chloramphenicol or tetracycline (if the strain is susceptible in vitro). Quinupristin/dalfopristin (Synercid) is a streptogramin with in vitro activity against *E. faecium*, including vancomycin-resistant isolates.

OUTPATIENT/HOME CARE CONSIDERATIONS

Persons with group A streptococcal pharyngitis and impetigo may be treated as outpatients with oral antibiotics. More serious infections, including cellulitis, mandate hospitalization and parenteral antibiotic therapy. Pts who exhibit a good response to parenteral antibiotic therapy (including resolution of signs of acute inflammation) may be switched to an oral regimen and complete their therapy as outpatients. Once their condition has stabilized, their fever has resolved, and their bacteremia has cleared, pts with viridans streptococcal endocarditis who show no signs of complications (such as embolization, heart block, or valvular failure) may complete their parenteral antibiotic therapy at home when this alternative is logistically feasible.

DIPHTHERIA

Diphtheria is a localized infection of mucous membranes or skin caused by *Corynebacterium diphtheriae*. Its incidence is increased among alcoholics, persons in lower socioeconomic groups, and Native Americans as well as under conditions of crowding. Its usual method of spread is by droplet. After an incubation period of 2–5 d, the illness manifests as low-grade fever and oropharyngeal pain, with the development of a thick gray membrane that covers the tonsils and pharynx and may extend over the larynx and cause airway obstruction. Dislodging of the membrane usually causes bleeding and occasionally causes obstruction of the respiratory tract. The major toxic manifestations of diphtheria are myocarditis and polyneuritis. Bulbar dysfunction develops in the first 2 weeks and peripheral polyneuritis in the 1–3 months after onset. Pneumonia occurs in more than half of fatal cases of diphtheria. Diagnosis of diphtheria of the respiratory tract is based on clinical suspicion; definitive diagnosis requires isolation of the organism. Cutaneous diphtheria may involve preexisting wounds, burns, or abrasions. A diagnosis is made by Gram's staining of the lesion, which reveals characteristic club-shaped, gram-positive rods in palisades or a "Chinese character" configuration, or by culture of the organism on selective tellurite medium.

TREATMENT

Treatment requires antitoxin, which must be administered in the following doses as early as possible after the diagnosis is suspected: for mild or early (≤48 h) pharyngeal or laryngeal disease, 20,000–40,000 U; for nasopharyngeal involvement, 40,000–60,000 U; and for disease that is extensive, of ≥3 d duration, or accompanied by diffuse swelling of the neck, 80,000–100,000 U. The pt should first be tested for hypersensitivity to horse serum, and the antiserum should then be administered IV in saline over 60 min. In addition, erythromycin (500 mg PO/IV qid for 14 d) or procaine penicillin G (600,000 units IM q12h) should be given for eradication of the organism in acute respiratory illness. Pts with cutaneous diphtheria and carriers can be treated with erythromycin (500 mg PO qid) or rifampin (600 mg PO qd) for a 7-d course. Diphtheria is preventable by immunization with DTaP or DT in childhood (for appropriate dosing schedule, see HPIM-15, Chap. 122) and reimmunization with Td every 10 years in adulthood.

For a more detailed discussion, see Wessels MR: Streptococcal and Enterococcal Infections, Chap. 140, p. 901; and Holmes RK: Diphtheria, Other Corynebacterial Infections, and Anthrax, Chap. 141, p. 909, in HPIM-15.

91

MENINGOCOCCAL AND LISTERIAL INFECTIONS

MENINGOCOCCAL INFECTIONS

EPIDEMIOLOGY   *Neisseria meningitidis* causes two life-threatening diseases: meningococcal meningitis and fulminant meningococcemia. Meningococci also cause pneumonia, septic arthritis, pericarditis, urethritis, and conjunctivitis.

N. meningitidis is a gram-negative diplococcus with a polysaccharide capsule. Humans are the only host for the organism, and transmission is via droplet respiratory secretions. Meningococcal colonization of the nasopharynx is more common than invasive disease and can persist for months; in nonepidemic periods, ~10% of healthy individuals are colonized. Factors predisposing to colonization include residence in a household with a person who has meningococcal disease or is a carrier, household or institutional crowding, active or passive exposure to tobacco smoke, and a recent viral URI. These factors are also associated with an increased risk of invasive disease. The attack rate for sporadic meningococcal disease is ~1 case per 100,000 persons per year; the peak incidence coincides with the winter peak of respiratory viral illnesses. Attack rates are higher for children than for adults and are highest among infants 3–9 months of age. There is a second peak of incidence among teenagers. The secondary attack rate among households is 400 to 1000 cases per 100,000 household members. Most secondary cases occur within 2 weeks of the primary case, but some develop up to several months later.

Meningococcal disease occurs worldwide as sporadic cases, institutional or community outbreaks, and large epidemics. Meningococci are classified traditionally by the serogroup method, which reflects the antigenicity of their capsular polysaccharides. Five serogroups (A, B, C, Y, and W-135) account for >90% of cases. In the U.S., endemic disease is caused most often by serogroup B, while serogroup C is a more frequent cause of outbreaks. Serogroup Y has been isolated from almost one-third of cases in the U.S.; the pts involved are generally older and have underlying illnesses. Other meningococcal classification methods are based on molecular typing and genomic sequencing.

PATHOGENESIS Meningococci that colonize the respiratory tract rarely traverse the mucosa to enter the bloodstream. If multiplication in the blood occurs slowly, the bacteria seed local sites (e.g., meninges, joints). More rapid multiplication is associated with DIC and shock. *N. meningitidis* has a striking tropism for the meninges. Host defense mechanisms include serogroup-specific bactericidal antibodies and complement.

CLINICAL MANIFESTATIONS *Meningococcemia* Between 10 and 30% of pts who develop meningococcal disease have bacteremia without meningitis. Occasionally, there is a prodromal syndrome of sore throat and upper respiratory symptoms. Manifestations of meningococcemia include fever, chills, nausea, vomiting, and myalgias. Rash is the most distinctive feature, with erythematous macules that rapidly become petechial and, in severe cases, purpuric. The lesions are typically located on the trunk and lower extremities but may also occur on the face, arms, and mucous membranes. Fulminant disease (the Waterhouse-Friderichsen syndrome) is marked by shock, DIC-induced microthrombosis, hemorrhage, and tissue injury. Chronic meningococcemia is a rare syndrome of episodic fever, maculopapular or petechial rash, and arthralgias that can last from weeks to months. If untreated or treated with glucocorticoids, it may evolve into meningitis, fulminant meningococcemia, or (rarely) endocarditis.

Meningitis In general, pts with meningococcal meningitis have been sick for ≥24 h before seeking medical attention. Symptoms are similar to those caused by other meningeal pathogens and include nausea, vomiting, headache, neck stiffness, lethargy, and confusion. Many pts have concurrent meningococcemia, and the associated skin lesions may suggest the diagnosis.

Other Manifestations Arthritis occurs in ~10% of pts with meningococcal disease and may be due to direct bacterial invasion of the joint or immune complex deposition. Rare manifestations of meningococcal infection include conjunctivitis, pneumonia (associated with serogroup Y), pericarditis, endocarditis, and urethritis.

DIAGNOSIS Early recognition of meningococcal disease depends on distinguishing it from the other acute systemic infections that it resembles. The detection of a petechial or purpuric rash should raise diagnostic suspicion. Diagnosis depends on recovering *N. meningitidis*, its antigens, or its DNA from normally sterile fluids, such as blood, CSF, or synovial fluid, or from skin lesions. A Gram's stain of CSF reveals intra- or extracellular organisms in ~85% of pts with meningococcal meningitis. The latex agglutination test for meningococcal polysaccharides is somewhat less sensitive. PCR amplification of DNA in buffy coat or CSF may be more sensitive than other tests and is not affected by prior antibiotic therapy.

 TREATMENT

Initial therapy (before the diagnosis is known) consists of cefotaxime (2 g IV q8h) or ceftriaxone (1 g IV q12h), since these drugs cover other likely bacterial pathogens besides meningococci. Penicillin G (4 million U IV q4h) is an acceptable alternative, with high-level resistance reported only in Spain. Chloramphenicol (75–100 mg/kg PO q6h) is an alternative in the β-lactam-allergic pt. Most pts with meningococcal meningitis should be treated for at least 5 days. Adjuvant glucocorticoid therapy for meningitis in adults is controversial. Pts with fulminant meningococcemia require additional IV fluids, elective ventilation, pressors, and control of bleeding.

PREVENTION Pts who are hospitalized with meningococcal disease should be placed in respiratory isolation for the first 24 h of antibiotic therapy. Meningococcal disease in close contacts of cases (e.g., household contacts, day care center contacts, anyone with direct exposure to the pt's secretions) can be prevented with rifampin (600 mg PO q12h for 4 doses). A single oral dose of ciprofloxacin (500 mg) or ofloxacin (400 mg) is an acceptable alternative in nonpregnant adults but not in children or pregnant women. A single dose of 250 mg of ceftriaxone IM is recommended for pregnant contacts. Casual contacts are not at increased risk. A polysaccharide vaccine active against serogroups A, C, Y, and W-135 is used to prevent infections in military recruits, persons with functional or anatomic asplenia, persons with complement deficiencies, and travelers to areas with epidemic disease and to prevent late infections in close contacts of cases.

LISTERIAL INFECTIONS

EPIDEMIOLOGY AND PATHOGENESIS *Listeria monocytogenes*, a motile gram-positive bacillus, is responsible for food-borne invasive infections, primarily sepsis and meningitis. Cases may occur sporadically or in outbreaks associated with particular foods. Implicated foods have included Mexican-style and other soft cheeses, coleslaw, pasteurized milk, and food from delicatessens. The incubation period for disease following consumption of contaminated food can be 2–6 weeks. At highest risk are pregnant women and persons immunocompromised by disease (solid or hematologic malignancies, diabetes mellitus, renal or hepatic disease, AIDS) or drugs (chronic glucocorticoid therapy), although infection occasionally occurs in immunocompetent adults, particularly elderly persons.

CLINICAL MANIFESTATIONS Immunocompromised hosts most often present with bacteremia without an evident focus; CNS infection is less commonly the initial symptom. Pts are usually febrile and may have myalgias, nausea, vomiting, and diarrhea. Cases of bacteremia and meningitis due to *Listeria* cannot be distinguished clinically from those caused by other organisms. Pregnancy-associated listeriosis develops most often in the third trimester but may occur at any time; 50–66% of pregnant women have a mild illness, with fever, myalgias, malaise, and occasional GI complaints. Transplacental spread of infection can lead to chorioamnionitis, premature labor, fetal demise, or neonatal infection. Neonatal infection may be of early (<7 days) or late onset. Early-onset infection usually occurs within the first 2 days of life, with sepsis, respiratory distress, skin lesions, or disseminated abscesses involving mutliple organs. Infants with late-onset infection are more likely to have meningitis. Recent studies of common-source outbreaks have indicated that *Listeria* is an occasional cause of an acute diarrhea syndrome in immunocompetent persons. *Listeria* may also cause encephalitis, cerebritis, intracranial abscesses, and (rarely) endocarditis and other focal infections.

DIAGNOSIS Listeriosis is diagnosed by culture of the organism from a normally sterile body site (e.g., CSF or blood). Culture from stool or vagina is not reliable because ~5% of healthy individuals carry the organism.

Ɍ **TREATMENT**

Nonpregnant adults with listeriosis should be treated with ampicillin (2 g IV q4h) or penicillin G (15–20 million units/d IV in 6 divided doses); immunosuppressed pts with meningitis can also receive gentamicin for synergy (1.3 mg/kg IV q8h). Penicillin-allergic pts can receive TMP-SMZ (15/75 mg/kg IV daily in 3 divided doses). Therapy for meningitis in an immunocompetent pt should continue for 2–3 weeks following defervescence. Immunosuppressed pts should probably receive 4–6 weeks of therapy. Listeriosis in pregnancy is treated with ampicillin (1–1.5 g IV q6h for 2 weeks); erythromycin may be used as an alternative in the penicillin-allergic pt during the last month of pregnancy. Treatment of maternal bacteremia during pregnancy can prevent neonatal infection. For neonatal listeriosis, treatment consists of a 2-week course of ampicillin. In infants weighing <2000 g, the dose is 100 mg/kg daily in 2 divided doses during the first week of life and 150 mg/kg daily during the second week. Infants weighing ≥2000 g should receive 150 (mg/kg)/d in 3 equal doses during the first week of life and 200 (mg/kg)/d during the second week. Gentamicin can be added for neonatal listeriosis at 5 mg/kg daily in 2 divided doses during the first week of life and 7.5 (mg/kg)/d in 3 divided doses during the second week.

PREVENTION Prevention of listeriosis requires dietary counseling of those at high risk of disease and measures to reduce the contamination of food sources.

For a more detailed discussion, see Munford RS: Meningococcal Infections, Chap. 146, p. 927; and Schuchat A, Broome CV: Infections Caused by *Listeria monocytogenes*, Chap. 142, p. 915, in HPIM-15.

92

INFECTIONS CAUSED BY *HAEMOPHILUS*, *BORDETELLA*, *MORAXELLA*, AND HACEK GROUP ORGANISMS

HAEMOPHILUS INFLUENZAE

ETIOLOGY *H. influenzae* is a small pleomorphic coccobacillary gram-negative pathogen that often stains only faintly with phenosafranin and therefore can easily be overlooked. The six capsular polysaccharide–based serotypes are designated *a* through *f*. *H. influenzae* type b (Hib) and unencapsulated strains, termed *nontypable H. influenzae* (NTHi), are the most frequently isolated pathogens.

PATHOGENESIS *H. influenzae* is part of the normal oropharyngeal flora and causes systemic disease by invasion and hematogenous spread to distant sites such as the meninges, bones, and joints. The type b capsular polysaccharide is an antiphagocytic barrier. NTHi strains cause disease by local invasion of mucosal surfaces. The incidence of invasive disease caused by nontypable strains is low but increasing.

EPIDEMIOLOGY *H. influenzae* is spread by airborne droplets or by direct contact with secretions or fomites. NTHi strains colonize up to 75% of healthy adults. Since 1991, vaccines of type b capsular polysaccharide conjugated to carrier proteins have greatly reduced rates of Hib meningitis among children. The rate of nasopharyngeal colonization by Hib strains has similarly decreased.

CLINICAL MANIFESTATIONS *H. influenzae* is the second most common cause of community-acquired pneumonia, especially in elderly adults, pts with chronic lung disease or prolonged tobacco use, and pts with HIV infection. More than 80% of isolates from cases of pneumonia are NTHi. Obstetric infections caused by NTHi are severe and are an important source of neonatal bacteremia. NTHi causes sinusitis in adults and children. In addition, it is a less common cause of empyema, adult epiglottitis, pericarditis, cellulitis, septic arthritis, osteomyelitis, endocarditis, cholecystitis, intraabdominal infection, UTI, mastoiditis, aortic graft infection, and bacteremia without a detectable focus.

Hib is a pathogen affecting mainly children, causing meningitis, epiglottitis, cellulitis, and pneumonia.

DIAGNOSIS The most reliable method for diagnosing *H. influenzae* infection is culture. Agglutination assays, immunoelectrophoresis, and ELISA are useful for antigen detection in clinical specimens.

 TREATMENT

Initial therapy for meningitis due to Hib in adults should consist of 1–2 weeks of ceftriaxone (2 g q12h IV) or cefotaxime (2 g q4–6h IV); pediatric doses are 75–100 (mg/kg)/d of ceftriaxone, given in 2 doses 12 h apart, and 200 (mg/kg)/d of cefotaxime, given in 4 doses 6 h apart. An alternative regimen is ampicillin (200–300 mg/kg qd in 4 divided doses) plus chloramphenicol (75–100 mg/kg qd in 4 divided doses). Early administration of glucocorticoids (dexamethasone, 0.6 mg/kg IV qd for 2 d) protects against hearing loss in children with Hib meningitis. Invasive infections other than meningitis are treated with the same regimens. Approximately 25% of NTHi strains produce β-lactamase and are resistant to ampicillin. Infections caused by ampicillin-resistant strains can be treated with trimethoprim-sulfamethoxazole (TMP-SMZ), amoxicillin/clavulanic acid, various extended-spectrum cephalosporins, clarithromycin, and azithromycin. Fluoroquinolones are highly active against *H. influenzae* but are not currently recommended for treatment of children or pregnant women. Unvaccinated school and household contacts of children infected with Hib should receive prophylaxis with rifampin (20 mg/kg qd, up to 600 mg, for 4 d). All children should be immunized with an Hib conjugate vaccine.

BORDETELLA PERTUSSIS

ETIOLOGY Humans are the sole host for the gram-negative coccobacillus *B. pertussis*, which grows slowly on selective media.

PATHOGENESIS *B. pertussis* attaches to the ciliated epithelial cells of the nasopharynx, adhering via filamentous hemagglutinin and pertactin. The organism elaborates pertussis toxin, which exerts a number of biologic effects and probably plays a role in producing the pertussis clinical syndrome.

EPIDEMIOLOGY Pertussis (whooping cough) is probably underdiagnosed. Rates of communicability to nonimmune household contacts of pertussis pts are 80–100%. There is an increasing incidence of pertussis among adolescents and adults. A number of studies suggest that pertussis may be the etiology in 12–30% of adults with cough that does not improve within 2 weeks. Severe morbidity and mortality are virtually restricted to infants.

CLINICAL MANIFESTATIONS Pertussis infection incubates for 7–10 d. The three stages of illness are *catarrhal* (1–2 weeks), *paroxysmal* (2–4 weeks), and *convalescent* (1–3 months). Coughing is distinctive: 5–10 coughs per spasm, which may be terminated by an audible whoop. Features predictive of pertussis are vomiting with cough, nighttime cough, and exposure to persons with a prolonged coughing illness.

DIAGNOSIS In the absence of classic symptoms, distinguishing pertussis from other causes of respiratory tract infection is difficult. Lymphocytosis is common only in young children. For the isolation of *B. pertussis*, a nasopharyngeal swab or aspirate is immediately inoculated onto selective media. Polymerase chain reaction of nasopharyngeal specimens may increase the yield and is helpful in pts treated with antibiotics. At present, no serologic test is commercially available, and no specific serologic criteria are defined.

℞ TREATMENT

Treatment does not alter the clinical course unless given early in the catarrhal phase; thus the purpose of therapy is to eradicate *B. pertussis* from the nasopharynx. Erythromycin (preferably estolate), at 50 (mg/kg)/d (maximum, 2 g/d) in 3 divided doses, is the recommended regimen; 1 g/d is effective and may be better tolerated. A 7-d course of therapy is as effective as a 2-week course. It is recommended that household and other close contacts be treated with the same regimen, regardless of age and immunization status. The average estimated efficacy for whole-cell vaccine is 85%. New acellular vaccines cause fewer adverse reactions.

MORAXELLA CATARRHALIS

ETIOLOGY/EPIDEMIOLOGY *Moraxella (Branhamella)* is a gram-negative diplococcus that colonizes the upper airways of 50% of healthy schoolchildren and 7% of adults. The incidence of infections peaks in late winter/early spring.

CLINICAL MANIFESTATIONS *M. catarrhalis* causes otitis media, tracheobronchitis, pneumonia, and rare cases of empyema, bacteremia, septic arthritis, meningitis, and endocarditis. The majority of respiratory infections occur in patients >50 years of age who have chronic pulmonary disease.

DIAGNOSIS Gram's staining of sputum reveals gram-negative diplo-cocci. *M. catarrhalis* is easily grown on blood or chocolate agar.

 TREATMENT

β-Lactamase production is detected in 85% of *M. catarrhalis* isolates. Amox-icillin/clavulanate, a second- or third-generation cephalosporin, erythromycin, quinolones, tetracycline, chloramphenicol, and TMP-SMZ are all effective against *M. catarrhalis* infection. A 5-day course cures respiratory infection.

HACEK GROUP ORGANISMS

ETIOLOGY *Haemophilus aphrophilus, H. paraphrophilus, H. parain-fluenzae, Actinobacillus actinomycetemcomitans, Cardiobacterium hominis, Ei-kenella corrodens,* and *Kingella kingae* are fastidious, CO_2-requiring pathogens.

PATHOGENESIS The HACEK organisms colonize the oral cavity and can cause severe systemic infections, most often endocarditis. In fact, up to 3% of endocarditis cases are caused by HACEK organisms, most commonly the *Haemophilus* species, *A. actinomycetemcomitans,* and *C. hominis.*

CLINICAL MANIFESTATIONS Endocarditis due to HACEK organisms can be insidious or complicated, with major emboli in 28–60% of cases.

DIAGNOSIS Blood cultures may require up to 30 days to become posi-tive, although most are positive in the first week.

 TREATMENT

Treatment with ceftriaxone (2 g/d IV) is a reasonable initial approach for HACEK endocarditis. Most cases of *C. hominis* endocarditis are treated with penicillin (16–18 million U/d IV in 6 divided doses) with or without an aminoglycoside (5–6 mg/kg qd IV in 3 divided doses). Treatment should be administered for 6 weeks. Unlike prosthetic valve endocarditis caused by other gram-negative rods, that due to HACEK organisms is often cured with antibiotics alone.

For a more detailed discussion, see Musher DM: *Moraxella catarrhalis* and Other *Moraxella* Species, Chap. 148, p. 938; Murphy TF: *Haemophilus* Infections, Chap. 149, p. 939; Kasper DL, Barlam TF: Infections due to the HACEK Group and Miscellaneous Gram-Negative Bacteria, Chap. 150, p. 942; and Halperin SA: Pertussis and Other *Bordetella* Infections, Chap. 152, p. 949, in HPIM-15.

93

DISEASES CAUSED BY GRAM-NEGATIVE ENTERIC BACTERIA, *PSEUDOMONAS,* AND *LEGIONELLA*

GRAM-NEGATIVE ENTERIC BACILLI

The gram-negative enteric bacilli are a diverse group of bacteria that reside in the human colon. Nearly every organ and body cavity can be infected with these organisms. The mortality rate is significant in many gram-negative bacillary infections and correlates with the severity of illness.

Escherichia coli

PATHOGENESIS AND CLINICAL SYNDROMES   *E. coli* is a major cause of enteric infections and UTIs, a common component of polymicrobial intraabdominal infections, and an occasional cause (either alone or in combination with other pathogens) of a variety of other infections, including pneumonia, osteomyelitis, cellulitis, myositis, septic arthritis, and sinusitis. Hosts compromised by neutropenia, vascular disease, diabetes mellitus, or traumatic injury are at added risk for invasive infections. Bacteremia and sepsis syndrome are serious potential consequences of *E. coli* infections. Strains bearing the K1 capsular serotype are important agents of neonatal meningitis.

Strains producing enteric infections are classified as enterotoxigenic (ETEC), enteropathogenic (EPEC), enteroinvasive (EIEC), or Shiga toxin–producing (STEC)/enterohemorrhagic (EHEC). Enteroaggregative *E. coli* (EAEC) and diffusely adherent *E. coli* (DAEC) cause persistent diarrhea, mainly affecting young children in developing countries. ETEC strains are common agents of traveler's diarrhea, producing watery, noninflammatory diarrheal syndromes. EPEC strains are causes of childhood diarrhea, especially in developing countries. EIEC strains cause dysentery syndromes similar to that caused by *Shigella* species and are rare in the United States. EHEC strains, typically of serotype O157:H7, cause colitis in which stools lack inflammatory cells but may be grossly bloody. A minority of pts subsequently develop the hemolytic-uremic syndrome (HUS), in which Shiga-like cytotoxins are involved.

Acute UTIs usually occur in sexually active females; bacteria colonize the periurethral region and ascend the urethra. Sequelae may include asymptomatic bacteriuria, urethritis, cystitis, pyelitis, and pyelonephritis. Polymicrobial intraabdominal infections typically follow fecal spillage into the peritoneum; *E. coli* and other facultative enteric gram-negative organisms are responsible for the early peritonitis and sepsis syndrome that often follows such catastrophes. *E. coli* bacteremia usually originates from the bowel, biliary tree, or urinary tract.

DIAGNOSIS   The diagnosis of *E. coli* infection rests on the combination of suspicious clinical findings and laboratory isolation of the organism. Specific identification is generally made biochemically. Growth of *E. coli* from a normally sterile site (e.g., blood, CSF, pleural fluid) should be considered diagnostic of infection at that site. In contrast, isolation from a normally nonsterile site (e.g., the GI tract) must be interpreted thoughtfully. Gram's staining is not specific for *E. coli*. Diagnosis of ETEC, EPEC, EIEC, EAEC, and DAEC infection requires special assays and is rarely indicated since disease due to these organisms is self-limited. Screening for *E. coli* O157:H7 infection is conducted on sorbitol-MacConkey agar, and the pathogen is identified by serotyping. Tests for Shiga-like toxins or their corresponding genes, which would detect both O157 and non-O157 strains, are being developed.

TREATMENT

The frequency of ampicillin resistance precludes its empirical use, and rates of resistance to first-generation cephalosporins, trimethoprim-sulfamethoxazole (TMP-SMZ), amoxicillin/clavulanic acid, and piperacillin are also high in some populations. Rates of resistance are low to second-, third-, and fourth-generation cephalosporins; quinolones; monobactams; carbapenems; and aminoglycosides. Traveler's diarrhea is often self-limited but may be treated with a fluoroquinolone. Antibiotic treatment of STEC/EHEC infections may increase the incidence of HUS. Thus these infections are managed supportively; signs of HUS should be sought for 1 week after onset of diarrhea. In many circumstances, therapy for *E. coli* infections must be individualized; several weeks of treatment may be required for serious or deep-seated infections.

Klebsiella, Enterobacter, Serratia

ETIOLOGY   These genera, lactose-fermenting members of the tribe Klebsielleae, are opportunistic and nosocomial pathogens.

CLINICAL MANIFESTATIONS   *K. pneumoniae* causes a small proportion of cases of community-acquired lobar pneumonia, typically in alcoholic men >40 years of age who have comorbid conditions (e.g., diabetes, chronic obstructive pulmonary disease). The disease mimics pneumococcal pneumonia. Pulmonary necrosis and empyema occur with progression. A bulging fissure is a late radiographic finding. The Klebsielleae cause complicated UTIs, intraabdominal infections, cellulitis, surgical wound infections, and neonatal meningitis or meningitis associated with neurosurgery. *Klebsiella* infection at any site can result in bacteremia. *E. cloacae* and *E. aerogenes* are responsible for most *Enterobacter* infections and cause clinical syndromes similar to those caused by *Klebsiella* except for community-acquired pneumonia. These species are important causes of hospital-acquired infections and bacteremia in the setting of neutropenia. *S. marcescens* causes the majority of *Serratia* infections. Hospital-acquired lung, genitourinary tract, catheter, and wound infections are common.

DIAGNOSIS   Most *Klebsiella, Enterobacter,* and *Serratia* organisms are readily isolated and identified by standard culture techniques.

 TREATMENT

K. pneumoniae and *K. oxytoca* are intrinsically resistant to ampicillin and ticarcillin. There is an increasing degree of resistance to third-generation cephalosporins due to extended-spectrum β-lactamases (ESBLs). Strains with ESBLs often have linked resistance to aminoglycosides, tetracyclines, and TMP-SMZ and may have fluoroquinolone resistance as well. At this time, rates of resistance to quinolones, cephamycins (cefoxitin), fourth-generation cephalosporins, and amikacin are generally low. *Enterobacter* strains are often resistant to first-, second-, and third-generation cephalosporins but have largely retained their sensitivity to imipenem, fourth-generation cephalosporins, aminoglycosides, TMP-SMZ, and quinolones. Imipenem, amikacin, cefepime, and quinolones are the most active agents against *Serratia.*

Proteus, Morganella, Providencia

ETIOLOGY   *Proteus, Morganella,* and *Providencia,* of the tribe Proteeae, are actively motile bacteria that do not ferment lactose.

CLINICAL MANIFESTATIONS   *P. mirabilis* causes 90% of *Proteus* infections and is a frequent cause of complicated UTI and of UTI in the setting of an indwelling urinary catheter. Its urease activity alkalinizes the urine and promotes formation of struvite stones. *Proteus* occasionally causes pneumonia, sinusitis, abdominal abscesses, biliary infection, wound and soft tissue infection, and osteomyelitis. The urinary tract serves as the portal of entry in most cases of *Proteus* bacteremia.

   M. morganii, *P. stuartii*, and *P. rettgeri* are the strains of *Morganella* and *Providencia* responsible for human infections, mainly of the urinary tract and less commonly of wounds, soft tissue, lungs, catheter sites, and abdomen.

   DIAGNOSIS   Microbiologic isolation from a normally sterile site is necessary for diagnosis. *P. mirabilis* swarms on moist agar and is nearly always indole negative; virtually all other strains in the tribe Proteeae are indole positive.

 TREATMENT

P. mirabilis is sensitive to most antibiotics except tetracycline, although 10–20% of strains are resistant to ampicillin and first-generation cephalosporins. Infected struvite stones must often be removed. The indole-positive Proteeae tend to be more resistant to antibiotics than most *P. mirabilis* strains. *Morganella* and *Providencia* may be highly resistant to antibiotics. Imipenem, amikacin, and the fourth-generation cephalosporins are most active.

PSEUDOMONAS AND RELATED ORGANISMS

   ETIOLOGY   *Pseudomonas* spp. and phylogenetically related organisms are ubiquitous, free-living, opportunistic gram-negative pathogens. Of this group, *P. aeruginosa* is the most common agent of human disease. A small aerobic rod, it is widespread in nature and has a predilection for moist environments. *Burkholderia cepacia* and *Stenotrophomonas maltophilia* are occasional nosocomial pathogens. *B. pseudomallei* causes melioidosis; *B. mallei* causes glanders.

   PATHOGENESIS   *P. aeruginosa* infections occur after normal cutaneous or mucosal barriers are breached, immunologic defenses are compromised, or the normal flora is eradicated by broad-spectrum antibiotics.

   EPIDEMIOLOGY   *P. aeruginosa* causes hospital-acquired infections. Individuals with cystic fibrosis, diabetes mellitus, IV drug use, neutropenia, wounds, burns, and urinary catheterization are predisposed to infection. Rates of *Pseudomonas* infection, particularly pneumonia, are increasing among pts with advanced AIDS, although the secondary effects of highly active antiretroviral therapy may reverse this trend. *B. cepacia* causes infection in circumstances similar to those predisposing to *Pseudomonas* infection. Melioidosis is endemic to Southeast Asia. Glanders is associated with close contact with horses and other equines.

   CLINICAL MANIFESTATIONS   *P. aeruginosa* causes pneumonia, UTI, bacteremia with ecthyma gangrenosum, endocarditis, sinusitis, "swimmer's ear," malignant otitis externa (in diabetics), contact lens–associated keratitis, vertebral osteomyelitis associated with complicated UTI, sternoclavicular pyarthrosis associated with IV drug use, pyoderma, burn wound infection, and hot-tub folliculitis. Melioidosis and glanders present as acute or chronic pulmonary or nonpulmonary suppurative diseases or as acute septicemia.

DIAGNOSIS *P. aeruginosa* can be identified by Gram's staining and culture. Its blue-green pigment and fruity odor are distinctive. *B. pseudomallei* has a characteristic bipolar "safety-pin" appearance on staining with methylene blue. In addition to culture, serologic methods are available for diagnosis of *B. pseudomallei* and *B. mallei* infections.

 TREATMENT

Agents with antipseudomonal activity include aminoglycosides, selected third-generation cephalosporins (e.g., ceftazidime, cefoperazone), cefepime, selected extended-spectrum penicillins (e.g., ticarcillin, ticarcillin/clavulanate, mezlocillin, piperacillin, piperacillin/tazobactam), carbapenems (e.g., imipenem, meropenem), monobactams (e.g., aztreonam), and fluoroquinolones (e.g., ciprofloxacin, levofloxacin). Local patterns of antimicrobial susceptibility should influence the choice of initial empirical therapy, while the susceptibility profile of the isolate from a particular case should dictate definitive therapy. For most severe infections, two agents are used in combination for synergy—e.g., a β-lactam antibiotic such as ceftazidime (1–2 g) plus an aminoglycoside such as gentamicin (1–1.5 mg/kg) IV q8h. The appropriate duration of antibiotic therapy depends on the type, location, and severity of infection. Uncomplicated lower UTIs due to *P. aeruginosa* may be amenable to short-course treatment with a single agent. Surgical intervention is necessary for drainage and debridement of pus and necrotic material and for removal of infected foreign bodies. For left-sided *P. aeruginosa* endocarditis, valve replacement should be performed early. Chronic lung infection in cystic fibrosis requires frequent pulmonary toileting; antibiotics should be given for acute exacerbations. Delivery by the aerosolized route has been used successfully in some instances. Nonmalignant external otitis and *Pseudomonas* dermatitis associated with exposure to contaminated water are self-limited and usually require no specific therapy.

TMP-SMZ is the drug of choice for *S. maltophilia* infections. Ceftazidime or imipenem is the agent of choice for melioidosis and is given in conjunction with appropriate surgical drainage of abscesses. Treatment of *B. cepacia* infection is complicated by this organism's intrinsic resistance to many antibiotics.

LEGIONELLA INFECTIONS

ETIOLOGY Legionellae are aerobic, gram-negative bacilli whose natural habitats are fresh-water aquatic environments. They may multiply in man-made aquatic reservoirs. *L. pneumophila* causes 80–90% of human *Legionella* infections.

PATHOGENESIS The modes of transmission of *Legionella* to humans include aerosolization, aspiration, and direct instillation into the lung during respiratory tract manipulations. Direct human-to-human transmission is thought not to occur.

EPIDEMIOLOGY *Legionella* infections account for 3–15% of community-acquired pneumonias and for 10–50% of nosocomial pneumonias when a hospital's water supply is colonized with the organisms. Most sporadic cases probably go undiagnosed. Host-specific risk factors include cigarette smoking, chronic lung disease, advanced age, and immunosuppression. Pontiac fever occurs in epidemics, with high attack rates reflecting airborne transmission.

Table 93-1

Clinical Clues Suggestive of Legionnaires' Disease

Diarrhea
High fever ($>40°C$ or $>104°F$)
Numerous neutrophils but no organisms revealed by Gram's staining of respiratory secretions
Hyponatremia (serum sodium level of <131 meq/L)
Failure to respond to β-lactam drugs (penicillins or cephalosporins) and aminoglycoside antibiotics
Occurrence of illness in an environment in which the potable water supply is known to be contaminated with *Legionella*
Onset of symptoms within 10 days after discharge from the hospital

SOURCE: FY Chang, VL Yu: HPIM-15, p. 947.

CLINICAL MANIFESTATIONS *Legionella* pneumonia (Legionnaires' disease) features high fever, nonproductive cough, and GI symptoms. Shortness of breath and confusion are not uncommon. Clues to the diagnosis of Legionnaires' disease are presented in Table 93-1. Chest examination reveals rales early in the course and evidence of consolidation as the disease progresses. Abnormalities on CXR are virtually uniformly evident on presentation but are nonspecific. Pleural effusion is evident in one-third of cases. Pontiac fever, another disease syndrome linked to legionellae, is an acute, self-limited, flulike illness characterized by malaise, fatigue, myalgias, fever, and headache. Pneumonia does not develop. Extrapulmonary legionellosis may occur; the heart is the site most commonly involved.

DIAGNOSIS The utilities of special tests for the diagnosis of Legionnaires' disease are presented in Table 93-2.

℞ TREATMENT

Newer macrolides and quinolones are now the agents of choice (Table 93-3). For severely ill pts, rifampin (600 mg PO or IV q12h) is combined with a

Table 93-2

Utility of Special Laboratory Tests for the Diagnosis
of Legionnaires' Disease

Test	Sensitivity, %	Specificity, %
Culture		
Sputum[a]	80	100
Transtracheal aspirate	90	100
DFA staining of sputum	50–70	96–99
Urinary antigen testing[b]	70	100
Antibody serology[c]	40–60	96–99

[a] Use of multiple selective media with dyes.
[b] Serogroup 1 only.
[c] IgG and IgM testing of both acute- and convalescent-phase sera. A single titer of $\geq1{:}128$ is considered presumptive, while a single titer of $\geq1{:}256$ or fourfold seroconversion is considered definitive.
SOURCE: FY Chang, VL Yu: HPIM-15, p. 948.

Table 93-3

Antibiotic Therapy for *Legionella* Infection[a]

Antimicrobial Agent	Dose, mg[b]	Route[c]	Frequency
Azithromycin	500[d]	PO, IV	q24h
Clarithromycin	500	PO, IV[e]	q12h
Roxithromycin	300[e]	PO	q12h
Erythromycin[f]	1000 (1 g)	IV	q6h
	500	PO	q6h
Ciprofloxacin	400	IV	q8h
	750	PO	q12h
Levofloxacin	500[d]	PO, IV	q24h
Ofloxacin	400	PO, IV	q12h
Doxycycline	100[d]	PO, IV	q12h
Minocycline	100[d]	PO, IV	q12h
Tetracycline	500	PO, IV	q6h
Trimethoprim-sulfamethoxazole	160/800	IV	q8h
	160/800	PO	q12h
Rifampin	300–600	PO, IV	q12h

[a] Total duration of therapy should be 10–14 days in immunocompetent hosts and 3 weeks in immunosuppressed pts and in those with advanced disease.
[b] Except as indicated.
[c] IV therapy should be used until the pt's clinical condition improves, after which oral therapy can be substituted.
[d] Doubling of the first dose is recommended.
[e] Investigational in the United States.
[f] Now replaced by newer macrolides.
SOURCE: FY Chang, VL Yu: HPIM-15, p. 948.

newer macrolide or a quinolone for initial therapy. A clinical response usually occurs within 3–5 d, after which the pt may be switched to oral therapy to complete a 10- to 14-d course. Immunosuppressed pts with advanced disease should be given a 3-week course. Tetracyclines and TMP-SMZ are alternative agents. Pontiac fever is treated supportively, without antibiotics.

For a more detailed discussion, see Russo TA: Diseases Caused by Gram-Negative Enteric Bacilli, Chap. 153, p. 953; Ohl CA, Pollack M: Infections Due to *Pseudomonas* Species and Related Organisms, Chap. 155, p. 963; and Chang FY, Yu VL: *Legionella* Infection, Chap. 151, p. 945, in HPIM-15.

94

DISEASES CAUSED BY OTHER GRAM-NEGATIVE BACTERIA

BRUCELLOSIS

EPIDEMIOLOGY   Brucellosis is a zoonosis caused by four species of aerobic gram-negative bacilli. *Brucella melitensis*, the most common cause, is acquired from goats, sheep, and camels. *B. suis* is acquired from hogs, *B. abortus* from cattle, and *B. canis* from dogs. Humans become infected by exposure to animal tissues (e.g., slaughterhouse workers, butchers) or by ingestion of untreated milk or milk products or raw meat.

CLINICAL MANIFESTATIONS   The acute illness generally presents after a 7- to 21-d incubation period, although the incubation period may be as long as several months. The most common signs and symptoms are fever, chills, fatigue, anorexia, weight loss, and sweats. Other common manifestations include headaches, myalgias, low back pain, constipation, sore throat, and dry cough. Localized infections may occur as well, including osteomyelitis (especially of the lumbosacral vertebrae), arthritis, splenic abscess, epididymoorchitis, CNS infection, and endocarditis. Finally, brucellosis may present chronically, with generalized ill health for >1 year after its onset.

DIAGNOSIS   Most cases are diagnosed on the basis of potential exposure, compatible clinical features, and elevated levels of *Brucella* agglutinins (usually detected by a standard tube agglutination test). In nonendemic areas a titer of ≥1:160 is considered positive; in endemic areas a titer of 1:320 or 1:640 is significant, and IgM assays are positive in early infection. The most definitive evidence of infection is isolation of the organism from blood or bone marrow, optimally with special culture techniques. Cultures may take up to 6 weeks to become positive but ultimately are positive in 50–70% of cases. Samples in which the presence of *Brucella* is suspected should be so labeled to alert the laboratory to use special culture techniques and to be aware of the hazard posed by this material to laboratory personnel.

 TREATMENT

Optimal treatment consists of doxycycline (100 mg bid) plus an aminoglycoside—i.e., gentamicin (3–5 mg/kg IV qd in 3 divided doses), streptomycin (1 g IM qd in pts <45 years old, 500–750 mg IM qd in pts ≥45 years old), or netilmicin (2 mg/kg IV or IM q12h)—for 4 weeks followed by a combination of doxycycline and rifampin (600–900 mg PO qd) for 4–8 weeks. Young children and pregnant women may be treated with trimethoprim-sulfamethoxazole (TMP-SMZ; 2 or 3 single-strength tablets q12h) and rifampin for 8–12 weeks. Repeat blood cultures and IgG measurements should be performed every 3–6 months for 2 years.

TULAREMIA

EPIDEMIOLOGY   *Francisella tularensis* is a bipolar-staining, pleomorphic bacillus that is transmitted to humans by insect bites, skin contact, inhalation, or ingestion of material from multiple species of wild animals. In the U.S., transmission takes place primarily through skin contact with infected wild rabbits or by tick or deerfly bite. Tularemia is common in Arkansas, Oklahoma, and Missouri; these three states account for >50% of U.S. cases. Cases have been reported with increasing frequency from Scandinavia, eastern Europe, and Siberia.

CLINICAL MANIFESTATIONS Tularemia presents as several different clinical syndromes, most of which are associated with fever, chills, headache, and myalgias, after a 2- to 10-d incubation period. Ulceroglandular tularemia (75–85% of cases) follows skin inoculation of *F. tularensis*; a papule forms and evolves into a punched-out-appearing ulcer with a necrotic base. Large, tender regional lymph nodes develop. Oculoglandular disease develops after inoculation into the eye and presents as purulent conjunctivitis and regional lymphadenopathy. Pulmonary tularemia, which has a high mortality rate and may complicate other forms of the disease or follow inhalation of the organism, presents as nonproductive cough and bilateral patchy infiltrates. The typhoidal form, which is now thought to be rare in the U.S., presents as fever without skin lesions or adenopathy.

DIAGNOSIS Diagnosis is based on serologic agglutination tests. A fourfold rise in titer over 2–3 weeks is diagnostic of acute infection. A single titer of ≥1:160 constitutes presumptive evidence of infection. Gram's staining of material usually yields negative results; special stains and indirect fluorescent antibody may be revealing, although false-positives due to *Legionella* spp. have been reported. Culture and isolation of *F. tularensis* are difficult, pose a major risk to laboratory personnel, and should be attempted only in laboratories with adequate isolation techniques and experienced personnel.

℞ TREATMENT

The treatment of choice is streptomycin (7.5–10 mg/kg IM q12h) for 7–10 d; in severe infections, 15 mg/kg q12h may be used for the first 48–72 h. Gentamicin (1.7 mg/kg IV or IM q8h) also may be used. Chloramphenicol and tetracycline have been used to treat tularemia, with good initial response rates but unacceptable relapse rates.

PLAGUE

EPIDEMIOLOGY *Yersinia pestis*, a gram-negative coccobacillus, causes sporadic cases of human disease and is transmitted by the bite of the rodent flea, predominantly in the southwestern U.S. Plague occurs sporadically both in rural areas throughout the world and in a few urban areas of southern Asia. Less commonly, plague is contracted via airborne droplets. In its pulmonic form, plague can be transmitted from person to person.

CLINICAL MANIFESTATIONS Bubonic plague is characterized by rapid onset of fever, myalgias, arthralgias, and painful lymphadenopathy (the bubo) after a 2- to 6-d incubation period. Insect contact often is not recalled, but an eschar, papule, pustule, scab, or ulcer may indicate the point of inoculation. If left untreated, bubonic plague may progress to sepsis, hypotension, DIC, and death within 2–10 d. Secondary pneumonia develops in 10–20% of pts, characteristically with initially diffuse interstitial pneumonitis in which sputum production is scant. Primary *Y. pestis* pneumonia develops after an incubation period of 1–4 d, with acute onset of fever, chills, myalgia, headache, cough, and dyspnea (often accompanied by hemoptysis); CXR shows involvement of a single lobe progressing to multilobar involvement. The illness is fulminant, and death occurs within 2–6 d in the absence of treatment. Meningitis is a serious but unusual manifestation of plague.

DIAGNOSIS   Since plague is unusual in the U.S., a high index of clinical suspicion and a thorough epidemiologic history are required for timely diagnosis and prompt institution of specific therapy. The laboratory diagnosis is usually based on stains and cultures of blood, sputum, an aspirated bubo, or CSF. Stains reveal characteristic bipolar "safety-pin" forms. Culture is usually positive but requires 48–72 h. Serology may serve to confirm cases.

℞ TREATMENT

The drug of choice for plague is streptomycin (1 g IM q12h for 10 d). Gentamicin (1.0–1.7 mg/kg IV q8h) and tetracycline (500 mg PO or IV q6h) are alternatives. Pts with pneumonic plague should be placed in respiratory isolation, and contacts should receive prophylactic tetracycline (250–500 mg PO qid). Death is almost always due to a delay in treatment.

BARTONELLOSIS
Bartonella henselae and Bartonella quintana

CLINICAL MANIFESTATIONS   *Cat-Scratch Disease*   Cat-scratch disease follows a primary skin inoculation by the lick, scratch, or bite of a cat. *B. henselae*, a tiny gram-negative rod, is now thought to be the only causative agent of cat-scratch disease. Frequently, a skin lesion (papule or pustule) develops after 3–5 d at the primary site of inoculation. Tender lymphadenopathy occurs after 1–2 weeks (often after resolution of the skin lesion) and persists for 3–6 weeks or longer. Dissemination of infection is rare in immunocompetent hosts and causes meningoencephalitis, osteomyelitis, or hepatitis. Conjunctival infection with preauricular lymphadenopathy is referred to as *Parinaud's oculoglandular syndrome*.

Trench Fever   Trench fever is a febrile illness that has recently reemerged in homeless persons (in whom infection has been caused by *B. quintana*) and persons bitten by ticks (*B. henselae*). Fever, headache, and aseptic meningitis are common symptoms. Bacteremia can persist for weeks.

Bacillary Angiomatosis   In immunocompromised hosts, especially those with HIV infection, *B. henselae* may disseminate to involve virtually any organ system, causing a lobular proliferation of new blood vessels. On the skin, this condition is recognized as cutaneous bacillary angiomatosis (also called epithelioid angiomatosis). Characteristically, the lesions are red or purple, resembling Kaposi's sarcoma; they develop anywhere on the skin or mucous membranes. Disseminated bacillary angiomatosis may involve the liver, spleen, bone marrow, lymph nodes, and/or CNS. Dissemination causes persistent fever, abdominal pain, weight loss, and malaise. *B. henselae* is associated with peliosis of the liver or spleen, which may cause abdominal pain and the appearance of nodular lesions on CT or MRI of the organ. *B. quintana* is associated with osseous and SC infection.

DIAGNOSIS   *B. henselae* and *B. quintana* may be identified in tissue by Warthin-Starry silver stain. In addition, in cases involving immunocompromised hosts, the bacteria may be isolated from cultures of blood and other sites, although lengthy incubation (2–4 h) is required. Polymerase chain reaction testing of clinical specimens may be considered for definitive identification of *Bartonella* spp. Serology is positive in 70–90% of pts with cat-scratch disease.

TREATMENT

Cat-scratch disease is generally self-limited and resolves spontaneously. However, pts with dissemination should be treated with azithromycin (500 mg PO on day 1, 250 mg PO on days 2–5); ciprofloxacin and doxycycline may also be used. Cutaneous bacillary angiomatosis usually responds to treatment with erythromycin (500 mg PO qid) or doxycycline (100 mg PO bid) for 3 weeks; relapse may require prolonged therapy. Disseminated disease is treated with erythromycin (2 g IV qd) for a prolonged course (3 weeks to 2 months), with a switch to oral therapy after clinical improvement.

Bartonella bacilliformis

EPIDEMIOLOGY *B. bacilliformis* is a tiny gram-negative bacillus that causes Oroya fever and, in its chronic form, skin lesions called *verruga peruana*. The vector of these diseases is the sandfly found in the river valleys of the Andes Mountains of Peru, Ecuador, and Colombia.

CLINICAL MANIFESTATIONS Oroya fever is characterized by fever, chills, malaise, headache, altered mentation, and muscle and joint pains that may begin insidiously or acutely ~3 weeks after the bite of the sandfly vector. Profound anemia results from parasitization of erythrocytes, which are then phagocytosed and destroyed by the host. Red or purple cutaneous lesions called *verrugas*—either tiny or large and pedunculated—may develop during the convalescent phase.

 TREATMENT

Oroya fever is usually treated with chloramphenicol, although it also responds to tetracyclines, penicillin, or streptomycin. Intercurrent *Salmonella* infections are common.

OTHER GRAM-NEGATIVE RODS ASSOCIATED WITH ANIMAL INJURIES
Pasteurella multocida

This small gram-negative coccobacillus is transmitted by bites or scratches from animals, particularly cats and dogs. Infections are characterized by the rapid development of intense inflammation and purulent drainage. There is a high risk of deep tissue infections, including osteomyelitis, tendon sheath involvement, or septic arthritis. *Treatment* consists of ampicillin/sulbactam (1.5–3.0 g IV q6h), amoxicillin/clavulanic acid (500/125 mg PO tid), or—in the penicillin-allergic pt—TMP-SMZ (160/800 mg PO or IV q12h).

Capnocytophaga canimorsus

This fusiform gram-negative rod is associated with septicemia following dog bites, particularly in alcoholics, splenectomized pts, or pts taking steroids on a chronic basis. The incubation period averages 5 d. Pts present with fever that is sometimes accompanied by meningitis or endocarditis. In splenectomized pts, DIC, gangrene, adrenal hemorrhage, pulmonary hemorrhage, and fulminant sepsis may occur. The organism may be identified on Gram's or Wright's stain of buffy coat of blood from splenectomized individuals. *Treatment* of *C. canimorsus* sepsis consists of penicillin G (2–3 million U IV q4h for 14 d). Alternatives for use in the penicillin-allergic pt include clindamycin, third-generation cephalosporins, and fluoroquinolones.

For a more detailed discussion, see Madoff LC: Infectious Complications of Bites and Burns, Chap. 127, p. 817; Madkour MM, Kasper DL: Brucellosis, Chap. 160, p. 986; Jacobs RF: Tularemia, Chap. 161, p. 990; Campbell GL, Dennis DT: Plague and Other *Yersinia* Infections, Chap. 162, p. 993; and Tompkins LS: *Bartonella* Infections, Including Cat-Scratch Disease, Chap. 163, p. 1001, in HPIM-15.

95

ANAEROBIC INFECTIONS

TETANUS

EPIDEMIOLOGY Tetanus, while preventable by immunization, has a worldwide distribution. In the U.S., most disease occurs in elderly unimmunized or incompletely immunized pts and follows an acute injury such as a puncture wound, abrasion, or laceration with exposure to soil.

PATHOGENESIS Under conditions of low oxidation-reduction potential, germination and toxin production follow contamination of a wound with spores of *Clostridium tetani*. The toxin tetanospasmin is transported to the nerve cell body and migrates across the synapse to presynaptic terminals, blocking the release of inhibitory neurotransmitters. Rigidity results from increases in the resting firing rate of the alpha motor neuron with diminished inhibition.

CLINICAL MANIFESTATIONS The median incubation period after injury is 7 d. The first symptoms are increased tone in the masseter muscles (trismus or lockjaw) followed by dysphagia, stiffness, or pain in the neck, shoulder, and back muscles. Contraction of facial muscles produces risus sardonicus, and contraction of back muscles causes an arched back (opisthotonos). Muscle spasms may be violent, may be provoked by even the slightest stimulation, and may threaten ventilation. Fever may or may not develop; mentation is unimpaired. Autonomic dysfunction commonly complicates severe cases. Complications can include pneumonia, fractures, muscle rupture, deep vein thrombophlebitis, pulmonary emboli, decubitus ulcer, and rhabdomyolysis. Neonatal tetanus develops in children born to unimmunized mothers after unsterile treatment of the umbilical cord stump.

DIAGNOSIS The diagnosis of tetanus is made clinically. The organism frequently cannot be recovered from wounds of pts with tetanus and may be recovered from wounds of pts without tetanus.

℞ TREATMENT

Goals of treatment are to eliminate the source of toxin, neutralize unbound toxin, prevent muscle spasms, and provide support (especially respiratory) until after recovery. Pts should be admitted to a quiet room in intensive care. Antibiotic therapy is given to eradicate vegetative cells, the source of toxin. Although of unproven value, the use of penicillin G (10–12 million U qd IV for 10 d) has been recommended; metronidazole (500 mg q6h or 1 g q12h IV) is preferred by some experts on the basis of the latter drug's excellent antimicrobial activity and a survival rate higher than that obtained with penicillin in one nonrandomized trial. Additional specific antimicrobial therapy should be given for active infection with other organisms. Human tetanus immune globulin (TIG) at a dose of 3000–6000 units IM should be given promptly to neutralize circulating and unbound toxin. Pooled IV immunoglobulin may be an alternative to TIG. Diazepam is used to treat muscle spasms; large doses (≥250 mg/d) may be required. Mechanical ventilation and therapeutic paralysis with a nondepolarizing neuromuscular blocking agent may be required for severe spasms or laryngospasm. However, because prolonged paralysis after discontinuation of therapy with such agents has been described, both the need for continued therapeutic paralysis and the occurrence of complications should be assessed daily. Optimal therapy for sympathetic overactivity is not clear; labetalol, esmolol, clonidine, morphine sulfate, parenteral magnesium sulfate, and continuous spinal or epidural anesthesia have been used.

Pts must be actively immunized against tetanus, since natural disease does not induce immunity. The preventive regimen for adults is three doses of tetanus and diphtheria toxoids (Td), with the first and second doses administered IM 4–8 weeks apart and the third dose 6–12 months after the second. A booster dose is required every 10 years. For any wound, Td should be given if (1) the pt's immunization status is unknown, (2) fewer than three doses have been given in the past, (3) more than 10 years have elapsed since the administration of three doses, or (4) the pt has received three doses of fluid (nonadsorbed) vaccine. For contaminated or severe wounds, a booster is given if more than 5 years have elapsed since immunization. In addition, TIG (250 mg IM) should be administered for all but clean, minor wounds if the pt's immunization status is incomplete or unknown. Vaccine and TIG should be administered with separate syringes at separate sites.

BOTULISM

EPIDEMIOLOGY Botulism is caused by neurotoxins elaborated by *Clostridium botulinum*, an anaerobic gram-positive organism with subterminal spores. Human botulism occurs worldwide. *Food-borne botulism* is acquired from ingestion of food contaminated with preformed toxin—most commonly, home-canned food. *Wound botulism* develops when wounds, including those contaminated by soil, those of chronic IV drug users, and those related to cesarean delivery, are contaminated with *C. botulinum*. *Infant botulism* occurs when an infant ingests spores and toxin is elaborated in the intestine. Botulism of undetermined classification is produced in older children and adults by a mechanism similar to that described for infant botulism.

CLINICAL MANIFESTATIONS *Food-Borne Botulism* The incubation period for botulism is usually 18–36 h after ingestion of food containing toxin. Cranial nerve involvement marks the onset of symptoms, which usually consist of diplopia, dysarthria, and/or dysphagia. Paralysis is symmetric and descending and can lead to respiratory failure and death. Nausea, vomiting, and abdominal pain may precede or follow the onset of paralysis. Dizziness, blurred vision, dry mouth, and dry or sore throat are common. Fever usually is not documented. Ptosis is common; fixed or dilated pupils are noted in 50% of cases. The gag reflex can be suppressed, and deep tendon reflexes can be either normal or decreased. Paralytic ileus, severe constipation, and urinary retention are common.

Wound Botulism   The presentation of wound botulism is similar to that of food-borne disease except that the incubation period is longer (~10 d) and no GI symptoms develop.

DIAGNOSIS   The diagnosis of botulism must be suspected on clinical grounds in the context of an appropriate history. Conditions often confused with botulism include myasthenia gravis and Guillain-Barré syndrome. Definitive diagnosis is made by the demonstration of toxin in serum; however, the test may be negative despite infection and cannot be conducted in all laboratories. Other fluids that may yield toxin are vomitus, gastric fluid, and stool. Isolation of the organism from food is not diagnostic.

 TREATMENT

Pts should be monitored carefully, particularly for signs of respiratory failure. In food-borne illness, trivalent equine antitoxin (types A, B, and E) should be administered as soon as possible after laboratory specimens are collected. A repeat dose is probably not necessary but may be given after 2–4 h. Cathartics may be used unless there is ileus. Antibiotics are of unproven value. Wound botulism is treated with exploration and debridement of the wound and the administration of penicillin (to eradicate the organism) and equine antitoxin. Supportive treatment is undertaken for infant botulism. Antitoxin and management advice are available at any time from state health departments or the CDC (404-639-2206; emergency number, 404-639-2888).

OTHER CLOSTRIDIAL INFECTIONS

PATHOGENESIS   Despite the isolation of clostridial species from many severe traumatic wounds, the incidence of serious infections due to these organisms is low. Tissue necrosis and a low oxidation-reduction potential appear to be essential to the development of serious disease. Clostridial disease is mediated by toxins.

CLINICAL MANIFESTATIONS   ***Food Poisoning***   *C. perfringens* is the second or third most common cause of food poisoning in the U.S. Primary sources are recooked meats, meat products, and poultry. Symptoms develop 8–24 h after ingestion and include epigastric pain, nausea, and watery diarrhea lasting for 12–24 h. Fever and vomiting are uncommon.

Antibiotic-Associated Colitis   Strains of *C. difficile* that produce toxins detectable in the stool have been identified as the major cause of colitis in pts with antibiotic-associated diarrhea. Any antibiotic (including metronidazole and vancomycin, which are used to treat the infection) can cause this syndrome, which is defined as diarrhea that has no other cause and that develops during antibiotic treatment or within 4 weeks of its discontinuation. Diarrhea is usually watery, voluminous, and without gross blood or mucus. Most pts have abdominal cramps and tenderness, fever, and leukocytosis with a marked left shift. Four categories of diarrhea have been based on the appearance of the colon: (1) normal colonic mucosa; (2) mild erythema with some edema; (3) granular, friable, or hemorrhagic mucosa; and (4) pseudomembrane formation.

Suppurative Deep-Tissue Infection   Clostridia are recovered, with or without other organisms, in a variety of conditions with severe local inflammation but usually without systemic signs attributable to toxins. These conditions include intraabdominal sepsis, empyema, pelvic abscess, SC abscess, frostbite with gas gangrene, infection of stumps in amputees, brain abscess, prostatic abscess, perianal abscess, conjunctivitis, infection of renal cell carcinomas, and infection of aortic grafts. At least 50% of cases of emphysematous cholecystitis are caused by clostridial species.

Skin and Soft Tissue Infections

1. *Localized infections*: Localized clostridial infections of skin and soft tissues tend to be indolent and devoid of systemic signs of toxicity, pain, and edema. Typical examples include cellulitis, perirectal abscesses, and diabetic foot ulcers. Gas may be present in the wound and the immediate surrounding tissues but is not present intramuscularly. A form of suppurative myositis is found in heroin addicts.

2. *Spreading cellulitis and fasciitis with systemic toxicity*: This syndrome is abrupt in onset, with rapid spread of suppuration and gas through fascial planes. Myonecrosis is absent, but overwhelming toxemia develops and can be rapidly fatal. On examination, crepitance is prominent, but there is little localized pain. This syndrome is most common among pts with carcinoma, especially of the sigmoid or cecum. Massive hemolysis may be present.

3. *Clostridial myonecrosis (gas gangrene)*: Clostridial myonecrosis occurs in deep necrotic wounds, often following trauma or surgery. The incubation period is short—always <3 d, often <24 h. In contrast to spreading cellulitis, gas gangrene begins with sudden pain in the region of the wound. Local swelling and edema follow, accompanied by a thin hemorrhagic exudate. Toxemia, hypotension, renal failure, and crepitance ensue; the pt often has a heightened awareness of surroundings before death.

4. *Clostridial bacteremia and sepsis*: Clostridial bacteremia may occur transiently without clinical sepsis. The most common predisposing foci are the intestinal and biliary tracts and the uterus, although half of pts have an unrelated illness. Often, fever has resolved and the pt's clinical condition has improved by the time blood cultures become positive; thus the pt must be assessed clinically rather than simply treated on the basis of the culture result. Clostridial sepsis is uncommon but is almost always fatal and follows clostridial infections of the uterus (esp. after septic abortion), colon, or biliary tract. Pts develop sepsis 1–3 d after abortion, with fever, chills, malaise, headache, severe myalgias, abdominal pain, nausea, vomiting, and (occasionally) diarrhea. Oliguria, hypotension, jaundice, and hemoglobinuria secondary to hemolysis develop rapidly. Like those with gas gangrene, pts with clostridial septicemia exhibit increased alertness and apprehension. In cases with bowel or biliary-tree sources, localized infection may not develop. Pts have chills and fever, and 50% have intravascular hemolysis. In pts with malignancy, *C. septicum* causes rapidly fatal septicemia with fever, tachycardia, hypotension, abdominal pain, nausea, and vomiting. Only 20–30% of these pts develop hemolysis; death may occur within 12 h.

DIAGNOSIS The diagnosis of clostridial infection must be based primarily on clinical findings because the mere presence of clostridia in a wound does not necessarily indicate severe disease. The detection of gas by radiography provides a clue, but gas is sometimes documented in mixed anaerobic-aerobic infections as well. Clostridial myonecrosis can be diagnosed by examination of a frozen section of muscle. Pts may have hemolytic anemia, hemoglobinuria, and disseminated intravascular hemolysis. *C. difficile*–associated colitis is most often diagnosed by ELISA for toxin A. Tissue culture, with appropriate neutralization by antitoxin, is the "gold standard" but requires a tissue culture facility.

 TREATMENT

Until recently, penicillin G was the antibiotic of choice for clostridial infections of tissues. Studies in experimental models of infection demonstrated that protein synthesis inhibitors may be preferable to cell wall–active drugs. In these studies clindamycin treatment enhanced survival more than penicillin therapy, and the combination of clindamycin and penicillin was superior to penicillin alone. For severe clostridial sepsis, clindamycin may be used at a dose of 600 mg IV q6h in combination with high-dose penicillin (3–4 million U IV q4h). A number of other antibiotics can be considered in the case of penicillin allergy, but the sensitivity of the infecting strain to these alternative drugs should be evaluated. Drainage of infected sites or surgery is a mainstay of therapy for clostridial myonecrosis. Amputation may be required for rapidly spreading infection in a limb; repeated debridement is necessary for abdominal wall myonecrosis; and hysterectomy must be performed for uterine myonecrosis. *C. difficile* enterocolitis is treated by discontinuation of the offending antibiotic. Treatment with metronidazole (500 mg tid PO) or vancomycin (125 mg qid PO) for 10–14 d shortens the duration of symptoms. The dose of vancomycin may be increased to 500 mg qid PO in severe cases. If pts fail to respond to PO metronidazole after 48 h, it is reasonable to switch to vancomycin. Relapses are much more common than treatment failures. Multiple relapses have been treated with tapering doses of vancomycin or cholestyramine or by repopulating the colon with normal flora via *Saccharomyces boulardii* administration.

MIXED ANAEROBIC INFECTIONS

CLINICAL MANIFESTATIONS *Head and Neck* Infections of the head and neck that involve anaerobes include gingivitis (trench mouth, Vincent's stomatitis), pharyngeal infections (including Ludwig's angina), fascial infections in which oropharyngeal organisms from mucous membranes or sites of dental manipulation spread to potential spaces in the head and neck, sinusitis, and otitis. Complications of these infections include osteomyelitis of the skull or mandible, intracranial infection (such as brain abscess), mediastinitis, pleuropulmonary infection, and suppurative thrombophlebitis of the internal jugular vein (Lemierre's syndrome), often due to *Fusobacterium* spp.

Central Nervous System When sought by optimal bacteriologic methods, anaerobes are found in 85% of brain abscesses. Anaerobic gram-positive cocci predominate; fusobacteria and *Bacteroides* spp. are next most common.

Pleuropulmonary Sites Four clinical syndromes are associated with anaerobic pleuropulmonary infection produced by aspiration: aspiration pneumonia, necrotizing pneumonia, lung abscess, and empyema. Aspiration pneumonia generally develops slowly, with low-grade fever, malaise, and sputum production, in pts with a predisposition for aspirating. Necrotizing pneumonia can be indolent or fulminating and is characterized by numerous small abscesses. Pts with lung abscess typically present with a syndrome of fever, chills, malaise, weight loss, and foul-smelling sputum developing over a period of weeks. Empyema is a manifestation of long-standing anaerobic pulmonary infection and has a clinical presentation similar to that of lung abscess. Pts may also have pleuritic chest pain and chest wall tenderness. Empyema can result from subdiaphragmatic extension.

Intraabdominal Sites See Chap. 81.

Pelvic Sites Anaerobes are encountered frequently in tubo-ovarian abscess, septic abortion, pelvic abscess, endometritis, and postoperative wound infection, especially after hysterectomy.

Skin and Soft Tissue Anaerobes are sometimes isolated in cases of crepitant cellulitis, synergistic cellulitis, gangrene, necrotizing fasciitis, cutaneous abscess, rectal abscess, and axillary sweat gland infection (hidradenitis suppur-

Table 95-1

Antimicrobial Therapy for Infections Involving Commonly Encountered Anaerobic Gram-Negative Rods

Group 1 (<1% Resistance)	Group 2 (<15% Resistance)	Group 3 (Variable Resistance)	Group 4 (Resistance)
Metronidazole	Clindamycin	Penicillin	Aminoglycosides
[a]Ampicillin/ sulbactam	Cefoxitin	Cephalosporins	Quinolones
Ticarcillin/ clavulanic acid	High-dose anti-pseudomonal penicillins	Tetracycline	Monobactams
Piperacillin/ tazobactam		Vancomycin	
Imipenem		Erythromycin	
Meropenem			
Chloramphenicol			
[b]Clinafloxacin			

[a] Usually needs to be given in combination with aerobic bacterial coverage. For infections originating below the diaphragm, aerobic gram-negative coverage is essential. For infections from an oral source, aerobic gram-positive coverage is added. Metronidazole also is not active against *Actinomyces, Propionibacterium,* or other gram-positive non-spore-forming bacilli (e.g., *Eubacterium, Bifidobacterium*) and is unreliable against peptostreptococci.

[b] Chloramphenicol is probably not as effective as other group 1 antimicrobials in treating anaerobic infections.

SOURCE: DL Kasper: HPIM-15, p. 1016.

ativa). Synergistic (Meleney's) gangrene is a progressive, exquisitely painful skin process, with erythema, swelling, induration, and a central zone of necrosis. Anaerobic cocci and *Staphylococcus aureus* are common pathogens. While necrotizing fasciitis is usually attributed to group A streptococci, it can be caused by anaerobes, including *Peptostreptococcus* and *Bacteroides* spp. Fournier's gangrene involves cellulitis of the genital and perineal areas.

Bones and Joints Anaerobic osteomyelitis usually develops by extension of a soft tissue infection. Septic arthritis often is not polymicrobial and can arise from hematogenous seeding; the most common isolates are *Fusobacterium* spp.

Table 95-2

Doses and Schedules for Treatment of Serious Infections due to Commonly Encountered Anaerobic Gram-Negative Rods

First-Line Therapy	Dose	Schedule[a]
Metronidazole[b]	7.5 mg/kg	q6h
Ticarcillin/clavulanic acid	3.1 g	q4h
Piperacillin/tazobactam	3.375 g	q6h
Imipenem	0.5 g	q6h
Meropenem	1.0 g	q8h

[a] See disease-specific chapters for recommendations on duration of therapy.

[b] Should generally be used in conjunction with drugs active against aerobic or facultative organisms.

NOTE: All drugs are given by the intravenous route.

SOURCE: DL Kasper: HPIM-15, p. 1017.

Bacteremia *Bacteroides fragilis* is the most common anaerobic isolate from the blood. The clinical presentation of anaerobic bacteremia may be quite similar to that of sepsis due to aerobic gram-negative bacilli. Septic thrombophlebitis and septic shock are uncommon. Mortality increases with the age of the pt.

DIAGNOSIS When infections develop in proximity to mucosal surfaces normally harboring an anaerobic flora, anaerobes should be considered as potential etiologic agents. The presence of gas in tissues is highly suggestive but not diagnostic. Cultures of suspected sites should be processed for anaerobes, usually in a transport medium, and should be conveyed rapidly to the laboratory. Since laboratory isolation of the pathogen(s) can be time-consuming, diagnosis must sometimes be presumptive.

℞ TREATMENT

Successful therapy for anaerobic infection involves a combination of appropriate antibiotics, surgical resection, and drainage. If anaerobic infection is suspected, effective empirical treatment can nearly always be administered, since patterns of antimicrobial susceptibility are usually predictable. Antibiotics active against *Bacteroides, Prevotella, Porphyromonas*, and *Fusobacterium* spp. are listed according to their predicted activity in Table 95-1. Although most mild oral anaerobic infections respond to penicillin, serious infections should be treated as if penicillin-resistant organisms are involved. Clindamycin is superior in the treatment of lung abscess. For infections below the diaphragm, agents active against *Bacteroides* spp. (frequently penicillin-resistant) are listed under group 1 in Table 95-1. Recommended doses for commonly used group 1 drugs are listed in Table 95-2. Anaerobic infections that have failed to respond to treatment should be reassessed, with a consideration of antibiotic resistance, of the need for additional drainage, and of superinfection with aerobic organisms. Since most infections involving anaerobes are bacteriologically mixed and involve aerobic bacteria, therapy must also be directed at those organisms.

For a more detailed discussion, see Abrutyn E: Tetanus, Chap. 143, p. 918; Abrutyn E: Botulism, Chap. 144, p. 920; Kasper DL, Zaleznik DF: Gas Gangrene, Antibiotic-Associated Colitis, and Other Clostridial Infections, Chap. 145, p. 922; and Kasper DL: Infections due to Mixed Anaerobic Organisms, Chap. 167, p. 1011, in HPIM-15.

96

NOCARDIOSIS AND ACTINOMYCOSIS

NOCARDIOSIS

The term *nocardiosis* refers to invasive disease due to *Nocardia* species, aerobic actinomycetes that cause several characteristic syndromes. The two most common syndromes—pneumonia and disseminated infection—may follow inhalation of fragmented nocardial mycelia. Three other syndromes may follow transcutaneous inoculation: cellulitis, a lymphocutaneous syndrome, and actinomycetoma. Finally, nocardial keratitis may result from corneal trauma and nocardial inoculation.

EPIDEMIOLOGY Nocardiae are common inhabitants of soil worldwide. Of the ~1000 cases of nocardiosis that occur annually in the U.S., 85% are either pulmonary or systemic. The risk of pulmonary or systemic disease is increased in persons with impaired cell-mediated immunity, especially those who have lymphoma or AIDS or have undergone solid organ or bone marrow transplantation. Nocardiosis is also associated with pulmonary alveolar proteinosis, tuberculosis, and chronic granulomatous disease.

CLINICAL MANIFESTATIONS *Pulmonary Disease* Nocardial pneumonia is typically subacute. Cough is prominent and productive of scant, thick, purulent, nonmalodorous sputum. Fever, anorexia, weight loss, and malaise are common. Nodular pulmonary infiltrates and cavitation are frequently evident on radiographs. In half of all cases of pulmonary nocardiosis, extrapulmonary disease is also evident.

Extrapulmonary Dissemination Disseminated nocardiosis typically manifests as abscesses presenting subacutely. The most common site of dissemination is the CNS, where one or more abscesses—usually supratentorial and often multiloculated—may be found. Other common sites of dissemination include skin and supporting structures, kidneys, bone, and muscle. Around 80% of pts with disseminated nocardiosis have demonstrable concurrent pulmonary involvement.

Disease Following Transcutaneous Inoculation After transcutaneous inoculation, disease may take one of three forms: (1) cellulitis, a subacute illness characterized by painful, firm, warm, nonfluctuant, erythematous lesions; (2) a lymphocutaneous sporotrichoid form; and (3) actinomycetoma, a chronic, deforming, locally invasive entity with minimal systemic manifestations.

Keratitis *Nocardia* spp. are uncommon causes of keratitis. Nocardial keratitis develops subacutely after eye trauma.

DIAGNOSIS The diagnosis of nocardiosis is suggested by the finding of beaded, branching, gram-positive, weakly acid-fast organisms on stains of sputum or pus. Cultural confirmation usually requires selective media and may take 2–4 weeks.

 TREATMENT

Sulfonamides are the drugs of choice for the treatment of nocardiosis (Table 96-1). Once disease is controlled, the dose of sulfonamide (sulfadiazine or sulfisoxazole) may be decreased to 1 g qid, or, if TMP-SMZ is used, the dose may be reduced by half. In difficult cases, the dose should be adjusted to maintain serum sulfonamide levels at 100–150 μg/mL. Whether combination therapy is more effective than monotherapy is unknown. The exact duration of treatment is somewhat arbitrary and depends on both the condition being treated and the immune status of the host (Table 96-1). Nocardial abscesses that are large and surgically accessible should be drained.

ACTINOMYCOSIS

Actinomycosis is an indolent bacterial infection caused by any of several gram-positive, non-spore-forming anaerobic or microaerophilic rods, most but not all

Table 96-1

Treatment for Nocardiosis

Disease	Duration, Months	Drugs (Daily Dose)[a]
Pulmonary or systemic		Systemic therapy
Intact host defenses	6–12	Oral
Deficient host defenses	12[b]	1. Sulfonamides (6–8 g) or combination of trimethoprim (10–20 mg/kg) and sulfa-methoxazole (50–100 mg/kg)
CNS disease	12[c]	2. Minocycline (200–400 mg)
Cellulitis, lymphocutaneous syndrome	2	Parenteral
Osteomyelitis, arthritis, laryngitis, sinusitis	4	1. Amikacin (10–15 mg/kg)
Actinomycetoma	6–12, after clinical cure	2. Cefotaxime (6 g), ceftizoxime (6 g), ceftriaxone (2 g), imipenem (2 g)
Keratitis	Topical: Until apparent cure	1. Sulfonamide drops
	Systemic: Until 2–4 mo after apparent cure	2. Amikacin drops
		Drugs for systemic therapy as listed above

[a] For each category, choices are numbered in order of preference.
[b] In some pts with AIDS or chronic granulomatous disease, therapy for pulmonary or systemic disease must be continued indefinitely.
[c] If all apparent CNS disease has been excised, the duration of therapy may be reduced to 6 months.
SOURCE: GA Filice: HPIM-15, p. 1008.

of which are in the genus *Actinomyces*. Characteristic features of actinomycosis include the violation of normal tissue plane barriers by the spreading infection, the formation of draining sinus tracts, and the presence of actinomycotic sulfur granules (yellow aggregates of organisms) in drainage or pus. In certain circumstances, actinomycosis may be easily mistaken for malignancy.

EPIDEMIOLOGY AND PATHOGENESIS   The agents of actinomycosis are members of the normal oral flora and may also be found in the bronchi, GI tract, and female genital tract. A critical step in the development of actinomycosis is disruption of the mucosal barrier, which allows actinomycetes to invade beyond their endogenous habitat. Local infection, subsequent extension, and (in rare cases) hematogenous seeding may ensue. Actinomycosis is associated with poor dental hygiene, the use of intrauterine contraceptive devices, HIV infection, transplantation, and chemotherapy.

CLINICAL MANIFESTATIONS   Actinomycosis occurs most frequently at an oral, cervical, or facial site and should be considered in the differential diagnosis of any mass lesion or relapsing infection of the head and neck. "Woody" induration is a common finding. Other common presentations include thoracic, abdominal, pelvic, and musculoskeletal disease. CNS infection and disseminated disease are both rare.

DIAGNOSIS   The finding of macro- or microscopic actinomycotic sulfur granules in drainage or purulent material is highly suggestive of actinomycosis. The isolation of an actinomycete from granules or from a normally sterile site confirms the diagnosis but takes from 5 days to 4 weeks. Prior antimicrobial therapy greatly decreases the likelihood of isolating the organism. Isolation of the organism from secretions in the absence of sulfur granules indicates that the actinomycete is a commensal.

 TREATMENT

Treatment recommendations are listed in Table 96-2. Like nocardiosis, actinomycosis typically requires protracted treatment. For extensive or serious

Table 96-2

Antibiotic Therapy for Actinomycosis: Regimens Supported by Extensive Clinical Experience

Agent	Dosage
Penicillin	18–24 million units/d IV q4h
	1–2 g/d PO q6h
Erythromycin	2–4 g/d IV q6h
	1–2 g/d PO q6h
Tetracycline	1–2 g/d PO q6h
Doxycycline	200 mg/d IV or PO q12–24h
Minocycline	200 mg/d IV or PO q12h
Clindamycin	2.7 g/d IV q8h
	1.2–1.8 g/d PO q6–8h

NOTE: Additional coverage for concomitant "companion" bacteria may be required. Controlled evaluations have not been performed. Regimens must be individualized according to the site and extent of infection. As a general rule, a maximal antimicrobial dose given parenterally for 2 to 6 weeks, followed by oral therapy, with a total duration of 6 to 12 months, optimizes the likelihood of cure.
SOURCE: TA Russo: HPIM-15, p. 1010.

infection, IV therapy for 2–6 weeks followed by oral therapy for 6–12 months is suggested. For limited disease, less intensive therapy may suffice. Extending treatment beyond the resolution of demonstrable disease minimizes the likelihood of relapse. Adjunctive surgical treatment is warranted for pts critically ill with actinomycosis and for those infected at a critical site (e.g., the CNS).

For a more detailed discussion, see Filice GA: Nocardiosis, Chap. 165, p. 1006; and Russo TA: Actinomycosis, Chap. 166, p. 1008, in HPIM-15.

97

TUBERCULOSIS AND OTHER MYCOBACTERIAL INFECTIONS

Mycobacteria are distinguished by their surface lipids, which cause them to be acid-fast in the laboratory. They may be divided into several groups: the *M. tuberculosis* complex (*M. tuberculosis, M. bovis*, and *M. africanum*), members of which cause tuberculosis (TB); *M. leprae*, which causes leprosy; and the nontuberculous mycobacteria (*M. avium* and others), a heterogeneous group that causes disseminated disease in immunocompromised hosts and a variety of local infectious syndromes in both immunocompromised and immunocompetent individuals. The vast majority of TB cases are caused by *M. tuberculosis*.

TUBERCULOSIS

EPIDEMIOLOGY Beginning in the mid-1980s in many industrialized countries, the number of TB case notifications, which had been falling steadily, stabilized or began to increase. A number of factors were implicated in the resurgence of TB in the U.S. in 1986–1992, including the AIDS epidemic; immigration from high-prevalence areas of the world; social problems such as poverty, homelessness, and drug abuse; and the emergence of multidrug-resistant (MDR) TB. With the implementation of stronger control programs, the number of cases began to decrease in 1993. In 1998, 18,361 cases of TB were reported—a 31% decrease from the 1992 peak. Currently in the U.S., TB tends to be a disease of the elderly, of young adults with HIV infection, of immigrants, and of the economically disadvantaged. In certain developing areas of the world, the HIV epidemic is responsible for the doubling or even tripling of the numbers of TB cases reported over the past decade; if the worldwide TB control situation remains as it is, the annual incident cases of TB may increase by 40% by 2020. *M. tuberculosis* is transmitted from person to person by droplet nuclei that are aerosolized by coughing, sneezing, or speaking. The infectivity of a given case correlates with the concentration of organisms in expectorated sputum, the extent of pulmonary disease, the frequency of cough, and the intimacy and duration of contact.

PATHOGENESIS   After entry into the lungs in aerosolized droplets, tubercle bacilli are ingested by macrophages and transported to regional lymph nodes. From there, they disseminate widely. Whether in the lung, lymph nodes, or sites of dissemination, lesions are contained by a delayed-type hypersensitivity (DTH) response (the *tissue-damaging response*) and by the cell-mediated *macrophage-activating response*. The development of host immunity and DTH to *M. tuberculosis* is evidenced by acquisition of skin-test reactivity to tuberculin purified protein derivative (PPD). The PPD skin test is the only test that reliably detects *M. tuberculosis* infection in asymptomatic persons. With the development of specific immunity and the accumulation of large numbers of activated macrophages at the sites of infection, granulomatous lesions (tubercles) form. The organisms survive within macrophages or necrotic material but do not spread further; reactivation (postprimary disease) may occur at a later time. In some cases, the immune response is inadequate to contain the infection, and symptomatic, progressive primary disease develops.

CLINICAL MANIFESTATIONS   TB is usually classified as pulmonary or extrapulmonary. In the absence of HIV infection, >80% of cases involve the lungs only. In the presence of HIV, up to two-thirds of pts with TB have either extrapulmonary disease alone or both pulmonary and extrapulmonary disease.

Pulmonary TB   Pulmonary tuberculous disease may be categorized as primary or postprimary.

- *Primary disease* is often seen in children and is frequently localized to the middle and lower lung zones. In the majority of cases, the lesion heals spontaneously and may later be evident as a small calcified nodule (Ghon lesion). In children and in persons with impaired immunity (e.g., malnutrition, HIV infection), primary disease may progress rapidly and may evolve in different ways (pleural effusion, acute cavitation, bronchial compression by enlarging lymph nodes, miliary TB, or tuberculous meningitis).

- *Postprimary disease* results from endogenous reactivation of latent infection and is usually localized to the apical and posterior segments of the upper lobes; in addition, the superior segments of the lower lobes are frequently involved. The extent of parenchymal involvement varies greatly, from the development of small infiltrates to extensive cavitary disease. Massive involvement and coalescence of lesions may produce tuberculous pneumonia; up to one-third of untreated pts succumb within a few weeks or months, others experience spontaneous remission, and still others have disease that follows a chronic, progressively debilitating course ("consumption"). Early signs and symptoms are often nonspecific and insidious (fever, night sweats, malaise, weight loss). Cough and blood-streaked sputum eventually develop in the majority of cases. Massive hemoptysis may occur. Physical findings are of limited diagnostic utility. The classic tuberculous amphoric breath sounds may be heard over areas with large cavities.

Extrapulmonary TB   The extrapulmonary sites most commonly involved are the lymph nodes, pleura, genitourinary (GU) tract, bones and joints, meninges, and peritoneum. Virtually any organ system may be affected.

- *Tuberculous lymphadenitis* occurs in >25% of cases of extrapulmonary TB and is particularly common among HIV-infected pts. The involved nodes are most commonly those at cervical and supraclavicular sites and are swollen, discrete, and painless. Fistulous drainage of caseous debris may occur. Systemic symptoms usually develop only in HIV-infected pts. Concomitant pulmonary disease may or may not exist.

- *Pleural involvement* is common during primary TB and results from DTH to bacilli in the pleural space; these organisms are typically few in number.

The effusion produced may be small and asymptomatic or large with associated fever, pleuritic chest pain, and dyspnea. The pleural fluid is straw-colored, with a protein content that is >50% of the serum value, a normal or low glucose level, a pH of <7.2, and detectable WBCs (usually 500–2500/μL). Pleural biopsy is often required for diagnosis and reveals granulomas or a positive culture in up to 70% of cases. This form of pleural TB responds well to chemotherapy and may resolve spontaneously. Tuberculous empyema is less common, results from rupture of a tuberculous cavity into the pleura, and may lead to severe pleural fibrosis and restrictive lung disease.

- *Genitourinary TB* accounts for 15% of extrapulmonary cases, may involve any part of the GU tract, and is usually due to hematogenous seeding following primary infection. UA is abnormal in 90% of cases, with culture-negative pyuria and dysuria. Local symptoms predominate. In women, genital TB (fallopian tubes, endometrium) may cause infertility or menstrual irregularities. Men may develop epididymitis, orchitis, or prostatitis. These infections at GU sites respond well to chemotherapy.

- *Skeletal TB* is responsible for ~10% of extrapulmonary cases in the U.S. Weight-bearing joints (spine, hips, knees) are affected most often. Spinal TB (Pott's disease) often involves adjacent vertebral bodies and destroys the intervertebral disk. Spinal cord compression by a tuberculous abscess or lesion is a medical emergency. In advanced Pott's disease, vertebral collapse may lead to kyphosis. Skeletal TB responds to chemotherapy, although severe cases may require surgery.

- *Central nervous system TB* accounts for 5% of extrapulmonary cases and occurs most often in young children and in HIV-infected pts. Tuberculous meningitis results either from hematogenous spread or from rupture of a subependymal tubercle into the subarachnoid space. The disease may present acutely or subacutely. Cranial nerve palsies (particularly of ocular nerves) and hydrocephalus are common. CSF examination reveals lymphocytic pleocytosis (with PMNs sometimes predominating early on), an elevated protein level (100–800 mg/dL), and hypoglycorrhachia. Repeated CSF examinations increase the diagnostic yield; CSF culture is positive in up to 80% of cases. While the disease responds to chemotherapy, neurologic sequelae are common. Glucocorticoids enhance survival and decrease neurologic sequelae.

- *Gastrointestinal TB* may affect any portion of the GI tract. The terminal ileum and cecum are the sites most commonly involved. Abdominal pain, diarrhea, obstruction, hematochezia, and a palpable abdominal mass are common findings. Cases with intestinal-wall ulcerations and fistulae may simulate Crohn's disease. Surgical intervention is required in most cases. *Tuberculous peritonitis* presents as fever, abdominal pain, and ascites; ascitic fluid is exudative, with an elevated protein level and—in most cases—lymphocytic pleocytosis. Peritoneal biopsy is often needed to make the diagnosis.

- *Pericardial TB* is frequently a disease of the elderly but is also common in HIV-infected pts. An effusion often develops and is exudative with a high leukocyte count; culture reveals TB in ~30% of cases. Without treatment, pericardial TB is fatal. Despite treatment, chronic constrictive pericarditis may develop.

- *Miliary TB* is due to hematogenous spread and may represent either newly acquired infection or reactivation of latent disease. Clinical manifestations are nonspecific and protean. Fever, night sweats, anorexia, weakness, and weight loss characterize the majority of cases. Hepatomegaly, splenomegaly, lymphadenopathy, and choroidal (ocular) tubercles may occur. A high index of suspicion is required for the diagnosis; PPD results may be negative in up to 50% of untreated cases, and sputum smears are negative in 80%.

HIV-Associated TB TB is an important opportunistic infection among HIV-infected persons worldwide. As of 1997, ~10 million persons in developing countries were coinfected with HIV and tubercle bacilli. In the U.S., coinfection is common among IV drug users and some minorities. The manifestations of TB in HIV-infected pts vary with the stage of the HIV infection. When cell-mediated immunity is only partly compromised, pulmonary TB presents as typical upper-lobe cavitary disease. In late HIV infection, a primary TB-like pattern may be evident, with diffuse interstitial or miliary infiltrates, little or no cavitation, and intrathoracic lymphadenopathy. Extrapulmonary TB occurs frequently in HIV-infected pts (at a rate of 40–60% in some series). Common syndromes include lymph nodal, disseminated, pleural, and pericardial TB as well as mycobacteremia and tuberculous meningitis. In pts in whom highly active antiretroviral therapy (HAART) has recently been started, symptoms and signs of TB may be exacerbated as a consequence of improving immune function. The diagnosis of TB in HIV-infected pts may be rendered difficult by PPD anergy and atypical radiographic and histologic manifestations.

DIAGNOSIS Initial suspicion of pulmonary TB is often based on abnormal CXR findings in a symptomatic pt. The classic picture is that of upper lobe infiltrates and cavitary disease; however, virtually any pattern may be seen. A diagnosis of active infection is established by the demonstration of acid-fast organisms in sputum, bodily fluids, or tissues. The fluorescent auramine-rhodamine stain is used by most modern laboratories. Traditional acid-fast stains are also useful but are more time-consuming. Primary isolation in culture may require 4–8 weeks. Radiometric growth detection and nucleic acid probe identification make it possible to isolate the infecting organism and identify it to the species level within 2–3 weeks. Sputum induction may be useful when a pt is unable to produce a sputum sample spontaneously, and bronchoalveolar lavage increases the diagnostic yield over that obtained with expectorated sputum alone. Similarly, sampling of bodily fluids (pleural, pericardial, peritoneal, cerebrospinal) or tissue biopsy (of pleura, pericardium, peritoneum, liver, or bone marrow) is appropriate for suspected extrapulmonary or disseminated disease. Blood from HIV-infected pts with suspected TB should be cultured for the organism. The PPD skin test is useful in screening for prior mycobacterial infection. The Mantoux method is most reliable and should be read at 48–72 h as the transverse diameter of induration (*not* erythema) in millimeters.

PREVENTION The best way to prevent TB is to diagnose cases rapidly and administer appropriate treatment until cure. Preventive chemotherapy is of value; recommendations for the treatment of latent TB infection, based on PPD result, are given in Table 97-1.

 TREATMENT

Recommendations for the treatment of TB are summarized in Tables 97-2 and 97-3. Treatment generally consists of isoniazid (INH) for 9 months. Shorter-course rifampin-based treatment has been shown to be effective in HIV-infected pts. Symptoms are alleviated in most cases within 2–3 weeks, but sputum conversion may take 3 months. Drug resistance is a serious problem and may be either primary (i.e., infection caused by a strain that is resistant before the start of treatment) or acquired (i.e., resistance arising during treatment because the regimen is inadequate or the pt is noncompliant). Rates of resistance to both INH and rifampin (from MDR strains) are generally low in North America and Europe. Immigrants with TB acquired in certain developing areas (e.g., the former USSR, Haiti, Southeast Asia, and many parts

Table 97-1

Tuberculin Reaction Size and Treatment of Latent Tuberculosis Infection

Risk Group	Tuberculin Reaction, mm
HIV-infected persons	≥5
Close contacts of tuberculosis pts	≥5[a]
Persons with fibrotic lesions on CXR	≥5
Recently infected persons (≤2 years)	≥10
Persons with high-risk medical conditions[b]	≥10
High-risk group, <35 years of age[c]	≥10
Low-risk group, <35 years of age[d]	≥15

[a] Tuberculin-negative contacts, especially children, should receive prophylaxis for 2–3 months after contact ends and should then be retested with PPD. Those whose results remain negative should discontinue prophylaxis. HIV-infected contacts should receive a full course of treatment regardless of PPD results.
[b] Includes diabetes mellitus, prolonged therapy with systemic glucocorticoids, other immuno-suppressive therapy, some hematologic and reticuloendothelial diseases, injection drug use (with HIV seronegativity), end-stage renal disease, and clinical situations associated with rapid weight loss.
[c] Includes persons born in high-prevalence countries, members of medically underserved low-income populations, and residents of long-term-care facilities.
[d] Decision to treat should be based on individual considerations of risk/benefit.
SOURCE: MC Raviglione, RJ O'Brien: HPIM-15, p. 1034.

of Latin America) commonly have MDR disease. A high index of suspicion, prescription of adequate chemotherapeutic regimens, education of pts, direct observation of therapy, and close and careful follow-up of pts are all crucial in maximizing cure rates and minimizing the spread of MDR strains.

LEPROSY

ETIOLOGY Leprosy (Hansen's disease), which is caused by *M. leprae*, is a chronic granulomatous infection that attacks skin and peripheral nerves.

Table 97-2

Dosage Recommendations for Initial Treatment of Tuberculosis in Adults[a]

Drug	Dosage	
	Daily	Thrice Weekly[b]
Isoniazid	5 mg/kg, max. 300 mg	15 mg/kg, max. 900 mg
Rifampin	10 mg/kg, max. 600 mg	10 mg/kg, max. 600 mg
Pyrazinamide	15–30 mg/kg, max. 2 g	50–70 mg/kg, max. 3 g
Ethambutol	15–25 mg/kg	25–30 mg/kg
Streptomycin	15 mg/kg, max. 1 g	25–30 mg/kg, max. 1.5 g

[a] Dosages for children are similar, except that some authorities recommend higher doses of isoniazid (10–20 mg/kg daily; 20–40 mg/kg intermittent) and rifampin (10–20 mg/kg).
[b] Dosages for twice-weekly administration are the same, except for pyrazinamide (maximum, 4 g/d) and ethambutol (50 mg/kg).
SOURCE: MC Raviglione, RJ O'Brien: HPIM-15, p. 1031. Based on recommendations of the American Thoracic Society, Am J Respir Crit Care Med 149:1359, 1994, and the Centers for Disease Control and Prevention, 1994.

Table 97-3

Recommended Regimens for the Treatment of Tuberculosis

Indication	Initial Phase Duration, Months	Initial Phase Drugs	Continuation Phase Duration, Months	Continuation Phase Drugs
New smear- or culture-positive case	2	HRZE[a]	4	HR[a]
New culture-negative case	2	HRZE[a]	2 (or 4)	HR[a]
Pregnancy[b]	2	HRE	7	HR
Failure and relapse[c]	—	—	—	—
Standardized re-treatment (susceptibility testing unavailable)	3	HRZES[d]	5	HRE
Resistance to H + R	Throughout (12–18)	ZE + Q + S (or another injectable agent[e])	—	—
Resistance to all first-line drugs	Throughout (24)	1 injectable agent[e] + 3 of these 4: ethionamide, cycloserine, Q, PAS	—	—
Intolerance or resistance to H	2[f]	RZE[f]	7	RE
Intolerance to R	2	HES(Z)	16	HE
Intolerance to Z	2	HRE	7	HR

[a] All drugs can be given daily or intermittently (three times weekly throughout or twice weekly after an initial phase of daily therapy).
[b] See also Table 168-1 in HPIM-15.
[c] Regimen is tailored according to the results of drug susceptibility tests.
[d] Streptomycin treatment should be discontinued after 2 months.
[e] Amikacin, kanamycin, or capreomycin. Treatment with all of these agents should be discontinued after 2–6 months, depending upon the pt's tolerance and response.
[f] RZE can be used throughout (for 6 months).

NOTE: H, isoniazid; R, rifampin; Z, pyrazinamide; E, ethambutol; S, streptomycin; Q, quinolone; PAS, para-aminosalicylic acid.
SOURCE: MC Raviglione, RJ O'Brien: HPIM-15, p. 1031.

EPIDEMIOLOGY   There are currently 1.5–8 million pts with leprosy worldwide. Leprosy is almost exclusively a disease of the developing world, affecting areas of Asia, Africa, Latin America, and the Pacific. The disease most often affects the rural poor; cases in India, Brazil, Bangladesh, Indonesia, and Myanmar represent >80% of the total. About 100–200 new infections are diagnosed in the U.S. each year. Leprosy can present at any age, but peak onset is in the second and third decades of life. The route of transmission remains uncertain and may be multiple; nasal droplet infection, contact with infected soil, and insect vectors have been considered the prime candidates. The incubation period is usually 5–7 years but may be several decades.

CLINICAL MANIFESTATIONS   The wide spectrum of clinical and histologic manifestations of leprosy is attributable to the variability of the immune response to *M. leprae*. The spectrum from tuberculoid leprosy to lepromatous leprosy is associated with an evolution from localized to more generalized disease manifestations and an increasing bacterial load. Where a pt presents on the clinical spectrum largely determines prognosis, complications, and the intensity of antimicrobial therapy required.

Tuberculoid Leprosy   At the less severe end of the spectrum is tuberculoid leprosy, which encompasses polar tuberculoid (TT) and borderline tuberculoid (BT) disease. The hallmark of tuberculoid disease is one or a few hypopigmented, sharply demarcated macular lesions that enlarge by peripheral spread, are densely hypesthetic, and have lost sweat glands and hair follicles. Nerves become involved early and may be palpable. Neuritic pain may be prominent. On histologic section, bacilli are frequently absent or difficult to detect. TT leprosy may resolve spontaneously, but BT leprosy does not.

Lepromatous Leprosy   At the more severe end of the leprosy spectrum is lepromatous disease, which encompasses the polar lepromatous (LL) and borderline lepromatous (BL) forms. In lepromatous leprosy, bacilli are numerous in the skin, in peripheral nerves, in the circulating blood, and in all organs except the lungs and the CNS. However, pts remain afebrile and without major organ dysfunction. The initial lesions of lepromatous leprosy are skin-colored or slightly erythematous papules or nodules. New lesions may appear and coalesce. Later, pts present with symmetrically distributed skin nodules, raised plaques, or diffuse dermal infiltration, which, when on the face, results in leonine facies. Late manifestations include loss of eyebrows and eyelashes, pendulous earlobes, and dry scaling skin. Nerve enlargement and damage tend to be symmetric and are more insidious but ultimately more extensive than in tuberculoid leprosy. Pts with LL leprosy have symmetric acral distal peripheral neuropathy. They may also have symptoms related to involvement of the upper respiratory tract (nasal stuffiness, epistaxis, obstructed breathing), the anterior chamber of the eye, and the testes.

DIAGNOSIS   Leprosy should be suspected when a pt from an endemic area has suggestive skin lesions or peripheral neuropathy. The diagnosis should be confirmed by histology. Skin biopsy of lesions is generally diagnostic.

Rx **TREATMENT**

Pts are classified as multibacillary if they have ≥5 skin lesions and as paucibacillary if they have <5 skin lesions. The World Health Organization recommends that paucibacillary adults be treated with dapsone (100 mg PO qd) and (under supervision) with rifampin (600 mg PO each month) for 6 months. Multibacillary adults should be treated without supervision with dapsone (100 mg PO qd) plus clofazimine (50 mg PO qd) and under supervision with rifampin (600 mg each month) plus clofazimine (300 mg each month) for 1 year. With effective therapy, lesions of lepromatous leprosy flatten within 2 months and resolve in a few years, while those of tuberculoid leprosy may disappear, improve, or remain unchanged.

OTHER MYCOBACTERIAL INFECTIONS

Mycobacteria other than members of the *M. tuberculosis* complex and *M. leprae* are termed *atypical mycobacteria, mycobacteria other than tuberculosis* (MOTT), or *nontuberculous mycobacteria* (NTM). In contrast to *M. tuberculosis*, NTM are ubiquitous in the environment.

Disseminated NTM Infections in AIDS and Other Immunodeficiencies

ETIOLOGY The *M. avium* complex (MAC, consisting of *M. avium* and *M. intracellulare*) is a microbiologic designation retained in clinical practice but rendered obsolete by modern molecular diagnostic methods. The majority of mycobacterial infections in immunocompromised hosts in the U.S., including essentially all those formerly attributed to MAC, are caused by *M. avium*. *M. genavense* is an occasional cause of similar infections.

EPIDEMIOLOGY AND HOST FACTORS Infection is probably acquired by the oral route. There is no evidence for nosocomial person-to-person spread. Disseminated infections with NTM almost exclusively affect severely immunosuppressed pts, usually those with AIDS. Rare cases occur in transplant recipients and in pts with leukemia (especially hairy cell leukemia), lymphoma, or certain congenital immunodeficiencies. In pts with AIDS, NTM infection is a late event: AIDS pts whose CD4 cell counts have been $<10/\mu L$ for 1 year have a 40% probability of having a blood culture positive for NTM.

CLINICAL MANIFESTATIONS No distinctive diagnostic features exist. Disseminated NTM infection should be suspected on the basis of prolonged fever and weight loss. Abdominal lymphadenopathy and/or hepatosplenomegaly may be evident either clinically or radiographically; diarrhea and abdominal pain may also be present. Anemia and leukopenia are frequent concomitants and may or may not be etiologically related to NTM. Suspicion of the diagnosis should prompt the performance of blood cultures.

DIAGNOSIS Blood cultures on special media are the cornerstone for the diagnosis of NTM infection. Two or three such cultures are usually sufficient. With the liquid Bactec system, positive results may be obtained within 7–14 d; the detection of *M. genavense* may require much longer. Acid-fast stains of liver or bone marrow biopsy material may permit a more rapid presumptive diagnosis. The yield of liver biopsy approaches 50% in pts with unequivocally abnormal LFTs but is much lower in pts with negative blood cultures and normal or nearly normal LFTs.

℞ TREATMENT

The agents most active against MAC are the macrolides clarithromycin and azithromycin. Monotherapy may lead to resistance and should therefore be avoided. The preferred regimen for treatment of disseminated MAC infection is the combination of clarithromycin (1 g bid), ethambutol (900 mg qd), and rifabutin (300–600 mg qd). Alternative agents include clofazimine, rifampin, ciprofloxacin, and amikacin. It is not clear how long therapy needs to be administered. In pts whose symptoms have lessened, whose blood cultures have become negative, and whose CD4 lymphocyte counts have recovered to >100/μL with HAART, it is reasonable to discontinue antimycobacterial treatment. The best approach to prevention of MAC infections is the prevention and reversal of immunodeficiency by HAART. In pts without an adequate response to HAART and with a CD4 cell count of <100/μL, anti-MAC prophylaxis with rifabutin (300 mg qd), clarithromycin (500 mg qd or bid), or azithromycin (1200 mg weekly) is a reasonable choice.

Localized Infections due to NTM

PULMONARY DISEASE   Preexisting lung disease (e.g., chronic obstructive pulmonary disease, cancer, previous TB, bronchiectasis, cystic fibrosis, or silicosis) is the main predisposing factor for NTM pulmonary disease. The organisms most frequently involved are *M. intracellulare, M. avium,* and *M. kansasii.* Accurate identification to the species level is important; both clinical significance and therapeutic strategies differ with the organism. *M. avium* rarely causes significant pulmonary disease in pts with AIDS. Its isolation from sputum in the absence of radiographic changes is usually without significance. On the other hand, the isolation of *M. kansasii,* which causes a pulmonary TB-like illness, is clinically significant. Most pts with NTM lung infection present with chronic cough, low-grade fever, and malaise. Hemoptysis may develop. Minimal diagnostic criteria include a pulmonary infiltrate of indeterminate cause and the repeated isolation from sputum of multiple colonies of the same strain of NTM.

 TREATMENT

Pts with minimal disease do not need treatment. Likewise, solitary nodular NTM disease identified upon surgical resection requires no further treatment. Most other pts with pulmonary NTM disease are treated with antimicrobial agents; they may require surgery as well. The regimens used in therapy for disseminated MAC infection are preferred for the treatment of localized infection with *M. avium* or *M. intracellulare* as well. Infection with *M. kansasii* is treated with INH (300 mg/d), rifampin (600 mg/d), and ethambutol (15–25 mg/kg qd). Most pts are treated for 18–24 months.

LYMPHADENITIS   This disease occurs most often in children 1–5 years old and is characterized by painless swelling of one node or a group of nodes, with fistulas to the skin. The anterior cervical chain is often affected. *M. scrofulaceum* and MAC organisms are the most common agents. Once TB has been excluded, the treatment of choice is surgical excision.

SKIN DISEASES   *Swimming-Pool and Fish-Tank Granuloma*   The causative organism is almost always *M. marinum,* and the usual incubation period is 2–3 weeks. After contact with a contaminated tropical fish tank, swimming pool, or saltwater fish, a small violet nodule or pustule appears at a site of minor trauma. The lesion may evolve into a crusted ulcer or small abscess. Dissemination may occur. In cases of persistence or dissemination, rifampin (300–600 mg/d) in combination with ethambutol (15–25 mg/kg qd), TMP-SMZ (160/800 mg bid), or minocycline (100 mg/d) may be tried for at least 3 months.

Buruli Ulcer   This entity occurs in the tropics and is due to *M. ulcerans.* Disease begins as a pruritic nodule, which then ulcerates; the course is prolonged. Excision constitutes the usual therapy.

INFECTIONS LINKED TO INJECTIONS AND SURGERY Occasionally, mycobacteria are isolated from nodular skin lesions of hospitalized pts, particularly those who are immunosuppressed. Many cases are linked to injections (e.g., in diabetic pts) or follow surgery (e.g., in ophthalmologic or cardiac pts). These infections are usually due to the rapidly growing and notoriously resistant *M. fortuitum* complex (*M. fortuitum, M. chelonae,* or *M. abscessus*). Debridement is best combined with the administration of two or three antimicrobial agents (selected from amikacin, ciprofloxacin, sulfonamides, clofazimine, and clarithromycin).

For a more detailed discussion, see Raviglione MC, O'Brien RJ: Tuberculosis, Chap. 169, p. 1024; Gelber RH: Leprosy (Hansen's Disease), Chap. 170, p. 1035; and Hirschel B: Infections due to Nontuberculous Mycobacteria, Chap. 171, p. 1040, in HPIM-15.

98

LYME DISEASE AND OTHER SPIROCHETAL INFECTIONS

LYME BORRELIOSIS

ETIOLOGY *Borrelia burgdorferi*, a fastidious spirochete, is the causative agent of Lyme disease. Three groups of *B. burgdorferi* organisms exist and are generally responsible for causing diseases with different manifestations in different parts of the world.

EPIDEMIOLOGY Lyme disease is a tick-transmitted illness; the distribution parallels the geographic range of certain ixodid ticks. The major areas of disease include the northeastern U.S. and Wisconsin and Minnesota in the Midwest. The principal vector in these regions is *Ixodes scapularis* (also called *I. dammini*); >20% of these ticks are infected with *B. burgdorferi* in these areas. Lyme disease also occurs in the western U.S., Europe, Asia, and Australia. The ticks have different animal hosts; the host of the immature *I. scapularis* is the white-footed mouse, while that of the mature tick is the white-tailed deer. The incidence of disease peaks during the summer. More than 100,000 cases have been reported to the CDC since 1982.

CLINICAL MANIFESTATIONS *Early Infection: Stage 1 (Localized Infection)* The principal site of stage 1 infection is the skin. After a 3- to 32-d incubation period, erythema migrans (EM) appears in ~75% of cases. Usually beginning as a red macule or papule at the site of the tick bite, EM expands to form a large annular lesion, often with a bright-red outer border and partial central clearing. Ixodid ticks are so small that most pts do not notice the initial tick bite. The lesion is warm but not usually painful.

Early Infection: Stage 2 (Disseminated Infection) Within days of the on-set of EM, *B. burgdorferi* can spread hematogenously to many sites. Secondary annular skin lesions are similar in appearance to the primary lesion and are frequently accompanied by severe headache, mild neck stiffness, fever, chills, migratory musculoskeletal pain, arthralgias, and profound malaise and fatigue. These early symptoms usually resolve in several weeks, even without treatment. After several weeks or months, ~15% of pts develop neurologic abnormalities, including meningitis, subtle encephalitis, cranial neuritis (including facial palsy), motor or sensory radiculoneuropathy, mononeuritis multiplex, chorea, and/or myelitis. The CSF shows lymphocytic pleocytosis (~100 cells/μL), often with an elevated protein level and a normal or slightly low glucose level. Early neurologic abnormalities resolve completely in months, but chronic neurologic disease may occur later. Cardiac abnormalities develop in ~8% of pts within several weeks of onset of illness. The most common finding is fluctuating de-grees of atrioventricular block. Some pts have myopericarditis. Like early neu-rologic findings, cardiac involvement usually resolves but may recur. Muscu-loskeletal pain is common during stage 2, with migratory pain in joints, tendons, bursae, muscles, or bones and without joint swelling.

Late Infection: Stage 3 (Persistent Infection) Months after the initial in-fection, ~60% of untreated pts in the U.S. develop arthritis, typically intermit-tent attacks of oligoarticular arthritis in large joints (especially the knees) lasting for weeks or months. Most pts have fewer recurrent attacks each year, but a few develop chronic arthritis of one or both knees, with erosion of cartilage and bone. Less commonly, chronic neurologic or skin involvement may develop months or years after initial infection.

DIAGNOSIS Lyme disease is diagnosed by the recognition of a charac-teristic clinical picture with serologic confirmation. Several weeks after infec-tion, most pts develop an antibody response to *B. burgdorferi* that is detectable by ELISA. Western blotting in cases with equivocal or positive results is rec-ommended to identify false-positive ELISAs. The persistence of serologic pos-itivity in pts who have had Lyme disease is common and may cause confusion if another illness with similar manifestations develops. About 20–30% of acute-phase serum samples are positive. IgM- and IgG-specific assays are recom-mended in the first month of illness; thereafter, only IgG assays are of value. Polymerase chain reaction (PCR) for the organism may serve as a substitute for culture in cases of Lyme arthritis, with 85% of joint fluid samples PCR-positive in one study. The sensitivity of PCR for *B. burgdorferi* in the CSF is much lower, and there is little if any role for PCR in the testing of blood or urine samples.

 TREATMENT See Fig. 98-1.

YAWS AND PINTA

CLINICAL MANIFESTATIONS Yaws is a chronic infectious disease of childhood caused by *Treponema pallidum* ssp. *pertenue* and transmitted by direct contact. The disease is characterized by one or more initial skin lesions (often a papule on the leg) followed by relapsing, nondestructive secondary lesions of skin and bone. In the late stages, destructive lesions of skin, bone, and joints develop.

Pinta, an infectious disease of the skin, is caused by *Treponema carateum*. The initial lesion is a small papule, located most often on the extremities, face,

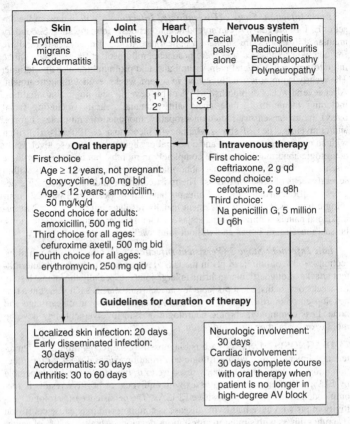

FIGURE 98-1 Algorithm for the treatment of the various acute or chronic manifestations of Lyme borreliosis. Relapse may occur with any of these regimens, and a second course of treatment may be necessary. AV, atrioventricular. *(From AC Steere: HPIM-15, p. 1064.)*

neck, or buttocks, that increases in size by peripheral extension and is accompanied by regional lymphadenopathy. Secondary pigmented lesions without adenopathy appear 1 month to 1 year after the initial lesion.

DIAGNOSIS Serologic tests are required for diagnosis of yaws, since clinical features have become less distinctive with the decreasing prevalence of the disease. However, there is no serologic test that can discriminate among the different treponemal infections. Nonvenereal treponemal infections should be considered in the evaluation of a reactive syphilis serology in any person who has immigrated from an endemic area.

℞ **TREATMENT**

Therapy with IM benzathine penicillin (1.2 million U for adults and 600,000 U for children) leads to rapid resolution of the lesions of yaws or pinta and prevents recurrence. Tetracycline, doxycycline, or erythromycin may be used in penicillin-allergic pts. Contacts of pts should be treated with antibiotics.

LEPTOSPIROSIS

EPIDEMIOLOGY   Leptospirosis is thought to be the most widespread zoonosis in the world, affecting at least 160 mammalian species. Infection in humans occurs mainly during the summer and fall in Western countries and in the tropics. Leptospirosis is acquired through incidental contact with contaminated water (two-thirds of cases) or through contact with urine or tissues of infected animals. Leptospiras enter through abraded skin or mucous membranes. Certain occupational groups are at especially high risk; included are veterinarians, agricultural workers, sewage workers, slaughterhouse employees, and workers in the fishing industry.

CLINICAL MANIFESTATIONS   The incubation period ranges from 2 to 26 d. Leptospirosis typically is a biphasic illness in which an acute leptospiremic phase is followed by an "immune" leptospiruric phase. The initial phase of leptospiremia is characterized by an abrupt onset of headache (usually frontal), severe muscle aches (most prominent in the thighs and the lumbar area), cutaneous hyperesthesia, chills, and fever. The most common physical findings include fever with conjunctival suffusion. Less common findings include muscle tenderness, lymphadenopathy, hepatosplenomegaly, pharyngeal injection, and skin rashes. Most pts become asymptomatic within 1 week. The "immune" phase follows an asymptomatic period of 1–3 d and coincides with the appearance of antibodies. Symptoms in this phase vary but include those seen earlier; symptoms and signs of meningitis are present in 15% of cases. Even in the absence of meningeal signs, CSF pleocytosis is evident after the seventh day in 50–90% of cases. Although often less pronounced in the second phase, fevers can recur; they usually last only 1–3 d. *Weil's syndrome*, the most severe form of leptospirosis, occurs in 5–10% of cases and is characterized by jaundice, renal dysfunction, hemorrhagic diathesis, and high mortality.

DIAGNOSIS   The diagnosis is made by culture or serology. Leptospiras can be cultured in special semisolid medium from blood or CSF during the initial phase or from urine during the second phase. Shedding in the urine may continue from months to years. Specimens can be mailed to a reference laboratory for culture, since leptospiras remain viable in anticoagulated blood for up to 11 days. Antibodies to the organism appear in the second week of illness. For presumptive diagnosis of leptospirosis, an antibody titer in the microscopic agglutination test (MAT) of ≥1:100 in the presence of a compatible clinical illness is required. ELISA can also be used. Serologic testing is not specific for the infecting serovar; thus it is important to culture for the organism.

 TREATMENT   See Table 98-1.

RELAPSING FEVER

EPIDEMIOLOGY   Two types of relapsing fever are caused by *Borrelia* species: louse-borne (LBRF) and tick-borne (TBRF). Louse-borne disease is endemic in Central and East Africa. Tick-borne disease has a worldwide distribution.

CLINICAL MANIFESTATIONS   The clinical manifestations of LBRF and TBRF are similar. After an incubation period of 2–18 d, the illness begins with an abrupt onset of rigors and fevers, headache, arthralgias, and myalgias. Fever is irregular in pattern. The pt develops dry mucous membranes and tender hepatosplenomegaly. Hemorrhagic complications can occur. Symptoms last 2–

Table 98-1

Treatment and Chemoprophylaxis of Leptospirosis

Purpose of Drug Administration	Regimen
Treatment	
Mild leptospirosis	Doxycycline, 100 mg PO bid
	or
	Ampicillin, 500–750 mg PO qid
	or
	Amoxicillin, 500 mg PO qid
Moderate/severe leptospirosis	Penicillin G, 1.5 million U IV qid
	or
	Ampicillin, 1 g IV qid
	or
	Amoxicillin, 1 g IV qid
	or
	Erythromycin, 500 mg IV qid
Chemoprophylaxis	Doxycycline, 200 mg PO once a week

NOTE: All regimens used for treatment are administered for 7 days.
SOURCE: From P Speelman: HPIM-15, p. 1058.

7 d and end in a crisis. Survivors have relapses after 5–10 d of feeling relatively well; TBRF is associated with more relapses than LBRF.

DIAGNOSIS   A definitive diagnosis is made by the demonstration of borreliae in peripheral blood films.

 TREATMENT

See Table 98-2. A Jarisch-Herxheimer reaction may develop within 1–4 h after the initiation of antibiotic therapy; its severity is correlated with the density of spirochetes in the blood.

Table 98-2

Antibiotic Treatment of Louse-Borne and Tick-Borne Relapsing Fever in Adults

Medication	Louse-Borne Relapsing Fever (Single Dose)	Tick-Borne Relapsing Fever (7-Day Schedule)
Oral		
Erythromycin	500 mg	500 mg q6h
Tetracycline	500 mg	500 mg q6h
Doxycycline	100 mg	100 mg q12h
Chloramphenicol	500 mg	500 mg q6h
Parenteral[a]		
Erythromycin	500 mg	500 mg q6h
Tetracycline	250 mg	250 mg q6h
Doxycycline	100 mg	100 mg q12h
Chloramphenicol	500 mg	500 mg q6h
Penicillin G (procaine)	600,000 IU	600,000 IU daily

[a] For tick-borne relapsing fever, parenteral therapy is used only until oral treatment is tolerated.
SOURCE: From DT Dennis, GL Campbell: HPIM-15, p. 1061.

For a more detailed discussion, see Lukehart SA: Endemic Treponemato-
ses, Chap. 173, p. 1053; Speelman P: Leptospirosis, Chap. 174, p. 1055;
Dennis DT, Campbell GL: Relapsing Fever, Chap. 175, p. 1058; and Steere
AC: Lyme Borreliosis, Chap. 176, p. 1061, in HPIM-15.

99

RICKETTSIAL INFECTIONS

The rickettsiae are obligate intracellular bacterial parasites that appear as gram-
negative coccobacilli and short bacilli. The majority of rickettsiae are maintained in nature by a cycle that involves an insect vector and an animal reservoir.
Except for louse-borne typhus, humans are incidental hosts. Only *Coxiella burnetii* (the agent of Q fever) can survive for an extended period outside the
mammalian reservoir or the insect vector.

TICK- AND MITE-BORNE SPOTTED FEVERS
Rocky Mountain Spotted Fever (RMSF)

EPIDEMIOLOGY   RMSF, so called because the first cases were described in the western U.S., has now been documented in 48 states and in
Canada, Mexico, Costa Rica, Panama, Colombia, and Brazil. In the U.S., two
types of ticks may transmit *Rickettsia rickettsii* to humans: the wood tick (*Der-
macentor andersoni*) and the dog tick (*D. variabilis*). The likelihood that an
individual tick carries *R. rickettsii* is small. From 1988 to 1997, the reported
incidence of RMSF was 0.16–0.26 cases per 100,000 population in the U.S.
The mortality rate (20–25% in the preantibiotic era) is now ~5% and is higher
among males than females.

CLINICAL MANIFESTATIONS   Fever, headache, malaise, myalgia,
nausea, vomiting, and anorexia are frequent but nonspecific manifestations during the first 3 d of clinical illness. Rash usually appears by the third day in half
of cases, beginning as pink macules on the wrists and ankles. Lesions spread
centripetally, convert to maculopapules that blanch on compression, and eventually become nonblanching and petechial. While diagnostically helpful when
present, the rash does not appear until day 6 or later in 20% of cases; 10% of
pts, including some with fatal cases, never develop a rash. Severe manifestations
begin by the second week: widespread microvascular damage leads to increased
vascular permeability, resulting in edema, hypovolemia, hypoalbuminemia, prerenal azotemia, and/or noncardiogenic pulmonary edema. Mechanical ventilation may be required—a poor prognostic sign. Encephalitis due to vascular
injury is apparent in 26–28% of cases, often presenting as confusion and lethargy; stupor, delirium, ataxia, coma, and seizures are signs of more severe involvement. CSF pleocytosis, typically mononuclear, occurs in about one-third
of cases. The CSF protein concentration may be elevated, but the CSF glucose
level is usually normal. Nonspecific GI disturbances are common, as are mildly
or moderately elevated serum aminotransferase concentrations (38%) and heme-

positive vomitus or stools (10%); hepatic failure does not occur. In ultimately fatal untreated cases, the pt usually dies within 8–15 d after the onset of illness.

DIAGNOSIS The diagnosis of RMSF during the acute stage is often difficult; early on, clinical and epidemiologic considerations (exposure within 12 d of onset to a potentially tick-infested environment during a season of possible tick activity) are more important than laboratory confirmation. During the acute phase, the only potentially diagnostic test is immunohistologic examination of a biopsy of involved skin. Serologic tests for RMSF are usually negative at presentation. Treatment should not be delayed while serologic results are pending. The most common confirmatory test is the indirect immunofluorescence assay, which is usually positive (titer, ≥1:64) by day 7–10. Moreover, latex agglutination is usually positive (titer, ≥1:128) at 1 week. Both tests are sensitive and highly specific. A solid-state enzyme immunoassay is also available. The Weil-Felix test is unreliable and should no longer be ordered.

 TREATMENT

Therapy is most effective when given early. The treatment of choice for children and nonpregnant adults with RMSF is doxycycline (100 mg PO or IV q12h). The oral route should be used unless precluded by the pt's condition. Tetracycline (25–50 mg/kg PO qd, divided q6h) is an equivalent alternative. For children with RMSF reinfection, up to 5 courses of doxycycline may be given without risk of dental staining. For pregnant women, chloramphenicol (50–75 mg/kg qd, divided q6h) can be used. ICU support may be necessary.

Mediterranean Spotted Fever (Boutonneuse Fever) and Other Spotted Fevers

EPIDEMIOLOGY AND CLINICAL MANIFESTATIONS A number of tick-borne rickettsial infections occur in the eastern hemisphere. *Mediterranean spotted fever* (*boutonneuse fever*), *Kenya tick typhus, Indian tick typhus, Israeli spotted fever*, and *Astrakhan spotted fever* are regional synonyms for the disease produced by *Rickettsia conorii*, which is prevalent in southern Europe, all of Africa, and southwestern and south-central Asia. High fever, rash, and—in most locales—an inoculation eschar at the site of the tick bite are characteristic. *R. africae* is prevalent in central, eastern, and southern Africa and causes *African tick-bite fever*, an illness milder than Mediterranean spotted fever. *R. japonica* causes *Japanese (Oriental) spotted fever*. *R. australis* causes *Queensland tick typhus*, an Australian illness characterized by maculopapular or vesicular rash and an inoculation eschar (a black necrotic area or crust with surrounding erythema).

DIAGNOSIS AND TREATMENT Table 99-1 summarizes the laboratory diagnosis and treatment of the tick-borne spotted fevers and other rickettsial diseases. The spotted fevers are diagnosed presumptively on clinical and epidemiologic grounds, and the diagnosis is generally confirmed serologically. In an endemic area, pts presenting with fever, rash, and an inoculation eschar should be considered to have one of the rickettsial spotted fevers.

Rickettsialpox

EPIDEMIOLOGY *Rickettsia akari*, the etiologic agent of rickettsialpox, infects mice and their mites and is transmitted to humans by mite bites. While formerly not uncommon in the northeastern U.S., the disease is now rarely diagnosed.

Table 99-1

Laboratory Diagnosis and Treatment of Selected Rickettsial Diseases

Disease(s)	Laboratory Diagnosis	Treatment
Mediterranean spotted fever, Japanese or Oriental spotted fever, Queensland tick typhus, Flinders Island spotted fever, African tick-bite fever	Isolation of rickettsiae by shell-vial culture; serology, IFA[a] (IgM, ≥1:64; or IgG, ≥1:128); PCR[a] amplification of DNA from tissue specimens (especially for *R. japonica*)	Doxycycline (100 mg bid PO for 1–5 d) *or* Ciprofloxacin (750 mg bid PO for 5 d) *or* Chloramphenicol (500 mg qid PO for 7–10 d) *or* (in pregnancy) Josamycin[b] (3 g/d PO for 5 d)
Rickettsialpox	IFA: seroconversion to a titer of ≥1:64 or a single titer of ≥1:128; cross-adsorption to eliminate antibodies to shared antigens necessary for a specific diagnosis of the spotted fever rickettsial species	Doxycycline (100 mg bid PO for 1–5 d) *or* Ciprofloxacin (750 mg bid PO for 5 d) *or* Chloramphenicol (500 mg qid PO for 7–10 d) *or* (in pregnancy) Josamycin[b] (3 g/d PO for 5 d)
Endemic (murine) typhus	IFA: fourfold rise to a titer of ≥1:64 or a single titer of ≥1:128; immunohistology: skin biopsy; PCR amplification of *R. typhi* or *R. felis* DNA from blood; dot ELISA[a] and immunoperoxidase methods also available	Doxycycline (100 mg bid PO for 7–15 d) *or* Chloramphenicol (500 mg qid for 7–15 d)
Epidemic typhus	IFA: titer of ≥1:128; necessary to use clinical and epidemiologic data to distinguish among louse-borne epidemic typhus, flying-squirrel typhus, and Brill-Zinsser disease	Doxycycline (200 mg PO as a single dose or until pt is afebrile for 24 h)

(continued)

Table 99-1 *(Continued)*

Laboratory Diagnosis and Treatment of Selected Rickettsial Diseases

Disease(s)	Laboratory Diagnosis	Treatment
Scrub typhus	IFA: titer of ≥1:200; PCR amplification of *Orientia tsutsugamushi* DNA from blood of febrile pts	Doxycycline (100 mg bid PO for 7–15 d)[c] *or* Chloramphenicol (500 mg qid PO for 7–15 d) *or* (for children) Chloramphenicol (150 mg/kg qd for 5 d)

[a] IFA, indirect immunofluorescence assay; PCR, polymerase chain reaction; ELISA, enzyme-linked immunosorbent assay.

[b] Not approved by the Food and Drug Administration.

[c] Azithromycin is more effective than doxycycline in vitro against both doxycycline-susceptible and doxycycline-resistant strains of *O. tsutsugamushi*.

SOURCE: D Walker et al: HPIM-15, p. 1068.

CLINICAL MANIFESTATIONS   The lesion at the site of the mite bite evolves from papular to vesicular and then to a painless black eschar with an erythematous halo. Regional lymphadenopathy is common. After a 10-d incubation period, malaise, chills, fever, headache, and myalgia begin. A macular rash begins 2–6 d later and evolves sequentially into papules, vesicles, and crusts that heal without scarring. Without treatment, the illness lasts for 6–10 d and is self-limited.

DIAGNOSIS AND TREATMENT   See Table 99-1.

FLEA- AND LOUSE-BORNE RICKETTSIAL DISEASES
Endemic (Murine) Typhus (Flea-Borne)

EPIDEMIOLOGY   Murine typhus is a global disease caused by two rickettsial species, *R. typhi* and *R. felis*. *R. typhi* is classically maintained in rats and is transmitted to humans by the Oriental rat flea (*Xenopsylla cheopis*). *R. felis* has been characterized more recently and is maintained in a cycle involving opossums and cat fleas (*Ctenocephalides felis*). Fewer than 100 cases of endemic typhus are reported annually in the U.S. and occur year-round, mainly in warm areas.

CLINICAL MANIFESTATIONS   The incubation period is 8–16 d. Prodromal symptoms of headache, myalgia, arthralgia, nausea, and malaise may occur. The onset of acute illness is characterized by the abrupt onset of chills and fever; nausea and vomiting are nearly universal. Rash occurs in somewhat more than half of pts. It most often appears about the sixth day of the illness and, in contrast to the rash of RMSF, is mostly confined to the trunk, with sparse involvement of the extremities, palms, soles, and face. Early lesions are macular and are hidden in the axillae and inner surfaces of the arms; later, a more generalized, discrete maculopapular rash involves the upper part of the abdomen, shoulders, chest, arms, and thighs. A hacking, nonproductive cough is a frequent finding. CXRs are abnormal in ~25% of cases. Without treatment, the illness lasts an average of 12 d. Pts recover rapidly after defervescing; the case-fatality rate is 1%.

DIAGNOSIS AND TREATMENT   See Table 99-1.

Epidemic Typhus (Louse-Borne)

EPIDEMIOLOGY   Epidemic typhus is caused by *R. prowazekii* and is transmitted to humans by the body louse (*Pediculus humanus corporis*), which lives on clothes and is associated with poor hygiene. Lice pass the infection from person to person. Epidemic typhus is associated with poverty, war, cold weather, and natural disasters. In the U.S., sporadic cases result from transmission by the fleas of flying squirrels. *Brill-Zinsser disease* is a recrudescent, mild form of epidemic typhus occurring years after the acute disease; *R. prowazekii* can remain dormant for years and reactivate if immunity wanes.

CLINICAL MANIFESTATIONS   Epidemic typhus resembles murine typhus but is more severe. The incubation period is ~7 d. Disease onset is abrupt, with prostration, severe headache, and rapidly mounting fever. Myalgias are usually severe. Rash appears by the fifth febrile day. It is initially macular and confined to the axillary folds but later involves the trunk and extremities and may become petechial and confluent. Photophobia, conjunctival injection, and ocular pain are frequent. In untreated cases, up to 40% of which are fatal, azotemia, multiorgan involvement, and digital gangrene may occur; 12% of such cases have prominent neurologic manifestations. Sporadic North American cases are much milder than epidemic cases. Brill-Zinsser disease resembles epidemic typhus. While it is not always mild, recovery is the rule.

DIAGNOSIS AND TREATMENT   See Table 99-1.

CHIGGER-BORNE SCRUB TYPHUS

EPIDEMIOLOGY   Scrub typhus is caused by *Orientia tsutsugamushi* and is transmitted to humans by the bites of infected trombiculid mite larvae (genus *Leptotrombidium*). The disease occurs in areas of heavy scrub vegetation, typically during the wet season when mites lay their eggs. It is endemic in eastern and southern Asia, in northern Australia, and in islands of the western Pacific.

CLINICAL MANIFESTATIONS   Scrub typhus varies in severity from mild to fatal. After an incubation period of 6–21 d, the illness begins with fever, headache, myalgia, cough, and GI symptoms. Classic but infrequently observed signs include an inoculation eschar, regional lymphadenopathy, and a maculopapular rash. In severe cases, vascular injury may lead to encephalitis and interstitial pneumonia.

DIAGNOSIS AND TREATMENT   See Table 99-1.

EHRLICHIOSIS

Ehrlichiae are small, gram-negative, obligately intracellular bacteria that grow as microcolonies in phagosomes. Visible vacuolar clusters of ehrlichiae within phagocytes are termed *morulae*. Two distinct *Ehrlichia* species cause human infections that can be severe and frequent. Their characteristics and treatment are listed in Table 99-2. Human monocytotropic ehrlichiosis (HME) is caused by *E. chaffeensis*, which infects predominantly mononuclear cells in blood and tissues. Human granulocytotropic ehrlichiosis (HGE) is caused by a member of the *E. phagocytophila* group, which infects cells of myeloid lineage.

Human Monocytotropic Ehrlichiosis

EPIDEMIOLOGY   The major vector for *E. chaffeensis* infection is the Lone Star tick (*Amblyomma americanum*); the white-tailed deer is an important reservoir host. Most U.S. cases have occurred in the south-central, southeastern,

Table 99-2

Comparison of Two Human Ehrlichioses: Human Monocytotropic Ehrlichiosis (HME) and Human Granulocytotropic Ehrlichiosis (HGE)

Variable	HME	HGE
Etiologic agent	*E. chaffeensis*	*E. phagocytophila* group
Tick vector(s)	*Amblyomma americanum, Dermacentor variabilis* (dog tick)	*Ixodes scapularis* (deer tick), *I. ricinus*, *I. pacificus*
Seasonality	April through September	Year-round (peak: May, June, and July)
Major target cell	Monocyte	Granulocyte
Morulae seen	Rarely	Frequently
Antigen used in IFA test	*E. chaffeensis*	HGE strains
Diagnostic titer	Fourfold rise or a single titer of ≥1:128; cutoff for negative titer, 1:64	Fourfold rise; cutoff for negative titer, 1:80
Treatment of choice	Doxycycline	Doxycycline
Mortality	2–3%	<1%

NOTE: IFA, indirect immunofluorescence assay.
SOURCE: D Walker et al: HPIM-15, p. 1070.

and mid-Atlantic regions. Cases have also been documented in Africa and Europe. Disease acquisition in the U.S. is most common in May–July and in rural areas. The median age of HME pts is 44 years, and 75% are male.

CLINICAL MANIFESTATIONS Clinical illness occurs in about one-third of persons who seroconvert. The median incubation period is 8 d, and the median duration of clinical illness is 23 d. Manifestations are nonspecific and include (in order of decreasing frequency) fever, headache, myalgia, malaise, GI involvement (nausea, vomiting, diarrhea), rash, cough, and confusion. Severe cases can include respiratory insufficiency, neurologic involvement, GI bleeding, and/or opportunistic viral or fungal infection. The mortality rate is 2–3%. Laboratory findings suggestive of the diagnosis include thrombocytopenia, leukopenia, and elevated serum levels of aminotransferases. Ehrlichial morular inclusions are seldom seen in peripheral blood. Bone marrow is hypercellular and may have noncaseating granulomas.

DIAGNOSIS Clinical suspicion of HME should be triggered by fever in the setting of tick exposure in an endemic area within the previous 3 weeks, leukopenia and/or thrombocytopenia, and increased aminotransferase concentrations in serum. PCR of peripheral blood may be positive for *E. chaffeensis* DNA during acute illness. Antibodies to the organism may be detected by indirect immunofluorescence during convalescence. A titer of ≥1:64 is considered positive.

 TREATMENT

Once HME has been presumptively identified, treatment should be initiated promptly. Tetracyclines (e.g., doxycycline, 100 mg q12h) shorten the course of illness and should be continued for 3–5 d after defervescence. Use of chloramphenicol is controversial.

Human Granulocytotropic Ehrlichiosis

EPIDEMIOLOGY   Most U.S. cases of HGE occur in the upper Midwest and in the Northeast, in May–July, and in a distribution similar to that of Lyme disease. *Ixodes* ticks—particularly *I. scapularis* (*dammini*) but also *I. pacificus* and *I. ricinus*—are probable vectors. Mammalian reservoir hosts are incompletely defined. HGE predominantly affects males and older persons.

CLINICAL MANIFESTATIONS   The incubation period is 4–8 d. HGE presents as a flulike illness, with fever, malaise, and headache. GI symptoms (nausea, vomiting, and diarrhea), cough, and confusion are less frequent. Rash is rare. Thrombocytopenia, leukopenia, anemia, and elevated serum aminotransferase levels are common. Morulae are commonly found in PMNs in the peripheral blood. The mortality rate is <1%, but nearly 7% of pts require management in the ICU. As in HME, opportunistic infections and respiratory insufficiency may occur. The possibility of coinfection with *Borrelia burgdorferi* (Lyme disease) or *Babesia microti* (babesiosis) should be entertained in all HGE cases, since the *I. scapularis* (*dammini*) vector is shared by all three agents.

DIAGNOSIS   HGE should be suspected in a pt with fever and flulike symptoms who has been exposed to an environment infested with the appropriate ticks, especially if thrombocytopenia is detected. PCR may be useful acutely. Serodiagnosis by indirect immunofluorescence assay may provide retrospective confirmation, with a convalescent *E. phagocytophila* group antibody titer of ≥1:80.

℞ TREATMENT

Doxycycline (100 mg PO bid) is therapeutically effective. Rifampin has been associated with clinical improvement in pregnant pts with HGE. Most treated pts defervesce within 24–48 h.

Q FEVER

EPIDEMIOLOGY   Q fever is a zoonosis caused by *C. burnetii*, an organism with a global distribution. The primary sources of human infection are infected cattle, sheep, and goats. In the infected female mammal, *C. burnetii* localizes to the uterus and mammary glands, reaches high concentrations in the placenta, and is dispersed as an aerosol at parturition. Infection follows inhalation of aerosolized organisms, ingestion of infected milk, or transfusion of infected blood. Abattoir workers and veterinarians are at particular risk. Rare cases of person-to-person transmission have followed delivery of an infant to an infected woman or autopsy of an infected cadaver.

CLINICAL MANIFESTATIONS   *Acute Q Fever*   With an incubation period of 3–30 d, Q fever may present in a variety of ways. Recognized syndromes include a flulike illness, prolonged fever, pneumonia, hepatitis, pericarditis, myocarditis, meningoencephalitis, and infection during pregnancy. Symptoms are nonspecific; fever, extreme fatigue, and severe headache are common. Chills, sweats, nausea, vomiting, diarrhea, cough, and nonspecific rash may also occur. Neurologic manifestations are infrequent. Thrombocytopenia is noted in ~25% of cases during the acute phase. Multiple rounded opacities on CXR are common and are highly suggestive of Q fever pneumonia in the appropriate epidemiologic setting.

Chronic Q Fever Chronic Q fever almost always implies endocarditis. This infection occurs in pts with previous valvular heart disease, immunosuppression, or chronic renal insufficiency. Nonspecific symptoms may exist for up to 1 year before diagnosis. Fever is absent or low-grade. Hepatomegaly and/or splenomegaly is usually detectable. The diagnosis should be considered in all pts with valvular heart disease, unexplained purpura, renal insufficiency, stroke, and/or progressive heart failure. A positive rheumatoid factor titer, an elevated ESR or C-reactive protein level, and/or an elevated gamma globulin concentration also suggests this diagnosis.

DIAGNOSIS Serology (CF, ELISA, or indirect immunofluorescence) is the diagnostic tool of choice. Indirect immunofluorescence is sensitive and specific and can be used to diagnose both acute and chronic Q fever. PCR can be used to amplify *C. burnetii* DNA from tissue specimens. Culture of the organism is possible but potentially dangerous.

 TREATMENT

Acute Q fever is treated with doxycycline (100 mg q12h for 14 d) or a quinolone. Chronic Q fever is treated with at least two active agents—e.g., doxycycline (100 mg q12h) plus rifampin (300 mg/d). A minimum treatment duration of 3 years is recommended. An alternative 18-month regimen—doxycycline plus hydroxychloroquine (600 mg/d)—is under investigation.

For a more detailed discussion, see Walker D, Raoult D, Dumler JS, Marrie T: Rickettsial Diseases, Chap. 177, p. 1065, in HPIM-15.

100

MYCOPLASMA INFECTIONS

Mycoplasmas, which are ubiquitous in nature, are the smallest free-living microorganisms and lack rigid cell walls.

MYCOPLASMA PNEUMONIAE

EPIDEMIOLOGY A common cause of upper and lower respiratory tract infection, *M. pneumoniae* is the most important pathogen of the *Mycoplasma* group. Infection is acquired by inhalation of aerosols, with an incubation period of 2–3 weeks. Although epidemics can occur in closed populations (e.g., those of schools and military installations), most cases occur sporadically or in families.

CLINICAL MANIFESTATIONS The most common clinical syndrome is acute or subacute tracheobronchitis accompanied by upper respiratory tract symptoms. Pneumonitis is also common. Symptoms generally include headache, malaise, fever [38.9–39.4°C (102–103°F)], sore throat, and a dry paroxysmal cough that later becomes productive. Extrapulmonary manifestations are unusual but may be the only clue that the respiratory infection is mycoplasmal. These manifestations can include otitis media, bullous myringitis, maculopapular rashes, erythema multiforme, and occasionally Stevens-Johnson syndrome. Cardiac abnormalities, including myocarditis and pericarditis, may develop. Neurologic conditions that have been associated with *M. pneumoniae* include meningoencephalitis, cerebellar ataxia, Guillain-Barré syndrome, transverse myelitis, and peripheral neuropathies. Arthralgias are not unusual, and arthritis can be seen in pts with hypogammaglobulinemia. *M. pneumoniae* infection may be particularly severe in pts with sickle cell disease, possibly because of functional asplenia.

DIAGNOSIS Clinical, radiologic, and laboratory findings in *M. pneumoniae* infection are not sufficiently distinctive for diagnostic purposes. The leukocyte count is somewhat elevated. The CXR may show reticulonodular or interstitial infiltrates, primarily in the lower lobes. However, these radiographic abnormalities may be more prominent than would be predicted by auscultation of the chest. Because it lacks a cell wall, *M. pneumoniae* cannot be seen on Gram's stain of sputum. Definitive diagnosis is difficult during acute infection, since most clinical laboratories do not have the capability to isolate the organism. Specific antibodies can be detected by ELISA, indirect immunofluorescence, or CF but do not develop early enough to aid in pt management. Examination of paired acute- and convalescent-phase serum specimens taken 2–4 weeks apart is required for good sensitivity and specificity. Cold agglutinins are nonspecific but develop within the first 7–10 days in >50% of pts with *M. pneumoniae* pneumonia. In a symptomatic pt, a cold agglutinin titer of ≥1:32 supports the diagnosis of mycoplasmal pneumonia.

℞ TREATMENT

Because most mycoplasmal infections are not specifically diagnosed, management is directed at one of two syndromes: URI or community-acquired pneumonia. URIs do not require antimicrobial treatment. Community-acquired pneumonia (Chap. 131) should be treated with antibiotics covering common and "atypical" bacteria. Recommended regimens for community-acquired pneumonia include a third-generation cephalosporin (e.g., ceftriaxone, 1 g IV qd) plus erythromycin (500 mg IV or PO qid). Newer agents that may be used as monotherapy include clarithromycin (500 mg PO bid), azithromycin (500 mg PO qd), and levofloxacin (500 mg PO qd). Pneumonia due to *M. pneumoniae* is usually self-limited, but appropriate antibiotic therapy shortens the course. Treatment of documented *M. pneumoniae* pneumonia is continued for 14–21 days.

GENITAL MYCOPLASMAS

EPIDEMIOLOGY *Mycoplasma hominis* and *Ureaplasma urealyticum* are the most prevalent genital mycoplasmas and cause genitourinary syndromes or perinatal infections. Both organisms may colonize the genital tract of healthy, sexually experienced adults without causing disease. Men have somewhat lower rates of genital colonization than women.

CLINICAL MANIFESTATIONS Manifestations include urethritis, epididymitis, prostatitis, and pelvic inflammatory disease. Occasionally, reactive arthritis (Reiter's disease) may be triggered by ureaplasmas. Pts with agammaglobulinemia develop joint inflammation that can be due to ureaplasmas or mycoplasmas. Infection with *M. hominis* has been documented in surgical wounds, at sites of trauma, and on prosthetic heart valves. Association of urea-plasmas with infertility in both men and women is controversial.

DIAGNOSIS   Diagnosis by culture usually requires that the specimen be sent to a reference laboratory, although *M. hominis* can be recovered in some routine blood culture systems. There is seldom any reason to examine specimens from the lower genital tract for mycoplasmas since the organisms are ubiquitous.

 TREATMENT

Treatment for *M. hominis* infection consists of tetracycline (250 mg PO qid) or clindamycin (150 mg PO qid); erythromycin is not effective. Up to 40% of *M. hominis* strains may now be resistant to tetracycline. For *Ureaplasma* infections, erythromycin or tetracycline may be used. Since a microbiologic diagnosis is seldom made, appropriate treatment should provide antimicrobial coverage for all potential pathogens.

For a more detailed discussion, see McCormack WM: *Mycoplasma* Infections, Chap. 178, p. 1073, in HPIM-15.

101

CHLAMYDIAL INFECTIONS

The genus *Chlamydia* contains three species: *C. psittaci, C. trachomatis*, and *C. pneumoniae* (formerly called TWAR). Chlamydiae are obligate intracellular bacteria. Different serovars are associated with different clinical syndromes. Chlamydiae cause conjunctival, genital, and respiratory infections.

C. TRACHOMATIS GENITAL INFECTIONS AND LYMPHOGRANULOMA VENEREUM
See Chap. 83.

TRACHOMA AND ADULT INCLUSION CONJUNCTIVITIS
EPIDEMIOLOGY   In trachoma-endemic areas, *C. trachomatis* (usually serovar A, B, Ba, or C) is the major preventable cause of blindness. Transmission is from eye to eye via hands, flies, or fomites. In nonendemic areas, disease is usually confined to inclusion conjunctivitis and is caused by serovars D–K, which are transmitted via infected secretions from the genital tract to the eye.

CLINICAL MANIFESTATIONS   Endemic trachoma usually begins as conjunctivitis with small lymphoid follicles in children <2 years old. It progresses to corneal involvement with inflammatory leukocytic infiltrations and superficial vascularization (pannus formation). Conjunctival scarring leads to distortion of the eyelids, inturned lashes that abrade and ulcerate the corneal epithelium, and subsequently corneal scarring and blindness. Eye infection with genital strains usually causes an acute onset of unilateral follicular conjunctivitis and preauricular lymphadenopathy in sexually active young adults.

DIAGNOSIS Classic trachoma is usually diagnosed clinically if two of the following signs are present: (1) lymphoid follicles on the upper tarsal conjunctiva, (2) typical conjunctival scarring, (3) vascular pannus, and (4) limbal follicles. The most sensitive laboratory tests are isolation of the organism in cell culture, newer antigen detection tests, and chlamydial polymerase chain reaction. Intracytoplasmic inclusions on Giemsa-stained conjunctival smears are diagnostic but are less sensitive. For adult inclusion conjunctivitis, culture or Giemsa or immunofluorescent staining of conjunctival smears is used and should be accompanied by genital examinations and cultures. Serum antibody tests are not diagnostic.

 TREATMENT

Therapy includes the topical application of tetracycline or erythromycin ointment for 21–60 d. Alternatively, tetracycline or erythromycin (500 mg qid PO for 3 weeks) may be used in adults and erythromycin (50 mg/kg PO daily for 3 weeks) in children. Treatment of sexual partners is important in genitally acquired infection. Topical therapy is not necessary if oral antibiotics are used.

PSITTACOSIS

EPIDEMIOLOGY Psittacosis (infection with *C. psittaci*) is transmitted via the respiratory route from many avian species, including psittacine birds (parrots, parakeets), pigeons, ducks, turkeys, chickens, and other birds. Occasionally, infection has resulted from contact with the environment previously occupied by an infected bird rather than from direct exposure to birds. Infected birds may not manifest symptoms. The incubation period is 7–14 d or longer.

CLINICAL MANIFESTATIONS Prominent headache, fevers increasing over a 3- to 4-d period, and a dry hacking cough occurring as late as 5 d after fevers begin are the most common manifestations. Pulmonary symptoms are usually more prominent than signs. Other symptoms may include myalgias, lethargy, agitation, mental depression (progressing to stupor or coma in severe cases), and GI symptoms such as abdominal pain, vomiting, and diarrhea. Splenomegaly is found in 10–70% of cases. Psittacosis should be considered strongly in pts with acute pneumonitis and splenomegaly.

DIAGNOSIS CXRs usually show diffuse, patchy infiltrates but may yield a variety of findings. The WBC count, ESR, and LFTs are usually normal. The diagnosis can be made only by isolating the organism (which is difficult in the laboratory) or by demonstrating a fourfold rise in CF antibody. Early antibiotic treatment may delay the convalescent antibody response by weeks or months.

C. psittaci, C. pneumoniae, and *C. trachomatis* share a genus-specific "group" antigen; a cross-reaction due to this antigen is the basis of the CF test. If there is doubt as to the interpretation, a micro-IF test can be used to distinguish the organisms based on different outer-membrane proteins.

 TREATMENT

Tetracycline (500 mg qid) usually leads to defervescence and alleviation of symptoms in 24–48 h. Treatment should be continued for at least 7–14 d after fever abates to avoid relapse. Erythromycin can be used for pts allergic to or intolerant of tetracycline.

C. PNEUMONIAE INFECTIONS

EPIDEMIOLOGY   Serologic studies indicate that *C. pneumoniae* infections are ubiquitous. Seroprevalence rates in adult populations exceed 40%. The route of transmission appears to be from person to person. Primary infection seems to occur in young adults, with less severe reinfection episodes in older adults. Epidemiologic studies have demonstrated an association between serologic evidence of *C. pneumoniae* infection and atherosclerotic disease of the coronary and other arteries. *C. pneumoniae* has been identified in atherosclerotic plaques by several techniques. Antimicrobial treatment of infected animals has been shown to reduce the increased risk of atherosclerosis. Larger trials in humans are needed to determine more definitively whether antibiotics affect the risk of atherosclerosis.

CLINICAL MANIFESTATIONS   The clinical spectrum includes acute pharyngitis, sinusitis, bronchitis, and pneumonitis. Upper respiratory tract symptoms usually precede fever and nonproductive cough. The pneumonitis often resembles *Mycoplasma pneumoniae* pneumonia. Pulmonary findings generally are minimal. Leukocytosis is typically absent. CXRs generally show small segmental infiltrates.

DIAGNOSIS   Diagnosis is difficult because culture and antigen detection techniques are not available. A rise in CF antibody between acute- and convalescent-phase serum samples can allow a retrospective diagnosis but does not distinguish *C. pneumoniae* from *C. trachomatis* and *C. psittaci*. The micro-IF test can be used to make these distinctions.

℞ TREATMENT

The recommended therapy consists of erythromycin or tetracycline (500 mg qid PO) for 10–14 d. Other macrolides, such as azithromycin, and some fluoroquinolones, such as levofloxacin, also appear to be effective.

For a more detailed discussion, see Stamm WE: Chlamydial Infections, Chap. 179, p. 1075, in HPIM-15.

102

HERPESVIRUS INFECTIONS

HERPES SIMPLEX VIRUSES

The genome of herpes simplex virus (HSV) is a linear, double-stranded DNA molecule that encodes for >75 gene products. Overall DNA sequence homology between HSV-1 and HSV-2 is ~50%. HSV infection of some neuronal cells does not result in cell death; instead, viral genomes are maintained by the cell in a repressed state known as *latency*. The process of activation of the viral genome that leads to viral replication and causes recurrent lesions is known as *reactivation*.

PATHOGENESIS   Exposure of mucosal surfaces or abraded skin to HSV permits entry of the virus and initiation of its replication in epidermal and dermal cells. Sensory or autonomic nerve endings may become infected whether or not clinically apparent lesions develop. Initially, virus replicates in ganglia and contiguous neural tissue; spread occurs via peripheral sensory nerves. While the mechanism of reactivation is not known, stimuli such as UV light, immunosuppression, and trauma to skin or ganglia are associated with reactivation.

EPIDEMIOLOGY   Infection with HSV-1 is acquired more frequently and at an earlier age than infection with HSV-2. By the fifth decade of life, >90% of adults have antibodies to HSV-1. Antibodies to HSV-2 are not routinely detected until puberty; their prevalence varies with the population studied. In obstetric and family planning clinic populations, 25% of women have antibody to HSV-2, although only 10% give a history of genital lesions. In heterosexual adults attending STD clinics, the prevalence of antibody to HSV-2 is up to 50%. The incubation period for HSV infection ranges from 1 to 26 d (median, 6–8 d). HSV can be transmitted by contact with active lesions or with an asymptomatic person excreting the virus; the efficiency of transmission is greater from active lesions.

CLINICAL MANIFESTATIONS   *Oral-Facial Infections*   Gingivostomatitis and pharyngitis are the most common clinical manifestations of first-episode HSV-1 infection and are most prevalent among children and young adults. Clinical symptoms and signs include fever, malaise, myalgias, inability to eat, irritability, and cervical adenopathy that may last 3–14 d. Lesions may involve the hard and soft palates, gingiva, tongue, lips, and facial area. Reactivation may lead to asymptomatic excretion in the saliva, intraoral mucosal ulcerations, or herpetic ulcerations of the vermilion border of the lip or external facial skin. In immunosuppressed pts, including those with AIDS, severe mucositis due to HSV can develop. Pts with eczema may develop severe oral-facial lesions (eczema herpeticum) with occasional visceral dissemination. HSV-1 has recently been implicated as a cause of Bell's palsy. Some evidence suggests that HSV infection is the precipitating event in ~75% of cases of erythema multiforme.

Rectal and Perianal Infections   HSV-1 and HSV-2 can cause symptomatic or asymptomatic rectal and perianal infections. Symptoms of HSV proctitis include anorectal pain, discharge, tenesmus, and constipation, with ulcerative lesions of the distal 10 cm of rectal mucosa. HSV proctitis is usually associated with rectal intercourse; however, subclinical perianal shedding can occur in persons who report no rectal intercourse.

Genital Infections   See Chap. 83.

Herpetic Whitlow   Clinical symptoms of herpetic whitlow (HSV infection of the finger) include an abrupt onset of edema, erythema, and localized tenderness of the infected finger after direct inoculation. Vesicular or pustular lesions, fever, and lymphadenitis make this infection clinically indistinguishable from a pyogenic infection. Surgical debridement may exacerbate the condition.

Herpes Gladiatorum   Mucocutaneous HSV infections of the thorax, ears, face, and hands have been described among wrestlers.

Herpetic Eye Infections   HSV infection is the most common cause of corneal blindness in the U.S. Herpetic keratitis presents as an acute onset of pain, blurring of vision, chemosis, conjunctivitis, and characteristic dendritic lesions of the cornea. Chorioretinitis occurs in neonates or HIV-infected pts, usually as a manifestation of disseminated infection. Acute necrotizing retinitis is a rare but serious manifestation of HSV and varicella-zoster virus (VZV) infection.

Central and Peripheral Nervous System Infections   HSV is the most common cause of acute sporadic viral encephalitis in the U.S., accounting for 10–20% of cases. HSV-1 causes >95% of cases, with peaks at 5–30 years and >50 years of age. Clinical manifestations include an acute onset of fever and focal neurologic (especially temporal lobe) symptoms. The diagnosis can be made by brain biopsy; the most sensitive early noninvasive method is demonstration of HSV DNA in the CSF by PCR. Treatment with IV acyclovir is started for a presumptive diagnosis. HSV meningitis, usually seen in association with primary genital HSV infection, is a self-limited disease, with headache, fever, and mild photophobia but no neurologic sequelae. Autonomic nervous system dysfunction, especially of the sacral region, is associated with both HSV and VZV infections. Symptoms include numbness, tingling of the buttock or perineal areas, urinary retention, constipation, CSF pleocytosis, and (in males) impotence; these symptoms resolve slowly over days or weeks. In rare instances, HSV infection is associated with transverse myelitis, manifested by rapidly progressive symmetric lower-extremity paralysis or Guillain-Barré syndrome. Peripheral nervous system involvement includes Bell's palsy or cranial polyneuritis related to reactivation of HSV-1 infection.

Visceral Infections   Visceral HSV infection commonly involves multiple organs and results from viremia. HSV esophagitis presents as odynophagia, dysphagia, substernal pain, weight loss, and multiple oval ulcerations on an erythematous base with or without a patchy white pseudomembrane. The distal esophagus is most frequently involved. The diagnosis can be made only by endoscopic biopsy with cytology and culture. HSV pneumonitis mainly affects severely immunocompromised pts. Focal necrotizing pneumonitis results from the extension of herpetic tracheobronchitis. Hematogenous dissemination from mucocutaneous disease causes bilateral interstitial pneumonitis. The mortality rate from untreated HSV pneumonia in immunosuppressed pts is high (>80%). HSV is an uncommon cause of hepatitis. The presentation includes fever, abrupt elevations of serum levels of bilirubin and aminotransferases, and leukopenia. DIC may be present. Other rare disseminated manifestations include monarticular arthritis, adrenal necrosis, idiopathic thrombocytopenia, and glomerulonephritis. In immunocompromised pts, rare sites of organ involvement can include the adrenal glands, pancreas, small and large intestines, and bone marrow.

Neonatal Infections   Infants <6 weeks of age have the highest frequency of visceral and/or CNS infection due to HSV. Without treatment, the overall rate of death from neonatal herpes is 65%. Neonatal cases almost always result from contact with infected genital secretions at delivery; 70% of cases are caused by HSV-2.

DIAGNOSIS   A clinical diagnosis can be made by scraping the base of lesions and demonstrating multinucleated giant cells with Wright's stain or Giemsa's stain (Tzanck preparation) or characteristic giant cells or intranuclear inclusions by cytology (Papanicolaou's stain). Cultures become positive in 48–96 h. Methods such as immunofluorescence assay, ELISA, and some DNA hybridization techniques are almost as sensitive as viral isolation from genital or orolabial lesions; however, they are only 50% as sensitive as viral culture for cervical lesions or salivary secretions. PCR is more sensitive than culture for CNS infections and late-stage ulcerative lesions. Seroconversion can be used to document primary infections, but only 5% of pts with reactivation of HSV infection have a fourfold or greater rise in antibody titer.

℞ TREATMENT   See Table 102-1.

VARICELLA-ZOSTER VIRUS

VZV is a herpesvirus that causes two distinct clinical entities: varicella (chickenpox) and herpes zoster (shingles).

PATHOGENESIS   Primary infection occurs via the respiratory route and is followed by viremia. Reactivation results in herpes zoster by mechanisms that are unknown. It is presumed that VZV infects the dorsal root ganglia during chickenpox and remains latent at that site until reactivated.

EPIDEMIOLOGY   Attack rates for chickenpox are at least 90% among susceptible pts. Cases occur throughout the year, but the disease is epidemic during the late winter and early spring in temperate climates. Children 5–9 years of age account for 50% of cases. The incubation period ranges between 10 and 21 d but is usually 14–17 d. Pts are infectious 48 h before vesicles erupt, during vesicle formation (usually 4–5 d), and until all vesicles are crusted. The incidence of herpes zoster is highest in the sixth through eighth decades of life, but the disease can occur at any age. Most pts with herpes zoster have no exposure to other persons infected with VZV.

CLINICAL MANIFESTATIONS   *Chickenpox*   Low-grade fever and malaise may precede the exanthem by 24–48 h. Fever and lassitude generally last 3–5 d in immunocompetent hosts. The rash consists of maculopapules, vesicles, and scabs in various stages of evolution. Crops of lesions develop over 2–4 d. Lesions may be found on the pharyngeal or vaginal mucosa. Younger pts tend to have fewer lesions overall than older individuals. Lesions of immunocompromised pts, especially those with leukemia, may be more numerous, may be hemorrhagic, and may take longer to resolve; these pts may be at greater risk of visceral complications. The most common complication of varicella is bacterial superinfection of the skin, usually caused by *Streptococcus pyogenes* or *Staphylococcus aureus*. In children, CNS involvement is the most common extracutaneous manifestation. A syndrome of cerebellar ataxia and meningeal irritation generally develops ~21 d after the onset of rash, is usually self-limited, and does not require hospitalization. Other CNS manifestations include aseptic meningitis, encephalitis, transverse myelitis, Guillain-Barré syndrome, and Reye's syndrome. Varicella pneumonia is the most common serious complication of chickenpox, occurring more frequently among adults (in up to 20% of cases) than among children. Usually developing 3–5 d into the illness, varicella pneumonia is associated with tachypnea, cough, dyspnea, and fever. CXR findings include nodular infiltrates and interstitial pneumonitis. Other complications include myocarditis, corneal lesions, nephritis, arthritis, bleeding diatheses, acute glomerulonephritis, and hepatitis. Hepatic involvement distinct from Reye's syndrome is common, is usually characterized by elevation of serum aminotransferase levels, and is generally asymptomatic. Perinatal varicella is most severe when maternal disease develops within 5 d before or 48 h after delivery. Congenital varicella is extremely uncommon.

Herpes Zoster   Herpes zoster is characterized by a unilateral vesicular eruption within a dermatome accompanied by severe local pain. Pain heralds

Table 102-1

Antiviral Chemotherapy for HSV Infection

Mucocutaneous HSV infections
 Infections in immunosuppressed pts
  Acute symptomatic first or recurrent episodes: IV acyclovir (5 mg/kg q8h)
   or oral acyclovir (400 mg qid for 7–10 d) relieves pain and speeds healing.
  Suppression of reactivation disease: IV acyclovir (5 mg/kg q12h) or oral
   acyclovir (400–800 mg 3–5 times/d) prevents recurrences during high-
   risk periods, e.g., the immediate posttransplantation period. In HIV-
   infected persons, oral famciclovir (500 mg bid) or valacyclovir (500 mg
   bid) is also effective.
 Genital herpes
  First episodes: Oral acyclovir (200 mg 5 times/d or 400 mg tid) is given.
   Oral valacyclovir (1000 mg bid) or famciclovir (250 mg tid) for 10–14
   d is effective. IV acyclovir (5 mg/kg q8h for 5 d) is given for severe
   disease or neurologic complications such as aseptic meningitis.
  Symptomatic recurrent genital herpes: Oral acyclovir (200 mg 5 times/d
   or 400 mg tid for 5 d), valacyclovir (500 mg bid), or famciclovir (125
   mg bid) is effective in shortening lesion duration and viral excretion time.
  Suppression of recurrent genital herpes: Oral acyclovir (200-mg capsules;
   400 mg bid or 800 mg qd), famciclovir (250 mg bid), or valacyclovir
   (250 or 500 mg bid or 1000 mg qd) prevents symptomatic reactivation.
 Oral-labial HSV infections
  First episode: Oral acyclovir (200 mg) is given 4 or 5 times/d. Famciclovir
   (250 mg bid) or valacyclovir (1000 mg bid) has been used clinically.
  Recurrent episodes: Topical penciclovir cream is effective in speeding the
   healing of oral-labial HSV. Topical acyclovir cream is licensed in Europe.
   The ointment formulation of acyclovir available in the U.S. has no clinical
   benefit. Oral valacyclovir has some benefit. Oral acyclovir has minimal
   benefit.
  Suppression of reactivation of oral-labial HSV: Oral acyclovir (400 mg
   bid), if started before exposure and continued for the duration of exposure
   (usually 5–10 d), prevents reactivation of recurrent oral-labial HSV infection associated with severe sun exposure.
 Herpetic whitlow: Oral acyclovir (200 mg) is given 5 times/d for 7–10 d.
 HSV proctitis: Oral acyclovir (400 mg 5 times/d) is useful in shortening the
  course of infection. In immunosuppressed pts or in pts with severe infection,
  IV acyclovir (5 mg/kg q8h) may be useful.
 Herpetic eye infections: In acute keratitis, topical trifluorothymidine, vidar-
  abine, idoxuridine, acyclovir, penciclovir, and interferon are all beneficial.
  Debridement may be required; topical steroids may worsen disease.
CNS HSV infections
 HSV encephalitis: IV acyclovir (10 mg/kg q8h; 30 mg/kg qd) for 10 d is
  preferred.
 HSV aseptic meningitis: No studies of systemic antiviral chemotherapy exist.
  If therapy is to be given, IV acyclovir (15–30 mg/kg qd) should be used.
 Autonomic radiculopathy: No studies are available.
Neonatal HSV infections: Acyclovir (60 mg/kg qd, divided into 3 doses) is
 given. The recommended duration of treatment is 21 d.
Visceral HSV infections
 HSV esophagitis: IV acyclovir (5 mg/kg q8h) is given. In some pts with
  milder forms of immunosuppression, oral therapy with valacyclovir or fam-
  ciclovir is effective.

(continued)

Table 102-1 *(Continued)*

Antiviral Chemotherapy for HSV Infection

   HSV pneumonitis: No controlled studies exist. IV acyclovir (15 mg/kg qd) should be considered.

   Surgical prophylaxis: IV acyclovir (5 mg/kg q12h) or oral acyclovir (800 mg bid), famciclovir (250 mg bid), or valacyclovir (500 mg bid) is given 2–3 d before laser resurfacing or other neurologic procedures.

Disseminated HSV infections: No controlled studies exist. IV acyclovir nevertheless should be tried. No definite evidence indicates that therapy decreases the risk of death.

Erythema multiforme associated with HSV: Anecdotal observations suggest that oral acyclovir (400 mg bid or tid) suppresses erythema multiforme.

Infections due to acyclovir-resistant HSV: Foscarnet (40 mg/kg IV q8h) should be given until lesions heal. The optimal duration of therapy and the usefulness of its continuation to suppress lesions are unclear. Some pts may benefit from cutaneous application of trifluorothymidine or 5% cidofovir gel.

SOURCE: Corey L: HPIM-15, p. 1105.

infection and may precede the development of lesions by 48–72 h. Erythematous maculopapules evolve rapidly into vesicles. The most debilitating consequences of herpes zoster are acute neuritis and postherpetic neuralgia, both of which are more common among adults than among children and the latter of which is increasingly common with advancing age. At least 50% of pts >50 years old with zoster report pain months after resolution of cutaneous disease. Zoster ophthalmicus is an infection involving the ophthalmic division of the trigeminal nerve. Ramsay Hunt syndrome occurs with involvement of the sensory branch of the facial nerve and is characterized by lesions on the ear canal, ipsilateral facial palsy, and loss of taste in the anterior two-thirds of the tongue. CNS involvement includes asymptomatic CSF pleocytosis; symptomatic meningoencephalitis with headache, fever, photophobia, meningitis, and vomiting; and, in rare instances, granulomatous angiitis with contralateral hemiplegia. Transverse myelitis with or without paralysis may also develop. In immunocompromised pts, especially those with Hodgkin's or non-Hodgkin's lymphoma, the clinical syndrome is more severe and the risk of disseminated skin lesions—or even visceral dissemination—is greater. Cutaneous dissemination occurs in ~40% of these pts. Visceral dissemination, including pneumonitis, meningoencephalitis, and hepatitis, occurs in 5–10% of pts with cutaneous dissemination. Even disseminated infection is rarely fatal.

   DIAGNOSIS   The diagnosis of both chickenpox and herpes zoster can be made clinically on the basis of the epidemiology, appearance, and distribution of lesions. The Tzanck preparation has a sensitivity of only ~60% and does not distinguish VZV from HSV infection. Serologic tests include fluorescent antibody to membrane antigen (FAMA) and ELISA. Confirmation is possible with viral isolation in tissue culture. VZV takes longer to isolate than HSV. PCR is available in a limited number of diagnostic laboratories.

 TREATMENT

   For chickenpox of ≤24 h duration in adolescents or adults, acyclovir (800 mg PO 5 times daily for 5–7 d) is recommended. When initiated early, therapy with acyclovir at a dose of 20 mg/kg q6h also may be of benefit to children <12 years old. Aspirin should not be administered to children because of its

Table 102-2

Recommendations for VZIG Administration

Exposure criteria
1. Both exposure to person with chickenpox or zoster as
   a. Continuous household contact
   b. Playmate for >1 h indoors
   c. Hospital contact (same room or prolonged face-to-face)
   d. Mother (see 3 below)
2. And time elapsed ≤96 h (preferably ≤72 h)

Candidates (provided they have significant exposure) include
1. Immunocompromised susceptible children
2. Immunocompetent susceptible adolescents (≥15 years old) and adults, especially pregnant women
3. Newborn infants of mothers with onset of chickenpox <5 days before or <2 days after delivery
4. Hospitalized premature infants
   a. ≥28 weeks of gestation when mother has no history of chickenpox
   b. <28 weeks of gestation and/or birth weight of ≤1000 g, regardless of maternal history

SOURCE: Adapted (by Whitley RJ: HPIM-15, p. 1108) from American Academy of Pediatrics, in Red Book, Report of the Committee on Infectious Diseases, G Peter (ed), Elk Grove Village, IL, American Academy of Pediatrics, 1997.

association with Reye's syndrome. Palliative measures are directed at the control of itching and drying lesions. For herpes zoster, acyclovir (800 mg PO 5 times daily for 7–10 d) speeds the healing of skin lesions and decreases acute pain but does not alter the incidence of postherpetic neuralgia. Famciclovir (500 mg tid for 7 d) is at least as effective as acyclovir and may accelerate resolution of postherpetic neuralgia. Valacyclovir (1 g tid for 5–7 d) is superior to acyclovir in accelerating healing and resolution of zoster-associated pain. Pts with zoster ophthalmicus should see an ophthalmologist in addition to receiving acyclovir. Postherpetic neuralgia is extremely difficult to treat; analgesics, amitriptyline hydrochloride, and fluphenazine hydrochloride are used. For immunocompromised pts with either chickenpox or herpes zoster, IV acyclovir is recommended at a dose of 10–12.5 mg/kg q8h for 7 d; oral therapy should not be used. Indications for the administration of varicella-zoster immune globulin (VZIG) are summarized in Table 102-2. A live attenuated vaccine is now available for the prevention of VZV infection and is recommended for routine immunization of children and for vaccination of susceptible adults.

HUMAN HERPESVIRUS TYPES 6, 7, AND 8

HHV-6 is a T-lymphotropic virus that causes exanthem subitum (roseola), a common childhood illness characterized by fever and subsequent rash. HHV-6 has also been associated with febrile seizures (without rash) during infancy and, in older age groups, with mononucleosis syndromes and focal encephalitis. It causes pneumonitis and disseminated disease in immunocompromised hosts. HHV-7 is frequently acquired during childhood and is present in saliva but has not been definitively linked with any known disease. HHV-8 has been assigned a putative etiologic role in Kaposi's sarcoma and body-cavity lymphoma in AIDS pts.

For a more detailed discussion, see Corey L: Herpes Simplex Viruses, Chap. 182, p. 1100; Whitley RJ: Varicella-Zoster Virus Infections, Chap. 183, p. 1106; and Hirsch MS: Cytomegalovirus and Human Herpesvirus Types 6, 7, and 8, Chap. 185, p. 1111, in HPIM-15.

103

CYTOMEGALOVIRUS AND EPSTEIN-BARR VIRUS INFECTIONS

CYTOMEGALOVIRUS (CMV) INFECTIONS

CMV, a member of the β-herpesvirus group, has double-stranded DNA, a protein capsid, and a lipoprotein envelope.

EPIDEMIOLOGY   CMV has a worldwide distribution, with infection common in the perinatal and childhood periods. In the U.S., ~1% of newborns are infected. Spread does not occur casually but rather takes place through repeated or prolonged intimate exposure. Transmission occurs in day-care centers, through sexual contact, and after transfusion of blood products (at a frequency of 0.14–10% per unit transfused). When an infected child introduces CMV into a household, the seroconversion rate is 50% among susceptible household contacts within 6 months.

PATHOGENESIS   Once acquired during asymptomatic or symptomatic primary infection, CMV persists indefinitely in latent form in tissues. If T cell function of the host becomes compromised, the virus can be reactivated to cause a variety of syndromes.

CLINICAL MANIFESTATIONS   *Congenital CMV Infection*   Most congenital CMV infections are not apparent at birth; 5–25% of asymptomatically infected infants develop psychomotor, hearing, ocular, or dental abnormalities over the next several years. Cytomegalic inclusion disease develops in ~5% of infected fetuses, almost exclusively in those whose mothers have acquired primary infection during pregnancy. Petechiae, hepatosplenomegaly, and jaundice are the most common signs (60–80% of cases). Microcephaly (with or without cerebral calcifications), intrauterine growth retardation, and prematurity are seen in 30–50% of cases. Mortality rates are as high as 20–30% among the most severely affected infants.

Perinatal Infection   The majority of infants infected at or after delivery remain asymptomatic. Infection is contracted by passage through an infected birth canal or, after birth, via maternal milk. CMV causes rare cases of protracted interstitial pneumonia in premature infants.

CMV Mononucleosis   Heterophile-negative mononucleosis is the most common manifestation of CMV infection in normal hosts beyond the neonatal period. The incubation period is 20–60 d, with clinical illness generally lasting 2–6 weeks. CMV mononucleosis is characterized by prolonged high fevers, sometimes with chills, fatigue, and malaise. While myalgias, headache, and splenomegaly are frequent, exudative pharyngitis and cervical lymphadenopathy are rare (in contrast to Epstein-Barr virus mononucleosis, in which these findings are prominent). The major laboratory finding is relative peripheral lymphocytosis with >10% atypical lymphocytes. Moderately elevated serum levels of aminotransferases and alkaline phosphatase are common; jaundice is rare.

CMV Infection in the Immunocompromised Host CMV is the most common and important viral pathogen affecting organ transplant recipients. Infections in these hosts include fever and leukopenia, hepatitis, pneumonitis, esophagitis, gastritis, colitis, and retinitis. The period of maximal risk is 1–4 months after transplantation. The greatest risk of disease appears to follow primary infection. The transplanted organ seems to be particularly susceptible, with CMV hepatitis common among liver transplant recipients and CMV pneumonitis among lung transplant recipients. CMV pneumonitis also occurs in 15–20% of bone marrow transplant recipients, most frequently 5–13 weeks after transplantation; the case-fatality rate is 84–88%. CMV is a significant pathogen in pts with advanced HIV infection, generally causing clinical syndromes at CD4 cell counts of <100/μL. Retinitis, esophagitis, colitis, encephalitis, and polyradiculopathy are the most common manifestations of CMV infection in this group. Successful treatment of HIV has decreased the incidence of CMV infection in HIV-positive pts.

DIAGNOSIS Diagnosis requires the isolation of CMV in culture or the detection of CMV antigens or DNA in clinical specimens, together with the documentation of a rise in or persistently elevated antibody titer. Recovery of CMV in culture may take only a few days if the titer of virus is high (e.g., congenital infection or AIDS) but may also take several weeks (e.g., CMV mononucleosis). To expedite this process, many laboratories use a shell-vial technique on overnight tissue cultures, which employs monoclonal antibodies and immunocytochemical detection of early antigens. Viral isolation from urine or saliva does not confirm infection, since shedding may continue for months or even years after infection; detection of CMV viremia by pp65 antigen testing of peripheral blood leukocytes is a good predictor of subsequent culture-positive CMV infection. PCR of CSF is useful in the diagnosis of CMV-related neurologic disease. While a fourfold rise in antibody titer can confirm a primary infection, antibody rises may take up to 4 weeks, and titers may remain high for years.

℞ **TREATMENT**

Ganciclovir has produced response rates of 70–90% among AIDS pts treated for CMV retinitis or colitis. The induction dose of ganciclovir (5 mg/kg bid IV for 14–21 d) is followed by maintenance therapy (5 mg/kg qd IV, 6 mg/ kg IV 5 d/week, or 3 g/d PO). Neutropenia, the major toxic effect, develops in 16–29% of pts; its severity can be lessened by the use of colony-stimulating factors. Oral ganciclovir is inferior to IV ganciclovir for induction therapy. The use of oral ganciclovir in HIV-infected pts for prophylaxis of CMV infection is controversial. A ganciclovir intraocular implant in combination with systemic therapy is another treatment alternative. In bone marrow transplant recipients, ganciclovir plus CMV immune globulin have elicited a favorable clinical response in 50–70% of episodes of CMV pneumonitis. For ganciclovir-resistant strains, foscarnet is active and compares favorably with ganciclovir in the treatment of CMV retinitis in AIDS. The induction dose of foscarnet (60 mg/kg q8h or 90 mg/kg q12h for 14 d) is followed by maintenance infusions of 90–120 mg/kg qd. Foscarnet exerts considerable toxicity: renal dysfunction, hypomagnesemia, hypokalemia, hypocalcemia, seizures, fever, and rash are each seen in >5% of pts. Cidofovir is an alternative that allows intermittent IV administration. Induction doses of 5 mg/kg weekly for 2 weeks are followed by 3–5 mg/kg every 2 weeks. Renal toxicity is the major adverse effect.

EPSTEIN-BARR VIRUS (EBV) INFECTIONS

EBV is a human herpesvirus that consists of a linear double-stranded DNA core surrounded by an icosahedral nucleocapsid and a glycoprotein-containing envelope. It is cytotropic for B lymphocytes.

EPIDEMIOLOGY EBV is transmitted primarily in saliva and occasionally by blood transfusion and is not highly contagious. Primary infection tends to occur at an early age in lower socioeconomic groups and in developing countries. Primary EBV infection among adolescents and young adults accounts for most cases of infectious mononucleosis (IM). By adulthood, >90% of individuals are seropositive for EBV. The virus is shed from the oropharynx for up to 18 months after primary infection and intermittently thereafter in the absence of clinical illness.

CLINICAL MANIFESTATIONS *Infection in Infants and Young Children* EBV infection in this group is generally asymptomatic or presents as mild pharyngitis with or without tonsillitis.

Infectious Mononucleosis The incubation period for IM is 4–6 weeks. Prodromal symptoms of malaise, fatigue, and myalgia frequently precede the onset of pharyngitis, fever, and lymphadenopathy by a few days. Common signs and symptoms are listed along with their frequencies in Table 103-1. After ampicillin administration, most pts with IM develop a pruritic maculopapular eruption that is not predictive of future penicillin allergy. Symptoms usually last for 2–4 weeks, but malaise and difficulty concentrating may persist for months. Complications are infrequent but may be dramatic and include auto-

Table 103-1

Signs and Symptoms of Infectious Mononucleosis

Manifestation	Median Percentage of Pts (Range)
Symptoms	
Sore throat	75 (50–87)
Malaise	47 (42–76)
Headache	38 (22–67)
Abdominal pain, nausea, or vomiting	17 (5–25)
Chills	10 (9–11)
Signs	
Lymphadenopathy	95 (83–100)
Fever	93 (60–100)
Pharyngitis or tonsillitis	82 (68–90)
Splenomegaly	51 (43–64)
Hepatomegaly	11 (6–15)
Rash	10 (0–25)
Periorbital edema	13 (2–34)
Palatal enanthem	7 (3–13)
Jaundice	5 (2–10)

SOURCE: Cohen JI: HPIM-15, p. 1109.

immune hemolytic anemia, thrombocytopenia, granulocytopenia, splenic rupture, cranial nerve palsies, encephalitis, hepatitis, pericarditis, myocarditis, coronary artery spasm, and airway obstruction from pharyngeal or paratracheal adenopathy.

Other Diseases Associated with EBV Infection EBV-associated lymphoproliferative disease occurs in pts with congenital or acquired immunodeficiency, including AIDS, severe combined immunodeficiency, and transplantation. Pts present with fever and lymphadenopathy or GI symptoms. X-linked lymphoproliferative syndrome (Duncan's syndrome), a disorder in immune responsiveness to EBV, permits overwhelming EBV infection in young boys. Oral hairy leukoplakia, an early feature in pts with HIV infection that is characterized by raised white corrugated tongue lesions, is caused by EBV. A rare chronic form of EBV infection (distinct from chronic fatigue syndrome) is characterized by multiple organ involvement, including hepatosplenomegaly, lymphadenopathy, and pneumonitis, uveitis, or neurologic disease.

EBV-Associated Malignancy First described in association with 90% of cases of African Burkitt's lymphoma, EBV has been associated with American Burkitt's lymphoma (15% of cases), anaplastic nasopharyngeal carcinoma, and B cell lymphomas, especially in pts immunosuppressed as a result of organ allografts and AIDS.

DIAGNOSIS Heterophile antibodies (antibodies to sheep, horse, or cow erythrocytes) are present in 40% of pts with IM during the first week and in 80–90% during the third week (Table 103-2). The test usually remains positive for 3 months after the illness, but positivity can persist for up to 1 year. The commercially available monospot test for heterophile antibodies is somewhat more sensitive than the classic heterophile test. While more specific EBV antibodies can be measured, these studies are rarely required for the diagnosis of IM except in heterophile-negative or atypical cases (Table 103-2). IgM anti-

Table 103-2

Serologic Features of EBV-Associated Diseases

		Result in Indicated Test[a]				
		Anti-VCA		Anti-EA		
Condition	Heterophile	IgM	IgG	EA-D	EA-R	Anti-EBNA
Acute infectious mononucleosis	+	+	++	+	−	−
Convalescence	±	−	+	−	±	+
Past infection	−	−	+	−	−	+
Reactivation with immunodeficiency	−	−	++	+	+	±
Burkitt's lymphoma	−	−	+++	±	++	+
Nasopharyngeal carcinoma	−	−	+++	++	±	+

[a] VCA, viral capsid antigen; EA, early antigen; EA-D antibody, antibody to early antigen, diffuse pattern in nucleus and cytoplasm of infected cells; EA-R antibody, antibody to early antigen, restricted to the cytoplasm; and EBNA, Epstein-Barr nuclear antigen.
SOURCE: Adapted from M Okano et al: Clin Microbiol Rev 1:300, 1988.

bodies to viral capsid antigen (VCA) are diagnostic of primary EBV infection and persist for only 2 months; IgG antibodies to VCA develop early in infection and persist for life. Antibodies to Epstein-Barr nuclear antigen (EBNA) appear at about 6–8 weeks and persist for life. The presence of IgM antibody to VCA and seroconversion to EBNA are diagnostic of primary EBV infection. PCR for EBV DNA in the CSF is used in the diagnosis of CNS lymphoma in AIDS pts. Culture of EBV from the throat is not diagnostic of acute infection since this virus is commonly shed from the oropharynx for the lifetime of the infected individual.

 TREATMENT

The treatment of IM is supportive. Excessive physical activity should be avoided for 6–8 weeks to avert splenic rupture. Glucocorticoids are indicated for airway obstruction and severe hemolytic anemia or thrombocytopenia. Occasional pts with protracted illness may also benefit from a short course of prednisone, but routine steroid use is not advised. Antiviral agents are not useful in the treatment of IM.

For a more detailed discussion, see Cohen JI: Epstein-Barr Virus Infections, Including Infectious Mononucleosis, Chap. 184, p. 1109; and Hirsch
MS: Cytomegalovirus and Human Herpesvirus Types 6, 7, and 8, Chap.
185, p. 1111, in HPIM-15.

104

INFLUENZA AND OTHER VIRAL RESPIRATORY DISEASES

INFLUENZA

ETIOLOGY   Influenza viruses, members of the Orthomyxoviridae family, include types A, B, and C. Strains are designated according to the site of origin, isolate number, year of isolation, and (for influenza A virus) subtype, which is based on surface hemagglutinin (H) and neuraminidase (N) antigens. The genome of influenza A virus is segmented, consisting of eight single-stranded segments of RNA; this characteristic leads to a high frequency of gene reassortment.

EPIDEMIOLOGY   Outbreaks of influenza occur virtually every year, although their extent and severity vary widely. Localized outbreaks take place at variable intervals, usually every 1–3 years. Except for the past two decades, global epidemics or pandemics have occurred approximately every 10–15 years since the 1918–1919 pandemic. The most extensive and severe outbreaks are caused by influenza A virus because of the propensity of its antigens to undergo variation. Major antigenic variations, referred to as *antigenic shifts*, likely arise from genome segment reassortment between viral strains, which results in the expression of a different H and/or N antigen. Minor variations, referred to as *antigenic drifts*, probably arise from point mutations. In human infections, three major H antigens (H1, H2, and H3) and two N antigens (N1 and N2) have been recognized. Epidemics of influenza A begin abruptly, peak over 2–3 weeks, generally last 2–3 months, and often subside rapidly. These epidemics take place almost exclusively during the winter months in the temperate zones of the northern and southern hemispheres. In contrast, influenza occurs throughout the year in the tropics. Outbreaks of influenza B are generally less extensive and less severe. The H and N antigens of influenza B virus undergo less frequent and less extensive variation. Influenza B outbreaks are most common in schools and military camps. Influenza C virus appears to cause subclinical infection; the prevalence of antibody is high in the general population, but the virus is infrequently associated with human disease.

CLINICAL MANIFESTATIONS   Influenza is an acute respiratory illness characterized by the abrupt onset of headache, fevers, chills, myalgia, malaise, cough, and sore throat. In uncomplicated influenza, the acute illness generally resolves over 2–5 d, and most pts largely recover within 1 week.

The major problem posed by influenza consists of its complications, the most common of which is pneumonia—primary influenza viral pneumonia, secondary bacterial pneumonia, or mixed viral and bacterial pneumonia. Primary influenza pneumonia is the least common but most severe of the pneumonic complications. Fever persists, and pts develop progressive dyspnea, cough with scant sputum, and eventually cyanosis. CXR reveals diffuse interstitial infiltrates and/or acute respiratory distress syndrome. Pts with cardiac disease, especially mitral stenosis, appear to have a predilection for developing influenza pneumonia.

The hallmark of secondary bacterial pneumonia is the reappearance of fever, accompanied by productive cough and physical signs of consolidation, in a pt whose condition has improved for 2–3 d following acute influenza. *Streptococcus pneumoniae, Staphylococcus aureus,* and *Haemophilus influenzae* are common pathogens. Pts at particular risk for this complication include elderly individuals or persons with chronic pulmonary or cardiac disease.

Mixed viral and bacterial pneumonia may be the most common pneumonic complication and has clinical features of both primary and secondary pneumonia. This complication occurs primarily in pts with chronic cardiovascular or pulmonary disease.

Extrapulmonary complications include Reye's syndrome, myositis, rhabdomyolysis, and myoglobinuria. Encephalitis, transverse myelitis, and Guillain-Barré syndrome have been associated with influenza, but an etiologic role for influenza virus has not been established in these conditions. Reye's syndrome occurs in children as a serious complication of influenza B or—less often—of influenza A or varicella-zoster virus infection. The syndrome begins with 1–2 d of nausea and vomiting followed by CNS symptoms, including changes in mental status that range from lethargy to coma and can encompass delirium and seizures. Elevated serum aminotransferase levels, elevated serum ammonia concentrations, and hepatomegaly are common; serum bilirubin levels are usually normal. An epidemiologic association of Reye's syndrome with the ingestion of aspirin has been noted; the syndrome's incidence in this context has declined markedly with widespread warnings about aspirin use in children with viral infections.

DIAGNOSIS   Influenza can be diagnosed during its acute phase by isolation of virus from throat swabs, nasopharyngeal washes, or sputum in tissue culture within 48–72 h after inoculation. Viral antigens may be detected some-what earlier by immunodiagnostic techniques in tissue culture or in exfoliated nasopharyngeal cells obtained by washings; these techniques have sensitivities of 57–81% compared with tissue culture. Acute infection can be diagnosed retrospectively by fourfold or greater rises in titers of hemagglutination inhi-bition or CF antibody or by significant rises in ELISA antibody between the acute illness and 10–14 d after onset.

℞ TREATMENT

Treatment for uncomplicated influenza is for relief of symptoms only. Salic-ylates should be avoided in children (<18 years old) because of the associ-ation of their use with Reye's syndrome. Amantadine or rimantadine (either given at a dose of 200 mg/d PO for 3–7 d) reduces the duration of systemic and respiratory symptoms by 50% if given within 48 h of onset. These agents are active only against influenza A virus. Amantadine causes mild CNS side effects (jitteriness, anxiety, insomnia, difficulty concentrating) in 5–10% of pts. Rimantadine is less frequently associated with CNS side effects. Both agents are given at a reduced dose of ≤100 mg/d to the elderly and to persons with renal insufficiency. Zanamivir (10 mg inhaled bid for 5 d) and oselta-mivir (75 mg PO bid with food for 5 d) are active against both influenza A and influenza B. These agents have been shown to reduce the duration of symptoms and signs of influenza by 1–1.5 d if treatment is started within 2 d of the onset of illness. Zanamivir may exacerbate bronchospasm, and os-eltamivir has been associated with nausea and vomiting. Ribavirin has been reported to be effective against both type A and type B viruses when admin-istered as an aerosol but is relatively ineffective when administered orally. It is not known whether these antiviral agents are effective in the treatment of complications such as influenza pneumonia. Antibacterial therapy should be reserved for bacterial complications of influenza, such as bacterial pneumonia.

PROPHYLAXIS The most common preventive measure is yearly vac-cination against influenza A and B; an inactivated vaccine derived from strains circulating the previous year is used. Vaccination is recommended for individ-uals >6 months of age who are at increased risk for complications of influenza. Included are pts with chronic pulmonary or cardiovascular disorders, residents of nursing homes or chronic care facilities, all persons >55 years old, health care providers, and pts with diabetes, renal disease, hemoglobinopathies, or immunosuppression. Individuals who care for high-risk pts or who come into frequent contact with them (including household members) should also be vac-cinated to reduce the risk of transmission. Since the vaccine is "killed," it may be administered to immunosuppressed pts.

Amantadine and rimantadine are 70–100% effective in the prophylaxis of influenza A. Prophylaxis with one of these drugs (200 mg/d PO) is indicated for high-risk individuals who have not been vaccinated or over the duration of outbreaks caused by a strain not well covered by the current vaccine. Simulta-neous administration of amantadine and vaccine may offer additive protection. Zanamivir and oseltamivir are under review for prophylaxis.

OTHER VIRAL RESPIRATORY INFECTIONS

Acute viral respiratory illnesses are among the most common of human diseases, accounting for one-half or more of all acute illnesses. The syndromes most commonly associated with the major respiratory virus groups are summarized in Table 104-1.

Table 104-1

Illnesses Associated with Respiratory Viruses

Virus	Most Frequent
Rhinoviruses	Common cold
Coronaviruses	Common cold
Respiratory syncytial virus	Pneumonia and bronchiolitis in young children
Parainfluenza viruses	Croup and lower respiratory tract disease in young children
Adenoviruses	Common cold and pharyngitis in children
Influenza A viruses	Influenza[b]
Influenza B viruses	Influenza[b]
Enteroviruses[c]	Acute undifferentiated febrile illnesses[d]
Herpes simplex viruses[e]	Gingivostomatitis in children; pharyngotonsillitis in adults

[a] Serotypes 4 and 7.
[b] Fever, cough, myalgia, malaise.
[c] See Chap. 106.

Rhinovirus

Rhinoviruses, members of the Picornaviridae family, are small and nonenveloped and have a single-stranded RNA genome. One hundred distinct serotypes of rhinovirus have been recognized.

EPIDEMIOLOGY   Rhinoviruses have been isolated from 15–40% of adults with the common cold, with seasonal peaks in the early fall and spring. Infection rates are highest among infants and young children and decrease with age. The infection is spread by contact with infected secretions or respiratory droplets or by hand-to-hand contact, with subsequent self-inoculation of the conjunctival or nasal mucosa. Exposure to cold, fatigue, and sleep deprivation have not been associated with increased rates of rhinovirus-induced illness.

CLINICAL MANIFESTATIONS   After an incubation period of 1–2 d, pts develop rhinorrhea, sneezing, nasal congestion, and sore throat. Systemic symptoms, including fever, are unusual. The illness generally lasts 4–9 d and resolves spontaneously. Although bronchitis, bronchiolitis, and bronchopneumonia have been reported in children, rhinoviruses are not a major cause of pediatric lower respiratory tract disease. Rhinoviruses may cause exacerbations of asthma and chronic pulmonary disease in adults.

DIAGNOSIS   Because of the mild nature and short duration of the illness, a specific diagnosis is not commonly needed. If isolation of the virus is of interest, tissue culture of nasal washes or secretions is performed.

Frequency of Respiratory Syndromes	
Occasional	Infrequent
Exacerbation of chronic bronchitis and asthma	Pneumonia in children
Exacerbation of chronic bronchitis and asthma	Pneumonia and bronchiolitis
Common cold in adults	Pneumonia in elderly and immuno-suppressed pts
Pharyngitis and common cold	Tracheobronchitis in adults; lower respiratory tract disease in immuno-suppressed pts
Outbreaks of acute respiratory disease in military recruits[a]	Pneumonia in children; lower respi-ratory tract and disseminated dis-ease in immunosuppressed pts
Pneumonia and excess mortality in high-risk pts	Pneumonia in healthy individuals
Rhinitis and pharyngitis alone	Pneumonia
Rhinitis and pharyngitis	Pneumonia
Tracheitis and pneumonia in immu-nocompromised pts	Disseminated infection in immuno-compromised pts

[a] May or may not have a respiratory component.   [c] See Chap. 102.
SOURCE: Dolin R: HPIM-15, p. 1121.

 TREATMENT

Treatment is not usually required, and no specific antiviral therapy is avail-able. Antibiotics should not be used in uncomplicated infections but rather should be reserved for any bacterial superinfections (e.g., otitis media, sinus-itis) that develop.

Coronavirus

Coronaviruses are pleomorphic, single-stranded RNA viruses.

EPIDEMIOLOGY   Coronaviruses account for 10–20% of common colds. They are most active in late fall, winter, and early spring—a period when rhinovirus is relatively inactive.

CLINICAL MANIFESTATIONS   Symptoms are similar to those of rhi-novirus infections, but the incubation period is longer (3 d). The illness usually lasts 6–7 d.

 TREATMENT

The approach to the treatment of common colds caused by coronaviruses is similar to that for rhinovirus-induced illness.

Respiratory Syncytial Virus

Respiratory syncytial virus (RSV) is an enveloped virus of the Paramyxoviridae family with a single-stranded RNA genome. Two distinct subtypes, A and B, have been described.

EPIDEMIOLOGY RSV is the major respiratory pathogen of young children and is the foremost cause of lower respiratory disease in infants. Rates of illness peak at 2–3 months of age, when attack rates among susceptible individuals approach 100%. RSV accounts for 20–25% of hospital admissions of infants and young children for pneumonia and for up to 75% of cases of bronchiolitis in this age group. This virus is an important nosocomial pathogen in both children and adults. It is transmitted by close contact with contaminated fingers or fomites as well as through coarse (not fine) aerosols produced by coughing or sneezing. The incubation period is 4–6 d; viral shedding by children may last ≥2 weeks, with a shorter duration in adults.

CLINICAL MANIFESTATIONS In infants, RSV disease begins with rhinorrhea, low-grade fever, and mild systemic symptoms, often accompanied by cough and wheezing; 25–40% of cases include lower respiratory tract involvement. RSV illness is especially severe in children born prematurely and in those with congenital cardiac disease, bronchopulmonary dysplasia, nephrotic syndrome, or immunosuppression. The mortality rate for RSV pneumonia among infants with congenital cardiac disease was 37% in one study. In adults, the symptoms of RSV infection are usually the same as those of the common cold. RSV can cause severe pneumonia in immunocompromised or elderly adults.

DIAGNOSIS RSV can be isolated in tissue culture from sputum, throat swabs, or nasopharyngeal washes. Immunofluorescence microscopy of nasal washings or scrapings provides a rapid diagnosis. Serologic diagnosis requires a fourfold rise in antibody titer between acute- and convalescent-phase specimens and is therefore not useful during acute illness.

 TREATMENT

Treatment of upper respiratory tract infections due to RSV is similar to that for URIs of other etiologies. Therapy with aerosolized ribavirin has been beneficial in infants with RSV infection. No data exist on treatment in adults.

PROPHYLAXIS Monthly administration of human immunoglobulin with high titers of antibody to RSV (RSVIG) or of a chimeric mouse-human IgG antibody to RSV (palivizumab) is approved as prophylaxis in high-risk pts <2 years old. No data exist on prophylaxis in adults.

Parainfluenza Virus

Parainfluenza viruses are single-stranded RNA viruses of the Paramyxoviridae family.

EPIDEMIOLOGY In the U.S., parainfluenza viruses cause 4–22% of respiratory illnesses in children and <5% of respiratory illnesses in adults. Parainfluenza virus is an important cause of mild illnesses and of croup (laryngotracheobronchitis), bronchiolitis, and pneumonia. In young children, parainfluenza virus ranks second only to RSV as a cause of lower respiratory infection. In adults, parainfluenza infections are generally mild.

CLINICAL MANIFESTATIONS In adults and older children, parainfluenza virus infection presents as a mild common cold or hoarseness with cough. In young children, it may present as an acute febrile illness with coryza, sore throat, hoarseness, and cough. The brassy or barking cough of croup may progress to frank stridor. Most children recover in 1–2 d, but progressive airway obstruction and hypoxia occasionally ensue, and bronchiolitis or pneumonia may develop. Severe or even fatal infection has been reported in both children and adults with profound immunosuppression.

DIAGNOSIS The diagnosis is established by tissue culture of the virus from respiratory tract secretions, throat swabs, or nasopharyngeal washings or by immunofluorescence microscopy of exfoliated respiratory cells. Serologic diagnosis is available.

 TREATMENT

In mild illness, treatment is symptom-based. Mild croup may be treated with moisturized air from a vaporizer. More severe cases require hospitalization and close observation for development of respiratory distress. No specific antiviral treatment is available.

Adenovirus

Adenoviruses are complex DNA viruses belonging to the genus *Mastadenovirus*.

EPIDEMIOLOGY Infections with adenovirus occur most frequently in infants and children, accounting for 3–5% of respiratory infections in children and for <2% of respiratory illnesses in civilian adults. There is a seasonal distribution of fall to spring. Certain serotypes are associated with outbreaks of acute respiratory disease in military recruits. Transmission can take place via the inhalation of aerosolized virus, through the inoculation of the conjunctival sacs, and probably by the fecal-oral route.

CLINICAL MANIFESTATIONS The spectrum of clinical symptoms in children includes rhinitis and occasional cases of bronchiolitis and pneumonia. Adenovirus types 3 and 7 cause pharyngoconjunctival fever (bilateral conjunctivitis, low-grade fever, rhinitis, sore throat, and cervical adenopathy). Adenovirus types 4 and 7 cause the most frequent syndrome in adults (classically affecting military recruits): an acute respiratory illness with prominent sore throat, fever on the second or third day, cough, coryza, and regional lymphadenopathy. Adenoviruses have also been associated with pneumonia in immunosuppressed pts (including pts with AIDS) and with diseases outside the respiratory tract, including acute diarrhea in young children, hemorrhagic cystitis, and epidemic keratoconjunctivitis.

DIAGNOSIS The diagnosis is established by the isolation of the virus in tissue culture from the conjunctivae, oropharynx, sputum, urine, or stool. ELISA or nucleic acid hybridization techniques may also be used for detection of the virus in clinical specimens. Serologic diagnosis is available.

 TREATMENT

No specific antiviral therapy is available. A live oral vaccine is used to prevent outbreaks among military recruits. Purified subunit vaccines are under investigation.

For a more detailed discussion, see Dolin R: Common Viral Respiratory Infections, Chap. 189, p. 1120; and Dolin R: Influenza, Chap. 190, p. 1125, in HPIM-15.

105

RUBEOLA, RUBELLA, MUMPS, AND PARVOVIRUS INFECTIONS

MEASLES (RUBEOLA)

Measles is a highly contagious acute respiratory disease with a characteristic clinical picture and a pathognomonic enanthem. Measles virus is a member of the family Paramyxoviridae.

EPIDEMIOLOGY Measles has a worldwide distribution. The disease is transmitted by respiratory secretions, predominantly via exposure to aerosols but also through direct contact with larger droplets. It is highly contagious: an infected individual can transmit the virus during a period from 1–2 d before onset of symptoms to 4 d after the appearance of skin lesions. In the U.S., the number of cases decreased progressively after the advent of routine childhood vaccination, except for a brief upsurge in 1990. By the mid-1990s, the disease was once more brought under control, with only 508 cases reported to the CDC in 1996. Most cases have since resulted from international importations of the virus. Outbreaks have involved not only unvaccinated infants and preschool children but also high school and college students with vaccination rates of >95%.

CLINICAL MANIFESTATIONS The incubation period for measles is 8–12 d. Pts first experience 3–4 d of prodromal symptoms, including malaise, irritability, fever, conjunctivitis with excessive lacrimation, edema of the eyelids, photophobia, hacking cough, and nasal discharge. Koplik's spots, which are pathognomonic for measles, appear 1–2 d before the onset of rash and are small, red, irregular lesions with blue-white centers found on mucous membranes, especially opposite the second molars. The rash of measles appears first on the forehead and spreads downward over the face, neck, trunk, and feet. The lesions are erythematous maculopapules that coalesce over the face and upper trunk. Most other symptoms resolve within 1–2 d of the appearance of rash, but cough may persist.

Measles is usually a self-limited disease, but a number of complications may ensue. Important complications include croup, bronchitis, and bronchiolitis; rare instances of interstitial giant cell pneumonia in immunocompromised children; conjunctivitis with progression to corneal ulceration, keratitis, and blindness; myocarditis; hepatitis; transient acute glomerulonephritis; bacterial pneumonia; and encephalomyelitis. This last complication, with headache, high fever, drowsiness, and coma, occurs in 1 of every 1000 pts within days after the appearance of rash; the mortality rate is 10%. An extremely rare condition, subacute sclerosing panencephalitis, is a late complication of measles.

Atypical measles can develop in pts who have received formalin-inactivated measles vaccine (used in the U.S. in 1963–1967) and can present with a variety of rashes; pneumonia and high fever are common. Despite the severity of atypical measles, pts invariably recover after a convalescence that may be prolonged.

DIAGNOSIS Lymphopenia and neutropenia are common in measles; leukocytosis may herald a bacterial superinfection. Measles virus can be isolated by inoculation of sputum, nasal secretions, or urine onto cell cultures. Immunofluorescent antibody staining of infected respiratory or urinary epithelial cells can detect measles antigen. Serologic tests include complement fixation, enzyme immunoassay, immunofluorescence, and hemagglutination inhibition assays.

Specific IgM antibodies are detectable within 1–2 d after the appearance of a rash, and IgG titers rise significantly after 10 d.

 TREATMENT

No therapy is indicated for uncomplicated measles. Clinical trials suggest benefit from high doses of vitamin A in severe or potentially severe measles, especially in children <2 years; a dose of 200,000 IU is used for children >1 year. Ribavirin is effective against measles virus in vitro and may be considered for use in immunocompromised individuals.

PREVENTION Measles should be controlled by vaccination. Live attenuated measles vaccine is given to children as part of the measles-mumps-rubella (MMR) vaccine at 12–15 months and again at either 4–5 years (CDC) or 12 years (American Academy of Pediatrics). Vaccine can also be given as prophylaxis within 3 d of exposure. Pts who received killed measles vaccine between 1963 and 1967 should be considered unprotected and are at risk for atypical measles. Pts infected with HIV who are susceptible should be vaccinated against measles; actively immunosuppressed pts (including AIDS pts with <15% CD4 lymphocytes) should not receive live vaccine. Gamma globulin (0.25 mL/kg, not to exceed 15 mL) modifies or prevents acquisition of measles if given within 6 d of exposure.

RUBELLA (GERMAN MEASLES)

Rubella is an acute viral infection that characteristically includes rash, fever, and lymphadenopathy and has a broad spectrum of other possible manifestations. Rubella virus, a togavirus, is closely related to the alphaviruses. Transmission takes place via direct or droplet contact with nasopharyngeal secretions.

CLINICAL MANIFESTATIONS The time from exposure to appearance of the rash is 12–23 d. In adults, a prodrome of malaise, headache, fever, and anorexia may precede the rash by 1–7 d. Subclinical infection is common. The distribution of the rash in rubella is the same as that in measles, but lesions are lighter in hue in rubella and are usually discrete. The rash may be accompanied by mild coryza and conjunctivitis. Enlarged, tender lymph nodes become apparent before onset of the rash and are most impressive during the eruptive phase; postauricular and suboccipital nodes are strikingly involved. Arthralgias and slight swelling of the joints sometimes accompany rubella, especially in young women, and may persist for 1–14 d after other manifestations have disappeared. Recurrences of joint symptoms for a year or more have been reported.

The most important factor in the pathogenicity of rubella virus for the fetus is gestational age at the time of infection. Maternal infection in the first trimester is most dangerous, leading to fetal infection in about half of cases. The congenital rubella syndrome consists of heart malformations (patent ductus arteriosus, interventricular septal defect, or pulmonic stenosis), eye lesions (corneal clouding, cataracts, chorioretinitis, and microphthalmia), microcephaly, and deafness. The "expanded" rubella syndrome was defined after an American epidemic in 1964 and includes mental retardation, thrombocytopenic purpura, hepatosplenomegaly, intrauterine growth retardation, interstitial pneumonia, myocarditis or myocardial necrosis, and metaphyseal bone lesions as well as the previously described manifestations.

DIAGNOSIS The diagnosis is made by isolation of virus, which is difficult and expensive, or by documentation of changes in antibody titers. The most commonly used test is an ELISA for IgG and IgM antibodies. Rubella antibodies may be detectable by the second day of rash and increase in titer over the next 10–21 d. Biopsied tissues and/or blood and CSF have also been used for demonstrating rubella antigens with monoclonal antibodies and for detecting rubella RNA by in situ hybridization and polymerase chain reaction.

TREATMENT AND PREVENTION Rubella is a mild illness that does not require treatment. It is prevented by vaccination, the goal of which is the elimination of congenital infection. Live attenuated rubella vaccine is given as part of the MMR vaccine. Vaccination is contraindicated in immunosuppressed pts, but vaccine is given to children with HIV infection. Although no cases of congenital rubella syndrome have occurred in women inadvertently vaccinated during pregnancy, the vaccine should not be administered to pregnant women or to women who might become pregnant within 3 months.

MUMPS

Mumps is an acute, systemic, communicable viral infection whose most distinctive feature is a swelling of one or both parotid glands. The etiologic agent is a paramyxovirus.

ETIOLOGY AND EPIDEMIOLOGY Humans are the only reservoir for mumps virus. In 1968 (before widespread immunization), 185,691 cases of mumps were reported in the U.S. The 906 cases reported in 1995 represent a reduction in the number of cases by >99% from prevaccine levels. The incubation period for mumps is generally 14–18 d. Infection tends to occur in the spring, with an especially high frequency in April and May. The virus is transmitted in infected salivary secretions but may be spread via urine as well. Infectivity is greatest from 1 or 2 d before the onset of parotitis to 5 d after the appearance of glandular enlargement; pts generally are no longer contagious 9 d after the onset of parotid swelling.

CLINICAL MANIFESTATIONS *Salivary Adenitis* There is frequently a prodrome of fever, myalgia, malaise, and anorexia. The onset of parotitis is usually sudden and in many cases is the first sign of illness. Pain and tenderness are generally marked; warmth and erythema are unusual. In two-thirds of cases, swelling is bilateral, although the onset on the two sides may not be synchronous. The submaxillary and sublingual glands are involved less often than the parotid glands and are almost never involved alone.

Epididymoorchitis Orchitis is a complication of mumps in 20% of postpubertal males. Testicular involvement, which is bilateral in <15% of cases, usually appears 7–10 d after the onset of parotitis but may precede it or develop simultaneously. Occasionally, mumps orchitis occurs without parotitis. The testicle becomes swollen to several times its normal size and is acutely painful, with accompanying high fevers, shaking chills, malaise, and headache. In 50% of cases, orchitis is followed by atrophy; even with bilateral involvement, sterility is rare in the absence of atrophy. Oophoritis in women is far less common than orchitis in men.

Pancreatitis Pts with pancreatic involvement develop abdominal pain and tenderness; shock and pseudocyst formation are rare. While serum amylase levels are elevated in parotitis as well as in mumps pancreatitis, serum lipase levels are increased only in the latter.

CNS Involvement Up to 50% of pts with clinical mumps have lymphocytic pleocytosis of the CSF, with up to 1000 cells/μL; 5–25% have symptoms of meningitis (headache, stiff neck, drowsiness). CNS symptoms tend to occur 3–

10 d after onset of parotitis; in 30–40% of laboratory-proven cases, parotitis is absent. True encephalitis is unusual. Mumps can produce mild paralytic polio-myelitis and, in rare cases, transverse myelitis, cerebellar ataxia, or Guillain-Barré syndrome.

Other Manifestations Mumps virus can cause subacute thyroiditis, ocular manifestations (dacryoadenitis, optic neuritis, keratitis, iritis, conjunctivitis, and episcleritis), myocarditis, hepatitis (without jaundice), thrombocytopenic purpura, interstitial pneumonia (in young children), polyarthritis, and acute hemorrhagic glomerulonephritis.

DIAGNOSIS Definitive diagnosis depends on isolation of the virus from saliva, throat swabs, CSF, or urine. Rapid diagnosis can be made by immuno-fluorescence assay for viral antigen in oropharyngeal cells. The best serologic test is the ELISA. Acute mumps can be diagnosed either by examination of acute- and convalescent-phase sera for an increase in antibody titer or by demonstration of specific IgM in one serum specimen.

℞ TREATMENT

No treatment is generally needed. Therapy for parotitis and other manifestations of mumps is usually symptom-based. Glucocorticoids have no proven value for the treatment of severe orchitis. Anecdotal information on a small number of pts with orchitis suggests that the administration of interferon α may be helpful.

PREVENTION Live attenuated mumps vaccine is administered at 12–15 months of age and again at 4–12 years as part of the MMR vaccine. Vaccination is not recommended for pregnant women, for pts receiving glucocorticoids, or for other immunocompromised hosts. However, children with HIV infection who are not severely immunocompromised can be safely immunized against mumps.

PARVOVIRUS

ETIOLOGY One parvovirus, designated B19, is known to be a human pathogen. It is a small, nonenveloped, single-stranded DNA virus.

EPIDEMIOLOGY Although B19 infections occur year-round, outbreaks of erythema infectiosum occur in schools during winter and spring months. Symptomatic infection occurs in 20–60% of children in outbreaks; 10% of infections are asymptomatic. Pts with transient aplastic crisis are highly infectious. The route of transmission of parvovirus B19 is unknown but may be respiratory or through direct contact.

CLINICAL MANIFESTATIONS *Erythema Infectiosum* Erythema infectiosum, or fifth disease, is the most common manifestation of parvovirus B19 infection and is seen predominantly in children. The typical presentation is a facial rash with a "slapped cheek" appearance, sometimes preceded by low-grade fever. The rash also develops on the arms and legs, with a lacy, reticular, erythematous appearance. Arthralgias and arthritis are uncommon in children but common in adults; rash is often absent or nonspecific in adults.

Arthropathy Parvovirus B19 infection in adults most often involves arthralgias and arthritis, sometimes accompanied by rash. Wrists, hands, and knees are most frequently involved in symmetric, nondestructive arthritis. Symptoms usually last about 3 weeks but may persist for months (or even years) in a small percentage of cases.

Transient Aplastic Crisis   This syndrome develops in pts with chronic hemolytic disease, including sickle cell disease, erythrocyte enzyme deficiencies, hereditary spherocytosis, thalassemias, paroxysmal nocturnal hemoglobinuria, and autoimmune hemolysis. Pts develop sudden, severe anemia that can be life-threatening and can be accompanied by weakness, lethargy, and pallor. Bone marrow examination reveals an absence of erythrocyte precursors despite a normal myeloid series. Reticulocytopenia usually lasts for 7–10 d. Unlike pts with fifth disease or arthritis, these pts are viremic and infectious.

Chronic Anemia   Immunodeficient pts—e.g., those with HIV infection, congenital immunodeficiencies, or acute lymphocytic leukemia (during maintenance chemotherapy)—and recipients of bone marrow transplants may develop chronic, transfusion-dependent anemia due to parvovirus B19 infection, with destruction of erythroid precursors in the bone marrow.

Fetal Infection   Maternal infection usually does not adversely affect the fetus. Parents should be counseled as to the relatively low risk of infection to the fetus. Fewer than 10% of maternal B19 infections lead to fetal death; when fetal death occurs, the cause is nonimmune hydrops fetalis. There is no evidence that B19 infection causes congenital anomalies. Exposure of a pregnant woman to a child with fifth disease is unlikely to result in maternal infection, since the infectious stage of illness is probably over by the time the rash develops. Pregnant women with known exposure to B19 virus should have their serum monitored for IgM antibodies to the virus and for α-fetoprotein levels, and ultrasonic examinations of the fetus for hydrops should be conducted. Some hydropic fetuses survive B19 infection and appear normal at delivery.

DIAGNOSIS   Diagnosis relies on measurements of parvovirus B19–specific IgM and IgG antibodies. Pts with transient aplastic crisis may have IgM antibodies but nevertheless usually have high titers of virus and viral DNA in serum. Immunodeficient pts with chronic anemia lack antibody but have viral particles and viral DNA in serum. Viral DNA may be detected in amniotic fluid or fetal blood in cases of hydrops fetalis. Fetal infection may be recognized by hydrops fetalis and the presence of B19 DNA in amniotic fluid or fetal blood in association with maternal IgM antibodies to B19 virus.

℞ TREATMENT

Erythema infectiosum requires no treatment; arthritis can be treated with NSAIDs. Transient aplastic crisis is usually treated with erythrocyte transfusions. Anemia in immunodeficient pts appears to respond to treatment with commercial IV gamma globulin.

PREVENTION   Prophylaxis of B19 infection with immunoglobulin should be considered for pts with chronic hemolysis or immunodeficiency and for pregnant women. Pts hospitalized with transient aplastic crisis or chronic anemia that is suspected of being related to parvovirus B19 should be put in private rooms and managed with droplet precautions.

For a more detailed discussion, see Gershon A: Measles (Rubeola), Chap. 194, p. 1143; Rubella (German Measles), Chap. 195, p. 1145; and Mumps, Chap. 196, p. 1147; Blacklow NR: Parvovirus, Chap. 187, p. 1117, in HPIM-15.

106

ENTEROVIRAL INFECTIONS

Enteroviruses belong to the family of small, nonenveloped viruses with single-stranded RNA called *picornaviruses*. Their stability allows these viruses to survive in the presence of acid and standard disinfectants and to persist for days at room temperature. Enteroviruses include polioviruses, coxsackieviruses, echoviruses, and recently discovered agents so far designated simply as enteroviruses. Nearly 70 serotypes are known to infect humans via intestinal tract epithelium and lymphoid tissue. Although enteroviruses are shed in stool, the clinical syndromes they cause are not gastrointestinal.

EPIDEMIOLOGY Enteroviruses are distributed worldwide and commonly cause asymptomatic infection. In temperate climates, most infections occur in the late summer and fall. The common mode of transmission is via direct or indirect fecal-oral spread. Enterovirus infection is more common in areas of crowding and with poor hygiene. Incubation periods can be 2–14 d long but generally last for <1 week. More is known about poliovirus than about other enteroviruses. Poliovirus can persist in the oropharynx for up to 3 weeks after infection and can be shed in stool for up to 8 weeks; shedding by immunocompromised pts can persist for much longer.

POLIOVIRUS INFECTIONS
PATHOGENESIS After ingestion, poliovirus is thought to infect epithelial cells in the mucosa of the GI tract and then to spread to submucosal lymphoid tissue. After spread to regional lymph nodes, the first (minor) viremic phase occurs, with replication in organs of the reticuloendothelial system. In some cases a secondary (major) viremic phase occurs. Virus enters the CNS either during viremia or via peripheral nerves.

CLINICAL MANIFESTATIONS Most poliovirus infections are mild or asymptomatic. Disease falls into three classes: (1) abortive poliomyelitis, a nonspecific febrile illness of 2–3 days' duration with no signs of CNS localization; (2) nonparalytic poliomyelitis, aseptic meningitis with complete recovery in a few days (~1% of pts); and (3) paralytic poliomyelitis, the least common presentation. In paralytic poliomyelitis, signs of aseptic meningitis are followed after one or several days by severe back, neck, and muscle pain and by the development of motor weakness. In some cases the disease appears to be biphasic, with a period of apparent recovery following the aseptic meningitis. Weakness is generally asymmetric and may involve the legs, the arms, or the abdominal, thoracic, or bulbar muscles. Paralytic disease is more common among older individuals, pregnant women, and persons with muscle trauma (including that incurred by strenuous exercise) at the time of CNS symptoms. Paralysis develops during the febrile phase of the illness, and many pts recover some or all function. Findings include weakness, fasciculations, and absent or decreased deep-tendon reflexes; sensation is intact. Postpolio syndrome consists of progressive muscle weakness beginning 20–40 years after the original infection and is thought not to involve persistent or reactivated infection.

COXSACKIEVIRUS, ECHOVIRUS, AND OTHER ENTEROVIRAL INFECTIONS
Between 5 and 10 million symptomatic enteroviral infections occur in the U.S. each year, with different serotypes accounting for different types of disease.

CLINICAL MANIFESTATIONS *Nonspecific Febrile Illness* In contrast to other respiratory viral infections, enteroviral febrile illness generally occurs in the summer. After an incubation period of 3–6 d, pts present with an acute onset of fever, malaise, and headache, often accompanied by upper respiratory symptoms and sometimes by nausea and vomiting. Symptoms generally persist for 3–4 d; most resolve within a week.

Aseptic Meningitis Enteroviruses cause up to 90% of the cases of aseptic meningitis in children and young adults in which an etiology is identified. Pts present with fever, headache, photophobia, and stiff neck and may have signs of meningeal irritation and drowsiness or irritability but no localizing neurologic findings. CSF analysis shows pleocytosis, with an early predominance of PMNs sometimes making it difficult to exclude a diagnosis of bacterial meningitis (particularly if the infection has been partially treated). In enteroviral meningitis, a shift to lymphocyte predominance occurs within 24 h of presentation, and the total WBC count is generally <1000/μL. The CSF glucose level is usually normal, and the CSF protein concentration is normal or only slightly elevated. Symptoms generally resolve within a week, but CSF abnormalities may persist for several weeks. Enteroviral encephalitis occurs less commonly and generally carries a good prognosis except in immunocompromised pts, who may develop chronic meningitis or encephalitis.

Acute Myocarditis/Pericarditis Enteroviruses, most commonly coxsackievirus B, cause an estimated one-third of cases of acute myocarditis/pericarditis.

Generalized Disease of the Newborn Enteroviral infection of the heart, liver, adrenals, brain, and other organs may resemble bacterial sepsis and is highly lethal. Most disease occurs during the first week of life, although cases may occur up to 3 months of age.

Herpangina Usually caused by coxsackievirus A serotypes, herpangina involves mucous membranes and is characterized by the acute onset of fever and sore throat and the appearance of small white papules or vesicles over the posterior half of the palate.

Pleurodynia (Bornholm Disease) An acute onset of fever and intense lower thoracic or abdominal pain aggravated by breathing or movement characterizes this syndrome, which is usually caused by coxsackievirus B.

Hand-Foot-and-Mouth Disease This illness, often caused by coxsackievirus A16 or enterovirus 71, is characterized by fever, anorexia, and malaise followed by the development of vesicular lesions in the oral cavity and on the dorsum or palm of the hands. The disease is highly infectious, with attack rates close to 100% among young children. The lesions usually resolve in 1 week.

Other Illnesses Enteroviruses commonly cause exanthems in children in summer and early fall. A sudden onset of severe eye pain, blurred vision, photophobia, and watery discharge from the eye characterizes acute hemorrhagic enteroviral conjunctivitis, which is often caused by enterovirus 70 and coxsackievirus A24. Enteroviruses are uncommon causes of childhood pneumonia and the common cold.

DIAGNOSIS Enteroviral infections are most often diagnosed by isolation of virus from throat swabs, stool, or rectal swabs. However, isolation of virus from these sites does not prove an association with disease since many pts with subclinical infections are colonized. Isolation of virus from normally sterile body fluids (CSF, pleural or pericardial fluid) or from tissues is less common but diagnostic. PCR of CSF is highly sensitive and specific and is more rapid than culture. Serologic testing is usually reserved for epidemiologic studies since the large number of serotypes makes it expensive and cumbersome and the result has little clinical utility.

TREATMENT AND PREVENTION   *Treatment* is supportive and directed at symptoms. Use of IV immunoglobulin remains controversial. Glucocorticoids are contraindicated. For polio, prevention is key. Two vaccines are licensed in the U.S.: inactivated (IPV) and live, oral, attenuated (OPV). OPV offers several advantages, including ease of administration, low cost, high efficacy, and induction of intestinal immunity. However, vaccine-associated paralytic poliomyelitis occurs at a rate of about 1 case per 2.6 million doses of OPV (a figure accounting for all cases of paralytic polio in the U.S.), and OPV must be avoided in immunosuppressed pts, including those infected with HIV and their family members. As of January 2000, the Advisory Committee for Immunization Practices suggested that children receive IPV for all four doses to further reduce the risk of vaccine-associated polio. OPV is to be used only in special circumstances (e.g., mass immunization campaigns).

For a more detailed discussion, see Cohen JI: Enteroviruses and Reoviruses, Chap. 193, p. 1138, in HPIM-15.

107

INSECT- AND ANIMAL-BORNE VIRAL INFECTIONS

RABIES
Rabies virus is an enveloped, bullet-shaped, single-stranded RNA virus belonging to the family Rhabdoviridae. The binding of viral glycoproteins to acetylcholine receptors contributes to neurovirulence.

EPIDEMIOLOGY   Rabies exists in two epidemiologic forms: urban rabies (propagated by unimmunized domesticated dogs and cats) and sylvatic rabies (propagated by skunks, foxes, raccoons, mongooses, wolves, and bats). The virus is transmitted in saliva. Since 1980, 36 human cases of rabies have been diagnosed in the U.S.; 58% of these cases were associated with exposure to bats, while one-third were acquired through dog bites sustained outside the U.S. Most persons with proven rabies in the U.S. report no Hx of animal bite. More than one-third of recent cases have been diagnosed after death. Most cases of postexposure prophylaxis are associated with domesticated animals, such as dogs and cats. Because of delayed diagnosis, postexposure prophylaxis of health care workers and close contacts of cases is common.

CLINICAL MANIFESTATIONS   The incubation period for rabies is variable, probably depending on the amount of virus introduced, the distance of the inoculation site from the CNS, and the host's defense status. The mean incubation period is 1–2 months, but the range is 7 d to >1 year.

A *prodromal* period of 1–4 d is marked by fever, headache, malaise, myalgias, increased fatigability, anorexia, nausea and vomiting, sore throat, and nonproductive cough. Paresthesia and/or fasciculations at or near the site of viral inoculation are found in 50–80% of cases in the prodromal stage and constitute the only symptom suggestive of rabies. An *encephalitic* phase follows, with periods of excessive motor activity, excitation, and agitation. Confusion, combativeness, aberrations of thought, muscle spasms, seizures, focal paralysis, and fever are interspersed with shortening periods of lucidity. *Hyperesthesia* (excessive sensitivity to light, noise, and touch) is very common. Hydrophobia or aerophobia has been seen in around two-thirds of recent cases and increases the likelihood of antemortem diagnosis. Signs may include hyperthermia, autonomic dysfunction, upper motor neuron paralysis, and vocal cord paralysis. *Brainstem dysfunction* becomes apparent shortly after the encephalitic phase begins. Manifestations include cranial nerve involvement (diplopia, facial palsies, optic neuritis, and difficulty with deglutition, which, combined with excessive salivation, produces characteristic "foaming at the mouth"); hydrophobia; painful violent involuntary contractions of the diaphragm and of accessory respiratory, pharyngeal, and laryngeal muscles initiated by swallowing liquids (seen in 50% of cases); priapism; and spontaneous ejaculation. The prominence of early brainstem dysfunction distinguishes rabies from other viral encephalitides. The median period of survival after the onset of symptoms is 4 d. With respiratory support, late complications may appear, including inappropriate secretion of vasopressin, diabetes insipidus, cardiac arrhythmias, vascular instability, ARDS, GI bleeding, thrombocytopenia, and paralytic ileus. Recovery is extremely rare.

DIAGNOSIS The specific diagnosis of rabies can be made by several techniques, including (1) isolation of the virus from saliva, CSF, or brain tissue by mouse inoculation; (2) detection of viral antigen in infected tissue samples, such as corneal impression smears, skin biopsies, or brain biopsies, by fluorescent antibody (FA) staining; (3) documentation of a fourfold rise in neutralizing antibody titer; or (4) detection of rabies virus RNA by PCR. Isolation of virus from saliva, demonstration of viral nucleic acid in saliva, or detection of viral antigen in a nuchal skin biopsy specimen is most sensitive. Brain tissue should be sent for virus culture, FA staining for antigen, histologic and/or electron microscopic examination for Negri bodies, or PCR. Pts receiving postexposure rabies prophylaxis usually have serum and CSF antibody titers of <1:64, whereas in human rabies CSF antibody titers may vary from 1:200 to 1:160,000.

 TREATMENT

An algorithm for *postexposure rabies prophylaxis* is shown in Fig. 107-1. Postexposure prophylaxis includes local wound treatment (mechanical and chemical cleansing, administration of tetanus toxoid and antibiotics); passive immunization [human rabies immune globulin (HRIG), 20 U/kg, with the full dose given by local infiltration into the wound and any remaining portion injected IM at a site distant from the vaccination site]; and active immunization [human diploid cell vaccine (HDCV), rabies vaccine adsorbed (RVA), or purified chick embryo vaccine], with five 1-mL doses given IM on days 0, 3, 7, 14, and 28 after exposure. The vaccine should be administered in the deltoid or anterolateral thigh; the gluteal area should not be used. An equine antiserum is also available for passive immunization at a dose of 40 U/kg but

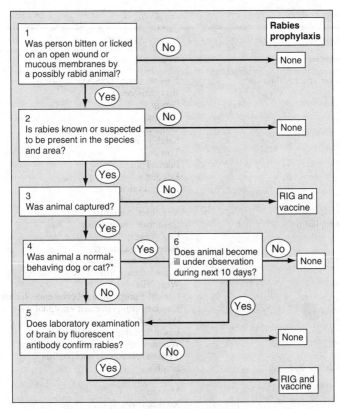

FIGURE 107-1 Postexposure rabies prophylaxis algorithm. *Instances of exposure to livestock or to normal-behaving, unvaccinated dogs or cats should be considered individually, and local and state public health officials should be consulted. (*From L Corey: HPIM-15, p. 1150.*)

is more likely than human antiserum to result in serum sickness. Postexposure prophylaxis for persons who have received preexposure prophylaxis consists of two doses of HDCV (1 mL IM) on days 0 and 3.

PREVENTION *Preexposure prophylaxis* should be given to individuals at high risk of exposure, such as veterinarians, cave explorers, laboratory workers, and animal handlers. Three doses of HDCV (1 mL IM or 0.1 mL intradermally) are given on days 0, 7, and 21 or 28, respectively. Serologic testing should be conducted after the series and then every 2–6 years, depending on risk. When antibody titers fall below 1:5, a booster dose of HDCV (1 mL IM or 0.1 mL intradermally) should be given.

INFECTIONS CAUSED BY ARTHROPOD- AND RODENT-BORNE VIRUSES

Arthropod- and rodent-borne viruses are transmitted by a variety of vectors. Table 107-1 lists the syndromes and major viruses causing human disease in this category.

Table 107-1

Syndromes and Major Viruses Transmitted by Arthropods and Rodents

Syndrome	Virus
Fever and myalgia	Lymphocytic choriomeningitis
	Bunyamwera
	Group C
	Tahyna
	Oropouche
	Sandfly fever
	Toscana
	Punta Toro
	Dengue
	Colorado tick fever
	Orbivirus
	Vesicular stomatitis
Encephalitis	California encephalitis
	La Crosse
	Jamestown Canyon
	St. Louis encephalitis
	Japanese encephalitis
	West Nile
	Central European tick-borne encephalitis
	Russian spring-summer encephalitis
	Powassan
	Eastern equine encephalitis
	Western equine encephalitis
	Venezuelan equine encephalitis
Arthritis and rash	Sindbis
	Chikungunya
	Mayaro
	Ross River
Hemorrhagic fever	Lassa
(HF)	South American HF
	Rift Valley fever
	Crimean Congo HF
	Hantavirus
	Hantaan
	Puumala
	Marburg
	Ebola
	Yellow fever
	Dengue
	Kyasanur Forest

Viruses Causing Fever and Myalgia

Fever and myalgia constitute the syndrome most commonly associated with zoonotic virus infection. The syndrome, which is caused by many agents belonging to the seven major families of zoonotic viruses, typically begins with the abrupt onset of fever, chills, intense myalgia, and malaise. Arthralgias are frequent, but arthritis is not. Anorexia is characteristic and is frequently associated with nausea and vomiting. Headache may be severe. Some viruses cause a maculopapular rash and others aseptic meningitis. Most pts recover completely with only supportive therapy.

LYMPHOCYTIC   CHORIOMENINGITIS   (LCM)   *Epidemiology*
The common house mouse is the primary host for LCM, which is worldwide
in distribution. Human infections are secondary to contact with an infected
rodent, with transmission thought to be via airborne spread or contact with
infected excrement.

Clinical Manifestations   The most common clinical pattern is an influenza-
like illness. In one-fourth of pts, the illness may be biphasic, with initial fever
and subsequent aseptic meningitis or encephalitis. Fever, malaise, weakness,
myalgia (especially lumbar), retroorbital headache, photophobia, anorexia, nausea, and light-headedness are common. Physical findings may include skin rash,
pharyngeal injection without exudate, mild cervical or axillary lymphadenopathy, alopecia, or meningeal signs. Testicular pain or frank orchitis may be
present. LCM virus infection in pregnant women may lead to congenital hydrocephalus and fetal chorioretinitis.

Diagnosis   Leukopenia and thrombocytopenia are observed during the first
week of illness. The CSF of pts with meningeal signs usually contains several
hundred cells per microliter, with a lymphocytic predominance. Typical CSF
findings are mononuclear cell counts of >1000/μL, elevated protein levels, and
low glucose levels. Recovery of LCM virus from blood or spinal fluid is most
likely in the initial phases of the illness. The most direct method for the diagnosis of LCM, therefore, is IgM-capture ELISA of serum or CSF; recently,
reverse transcription (RT)-PCR assays have been developed for application to
CSF.

 TREATMENT

There is no specific treatment for LCM.

DENGUE FEVER   Dengue viruses are flaviviruses. Four serotypes have
been identified.

Epidemiology   Dengue is transmitted by *Aedes* mosquitoes and is endemic
over large areas of the tropics and subtropics, Asia, Oceania, Africa, Australia,
and the Americas, including the Caribbean. Classic dengue, also known as
breakbone fever, usually occurs in nonimmune individuals, children, and adults
who do not reside in an endemic area. Dengue hemorrhagic fever (DHF) occurs
almost exclusively in indigenous populations and is thought to be immunologically mediated, with enhanced infection of the target cells (macrophages and
monocytes) more likely in the presence of antibody from a previous infection.

Clinical Manifestations   Dengue viruses frequently produce inapparent infection. When symptoms develop, three clinical patterns are seen: classic dengue, a mild atypical form, and DHF.

1.   *Classic dengue*: After an incubation period of 5–8 d, a short prodrome
of mild conjunctivitis or coryza may precede by a few hours the abrupt onset
of severe headache, retroorbital pain, backache (especially lumbar), and leg and
joint pains. Ocular soreness, anorexia, and weakness are common; cough is rare.
Skin rashes that vary in appearance are common, as is lymphadenopathy. The
fever may follow a diphasic course. The febrile illness usually lasts for 5–6 d
and terminates abruptly.

2.   *Atypical dengue*: Symptoms of mild atypical illness include fever, anorexia, headache, and myalgia. An evanescent rash may develop; lymphadenopathy is absent. Symptoms usually last for <72 h.

3. *DHF*: Illness begins abruptly with a relatively mild stage (2–4 d) consisting of fever, cough, pharyngitis, headache, anorexia, nausea, vomiting, and abdominal pain, which may be severe. Myalgia, arthralgia, and bone pain, which are common in classic dengue, are unusual in DHF. Hemorrhagic manifestations include a positive tourniquet test, petechiae, purpura, ecchymoses, epistaxis, bleeding gums, hematemesis, melena, enlargement of the liver, thrombocytopenia, hemoconcentration, and hematocrit increased by ≥20%. Dengue shock syndrome (DSS) is diagnosed when there is a rapid weak pulse with narrowing of the pulse pressure to ≤20 mmHg or hypotension with cold clammy skin and restlessness.

Diagnosis   Primary viral isolation may be accomplished by inoculation of blood obtained in the first 3–5 d of illness into mosquitoes or mosquito cell cultures. Serologic diagnosis can be made by IgM ELISA or testing of paired serum specimens during recovery or by antigen-detection ELISA or RT-PCR during the acute phase.

 TREATMENT

Treatment is supportive, with close monitoring and administration of oxygen and IV fluids. Overall mortality at an experienced center in the tropics is probably as low as 1%.

Arboviruses Causing Encephalitis

EPIDEMIOLOGY   Since arboviruses causing encephalitis are transmitted by mosquitoes, infections occur during peak mosquito season (late spring to early fall). Table 107-2 lists prominent features of arboviral encephalitis.

CLINICAL MANIFESTATIONS   Features of arboviral encephalitis differ among age groups and depend on the specific infecting virus. In adults, initial symptoms include fever, abdominal pain, sore throat, vertigo, and respiratory symptoms followed by headache, meningeal signs, photophobia, and vomiting. Disturbances in mentation are the most prominent neurologic findings, ranging from subtle abnormalities detected by cerebral function tests to coma. Other findings include tremor, cranial nerve abnormalities, reflex abnormalities, paresis, and frontal lobe signs. Fever and neurologic symptoms and signs vary in duration from a few days to as long as 2–3 weeks; however, the time to full recovery may be weeks or months.

DIAGNOSIS   CSF findings include pleocytosis (usually several hundred cells per microliter, but occasionally >1000 cells/μL), with an initial neutrophil predominance shifting after several days to a lymphocyte predominance. The CSF protein level is usually slightly elevated and may increase with time; the CSF glucose concentration is normal. A specific diagnosis rests on demonstration of a rise in antibody level between acute- and convalescent-phase sera. A humoral immune response is usually detectable at the clinical onset of the disease; both serum and CSF should be examined for IgM. Virus generally cannot be isolated from blood or CSF. However, there is a heterogeneous distribution of virus and viral antigen in brain tissue.

 TREATMENT

Treatment is supportive.

Alphaviruses Causing Arthritis and Rash

True arthritis is a common accompaniment of several viral diseases, such as rubella, parvovirus B19 infection, and hepatitis B. In addition, the alphaviruses cause true arthritis and a maculopapular rash.

SINDBIS VIRUS INFECTION *Epidemiology* Sindbis virus is transmitted among birds by mosquitoes. Infections with the northern European and genetically related southern African strains are particularly likely to cause an arthritis-rash syndrome.

Clinical Manifestations The incubation period is <1 week. Clinical symptoms begin with rash and arthralgia. The rash lasts about a week and spreads from the trunk to the extremities, evolving from macules to papules that frequently vesiculate. The arthritis is multiarticular, migratory, and incapacitating.

 TREATMENT

There is no specific therapy.

CHIKUNGUNYA VIRUS INFECTION *Epidemiology* Chikungunya virus is transmitted among humans by *Aedes* mosquitoes. The virus is endemic in rural Africa and is intermittently epidemic in towns and cities of Africa and Asia.

Clinical Manifestations The incubation period is 2–3 d. Fever and severe arthralgia are accompanied by chills and constitutional symptoms such as headache, photophobia, conjunctival injection, anorexia, nausea, and abdominal pain. Migratory arthritis primarily affects small joints.

 TREATMENT

No specific therapy is available.

EPIDEMIC POLYARTHRITIS *Epidemiology* Ross River virus causes epidemics of distinctive disease in Australia, New Guinea, and the eastern Pacific islands. This virus is transmitted among humans by *Aedes* mosquitoes.

Clinical Manifestations The incubation period is 7–11 d, and the onset of illness is sudden, with joint pain usually ushering in the disease. The rash develops around the same time. Most pts are incapacitated for considerable periods by joint involvement. Joint fluid contains 1000–60,000 mononuclear cells/μL. The detection of IgM antibodies is valuable, although these antibodies occasionally persist for years.

 TREATMENT

No specific therapy is available.

Viruses Causing Hemorrhagic Fevers

LASSA FEVER *Epidemiology* Lassa fever is a highly contagious arenavirus first described in Lassa, a town in northeastern Nigeria, in 1969 and subsequently found in Sierra Leone, Guinea, and Liberia. The virus is carried

Table 107-2

Prominent Features of Arboviral Encephalitis

Virus	Incubation Period, Days	Annual No. of Cases	Case-to-Infection Ratio
La Crosse	~3–7	70 (U.S.)	<1:1000
St. Louis	4–21	85, with hundreds to thousands in epidemic years (U.S.)	<1:200
Japanese	5–15	>25,000	1:200–300
West Nile	3–6	?	Very low
Central European	7–14	Thousands	1:12
Russian spring-summer	7–14	Hundreds	—
Powassan	~10	~1 (U.S.)	—
Eastern equine	~5–10	5 (U.S.)	1:40 adult 1:17 child
Western equine	~5–10	~20 (U.S.)	1:1000 adult 1:50 child 1:1 infant
Venezuelan equine (epidemic)	1–5	?	1:250 adult 1:25 child (approximate)

SOURCE: Adapted from CJ Peters: HPIM-15, p. 1157.

in a species of rat that is widespread in Africa. Spread takes place through small-particle aerosols, but person-to-person transmission also occurs.

Clinical Manifestations The incubation period is 7–18 d. The onset of illness is insidious, with fevers, rigors, headache, malaise, and myalgia. The average case has a gradual onset that gives way to more constitutional symptoms and prostration. Bleeding occurs in 15–30% of cases, a maculopapular rash is noted in light-skinned pts, and effusions (especially pericarditis in males) are seen. Deafness occurs in 20% of cases and is occasionally permanent. The WBC count may be slightly high, and platelet counts may be somewhat low. High aspartate aminotransferase (AST) levels predict a fatal outcome, and AST levels of >150 IU/mL warrant treatment with IV ribavirin.

Diagnosis The diagnosis can be made by the demonstration of a fourfold rise in antibody titer between acute- and convalescent-phase sera. The diagnosis is unlikely if IgM antibodies are absent by day 14 of illness.

Age of Cases	Case-Fatality Rate, %	Residua
<15 years	<0.5	Recurrent seizures in ~10%; severe deficits in rare cases; decreased school performance and behavioral change suspected in small proportion
Milder cases in the young; more severe cases in adults >40 years old, particularly the elderly	7	Common in the elderly
All ages; children in highly endemic areas	20–50	Common (approximately half of cases); may be severe
Mainly the elderly and children	—	Uncommon
All ages; milder in children	1–5	20%
All ages; milder in children	20	Approximately half of cases; often severe; limb-girdle paralysis
All ages; some predilection for children	~10	Common (approximately half of cases)
All ages; predilection for children	50–75	Common
All ages; predilection for children <2 years old (increased mortality in elderly)	3–7	Common only among infants <1 year old
All ages; predilection for children	~10	—

℞ **TREATMENT**

Ribavirin appears to be effective in reducing mortality rates and should be administered to pts with AST levels of >150 IU/mL. The drug should be given by slow IV infusion in a dose of 32 mg/kg; this dose should be followed by 16 mg/kg q6h for 4 d and then by 8 mg/kg q8h for 6 d.

HANTAVIRUS PULMONARY SYNDROME *Epidemiology* The causative agents of hantavirus pulmonary syndrome are hantaviruses associated with the rodent subfamily Sigmodontinae. Sin Nombre virus chronically infects the deer mouse and is the most important virus causing hantavirus pulmonary syndrome in the U.S.

Clinical Manifestations The disease begins with a prodrome of 3–4 d comprising fever, myalgia, malaise, and (in many cases) GI disturbances. Pts usually present as the pulmonary phase begins. Typical findings include slightly lowered blood pressure, tachycardia, tachypnea, mild hypoxemia, and early pulmonary edema. Over several hours, decompensation progresses rapidly to respiratory failure.

Diagnosis   A specific diagnosis is made by IgM testing of acute-phase serum. RT-PCR is usually positive when used to test blood clots or tissues in the first 7–9 d of illness.

 TREATMENT

Appropriate management during the first few hours after presentation is critical. The goal is to prevent severe hypoxemia with oxygen therapy and, if needed, intubation and intensive respiratory management. Mortality remains at ~30–40% with good management. Ribavirin inhibits the virus in vitro but did not have a marked clinical effect on pts in an open-label study.

DENGUE HEMORRHAGIC FEVER/DENGUE SHOCK SYNDROME
See "Dengue Fever," above.

MARBURG AND EBOLA VIRUSES

EPIDEMIOLOGY   Marburg and Ebola viruses are antigenically and genetically distinct viruses in the family Filoviridae. Of the 25 cases of primary Marburg infection, 7 ended in death. Isolated cases have been reported in Africa. In a 1976 epidemic of severe hemorrhagic fever due to Ebola virus in Zaire and Sudan, there were >470 deaths among 550 cases. The virus was spread by close person-to-person contact and reuse of needles for injections. Another Ebola epidemic occurred in the Democratic Republic of Congo in 1995, and smaller epidemics took place in Gabon in 1994–1996; these epidemics included 317 cases, with a mortality rate of 88%. Strict quarantine measures arrested the Congo epidemic. The reservoirs for the filoviruses are unknown, although evidence points to a nonprimate reservoir.

CLINICAL MANIFESTATIONS   After an incubation period ranging from 3 to 16 d, pts develop fever, severe headache, malaise, myalgias, nausea, and vomiting. Between 1 and 3 d after onset, watery diarrhea, lethargy, and a change in mentation are noted. A nonpruritic maculopapular rash begins on the fifth to seventh day and is followed by desquamation. Hemorrhagic manifestations develop at about this time; bleeding can be apparent from any mucosal site, although it does not always occur and has been absent even in fatal cases. The temperature response is frequently biphasic, with lysis after the first 10–12 d and a recurrence that may be associated with secondary bacterial infections or possibly with localized viral persistence.

DIAGNOSIS   Leukopenia and thrombocytopenia are typical, and pts with fatal cases develop DIC. AST and alanine aminotransferase levels progressively rise, and jaundice is evident in some cases. Amylase levels may be elevated. Renal insufficiency is proportional to shock; proteinuria is common. Antigen-detection ELISA–based IgM and IgG tests are positive in recovering pts. Antigen detection in skin biopsies is a useful postmortem diagnostic tool.

 TREATMENT

Supportive care is all that can currently be offered. Barrier nursing precautions can decrease the spread of the virus.

For a more detailed discussion, see Corey L: Rabies Virus and Other Rhab-
doviruses, Chap. 197, p. 1149; Peters CJ: Infections Caused by Arthropod-
and Rodent-Borne Viruses, Chap. 198, p. 1152; and Peters CJ: Filoviridae
(Marburg and Ebola Viruses), Chap. 199, p. 1166, in HPIM-15.

108

FUNGAL INFECTIONS

Fungi can appear microscopically as either yeasts or molds. Most pathogenic
fungi are saprophytic in nature; they cause infection when airborne spores reach
the lung or paranasal sinus or when hyphae or spores are accidentally inoculated
into the skin or cornea. Acquisition of infection from another person is rare.

CRYPTOCOCCOSIS

EPIDEMIOLOGY/PATHOGENESIS   The yeastlike fungus *Cryptococcus neoformans* elaborates a large polysaccharide capsule. Humans become infected by inhalation of the fungus. Pulmonary infection is frequently asymptomatic. Dissemination, including that to the CNS, occurs via the bloodstream.
Pts with late-stage HIV infection are at substantial risk for this infection, as are
pts who have undergone solid organ transplantation, those with sarcoidosis, and
those receiving glucocorticoid therapy.

CLINICAL MANIFESTATIONS   *Meningoencephalitis*   Headache,
nausea, staggering gait, dementia, irritability, confusion, and blurred vision are
common early symptoms. One-third of pts have papilledema at diagnosis. Fever
and nuchal rigidity are often mild or lacking. Cranial nerve palsies, typically
asymmetric, occur in about one-fourth of cases. With progression of the infection, deepening coma and signs of brainstem compression appear.

Pulmonary Infection   Chest pain occurs in 40% of cases and cough in
20%. CXRs commonly show one or more dense infiltrates, which are often well
circumscribed.

Disseminated Infection   Some 10% of pts with cryptococcosis have skin
lesions, and the vast majority of those who do also have disseminated infection.
Cutaneous findings begin with one or more papular lesions, which tend eventually to ulcerate. Rare manifestations of disseminated disease include prostatitis, osteomyelitis, endophthalmitis, hepatitis, pericarditis, endocarditis, and renal abscess.

DIAGNOSIS   LP is the single most useful diagnostic test for cryptococcal
meningitis. The India ink smear is positive in >50% of cases. Among non-
AIDS pts, hypoglycorrhachia is present half of the time, and elevated CSF
protein levels and lymphocytic pleocytosis are also common. Among AIDS pts,
CSF abnormalities are less pronounced but the India ink smear is more often
positive. A CSF or serum latex agglutination test is positive in 90% of cases of
cryptococcal meningitis. Fungemia develops in 10–30% and is particularly
common among persons with AIDS. For the diagnosis of pulmonary or dissem-

inated cryptococcosis, biopsy (with culture) is usually required. Sputum culture is positive in only 10% of cases of cryptococcal pneumonia and serum latex agglutination in only one-third.

 TREATMENT

For pts with AIDS and cryptococcosis, therapy begins with IV amphotericin B (0.7 mg/kg qd), which is administered for at least 2 weeks and until the clinical condition is stable. Thereafter, these pts receive oral fluconazole (400 mg/d). The addition of flucytosine to the amphotericin B regimen for 2 weeks has minimal impact on morbidity and mortality; its addition to fluconazole only increases GI intolerance. After infection is controlled, suppressive therapy with oral fluconazole (200 mg/d) is continued indefinitely. It is not yet known whether pts with a sustained rise in CD4+ T lymphocyte counts can safely discontinue fluconazole maintenance therapy. Surgical excision of a solitary lesion, without systemic therapy, may be appropriate for selected immunocompetent pts with no cryptococci in blood, CSF, or urine. In non-AIDS pts, the goal of therapy is to cure the infection, not merely to control its symptoms. A single intensive course is given until cultures from all previously positive sites are negative. Amphotericin B is administered either alone (0.6–0.7 mg/kg IV qd for ≥10 weeks) or with flucytosine (25–37.5 mg/kg q6h). Flucytosine accelerates culture response, but grave toxicity can result unless serum levels are kept below 100 μg/mL. Use of liposomal formulations of amphotericin B for treatment of cryptococcal meningitis in pts without HIV infection is controversial.

CANDIDIASIS

ETIOLOGY/PATHOGENESIS *Candida* spp., common commensals of humans, are found most often in the mouth, stool, and vagina. Candidiasis is often preceded by expansion of the commensal population as a result of broad-spectrum antibiotic therapy. Additional host factors, both local and systemic, favor infection. Examples include diabetes mellitus, HIV infection, and denture wear, all of which favor the development of oropharyngeal thrush; macerated skin (regardless of etiology), which favors the development of cutaneous candidiasis; and the third trimester of pregnancy, during which vulvovaginal candidiasis is especially common. *Candida* can pass from colonized surfaces to deep tissues when the integrity of the mucosa or skin is violated (as a consequence, for example, of GI perforation by trauma or surgery, use of an indwelling catheter, or mucosal damage from cytotoxic chemotherapy). Hosts who are particularly susceptible to *Candida* once it has traversed the integumentary barrier include neonates of very low birth weight, people with neutropenia, and pts who are using or have recently used high-dose glucocorticoids. Hematogenous seeding is particularly evident in the retinas, kidneys, spleen, and liver.

CLINICAL MANIFESTATIONS *Oral thrush* presents as discrete and confluent adherent white plaques in the mouth and on the tongue. *Cutaneous candidiasis* presents as redness and maceration in intertriginous areas. *Vulvovaginal thrush* causes pruritus and discharge and is sometimes responsible for dyspareunia or dysuria. Oral and vaginal thrush, circumscribed hyperkeratotic skin lesions, dystrophic nails, and partial alopecia characterize *chronic mucocutaneous candidiasis*. A variety of defects in T cell function have been described in pts with this condition, who may also exhibit hypofunction of the parathyroid, adrenal, or thyroid gland. Dysphagia or substernal chest pain occurs in *esophageal candidiasis*, the most common type of GI candidiasis. Endoscopic findings include areas of redness and edema, focal white patches, and/or ulcers. *Hematogenous dissemination* presents with varied severity, ranging from fever alone to septic shock. Other findings may include retinal lesions, multiple small hepatosplenic abscesses, nodular pulmonary infiltrates, endocarditis, chronic meningitis or arthritis, and (in rare cases) focal manifestations such as osteomyelitis, pustular skin lesions, myositis, and brain abscess.

DIAGNOSIS   Demonstration of pseudohyphae on wet smear with confirmation by culture is the procedure of choice for diagnosing superficial candidiasis. Deeper lesions due to *Candida* may be diagnosed by histologic section of biopsy specimens or by culture of blood, CSF, joint fluid, or surgical specimens. Serologic tests for antibody or antigen are not useful.

 TREATMENT

For cutaneous candidiasis, nystatin powder or a cream containing ciclopirox or an azole is applied topically. For vulvovaginal candidiasis, vaginal azole formulations are therapeutically superior to nystatin suppositories. A single oral dose of fluconazole (150 mg) is a convenient alternative but is more likely to cause adverse effects. Oral or esophageal candidiasis responds better to clotrimazole troches taken five times a day than to nystatin suspension swished and swallowed. Oral fluconazole (100–200 mg/d) is more convenient and effective in esophagitis than clotrimazole troches. Esophagitis not responding to fluconazole may warrant repeat endoscopy to exclude other conditions. Itraconazole suspension (100–200 mg/d) alleviates *Candida* esophagitis in some pts when fluconazole treatment fails. Pts with AIDS and recurrent oropharyngeal or esophageal candidiasis may develop azole resistance. For AIDS pts with azole-resistant disease, amphotericin B (0.3–0.5 mg/kg IV qd) may be used. Bladder thrush responds to bladder irrigation with amphotericin B (50 mg/L for 5 d); oral fluconazole may be substituted in the treatment of noncatheterized pts with candiduria. For disseminated disease, amphotericin B (0.5–0.7 mg/kg qd) is the treatment of choice. In immunocompetent pts with catheter-acquired *C. albicans* fungemia, the catheter should be removed in conjunction with the administration of fluconazole (400 mg/d) or amphotericin B (0.5 mg/kg qd). Therapy for candidemia should be continued for 2 weeks after the pt becomes afebrile. The *Candida* species involved should be considered in choosing between fluconazole and amphotericin B. For example, *C. krusei* is resistant to fluconazole in vitro, *C. glabrata* is intermediately sensitive to fluconazole, and strains of *C. lusitaniae* are resistant to amphotericin B. Oral fluconazole (400 mg/d) is used prophylactically against invasive candidiasis in recipients of allogeneic bone marrow transplants.

ASPERGILLOSIS

EPIDEMIOLOGY/PATHOGENESIS   *Aspergillus* is a mold with septate hyphae ~2–4 μm in diameter. *Aspergillus* species are ubiquitous in the environment and cause several syndromes, including allergic bronchopulmonary aspergillosis, aspergilloma, and invasive aspergillosis. Invasive disease originates in the lung after inhalation of *Aspergillus* spores and is confined almost entirely to immunosuppressed hosts. In roughly 90% of such cases, two of the following risk factors are present: neutropenia (granulocyte count <500/μL), history of high-dose glucocorticoid therapy, or history of treatment with cytotoxic drugs. Invasive infection, which may also complicate AIDS, is characterized by hyphal invasion of blood vessels, thrombosis, necrosis, and hemorrhagic infarction.

CLINICAL MANIFESTATIONS   *Allergic bronchial aspergillosis* presents in pts with preexisting asthma as eosinophilia, fleeting pulmonary infiltrates, and demonstrable IgE antibody to *Aspergillus. Endobronchial saprophytic pulmonary aspergillosis* presents as chronic productive cough, often with hemoptysis, in pts with prior chronic lung disease, such as tuberculosis, sarcoidosis, or bronchiectasis. The term *aspergilloma* refers to a ball of hyphae that forms within a preexisting pulmonary cyst or cavity, usually in an upper lobe. *Invasive aspergillosis* in the immunocompromised host presents as an acute, rapidly progressive, densely consolidated pulmonary infiltrate. In the pt recovering from neutropenia, cavitation is a classic occurrence. Infection may spread hematogenously or by direct extension.

DIAGNOSIS   The repeated isolation of *Aspergillus* from sputum implies colonization or infection. The diagnosis of invasive aspergillosis is suggested by even a single isolation of *Aspergillus* from the sputum of a neutropenic pt with pneumonia. A biopsy and culture are usually required for definitive diagnosis, the latter for confirmation and speciation. Blood cultures are rarely positive. A fungus ball in the lung is usually detectable by CXR. CT is particularly valuable in diagnosing invasive aspergillosis in pts with neutropenia. The earliest finding is of an enlarging pulmonary nodule surrounded by a hazy rim of edema or hemorrhage (*halo sign*). With the recovery of the bone marrow, the infarcted central core cavitates, forming the *crescent sign*. Serum IgG antibodies to *Aspergillus* are often found in pts colonized with the organism and are nearly universally present in those with aspergilloma.

 TREATMENT

Pts with pulmonary aspergilloma and severe hemoptysis may benefit from lobectomy. Systemic therapy is of no value in endobronchial or endocavitary aspergillosis. Treatment with IV amphotericin B (1.0–1.5 mg/kg qd) has resulted in the arrest or cure of invasive aspergillosis when immunosuppression is not severe. Itraconazole (200 mg bid) may be used judiciously by pts who are not severely immunosuppressed and who have indolent or slowly progressive invasive infection.

HISTOPLASMOSIS

EPIDEMIOLOGY/PATHOGENESIS   *Histoplasma capsulatum* is a dimorphic fungus found in moist surface soil, particularly soil enriched by droppings of certain birds and bats. In the U.S., infection is most common in the southeastern, mid-Atlantic, and central states. Case clusters have occurred among groups of people exposed to dust (e.g., while raking; cleaning dirt-floored chicken coops; spelunking; or cleaning, remodeling, or demolishing old buildings). Infection follows inhalation of the organism and is usually a self-limited condition.

CLINICAL MANIFESTATIONS   In the vast majority of cases, *acute pulmonary histoplasmosis* is either asymptomatic or mild. Symptoms and signs may include cough, fever, malaise, and CXR findings of hilar adenopathy, with or without areas of pneumonitis. Erythema nodosum and erythema multiforme have been reported in a few outbreaks. *Chronic pulmonary histoplasmosis* is characterized by subacute onset of productive cough, weight loss, and night sweats. CXRs show uni- or bilateral fibronodular apical infiltrates. In one-third of pts, the disease stabilizes or improves spontaneously. In the remainder, it progresses insidiously and may terminate in death from cor pulmonale, bacterial pneumonia, or histoplasmosis itself. The findings in *acute disseminated histo-*

plasmosis, which resemble those in miliary tuberculosis, include fever, hepatosplenomegaly, lymphadenopathy, jaundice, and pancytopenia. Indurated ulcers of the mouth, tongue, nose, or larynx occur in about one-fourth of cases. AIDS pts may develop disseminated disease years after exposure in an endemic area. CXRs are abnormal in 50% of cases, showing discrete nodules or a miliary pattern.

DIAGNOSIS Culture of *H. capsulatum* is the preferred diagnostic method but is often difficult. Blood should be cultured by the lysis-centrifugation technique and plates held at 30°C for at least 2 weeks. Cultures of bone marrow, mucosal lesions, liver, and bronchoalveolar lavage fluid are useful in disseminated disease. Sputum culture is preferred for suspected chronic pulmonary histoplasmosis, but visible growth requires 2–4 weeks. Histologic diagnosis is possible but requires considerable expertise. An assay for *Histoplasma* antigen in blood or urine is commercially available and is useful for diagnosis and monitoring of the response to therapy in AIDS pts with disseminated infection. Serology is of limited value, and histoplasmin skin testing is of no clinical utility.

 TREATMENT

Acute pulmonary histoplasmosis does not require therapy. Pts with disseminated or chronic pulmonary histoplasmosis should receive chemotherapy. Amphotericin B (0.6 mg/kg qd) is the agent of choice for pts who are severely ill, who are immunosuppressed, or whose infection involves the CNS. The regimen can be changed to itraconazole (200 mg bid) once improvement becomes evident. The measurement of itraconazole trough blood levels should be considered in pts who may not be absorbing the drug well (e.g., AIDS pts). Itraconazole suspension is better absorbed than the capsule formulation. Immunocompetent pts with mild or moderate disease can immediately be given itraconazole (200 mg bid) and are generally treated for 6–12 months. Ketoconazole (400–800 mg/d) is an alternative for these pts if CNS disease is absent, but side effects are more frequent. A third alternative for immunocompetent pts is amphotericin B (0.5 mg/kg qd) for 10 weeks. Maintenance therapy with itraconazole (200 mg/d) is continued for life in AIDS pts who have responded to 10 weeks of therapy.

BLASTOMYCOSIS

EPIDEMIOLOGY/PATHOGENESIS Blastomycosis is acquired by inhalation of the dimorphic fungus *Blastomyces dermatitidis* from soil, decomposed vegetation, or rotting wood. The disease is uncommon in any locality; the majority of cases occur in the southeastern, central, and mid-Atlantic areas of the U.S.

CLINICAL MANIFESTATIONS A minority of pts have acute, self-limited pneumonia. Most cases, however, have an indolent onset and a chronically progressive course. Fever, cough, weight loss, lassitude, chest ache, and skin lesions are common. The skin lesions enlarge over many weeks from pimples to verrucous, crusted, or ulcerated forms. CXR findings are abnormal in two-thirds of cases, revealing one or more nodular or pneumonic infiltrates. Infection may spread to the brain or meninges. Osteolytic lesions, which may be found in nearly any bone, present as cold abscesses or draining sinuses. Prostatic and epididymal lesions resemble those of tuberculosis.

DIAGNOSIS The diagnosis is made by culture of *B. dermatitidis* from sputum, pus, or urine or by wet smear or histology.

TREATMENT

Every pt should receive chemotherapy. As with histoplasmosis, severe disease should be treated with amphotericin B. Skin and noncavitary lung lesions should be treated for 8–10 weeks (cumulative dose, 2.0 g). Cavitary lung disease and disease extending beyond the lungs and skin should be treated for 10–12 weeks (total dose, ≥2.5 g). Itraconazole (200 mg bid) is the drug of choice for indolent, nonmeningeal blastomycosis of mild to moderate severity in compliant pts. Ketoconazole (400–800 mg/d) is an effective alternative. Itraconazole or ketoconazole should be given for 6–12 months.

COCCIDIOIDOMYCOSIS

EPIDEMIOLOGY/PATHOGENESIS *Coccidioides immitis* is a soil saprophyte with a mold and a spherule form that is found in certain arid regions of the U.S., Mexico, and Central and South America. Infection results from inhalation of windborne arthrospores from soil. Within the U.S., most cases are acquired in California, Arizona, and western Texas.

CLINICAL MANIFESTATIONS *Primary pulmonary coccidioidomycosis* is symptomatic in ~40% of cases. When present, symptoms include fever, cough, chest pain, and malaise. Hypersensitivity reactions (e.g., erythema nodosum, erythema multiforme, toxic erythema) sometimes occur. CXRs may show an infiltrate, hilar adenopathy, or pleural effusion. Mild peripheral eosinophilia may be present. Recovery usually begins after several days to 2 weeks of illness and is usually complete. *Chronic progressive pulmonary coccidioidomycosis* causes cough, sputum production, variable degrees of fever, and weight loss. *Disseminated coccidioidomycosis* is characterized by malaise, fever, and hilar or paratracheal lymphadenopathy, with serologic evidence of abnormal fungal persistence. With time, lesions appear in bone, skin, subcutaneous tissue, meninges, joints, and other sites. Disseminated coccidioidomycosis can progress rapidly in pts with advanced HIV infection.

DIAGNOSIS The diagnosis is made by wet smear and culture of sputum, urine, or pus. The suspicion of coccidioidomycosis should be clearly indicated on the requisition to ensure that laboratory personnel exercise appropriate caution. Serology is also helpful; a positive CF test of unconcentrated CSF is diagnostic of coccidioidal meningitis. Seroconversion may be delayed for up to 8 weeks, however. Skin test conversion occurs 3–21 d after the onset of symptoms, but skin testing for the diagnosis of acute infection is of limited utility since results remain positive after remote exposure and may be negative in thin-walled pulmonary cavitary or disseminated disease.

 TREATMENT

Pts with disseminated disease should be treated. Pts with severe or rapidly progressive disseminated cases should receive amphotericin B (0.5–0.7 mg/kg qd). Once improvement occurs or when an infection is relatively indolent, itraconazole (200 mg bid) or fluconazole (400–600 mg/d) may be given. Oral therapy is continued for years. Coccidioidal meningitis is treated with fluconazole (400–800 mg/d) but may also require intrathecal amphotericin B. Single, thin-walled pulmonary cavities are poorly responsive to chemotherapy but tend to close spontaneously.

PARACOCCIDIOIDOMYCOSIS

EPIDEMIOLOGY Paracoccidioidomycosis, formerly called South American blastomycosis, follows inhalation of spores of *Paracoccidioides bra-*

siliensis (a dimorphic fungus). Infection is acquired only in South or Central America or in Mexico.

CLINICAL MANIFESTATIONS Signs include indurated ulcers of the mouth, oropharynx, larynx, and nose; enlarged and draining lymph nodes; lesions of the skin (particularly that of the genitalia); productive cough, dyspnea, and weight loss; and, in some cases, fever. CXRs most frequently show bilateral patchy infiltrates.

DIAGNOSIS Cultures of sputum, pus, or mucosal lesions are often diagnostic. Serology may provide an initial clue to the diagnosis.

 TREATMENT

Mild cases may be cured by 1 year of oral ketoconazole or itraconazole (200–400 mg/d). More advanced cases are treated with IV amphotericin B followed by an oral agent.

MUCORMYCOSIS

EPIDEMIOLOGY/PATHOGENESIS *Mucormycosis* refers to infection by any of several fungal genera, the most common of which in human disease are *Rhizopus, Rhizomucor*, and *Cunninghamella*. The organisms are ubiquitous in nature; person-to-person spread does not take place. The disease is largely confined to pts with serious preexisting conditions. Mucormycosis originating in the paranasal sinuses and nose (*rhinocerebral mucormycosis*) classically occurs in pts with poorly controlled diabetes mellitus. Pts who have undergone organ transplantation, who have a hematologic malignancy, or who have received long-term deferoxamine therapy are predisposed to *sinus* or *pulmonary mucormycosis*. *GI mucormycosis* may occur in a variety of settings, including uremia, severe malnutrition, and diarrheal disease. Regardless of the anatomic location of the infection, vascular hyphal invasion is prominent and leads to hemorrhagic or ischemic necrosis.

CLINICAL MANIFESTATIONS Disease arising in the nose and paranasal sinuses produces the characteristic clinical picture of low-grade fever, dull sinus pain, and sometimes a thin bloody nasal discharge; following in a few days are double vision, increasing fever, and obtundation. On examination, a unilateral generalized reduction of ocular motion, chemosis, proptosis, a dusky red or necrotic nasal turbinate on the affected side, and a sharply demarcated area of necrosis on the hard palate (strictly respecting the midline) may be present. Invasion of the globe or ophthalmic artery may lead to blindness and that of the orbit to cavernous sinus thrombosis. Pulmonary mucormycosis manifests as progressive, severe necrotizing pneumonia.

DIAGNOSIS The diagnosis is typically made histologically. The agents of mucormycosis appear as broad, rarely septate hyphae 6–50 μm in diameter. Culture should be attempted, but the yield is low. CT and MRI are helpful in assessing the extent of sinusitis preoperatively and in evaluating the pt postoperatively.

 TREATMENT

Regulation of diabetes and reduction of immunosuppression facilitate the treatment of mucormycosis. Craniofacial lesions are treated with extensive surgical debridement and 10–12 weeks of IV amphotericin B at maximal doses (1–1.5 mg/kg qd). Cure may be achieved in 50% of cases.

MISCELLANEOUS MYCOSES
Fusariosis

Fusarium spp. can cause localized or hematogenously disseminated infection, the latter almost exclusively affecting pts with hematologic malignancy and neutropenia. In disseminated infection, an abrupt onset of fever is followed in two-thirds of cases by the appearance of distinctive skin lesions that resemble ecthyma gangrenosum. Blood cultures have been positive in 59% of pts. Amphotericin B should be given, but recovery depends on reduction in the severity of neutropenia.

Malassezia Infection

Malassezia furfur is a component of the normal skin flora but can cause tinea (pityriasis) versicolor or catheter-related sepsis. The latter infection occurs predominantly in pts receiving IV lipid and is cured by catheter removal.

Pseudallescheriasis

Pseudallescheria boydii (also called *Petriellidium boydii*) is a mold frequently found in soil. Infection may follow inhalation or direct inoculation. The clinical and histologic manifestations of pseudallescheriasis resemble those of aspergillosis, which is much more common. *P. boydii* can cause fungus balls in the lungs or paranasal sinuses and can invade the globe, the soft tissues, the joints, or the bones after trauma or surgery. In the U.S., *P. boydii* is the foremost cause of mycetoma, a chronic suppurative infection of subcutaneous tissue. The diagnosis is based on the demonstration of hyphae in tissues. Cultural confirmation is required to distinguish *P. boydii* from *Aspergillus* spp. Therapy with itraconazole at the maximal tolerated doses is the regimen of choice; the response is typically poor. Surgical drainage or debridement can be helpful.

Sporotrichosis

Sporotrichosis results from the inoculation of *Sporothrix schenckii* into subcutaneous tissue via minor trauma. Nursery workers, florists, and gardeners acquire the illness from roses, peat moss, and other plants. Lymphangitic sporotrichosis, by far the most common form, is characterized by the appearance of a nearly painless red papule at the site of inoculation. Over the next several weeks, similar lesions form along proximal lymphatic channels. Spread beyond an extremity is rare. Diagnosis is made by culture of a skin biopsy sample or of draining pus. A saturated solution of potassium iodide, given orally in increasing divided daily doses up to 4.5–9 mL/d for adults, may be curative. Therapy should be continued for a month after the resolution of all lesions. Itraconazole (100–200 mg/d) is an effective and better-tolerated alternative. For extracutaneous disease, a prolonged course of amphotericin B may be curative.

For a more detailed discussion, see Bennett JE: Diagnosis and Treatment of Fungal Infections, Chap. 200, p. 1168; Histoplasmosis, Chap. 201, p. 1171; Coccidioidomycosis, Chap. 202, p. 1172; Blastomycosis, Chap. 203, p. 1173; Cryptococcosis, Chap. 204, p. 1174; Candidiasis, Chap. 205, p. 1176; Aspergillosis, Chap. 206, p. 1178; Mucormycosis, Chap. 207, p. 1179; and Miscellaneous Mycoses and Algal Infections, Chap. 208, p. 1180, in HPIM-15.

109

PNEUMOCYSTIS CARINII INFECTION

Etiology

Pneumocystis carinii is a eukaryotic organism that causes disease in immuno-compromised hosts, particularly those with HIV infection. Although its taxonomy has been controversial, recent molecular studies clearly place the organism among the fungi.

Epidemiology

P. carinii has a worldwide distribution. It is transmitted by airborne inhalation; person-to-person transmission has been suggested in some instances. People at risk for pneumocystosis have defects in cellular and humoral immunity; at-risk groups include premature malnourished infants, children with primary immunodeficiency diseases, pts receiving immunosuppressive therapy (especially glucocorticoids) for cancer and organ transplantation, and pts infected with HIV. In HIV infection, the incidence of *P. carinii* pneumonia (PCP) rises dramatically when the CD4+ cell count falls below 200/μL.

Clinical Manifestations

P. carinii Pneumonia   Pts with PCP have dyspnea, fever, and nonproductive cough. In HIV-infected pts, the symptoms may be more subtle with insidious onset, and pts are often ill for several weeks. In pts not infected with HIV, symptoms commonly begin after the glucocorticoid dose has been tapered and last ~1–2 weeks. Physical findings include tachypnea, tachycardia, and cyanosis, but lung auscultation reveals few abnormalities. CXR classically demonstrates bilateral diffuse infiltrates, but many other patterns have been associated with PCP, including nodular densities, cavitary lesions, upper lobe infiltrates (particularly in pts receiving aerosolized pentamidine prophylaxis), and pneumothorax. Early in the course, the CXR may be normal. Evaluation of arterial blood gas reveals hypoxia and an increase in alveolar-arterial oxygen gradient. Gallium scan demonstrates increased uptake in the lungs.

Extrapulmonary Infection   Infection usually remains confined to the lungs, but extrapulmonary infection has been described. One risk factor for extrapulmonary spread in pts with HIV infection is the administration of aerosolized pentamidine prophylaxis. The organs most frequently involved include lymph nodes, liver, spleen, and bone marrow. Clinical manifestations range from incidental findings at autopsy to specific organ involvement.

Diagnosis

As the clinical presentation may vary, the level of suspicion of infection must be high in populations most at risk. The diagnosis is made by demonstration of the organism with stains, including methenamine silver, toluidine blue, and cresyl echt violet. The immunofluorescence and immunoperoxidase staining procedures, based on commercially available monoclonal antibodies, are sensitive and are used in many laboratories. The mainstay of diagnosis is the staining of specimens obtained by fiberoptic bronchoscopy with bronchoalveolar lavage (BAL). In HIV-infected pts, in whom the burden of organisms is high, induced sputum may yield a diagnosis. While this technique is simple and non-invasive, its success has varied at different institutions. Transbronchial and open lung biopsy now are reserved for situations in which BAL is not diagnostic.

℞ TREATMENT

Trimethoprim-sulfamethoxazole (TMP-SMZ) is the drug of choice for all forms of pneumocystosis. It is administered PO or IV at a TMP dosage of 15–20 (mg/kg)/d in three or four divided doses. Because TMP-SMZ is poorly tolerated by >50% of pts with HIV infection, resulting in fever, rash, neutropenia, thrombocytopenia, hepatitis, or hyperkalemia, alternative regimens are often required. For the treatment of mild to moderate cases of PCP, alternative regimens include TMP [15 (mg/kg)/d PO] plus dapsone (100 mg/d PO), clindamycin (600 mg q6h IV or 300–450 mg q6h PO) plus primaquine (15–30 mg of base/d PO), or atovaquone alone (750 mg twice daily PO). For the treatment of moderate to severe forms of pneumocystosis, two drugs are available. Pentamidine isethionate—4 (mg/kg)/d given as a single slow IV infusion—is about as effective as TMP-SMZ but exerts some toxic effects in most recipients, including hypotension, dysglycemia, azotemia, and cardiac arrhythmias. Alternatively, trimetrexate is given (45 mg/m^2 IV once daily) with folinic acid (20 mg/m^2 q6h PO or IV) to prevent bone marrow suppression. Because respiratory decompensation frequently follows initiation of treatment in HIV-infected pts with moderate to severe PCP, glucocorticoids (e.g., prednisone, 40 mg PO bid tapered to 20 mg PO qd over 3 weeks) are given adjunctively to pts with PA$_{O_2}$ values ≤70 mmHg or an alveolar-arterial oxygen gradient ≥35 mmHg and have been shown to improve survival. The use of glucocorticoids has not been studied in PCP unrelated to HIV infection. The duration of therapy is 14 d for non-HIV-infected pts and 21 d for HIV-infected pts.

Prevention

Pts with HIV infection should receive prophylactic therapy for life after an episode of PCP (secondary prophylaxis). Primary prophylaxis is given to HIV-infected pts with CD4+ cell counts <200/μL, unexplained fever for ≥2 weeks, or a history of oropharyngeal candidiasis. The prophylactic regimen of choice is TMP-SMZ (one double-strength tablet qd). Alternative regimens, necessitated by the high rate of adverse reactions to TMP-SMZ in HIV infection, include TMP-SMZ at reduced dose or frequency; dapsone alone; dapsone, pyrimethamine, and leucovorin; or aerosolized pentamidine in a Respirgard II nebulizer. Indications for prophylaxis of PCP in immunocompromised pts without HIV infection are less clear, but prophylaxis should be given to all such pts after recovery from PCP.

Outpatient/Home Care Considerations

Pts with mild PCP who can tolerate oral therapy may be managed as outpatients. Hospitalized pts may be discharged to complete therapy at home when they are able to breathe room air and tolerate oral therapy.

For a more detailed discussion, see Walzer PD: *Pneumocystis carinii* **Infec-tion, Chap. 209, p. 1182, in HPIM-15.**

110

PROTOZOAL INFECTIONS

AMEBIASIS

EPIDEMIOLOGY   Amebiasis is the third leading cause of death from parasitic disease worldwide. The areas of highest incidence include most developing countries in the tropics, particularly Mexico, India, and the nations of Central and South America, tropical Asia, and Africa. The main groups at risk in developed countries are travelers, recent immigrants, homosexual men, and residents of institutions. *Entamoeba histolytica*, the intestinal protozoan that causes amebiasis, is acquired by ingestion of viable cysts from fecally contaminated water, food, or hands. Food-borne exposure is most common. Less common modes of transmission include oral and anal sexual practices; rare cases are transmitted by direct rectal inoculation through colonic irrigating devices.

PATHOGENESIS   After ingestion, cysts release trophozoites (the only form that invades tissue) into the lumen of the small intestine. While cysts can persist in a moist environment for several weeks, trophozoites are killed rapidly by exposure to air. In most pts trophozoites are harmless commensals, but in some they invade the bowel mucosa, causing symptomatic colitis. In yet other pts, trophozoites invade the bloodstream, causing distant abscesses of the liver, lungs, or brain. Numerous virulence factors, including extracellular proteinase, have been linked to the ability of amebas to invade through interglandular epithelium.

CLINICAL MANIFESTATIONS   *Intestinal Amebiasis*   The most common type of amebic infection is asymptomatic cyst passage. Symptomatic amebic colitis develops 2–6 weeks after ingestion of infectious cysts. Lower abdominal pain and mild diarrhea develop gradually and are followed by malaise, weight loss, and diffuse lower-abdominal or back pain. Cecal involvement may mimic appendicitis. In full-blown dysentery, pts may daily pass 10–12 stools consisting of blood and mucus but little fecal material. Virtually all pts have heme-positive stools; <40% are febrile. Rarely (most often in children), a more fulminant form occurs, with high fevers, severe abdominal pain, and profuse diarrhea. Pts may develop toxic megacolon. Pts receiving glucocorticoids are at risk for more severe amebiasis. Uncommonly, pts develop a more chronic form of amebiasis, which can be confused with inflammatory bowel disease. *Amebomas* are inflammatory mass lesions due to chronic intestinal amebiasis.

Amebic Liver Abscess   Extraintestinal amebic infection frequently involves the liver. Most pts develop symptoms within 5 months. The majority of these pts are febrile and have RUQ pain, which may be dull or pleuritic and may radiate to the shoulder. Point tenderness of the liver and right pleural effusion are common; jaundice is rare. Fewer than one-third of pts have accompanying diarrhea. In some pts, especially those who are older, the illness can have a subacute course with weight loss and hepatomegaly. Only about one-third of pts with chronic presentations are febrile. Amebic liver abscess must be considered in the differential diagnosis of fever of unknown origin, as 10–15% of pts present with fever only. Complications of amebic liver abscesses include pleuropulmonary involvement in 20–30% of pts with sterile effusions, contiguous spread from the liver, and frank rupture into the pleural space, the peritoneum, or the pericardium. Rupture of an amebic abscess, which may occur during medical therapy, usually requires drainage.

Other Extraintestinal Sites Besides the liver, extraintestinal sites of amebiasis include the genitourinary tract (with painful genital ulcers) and the cerebrum (in <0.1% of pts).

DIAGNOSIS The definitive diagnosis of amebic colitis relies on the demonstration of trophozoites of *E. histolytica* on wet mount, iodine-stained concentrates of stool, or trichrome stains of stool or concentrates. A combination of these procedures is positive in 75–95% of cases. At least three fresh stool specimens should be examined. Experience in distinguishing *E. histolytica* from *Entamoeba hartmanni*, *Entamoeba coli*, and *Endolimax nana* is important as the latter parasites do not cause clinical disease and do not need to be treated. Commercially available serologic tests are positive in >90% of cases of invasive disease, including colitis. A positive test suggests active infection, since serologies usually revert to negative in 6–12 months. Liver scans, ultrasound, CT, and MRI are all useful for the detection of liver abscess. Barium enemas and sigmoidoscopy with biopsy are potentially dangerous in acute amebic colitis because of a risk of perforation.

 TREATMENT

Asymptomatic cyst carriers should be treated with a luminal amebicide that is poorly absorbed. Two luminal drugs are available in the U.S.—iodoquinol (650 mg PO tid for 20 d) and paromomycin (500 mg PO tid for 10 d). Pts with colitis or liver abscess should receive a tissue amebicide and a luminal agent. Metronidazole (750 mg PO or IV tid for 5–10 d) is used for the treatment of amebic colitis or liver abscess. Clinical response occurs within 72 h in >90% of pts with liver abscesses. Except in the case of rupture, amebic liver abscesses rarely require drainage. Indications for abscess aspiration include (1) the need to rule out a pyogenic process, (2) failure to respond to therapy in 3–5 d, (3) the threat of imminent rupture, and (4) the need to prevent left-lobe abscess rupture into the pericardium.

MALARIA

ETIOLOGY Four species of the genus *Plasmodium* infect humans: *P. vivax*, *P. ovale*, *P. malariae*, and *P. falciparum*. This last species is responsible for most deaths due to malaria.

EPIDEMIOLOGY Malaria is the most important parasitic disease of humans, causing 1–3 million deaths annually. The disease is found throughout the tropical regions of the world. *P. falciparum* predominates in Africa, New Guinea, and Haiti. *P. vivax* is more common in Central America and the Indian subcontinent, but *P. falciparum* has been found with increasing frequency in India over the past decade. *P. falciparum* and *P. vivax* are equally prevalent in South America, eastern Asia, and Oceania. *P. malariae* is less common but is found in most areas (especially sub-Saharan Africa). *P. ovale* is uncommon outside of Africa. Malaria is transmitted by the bite of the female anopheline mosquito.

PATHOGENESIS Human infection begins with the transfer of sporozoites from the mosquito's salivary glands to the bloodstream during a blood meal. After a period of asexual reproduction of the parasite in liver cells, the swollen cells rupture, releasing merozoites into the bloodstream and initiating the symptomatic phase of infection. In *P. vivax* and *P. ovale* infection, some intrahepatic forms remain dormant for months and can cause relapses after treatment. Merozoites attach to specific erythrocyte surface receptors and then invade the cell. In *P. vivax* infection, this receptor is related to the Duffy group antigen, whose absence in most West Africans renders them resistant to this form of malaria. After invading the erythrocyte, the parasite grows progressively, consumes and degrades intracellular proteins (principally hemoglobin), and alters the cell membrane.

Host defense also plays a role in malaria. In the nonimmune individual, infection triggers nonspecific host defense mechanisms such as splenic filtration. When parasitized erythrocytes that have evaded splenic filtration rupture, the material released activates macrophages, which release proinflammatory cytokines that cause fever and exert other pathologic effects. The distribution of malaria before the introduction of mosquito control programs paralleled the distribution of sickle cell disease, thalassemia, and G6PD deficiency. These diseases may confer protection against death due to falciparum malaria, as has been demonstrated with the sickle cell trait. With repeated exposure to malaria, a specific immune response develops and limits the degree of parasitemia. Over time, pts are rendered immune to disease but remain susceptible to infection.

CLINICAL MANIFESTATIONS The first symptoms are nonspecific and include malaise, headache, fatigue, abdominal discomfort, and muscle aches, followed by fever and chills. Nausea, vomiting, and orthostatic hypotension are common. The classic malaria paroxysms, in which fever spikes, chills, and rigors occur at regular intervals, suggest infection with *P. vivax* or *P. ovale*. Most often, the fever is irregular at first. In uncomplicated malaria, mild anemia and a palpable spleen may be the only clinical abnormalities identified. The complications of falciparum malaria include cerebral malaria (obtundation, delirium, or gradual or sudden onset of coma, with seizures common as well), hypoglycemia, lactic acidosis, noncardiogenic pulmonary edema, renal impairment (seen mainly in adults and resembling acute tubular necrosis), hematologic abnormalities (anemia, coagulation defects, DIC in pts with cerebral malaria, and so-called blackwater fever, in which massive hemolysis causes hemoglobinemia, black urine, and renal failure), and aspiration pneumonia.

DIAGNOSIS The diagnosis of malaria rests on the demonstration of the asexual form of the parasite in thick or thin smears of peripheral blood. Giemsa is the preferred staining method. The level of parasitemia, which can be determined from either type of smear, is expressed as the number of parasitized erythrocytes per 1000 cells; this figure is then used to derive the number of infected erythrocytes per microliter of blood. A thick smear concentrates the parasites and increases diagnostic specificity but should be interpreted with care as artifacts are common. Smears should be examined every 12 h for 2 d before a diagnosis of malaria is excluded. It is important to diagnose probable or possible *P. falciparum* infection. Features on smear suggestive of falciparum malaria include double-chromatin dots, multiple infected erythrocytes of normal size, banana-shaped gametocytes, and a parasitemia level of >5%. *P. vivax* infection is characterized by the presence of Schüffner's dots in enlarged erythrocytes; *P. ovale* infection is typified by Schüffner's dots in minimally enlarged erythrocytes that are slightly oval in shape and may have fringed edges. A simple, sensitive, and specific diagnostic test that detects *P. falciparum* histidine-rich protein 2 in fingerprick blood samples has been introduced.

 TREATMENT

Table 110-1 summarizes malaria therapy. Severe falciparum malaria constitutes a medical emergency. The antiarrhythmic agent quinidine gluconate is as effective as quinine in these cases and is more readily available; thus quinidine infusion can be used with cardiovascular monitoring (acceptable QT_c,

Table 110-1

Recommended Therapeutic Doses of Antimalarial Drugs

Drug	Severe Malaria[a] (Parenteral)
Chloroquine	10 mg of base/kg by constant-rate infusion over 8 h followed by 15 mg/kg over 24 h *or* by 3.5 mg of base/kg by IM or SC injection every 6 h (total dose, 25 mg/kg)[b]
Sulfadoxine/ pyrimethamine	—
Mefloquine	—
Quinine	20 mg of salt/kg by IV infusion over 4 h[d] followed by 10 mg/kg infused over 2–8 h every 8 h
Quinidine gluconate	10 mg of base/kg by constant-rate infusion over 1–2 h followed by 0.02 mg/kg per min, with ECG monitoring[f]
Artesunate	2.4 mg/kg IV or IM stat followed by 1.2 mg/kg at 12 and 24 h and then daily
Artemether	3.2 mg/kg IM stat followed by 1.6 mg/kg per day
Atovaquone-proguanil	—
Artemether-lumefantrine	—

[a] Oral treatment should be substituted for parenteral therapy as soon as the pt can take tablets by mouth.
[b] Chloroquine-resistant *P. falciparum* is now very widespread.
[c] In Oceania and Southeast Asia, the dose should be 0.33 to 0.5 mg of base/kg. This regimen should not be used in pts with severe variants of G6PD deficiency.
[d] Alternatively, infusion of 7 mg of salt/kg over 30 min can be followed by 10 mg of salt/kg over 4 h.

<0.65; acceptable QRS widening, <25% of baseline). In addition to antimalarial agents, the pt should be given phenobarbital (a single dose of 5–20 mg/kg) to prevent seizures. In comatose pts, the blood glucose level should be measured every 4–6 h; those with levels <40 mg/dL should receive IV dextrose. Exchange transfusion is indicated for vital organ dysfunction and a parasitemia level of >15% and should be considered for pts with parasitemia levels of 5–15%. Glucocorticoids, urea, heparin, and dextran are of no value.

PREVENTION   Table 110-2 summarizes malaria prophylaxis.

LEISHMANIASIS

EPIDEMIOLOGY   Leishmaniasis is spread by female phlebotomine sandflies. Rodents, small mammals, and canines are the common reservoir hosts of *Leishmania* spp; humans are incidental hosts.

CLINICAL MANIFESTATIONS   *Visceral Leishmaniasis (Kala-Azar)* Visceral leishmaniasis is most often caused by *Leishmania donovani*. Visceral infection may remain subclinical or become symptomatic, with an acute, subacute, or chronic course. The incubation period usually ranges from weeks to months but can be years. In some settings, inapparent infections far outnumber clinically apparent ones; malnutrition is a risk factor for the development of disease. The term *kala-azar* refers to the classic image of the profoundly cachectic, febrile pt who is heavily parasitized and has life-threatening disease.

Uncomplicated Malaria (Oral)

10 mg of base/kg followed by 10 mg/kg at 24 h and 5 mg/kg at 48 h *or* by 5 mg/kg at 12, 24, and 36 h (total dose, 25 mg/kg); for *P. vivax* or *P. ovale*, primaquine (0.25 mg of base/kg per day for 14 days[c]) added for radical cure
25/1.25 mg/kg, single oral dose (3 tablets for adults)

15 mg/kg followed 8–12 h later by second dose of 10 mg/kg
10 mg of salt/kg q8h for 7 days combined with tetracycline[e] (4 mg/kg qid) or doxycycline (3 mg/kg once daily) or clindamycin (10 mg/kg bid) for 7 days
—

In combination with 25 mg of mefloquine/kg, 12 mg/kg given in divided doses over 3–5 days (e.g., 4 mg/kg for 3 days or 4 mg/kg followed by 2 mg/kg per day for 4 days); if used alone, give for 7 days (usually 4 mg/kg initially followed by 2 mg/kg daily)
Same regimen as for artesunate
For adults >40 kg, each dose comprises 4 tablets (each containing atovaquone 250 mg and proguanil 100 mg) taken once daily for 3 days with food
For adults ≥35 kg, each dose comprises 4 tablets (each containing artemether 20 mg and lumefantrine 120 mg) at 0, 8, 24, and 48 h (semi-immunes) or at 0, 8, 24, 36, 48, and 60 h (nonimmunes) taken after food

[e] Neither tetracycline nor doxycycline should be given to pregnant women or to children <8 years old.
[f] Some authorities recommend a lower dose of IV quinidine: 6.2 mg of base/kg over 1–2 h followed by 0.0125 mg/kg per min.
NOTE: In severe malaria, quinine or quinidine should be used if there is any doubt about the infecting strain's sensitivity to chloroquine.
SOURCE: NJ White, JG Breman: HPIM-15, p. 1211.

Splenomegaly is typically more impressive than hepatomegaly and can be massive. Peripheral lymphadenopathy may also be detected. With advanced disease, pancytopenia, hypergammaglobulinemia, and hypoalbuminemia may develop.

Visceral leishmaniasis is becoming an important opportunistic infection in HIV pts from *Leishmania*-endemic areas; most dual infections have been reported from southern Europe. Such cases may represent newly acquired or reactivated infections. In these hosts, even relatively avirulent leishmanial strains may disseminate to the viscera. The CD4 cell count is usually <200/μL when disease becomes clinically evident.

Cutaneous Leishmaniasis Cutaneous leishmaniasis has traditionally been classified as New World (American) or Old World. New World leishmaniasis occurs from southern Texas to northern Argentina; it is usually caused by the *L. mexicana* complex or the *Viannia* subgenus but can also be attributable to *L. major*–like organisms and *L. chagasi*. Old World disease is caused by *L. tropica, L. major, L. aethiopica, L. infantum,* and *L. donovani.* The incubation period ranges from weeks to months. The lesion usually begins as a single papule at the site of a sandfly bite and evolves to a nodular and then an ulcerative form, with a central depression surrounded by a raised indurated border. Multiple primary lesions, satellite lesions, regional lymphadenopathy, sporotrichoid subcutaneous nodules, lesional pain or pruritus, and secondary bacterial infection are variably present. Spontaneous resolution of the lesions may require weeks, months, or years; reactivation may occur. *Diffuse cutaneous leishman-*

Table 110-2

Prophylaxis for Malaria

Drug	Usage	Adult Dosage
Mefloquine	Used in areas where chloroquine-resistant malaria has been reported	228 mg of base (250 mg of salt) orally, once/week[a]
Doxycycline[b]	Used as alternative to mefloquine	100 mg orally, once/day
Chloroquine	Used in areas where chloroquine-resistant malaria has *not* been reported	300 mg of base (500 mg of salt) orally, once/week
Proguanil (not available in U.S.)	Used simultaneously *with* chloroquine as alternative to mefloquine or doxycycline	200 mg orally, once/day, in combination with weekly chloroquine
Primaquine[c]	Used for travelers only after testing for G6PD deficiency; postexposure prevention for relapsing malaria or prophylaxis	Postexposure: 15 mg of base (26.3 mg of salt) orally, once/day for 14 days Prophylaxis: 30 mg of base daily
Atovaquone-proguanil[c]	Used as alternative to mefloquine	250/100 mg orally, once/day

[a] Tablets manufactured outside the U.S. contain 250 mg of base.
[b] Not in pregnant women or children <8 years old.
[c] Primaquine and atovaquone-proguanil have both proved safe and effective for antimalarial chemoprophylaxis in areas with chloroquine-resistant falciparum malaria, but more data are needed, particularly in children. These drugs should not be used in pregnancy.
SOURCE: NJ White, JG Breman: HPIM-15, p. 1209.

iasis (DCL) develops in the context of *Leishmania*-specific anergy and manifests as chronic nonulcerative skin lesions. *Leishmaniasis recidivans*, a hyperergic variant with scarce parasites, manifests as a chronic solitary lesion on the cheek that expands slowly despite central healing.

DIAGNOSIS   The diagnosis of leishmaniasis requires demonstration of amastigotes by smear or culture of aspirates or biopsy specimens (e.g., spleen, liver, bone marrow, or lymph node for visceral disease). Organism density on histologic exam decreases as the lesion ages. Serologic testing shows elevated antibody titers only in pts with DCL. In contrast, skin testing is usually positive in simple cutaneous or recidivans leishmaniasis but not in DCL. The sensitivity of antibody testing is only ~50% in pts with visceral disease who are coinfected with HIV.

 TREATMENT

Drug regimens for treatment of leishmaniasis are listed in Table 110-3. Local or topical therapy (paromomycin ointment, intralesional Sb[v], heat therapy, or cryotherapy) should be considered only for infections that do not have the potential to disseminate.

Table 110-3

Drug Regimens for Treatment of Leishmaniasis[a]

Clinical Syndrome, Drug	Route of Administration	Regimen
VISCERAL LEISHMANIASIS		
First-line		
Pentavalent antimony[b]	IV, IM	20 mg Sb^V/kg qd for 28 d
Amphotericin B, lipid formulation[c]	IV	2–5 mg/kg qd (total: usually ~15–21 mg/kg)
Alternatives		
Amphotericin B (deoxycholate)	IV	0.5–1 mg/kg qod or qd (total: usually ~15–20 mg/kg)
Paromomycin sulfate[d]	IV, IM	15–20 mg/kg qd for ~21 d
Pentamidine isethionate	IV, IM	4 mg/kg qod or thrice weekly for ~15–30 doses
CUTANEOUS LEISHMANIASIS		
First-line		
Pentavalent antimony[b]	IV, IM	20 mg Sb^V/kg qd for 20 d
Parenteral alternatives		
Pentamidine isethionate	IV, IM	3 mg/kg qod for 4 doses or 2 mg/kg qod for 7 doses
Amphotericin B (deoxycholate)	IV	0.5–1 mg/kg qod or qd (total: up to ~20 mg/kg)
Oral alternatives		
Ketoconazole	PO	600 mg/d for 28 d[e]
Itraconazole	PO	200 mg bid for 28 d[e]
Dapsone	PO	100 mg bid for 6 weeks[e]
MUCOSAL LEISHMANIASIS		
First-line		
Pentavalent antimony[b]	IV, IM	20 mg Sb^V/kg qd for 28 d
Alternatives		
Amphotericin B (deoxycholate)	IV	1 mg/kg qod or qd (total: usually ~20–40 mg/kg)
Pentamidine isethionate	IV, IM	2–4 mg/kg qod or thrice weekly for ≥15 doses

[a] See HPIM-15, Chap. 215, for additional details. To maximize effectiveness and minimize toxicity, the listed regimens should be individualized according to the particularities of the case.
[b] The Centers for Disease Control and Prevention (CDC) provides the pentavalent antimonial (Sb^V) compound sodium stibogluconate (Pentostam; Glaxo Wellcome, PLC, United Kingdom; 100 mg Sb^V/mL) to U.S.-licensed physicians through the CDC Drug Service (404-639-3670). The other widely used pentavalent antimonial compound, meglumine antimonate (Glucantime; Rhône Poulenc, France; 85 mg Sb^V/mL), is available primarily in Spanish- and French-speaking areas of the world.
[c] The lipid formulations of amphotericin B include liposomal amphotericin B, amphotericin B lipid complex, and amphotericin B cholesteryl sulfate. The U.S. Food and Drug Administration recently approved the following regimen of liposomal amphotericin B for immunocompetent pts: 3 mg/kg qd on days 1–5, 14, and 21, for a total of 21 mg/kg; for immunosuppressed pts, the approved regimen is 4 mg/kg qd on days 1–5, 10, 17, 24, 31, and 38, for a total of 40 mg/kg. Alternative regimens that have been proposed for immunocompetent pts include treatment on days 1–5 and 10 with 3–4 mg/kg qd for cases from Europe or Brazil, with 3 mg/kg qd for cases from Africa, and with 2–3 mg/kg qd for cases from India.
[d] Not commercially available as of this writing.
[e] Adult dosage.
SOURCE: BL Herwaldt: HPIM-15, p. 1215.

TRYPANOSOMIASIS
Chagas' Disease

EPIDEMIOLOGY   Chagas' disease (American trypanosomiasis) is a zoonosis caused by *Trypanosoma cruzi*, a parasite found only in the Americas. The disease is transmitted to humans primarily by infected reduviid bugs, which are spottily distributed from the southern U.S. to southern Argentina. Infection can also be transmitted by transfusion of infected blood as well as vertically from mother to fetus. Human *T. cruzi* infection is a health problem primarily among the rural poor of Central and South America.

CLINICAL MANIFESTATIONS   The first signs of acute Chagas' disease begin at least 1 week after infection. An indurated area of erythema and swelling (the *chagoma*), accompanied by lymphadenopathy, may appear. *Romaña's sign* (unilateral painless palpebral and periocular edema) occurs when the conjunctiva is the portal of entry. Local signs are followed by fever, anorexia, and edema of the face and lower extremities. Severe myocarditis is a rare but potentially fatal complication. Acute symptoms resolve spontaneously, after which pts enter the asymptomatic or indeterminate phase of chronic *T. cruzi* infection. Symptomatic, chronic Chagas' disease develops years or even decades later, with manifestations attributable principally to cardiac and/or GI involvement. Cardiomyopathy, rhythm disturbances, or thromboemboli may occur. RBBB is the most common ECG abnormality. GI manifestations include megaesophagus (causing dysphagia, odynophagia, chest pain, and regurgitation) and megacolon (leading to abdominal pain, chronic constipation, obstruction, perforation, septicemia, and even death).

DIAGNOSIS   The diagnosis of acute Chagas' disease requires the detection of parasites, which may be found by examination of fresh blood or buffy coat or of thick or thin blood smears. Mouse inoculation and culture of blood in special media can be attempted if efforts at direct visualization are unsuccessful. Chronic disease is diagnosed by serology. CF, immunofluorescence, and ELISA are all available, but their utility is limited by false-positive results. For this reason, it is recommended that positivity in one assay be confirmed by two other tests.

 TREATMENT

Nifurtimox, the only drug active against *T. cruzi* that is available in the U.S., reduces the duration and severity of acute disease, but its efficacy in eradicating parasites is low, with only ~70% of acute infections parasitologically cured. Treatment should be started as early as possible at a daily dose of 8–10 mg/kg for adults, 12.5–15 mg/kg for adolescents, and 15–20 mg/kg for children 1–10 years of age. Treatment is given orally in four divided doses each day for 90–120 d. Nifurtimox may be obtained from the CDC (tel. no. 770-639-3670). Although the point has been debated for years, it is currently recommended that pts infected with *T. cruzi* be treated, regardless of their clinical status or the duration of infection.

Sleeping Sickness

EPIDEMIOLOGY   Sleeping sickness (African trypanosomiasis) is caused by parasites of the *Trypanosoma brucei* complex and is transmitted to humans by tsetse flies.

CLINICAL MANIFESTATIONS   A painful chancre may appear at the site of inoculation. The disease is divided into stages. Stage I, during which hematogenous and lymphatic dissemination occurs, is characterized by fever, lymphadenopathy, pruritus, and circinate rash. Stage II (CNS invasion) is characterized by the insidious development of neurologic manifestations, such as daytime somnolence, halting speech, extrapyramidal signs, and ataxia, and by progressive CSF abnormalities. Neurologic impairment eventually ends in coma and death. East African trypanosomiasis (caused by *T. brucei rhodesiense*) follows a more acute course than West African trypanosomiasis (caused by *T. brucei gambiense*).

DIAGNOSIS   Definitive diagnosis requires detection of the parasite in expressed fluid from the chancre, thin or thick blood smear, buffy coat, lymph node aspirates, bone marrow biopsies, or CSF. CSF examination is mandatory in all pts in whom African trypanosomiasis is suspected. Serology is variably sensitive and specific and is most useful for epidemiologic surveys.

℞ TREATMENT

Drugs for the treatment of this infection include suramin (1 g IV on days 1, 3, 7, 14, and 21 after a test dose of 100–200 mg), eflornithine (400 mg/kg qd in four divided doses for 2 weeks), or pentamidine (4 mg/kg qd IM or IV for 10 d). Suramin and eflornithine are available through the CDC. The choice of regimens is based on the stage of disease and the parasite subspecies.

TOXOPLASMOSIS

EPIDEMIOLOGY   Cats are the definitive host for *Toxoplasma gondii*, which is transmitted to humans by ingestion of contaminated oocysts from the soil or of bradyzoites in undercooked meat. In the U.S., mutton and pork are far more likely to be contaminated than is beef. The seroprevalence of antibody to *T. gondii* varies by geographic location and population age. Transplacental transmission occurs overall in about one-third of cases in which the mother acquires infection during pregnancy. The risk of transmission and the potential consequences for the fetus vary according to the time in pregnancy at which maternal infection occurs. Only ~15% of women infected in the first trimester transmit infection, but neonatal disease is most severe in these cases; 65% of women infected in the third trimester transmit infection, but the infant is usually asymptomatic at birth.

CLINICAL MANIFESTATIONS   *Immunocompetent Patients*   Acute infection is usually asymptomatic and may go unrecognized in 80–90% of children and adults who acquire infection postnatally. Acute toxoplasmosis is characterized by lymphadenopathy, which, while most often cervical, is generalized in 20–30% of symptomatic pts. Headache, malaise, fatigue, and fever develop in 20–40% of pts with lymphadenopathy. Symptoms usually resolve within several weeks. Lymphadenopathy may persist for months.

Ocular Infection   *T. gondii* causes 35% of cases of chorioretinitis in the U.S. and Europe. Most such infections are acquired congenitally.

Immunocompromised Patients   Pts who have AIDS or who are receiving chemotherapy for a lymphoproliferative disorder are at greatest risk for acute infection. More than 95% of toxoplasmosis cases in AIDS pts represent reactivated latent infection. Encephalitis occurs in most of these cases, typically when CD4 cell counts are $<100/\mu L$. Manifestations referable to CNS disease occur in >50% of immunocompromised hosts with acute toxoplasmosis. Symptoms and signs include altered mental status (75%), fever (10–72%), seizures

(33%), headaches (56%), and focal neurologic abnormalities (60%) and are attributable to encephalopathy, meningoencephalitis, and/or mass lesions.

Congenital Infection Each year in the U.S., 400 to 4000 infants are born with congenital toxoplasmosis. Although many of these transplacentally infected infants are asymptomatic at birth, reactivation of infection years or even decades later can result in disease and disabilities that are often relatively severe and include chorioretinitis, strabismus, epilepsy, and psychomotor retardation. Appropriate treatment (see below) is followed by normal development in upwards of 70% of children.

DIAGNOSIS Serologic testing is the routine diagnostic method. The Sabin-Feldman dye test, the indirect fluorescent antibody test, and the ELISA all satisfactorily measure circulating IgG antibody, which can appear as early as 2–3 weeks after infection and persists for life. Simultaneous testing for IgM antibody is necessary to determine the timing of infection; the methods used are double-sandwich IgM-ELISA and IgM-immunosorbent assay. The former is more sensitive for detecting fetal and neonatal infections. In AIDS pts, a positive IgG serology and compatible neuroradiographic findings are sufficient for a presumptive diagnosis. On CT or MRI, pts with *Toxoplasma* encephalitis have focal or multifocal lesions, usually in the basal ganglia or at the corticomedullary junction; these lesions are usually ring-enhancing on CT. These findings are not pathognomonic of *Toxoplasma* infection since 40% of CNS lymphomas are multifocal and 50% are ring-enhancing. If presumptive therapy for toxoplasmosis fails to result in early radiologic improvement, a brain biopsy should be considered. The persistence of IgG antibody or a positive IgM titer after the first week of life is suggestive of congenitally acquired infection. However, up to 25% of infected newborns may be seronegative and have normal routine physical exams. Thus, specific end-organ assessment (eye, brain) may be necessary to establish the diagnosis.

 TREATMENT

Immunocompetent pts with lymphadenopathy due to toxoplasmosis generally do not require therapy. For immunocompromised pts, the preferred regimen is pyrimethamine (a 200-mg PO loading dose followed by 50–75 mg/d) plus sulfadiazine (4–6 g/d PO, divided qid), along with leucovorin (10–15 mg/d). Hypersensitivity develops in up to 20% and toxicity in 40% of pts given this dual regimen. Pyrimethamine (75 mg/d) plus clindamycin (450 mg tid) is an alternative. Glucocorticoids are often used to treat intracerebral edema. After 4–6 weeks (or when radiographic improvement becomes evident), the pt may be switched to chronic suppressive therapy with pyrimethamine (25–50 mg/d) plus sulfadiazine (2–4 g/d) or pyrimethamine (75 mg/d) plus clindamycin (450 mg tid); pyrimethamine alone (50–75 mg/d) may be sufficient. Pts with ocular infection can be treated for 1 month. Congenitally infected neonates are treated with daily pyrimethamine (0.5–1 mg/kg) and sulfadiazine (100 mg/kg) for 1 year. A variety of other regimens are available for pts in whom long-term therapy is limited by toxicity. Dapsone may be substituted for sulfadiazine. For pts with AIDS and *Toxoplasma* encephalitis, pyrimethamine (25–75 mg/d) plus clindamycin (300–1200 mg IV qid) is effective, as is pyrimethamine plus clarithromycin. Atovaquone (750 mg tid or qid) is an optional agent. For prophylaxis in AIDS pts with CD4 counts of <100/μL, TMP-SMZ alone or the combination of pyrimethamine, dapsone, and leucovorin may be used.

PROTOZOAL INTESTINAL INFECTIONS
Giardiasis
EPIDEMIOLOGY Giardiasis is one of the most common parasitic infections worldwide and is the most common cause of waterborne epidemics of gastroenteritis in the U.S. Infection follows ingestion of the cyst form of *Giardia lamblia*. Person-to-person transmission may take place (e.g., among children in day-care centers, among residents of institutions where fecal hygiene is poor, and during sexual contact). Food-borne transmission has also been documented.

CLINICAL MANIFESTATIONS Manifestations may range from asymptomatic infection to fulminant diarrhea and malabsorption. The usual incubation period is 1–3 weeks; symptoms may develop suddenly or gradually. Early symptoms include diarrhea, abdominal pain, bloating, belching, flatus, nausea, and vomiting. Diarrhea is common, but upper intestinal manifestations may predominate. The duration of acute symptoms is usually >1 week; diarrhea may abate earlier. In chronic giardiasis, diarrhea may not be prominent, but increased flatus, loose stools, sulfurous burping, and (in some cases) weight loss occur. Fever is uncommon, as is the presence of blood or mucus in the stool.

DIAGNOSIS Giardiasis is diagnosed by the identification of cysts in the feces or of trophozoites in the feces or small intestine. Repeat examinations of stool or examination of aspirated duodenal fluid or of tissue from a small-intestinal biopsy may be required. A sensitive and specific alternative is to test for parasitic antigen in stool.

℞ TREATMENT

Metronidazole (250 mg PO tid for 5 d) is curative in >80% of cases. Furazolidone (100 mg PO qid for 7–10 d) is somewhat less effective but more palatable to children. Pts in whom initial treatment fails can be re-treated with a longer course. Those who remain infected should be evaluated for reinfection through close personal contacts or environmental sources and for hypogammaglobulinemia. In particularly refractory cases, prolonged treatment with metronidazole (750 mg PO tid for 21 d) has been successful. Paromomycin can be used in pregnant pts with symptomatic giardiasis.

Cryptosporidiosis
EPIDEMIOLOGY Cryptosporidiosis is acquired by ingestion of oocysts. Water is the primary source in outbreaks; the oocysts are resistant to killing by routine chlorination. Cryptosporidial infection may cause symptomatic diarrhea in immunocompetent hosts, but pts with immunodeficiencies (especially AIDS) are at greatest risk.

CLINICAL MANIFESTATIONS The diarrhea of cryptosporidiosis characteristically is watery, nonbloody, and profuse. Abdominal pain, nausea, anorexia, fever, and weight loss may occur. In immunocompetent hosts, diarrhea resolves in 1–2 weeks. In immunocompromised hosts, especially AIDS pts, diarrhea may be chronic and profuse and may cause significant fluid and electrolyte losses. Stool volumes may reach 25 L/d.

DIAGNOSIS The diagnosis is made by the demonstration of oocysts in stool. Concentration methods as well as modified acid-fast or immunofluorescent staining enhance detection. Small-intestinal biopsy may also be useful.

TREATMENT

There is no effective therapy for this infection, although paromomycin (500–750 mg qid) may be partially effective for some HIV-infected pts. Supportive treatment is used, including fluid and electrolyte replacement and the administration of antidiarrheal agents.

Isosporiasis

CLINICAL MANIFESTATIONS Acute infection with *Isospora belli* begins abruptly with fever, abdominal pain, and watery nonbloody diarrhea and may last for weeks or months. In AIDS and other immunocompromised pts, the infection may not be self-limited but rather may resemble cryptosporidiosis, with chronic profuse watery diarrhea. Eosinophilia, not found in other enteric protozoan infections, may develop.

DIAGNOSIS The diagnosis is made by the demonstration in stool of large oocysts revealed by modified acid-fast staining. Repeated stool examinations, sampling of duodenal contents by aspiration or a string test, or even small-bowel biopsy may be required.

 TREATMENT

I. belli does respond to treatment. TMP-SMZ (160/800 mg PO qid for 10 d, then bid for 3 weeks) has proved effective. Pyrimethamine (50–75 mg/d PO) may be used in pts with sulfonamide intolerance. Relapses can occur in AIDS pts, necessitating maintenance therapy with TMP-SMZ (160/800 mg) three times a week or with sulfadoxine (500 mg) plus pyrimethamine (25 mg) once a week.

Cyclosporiasis

CLINICAL MANIFESTATIONS *Cyclospora cayetanensis* is globally distributed. Waterborne transmission is one means of its acquisition by humans. Infection may be asymptomatic or may manifest as diarrhea, a flulike illness, flatulence, and burping. The illness may be self-limited, may wax and wane, or may persist for >1 month.

DIAGNOSIS The diagnosis can be made by detection of spherical 8- to 10-μm oocysts in the stool. The oocysts are refractile, are variably acid-fast, and fluoresce under UV light.

 TREATMENT

Cyclosporiasis is effectively treated with TMP-SMZ (160/800 mg PO bid for 7 d). HIV-infected pts may require suppressive maintenance therapy.

Microsporidiosis

ETIOLOGY AND CLINICAL MANIFESTATIONS Microsporidia are obligate intracellular spore-forming protozoa that have recently been recognized as agents of human disease, especially among people infected with HIV. Six genera are recognized. *Enterocytozoon bieneusi* and *Encephalitozoon intestinalis* cause chronic diarrhea and wasting in AIDS pts; these organisms are found in 10–40% of pts with chronic diarrhea. Disseminated disease due to *E. intestinalis* may also occur, with fever, diarrhea, sinusitis, cholangitis, and bronchiolitis.

DIAGNOSIS   The diagnosis of tissue infection may require electron microscopy, although intracellular spores (0.5–2 μm × 1–4 μm) may be seen in tissue sections stained with hematoxylin and eosin, Giemsa, or Gram's stain.

 TREATMENT

Definitive therapies for microsporidial infections remain to be established.

For a more detailed discussion, see Reed SL: Amebiasis and Infection with Free-Living Amebas, Chap. 213, p. 1199; White NJ, Breman JG: Malaria and Babesiosis: Diseases Caused by Red Blood Cell Parasites, Chap. 214, p. 1203; Herwaldt BL: Leishmaniasis, Chap. 215, p. 1213; Kirchhoff LV: Trypanosomiasis, Chap. 216, p. 1218; Kasper LH: *Toxoplasma* Infection, Chap. 217, p. 1222; and Weller PF: Protozoal Intestinal Infections and Trichomoniasis, Chap. 218, p. 1227, in HPIM-15.

111

HELMINTHIC INFECTIONS AND ECTOPARASITE INFESTATIONS

TRICHINELLOSIS

EPIDEMIOLOGY   *Trichinella* spp. infect carnivorous and omnivorous animals worldwide. Both humans and animals acquire the infection by ingesting meat containing encysted *Trichinella* larvae. Swine are the most common human vector. Around 40 human cases are reported in the U.S. each year; however, most mild cases probably remain undiagnosed. Recent U.S. outbreaks have been attributed to undercooked pork, homemade and commercial sausage, wild boar, and walrus meat.

PATHOGENESIS AND CLINICAL MANIFESTATIONS   Light infections (<10 larvae per gram of muscle) are usually asymptomatic. With heavy infection (>50 larvae per gram of muscle), clinical symptoms parallel the stages of the parasite's life cycle: Enteric invasion during the first week may cause diarrhea or constipation, abdominal pain, nausea, and vomiting. Larval migration during the second week is associated with fever, hypereosinophilia, periorbital and facial edema, and splinter hemorrhages. Maculopapular rash, myocarditis, pneumonitis, or encephalitis may develop. Encystment of larvae in muscle beginning in the second to third week is associated with myalgia, muscle edema, and weakness. The most commonly involved muscle groups are the extraocular muscles, the biceps, and the muscles of the jaw, neck, lower back, and diaphragm.

DIAGNOSIS   The diagnosis is made histologically by the finding of larvae in a fresh specimen of muscle, which should be compressed between glass slides and examined microscopically. At least 1 g of involved muscle should be biopsied. The yield is highest near tendinous insertions. A rise in the titer of parasite-specific antibody may also be diagnostic but usually does not occur until after the third week of infection. Eosinophilia may peak at >50% between 2 and 4 weeks after infection. Serum levels of IgE, creatine phosphokinase, lactate dehydrogenase, and aspartate aminotransferase are elevated in most symptomatic pts.

TREATMENT

No agents are currently available for the treatment of *Trichinella* larvae in muscle. Thiabendazole (25 mg/kg PO bid for 5–7 d) and mebendazole (400 mg PO tid) are active against the early, enteric stage of the infection. For cases with severe myositis or myocarditis, prednisone (1 mg/kg PO qd for 5 d) is beneficial. Most lightly infected pts recover uneventfully.

PREVENTION   Larvae encysted in pork may be killed by cooking the meat until it is no longer pink or by freezing it at −15°C for 3 weeks. *T. nativa*, the species prevalent among arctic carnivores, is relatively tolerant of freezing.

VISCERAL AND OCULAR LARVA MIGRANS

PATHOGENESIS AND EPIDEMIOLOGY   Visceral larva migrans (toxocariasis) is a syndrome caused by nematodes parasitic for nonhuman species. Human infection is a dead end for the parasite. The nematode larvae do not develop into adult worms. Instead, their migration through host tissues elicits an eosinophilic inflammatory response. Humans acquire toxocariasis mainly by eating soil contaminated with puppy feces containing infective *Toxocara canis* eggs. Seropositivity rates may exceed 20% among U.S. kindergarten children.

CLINICAL MANIFESTATIONS   Most light infections are asymptomatic; eosinophilia may be the lone clue. Characteristic manifestations of heavier infection include fever, malaise, anorexia, weight loss, cough, wheezing, rash, and hepatosplenomegaly. Extraordinary eosinophilia is often present; eosinophils may constitute 90% of the WBCs. Half of pts with symptomatic pneumonitis have transient pulmonary infiltrates. Ocular disease occurs when larvae invade the eye. A granulomatous mass develops around the larvae and may be mistaken for retinoblastoma. The spectrum of ocular involvement also includes endophthalmitis, uveitis, and chorioretinitis.

DIAGNOSIS   The clinical diagnosis of toxocariasis is confirmed by an ELISA positive for toxocaral antibodies. Since *Toxocara* larvae do not develop into adult worms in humans, eggs are not found in the stool.

TREATMENT

Available anthelmintic drugs have not been shown conclusively to alter the course of larva migrans. In pts with severe disease, glucocorticoids may be used to reduce inflammatory complications. For ocular disease, treatment is unsatisfactory; the roles of glucocorticoids and anthelmintics are controversial.

CUTANEOUS LARVA MIGRANS

Cutaneous larva migrans ("creeping eruption") is a serpiginous skin eruption caused by burrowing larvae of animal hookworms, most commonly *Ancylostoma braziliense*.

PATHOGENESIS AND CLINICAL MANIFESTATIONS Larvae hatch from eggs passed in canine or feline feces and mature in the soil, after which they can penetrate human skin to initiate infection. Erythematous, pruritic lesions form along the tortuous tracks of their migration; the larvae may advance several centimeters per day.

DIAGNOSIS The diagnosis is readily made on clinical grounds. A skin biopsy rarely yields diagnostic material.

 TREATMENT

Without treatment, larvae die out after several weeks. Symptoms are alleviated by treatment with thiabendazole (25 mg/kg PO bid or a 10% suspension applied topically for 2–5 d), ivermectin (a single dose of 150–200 μg/kg), or albendazole (200 mg bid for 2 d).

ASCARIASIS

Ascaris lumbricoides (roundworm) is the largest intestinal nematode parasite of humans, reaching up to 40 cm in length.

EPIDEMIOLOGY *Ascaris* is widely distributed in tropical and subtropical regions and in other humid areas, such as the rural southeastern U.S. Younger children in impoverished rural areas are most affected.

PATHOGENESIS Infective eggs present in soil are ingested. Larvae hatch in the intestine, traverse the mucosa to gain access to the bloodstream, and are transported to the lung, where they break into the alveoli, ascend the bronchial tree, are swallowed, and return to the small intestine. There they become adult worms. Mature females produce many thousands of eggs each day.

CLINICAL MANIFESTATIONS Clinical disease arises from pulmonary hypersensitivity or from intestinal events. Fever, cough, and eosinophilia may develop during the stage of pulmonary migration. Eosinophilic pneumonitis (Loeffler's syndrome) may be evident on CXR. Light intestinal infection is usually asymptomatic. A heavy intestinal burden of adult worms may cause obstruction and malabsorption. A lone worm migrating to aberrant sites (e.g., the biliary tree) may also cause disease. Migration of a worm up the esophagus can cause coughing and oral expulsion.

DIAGNOSIS The characteristic eggs may be seen on microscopic examination of stool. Adult worms may be passed in the stool or through the mouth or nose. Larvae can be found in the sputum during the transpulmonary migratory phase. Large adult worms may be serendipitously visualized on contrast studies of the GI tract.

 TREATMENT

Mebendazole and albendazole are effective, but their use is contraindicated in pregnancy or for heavy infection. Pyrantel pamoate and piperazine citrate are safe in pregnancy. Intestinal obstruction should be managed by nasogastric suction, IV fluid administration, and instillation of piperazine through the nasogastric tube. Worms in the biliary tract may require extraction via endoscopy.

STRONGYLOIDIASIS

Strongyloides stercoralis is distinguished by a capacity, unusual among helminths, to replicate in humans. This capacity permits ongoing cycles of autoinfection from endogenously produced larvae. Strongyloidiasis can thus persist for decades; at times of host immunocompromise, the larvae may disseminate widely, with catastrophic results (autoinfection syndrome).

EPIDEMIOLOGY   *S. stercoralis* is spottily distributed in tropical areas and other hot, humid regions. It is endemic in parts of the southern U.S. This nematode is also found among residents of mental institutions, where hygiene may be poor, and among persons who have lived in endemic areas abroad.

PATHOGENESIS   Filariform larvae in fecally contaminated soil penetrate human skin, travel via the bloodstream to the lung, penetrate into the alveoli, ascend the airway, are swallowed, reach the small bowel, and there mature into adult worms. In autoinfection, larvae invade through the colonic wall or perianal skin.

CLINICAL MANIFESTATIONS   In uncomplicated strongyloidiasis, pts may be asymptomatic or have mild cutaneous and/or abdominal symptoms, including recurrent urticaria (especially involving the wrists and/or buttocks), "larva currens" (a pathognomonic response to subcutaneous migrating larvae, which may advance up to 10 cm/h), nausea, diarrhea, GI bleeding, and epigastric pain aggravated by eating. Eosinophilia is common and may fluctuate with time. Pulmonary symptoms are rare. In autoinfection syndrome, larvae may invade the GI tract, lungs, CNS, liver, kidneys, and peritoneum and may facilitate the development of gram-negative sepsis, pneumonia, or meningitis. Disseminated strongyloidiasis, especially in pts who are given steroids, can be fatal.

DIAGNOSIS   In uncomplicated strongyloidiasis, the finding of rhabditiform larvae in stool or intestinal aspirates is diagnostic. Eggs are almost never detectable in the stool. A sensitive ELISA for *Strongyloides* antigens is available. For suspected disseminated strongyloidiasis, filariform larvae should be sought in stool, sputum, and other sites of potential dissemination.

 TREATMENT

Even in the asymptomatic state, strongyloidiasis should be treated. Ivermectin (200 μg/kg qd for 1–2 d) is more effective and better tolerated than thiabendazole (25 mg/kg PO bid for 2 d). For disseminated infection, treatment should be extended for at least 5–7 d.

LYMPHATIC FILARIASIS
PATHOGENESIS AND EPIDEMIOLOGY   The agents of lymphatic filariasis (*Wuchereria bancrofti* throughout the tropics and subtropics, *Brugia malayi* in India and the Far East, and *Brugia timori* in Indonesia) are transmitted by mosquitoes. An estimated 115 million people are affected. The adult filariae reside in lymphatics and lymph node sinuses. The presence of the worms and the host's inflammatory response to them lead to lymphatic compromise. Death of the worms enhances inflammation and fibrosis, ultimately causing lymphatic obstruction and lymphedema.

CLINICAL MANIFESTATIONS   Common manifestations include asymptomatic microfilaremia, hydrocele, acute adenolymphangitis, chronic lymphatic disease, and lymphatic obstruction and the permanent changes associated with elephantiasis.

DIAGNOSIS   A definitive diagnosis is made only by detection of the parasite, which can be difficult. By virtue of their location in lymphatics, the adults are inaccessible. Microfilariae should be sought in blood and hydrocele fluid.

The timing of blood sampling is critical and should be based on the periodicity of the microfilariae suspected to be involved. Assays for circulating antigens of *W. bancrofti* are highly sensitive and specific. Antibody assays are complicated by cross-reactivity with other helminths. PCR-based assays have been developed for *W. bancrofti* and *B. malayi*.

 TREATMENT

Therapy with diethylcarbamazine (DEC, 6 mg/kg daily in either single or divided doses for 12 d) clears microfilariae. To minimize acute reactions to antigens released by dying filariae, gradual upward titration of the DEC dose or premedication with glucocorticoids may be useful.

ONCHOCERCIASIS

EPIDEMIOLOGY   Onchocerciasis ("river blindness") is caused by the filarial nematode *Onchocerca volvulus*. Some 13 million people are infected in equatorial Africa and Latin America. Onchocerciasis is the second leading infectious cause of blindness worldwide.

PATHOGENESIS   Infective larvae are deposited on human skin by the bites of infected blackflies. The larvae develop into adults, which reside in subcutaneous nodules. After an interval ranging from months to ~3 years, microfilariae begin to be released, migrate out of the nodule and throughout the tissues, and concentrate in the dermis. Onchocerciasis affects primarily the skin, eyes, and lymph nodes. The damage is elicited by the microfilariae, not by the adult worms.

CLINICAL MANIFESTATIONS   Pruritus and generalized papular rash are common; the pruritus can be incapacitating. Subcutaneous onchocercomata contain adult worms. Lesions may develop in any part of the eye. Ocular lesions include sclerosing keratitis (the leading cause of onchocercal blindness in Africa), anterior uveitis, iridocyclitis, and chorioretinal atrophy. Secondary glaucoma or optic atrophy may occur.

DIAGNOSIS   Definitive diagnosis depends on detection of an adult worm in an excised nodule or of microfilariae in a skin snip. For identification of the latter form, snips should be incubated for 2–4 h in tissue culture medium or in saline on a glass slide or a flat-bottomed microtiter plate and examined by low-power microscopy. Antibody detection as well as PCR are highly sensitive and specific and are used in specialized laboratories.

 TREATMENT

The main goals of therapy are to prevent the development of irreversible lesions and to ease symptoms. Nodules on the head must be excised to avoid ocular infection. Ivermectin is administered orally in a single dose of 150 μg/kg, either annually or semiannually. Contraindications to treatment include pregnancy, breast-feeding, CNS disorders that compromise the blood-brain barrier, and an age of <5 years. Ivermectin does not kill adult worms.

SCHISTOSOMIASIS

EPIDEMIOLOGY   *Schistosoma mansoni* is found in parts of South America, Africa, and the Middle East; *S. japonicum*, in China, the Philippines, and Indonesia; *S. haematobium*, in Africa and the Middle East; and *S. mekongi*, along the Mekong River in Southeast Asia. Worldwide, some 200–300 million people may be infected with schistosomes. Only a small minority of them develop significant disease.

PATHOGENESIS Cercariae, released from freshwater snails, penetrate unbroken human skin. As they mature into schistosomes, they reach the portal vein, where males and females pair. They then migrate to the venules of the bladder and ureters (*S. haematobium*) or mesentery (*S. mansoni, S. japonicum, S. mekongi*) and begin to deposit eggs. Some mature ova are extruded into the intestinal or urinary lumina, from which they may reach water and perpetuate the life cycle. The persistence of other ova in tissues leads to a granulomatous host response and fibrosis. Factors governing disease manifestations include the intensity and duration of infection, the location of egg deposition, and the genetic characteristics of the host.

CLINICAL MANIFESTATIONS Dermatitis ("swimmer's itch") may result from cercarial invasion by *S. mansoni* and *S. japonicum*. Acute schistosomiasis, or Katayama fever, is a serum sickness–like syndrome associated with fever, lymphadenopathy, and hepatosplenomegaly; it occurs in visitors to endemic areas and lasts up to 3 months. Chronic infection with *S. mansoni, S. japonicum,* or *S. mekongi* manifests as an initial intestinal phase of colicky abdominal pain and bloody diarrhea followed by hepatomegaly from granulomatous liver lesions and eventually peripheral fibrosis with portal hypertension, splenomegaly, and esophageal varices. *S. haematobium* prefers the veins of the urinary tract. It may cause hematuria and dysuria at all stages of infection and may produce ureteral and vesicular fibrosis and calcification in the chronic stage. Squamous cell carcinoma of the bladder has been associated with *S. haematobium* infection.

DIAGNOSIS Two serologic tests available through the CDC are highly sensitive and specific. In some instances, examination of the stool or urine for ova may yield positive results.

 TREATMENT

Praziquantel results in parasitologic cure in ~85% of cases. Recommended doses are 20 mg/kg bid for *S. mansoni* and *S. haematobium* infections and 20 mg/kg tid for *S. japonicum* and *S. mekongi* infections.

TAENIASIS AND DIPHYLLOBOTHRIASIS

PATHOGENESIS Cysticercal larvae are ingested in undercooked beef (*Taenia saginata*), pork (*Taenia solium*), or fish (*Diphyllobothrium latum*) and develop into mature tapeworms within the definitive human host. For *T. solium,* humans can also be the intermediate host: ingestion of *T. solium* eggs, their embryonation, and dissemination of the larvae lead to cysticercosis.

CLINICAL MANIFESTATIONS *T. saginata* and *T. solium* infections may be asymptomatic or may cause mild abdominal discomfort, nausea, change in appetite, and/or weight loss. Proglottids may be visible in stool. *D. latum* infections are associated with vitamin B_{12} deficiency. Cysticerci of *T. solium* can be found anywhere in the body, most commonly in the brain and skeletal muscle. CNS cysticercosis can result in seizures, hydrocephalus, and signs of elevated intracranial pressure.

DIAGNOSIS Infections with *T. saginata* and *T. solium* are diagnosed by detecting eggs or proglottids in the stool; distinguishing between the two species requires examination of mature proglottids or the scolex. The diagnostic criteria for cysticercosis are listed in Table 111-1.

Table 111-1

Proposed Diagnostic Criteria for Human Cysticercosis, 1996

1. Absolute criteria
   a. Demonstration of cysticerci by histologic or microscopic examination of biopsy material
   b. Visualization of the parasite in the eye by funduscopy
   c. Neuroradiologic demonstration of cystic lesions containing a scolex
2. Major criteria
   a. Neuroradiologic lesions suggestive of neurocysticercosis
   b. Demonstration of antibodies to cysticerci in serum by immunoblot or in CSF by immunoblot or ELISA
   c. Identification of characteristic "cigar-shaped" calcifications on soft tissue x-rays
3. Minor criteria
   a. Presence of subcutaneous nodules suggestive of cysticerci
   b. Punctate calcifications on radiographic studies
   c. Clinical manifestations suggestive of neurocysticercosis
   d. Disappearance of intracranial lesions during treatment with anticysticercal drugs
4. Epidemiologic criteria
   a. Residence in a cysticercosis-endemic area
   b. Frequent travel to a cysticercosis-endemic area
   c. Household contact with an individual infected with *Taenia solium*

SOURCE: AC White Jr, PF Weller: HPIM-15, p. 1249 (modified from Del Brutto et al.).

 TREATMENT

For infection with adult worms, a single dose of praziquantel (5–10 mg/kg) is highly effective. Vitamin B_{12} should be given parenterally if the pt is B_{12} deficient. Four placebo-controlled trials failed to identify any clinical advantage of antiparasitic drugs for parenchymal neurocysticercosis. However, some authorities favor treatment of these cases in light of trends toward faster resolution of neuroradiologic abnormalities. Treatment of the symptoms of neurocysticercosis consists of praziquantel (50–60 mg/kg qd in 3 doses for 15 d or 100 mg/kg given in three doses over a single day) or albendazole (15 mg/kg qd in 3 doses for 8–28 d); hospitalization and concomitant glucocorticoid therapy are advisable if symptoms worsen during treatment. Ocular, spinal, or cerebral ventricular lesions may require excision.

ECHINOCOCCOSIS

PATHOGENESIS AND EPIDEMIOLOGY Infection occurs through human ingestion of eggs of the dog tapeworms. Embryos penetrate the intestinal mucosa, enter the portal circulation, and disseminate to various organs, especially the liver and lungs. Brood capsules and daughter cysts develop within hydatid cysts. New larvae, called *scolices*, develop within the brood capsules. *Echinococcus granulosus* occurs in livestock-raising regions outside North America. *E. multilocularis* predominates in arctic and subarctic zones. *E. vogeli* is found only in Central and South America. *E. multilocularis* vesicles are locally invasive.

CLINICAL MANIFESTATIONS Enlargement of cysts may progress for 5–20 years before the development of symptoms, which are typically related to compressive or mass effects. Hepatic echinococcosis may present as abdominal pain, a palpable RUQ mass, or biliary obstruction. Cyst rupture may produce fever, pruritus, urticaria, or anaphylaxis and leads to multifocal dissemination. *E. multilocularis* infection mimics hepatic malignancy, with liver destruction, extension into vital structures, and (in occasional cases) metastasis.

DIAGNOSIS   The CT finding of daughter cysts within the larger cyst is pathognomonic for *E. granulosus* infection. MRI, ultrasound, and—for pulmonary disease—plain films may be diagnostically helpful. Calcification may be evident in liver cyst walls. Serology is negative in up to 50% of pts with pulmonary echinococcosis but is positive in ~90% of cases with liver involvement. Aspiration poses a risk of rupture and dissemination and is not usually recommended; however, if aspiration is performed, demonstration of scoliceal hooklets solidifies the diagnosis.

 TREATMENT

Both surgical excision and repeated aspiration and instillation of scolicidal agents have been advocated to remove the cyst. Albendazole (15 mg/kg qd in two divided doses) should be administered before the procedure and continued thereafter for several weeks in *E. granulosus* infection and for up to 2 years in *E. multilocularis* infection. Albendazole therapy results in cure in ~30% of cases. Multiple courses of treatment may be necessary.

ECTOPARASITE INFESTATIONS

Ectoparasites are arthropods or helminths that infest the skin of other animals from which they derive sustenance. They damage their hosts by inflicting direct injury, eliciting hypersensitivity, or inoculating toxins or pathogens.

Scabies

The human itch mite, *Sarcoptes scabiei*, infests 300 million persons per year. Itching and rash are the results of a sensitization reaction to the excreta of female mites that burrow beneath the stratum corneum to deposit eggs. Intimate contact is generally required for person-to-person transmission; sharing of contaminated garments is an infrequent mode of transmission. Burrows appear as dark wavy lines in the epidermis, at one end of which is a small bleb containing the female mite. Excoriated papules and vesicles are symmetrically distributed over the volar wrists, between the fingers, on the penis, and in skin folds. Hyperinfestation may occur in immunodeficient pts and results in thick keratotic crusts with fissuring, a condition known as *Norwegian scabies* or *crusted scabies*. Bacteremia may result from secondary infection of the lesions. Diagnosis is made by microscopic demonstration of the mite, its eggs, and its feces in scrapings of lesions. For treatment, 5% permethrin cream is less toxic than 1% lindane and is effective against lindane-tolerant infestations. Both agents are applied behind the ears and from the neck down, left on for 8 h, and washed off. Lindane should not be used in childhood or pregnancy. Alternatives are crotamiton cream, benzyl benzoate, and sulfur ointments. A single oral dose of ivermectin (200 μg/kg) is effective for treatment of scabies in healthy persons but has not yet been approved by the FDA. Treated pts become noninfectious within a day, although itching may persist for weeks or months and should be treated with antipruritics. Bedding and clothing should be washed, and all close contacts should be treated regardless of symptoms.

Pediculosis

All three species of human louse—*Pediculus humanus* var. *capitis* (the head louse), *P. humanus* var. *corporis* (the body louse, which infests clothing), and

Phthirus pubis (the pubic louse)—feed at least once a day on human blood. Itching results from sensitization to the saliva of the lice. Head lice are transmitted between schoolchildren, body lice are transmitted between persons who do not change their clothes often, and pubic lice are usually sexually transmitted. Body lice can transmit typhus, relapsing fever, or trench fever. Diagnosis is made by observation of the 2- to 4-mm-long lice or their nits, which are white or cream colored (head and body lice) or dark brown (pubic lice). The preferred treatment is a single application of 1% permethrin cream rinse, which kills both lice and eggs; 0.5% malathion is an alternative but must be left on for 8–12 h. Lindane (1%) and pyrethrins are not ovicidal and require a second application 1 week after the first. The hair should be combed with a fine-toothed comb to remove nits. Pediculicides must be applied from head to foot to remove body lice. Clothes and bedding should be deloused by placement in a hot dryer for 30 min or by fumigation.

Tungiasis

Tunga penetrans is also known as the jigger, sand flea, or chigoe flea. Adults live in sandy soil and burrow under the skin between toes, under nails, or on the soles of the feet. Lesions resemble a white pustule with a central black depression and may be pruritic or painful. Treatment entails removal of the intact flea with a needle or scalpel, tetanus prophylaxis, and topical antibiotic application.

For a more detailed discussion, see Weller PF, Liu LX: *Trichinella* and Other Tissue Nematodes, Chap. 219, p. 1231; Weller PF, Nutman TB: Intestinal Nematodes, Chap. 220, p. 1233; Nutman TB, Weller PF: Filariasis and Related Infections (Loiasis, Onchocerciasis, and Dracunculiasis), Chap. 221, p. 1237; Mahmoud AAF: Schistosomiasis and Other Trematode Infections, Chap. 222, p. 1242; White AC Jr, Weller PF: Cestodes, Chap. 223, p. 1248; and Maguire JH, Spielman A: Ectoparasite Infestations, Arthropod Bites and Stings, Chap. 398, p. 2622, in HPIM-15.

112

PHYSICAL EXAMINATION OF THE HEART

General examination of a pt with suspected heart disease should include vital signs (respiratory rate, pulse, blood pressure), skin color, clubbing, edema, evidence of decreased perfusion (cool and sweaty skin), and hypertensive changes in optic fundi. Important findings on cardiovascular examination include:

CAROTID ARTERY PULSE (Fig. 112-1)

1. *Pulsus parvus:* Weak upstroke due to decreased stroke volume (hypovolemia, LV failure, aortic or mitral stenosis).
2. *Pulsus tardus:* Delayed upstroke (aortic stenosis).
3. *Bounding pulse:* Hyperkinetic circulation, aortic regurgitation, patent ductus arteriosus, marked vasodilatation.
4. *Pulsus bisferiens:* Double systolic pulsation in aortic regurgitation, hypertrophic cardiomyopathy.
5. *Pulsus alternans:* Regular alteration in pulse pressure amplitude (severe LV dysfunction).
6. *Pulsus paradoxus:* Exaggerated inspiratory fall (>10 mmHg) in systolic bp (pericardial tamponade, severe obstructive lung disease).

JUGULAR VENOUS PULSATION (JVP) (Fig. 112-2)   Jugular venous distention develops in right-sided heart failure, constrictive pericarditis, pericardial tamponade, obstruction of superior vena cava. JVP normally *falls* with inspiration but may *rise* (Kussmaul's sign) in constrictive pericarditis. Abnormalities in examination include:

1. *Large "a" wave:* Tricuspid stenosis (TS), pulmonic stenosis, AV dissociation (right atrium contracts against closed tricuspid valve).
2. *Large "v" wave:* Tricuspid regurgitation, atrial septal defect.
3. *Steep "y" descent:* Constrictive pericarditis.
4. *Slow "y" descent:* Tricuspid stenosis.

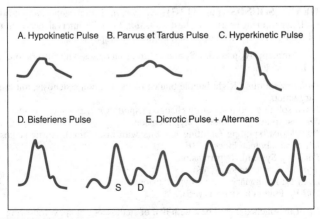

A. Hypokinetic Pulse   B. Parvus et Tardus Pulse   C. Hyperkinetic Pulse

D. Bisferiens Pulse   E. Dicrotic Pulse + Alternans

S   D

FIGURE 112-1   Carotid artery pulse patterns.

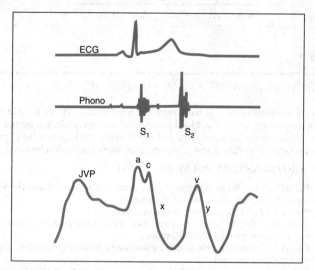

FIGURE 112-2   Normal jugular venous pressure recording.

PRECORDIAL PALPATION   Cardiac apical impulse is normally localized in the fifth intercostal space, midclavicular line (Fig. 112-3). Abnormalities
include:

1. *Forceful apical thrust:* Left ventricular hypertrophy.
2. *Lateral and downward displacement of apex impulse:* Left ventricular dil-
    atation.
3. *Prominent presystolic impulse:* Hypertension, aortic stenosis, hypertrophic
    cardiomyopathy.
4. *Double systolic apical impulse:* Hypertrophic cardiomyopathy.
5. *Sustained "lift" at lower left sternal border:* Right ventricular hypertrophy.
6. *Dyskinetic (outward bulge) impulse:* Ventricular aneurysm, large dyski-
    netic area post MI, cardiomyopathy.

AUSCULTATION

HEART SOUNDS (Fig. 112-3) S_1 *Loud:* Mitral stenosis, short PR
interval, hyperkinetic heart, thin chest wall. *Soft:* Long PR interval, heart failure,
mitral regurgitation, thick chest wall, pulmonary emphysema.

S_2 Normally A_2 precedes P_2 and splitting increases with inspiration; abnormalities include:

• *Widened* splitting: Right bundle branch block, pulmonic stenosis, mitral re-
  gurgitation.
• *Fixed* splitting (no respiratory change in splitting): Atrial septal defect.
• *Narrow* splitting: Pulmonary hypertension.
• *Paradoxical* splitting (splitting *narrows* with inspiration): Aortic stenosis,
  left bundle branch block, CHF.
• *Loud* A_2: Systemic hypertension.
• *Soft* A_2: Aortic stenosis (AS).
• *Loud* P_2: Pulmonary arterial hypertension.
• *Soft* P_2: Pulmonic stenosis (PS).

S_3 Low-pitched, heard best with bell of stethoscope at apex, following S_2;
normal in children; after age 30–35, indicates LV failure or volume overload.

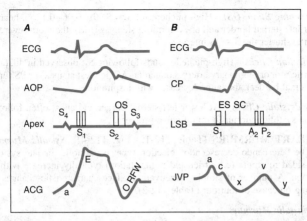

FIGURE 112-3   *A*. Schematic representation of electrocardiogram, aortic pressure pulse (AOP), phonocardiogram recorded at the apex, and apex cardiogram (ACG). On the phonocardiogram, S_1, S_2, S_3, and S_4 represent the first through fourth heart sounds; OS represents the opening snap of the mitral valve, which occurs coincident with the O point of the apex cardiogram. S_3 occurs coincident with the termination of the rapid-filling wave (RFW) of the ACG, while S_4 occurs coincident with the *a* wave of the ACG. *B*. Simultaneous recording of electrocardiogram, indirect carotid pulse (CP), phonocardiogram along the left sternal border (LSB), and indirect jugular venous pulse (JVP). ES, ejection sound; SC, systolic click.

S_4 Low-pitched, heard best with bell at apex, preceding S_1; reflects atrial contraction into a noncompliant ventricle; found in AS, hypertension, hypertrophic cardiomyopathy, and CAD.

Table 112-1

Heart Murmurs	
SYSTOLIC MURMURS	
Ejection-type	Aortic outflow tract Aortic valve stenosis Hypertrophic obstructive cardiomyopathy Aortic flow murmur Pulmonary outflow tract Pulmonic valve stenosis Pulmonic flow murmur
Holosystolic	Mitral regurgitation Tricuspid regurgitation Ventricular septal defect
Late-systolic	Mitral or tricuspid valve prolapse
DIASTOLIC MURMURS	
Early diastolic	Aortic valve regurgitation Pulmonic valve regurgitation
Mid-to-late diastolic	Mitral or tricuspid stenosis Flow murmur across mitral or tricuspid valves
Continuous	Patent ductus arteriosus Coronary AV fistula Ruptured sinus of Valsalva aneurysm

Opening Snap (OS) High-pitched; follows S_2 (by 0.06–0.12 s), heard at lower left sternal border and apex in mitral stenosis (MS); the more severe the MS, the shorter the S_2–OS interval.

Ejection Clicks High-pitched sounds following S_1; observed in dilatation of aortic root or pulmonary artery, congenital AS (loudest at apex) or PS (upper left sternal border); the latter decreases with inspiration.

Midsystolic Clicks At lower left sternal border and apex, often followed by late systolic murmur in mitral valve prolapse.

HEART MURMURS (Table 112-1, Fig. 112-4) *Systolic Murmurs* May be "crescendo-decrescendo" ejection type, pansystolic, or late systolic; right-sided murmurs (e.g., tricuspid regurgitation) typically increase with inspiration. A number of simple maneuvers produce characteristic changes depending on cause of murmur (Table 112-2).

Diastolic Murmurs

1. *Early diastolic murmurs:* Begin immediately after S_2, are high-pitched, and are usually caused by aortic or pulmonary regurgitation.

2. *Mid-to-late diastolic murmurs:* Low-pitched, heard best with bell of stethoscope; observed in MS or TS; less commonly due to atrial myxoma.

3. *Continuous murmurs:* Present in systole and diastole (envelops S_2); found in patent ductus arteriosus and sometimes in coarctation of aorta; less common causes are systemic or coronary AV fistula, aortopulmonary septal defect, ruptured aneurysm of sinus of Valsalva.

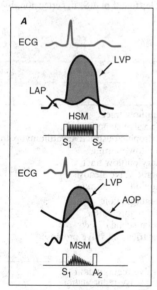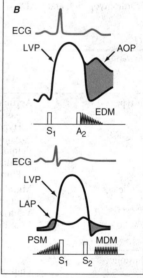

FIGURE 112-4 *A.* Schematic representation of ECG, aortic pressure (AOP), left ventricular pressure (LVP), and left atrial pressure (LAP). The hatched areas indicated a transvalvular pressure difference during systole. HSM, holosystolic murmur; MSM, midsystolic murmur. *B.* Graphic representation of ECG, aortic pressure (AOP), left ventricular pressure (LVP), and left atrial pressure (LAP) with hatched areas indicating transvalvular diastolic pressure difference. EDM, early diastolic murmur; PSM, presystolic murmur; MDM, middiastolic murmur.

Table 112-2

Heart Murmurs and Responsible Lesions

Lesion	Type of murmur	Maneuver			
		Valsalva	Hand Grip	Squat	Stand
Aortic stenosis	Crescendo-decrescendo	↓	↓	↑	↓
Mitral regurgitation	Holosystolic	↓	↑	↑	↓
Ventricular septal defect	Holosystolic	↓	↑	↑	↓
Mitral valve prolapse	Late systolic (follows click)	↑	↓	↓	↑
Hypertrophic obstructive cardiomyopathy	Harsh, diamond-shaped at left sternal border; holosystolic at apex	↑	↓	↓	↑

For a more detailed discussion, see O'Gara PT, Braunwald E: Approach to the Patient with a Heart Murmur, Chap. 34, p. 207; and O'Rourke RA, Braunwald E: Physical Examination of the Cardiovascular System, Chap. 225, p. 1255, in HPIM-15.

113

ELECTROCARDIOGRAPHY AND ECHOCARDIOGRAPHY

STANDARD APPROACH TO THE ECG

Normally, standardization is 1.0 mV per 10 mm, and paper speed is 25 mm/s (each horizontal small box = 0.04 s).

HEART RATE   Beats/min = 300 divided by the number of *large* boxes (each 5 mm apart) between consecutive QRS complexes. For faster heart rates, divide 1500 by number of *small* boxes (1 mm apart) between each QRS.

RHYTHM   *Sinus rhythm* is present if every P wave is followed by a QRS, PR interval ≥0.12 s, every QRS is preceded by a P wave, and the P wave is upright in leads I, II, and III. Arrhythmias are discussed in Chap. 115.

MEAN AXIS   If QRS is primarily positive in limb leads I and II, then axis is *normal*. Otherwise, find limb lead in which QRS is most isoelectric (R = S). The mean axis is perpendicular to that lead (Fig. 113-1). If the QRS complex is *positive* in that perpendicular lead, then mean axis is in the direction of that lead; if *negative*, then mean axis points directly away from that lead.

Left-axis deviation (≤30°) occurs in diffuse left ventricular disease, inferior MI; also in left anterior hemiblock (small R, deep S in leads II, III, and aVF).

Right-axis deviation (>90°) occurs in right ventricular hypertrophy (R > S in V₁) and left posterior hemiblock (small Q and tall R in leads II, III, and aVF). Mild right-axis deviation is seen in thin, healthy individuals (up to 110°).

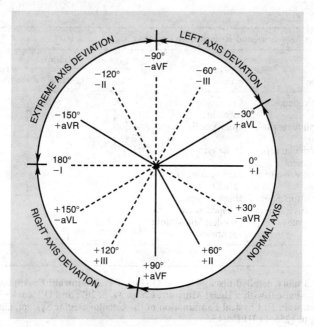

FIGURE 113-1 Electrocardiographic lead systems: The hexaxial frontal plane reference system to estimate electrical axis. Determine leads in which QRS deflections are maximum and minimum. For example, a maximum positive QRS in I which is isoelectric in aVF is oriented to 0°. Normal axis ranges from −30° to +90°. An axis > +90° is right axis deviation and < −30° is left axis deviation.

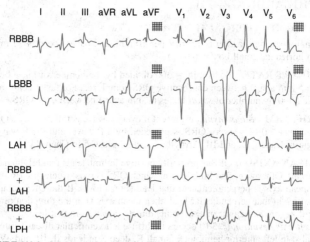

FIGURE 113-2 Intraventricular conduction abnormalities. Illustrated are right bundle branch block (RBBB); left bundle branch block (LBBB); left anterior hemiblock (LAH); right bundle branch block with left anterior hemiblock (RBBB + LAH); and right bundle branch block with left posterior hemiblock (RBBB + LPH). (*Reproduced from RJ Myerburg: HPIM-12.*)

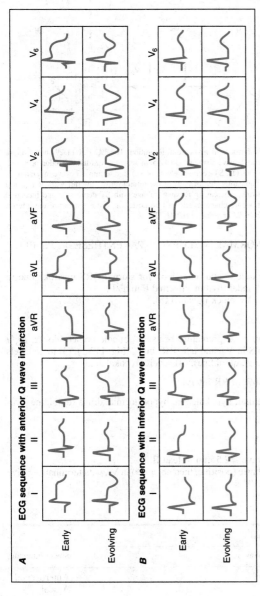

FIGURE 113-3 Sequence of depolarization and repolarization changes with (*A*) acute anterior and (*B*) acute inferior wall Q-wave infarctions. With anterior infarcts, ST elevation in leads I, aVL, and the precordial leads may be accompanied by reciprocal ST depressions in leads II, III, and aVF. Conversely, acute inferior (or posterior) infarcts may be associated with reciprocal ST depressions in leads V₁ to V₃. (*After AL Goldberger, E Goldberger: Clinical Electrocardiography: A Simplified Approach, 6th ed. St. Louis, Mosby-Year Book, 1999.*)

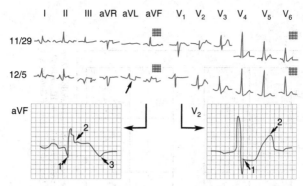

FIGURE 113-4 Acute inferior wall myocardial infarction. The ECG of 11/29 shows minor nonspecific ST-segment and T-wave changes. On 12/5 an acute myocardial infarction occurred. There are pathologic Q waves (1), ST-segment elevation (2), and terminal T-wave inversion (3) in leads II, III, and aVF indicating the location of the infarct on the inferior wall. Reciprocal changes in aVL (small arrow). Increasing R-wave voltage with ST depression and increased voltage of the T wave in V_2 are characteristic of true posterior wall extension of the inferior infarction. (*Reproduced from RJ Myerburg: HPIM-12.*)

INTERVALS (NORMAL VALUES IN PARENTHESES) *PR* (0.12–0.20 s)

- *Short:* (1) preexcitation syndrome (look for slurred QRS upstroke due to "delta" wave), (2) nodal rhythm (inverted P in aVF).
- *Long:* first-degree AV block (Chap. 115).

    QRS (0.06–0.10 s)

- *Widened:* (1) ventricular premature beats, (2) bundle branch blocks: *right* (RsR′ in V_1, deep S in V_6) and *left* (RR′ in V_6 (Fig. 113-2), (3) toxic levels of certain drugs (e.g., quinidine), (4) severe hypokalemia.

    QT (≤0.43 s; <50% of RR interval)

- *Prolonged:* congenital, hypokalemia, hypocalcemia, drugs (quinidine, procainamide, tricyclics).

HYPERTROPHY

- *Right atrium:* P wave ≥2.5 mm in lead II.
- *Left atrium:* P biphasic (positive, then negative) in V_1, with terminal negative force wider than 0.04 s.

Table 113-1

Leads with Abnormal Q Waves in MI

Leads with Abnormal Q Waves	Site of Infarction
V_1–V_2	Anteroseptal
V_3–V_4	Apical
I, aVL, V_5–V_6	Anterolateral
II, III, aVF	Inferior
V_1–V_2 (tall R, *not* deep Q)	True posterior

Table 113-2

Differential Diagnosis of Q Waves (with Selected Examples)

Physiologic or positional factors
1. Normal variant "septal" Q waves
2. Normal variant Q waves in V_1 to V_2, aVL, III, and aVF
3. Left pneumothorax or dextrocardia

Myocardial injury or infiltration
1. Acute processes: myocardial ischemia or infarction, myocarditis, hyperkalemia
2. Chronic processes: myocardial infarction, idiopathic cardiomyopathy, myocarditis, amyloid, tumor, sarcoid, scleroderma

Ventricular hypertrophy/enlargement
1. Left ventricular (poor R-wave progression)[a]
2. Right ventricular (reversed R-wave progression)
3. Hypertrophic cardiomyopathy

Conduction abnormalities
1. Left bundle branch block
2. Wolff-Parkinson-White patterns

[a] Small or absent R waves in the right to midprecordial leads.
SOURCE: After AL Goldberger: *Myocardial Infarction: Electrocardiographic Differential Diagnosis*, 4th ed. St. Louis, Mosby–Year Book, 1991.

- *Right ventricle:* R > S in V_1 and R in V_1 > 5 mm; deep S in V_6; right-axis deviation.
- *Left ventricle:* S in V_1 plus R in V_5 or $V_6 \geq 35$ mm or R in aVL > 11 mm.

INFARCTION (Figs. 113-3 and 113-4) *Q-wave MI:* Pathologic Q waves (≥ 0.04 s and $\geq 25\%$ of total QRS height) in leads shown in Table 113-1; acute *non-Q-wave MI* shows ST-T changes in these leads without Q wave development. A number of conditions (other than acute MI) can cause Q waves (Table 113-2).

ST-T WAVES

- *ST elevation:* Acute MI, coronary spasm, pericarditis (concave upward), LV aneurysm.
- *ST depression:* Digitalis effect, strain (due to ventricular hypertrophy), ischemia, or nontransmural MI.
- *Tall peaked T:* Hyperkalemia; acute MI ("hyperacute T").
- *Inverted T:* Non-Q-wave MI, ventricular "strain" pattern, drug effect (e.g., digitalis), hypokalemia, hypocalcemia, increased intracranial pressure (e.g., subarachnoid bleed).

INDICATIONS FOR ECHOCARDIOGRAPHY (Fig. 113-5)

VALVULAR STENOSIS Both native and artificial valvular stenosis can be evaluated, and severity can be determined by Doppler [peak gradient = 4 × (peak velocity)^2].

VALVULAR REGURGITATION Structural lesions (e.g., flail leaflet, vegetation) resulting in regurgitation may be identified. Echo can demonstrate whether ventricular function is normal; Doppler (Fig. 113-6) can identify and estimate severity of regurgitation through each valve.

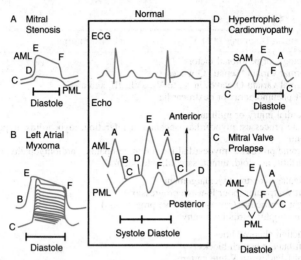

FIGURE 113-5 A schematic presentation of the normal M-mode echocardiographic (Echo) recording of anterior (AML) and posterior mitral leaflet (PML) motion is shown in the center with the simultaneous ECG. Abnormal mitral echocardiograms which occur in (*A*) mitral stenosis, (*B*) left atrial myxoma, (*C*) mitral valve prolapse, and (*D*) obstructive hypertrophic cardiomyopathy are also depicted. In the ECHO, the A point represents the end of anterior movement resulting from left atrial contraction, the CD segment represents the closed position of both mitral leaflets during ventricular systole, and point E ends the anterior movement as the leaflet opens. The slope EF results from posterior motion of the AML during rapid ventricular filling. In obstructive hypertrophic cardiomyopathy, SAM represents systolic anterior movement. (*Reproduced from J Wynne, RA O'Rourke, E Braunwald: HPIM-10, p. 1333.*)

VENTRICULAR PERFORMANCE Global and regional wall motion abnormalities of both ventricles can be assessed; ventricular hypertrophy/infiltration may be visualized; evidence of pulmonary hypertension may be obtained.

CARDIAC SOURCE OF EMBOLISM May visualize atrial or ventricular thrombus, intracardiac tumors, and valvular vegetations. Yield of identifying cardiac source of embolism is *low* in absence of cardiac history or physical findings. Transesophageal echocardiography is more sensitive than standard transthoracic study for this purpose.

ENDOCARDITIS Vegetation visualized in more than half of pts (transesophageal echo has much higher sensitivity), but management is generally based on clinical findings, not echo. Complications of endocarditis (e.g., valvular regurgitation) may be evaluated.

CONGENITAL HEART DISEASE Echo, Doppler, and contrast echo (rapid IV injection of saline) are noninvasive procedures of choice in identifying congenital lesions.

AORTIC ROOT Aneurysm and dissection of the aorta may be evaluated and complications (aortic regurgitation, tamponade) assessed (Chap. 125).

HYPERTROPHIC CARDIOMYOPATHY, MITRAL VALVE PROLAPSE, PERICARDIAC EFFUSION Echo is the diagnostic technique of choice for identifying these conditions.

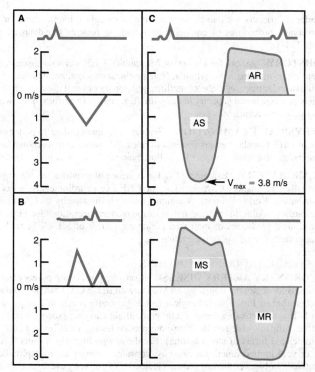

FIGURE 113-6 Schematic presentation of normal Doppler flow across the aortic (*A*) and mitral valves (*B*). Abnormal continuous wave Doppler profiles are depicted in *C*. Aortic stenosis (AS) [peak transaortic gradient $= 4 \times V_{max}^2 = 4 \times (3.8)^2 = 58$ mmHg] and regurgitation (AR). *D*. Mitral stenosis (MS) and regurgitation (MR).

For a more detailed discussion, see Goldberger AL: Electrocardiography, Chap. 226, p. 1262; and Nishimura RA, Gibbons RJ, Tajik AJ: Noninvasive Cardiac Imaging: Echocardiography and Nuclear Cardiology, Chap. 227, p. 1271, in HPIM-15.

114

PREOPERATIVE EVALUATION OF CARDIOVASCULAR DISEASE

Goal is to determine if cardiovascular disease is present, assess its severity and stability, and intervene if necessary to minimize surgical risk. Greatest cardiovascular risk occurs with aortic (or other major vascular), intrathoracic, or intraperitoneal procedures or emergent operations in patients of advanced age (Table 114-1).

HISTORY   Assess for history of MI, angina, CHF, valvular disease, hypertension, symptomatic arrhythmia. Note pertinent concomitant illnesses (e.g., cerebrovascular disease, diabetes mellitus, pulmonary or renal disease, anemia). Review pt's functional capacity in daily life (e.g., ability to perform housework, climb stairs, exercise).

PHYSICAL EXAMINATION   Evaluate for uncontrolled hypertension, signs of CHF (jugular venous distention, rales, S_3), previously unknown heart murmurs, carotid bruits. Inspect for pallor, cyanosis, poor nutritional state.

LABORATORY   Examine *ECG* for evidence of previous MI (Q waves) or arrhythmias. Inspect *CXR* for signs of CHF (e.g., cardiomegaly, vascular redistribution, Kerley B lines). Additional testing is dictated by specific underlying cardiovascular disease and nature of the planned operation. See Fig. 114-1 for clinical predictors of increased perioperative risk of MI, CHF, or death and approaches to preoperative evaluation.

SPECIFIC CARDIAC CONDITIONS

CORONARY ARTERY DISEASE   Consider postponing purely elective operations for 6 months following an MI. Pts with stable CAD can be evaluated per algorithm in Fig. 114-1. Surgical risk is generally acceptable in pts with class I–II symptoms (e.g., able to climb one flight carrying grocery bags) and in those with low-risk results from noninvasive testing (see Table 122-1 for recommended forms of stress testing). For those with high-risk results (Chap. 122) or very limited functional capacity, consider coronary angiography. Perioperative beta-blocker therapy reduces incidence of coronary events and should be included in medical regimen if no contraindications (Chap. 122).

HEART FAILURE   This is a major predictor of perioperative risk. Regimen of ACE inhibitor and diuretics should be optimized preoperatively to minimize risk of either pulmonary congestion or intravascular volume depletion postoperatively.

ARRHYTHMIAS   These are often markers for underlying CHF, CAD, drug toxicities (e.g., digitalis), or metabolic abnormalities (e.g., hypokalemia,

Table 114-1

Cardiac Risk of Noncardiac Procedures

Risk	Procedure
High (>5%)	Aortic (or other major vascular) operations
	Emergent operation in patient of advanced age
Intermediate (<5%)	Intrathoracic or intraperitoneal procedures
	Carotid endarterectomy
	Orthopedic operations
	Prostate surgery
Low (<1%)	Endoscopy
	Cataract surgery
	Breast procedures
	Superficial skin operations

SOURCE: Modified from KA Eagle et al: Circulation 93:1278, 1996, with permission.

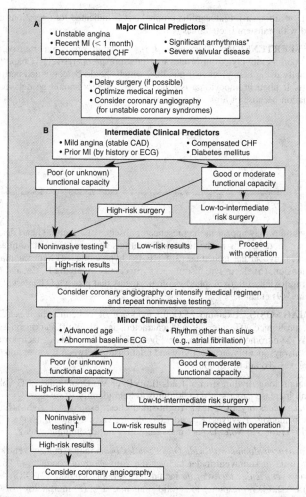

A **Major Clinical Predictors**
- Unstable angina
- Recent MI (< 1 month)
- Decompensated CHF
- Significant arrhythmias*
- Severe valvular disease

↓

- Delay surgery (if possible)
- Optimize medical regimen
- Consider coronary angiography
  (for unstable coronary syndromes)

B **Intermediate Clinical Predictors**
- Mild angina (stable CAD)
- Prior MI (by history or ECG)
- Compensated CHF
- Diabetes mellitus

Poor (or unknown) functional capacity | Good or moderate functional capacity

High-risk surgery | Low-to-intermediate risk surgery

Noninvasive testing† — Low-risk results → Proceed with operation

High-risk results ↓

Consider coronary angiography or intensify medical regimen and repeat noninvasive testing

C **Minor Clinical Predictors**
- Advanced age
- Abnormal baseline ECG
- Rhythm other than sinus (e.g., atrial fibrillation)

Poor (or unknown) functional capacity | Good or moderate functional capacity

High-risk surgery | Low-to-intermediate risk surgery

Noninvasive testing† — Low-risk results → Proceed with operation

High-risk results ↓

Consider coronary angiography

FIGURE 114-1 Approach to preoperative cardiac evaluation. *Significant arrhythmias include: (1) High-grade AV block, (2) symptomatic ventricular arrhythmias, and (3) supraventricular arrhythmias with uncontrolled ventricular rate. †Exercise testing is preferred (treadmill, bicycle, arm ergometry). Perform with echo or nuclear scintigraphy if baseline ST-T waves preclude ECG interpretation. If unable to exercise, consider pharmacologic (e.g., dobutamine or adenosine) test with echo or nuclear imaging, or ambulatory ECG monitoring, if baseline ST-T waves normal. (*Modified from KA Eagle et al: Circulation 93:1278, 1996, with permission.*)

hypomagnesemia), which should be identified and corrected. Indications for antiarrhythmic therapy or pacemakers are same as in nonsurgical situations (Chap. 115). Notably, asymptomatic ventricular premature beats generally do not require suppressive therapy preoperatively.

VALVULAR DISEASES Those portending greatest surgical risk are advanced aortic or mitral stenosis (Chap. 118), which should be repaired, if severe or symptomatic, prior to elective surgery. Ensure adequate ventricular rate control in mitral stenosis with atrial fibrillation (using beta blocker, digoxin, verapamil, or diltiazem). Endocarditis prophylaxis is indicated for operations associated with transient bacteremias (Chap. 80).

HYPERTENSION This carries a risk of labile bp or hypertensive episodes perioperatively. Control elevated pressure preoperatively (Chap. 124), especially using beta blocker if possible, which should be continued perioperatively. If pheochromocytoma is a possibility, surgery should be delayed for evaluation because of high anesthetic risk.

115

ARRHYTHMIAS

Arrhythmias may appear in the presence or absence of structural heart disease; they are more serious in the former. Conditions that provoke arrhythmias include (1) myocardial ischemia, (2) CHF, (3) hypoxemia, (4) hypercapnia, (5) hypotension, (6) electrolyte disturbances (especially involving K, Ca, and Mg), (7) drug toxicity (digoxin, pharmacologic agents that prolong QT interval), (8) caffeine, (9) ethanol.

DIAGNOSIS Examine ECG for evidence of ischemic changes (Chap. 113), prolonged QT interval, and characteristics of Wolff-Parkinson-White (WPW) syndrome (see below). See Fig. 115-1 for diagnosis of tachyarrhythmias; always identify atrial activity and relationship between P waves and QRS complexes. To aid the diagnosis:

- Obtain long rhythm strip of leads II, aVF, or V_1. Double the ECG voltage and increase paper speed to 50 mm/s to help identify P waves.
- Place accessory ECG leads (right-sided chest, esophageal, right-atrial) to help identify P waves. Record ECG during carotid sinus massage (Table 115-1) for 5 s. *Note:* Do not massage both carotids simultaneously.

Tachyarrhythmias with wide QRS complex beats may represent ventricular tachycardia or supraventricular tachycardia with aberrant conduction. Factors favoring *ventricular tachycardia* include (1) AV dissociation, (2) QRS >0.14 s, (3) LAD, (4) no response to carotid sinus massage, (5) morphology of QRS similar to that of previous ventricular premature beats (Table 115-2).

℞ TREATMENT

Tachyarrhythmias (Tables 115-1 and 115-3) Precipitating causes (listed above) should be corrected. If pt is hemodynamically compromised (angina, hypotension, CHF), proceed to immediate cardioversion. *Note:* Do not cardiovert sinus tachycardia; exercise caution if digitalis toxicity is suspected. Initiate drugs as indicated in the tables; follow drug levels and ECG intervals (esp. QRS and QT). Reduce dosage for pts with hepatic and renal dysfunction as indicated in Table 115-3. Drug efficacy is confirmed by ECG (or Holter) monitoring, stress testing, and in special circumstances, invasive electrophysiologic study.

Antiarrhythmic agents all have potential toxic side effects, including *provocation* of ventricular arrhythmias, esp. in pts with LV dysfunction or history of sustained ventricular arrhythmias. Drug-induced QT prolongation and as-

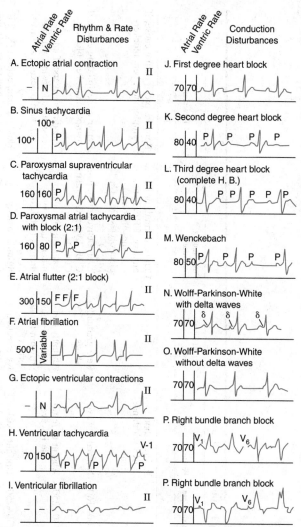

FIGURE 115-1 Tachyarrhythmias. (*Reproduced by BE Sobel, E Braunwald: HPIM-9, p. 1052.*)

sociated torsades de pointes ventricular tachycardia (Table 115-1) is most common with group IA agents; the drug should be discontinued if the QTc interval (QT divided by square root of RR interval) increases by >25%. Antiarrhythmic drugs should be avoided in pts with asymptomatic ventricular arrhythmias after MI, since mortality risk increases.

Chronic Atrial Fibrillation Evaluate potential underlying cause (e.g., thyrotoxicosis, mitral stenosis, excessive ethanol consumption, pulmonary embolism). Pts with risk factors for stroke (e.g., valvular heart disease, hypertension, CAD, CHF, age >75) should receive warfarin anticoagulation (INR 2.0– 3.0; use caution to keep INR < 3.0 in pts >age 75). Substitute

Table 115-1

Clinical and Electrocardiographic Features of Common Arrhythmias

Rhythm	Example (Fig. 115-1)	Atrial Rate	Features	Carotid Sinus Massage	Precipitating Conditions	Initial Treatment
NARROW QRS COMPLEX						
Atrial premature beats	A	—	P wave abnormal; QRS width normal	—	Can be normal; or due to anxiety, CHF, hypoxia, caffeine, abnormal electrolytes (K^+, Ca^{2+}, Mg^{2+})	Remove precipitating cause; if symptomatic: beta blocker
Sinus tachycardia	B	100–160	Normal P wave	Rate gradually slows	Fever, dehydration, pain, CHF, hyperthyroidism, COPD	Remove precipitating cause; if symptomatic: beta blocker
Paroxysmal SVT (reentrant)	C	140–250	Absent or retrograde P wave	Abruptly converts to sinus rhythm (or no effect)	Healthy individuals; preexcitation syndromes (see text)	Vagal maneuvers; if unsuccessful: adenosine, verapamil, beta blocker, cardioversion (150 J)
Paroxysmal atrial tachycardia with block	D	130–250	Upright "peaked" P; 2:1, 3:1, 4:1 block	No effect on atrial rate; block may ↑	Digitalis toxicity	Hold digoxin, correct $[K^+]$; if persists: phenytoin (250 mg IV over 5 min)

Arrhythmia		Rate	ECG features	Carotid massage/vagal response	Associated conditions	Treatment
Atrial flutter	E	250–350	"Sawtooth" flutter waves; 2:1, 4:1 block	↑ Block; ventricular rate ↓	Mitral valve disease, hypertension, pulmonary embolism, pericarditis, postcardiac surgery, hyperthyroidism; obstructive lung disease, EtOH, idiopathic	1. Slow the ventricular rate: beta blocker, verapamil, or digoxin 2. Convert to NSR (after anticoagulation if chronic) with IV Ibutilide or orally with group IC, III, or IA[a] agent; may require electrical cardioversion (flutter: 50 J; fib: 100–200 J). Atrial flutter may respond to rapid atrial pacing, and radio frequency ablation highly effective for common types
Atrial fibrillation	F	>350	No discrete P; irregularly spaced QRS	Ventricular rate ↓		
Multifocal atrial tachycardia		100–220	More than 3 different P wave shapes with varying PR intervals	No effect	Severe respiratory insufficiency	Treat underlying lung disease; verapamil may be used to slow ventricular rate
WIDE QRS COMPLEX						
Ventricular premature beats	G		Fully compensatory pause between normal beats	No effect	Coronary artery disease, myocardial infarction, CHF, hypoxia, hypokalemia, digitalis toxicity, prolonged QT interval (congenital or drugs: quinidine and other antiarrhythmics, tricyclics, phenothiazines)	May not require therapy;[b] use beta blocker or same drugs as ventricular tachycardia.
Ventricular tachycardia	H		QRS rate 100–250; slightly irregular rate	No effect		If unstable: electrical conversion (100 J); otherwise: Acute (IV): procainamide, amiodarone, lidocaine; chronic (PO) prevention: group IA, IB, IC, III drugs[a]

(continued)

559

Table 115-1 *(Continued)*

Clinical and Electrocardiographic Features of Common Arrhythmias

Rhythm	Example (Fig. 115-1)	Atrial Rate	Features	Carotid Sinus Massage	Precipitating Conditions	Initial Treatment
Ventricular fibrillation	1		Erratic electrical activity only	No effect	Prolonged QT interval (congenital or drugs: quinidine and other antiarrhythmics, tricyclics, phenothiazines)	Immediate defibrillation (200–400 J)
Torsades de pointes			Ventricular tachycardia with sinusoidal oscillations of QRS height	No effect	Etiologies of the respective supraventricular rhythms listed above; atrial fibrillation with rapid, wide QRS may be due to preexcitation (WPW)	IV magnesium (1–2 g bolus); overdrive pacing; lidocaine; isoproterenol (unless CAD present); lidocaine. Drugs that prolong QT interval (e.g., quinidine) are contraindicated.
Supraventricular tachycardias with aberrant ventricular conduction			P wave typical of the supraventricular rhythm; wide QRS complex due to conduction through partially refractory pathways			Same as treatment of respective supraventricular rhythm; if ventricular rate rapid (>200), treat as WPW (see text)

a Antiarrhythmic drug groups listed in Table 115–3.
b Indications for treating VPCs listed in Chap. 121.

Table 115-2

Wide Complex Tachycardia

ECG CRITERIA THAT FAVOR VENTRICULAR TACHYCARDIA

1. AV dissociation
2. QRS width: >0.14 s with RBBB configuration
                >0.16 s with LBBB configuration
3. QRS axis: Left axis deviation with RBBB morphology
                Extreme left axis deviation (northwest axis) with LBBB morphology
4. Concordance of QRS in precordial leads
5. Morphologic patterns of the QRS complex
        RBBB: Mono- or biphasic complex in V_1
                RS (*only with left axis deviation*) or QS in V_6

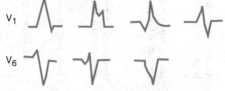

        LBBB: Broad R wave in V_1 or V_2 ≥0.04 s
                Onset of QRS to nadir of S wave in V_1 or V_2 of ≥0.07 s
                Notched downslope of S wave in V_1 or V_2
                Q wave in V_6

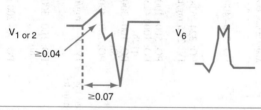

NOTE: AV, atrioventricular; BBB, bundle branch block.

aspirin 325 mg/d for pts without these risk factors or if contraindication to warfarin exists. Control ventricular rate (60–80 bpm at rest, <100 bpm with mild exercise) with beta blocker, digoxin, or calcium channel blocker (verapamil, diltiazem). Consider cardioversion (after ≥3 weeks therapeutic anticoagulation or if no evidence of left atrial thrombus by transesophageal echo), especially if symptomatic despite rate control: use group IA, IC, or III agent (usually initiate with inpatient monitoring), followed, within a few days, by electrical cardioversion (usually 100–200 J). Type IC (Table 115-3) drugs are preferred in pts without structural heart disease and type III drugs are recommended in presence of left ventricular dysfunction or CAD (Fig. 115-2). Anticoagulation should be continued for an additional 3 weeks after successful cardioversion.

Preexcitation Syndrome (WPW)

Conduction occurs through an accessory pathway between atria and ventricles. Baseline ECG typically shows a short PR interval and slurred upstroke of the

Table 115-3

Antiarrhythmic Drugs

Drug	Loading Dose	Maintenance Dose	Side Effects	Excretion
Group IA				
Quinidine sulfate		PO: 200–400 mg q6h	Diarrhea, tinnitus, QT prolongation, hypotension, anemia, thrombocytopenia	Hepatic
Quinidine gluconate		PO: 324–628 mg q8h		Hepatic
Procainamide	IV: 500–1000 mg	IV: 2–5 mg/min	Nausea, lupus-like syndrome, agranulocytosis, QT prolongation	Renal and hepatic
		PO: 500–1000 mg q4h		
Sustained-release:		PO: 1000–2500 mg q12h		
Disopyramide		PO: 100–300 mg q6–8h	Myocardial depression, AV block, QT prolongation anticholinergic effects	Renal and hepatic
Sustained-release:		PO: 200–400 mg q12h		
Group IB				
Lidocaine	IV: 1 mg/kg bolus followed by 0.5 mg/kg bolus q8–10 min to total 3 mg/kg	IV: 1–4 mg/min	Confusion, seizures, respiratory arrest	Hepatic
Mexiletine		PO: 100–300 mg q6–8h	Nausea, tremor, gait disturbance	Hepatic
Group IC				
Flecainide		PO: 50–200 mg q12h	Nausea, exacerbation of ventricular arrhythmia, prolongation of PR and QRS intervals	Hepatic and renal
Propafenone		PO: 150–300 mg q8h		Hepatic and renal

562

Drug	IV	PO / Maintenance	Adverse effects	Elimination
Group II				
Metoprolol	IV: 5–10 mg q5min × 3	PO: 25–100 mg bid	CHF, bradycardia, AV block, bronchospasm	Hepatic
Group III				
Amiodarone	PO: 800–1600 mg qd × 1–2 weeks, then 400–600 mg/d × 3 weeks; IV: 150 mg over 10 min	PO: 200–400 mg qd; IV: 1 mg/min × 6 h, then 0.5 mg/min	Thyroid abnormalities, pulmonary fibrosis, hepatitis, corneal microdeposits, bluish skin, QT prolongation	—
Ibutilide	IV (≥60 kg): 1 mg over 10 min, can repeat after 10 min	—	Torsades de pointes, hypotension, nausea	Hepatic
Dofetilide		PO: 125–500 µg mcg bid	Torsades de pointes, headache, dizziness	Renal
Bretylium	IV: 5–10 mg/kg	IV: 0.5–2.0 mg/min	Hypertension, orthostatic hypotension, nausea, parotid pain	Renal
Sotalol		PO: 80–320 mg q12h	Fatigue, bradycardia, exacerbation of ventricular arrhythmia	Renal
Group IV				
Verapamil	IV: 2.5–10 mg	PO: 120–480 mg qd	AV block, CHF, hypotension, constipation	Hepatic
Diltiazem	IV: 0.25 mg/kg over 2 min; can repeat with 0.35 mg/kg after 15 min	IV: 5–15 mg/h; PO: 120–360 mg/d	—	—
Other				
Digoxin	IV, PO: 0.75–1.5 mg over 24 h	IV, PO: 0.125–0.25 mg qd	Nausea, AV block, ventricular and supraventricular arrhythmias	Renal
Adenosine	IV: 6-mg bolus; if no effect then 12-mg bolus	—	Transient hypotension or atrial standstill	—

563

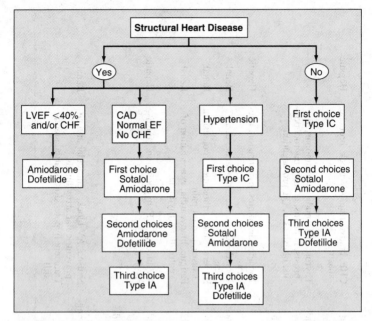

FIGURE 115-2 Recommendations for the selection of antiarrhythmic medications to prevent the recurrence of atrial fibrillation. See Table 115-3 for definition of types IA and IC drugs. An atrioventricular nodal blocking agent (i.e., beta blocker, calcium channel blocker, or digoxin) should be added to all type IC and IA agents as well as to dofetilide. LVEF, left ventricular ejection fraction; CHF, congestive heart failure; CAD, coronary artery disease; EF, ejection fraction.

QRS ("delta" wave) (Fig. 115-1*N*). Associated tachyarrhythmias are of two types:

- *Narrow QRS complex tachycardia* (antegrade conduction through AV node): usually paroxysmal supraventricular tachycardia. Treat cautiously with IV verapamil, digoxin, or propranolol (Table 115-3).
- *Wide QRS complex tachycardia* (antegrade conduction through accessory pathway): often associated with AF with a very *rapid* (>250/min) ventricular rate (which may degenerate into VF). If hemodynamically compromised, immediate cardioversion is indicated; otherwise, treat with IV procainamide, *not* digoxin, beta blocker, or verapamil.

AV Block

FIRST DEGREE (See Fig. 115-1*J*) Prolonged, constant PR interval (>0.20 s). May be normal or secondary to increased vagal tone or digitalis; no treatment required.

SECOND DEGREE *Mobitz I (Wenckebach)* (See Fig. 115-1*M*) Narrow QRS, progressive increase in PR interval until a ventricular beat is dropped, then sequence is repeated. Seen with drug intoxication (digitalis, beta blockers), increased vagal tone, inferior MI. Usually transient, no therapy required; if symptomatic, use atropine (0.6 mg IV, repeated × 3–4) or temporary pacemaker.

Mobitz II (See Fig. 115-1*K*) Fixed PR interval with occasional dropped beats, in 2:1, 3:1, or 4:1 pattern; the QRS complex is usually wide. Seen with MI or degenerative conduction system disease; a dangerous rhythm—may progress suddenly to complete AV block; pacemaker is indicated.

THIRD DEGREE (COMPLETE AV BLOCK) (See Fig. 115-1*L*) Atrial activity is not transmitted to ventricles; atria and ventricles contract independently. Seen with MI, digitalis toxicity, or degenerative conduction system disease. Permanent pacemaker is indicated, except when associated transiently with inferior MI or in asymptomatic congenital heart block.

For a more detailed discussion, see Josephson ME, Zimetbaum P: Bradyarrhythmias, Chap. 229, p. 1283; and The Tachyarrhythmias, Chap. 230, p. 1292, in HPIM-15.

116

CONGESTIVE HEART FAILURE AND COR PULMONALE

HEART FAILURE

DEFINITION Heart failure is a condition in which the heart is unable to pump sufficient blood for metabolizing tissues or can do so only from an abnormally elevated filling pressure. It is important to identify the *underlying* nature of the cardiac disease and the factors that precipitate acute CHF.

UNDERLYING CARDIAC DISEASE Includes states that depress ventricular function (coronary artery disease, hypertension, dilated cardiomyopathy, valvular disease, congenital heart disease) and states that restrict ventricular filling (mitral stenosis, restrictive cardiomyopathy, pericardial disease).

ACUTE PRECIPITATING FACTORS Include (1) increased Na intake, (2) noncompliance with anti-CHF medications, (3) acute MI (may be silent), (4) exacerbation of hypertension, (5) acute arrhythmias, (6) infections and/or fever, (7) pulmonary embolism, (8) anemia, (9) thyrotoxicosis, (10) pregnancy, and (11) acute myocarditis or infective endocarditis.

SYMPTOMS Due to inadequate perfusion of peripheral tissues (fatigue, dyspnea) and elevated intracardiac filling pressures (orthopnea, paroxysmal nocturnal dyspnea, peripheral edema).

PHYSICAL EXAMINATION Jugular venous distention, S_3, pulmonary congestion (rales, dullness over pleural effusion, peripheral edema, hepatomegaly, and ascites).

LABORATORY CXR can reveal cardiomegaly, pulmonary vascular redistribution, Kerley B lines, pleural effusions. Left ventricular contraction can be assessed by *echocardiography* or *radionuclide ventriculography*. In addition, echo can identify underlying valvular, pericardial, or congenital heart disease, as well as regional wall motion abnormalities typical of coronary artery disease.

CONDITIONS THAT MIMIC CHF *Pulmonary Disease* Chronic bronchitis, emphysema, and asthma (Chaps. 128 and 130); look for sputum production and abnormalities on CXR and pulmonary function tests.

Other Causes of Peripheral Edema Liver disease, varicose veins, and cyclic edema, none of which results in jugular venous distention. Edema due to renal dysfunction is often accompanied by elevated serum creatinine and abnormal urinalysis (Chap. 17).

 TREATMENT

Aimed at symptomatic relief, removal of precipitating factors, and control of underlying cardiac disease. Overview of treatment shown in Table 116-1; notably, ACE inhibitor should be begun early, even in pts with asymptomatic LV dysfunction. Once symptoms develop:

1. *Decrease cardiac workload:* Reduce physical activity; include periods of bed rest. Prevent deep venous thrombosis of immobile pts with heparin 5000 U SC bid.

Table 116-1

Therapy for Heart Failure

1. General measures
   a. Restrict salt intake
   b. Avoid antiarrhythmics for asymptomatic arrhythmias
   c. Avoid NSAIDs
   d. Immunize against influenza and pneumococcal pneumonia
2. Diuretics
   a. Use in volume-overloaded pts to achieve normal JVP and relief of edema
   b. Weigh daily to adjust dose
   c. For diuretic resistance, administer IV or use 2 diuretics in combination (e.g., furosemide plus metolazone)
   d. Low-dose dopamine to enhance renal flow
3. ACE inhibitors
   a. For all patients with LV systolic heart failure or asymptomatic LV dysfunction
   b. Contraindications: Serum K^+ > 5.5, advanced renal failure (e.g., creatinine > 3 mg/dL), bilateral renal artery stenosis, pregnancy
4. Beta blockers
   a. For patients with class II–III heart failure, combined with ACE inhibitor and diuretics
   b. Contraindications: Bronchospasm, symptomatic bradycardia or advanced heart block, unstable heart failure or class IV symptoms
5. Digitalis
   a. For persistently symptomatic pts with systolic heart failure (especially if atrial fibrillation present) added to ACE inhibitor, diuretics, beta blocker
6. Other measures
   a. Consider angiotensin receptor blocker or combination of hydralazine plus isosorbide dinitrate if not tolerant of ACE inhibitor
   b. Consider spironolactone in class IV heart failure

SOURCE: Modified from E Braunwald: HPIM-15, p. 1318

2. *Control excess fluid retention:* (a) *Dietary sodium restriction* (eliminate salty foods, e.g., potato chips, canned soups, bacon, salt added at table); more stringent requirements (<2 g NaCl/d) in advanced CHF. If dilutional hyponatremia present, restrict fluid intake (<1000 mL/d). (b) *Diuretics* (see Table 17-1): *Loop diuretics* (e.g., furosemide 20–120 mg/d PO or IV) are most potent and unlike thiazides remain effective when GFR <25 mL/min. Combine loop diuretic with thiazide or metolazone for augmented effect. Potassium-sparing diuretics are useful adjunct to reduce potassium loss; should be used cautiously when combined with ACE inhibitor to avoid hyperkalemia.

During diuresis, obtain daily weights aiming for loss of 1–1.5 kg/d.

3. *Vasodilators* (Table 116-2): ACE inhibitors recommended as standard initial CHF therapy. ACE inhibitors are mixed (arterial and venous) dilators and are particularly effective and well tolerated. They, and to a lesser extent the combination of hydralazine plus nitrates, have been shown to prolong life in pts with symptomatic CHF. ACE inhibitors also have been shown to delay the onset of CHF in pts with asymptomatic LV dysfunction and to lower mortality when begun soon after acute MI. Vasodilators may result in significant hypotension in pts who are volume depleted, so start at lowest dosage (e.g., captopril 6.25 mg PO tid); pt should remain supine for 2–4 h after the initial doses. Angiotensin receptor blocker (Table 124-4) may be substituted if pt is intolerant of ACE inhibitor (e.g., cough, angioedema).

In sicker, hospitalized pts, IV vasodilator therapy (Table 116-2) is monitored by placement of a pulmonary artery catheter and indwelling arterial line. Nitroprusside is a potent mixed vasodilator for pts with markedly elevated SVR. It is metabolized to thiocyanate, then excreted via the kidneys. To avoid thiocyanate toxicity (seizures, altered mental status, nausea), follow thiocyanate levels in pts with renal failure or if administered for more than 2 d.

Table 116-2

Vasodilators for Treatment of CHF

Drug and Site of Action[a]	Dose	Adverse Effects
IV AGENTS		
Nitroprusside, V = A	0.5–10 (μg/kg)/min	Thiocyanate toxicity (blurred vision, tinnitus, delirium) can occur during prolonged therapy or in renal failure
Nitroglycerin, V > A	10 μg/min–10 (μg/kg)/min	May cause hypotension if LV filling pressure is low
ORAL AGENTS		
ACE inhibitors, V = A		Angioedema, cough, hyperkalemia, leukopenia. Reduce diuretic dosage to prevent azotemia
Captopril	6.25–50 mg tid	
Enalapril	2.5–10 mg bid	
Lisinopril	5–40 mg tid	
Hydralazine,[b] A	50–200 mg tid	May cause drug-induced lupus or angina due to reflex tachycardia
Nitrates,[b] V (e.g., isosorbide dinitrate)	10–40 mg tid	Drug tolerance may develop with more frequent administration

[a] V, venous; A, arterial.
[b] Hydralazine and nitrates are often used together to achieve combined venous and arterial effect.

4. *Beta blockers* administered in gradually augmented dosage improve symptoms and prolong survival in patients with moderate (NYHA class II–III) heart failure. Begin at low dosage and increase gradually [e.g., carvedilol 3.125 mg bid, double q2 weeks as tolerated to maximum of 25 mg bid (for weight < 85 kg) or 50 mg bid (weight > 85 kg)].

5. *Digoxin* is useful in heart failure due to (a) marked systolic dysfunction (LV dilatation, low ejection fraction, S_3) and (b) heart failure associated with atrial fibrillation and rapid ventricular rate. Unlike ACE inhibitors, digoxin does not prolong survival in heart failure pts. Not indicated in CHF due to pericardial disease, restrictive cardiomyopathy, or mitral stenosis (unless atrial fibrillation is present). Digoxin is contraindicated in hypertrophic cardiomyopathy and in pts with AV conduction blocks.

Digoxin loading dose is administered over 24 h (0.5 mg PO/IV, followed by 0.25 mg q6h to achieve total of 1.0–1.5 mg). Subsequent dose (0.125–0.25 mg qd) depends on age, weight, and renal function and is guided by measurement of serum digoxin level. The addition of quinidine increases serum digoxin level; therefore, digoxin dosage should be halved. Verapamil, amiodarone, propafenone, and spironolactone also increase serum digoxin level.

Digitalis toxicity may be precipitated by hypokalemia, hypoxemia, hypercalcemia, hypomagnesemia, hypothyroidism, or myocardial ischemia. Early signs of toxicity include anorexia, nausea, and lethargy. *Cardiac toxicity* includes ventricular extrasystoles and ventricular tachycardia and fibrillation; atrial tachycardia with block; sinus arrest and sinoatrial block; all degrees of AV block. *Chronic* digitalis intoxication may cause cachexia, gynecomastia, "yellow" vision, or confusion. At first sign of digitalis toxicity, discontinue the drug; maintain serum K concentration between 4.0 and 5.0 mmol/L. Bradyarrhythmias and AV block may respond to atropine (0.6 mg IV); otherwise, a temporary pacemaker may be required. Digitalis-induced ventricular arrhythmias are treated with lidocaine or phenytoin (Chap. 115). Antidigoxin antibodies are available for massive overdose.

6. The aldosterone antagonist *spironolactone*, 25 mg/d, added to standard therapy in patients with advanced heart failure has been shown to reduce mortality. Its diuretic properties may also be beneficial, and it should be considered in patients with class IV heart failure symptoms.

7. *IV sympathomimetic amines* (Table 121-2) are administered to hospitalized pts for refractory symptoms or acute exacerbation of CHF. They are contraindicated in hypertrophic cardiomyopathy. *Dobutamine* [2.5–10 (µg/kg)/min], the preferred agent, augments cardiac output without significant peripheral vasoconstriction or tachycardia. *Dopamine* at low dosage [1–5 (µg/kg)/min] facilitates diuresis; at higher dosage [5–10(µg/kg)/min] positive inotropic effects predominate; peripheral vasoconstriction is greatest at dosage greater than 10 (µg/kg)/min. *Amrinone* [5–10 (µg/kg)/min after a 0.75 mg/kg bolus] is a nonsympathetic positive inotrope and vasodilator. Vasodilators and inotropic agents may be used together for additive effect.

Patients with severe refractory CHF with <6 months expected survival, who meet stringent criteria, may be candidates for cardiac transplantation.

COR PULMONALE

Right ventricular enlargement resulting from *primary* lung disease; leads to RV hypertrophy and eventually to RV failure. Etiologies include the following:

- *Pulmonary parenchymal or airway disease.* Chronic obstructive lung disease (COPD), interstitial lung diseases, bronchiectasis, cystic fibrosis (Chaps. 130 and 133).
- *Pulmonary vascular disease.* Recurrent pulmonary emboli, primary pulmonary hypertension (PHT), vasculitis, sickle cell anemia.
- *Inadequate mechanical ventilation.* Kyphoscoliosis, neuromuscular disorders, marked obesity, sleep apnea.

SYMPTOMS   Depend on underlying disorder but include dyspnea, cough, fatigue, and sputum production (in parenchymal diseases).

PHYSICAL EXAMINATION   Tachypnea, cyanosis, clubbing are common. RV impulse along left sternal border, loud P_2, right-sided S_4. If RV failure develops, elevated jugular venous pressure, hepatomegaly with ascites, pedal edema.

LABORATORY   *ECG*   RV hypertrophy and RA enlargement (Chap. 113); tachyarrhythmias are common.

CXR   RV and pulmonary artery enlargement; if PHT present, tapering of the pulmonary artery branches. Pulmonary function tests and ABGs characterize intrinsic pulmonary disease.

Echocardiogram   RV hypertrophy; LV function typically normal. RV systolic pressure can be estimated from Doppler measurement of tricuspid regurgitant flow. If imaging is difficult because of air in distended lungs, RV volume and wall thickness can be evaluated by MRI. If pulmonary emboli suspected, obtain radionuclide lung scan.

R͟x͟ TREATMENT

Aimed at underlying pulmonary disease and may include bronchodilators, antibiotics, and oxygen administration. If RV failure is present, treat as CHF, instituting low-sodium diet and diuretics; digoxin must be administered cautiously (toxicity increased due to hypoxemia, hypercapnia, acidosis). Loop diuretics must also be used with care to prevent significant metabolic alkalosis that blunts respiratory drive. Supraventricular tachyarrhythmias are common and treated with digoxin or verapamil (*not* beta blockers). Chronic anticoagulation with warfarin is indicated when pulmonary hypertension is accompanied by RV failure. In selected pts, inhalation of nitric oxide and infusion of prostacyclin reduce pulmonary hypertension and are undergoing evaluation for this purpose.

For a more detailed discussion, see Braunwald E: Heart Failure, Chap. 232, p. 1318; and Cor Pulmonale, Chap. 237, p. 1355, in HPIM-15.

117

CONGENITAL HEART DISEASE IN THE ADULT

ATRIAL SEPTAL DEFECT (ASD)

HISTORY   Usually asymptomatic until third or fourth decades, when exertional dyspnea, fatigue, and palpitations may develop. Symptoms often associated with pulmonary hypertension (see below).

PHYSICAL EXAMINATION   Parasternal RV lift, wide fixed splitting of S_2, systolic flow murmur along sternal border, diastolic flow rumble across tricuspid valve, prominent jugular venous v wave.

ECG   Incomplete RBBB. LAD common with ostium primum (lower septal) defect.

CXR   Increased pulmonary vascular markings, prominence of RV and main pulmonary artery (LA enlargement *not* usually present).

ECHOCARDIOGRAM   RA and RV enlargement; Doppler shows abnormal turbulent transatrial flow. Echo contrast (agitated saline) injection into peripheral vein may visualize transatrial shunt. Transesophageal echo is indicated if transthoracic echo is ambiguous.

 TREATMENT

In the absence of contraindications an ASD with pulmonary-to-systemic flow ratio (PF:SF) >1.5:1.0 should be surgically repaired. Surgery is contraindicated with significant pulmonary hypertension and PF:SF <1.2:1.0. Medical management includes antiarrhythmic therapy for associated atrial fibrillation or supraventricular tachycardia (Chap. 115) and standard therapy for symptoms of CHF (Chap. 116).

VENTRICULAR SEPTAL DEFECT (VSD)
Congenital VSDs may close spontaneously during childhood. Symptoms relate to size of the defect and pulmonary vascular resistance.

HISTORY   CHF in infancy. Adults may be asymptomatic or develop fatigue and reduced exercise tolerance.

PHYSICAL EXAMINATION   Systolic thrill and holosystolic murmur at lower left sternal border, loud P_2, S_3; flow murmur across mitral valve.

ECG   Normal with small defects. Large shunts result in LA and LV enlargement.

CXR   Enlargement of main pulmonary artery, LA, and LV, with increased pulmonary vascular markings.

ECHOCARDIOGRAM   LA and LV enlargement; defect may be visualized. Color Doppler usually demonstrates flow across the defect.

 TREATMENT

Fatigue and mild dyspnea are treated with diuretics and afterload reduction (Chap. 116). Surgical closure is indicated if PF:SF > 1.5:1. Antibiotic prophylaxis for endocarditis is important.

PATENT DUCTUS ARTERIOSUS (PDA)
Abnormal communication between the descending aorta and pulmonary artery; associated with birth at high altitudes and maternal rubella.

HISTORY   Asymptomatic or dyspnea on exertion and fatigue.

PHYSICAL EXAMINATION   Hyperactive LV impulse; loud systolic-diastolic "machinery" murmur at upper left sternal border. If pulmonary hypertension develops, diastolic component of the murmur may disappear.

ECG LV hypertrophy is common; RV hypertrophy with pulmonary hypertension.

CXR Increased pulmonary vascular markings; enlarged main pulmonary artery, ascending aorta, LV; occasional calcification of ductus.

ECHOCARDIOGRAPHY Hyperdynamic, enlarged LV; the PDA can often be visualized on two-dimensional echo; Doppler demonstrates abnormal flow contained within it.

 TREATMENT

In absence of pulmonary hypertension, PDA should be ligated to prevent infective endocarditis, LV dysfunction, and pulmonary hypertension. Transcatheter closure may be possible in selected pts.

PROGRESSION TO PULMONARY HYPERTENSION (PHT)

Pts with significant, uncorrected ASD, VSD, or PDA may develop progressive, irreversible PHT with shunting of desaturated blood into the arterial circulation (right-to-left shunting). Fatigue, light-headedness, and chest pain due to RV ischemia are common, accompanied by cyanosis, clubbing of digits, loud P_2, murmur of pulmonary valve regurgitation, and signs of RV failure. ECG and echocardiogram show RV hypertrophy. Surgical correction of congenital defects contraindicated with severe PHT and right-to-left shunting.

PULMONIC STENOSIS (PS)

A transpulmonary valve gradient <50 mmHg rarely causes symptoms, and progression tends not to occur. Higher gradients result in dyspnea, fatigue, light-headedness, chest pain (RV ischemia).

PHYSICAL EXAMINATION Shows jugular venous distention with prominent *a* wave, RV parasternal impulse, wide splitting of S_2 with soft P_2, ejection click followed by "diamond-shaped" systolic murmur at upper left sternal border, S_4.

ECG RA and RV enlargement in advanced PS.

CXR Often shows poststenotic dilatation of the pulmonary artery and RV enlargement.

ECHOCARDIOGRAPHY RV hypertrophy and "doming" of the pulmonic valve. Doppler accurately measures transvalvular gradient.

 TREATMENT

Prophylaxis for infective endocarditis is mandatory. Moderate or severe stenosis (gradient >50 mmHg) requires surgical (or balloon) valvuloplasty.

COARCTATION OF THE AORTA

Aortic constriction just distal to the origin of the left subclavian artery is a surgically correctable form of hypertension (Chap. 124). Usually asymptomatic, but it may cause headache, fatigue, or claudication of lower extremities.

PHYSICAL EXAMINATION Hypertension in upper extremities; delayed femoral pulses with decreased pressure in lower extremities. Pulsatile collateral arteries can be palpated in the intercostal spaces. Systolic (and sometimes diastolic) murmur is best heard over the mid-upper back.

ECG   LV hypertrophy.

CXR   Notching of the ribs due to collateral arteries; "figure 3" appearance of distal aortic arch.

 TREATMENT

Surgical correction, although hypertension may persist. Antibiotic prophylaxis against endocarditis is required even after correction. Recoarctation after surgical repair may be amenable to percutaneous balloon dilatation.

For a more detailed discussion, see Friedman WF, Child JS: Congenital Heart Disease in the Adult, Chap. 234, p. 1331, HPIM-15.

118

VALVULAR HEART DISEASE

MITRAL STENOSIS (MS)

ETIOLOGY   Most commonly rheumatic, although history of acute rheumatic fever is now uncommon; congenital MS is an uncommon cause, observed primarily in infants.

HISTORY   Symptoms most commonly begin in the fourth decade, but MS often causes severe disability by age 20 in economically deprived areas. Principal symptoms are dyspnea and pulmonary edema precipitated by exertion, excitement, fever, anemia, paroxysmal tachycardia, pregnancy, sexual intercourse, etc.

PHYSICAL EXAMINATION   Right ventricular lift; palpable S_1; opening snap (OS) follows A_2 by 0.06 to 0.12 s; $OS-A_2$ interval inversely proportional to severity of obstruction. Diastolic rumbling murmur with presystolic accentuation in sinus rhythm. Duration of murmur correlates with severity of obstruction.

COMPLICATIONS   Hemoptysis, pulmonary embolism, pulmonary infection, systemic embolization; endocarditis is *uncommon* in pure MS.

LABORATORY   *ECG*   Typically shows atrial fibrillation (AF) or left atrial (LA) enlargement when sinus rhythm is present. Right-axis deviation and RV hypertrophy in the presence of pulmonary hypertension.

CXR   Shows LA and RV enlargement and Kerley B lines.

ECHOCARDIOGRAM   Most useful noninvasive test; shows inadequate separation, calcification and thickening of valve leaflets, and LA enlargement.

Doppler echocardiogram allows estimation of transvalvular gradient and mitral valve area (Chap. 113).

℞ **TREATMENT**

(See Fig. 118-1) Pts should receive prophylaxis for rheumatic fever (penicillin) and infective endocarditis (Chap. 80). In the presence of dyspnea, medical therapy for heart failure; digitalis, beta blockers, or verapamil to slow ventricular rate in AF; diuretics, and sodium restriction. Anticoagulants for pts with AF and/or history of systemic and pulmonic emboli. Mitral valvotomy in the presence of symptoms and mitral orifice ≤ approximately 1.6 cm². In uncomplicated MS, percutaneous balloon valvuloplasty is the procedure of choice; if not feasible, then open surgical valvotomy.

MITRAL REGURGITATION (MR)

ETIOLOGY Rheumatic heart disease in approximately 33%. Other causes: mitral valve prolapse, ischemic heart disease with papillary muscle dysfunction, LV dilatation of any cause, mitral annular calcification, hypertrophic cardiomyopathy, infective endocarditis, congenital.

CLINICAL MANIFESTATIONS Fatigue, weakness, and exertional dyspnea. Physical examination: sharp upstroke of arterial pulse, LV lift, S_1 diminished: wide splitting of S_2; S_3; loud holosystolic murmur and often a brief early-mid-diastolic murmur.

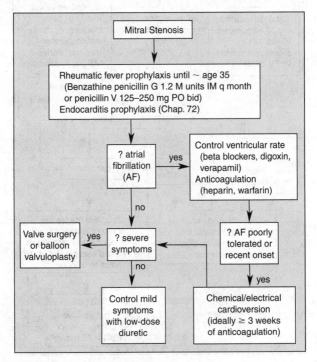

FIGURE 118-1 Management of mitral stenosis.

ECHOCARDIOGRAM   Enlarged LA, hyperdynamic LV; Doppler echocardiogram helpful in diagnosing and assessing severity of MR.

 TREATMENT

(See Fig. 118-2) As for heart failure (Chap. 116), including diuretics and digoxin. Afterload reduction (ACE inhibitors, hydralazine, or IV nitroprusside) decreases the degree of regurgitation, increases forward cardiac output, and improves symptomatology. Endocarditis prophylaxis is indicated, as is anticoagulation in the presence of atrial fibrillation. Surgical treatment, either valve repair or replacement, is indicated in the presence of symptoms or evidence of progressive LV dysfunction (LVEF < 60% or end-systolic LV diameter by echo >45 mm/m²). Operation should be carried out *before* development of severe chronic heart failure.

MITRAL VALVE PROLAPSE (MVP)

ETIOLOGY   Most commonly idiopathic; ?familial; may accompany rheumatic fever, ischemic heart disease, atrial septal defect, the Marfan syndrome.

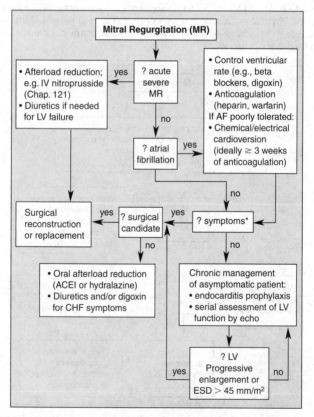

FIGURE 118-2   Management of advanced mitral regurgitation. *Including class II; ACEI, angiotensin converting-enzyme inhibitors; ESD, end-systolic diameter.

PATHOLOGY Redundant mitral valve tissue with myxedematous degeneration and elongated chordae tendineae.

CLINICAL MANIFESTATIONS More common in females. Most pts are asymptomatic and remain so. Most common symptoms are atypical chest pain and a variety of supraventricular and ventricular arrhythmias. Most important complication is severe MR resulting in LV failure. Rarely, systemic emboli from platelet-fibrin deposits on valve. Sudden death is a *very rare* complication.

PHYSICAL EXAMINATION Mid or late systolic click(s) followed by late systolic murmur; exaggeration by Valsalva maneuver, reduced by squatting and isometric exercise (Chap. 112).

ECHOCARDIOGRAM Shows posterior displacement of posterior (occasionally anterior) mitral leaflet late in systole.

℞ TREATMENT

Asymptomatic pts should be reassured, but if systolic murmur is present and/or typical echocardiographic findings with significant MR, prophylaxis for infective endocarditis is indicated. Valve repair or replacement for pts with severe mitral regurgitation; anticoagulants for pts with history of embolization.

AORTIC STENOSIS (AS)

ETIOLOGY Often congenital; rheumatic AS is usually associated with rheumatic mitral valve disease. Idiopathic, calcific AS is a degenerative disorder common in the elderly and usually mild.

SYMPTOMS Dyspnea, angina, and syncope are cardinal symptoms; they occur late, after years of obstruction.

PHYSICAL EXAMINATION Weak and delayed arterial pulses with carotid thrill. Double apical impulse; A_2 soft or absent; S_4 common. Diamond-shaped systolic murmur ≥grade 3/6, often with systolic thrill.

LABORATORY *ECG and CXR* Often show LV hypertrophy, but not useful for predicting gradient.

ECHOCARDIOGRAM Shows thickening of LV wall, calcification and thickening of aortic valve cusps. Dilatation and reduced contraction of LV indicate poor prognosis. Doppler useful for estimating gradient and calculating valve area.

℞ TREATMENT

Avoid strenuous activity in severe AS, even in asymptomatic phase. Treat heart failure in standard fashion (Chap. 116), but *avoid afterload reduction.* Valve replacement is indicated in adults with symptoms resulting from AS and hemodynamic evidence of severe obstruction. Operation should be carried out *before* frank failure has developed.

AORTIC REGURGITATION (AR)

ETIOLOGY Rheumatic in 70%; also may be due to infective endocarditis, syphilis, aortic dissection, or aortic dilatation due to cystic medial necrosis; three-fourths of pts are males.

CLINICAL MANIFESTATIONS Exertional dyspnea and awareness of heart beat, angina pectoris, and signs of LV failure. Wide pulse pressure, waterhammer pulse, capillary pulsations (Quincke's sign), A_2 soft or absent, S_3 common. Blowing, decrescendo diastolic murmur along left sternal border (along right sternal border with aortic dilatation). May be accompanied by systolic murmur of augmented blood flow.

LABORATORY *ECG and CXR* LV enlargement.

ECHOCARDIOGRAM Increased excursion of posterior LV wall, LA enlargement, LV enlargement, high-frequency diastolic fluttering of mitral valve. Doppler studies useful in detection and quantification of AR.

 TREATMENT

Standard therapy for LV failure (Chap. 116). Surgical valve replacement should be carried out in pts with severe AR when symptoms develop or in asymptomatic pts with LV dysfunction (LV ejection fraction <55%, LV end-systolic volume >55 mL/m², or end-systolic diameter >55 mm) by echocardiography.

TRICUSPID STENOSIS (TS)

ETIOLOGY Usually rheumatic; most common in females; almost invariably associated with MS.

CLINICAL MANIFESTATIONS Hepatomegaly, ascites, edema, jaundice, jugular venous distention with slow γ descent (Chap. 112). Diastolic rumbling murmur along left sternal border increased by inspiration with loud presystolic component. Right atrial and superior vena caval enlargement on x-ray.

 TREATMENT

In severe TS, surgical relief is indicated and usually requires valve replacement.

TRICUSPID REGURGITATION (TR)

ETIOLOGY Usually functional and secondary to marked RV dilatation of any cause and often associated with pulmonary hypertension.

CLINICAL MANIFESTATIONS Severe RV failure, with edema, hepatomegaly, and prominent *v* waves in jugular venous pulse with rapid *y* descent (Chap. 112). Systolic murmur along sternal edge is increased by inspiration.

 TREATMENT

Intensive diuretic therapy. In severe cases (in absence of severe pulmonary hypertension), surgical treatment consists of tricuspid annuloplasty or valve replacement.

For a more detailed discussion, see Braunwald E: Valvular Heart Disease, Chap. 236, p. 1343, in HPIM-15.

119

CARDIOMYOPATHIES AND MYOCARDITIS

DILATED CARDIOMYOPATHY (CMP)

Symmetrically dilated left ventricle (LV), with poor systolic contractile function; right ventricle (RV) commonly involved.

ETIOLOGY Previous myocarditis or "idiopathic" most common; also toxins (ethanol, doxorubicin), connective tissue disorders, muscular dystrophies, "peripartum." Severe coronary disease/infarctions or chronic aortic/mitral regurgitation may behave similarly.

SYMPTOMS Congestive heart failure (Chap. 116); tachyarrhythmias and peripheral emboli from LV mural thrombus occur.

PHYSICAL EXAMINATION Jugular venous distention (JVD), rales, diffuse and dyskinetic LV apex, S_3, hepatomegaly, peripheral edema; murmurs of mitral and tricuspid regurgitation are common.

LABORATORY *ECG* Left bundle branch block and ST-T-wave abnormalities common.

CXR Cardiomegaly, pulmonary vascular redistribution, pulmonary effusions common.

Echocardiogram LV and RV enlargement with globally impaired contraction. *Regional* wall motion abnormalities suggest coronary artery disease rather than primary cardiomyopathy.

℞ TREATMENT

Standard therapy of CHF (Chap. 116); vasodilator therapy with ACE inhibitor (preferred) or hydralazine-nitrate combination shown to improve longevity. Add beta blocker in ambulatory pts (Chap. 116). Chronic anticoagulation with warfarin, recommended for very low ejection fraction (<25%), if no contraindications. Antiarrhythmic drugs (Chap. 115) e.g., amiodarone, indicated for symptomatic or sustained arrhythmias but may cause proarrhythmic side effects; implanted internal defibrillator is often a better alternative. Possible trial of immunosuppressive drugs, if active myocarditis present on RV biopsy (controversial as long-term efficacy has not been demonstrated). In selected pts, consider cardiac transplantation.

RESTRICTIVE CARDIOMYOPATHY

Increased myocardial "stiffness" impairs ventricular relaxation; diastolic ventricular pressures are elevated. Etiologies include infiltrative disease (amyloid, sarcoid, hemochromatosis, eosinophilic disorders), myocardial fibrosis, and fibroelastosis.

SYMPTOMS Are of CHF, although right-sided heart failure often predominates, with peripheral edema and ascites.

PHYSICAL EXAMINATION Signs of right-sided heart failure: JVD, hepatomegaly, peripheral edema, murmur of tricuspid regurgitation. Left-sided signs may also be present.

LABORATORY *ECG* Low limb lead voltage, sinus tachycardia, ST-T-wave abnormalities.

CXR Mild LV enlargement.

Echocardiogram Bilateral atrial enlargement; increased ventricular thickness ("speckled pattern") in infiltrative disease, especially amyloidosis. Systolic function is usually normal, but may be mildly reduced.

Cardiac Catheterization Increased LV and RV diastolic pressures with "dip and plateau" pattern; RV biopsy useful in detecting infiltrative disease (rectal or fat pad biopsy useful in diagnosis of amyloidosis).

Note: Must distinguish restrictive cardiomyopathy from constrictive pericarditis, which is surgically correctable (Table 119-1).

 TREATMENT

Salt restriction and diuretics ameliorate pulmonary and systemic congestion; digitalis is not indicated unless systolic function impaired or atrial arrhythmias present. *Note:* Increased sensitivity to digitalis in amyloidosis. Anticoagulation often indicated, particularly in pts with eosinophilic endomyocarditis. For specific therapy of hemochromatosis and sarcoidosis, see Chaps. 345 and 318, respectively, in HPIM-15.

HYPERTROPHIC OBSTRUCTIVE CARDIOMYOPATHY (HOCM)

Marked LV hypertrophy; often asymmetric, without underlying cause. Systolic function is normal; increased LV stiffness results in elevated diastolic filling pressures.

SYMPTOMS Secondary to elevated diastolic pressure, dynamic LV outflow obstruction, and arrhythmias; dyspnea on exertion, angina, and presyncope; sudden death may occur.

PHYSICAL EXAMINATION Brisk carotid upstroke with pulsus bisferiens; S_4, harsh systolic murmur along left sternal border, blowing murmur of mitral regurgitation at apex; murmur changes with Valsalva and other maneuvers (Chap. 112).

Table 119-1

Constrictive Pericarditis vs. Restrictive Cardiomyopathy

	Constrictive Pericarditis	Restrictive Cardiomyopathy
Prominent palpable cardiac apex	No	Often present
Cardiac size	Normal	May be enlarged
S_3, S_4	Absent (pericardial knock possible)	Often present
Calcification of pericardium on x-ray	Frequent	Absent
Systolic function	Normal	May be depressed
"Dip and plateau"	Yes	Yes
LV vs. RV diastolic pressure	Equal	LV usually higher
RV biopsy	Normal	Abnormal: may show infiltrative disease
CT or MRI	Thickened pericardium	Normal pericardium

LABORATORY *ECG* LV hypertrophy with prominent "septal" Q waves in leads I, aVL, V_{5-6}. Periods of atrial fibrillation or ventricular tachycardia are often detected by Holter monitor.

Echocardiogram LV hypertrophy, often with asymmetric septal hypertrophy (ASH) and ≥1.3 × thickness of LV posterior wall; LV contractile function excellent with small end-systolic volume. If LV outflow tract obstruction is present, systolic anterior motion (SAM) of mitral valve and midsystolic partial closure of aortic valve are present. Doppler shows early systolic accelerated blood flow through LV outflow tract. Carotid pulse tracing shows "spike and dome" configuration.

 TREATMENT

Strenuous exercise should be avoided. Beta blockers, verapamil, or disopyramide used individually to reduce symptoms. Digoxin, other inotropes, diu-

Table 119-2

Characteristics of the Cardiomyopathies

Dilated	Restrictive	Hypertrophic
VENTRICULAR CHARACTERISTICS		
LV (and usually RV) chamber dilatation	Impaired relaxation (reduced compliance); often due to ventricular infiltration	Marked hypertrophy, often asymmetric with septal thickness > LV free wall
PHYSICAL EXAMINATION		
Dyskinetic LV apex with biventricular CHF: rales, S_3, JVD, peripheral edema; may have murmurs of mitral and tricuspid regurgitation	Predominant right-sided CHF: JVD, hepatomegaly, peripheral edema	Brisk carotid upstroke; prominent S_4, harsh systolic murmur at left sternal border plus apical murmur of mitral regurgitation
CHEST X-RAY		
Four-chamber cardiac enlargement; pulmonary vascular redistribution	Mild cardiac enlargement	Mild cardiac enlargement
ECHOCARDIOGRAM		
Ventricular dilatation and global contractile impairment	Systolic function usually normal or mildly decreased; increased ventricular wall thickness in infiltrative disease; marked biatrial enlargement typical	Left ventricular hypertrophy, often asymmetric (septal thickness ≥1.3 × LV free wall); systolic anterior motion of mitral valve; mitral regurgitation and outflow gradient by Doppler

retics, and vasodilators are *contraindicated*. Endocarditis antibiotic prophylaxis (Chap. 80) is necessary when outflow obstruction or mitral regurgitation is present. Antiarrhythmic agents, especially amiodarone, may suppress atrial and ventricular arrhythmias. In selected pts, LV outflow gradient can be reduced by dual-chamber permanent pacemaker or controlled septal infarction by ethanol injection into the septal artery. Consider implantable automatic defibrillator for pts with high-risk ventricular arrhythmias. Surgical myectomy may be useful in pts refractory to medical therapy.

Table 119-2 summarizes distinguishing features of the cardiomyopathies.

MYOCARDITIS

Inflammation of the myocardium most commonly due to acute viral infection; may progress to chronic dilated cardiomyopathy. Myocarditis may develop in pts with HIV infection or Lyme disease.

HISTORY   Fever, fatigue, palpitations; if LV dysfunction is present, then symptoms of CHF are present. Viral myocarditis may be preceded by URI.

PHYSICAL EXAMINATION   Fever, tachycardia, soft S_1; S_3 common.

LABORATORY   CK-MB isoenzyme may be elevated in absence of MI. Convalescent antiviral antibody titers may rise.

ECG   Transient ST-T-wave abnormalities.

CXR   Cardiomegaly

Echocardiogram   Depressed LV function; pericardial effusion present if accompanying pericarditis present.

 TREATMENT

Rest; treat as CHF (Chap. 116); immunosuppressive therapy (steroids and azathioprine) may be considered if RV biopsy shows active inflammation, but long-term efficacy not demonstrated.

For a more detailed discussion, see Wynne J, Braunwald E: The Cardiomyopathies and Myocarditides, Chap. 238, p. 1359, in HPIM-15.

120

PERICARDIAL DISEASE

ACUTE PERICARDITIS
CAUSES   See Table 120-1
HISTORY   Chest pain, which may be intense, mimicking acute MI, but characteristically sharp, pleuritic, and positional (relieved by leaning forward); fever and palpitations are common.

Table 120-1

Most Common Causes of Pericarditis

Idiopathic
Infections (particularly viral)
Acute myocardial infarction
Metastatic neoplasm
Radiation therapy for tumor (up to 20 years earlier)
Chronic renal failure
Connective tissue disease (rheumatoid arthritis, SLE)
Drug reaction (e.g., procainamide, hydralazine)
"Autoimmune" following heart surgery or myocardial infarction (several weeks/
  months later)

PHYSICAL EXAMINATION Rapid or irregular pulse, coarse pericardial friction rub, which may vary in intensity and is loudest with pt sitting
forward.

LABORATORY *ECG* (See Table 120-2 and Fig. 120-1) Diffuse
ST elevation (concave upward) usually present in all leads except aVR and V_1;
PR-segment depression may be present; *days* later (unlike acute MI), ST returns
to baseline and T-wave inversion develops. Atrial premature beats and atrial
fibrillation may appear. Differentiate from ECG of early repolarization variant
(ERV) (ST-T ratio <0.25 in ERV, but >0.25 in pericarditis).

CXR Increased size of cardiac silhouette if large (>250 mL) pericardial
effusion is present, with "water bottle" configuration.

Echocardiogram Most sensitive test for detection of pericardial effusion,
which commonly accompanies acute pericarditis.

℞ TREATMENT

Aspirin 650–975 mg qid or NSAIDs (e.g., indomethacin 25–75 mg qid); for
severe, refractory pain, prednisone 40–60 mg/d is used and tapered over

Table 120-2

ECG in Acute Pericarditis vs. Acute (Q-wave) MI

ST-Segment Elevation	ECG Lead Involvement	Evolution of ST and T Waves	PR-Segment Depression
PERICARDITIS			
Concave upward	All leads involved except aVR and V_1	ST remains elevated for several days; after ST returns to baseline, T waves invert	Yes, in majority
ACUTE MI			
Convex upward	ST elevation over infarcted region only; reciprocal ST depression in opposite leads	T waves invert within hours, while ST still elevated; followed by Q wave development	No

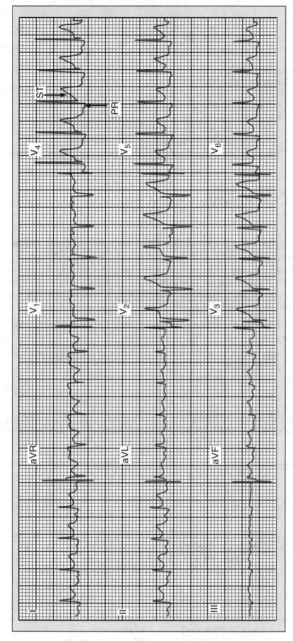

FIGURE 120-1 Electrocardiogram in acute pericarditis. Note diffuse ST-segment elevation and PR-segment depression.

several weeks or months. Intractable, prolonged pain or frequently recurrent episodes may require pericardiectomy. Anticoagulants are relatively contra-indicated in acute pericarditis because of risk of pericardial hemorrhage.

CARDIAC TAMPONADE

Life-threatening emergency resulting from accumulation of pericardial fluid under pressure; impaired filling of cardiac chambers and decreased cardiac output.

ETIOLOGY Previous pericarditis (most commonly metastatic tumor, uremia, acute MI, viral or idiopathic pericarditis), cardiac trauma, or myocardial perforation during catheter or pacemaker placement.

HISTORY Hypotension may develop suddenly; subacute symptoms include dyspnea, weakness, confusion.

PHYSICAL EXAMINATION Tachycardia, hypotension, pulsus paradoxus (inspiratory fall in systolic blood pressure >10 mmHg), jugular venous distention with preserved x descent, but loss of y descent; heart sounds distant. If tamponade develops subacutely, peripheral edema, hepatomegaly, and ascites are frequently present.

LABORATORY *ECG* Low limb lead voltage; large effusions may cause electrical alternans (alternating size of QRS complex due to swinging of heart).

CXR Enlarged cardiac silhouette if large (>250 mL) effusion present.

Echocardiogram Swinging motion of heart within large effusion; prominent respiratory alteration of RV dimension with RA and RV collapse during diastole.

Cardiac Catheterization Confirms diagnosis; shows equalization of diastolic pressures in all four chambers; pericardial = RA pressure.

 TREATMENT

Immediate pericardiocentesis and IV volume expansion.

CONSTRICTIVE PERICARDITIS

Rigid pericardium leads to impaired cardiac filling, elevation of systemic and pulmonary venous pressures, and decreased cardiac output. Results from healing and scar formation in some pts with previous pericarditis. Viral, tuberculosis, previous cardiac surgery, uremia, neoplastic pericarditis are most common causes.

HISTORY Gradual onset of dyspnea, fatigue, pedal edema, abdominal swelling; symptoms of LV failure uncommon.

PHYSICAL EXAMINATION Tachycardia, jugular venous distention (prominent y descent), which increases further on inspiration (Kussmaul's sign); hepatomegaly, ascites, peripheral edema are common; sharp diastolic sound, "pericardial knock" following S_2 sometimes present.

LABORATORY *ECG* Low limb lead voltage; atrial arrhythmias are common.

CXR Rim of pericardial calcification in up to 50% of pts.

Echocardiogram Thickened pericardium, normal ventricular contraction; abrupt halt in ventricular filling in early diastole.

CT or MRI More precise than echocardiogram in demonstrating thickened pericardium.

Cardiac Catheterization Equalization of diastolic pressures in all chambers; ventricular pressure tracings show "dip and plateau" appearance (to distinguish from restrictive cardiomyopathy; Table 119-1). Pts with constrictive pericarditis should be investigated for tuberculosis (Chap. 97).

℞ TREATMENT

Surgical stripping of the pericardium. Progressive improvement ensues over several months.

——————————— *Approach to the Patient* ———————————
With Asymptomatic Pericardial Effusion of Unknown Cause

If careful history and physical exam do not suggest etiology, the following may lead to diagnosis:

* Skin test and cultures for tuberculosis (Chap. 97)
* Serum albumin and urine protein measurement (nephrotic syndrome)
* Serum creatinine and BUN (renal failure)
* Thyroid function tests (myxedema)
* ANA (SLE and other collagen-vascular disease)
* Search for a primary tumor (especially lung and breast)

For a more detailed discussion, see Braunwald E: Pericardial Disease, Chap. 239, p. 1365, in HPIM-15.

121

ACUTE MYOCARDIAL INFARCTION

Early recognition and immediate treatment of acute MI are essential; diagnosis is based on characteristic history, ECG, and evolution of cardiac enzymes.

SYMPTOMS Chest pain similar to angina (Chap. 2) but more intense and persistent (>30 min); not fully relieved by rest or nitroglycerin, often accompanied by nausea, sweating, apprehension. However, 25% of MIs are clinically silent.

PHYSICAL EXAMINATION Pallor, diaphoresis, tachycardia, S_4, dyskinetic cardiac impulse may be present. If CHF exists: rales, S_3. Jugular venous distention is common in right ventricular infarction.

ECG *Q-wave MI* ST elevation, followed by T-wave inversion, then Q-wave development (Chap. 113) over several hours.

Non-Q-wave MI ST depression followed by persistent ST-T-wave changes *without* Q-wave development. Comparison with old ECG helpful.

CARDIAC ENZYMES Time course is important for diagnosis; creatine phosphokinase (CK) level should be checked every 8 h for first day: CK rises within 4–8 h, peaks at 24 h, returns to normal by 48–72 h. CK-MB isoenzyme is more specific for MI but may also be elevated with myocarditis or after electrical cardioversion. Total CK (but not CK-MB) rises (two- to threefold) after IM injection, vigorous exercise, or other skeletal muscle trauma. A ratio of CK-MB mass: CK activity ≥2.5 suggests acute MI. CK-MB peaks earlier (about 8 h) following acute reperfusion therapy (see below). Cardiac-specific troponin T and troponin I are highly specific for myocardial injury and are the preferred biochemical markers for acute MI. They remain elevated for 1–2 weeks.

NONINVASIVE IMAGING TECHNIQUES Useful when diagnosis of MI is not clear. *Echocardiography* detects infarct-associated regional wall motion abnormalities (but cannot distinguish acute MI from a previous myocardial scar). Echo is also useful in detecting RV infarction, LV aneurysm, and LV thrombus. *Myocardial perfusion imaging* (thallium 201 or technetium 99m-sestamibi) is sensitive for regions of decreased perfusion but is not specific for acute MI.

 TREATMENT

Initial Therapy

Goal is to relieve pain, minimize extent of infarcted tissue, and prevent/treat arrhythmias and mechanical complications. Aspirin (160–325 mg chewed at presentation, then 160–325 mg po qd) should be administered immediately. For Q-wave MI (ST-segment elevation MI), early thrombolytic therapy with streptokinase, reteplase (rPA), or tissue plasminogen activator (tPA) can reduce infarct size and mortality and limit LV dysfunction. In appropriate candidates (Figs. 121-1 and 121-2), thrombolysis should be initiated as quickly as possible (ideally within 30 min) in the emergency room or coronary care unit (CCU); pts treated within 3 h of initial symptoms benefit the most. Complications include bleeding, reperfusion arrhythmias, and, in the case of streptokinase, allergic reactions. Anticoagulation with heparin [60 U/kg, then 12 (U/kg)/h] is begun concurrently with the thrombolytic agent (Fig. 121-1). Subsequent coronary arteriography is reserved for pts with recurrent angina or positive exercise test prior to discharge. In pts with contraindications to thrombolytic therapy (Fig. 121-1), primary percutaneous transluminal coronary angioplasty (PTCA) and/or stenting can be undertaken to restore coronary flow. Primary PTCA may be preferred over thrombolytic therapy in cardiogenic shock, in pts of advanced age (>70), and in some highly experienced centers, especially if delay can be minimized.

The initial management of non-ST-segment elevation MI (non-Q MI) is different (Fig. 121-3). Thrombolytic therapy should not be administered. Begin aspirin and antithrombin therapy: either low-molecular-weight heparin (e.g., enoxaparin 1 mg/kg SC q12h) or IV heparin [60 U/kg followed by 12(U/kg)/h, then adjust to maintain PTT at 2 × control). Begin beta blocker and IV nitroglycerin (Table 121-1) for control of ischemic pain. In high-risk patients, add IV glycoprotein IIb/IIIa inhibitor [e.g., tirofiban, 0.4 (μg/kg)/min × 30 min then 0.1 (μg/kg)/min, *or* eptifibatide, 180 μg/kg then 2 (μg/kg)/min] and consider cardiac catheterization/revascularization.

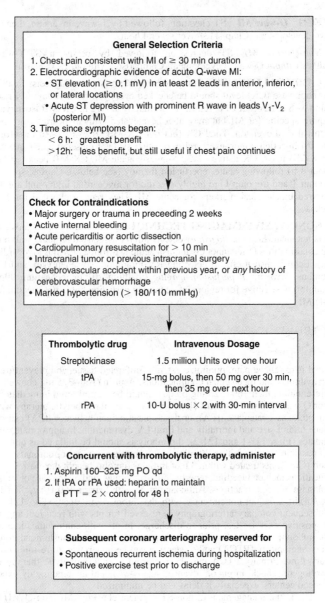

FIGURE 121-1   Approach to thrombolytic therapy of pts with acute MI.

Additional Standard Treatment

(Whether or not thrombolytic therapy is administered):

1. *Hospitalize in CCU* with continuous ECG monitoring.
2. *IV line* for emergency arrhythmia treatment.

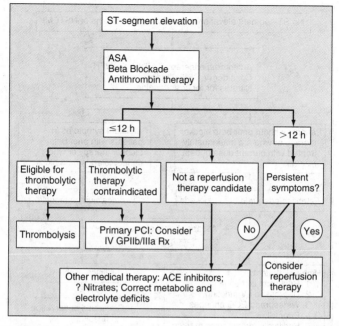

FIGURE 121-2 Management strategy for pts suspected of having an ST-segment elevation. Acute MI pts should receive aspirin (ASA), beta blockers (in the absence of contraindications), and an antithrombin (particularly if a relatively fibrin-specific thrombolytic agent is used). Adjunctive antithrombin therapy is probably not required for pts receiving streptokinase. Pts treated within 12 h who are eligible for thrombolytic therapy should expeditiously receive such treatment or be considered for primary percutaneous transluminal coronary angioplasty (PCI). Immediate, primary PCI is also to be considered when lytic therapy is contraindicated. An intravenous glycoprotein IIb/IIIa (GPIIb/IIIa) inhibitor may be helpful for reducing thrombotic complications during primary PCI. Pts treated after 12 h should receive the initial medical therapy noted above and, on an individual basis, may be candidates for ACE inhibitors (particularly if LV function is impaired).

3. *Pain control*: (a) Morphine sulfate 2–4 mg IV q5–10 min until pain is relieved or side effects develop [nausea, vomiting, respiratory depression (treat with naloxone 0.4–1.2 mg IV), hypotension (if bradycardic, treat with atropine 0.5 mg IV; otherwise use careful volume infusion)]; (b) nitroglycerin 0.3 mg SL if systolic bp >100 mmHg; for refractory pain: IV nitroglycerin (begin at 10 μg/min, titrate upward to maximum of 200 μg/min, monitoring bp closely); (c) β-adrenergic antagonists (see below).

4. *Oxygen* 2–4 L/min by nasal cannula (maintain O_2 saturation >90%).

5. Mild *sedation* (e.g., diazepam 5 mg PO qid).

6. *Soft diet* and stool softeners (e.g., docusate sodium 100–200 mg/d).

7. *β-Adrenergic blockers* (Chap. 124) reduce myocardial O_2 consumption, limit infarct size, and reduce mortality. Especially useful in pts with hypertension, tachycardia, or persistent ischemic pain; contraindications include CHF, systolic bp <95 mmHg, heart rate <50 beats/min, AV block, or history of bronchospasm. Administer IV (e.g., metoprolol 5 mg q5–10 min to total dose of 15 mg), followed by PO regimen (e.g., metoprolol 25–100 mg bid).

8. *Anticoagulation/antiplatelet agents:* Pts who receive thrombolytic therapy are begun on heparin and aspirin. In absence of thrombolytic therapy,

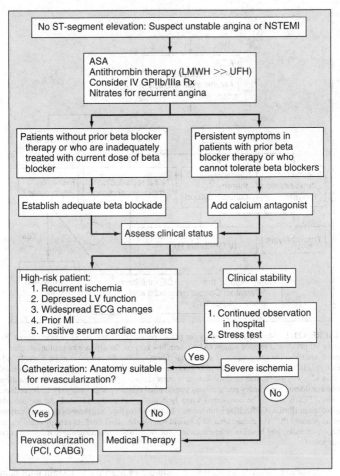

No ST-segment elevation: Suspect unstable angina or NSTEMI

ASA
Antithrombin therapy (LMWH >> UFH)
Consider IV GPIIb/IIIa Rx
Nitrates for recurrent angina

Patients without prior beta blocker therapy or who are inadequately treated with current dose of beta blocker

Persistent symptoms in patients with prior beta blocker therapy or who cannot tolerate beta blockers

Establish adequate beta blockade

Add calcium antagonist

Assess clinical status

High-risk patient:
1. Recurrent ischemia
2. Depressed LV function
3. Widespread ECG changes
4. Prior MI
5. Positive serum cardiac markers

Clinical stability

1. Continued observation in hospital
2. Stress test

Catheterization: Anatomy suitable for revascularization?

Yes

Severe ischemia

No

Yes   No

Revascularization (PCI, CABG)   Medical Therapy

FIGURE 121-3 Management strategy for pts with unstable angina and acute MI without ST-segment elevation. These pts should be treated with an antithrombin and aspirin. Nitrates should be administered for recurrent episodes of angina. The risk of death and cardiac ischemic events may be reduced in high-risk pts if an intravenous GPIIb/IIIa inhibitor is administered. Adequate beta blockade should be established; when that is not possible or contraindications exist, a calcium antagonist can be considered. Pts at high risk should be triaged to cardiac catheterization with plans for revascularization if clinically suitable; pts who are clinically stable can be treated more conservatively with continued observation in the hospital and consideration of a stress test to screen for any provocable myocardial ischemia. CABG, coronary artery bypass grafting; LV, left ventricular. *[Modified from EM Antman, in RM Califf (ed): Acute Myocardial Infarction and Other Acute Ischemic Syndromes, in E Braunwald (Series ed): Atlas of Heart Diseases, vol. 8. Philadelphia, Current Medicine 1996.]*

administer aspirin 160–325 mg qd and low-dose heparin (5000 U SC q12h). Full-dose IV heparin (PTT 2 × control) or low-molecular-weight heparin (e.g., enoxaparin 1 mg/kg SC q12h) followed by oral anticoagulants is recommended for pts with severe CHF, presence of ventricular thrombus by echocardiogram, or large dyskinetic region in anterior MI. Oral anticoagulants are continued for 3 to 6 months, then replaced by aspirin.

Table 121-1

Intravenous Vasodilators and Inotropic Drugs Used in Acute MI

Drug	Usual Dosage Range	Comment
Nitroglycerin	5–100 μg/min	May improve coronary blood flow to ischemic myocardium
Nitroprusside	0.5–10 (μg/kg)/min	More potent vasodilator, but improves coronary blood flow less than nitroglycerin With therapy >24 h or in renal failure, watch for thiocyanate toxicity (blurred vision, tinnitus, delirium)
Dobutamine	2–20 (μg/kg)/min	Results in ↑ cardiac output, ↓ PCW, but does not raise bp
Dopamine	2–10 (μg/kg)/min (sometimes higher)	More appropriate than dobutamine if hypotensive Hemodynamic effect depends on dose: (μg/kg)/min <5:↑ renal blood flow 2.5–10:positive inotrope >10:vasoconstriction
Amrinone	0.75 mg/kg bolus, then 5–15 (μg/kg)/min	Positive inotrope and vasodilator Can combine with dopamine or dobutamine May result in thrombocytopenia
Milrinone	50 mg/kg bolus, then 0.375–0.75 (μg/kg)/min	Ventricular arrhythmias may result

9.   *ACE inhibitors* reduce mortality in pts following acute MI and should be prescribed within 24 h of hospitalization for pts with CHF and those who are hemodynamically stable with ST-segment elevation MI or left bundle branch block—e.g., captopril (6.25 mg PO test dose) advanced to 50 mg PO tid. ACE inhibitors should be continued indefinitely in pts with CHF or those with asymptomatic LV dysfunction [ejection fraction (EF) ≤40%].

10.   *Serum magnesium* level should be measured and repleted if necessary to reduce risk of arrhythmias.

COMPLICATIONS

VENTRICULAR ARRHYTHMIAS   Isolated ventricular premature beats (VPBs) occur frequently. Precipitating factors should be corrected [hypoxemia, acidosis, hypokalemia (maintain serum K$^+$ ~ 4.5 mmol/L), hypercalcemia, hypomagnesemia, CHF, arrhythmogenic drugs]. Routine beta-blocker administration (see above) diminishes ventricular ectopy. Other in-hospital antiarrhythmic therapy should be reserved for pts with sustained ventricular arrhythmias.

VENTRICULAR TACHYCARDIA

If hemodynamically unstable, perform immediate electrical countershock (unsynchronized discharge of 200–300 J). If hemodynamically tolerated, use IV lidocaine [bolus of 1.0–1.5 mg/kg, infusion of 20–50 (μg/kg)/min; use lower infusion rate ($\approx$ 1 mg/min) in pts of advanced age or those with CHF or liver disease], IV procainamide (bolus of 15 mg/kg over 20–30 min; infusion of 1–4 mg/min) or IV amiodarone (bolus of 75–150 mg over 10–15 min; infusion of 1.0 mg/min for 6 h, then 0.5 mg/min).

VENTRICULAR FIBRILLATION VF requires immediate defibrillation (200–400 J). If unsuccessful, initiate CPR and standard resuscitative measures (Chap. 29). Ventricular arrhythmias that appear several days or weeks following MI often reflect pump failure and may warrant invasive electrophysiologic study.

ACCELERATED IDIOVENTRICULAR RHYTHM Wide QRS complex, regular rhythm, rate 60–100 beats/min is common and usually benign; if it causes hypotension, treat with atropine 0.6 mg IV.

SUPRAVENTRICULAR ARRHYTHMIAS *Sinus tachycardia* may result from CHF, hypoxemia, pain, fever, pericarditis, hypovolemia, administered drugs. If no cause is identified, may treat with beta blocker (Table 124-1). For persistent sinus tachycardia (>120), use Swan-Ganz catheter to differentiate CHF from decreased intravascular volume (Table 121-2). Other *supraventricular arrhythmias* (paroxysmal supraventricular tachycardia, atrial flutter, and fibrillation) are often secondary to CHF, in which digoxin (Chap. 116) is treatment of choice. In absence of CHF, may also use verapamil or beta blocker (Chap. 115). If hemodynamically unstable, proceed with electrical cardioversion.

BRADYARRHYTHMIAS AND AV BLOCK (See Chap. 115) In *inferior MI*, usually represent heightened vagal tone or discrete AV nodal ischemia. If hemodynamically compromised (CHF, hypotension, emergence of ventricular arrhythmias), treat with atropine 0.5 mg IV q5min (up to 2 mg). If no response, use temporary external or transvenous pacemaker. Isoproterenol should be avoided. In *anterior MI*, AV conduction defects usually reflect extensive tissue necrosis. Consider temporary external or transvenous pacemaker for (1) complete heart block, (2) Mobitz type II block (Chap. 115), (3) new bifascicular block (LBBB, RBBB + left anterior hemiblock, RBBB + left posterior hemiblock), (4) any bradyarrhythmia associated with hypotension or CHF.

CONGESTIVE HEART FAILURE CHF may result from systolic "pump" dysfunction, increased LV diastolic "stiffness," and/or acute mechanical complications.

Symptoms Dyspnea, orthopnea, tachycardia.

Examination Jugular venous distention, S_3 and S_4 gallop, pulmonary rales; systolic murmur if acute mitral regurgitation or ventricular septal defect (VSD) have developed.

Table 121-2

Indications for Swan-Ganz Catheter in Acute Myocardial Infarction

1. Moderate to severe CHF
2. Hypotension not corrected by volume infusion
3. Unexplained sinus tachycardia or tachypnea
4. Suspected acute mitral regurgitation or ventricular septal rupture
5. To manage IV vasodilator therapy

R̶x̶ TREATMENT

(See Chaps. 32 and 116) Initial therapy includes diuretics (begin with furosemide 10–20 mg IV), inhaled O_2, and vasodilators, particularly nitrates [PO, topical, or IV (Chap. 116) unless pt is hypotensive (systolic bp <100 mmHg)]; digitalis is usually of little benefit in acute MI unless supraventricular arrhythmias are present. Diuretic, vasodilator, and inotropic therapy (Table 121-1) best guided by invasive hemodynamic monitoring (Swan-Ganz pulmonary artery catheter, arterial line) particularly in pts with accompanying hypotension (Tables 121-2 and 121-3; Fig. 121-4). In acute MI, optimal pulmonary capillary wedge pressure (PCW) is 15–20 mmHg; in the absence of hypotension, PCW >20 mmHg is treated with diuretic plus vasodilator therapy [IV nitroglycerin (begin at 10 μg/min) or nitroprusside (begin at 0.5 μg/kg per min)] and titrated to optimize bp, PCW, and systemic vascular resistance (SVR).

$$SVR = \frac{(\text{mean arterial pressure} - \text{mean RA pressure}) \times 80}{\text{cardiac output}}$$

Normal SVR = 900 – 1350 dyn · s/cm⁵. If PCW > 20 mmHg and pt is hypotensive (Table 121-3 and Fig. 121-4), evaluate for VSD or acute mitral regurgitation, add dobutamine [begin at 1–2 (μg/kg)/min], titrate upward to maximum of 10 (μg/kg)/min; beware of drug-induced tachycardia or ventricular ectopy.

If CHF improves on parenteral vasodilator therapy, oral therapy follows with ACE inhibitor (e.g., captopril, enalapril, or lisinopril–Chap. 124) or the combination of nitrates plus hydralazine (Chap. 116).

CARDIOGENIC SHOCK   Severe LV failure with hypotension (bp <80 mmHg *and* elevated PCW (>20 mmHg), accompanied by oliguria (<20 mL/ h), peripheral vasoconstriction, dulled sensorium, and metabolic acidosis.

R̶x̶ TREATMENT

(See Chap. 30) Swan-Ganz catheter and intraarterial bp monitoring are essential; aim for mean PCW of 18–20 mmHg with adjustment of volume (diuretics or infusion) as needed. Intraaortic balloon counterpulsation may be necessary to maintain bp and reduce PCW. Administer high concentration of O_2 by mask; if pulmonary edema coexists, intubation and mechanical ventilation should be considered. Acute mechanical complications (see below) should be sought and promptly treated.

If cardiogenic shock develops within 4 h of first MI symptoms, acute reperfusion by PTCA may markedly improve LV function.

Hypotension may also result from *RV MI*, which should be suspected in the setting of inferior or posterior MI, if jugular venous distention and elevation of right-heart pressures predominate (rales are typically absent and PCW may be normal); right-sided ECG leads typically show ST elevation, and echocardiography may confirm diagnosis. *Treatment* consists of volume infusion, gauged by PCW and arterial pressure. Noncardiac causes of hypotension should be considered: hypovolemia, acute arrhythmia, or sepsis.

ACUTE MECHANICAL COMPLICATIONS   Ventricular septal rupture and acute mitral regurgitation due to papillary muscle ischemia/infarct develop during the first week following MI and are characterized by sudden onset of CHF and new systolic murmur. Echocardiography with Doppler can confirm presence of these complications. PCW tracings may show large *v* waves in either

Table 121-3

Hemodynamic Complications in Acute MI

Condition	Cardiac Index, (L/min)/m²	PCW, mmHg	Systolic bp, mmHg	Treatment
Uncomplicated	>2.5	≤18	>100	—
Hypovolemia	<2.5	<15	<100	Successive boluses of normal saline In setting of inferior wall MI, consider RV infarction (esp. if RA pressure >10)
Volume overload	>2.5	>20	>100	Diuretic (e.g., furosemide 10–20 mg IV) Nitroglycerin, topical paste or IV (Table 121-1)
LV failure	<2.5	>20	>100	Diuretic (e.g., furosemide 10–20 mg IV) IV nitroglycerin (or if hypertensive, use IV nitroprusside)
Severe LV failure	<2.5	>20	<100	If bp ≥90: IV dobutamine ± IV nitroglycerin or sodium nitroprusside If bp <90: IV dopamine If accompanied by pulmonary edema: attempt diuresis with IV furosemide; may be limited by hypotension If new systolic murmur present, consider acute VSD or mitral regurgitation
Cardiogenic shock	<1.8	>20	<90 with oliguria and confusion	IV dopamine Intraaortic balloon pump Coronary angioplasty may be life-saving

NOTE: PCW, pulmonary artery wedge pressure; RV, right ventricle; LV, left ventricle; VSD, ventricular septal defect.

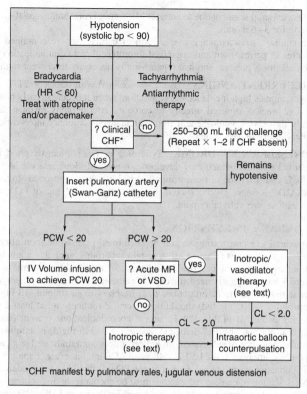

FIGURE 121-4 Approach to hypotension in pts with acute myocardial infarction; PCW, pulmonary capillary wedge pressure.

condition, but an oxygen "step-up" as the catheter is advanced from RA to RV suggests septal rupture. Acute medical therapy of these conditions includes vasodilator therapy (IV nitroprusside: begin at 10 μg/min and titrate to maintain systolic bp $\cong$100 mmHg); intraaortic balloon pump may be required to maintain cardiac output. Surgical correction is postponed for 4–6 weeks after acute MI if pt is stable; surgery should not be deferred if pt is unstable. Acute ventricular free-wall rupture presents with sudden loss of bp, pulse, and consciousness, while ECG shows an intact rhythm; emergent surgical repair is crucial, and mortality is high.

PERICARDITIS Characterized by *pleuritic, positional* pain and pericardial rub (Chap. 120); atrial arrhythmias are common; must be distinguished from recurrent angina. Often responds to aspirin 650 mg PO qid. Anticoagulants should be withheld when pericarditis is suspected to avoid development of tamponade.

VENTRICULAR ANEURYSM Localized "bulge" of LV chamber due to infarcted myocardium. *True aneurysms* consist of scar tissue and do not rupture. However, complications include CHF, ventricular arrhythmias, and thrombus formation. Typically, ECG shows persistent ST-segment elevation, >2 weeks after initial infarct; aneurysm is confirmed by echocardiography and by left ventriculography. The presence of thrombus within the aneurysm, or a large aneurysmal segment due to anterior MI, warrants oral anticoagulation with warfarin for 3–6 months.

In contrast, *pseudoaneurysm* is a form of cardiac rupture contained by a local area of pericardium and organized thrombus; direct communication with the LV cavity is present; surgical repair usually necessary to prevent rupture.

RECURRENT ANGINA Usually associated with transient ST-T wave changes; signals high incidence of reinfarction; when it occurs in early post-MI period (2 weeks), proceed directly to coronary arteriography in most pts, to identify those who would benefit from percutaneous coronary intervention or coronary artery bypass surgery.

DRESSLER'S SYNDROME Syndrome of fever, pleuritic chest pain, pericardial effusion, which may develop 2–6 weeks following acute MI; pain and ECG characteristic of pericarditis (Chap. 120); usually responds to aspirin or NSAIDs. Reserve glucocorticoid therapy (prednisone 1 mg/kg PO qd) for those with severe, refractory pain.

SECONDARY PREVENTION

Submaximal exercise testing should be performed prior to or soon after discharge. A positive test (Chap. 122) in certain subgroups (angina at a low workload, a large region of provocable ischemia, or provocable ischemia with a reduced LVEF) suggests need for cardiac catheterization to evaluate myocardium at risk of recurrent infarction. *Beta blockers* (e.g., timolol, 10 mg bid; metoprolol, 25–100 mg bid) should be prescribed routinely for at least 2 years following acute MI (Table 124-1), unless contraindications present (asthma, CHF, bradycardia, "brittle" diabetes). Aspirin (80–325 mg/d) is administered to reduce incidence of subsequent infarction, unless contraindicated (e.g., active peptic ulcer, allergy). If the LVEF ≤40%, an ACE inhibitor (e.g., captopril 6.25 mg PO tid, advanced to target dose of 50 mg PO tid) should be used indefinitely.

Modification of cardiac risk factors must be encouraged: discontinue smoking; control hypertension, diabetes, and serum lipids (target LDL ≤100 mg/dL) (Chap. 178); and pursue graduated exercise.

For a more detailed discussion, see Antman EM, Braunwald E: Acute Myocardial Infarction, Chap. 243, p. 1386, in HPIM-15.

122

CHRONIC CORONARY ARTERY DISEASE AND UNSTABLE ANGINA

Angina pectoris, the most common clinical manifestation of CAD, results from an imbalance between myocardial O_2 supply and demand, most commonly resulting from atherosclerotic coronary artery obstruction. Other major conditions that upset this balance and result in angina include aortic valve disease (Chap. 118), hypertrophic cardiomyopathy (Chap. 119), and coronary artery spasm (see below).

SYMPTOMS   Angina is typically associated with extension or emotional upset; relieved quickly by rest or nitroglycerin (Chap. 2). Major risk factors are cigarette smoking, hypertension, hypercholesterolemia ($\uparrow$LDL fraction; $\downarrow$HDL), diabetes, and family history of CAD below age 55.

PHYSICAL EXAMINATION   Often normal; arterial bruits or retinal vascular abnormalities suggest generalized atherosclerosis; S_4 is common. During acute anginal episode, other signs may appear: loud S_3 or S_4, diaphoresis, rales, and a transient murmur of mitral regurgitation due to papillary muscle ischemia.

LABORATORY   *ECG*   May be normal between anginal episodes or show old infarction (Chap. 113). During angina, ST- and T-wave abnormalities typically appear (ST-segment depression reflects subendocardial ischemia; ST-segment elevation may reflect acute infarction or transient coronary artery spasm). Ventricular arrhythmias frequently accompany acute ischemia.

Stress Testing   Enhances diagnosis of CAD (Fig. 122-1). Exercise is performed on treadmill or bicycle until target heart rate is achieved or pt becomes symptomatic (chest pain, light-headedness, hypotension, marked dyspnea, ventricular tachycardia) or develops diagnostic ST-segment changes. useful information includes duration of exercise achieved; peak heart rate and bp; depth, morphology, and persistence of ST-segment depression; and whether and at which level of exercise pain, hypotension, or ventricular arrhythmias develop. *Thallium 201* (or 99m-technetium sestamibi) imaging increases sensitivity and specificity and is particularly useful if baseline ECG abnormalities prevent interpretation of test (e.g., LBBB). *Note:* Exercise testing should not be performed in pts with acute MI, unstable angina, or severe aortic stenosis. If the pt is unable to exercise, intravenous dipyridamole (or adenosine) testing can be performed in conjunction with thallium or sestamibi imaging or a dobutamine echocardiographic study can be obtained (Table 122-1).

Some pts do not experience chest pain during ischemic episodes with exertion ("silent ischemia") but are identifed by transient ST-T-wave abnormalities during stress testing or Holter monitoring (see below).

Coronary Arteriography   The definitive test for assessing severity of CAD; major indications are (1) angina refractory to medical therapy, (2) markedly positive exercise test ($\geq$2-mm ST-segment depression or hypotension with exercise) suggestive of left main or three-vessel disease, (3) recurrent angina or positive exercise test after MI, (4) to assess for coronary artery spasm, and (5) to evaluate pts with perplexing chest pain in whom noninvasive tests are not diagnostic.

 TREATMENT

General

- Identify and treat risk factors: mandatory cessation of smoking; treatment of diabetes, hypertension, and lipid disorders (Chap. 178).
- Correct exacerbating factors contributing to angina: marked obesity, CHF, anemia, hyperthyroidism.
- Reassurance and pt education.

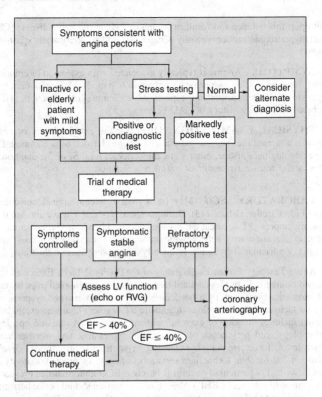

FIGURE 122-1A Role of exercise testing in management of CAD, RVG, radionuclide ventriculogram; EF, left ventricular ejection fraction. [*Modified from LS Lilly, in Textbook of Primary Care Medicine, J Nobel (ed.) St. Louis Mosby, 1996, p. 224.*]

Drug Therapy

Sublingual nitroglycerin (TNG 0.3–0.6 mg); may be repeated at 5-min intervals; warn pts of possible headache or light-headedness; teach prophylactic use of TNG prior to activity that regularly evokes angina. If chest pain persists for more than 10 min despite 2–3 TNG, pt should report promptly to nearest medical facility for evaluation of possible unstable angina or acute MI.

Long-Term Angina Supresion

Three classes of drugs are used, frequently in combination:

Long-Acting Nitrates May be administered by many routes (Table 122-2); start at the lowest dose and frequency to limit tolerance and side effects of headache, light-headedness, tachycardia.

Beta Blockers (See Table 124-1) All have antianginal properties; β_1-selective agents are less likely to exacerbate airway or peripheral vascular disease. Dosage should be titrated to resting heart rate of 50–60 beats/min. *Contraindications* to beta blockers include CHF, AV block, bronchospasm, "brittle" diabetes. Side effects include fatigue, bronchospasm, depressed LV function, impotence, depression, and masking of hypoglycemia in diabetics.

Calcium Antagonists (See Table 124-4) Useful for stable and unstable angina, as well coronary vasospasm. Combination with other antianginal

Table 122-1

Stress Testing Recommendations

Subgroup	Recommended Study
Patient able to exercise	
If baseline ST-T on ECG is iso-electric	Standard exercise test (treadmill, bicycle, or arm ergometry)
If baseline ST-T impairs test interpretation (e.g., LBBB, LVH with strain, digoxin)	Standard exercise test (above) combined with *either*
	Perfusion scintigraphy (thallium 201 or Tc99m-sestamibi) *or* Echocardiography
Patient *not* able to exercise (regardless of baseline ST-T abnormality)	Pharmacologic stress test (IV dobutamine, dipyridamole, or adenosine combined with *either*
	Perfusion scintigraphy (thallium 201 or Tc99m-sestamibi) *or* Echocardiography
Alternative choice (if baseline ST-T normal)	Ambulatory ECG monitor

agents is beneficial, but verapamil should be administered very cautiously or not at all to pts on beta blockers or disopyramide (additive effects on LV dysfunction). Use sustained-release, not short-acting, calcium antagonists; the latter increase coronary mortality.

Aspirin   80–325 mg/d reduces the incidence of MI in chronic stable angina, following MI, and in asymptomatic men. It is recommended in pts

Table 122-2

Examples of Commonly Used Nitrates

	Usual Dose	Recommended Dosing Frequency
SHORT-ACTING AGENTS		
Sublingual TNG	0.3–0.6 mg	As needed
Aerosol TNG	0.4 mg (1 inhalation)	As needed
Sublingual ISDN	2.5–10 mg	As needed
LONG-ACTING AGENTS		
ISND		
Oral	5–30 mg	tid
Sustained-action	40 mg	bid (once in **A.M.**, then 7 h later)
TNG ointment (2%)	0.5–2	qid (with one 7- to 10-h nitrate-free interval)
TNG skin patches	0.1–0.6 mg/h	Apply in morning, remove at bedtime
ISMO		
Oral	20–40 mg	bid (once in **A.M.**, then 7 h later)
Sustained-action	30–240 mg	qd

NOTE: TNG, nitroglycerin; ISDN, isosorbide dinatrate; ISMO, isosorbide mononitrate.

Table 122-3

Comparison of Revascularization Procedures in Multivessel Disease

Procedure	Advantages	Disadvantages
Percutaneous coronary revascularization (angioplasty and/or stenting)	Less invasive Shorter hospital stay Lower initial cost Easily repeated Effective in relieving symptoms	Restenosis High incidence of incomplete revascularization Unknown outcomes in pts with severe left ventricular dysfunction Limited to specific anatomic subsets Poor outcome in diabetics with 2–3 vessel coronary disease
Coronary artery bypass grafting	Effective in relieving symptoms Improved survival in certain subsets, including diabetics Ability to achieve complete revascularization	Cost Increased risk of a repeat procedure due to late graft closure Morbidity and mortality of major surgery

SOURCE: Modified from DP Faxon, in GA Beller (ed), *Chronic Ischemic Heart Disease*, in E Braunwald (series ed), *Atlas of Heart Disease*, Philadelphia, Current Medicine, 1994.

with CAD in the absence of contraindications (GI bleeding or allergy). Consider clopidogrel (75 mg/d) for aspirin-intolerant individuals.

Mechanical Revascularization

Percutaneous Coronary Intervention (PCI) Includes percutaneous transluminal angioplasty (PTCA) and/or stenting. Performed on anatomically suitable stenoses of native vessels and bypass grafts; more effective than medical therapy for relief of angina. Has not been shown to reduce risk of MI or death; should not be performed on asymptomatic or only mildly symptomatic individuals. With PCI initial relief of angina occurs in 95% of pts; however, with PTCA stenosis recurs in 30–45% within 6 months (more commonly in pts with initial unstable angina, incomplete dilation, diabetes, or stenoses containing thrombi). If restenosis occurs, PTCA can be repeated with success and risks like original procedure. Potential complications include dissection or thrombosis of the vessel and uncontrolled ischemia or CHF. Complications are most likely to occur in pts with CHF, long eccentric stenoses, calcified plaque, female gender, and dilation of an artery that perfuses a large segment of myocardium with inadequate collaterals. Placement of an intracoronary stent in suitable pts reduces the restenosis rate to 10–30% at 6 months. PCI has also been successful in some pts with recent *total* coronary occlusion (<3 months).

Coronary Artery Bypass Surgery (CABG) For angina refractory to medical therapy or when the latter is not tolerated (and when lesions are not amenable to PCI) or if severe CAD is present (left main, three-vessel disease with impaired LV function). CABG is preferred over PTCA in diabetics with CAD in ≥ 2 vessels because of better survival.

The relative advantages of PTCA and CABG are summarized in Table 122-3.

UNSTABLE ANGINA

Includes (1) new onset (<2 months) of severe angina, (2) angina at rest or with minimal activity, (3) recent increases in frequency and intensity of chronic angina, (4) recurrent angina within several days of acute MI without reelevation of cardiac enzymes.

℞ TREATMENT

- Admit to continuous ECG-monitored floor.
- Identify and treat exacerbating factors (hypertension, arrhythmias, CHF, acute infection).
- Anticoagulation: IV heparin (aim for PTT 2 × control) or low-molecular-weight heparin (e.g., enoxaparin 1 mg/kg SC bid) × 3–5 d; plus aspirin 325 mg/d. In high-risk patients (Fig. 122-2) add GpIIb/IIIa inhibitor [e.g., eptifibatide, 180 μg/kg, then 2 (μg/kg)/min].
- Rule out MI by ECG and cardiac enzymes.
- Maximize therapy with oral nitrates, beta blockers (to reduce heart rate to 50–70 beats per min). Reserve use of calcium antagonists for those with refractory pain.
- For refractory pain: IV TNG (begin at 10 μg/min); titrate dosage to alleviate pain, but maintain systolic bp ≥ 100 mmHg.
- Refractory unstable angina warrants coronary arteriography and possible PCI or CABG. If symptoms are controlled on medical therapy, a predischarge exercise test should be performed to assess need for coronary arteriography.

CORONARY VASOSPASM

Intermittent focal spasm of coronary artery; often associated with atherosclerotic lesion near site of spasm. Chest discomfort is similar to angina but more severe and occurs typically at rest, with transient ST-segment elevation. Acute infarction or malignant arrhythmias may develop during spasm-induced ischemia. Evaluation includes observation of ECG (or ambulatory Holter monitor) for transient ST elevation; diagnosis confirmed at coronary angiography using provocative (e.g., IV acetylcholine) testing. *Treatment* consists of long-acting nitrates and calcium antagonists. Prognosis is better in pts with anatomically normal coronary arteries than those with fixed coronary stenoses.

SILENT ISCHEMIA

Myocardial ischemia that develops without anginal symptoms; detected by Holter monitoring or exercise electrocardiography; occurs mainly in pts who also have *symptomatic* ischemia but is sometimes demonstrated in totally asymptomatic individuals. *Management* is guided by exercise electrocardiography, often with radionuclide scintigraphy, to assess severity of myocardial ischemia. Pts with evidence of severe silent ischemia are candidates for coronary arteriography. It has *not* been demonstrated that pts with silent ischemia without marked abnormalities on exercise testing require chronic anti-ischemic therapy. However, aspirin and lipid-lowering therapy (if LDL > 130 mg/dL) are recommended.

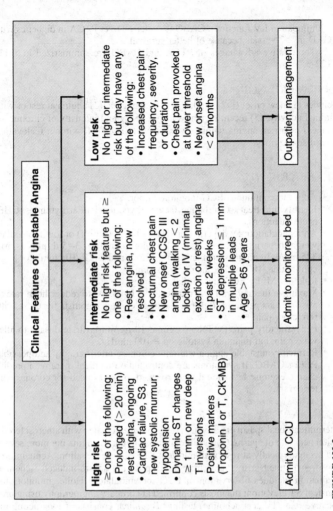

Clinical Features of Unstable Angina

High risk
≥ one of the following:
• Prolonged (> 20 min) rest angina, ongoing
• Cardiac failure, S3, new systolic murmur, hypotension
• Dynamic ST changes ≥ 1 mm or new deep T inversions
• Positive markers (Troponin I or T, CK-MB)

Intermediate risk
No high risk feature but one of the following:
• Rest angina, now resolved
• Nocturnal chest pain
• New onset CCSC III angina (walking < 2 blocks) or IV (minimal exertion or rest) angina in past 2 weeks
• ST depression ≤ 1 mm in multiple leads
• Age > 65 years

Low risk
No high or intermediate risk but may have any of the following:
• Increased chest pain frequency, severity, or duration
• Chest pain provoked at lower threshold
• New onset angina < 2 months

Admit to CCU

Admit to monitored bed

Outpatient management

FIGURE 122-2

600

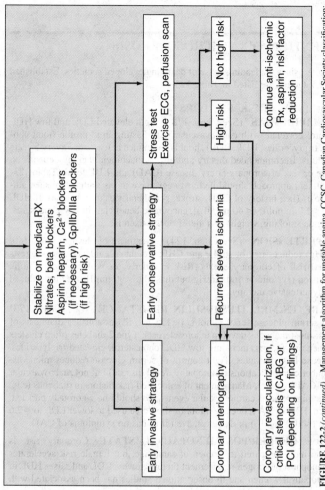

FIGURE 122-2 *(continued)* Management algorithm for unstable angina. CCSC, Canadian Cardiovascular Society classification; CCU, coronary care unit; CABG, coronary artery bypass grafting; PCI, percutaneous coronary intervention. *(Modified from E Braunwald et al, Circulation 90: 613, 1994.)*

For a more detailed discussion, see Selwyn AP, Braunwald E: Ischemic Heart Disease, Chap. 244 p. 1399; and Baim DS: Percutaneous Coronary Revascularization, Chap. 245, p. 1410, in HPIM-15.

123

PREVENTION OF ATHEROSCLEROSIS

Atherosclerosis is the leading cause of death in developed societies. Established major risk factors are listed in Table 123-1.

ESTABLISHED RISK FACTORS

DYSLIPIDEMIAS (See Chap. 178) Both elevated LDL and low HDL cholesterol correlate with cardiovascular risk. Fasting lipid profile (total cholesterol, triglycerides, HDL, LDL) should be obtained at least once every 5 years in all adults. Recommended dietary and/or pharmacologic therapy depends on presence or risk of coronary artery disease (CAD) and LDL level (Table 123-2). Treatment approach should be most aggressive in pts with established atherosclerosis (i.e., history of CAD, stroke, peripheral vascular disease). If HDL is low [<1.0 mmol/L (<40 mg/dL)], encourage beneficial life-style measures: discontinue smoking, weight-loss diet if obese, exercise.

HYPERTENSION (See Chap. 124) Treatment of elevated bp (>140/90 mmHg) reduces risk of stroke and CHF; weight of evidence also suggests decreased risk of coronary events. Risk in elderly pts with isolated systolic hypertension (systolic > 160 mmHg but diastolic <90 mmHg) is also reduced by antihypertensive therapy.

DIABETES MELLITUS/INSULIN RESISTANCE (See Chap. 173) Fasting serum glucose ≥6.9 mmol/L (≥125 mg/dL) establishes diagnosis of diabetes; most diabetics develop atherosclerosis. Type 2 diabetes often clusters with other risk factors, including low HDL cholesterol, elevated triglycerides, small dense LDL particles. Tight control of serum glucose reduces microvascular diabetic complications (retinopathy, renal disease) but not macrovascular disease (CAD, stroke). Management of associated risk factors in diabetics (e.g., dyslipidemia) reduces cardiovascular events and should be vigorously pursued. If needed, HMG-CoA reductase inhibitor should be used to lower LDL to <2.6 mmol/L (<100 mg/dL) in diabetics, even if pt has no symptoms of CAD.

MALE GENDER/POSTMENOPAUSAL STATE Coronary risk is greater in men compared to women of same age, but female risk accelerates after menopause. Estrogen replacement therapy lowers LDL and raises HDL in postmenopausal women and in observational studies has been associated with

Table 123-1

Major Risk Factors of Atherosclerosis

MODIFIABLE RISK FACTORS

Dyslipidemias (↑LDL or ↓HDL)
Hypertension
Diabetes/insulin resistance
Smoking
Obesity
Sedentary life-style

UNMODIFIABLE RISK FACTORS

↑Age
Male gender

Table 123-2

Treatment Decisions Based on LDL Cholesterol

Patient Category	Initiation Level, mg/dL (mmol/L)		LDL Goal, mg/dL
	Dietary Therapy	Drug Treatment	
Without CAD and < 2 risk factors	≥160 (4.1)	≥190 (4.9)	<160 (4.1)
Without CAD and ≥ 2 risk factors	≥130 (3.4)	≥160 (4.1)	<130 (3.4)
With CAD	>100 (2.6)	≥130 (3.4)	≤100 (2.6)

NOTE: LDL, low-density lipoprotein; CAD, coronary artery disease.

reduced coronary events. However, recent rigorous clinical trials do not support such a benefit, and hormone replacement therapy should not be prescribed routinely for purpose of cardiovascular risk reduction.

LIFE-STYLE MODIFICATIONS   For cardiac risk reduction, encourage smoking cessation, good exercise habits (>30 min moderate intensity physical activity daily), and sensible diet (low in saturated and trans fat, high in fruits, vegetables, and low-fat dairy products). Encourage elimination of obesity (Chap. 55).

EMERGING RISK FACTORS
May be useful in assessing pts without the above traditional risk factors who have premature vascular disease or a strong family history of premature vascular disease.

HOMOCYSTEINE   There is a graded correlation between serum homocysteine levels and risk of cardiovascular events and stroke. Folic acid and other B vitamins lower serum levels, but no study has yet evaluated if such reduction improves cardiovascular risk. For pts with hyperhomocystinemia, folic acid supplements are safe, starting at 400 μg/d; avoid doses > 1 mg/d unless serum B_{12} has been evaluated (higher dose folic acid could mask presence of pernicious anemia).

OTHER POTENTIAL RISK FACTORS   C-reactive protein is a marker of inflammation that prospectively predicts risk of MI; its usefulness and role in prevention is currently being defined. Potential benefits of assessing other emerging risk factors [e.g., lipoprotein(a), fibrinogen, infections by *Chlamydia* or CMV] remain unproven and controversial.

For a more detailed discussion, see Libby P: Prevention and Treatment of Atherosclerosis, Chapter 242, p. 1382, in HPIM-15.

124

HYPERTENSION

DEFINITION   Chronic elevation in bp >140/90; etiology unknown in 90–95% of pts ("essential hypertension"). Always consider a secondary correctable form of hypertension, especially in pts under age 30 or those who become hypertensive after 55. Isolated systolic hypertension (systolic >160, diastolic <90) most common in elderly pts, due to reduced vascular compliance.

SECONDARY HYPERTENSION

RENAL ARTERY STENOSIS   Due either to atherosclerosis (older men) or fibromuscular dysplasia (young women). Presents with sudden onset of hypertension, refractory to usual antihypertensive therapy. Abdominal bruit often audible; mild hypokalemia due to activation of the renin-angiotensin-aldosterone system may be present.

RENAL PARENCHYMAL DISEASE   Elevated serum creatinine and/or abnormal urinalysis, containing protein, cells, or casts.

COARCTATION OF AORTA   Presents in children or young adults; constriction is usually present in aorta at origin of left subclavian artery. Exam shows diminished, delayed femoral pulsations; late systolic murmur loudest over the midback. CXR shows indentation of the aorta at the level of the coarctation and rib notching (due to development of collateral arterial flow).

PHEOCHROMOCYTOMA   A catecholamine-secreting tumor, typically of the adrenal medulla, that presents as paroxysmal or sustained hypertension in young to middle-aged pts. Sudden episodes of headache, palpitations, and profuse diaphoresis are common. Associated findings include chronic weight loss, orthostatic *hypotension*, and impaired glucose tolerance. Pheochromocytomas may be localized to the bladder wall and may present with micturition-associated symptoms of catecholamine excess. Diagnosis is suggested by elevated urinary catecholamine metabolites in a 24-h urine collection (see below); the tumor is then localized by CT scan or angiography.

HYPERALDOSTERONISM   Due to aldosterone-secreting adenoma or bilateral adrenal hyperplasia. Should be suspected when hypokalemia is present in a hypertensive pt off diuretics (Chap. 172).

OTHER CAUSES   Oral contraceptive usage, Cushing's and adrenogenital syndromes (Chap. 172), thyroid disease (Chap. 171), hyperparathyroidism (Chap. 176), and acromegaly (Chap. 169).

_____ *Approach to the Patient* _____

History

Most pts are asymptomatic. Severe hypertension may lead to headache, epistaxis, or blurred vision.
   Clues to Specific Forms of Secondary Hypertension   Use of birth control pills or glucocorticoids; paroxysms of headache, sweating, or tachycardia (pheochromocytoma); history of renal disease or abdominal traumas (renal hypertension).

Physical Examination

Measure bp with appropriate-sized cuff (large cuff for large arm). Measure bp in both arms as well as a leg (to evaluate for coarctation). Signs of hypertension include retinal arteriolar changes (narrowing/nicking); left ventricular lift, loud A_2, S_4. Clues to secondary forms of hypertension include cushingoid appearance, thyromegaly, abdominal bruit (renal artery stenosis), delayed femoral pulses (coarctation of aorta).

Laboratory Workup

Screening Tests for Secondary Hypertension Should be carried out on all pts with documented hypertension: (1) serum creatinine, BUN, and urinalysis (renal parenchymal disease); (2) serum K measured off diuretics (hypokalemia prompts workup for hyperaldosteronism or renal artery stenosis); (3) CXR (rib notching or indentation of distal aortic arch in coarctation of the aorta); (4) ECG (LV hypertrophy suggests chronicity of hypertension); (5) other useful screening blood tests include CBC, glucose, cholesterol, triglycerides, calcium, uric acid.

Further Workup Indicated for specific diagnoses if screening tests are abnormal or bp is refractory to antihypertensive therapy: (1) renal artery stenosis: magnetic resonance angiography, captopril renogram, renal duplex ultrasound, digital subtraction angiography, renal arteriography, and measurement of renal vein renin; (2) Cushing's syndrome: dexamethasone suppression test (Chap. 172); (3) pheochromocytoma: 24-h urine collection for catecholamines, metanephrines, and vanillylmandelic acid; (4) primary hyperaldosteronism: depressed plasma renin activity and hypersecretion of aldosterone, both of which fail to change with volume expansion; (5) renal parenchymal disease (Chaps. 137–147).

 TREATMENT

Drug Therapy of Essential Hypertension

Goal is to control hypertension with minimal side effects using a single drug if possible. First-line agents include ACE inhibitors, calcium antagonists, beta blockers, diuretics, and α-adrenergic receptor blockers.

Beta Blockers (Table 124-1) Particularly effective in young pts with "hyperkinetic" circulation. Begin with low dosage (e.g., atenolol 25 mg qd). Relative contraindications: bronchospasm, CHF, AV block, bradycardia, and "brittle" insulin-dependent diabetes.

ACE Inhibitors (Table 124-2) Well tolerated with low frequency of side effects. May be used as monotherapy or in combination with beta blockers, calcium antagonists, or diuretics. Side effects are uncommon and include rash, angioedema, proteinuria, or leukopenia, particularly in pts with elevated serum creatinine. A nonproductive cough may develop in the course of therapy, requiring an alternative regimen. Note that renal function may deteriorate as a result of ACE inhibitors in pts with bilateral renal artery stenosis.

Potassium supplements and potassium-sparing diuretics should be used cautiously with ACE inhibitors to prevent hyperkalemia. If pt is intravascularly volume depleted, hold diuretics for 2–3 d prior to initiation of ACE inhibitor, which should then be administered at very low dosage (e.g., captopril 6.25 mg bid).

For pts who do not tolerate ACE inhibitors because of cough or angioedema, consider angiotensin receptor antagonists (Table 124-3) instead.

Calcium Antagonists (Table 124-4) Direct arteriolar vasodilators; all have negative inotropic effects (particularly verapamil) and should be used cautiously if LV dysfunction is present. Verapamil, and to a lesser extent diltiazem, can result in bradycardia and AV block so combination with beta blockers is generally avoided. Use sustained-release formulations, as short-

Table 124-1

Beta Blockers

	Usual Dose (PO)
NONSELECTIVE AGENTS	
Carteolol[a]	2.5–10 mg qd
Carvedilol[b]	6.25–25 mg bid
Labetolol[b]	100–600 mg bid
Nadolol	20–120 mg qd
Penbutolol[a]	20 mg qd
Pindolol[a]	5–30 mg bid
Propranolol, sustained-action	20–60 mg qid
	80–160 mg qd
Timolol	5–15 mg bid
BETA$_1$-SELECTIVE AGENTS	
Acebutolol[a]	200–600 mg bid
Atenolol	25–100 mg qd
Betaxolol	10–20 mg qd
Metoprolol, sustained-action	25–150 mg bid
	50–300 mg qd

[a] Also has beta-agonist activity.
[b] Also has alpha$_1$ blocking properties.
Side-effects: Bradycardia (less common in those with beta-agonist activity), GI discomfort, CHF, bronchospasm (less common with beta$_1$-selective agents), exacerbation of diabetes or impaired response to insulin-induced hypoglycemia, impotence.

acting dihydropyridine calcium channel blockers may increase incidence of coronary events.

Diuretics (Table 17-1)   Thiazides preferred over loop diuretics because of longer duration of action; however, the latter are more potent when GFR < 25 mL/min. Major side effects include hypokalemia, hyperglycemia, and hyperuricemia, which can be minimized by using low dosage (e.g., hydrochlorothiazide 12.5–50 mg qd). Diuretics are particularly effective in elderly

Table 124-2

ACE Inhibitors

	Dose (PO)
Captopril	12.5–75 mg bid
Enalapril	2.5–40 mg qd
Lisinopril	5–40 mg qd
Benazapril	10–40 mg qd
Fosinopril	10–40 mg qd
Quinapril	10–80 mg qd
Ramipril	2.5–20 mg qd
Moexipril	7.5–30 mg qd
Trandolapril	2–4 mg qd

NOTE: Dosage of ACE inhibitors (except fosinopril) should be reduced in pts with renal failure.
Side effects: Hypotension, angiodema, cough, rash, azotemia, hyperkalemia.

Table 124-3

Angiotensin II Receptor Antagonists

	Usual Dose (PO)
Candesartan	8–32 mg qd
Eprosartan	400–800 mg qd
Irbesartan	75–300 mg qd
Losartan	25–100 mg qd
Telmisartan	20–80 mg qd
Valsartan	80–320 mg qd

and black pts. Prevention of hypokalemia is especially important in pts on digitalis glycosides.

If bp proves refractory to drug therapy, work up for secondary forms of hypertension, especially renal artery stenosis and pheochromocytoma (see HPIM-15, Table 246-6, p. 1424) for detailed list of antihypertensives).

Special Circumstances

Pregnancy   Safest antihypertensives include methyldopa (250–1000 mg PO bid-tid) and hydralazine (10–150 mg PO bid-tid). Calcium channel blockers also appear to be safe in pregnancy. Beta blockers need to be used cautiously—fetal hypoglycemia and low birth weights have been reported. ACE inhibitors and angiotensin receptor antagonists are contraindicated in pregnancy.

Renal Failure   Standard thiazide diuretics may not be effective. Consider metolazone, furosemide, or bumetanide, alone or in combination.

Malignant Hypertension   Diastolic bp > 120 mmHg is a medical emergency. Immediate therapy is mandatory if there is evidence of cardiac decompensation (CHF, angina), encephalopathy (headache, seizures, visual disturbances), or deteriorating renal function. Drugs to treat hypertensive crisis are

Table 124-4

Calcium Channel Antagonists

	Usual Dose (PO)	Adverse Effects
Verapamil	40–120 mg tid-qid	Hypotension, bradycardia AV
SR formulation	120–480 mg qd-bid	block, heart failure, constipation, ↑ digoxin level
Diltiazem	30–90 mg tid-qid	Hypotension, peripheral edema,
SR formulation	60–180 mg bid	bradycardia, AV block, heart
CD formulation	180–300 mg qd	failure
Dihydropyridines		Tachycardia, hypotension, peripheral edema, headache, flushing
Nifedipine XL	30–90 mg qd	
Nicardipine[a]	20–40 mg tid	
Isradipine[a]	2.5–10 mg bid	
Felodipine[a]	5–10 mg qd	
Amlodipine[a]	2.5–10 mg qd	

[a] Least negatively inotropic agents.

Table 124-5

Treatment of Malignant Hypertension and Hypertensive Crisis

	Dosage	Adverse Effects
Nitroprusside[a]	IV: 0.5–8.0 (μg/kg)/min	Hypotension; after 24 h watch for thiocyanate toxicity (tinnitus, blurred vision, altered mental state)
Nitroglycerin[a]	IV: 5–100 μg/min	Hypotension, headache
Labetolol	IV: 20–80 mg q10min (maximum of 300 mg) *or* 20 mg IV bolus, then 1–2 mg/min infusion	Hypotension, bradycardia, AV block, bronchospasm
Enalaprilat	IV: 1.25 mg q6h	Angioedema, hyperkalemia
Hydralazine	IV: 5–10 mg IV q10–15min (maximum of 50 mg)	Reflex tachycardia, avoid in pts with CAD or suspected aortic dissection
Diazoxide	IV: 50 mg q5–10min (max of 600 mg)	Na$^+$ retention[b], hyperglycemia
Fenoldopam	IV: 0.1–0.3 (μg/kg)/min	Hypotension, tachycardia, headache, flushing

[a] Intraarterial bp monitoring recommended to avoid rapid fluctuations in bp.
[b] Administer furosemide 20–80 mg IV concurrently to prevent Na$^+$ retention.

listed in Table 124-5. Replace with PO antihypertensive as pt becomes asymptomatic and diastolic bp improves.

For a more detailed discussion, see Williams GH: Approach to the Patient with Hypertension, Chap. 35, p. 211, and Hypertensive Vascular Disease, Chap. 246, p. 1414, in HPIM-15.

125

DISEASES OF THE AORTA

AORTIC ANEURYSM

Abnormal widening of the abdominal or thoracic aorta; in ascending aorta most commonly secondary to cystic medial necrosis or atherosclerosis; aneurysms of descending thoracic and abdominal aorta are primarily atherosclerotic.

HISTORY   May be clinically silent, but thoracic aortic aneurysms often result in deep, diffuse chest pain, dysphagia, hoarseness, hemoptysis, dry cough;

abdominal aneurysms result in abdominal pain or thromboemboli to the lower extremities.

PHYSICAL EXAMINATION　Abdominal aneurysms are often palpable, most commonly in periumbilical area. Pts with ascending thoracic aneurysms may show features of the Marfan syndrome (HPIM-15, Chap. 351).

LABORATORY　*CXR*: Enlarged aortic silhouette (thoracic aneurysm); confirm abdominal aneurysm by *abdominal plain film* (rim of calcification), *ultrasound, CT scan,* or *MRI.* Contrast aortography is often performed preoperatively. If clinically suspected, obtain serologic test for syphilis, especially if ascending thoracic aneurysm shows thin shell of calcification.

 TREATMENT

Control of hypertension (Chap. 124) is essential. Surgical resection of thoracic aortic aneurysms >6 cm in diameter (abdominal aortic aneurysms >5 cm), for persistent pain despite bp control, or for evidence of rapid expansion. In pts with the Marfan syndrome, thoracic aortic aneurysms >5 cm usually warrant repair.

AORTIC DISSECTION　(Fig. 125-1)

Potentially life-threatening condition in which disruption of aortic intima allows dissection of blood into vessel wall; may involve ascending aorta (type II), descending aorta (type III), or both (type I). Alternative classification: Type A—dissection involves ascending aorta; type B—limited to descending aorta. Involvement of the ascending aorta is most lethal form.

ETIOLOGY　Ascending aortic dissection associated with hypertension, cystic medial necrosis, the Marfan syndrome; descending dissections commonly associated with atherosclerosis or hypertension. Incidence is increased in pts with coarctation of aorta, bicuspid aortic valve, and rarely in third trimester of pregnancy in otherwise normal women.

SYMPTOMS　Sudden onset of severe anterior or posterior chest pain, with "ripping" quality; maximal pain may travel if dissection propagates. Additional symptoms relate to obstruction of aortic branches (stroke, MI), dyspnea (acute aortic regurgitation), or symptoms of low cardiac output due to cardiac tamponade (dissection into pericardial sac).

PHYSICAL EXAMINATION　Sinus tachycardia common; if cardiac tamponade develops, hypotension, pulsus paradoxus, and pericardial rub appear. Asymmetry of carotid or brachial pulses, aortic regurgitation, and neurologic abnormalities associated with interruption of carotid artery flow are common findings.

LABORATORY　*CXR*: Widening of mediastinum; dissection can be confirmed by *CT scan, MRI,* or *ultrasound* (esp. transesophageal echocardiography). Aortography recommended if results of these imaging techniques are not definitive.

 TREATMENT

Reduce cardiac contractility and treat hypertension to maintain systolic bp between 100 and 120 mmHg using IV agents (Table 125-1), e.g., sodium nitroprusside accompanied by a beta blocker (aiming for heart rate of 60 beats per min), followed by oral therapy. If beta blocker contraindicated, consider

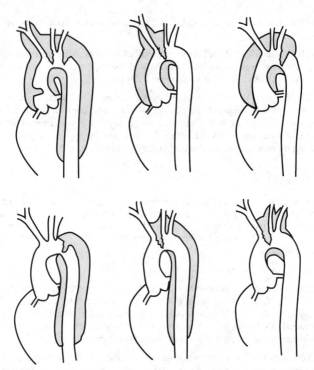

FIGURE 125-1 Classification of aortic dissections. Stanford classification: Top panels illustrate type A dissections that involve the ascending aorta independent of site of tear and distal extension; type B dissections (bottom panels) involve transverse and/or descending aorta without involvement of the ascending aorta. DeBakey classification: Type I dissection involves ascending to descending aorta (top left); type II dissection is limited to ascending or transverse aorta, without descending aorta (top center + top right); type III dissection involves descending aorta only (bottom left). [*From DC Miller, in RM Doroghazi, EE Slater (eds.) Aortic Dissection. New York, McGraw-Hill, 1983, with permission.*]

IV verapamil or diltiazem (Table 115-3). Direct vasodilators (hydralazine, diazoxide) are contraindicated because they may increase shear stress. Ascending aortic dissection (type A) requires surgical repair emergently or, if pt can be stabilized with medications, semielectively. Descending aortic dissections are stabilized medically (maintain systolic bp between 110 and 120 mmHg) with oral antihypertensive agents (esp. beta blockers); immediate surgical repair is not necessary unless continued pain or extension of dissection is observed (serial MRI or CT scans).

OTHER ABNORMALITIES OF THE AORTA

ATHEROSCLEROSIS OF ABDOMINAL AORTA   Particularly common in presence of diabetes mellitus or cigarette smoking. Symptoms include intermittent claudication of the buttocks and thighs and impotence (Leriche syndrome); femoral and other distal pulses are absent. Diagnosis is established by noninvasive leg pressure measurements and Doppler velocity analysis, and confirmed by aortography. Aortic-femoral bypass surgery is required for symptomatic treatment.

Table 125-1

Treatment of Aortic Dissection

Preferred Regimen	Dose
Sodium nitroprusside *plus* a beta blocker:	20–400 μg/min IV
Propranolol *or*	0.5 mg IV; then 1 mg q5min, to total of 0.15 mg/kg
Esmolol *or*	500 μg/kg IV over 1 min; then 50–200 (μg/kg)/min
Labetolol	20 mg IV over 2 min, then 40–80 mg q10–15min to max of 300 mg

TAKAYASU'S ("PULSELESS") DISEASE   Arteritis of aorta and major branches in young women. Anorexia, weight loss, fever, and night sweats occur. Localized symptoms relate to occlusion of aortic branches (cerebral ischemia, claudication, and loss of pulses in arms). ESR is increased; diagnosis confirmed by aortography. Glucocorticoid and immunosuppressive therapy may be beneficial, but mortality is high.

For a more detailed discussion, see Dzau VJ, Creager MA: Diseases of the Aorta, Chap. 247, p. 1430, in HPIM-15.

126

PERIPHERAL VASCULAR DISEASE

Occlusive or inflammatory disease that develops within the peripheral arteries, veins, or lymphatics.

ARTERIOSCLEROSIS OF PERIPHERAL ARTERIES

HISTORY   *Intermittent claudication* is muscular cramping with exercise; quickly relieved by rest. Pain in buttocks and thighs suggests aortoiliac disease; calf muscle pain implies femoral or popliteal artery disease. More advanced arteriosclerotic obstruction results in pain at rest; painful ulcers of the feet (painless in diabetics) may result.

PHYSICAL EXAMINATION   Decreased peripheral pulses, blanching of affected limb with elevation, dependent rubor (redness). Ischemic ulcers or gangrene of toes may be present.

LABORATORY   Doppler ultrasound of peripheral pulses before and during exercise localizes stenoses; contrast arteriography performed only if reconstructive surgery or angioplasty is considered.

Rx TREATMENT

Most pts can be managed medically with daily exercise program, careful foot care (esp. in diabetics), treatment of hypercholesterolemia, and local debridement of ulcerations. Abstinence from cigarettes is mandatory. Some, but not all, pts note symptomatic improvement with drug therapy (pentoxifylline or cilostazol). Pts with severe claudication, rest pain, or gangrene are candidates for arterial reconstructive surgery; percutaneous transluminal angioplasty can be performed in selected pts.

Other Conditions That Impair Peripheral Arterial Flow

ARTERIAL EMBOLISM   Due to thrombus or vegetation within the heart or aorta or paradoxically from a venous thrombus through a right-to-left intracardiac shunt.

History   Sudden pain or numbness in an extremity in absence of previous history of claudication.

Physical Exam   Absent pulse, pallor, and decreased temperature of limb distal to the occlusion. Lesion is identified by angiography.

Rx TREATMENT

Intravenous heparin to prevent propagation of clot. For acute severe ischemia, immediate surgical embolectomy is indicated. Thrombolytic therapy (e.g., tPA, streptokinase, urokinase) may be effective for thrombus within atherosclerotic vessel or arterial bypass graft.

VASOSPASTIC DISORDERS   Manifest by Raynaud's phenomenon in which cold exposure results in triphasic color response: blanching of the fingers, followed by cyanosis, then redness. Usually a benign disorder. However, suspect an underlying disease (e.g., scleroderma) if tissue necrosis occurs, if disease is unilateral, or if it develops after age 50.

Rx TREATMENT

Keep extremities warm; calcium channel blockers (nifedipine 30–90 mg PO qd or α-adrenergic antagonists (e.g., prazocin 1–5 mg tid) may be effective.

THROMBOANGIITIS OBLITERANS (BUERGER'S DISEASE)   Occurs in young men who are heavy smokers and involves both upper and lower extremities; nonatheromatous inflammatory reaction develops in veins and small arteries leading to superficial thrombophlebitis and arterial obstruction with ulceration or gangrene of digits. Abstinence from tobacco is essential.

VENOUS DISEASE

SUPERFICIAL THROMBOPHLEBITIS   Benign disorder characterized by erythema, tenderness, and edema along involved vein. Conservative therapy includes local heat, elevation, and anti-inflammatory drugs such as aspirin. More serious conditions such as cellulitis or lymphangitis may mimic this, but these are associated with fever, chills, lymphadenopathy, and red superficial streaks along inflamed lymphatic channels.

DEEP VENOUS THROMBOSIS (DVT)   More serious condition that may lead to pulmonary embolism (Chap. 132). Particularly common in pts on prolonged bed rest, those with chronic debilitating disease, and those with malignancies (Table 126-1).

History   Pain or tenderness in calf or thigh, usually unilateral; may be asymptomatic, with pulmonary embolism as primary presentation.

Physical Exam   Often normal; local swelling or tenderness to deep palpation may be present over affected vein.

Laboratory   Most helpful noninvasive testing is ultrasound imaging of the deep veins. Doppler studies or impedance plethysmography may also be useful. These noninvasive studies are most sensitive for proximal (upper leg) DVT, less sensitive for calf DVT. Invasive venography is used when diagnosis not clear. MRI may be useful for diagnosis of proximal DVT and DVT within the pelvic veins or in the superior or inferior vena cavae.

℞ TREATMENT

Systemic anticoagulation with heparin (5000- to 10,000-U bolus, followed by continuous IV infusion to maintain a PTT at 2× normal) or low-molecular-weight heparin (e.g., enoxaperin 1 mg/kg SC bid), followed by warfarin PO (overlap with heparin for at least 3–4 d and continue for at least 3 months if proximal deep veins involved). Adjust warfarin dose to maintain prothrombin time at INR 2.0–3.0.

DVT can be prevented by early ambulation following surgery or with low-dose heparin during prolonged bed rest (5000 U SC bid-tid), supplemented by pneumatic compression boots. Following knee or hip surgery, warfarin (INR 2.0–3.0) is an effective regimen. Low-molecular-weight heparins are also effective in preventing DVT after general or orthopedic surgery.

LYMPHEDEMA

Chronic, painless edema, usually of the lower extremities; may be primary (inherited) or secondary to lymphatic damage or obstruction (e.g., recurrent lymphangitis, tumor, filariasis).

Table 126-1

Conditions Associated with an Increased Risk for Development of Venous Thrombosis

Surgery
   Orthopedic, thoracic, abdominal, and genitourinary procedures
Neoplasms
   Pancreas, lung, ovary, testes, urinary tract, breast, stomach
Trauma
   Fractures of spine, pelvis, femur, tibia
Immobilization
   Acute MI, CHF, stroke, postoperative convalescence
Pregnancy
   Estrogen use (for replacement or contraception)
Hypercoagulable states
   Resistance to activated protein C; deficiencies of antithrombin III, protein C, or protein S; circulating lupus anticoagulant; myeloproliferative disease; dysfibrinogenemia; DIC
Venulitis
   Thromboangiitis obliterans, Behçet's disease, homocysteinuria
Previous deep vein thrombosis

PHYSICAL EXAMINATION Marked pitting edema in early stages; limb becomes indurated with *non*pitting edema chronically. Differentiate from chronic *venous* insufficiency, which displays hyperpigmentation, stasis dermatitis, and superficial venous varicosities.

LABORATORY Abdominal and pelvic ultrasound or CT or MRI to identify obstructing lesions. Lymphangiography or lymphoscintigraphy (rarely done) to confirm diagnosis. If *unilateral* edema, differentiate from DVT by noninvasive venous studies (above).

 TREATMENT

(1) Meticulous foot hygiene to prevent infection, (2) leg elevation, (3) compression stockings and/or pneumatic compression boots. Diuretics should be *avoided* to prevent intravascular volume depletion.

For a more detailed discussion, see Creager MA, Dzau VJ: Vascular Diseases of the Extremities, Chap. 248, p. 1434, in HPIM-15.

127

RESPIRATORY FUNCTION AND DIAGNOSIS OF PULMONARY DISEASE

DISTURBANCES OF RESPIRATORY FUNCTION

The respiratory system includes not only the lungs but also the CNS, chest wall (diaphragm, abdomen, intercostal muscles), and pulmonary circulation. Prime function of the system is to exchange gas between inspired air and venous blood.

DISTURBANCES IN VENTILATORY FUNCTION (Figs. 127-1 and 127-2) Ventilation is the process whereby lungs deliver fresh air to alveoli. Measurements of ventilatory function consist of quantification of air in the lungs [total lung capacity (TLC), residual volume (RV)] and the rate at which air can be expelled from the lungs [forced vital capacity (FVC), forced expiratory volume in 1 s (FEV_1)] during a forced exhalation from TLC. Expiratory flow rates may be plotted against lung volumes yielding a flow-volume curve (HPIM-15, Fig. 250-4, p. 1448).

Two major patterns of abnormal ventilatory function are restrictive and obstructive patterns (Tables 127-1 and 127-2).

In obstructive pattern:

- Hallmark is decrease in expiratory flow rate, i.e., FEV_1.
- Ratio FEV_1/FVC is reduced.
- TLC is normal or increased.
- RV is elevated due to trapping of air during expiration.

In restrictive disease:

- Hallmark is decrease in TLC.
- May be caused by pulmonary parenchymal disease or extraparenchymal (neuromuscular such as myasthenia gravis or chest wall such as kyphoscoliosis).
- Pulmonary parenchymal disease usually occurs with a reduced RV, but extraparenchymal disease (with expiratory dysfunction) occurs with an increased RV.

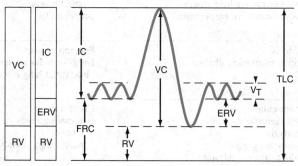

FIGURE 127-1 Lung volumes, shown by block diagrams (*left*) and by a spirographic tracing (*right*). TLC, total lung capacity; VC, vital capacity; RV, residual volume; IC, inspiratory capacity; ERV, expiratory reserve volume; FRC, functional residual capacity; V_T, tidal volume. (*From SE Weinberger, JM Drazen: HPIM-15, 1447.*)

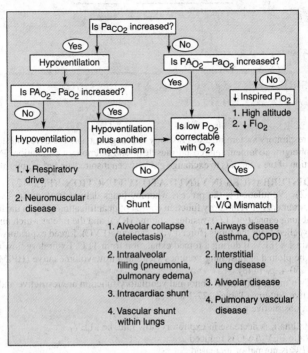

FIGURE 127-2 Flow diagram outlining the diagnostic approach to the pt with hypoxemia ($Pa_{O_2} < 80$ mmHg). $PA_{O_2} - Pa_{O_2}$ is usually <15 mmHg for subjects ≤ 30 years old, and increases ~ 3 mmHg per decade after age 30.

Table 127-1

Common Respiratory Diseases by Diagnostic Categories

OBSTRUCTIVE

Asthma	Bronchiectasis
Chronic obstructive lung disease (chronic bronchitis, emphysema)	Cystic fibrosis
	Bronchiolitis

RESTRICTIVE—PARENCHYMAL

Sarcoidosis	Pneumoconiosis
Idiopathic pulmonary fibrosis	Drug- or radiation-induced interstitial lung disease

RESTRICTIVE—EXTRAPARENCHYMAL

Neuromuscular	Chest wall
Diaphragmatic weakness/ paralysis	Kyphoscoliosis
Myasthenia gravis[a]	Obesity
Guillain-Barré syndrome[a]	Ankylosing spondylitis[a]
Muscular dystrophies[a]	
Cervical spine injury[a]	

[a] Can have inspiratory and expiratory limitation (see text).

Table 127-2

Alterations in Ventilatory Function

	TLC	RV	VC	FEV$_1$/FVC
Obstructive	N to ↑	↑	↓	↓
Restrictive				
Pulmonary parenchymal	↓	↓	↓	N to ↑
Extraparenchymal—inspiratory	↓	N to ↓	↓	N
Extraparenchymal—inspiratory + expiratory	↓	↑	↓	Variable

NOTE: N, normal.
SOURCE: Adapted from SE Weinberger, JM Drazen: HPIM-15, p. 1449.

DISTURBANCES IN PULMONARY CIRCULATION Pulmonary vasculature transmits the RV output, ~5 L/min at a low pressure. Perfusion of lung greatest in dependent portion. Assessment requires measuring pulmonary vascular pressures and cardiac output to derive pulmonary vascular resistance. Pulmonary vascular resistance rises with hypoxia, intraluminal thrombi, scarring, or loss of alveolar beds.

All diseases of the respiratory system causing hypoxia are capable of causing pulmonary hypertension. However, pts with hypoxemia due to chronic obstructive lung disease, interstitial lung disease, chest wall disease, and obesity-hypoventilation–sleep apnea are particularly likely to develop pulmonary hypertension.

DISTURBANCES IN GAS EXCHANGE Primary functions of the respiratory system are to remove CO_2 and provide O_2. Normal tidal volume is about 500 mL, and normal frequency is 15 breaths per minute for a total ventilation of 7.5 L/min. Because of dead space, alveolar ventilation is 5 L/min.

Partial pressure of CO_2 in arterial blood (Pa_{CO_2}) is directly proportional to amount of CO_2 produced each minute ($\dot{V}_{CO_2}$) and inversely proportional to alveolar ventilation ($\dot{V}A$).

$$Pa_{CO_2} = 0.863 \times \dot{V}_{CO_2}/\dot{V}A$$

Gas exchange is critically dependent on proper matching of ventilation and perfusion.

Assessment of gas exchange requires measurement of ABGs. The actual content of O_2 in blood is determined by both P_{O_2} and hemoglobin.

Arterial P_{O_2} can be used to measure alveolar-arterial O_2 difference (A−a gradient). Increased A−a gradient (normal <15 mmHg, rising by 3 mmHg each decade after age 30) indicates impaired gas exchange.

In order to calculate A−a gradient, the alveolar P_{O_2} (PA_{O_2}) must be calculated:

$$PA_{O_2} = FI_{O_2} \times (PB - P_{H_2O}) - Pa_{CO_2}/R$$

where FI_{O_2} = fractional concentration of inspired O_2 (0.21 breathing room air), PB = barometric pressure (760 mmHg at sea level), P_{H_2O} = water vapor pressure (47 mmHg when air is saturated at 37°C), and R = respiratory quotient (the ratio of CO_2 production to O_2 consumption, usually assumed to be 0.8).

Adequacy of CO_2 removal is reflected in the partial pressure of CO_2 in arterial blood.

Because measurement of ABGs necessitates arterial puncture, noninvasive techniques may be useful, particularly to determine trends in gas exchange over time. The pulse oximeter measures oxygen saturation Sa_{O_2} rather than Pa_{O_2}. While widely used, clinicians must be aware that (1) the relationship between Sa_{O_2} and Pa_{O_2} is curvilinear, flattening above a Pa_{O_2} of 60 mmHg; (2) poor peripheral perfusion may interfere with the oximeter's function; and (3) the oximeter provides no information about P_{CO_2}.

Ability of gas to diffuse across the alveolar-capillary membrane is assessed by the diffusing capacity of the lung (DL_{CO}). Carried out with low concentration of carbon monoxide during a single 10-s breath-holding period or during 1 min of steady breathing. Value depends on alveolar-capillary surface area, pulmonary capillary blood volume, degree of ventilation-perfusion ($\dot{V}/\dot{Q}$) mismatching, and thickness of alveolar-capillary membrane.

MECHANISMS OF ABNORMAL FUNCTION Four basic mechanisms of hypoxemia are (1) ↓ inspired P_{O_2}, (2) hypoventilation, (3) shunt, and (4) $\dot{V}/\dot{Q}$ mismatch. Diffusion block contributes to hypoxemia only under selected circumstances. Approach to the hypoxemic pt is shown in Fig. 127-2.

The essential mechanism underlying all cases of hypercapnia is inadequate alveolar ventilation. Potential contributing factors include (1) increased CO_2 production, (2) decreased ventilatory drive, (3) malfunction of the respiratory pump or increased airways resistance, and (4) inefficiency of gas exchange (increased dead space or $\dot{V}/\dot{Q}$ mismatch) necessitating a compensatory increase in overall minute ventilation.

DIAGNOSTIC PROCEDURES

NONINVASIVE PROCEDURES *Radiography* No CXR pattern is sufficiently specific to *establish* a diagnosis; instead, the CXR serves to *detect* disease, assess magnitude, and guide further diagnostic investigation. Thoracic CT is now routine in evaluation of pts with pulmonary nodules and masses. CT is especially helpful in the assessment of pleural lesions. Contrast enhancement also makes thoracic CT useful in differentiating tissue masses from vascular structures. High-resolution CT has largely replaced bronchography in the evaluation of surgical bronchiectasis and is useful in evaluation of pts with interstitial lung disease. Spiral or helical CT is increasingly used in the diagnosis of pulmonary thromboembolism. MRI is generally less useful than CT but is preferred in evaluation of abnormalities at the lung apex, adjacent to the spine, and at the thoracoabdominal junction.

Skin Tests Specific skin test antigens are available for tuberculosis, histoplasmosis, coccidioidomycosis, blastomycosis, trichinosis, toxoplasmosis, and aspergillosis. A positive delayed reaction (type IV) to a tuberculin test indicates only prior infection, not active disease. Immediate (type I) and late (type III) dermal hypersensitivity to *Aspergillus* antigen supports diagnosis of allergic bronchopulmonary aspergillosis in pts with a compatible clinical illness.

Sputum Exam Sputum is distinguished from saliva by presence of bronchial epithelial cells and alveolar macrophages. Sputum exam should include gross inspection for blood, color, and odor, as well as microscopic inspection of carefully stained smears. Culture of expectorated sputum may be misleading owing to contamination with oropharyngeal flora. Sputum samples induced by inhalation of nebulized, warm, hypertonic saline can be stained using immunofluorescent techniques for the presence of *Pneumocystis carinii*.

Pulmonary Function Tests May indicate abnormalities of airway function, alterations of lung volume, and disturbances of gas exchange. Specific patterns of pulmonary function may assist in differential diagnosis. PFTs may also provide objective measures of therapeutic response, e.g., to bronchodilators.

Pulmonary Scintigraphy Scans of pulmonary ventilation and perfusion aid in the diagnosis of pulmonary embolism. Quantitative ventilation-perfusion scans are also used to assess surgical resectability of lung cancer in pts with diminished respiratory function. *Gallium scanning* may be used to identify inflammatory disease of the lungs or mediastinal lymph nodes. Inflammatory activity of the lungs detected with gallium may be associated with diffuse interstitial infections. Gallium uptake by the lungs may also occur in *P. carinii* pneumonia (PCP).

INVASIVE PROCEDURES *Bronchoscopy* Permits visualization of airways, identification of endobronchial abnormalities, and collection of diagnostic specimens by lavage, brushing, or biopsy. The fiberoptic bronchoscope permits exam of smaller, more peripheral airways than the rigid bronchoscope, but the latter permits greater control of the airways and provides more effective suctioning. These features make rigid bronchoscopy particularly useful in pts with central obstructing tumors, foreign bodies, or massive hemoptysis. The fiberoptic bronchoscope increases the diagnostic potential of bronchoscopy, permitting biopsy of peripheral nodules and diffuse infiltrative diseases as well as aspiration and lavage of airways and airspaces. Fiberoptic biopsy is particularly useful in diagnosing diffuse infectious processes, lymphangitic spread of cancer, and granulomatous diseases.

Video-Assisted Thoracic Surgery Now commonly used for diagnosis of pleural lesions as well as peripheral parenchymal infiltrates and nodules. Has largely replaced "open biopsy"; may be used therapeutically.

Percutaneous Needle Aspiration of the Lung Usually performed under CT guidance to obtain cytologic or microbiologic specimens from local pulmonary lesions.

Bronchoalveolar Lavage (BAL) An adjunct to fiberoptic bronchoscopy permitting collection of cells and liquid from distal air spaces. Useful in diagnosis of PCP, other infections, and some interstitial diseases.

Thoracentesis and Pleural Biopsy Thoracentesis should be performed as an early step in the evaluation of any pleural effusion of uncertain etiology. Analysis of pleural fluid helps differentiate transudate from exudate (Chap. 134). (Exudate: pleural fluid LDH >200 IU, pleural fluid/serum protein >0.5, pleural fluid/serum LDH >0.6.) Pleural fluid pH <7.2 suggests that an exudate associated with an infection is an empyema and will almost certainly require drainage. WBC count and differential; glucose, P_{CO_2}, amylase, Gram stain, culture, and cytologic exam should be performed on all specimens. Rheumatoid factor and complement may also be useful. Closed pleural biopsy can also be done when a pleural effusion is present, but has largely been replaced by video-assisted thoracoscopy.

Pulmonary Angiography The definitive test for pulmonary embolism; may also reveal AV malformations.

Mediastinoscopy Diagnostic procedure of choice in pts with disease involving mediastinal lymph nodes. However, lymph nodes in left superior mediastinum must be approached via *mediastinotomy*.

For a more detailed discussion, see Weinberger SE, Drazen JM: Disturbances of Respiratory Function, Chap. 250, p. 1446, and Diagnostic Procedures in Respiratory Diseases, Chap. 251, p. 1453, in HPIM-15.

128

ASTHMA AND HYPERSENSITIVITY PNEUMONITIS

ASTHMA

DEFINITION   Increased responsiveness of lower airways to multiple
stimuli; episodic, and with reversible obstruction; may range in severity from
mild without limitation of pt's activity to severe and life-threatening. Severe
obstruction persisting for days or weeks is known as *status asthmaticus.*

EPIDEMIOLOGY AND ETIOLOGY   Some 4–5% of adults and up to
10% of children are estimated to experience episodes of asthma. Basic abnormality is airway hyperresponsiveness to both specific and nonspecific stimuli.
All pts demonstrate enhanced bronchoconstriction in response to inhalation of
methacholine or histamine (nonspecific bronchoconstrictor agents). Some pts
may be classified as having *allergic asthma*; these experience worsening of
symptoms on exposure to pollens or other allergens. They characteristically give
personal and/or family history of other allergic diseases, such as rhinitis, urticaria, and eczema. Skin tests to allergens are positive; serum IgE may be ↑.
Bronchoprovocation studies may demonstrate positive responses to inhalation
of specific allergens.

A significant number of asthmatic pts have negative allergic histories and
do not react to skin or bronchoprovocation testing with specific allergens. Many
of these develop bronchospasm after a URI. These pts are said to have *idiosyncratic asthma*.

Some pts experience worsening of symptoms on exercise or exposure to
cold air or occupational stimuli. Many note increased wheezing following viral
URI or in response to emotional stress.

PATHOGENESIS   Common denominator underlying the asthmatic diathesis is nonspecific hyperirritability of the tracheobronchial tree. The etiology of
airway hyperresponsiveness in asthma is unknown, but airway inflammation is
believed to play a fundamental role. Airway reactivity may fluctuate, and fluctuations correlate with clinical symptoms. Airway reactivity may be increased
by a number of factors: allergenic, pharmacologic, environmental, occupational,
infectious, exercise-related, and emotional. Among the more common are airborne allergens, aspirin, β-adrenergic blocking agents (e.g., propranolol, timolol), sulfites in food, air pollution (ozone, nitrogen dioxide), and respiratory
infections.

_____ *Approach to the Patient* _____

History   Symptoms: wheezing, dyspnea, cough, fever, sputum production,
other allergic disorders. Possible precipitating factors (allergens, infection, etc.);

asthma attacks often occur at night. Response to medications. Course of previous attacks (e.g., need for hospitalization, steroid treatment).

Physical Exam General: tachypnea, tachycardia, use of accessory respiratory muscles, cyanosis, pulsus paradoxus (accessory muscle use and pulsus paradoxus correlate with severity of obstruction). Lungs: adequacy of aeration, symmetry of breath sounds, wheezing, prolongation of expiratory phase, hyperinflation. Heart: evidence for CHF. ENT/skin: evidence of allergic nasal, sinus, or skin disease.

Laboratory While PFT findings are not diagnostic, they are very helpful in judging severity of airway obstruction and in following response to therapy in both chronic and acute situations. Forced vital capacity (FVC), FEV_1, maximum mid- and peak expiratory flow rate (MMEFR, PEFR), FEV_1/FVC are decreased; residual volume and TLC increased during episodes of obstruction; DL_{CO} usually normal or slightly increased. Reduction of FEV_1 to <25% predicted or <0.75 L after administration of a bronchodilator indicates severe disease. CBC may show eosinophilia. IgE may show mild elevations; marked elevations may suggest evidence of allergic bronchopulmonary aspergillosis (ABPA). Sputum examination: eosinophilia, Curschmann's spirals (casts of small airways), Charcot-Leyden crystals; presence of large numbers of neutrophils suggests bronchial infection. ABGs: uniformly show hypoxemia during attacks; usually hypocarbia and respiratory alkalosis present; normal or elevated P_{CO_2} worrisome as it may suggest severe respiratory muscle fatigue and airways obstruction. CXR not always necessary: may show hyperinflation, patchy infiltrates due to atelectasis behind plugged airways; important when complicating infection is a consideration.

Differential diagnosis "All that wheezes is not asthma": CHF; chronic bronchitis/emphysema; upper airway obstruction due to foreign body, tumor, laryngeal edema; carcinoid tumors (usually associated with stridor, not wheezing); recurrent pulmonary emboli; eosinophilic pneumonia; vocal cord dysfunction; systemic vasculitis with pulmonary involvement.

℞ TREATMENT

Removal of inciting agent, if possible, is most successful treatment. Desensitization or immunotherapy, although popular, has limited scientific support and minimal clinical effectiveness.

Pharmacologic agents for treating asthma can be divided into two general categories: (1) drugs that inhibit smooth-muscle contraction, "quick relief medications" (β-adrenergic agonists, methylxanthines, and anticholinergics); and (2) agents that prevent or reverse inflammation, "long-term control medications" (glucocorticoids, leukotriene inhibitors and receptor antagonists, and mast cell–stabilizing agents).

1. *β-Adrenergic agonists*: Inhaled route provides most rapid effect and best therapeutic index; resorcinols (metaproterenol, terbutaline, fenoterol), saligenins (albuterol), and catecholamines (isoproterenol, isoetharine) may be given by nebulizer or metered-dose inhaler. Epinephrine, 0.3 mL of 1:1000 solution SC (for use in acute situations in absence of cardiac history). Salmeterol, a very long-acting congener of albuterol (9–12 mL), is not recommended for acute attacks but may be helpful for nocturnal or exercise-induced asthma. IV administration of β-adrenergic agents for severe asthma is not considered justified due to the risk of toxicity.

2. *Methylxanthines*: Theophylline and various salts; adjust dose to maintain blood level between 5 and 15 $\mu g/mL$; may be given PO or IV (as aminophylline). Theophylline clearance varies widely and is reduced with age,

hepatic dysfunction, cardiac decompensation, cor pulmonale, febrile illness. Many drugs also alter theophylline clearance (decrease half-life: cigarettes, phenobarbital, phenytoin; increase half-life: erythromycin, allopurinol, cimetidine, propranolol). Long-acting oral compounds permit qd or bid dosing. Single dose at nighttime reduces nocturnal symptoms. For acute therapy, intravenous therapy is used. In children and young-adult smokers, a loading dose of 6 mg/kg is given, followed by an infusion of 1.0(mg/kg)/h for 12 h, after which the infusion is reduced to 0.8(mg/kg)/h. In other pts not on theophylline, the loading dose remains the same, but the infusion rate is reduced to 0.1–0.5 (mg/kg)/h. In pts already taking theophylline, the loading dose is withheld or reduced. Theophylline compounds have lost favor in asthma therapy due to narrow toxic-therapeutic margin.

3. *Anticholinergics*: Aerosolized atropine and related compounds, such as ipratropium, a nonabsorbable quaternary ammonium. May enhance the bronchodilation achieved by sympathomimetics but is slow acting (60–90 min to peak bronchodilation). Ipratropium may be given by metered-dose inhaler, 2 puffs up to every 6 h. Expectorants and mucolytic agents add little to the management of acute or chronic asthma.

4. *Glucocorticoids*: Systemic or oral administration most beneficial for severe or refractory asthma. For hospitalized patients, methylprednisolone 40–60 mg q6h IV is usual. Prednisone 60 mg q6h orally is equivalent. Lower doses may be equally effective with fewer side effects. Steroids in acute asthma require ≥6h to have an effect.

For exacerbations of asthma in the outpatient setting, prednisone 40–60 mg PO daily, followed by tapering schedule of 50% reduction every 3–5 d. Inhaled glucocorticoid preparations are important adjuncts to chronic therapy; not useful in acute attacks. Effects of inhaled steroids are dose-dependent. Inhaled steroids are a mainstay of outpatient management and should be started in any pt not easily controlled with occasional use of inhaled adrenergic agents. Agents available include beclamethasone, budesonide, flunisolide, fluticasone proprionate, and triamcinolone acetonide. Dosing should be adjusted to disease activity, with frequent attempts to taper to low maintenance (1–2 puffs, 1–2 times/day). In addition to local symptoms (dysphonia, thrush), systemic effects may occur (e.g., adrenal suppression, cataracts, bone loss).

5. *Cromolyn sodium and Nedocromil sodium*: Not bronchodilators; useful in chronic therapy for prevention, not useful during acute attacks; administered as metered-dose inhaler or nebulized powder, 2 puffs daily. A trial of 4–6 weeks is often necessary to determine effectiveness in chronic asthma. Because the drugs may block acute bronchoconstriction when administered 15–20 min before exposure to antigens, chemicals, or exercise, they may be of use in selected pts who have predictable attacks of extrinsic asthma.

6. *Leukotriene modifiers*: The 5-lipoxygenase inhibitor, zileuton, and the LTD_4 receptor antagonists, zafirlukast and monteleukast, are recent additions to anti-inflammatory therapy of asthma. The LTD_4 receptor antagonists are long-acting, permitting qd or bid dosing. Effective in about one-half of pts. Modest bronchodilators with action against exercise-induced asthma. May reduce nocturnal symptoms.

Framework for Management

Emergencies   Aerosolized β_2 agonists are the primary therapy of acute episodes of asthma. Give every 20 min for 3 doses, then every 2 h until attack subsides. Aminophylline may speed resolution after first hour in 5–10% of pts. Paradoxical pulse, accessory muscle use, and marked hyperinflation indicate severe disease and mandate ABG measurement and monitoring of PEFR or FEV_1. PEFR ≥20% predicted on presentation with failure to double after 60 min of treatment suggests addition of steroid therapy. Failure of PEFR to improve to ≥70% of baseline with emergency treatment suggests need for hospitalization, with final decision made on individual factors (symptoms, past history, etc.). PEFR ≤40% after emergency treatment mandates admission.

Chronic Treatment   First-line therapy for intermittent asthma consists of β_2 agonists. Persistence of symptoms should prompt addition of an anti-inflammatory agent (glucocorticoids or a mast cell–stabilizing agent). Medication adjustments should be based on objective measurement of lung function (PEFR, FEV_1), and pts should monitor PEFR regularly.

HYPERSENSITIVITY PNEUMONITIS

DEFINITION   Hypersensitivity pneumonitis (HP), or extrinsic allergic alveolitis, is an immunologically mediated inflammation of lung parenchyma involving alveolar walls and terminal airways secondary to repeated inhalation of a variety of organic dusts by a susceptible host.

ETIOLOGY   A number of inhaled substances have been implicated (Table 253-1, p. 1464 in HPIM-15). These substances are usually organic antigens, particularly thermophilic actinomycetes, but may include inorganic compounds such as isocyanates.

CLINICAL MANIFESTATIONS   Symptoms may be acute, subacute, or chronic depending on the frequency and intensity of exposure to the causative agent; in acute form, cough, fever, chills, dyspnea appear 6–8 h after exposure to antigen; in subacute and chronic forms, temporal relationship to antigenic exposure may be lost, and insidiously increasing dyspnea may be predominant symptom.

DIAGNOSIS   *History*   Occupational history and history of possible exposures and relationship to symptoms are very important.

Physical Exam   Nonspecific; may reveal rales in lung fields, cyanosis in advanced cases.

Laboratory   Serum precipitins to offending antigen may be present but are not specific. After acute exposure to antigen, neutrophilia and lymphopenia are common, as are increased nonspecific tests of inflammation (C-reactive protein, rheumatoid factor, serum immunoglobulins).

CXR: nonspecific changes in interstitial structures; pleural changes or hilar adenopathy rare. High-resolution chest CT may show characteristic constellation of findings: (1) global lung involvement with ↑ lung density, (2) prominence of medium-sized bronchial walls, (3) patchy airspace consolidation, and (4) absence of lymphadenopathy. *PFTs and ABGs*: restrictive pattern possibly associated with airway obstruction; diffusing capacity decreased; hypoxemia at rest or with exercise. Bronchoalveolar lavage may show increased lymphocytes of suppressor-cytotoxic phenotype. Lung biopsy may be necessary in some pts who do not have sufficient other criteria; transbronchial biopsy may suffice, but open lung biopsy is frequently necessary.

DIFFERENTIAL DIAGNOSIS   Other interstitial lung diseases, including sarcoidosis, idiopathic pulmonary fibrosis, lung disease associated with collagen-vascular diseases, drug-induced lung disease; eosinophilic pneumonia; allergic bronchopulmonary aspergillosis; silo-fillers' disease; "pulmonary mycotoxicosis" or "atypical" farmer's lung; infection.

 TREATMENT

Avoidance of offending antigen is essential. Chronic form may be partially irreversible at the time of diagnosis. Prednisone 1(mg/dg)/d for 7–14 d, followed by tapering schedule over 2–4 weeks to lowest possible dose. Subacute form may have severe physiologic impairment and may progress for several days in hospital. Prednisone therapy is used at the same initial dose, tapered after 7–14 d over 5–6 weeks at a rate dictated by Sx. Pts with acute form usually recover without glucocorticoids.

For a more detailed discussion, see Mcfadden ER Jr: Asthma, Chap. 252, p. 1456; and Kline JN, Hunninghake GW: Hypersensitivity Pneumonitis and Pulmonary Infiltrates with Eosinophilia, Chap. 253, p. 1463, in HPIM-15.

129

ENVIRONMENTAL LUNG DISEASES

―――――――――――― *Approach to the Patient* ――――――――――

Ask about workplace and work history in detail: Specific contaminants? Availability and use of protective devices? Ventilation? Do co-workers have similar complaints? Ask about every job; short-term exposures may be significant. CXR is very valuable but may over- or underestimate functional impact of pneumoconioses. PFTs may both quantify impairment and suggest the nature of exposure.

An individual's dose of an environmental agent is influenced by intensity as well as by physiologic factors (ventilation rate and depth).

OCCUPATIONAL EXPOSURES AND PULMONARY DISEASE

INORGANIC DUSTS *Asbestosis* Exposures may occur in mining, milling, and manufacture of asbestos products; construction trades (pipefitting, boilermaking); and manufacture of safety garments, filler for plastic material, and friction materials (brake and clutch linings). Major health effects of asbestos include pulmonary fibrosis (asbestosis) and cancers of the respiratory tract, pleura, and peritoneum.

Asbestosis is a diffuse interstitial fibrosing disease of the lung that is directly related to intensity and duration of exposure, usually requiring ≥10 years of moderate to severe exposure. PFTs show a restrictive pattern. CXR reveals irregular or linear opacities, greatest in lower lung fields. High-resolution CT may show distinct changes of subpleural curvilinear line 5–10 cm in length. *Pleural plaques* indicate past exposure. Excess frequency of *lung cancer* occurs 15 to 20 years after first asbestos exposure. Smoking substantially increases risk of lung cancer after asbestos exposure but does not alter risk of *mesotheliomas*, which peaks 30 to 50 years after (an often brief) initial exposure.

Silicosis Exposure to free silica (crystalline quartz) occurs in mining, stone cutting, abrasive industries, blasting, quarrying. Short-term, high-intensity exposures (as brief as 10 months) may produce acute silicosis—rapidly fatal pulmonary fibrosis with radiographic picture of profuse miliary infiltration or consolidation. Longer-term, less-intense exposures are associated with upper lobe fibrosis and hilar adenopathy ≥15 years after exposure. Fibrosis is nodular and may lead to pulmonary restriction and airflow obstruction. Pts with silicosis are at higher than normal risk for tuberculosis, and pts with chronic silicosis and a positive PPD warrant antituberculous treatment.

Coal Worker's Pneumoconiosis (CWP) Symptoms of simple CWP are additive to the effects of cigarette smoking on chronic bronchitis and obstructive lung disease. X-ray signs of simple CWP are small, irregular opacities (reticular pattern) that may progress to small, rounded opacities (nodular pattern). Complicated CWP is indicated by roentgenographic appearance of nodules >1 cm in diameter in upper lung fields; DL_{CO} is reduced.

Berylliosis Beryllium exposure may produce acute pneumonitis or chronic interstitial pneumonitis. Histology is indistinguishable from sarcoidosis (noncaseating granulomas).

ORGANIC DUSTS *Cotton Dust (Byssinosis)* Exposures occur in production of yarns for cotton, linen, and rope making. (Flax, hemp, and jute produce a similar syndrome.) Chest tightness occurs typically on first day of work week. In 10–25% of workers, disease may be progressive with chest tightness persisting throughout the work week. After 10 years, recurrent symptoms are associated with irreversible airflow obstruction. Therapy includes bronchodilators, antihistamines, and elimination of exposure.

Grain Dust Farmers and grain elevator operators are at risk. Symptoms are those of cigarette smokers—cough, mucus production, wheezing, and airflow obstruction.

Farmer's Lung Persons exposed to mold hay with spores of thermophilic actinomycetes may develop a hypersensitivity pneumonitis. Acute farmer's lung causes fever, chills, malaise, cough, and dyspnea 4–8 h after exposure. Chronic low-intensity exposure causes interstitial fibrosis.

TOXIC CHEMICALS Many toxic chemicals can affect the lung in the form of vapor and gases.

Smoke inhalation kills more fire victims than does thermal injury. Severe cases may develop pulmonary edema. CO poisoning causing O_2 desaturation may be fatal. Early endoscopy may distinguish thermal upper airway injury from diffuse lower airway damage due to toxic constituents of inhaled smoke.

Agents used in the manufacture of synthetic materials may produce sensitizaton to isocyanates, aromatic amines, and aldehydes. Repeated exposure causes some workers to develop productive cough, asthma, or low-grade fever and malaise.

Fluorocarbons, transmitted from a worker's hands to cigarettes, may be volatilized. The inhaled agent causes fever, chills, malaise, and sometimes wheezing. Occurring in plastic workers, the syndrome is termed *polymer fume fever*.

℞ TREATMENT

Treatment of environment lung diseases almost invariably involves avoidance of toxic substance. Inorganic dust inhalation produces fibrosis without inflammation, unresponsive to pharmacologic treatment. Acute organic dust exposures may respond to glucocorticoids.

GENERAL ENVIRONMENTAL EXPOSURES

Air Pollution Difficult to relate specific health effects to any single pollutant. Symptoms and diseases of air pollution are also the nononcogenic conditions associated with cigarette smoking (respiratory infections, airway irritation).

Passive Cigarette Smoking Increased respiratory illness and reduced lung function have been found in children of smoking parents. Lung cancer risk is elevated in adults exposed to passive smoke.

Radon Risk factor for lung cancer, exacerbated by cigarette smoke.

PRINCIPLES OF MANAGEMENT

With many environmental agents, lung disease occurs years after exposure. If exposure continues, inciting agent must be eliminated, usually by removing pt from workplace. Pulmonary fibrosis (e.g., asbestosis, CWP) is not responsive to glucocorticoids. Therapy of occupational asthma follows usual guidelines (Chap. 128). Lung cancer screening has not yet proven effective, even in high-risk occupations.

For a more detailed discussion, see Speizer FE: Environmental Lung Diseases, Chap. 254, p. 1467, in HPIM-15.

130

CHRONIC BRONCHITIS, EMPHYSEMA, AND ACUTE OR CHRONIC RESPIRATORY FAILURE

Natural History

Chronic obstructive pulmonary disease (COPD) is a progressive disorder even when contributing factors are eliminated and aggressive therapy is instituted. Progression is inevitable, since loss of elastic tissue is a normal part of the aging process. In normal individuals, forced expiratory volume in 1 s (FEV_1) reaches lifetime peak around 25 years and declines on average approx 35 milliliters per year thereafter. Annual loss among susceptible individuals with COPD is 50–100 mL/year. Greater rates of decline are associated with mucus hypersecretion (men) and with airway hyperreactivity. Symptoms occur only in association with moderate or severe COPD. Typically, dyspnea occurs when FEV_1 falls below ~40% of predicted. Hypercarbia is most common after FEV_1 has fallen to <25% of predicted. Some pts whose symptoms are out of proportion to the decrease in FEV_1 have marked reductions in diffusing capacity for carbon monoxide.

Clinical Manifestations

HISTORY Pts with COPD usually have an exposure to tobacco of ≥ 20 pack years. Onset is typically in the fifth decade or later. Exertional dyspnea and productive cough are typical early symptoms. Functional limitation may correlate poorly with reduction in FEV_1. Sputum volume is usually small; production of >60 mL/d should prompt investigation for bronchiectasis. Weight loss is common in advanced disease. Hypoxemia and hypercarbia may result in fluid retention, morning headaches, sleep disruption, erythrocytosis, and cyanosis. Exacerbations are more frequent as disease progresses and are most often triggered by respiratory infections, often with a bacterial component. They may also be precipitated by left ventricular failure, cardiac arrhythmia, pneumothorax, pneumonia, and pulmonary thromboembolism.

PHYSICAL FINDINGS These correlate poorly with disease severity. Exam may be normal early. As disease progresses, signs of hyperinflation become more prominent. Mid-inspiratory crackles may reflect disease of moderate-size airways. Pursed-lip breathing may reduce dyspnea and dynamic hyperinflation. Wheezing is an inconstant finding and does not predict degree of obstruction or response to therapy.

RADIOGRAPHIC FINDINGS Plain CXR may show hyperinflation, emphysema, and pulmonary hypertension. Local radiolucencies (>1 cm) may indicate bullae. CT scan has greater sensitivity for emphysema but is not necessary for diagnosis.

PULMONARY FUNCTION TESTS Objective documentation of airflow obstruction is essential for diagnosis of COPD. Forced vital capacity (FVC) is typically decreased, but FEV_1 is decreased more so that the ratio of $FEV_1/$FVC is reduced. Exhalation may be incomplete even after a 10-s forced attempt. The American Thoracic Society grades COPD by FEV_1: stage I, mild disease $FEV_1 \geq 50\%$ predicted; stage II, moderate disease, FEV_1 35–49% predicted; stage III, severe disease, $FEV_1 < 35\%$ predicted. Reversibility of obstruction is determined by a trial of inhaled bronchodilators.

℞ TREATMENT

Smoking Cessation Elimination of tobacco has been convincingly shown to prolong survival in patients with COPD. Although lost lung function is not regained, the rate of decline in FEV_1 reverts rapidly to that of nonsmokers. Use of nicotine replacement therapy (patch, gum) can increase rates of cessation in motivated pts. Oral bupropion (150 mg bid) produces significant additional benefit.

Bronchodilators (Table 130-1) These do not influence longevity in pts with COPD but may significantly reduce symptoms. Short- and long-acting β-adrenergic agonists, anticholinergics, and theophylline derivatives may all be used. Although oral medications are associated with greater rates of adherence, inhaled medications generally have fewer side effects. Pts with mild disease can usually be managed with an inhaled short-acting β agonist such as albuterol. Anticholinergic therapy, e.g., inhaled ipatroprium, may be added to more symptomatic pts with moderate disease. Long-acting β agents, e.g., inhaled salmeterol or oral sustained-release albuterol, should be added in pts with severe disease. The narrow toxic-therapeutic ratio of theophylline compounds limits their use.

Glucocorticoids Unlike pts with asthma, patients with COPD respond unpredictably to glucocorticoids. Approximately 10% of pts will have a sig-

Table 130-1

Recommended Bronchodilator Therapy for Chronic Obstructive Pulmonary Disease

Stage	FEV$_1$, % Predicted	Treatment
I	> 50	β_2-Agonist prn
II	35–49	Combined anticholinergic and β_2-agonist
III	<35	Above plus long-acting β_2-agonist and/or sustained release theophylline Consider oral glucocorticoid trial

SOURCE: B Celli et al: Am J Respir Crit Care Med 152: S77, 1995; M Pearson et al: Thorax 52(Suppl5):S1, 1997.

nificant response as assessed by symptoms and FEV$_1$. Responders cannot be predicted by clinical characteristics. Systemic steroids have substantial side effects, so their use should be restricted. The role of inhaled steroids is uncertain, but some evidence suggests they may reduce the severity of exacerbations. However, they do not slow progression of disease.

Oxygen   Long-term domicilary O$_2$ therapy has been shown to reduce symptoms and improve survival in pts who are chronically hypoxemic, if they have stopped smoking. Documentation of the need for O$_2$ requires a measurement of Pa$_{O_2}$ or oxygen saturation (Sa$_{O_2}$) after a period of stability. Pts with a Pa$_{O_2} \leq 55$ mmHg or Sa$_{O_2} \leq 88\%$ should receive O$_2$ to raise the Sa$_{O_2} \geq 90\%$. O$_2$ is also indicated for pts with Pa$_{O_2}$ of 56–59 mmHg or Sa$_{O_2} \leq 89\%$ if associated with signs and symptoms of pulmonary hypertension or cor pulmonale. O$_2$ may also be prescribed for selected pts who desaturate with exercise or during sleep.

Transplantation   Lung transplantation should be considered for pts with severe COPD whose FEV$_1$ is < 25% predicted despite maximal therapy, particularly if associated with hypoxemia and cor pulmonale.

Lung Volume Reduction Surgery   This procedure, which removes emphysematous lung tissue to allow expansion of the remaining pulmonary parenchyma, is currently being studied in pts with disabling dyspnea. Indications and potential for long-term benefit remain controversial.

Mild Exacerbations

These may be managed with bronchodilators, antibiotics, and short courses of systemic glucocorticoids. Short-acting β-adrenergic agonists such as albuterol may be used up to every 1–2 h by metered dose inhaler (MDI). Anticholinergics such as ipatroprium by MDI should not be used more frequently than every 4–6 h, however. With increased sputum volume or change in character, antibiotic therapy should be administered. Trimethoprim-sulfamethoxazole, doxycycline, and amoxicillin are all acceptable choices. Evidence for effectiveness of systemic glucocorticoids in outpatient management of exacerbations is lacking, but usual practice is to administer 20–40 mg of prednisone daily for 7–10 days.

Acute Respiratory Failure

Diagnosis is made on the basis of decrease in Pa$_{O_2}$ by 10–15 mmHg from baseline or increase in Pa$_{CO_2}$ associated with a pH ≤ 7.30.

Rx TREATMENT

Precipitating factors should be sought, especially the presence of left ventricular failure. Clinical signs of CHF are often difficult to identify, so empirical therapy with a diuretic (furosemide 10–60 mg IV) is appropriate if peripheral edema is present.

Bronchodilators Administer short-acting β-adrenergic agonists by inhalation (e.g., albuterol q1–2h; may be administered as frequently as q20mins initially). Because absorption is unpredictable when pts are in distress, dosing should be dictated by side effects. Addition of anticholinergics is likely of benefit (ipatroprium q4–6h).

Glucocorticoids Evidence is convincing that systemic steroids may hasten resolution of symptoms. Dosing is not well worked out, but 30–60 mg of prednisone daily (or IV equivalent) is standard, with a total course of 14 days.

Oxygen Supplemental O_2 should be administered to maintain $Sa_{O_2} \geq$ 90%. Delivery systems include nasal prongs 1–2 1pm or 24% Venturi mask.

Ventilatory Support Numerous studies suggest noninvasive mask ventilation can improve outcomes in acute exacerbations. Pts with marked respiratory distress (respiratory rate > 30 breaths/min) should have a trial of mask ventilation. Success is indicated by a reduction in respiratory rate to < 25 breaths/min after 30–60 min. Progressive hypercarbia, refractory hypoxemia, or alteration in mental status that compromises ability to comply with therapy may necessitate endotracheal intubation.

For a more detailed discussion, see Honig EG, Ingram RH Jr: Chronic Bronchitis, Emphysema, and Airways Obstruction, Chap. 258, p. 1491, in HPIM-15.

131

PNEUMONIA AND LUNG ABSCESS

PNEUMONIA

ETIOLOGY Pneumonia is an infection of the pulmonary parenchyma caused by various bacterial species (including mycoplasmas, chlamydiae, and rickettsiae), viruses, fungi, and parasites. Compromised hosts are particularly vulnerable to pulmonary infections caused by a variety of pathogens.

EPIDEMIOLOGY Factors such as travel history, exposure to pets, exposure to other people who are ill, occupation, age, presence or absence of teeth, season of the year, geographic location, setting (community vs. hospital acquisition), smoking status, and HIV status all influence the types of pathogens to consider in the etiology of pneumonia.

PATHOGENESIS The most common mechanism for acquiring pneumonia is aspiration of organisms from the oropharynx. The usual organisms are

Table 131-1

Treatment of Pneumonia

Syndrome	Common Organisms	Antibiotic(s)
Community-acquired		
Lobar	*S. pneumoniae, H. influenzae, M. catarrhalis*	Penicillin,[a] erythromycin, SGC, TGC, ampicillin/sulbactam[b]
Atypical	*M. pneumoniae, Legionella* spp., *C. pneumoniae*	Erythromycin, clarithromycin
Aspiration (mixed flora)	Anaerobes	Clindamycin, ampicillin/sulbactam, amoxicillin + metronidazole
Hospital-acquired	*S. aureus*	Nafcillin, vancomycin
	Enteric gram-negative bacilli or *P. aeruginosa*	Ceftazidime ± antipseudomonal aminoglycoside, ticarcillin/clavulanate ± aminoglycoside, imipenem, ciprofloxacin
	Mixed flora	Ceftazidime + clindamycin (or metronidazole) ± aminoglycoside, imipenem ± aminoglycoside, ticarcillin/clavulanate or piperacillin/tazobactam ± aminoglycoside
Postinfluenza	*S. pneumoniae, S. aureus*	Nafcillin, vancomycin

[a] For susceptible strains of *S. pneumoniae*. When resistance is suspected, use TGC; in life-threatening cases, add vancomycin.

[b] Ampicillin/sulbactam does not cover penicillin-resistant *S. pneumoniae*.

ABBREVIATIONS: SGC, second-generation cephalosporin; TGC, third-generation cephalosporin.

aerobic gram-positive cocci and anaerobes that colonize the oropharynx. Normally, 50% of adults aspirate during sleep. Aspiration increases with impaired consciousness—e.g., in alcoholics and drug users; in pts with stroke or seizure, other neurologic or swallowing disorders, or nasogastric or endotracheal tubes; and during or after anesthesia. Aerobic gram-negative bacilli colonize the oropharynx or stomach more frequently in hospitalized or institutionalized pts than in other individuals. Other routes of transmission for pneumonia include inhalation of infected particles (diameter <5 μm), hematogenous spread, contiguous spread from another infected site, and direct inoculation from open trauma to the chest.

CLINICAL MANIFESTATIONS The "typical" pneumonia syndrome is characterized by the sudden onset of fever, cough productive of purulent sputum, and pleuritic chest pain; signs of pulmonary consolidation; and a lobar infiltrate on CXR. This syndrome is most commonly caused by *Streptococcus pneumoniae* and other bacterial pathogens. The "atypical" pneumonia syndrome is characterized by a more gradual onset, a dry cough, a prominence of extrapulmonary symptoms (e.g., headache, malaise, myalgias, sore throat, GI distress), and minimal signs on physical exam (other than rales) despite an abnor-

Table 131-2

Dosage of Antimicrobial Agents for the Treatment of Pneumonia in Hospitalized Patients[a]

Drug	Dosage
Ampicillin/sulbactam	3 g IV q6h
Aztreonam	2 g IV q8h
Cefazolin	1–2 g IV q8h
Cefepime	2 g IV q8h
Cefotaxime, ceftizoxime	1–2 g IV q8–12h
Ceftazidime	2 g IV q8h
Ceftriaxone	1–2 g IV q12h
Cefuroxime	750 mg IV q8h
Ciprofloxacin	400 mg IV or 750 mg PO q12h
Clindamycin	600–900 mg IV q8h
Erythromycin	0.5–1.0 g IV q6h
Gentamicin (or tobramycin)	5 (mg/kg)/d in 3 equally divided doses IV q8h
Imipenem	500 mg IV q6h
Levofloxacin	500 mg IV or PO q24h
Metronidazole	500 mg IV or PO q6h
Nafcillin	2 g IV q4h
Penicillin G	3 million U IV q4–6h
Piperacillin/tazobactam	4.5 g IV q6h
Ticarcillin/clavulanate	3.1 g IV q4h
Vancomycin	1 g (15 mg/kg) IV q12h

[a] Dosage must be modified for pts with renal failure.
SOURCE: ME Levison: HPIM-15, p. 1483.

mal, often patchy or diffuse pattern on CXR. Atypical pneumonia is classically caused by *Mycoplasma pneumoniae* but may also be due to *Legionella pneumophila*, *Chlamydia pneumoniae*, oral anaerobes, *Pneumocystis carinii*, and *S. pneumoniae*.

Other, rarer pathogens causing atypical pneumonia include *Chlamydia psittaci*, *Coxiella burnetii*, *Francisella tularensis*, *Histoplasma capsulatum*, and *Coccidioides immitis*. While recent data suggest that the distinction between typical and atypical pneumonia syndromes may be less reliable than was once thought, the differences are of some diagnostic value. Certain viruses, including influenza virus, respiratory syncytial virus, measles virus, varicella-zoster virus, and cytomegalovirus, may produce an atypical pneumonia. Hantavirus causes an initial febrile prodrome followed by rapidly progressive respiratory failure and diffuse pulmonary infiltrates.

DIAGNOSIS *Radiography* Findings on CXR range from lobar consolidation with air bronchograms to diffuse patchy interstitial infiltrates. Other findings include multiple nodules suspicious for septic emboli, cavitation, pleural effusion, and hilar adenopathy.

Sputum Examination Whenever possible, sputum should be obtained and evaluated grossly for purulence and blood and by Gram's stain. The presence of >25 PMNs and <10 epithelial cells per high-power field suggests that the specimen is adequate. The finding of mixed flora on Gram's stain suggests anaerobic infection. The presence of a single, predominant type of organism suggests the etiology of the pneumonia. Sputum may also be examined directly

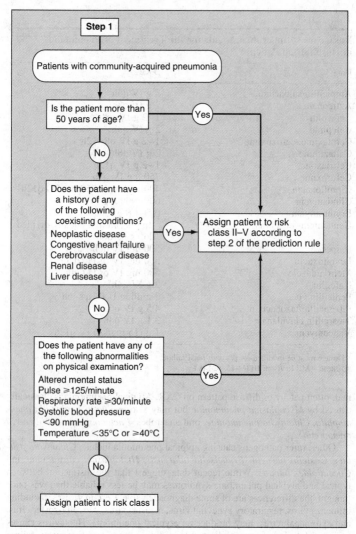

FIGURE 131-1 Criteria for hospitalization of pts with pneumonia: the PORT score. *A risk score (total point score) for a given pt is obtained by summing the pt's age in years (age minus 10 for females) and the points for each applicable pt characteristic. (*From: ME Levison: HPIM-15, p. 1480.*)

for acid-fast organisms and by special stain or immunofluorescence for *Legionella* or *Pneumocystis*. Sputum culture may yield the causative agent but is usually less sensitive than Gram's stain.

Blood Cultures Since sputum examination and culture do not always reveal a pathogen, blood for cultures should be obtained before therapy begins.

Other Diagnostic Maneuvers Sputum induction (with ultrasonic nebulization of 3% saline), bronchoscopy with bronchoalveolar lavage or protected

Step 2

Characteristic	Points Assigned*
Demographic factor	
Age	
Men	Age (yr)
Women	Age (yr) − 10
Nursing home resident	+10
Coexisting illnesses	
Neoplastic disease	+30
Liver disease	+20
Congestive heart failure	+10
Cerebrovascular disease	+10
Renal disease	+10
Physical examination findings	
Altered mental status	+20
Respiratory rate ≥30/min	+20
Systolic blood pressure <90 mmHg	+20
Temperature <35°C or ≥40°C	+15
Pulse ≥125/min	+10
Laboratory and radiographic findings	
Arterial pH <7.35	+30
Blood urea nitrogen >30 mg/dL (11 mmol/L)	+20
Sodium <130 mmol/L	+20
Glucose >250 mg/dL (14 mmol/L)	+10
Hematocrit <30%	+10
Partial pressure of arterial oxygen <60 mmHg or O_2 saturation <90%	+10
Pleural effusion	+10

Risk class	No. of points	Recommendations for site of care
I	No predictors	Outpatient
II	≤70	Outpatient
III	71–90	Inpatient (briefly)
IV	91–130	Inpatient
V	>130	Inpatient

FIGURE 131-1

brush specimens, transtracheal aspiration, thoracentesis, percutaneous lung puncture, open-lung biopsy, acute and convalescent serologies, and chest CT are all useful in selected cases.

Rx TREATMENT

Initial antibiotic treatment for pneumonia is often empirical. However, establishing a specific microbial etiology is important, for it allows institution of specific pathogen-directed antimicrobial therapy, exposes the pt to fewer potential adverse drug effects, and reduces the pressure for selection of antimicrobial resistance. See Table 131-1 for clinical syndromes, likely organisms, and antibiotic choices. See Table 131-2 for doses of antibiotics used for inpatient treatment of pneumonia.

Outpatient and Home Care Considerations Some persons with pneumonia may be treated as outpatients with oral antibiotics. Criteria for hospitalization of pts with pneumonia are listed in Fig. 131-1. These criteria are from the Pneumonia Patient Outcomes Research Team (PORT) and attempt to stratify pts into five risk classes for death and other adverse outcomes on the basis of a cumulative point score. Outpatient management is appropriate for many pts in the low-risk groups (I and II).

LUNG ABSCESS
CLINICAL MANIFESTATIONS Lung abscess is usually a complication of the aspiration of oral anaerobes. In most pts it is a subacute disease with an indolent presentation. The pt usually has a cough that may or may not be productive of large quantities of purulent, foul-smelling sputum and often has fevers, night sweats, and weight loss. Pleuritic chest pain and blood-streaked sputum also may be noted.

DIAGNOSIS CXR usually shows a cavitary lesion with an air-fluid level, often in dependent, poorly ventilated portions of the lung. The sputum is not necessarily foul-smelling but usually contains a mixed flora revealed by Gram's stain.

 TREATMENT

The treatment of choice is clindamycin (600 mg q8h IV, then 300–450 mg PO); ampicillin (2 g IV q6h) or amoxicillin (500 mg PO tid) with metronidazole (500 mg PO q6h); ampicillin/sulbactam; or amoxicillin/clavulanate. Antibiotics rarely need to be directed at each organism isolated if the abscess is aspirated. Treatment should be continued until CXR findings have resolved, which may require months.

For a more detailed discussion, see Levison ME: Pneumonia, Including Necrotizing Pulmonary Infections (Lung Abscess), Chap. 255, p. 1475, in HPIM-15.

132

PULMONARY THROMBOEMBOLISM AND PRIMARY PULMONARY HYPERTENSION

PULMONARY EMBOLISM (PE) (See Fig. 132-1)
NATURAL HISTORY Immediate result is obstruction of pulmonary blood flow to the distal lung. Respiratory consequences include (1) wasted ven-

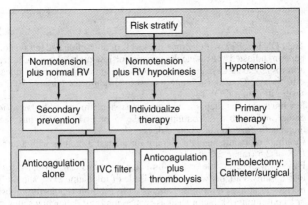

FIGURE 132-1 Acute PTE management: Risk stratification. RV, right ventricular; IVC, inferior vena cava. (*From Goldhaber SZ: HPIM-15.*)

tilation (lung ventilated but not perfused), (2) atelectasis that occurs 2–24 h following PE, and (3) widened alveolar-arterial P_{O_2} gradient, usually with arterial hypoxemia. Hemodynamic consequences may include (1) pulmonary hypertension, (2) acute RV failure, and (3) decline in cardiac output. These occur only when significant fraction of pulmonary vasculature is obstructed. Infarction of lung tissue is uncommon, occurring only with underlying cardiac or pulmonary disease.

SYMPTOMS   Sudden onset of dyspnea most common; chest pain, hemoptysis accompany infarction; syncope may indicate massive embolism.

PHYSICAL EXAMINATION   Tachypnea and tachycardia common; RV gallop; loud P_2 and prominent jugular *a* waves suggest RV failure; temperature >39°C uncommon. Hypotension suggests massive PE.

LABORATORY FINDINGS   Routine studies contribute little to diagnosis; normal D-dimer level (<500 μg/ml by ELISA) essentially rules out PE, particularly in younger, ambulatory pts, but normal CXR does not exclude PE. Impedance plethysmography and femoral ultrasonography are sensitive tests for deep venous thrombosis when the pt has local symptoms. Likelihood of PE with ventilation-perfusion scan is dependent on clinical suspicion. With high clinical suspicion, high probability scan is very specific (>90%). A normal scan essentially excludes clinically significant PE. Many scans are "intermediate," necessitating further evaluation. Spiral or helical CT, with a multidetector scanner, has a sensitivity of >90% compared to pulmonary angiography, the definitive test.

℞ TREATMENT   (See Fig. 132-1 and Guidelines)

IV heparin [18 (U/kg)/h] by continuous infusion is therapy for most pts after an initial bolus of 80 U/kg. Documentation of effectiveness (activated PTT 1.5–2.0 × control) is essential as delay in reaching therapeutic level increases risk of recurrence. Heparin is continued 7 to 10 d for deep venous thrombosis (DVT) and 10 d for thromboembolism. Low-molecular-weight heparin (enoxaparin 1 mg/kg q12h) may be an alternative for DVT and in pts with minimally symptomatic PE. Most pts receive minimum of 3 months of oral coumadin therapy after PE. Thrombolytic therapy hastens resolution of venous thrombi and is probably indicated for pts with massive embolism and systemic

Guidelines for the Treatment of Pulmonary Embolism

1. Treat DVT or PTE with therapeutic levels of unfractionated intravenous heparin, adjusted subcutaneous heparin, or low-molecular-weight heparin for at least 5 days and overlap with oral anticoagulation for at least 4 to 5 days. Consider a longer course of heparin for massive PTE or severe iliofemoral DVT.

2. For most patients, heparin and oral anticoagulation can be started together and heparin discontinued on day 5 or 6 if the INR has been therapeutic for two consecutive days.

3. Continue oral anticoagulant therapy for at least 3 months with a target INR of 2.5 (range 2.0 to 3.0).

4. Patients with reversible or time-limited risk factors can be treated for 3 to 6 months. Patients with a first episode of idiopathic DVT should be treated for at least 6 months. Patients with recurrent venous thrombosis or a continuing risk factor such as cancer, inhibitor deficiency states, or antiphospholipid antibody syndrome should be treated indefinitely.

5. Isolated calf vein DVT should be treated with anticoagulation for at least 3 months.

6. The use of thrombolytic agents continues to be highly individualized, and clinicians should have some latitude in using these agents. Patients with hemodynamically unstable PTE or massive iliofemoral thrombosis are the best candidates.

7. Inferior vena caval filter placement is recommended when there is a contraindication to or failure of anticoagulation, for chronic recurrent embolism with pulmonary hypertension, and with concurrent performance of surgical pulmonary embolectomy or pulmonary endarterectomy.

* Modified from TM Hyers et al: Antithrombotic therapy for venous thromboembolic disease. Chest 114:561S, 1998.

hypotension. Surgical therapy is rarely employed for DVT or acute PE. IVC interruption (clip or filter) is used in pts with recurrent PE despite anticoagulants and in those who cannot tolerate anticoagulants. Surgical extraction of old emboli may be helpful in pts with chronic pulmonary hypertension due to repeated PE without spontaneous resolution.

PRIMARY PULMONARY HYPERTENSION (PPH)

HISTORY Uncommon condition. Typical pt is female aged 20–40. At presentation, symptoms are usually of recent onset, and natural history is ordinarily <5 years. Familial clusters occur. Early symptoms are nonspecific—hyperventilation, chest discomfort; anxiety, weakness, fatigue. Later, dyspnea develops and precordial pain on exertion occurs in 25–50%. Effort syncope occurs very late and signifies ominous prognosis.

PHYSICAL EXAMINATION Prominent *a* wave in jugular venous pulse, right ventricular heave, narrowly split S_2 with accentuated P_2. Terminal course is characterized by signs of right-sided heart failure. CXR: RV and central pulmonary arterial prominence. Pulmonary arteries taper sharply. PFT: usually normal or mild restrictive defect. ECG: RV enlargement, right axis deviation, and RV hypertrophy. Echocardiogram: RA and RV enlargement and tricuspid regurgitation (Fig. 132-2).

DIFFERENTIAL DIAGNOSIS Other disorders of heart, lungs, and pulmonary vasculature must be excluded. Lung function studies will identify

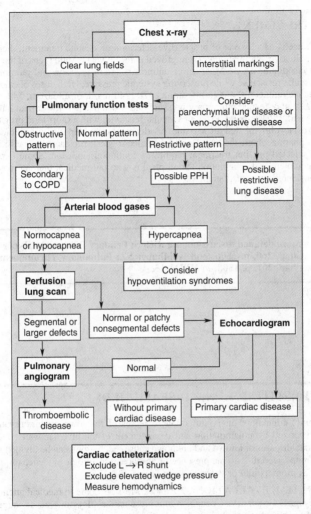

FIGURE 132-2 An algorithm for the workup of a pt with unexplained pulmonary hypertension. (*Adapted with permission from Rich S: HPIM-15.*)

chronic pulmonary disease causing pulmonary hypertension and cor pulmonale. Interstitial diseases (PFTs, CT scan) and hypoxic pulmonary hypertension (ABGs, Sa_{O_2}) should be excluded. Perfusion lung scan should be performed to exclude chronic PE. Spiral CT scan, pulmonary arteriogram, and even open-lung biopsy may be required to distinguish PE from PPH. Rarely, pulmonary hypertension is due to parasitic disease (schistosomiasis, filariasis). Cardiac disorders to be excluded include pulmonary artery and pulmonic valve stenosis. Pulmonary artery and ventricular and atrial shunts with pulmonary vascular disease (Eisenmenger reaction) should be sought. Silent mitral stenosis should be excluded by echocardiography.

℞ **TREATMENT**

Course is usually one of progressive deterioration despite treatment; therapy is palliative, but treatment has improved in recent years. Main focus of therapy is vasodilator drugs. Must lower pulmonary artery pressure and pulmonary vascular resistance while preserving systemic pressure. High doses of calcium channel antagonists (e.g., nifedipine, 120–240 mg/d, or diltiazem, 540–900 mg/d) may reduce pulmonary pressure and resistance, but fewer than half of pts with PPH respond. Proof of vascular reactivity with a short-term drug trial (prostacyclin, inhaled nitric oxide, or adenosine) can help identify candidates for pharmacologic therapy. Recent evidence suggests prostacyclin is effective in selected pts, but treatment requires a continuous infusion. Some experts recommend anticoagulation for all pts. Pts who fail medical therapy may be considered for transplantation.

For a more detailed discussion, see Rich S: Primary Pulmonary Hypertension, Chap. 260, p. 1506; and Goldhaber SZ: Pulmonary Thromboembolism, Chap. 261, p. 1508, in HPIM-15.

133

INTERSTITIAL LUNG DISEASE (ILD)

Chronic, nonmalignant, noninfectious diseases of the lower respiratory tract characterized by inflammation and derangement of the alveolar walls; >200 separate diseases of known and unknown cause. Each group can be divided into subgroups according to the presence or absence of histologic evidence of granulomas in interstitial or vascular areas (Table 133-1).

INITIAL EVALUATION *History* Most pts come to medical attention for dyspnea or persistent cough. Acute presentation (days to weeks) suggests allergy (drugs, fungi, helminths), acute idiopathic interstitial pneumonia, eosinophilic pneumonia, or hypersensitivity. Pts with pulmonary Langerhans cell histiocytosis, desquamative interstitial pneumonitis, Goodpasture's syndrome, and respiratory bronchiolitis are almost invariably current or former smokers. A careful occupational history is essential. Familial associations have been identified with tuberculous sclerosis and neurofibromatosis, and family clusters are seen with sarcoidosis and familial pulmonary fibrosis.

Physical Examination Usually reveals tachypnea and end-inspiratory crackles.

Chest Imaging X-ray most commonly reveals bibasilar reticular pattern. Honeycombing portends a poor prognosis. High-resolution CT may be sufficiently specific to avoid a need for histologic examination (sarcoidosis, hypersensitivity pneumonitis, lymphangitic carcinoma, asbestosis, pulmonary Langerhans cell histiocytosis).

Table 133-1

Major Categories of Alveolar and Interstitial Inflammatory Lung Disease

Lung Response: Alveolitis, Interstitial Inflammation, and Fibrosis

KNOWN CAUSE

Asbestos	Radiation
Fumes, gases	Aspiration pneumonia
Drugs (antibiotics, amiodarone, gold) and chemotherapy drugs	Residual of adult respiratory distress syndrome

UNKNOWN CAUSE

Idiopathic interstitial pneumonias	Pulmonary alveolar proteinosis
Idiopathic pulmonary fibrosis (usual interstitial pneumonia)	Lymphocytic infiltrative disorders (lymphocytic interstitial pneumonitis associated with connective tissue disease)
Desquamative interstitial pneumonia	Eosinophilic pneumonias
Respiratory bronchiolitis-associated interstitial lung disease	Lymphangioleiomyomatosis Amyloidosis
Acute interstitial pneumonia (diffuse alveolar damage)	Inherited diseases Tuberous sclerosis, neurofibromatosis, Niemann-Pick disease, Gaucher's disease, Hermansky-Pudlak syndrome
Cryptogenic organizing pneumonia (bronchiolitis obliterans with organizing pneumonia)	Gastrointestinal or liver diseases (Crohn's disease, primary biliary cirrhosis, chronic active hepatitis, ulcerative colitis)
Nonspecific interstitial pneumonia	
Connective tissue diseases Systemic lupus erythematosus, rheumatoid arthritis, ankylosing spondylitis, systemic sclerosis, Sjögren's syndrome, polymyositis-dermatomyositis	Graft-vs.-host disease (bone marrow transplantation; solid organ transplantation)
Pulmonary hemorrhage syndromes Goodpasture's syndrome, idiopathic pulmonary hemosiderosis, isolated pulmonary capillaritis	

Lung Response: Granulomatous

KNOWN CAUSE

Hypersensitivity pneumonitis (organic dusts)	Inorganic dusts: beryllium silica

UNKNOWN CAUSE

Sarcoidosis	Bronchocentric granulomatosis
Langerhans cell granulomatosis (eosinophilic granuloma of the lung)	Lymphomatoid granulomatosis
Granulomatous vasculitides	
Wegener's granulomatosis, allergic granulomatosis of Churg-Strauss	

Tissue and Cellular Examination Rarely, clinical syndrome can be related to a causative agent, but histologic exam is usually necessary. With exception of sarcoidosis, which can often be diagnosed by transbronchial biopsy, most infiltrative diseases require open-lung biopsy for diagnosis. Gallium scans and bronchoalveolar lavage do not yield a specific diagnosis but help to document the extent and character of inflammation.

INDIVIDUAL ILDS

IDIOPATHIC PULMONARY FIBROSIS *History* Average age of 50 at presentation; sometimes familial. First manifestations are dyspnea, effort intolerance, and dry cough. Dyspnea and coughing often accompanied by constitutional symptoms (fatigue, anorexia, weight loss). One-third of pts date symptoms to aftermath of viral respiratory infection. Smoking history is common.

Physical Exam Late inspiratory crackles at posterior lung bases. Signs of pulmonary hypertension and clubbing occur late in course.

Laboratory Findings ESR may be elevated. Hypoxemia is common, but polycythemia is rare. Circulating immune-complex titers and serum immunoglobulin levels may be elevated.

Imaging Studies CXR usually reveals patchy, predominantly peripheral reticulonodular markings, prominent in lower lung zones. About 14% of biopsy-proven cases have normal CXR. High-resolution CT may show abnormalities when CXR is normal, such as ground glass opacities with traction bronchiectasis or honeycombing.

PFTs Typically restrictive pattern (Fig. 127-1) with reduced total lung capacity. DL_{CO} often decreased; mild hypoxemia, which worsens with exercise.

Histologic Findings Surgical biopsy usually required. Evidence of usual interstitial pneumonia (UIP) required. Characteristic is heterogeneous appearance of normal lung, interstitial inflammation, fibrosis, and honeycomb change.

Prognosis 5-year survival from diagnosis is 30–50%. No compelling evidence any therapy alters outcome, although glucocorticoids with or without cytotoxic agents (azathioprine, cyclophosphamide) or antifibrotics (colchicine, perfenidone, or interferon γ1b) may provide symptomatic benefit.

DESQUAMATIVE INTERSTITIAL PNEUMONIA (DIP) Rare. Found exclusively in smokers in fourth and fifth decades. Better prognosis than idiopathic pulmonary fibrosis (10-year survival ∼ 70%).

ILD ASSOCIATED WITH COLLAGEN VASCULAR DISORDERS Usually follows development of collagen-vascular disorder; typically mild but occasionally fatal.

Rheumatoid Arthritis (RA) 50% of pts with RA have abnormal lung function, 25% have abnormal CXR. Rarely causes symptoms. Males more commonly affected than females.

Progressive Systemic Sclerosis Fibrosis with little inflammation; poor prognosis. Must be distinguished from pulmonary vascular disease.

SLE Uncommon complication. When it occurs, it is most often an acute, inflammatory patchy process.

LANGERHANS CELL PULMONARY HISTIOCYTOSIS (EOSINO-PHILIC GRANULOMA OR HISTIOCYTOSIS X) Disorder of the dendritic cell system, related to Letterer-Siwe and Hand-Schuller-Christian disease. Develops between 20 and 40 years of age; 90% are present or former smokers. Complicated frequently by pneumothorax. No therapy available.

CHRONIC EOSINOPHILIC PNEUMONIA Affects females predominantly; often a history of chronic asthma. Symptoms include weight loss, fever, chills, fatigue, dyspnea. CXR shows "photonegative pulmonary edema" pattern with central sparing. Very responsive to glucocorticoids.

IDIOPATHIC PULMONARY HEMOSIDEROSIS Characterized by recurrent pulmonary hemorrhage; may be life-threatening. Not associated with renal disease.

GOODPASTURE'S SYNDROME Relapsing pulmonary hemorrhage, anemia, and renal failure. Adult males most commonly affected. Circulating anti-basement membrane antibodies.

INHERITED DISORDERS ILD may be associated with tuberous sclerosis, neurofibromatosis, Gaucher's disease, Hermansky-Pudlak syndrome, and Niemann-Pick disease.

℞ TREATMENT

Most important is removal of causative agent. With exception of pneumoconioses, which are generally not treated except for discontinuation of further exposure and some other specific disorders, therapy is directed toward suppressing the inflammatory process, usually with glucocorticoids. After diagnosis, pts are given oral prednisone, 1 (mg/kg)/d, for 8–12 weeks. Response is assessed by symptoms and PFTs. For idiopathic pulmonary fibrosis and some other disorders, consider immunosuppressive therapy with cyclophosphamide, 1.0 (mg/kg)/d, added to prednisone, 0.25 (mg/kg)/d. Smoking cessation, supplemental oxygen (when $Pa_{O_2} < 55$ mmHg), and therapy for right-sided heart failure and bronchospasm may all improve symptoms.

For a more detailed discussion, see King TE Jr: Interstitial Lung Diseases, Chap. 259, p. 1499, in HPIM-15.

134

DISEASES OF THE PLEURA, MEDIASTINUM, AND DIAPHRAGM

PLEURAL DISEASE

PLEURITIS Inflammation of pleura may occur with pneumonia, tuberculosis, pulmonary infarction, and neoplasm. Pleuritic pain without physical and x-ray findings suggests epidemic pleurodynia (viral inflammation of intercostal muscles); hemoptysis and parenchymal involvement on CXR suggest infection or infarction. Pleural effusion without parenchymal disease suggests postprimary tuberculosis, subdiaphragmatic abscess, mesothelioma, connective tissue disease, or primary bacterial infection of pleural space.

PLEURAL EFFUSION May or may not be associated with pleuritis. In general, effusions due to pleural disease resemble plasma (exudates); effusions with normal pleura are ultrafiltrates of plasma (transudates). Exudates have at least one of the following criteria: high total fluid/serum protein ratio (>0.5), pleural fluid LDH greater than two-thirds of the normal upper limit, or pleural/serum LDH activity ratio >0.6. Leading causes of transudative pleural effusions in the U.S. are left ventricular failure, pulmonary embolism, and cirrhosis. Leading causes of exudative effusions are bacterial pneumonia, malignancy, viral infection, and pulmonary embolism. With empyema, pH < 7.2, WBCs ↑ (>1000/mL), and glucose ↓. If neoplasm or tuberculosis is considered, closed pleural biopsy or thoracoscopic biopsy should be performed (Tables 134-1 and 134-2; and Fig. 134-1). Despite full evaluation, no cause for effusion will be found in 25% of pts.

POSTPRIMARY TUBERCULOSIS EFFUSIONS   Fluid is exudative with predominant lymphocytosis; bacilli are rarely seen on smear, and fluid

Table 134-1

Differential Diagnoses of Pleural Effusions

TRANSUDATIVE PLEURAL EFFUSIONS

1. Congestive heart failure
2. Cirrhosis
3. Pulmonary embolization
4. Nephrotic syndrome
5. Peritoneal dialysis
6. Superior vena cava obstruction
7. Myxedema
8. Urinothorax

EXUDATIVE PLEURAL EFFUSIONS

1. Neoplastic diseases
   a. Metastatic disease
   b. Mesothelioma
2. Infectious diseases
   a. Bacterial infections
   b. Tuberculosis
   c. Fungal infections
   d. Viral infections
   e. Parasitic infections
3. Pulmonary embolization
4. Gastrointestinal disease
   a. Esophageal perforation
   b. Pancreatic disease
   c. Intraabdominal abscesses
   d. Diaphragmatic hernia
   e. After abdominal surgery
   f. Endoscopic variceal sclerotherapy
   g. After liver transplant
5. Collagen-vascular diseases
   a. Rheumatoid diseases
   b. Systemic lupus erythematosus
   c. Drug-induced lupus
   d. Immunoblastic lymphadenopathy
   e. Sjögren's syndrome
   f. Wegener's granulomatosis
   g. Churg-Strauss syndrome
6. Post-coronary artery bypass surgery
7. Asbestos exposure
8. Sarcoidosis
9. Uremia
10. Meigs' syndrome
11. Yellow nail syndrome
12. Drug-induced pleural disease
    a. Nitrofurantoin
    b. Dantrolene
    c. Methysergide
    d. Bromocriptine
    e. Procarbazine
    f. Amiodarone
13. Trapped lung
14. Radiation therapy
15. Post-cardiac injury syndrome
16. Hemothorax
17. Iatrogenic injury
18. Ovarian hyperstimulation syndrome
19. Pericardial disease
20. Chylothorax

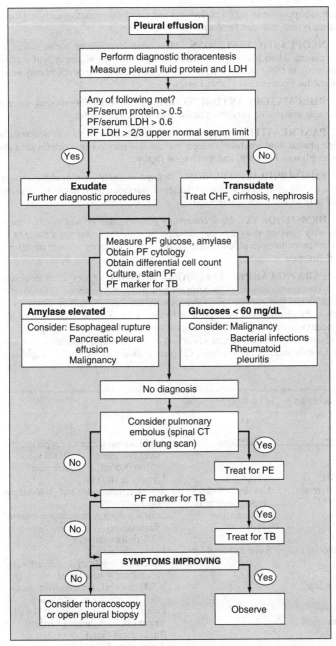

FIGURE 134-1 Approach to the diagnosis of pleural effusions. The special tests are summarized in Table 134-1. PF, pleural fluid; PE, pulmonary embolism. (*From RW Light: HPIM-15.*)

culture is positive in <20%; tuberculin test may be nonreactive early in illness; closed biopsy required for diagnosis.

NEOPLASTIC EFFUSIONS Most often lung cancer, breast cancer, or lymphoma. Fluid is exudative; fluid cytology and pleural biopsy will confirm diagnosis in 60%; pleural sclerosis with bleomycin or minocycline may be required for management (Table 134-2).

RHEUMATOID ARTHRITIS (RA) Exudative effusions may precede articular symptoms; very low glucose and pH; usually males.

PANCREATITIS Typically left-sided; up to 15% of pts with pancreatitis; high pleural fluid amylase is suggestive but also may occur with effusions due to neoplasms, infection, and esophageal rupture.

EOSINOPHILIC EFFUSION Defined as >10% eosinophils; nonspecific finding may occur with viral, bacterial, traumatic, and pancreatic effusions and may follow prior thoracentesis.

HEMOTHORAX Most commonly follows blunt or penetrating trauma. Pts with bleeding disorders may develop hemothorax following trauma or invasive procedures on pleura. Adequate drainage mandatory to avoid fibrothorax and "trapped" lung.

PARAPNEUMONIC EFFUSION/EMPYEMA An effusion associated with contiguous infection. The term *complicated parapneumonic effusion* refers to effusions that require tube thoracostomy for their resolution. Empyema is pus in the pleural space with positive Gram's stain. Tube thoracostomy of parapneumonic effusions is likely indicated if any of the following applies (descending order of importance): (1) gross pus is present, (2) organisms are visible on Gram's stain of pleural fluid, (3) pleural fluid glucose is <60 mg/dL, (4)

Table 134-2

Special Tests for Pleural Effusions

	Transudate	Exudate
RBC	<10,000/mL	>100,00/mL suggests neoplasm, infarction, trauma; >10,000 to <100,000/mL is indetermine
WBC	<100/mL	Usually >1000/mL
Differential WBC	Usually >50% lypmphocytes or mononuclear cells	>50% lymphocytes (tuberculosis, neoplasm) >50% polymorphonuclear (acute inflammation)
pH	>7.3	>7.3 (inflammatory)
Glucose	Same as blood (±)	Low (infection) Extremely low (rheumatoid arthritis, occasionally neoplasm)
Amylase		>500 units/mL (pancreatitis; occasionally neoplasm, infection)
Specific proteins		Low C3, C4 components of complement (SLE, rheumatoid arthritis) Rheumatoid factor Antinuclear factor

SOURCE: From Ingram RH Jr, HPIM-11, p. 1125.

pleural fluid pH is <7.20 and 0.15 units less than arterial pH, or (5) there is loculated pleural fluid. If closed drainage does not result in complete removal of fluid, streptokinase, 250,000 units, can be instilled through the tube. If fluid persists, open drainage is indicated, usually accomplished through a videoscope.

PNEUMOTHORAX (PNTX)   Spontaneous PNTX most commonly occurs between 20 and 40 years of age; causes sudden, sharp chest pain and dyspnea. Treatment depends on size—if small, observation is sufficient; if large, closed drainage with chest tube is necessary. 50% suffer recurrence, and pleural abrasion by thoracotomy or thoracostomy may be required so that surfaces become adherent (pleurodesis). Complications include hemothorax, cardiovascular compromise secondary to tension PNTX, and bronchopleural fistula. Many interstitial and obstructive lung diseases may predispose to PNTX.

MEDIASTINAL DISEASE

MEDIASTINITIS   Usually infectious. Routes of infection include esophageal perforation or tracheal disruption (trauma, instrumentation, eroding carcinoma). Radiographic hallmarks include mediastinal widening, air in mediastinum, pneumo- or hydropneumothorax. Therapy usually involves surgical drainage and antibiotics.

TUMORS AND CYSTS   Most common mediastinal masses in adults are metastatic carcinomas and lymphomas. Sarcoidosis, infectious mononucleosis, and AIDS may produce mediastinal lymphadenopathy. Neurogenic tumors, teratodermoids, thymomas, and bronchogenic cysts account for two-thirds of remaining mediastinal masses. Specific locations for specific etiologies (Table 134-3). Evaluation includes CXR, CT, and when diagnosis remains in doubt, mediastinoscopy and biopsy.

Neurogenic Tumors   Most common primary mediastinal neoplasms; majority are benign; vague chest pain and cough.

Teratodermoids   Anterior mediastinum; 10–20% undergo malignant transformation.

Thymomas   10% primary mediastinal neoplasms; one-quarter are malignant; myasthenia gravis occurs in half.

SUPERIOR VENA CAVA SYNDROME   Dilation of veins of upper thorax and neck, plethora, facial and conjunctival edema, headache, visual disturbances, and reduced state of consciousness; most often due to malignant disease—75% bronchogenic carcinoma, most others lymphoma.

Table 134-3

Nature of Masses in Various Locations in Mediastinum

Superior	Anterior and Middle	Posterior
Lymphoma	Lymphoma	Neurogenic tumors
Thymoma	Metastatic carcinoma	Lymphoma
Retrosternal thyroid	Teratodermoid	Hernia (Bochdalek)
Metastatic carcinoma	Bronchogenic cyst	Aortic aneurysm
Parathyroid tumors	Aortic aneurysm	
Zenker's diverticulum	Pericardial cyst	
Aortic aneurysm		

DISORDERS OF DIAPHRAGM

DIAPHRAGMATIC PARALYSIS *Unilateral Paralysis* Usually caused by phrenic nerve injury due to trauma or mediastinal tumor, but nearly half are unexplained; usually asymptomatic; suggested by CXR, confirmed by fluoroscopy.

Bilateral Paralysis May be due to high cervical cord injury, motor neuron disease, poliomyelitis, polyneuropathies, bilateral phrenic involvement by mediastinal lesions, after cardiac surgery, dyspnea; paradoxical abdominal motion should be sought in supine pts.

For a more detailed discussion, see Light, RW: Disorders of the Pleura, Mediastinum, and Diaphragm, Chap. 262, p. 1513, in HPIM-15.

135

DISORDERS OF VENTILATION, INCLUDING SLEEP APNEA

ALVEOLAR HYPOVENTILATION Exists when arterial P_{CO_2} increases above the normal 37–43 mmHg. In most clinically important chronic hypoventilation syndromes, Pa_{CO_2} is 50–80 mmHg.

Cause Alveolar hypoventilation always is (1) a defect in the metabolic respiratory control system, (2) a defect in the respiratory neuromuscular system, or (3) a defect in the ventilatory apparatus (Table 135-1).

Disorders associated with impaired respiratory drive, defects in respiratory neuromuscular system, and upper airway obstruction produce an increase in Pa_{CO_2}, despite normal lungs, because of a decrease in overall minute ventilation.

Disorders of chest wall, lower airways, and lungs produce an increase in Pa_{CO_2}, despite a normal or increased minute ventilation.

Increased Pa_{CO_2} leads to respiratory acidosis, compensatory increase in HCO_3^-, and decrease in Pa_{O_2}.

Hypoxemia may induce secondary polycythemia, pulmonary hypertension, right heart failure. Gas exchange worsens during sleep, resulting in morning headache, impaired sleep quality, fatigue, daytime somnolence, mental confusion (Fig. 135-1).

HYPOVENTILATION SYNDROMES

PRIMARY ALVEOLAR Cause unknown; rare; thought to arise from defect in metabolic respiratory control system; key diagnostic finding is chronic respiratory acidosis without respiratory muscle weakness or impaired ventilatory mechanics. Some pts respond to respiratory stimulants and supplemental O_2.

Table 135-1

Chronic Hypoventilation Syndromes

Mechanism	Site of Defect	Disorder
Impaired respiratory drive	Peripheral and central chemoreceptors	Carotid body dysfunction, trauma
	Brainstem respiratory neurons	Prolonged hypoxia
		Metabolic alkalosis
		Bulbar poliomyelitis, encephalitis
		Brainstem infarction, hemorrhage, trauma
		Brainstem demyelination, degeneration
		Chronic drug administration
		Primary alveolar hypoventilation syndrome
Defective respiratory neuromuscular system	Spinal cord and peripheral nerves	High cervical trauma
		Poliomyelitis
		Motor neuron disease
		Peripheral neuropathy
	Respiratory muscles	Myasthenia gravis
		Muscular dystrophy
		Chronic myopathy
Impaired ventilatory apparatus	Chest wall	Kyphoscoliosis
		Fibrothorax
		Thoracoplasty
		Ankylosing spondylitis
		Obesity-hypoventilation
	Airways and lungs	Laryngeal and tracheal stenosis
		Obstructive sleep apnea
		Cystic fibrosis
		Chronic obstructive pulmonary disease

SOURCE: EA Phillipson: HPIM-15, p. 1517.

RESPIRATORY NEUROMUSCULAR Several primary neuromuscular disorders produce chronic hypoventilation (Table 135-1). Hypoventilation usually develops gradually, but acute, superimposed respiratory loads (e.g., viral bronchitis with airways obstruction) may precipitate respiratory failure. Diaphragm weakness is a common feature, with orthopnea and paradoxical abdominal movement in supine posture. Testing reveals low maximum voluntary ventilation and reduced maximal inspiratory and expiratory pressures. Therapy involves treatment of underlying condition. Many pts benefit from mechanical ventilatory assistance at night (often through nasal mask) or the entire day (typically through tracheostomy).

OBESITY-HYPOVENTILATION Massive obesity imposes a mechanical load on the respiratory system. Small percentage of morbidly obese pts develop hypercapnia, hypoxemia, and ultimately polycythemia, pulmonary hypertension, and right heart failure. Most pts have mild to moderate airflow obstruction. Treatment includes weight loss, smoking cessation, and pharmacologic respiratory stimulants such as progesterone.

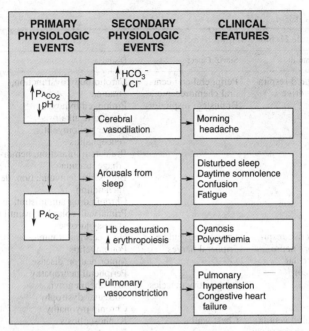

FIGURE 135-1 Physiologic and clinical features of alveolar hypoventilation. PA_{CO_2} alveolar P_{CO_2}. (*After EA Phillipson: HPIM-15.*)

SLEEP APNEA

By convention, apnea is defined as cessation of airflow for >10 s. Hypopnea is defined as reduction in airflow resulting in arousal from sleep or oxygen desaturation. Minimum number of events per night for diagnosis is uncertain, but most pts have at least 10–15/h of sleep. Prevalence estimates vary depending on threshold for diagnosis (events/h) and on definition of hypopnea (degree of desaturation required), but conservative figures are 10% of working-age men & 4% of women. Some pts have *central apnea* with transient loss of neural drive to respiratory muscles during sleep. Vast majority have primarily *obstructive apnea* with occlusion in the upper airway. Sleep plays a permissive role in collapse of upper airway. Alcohol and sedatives exacerbate the condition. Most pts have structural narrowing of upper airway. Obesity is frequent, but many pts have normal body habitus. Most pts have obstruction at nasal or palatal level. Mandibular deformities (retrognathia) also predispose. Symptoms include snoring, excessive daytime sleepiness, memory loss, and impotence. Sleepiness increases risk of automobile accidents. Nocturnal hypoxia, a consequence of apnea, may contribute to systemic hypertension, arrhythmias, and right ventricular hypertrophy. Sleep apnea, in the absence of co-morbidity causing daytime hypoxia, is not a cause of substantial pulmonary hypertension or right heart failure.

Diagnosis This requires overnight observation of the pt. The definitive test for obstructive sleep apnea is overnight polysomnography, including sleep staging and respiratory monitoring.

Table 135-2

Management of Obstructive Sleep Apnea (OSA)

Mechanism	Mild to Moderate OSA	Moderate to Severe OSA
↑ Upper airway muscle tone	Avoidance of alcohol, sedatives	
↑ Upper airway lumen size	Weight reduction	Uvulopalatopharyngoplasty
	Avoidance of supine posture	
	Oral prosthesis	
↓ Upper airway subatmospheric pressure	Improved nasal patency	Nasal continuous positive airway pressure
Bypass occlusion		Tracheostomy

SOURCE: EA Phillipson: HPIM-15, p. 1522.

 TREATMENT

(See Table 135-2) Therapy is directed at increasing upper airway size, increasing upper airway tone, and minimizing upper airway collapsing pressures. Weight loss often reduces disease severity. Majority of pts with severe sleep apnea require nasal continuous positive airway pressure (nasal C-PAP). Mandibular positioning device (dental) may treat pts with mild or moderate disease. Surgery (uvulopalatopharyngoplasty) is usually reserved for pts who fail other therapies, as failure rate is high (>50%) and surgery may compromise later therapy with CPAP.

HYPERVENTILATION

Increased ventilation, causing Pa_{CO_2} <37 mmHg. Causes include lesions of the CNS, metabolic acidosis, anxiety, drugs (e.g., salicylates), hypoxemia, hypoglycemia, hepatic coma, and sepsis. Hyperventilation may also occur with some types of lung disease, particularly interstitial disease and pulmonary edema.

For a more detailed discussion, see Phillipson EA: Disorders of Ventilation, Chap. 263, p. 1517, and Sleep Apnea, Chap. 264, p. 1520, in HPIM-15.

136

PULMONARY INSUFFICIENCY AND ACUTE RESPIRATORY DISTRESS SYNDROME (ARDS)

ARDS is a descriptive term applied to many acute, diffuse infiltrative lung lesions of diverse etiologies (Table 136-1) with severe arterial hypoxemia. Acute lung injury (ALI) is a mild form of ARDS.

Table 136-1

Conditions That May Lead to the Acute Respiratory Distress Syndrome

1. Diffuse pulmonary infections (e.g., viral, bacterial, fungal, *Pneumocystis*)
2. Aspiration (e.g., gastric contents with Mendelson's syndrome, water with near drowning)
3. Inhalation of toxins and irritants (e.g., chlorine gas, NO_2, smoke, ozone, high concentrations of oxygen)
4. Narcotic overdose pulmonary edema (e.g., heroin, methadone, morphine, dextropropoxyphene)
5. Nonnarcotic drug effects (e.g., nitrofurantoin)
6. Immunologic response to host antigens (e.g., Goodpasture's syndrome, systemic lupus erythematosus)
7. Effects of nonthoracic trauma with hypotension
8. In association with systemic reactions to processes initiated outside the lung (e.g., gram-negative septicemia, hemorrhagic pancreatitis, amniotic fluid embolism, fat embolism)
9. Postcardiopulmonary bypass ("pump lung," "postperfusion lung")

SOURCE: Adapted from M Moss, RH Ingram, Jr: HPIM-15, p. 1524.

Clinical Characteristics and Pathophysiology

Earliest sign is often tachypnea followed by dyspnea. Arterial blood gas shows reduction of P_{O_2} and P_{CO_2} with widened alveolar-arterial O_2 difference. Physical exam and CXR may be normal initially. With progression, pt becomes cyanotic, dyspneic, and increasingly tachypneic. Crackles become audible diffusely, and CXR shows diffuse, bilateral, interstitial and alveolar infiltrates.

ARDS increases lung water without increasing hydrostatic forces. Toxic gases (chlorine, NO_2, smoke) and gastric acid aspiration damage the alveolar-capillary membrane directly, whereas sepsis increases alveolar-capillary permeability by producing activation and aggregation of formed blood elements. Though radiologically diffuse, regional lung dysfunction is non-homogeneous, with severe ventilation-perfusion imbalance and actual shunting of blood through collapsed alveoli.

℞ TREATMENT

Early in illness, supplemental O_2 may be sufficient to correct hypoxemia, but with progression mechanical ventilatory support is necessary. Goal of therapy is to provide adequate tissue O_2 delivery—determined by arterial oxygen saturation (Sa_{O_2}), hemoglobin (Hb), cardiac output, and blood flow distribution. Reasonable objective is to achieve 90% saturation (Pa_{O_2} 8 kPa, or 60 mmHg) with the lowest inspired O_2 concentration practical to avoid O_2 toxicity ($FI_{O_2} < 0.6$). Hb should be ≥ 100 g/L (≥ 10 g/dL).

- Cardiac output is supported as necessary with IV fluids and inotropic agents. Pulmonary artery catheter insertion may be necessary for accurate assessment of ventricular filling pressures, hemodynamics, and O_2 transport.
- Because airspace disease is nonhomogeneous, large-volume breaths are administered preferentially to normal areas of lung, causing alveolar overdistention and furthering lung injury ("volutrauma"). Avoidance of overdistention is accomplished by using pressure-cycled mechanical ventilation with maximal distending pressure of 35 cmH_2O or by using low tidal volumes (5–7 mL/kG ideal body weight) with the ventilator in vol-

ume-cycled mode. Positive end-expiratory pressure (PEEP, >12 cmH$_2$O) is used to prevent alveolar collapse.
• Pressure or volume limitation frequently results in hypoventilation and hypercarbia. Inadequate oxygenation is corrected with: (1) prone positioning, which improves gas exchange; and (2) prolonged inspiratory times (inverse ratio ventilation), which increases mean lung volumes. Recruitment breaths (sustained large-volume breaths lasting >30 sec) may also markedly improve oxygenation. Techniques such as inhaled nitric oxide or partial liquid ventilation have not been shown to improve outcome.

Complications

1. *LV failure* is a common, easily missed complication, particularly in pts receiving mechanical ventilation.
2. *Secondary bacterial infection* may be obscured by the diffuse roentgenographic changes.
3. *Bronchial obstruction* may be caused by endotracheal or tracheostomy tubes.
4. *Pneumothorax and pneumomediastinum* may cause abrupt deterioration in pts receiving mechanical ventilation.

Prognosis

Overall mortality rate is 50% and varies with the intrinsic mortality of the underlying condition, but preliminary studies suggest new ventilator strategies reduce mortality. If ARDS occurs as a result of extrapulmonic sepsis, multiple organ failure may supervene.

For a more detailed discussion, see Moss M, Ingram RH Jr: Acute Respiratory Distress Syndrome, Chap. 265, p. 1523, HPIM-15.

137

APPROACH TO THE PATIENT WITH RENAL DISEASE

The approach to renal disease begins with recognition of particular syndromes on the basis of findings such as presence or absence of azotemia, proteinuria, hypertension, edema, abnormal urinalysis, electrolyte disorders, abnormal urine volumes, or infection (Table 137-1).

Acute Renal Failure   (See Chap. 138)

Clinical syndrome is characterized by a rapid, severe decrease in GFR (rise in serum creatinine and BUN), usually with reduced urine output. Extracellular fluid expansion leads to edema, hypertension, and occasionally to CHF. Hyperkalemia, hyponatremia, and acidosis are common. Etiologies include ischemia; nephrotoxic injury due to drugs, toxins, or endogenous pigments; sepsis; severe renovascular disease; or conditions related to pregnancy. Prerenal and postrenal failure are potentially reversible causes.

RAPIDLY PROGRESSIVE GLOMERULONEPHRITIS   Loss of renal function occurs over weeks to months. Pts are initially nonoliguric and may have recent flulike symptoms; later, oliguric renal failure with uremic symptoms supervenes. Hypertension is common. Pulmonary manifestations range from asymptomatic infiltrates to life-threatening hemoptysis. Urinalysis typically shows hematuria, proteinuria, and RBC casts.

ACUTE GLOMERULONEPHRITIS   (See Chap. 142)   An acute illness with sudden onset of hematuria, edema, hypertension, oliguria, and elevated BUN and creatinine. Mild pulmonary congestion may be present. An antecedent or concurrent infection or multisystem disease may be causative, or glomerular disease may exist alone. Hematuria, proteinuria, and pyuria are usually present, and RBC casts confirm the diagnosis. Serum complement may be decreased in certain conditions.

Chronic Renal Failure   (See Chap. 139)

Progressive permanent loss of renal function over months to years does not cause symptoms of uremia until GFR is reduced to about 10–15% of normal. Hypertension may occur early. Later, manifestations include anorexia, nausea, vomiting, insomnia, weight loss, weakness, paresthesia, bleeding, serositis, anemia, acidosis, and hyperkalemia. Causes include diabetes mellitus, severe hypertension, glomerular disease, urinary tract obstruction, interstitial nephritis. Indications of chronicity include long-standing azotemia, anemia, hyperphosphatemia, hypocalcemia, shrunken kidneys, renal osteodystrophy by x-ray, or findings on renal biopsy.

Nephrotic Syndrome   (See Chap. 142)

Defined as heavy albuminuria (>3.5 g/d in the adult) with or without edema, hypoalbuminemia, hyperlipidemia, and varying degrees of renal insufficiency. Can be idiopathic or due to drugs, infections, neoplasms, multisystem or hereditary diseases. Complications include severe edema, thromboembolic events, infection, and protein malnutrition.

Table 137-1

Initial Clinical and Laboratory Data Base for Defining Major Syndromes in Nephrology

Syndromes	Important Clues to Diagnosis	Common Findings
Acute or rapidly progressive renal failure	Anuria Oliguria Documented recent decline in GFR	Hypertension, hematuria Proteinuria, pyuria Casts, edema
Acute nephritis	Hematuria, RBC casts Azotemia, oliguria Edema, hypertension	Proteinuria Pyuria Circulatory congestion
Chronic renal failure	Azotemia for >3 months Prolonged symptoms or signs of uremia Symptoms or signs of renal osteodystrophy Kidneys reduced in size bilaterally Broad casts in urinary sediment	Hematuria, proteinuria Casts, oliguria Polyuria, nocturia Edema, hypertension Electrolyte disorders
Nephrotic syndrome	Proteinuria >3.5 g per 1.73 m^2 per 24 h Hypoalbuminemia Hyperlipidemia Lipiduria	Casts Edema
Asymptomatic urinary abnormalities	Hematuria Proteinuria (below nephrotic range) Sterile pyuria, casts	
Urinary tract infection	Bacteriuria >10^5 colonies per milliliter Other infectious agent documented in urine Pyuria, leukocyte casts Frequency, urgency Bladder tenderness, flank tenderness	Hematuria Mild azotemia Mild proteinuria Fever
Renal tubule defects	Electrolyte disorders Polyuria, nocturia Symptoms or signs of renal osteodystrophy Large kidneys Renal transport defects	Hematuria "Tubular" proteinuria Enuresis
Hypertension	Systolic/diastolic hypertension	Proteinuria Casts Azotemia
Nephrolithiasis	Previous history of stone passage or removal Previous history of stone seen by x-ray Renal colic	Hematuria Pyuria Frequency, urgency

(continued)

Table 137-1 *(Continued)*

Initial Clinical and Laboratory Data Base for Defining Major Syndromes in Nephrology

Syndromes	Important Clues to Diagnosis	Common Findings
Urinary tract obstruction	Azotemia, oliguria, anuria Polyuria, nocturia, urinary retention Slowing of urinary stream Large prostrate, large kidneys Flank tenderness, full bladder after voiding	Hematuria Pyuria Enuresis, dysuria

SOURCE: Modified from FL Coe, BM Brenner: HPIM-14.

Asymptomatic Urinary Abnormalities

Hematuria may be due to neoplasms, stones, infection at any level of the urinary tract, sickle cell disease, or analgesic abuse. Renal parenchymal causes are suggested by RBC casts, proteinuria, or dysmorphic RBCs in urine. Pattern of gross hematuria may be helpful in localizing site. Hematuria with low-grade proteinuria may be due to benign recurrent hematuria or IgA nephropathy. Modest *proteinuria* may be an isolated finding due to fever, exertion, CHF, or upright posture. Renal causes include diabetes mellitus, amyloidosis, or other causes of glomerular disease. *Pyuria* can be caused by UTI, interstitial nephritis, glomerulonephritis, or renal transplant rejection. "Sterile" pyuria is associated with UTI treated with antibiotics, glucocorticoid therapy, acute febrile episodes, cyclophosphamide therapy, pregnancy, renal transplant rejection, genitourinary trauma, prostatitis, cystourethritis, tuberculosis and other mycobacterial infections, fungal infection, *Haemophilus influenzae*, anaerobic infection, fastidious bacteria, and bacterial L forms.

Urinary Tract Infection (See Chap. 144)

Generally defined as $>10^5$ bacteria per mL of urine. Levels between 10^2 and 10^5/mL may indicate infection but are usually due to poor sample collection, especially if mixed flora are present. Adults at risk are sexually active women or anyone with urinary tract obstruction, vesicoureteral reflux, bladder catheterization, neurogenic bladder (associated with diabetes mellitus), or primary neurologic diseases. Prostatitis, urethritis, and vaginitis may be distinguished by quantitative urine culture. Flank pain, nausea, vomiting, fever, and chills indicate kidney infection. UTI is a common cause of sepsis, especially in the elderly and institutionalized.

Renal Tubular Defects (See Chap. 143)

Generally inherited, they include anatomic defects (polycystic kidneys, medullary cystic disease, medullary sponge kidney) detected in the evaluation of hematuria, flank pain, infection, or renal failure of unknown cause and disorders of tubular transport that cause glucosuria, aminoaciduria, stones, or rickets. Fanconi syndrome is a generalized tubular defect that can be hereditary or acquired, due to drugs, heavy metals, multiple myeloma, amyloidosis, or renal transplantation. Nephrogenic diabetes insipidus (polyuria, polydypsia, hypernatremia, hypernatremic dehydration) and renal tubular acidosis are additional causes.

Hypertension   (See Chap. 124)

Blood pressure >140/90 mmHg affects 20% of the U.S. adult population; when inadequately controlled, it is an important cause of cerebrovascular accident, MI, and CHF and can contribute to the development of renal failure. Hypertension is usually asymptomatic until cardiac, renal, or neurologic symptoms appear. In most cases hypertension is idiopathic and becomes evident between ages 25 and 45.

Nephrolithiasis   (See Chap. 146)

Causes colicky pain, UTI, hematuria, dysuria, or unexplained pyuria. Stones may be found on routine x-ray. Most are radiopaque Ca stones and are associated with high levels of urinary Ca, and/or oxalate excretion, and/or low levels of urinary citrate excretion. Staghorn calculi are large, branching radiopaque stones within the renal pelvis due to recurrent infection. Uric acid stones are radiolucent. Urinalysis may reveal hematuria, pyuria, or pathologic crystals.

Urinary Tract Obstruction   (See Chap. 147)

Causes variable symptoms depending on whether it is acute or chronic, unilateral or bilateral, complete or partial, and on underlying etiology. It is an important reversible cause of unexplained renal failure. Upper tract obstruction may be silent or produce flank pain, hematuria, and renal infection. Bladder symptoms may be present in lower tract obstruction. Functional consequences include polyuria, anuria, nocturia, acidosis, hyperkalemia, and hypertension. A flank or suprapubic mass may be found on physical exam.

For a more detailed discussion, see Part 10: Disorders of the Kidney and Urinary Tract, pp. 1535–1629, in HPIM-15.

138

ACUTE RENAL FAILURE

Definition

Acute renal failure (ARF), defined as a measurable increase in the serum creatinine (Cr) concentration (usually relative increase of 50% or absolute increase of 0.5 to 1.0 mg/dL), occurs in ~ 5% of hospitalized pts. It is associated with a substantial increase in in-hospital mortality and morbidity. ARF can be anticipated in some clinical circumstances (e.g., after radiocontrast exposure or major surgery), and there are no specific pharmacologic therapies proven helpful at preventing or reversing the condition. Maintaining optimal renal perfusion and intravascular volume appears to be important in most clinical circumstances.

Differential Diagnosis

The separation into three broad categories (prerenal, intrinsic renal, and post-renal failure) is of great clinical utility (Table 138-1). *Prerenal failure* is most common among hospitalized pts. It may result from true volume depletion (e.g., diarrhea, vomiting, GI or other hemorrhage) or "effective circulatory volume" depletion, i.e., reduced renal perfusion in the setting of adequate or excess blood volume. Reduced renal perfusion may be seen in CHF (due to reduced cardiac output and/or potent vasodilator therapy), hepatic cirrhosis (due most likely to arteriovenous shunting), nephrotic syndrome and other states of severe hypoproteinemia (total serum protein <5 g/dL), and renovascular disease (because of fixed stenosis at the level of the main renal artery or large branch vessels). Several drugs can reduce renal perfusion, most notably NSAIDs. ACE inhibitors and angiotensin II receptor antagonists may reduce GFR but do not tend to reduce renal perfusion.

Causes of *intrinsic renal failure* depend on the clinical setting. Among hospitalized pts, especially on surgical services or in intensive care units, acute tubular necrosis (ATN) is the most common diagnosis. Allergic interstitial nephritis, usually due to antibiotics (e.g., penicillins, cephalosporins, sulfa drugs, quinolones, and rifampin) may also be responsible. These conditions are relatively uncommon in the outpatient setting. There, intrinsic disease due to glomerulonephritis or pyelonephritis predominates.

Postrenal failure is due to urinary tract obstruction, which is also more common among ambulatory rather than hospitalized pts. More common in men than women, it is most often caused by ureteral or urethral blockade. Occasionally, stones or renal papillae may cause more proximal obstruction.

Characteristic Findings and Diagnostic Workup

All pts with ARF manifest some degree of azotemia (increased BUN and Cr). Other clinical features depend on the etiology of renal disease. Pts with prerenal azotemia due to volume depletion usually demonstrate orthostatic hypotension, tachycardia, low JVP, and dry mucous membranes. Pts with prerenal azotemia and CHF may show jugular venous distention, an S_3 gallop, and peripheral and pulmonary edema. Therefore, the physical exam is critical in the workup of pts with prerenal ARF. In general, the BUN/Cr ratio tends to be high (>20:1), more so with volume depletion and CHF than with cirrhosis. The uric acid may also be disproportionately elevated in noncirrhotic prerenal states (due to increased proximal tubular absorption overall). Urine chemistries tend to show low urine [Na$^+$] (< 10–20 mmol/L, <<10 with hepatorenal syndrome) and a fractional excretion of sodium (FEN$_a$) << 1% (Table 138-2). The UA typically shows hyaline and a few granular casts, without cells or cellular casts. Renal ultrasonography is usually normal.

Pts with intrinsic renal disease present with varying complaints. Glomerulonephritis (GN) is often accompanied by hypertension and mild to moderate edema (associated with Na retention and proteinuria, and sometimes with hematuria). The urine chemistries may be indistinguishable from those in pts with prerenal failure; in fact, some pts with GN have renal hypoperfusion (due to glomerular inflammation and ischemia) with resultant hyperreninemia leading to hypertension. The urine sediment is most helpful in these cases. RBC, WBC, and cellular casts are characteristic of GN; RBC casts are rarely seen in other conditions (i.e., high specificity). In the setting of inflammatory nephritis (GN or interstitial nephritis, see below), there may be increased renal echogenicity on ultrasonography, so-called medical renal disease. Unlike pts with GN, pts with interstitial diseases are less likely to have hypertension or proteinuria.

Table 138-1

Common Causes of Acute Renal Failure

PRERENAL

Volume depletion
  Blood loss
  GI fluid loss (e.g., vomiting, diarrhea)
  Overzealous diuretic use
Volume overload with reduced renal perfusion
  Congestive heart failure
    Low-output with systolic dysfunction
    "High-output" (e.g., anemia, thyrotoxicosis)
  Hepatic cirrhosis
  Severe hypoproteinemia
Renovascular disease
Drugs
  NSAIDs, cyclosporine, amphotericin B
Other
  Hypercalcemia, "third spacing" (e.g., pancreatitis, systemic inflammatory
    response), hepatorenal syndrome

INTRINSIC

Acute tubular necrosis (ATN)
  Hypotension or shock, prolonged prerenal azotemia, post-operative
    sepsis syndrome, rhabdomyolysis, hemolysis, drugs
    Radiocontrast, aminoglycosides, cisplatin
Other tubulointerstitial disease
  Allergic interstitial nephritis
  Pyelonephritis (bilateral, or unilateral in single functional kidney)
  Heavy metal poisoning
Atheroembolic disease
Glomerulonephritis
  "Rapidly progressive"
    Wegener's granulomatosis
    Anti-GBM disease (Goodpasture's syndrome)
    PAN and other pauci-immune GN
  Immune complex-mediated
    Subacute bacterial endocarditis, SLE, cryoglobulinemia (with or
      without hepatitis C infection), postinfectious GN
  Other
    IgA nephropathy (Henoch-Schönlein purpura), preeclampsia

POSTRENAL (URINARY TRACT OBSTRUCTION)

Bladder neck obstruction, bladder calculi
Prostatic hypertrophy
Ureteral obstruction due to compression
  Pelvic or abdominal malignancy, retroperitoneal fibrosis
Nephrolithiasis
Papillary necrosis with obstruction

NOTE: GBM, glomerular basement membrane; PAN, polyarteritis nodosa.

Table 138-2

Urine Diagnostic Indices in Differentiation of Prerenal versus Intrinsic Renal Azotemia

Diagnostic Index	Typical Findings	
	Prerenal Azotemia	Intrinsic Renal Azotemia
Fractional excretion of sodium (%)* $$\frac{U_{Na} \times P_{Cr}}{P_{Na} \times U_{Cr}} \times 100$$	<1	>1
Urine sodium concentration (mmol/L)	<10	>20
Urine creatinine to plasma creatinine ratio	>40	>20
Urine urea nitrogen to plasma urea nitrogen ratio	>8	<3
Urine specific gravity	>1.018	<1.015
Urine osmolality (mosmol/kg H_2O	>500	<300
Plasma BUN/creatinine ratio	>20	<10–15
Renal failure index $$\frac{U_{Na}}{U_{Cr}/P_{cr}}$$	<1	>1
Urinary sediment	Hyaline casts	Muddy brown granular casts

* Most sensitive indices.
NOTE: U_{Na}, urine sodium concentration; P_{Cr}, plasma creatinine concentration; P_{Na}, plasma sodium concentration; U_{Cr}, urine creatinine concentration.

Hematuria and pyuria may present on UA; the classic sediment finding in allergic interstitial nephritis is a predominance (>10%) of urinary eosinophils with Wright's or Hansel's stain. WBC casts may also be seen, particularly in cases of pyelonephritis.

Pts with postrenal ARF due to urinary tract obstruction are usually less severely ill than pts with prerenal or intrinsic renal disease, and their presentation may be delayed until azotemia is markedly advanced (BUN > 150, Cr > 12–15 mg/dL). An associated impairment of urinary concentrating ability often "protects" the pt from complications of volume overload. Urinary electrolytes typically show a FEN_a > 1%, and microscopic examination of the urinary sediment is usually bland. Ultrasonography is the key diagnostic tool. More than 90% of pts with postrenal ARF show obstruction of the urinary collection system on ultrasound (e.g., dilated ureter, calyces); false negatives include hyperacute obstruction and encasement of the ureter and/or kidney by tumor, functionally obstructing urinary outflow without structural dilatation.

 TREATMENT

This should focus on providing etiology-specific supportive care. For example, pts with prerenal failure due to GI fluid loss may experience relatively rapid correction of ARF after the administration of IV fluid to expand volume. The same treatment in prerenal pts with CHF would be counterproductive; in this case, treatment of the underlying disease with vasodilators and/or inotropic agents would more likely be of benefit.

There are relatively few intrinsic renal causes of ARF for which there is safe and effective therapy. ARF associated with vasculitis may respond to high-dose glucocorticoids and cytotoxic agents (e.g., cyclophosphamide); plasmapheresis and plasma exchange may be useful in other selected circumstances [e.g., Goodpasture's syndrome and hemolytic-uremic syndrome/ thrombotic thrombocytopenic purpura (HUS/TTP), respectively]. Antibiotic therapy may be sufficient for the treatment of ARF associated with pyelonephritis or endocarditis. There are conflicting data regarding the utility of glucocorticoids in allergic interstitial nephritis. Many practitioners advocate their use with clinical evidence of progressive renal insufficiency despite discontinuation of the offending drug, or with biopsy evidence of potentially reversible, severe disease.

The treatment of urinary tract obstruction often involves consultation with a urologist. Interventions as simple as Foley catheter placement or as complicated as multiple ureteral stents and/or nephrostomy tubes may be required.

Dialysis for ARF and Recovery of Renal Function Most cases of community- and hospital-acquired ARF resolve with conservative supportive measures, time, and patience. If nonprerenal ARF continues to progress, dialysis must be considered. Traditional indications include: volume overload refractory to diuretic agents; hyperkalemia; encephalopathy not otherwise explained; pericarditis, pleuritis, or other inflammatory serositis; and severe metabolic acidosis, compromising respiratory or circulatory function. The inability to provide requisite fluids for antibiotics, inotropes and other drugs, and/or nutrition should also be considered an indication for dialysis.

Dialytic options for ARF include (1) intermittent hemodialysis (IHD), (2) peritoneal dialysis (PD), and (3) continuous renal replacement therapy (CRRT, i.e., continuous arteriovenous or venovenous hemodiafiltration). Most pts are treated with IHD. The use of a noncellulosic membrane for IHD may limit renal injury in selected pt groups and has been associated with enhanced renal recovery. At many centers, CRRT is prescribed only in pts intolerant of IHD, usually because of hypotension; other centers use it as the modality of choice for pts in intensive care units.

For a more detailed discussion, see Brady HR, Brenner BM: Acute Renal Failure, Chap. 269, p. 1541, in HPIM-15.

139

CHRONIC RENAL FAILURE (CRF) AND UREMIA

Epidemiology

The prevalence of CRF, defined as a long-standing, irreversible impairment of renal function, is thought to be substantially greater than the number of pts with

Table 139-1

___

Common Causes of Chronic Renal Failure

___

Diabetic nephropathy
Hypertensive nephrosclerosis*
Glomerulonephritis
Renovascular disease (ischemic nephropathy)
Polycystic kidney disease
Reflux nephropathy and other congenital renal diseases
Interstitial nephritis, including analgesic nephropathy
HIV-associated nephropathy
Transplant allograft failure ("chronic rejection")

___

* Often diagnosis of exclusion; very few pts undergo renal biopsy; may be occult renal disease
  with hypertension.

___

end-stage renal disease (ESRD), now ≥300,000 in the U.S. There is a spectrum of disease related to decrements in renal function; clinical and therapeutic issues differ greatly depending on whether the GFR reduction is moderate (e.g., 20–60 mL/min) or severe (<20 mL/min). Dialysis is usually required to control symptoms of uremia with GFR < 5–10 mL/min. Common causes of CRF are outlined in Table 139-1.

Differential Diagnosis

The first step in the differential diagnosis of CRF is establishing its chronicity, i.e., disproving a major acute component. The two most common means of determining disease chronicity are the history (if available) and the renal ultrasound, which is used to measure kidney size. In general, kidneys that have shrunk (<10–11.5 cm, depending on body size) are more likely affected by chronic disease. While reasonably specific (few false positives), reduced kidney size is only a moderately sensitive marker for CRF, i.e., there are several relatively common conditions in which kidney disease may be chronic, without any reduction in renal size. Diabetic nephropathy, HIV-associated nephropathy, and infiltrative diseases such as multiple myeloma may be associated with relatively large kidneys despite chronicity. Renal biopsy is a more reliable means of proving chronicity; a predominance of glomerulosclerosis or interstitial fibrosis argues strongly for chronic disease. Hyperphosphatemia and other metabolic derangements are not reliable indicators in distinguishing acute from chronic disease.

Once chronicity has been established, clues from the physical exam, laboratory panel, and urine sediment evaluation can be used to determine etiology. A detailed Hx will identify important comorbid conditions, such as diabetes, HIV seropositivity, or peripheral vascular disease. The family Hx is paramount in the workup of autosomal dominant polycystic kidney disease or hereditary nephritis (Alport's syndrome). An occupational Hx may reveal exposure to environmental toxins or culprit drugs (including over-the-counter agents, such as analgesics or Chinese herbs).

Physical exam may demonstrate abdominal masses (i.e., polycystic kidneys), diminished pulses (i.e., atherosclerotic peripheral vascular disease), or an abdominal bruit (i.e., renovascular disease). The Hx and exam may also yield important data regarding severity of disease. The presence of foreshortened fingers (due to resorption of the distal phalangeal tufts) and/or subcutaneous nodules may be seen with advanced renal failure and secondary hyperparathyroidism. Excoriations (uremic pruritus), pallor (anemia), muscle wasting, and a

nitrogenous fetor are all signs of advanced chronic renal disease, as are pericarditis, pleuritis, and asterixis, complications of particular concern that usually
prompt the initiation of dialysis.

LABORATORY FINDINGS Serum and urine laboratory findings typically provide additional information useful in determining the etiology and severity of CRF. Heavy proteinuria (>3.5 g/d), hypoalbuminemia, hypercholesterolemia, and edema suggest nephrotic syndrome (see Chap. 142). Diabetic
nephropathy, membranous nephropathy, focal segmental glomerulosclerosis,
minimal change disease, amyloid, and HIV-associated nephropathy are principal
causes. Proteinuria may decrease slightly with decreasing GFR but rarely to
normal levels. Hyperkalemia and metabolic acidosis may complicate all forms
of CRF eventually but are more prominent in pts with interstitial renal diseases.

The Uremic Syndrome

The culprit toxin(s) responsible for the uremic syndrome remain elusive. The
serum creatinine (Cr) is the most common laboratory surrogate of renal function.
The creatinine clearance (Cr_{Cl}) is calculated as the urine concentration divided
by serum concentration multiplied by the urine flow rate; it approximates the
GFR and is a more reliable indicator of renal function than the serum Cr alone.
Uremic symptoms tend to develop with serum Cr > 530–710 μmol/L (> 6–
8 mg/dL) or Cr_{Cl} < 10 mL/min, although these values vary widely.

Symptoms of advanced uremia include anorexia, weight loss, dyspnea, fatigue, pruritus, sleep and taste disturbance, and confusion and other forms of
encephalopathy. Key findings on physical exam include hypertension, jugular
venous distention, pericardial and/or pleural friction rub, muscle wasting, asterixis, excoriations, and ecchymoses. Laboratory abnormalities may include:
hyperkalemia, hyperphosphatemia, metabolic acidosis, hypocalcemia, hyperuricemia, anemia, and hypoalbuminemia. Most of these abnormalities eventually resolve with initiation of dialysis or renal transplantation (Chaps. 140, 141).

℞ TREATMENT

Hypertension complicates most forms of CRF and warrants aggressive treatment to reduce the risk of stroke and potentially to slow the progression of
renal disease (see below). Volume overload contributes to hypertension in
many cases, and potent diuretic agents are frequently required. Anemia can
be reversed with recombinant human erythropoetin (rHuEPO); 2000–6000
units subcutaneously once or twice weekly can increase Hb concentrations
toward the normal range in most pts.

Hyperphosphatemia can be controlled with judicious restriction of dietary
potassium and the use of postprandial phosphate binders, usually calcium-
based salts (calcium carbonate or acetate). Newer non-calcium-, non-alumi-
num-containing resins (e.g., sevelamer) are also used. Hyperkalemia should
be controlled with dietary potassium restriction. Sodium polystyrene sulfonate
(Kayexalate) can be used in refractory cases, although dialysis should be
considered if the potassium >6 mmol/L on repeated occasions. If these conditions cannot be conservatively controlled, dialysis should be instituted
(Chap. 140). It is also advisable to begin dialysis if severe anorexia, weight
loss, and/or hypoalbuminemia develop, as it has been definitively shown that
outcomes for dialysis pts with malnutrition are particularly poor.

Slowing Progression of Renal Disease Prospective clinical trials
have explored the roles of blood pressure control and dietary protein restriction on the rate of progression of renal failure. Control of hypertension is of
some benefit, although ACE inhibitors may exert unique beneficial effects,

most likely due to their effects on intrarenal hemodynamics. Angiotensin receptor antagonists have similar effects; the effects of other drugs (e.g., calcium channel blockers) on intrarenal hemodynamics are relatively minor. The effects of ACE inhibitors and related drugs are most pronounced in pts with diabetic nephropathy and in those without diabetes but with significant proteinuria (>1 g/d). Dietary protein restriction may offer an additional benefit, particularly in these same subgroups.

For a more detailed discussion, see Skorecki K, Green J, Brenner BM: Chronic Renal Failure, Chap. 270, p. 1551, in HPIM-15.

140

DIALYSIS

Overview

Initiation of dialysis usually depends on a combination of the pt's symptoms, comorbid conditions, and laboratory parameters. Unless a living donor is identified, transplantation is deferred by necessity, due to the scarcity of cadaveric donor organs (median waiting time 2–5 years at most transplant centers). Dialytic options include (in order of prevalence in U.S.): in-center hemodialysis, continuous ambulatory peritoneal dialysis (PD), nocturnal cycled PD, and home-hemodialysis. Roughly 75% of U.S. pts are started on hemodialysis.

Absolute indications for dialysis include: severe volume overload refractory to diuretic agents, severe hyperkalemia and/or acidosis, encephalopathy not otherwise explained, and pericarditis or other serositis. *Additional indications* for dialysis include symptomatic uremia (Chap. 139) (e.g., intractable fatigue, anorexia, nausea, vomiting, pruritus, difficulty maintaining attention and concentration), and protein-energy malnutrition/failure to thrive without other overt cause. No absolute serum creatinine, BUN, creatinine or urea clearance, or glomerular filtration rate (GFR) is used as an absolute cut-off for requiring dialysis, although most individuals experience, or will soon develop, symptoms and complications when the GFR is below ~10 mL/min.

Hemodialysis

This requires direct access to the circulation, either via a native arteriovenous fistula (the preferred method of vascular access), usually at the wrist (a "Brescia-Cimino" fistula); an arteriovenous graft, usually made of polytetrafluoroethylene; a large-bore intravenous catheter; or a subcutaneous device attached to intravascular catheters. Blood is pumped though hollow fibers of an artificial kidney (the "dialyzer") and bathed with a solution of favorable chemical composition (isotonic, free of urea and other nitrogenous compounds, and generally low in potassium). Most pts undergo dialysis thrice weekly, usually for 3–4 h. The efficiency of dialysis is largely dependent on the duration of dialysis, the

Table 140-1

Complications of Hemodialysis	
Hypotension	Dialysis-related amyloidosis
Accelerated vascular disease	Protein-calorie malnutrition
Rapid loss of residual renal function	Hemorrhage
Access thrombosis	Dyspnea/hypoxemia[a]
Access or catheter sepsis	Leukopenia[a]

[a] Particularly with first use of conventional modified cellulosic dialyzer.

blood flow rate, dialysate flow rate, and surface area of the dialyzer. More intense dialysis is generally associated with reduced morbidity and mortality.

Complications of hemodialysis are outlined in Table 140-1. Many of these relate to the process of hemodialysis as an intense, intermittent therapy. In contrast to the native kidney or to PD, both major dialytic functions (i.e., clearance of solutes and fluid removal, or "ultrafiltration") are accomplished over relatively short time periods. The rapid flux of fluid can cause hypotension, even without a pt reaching "dry weight." Hemodialysis-related hypotension is common in diabetic pts whose neuropathy prevents the compensatory responses (vasoconstriction and tachycardia) to intravascular volume depletion. Occasionally, confusion or other CNS symptoms will occur. The dialysis "disequilibrium syndrome" refers to the development of headache, confusion, and rarely seizures, in association with rapid solute removal early in the pt's dialysis history, before adaptation to the procedure.

Peritoneal Dialysis

This does not require direct access to the circulation; rather, it obligates placement of a peritoneal ("Tenckoff") catheter that allows infusion of a dialysate solution into the abdominal cavity, which allows transfer of solutes (i.e., urea, potassium, other uremic molecules) across the peritoneal membrane, which serves as the "artificial kidney." This solution is similar to that used for hemodialysis, except that it must be sterile, and uses lactate, rather than bicarbonate, to provide base equivalents. PD is far less efficient at cleansing the bloodstream than hemodialysis and therefore requires a much longer duration of therapy. Pts generally have the choice of performing their own "exchanges" (2–3 L of dialysate, 4–5 times during daytime hours) or using an automated device at night. Compared with hemodialysis, PD offers the major advantages of (1) independence and flexibility, and (2) a more gentle hemodynamic profile.

Complications are outlined in Table 140-2. Peritonitis is the most important complication. In addition to the ill effects of the systemic inflammatory response, protein loss is magnified severalfold during the peritonitis episode. If severe or prolonged, an episode of peritonitis may prompt removal of the Tenckoff catheter or even discontinuation of the modality (i.e., switch to hemodial-

Table 140-2

Complications of Peritoneal Dialysis	
Peritonitis	Dialysis-related amyloidosis
Hyperglycemia	Insufficient clearance due to vascular disease or other
Hypertriglyceridemia	factors
Obesity	Uremia secondary to loss of residual renal function
Hypoproteinemia	

ysis). Gram-positive organisms (especially *Staphylococcus aureus* and other *Staph* spp.) predominate; *Pseudomonas* or fungal (usually *Candida*) infections tend to be more resistant to medical therapy. Antibiotic administration may be intravenous or intraperitoneal when intensive therapy is required.

For a more detailed discussion, see Singh AK, Brenner B: Dialysis in the Treatment of Renal Failure: Chap. 271, p. 1562, in HPIM-15.

141

RENAL TRANSPLANTATION

With the advent of more potent and well-tolerated immunosuppressive regimens and further improvements in short-term graft survival, renal transplantation remains the treatment of choice for most pts with end-stage renal disease. Results are best with living-related transplantation, in part because of optimized tissue matching and in part because waiting time can be minimized. Many centers have recently begun to perform living-unrelated donor (e.g., spousal) transplants. Graft survival in these cases has been superior to that observed with cadaveric transplants, although less favorable than living-related transplants. Factors that influence graft survival are outlined in Table 141-1. Contraindications to renal transplantation are outlined in Table 141-2.

Rejection

Immunologic rejection is the major hazard to the short-term success of renal transplantation. Rejection may be (1) hyperacute (immediate graft dysfunction due to presensitization) or (2) acute (sudden change in renal function occurring within weeks to months). Rejection is characterized by a rise in serum Cr, hypertension, fever, reduced urine output, and occasionally graft tenderness. A

Table 141-1

Some Factors That Influence Graft Survival in Renal Transplantation

HLA mismatch	↓
Presensitization (preformed antibodies)	↓
Pretransplant blood transfusion	↑
Very young or older donor age	↓
Female donor sex	↓
African-American donor race (compared with Caucasian)	↓
Older recipient age	↓
African-American recipient race (compared with Caucasian)	↓
Prolonged cold ischemia time	↓
Large recipient body size	↓

Table 141-2

Contraindications to Renal Transplantation

ABSOLUTE CONTRAINDICATIONS

Active glomerulonephritis
Active bacterial or other infection
Active or very recent malignancy
HIV infection
Hepatitis B surface antigenemia
Severe degrees of comorbidity (e.g., advanced atherosclerotic vascular disease)

RELATIVE CONTRAINDICATIONS

Age > 70 years
Severe psychiatric disease
Moderately severe degrees of comorbidity
Hepatitis C infection with chronic hepatitis or cirrhosis
Noncompliance with dialysis or other medical therapy
Primary renal diseases
    Primary focal sclerosis with prior recurrence in transplant
    Multiple myeloma
    Amyloid
    Oxalosis

percutaneous renal transplant biopsy confirms the diagnosis. Treatment usually consists of a "pulse" of methylprednisolone (500–1000 mg/d for 3 days). In refractory or particularly severe cases, 7–10 days of a monoclonal antibody directed at human T lymphocytes may be given.

Immunosuppression

Maintenance immunosuppressive therapy usually consists of a two- or three-drug regimen, with each drug targeted at a different stage in the immune response. Cyclosporine is the cornerstone of immunosuppressive therapy. The most potent of orally available agents, its routine use has markedly improved short-term graft survival. Side effects of cyclosporine include hypertension, hyperkalemia, resting tremor, hirsutism, gingival hypertrophy, hyperlipidemia, hyperuricemia, and a slowly progressive loss of renal function with characteristic histopathologic patterns (also seen in exposed recipients of heart and liver transplants).

Prednisone is frequently used in conjunction with cyclosporine, at least for the first several years following successful graft function. Side effects of prednisone include hypertension, glucose intolerance, Cushingoid features, osteoporosis, hyperlipidemia, acne, and depression and other mood disturbances.

Until relatively recently, azathioprine was the most commonly used "third drug" in combination with cyclosporine and prednisone, although mycophenolate mofetil has become more popular than azathioprine in the past 2–3 years. Azathioprine is generally well tolerated; side effects include leukopenia (and occasionally anemia and thrombocytopenia), liver dysfunction, alopecia, and squamous cell carcinoma of the skin. The drug-drug interaction between azathioprine and allopurinol may complicate treatment of gout (a frequent complication of cyclosporine therapy). Mycophenolate mofetil has a similar mode of action as azathioprine but is more effective at preventing or reversing rejection. The major side effects of mycophenolate mofetil are gastrointestinal (i.e., abdominal discomfort, diarrhea).

Tacrolimus (FK-506) is similar in efficacy and side-effect profile to cyclosporine although it has been used more widely in liver than kidney transplantation. It is occasionally employed in pts with subacute or chronic rejection poorly controlled with cyclosporine. Sirolimus is gaining popularity in multidrug regimens or in refractory rejection. Treatment can be complicated by severe hyperlipidemia.

Other Complications

Infection and neoplasia are important complications of renal transplantation. Infection is common in the heavily immunosuppressed host (e.g., cadaveric transplant recipient with multiple episodes of rejection requiring steroid pulses or monoclonal antibody treatment). The culprit organism depends in part on characteristics of the donor and recipient and timing following transplantation. In the first month, bacterial organisms predominate. After 1 month, there is a significant risk of systemic infection with CMV, particularly in recipients without prior exposure whose donor was CMV positive. Prophylactic use of ganciclovir or valacyclovir can reduce the risk of disease. Later on, there is a substantial risk of fungal and related infections, especially in pts who are unable to taper prednisone to <20–30 mg/d. Daily low-dose trimethoprim-sulfamethoxazole is effective at reducing the risk of *Pneumocystis carinii* infection.

EBV-associated lymphoproliferative disease is the most important neoplastic complication of renal transplantation, especially in pts who receive polyclonal (antilymphocyte globulin, used at some centers for induction of immunosuppression) or monoclonal antibody therapy. Non-Hodgkin's lymphoma and squamous cell carcinoma of the skin are also more common in this population.

For a more detailed discussion, see Carpenter CB, Milford EL, Sayegh MH: Transplantation in the Treatment of Renal Failure: Chap. 272, p. 1567, in HPIM-15.

142

GLOMERULAR DISEASES

ACUTE GLOMERULONEPHRITIS (GN)

Characterized by development, over days, of azotemia, hypertension, edema, hematuria, proteinuria, and sometimes oliguria. Salt and water retention are due to reduced GFR and may result in circulatory congestion. RBC casts on UA confirm Dx. Proteinuria usually <3 g/d. Most forms of acute GN are mediated by humoral immune mechanisms. Clinical course depends on underlying lesion (Table 142-1).

Table 142-1

Causes of Acute Glomerulonephritis

I. Infectious diseases
   A. Poststreptococcal glomerulonephritis[a]
   B. Nonstreptococcal postinfectious glomerulonephritis
      1. Bacterial: infective endocarditis, "shunt nephritis," sepsis, pneumococcal pneumonia, typhoid fever, secondary syphilis, meningococcemia
      2. Viral: hepatitis B, infectious mononucleosis, mumps, measles, varicella, vaccinia, echovirus, and coxsackievirus
      3. Parasitic: malaria, toxoplasmosis
II. Multisystem diseases: SLE, vasculitis, Henoch-Schönlein purpura, Goodpasture's syndrome
III. Primary glomerular diseases: mesangiocapillary glomerulonephritis, Berger's disease (IgA nephropathy), "pure" mesangial proliferative glomerulonephritis
IV. Miscellaneous: Guillain-Barré syndrome, irradiation of Wilm's tumor, self-administered diptheria-pertussis-tetanus vaccine, serum sickness

[a] Most common causes.
SOURCE: RJ Glassock, BM Brenner: HPIM-13.

ACUTE POSTSTREPTOCOCCAL GN The prototype and most common cause in childhood. Nephritis develops 1–3 weeks after pharyngeal or cutaneous infection with "nephritogenic" strains of group A β-hemolytic streptococci. Dx depends on a positive pharyngeal or skin culture, rising antibody titers, and hypocomplementemia. Renal biopsy reveals diffuse proliferative GN. Treatment consists of correction of fluid and electrolyte imbalance. In most cases the disease is self-limited, although the prognosis is less favorable and urinary abnormalities are more likely to persist in adults.

POSTINFECTIOUS GN May follow other bacterial, viral, and parasitic infections. Examples are bacterial endocarditis, sepsis, hepatitis B, and pneumococcal pneumonia. Features are milder than with poststreptococcal GN. Control of primary infection usually produces resolution of GN.

SLE (LUPUS) Renal involvement is due to deposition of circulating immune complexes. Clinical features of SLE with or without renal involvement include arthralgias, "butterfly" skin rash, serositis, alopecia (hair loss), and CNS disease. Nephrotic syndrome with renal insufficiency is common. Renal biopsy reveals mesangial, focal, or diffuse GN and/or membranous nephropathy. Diffuse GN, the most common finding, is characterized by an active sediment, severe proteinuria, and progressive renal insufficiency and may have an ominous prognosis. Pts have a positive ANA, anti-dsDNA, and complement. Treatment includes glucocorticoids and cytotoxic agents. Oral or IV monthly cyclophosphamide is most commonly employed. Mycophenolate mofetil or azathioprine may be of benefit in some pts, especially those unable to be easily tapered off prednisone.

GOODPASTURE'S SYNDROME Characterized by lung hemorrhage, GN, and circulating antibody to basement membrane, usually in young men. Hemoptysis may precede nephritis. Rapidly progressive renal failure is typical. Circulating antiglomerular basement membrane (GBM) antibody and linear immunofluorescence on renal biopsy establish Dx. Linear IgG is also present on lung biopsy. Plasma exchange may produce remission. Severe lung hemorrhage is treated with IV glucocorticoids (e.g., 1 g/d × 3 d). Disease isolated to the kidney ("anti-GBM disease") may also occur.

HENOCH-SCHÖNLEIN PURPURA A generalized vasculitis causing GN, purpura, arthralgias, and abdominal pain; occurs mainly in children. Renal involvement is manifested by hematuria and proteinuria. Serum IgA is increased in half of pts. Renal biopsy is useful for prognosis. Treatment is symptomatic.

VASCULITIS Polyarteritis nodosa causes hypertension, arthralgias, neuropathy, and renal failure. Similar features plus palpable purpura and asthma are common in hypersensitivity angiitis. Wegener's granulomatosis involves upper respiratory tract and kidney and responds well to IV or oral cyclophosphamide.

RAPIDLY PROGRESSIVE GLOMERULONEPHRITIS
Characterized by gradual onset of hematuria, proteinuria, and renal failure, which progresses over a period of weeks to months. Crescentic GN is usually found on renal biopsy. The causes are outlined in Table 142-2. Prognosis for

Table 142-2

Causes of Rapidly Progressive Glomerulonephritis

I. Infectious diseases
    A. Poststreptococcal glomerulonephritis[a]
    B. Infective endocarditis
    C. Occult visceral sepsis
    D. Hepatitis B infection (with vasculitis and/or cryoglobulinemia)
    E. HIV infection (?)
II. Multisystem diseases
    A. Systemic lupus erythematosus
    B. Henoch-Schönlein purpura
    C. Systemic necrotizing vasculitis (including Wegener's granulomatosis)
    D. Goodpasture's syndrome
    E. Essential mixed (IgG/IgM) cryoglobulinemia
    F. Malignancy
    G. Relapsing polychondritis
    H. Rheumatoid arthritis (with vasculitis)
III. Drugs
    A. Penicillamine
    B. Hydralazine
    C. Allopurinol (with vasculitis)
    D. Rifampin
IV. Idiopathic or primary glomerular disease
    A. Idiopathic crescentic glomerulonephritis
        1. Type I—with linear deposits of Ig (anti-GBM antibody-mediated)
        2. Type II—with granular deposits of Ig (immune complex-mediated)
        3. Type III—with few or no immune deposits of Ig ("pauci-immune")
        4. Antineutrophil cytoplasmic antibody-induced, ? forme fruste of vasculitis
    B. Superimposed on another primary glomerular disease
        1. Mesangiocapillary (membranoproliferative glomerulonephritis) (especially type II)
        2. Membranous glomerulonephritis Berger's disease (IgA nephropathy)

[a] Most common causes.
SOURCE: RJ Glassock, BM Brenner: HPIM-13.

preservation of renal function is poor. Some 50% of pts require dialysis within 6 months of diagnosis. Combinations of glucocorticoids in pulsed doses, cyclophosphamide, and intensive plasma exchange may be useful, although few prospective clinical trial data are available.

NEPHROTIC SYNDROME (NS)

Characterized by albuminuria (>3.5 g/d) and hypoalbuminemia (<30 g/L) and accompanied by edema, hyperlipidemia, and lipiduria. Complications include renal vein thrombosis and other thromboembolic events, infection, vitamin D deficiency, protein malnutrition, and drug toxicities due to decreased protein binding.

In adults, a minority of cases are secondary to diabetes mellitus, SLE, amyloidosis, drugs, neoplasia, or other disorders (Table 142-3). By exclusion, the remainder are idiopathic. Renal biopsy is required to make the diagnosis and determine therapy in idiopathic NS.

MINIMAL CHANGE DISEASE   Causes about 10–15% of idiopathic NS in adults. Blood pressure is normal; GFR is normal or slightly reduced; urinary sediment is benign or may show few RBCs. Protein selectivity is variable in adults. Recent URI, allergies, or immunizations are present in some cases. ARF may rarely occur, particularly among elderly persons. Renal biopsy shows only foot process fusion on electron microscopy. Remission of proteinuria with glucocorticoids carries a good prognosis; cytotoxic therapy may be required for relapse. Progression to renal failure is uncommon. Focal sclerosis has been suspected in some cases refractory to steroid therapy.

MEMBRANOUS GN   Characterized by subepithelial IgG deposits; accounts for ~ 45% of adult NS. Pts present with edema and nephrotic proteinuria. Blood pressure, GFR, and urine sediment are usually normal at initial presentation. Hypertension, mild renal insufficiency, and abnormal urine sediment develop later. Renal vein thrombosis is relatively common, more so than with other forms of nephrotic syndrome. Underlying diseases such as SLE, hepatitis B, and solid tumors and exposure to such drugs as high-dose captopril or penicillamine should be sought. Some pts progress to end-stage renal disease (ESRD); men and persons with very heavy proteinuria are at highest risk—

Table 142-3

Causes of Nephrotic Syndrome (NS)

Systemic Causes (25%)	Glomerular Disease (75%)
Diabetes mellitus, SLE, amyloidosis, HIV-associated nephropathy	Membranous (40%)
	Minimal change disease (15%)
Drugs: gold, penicillamine, probenecid, street heroin, captopril, NSAIDs	Focal glomerulosclerosis (15%)
	Membranoproliferative GN (7%)
Infections: bacterial endocarditis, hepatitis B, shunt infections, syphilis, malaria, hepatic schistosomiasis	Mesangioproliferative GN (5%)
Malignancy: Multiple myeloma, light-chain deposition disease, Hodgkin's and other lymphomas, leukemia, carcinoma of breast, GI tract	

SOURCE: Modified from RJ Glassock, BM Brenner: HPIM-13.

glucocorticoids are frequently prescribed but are rarely effective. Cytotoxic agents (chlorambucil or cyclophosphamide) may promote complete or partial remission in some pts. There is less experience, but some positive reports, using cyclosporine.

FOCAL GLOMERULOSCLEROSIS (FGS)   Can be primary or secondary. Primary tends to be more acute, similar to minimal change disease in abruptness of nephrotic syndrome, but with added features of hypertension, renal insufficiency, and hematuria. Involves fibrosis of portions of some (primarily juxtamedullary) glomeruli and is found in 15% of pts with NS. African-Americans are disproportionately affected. HIV-associated nephropathy and collapsing nephropathy have similar pathologic features; both tend to be more rapidly progressive than typical cases. Fewer than half of pts with primary FGS undergo remission with glucocorticoids; half progress to renal failure in 10 years. FGS may recur in a renal transplant. Presence of azotemia or hypertension reflects poor prognosis.

Secondary FGS can occur in the late stages of any form of kidney disease associated with nephron loss (e.g., remote GN, pyelonephritis, vesicoureteral reflux). Typically responds to ACE inhibition and blood pressure control. No benefit of glucocorticoids in secondary FGS. Clinical history, kidney size, and associated conditions usually allow differentiation of primary vs. secondary causes.

MEMBRANOPROLIFERATIVE GLOMERULONEPHRITIS (MPGN)
Mesangial expansion and proliferation extend into the capillary loop. Two ultrastructural variants exist. In MPGN I, subendothelial electron-dense deposits are present, C3 is deposited in a granular pattern indicative of immune-complex pathogenesis, and IgG and the early components of complement may or may not be present. In MPGN II, the lamina densa of the GBM is transformed into an electron-dense character, as is the basement membrane in Bowman's capsule and tubules. C3 is found irregularly in the GBM. Small amounts of Ig (usually IgM) are present, but early components of complement are absent. Serum complement levels are decreased. MPGN affects young adults. Blood pressure and GFR are abnormal, and the urine sediment is active. Some have acute nephritis or hematuria. Similar lesions occur in SLE and hemolytic-uremic syndrome. Infection with hepatitis C virus has been linked to MPGN. Treatment with interferon α and ribavirin has resulted in remission of renal disease in some cases, depending on HCV serotype. Glucocorticoids, cytotoxic agents, antiplatelet agents, and plasmapheresis have been used with limited success. MPGN may recur in allografts.

DIABETIC NEPHROPATHY   Common cause of NS. Pathologic changes include diffuse and/or nodular glomerulosclerosis, nephrosclerosis, chronic pyelonephritis, and papillary necrosis. Clinical features include proteinuria, hypertension, azotemia, and bacteriuria. Although prior duration of diabetes mellitus (DM) is variable, proteinuria may develop 10–15 years after onset, progress to NS, and then lead to renal failure over 3–5 years. Other complications of DM are common; retinopathy is nearly universal. Treatment with ACE inhibitors delays the onset of nephropathy and should be instituted in all pts tolerant to that class of drug.

If a cough develops in a pt treated with an ACE inhibitor, an angiotensin (AII) receptor antagonist is the next best choice. If hyperkalemia develops and cannot be controlled with (1) optimizing glucose control, (2) loop diuretics, or (3) occasional polystyrene sulfonate (Kayexalate), then tight control of blood pressure with alternative agents is warranted. The combination of ACE inhibitor and AII receptor antagonist may be more effective than either agent alone,

Table 142-4

Evaluation of Nephrotic Syndrome

24-h urine for protein; creatinine clearance
Serum albumin, cholesterol, complement
Urine protein electrophoresis
Rule out SLE, diabetes mellitus
Review drug exposure
Renal biopsy
Consider malignancy (in elderly pt with membranous GN or minimal change disease)
Consider renal vein thrombosis (if membranous GN or symptoms of pulmonary embolism are present)

especially if there is an additive effect on blood pressure. Modest restriction of dietary protein may also slow decline of renal function.

Evaluation of NS is shown in Table 142-4.

ASYMPTOMATIC URINARY ABNORMALITIES

Proteinuria in the nonnephrotic range and/or hematuria unaccompanied by edema, reduced GFR, or hypertension can be due to multiple causes (Table 142-5).

Table 142-5

Glomerular Causes of Asymptomatic Urinary Abnormalities

I. Hematuria with or without proteinuria
  A. Primary glomerular diseases
    1. Berger's disease (IgA nephropathy)[a]
    2. Mesangiocapillary glomerulonephritis
    3. Other primary glomerular hematurias accompanied by "pure" mesangial proliferation, focal and segmental proliferative glomerulonephritis, or other lesions
    4. "Thin basement membrane" disease (? forme fruste of Alport's syndrome)
  B. Associated with multisystem or hereditary diseases
    1. Alport's syndrome and other "benign" familial hematurias
    2. Fabry's disease
    3. Sickle cell disease
  C. Associated with infections
    1. Resolving poststreptococcal glomerulonephritis
    2. Other postinfectious glomerulonephritides
II. Isolated nonnephrotic proteinuria
  A. Primary glomerular diseases
    1. "Orthostatic" proteinuria
    2. Focal and segmental glomerulosclerosis
    3. Membranous glomerulonephritis
  B. Associated with multisystem or heredofamilial diseases
    1. Diabetes mellitus
    2. Amyloidosis
    3. Nail-patella syndrome

[a] Most common.
SOURCE: RJ Glassock, BM Brenner: HPIM-13.

Table 142-6

Serologic Findings in Selected Multisystem Diseases Causing Glomerular Disease

Disease	C3	Ig	FANA	Anti-dsDNA	Anti-GBM	Cryo-Ig	CIC	ANCA
SLE	↓↓	↑IgG	+++	++	-	++	++	±
Goodpasture's syndrome	-	-	-	-	+++	-	±	-
Henoch-Schönlein purpura	-	↑IgA	-	-	-	++	++	-
Polyarteritis	↑↓	↑IgG	+ -	±	-	±	++	++
Wegener's granulomatosis	→→	↑IgA, IgE	-	-	-	++	++	++
Cryoglobulinemia		↓↑ IgG, IgA, IgD, IgE				+++	++	-
Multiple myeloma	-	IgE	-	-	-	+	-	-
Waldenström's macroglobulinemia	-	↑IgM	-	-	-	-	-	-
Amyloidosis	-	± Ig	-	-	-	-	-	-

SOURCE:: RJ Glassock, BM Brenner: HPIM-13.

NOTE:: C3, C3 component; Ig, immunoglobulin levels; FANA, fluorescent antinuclear antibody assay; anti-dsDNA, antibody to double-stranded (native) DNA; anti-GBM, antibody to glomerular basement membrane antigens; cryo-Ig, cryoimmunoglobulin; CIC, circulating immune complexes; ANCA, antineutrophil cytoplasmic antibody; -, normal; +, occasionally slightly abnormal; ++, often abnormal; +++, severely abnormal.

BERGER'S DISEASE, IGA NEPHROPATHY The most common cause of recurrent hematuria of glomerular origin; is most frequent in young men. Episodes of macroscropic hematuria are present with flulike symptoms, without skin rash, abdominal pain, or arthritis. Renal biopsy shows diffuse mesangial deposition of IgA, often with lesser amounts of IgG, nearly always by C3 and properdin but not by C1q or C4. Prognosis is variable; 50% develop ESRD within 25 years; men with hypertension and heavy proteinuria are at highest risk. Glucocorticoids and other immunosuppressive agents have not proved successful. A randomized clinical trial of fish oil supplementation suggested a modest therapeutic benefit. Rarely recurs in allografts.

CHRONIC GLOMERULONEPHRITIS Characterized by persistent urinary abnormalities, slow progressive impairment of renal function, symmetrically contracted kidneys, moderate to heavy proteinuria, abnormal urinary sediment (especially RBC casts), and x-ray evidence of normal pyelocalyceal systems. The time to progression to ESRD is variable, hastened by uncontrolled hypertension and infections. Control of blood pressure is of paramount importance and is the most important factor influencing the pace of progression. While ACE inhibitors may be the most effective agents, additional agents should be added to ACE inhibitors if blood pressure is not optimally controlled with ACE inhibitors alone. Diuretics, non-dihydropyridine calcium antagonists, and β-adrenergic blockers have been successfully used in a variety of clinical settings.

GLOMERULOPATHIES ASSOCIATED WITH MULTISYSTEM DISEASE (See Table 142-6)

For a more detailed discussion, see Brady HR, O'Meara YM, Brenner BM: The Major Glomerulopathies, Chap. 274, p. 1580; and O'Meara YM, Brady HR, Brenner BM: Glomerulopathies Associated with Multisystem Diseases, Chap. 275, p. 1590, in HPIM-15.

143

RENAL TUBULAR DISEASE

Tubulointerstitial diseases constitute a diverse group of acute and chronic, hereditary and acquired disorders involving renal tubules and supporting structures (Table 143-1). Functionally, they may result in nephrogenic diabetes insipidus (DI) with polyuria, nocturia, non-anion-gap metabolic acidosis, salt-wasting, and hypo- or hyperkalemia. Azotemia is common, owing to associated glomerular fibrosis and/or ischemia. Compared with glomerulopathies, proteinuria and hematuria are less dramatic, and hypertension is less common. Functional consequences of tubular dysfunction are outlined in Table 143-2.

Table 143-1

| Principal Causes of Tubulointertitial Disease of the Kidney |

TOXINS

Endogenous toxins
  Analgesic nephropathy[a]
  Lead nephropathy
  Miscellaneous nephrotoxins (e.g., antibiotics, cyclosporine, radiographic
    contrast media, heavy metals)[a,b]
Metabolic toxins
  Acute uric acid nephropathy
  Gouty nephropathy[a]
  Hypercalcemic nephropathy
  Hypokalemic nephropathy
  Miscellaneous metabolic toxins (e.g., hyperoxaluria, cystinosis, Fabry's
    disease

NEOPLASIA

| Lymphoma | Multiple myeloma |
| Leukemia | |

IMMUNE DISORDERS

Hypersensitivity nephropathy[a,b]	Transplant rejection
Sjögren's syndrome	HIV-associated nephropathy
Amyloidosis	

VASCULAR DISORDERS

Arteriolar nephrosclerosis[a]	Medullary cystic disease
Atheroembolic disease	Medullary sponge kidney
Sickle cell nephropathy	Polycystic kidney disease
Acute tubular necrosis[a,b]	

HEREDITARY RENAL DISEASES

Hereditary nephritis (Alport's syndrome)

INFECTIOUS INJURY

| Acute pyelonephritis[a,b] | Chronic pyelonephritis |

MISCELLANEOUS DISORDERS

| Chronic urinary tract obstruction[a] | Radiation nephritis |
| Vesicoureteral reflux[a] | |

[a] Common.
[b] Typically acute.

ACUTE (ALLERGIC) INTERSTITIAL NEPHRITIS (AIN)

Drugs are a leading cause of this type of renal failure, usually identified by a gradual rise in the serum creatinine at least several days after the institution of therapy, occasionally accompanied by fever, eosinophilia, rash, and arthralgias. In addition to azotemia, there may be evidence of tubular dysfunction (e.g., hyperkalemia, metabolic acidosis). Drugs that commonly cause AIN include: anti-staphyloccal (i.e., methicillin, oxacillin, or nafcillin) and other penicillins, cephalosporins, sulfonamides, quinolones, rifampin, allopurinol, and cimetidine; NSAIDs may cause AIN with or without nephrotic syndrome. UA shows hematuria, pyuria, and eosinophiluria on Hansel's or Wright's stain.

Table 143-2

Transport Dysfunction of Tubulointerstitial Disease

Defect	Cause(s)
Reduced GFR[a]	Obliteration of microvasculature and obstruction of tubules
Fanconi syndrome	Damage to proximal tubular reabsorption of glucose, amino acids, phosphate, and bicarbonate
Hyperchloremic acidosis[a]	1. Reduced ammonia production 2. Inability to acidify the collecting duct fluid (distal renal tubular acidosis) 3. Proximal bicarbonate wasting
Tubular or small molecular-weight proteinuria[a]	Failure of proximal tubule protein reabsorption
Polyuria, isothenuria[a]	Damage to medullary tubules and vasculature
Hyperkalemia[a]	Potassium secretory defects including aldosterone resistance
Salt wasting	Distal tubular damage with impaired sodium reabsorption

[a] Common

Renal dysfunction usually improves after withdrawal of the offending drug, but complete recovery may be delayed and incomplete. In uncontrolled studies, glucocorticoids have been shown to promote earlier recovery of renal function. Other than kidney biopsy, no specific diagnostic tests are available. Acute pyelonephritis may also cause AIN, although it is rarely associated with renal failure, unless bilateral (or present in a single functioning kidney) or complicated by urinary tract obstruction, sepsis syndrome, or volume depletion.

CHRONIC INTERSTITIAL NEPHRITIS (IN)
Analgesic nephropathy is an important cause of chronic renal failure (CRF) that results from the cumulative (in quantity and duration) effects of combination analgesic agents, usually phenacetin and aspirin. It is thought to be a more common cause of end-stage renal disease in Australia/New Zealand than elsewhere owing to the larger per capita ingestion of analgesic agents in that region of the world. Transitional cell carcinoma may develop. Analgesic nephropathy should be suspected in pts with a history of chronic headache or back pain with CRF that is otherwise unexplained. Manifestations include papillary necrosis, calculi, sterile pyuria, and azotemia. Metabolic causes of chronic IN include: hypercalcemia (with nephrocalcinosis), oxalosis (primary or secondary, e.g., with intestinal malabsorption, leading to nephrocalcinosis), hypokalemia, and hyperuricemia or hyperuricosuria. Chronic IN can occur in association with several systemic diseases, including sarcoidosis, Sjögren's syndrome, and tuberculosis, and following radiation or chemotherapy exposure (e.g., ifosfamide, cisplatin).

POLYCYSTIC KIDNEY DISEASE
Autosomal dominant polycystic kidney disease (ADPKD) is the most important hereditary renal disease (except perhaps for "essential" hypertension). It is char-

acterized clinically by episodic flank pain, hematuria (often gross), hypertension, and/or urinary infection in the third or fourth decade. The kidneys are often palpable and occasionally of very large size. Hepatic cysts and intracranial Berry aneurysms may also be present.

The expression of ADPKD is variable. Some persons discover the disease incidentally in late adult life, having had mild to moderate hypertension earlier. More often, azotemia is progressive and unfortunately does not appear to respond as favorably to ACE inhibition or to the restriction of dietary protein intake as other causes of renal disease. The diagnosis is usually made by ultrasonography. Renal cysts are common (50% of persons >50 years have at least one cyst), and multiple renal cysts do not necessarily indicate the presence of ADPKD.

RENAL TUBULAR ACIDOSIS (RTA)

This describes a number of pathophysiologically distinct entities of tubular function whose common feature is the presence of a non-anion-gap metabolic acidosis. Diarrhea and RTA together constitute the vast majority of cases of non-anion-gap metabolic acidosis.

DISTAL (TYPE 1) RTA Pts are unable to acidify the urine despite acidosis; it may be inherited (autosomal dominant) or acquired due to autoimmune and inflammatory diseases (e.g., Sjögren's syndrome, sarcoidosis), urinary tract obstruction, or amphotericin B therapy. Type I RTA may be associated with hypokalemia, hypercalciuria, and osteomalacia.

PROXIMAL (TYPE II) RTA There is a defect in bicarbonate reabsorption, usually associated with glycosuria, aminoaciduria, phosphaturia, and uricosuria (indicating proximal tubular dysfunction); it may be inherited or acquired due to myeloma, renal transplantation, or drugs (e.g., ifosfamide, L-lysine). Treatment requires large doses of bicarbonate, which may aggravate hypokalemia, and repletion of phosphorus to prevent bone disease.

TYPE IV RTA Due to a defect in ammonium excretion, acidosis is accompanied by hyperkalemia and usually with low renin and aldosterone levels (and minimal response to exogenous mineralocorticoid). It is associated with diabetes, other forms of glomerulosclerosis, and many forms of advanced CRF (especially with tubulointerstitial component).

℞ **TREATMENT**

Tubulointerstitial diseases associated with exogenous toxins (e.g., analgesic nephropathy, lead and other heavy metal nephropathy) should be treated by withdrawal of the offending toxin. Primary oxalosis may require liver (or combined liver-kidney) transplantation, but secondary oxalosis can be improved with a low-oxalate diet, generous fluid intake, and supplemental calcium salts (calcium carbonate or calcium citrate) with meals to bind intestinal oxalate and prevent hyperoxalemia/hyperoxaluria. Calcium citrate affords additional protection against nephrolithiasis (correcting hypocitraturia). Hypercalcemia due to multiple causes (e.g., primary hyperparathyroidism, vitamin D excess, thiazide therapy, milk-alkali syndrome) can usually be corrected once recognized. Pts with pyelonephritis due to reflux or recurrent UTI with ADPKD may benefit from suppressive antibiotic therapy. The treatment of RTA depends on type but focuses on correction of the acidosis and prevention of nephrolithiasis (type I), vitamin D deficiency and other metabolic complications (type II), and severe hyperkalemia (type IV).

For a more detailed discussion, see Yu ASL, Brenner B: Tubulointerstitial Diseases of the Kidney, Chap. 277, p. 1606, in HPIM-15.

144

URINARY TRACT INFECTIONS

URETHRITIS, CYSTITIS, AND PYELONEPHRITIS

ETIOLOGY *Escherichia coli* causes ~80% of uncomplicated UTIs (those unassociated with catheters, urologic abnormalities, or calculi); *Proteus, Klebsiella,* and *Enterobacter* account for lesser percentages of cases. *Staphylococcus saprophyticus* causes 10–15% of acute symptomatic UTIs in young women. Pathogens in recurrent or catheter-associated infections, in infections following urologic manipulation, and in the setting of genitourinary (GU) obstruction or calculi include *E. coli, Proteus, Klebsiella, Enterobacter, Pseudomonas,* and *Serratia.* Isolation of *Staphylococcus aureus* from the urine should always arouse suspicion of staphylococcal bacteremia and secondary infection of the kidney. Agents causing acute urinary symptoms and pyuria in the absence of demonstrable bacteriuria include *Chlamydia trachomatis, Neisseria gonorrhoeae,* and herpes simplex virus. *Candida* and other fungal species commonly colonize the urine of catheterized or diabetic pts.

PATHOGENESIS In the vast majority of UTIs, bacteria gain access to the bladder via the urethra. Ascent of bacteria from the bladder may follow and may lead to upper tract disease. Risk factors for UTIs include female gender, sexual activity, pregnancy, GU obstruction, neurogenic bladder dysfunction, and vesicoureteral reflux. Hematogenous pyelonephritis occurs most often in debilitated pts. Staphylococcemia or candidemia may lead to metastatic renal parenchymal infection.

EPIDEMIOLOGY UTIs may be categorized as catheter-associated (nosocomial) or non-catheter-associated (community-acquired). Acute infections are very common; the vast majority of symptomatic cases involve young women, for whom sexual activity augments the risk of infection. UTIs are rare among men under the age of 50. The development of asymptomatic bacteriuria parallels that of symptomatic infection: it, too, is rare among men under age 50 but common among women between ages 20 and 50 and very common among the elderly of either sex. Bacteriuria develops in at least 10–15% of hospitalized pts with indwelling urethral catheters; the risk of infection is about 3–5% per day of catheterization.

CLINICAL MANIFESTATIONS Bacteriuria can be asymptomatic. Dysuria, frequency, urgency, and suprapubic pain signal cystitis. One-third of pts with such symptoms and significant bacteriuria have concomitant, clinically silent upper tract disease. On the other hand, ~30% of women with acute dysuria do not have significant bacteriuria; some of them have urethritis due to a sexually transmitted pathogen (e.g., *N. gonorrhoeae, C. trachomatis,* or herpesvirus). Manifestations of acute pyelonephritis may include fever, shaking chills, nausea, vomiting, and diarrhea as well as flank pain and dysuria. Most catheter-associated infections cause minimal symptoms. The frequency of upper tract infection with catheter-induced bacteriuria is unknown, although the catheterized urinary tract is the most common source of gram-negative bacteremia in hospitalized pts, accounting for approximately one-third of cases.

DIAGNOSIS   Women with symptoms characteristic of acute uncomplicated cystitis may reasonably be treated empirically, either on the basis of Hx and physical findings alone or after confirmatory microscopy or leukocyte esterase determination. Urine should be cultured, however, when the diagnosis of cystitis is uncertain, when upper tract infection is suspected, or when any complicating factors are present. A colony count of $\geq 10^5$/mL in a voided midstream specimen generally indicates infection, as does bacteriuria to any degree in a suprapubic aspirate or the presence of $\geq 10^2$ bacteria/mL in urine obtained by catheterization. Microscopy of urine from symptomatic pts can be of great value: the finding of bacteria on a gram-stained, unspun specimen indicates a colony count of at least 10^5/mL. The finding of bacteriuria with leukocyte casts suggests pyelonephritis. Asymptomatic bacteriuria should be documented twice before treatment is instituted. All males with UTI and any pt with obstructive disease and non-catheter-associated infection should be evaluated urologically.

 TREATMENT

Principles underlying the treatment of UTIs are listed in Table 144-1. Treatment regimens for bacterial UTIs are listed in Table 144-2. Recurrent symp-

Table 144-1

Principles Underlying the Treatment of UTIs

1. Except in acute uncomplicated cystitis in women, a quantitative urine culture, Gram's staining, or an alternative rapid diagnostic test should be performed to confirm infection before treatment is begun. When culture results become available, antimicrobial sensitivity testing should be used to direct therapy.
2. Factors predisposing to infection, such as obstruction and calculi, should be identified and corrected if possible.
3. Relief of clinical symptoms does not always indicate bacteriologic cure.
4. Each course of treatment should be classified after its completion as a failure (symptoms and/or bacteriuria not eradicated during therapy or in the immediate posttreatment culture) or a cure (resolution of symptoms and elimination of bacteriuria). Recurrent infections should be classified as same-strain or different-strain and as early (occurring within 2 weeks of the end of therapy) or late.
5. In general, uncomplicated infections confined to the lower urinary tract respond to short courses of therapy, while upper tract infections require longer treatment. After therapy, early recurrences due to the same strain may result from an unresolved upper tract focus of infection but often (especially after short-course therapy for cystitis) result from persistent vaginal colonization. Recurrences >2 weeks after the cessation of therapy nearly always represent reinfection with a new strain or with the previously infecting strain that has persisted in the vaginal and rectal flora.
6. Despite increasing resistance, community-acquired infections, especially initial infections, are usually due to more antibiotic-sensitive strains.
7. In pts with repeated infections, instrumentation, or recent hospitalization, the presence of antibiotic-resistant strains should be suspected.

SOURCE: Adapted from WE Stamm: HPIM-15, p. 1623.

Table 144-2

Treatment Regimens for Bacterial UTIs

Condition	Characteristic Pathogens
Acute uncomplicated cystitis in women	*Escherichia coli, Staphylococcus saprophyticus, Proteus mirabilis, Klebsiella pneumoniae*
Acute uncomplicated pyelonephritis in women	*E. coli, P. mirabilis, S. saprophyticus*
Complicated UTI in men and women	*E. coli, Proteus, Klebsiella, Pseudomonas, Serratia*, enterococci, staphylococci

[a] Treatments listed are those to be prescribed before the etiologic agent is known; Gram's staining can be helpful in the selection of empirical therapy. Such therapy can be modified once the infecting agent has been identified. Fluoroquinolones should not be used in pregnancy. TMP-SMZ, although not approved for use in pregnancy, has been widely used. Gentamicin should be used with caution in pregnancy because of its possible toxicity to eighth-nerve development in the fetus.

[b] Multiday oral regimens for cystitis are as follows: TMP-SMZ, 160/800 mg q12h; TMP, 100 mg q12h; norfloxacin, 400 mg q12h; ciprofloxacin, 250 mg q12h; ofloxacin, 200 mg q12h; lomefloxacin, 400 mg/d; enoxacin, 400 mg q12h; macrocrystalline nitrofurantoin, 100 mg qid; amoxicillin, 250 mg q8h; cefpodoxime proxetil, 100 mg q12h.

tomatic UTI ($\geq$3 infections per year) warrants prophylaxis daily or thrice weekly with agents such as nitrofurantoin (50 mg), TMP-SMZ (80/400 mg), or TMP alone (100 mg).

PROSTATITIS

ETIOLOGY In non-catheter-associated cases, acute bacterial prostatitis is usually due to common gram-negative urinary tract pathogens (*E. coli* or *Klebsiella*). In catheter-associated cases, nosocomially acquired gram-negative rods or enterococci may also be involved. *E. coli, Klebsiella, Proteus,* or other uropathogenic organisms may also cause chronic prostatitis. Evidence for caus-

Mitigating Circumstances	Recommended Empirical Treatment[a]
None	3-Day regimens: oral TMP-SMZ, TMP, quinolone; 7-day regimen: macrocrystalline nitrofurantoin[b]
Diabetes, symptoms for >7 d, recent UTI, use of diaphragm, age >65 years	Consider 7-day regimen: oral TMP-SMZ, TMP, quinolone[b]
Pregnancy	Consider 7-day regimen: oral amoxicillin, macrocrystalline nitrofurantoin, cefpodoxime proxetil, or TMP-SMZ[b]
Mild to moderate illness, no nausea or vomiting: outpatient therapy	Oral[c] quinolone for 7–14 d (initial dose given IV if desired); or single-dose ceftriaxone[d] or gentamicin[d] IV followed by oral TMP-SMZ[b] for 14 d
Severe illness or possible urosepsis: hospitalization required	Parenteral[d] ceftriaxone, quinolone, gentamicin (± ampicillin), or aztreonam until defervescence; then oral[c] quinolone, cephalosporin, or TMP-SMZ for 14 d
Mild to moderate illness, no nausea or vomiting: outpatient therapy	Oral[c] quinolone for 10–14 d
Severe illness or possible urosepsis: hospitalization required	Parenteral[d] ampicillin and gentamicin, quinolone, ceftriaxone, aztreonam, ticarcillin/clavulanate, or imipenem-cilastatin until defervescence; then oral[c] quinolone or TMP-SMZ for 10–21 d

[c] Oral regimens for pyelonephritis and complicated UTI are as follows: TMP-SMZ, 160/800 mg q12h; ciprofloxacin, 500 mg q12h; ofloxacin, 200–300 mg q12h; lomefloxacin, 400 mg/d; enoxacin, 400 mg q12h; amoxicillin, 500 mg q8h; cefpodoxime proxetil, 200 mg q12h.

[d] Parenteral regimens are as follows: ciprofloxacin, 200–400 mg q12h; ofloxacin, 200–400 mg q12h; gentamicin, 1 mg/kg q8h; ceftriaxone, 1–2 g/d; ampicillin, 1 g q6h; imipenem-cilastatin, 250–500 mg q6–8h; ticarcillin/clavulanate, 3.2 g q8h; aztreonam, 1 g q8–12h.

SOURCE: WE Stamm: HPIM-15, p. 1624.

ative roles of *Ureaplasma urealyticum* and *C. trachomatis* in chronic prostatitis is inconclusive.

CLINICAL MANIFESTATIONS Acute bacterial prostatitis is characterized by fever, chills, dysuria, and extreme prostatic tenderness. It may occur spontaneously (generally in young men) or in association with an indwelling urethral catheter. Chronic bacterial prostatitis is often asymptomatic, and the prostate usually feels normal on palpation; perineal or lower back pain or obstructive symptoms develop in some cases. A pattern of relapsing cystitis in a middle-aged man suggests the diagnosis and is due to intermittent spread of the prostatic infection.

DIAGNOSIS Cultures of urine usually yield the bacterial pathogen. Vigorous prostatic massage should be avoided. Gram's staining of urine may be particularly useful in guiding empirical therapy for catheter-associated cases.

TREATMENT

For acute prostatitis in which gram-negative pathogens are detected in the urine, initially use a fluoroquinolone, a third-generation cephalosporin, or an aminoglycoside; for cases in which gram-positive cocci are detected, use nafcillin or a cephalosporin. For catheter-associated acute prostatitis, use imipenem, a fluoroquinolone, a third-generation cephalosporin, or an aminoglycoside until the etiologic agent has been isolated and tested for sensitivity. For treatment of chronic prostatitis, fluoroquinolones (e.g., ciprofloxacin, 500 mg bid) have been more successful than other agents but must be given for at least 12 weeks to be effective.

For a more detailed discussion, see Stamm WE: Urinary Tract Infections and Pyelonephritis, Chap. 280, p. 1620, in HPIM-15.

145

RENOVASCULAR DISEASE

Ischemic injury to the kidney depends on the rate, site, severity, and duration of vascular compromise. Manifestations range from painful infarction to acute renal failure (ARF), impaired GFR, hematuria, or tubular dysfunction. Renal ischemia of any etiology may cause renin-mediated hypertension.

Acute Occlusion of a Renal Artery

Can be due to thrombosis or embolism (from valvular disease, endocarditis, mural thrombi, or atrial arrhythmias).

Thrombosis of Renal Arteries   Large renal infarcts cause pain, vomiting, nausea, hypertension, fever, proteinuria, hematuria, and elevated LDH (with "flipping" of the LDH isoenzyme 1:2 ratio) and AST. In unilateral lesion, renal functional loss depends on contralateral function. IVP or radionuclide scan shows unilateral hypofunction; ultrasound is typically normal until scarring develops. Renal arteriography establishes diagnosis. With occlusions of large arteries, surgery may be the initial therapy; anticoagulation should be used for occlusions of small arteries.

Renal Atheroembolism   Usually arises when aortic angiography or surgery causes cholesterol embolization of small renal vessels. Renal insufficiency may develop suddenly or gradually. Pace may be progressive or "stuttering." Associated findings are GI or retinal ischemia with cholesterol emboli visible on fundoscopic examination, pancreatitis, neurologic deficits (especially confusion), livedo reticularis, toe gangrene, and hypertension. Skin or renal biopsy may be necessary for diagnosis. Heparin and other anticoagulants are contraindicated. Should be suspected when renal function does not improve more than 1 week after radiocontrast exposure with presumed contrast nephropathy.

Renal Vein Thrombosis

This occurs in a variety of settings, including pregnancy, oral contraceptive use, trauma, nephrotic syndrome (especially membranous nephropathy, see Chap. 142), dehydration (in infants), extrinsic compression of the renal vein (lymph nodes, aortic aneurysm, tumor), and invasion of the renal vein by renal cell carcinoma. Definitive Dx is established by selective renal renography. Streptokinase may be effective. Oral anticoagulants (warfarin) usually prescribed for longer term.

Renal Artery Stenosis

Main cause of renovascular hypertension; due to (1) atherosclerosis (two-thirds of cases; usually men aged >60 years, advanced retinopathy) or (2) fibromuscular dysplasia (a third of cases; usually white women aged <45 years, brief history of hypertension). Renal hypoperfusion activates renin-angiotensin-aldosterone (RAA) axis. Suggestive clinical features include onset of hypertension <30 or >50 years of age, abdominal or femoral bruits, hypokalemic alkalosis, acute onset of hypertension or malignant hypertension, and hypertension resistant to medical therapy. Malignant hypertension (Chap. 124) may also be caused by renal vascular occlusion. Nitroprusside, labetalol, or calcium antagonists are generally effective in lowering bp acutely, although inhibitors of the RAA axis [e.g., ACE inhibitors, angiotensin II (AII) receptor antagonists] are most effective long-term treatment, if disease is not bilateral.

The "gold standard" in diagnosis of renal artery stenosis is conventional arteriography. Magnetic resonance angiography is used in experienced centers, especially among pts with renal insufficiency at higher risk for contrast nephropathy. The least invasive and most reliable preliminary test in pts with normal renal function and hypertension is the captopril (or enalaprilat) renogram. Lateralization of renal function [accentuation of the difference between affected and unaffected (or "less affected" sides] is suggestive of significant vascular disease. Test results may be falsely negative in the presence of bilateral disease. Measurement of renal vein renins may be necessary to demonstrate functional significance of a lesion.

Surgical revascularization appears to be superior for ostial lesions characteristic of atherosclerosis. The relative efficacy of surgery compared with angioplasty (especially with stenting) for fibromuscular dysplasia or for nonocclusive, nonostial atherosclerotic disease is unclear. Angioplasty (with or without stenting) tends to be most effective for mid-vessel or more distal lesions. No studies have adequately compared revascularization with medical therapy. ACE inhibitors or AII receptor antagonists are ideal agents for hypertension associated with renal artery stenosis, except in pts with bilateral disease (see "Ischemic Nephropathy," below) or disease in a solitary kidney (including an allograft).

Ischemic Nephropathy

In addition to the association between renal artery stenosis and hypertension, there is an important (and less well recognized) association between renal artery stenosis and progressive chronic renal failure. Because most pts do not undergo either kidney biopsy or angiography prior to the initiation of dialysis, it is difficult to estimate the incidence of renovascular disease as a primary cause of end-stage renal disease (ESRD) (some have suggested up to 15–20%, even greater among elderly). Indeed, many individuals diagnosed with ESRD due to hypertension or diabetes suffer from ischemic nephropathy, with diabetes being a secondary causes and hypertension, a consequence, rather than a cause.

The presence of widespread atherosclerotic vascular disease, asymmetric kidney size and function, and hypertension suggest renovascular disease; episodic "flash" pulmonary edema, renal insufficiency, and ARF in response to a trial of ACE inhibitors suggests that the disease may be severe and bilateral.

Revascularization with the goal of preservation of renal function is sometimes entertained. Angioplasty is less often successful than for fibromuscular dysplasia, although stenting may offer the potential for better "noninvasive" results. Whether with surgical or angiographic intervention, it appears that kidneys <8 cm in size are unlikely to recover substantial renal function. The use of aspirin and lipid-lowering agents is advisable in pts with evidence of renovascular disease, regardless of revascularization options.

Scleroderma

May cause sudden oliguric renal failure and severe hypertension due to small-vessel occlusion in previously stable pts. Aggressive control of bp with ACE inhibitors and dialysis, if necessary, improve survival and may restore renal function.

Arteriolar Nephrosclerosis

Persistent hypertension causes arteriosclerosis of the renal arterioles and loss of renal function (nephrosclerosis). "Benign" nephrosclerosis is associated with loss of cortical kidney mass and thickened afferent arterioles and mild to moderate impairment of renal function. Malignant nephrosclerosis is characterized by accelerated rise in bp and the clinical features of malignant hypertension, including renal failure (Chap. 124). Agressive control of the bp can usually halt or reverse the deterioration of renal function, and some pts have a return of renal function to near normal.

Hemolytic-Uremic Syndrome

Characterized by ARF, microangiopathic hemolytic anemia, and thrombocytopenia; increasingly recognized in adults; may be preceded by a prodrome of bloody diarrhea and abdominal pain. Fibrin deposition leads to small-vessel occlusion. Lack of fever or CNS involvement helps to distinguish it from thrombotic thrombocytopenic purpura. Plasmapheresis may be of benefit; prognosis for recovery of renal function is generally poor.

Toxemias of Pregnancy

Preeclampsia is characterized by hypertension, proteinuria, edema, consumptive coagulopathy, sodium retention, and hyperreflexia; eclampsia is the further development of seizures. Glomerular swelling and/or ischemia causes renal insufficiency. Coagulation abnormalities and ARF may occur. Treatment consists of bed rest, sedation, control of neurologic manifestations with magnesium sulfate, control of hypertension with vasodilators and other anti-hypertensive agents proved safe in pregnancy, and delivery of the infant.

Vasculitis

Renal complications are frequent and severe in polyarteritis nodosa, hypersensitivity angiitis, Wegener's granulomatosis, and other forms of vasculitis (Chap. 160). Therapy is directed toward the underlying disease.

Sickle Cell Nephropathy

The hypertonic and relatively hypoxic renal medulla coupled with slow blood flow in the vasa recta favors sickling. Papillary necrosis, cortical infarcts, functional tubule abnormalities (nephrogenic diabetes insipidus), glomerulopathy, nephrotic syndrome, and, rarely, ESRD may be complications.

For a more detailed discussion, see Badr KF, Brenner BM: Vascular Injury to the Kidney, Chap. 278, p. 1610, in HPIM-15.

146

NEPHROLITHIASIS

Renal calculi are common, affecting ~1% of the population, and recurrent in more than half of pts. Stone formation begins when urine becomes supersaturated with insoluble components due to (1) low volume, (2) excessive excretion of selected compounds, or (3) other factors (e.g., urinary pH) that diminish solubility. Approximately 75% of stones are Ca-based (the majority are Ca oxalate; also Ca phosphate and other mixed stones), 15% struvite (magnesium-ammonium-phosphate), 5% uric acid, and 1% cystine, depending on the metabolic disturbance(s) from which they arise.

Signs and Symptoms

Stones in the renal pelvis may be asymptomatic or cause hematuria alone; with passage, obstruction may occur at any site along the collecting system. Obstruction related to the passing of a stone leads to severe pain, often radiating to the groin, sometimes accompanied by intense visceral symptoms (i.e., nausea, vomiting, diaphoresis, light-headedness), hematuria, pyuria, UTI, and, rarely, hydronephrosis. Staghorn calculi are associated with recurrent UTI with urea-splitting organisms (*Proteus, Klebsiella, Providencia, Morganella,* and others).

Stone Composition

Most stones are composed of Ca oxalate. These may be associated with hypercalciuria or hyperoxaluria. Hypercalciuria can be seen in association with a very high Na diet (or exogenous saline administration), furosemide or other loop diuretic therapy, distal (type I) renal tubular acidosis (RTA), sarcoidosis, Cushing's syndrome, conditions associated with hypercalcemia (e.g., primary hyperparathyroidism, vitamin D excess, milk-alkali syndrome), or may be idiopathic.

Hyperoxaluria may be seen with intestinal (especially ileal) malabsorption syndromes (e.g., inflammatory bowel disease, pancreatitis), due to the binding of intestinal Ca by fatty acids within the bowel lumen to form soaps, allowing free oxalate to be absorbed (and then excreted via the urinary tract). Ca oxalate stones may also form due to (1) a deficiency of urinary citrate, an inhibitor of stone formation that is underexcreted with metabolic acidosis; and (2) hyperuricosuria (see below). Ca phosphate stones are much less common and tend to

Table 146-1

Workup for an Outpatient with a Renal Stone

1. Dietary and fluid intake history
2. Careful medical history and physical examination, focusing on systemic diseases
3. Abdominal flat plate examination
4. Serum chemistries: BUN, creatinine (Cr), uric acid, calcium, phosphate, chloride, bicarbonate
5. Timed urine collections (at least one day during week, one day on weekend): Cr, Na, K, urea nitrogen, uric acid, calcium, phosphate, oxalate, citrate, magnesium

occur in the setting of an abnormally high urinary pH (7–8), usually in association with a complete or partial distal (type I) RTA.

Struvite stones form in the collecting system when infection with urea-splitting organisms is present. Struvite is the most common component of staghorn calculi and obstruction. Risk factors include previous UTI, nonstruvite stone disease, urinary catheters, neurogenic bladder (e.g., with diabetes or multiple sclerosis), and instrumentation.

Uric acid stones develop when the urine is saturated with uric acid in the presence of dehydration and an acid urine pH. Pts with myeloproliferative disorders (esp. after treatment with chemotherapy), gout, acute and chronic renal failure, and following cyclosporine therapy often develop hyperuricemia and hyperuricosuria and are at risk for stones if the urine volume diminishes. Hy-

Table 146-2

Specific Therapies for Nephrolithiasis

Stone Type	Dietary Modifications	Other
Calcium oxalate	Increase fluid intake Moderate sodium intake Moderate oxalate intake Moderate protein intake Moderate fat intake	Citrate supplementation (calcium or potassium salts > sodium) Cholestyramine or other therapy for fat malabsorption Thiazides if hypercalciuric Allopurinol if hyperuricosuric
Calcium phosphate	Increase fluid intake Moderate sodium intake	Thiazides if hypercalciuric
Struvite	Increase fluid intake; same as calcium oxalate if evidence of calcium oxalate nidus for struvite	Mandelamine and vitamin C or daily suppressive antibiotic therapy (e.g., trimethoprimsulfamethoxazole)
Uric acid	Increase fluid intake Moderate dietary protein intake	Allopurinol
Cystine	Increase fluid intake	Alkali therapy Penicillamine

NOTE: Sodium excretion correlates with calcium excretion.

peruricosuria without hyperuricemia may be seen in association with certain drugs (e.g., probenecid, high-dose salicylates).

Cystine stones are the result of a rare inherited defect of renal and intestinal transport resulting in overexcretion of cystine. Stones begin in childhood and are a rare cause of staghorn calculi; they occasionally lead to end-stage renal disease. Stones are more likely to form in acidic urinary pH.

Workup

Although some have advocated a complete workup after a first stone episode, others would defer that evaluation until there has been evidence of recurrence or if there is no obvious cause (e.g., low fluid intake during the summer months with obvious dehydration). Table 146-1 outlines a reasonable workup for an outpatient with an uncomplicated kidney stone.

 TREATMENT

Treatment of renal calculi is often empirical, based on odds (Ca oxalate most common stones) or clinical Hx. Sometimes a stone is recovered and can be analyzed for content. Stone analysis is advisable, especially for pts with more complex presentations or recurrent disease. An increase in fluid intake to at least 2.5–3 L/d is advisable, regardless of the type of stone. Conservative recommendations for pts with Ca oxalate stones (i.e., low salt, low fat, moderate protein diet) are thought to be healthful in general and therefore probably advisable in pts whose condition is otherwise uncomplicated. Table 146-2 outlines stone-specific therapies for pts with complex or recurrent nephrolithiasis.

For a more detailed discussion, see Asplin JR, Coe FL, Favus MJ: Nephrolithiasis, Chap. 279, p. 1615, in HPIM-15.

147

URINARY TRACT OBSTRUCTION

Urinary tract obstruction (UTO), a potentially reversible cause of renal failure (RF), should be considered in all cases of acute or abrupt worsening of chronic RF. Consequences depend on duration and severity and whether the obstruction is unilateral or bilateral. UTO may occur at any level from collecting tubule to urethra. It is preponderant in women (pelvic tumors), elderly men (prostatic disease), diabetic pts (papillary necrosis), pts with neurologic diseases (spinal cord injury or multiple sclerosis, with neurogenic bladder), or in individuals with retroperitoneal lymphadenopathy or fibrosis, vesicoureteral reflux, nephrolithiasis, or other causes of functional urinary retention (e.g., anticholinergic drugs).

Clinical Manifestations

Pain can occur in some settings (obstruction due to stones) but is not common. In men, there is frequently a history of prostatism. Physical exam may reveal an enlarged bladder by percussion over the lower abdominal wall. Other findings depend on the clinical scenario. Prostatic hypertrophy can be determined by digital rectal examination. A bimanual examination in women may show a pelvic or rectal mass. The workup of pts with RF suspected of having UTO is shown in Fig. 147-1. Laboratory studies may show marked elevations of BUN and creatinine; if the obstruction has been of sufficient duration, there may be evidence of tubulointerstitial disease (e.g., hyperkalemia, non-anion-gap metabolic acidosis, mild hypernatremia). Urinalysis is most often benign or with a small number of cells; heavy proteinuria is rare. An opaque (all but uric acid) stone may be visualized on abdominal radiography.

Ultrasonography can be used to assess the degree of hydronephrosis and the integrity of the renal parenchyma; CT or intravenous urography may be required

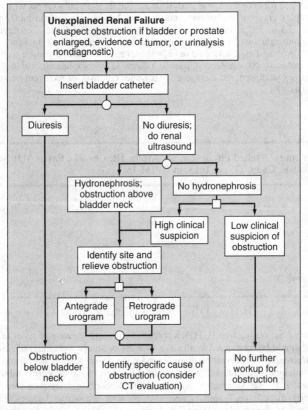

FIGURE 147-1   Diagnostic approach for urinary tract obstruction in unexplained renal failure. Circles represent diagnostic procedures and squares indicate clinical decisions based on available data. CT, computed tomography.

to localize the level of obstruction. Calyceal dilation is commonly seen; it may be absent with hyperacute obstruction, upper tract encasement by tumor or retroperitoneal fibrosis, or indwelling staghorn calculi. Kidney size may indicate the duration of obstruction. It should be noted that unilateral obstruction may be prolonged and severe (ultimately leading to loss of renal function in the obstructed kidney), with no hint of abnormality on physical exam and laboratory survey.

 TREATMENT

Management of acute RF associated with UTO is dictated by (1) the level of obstruction (upper vs. lower tract), and (2) the acuity of the obstruction and its clinical consequences, including renal dysfunction and infection. Benign causes of UTO, including bladder outlet obstruction and nephrolithiasis, should be ruled out as conservative management, including Foley catheter placement and IV fluids, respectively, will usually relieve the obstruction in most cases.

Among more seriously ill pts, ureteral obstruction due to tumor is the most common and concerning cause of UTO. If technically feasible, ureteral obstruction due to tumor is best managed by cystoscopic placement of a ureteral stent. Otherwise, the placement of nephrostomy tubes with external drainage may be required. IV antibiotics should also be given if there are signs of pyelonephritis or urosepsis. Fluid and electrolyte status should be carefully monitored after obstruction is relieved. There may be a physiologic natriuresis/diuresis related to volume overload. However, there may be an "inappropriate" natriuresis/diuresis related to (1) elevated urea nitrogen, leading to an osmotic diuresis; and (2) acquired nephrogenic diabetes insipidus. Hypernatremia, sometimes to a severe degree, may develop.

For a more detailed discussion, see Seifter JL, Brenner BM: Urinary Tract Obstruction, Chap. 281, p. 1627, in HPIM-15.

PEPTIC ULCER AND RELATED DISORDERS

PEPTIC ULCER DISEASE (PUD)

PUD occurs most commonly in duodenal bulb (duodenal ulcer—DU) and stomach (gastric ulcer—GU). It may also occur in esophagus, pyloric channel, duodenal loop, jejunum, Meckel's diverticulum. PUD results when "aggressive" factors (gastric acid, pepsin) overwhelm "defensive" factors involved in mucosal resistance (gastric mucus, bicarbonate, microcirculation, prostaglandins, mucosal "barrier"), and from effects of *Helicobacter pylori*.

CAUSES AND RISK FACTORS *General* Major role for *H. pylori*, spiral urease-producing organism that colonizes gastric antral mucosa in up to 100% of persons with DU and 80% with GU. Also found in normals (increasing prevalence with age) and those of low socioeconomic status. Invariably associated with histologic evidence of active chronic gastritis, which over years can lead to atrophic gastritis and gastric cancer. Other major cause of ulcers is NSAIDs (those not due to *H. pylori*). Fewer than 1% are due to gastrinoma (Zollinger-Ellison syndrome). Other risk factors and associations: hereditary (? increased parietal cell number), smoking, hypercalcemia, mastocytosis, blood group O (antigens may bind *H. pylori*). Unproven: stress, coffee, alcohol.

DU Mild gastric acid hypersecretion resulting from (1) increased release of gastrin, presumably due to (a) stimulation of antral G cells by cytokines released by inflammatory cells and (b) diminished production of somatostatin by D cells, both resulting from *H. pylori* infection; and (2) an exaggerated acid response to gastrin due to an increased parietal cell mass resulting from gastrin stimulation. These abnormalities reverse rapidly with eradication of *H. pylori*. However, a mildly elevated maximum gastric acid output in response to exogenous gastrin persists in some pts long after eradication of *H. pylori*, suggesting that gastric acid hypersecretion may be, in part, genetically determined. *H. pylori* may also result in elevated serum pepsinogen levels. Mucosal defense in duodenum is compromised by toxic effects of *H. pylori* infection on patches of gastric metaplasia that result from gastric acid hypersecretion or rapid gastric emptying. Other risk factors include glucocorticoids, NSAIDs, chronic renal failure, renal transplantation, cirrhosis, chronic lung disease.

GU *H. pylori* is also principal cause. Gastric acid secretory rates usually normal or reduced, possibly reflecting earlier age of infection by *H. pylori* than in DU pts. Gastritis due to reflux of duodenal contents (including bile) may play a role. Chronic salicylate or NSAID use may account for 15–30% of GUs and increase risk of associated bleeding, perforation.

CLINICAL FEATURES *DU* Burning epigastric pain 90 min to 3 h after meals, often nocturnal, relieved by food.

GU Burning epigastric pain made worse by or unrelated to food; anorexia, food aversion, weight loss (in 40%). Great individual variation. Similar symptoms may occur in persons without demonstrated peptic ulcers ("nonulcer dyspepsia"); less responsive to standard therapy.

COMPLICATIONS Bleeding, obstruction, penetration causing acute pancreatitis, perforation, intractability.

DIAGNOSIS *DU* Upper endoscopy or upper GI barium radiography.

GU Upper endoscopy preferable to exclude possibility that ulcer is malignant (brush cytology, ≥6 pinch biopsies of ulcer margin). Radiographic features suggesting malignancy: ulcer within a mass, folds that do not radiate from ulcer margin, a large ulcer (>2.5–3 cm).

DETECTION OF *H. PYLORI* Detection of antibodies in serum (inexpensive, preferred when endoscopy is not required); rapid urease test of antral biopsy (when endoscopy is required). Urea breath test generally used to confirm eradication of *H. pylori*, if necessary (Table 148-1).

 TREATMENT

Medical

Objectives: pain relief, healing, prevention of complications, prevention of recurrences. For GU, exclude malignancy (follow endoscopically to healing). Dietary restriction unnecessary with contemporary drugs; discontinue NSAIDs; smoking may prevent healing and should be stopped. Eradication of *H. pylori* markedly reduces rate of ulcer relapse and is indicated for all DUs and GUs associated with *H. pylori* (Table 148-2). Acid suppression is generally included in regimen. Standard drugs (H2-receptor blockers, sucralfate, antacids) heal 80–90% of DUs and 60% of GUs in 6 weeks; healing is more rapid with omeprazole (20 mg/d).

Surgery

For complications (persistent or recurrent bleeding, obstruction, perforation) or, uncommonly, intractability (first screen for surreptitious NSAID use and gastrinoma). For DU, see Table 148-3. For GU, perform subtotal gastrectomy.

Table 148-1

Tests for Detection of *H. pylori*

Test	Sensitivity/Specificity, %	Comments
INVASIVE (ENDOSCOPY/BIOPSY REQUIRED)		
Rapid urease	80–95/95–100	Simple; false negative with recent use of PPIs, antibiotics, or bismuth compounds
Histology	80–90/>95	Requires pathology processing and staining; provides histologic information
Culture	—/—	Time-consuming, expensive, dependent on experience; allows determination of antibiotic susceptibility
NONINVASIVE		
Serology	>80/>90	Inexpensive, convenient; not useful for early follow-up
Urea breath test	>90/>90	Simple, rapid; useful for early follow-up; false negative with recent therapy (see rapid urease test)

NOTE: PPI, proton pump inhibitor.

Table 148-2

Regimens Recommended for Eradication of *H. pylori* Infection

Drug	Dose
TRIPLE THERAPY	
1. Bismuth subsalicylate *plus*	2 tablets qid
Metronidazole *plus*	250 mg qid
Tetracycline[a]	500 mg qid
2. Ranitidine bismuth citrate *plus*	400 mg bid
Tetracycline *plus*	500 mg bid
Clarithromycin *or* metronidazole	500 mg bid
3. Omeprazole (lansoprazole) *plus*	20 mg bid (30 mg bid)
Clarithromycin *plus*	250 or 500 mg bid
Metronidazole[b] *or*	500 mg bid
Amoxicillin[c]	1 g bid
QUADRUPLE THERAPY	
Omeprazole (lansoprazole)	20 mg (30 mg) daily
Bismuth subsalicylate	2 tablets qid
Metronidazole	250 mg qid
Tetracycline	500 mg qid

[a] Alternative: use prepacked Helidac (see text).
[b] Alternative: use prepacked Prevpac (see text).
[c] Use either metronidazole or amoxicillin, but not both.

Complications of Surgery (1) Obstructed afferent loop (Billroth II), (2) bile reflux gastritis, (3) dumping syndrome (rapid gastric emptying with abdominal distress + postprandial vasomotor symptoms), (4) postvagotomy diarrhea, (5) bezoar, (6) anemia (iron, B_{12}, folate malabsorption), (7) malabsorption (poor mixing of gastric contents, pancreatic juices, bile; bacterial overgrowth), (8) osteomalacia and osteoporosis (vitamin D and Ca malabsorption), (9) gastric remnant carcinoma.

Approach to the Patient

Optimal approach is uncertain. Serologic testing for *H. pylori* and treating, if present, may be cost-effective. Other options include trial of acid-suppressive therapy, endoscopy only in treatment failures, or initial endoscopy in all cases.

Table 148-3

Surgical Treatment of Duodenal Ulcer

Operation	Recurrence Rate	Complication Rate
Vagotomy + antrectomy (Billroth I or II)[a]	1%	Highest
Vagotomy and pyloroplasty	10%	Intermediate
Parietal cell (proximal gastric, superselective) vagotomy	≥10%	Lowest

[a] Billroth I, gastroduodenostomy; Billroth II, gastrojejunostomy.

GASTROPATHIES

EROSIVE GASTROPATHIES Hemorrhagic gastritis, multiple gastric erosions. Caused by aspirin and other NSAIDs (lower risk with newer agents, e.g., nabumetone and etodolac, which do not inhibit gastric mucosal prostaglandins) or severe stress (burns, sepsis, trauma, surgery, shock, or respiratory, renal, or liver failure). May be asymptomatic or associated with epigastric discomfort, nausea, hematemesis, or melena. Diagnosis by upper endoscopy.

℞ TREATMENT

Removal of offending agent and maintenance of O_2 and blood volume as required. For prevention of stress ulcers in critically ill pts, hourly oral administration of liquid antacids (e.g., Maalox 30 mL), IV H_2-receptor antagonist (e.g., cimetidine, 300-mg bolus + 37.5–50 mg/h IV), or both is recommended to maintain gastric pH >4. Alternatively, sucralfate slurry, 1 g PO q6h, can be given; does not raise gastric pH and may thus avoid increased risk of aspiration pneumonia associated with liquid antacids. Misoprostol, 200 μg PO qid, or profound acid suppression (e.g., famotidine, 40 mg PO bid) can be used with NSAIDs to prevent NSAID-induced ulcers.

CHRONIC GASTRITIS Identified histologically by an inflammatory cell infiltrate dominated by lymphocytes and plasma cells with scant neutrophils. In its early stage, the changes are limited to the lamina propria (*superficial gastritis*). When the disease progresses to destroy glands, it becomes *atrophic gastritis*. The final stage is *gastric atrophy* in which the mucosa is thin and the infiltrate sparse. Chronic gastritis can be classified based on predominant site of involvement.

Type A Gastritis This is the body-predominant and less common form. Generally asymptomatic, common in elderly; autoimmune mechanism may be associated with achlorhydria, pernicious anemia, and increased risk of gastric cancer (value of screening endoscopy uncertain). Antibodies to parietal cells present in >90%.

Type B Gastritis This is antral-predominant disease and caused by *H. pylori*. Often asymptomatic but may be associated with dyspepsia. May also lead to atrophic gastritis, gastric atrophy, gastric lymphoid follicles, and low-grade gastric B cell lymphomas. Infection early in life or in setting of malnutrition or low gastric acid output is associated with gastritis of entire stomach (including body) and increased risk of gastric cancer. Eradication of *H. pylori* (Table 148-2) not routinely recommended unless PUD or low-grade MALT lymphoma is present.

SPECIFIC TYPES OF GASTROPATHY OR GASTRITIS Alcoholic gastropathy (submucosal hemorrhages), Ménétrier's disease (hypertrophic gastropathy), eosinophilic gastritis, granulomatous gastritis, Crohn's disease, sarcoidosis, infections (tuberculosis, syphilis, fungi, viruses, parasites), pseudolymphoma, radiation, corrosive gastritis.

ZOLLINGER-ELLISON (Z-E) SYNDROME (GASTRINOMA)

Consider when ulcer disease is severe, refractory to therapy, associated with ulcers in atypical locations, or associated with diarrhea. Tumors usually pancreatic or in duodenum (submucosal, often small), may be multiple, slowly growing; >60% malignant; 25% associated with MEN 1, i.e., multiple endo-

Table 148-4

Differential Diagnostic Tests

Condition	Fasting Gastrin	Gastrin Response to	
		IV Secretin	Food
DU	N ($\leq$150 ng/L)	NC	Slight ↑
Z-E	↑↑↑	↑↑↑	NC
Antral G (gastrin) cell hyperplasia	↑	↑, NC	↑↑↑

NOTE: N, normal; NC, no change.

crine neoplasia type 1 (gastrinoma, hyperparathyroidism, pituitary neoplasm), often duodenal, small, multicentric, less likely to metastasize to liver than pancreatic gastrinomas but often metastasize to local lymph nodes.

DIAGNOSIS   *Suggestive*   Basal acid output >15 mmol/h; basal/maximal acid output >60%; large mucosal folds on endoscopy or upper GI radiograph.

Confirmatory   Serum gastrin >1000 ng/L or rise in gastrin of 200 ng/L following IV secretin and, if necessary, rise of 400 ng/L following IV calcium (Table 148-4).

DIFFERENTIAL DIAGNOSIS   *Increased Gastric Acid Secretion*   Z-E syndrome, antral G cell hyperplasia or hyperfunction (? due to *H. pylori*), postgastrectomy retained antrum, renal failure, massive small bowel resection, chronic gastric outlet obstruction.

Normal or Decreased Gastric Acid Secretion   Pernicious anemia, chronic gastritis, gastric cancer, vagotomy, pheochromocytoma.

℞ TREATMENT

Omeprazole, beginning at 60 mg PO qAM and increasing until maximal gastric acid output is <10 mmol/h before next dose, is drug of choice during evaluation and in pts who are not surgical candidates; dose can often be reduced over time. Radiolabeled octreotide scanning has emerged as the most sensitive test for detecting primary tumors and metastases; may be supplemented by endoscopic ultrasonography. Exploratory laparotomy with resection of primary tumor and solitary metastases when possible. In pts with MEN 1, tumor is often multifocal and unresectable; treat hyperparathyroidism first (hypergastrinemia may improve). For unresectable tumors, parietal cell vagotomy may enhance control of ulcer disease by drugs. Chemotherapy for metastatic tumor to control symptoms (e.g., streptozotocin, 5-fluorouracil, doxorubicin, or interferon α); 40% partial response rate.

For a more detailed discussion, see Del Valle J: Peptic Ulcer Disease and Related Disorders, Chap. 285, p. 1649, in HPIM-15.

149

INFLAMMATORY BOWEL DISEASES

Inflammatory bowel diseases (IBD) are chronic inflammatory disorders of unknown etiology involving the GI tract. Peak occurrence between ages 15 and 30 and between ages 60 and 80, but onset may occur at any age. Pathogenesis of IBD involves activation of immune cells by unknown inciting agent (?microorganism, dietary component, bacterial or self-antigen) leading to release of cytokines and inflammatory mediators. Genetic component suggested by increased risk in first-degree relatives of pts with IBD and concurrence of type of IBD, location of Crohn's disease, and clinical course. Reported associations include HLA-DR2 in Japanese patients with ulcerative colitis and a Crohn's disease–related gene on chromosome 16. Other potential pathogenic factors include serum antineutrophil cytoplasmic antibodies (ANCA) in 70% of pts with ulcerative colitis and granulomatous angiitis (vasculitis) in Crohn's disease. Acute flares may be precipitated by infections, NSAIDs, stress. Onset of ulcerative colitis often follows cessation of smoking.

ULCERATIVE COLITIS (UC)

PATHOLOGY   Colonic mucosal inflammation; rectum almost always involved, with inflammation extending continuously (no skip areas) proximally for a variable extent; histologic features include epithelial damage, inflammation, crypt abscesses, loss of goblet cells.

CLINICAL MANIFESTATIONS   Bloody diarrhea, mucus, fever, abdominal pain, tenesmus, weight loss; spectrum of severity (majority of cases are mild, limited to rectosigmoid). In severe cases dehydration, anemia, hypokalemia, hypoalbuminemia.

COMPLICATIONS   Toxic megacolon, colonic perforation; cancer risk related to extent and duration of colitis; often preceded by or coincident with dysplasia, which may be detected on surveillance colonoscopic biopsies.

DIAGNOSIS   Sigmoidoscopy/colonoscopy: mucosal erythema, granularity, friability, exudate, hemorrhage, ulcers, inflammatory polyps (pseudopolyps). Barium enema: loss of haustrations, mucosal irregularity, ulcerations.

CROHN'S DISEASE (CD)

PATHOLOGY   Any part of GI tract, usually terminal ileum and/or colon; transmural inflammation, bowel wall thickening, linear ulcerations, and submucosal thickening leading to cobblestone pattern; discontinuous (skip areas); histologic features include transmural inflammation, granulomas (often absent), fissures, fistulas.

CLINICAL MANIFESTATIONS   Fever, abdominal pain, diarrhea (often without blood), fatigue, weight loss, growth retardation in children; acute ileitis mimicking appendicitis; anorectal fissures, fistulas, abscesses. Clinical course falls into three broad patterns: (1) inflammatory, (2) stricturing, and (3) fistulizing.

COMPLICATIONS   Intestinal obstruction (edema vs. fibrosis); rarely toxic megacolon or perforation; intestinal fistulas to bowel, bladder, vagina, skin, soft tissue, often with abscess formation; bile salt malabsorption leading to cholesterol gallstones and/or oxalate kidney stones; intestinal malignancy; amyloidosis.

DIAGNOSIS   Sigmoidoscopy/colonoscopy, barium enema, upper GI and small-bowel series: nodularity, rigidity, ulcers that may be deep or longitudinal, cobblestoning, skip areas, strictures, fistulas. CT may show thickened, matted bowel loops or an abscess.

DIFFERENTIAL DIAGNOSIS

INFECTIOUS ENTEROCOLITIS   *Shigella, Salmonella, Campylobacter, Yersinia* (acute ileitis), *Plesiomonas shigelloides, Aeromonas hydrophilia, E. coli* serotype O157:H7, *Gonorrhea, Lymphogranuloma venereum, Clostridium difficile* (pseudomembranous colitis), tuberculosis, amebiasis, cytomegalovirus, AIDS.

OTHERS   Ischemic bowel disease, appendicitis, diverticulitis, radiation enterocolitis, bile salt–induced diarrhea (ileal resection), drug-induced colitis (e.g., NSAIDs), bleeding colonic lesion (e.g., neoplasm), irritable bowel syndrome (no bleeding), microscopic (lymphocytic) or collagenous colitis (chronic watery diarrhea)—normal colonoscopy, but biopsies show superficial colonic epithelial inflammation and, in collagenous colitis, a thick subepithelial layer of collagen; response to aminosalicylates and glucocorticoids variable.

EXTRAINTESTINAL MANIFESTATIONS   (UC and CD)

1. *Joint*: Peripheral arthritis—parallels activity of bowel disease; ankylosing spondylitis and sacroiliitis (associated with HLA-B27)—activity independent of bowel disease.
2. *Skin*: Erythema nodosum, aphthous ulcers, pyoderma gangrenosum, cutaneous Crohn's disease.
3. *Eye*: Episcleritis, iritis, uveitis.
4. *Liver*: Fatty liver, "pericholangitis" (intrahepatic sclerosing cholangitis), primary sclerosing cholangitis, cholangiocarcinoma, chronic hepatitis.
5. *Others*: Autoimmune hemolytic anemia, phlebitis, pulmonary embolus (hypercoagulable state).

℞ TREATMENT   (See Table 149-1)

Supportive   Antidiarrheal agents (diphenoxylate and atropine, loperamide) in mild disease; IV hydration and blood transfusions in severe disease; parenteral nutrition or defined enteral formulas—effective as primary therapy in CD, although high relapse rate when oral feeding is resumed; should not replace drug therapy; important role in preoperative preparation of malnourished pt; emotional support.

Sulfasalazine and Aminosalicylates   Active component of sulfasalazine is 5-aminosalicylic acid (5-ASA) linked to sulfapyridine carrier; useful in colonic disease of mild to moderate severity (1–1.5 g PO qid); efficacy in maintaining remission demonstrated only for UC (500 mg PO qid). Toxicity (generally due to sulfapyridine component): dose-related—nausea, headache, rarely hemolytic anemia—may resolve when drug dose is lowered; idiosyncratic—fever, rash, neutropenia, pancreatitis, hepatitis, etc.; miscellaneous—oligospermia. Newer aminosalicylates are as effective as sulfasalazine but with fewer side effects. Enemas containing 4 g of 5-ASA (mesalamine) may be used in distal UC, 1 nightly retained qhs until remission, then q2hs or q3hs. Suppositories containing 500 mg of 5-ASA may be used in proctitis.

Glucocorticoids   Useful in severe disease and ileal or ileocolonic CD. Prednisone, 40–60 mg PO qd, then taper; IV hydrocortisone, 100 mg tid or equivalent, in hospitalized pts; IV ACTH drip (120 U qd) may be preferable

Table 149-1

Medical Management of IBD

ULCERATIVE COLITIS: ACTIVE DISEASE

	Mild
Distal	5-ASA oral and/or enema
Extensive	5-ASA oral or enema

ULCERATIVE COLITIS: MAINTENANCE THERAPY

Distal	5-ASA oral and/or enema 6-MP or azathioprine
Extensive	5-ASA oral and/or enema 6-MP or azathioprine

CROHN'S DISEASE: ACTIVE DISEASE

Mild–Moderate	Severe
5-ASA oral or enema Metronidazole and/or ciprofloxacin Oral glucocorticoids Azathioprine or 6-MP Infliximab	5-ASA oral or enema Metronidazole and/or ciprofloxacin Oral or IV glucocorticoids Azathioprine or 6-MP Infliximab TPN or elemental diet Intravenous cyclosporine

CROHN'S DISEASE: MAINTENANCE THERAPY

Inflammatory	Perianal or Fistulizing Disease
5-ASA oral or enema Metronidazole and/or ciprofloxacin Azathioprine or 6-MP	Metronidazole and/or ciprofloxacin Azathioprine or 6-MP

NOTE: CSA, cyclosporine; 6-MP, 6-mercaptopurine; TPN, total parenteral nutrition

in first attacks of UC. Nightly hydrocortisone retention enemas in proctosigmoiditis. Numerous side effects make long-term use problematic.

Immunosuppressive Agents Azathioprine, 6-mercaptopurine 50 mg PO qd up to 2.0 or 1.5 mg/kg qd, respectively. Useful as steroid-sparing agents and in intractable or fistulous CD (may require 2- to 6-month trial before efficacy seen). Toxicity—immunosuppression, pancreatitis, ? carcinogenicity. Avoid in pregnancy.

Metronidazole Appears effective in colonic CD (500 mg PO bid) and refractory perineal CD (10–20 mg/kg PO qd). Toxicity—peripheral neuropathy, metallic taste, ? carcinogenicity. Avoid in pregnancy. Other antibiotics

Moderate	Severe	Fulminant
5-ASA oral and/or enema	5-ASA oral and/or enema	Intravenous glucocorticoid
Glucocorticoid enema	Glucocorticoid enema	Intravenous CSA
Oral glucocorticoid	Oral or IV glucocorticoid	
5-ASA oral and/or enema	5-ASA oral and/or enema	Intravenous glucocorticoid
Glucocorticoid enema	Glucocorticoid enema	Intravenous CSA
Oral glucocorticoid	Oral or IV glucocorticoid	

Perianal or Fistulizing Disease
Metronidazole and/or ciprofloxacin
Azathioprine or 6-MP
Infliximab
Intravenous CSA

(e.g., ciprofloxacin 500 mg PO bid) may be of value in terminal ileal and perianal CD, and broad-spectrum IV antibiotics are indicated for fulminant colitis and abscesses.

Others Cyclosporine [potential value in a dose of 4 (mg/kg)/d IV for 7–14 d in severe UC and possibly intractable Crohn's fistulas]; experimental—methotrexate, chloroquine, fish oil, nicotine, others.

Surgery UC: Colectomy (curative) for intractability, toxic megacolon (if no improvement with aggressive medical therapy in 24–48 h), cancer, dysplasia. Ileal pouch–anal anastomosis is operation of choice in UC but contraindicated in CD and in elderly. CD: Resection for fixed obstruction (or stricturoplasty), abscesses, persistent symptomatic fistulas, intractability.

For a more detailed discussion, see Friedman S, Blumberg RS: **Inflammatory Bowel Disease, Chap. 287, p. 1679, in HPIM-15.**

150

COLONIC AND ANORECTAL DISEASES

IRRITABLE BOWEL SYNDROME (IBS)

Characterized by altered bowel habits, abdominal pain, and absence of detectable organic pathology. Most common GI disease in clinical practice. Three types of clinical presentations: (1) spastic colon (chronic abdominal pain and constipation), (2) alternating constipation and diarrhea, or (3) chronic, painless diarrhea.

PATHOPHYSIOLOGY Visceral hyperalgesia to mechanoreceptor stimuli is common. Reported abnormalities include altered colonic motility at rest and in response to stress, cholinergic drugs, cholecystokinin; altered small-intestinal motility; enhanced visceral sensation (lower pain threshold in response to gut distention); and abnormal extrinsic innervation of the gut. Patients presenting with IBS to a physician have an increased frequency of psychological disturbances—depression, hysteria, obsessive-compulsive disorder. Specific food intolerances and malabsorption of bile acids by the terminal ileum may account for a few cases.

CLINICAL MANIFESTATIONS Onset often before age 30; females/males = 2:1. Abdominal pain and irregular bowel habits. Additional symptoms often include abdominal distention, relief of abdominal pain with bowel movement, increased frequency of stools with pain, loose stools with pain, mucus in stools, and sense of incomplete evacuation. Associated findings include pasty stools, ribbony or pencil-thin stools, heartburn, bloating, back pain, weakness, faintness, palpitations, urinary frequency.

DIAGNOSIS IBS is a diagnosis of exclusion. Rome criteria for diagnosis are shown in Table 150-1. Consider sigmoidoscopy and barium radiographs to exclude inflammatory bowel disease or malignancy; consider excluding giardiasis, intestinal lactase deficiency, hyperthyroidism.

℞ TREATMENT

Reassurance and supportive physician-patient relationship, avoidance of stress or precipitating factors, dietary bulk (fiber, psyllium extract, e.g., Metamucil 1 tbsp daily or bid); for diarrhea, trials of loperamide (2 PO qA.M. then 1 PO after each loose stool to a maximum of 8/d, then titrate), diphenoxylate (Lomotil) (up to 2 PO qid), or cholestyramine (up to 1 packet mixed in water PO qid); for pain, anticholinergics (e.g., dicyclomine HCl 10–40 mg PO qid) or hyoscyamine as Levsin 1–2 PO q4h prn. Amitryptiline 25–50 mg PO qhs or other antidepressants in low doses may relieve pain. Leuprolide

Table 150-1

Rome Criteria for the Diagnosis of IBS

Abdominal Pain/Discomfort[a]	*AND*	Two or More at Least 25% of the Time[a]
Relieved with defecation		Change in stool frequency
and/or		Change in consistency
With change in stool frequency		Difficult stool passage
and/or		Sense of incomplete evacuation
With change in stool consistency		Presence of mucus in stool

[a] Symptoms must have been present for > 3 months.

acetate (gonadotropin-releasing hormone analogue), psychotherapy, hypnotherapy of possible benefit in severe refractory cases.

DIVERTICULAR DISEASE
Herniations or saclike protrusions of the mucosa through the muscularis at points of nutrient artery penetration; possibly due to increased intraluminal pressure, low-fiber diet; most common in sigmoid colon.

CLINICAL PRESENTATION
1. *Asymptomatic* (detected by barium enema or colonoscopy).
2. *Pain*: Recurrent left lower quadrant pain relieved by defecation; alternating constipation and diarrhea. Diagnosis by barium enema.
3. *Diverticulitis*: Pain, fever, altered bowel habits, tender colon, leukocytosis. Best confirmed and staged by CT after opacification of bowel. (In pts who recover with medical therapy, perform elective barium enema or colonoscopy in 4–6 weeks to exclude cancer.) Complications: pericolic abscess, perforation, fistula (to bladder, vagina, skin, soft tissue), liver abscess, stricture. Frequently require surgery or, for abscesses, percutaneous drainage.
4. *Hemorrhage*: Usually in absence of diverticulitis, often from ascending colon and self-limited. If persistent, manage with mesenteric arteriography and intraarterial infusion of vasopressin, or surgery (Chap. 22).

℞ TREATMENT

Pain High-fiber diet, psyllium extract (e.g., Metamucil 1 tbsp PO qd or bid), anticholinergics (e.g., dicyclomine HCl 10–40 mg PO qid).

Diverticulitis NPO, IV fluids, antibiotics (e.g., cefoxitin 2 g IV q6h or imipenem 500 mg IV q6–8h); for ambulatory pts, ampicillin or tetracycline 500 mg PO qid (clear liquid diet); surgical resection in refractory or frequently recurrent cases, young persons (<age 50), immunosuppressed pts, or when there is inability to exclude cancer.

INTESTINAL PSEUDOOBSTRUCTION
Recurrent attacks of nausea, vomiting, and abdominal pain and distention mimicking mechanical obstruction; may be complicated by steatorrhea due to bacterial overgrowth.

CAUSES *Primary*: Familial visceral neuropathy, familial visceral myopathy, idiopathic. *Secondary*: Scleroderma, amyloidosis, diabetes, celiac disease, parkinsonism, muscular dystrophy, drugs, electrolyte imbalance, postsurgical.

TREATMENT

For acute attacks: intestinal decompression with long tube. Oral antibiotics for bacterial overgrowth (e.g., metronidazole 250 mg PO tid, tetracycline 500 mg PO qid, or ciprofloxacin 500 mg bid 1 week out of each month, usually in an alternating rotation of at least two antibiotics). Avoid surgery. In refractory cases, consider long-term parenteral hyperalimentation.

VASCULAR DISORDERS (SMALL AND LARGE INTESTINE)

MECHANISMS OF MESENTERIC ISCHEMIA (1) Occlusive: embolus (atrial fibrillation, valvular heart disease); arterial thrombus (atherosclerosis); venous thrombosis (trauma, neoplasm, infection, cirrhosis, oral contraceptives, antithrombin-III deficiency, protein S or C deficiency, lupus anticoagulant, factor V Leiden mutation, idiopathic); vasculitis (SLE, polyarteritis, rheumatoid arthritis, Henoch-Schönlein purpura); (2) nonocclusive: hypotension, heart failure, arrhythmia, digitalis (vasoconstrictor).

ACUTE MESENTERIC ISCHEMIA Periumbilical pain out of proportion to tenderness; nausea, vomiting, distention, GI bleeding, altered bowel habits. Abdominal x-ray shows bowel distention, air-fluid levels, thumbprinting (submucosal edema) but may be normal early in course. Peritoneal signs indicate infarcted bowel requiring surgical resection. Early celiac and mesenteric arteriography is recommended in all cases following hemodynamic resuscitation (avoid vasopressors, digitalis). Intraarterial vasodilators (e.g., papaverine) can be administered to reverse vasoconstriction. Laparotomy indicated to restore intestinal blood flow obstructed by embolus or thrombosis or to resect necrotic bowel. Postoperative anticoagulation indicated in mesenteric venous thrombosis, controversial in arterial occlusion.

CHRONIC MESENTERIC INSUFFICIENCY "Abdominal angina": dull, crampy periumbilical pain 15–30 min after a meal and lasting for several hours; weight loss; occasionally diarrhea. Evaluate with mesenteric arteriography for possible bypass graft surgery.

ISCHEMIC COLITIS Usually due to nonocclusive disease in pt with atherosclerosis. Severe lower abdominal pain, rectal bleeding, hypotension. Abdominal x-ray shows colonic dilatation, thumbprinting. Sigmoidoscopy shows submucosal hemorrhage, friability, ulcerations; rectum often spared. Conservative management (NPO, IV fluids); surgical resection for infarction or postischemic stricture.

COLONIC ANGIODYSPLASIA

In persons over age 60, vascular ectasias, usually in right colon, account for up to 40% of cases of chronic or recurrent lower GI bleeding. May be associated with aortic stenosis. Diagnosis is by arteriography (clusters of small vessels, early and prolonged opacification of draining vein) or colonoscopy (flat, bright red, fernlike lesions). For bleeding, treat by colonoscopic electro- or laser coagulation, band ligation, arteriographic embolization, or, if necessary, right hemicolectomy (Chap. 22).

ANORECTAL DISEASES

HEMORRHOIDS Due to increased hydrostatic pressure in hemorrhoidal venous plexus (associated with straining at stool, pregnancy). May be external, internal, thrombosed, acute (prolapsed or strangulated), or bleeding. Treat pain with bulk laxative and stool softeners (psyllium extract, dioctyl sodium sulfosuccinate 100–200 mg/d), sitz baths 1–4/d, witch hazel compresses, analgesics as needed. Bleeding may require rubber band ligation or injection sclerotherapy. Operative hemorrhoidectomy in severe or refractory cases.

ANAL FISSURES   Medical therapy as for hemorrhoids. Internal anal sphincterotomy in refractory cases.

PRURITUS ANI   Often of unclear cause; may be due to poor hygiene, fungal or parasitic infection. Treat with thorough cleansing after bowel movement, topical glucocorticoid, antifungal agent if indicated.

ANAL CONDYLOMAS (GENITAL WARTS)   Wart-like papillomas due to sexually transmitted papillomavirus. Treat with cautious application of liquid nitrogen or podophyllotoxin or with intralesional interferon-α. Tend to recur.

For a more detailed discussion, see Owyang C: Irritable Bowel Syndrome, Chap. 288, p. 1692; and Isselbacher KJ, Epstein A: Diverticular, Vascular, and Other Disorders of the Intestine and Peritoneum, Chap. 289, p. 1695, in HPIM-15.

151

CHOLELITHIASIS, CHOLECYSTITIS, AND CHOLANGITIS

CHOLELITHIASIS

There are three major types of gallstones: cholesterol, pigment, and mixed stones. Mixed and cholesterol gallstones contain >70% cholesterol monohydrate. Pigment stones have <10% cholesterol and are composed primarily of calcium bilirubinate. In the U.S., 80% of stones are cholesterol or mixed, 20% pigment.

EPIDEMIOLOGY   One million new cases of cholelithiasis per year in the U.S. Predisposing factors include demographic/genetics (increased prevalence in American Indians), obesity, weight loss, diabetes, ileal disease, pregnancy, estrogen or oral contraceptive use, type IV hyperlipidemia, and cirrhosis. Females/males = 4:1.

SYMPTOMS AND SIGNS   Many gallstones are "silent," i.e., present in asymptomatic pts. Symptoms occur when stones produce inflammation or obstruction of the cystic or common bile ducts. Major symptoms: (1) biliary colic — a severe steady ache in the RUQ or epigastrium that begins suddenly; often occurs 30–90 min after meals, lasts for several hours, and occasionally radiates to the right scapula or back; (2) nausea, vomiting. Physical exam may be normal or show epigastric or RUQ tenderness.

LABORATORY   Occasionally, mild and transient elevations in bilirubin [<85 μmol/L (<5 mg/dL)] accompany biliary colic.

IMAGING   Only 10% of gallstones are radiopaque. Ultrasonography is best diagnostic test. The oral cholecystogram requires a functioning gallbladder and serum bilirubin <51 μmol/L (<3 mg/dL) (Table 151-1).

DIFFERENTIAL DIAGNOSIS   Includes peptic ulcer disease (PUD), gastroesophageal reflux, irritable bowel syndrome, and hepatitis.

 TREATMENT

In asymptomatic pts, risk of developing complications requiring surgery is small. Elective cholecystectomy should be reserved for: (1) symptomatic pts (i.e., biliary colic despite low-fat diet); (2) persons with previous complications of cholelithiasis (see below); and (3) asymptomatic pts with an increased risk of complications (calcified or nonfunctioning gallbladder, cholesterolosis, adenomyomatosis). Pts with gallstones >2 cm or with an anomalous gallbladder containing stones should also be considered for surgery. Laparoscopic cholecystectomy is minimally invasive and is the procedure of choice for most pts undergoing elective cholecystectomy. Oral dissolution agents (chenodeoxycholic acid, ursodeoxycholic acid) partially or completely dissolve small radiolucent stones in 50% of selected pts but are ineffective in dissolving large, radiopaque, or pigment stones and those within a poorly opacified gallbladder following oral cholecystography. Recurrence is likely if the medication is stopped. Extracorporeal shockwave lithotripsy followed by medical

Table 151-1

Radiologic and Imaging Modalities for Biliary Tract Disease

Plain films of abdomen	Rarely useful for diagnosis of gallstones
	Can exclude other causes of abdominal pain (intestinal obstruction, perforated ulcer)
Ultrasound	High sensitivity/specificity for detecting gallstones
	Dilated ducts suggest ductal obstruction
	Intramural gas, pericholecystic fluid suggest gallbladder inflammation or infection
	Cannot definitively exclude choledocholithiasis
Scintigraphy (HIDA)	High sensitivity/specificity for acute cholecystitis
Oral cholecystogram	Seldom used for diagnosis of gallstone disease
	Can help select pts for nonsurgical therapy
CT scan	Useful if suspicion of cancer is high
Endoscopic retrograde cholangiopancreatography	Delineates lower limit of common bile duct (CBD) obstruction
	Therapeutic intervention possible
Percutaneous transhepatic cholangiography	Delineates upper limit of CBD obstruction
MR cholangiography	Useful for visualizing pancreatic and biliary ducts

litholytic therapy is effective in selected pts with solitary radiolucent gallstones.

COMPLICATIONS   Cholecystitis, pancreatitis, cholangitis.

ACUTE CHOLECYSTITIS

Acute inflammation of the gallbladder usually caused by cystic duct obstruction by an impacted stone.

ETIOLOGY   90% calculous; 10% acalculous; latter associated with higher complication rate and caused by prolonged acute illness (i.e.,: burns, trauma, major surgery), fasting, hyperalimentation leading to gallbladder stasis, vasculitis, carcinoma of gallbladder or common bile duct, some gallbladder infections (*Leptospira, Streptococcus*, parasitic etc.).

SYMPTOMS AND SIGNS   (1) Attack of bilary colic (RUQ or epigastric pain) that progressively worsens; (2) nausea, vomiting, anorexia; and (3) fever. Examination typically reveals RUQ tenderness; palpable RUQ mass found in 20% of pts. *Murphy's sign* is present when deep inspiration or cough during palpation of the RUQ produces increased pain or inspiratory arrest.

LABORATORY   Mild leukocytosis; serum bilirubin, alkaline phosphatase, and AST may be mildly elevated.

IMAGING   Ultrasonography is useful for demonstrating gallstones and occasionally a phlegmonous mass surrounding the gallbladder. Radionuclide scans (HIDA, DIDA, DISIDA, etc.) may identify cystic duct obstruction.

DIFFERENTIAL DIAGNOSIS   Includes acute pancreatitis, appendicitis, pyelonephritis, PUD, hepatitis, and hepatic abscess.

℞ **TREATMENT**

No oral intake, nasogastric suction, IV fluids and electrolytes, analgesia (meperidine or NSAIDS), and antibiotics (ampicillin, cephalosporins; consider combination with aminoglycosides in diabetic pt or others with signs of gram-negative sepsis). Acute symptoms will resolve in 75% of pts. Surgery is definitive and should be performed as soon as feasible (within 24–48 h of admission). Delayed surgery is reserved for pts with high risk of emergent surgery and where the diagnosis is in doubt.

COMPLICATIONS   Empyema, hydrops, gangrene, perforation, fistulization, gallstone ileus, porcelain gallbladder.

CHRONIC CHOLECYSTITIS

ETIOLOGY   Chronic inflammation of the gallbladder; almost always associated with gallstones. Results from repeated acute/subacute cholecystitis or prolonged mechanical irritation of gallbladder wall.

SYMPTOMS AND SIGNS   Often nonspecific; include dyspepsia, fatty food intolerance, and abdominal pain.

LABORATORY   Tests are usually normal.

IMAGING   Ultrasonography preferred; usually shows gallstones within a contracted gallbladder (Table 151-1).

DIFFERENTIAL DIAGNOSIS   PUD, esophagitis, irritable bowel syndrome.

TREATMENT

Surgery indicated if pt is symptomatic.

CHOLEDOCHOLITHIASIS/CHOLANGITIS

ETIOLOGY   In pts with cholelithiasis, passage of gallstones into common bile duct occurs in 10–15%; increases with age. At cholecystectomy, undetected stones are left behind in 1–5% of pts.

SYMPTOMS AND SIGNS   Choledocholithiasis may present as an incidental finding, biliary colic, obstructive jaundice, cholangitis, or pancreatitis. Cholangitis usually presents as fever, RUQ pain, and jaundice (*Charcot's triad*).

LABORATORY   Elevations in serum bilirubin, alkaline phosphatase, and aminotransferases. Leukocytosis usually accompanies cholangitis; blood cultures are frequently positive. Amylase is elevated in 15% of cases.

IMAGING   Diagnosis usually made by cholangiography either preoperatively by endoscopic retrograde cholangiopancreatography (ERCP) or intraoperatively at the time of cholecystectomy. Ultrasonography may reveal dilated bile ducts but is not sensitive for detecting common duct stones (Table 151-1).

DIFFERENTIAL DIAGNOSIS   Acute cholecystitis, renal colic, perforated viscus, pancreatitis.

 TREATMENT

Laparoscopic cholecystectomy and ERCP have decreased the need for choledocholithotomy and T-tube drainage of the bile ducts. Endoscopic biliary sphincterotomy followed by spontaneous passage or stone extraction is the treatment of choice in the management of pts with common duct stones, especially in elderly or high-risk pts. Preoperative ERCP is indicated in gallstone pts with (1) history of jaundice or pancreatitis, (2) abnormal LFT, and (3) ultrasound evidence of a dilated common bile duct or stones in the duct. Cholangitis treated like acute cholecystitis; no oral intake, hydration, and analgesia are the mainstays; stones should be removed surgically or endoscopically.

COMPLICATIONS   Cholangitis, obstructive jaundice, gallstone-induced pancreatitis, and secondary biliary cirrhosis.

PRIMARY SCLEROSING CHOLANGITIS (PSC)

PSC is a sclerosing inflammatory process involving the biliary tree.

ETIOLOGY   Males outnumber females and most patients are 25–45 years old. Associations: inflammatory bowel disease (ulcerative colitis—70% of cases of PSC), AIDS, rarely retroperitoneal fibrosis.

SYMPTOMS AND SIGNS   Pruritus, RUQ pain, jaundice, fever, weight loss, and malaise. May progress to cirrhosis with portal hypertension.

LABORATORY   Evidence of cholestasis (elevated bilirubin and alkaline phosphatase) common.

RADIOLOGY/ENDOSCOPY   Transhepatic or endoscopic cholangiograms reveal stenosis and dilation of the intra- and extrahepatic bile ducts.

DIFFERENTIAL DIAGNOSIS   Cholangiocarcinoma, Caroli's disease (cystic dilation of bile ducts), *Fasciola hepatica* infection, echinococcosis, and ascariasis.

℞ TREATMENT

No satisfactory therapy. Cholangitis should be treated as outlined above. Cholestyramine may control pruritus. Supplemental vitamin D and calcium may retard bone loss. Glucocorticoids, methotrexate, and cyclosporine have not been shown to be effective. Urodeoxycholic acid improves liver tests but has not been shown to affect survival. Surgical relief of biliary obstruction may be appropriate but has a high complication rate. The efficacy of colectomy for pts with ulcerative colitis is uncertain. Liver transplantation should be considered in pts with endstage cirrhosis.

For a more detailed discussion, see Greenberger NJ, Paumgartner G: Diseases of the Gallbladder and Bile Ducts, Chap. 302, p. 1776, in HPIM-15.

152

PANCREATITIS

ACUTE PANCREATITIS

The differentiation between acute and chronic pancreatitis is based on clinical criteria. In acute pancreatitis, there is restoration of normal pancreatic function; in the chronic form, there is permanent loss of function and pain may predominate. There are two pathologic types of acute pancreatitis: *edematous* and *necrotizing*.

ETIOLOGY Most common causes in the U.S. are alcohol and cholelithiasis. Others include abdominal trauma; postoperative or postendoscopic retrograde cholangiopancreatography (ERCP); metabolic (e.g., hypertriglyceridemia, hypercalcemia, renal failure); hereditary pancreatitis; infection (e.g., mumps, viral hepatitis, coxsackievirus, ascariasis, *Mycoplasma*); opportunistic infections (CMV, *Cryptococcus, Candida*, TB); medications (e.g., azathioprine, sulfonamides, thiazides, furosemide, estrogens, tetracycline, valproic acid, pentamidine, dideoxyinosine); connective tissue diseases/vasculitis (e.g., lupus, necrotizing angiitis, thrombotic thrombocytopenic purpura); penetrating peptic ulcer; obstruction of the ampulla of Vater (e.g., regional enteritis); pancreas divisum.

CLINICAL FEATURES Can vary from mild abdominal pain to shock. *Common symptoms*: (1) steady, boring midepigastric pain radiating to the back that is frequently increased in the supine position; (2) nausea, vomiting.

Physical exam: (1) low-grade fever, tachycardia, hypotension; (2) erythematous skin nodules due to subcutaneous fat necrosis; (3) basilar rales, pleural effusion (often on the left); (4) abdominal tenderness and rigidity, diminished bowel sounds, palpable upper abdominal mass; (5) Cullen's sign: blue discoloration in the periumbilical area due to hemoperitoneum; (6) Turner's sign:

blue-red-purple or green-brown discoloration of the flanks due to tissue catabolism of hemoglobin.

LABORATORY

1. *Serum amylase*: Large elevations ($>3 \times$ normal) virtually assure the
diagnosis if salivary gland disease and intestinal perforation/infarction are excluded. However, normal serum amylase does not exclude the diagnosis of acute
pancreatitis, and the degree of elevation does not predict severity of pancreatitis.
Amylase levels typically return to normal in 48–72 h.

2. *Urinary amylase–creatinine clearance ratio* may be helpful in distinguishing between pancreatitis and other causes of hyperamylasemia (e.g., mac-
roamylasemia) but is invalid in the presence of renal failure. Simultaneous serum and urine amylase values are used. $C_{am}/C_{Cr} = (am_{urine} \times Cr_{serum}) / (am_{serum}$
$\times Cr_{urine})$. Normal value is $<4\%$.

3. *Serum lipase* level is more specific for pancreatic disease and remains
elevated for 7–14 d.

4. *Other tests:* Hypocalcemia occurs in ~25% of pts. *Leukocytosis*
($15,000–20,000/\mu L$) occurs frequently. *Hypertriglyceridemia* occurs in 15% of
cases and can cause a spuriously normal serum amylase level. *Hyperglycemia*
is common. *Serum bilirubin, alkaline phosphatase*, and *aspartame aminotransferase* can be transiently elevated. *Hypoalbuminemia* and marked elevations of
serum lactic dehydrogenase (LDH) are associated with an increased mortality
rate. *Hypoxemia* is present in 25% of pts. Arterial pH < 7.32 may spuriously
elevate serum amylase. The *ECG* may demonstrate ST-segment and T-wave
abnormalities.

IMAGING

1. *Abdominal radiographs* are abnormal in 50% of pts but are not specific
for pancreatitis. Common findings include total or partial ileus ("sentinel loop")
and spasm of transverse colon. Useful for excluding diagnoses such as intestinal
perforation.

2. *Ultrasound* often fails to visualize the pancreas because of overlying
intestinal gas but may detect gallstones or edema or enlargement of the pancreas.

3. *CT* can confirm diagnosis of pancreatitis (edematous pancreas) and is
useful for predicting and identifying late complications. Contrast-enhanced dynamic CT is indicated for clinical deterioration, ≥ 3 Ransom/Imrie signs (Table
152-1), other features of serious illness.

DIFFERENTIAL DIAGNOSIS Intestinal perforation (especially peptic
ulcer), cholecystitis, acute intestinal obstruction, mesenteric ischemia, renal
colic, myocardial ischemia, aortic dissection, connective tissue disorders, pneumonia, and diabetic ketoacidosis.

 TREATMENT

Most (90%) cases subside over a period of 3–7 d. Conventional measures:
(1) analgesics, such as meperidine; (2) IV fluids and colloids; (3) no oral
alimentation; (4) treatment of hypocalcemia, if symptomatic; (5) antibiotics
if there is established infection or prophylactically in severe acute pancreatitis—carbapenem agents cover a broad range of organisms and penetrate
well into pancreatic tissue. Not effective: cimetidine (or related agents), nasogastric suction, glucagon, peritoneal lavage, and anticholinergic medications. Precipitating factors (alcohol, medications) must be eliminated. In mild
or moderate pancreatitis, a clear liquid diet can usually be started after 3–
6 d. Pts with severe gallstone-induced pancreatitis often benefit from early
(<3 d) papillotomy.

Table 152-1

Factors That Adversely Affect Survival in Acute Pancreatitis

Ranson/Imrie criteria
  At admission or diagnosis
    Age >55 years
    Leukocytosis >16,000/μL
    Hyperglycemia >11 mmol/L (>200 mg/dL)
    Serum LDH >400 IU/L
    Serum AST >250 IU/L
  During initial 48 h
    Fall in hematocrit by >10%
    Fluid deficit of >4000 mL
    Hypocalcemia [calcium concentration <1.9 mmol/L (<8.0 mg/dL)]
    Hypoxemia (P_{O_2} <60 mmHg)
    Increase in BUN to >1.8 mmol/L (>5 mg/dL) after IV fluid
      administration
    Hypoalbuminemia [albumin level <32 g/L (<3.2 g/dL)]
Acute physiology and chronic health evaluation (APACHE II) score > 12
Hemorrhagic peritoneal fluid
Obesity [body mass index (BMI) > 29]
Key indicators of organ failure
  Hypotension (blood pressure <90 mmHg) or tachycardia >130 beats per
    minute
  P_{O_2} <60 mmHg
  Oliguria (<50 mL/h) or increasing blood urea nitrogen (BUN), creatinine
  Metabolic indicators: serum calcium <1.9 mmol/L (<8.0 mg/dL) or
    serum albumin <32 g/L (<3.2 g/dL)

COMPLICATIONS   It is important to identify pts who are at risk of poor outcome. Increased mortality has been observed with the presence of ≥3 Ransom/Imrie prognostic criteria at admission or within 48 h (Table 152-1). Fulminant pancreatitis requires aggressive fluid support and meticulous management. Mortality is largely due to infection.

Systemic   Shock, GI bleeding, common duct obstruction, ileus, splenic infarction or rupture, DIC, subcutaneous fat necrosis, ARDS, pleural effusion, acute renal failure, sudden blindness.

Local

1. Sterile or infected *pancreatic necrosis*—necrosis may become secondarily infected in 40–60% of pts; typically within 1–2 weeks after the onset of pancreatitis. Most frequent organisms: gram-negative bacteria of alimentary origin, but intraabdominal *Candida* infection increasing in frequency. Necrosis can be visualized by contrast-enhanced dynamic CT with infection diagnosed by CT-guided needle aspiration. Laparotomy with removal of necrotic material and adequate drainage should be considered for pts with sterile acute necrotic pancreatitis if pt continues to deteriorate despite conventional therapy. Infected pancreatic necrosis requires aggressive surgical debridement and antibiotics.

2. *Pancreatic pseudocysts* develop over 1–4 weeks in 15% of pts. Abdominal pain is the usual complaint, and a tender upper abdominal mass may be present. Can be detected by abdominal ultrasound or CT. In pts who are stable and uncomplicated, treatment is supportive; if there is no resolution within 6 weeks, consider CT-guided needle aspiration/drainage, surgical drain-

age, or resection. In pts with an expanding pseudocyst or complicated by hemorrhage, rupture, or abscess, surgery should be performed.

3. *Pancreatic abscess*—ill defined liquid collection of pus that evolves over 4–6 weeks. Can be treated surgically or in selected cases by percutaneous drainage.

4. *Pancreatic ascites and pleural effusions* are usually due to disruption of the main pancreatic duct. Treatment involves nasogastric suction and parenteral alimentation for 2–3 weeks. If medical management fails, pancreatography followed by surgery should be performed.

CHRONIC PANCREATITIS Chronic pancreatitis may occur as recurrent episodes of acute inflammation superimposed upon a previously injured pancreas or as chronic damage with pain and malabsorption.

ETIOLOGY Chronic alcoholism most frequent cause of pancreatic exocrine insufficiency in U.S. adults; also hypertriglyceridemia, hypercalcemia, hereditary pancreatitis, hemochromatosis. Cystic fibrosis most frequent cause in children. In 25% of adults, etiology is unknown.

SYMPTOMS AND SIGNS *Pain* is cardinal symptom. Weight loss, steatorrhea, and other signs and symptoms of malabsorption common. Physical exam often unremarkable.

LABORATORY No specific laboratory test for chronic pancreatitis. Serum amylase and lipase levels are often normal. Serum bilirubin and alkaline phosphatase may be elevated. Steatorrhea (fecal fat concentration $\geq 9.5\%$) late in the course. The bentiromide test, a simple, effective test of pancreatic exocrine function, may be helpful. D-Xylose urinary excretion test is usually normal. Impaired glucose tolerance is present in $>50\%$ of pts. Secretin stimulation test is a relatively sensitive test for pancreatic exocrine deficiency.

IMAGING *Plain films of the abdomen* reveal pancreatic calcifications in 30–60%. *Ultrasound* and *CT scans* may show dilation of the pancreatic duct. *ERCP* often reveals irregular dilation of the main pancreatic duct and pruning of the branches.

DIFFERENTIAL DIAGNOSIS Important to distinguish from pancreatic carcinoma; may require radiographically guided biopsy.

 TREATMENT

Aimed at controlling pain and malabsorption. Intermittent attacks treated like acute pancreatitis. Alcohol and large, fatty meals must be avoided. Narcotics for severe pain, but subsequent addiction is common. Pts unable to maintain adequate hydration should be hospitalized, while those with milder symptoms can be managed on an ambulatory basis. Surgery may control pain if there is a ductal stricture. Subtotal pancreatectomy may also control pain but at the cost of exocrine insufficiency and diabetes. Malabsorption is managed with a low-fat diet and pancreatic enzyme replacement (8 conventional tablets or 3 enteric-coated tablets with meals). Because pancreatic enzymes are inactivated by acid, agents that reduce acid production (e.g., omeprazole or sodium bicarbonate) may improve their efficacy (but should not be given with enteric-coated preparations). Insulin may be necessary to control serum glucose.

COMPLICATIONS Vitamin B_{12} malabsorption in 40% of alcohol-induced and all cystic fibrosis cases. Impaired glucose tolerance. Nondiabetic retinopathy due to vitamin A and/or zinc deficiency. GI bleeding, icterus, effusions, subcutaneous fat necrosis, and bone pain occasionally occur. Increased risk for pancreatic carcinoma. Narcotic addiction common.

For a more detailed discussion, see Greenberger NJ, Toskes PP: Acute and Chronic Pancreatitis, Chap. 304, p. 1792;, Toskes PP, Greenberger NJ: Approach to the Patient with Pancreatic Disease, Chap. 303, p. 1788, in HPIM-15.

153

ACUTE HEPATITIS

VIRAL HEPATITIS

Clinically characterized by malaise, nausea, vomiting, diarrhea, and low-grade fever followed by dark urine, jaundice, and tender hepatomegaly; may be subclinical and detected on basis of elevated aspartate and alanine aminotransferase (AST and ALT) levels. Hepatitis B may be associated with immune-complex phenomena, including arthritis, serum-sickness–like illness, glomerulonephritis, and polyarteritis nodosa. Hepatitis-like illnesses may be caused not only by hepatotropic viruses (A, B, C, D, E) but also by other viruses (Epstein-Barr, CMV, coxsackievirus, etc.), alcohol, drugs, hypotension and ischemia, and biliary tract disease (Table 153-1).

HEPATITIS A (HAV)   27-nm picornavirus (hepatovirus) with single-stranded RNA genome. Clinical course: See Fig. 153-1

Outcome   Recovery within 6–12 months, occasionally after one or two apparent clinical and serologic relapses; in some cases, pronounced cholestasis suggesting biliary obstruction may occur; rare fatalities (fulminant hepatitis), no chronic carrier state.

Diagnosis   IgM anti-HAV in acute or early convalescent serum sample.

Epidemiology   Fecal-oral transmission; endemic in underdeveloped countries; food-borne and waterborne epidemics; outbreaks in day-care centers, residential institutions.

Prevention   *After exposure*: immune globulin 0.02 mL/kg IM within 2 weeks to household and institutional contacts (not casual contacts at work). *Before exposure*: inactivated HAV vaccine 0.5–1 mL IM (dose depends on formulation); half dose to children; repeat at 6–12 months; target travelers, military recruits, animal handlers, day-care personnel.

HEPATITIS B (HBV)   42-nm hepadnavirus with outer surface coat (HBsAg), inner nucleocapsid core (HBcAg), DNA polymerase, and partially double-stranded DNA genome of 3200 nucleotides. Circulating form of HBcAg is HBeAg, a marker of viral replication and infectivity. Multiple serotypes and genetic heterogeneity. Course: See Fig. 153-2.

Table 153-1

The Hepatitis Viruses

	HAV	HBV	HCV	HDV	HEV	HGV
Viral Properties						
Size nm	27	42	~55	~36	~32	?
Nucleic acid	RNA	DNA	RNA	RNA	RNA	RNA
Genome length, kb	7.5	3.2	9.4	1.7	7.5	9.4
Classification	Picornavirus	Hepadnavirus	Flavivirus-like	—	Calicivirus-like or al- pha-virus-like	Flavivirus
Incubation, days	15–45	30–180	15–160	21–140	14–63	?
Transmission						
Fecal-oral	+++	—	—	—	+++	?
Percutaneous	Rare	+++	+++	+++	—	++
Sexual	?	++	Uncommon	++	—	?
Perinatal	—	+++	Uncommon	+	—	?
Clinical Features						
Severity	Usually mild	Moderate	Mild	May be severe	Usually mild	Mild
Chronic infection	No	1–10%; up to 90% in neonates	80–90%	Common	No	Yes
Carrier state	No	Yes	Yes	Yes	No	Yes
Fulminant hepatitis	0.1%	1%	Rare	Up to 20% in super- infection	10–20% in pregnant women	?
Hepatocellular carcinoma	No	Yes	Yes	?	No	?
Prophylaxis	IG; vaccine	HBIG; vaccine	None	None (HBV vaccine for susceptibles)	None	None

NOTE: HAV, hepatitis A virus; HBV, hepatitis B virus; HCV, hepatitis C virus; HDV, hepatitis D virus; HEV, hepatitis E virus; HGV, hepatitis G virus; IG, immune globulin; + +, sometimes; + + +, often; ?, possibly.

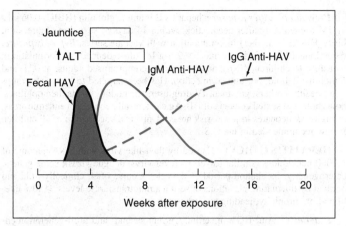

FIGURE 153-1 Scheme of typical clinical and laboratory features of HAV. (*Reproduced from Dienstag JL, Isselbacher KJ, HPIM-15, p. 1721*).

Outcome Recovery >90%, fulminant hepatitis (<1%), chronic hepatitis or carrier state (only 1–2% of immunocompetent adults; higher in neonates, elderly, immunocompromised), cirrhosis, and hepatocellular carcinoma (especially following chronic infection beginning in infancy or early childhood) (Chap. 155).

Diagnosis HBsAg in serum (acute or chronic infection); IgM anti-HBc (early anti-HBc indicative of acute or recent infection). Most sensitive test is detection of HBV DNA in serum; not generally required for routine diagnosis.

Epidemiology Percutaneous (needlestick), sexual, or perinatal transmission. Endemic in sub-Saharan Africa and Southeast Asia, where up to 20% of population acquire infection, usually early in life.

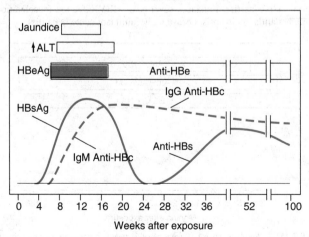

FIGURE 153-2 Scheme of typical clinical and laboratory features of HBV. (*Reproduced from Dienstag JL, Isselbacher KJ, HPIM-15, p. 1721*)

Prevention *After exposure*: hepatitis B immune globulin (HBIG) 0.06 mL/ kg IM immediately after needlestick, within 14 days of sexual exposure, or at birth (HbsAg+ mother) in combination with vaccine series. *Before exposure*: recombinant hepatitis B vaccine 10–20µg IM (dose depends on formulation); half dose to children, 40-µg dose to immunocompromised adults; at 0, 1, and 6 months; deltoid, not gluteal injection. Has been targeted to high-risk groups (e.g., health workers, gay men, IV drug users, hemodialysis pts, hemophiliacs, household and sexual contacts of HBsAg carriers, all neonates in endemic areas, or high-risk neonates in lower-risk areas). Universal vaccination of all children is now recommended in the U.S.

HEPATITIS C (HCV)   Caused by flavi-like virus with RNA genome of >9000 nucleotides (similar to yellow fever virus, dengue virus); some genetic heterogeneity. Incubation period 7–8 weeks. Course often clinically mild and marked by fluctuating elevations of serum aminotransferase levels; >50% likelihood of chronicity, leading to cirrhosis in >20%.

Diagnosis   Anti-HCV in serum. Current second- and third-generation enzyme immunoassay detects antibody to epitopes designated C200, C33c, C22-3; may appear after acute illness but generally present by 3–5 months after exposure. A positive enzyme immunoassay can be confirmed by recombinant immunoblot assay (RIBA) or by detection of HCV RNA in serum (Fig. 153-3).

Epidemiology   Percutaneous transmission accounts for >90% of transfusion-associated hepatitis cases. IV drug use accounts >50% of reported cases. Little evidence for frequent sexual or perinatal transmission.

Prevention   Exclusion of paid blood donors, testing of donated blood for anti-HCV. Anti-HCV detected by enzyme immunoassay in blood donors with normal ALT is often falsely positive (30%); result should be confirmed with RIBA, which correlates with presence of HCV RNA in serum.

HEPATITIS D (HDV, DELTA AGENT)   Defective 37-nm RNA virus that requires HBV for its replication; either coinfects with HBV or superinfects a chronic HBV carrier. Enhances severity of HBV infection (acceleration of chronic hepatitis to cirrhosis, occasionally fulminant acute hepatitis).

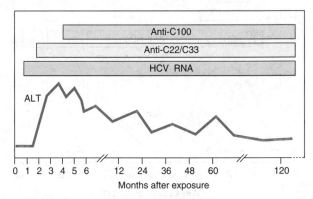

FIGURE 153-3   Serologic course of acute hepatitis type C progressing to chronicity. HCV RNA is detectable before the ALT elevation. Antibody to C22 and anti-C33 appears during acute hepatitis C, whereas antibody to C100 appears 1 to 3 months later. (*Reproduced from Dienstag JL, Isselbacher KJ, HPIM-15, p. 1721*)

Diagnosis Anti-HDV in serum (acute hepatitis D—often in low titer, is transient; chronic hepatitis D—in higher titer, is sustained).

Epidemiology Endemic among HBV carriers in Mediterranean basin, areas of South America, etc. Otherwise spread percutaneously among HbsAg+ IV drug users or by transfusion in hemophiliacs and to a lesser extent among HbsAg+ gay men.

Prevention Hepatitis B vaccine (noncarriers only).

HEPATITIS E (HEV) Caused by 29- to 32-nm agent thought to be related to caliciviruses. Enterically transmitted and responsible for waterborne epidemics of hepatitis in India, parts of Asia and Africa, and Central America. Self-limited illness with high (10–20%) mortality rate in pregnant women.

HEPATITIS G (HGV) Recently identified flavivirus with RNA genome of >9000 nucleotides (distantly related to HCV). Though common (detected in 1.7% of U.S. blood donors) and associated with viremia lasting for years, HGV does not appear to cause significant liver disease.

 TREATMENT

Activity as tolerated, high-calorie diet (often tolerated best in morning), IV hydration for severe vomiting, cholestyramine up to 4 g PO qid for severe pruritus, avoid hepatically metabolized drugs; no role for glucocorticoids. Liver transplantation for fulminant hepatic failure and grades III–IV encephalopathy.

TOXIC AND DRUG-INDUCED HEPATITIS

DOSE-DEPENDENT (DIRECT HEPATOTOXINS) Onset is within 48 h, predictable, necrosis around terminal hepatic venule—e.g., carbon tetrachloride, benzene derivatives, mushroom poisoning, acetaminophen, or microvesicular steatosis (e.g., tetracyclines, valproic acid).

IDIOSYNCRATIC Variable dose and time of onset; small number of exposed persons affected; may be associated with fever, rash, arthralgias, eosinophilia. In many cases, mechanism may actually involve toxic metabolite, possibly determined on genetic basis—e.g., isoniazid, halothane, phenytoin, methyldopa, carbamazepine, diclofenac, oxacillin, sulfonamides.

 TREATMENT

Supportive as for viral hepatitis; withdraw suspected agent. Liver transplantation if necessary.

ACUTE HEPATIC FAILURE

Massive hepatic necrosis with impaired consciousness occurring within 8 weeks of the onset of illness.

CAUSES Infections (viral, including HAV, HBV, HCV (rarely), HDV, HEV, bacterial, rickettsial, parasitic), drugs and toxins, ischemia (shock), Budd-Chiari syndrome, idiopathic chronic active hepatitis, acute Wilson's disease, microvesicular fat syndromes (Reye's syndrome, acute fatty liver of pregnancy).

CLINICAL MANIFESTATIONS Neuropsychiatric changes—delirium, personality change, stupor, coma; cerebral edema—suggested by profuse sweating, hemodynamic instability, tachyarrhythmias, tachypnea, fever, papilledema, decerebrate rigidity (though all may be absent); deep jaundice, coagulopathy, bleeding, renal failure, acid-base disturbance, hypoglycemia, acute pancreatitis, cardiorespiratory failure, infections (bacterial, fungal).

ADVERSE PROGNOSTIC INDICATORS Age <10 or >40, certain causes (e.g., halothane, hepatitis C), duration of jaundice >7 d before onset of encephalopathy, serum bilirubin >300 μmol/L (>18 mg/dL), coma (survival <20%), rapid reduction in liver size, respiratory failure, marked prolongation of PT, factor V level <20%. In acetaminophen overdose, adverse prognosis is suggested by blood pH <7.30, serum creatinine >266 μmol/L (>3 mg/dL), markedly prolonged PT.

℞ TREATMENT

Endotracheal intubation often required. Monitor serum glucose—IV D10 or D20 as necessary. Prevent gastrointestinal bleeding with H_2-receptor antagonists and antacids (maintain gastric pH ≥3.5). In many centers intracranial pressure is monitored—more sensitive than CT in detecting cerebral edema. Value of dexamethasone for cerebral edema unclear; IV mannitol may be beneficial. Liver transplantation should be considered in pts with grades III–IV encephalopathy and other adverse prognostic indicators.

For a more detailed discussion, see Dienstag JL, Isselbacher KJ: Acute Viral Hepatitis, Chap. 295, p. 1721, in HPIM-15.

154

CHRONIC HEPATITIS

A group of disorders characterized by a chronic inflammatory reaction in the liver for at least 6 months.

OVERVIEW
ETIOLOGY Hepatitis B virus (HBV), hepatitis C virus (HCV), hepatitis D virus (HDV, delta agent), drugs (methyldopa, nitrofurantoin, isoniazid, dantrolene), autoimmune hepatitis, Wilson's disease, hemochromatosis, alpha$_1$ antitrypsin deficiency.

HISTOLOGIC CLASSIFICATION See Table 154-1
PRESENTATION Wide clinical spectrum ranging from asymptomatic serum aminotransferase elevations to apparently acute, even fulminant, hepatitis. Common symptoms include fatigue, malaise, anorexia, low-grade fever; jaundice is frequent in severe disease. Some pts may present with complications of cirrhosis: ascites, variceal bleeding, encephalopathy, coagulopathy, and hypersplenism. In chronic hepatitis B or C and autoimmune hepatitis, extrahepatic features may predominate.

Table 154-1

Histologic Classification of Chronic Hepatitis

	Inflammatory Activity			Degree of Fibrosis
Grade	Portal Tracts	Hepatic Lobule	Stage	Fibrosis
0	None or minimal	None	1	No fibrosis or limited to within expanded portal tracts
1	Portal inflammation	Inflammation, no necrosis	2	Periportal fibrosis or portal-to-portal septa with intact architecture
2	Mild limiting plate necrosis	Focal necrosis	3	Septal fibrosis with architectural distortion
3	Moderate limiting plate necrosis	Severe focal cell damage	4	Cirrhosis
4	Severe limiting plate necrosis	Bridging necrosis		

CHRONIC HEPATITIS B

Follows up to 1–2% of cases of acute hepatitis B in immunocompetent hosts; more frequent in immunocompromised hosts. Spectrum of disease: asymptomatic antigenemia, chronic hepatitis, cirrhosis hepatocellular cancer; early phase often associated with continued symptoms of hepatitis, elevated aminotransferase levels, presence in serum of HBeAg and HBV DNA, and presence in liver of replicative form of HBV; later phase in some pts may be associated with clinical and biochemical improvement, disappearance of HBeAg and HBV DNA and appearance of anti-HBe in serum, and integration of HBV DNA into host hepatocyte genome. In Mediterranean area, a frequent variant is characterized by a severe and rapidly progressive course and HBV DNA with anti-HBe in serum, due to a mutation in the pre-C region of the HBV genome that prevents HBeAg synthesis (may appear during course of chronic wild-type HBV infection as a result of immune pressure and may also account for some cases of fulminant hepatitis B). Chronic hepatitis B ultimately leads to cirrhosis in 25–40% of cases (particularly in pts with HDV superinfection or the pre-C mutation) and hepatocellular carcinoma in many of these pts (particularly when chronic infection is acquired early in life).

EXTRAHEPATIC MANIFESTATIONS (IMMUNE-COMPLEX–MEDIATED) Rash, urticaria, arthritis, polyarteritis, polyneuropathy, glomerulonephritis.

 TREATMENT

Standard approach is interferon α 5 million units qd or 10 million units three times per week × 4 months for serum HBeAg/HBV-DNA-positive pts with symptoms, elevated aminotransferase levels, and biopsy evidence of chronic hepatitis. Results in anti-HBe seroconversion with clinical, biochemical, and histologic improvement in up to 40% of cases. Best predictors of response are serum HBV DNA level <200 ng/L and substantial elevations of aminotransferases (>100 units). Poor responders: pts positive for anti-HDV or HIV, adult carriers infected in childhood, immunocompromised pts, persons infected with HBeAg-negative "pre-core" mutant. Side effects: flulike reactions (common), bone marrow depression, precipitation of autoimmune diseases including thyroid disease, CNS symptoms, anorexia, sleep disturbance. In pts with lower aminotransferase levels (<100 U/L), efficacy of interferon may be enhanced by a priming prednisone course, 60 mg PO qd, tapering over 6 weeks, but this approach may result in fatal flare of hepatitis B and is not recommended. Avoid interferon in pts with decompensated cirrhosis (e.g., ascites, jaundice, coagulopathy, encephalopathy). The nucleoside analogue lamivudine (3TC) has recently been approved by the FDA for the treatment of chronic HBV. Treatment with lamivudine (100 mg/d) results in significant biochemical and histologic improvement in >50% of pts and anti-HBe seroconversion in 16–20%. Lamivudine is associated with minimal side effects in HBV-infected pts. Flares of HBV, which can potentially lead to decompensation of liver disease, can occur on stopping lamivudine, with development of lamivudine resistance mutations, and with seroconversion. Lamivudine should be considered as first-line therapy in pts with evidence of active hepatitis and viral replication who fall into one of the following groups: contraindications to interferon (especially decompensated cirrhosis); pts with pre-core mutations; pts with chronic immunosuppression; or pts not responsive to interferon.

CHRONIC HEPATITIS C

Follows 80% of cases of transfusion-associated and sporadic hepatitis C. Clinically mild, often waxing and waning aminotransferase elevations; mild chronic hepatitis on liver biopsy. Associated with essential mixed cryoglobulinemia, porphyria cutanea tarda, membranoproliferative glomerulonephritis, and lymphocytic sialadenitis. Diagnosis confirmed by detecting anti-HCV in serum. May lead to cirrhosis in ≥20% of cases after 20 years.

℞ TREATMENT

Therapy with interferon α 3 million units 3 times per week for 12–18 months should be considered in pts with aminotransferase elevations, biopsy evidence of moderate or severe chronic hepatitis, HCV RNA in serum; 50% achieve clinical and biochemical remission or improvement; however, at least 50% of pts relapse within 12 months of treatment and may require retreatment. Higher doses do not improve sustained response rate and cause more side effects. Sustained response is associated with loss of HCV RNA from serum. Poorer response rates are associated with cirrhosis, high serum HCV RNA levels, and HCV genotypes 1a and 1b, which are prevalent in U.S. Benefit in pts with normal or nearly normal serum aminotransferase levels or decompensated cirrhosis is doubtful. The efficacy and tolerability of a long-acting form of interferon α (PEG-Interferon) is under study.

The guanosine nucleoside analogue ribavirin is ineffective when used alone to treat chronic HCV. However, treatment with the combination of ribavirin with interferon α for 1 year yields a sustained response rate of 40% (twice as high as with interferon α alone). Response rates are even higher in pts with low viral loads and genotypes other than type 1. In pts with non-1 genotypes, 6 months of combination therapy yields sustained response rates comparable to 12 months of combination therapy. Thus, pts with low viral loads and non-1 genotypes may be treated with 6 months of combination therapy. The side effect profile of combination interferon and ribavirin therapy is similar to interferon monotherapy. Ribavirin therapy is associated with some degree of hemolysis, but the resultant modest reduction in hemoglobin is not of clinical importance in most pts.

AUTOIMMUNE HEPATITIS

CLASSIFICATION   *Type I*: classic autoimmune hepatitis, anti-smooth muscle and/or antinuclear antibodies. *Type II*: associated with anti-liver/kidney microsomal (anti-LKM) antibodies, which are directed against cytochrome P450IID6 (seen primarily in southern Europe). *Type III* patients lack antinuclear antibodies and anti-LKM, have antibodies reactive with hepatocyte cytokeratins; clinically similar to type I.

CLINICAL MANIFESTATIONS   Classic autoimmune hepatitis (type I): 80% women, third to fifth decades. Abrupt onset (acute hepatitis) in a third. Insidious onset in two-thirds: progressive jaundice, anorexia, hepatomegaly, abdominal pain, epistaxis, fever, fatigue, amenorrhea. Leads to cirrhosis; >50% 5-year mortality if untreated.

EXTRAHEPATIC MANIFESTATIONS   Rash, arthralgias, keratoconjunctivitis sicca, thyroiditis, hemolytic anemia, nephritis.

SEROLOGIC ABNORMALITIES   Hypergammaglobulinemia, smooth-muscle antibody (40–80%), ANA (20–50%), antimitochondrial antibody (10–20%), false-positive anti-HCV enzyme immunoassay but usually not recombinant immunoblot assay (RIBA). Type II: anti-LKM antibody.

℞ **TREATMENT**

Indicated for symptomatic disease with biopsy evidence of severe chronic hepatitis (bridging necrosis), marked aminotransferase elevations (5- to 10-fold), and hypergammaglobulinemia. Prednisone or prednisolone 30–60 mg PO qd tapered to 10–15 mg qd over several weeks; often azathioprine 50 mg PO qd is also administered to permit lower glucocorticoid doses and avoid steroid side effects. Monitor LFTs monthly. Symptoms may improve rapidly, but biochemical improvement may take weeks or months and subsequent histologic improvement (to lesion of mild chronic hepatitis or normal biopsy) up to 18–24 months. Withdrawal of glucocorticoids can be attempted following clinical, biochemical, and histologic remission; relapse occurs in 50–90% of cases (re-treat). For frequent relapses, consider maintenance therapy with low-dose glucocorticoids or azathioprine 2(mg/kg)/d.

Although hepatitis A rarely causes fulminant hepatic failure, it may do so more frequently in pts with chronic liver disease—especially those with chronic hepatitis B or C. The hepatitis A vaccine is immunogenic and well tolerated in pts with chronic hepatitis. Thus, pts with chronic liver disease, especially those with chronic hepatitis B or C, should be vaccinated against hepatitis A.

For a more detailed discussion, see **Dienstag JL, Isselbacher KJ: Chronic Hepatitis, Chap. 297, p. 1742, in HPIM-15.**

155

CIRRHOSIS AND ALCOHOLIC LIVER DISEASE

CIRRHOSIS

Chronic disease of the liver characterized by fibrosis, disorganization of the lobular and vascular architecture, and regenerating nodules of hepatocytes.

CAUSES　Alcohol, viral hepatitis (B, C, D), primary or secondary biliary cirrhosis, hemochromatosis, Wilson's disease, α_1 antitrypsin deficiency, autoimmune hepatitis, Budd-Chiari syndrome, chronic CHF (cardiac cirrhosis), drugs and toxins, schistosomiasis, cryptogenic.

CLINICAL MANIFESTATIONS　May be absent.

Symptoms　Anorexia, nausea, vomiting, diarrhea, fatigue, weakness, fever, jaundice, amenorrhea, impotence, infertility.

Signs　Spider telangiectases, palmar erythema, parotid and lacrimal gland enlargement, nail changes (Muehrcke lines, Terry's nails), clubbing, Dupuytren's contracture, gynecomastia, testicular atrophy, hepatosplenomegaly, ascites, gastrointestinal bleeding (e.g., varices), hepatic encephalopathy.

Laboratory Findings　Anemia (microcytic due to blood loss, macrocytic due to folate deficiency), pancytopenia (hypersplenism), prolonged PT, rarely overt DIC; hyponatremia, hypokalemic alkalosis, glucose disturbances, hypoalbuminemia, hypoxemia (hepatopulmonary syndrome).

Other Associations　Gastritis, duodenal ulcer, gallstones. Altered drug metabolism because of decreased drug clearance, metabolism (e.g., by cytochrome P450), and elimination; hypoalbuminemia; and portosystemic shunting.

DIAGNOSTIC STUDIES　Depend on clinical setting. Serum: HBsAg, anti-HBc, anti-HBs, anti-HCV, anti-HDV, Fe, total iron-binding capacity, ferritin, antimitochondrial antibody (AMA), smooth-muscle antibody (SMA), anti-KLM antibody, ANA, ceruloplasmin, α_1 antitrypsin (and pi typing); abdominal ultrasound with doppler study, CT or MRI (may show cirrhotic liver, splenomegaly, collaterals, venous thrombosis), portal venography, and wedged hepatic vein pressure measurement. Definitive diagnosis often depends on liver biopsy (percutaneous, transjugular, or open).

ALCOHOLIC LIVER DISEASE

Three forms: fatty liver, alcoholic hepatitis, cirrhosis; may coexist. History of excessive alcohol use often denied. Severe forms (hepatitis, cirrhosis) associated with ingestion of 80–160 g/d for >5–10 years; women more susceptible than men because of lower levels of gastric alcohol dehydrogenase; polymorphisms of alcohol dehydrogenase and acetaldehyde dehydrogenase genes may also affect susceptibility. Hepatitis B and C may be cofactors in the development of liver disease. Malnutrition may contribute to development of cirrhosis.

FATTY LIVER　May follow even brief periods of ethanol use. Often presents as asymptomatic hepatomegaly and mild elevations in biochemical liver tests. Reverses on withdrawal of ethanol; does not lead to cirrhosis.

ALCOHOLIC HEPATITIS　Clinical presentation ranges from asymptomatic to severe liver failure with jaundice, ascites, GI bleeding, and encephalopathy. Typically anorexia, nausea, vomiting, fever, jaundice, tender hepatomegaly. Occasional cholestatic picture mimicking biliary obstruction.

Aspartate aminotransferase (AST) usually <300 U and more than twofold higher than alanine aminotransferase (ALT). Bilirubin may be >170 μmol/L (>10 mg/dL). WBC may be as high as 20,000/μL. Diagnosis defined by liver biopsy findings: hepatocyte swelling, alcoholic hyaline (Mallory bodies), infiltration of PMNs, necrosis of hepatocytes, pericentral venular fibrosis.

Other Metabolic Consequences of Alcoholism   Increased NADH/NAD ratio leads to lacticacidemia, ketoacidosis, hyperuricemia, hypoglycemia. Hypomagnesemia, hypophosphatemia. Also mitochondrial dysfunction, induction of microsomal enzymes resulting in altered drug metabolism, lipid peroxidation leading to membrane damage, hypermetabolic state; many features of alcoholic hepatitis are attributable to toxic effects of acetaldehyde and cytokines (IL-1, IL-6, and TNF, released because of impaired detoxification of endotoxin).

Adverse Prognostic Factors   Short-term: PT > 5 s above control despite vitamin K, bilirubin > 170 μmmol/L (>10 mg/dL), encephalopathy, hypoalbuminemia, azotemia. Mortality is >35% if (pt's PT in seconds) − (control PT in seconds) $\times$ 4.6 + serum bilirubin (mg/dL) = > 32.

Long-term: severe hepatic necrosis and fibrosis, portal hypertension, continued alcohol consumption.

 TREATMENT

Abstinence is essential; 8500–12,500 kJ (2000–3000 kcal) diet with 1 g/kg protein (less if encephalopathy). Daily multivitamin, thiamine 100 mg, folic acid 1 mg. Correct potassium, magnesium, and phosphate deficiencies. Transfusions of packed red cells, plasma as necessary. Monitor glucose (hypoglycemia in severe liver disease). Prednisone 40 mg or prednisolone 32 mg PO qd $\times$ 1 month may be beneficial in severe alcoholic hepatitis with encephalopathy (in absence of GI bleeding, renal failure, infection). Colchicine 0.6 mg PO bid may slow progression of alcoholic liver disease. Experimental: amino acid infusions, propylthiouracil, insulin and glucagon, anabolic steroids. Liver transplantation in carefully selected pts who have been abstinent >6 months.

PRIMARY BILIARY CIRRHOSIS

Progressive nonsuppurative destructive intrahepatic cholangitis. Affects middle-aged women. Presents as asymptomatic elevation in alkaline phosphatase (better prognosis) or with pruritus, progressive jaundice, consequences of impaired bile excretion, and ultimately cirrhosis and liver failure.

CLINICAL MANIFESTATIONS   Pruritus, jaundice, xanthelasma, xanthomata, osteoporosis, steatorrhea, skin pigmentation, hepatosplenomegaly, portal hypertension; elevations in serum alkaline phosphatase, bilirubin, cholesterol, and IgM levels.

ASSOCIATED DISEASES   Sjögren's syndrome, collagen vascular diseases, thyroiditis, glomerulonephritis, pernicious anemia, renal tubular acidosis.

DIAGNOSIS   AMA in >90–95% (directed against the E_2 component of pyruvate dehydrogenase and other 2-oxo-acid dehydrogenase mitochondrial enzymes). Liver biopsy: stage 1—destruction of interlobular bile ducts, granulomas; stage 2—ductular proliferation; stage 3—fibrosis; stage 4—cirrhosis.

PROGNOSIS   Correlates with age, serum bilirubin, serum albumin, prothrombin time, edema.

℞ TREATMENT

Cholestyramine 4 g PO with meals for pruritus; in refractory cases consider rifampin, phototherapy with UVB light, naloxone infusion, plasmapheresis. Vitamin K 10 mg IM qd × 3 (then once a month) for elevated PT due to intestinal bile-salt deficiency. Vitamin D 100,000 U IM q 4 weeks plus oral calcium 1 g qd for osteoporosis (often unresponsive). Vitamin A 25,000—50,000 U PO qd or 100,000 U IM q 4 weeks and zinc 220 mg PO qd may help night blindness. Vitamin E 10 mg IM or PO qd. Substituting dietary fat with medium-chain triglycerides (MCTs) may reduce steatorrhea. Glucocorticoids, D-penicillamine, azathioprine, chlorambucil, cyclosporine of no value. Most widely used agent is ursodeoxycholic acid 10–15(mg/kg)/d PO in 2 divided doses—improves symptoms and LFTs and slows progression, delaying need for liver transplantation. Colchicine less effective, and methotrexate requires more study. Liver transplantation for end-stage disease.

LIVER TRANSPLANTATION

Consider for chronic, irreversible, progressive liver disease or fulminant hepatic failure when no alternative therapy is available. (Also indicated to correct certain congenital enzyme deficiencies and inborn errors of metabolism.)

CONTRAINDICATIONS *Absolute* Extrahepatobiliary sepsis or malignancy, severe cardiopulmonary disease, preexisting advanced cardiovascular or pulmonary disease, active alcoholism or drug abuse, AIDS.

Relative Age >70, HIV infection, extensive previous abdominal surgery, portal and superior mesenteric vein thrombosis, lack of pt understanding.

INDICATIONS Guidelines: expected death in 2 years; preferably in anticipation of major complication (variceal bleeding, irreversible encephalopathy, severe malnutrition and incapacitating weakness, hepatorenal syndrome); refractory ascites, progressive bone disease, severe pruritus, recurrent bacterial cholangitis, intractable coagulopathy; hepatopulmonary syndrome (intrapulmonary vascular dilatations with increased alveolar-arterial gradient), once considered a contraindication, may reverse with transplantation; bilirubin >170–340 μmol/L (>10–20 mg/dL), albumin <20 g/L (<2 g/dL), worsening coagulopathy; poor quality of life. In fulminant hepatic failure consider for grade III–IV coma (before cerebral edema develops).

SELECTION OF DONOR Matched for ABO blood group compatibility and liver size (reduced-size grafts may be used, esp. in children). Should be negative for HIV, HBV, and HCV.

IMMUNOSUPPRESSION Various combinations of tacrolimus or cyclosporine and glucocorticoids, mycophenolate mofetil, azathioprine, or OKT3 (monoclonal antithymocyte globulin).

MEDICAL COMPLICATIONS AFTER TRANSPLANTATION Liver graft dysfunction (primary nonfunction, acute or chronic rejection, ischemia, hepatic artery thrombosis, biliary obstruction or leak, recurrent hepatitis B or C); infections (bacterial, viral, fungal, opportunistic); renal dysfunction; neuropsychiatric disorders.

SUCCESS RATE 70–80% long-term survival; less for certain conditions (e.g., chronic hepatitis B, hepatocellular carcinoma).

For a more detailed discussion, see Chung RT, Podolsky DK: Cirrhosis and Its Complications, Chap. 299, p. 1754; Dienstag JL: Liver Transplantation, Chap. 301, p. 1770, in HPIM-15.

156

PORTAL HYPERTENSION

An increase in portal vein pressure due to anatomic or functional obstruction to blood flow in the portal venous system. Normal portal vein pressure is 5–10 mmHg. Indicators of portal hypertension are (1) intraoperative portal vein pressure of >30 cm saline, (2) intrasplenic pressure of >17 mmHg, (3) wedged hepatic vein pressure of >4 mmHg above IVC pressure.

CLASSIFICATION   See Table 156-1.

CONSEQUENCES   (1) Increased collateral circulation between high-pressure portal venous system and low-pressure systemic venous system: lower esophagus/upper stomach (varices, portal hypertensive gastropathy), rectum (varices, portal hypertensive colopathy), anterior abdominal wall (caput Medusae; flow away from umbilicus), parietal peritoneum, splenorenal; (2) increased lymphatic flow; (3) increased plasma volume; (4) ascites; (5) splenomegaly, possible hypersplenism; (6) portosystemic shunting (including hepatic encephalopathy).

ESOPHAGOGASTRIC VARICES

Bleeding is major life-threatening complication; risk correlates with variceal size above minimal portal venous pressure >12 mmHg and presence on varices

Table 156-1

Pathophysiologic Classification of Portal Hypertension

Site of obstruction	Pressure		Examples
	Portal	Corrected wedged hepatic vein[a]	
Presinu- soidal	↑	Normal	Splenic AV fistula, portal or splenic vein thrombosis, schistosomiasis
Sinusoidal	↑	↑	Cirrhosis, hepatitis
Postsinu- soidal	↑	↑ (May be un-measurable due to hepatic vein occlusion)	Budd-Chiari syndrome, veno-occlusive disease

[a] Wedged hepatic vein minus inferior vena cava pressure.

of "red wales." Mortality correlates with severity of underlying liver disease (hepatic reserve), e.g., Child-Turcotte classification (Table 156-2).

DIAGNOSIS *Esophagogastroscopy*: procedure of choice for acute bleeding. *Upper GI series*: tortuous, beaded filling defects in lower esophagus. *Celiac and mesenteric arteriography*: when massive bleeding prevents endoscopy and to evaluate portal vein patency (portal vein also may be studied by ultrasound with Doppler and MRI).

℞ TREATMENT

See Chap. 22 for general measures to treat GI bleeding.

Control of Acute Bleeding Choice of approach depends on clinical setting and availability.

1. Endoscopic band ligation or sclerotherapy—procedure of choice (not always suitable for gastric varices); band ligation is now preferred because of lower complication rate and possibly greater efficacy—application of bands around "pseudopolyp" of varix created by endoscopic suction; sclerotherapy involves direct injection of sclerosant into varix; >90% success rate in controlling acute bleeding; complications (less frequent with band ligation than sclerotherapy)—esophageal ulceration and stricture, fever, chest pain, mediastinitis, pleural effusions, aspiration.

2. Intravenous vasopressin up to 0.1–0.4 U/min until bleeding is controlled for 12–24 h (50–80% success rate, but no effect on mortality), then discontinue or taper (0.1 U/min q6–12h); add nitroglycerin up to 0.6 mg SL q 30 min, 40–400 μg/min IV, or by transdermal patch 10 mg/24 h to prevent coronary and renal vasoconstriction. Maintain systolic bp >90 mmHg. Octreotide 50–250 μg bolus + 50–250 μg/h IV infusion as effective as vasopressin with fewer serious complications.

3. Blakemore-Sengstaken balloon tamponade: can be inflated for up to 24–48 h; complications—obstruction of pharynx, asphyxiation, aspiration, esophageal ulceration. Due to risk of aspiration, endotracheal intubation should be performed prior to placing Blakemore-Sengstaken tube. Generally reserved for massive bleeding, failure of vasopressin and/or endoscopic therapy.

4. Transjugular intrahepatic portosystemic shunt (TIPS)—radiologic portacaval shunt, reserve for failure of other approaches; risk of hepatic encephalopathy (20–30%), shunt stenosis or occlusion (30–60%), infection.

Table 156-2

Classification of Cirrhosis According to Child and Turcotte

	Class		
	A	B	C
Serum bilirubin, μmol/L (mg/dL)	<34 (<2)	34–51 (2–3)	>51 (>3)
Serum albumin, g/L (g/dL)	>35 (>3.5)	30–35 (3.0–3.5)	<30 (<3.0)
Ascites	None	Easily controlled	Poorly controlled
Encephalopathy	None	Mild	Advanced
Nutrition	Excellent	Good	Poor
Prognosis	Good	Fair	Poor

Prevention of Recurrent Bleeding
1. Repeated endoscopic band ligation or sclerotherapy (e.g., q2–4 weeks) until obliteration of varices. Decreases but does not eliminate risk of recurrent bleeding; effect on overall survival uncertain but compares favorably to shunt surgery.
2. Propranolol or nadolol—nonselective beta blockers that act as portal venous antihypertensives; most effective in well-compensated cirrhotics; generally given in doses that reduce heart rate by 25%.
3. Splenectomy (for splenic vein thrombosis).
4. TIPS—regarded as useful "bridge to" liver transplantation in pt awaiting a donor liver who has failed on pharmacologic therapy.
5. Portosystemic shunt surgery: portacaval (total decompression) or distal splenorenal (Warren) (selective; contraindicated in ascites; ? lower incidence of hepatic encephalopathy). Alternative procedure—devascularization of lower esophagus and upper stomach (Sugiura). Surgery is now generally reserved for pts with compensated cirrhosis (Child's class A) who fail nonsurgical therapy (e.g., band ligation). Liver transplantation should be considered in appropriate candidates. (A previous portosystemic shunt does not preclude subsequent liver transplantation, though best to avoid portacaval shunts in transplant candidates.)

Prevention of Initial Bleed Recommended for pts at high risk of variceal bleeding—large varices, "red wales." Beta blockers appear to be more effective than sclerotherapy; role of band ligation uncertain.

PROGNOSIS (AND SURGICAL RISK) Correlated with Child and Turcotte classification (see Table 156-2).

HEPATIC ENCEPHALOPATHY

A state of disordered CNS function associated with severe acute or chronic liver disease; may be acute and reversible or chronic and progressive.

CLINICAL FEATURES *Stage 1*: euphoria or depression, mild confusion, slurred speech, disordered sleep, asterixis (flapping tremor). *Stage 2*: lethargy, moderate confusion. *Stage 3*: marked confusion, sleeping but arousable, inarticulate speech. *Stage 4*: coma; initially responsive to noxious stimuli, later unresponsive. Characteristic EEG abnormalities.

PATHOPHYSIOLOGY Failure of liver to detoxify agents noxious to CNS, i.e., ammonia, mercaptans, fatty acids, γ-aminobutyric acid (GABA), due to decreased hepatic function and portosystemic shunting. Ammonia may deplete brain of glutamate, an excitatory neurotransmitter, to form glutamine. False neurotransmitters also may enter CNS due to increased aromatic and decreased branched-chain amino acid levels in blood. Endogenous benzodiazepine agonists may play a role. Blood ammonia most readily measured marker, although may not always correlate with clinical status.

PRECIPITANTS GI bleeding (100 mL = 14–20 g of protein), azotemia, constipation, high-protein meal, hypokalemic alkalosis, CNS depressant drugs (e.g., benzodiazepines and barbiturates), hypoxia, hypercarbia, sepsis.

℞ TREATMENT

Remove precipitants; reduce blood ammonia by decreasing protein intake (20–30 g/d initially, then 60–80 g/d, vegetable sources); enemas/cathartics to clear gut. Lactulose (converts NH_3 to unabsorbed NH_4^+, produces diarrhea, alters bowel flora) 30–60 mL PO qh until diarrhea, then 15–30 mL tid-qid prn titrated to produce 3–4 loose stools/d. In coma, give as enema (300 mL in 700 mL H_2O). Lactilol, a second-generation disaccharide that is less sweet than lactulose and can be dispensed as a powder, is not yet available in U.S. In refractory cases, add neomycin 0.5–1 g PO bid, metronidazole 250 mg PO tid, or vancomycin 1 g PO bid. Unproven: IV branched-chain amino acids, levodopa, bromocriptine, keto-analogues of essential amino acids. Flumazenil, a short-acting benzodiazepine receptor antagonist, may have a role in management of hepatic encephalopathy precipitated by benzodiazepine use. Liver transplantation when otherwise indicated.

For a more detailed discussion, see Chung, RT, Podolsky DK: Cirrhosis and Its Complications, Chap. 299, p. 1754; in HPIM-15.

ALLERGY, CLINICAL IMMUNOLOGY, AND RHEUMATOLOGY

157

DISEASES OF IMMEDIATE TYPE HYPERSENSITIVITY

DEFINITION   These diseases result from IgE-dependent release of mediators from sensitized basophils and mast cells on contact with appropriate antigen (allergen). Associated disorders include anaphylaxis, allergic rhinitis, urticaria, asthma, and eczematous (atopic) dermatitis. Atopic allergy implies a familial tendency to the development of these disorders singly or in combination.

PATHOPHYSIOLOGY   IgE binds to surface of mast cells and basophils through a high-affinity receptor. Cross-linking of this IgE by antigen causes cellular activation with the subsequent release of preformed and newly synthesized mediators. These include histamine, prostaglandins, leukotrienes (including C4, D4, and E4, collectively known as *slow-reacting substance of anaphylaxis*—SRS-A), acid hydrolases, neutral proteases, proteoglycans, and cytokines (Fig. 310-2, p. 1914, HPIM-15). The mediators have been implicated in many pathophysiologic events associated with immediate type hypersensitivity, such as vasodilatation, increased vasopermeability, smooth-muscle contraction, and chemotactic attraction of neutrophils and other inflammatory cells. The clinical manifestations of each allergic reaction depend largely on the anatomic site(s) and time course of mediator release.

URTICARIA AND ANGIOEDEMA

DEFINITION   May occur together or separately. *Urticaria* involves superficial dermis and presents as circumscribed wheals with raised serpiginous borders and blanched centers; wheals may coalesce. *Angioedema* involves deeper layers of skin and may include subcutaneous tissue. These disorders may be classified as (1) IgE-dependent, including atopic, secondary to specific allergens, and physical stimuli, especially cold; (2) complement-mediated (including hereditary angioedema and hives related to serum sickness or vasculitis); (3) nonimmunologic due to direct mast cell–releasing agents or drugs that influence mediator release; and (4) idiopathic.

PATHOPHYSIOLOGY   Characterized by massive edema formation in the dermis (and subcutaneous tissue in angioedema). Presumably the edema is due to increased vasopermeability caused by mediator release from mast cells or other cell populations.

DIAGNOSIS   History, with special attention to possible offending exposures and/or ingestion as well as the duration of lesions. Vasculitic urticaria typically persists >72 h, whereas conventional urticaria often has a duration <48 h.

- Skin testing to food and/or inhalant antigens.
- Physical provocation, e.g., challenge with vibratory or cold stimuli
- Laboratory exam: complement levels, ESR (neither an elevated ESR nor hypocomplementemia is observed in IgE-mediated urticaria or angioedema);

C1-esterase inhibitor levels if history suggests hereditary angioedema; cryoglobulins, hepatitis B antigen, and antibody studies; autoantibody screen.
- Skin biopsy may be necessary.

DIFFERENTIAL DIAGNOSIS Atopic dermatitis, cutaneous mastocytosis (urticaria pigmentosa), systemic mastocytosis.

PREVENTION Identification and avoidance of offending agent(s), if possible.

 TREATMENT

- H_1 and H_2 antihistamines may be helpful: e.g., ranitidine 150 mg PO bid; diphenhydramine 25–50 mg PO qid; hydroxyzine 25–50 mg PO qid.
- Cyproheptadine 4 mg PO tid may be helpful.
- Sympathomimetic agents occasionally are useful.
- Topical glucocorticoids are of no value in the management of urticaria and/or angioedema. Because of their long-term toxicity, systemic glucocorticoids should not be used in the treatment of idiopathic, allergen-induced, or physical urticaria.

ALLERGIC RHINITIS
DEFINITION An inflammatory condition of the nose characterized by sneezing, rhinorrhea, and obstruction of nasal passages; may be associated with conjunctival and pharyngeal itching, lacrimation, and sinusitis. Seasonal allergic rhinitis is commonly caused by exposure to pollens, especially from grasses, trees, weeds, and molds. Perennial allergic rhinitis is frequently due to contact with house dust (containing dust mite antigens) and animal danders.

PATHOPHYSIOLOGY Impingement of pollens and other allergens on nasal mucosa of sensitized individuals results in IgE-dependent triggering of mast cells with subsequent release of mediators that cause development of mucosal hyperemia, swelling, and fluid transudation. Inflammation of nasal mucosal surface probably allows penetration of allergens deeper into tissue, where they contact perivenular mast cells. Obstruction of sinus ostia may result in development of secondary sinusitis, with or without bacterial infection.

DIAGNOSIS Accurate history of symptoms correlated with time of pollenation of plants in a given locale; special attention must be paid to other potentially sensitizing antigens such as pets.

- Physical examination: nasal mucosa may be boggy or erythematous; nasal polyps may be present; sinuses may demonstrate decreased transillumination; conjunctivae may be inflamed or edematous; manifestations of other allergic conditions (e.g., asthma, eczema) may be present.
- Skin tests to inhalant and/or food antigens.
- Nasal smear may reveal large numbers of eosinophils; presence of neutrophils may suggest infection.
- Total and specific serum IgE (as assessed by immunoassay) may be elevated.

DIFFERENTIAL DIAGNOSIS Vasomotor rhinitis, URI, irritant exposure, pregnancy with nasal mucosal edema, rhinitis medicamentosa, nonallergic rhinitis with eosinophilia, rhinitis due to use of β-adrenergic agents.

PREVENTION Identification and avoidance of offending antigen(s).

TREATMENT

- Antihistamines, e.g., sustained-release chlorpheniramine 12 mg PO bid, terfenadine 60 mg PO bid, astemizole 10 mg PO qd, loratidine 10 mg PO qd. *Note*: life-threatening cardiac arrhythmias have occurred due to inhibition of the metabolism of terfenadine or astemizole by concomitantly administered macrolide antibiotics (such as erythromycin and clarithromycin) or broad-spectrum antifungal agents such as ketoconazole or itraconazole. The use of either terfenadine or astemizole is contraindicated in combination with these drugs and in individuals with concomitant medical illnesses that impair hepatic function or predispose to cardiac arrhythmias.
- Oral sympathomimetics, e.g., pseudoephedrine 30–60 mg PO qid; may aggravate hypertension; combination antihistamine/decongestant preparations may balance side effects and provide improved pt convenience.
- Topical vasoconstrictors—should be used sparingly due to rebound congestion and chronic rhinitis associated with prolonged use.
- Topical nasal steroids, e.g., beclomethasone 2 sprays in each nostril bid–tid.
- Topical nasal cromolyn sodium 1–2 sprays in each nostril qid.
- Hyposensitization therapy if more conservative therapy is unsuccessful.

SYSTEMIC MASTOCYTOSIS

DEFINITION A systemic disorder characterized by mast cell hyperplasia; generally recognized in bone marrow, skin, GI mucosa, liver, and spleen. Classified as: (1) indolent, (2) associated with concomitant hematologic disorder, (3) aggressive, and (4) mastocytic leukemia.

PATHOPHYSIOLOGY AND CLINICAL MANIFESTATIONS The clinical manifestations of systemic mastocytosis are due to tissue occupancy by the mast cell mass, the tissue response to that mass (fibrosis), and the release of bioactive substances acting both locally (urticaria pigmentosa, crampy abdominal pain, gastritis, peptic ulcer) and at distal sites (headache, pruritus, flushing, vascular collapse). Clinical manifestations may be aggravated by alcohol, use of narcotics (e.g., codeine), ingestion of NSAIDs.

DIAGNOSIS May be made by measurement of urinary or blood levels of mast cell products including histamine, histamine metabolites, prostaglandin D_2 (PGD_2) metabolites, or mast cell tryptase, and tissue or bone marrow biopsy demonstrating increased mast cell density. Other studies including bone scan, skeletal survey, GI contrast studies may be helpful. Other flushing disorders (e.g., carcinoid syndrome, pheochromocytoma) should be excluded.

 TREATMENT

- H_1 and H_2 antihistamines.
- Proton pump inhibitor for gastric hypersecretion.
- Oral cromolyn sodium for diarrhea and abdominal pain.
- NSAIDs (in nonsensitive pts) may help by blocking PGD2 production.
- Systemic glucocorticoids may help but frequently are associated with complications.

For a more detailed discussion, see Austen KF: Allergies, Anaphylaxis, and Systemic Mastocytosis, Chap. 310, p. 1913, in HPIM-15.

158

PRIMARY IMMUNODEFICIENCY DISEASES

DEFINITION

Disorders involving the cell-mediated (T cell) or antibody-mediated (B cell) pathways of the immune system; some disorders may manifest abnormalities of both pathways. Pts are prone to development of recurrent infections and, in certain disorders, lymphoproliferative neoplasms. *Primary disorders* may be congenital or acquired; some are familial in nature. *Secondary disorders* are not caused by intrinsic abnormalities of immune cells but may be due to infection (such as in AIDS; see HPIM-15, Chap. 309), treatment with cytotoxic drugs, radiation therapy, or lymphoreticular malignancies. Pts with disorders of antibody formation are chiefly prone to infection with encapsulated bacterial pathogens (e.g., streptococci, *Haemophilus*, meningococcus), and *Giardia*. Individuals with T cell defects are generally susceptible to infections with viruses, fungi, and protozoa.

CLASSIFICATION

Severe Combined Immunodeficiency (SCID)

Congenital (autosomal recessive or X-linked); affected infants rarely survive beyond 1 year without treatment. Dysfunction of both cellular and humoral immunity.

1. *Swiss-type*: Autosomal recessive; severe lymphopenia involving B and T cells. Some cases due to mutations in the RAG-1 or RAG-2 genes; the combined activities of which are needed for V(D)J recombination of the T and B cell antigen receptors.

2. *Adenosine deaminase (ADA) deficiency*: Autosomal recessive; has been treated with gene therapy.

3. *X-linked SCID*: Characterized by an absence of peripheral T cells and natural killer (NK) cells. B lymphocytes are present in normal numbers but are functionally defective. These pts have a mutation in the gene that encodes the gamma chain common to the interleukin (IL) -2, -4, -7, -9, -15 receptors, thus disrupting the action of these important lymphokines. The same phenotype seen in X-linked SCID can be inherited as an autosomal recessive disease due to mutations in the JAK3 protein kinase gene. This enzyme associates with the common gamma chain of the receptors for IL-2, -4, -9, and -15 and is a key element in the signal transduction pathways used by these receptors.

 TREATMENT

Bone marrow transplantation is useful in some SCID pts.

T Cell Immunodeficiency

1. *DiGeorge's syndrome*: Maldevelopment of organs derived embryologically from third and fourth pharyngeal pouches (including thymus); associated with congenital cardiac defects, parathyroid hypoplasia with hypocalcemic tetany, abnormal facies, thymic aplasia; serum Ig levels may be normal, but specific antibody responses are impaired.

2. *T cell receptor (TCR) complex deficiency*: Immunodeficiencies due to inherited mutations of the CD3γ and CD3ε components of the TCR complex have been identified. CD3γ mutations result in a selective defect in CD8 T cells, whereas CD3ε mutations lead to a preferential reduction in CD4 T cells.

3. *MHC class II deficiency*: Antigen-presenting cells from pts with this rare disorder fail to express the class II molecules DP, DQ, and DR on their surface, which results in limited development of CD4+ T cells in the thymus and defective interaction of CD4 T cells and antigen-presenting cells in the periphery. Affected pts experience recurrent bronchopulmonary infections, chronic diarrhea, and severe viral infections.

4. *Inherited deficiency of purine nucleoside phosphorylase*: Functions in same salvage pathway as ADA; cellular dysfunction may be related to intracellular accumulation of purine metabolites.

5. *Ataxia-telangiectasia*: Autosomal recessive; cerebellar ataxia, oculocutaneous telangiectasia, immunodeficiency; not all pts have immunodeficiency; lymphomas common; IgG subclasses may be abnormal.

℞ TREATMENT

Treatment for T cell disorders is complex and largely investigational. Live vaccines and blood transfusions containing viable T cells should be assiduously avoided. Preventive therapy for *Pneumocystis carinii* pneumonia should be considered in selected pts with severe T cell deficiency.

Immunoglobulin Deficiency Syndromes

1. *X-linked agammaglobulinemia*: Due to a mutation in the Bruton's tyrosine kinase (Btk) gene. Marked deficiency of circulating B lymphocytes; all Ig classes low; recurrent sinopulmonary infections and chronic enteroviral encephalitis, including vaccine-acquired poliomyelitis infection, are common complications.

2. *Transient hypogammaglobulinemia of infancy*: This occurs between 3 and 6 months of age as maternally derived IgG levels decline.

3. *Isolated IgA deficiency*: Most common immunodeficiency; the majority of affected individuals do not have increased infections; antibodies against IgA may lead to anaphylaxis during transfusion of blood or plasma; may be associated with deficiencies of IgG subclasses; often familial.

4. *IgG subclass deficiencies*: Total serum IgG may be normal, yet some individuals may be prone to recurrent sinopulmonary infections due to selective deficiencies of certain IgG subclasses.

5. *Common variable immunodeficiency*: Heterogeneous group of syndromes characterized by panhypogammaglobulinemia, deficiency of IgG and IgA, or selective IgG deficiency and recurrent sinopulmonary infections; associated conditions include chronic giardiasis, intestinal malabsorption, atrophic gastritis with pernicious anemia, benign lymphoid hyperplasia, lymphoreticular neoplasms, arthritis, and autoimmune diseases.

6. *X-linked immunodeficiency with increased IgM*: In most pts this syndrome results from genetic mutation in the gene encoding CD40 ligand, a transmembrane protein expressed by activated T cells and necessary for normal T and B cell cooperation, germinal center formation, and immunoglobulin isotype switching. Pts exhibit normal or increased serum IgM with low or absent IgG and IgA and recurrent sinopulmonary infections; pts also exhibit T lymphocyte abnormalities with increased susceptibility to infection with opportunistic pathogens (*P. carinii, Cryptosporidium*). Associated conditions include neutropenia and hepatobiliary tract disease.

℞ TREATMENT

Intravenous immunoglobulin administration (only for pts who have recurrent bacterial infections and are deficient in IgG):

Table 158-1

Laboratory Work-Up for Primary Immunodeficiency

INITIAL SCREENING ASSAYS[a]

Complete blood count with differential smear.
Serum immunoglobulin levels: IgM, IgG, IgA, IgD, IgE

OTHER READILY AVAILABLE ASSAYS

Quantification of blood mononuclear cell populations by immunofluorescence
assays employing monoclonal antibody markers[b]
  T cells: CD3, CD4, CD8, TCRα/β, TCRγ/δ
  B cells: CD19, CD20, CD21, Ig(μ, δ, γ, α, κ, λ), Ig-associated molecules
            (α, β)
  NK cells: CD16/CD56
  Monocytes: CD15
  Activation markers: HLA-DR, CD25, CD80 (B cells)
T cell functional evaluation
  1. Delayed hypersensitivity skin tests (PPD, *Candida, histoplasmin*, teta-
     nus toxoid)
  2. Proliferative response to mitogens (anti-CD3 antibody, phytohemagglu-
     tinin, concanavalin A) and allogeneic cells (mixed lymphocyte re-
     sponse)
  3. Cytokine production
B cell functional evaluation
  1. Natural or commonly acquired antibodies: isohemagglutinins; antibodies
     to common viruses (influenza, rubella, rubeola) and bacterial toxins
     (diphtheria, tetanus)
  2. Response to immunization with protein (tetanus toxoid) and carbohy-
     drate (pneumococcal vaccine) antigens
  3. Quantitative IgG subclass determinations
Complement
  1. CH50 assays (classic and alternative pathways)
  2. C3, C4, and other components
Phagocyte function
  1. Reduction of nitroblue tetrazolium
  2. Chemotaxis assays
  3. Bactericidal activity

[a] Together with a history and physical examination, these tests will identify more than 95 percent
   of pts with primary immunodeficiencies.
[b] The menu of monoclonal antibody markers may be expanded or contracted to focus on particular clinical questions.

- Starting dose 200–400 mg/kg given every 3–4 weeks
- Adjust dose to keep trough IgG level > 500 mg/dL
- Usually done in outpatient setting
- Decision to treat based on severity of clinical symptoms and response to
  antigenic challenge

MISCELLANEOUS IMMUNODEFICIENCY SYNDROMES

- Mucocutaneous candidiasis
- X-linked lymphoproliferative syndrome
- Immunodeficiency with thymoma
- Wiskott-Aldrich syndrome

- Hyper-IgE syndrome
- Metabolic abnormalities associated with immunodeficiency

For a more detailed discussion, see Cooper MD, Schroeder HW Jr: Primary Immune Deficiency Diseases, Chap. 308, p. 1843, in HPIM-15.

159

SLE, RA, AND OTHER CONNECTIVE TISSUE DISEASES

CONNECTIVE TISSUE DISEASE

DEFINITION   Heterogeneous disorders that share certain common features, including inflammation of skin, joints, and other structures rich in connective tissue, as well as altered patterns of immunoregulation, including production of autoantibodies and abnormalities of cell-mediated immunity. While certain distinct clinical entities may be defined, manifestations may vary considerably from one pt to the next, and overlap of clinical features between and among specific diseases is common.

SYSTEMIC LUPUS ERYTHEMATOSUS (SLE)

DEFINITION AND PATHOGENESIS   Disease of unknown etiology in which tissues and cells are damaged by deposition of pathogenic autoantibodies and immune complexes. Genetic, environmental, and sex hormonal factors are likely of pathogenic importance. T and B cell hyperactivity, production of autoantibodies with specificity for nuclear antigenic determinants, and abnormalities of T cell function occur.

CLINICAL MANIFESTATIONS   90% of cases are women, usually of child-bearing age; more common in blacks than whites. Course of disease is often one of periods of exacerbation and relative quiescence. May involve virtually any organ system and have a wide range of disease severity. Common features include:

- *Constitutional*—fatigue, fever, malaise, weight loss
- *Cutaneous*—rashes (especially malar "butterfly" rash), photosensitivity, vasculitis, alopecia, oral ulcers
- *Arthritis*—inflammatory, symmetric, nonerosive
- *Hematologic*—anemia (may be hemolytic), neutropenia, thrombocytopenia, lymphadenopathy, splenomegaly, venous or arterial thrombosis
- *Cardiopulmonary*—pleuritis, pericarditis, myocarditis, endocarditis
- *Nephritis*
- *GI*—peritonitis, vasculitis
- *Neurologic*—organic brain syndromes, seizures, psychosis, cerebritis

Drug-Induced Lupus A clinical and immunologic picture similar to spontaneous SLE may be induced by drugs; in particular: procainamide, hydralazine, isoniazid, chlorpromazine, methyldopa. Features are predominantly constitutional, joint, and pleuropericardial; CNS and renal disease are rare. All pts have antinuclear antibodies (ANA); antihistone antibodies may be present, but antibodies to dsDNA and hypocomplementemia are uncommon. Most pts improve following withdrawal of offending drug.

EVALUATION

- Hx and physical exam
- Presence of ANA is a cardinal feature, but a (+) ANA is not specific for SLE. Laboratory assessment should include: CBC, ESR, ANA and subtypes (antibodies to dsDNA, ssDNA, Sm, Ro, La, histone), complement levels (C3, C4, CH50), serum immunoglobulins, VDRL, PT, PTT, anticardiolipin antibody, lupus anticoagulant, UA.
- Appropriate radiographic studies
- ECG
- Consideration of renal biopsy if evidence of glomerulonephritis

DIAGNOSIS Made in the presence of four or more published criteria (Table 311-3, p. 1925, in HPIM-15).

℞ TREATMENT

Choice of therapy is based on type and severity of disease manifestations (Fig. 159-1). Goals are to control acute, severe flares and to develop maintenance strategies where symptoms are suppressed to an acceptable level. The toxicity of therapy must always be considered. Useful agents include:

- *NSAIDs* (e.g., ibuprofen 400–800 mg tid–qid).
- *Antimalarials*(hydroxychloroquine 400 mg/d)—may improve constitutional, cutaneous, articular manifestations. Ophthalmologic evaluation required before and during Rx to rule out ocular toxicity.
- *Systemic glucocorticoids*—may be necessary for life-threatening or severely disabling manifestations.
- *Cytotoxic agents*—beneficial in active glomerulonephritis; may be required for severe disease not successfully controlled by acceptable doses of steroids.

    1. Cyclophosphamide—most effective and most toxic; administered as IV pulse 10–15 mg/kg every 4 weeks. Daily oral dosing 1.5–2.5 (mg/kg)/d can also be used but has a greater risk of urinary bladder toxicity.
    2. Azathioprine 2–3 (mg/kg)/d—indicated in pts who cannot take cyclophosphamide.
    3. Mycophenolate mofetil 1000 mg bid—may be considered in selected pts.

- *Anticoagulation* may be indicated in pts with thrombotic complications.

RHEUMATOID ARTHRITIS (RA)

DEFINITION AND PATHOGENESIS A chronic multisystem disease of unknown etiology characterized by persistent inflammatory synovitis, usually involving peripheral joints in a symmetric fashion. Although cartilaginous destruction, bony erosions, and joint deformity are hallmarks, the course of RA can be variable. An association with HLA-DR4 has been noted; both genetic and environmental factors may play a role in initiating disease. The propagation

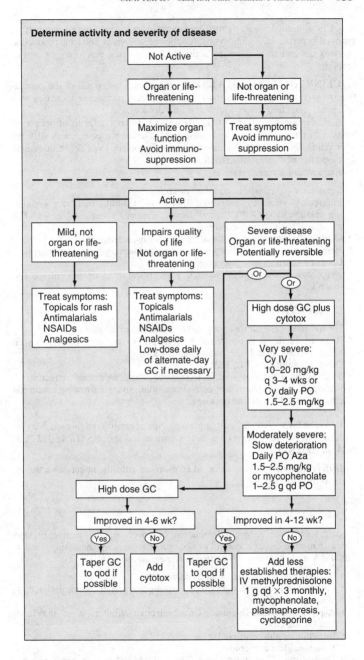

FIGURE 159-1   Algorithm for the treatment of SLE, GC, glucocorticoids; high-dose GC, methylprednisolone 1000 mg, IV, qd × 3, then 1 to 2 mg/kg prednisone per day orally, cytotox, cytotoxic drugs such as cyclophosphamide (Cy) and azathioprine (Aza); qod, alternate day therapy.

of RA is an immunologically mediated event in which joint injury occurs from synovial hyperplasia, lymphocytic infiltration of synovium, and local production of cytokines and chemokines by activated lymphocytes, macrophages, and fibroblasts.

CLINICAL MANIFESTATIONS RA occurs in ~0.8% of the population; women affected 3 times more often than men; prevalence increases with age, onset most frequent in fourth and fifth decades.

Articular manifestations—typically a symmetric polyarthritis of peripheral joints with pain, tenderness, and swelling of affected joints; morning stiffness is common; PIP and MCP joints frequently involved; joint deformities may develop after persistent inflammation.

Extraarticular manifestations:

- Cutaneous—rheumatoid nodules, vasculitis
- Pulmonary—nodules, interstitial disease, bronchiolitis obliterans-organizing pneumonia (BOOP), pleural disease, Caplan's syndrome [sero(+) RA associated with pneumoconiosis]
- Ocular—keratoconjunctivitis sicca, episcleritis, scleritis
- Hematologic—anemia, Felty's syndrome (splenomegaly and neutropenia)
- Cardiac—pericarditis, myocarditis
- Neurologic—myelopathies secondary to cervical spine disease, entrapment, vasculitis.

EVALUATION

- Hx and physical exam with careful examination of all joints.
- Rheumatoid factor is present in 85% of pts; its presence correlates with severe disease, nodules, extraarticular features.
- Other laboratories: CBC, ESR.
- Synovial fluid analysis—useful to rule out crystalline disease, infection.
- Radiographs—juxtaarticular osteopenia, joint space narrowing, marginal erosions. CXR should be obtained.

DIAGNOSIS Not difficult in pts with typical established disease. May be confusing early. New criteria are more sensitive and specific (Table 312-1, p. 1934, in HPIM-15).

Differential Diagnosis Gout, SLE, psoriatic arthritis, infectious arthritis, osteoarthritis, sarcoid.

R̲x̲ **TREATMENT**

Goals: lessen pain, reduce inflammation, improve/maintain function, prevent long-term joint damage, control of systemic involvement. Increasing trend to treat RA more aggressively earlier in disease course (Fig. 159-2).

- Pt education on disease, joint protection
- Physical and occupational therapy—strengthen periarticular muscles, consider assistive devices.
- Aspirin or NSAIDs (including Cox-2 selective inhibitors, which may have less GI toxicity).
- Intrarticular glucocorticoids.
- Systemic glucocorticoids.
- Disease-modifying antirheumatic drugs (DMARDs)—e.g., methotrexate; oral or IM gold salts; hydroxychloroquine; sulfasalazine; D-penicillamine. Each agent has individual toxicities—pt education and monitoring required. Have been used in combination but with increased toxicity.

- TNF-α neutralizing agents—consider in pts with moderate to severely active RA or DMARD-unresponsive disease.
- Immunosuppressive therapy—e.g., azathioprine, leflunomide, cyclosporine, and cyclophosphamide. Generally reserved for pts who have failed DMARDs.
- Surgery—may be considered for severe functional impairment due to deformity.

SYSTEMIC SCLEROSIS (SCLERODERMA, SSC)

DEFINITION AND PATHOGENESIS   Multisystem disorder characterized by inflammatory, vascular, and fibrotic changes of skin and various internal organ systems (chiefly GI tract, lungs, heart, and kidney). Pathogenesis unclear; involves immunologic mechanisms leading to vascular endothelial damage and activation of fibroblasts.

CLINICAL MANIFESTATIONS

- Cutaneous—edema followed by fibrosis of the skin (chiefly extremities, face, trunk); telangiectasis; calcinosis; Raynaud's phenomenon
- Arthralgias and/or arthritis
- GI—esophageal hypomotility; intestinal hypofunction
- Pulmonary—fibrosis, pulmonary hypertension, alveolitis.
- Cardiac—pericarditis, cardiomyopathy, conduction abnormalities
- Renal—hypertension; renal crisis/failure (leading cause of death).

Two main subsets can be identified:

1.   *Diffuse cutaneous scleroderma*—rapid development of symmetric skin thickening of proximal and distal extremity, face, and trunk. At high risk for development of visceral disease early in course.

2.   *Limited cutaneous scleroderma* or *CREST syndrome* (*c*alcinosis, *R*aynaud's, *e*sophageal dysmotility, *s*clerodactyly, *t*elangiectasias)—skin involvement limited to face and extremity distal to elbows; associated with better prognosis.

EVALUATION

- Hx and physical exam with particular attention to blood pressure (heralding feature of renal disease).
- Laboratories: ESR, ANA (anticentromere pattern associated with CREST), specific antibodies may include antitopoisomerase I (Scl-70), UA
- Radiographs: CXR, barium swallow if indicated, hand x-rays may show distal tuft resorption and calcinosis.
- Additional studies: ECG, consider skin biopsy.

℞ TREATMENT

- Education regarding warm clothing, smoking cessation, antireflux measures
- Calcium channel blockers (e.g., nifedipine) useful for Raynaud's phenomenon
- ACE inhibitors (e.g., captopril)—particularly important for controlling hypertension and limiting progression of renal disease.
- Antacids, H2 antagonists, omeprazole, and metoclopramide may be useful for esophageal reflux.
- D-Penicillamine—controversial benefit to reduce skin thickening and prevent organ involvement; no advantages to using doses >125 mg every other day.

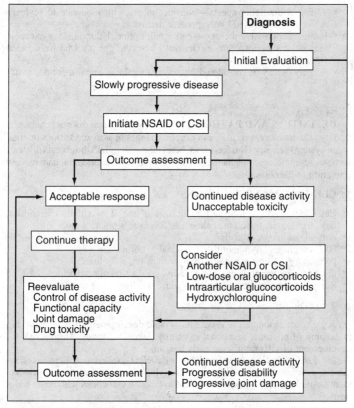

FIGURE 159-2 Algorithm for the medical management of rheumatoid arthritis. CSI, Cox-2 selective inhibitors; DMARD, disease-modifying antirheumatic drug; TNF-α, tumor necrosis factor α.

- Glucocorticoids—no efficacy in slowing progression of SSc; indicated for inflammatory myositis or pericarditis; high doses early in disease may be associated with development of renal crisis.
- Cyclophosphamide—improves lung function outcomes and survival in pts with alveolitis.
- Epoprostenol—may improve cardiopulmonary hemodynamics in pts with pulmonary hypertension.

MIXED CONNECTIVE TISSUE DISEASE (MCTD)

DEFINITION Syndrome characterized by a combination of clinical features similar to those of SLE, SSc, polymyositis, and RA; unusually high titers of circulating antibodies to a nuclear ribonucleoprotein (RNP) are found.

CLINICAL MANIFESTATIONS Raynaud's phenomenon, polyarthritis, swollen hands or sclerodactyly, esophageal dysfunction, pulmonary fibrosis, inflammatory myopathy. Renal involvement occurs in about 25%. Laboratory abnormalities include high-titer ANAs, very high titers of antibody to RNP, positive rheumatoid factor in 50% of pts.

EVALUATION Similar to that for SLE and SSc.

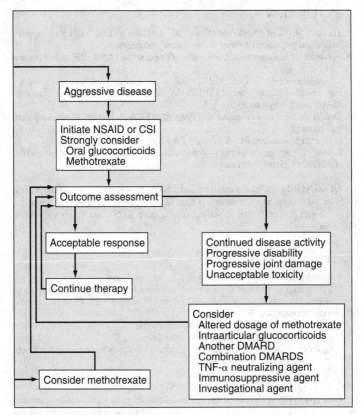

FIGURE 159-2

℞ TREATMENT

Little published data. Treat based upon manifestations with similar approach to that used if feature occurred in SLE/SSc/polymyositis/RA.

SJÖGREN'S SYNDROME

DEFINITION An immunologic disorder characterized by progressive lymphocytic destruction of exocrine glands most frequently resulting in symptomatic eye and mouth dryness; can be associated with extraglandular manifestations; predominantly affects middle-age females; may be primary or secondary when it occurs in association with other autoimmune diseases.

CLINICAL MANIFESTATIONS

- *Constitutional*—fatigue
- *Sicca symptoms*—keratoconjunctivitis sicca (KCS) and xerostomia
- *Dryness of other surfaces*—nose, vagina, trachea, skin
- *Extraglandular features*—arthralgia/arthritis, Raynaud's, lymphadenopathy, interstitial pneumonitis, vasculitis (usually cutaneous), nephritis, lymphoma.

EVALUATION

- Hx and physical exam—with special attention to oral, ocular, lymphatic exam and presence of other autoimmune disorders.
- Presence of autoantibodies is a hallmark of disease (ANA, RF, anti-Ro, anti-La)
- Other laboratories—ESR, CBC, renal, liver, and thyroid function tests, serum protein electrophoresis (SPEP) (hypergammaglobulinemia or monoclonal gammopathy common), UA.
- Ocular studies—to diagnose and quantitate KCS; Schirmer's test, Rose bengal staining.
- Oral exam—unstimulated salivary flow, dental exam.
- Labial salivary gland biopsy—demonstrates lymphocytic infiltration and destruction of glandular tissue.

DIAGNOSIS Criteria often include: KCS, xerostomia, (+) serologic features of autoimmunity. Positive lip biopsy considered necessary in some series—should be performed in setting of objective KCS/xerostomia with negative serologies.

 TREATMENT

- Regular follow-up with dentist and ophthalmologist.
- Symptomatic relief of dryness with artificial tears, ophthalmic lubricating ointments, nasal saline sprays, frequent sips of water, sugarless candy, moisturizing skin lotions.
- Pilocarpine—may help sicca manifestations.
- Hydroxychloroquine—may help arthralgias.
- Glucocorticoids—not effective for sicca Sx but may have role in treatment of extraglandular manifestations.

POLYMYOSITIS/DERMATOMYOSITIS

DEFINITION *Polymyositis* is a condition of presumed autoimmune etiology in which the skeletal muscle is damaged by an inflammatory process dominated by lymphocytic infiltration. *Dermatomyositis* is characterized by skin changes accompanying or preceding muscle weakness and inflammatory myopathy.

CLASSIFICATION

- *Group I: Primary idiopathic polymyositis*—female:male 2:1.
- *Group II: Primary idiopathic dermatomyositis*—skin changes may precede or follow muscle changes.
- *Group III: Dermatomyositis (or polymyositis) associated with neoplasia*—malignancy may precede or follow onset of myositis by up to 2 years; commonly associated malignancies: lung, ovary, breast, GI tract, myeloproliferative disorders.
- *Group IV: Childhood dermatomyositis (or polymyositis) associated with vasculitis*—vasculitis may involve skin and visceral organs.
- *Group V: Polymyositis (or dermatomyositis) associated with collagen-vascular disease*—RA, scleroderma, SLE, MCTD most frequently associated.

CLINICAL MANIFESTATIONS *Symptoms*

- Proximal muscle weakness—difficulty climbing stairs, combing hair, arising from chair
- Weakness of neck flexors—unable to raise head from pillow
- Muscle pain or tenderness

- Dysphagia—25% at presentation
- Dyspnea—respiratory impairment in 5%, interstitial lung disease in 10%
- Cardiac disturbances—conduction defects, tachyarrhythmias, cardiomyopathy.
- Systemic symptoms—fever, malaise, weight loss, arthralgias, Raynaud's phenomenon.

Physical Examination

- Muscle weakness proximal > distal
- Skin lesions: localized or diffuse erythema, maculopapular eruption, scaling eczematoid dermatitis, exfoliative dermatitis, classic lilac-colored (heliotrope) rash on eyelids, nose, cheeks, forehead, trunk, extremities, nailbeds, knuckles (Gottron rash)
- Subcutaneous calcification—see especially in childhood disease
- Complete evaluation is important to look for features suggestive of neoplasm or other connective tissue diseases.

EVALUATION

- CPK, aldolase, SGOT, SGPT, LDH usually elevated.
- In setting of very high CPK, check urine myoglobin and renal function.
- Autoantibodies—anti-Jo-1 seen in 50% of pts with polymyositis and 15% with dermatomyositis, other antibodies may be seen in association with other connective tissue diseases.
- ECG abnormal in 5–10% cases at presentation.
- EMG—abnormal in 40% of cases; short-duration, low-amplitude polyphasic units on voluntary activation and increased spontaneous activity with fibrillations, complex repetitive discharges, and positive sharp waves.
- MRI—may identify sites of muscle involvement and guide biopsy location.
- Skeletal muscle pathology—patchy process; inflammatory cells, destruction of muscle fibers with a phagocytic reaction, and perivascular inflammatory cell infiltration. The presence of perifascicular atrophy is diagnostic of dermatomyositis.
- Search for underlying malignancies—extent of search for occult neoplasm in dermatomyositis depends on the clinical circumstances. Tumors usually uncovered by abnormal history and exam and not through extensive blind searches. When malignancy is not apparent, consider complete annual physical exam with pelvic, breast, and rectal examination, urinalysis, CBC, blood chemistries, and CXR.

DIAGNOSIS Diagnosis strongly suggested by presence of muscle weakness, elevation of CK, abnormal EMG. Pts with dermatomyositis who have skin rash may not require muscle biopsy. In polymyositis, biopsy usually needed to make a firm diagnosis and rule out other myopathies.

DIFFERENTIAL DIAGNOSIS Metabolic myopathies, infectious myositis, toxic or drug-induced myopathies, neuromuscular disorders, endocrine and electrolyte disorders, myositis associated with sarcoidosis, polymyalgia rheumatica, eosinophilia myalgia syndrome.

Inclusion Body Myositis The most common inflammatory myopathy in pts ≥50. Weakness and atrophy occur in distal muscles. Characteristic appearance on muscle biopsy. Resistant to immunosuppressive therapies.

 TREATMENT

Goal is to improve muscle strength improving function in activities of daily living. When strength improves, CK falls but the reverse is not always true.

Therapy should be directed to improving muscle strength, not solely on lowering CK level.

- Prednisone 1–2 (mg/kg)/day, tapered after strength improves and CK declines. The onset of steroid-induced myopathy may complicate therapy.
- Cytotoxic agents: should be considered for severe disease, inadequate response to steroids, relapsing disease, steroid-induced complications. Methotrexate 7.5–15 mg/week, azathioprine 2.5–3.5(mg/kg)/day, mycophenolate mofetil, cyclophosphamide 1–2(mg/kg)/d reported to be beneficial but have significant side effects.
- Intravenous immunoglobulin—may bring about short-lived improvement in some pts.
- Physical therapy

For a more detailed discussion, see Hahn BH: Systemic Lupus Erythematosus, Chap. 311, p. 1922; Lipsky PE: Rheumatoid Arthritis, Chap. 312, p. 1928; Gilliland BC: Systemic Sclerosis (Scleroderma), Chap. 313, p. 1937; Moutsopoulos HM: Sjögren's Syndrome, Chap. 314, p. 1947; Dalakas MC Jr: Polymyositis, Dermatomyositis, and Inclusion Body Myositis, Chap. 382, p. 2524, in HPIM-15.

160

VASCULITIS

Definition and Pathogenesis

A clinicopathologic process characterized by inflammation of and damage to blood vessels, compromise of vessel lumen, and resulting ischemia. Clinical manifestations depend on size and location of affected vessel. Most vasculitic syndromes appear to be mediated in whole or in part by immune mechanisms. May be primary or sole manifestation of a disease or secondary to another disease process. Unique vasculitic syndromes can be identified that can differ greatly with regards to clinical features, disease severity, histology, and treatment.

Classification

CLASSIC POLYARTERITIS NODOSA (PAN) Medium-sized muscular arteries involved; frequently associated with arteriographic aneurysms; commonly affects renal arteries, liver, GI tract, peripheral nerves, skin, heart; can be associated with hepatitis B.

MICROSCOPIC POLYANGIITIS Small-vessel vasculitis that can affect the glomerulus and lungs; medium-sized vessels may also be affected.

WEGENER'S GRANULOMATOSIS Granulomatous vasculitis of upper and lower respiratory tracts together with glomerulonephritis; upper airway lesions affecting the nose and sinuses can cause purulent or bloody nasal discharge, mucosal ulceration, septal perforation, and cartilaginous destruction (saddlenose deformity). Lung involvement may be asymptomatic or cause cough, hemoptysis, dyspnea; eye involvement may occur; renal involvement accounts for most deaths.

ALLERGIC ANGIITIS AND GRANULOMATOSIS (CHURG-STRAUSS DISEASE)   Granulomatous vasculitis of multiple organ systems, particularly the lung; characterized by asthma, peripheral eosinophilia, eosinophilic tissue infiltration; glomerulonephritis can occur.

POLYANGIITIS OVERLAP SYNDROME   Primary systemic vasculitis that does not precisely fit into a single diagnostic category.

GIANT CELL (OR TEMPORAL) ARTERITIS   Inflammation of medium- and large-sized arteries; primarily involves temporal artery but systemic involvement may occur; symptoms include headache, jaw/tongue claudication, scalp tenderness, fever, musculoskeletal symptoms (polymyalgia rheumatica); sudden blindness from involvement of optic vessels is a dreaded complication.

TAKAYASU'S ARTERITIS   Vasculitis of the large arteries with strong predilection for aortic arch and its branches; most common in young women; presents with inflammatory or ischemic symptoms in arms and neck, systemic inflammatory symptoms, aortic regurgitation.

HENOCH-SCHÖNLEIN PURPURA   Characterized by involvement of skin, GI tract, kidneys; more common in children; may recur after initial remission.

PREDOMINANTLY CUTANEOUS VASCULITIS (HYPERSENSITIVITY VASCULITIS)   Heterogeneous group of disorders; common feature is small-vessel involvement; skin disease usually predominates.

Exogenous Stimuli Proved or Suspected

* Serum sickness and serum sickness–like reactions
* Drug-induced vasculitis
* Vasculitis associated with infectious diseases

Endogenous Antigens Likely Involved

* Vasculitis associated with neoplasms
* Vasculitis associated with connective tissue disorders
* Vasculitis associated with other underlying diseases
* Vasculitis associated with congenital deficiencies of complement system.

MISCELLANEOUS VASCULITIC SYNDROMES

* Mucocutaneous lymph node syndrome (Kawasaki disease)
* Isolated vasculitis of the central nervous system
* Thromboangiitis obliterans (Buerger's disease)
* Behçet's syndrome
* Cogan's syndrome
* Erythema elevatum diutinum

Evaluation   (See Fig. 160-1)

* Thorough Hx and physical exam—special reference to ischemic manifestations and systemic inflammatory signs/symptoms.
* Laboratories—important in assessing organ involvement: CBC with differential, ESR, renal function tests, UA. Should also be obtained to rule out

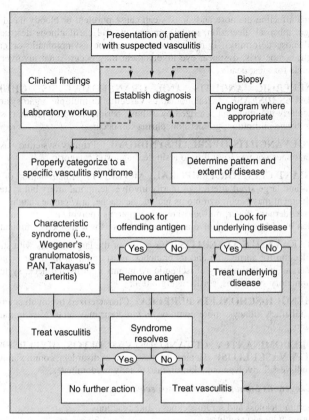

FIGURE 160-1 Algorithm for the approach to a pt with suspected diagnosis of vasculitis.

other diseases: ANA, rheumatoid factor, anti-GBM, hepatitis B/C serologies, HIV.
- Antineutrophil cytoplasmic autoantibodies (ANCA)—cytoplasmic pattern associated with Wegener's granulomatosis; presence of ANCA is adjunctive and should not be used in place of biopsy as a means of diagnosis.
- Radiographs—CXR should be performed even in the absence of symptoms.
- Diagnosis—can only be made by arteriogram or biopsy of affected organ(s).

Differential Diagnosis

Guided by organ manifestations. In many instances includes infections and neoplasms, which must be ruled out prior to beginning immunosuppressive therapy.

℞ TREATMENT

Therapy is based on the specific vasculitic syndrome and its manifestations. Immunosuppressive therapy should be avoided in disease that rarely results in irreversible organ system dysfunction or that usually does not respond to such agents (e.g., predominantly cutaneous vasculitis). Glucocorticoids alone may control temporal arteritis and Takayasu's arteritis. Cytotoxic agents are particularly important in syndromes with life-threatening organ system involvement, especially active glomerulonephritis. Frequently used agents:

- Prednisone 1 (mg/kg)/d initially, then tapered; convert to alternate-day regimen and discontinue.
- Cyclophosphamide 2 (mg/kg)/d, adjusted to avoid severe leukopenia. Morning administration with a large amount of fluid is important in minimizing bladder toxicity. Pulsed intravenous cyclophosphamide (1 g/m² per month) is less effective but may be considered in selected pts who cannot tolerate daily dosing.
- Methotrexate in weekly doses up to 25 mg/week may be used to induce remission in Wegener's granulomatosis pts who do not have immediately life-threatening disease or cannot tolerate cyclophosphamide. It may also be considered for maintaining remission after induction with cyclophosphamide.
- Azathioprine 2 (mg/kg)/d. Less effective in treating active disease but may be useful in maintaining remission in pts who become cyclophosphamide intolerant.
- Plasmapheresis may have an adjunctive role in management if manifestations not controlled by above measures.

For a more detailed discussion, see Fauci AS: The Vasculitis Syndromes, Chap. 317, p. 1956, in HPIM-15.

161

ANKYLOSING SPONDYLITIS

Definition

Chronic and progressive inflammatory disease of the axial skeleton with sacroiliitis (usually bilateral) as its hallmark. Involvement of limb joints other than hips and shoulders is uncommon. Most frequently presents in young men in second or third decade; strong association with histocompatibility antigen HLA-B27. In Europe, also known as Marie-Strumpell or Bechterew's disease.

Clinical Manifestations

- Back pain and stiffness—not relieved by lying down, often present at night forcing pt to leave bed, worse in the morning, improves with activity, insidious onset, duration >3 months (often called symptoms of "inflammatory" back pain).
- Peripheral joint pain (especially hip).
- Chest pain from involvement of thoracic skeleton and muscular insertions.
- Extra/juxtaarticular pain—due to "enthesitis": inflammation at insertion of tendons and ligaments into bone; frequently affects greater trochanter, iliac crests, ischial tuberosities, tibial tubercles, heels.

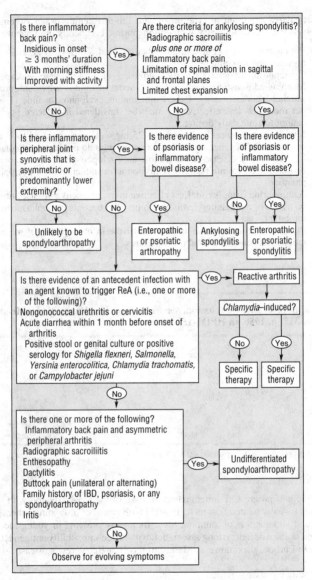

FIGURE 161-1 Algorithm for diagnosis of the spondyloarthropathies.

- Extraarticular findings include acute anterior uveitis in about 20% of pts, aortitis, aortic insufficiency, GI inflammation, cardiac conduction defects, amyloidosis, bilateral upper lobe pulmonary fibrosis.
- Constitutional symptoms may occur: fever, fatigue, weight loss.
- Neurologic complications related to spinal fracture/dislocation (can occur with even minor trauma), atlantoaxial subluxation, cauda equina syndrome.

Physical Examination

- Tenderness over involved joints
- Diminished chest expansion
- Diminished anterior flexion of lumbar spine (Schober test)

Evaluation

- ESR and C-reactive protein elevated in majority.
- Mild anemia.
- Rheumatoid factor and ANA negative.
- HLA-B27 may be helpful in pts with inflammatory back Sx but negative x-rays.
- Radiographs: early may be normal. Sacroiliac joints: usually symmetric; bony erosions with "pseudowidening" followed by fibrosis and ankylosis. CT can detect changes earlier than plain x-ray. Spine: squaring of vertebrae; syndesmophytes; ossification of annulus fibrosis and anterior longitudinal ligament causing "bamboo spine." Sites of enthesitis may ossify and be visible on x-ray.

Diagnosis

Modified New York criteria widely used: radiographic evidence of sacroiliitis plus one of: (1) Hx of inflammatory back pain symptoms, (2) lumbar motion limitation, (3) limited chest expansion.

DIFFERENTIAL DIAGNOSIS   Spondyloarthropathy associated with reactive arthritis, psoriatic arthritis, enteropathic arthritis (Fig. 161-1). Diffuse idiopathic skeletal hyperostosis.

℞ TREATMENT

- Exercise program to maintain posture and mobility is key to management.
- NSAIDs (e.g., indomethacin 75 mg slow-release qd or bid) useful in most pts.
- Sulfasalazine 2–3 g/d may be useful.
- No therapeutic role for systemic glucocorticoids or other immunosuppressive has been documented in ankylosing spondylitis.
- Adjunctive therapy includes intraarticular glucocorticoids for persistent enthesitis or peripheral synovitis; ocular glucocorticoids for uveitis; surgery for severely affected or deformed joints.

For a more detailed discussion, see Taurog JD, Lipsky PE: Ankylosing Spondylitis, Reactive Arthritis, and Undifferentiated Spondyloarthropathy, Chap. 315, p. 1949, in HPIM-15.

162

DEGENERATIVE JOINT DISEASE

Definition

Degenerative joint disease, or osteoarthritis (OA), is a disorder characterized by progressive deterioration and loss of articular cartilage accompanied by proliferation of new bone and soft tissue in and around involved joint.

- *Primary (idiopathic) OA*: no underlying cause is apparent.
- *Secondary OA*: a predisposing factor is present such as trauma, repetitive stress (occupation, sports), congenital abnormality, metabolic disorder, or other bone/joint disease.
- *Erosive OA*: term often applied to pts who have hand DIP/PIP OA associated with synovitis and radiographic central erosions of the articular surface.

Pathogenesis

Initial changes begin in cartilage, with change in arrangement and size of collagen fibers. Proteases lead to loss of cartilage matrix. Proteoglycan synthesis initially undergoes a compensatory increase but eventually falls off, leading to full-thickness cartilage loss.

Clinical Manifestations

OA is the most common form of joint disease. It can affect almost any joint, but usually occurs in weight-bearing and frequently used joints such as the knee, hip, spine, and hands. The hand joints that are typically affected are the DIP, PIP, or first CMC (thumb base); MCP involvement is rare.

SYMPTOMS

- Use-related pain affecting one or a few joints (rest and nocturnal pain less common)
- Stiffness after rest or in morning may occur but usually brief (< 30 min)
- Loss of joint movement or functional limitation
- Joint instability
- Joint deformity
- Joint crepitation ("crackling")

PHYSICAL EXAMINATION

- Chronic monarthritis or asymmetric oligo/polyarthritis
- Firm or "bony" swellings of the joint margins, e.g., Heberden's nodes (hand DIP) or Bouchard's nodes (hand PIP)
- Mild synovitis with a cool effusion can occur but is uncommon
- Crepitance—audible creaking or crackling of joint on passive or active movement
- Deformity, e.g., OA of knee may involve medial, lateral, or patellofemoral compartments resulting in varus or valgus deformities
- Restriction of movement, e.g., limitation of internal rotation of hip
- Objective neurologic abnormalities may be seen with spine involvement (may affect intervertebral disks, apophyseal joints, and paraspinal ligaments)

Evaluation

- Routine lab work usually normal.
- ESR usually normal but may be elevated in pts who have synovitis.
- Rheumatoid factor, ANA studies negative.

- Joint fluid is straw-colored with good viscosity; fluid WBCs <2000/μL; of value in ruling out crystal-induced arthritis or infection.
- Radiographs may be normal at first but as disease progresses may show joint space narrowing, subchondral bone sclerosis, subchondral cysts, and osteophytes. Erosions are distinct from those of rheumatoid and psoriatic arthritis as they occur subchondrally along the central portion of the joint surface.

Diagnosis

Usually established on basis of pattern of joint involvement, radiographic features, normal laboratory tests, and synovial fluid findings.

DIFFERENTIAL DIAGNOSIS Osteonecrosis, Charcot joint, rheumatoid arthritis, psoriatic arthritis, crystal-induced arthritides.

℞ **TREATMENT**

- Pt education, weight reduction, appropriate use of cane and other supports, isometric exercises to strengthen muscles around affected joints.
- Topical capsaicin cream may help relieve hand or knee pain.
- Acetaminophen, salicylates, or NSAIDs; consider Cox-2-specific NSAIDs for those at risk of GI toxicity.
- Tramadol—may be considered in pts whose symptoms are inadequately controlled with NSAIDs; as it is a synthetic opioid agonist, habituation is a potential concern.
- Intraarticular glucocorticoids—may provide symptomatic relief but should be performed infrequently as cartilage breakdown may be accelerated if performed too often.
- Intraarticular hyaluronin—indicated in pts who have not responded to nonpharmacologic therapy and analgesics; consider when NSAIDs contraindicated or ineffective.
- Tidal irrigation—invasive modality; role in treatment remains unclear.
- Glucosamine and chondroitin—proof of efficacy has not been established.
- Systemic glucocorticoids have no place in the treatment of OA.
- Surgery may be considered in pts with intractable pain and loss of function who are unresponsive to other measures.

For a more detailed discussion, see Brandt KD: Osteoarthritis, Chap. 321, p. 1987, in HPIM-15.

163

GOUT, PSEUDOGOUT, AND RELATED DISEASES

GOUT
Definition

The term *gout* is applied to a spectrum of manifestations that may occur singly or in combination. Hyperuricemia is the biologic hallmark of gout. When present, plasma and extracellular fluids become supersaturated with uric acid, which, under the right conditions, may crystallize and result in clinical gout.

Pathogenesis

Uric acid is the end product of purine nucleotide degradation; its production is closely linked to pathways of purine metabolism, with the intracellular concentration of 5-phosphoribosyl-1-pyrophosphate (PRPP) being the major determinant of the rate of uric acid biosynthesis. Uric acid is excreted primarily by the kidney through mechanisms of glomerular filtration, tubular secretion, and reabsorption. Hyperuricemia may thus arise in a wide range of settings that cause overproduction or reduced excretion of uric acid or a combination of the two (Table 347-2, p. 2269, HPIM-15).

ACUTE GOUTY ARTHRITIS Monosodium urate (MSU) crystals present in the joint are phagocytosed by leukocytes; release of inflammatory mediators and lysosomal enzymes leads to recruitment of additional phagocytes into the joint and to synovial inflammation.

Clinical Manifestations

* *Acute inflammatory arthritis*. Usually an exquisitely painful monarthritis but may be polyarticular and accompanied by fever; podagra (attack in the great toe) is the site of first attack in half and may occur eventually in 90%. Attack will generally subside spontaneously after days to weeks. Although some pts may have a single attack, 75% have a second attack within 2 years. Differential diagnosis includes septic arthritis, reactive arthritis, calcium pyrophosphate deposition (CPPD) disease, rheumatoid arthritis.
* *Tenosynovitis*.
* *Chronic tophaceous arthritis. Tophi*: aggregates of MSU crystals surrounded by a giant cell inflammatory reaction. Occurs in the setting of long-standing gout.
* *Extraarticular tophi*. Often occur in olecranon bursa, helix and anthelix of ears, ulnar surface of forearm, Achilles tendon.
* *Urate nephrosis*. Deposition of MSU crystals in interstitium and pyramids. Can cause chronic renal insufficiency.
* *Acute uric acid nephropathy*. Reversible cause of acute renal failure due to precipitation of urate in the tubules; pts receiving cytotoxic treatment for neoplastic disease are at risk.
* *Uric acid nephrolithiasis*. Responsible for 10% of renal stones in U.S.

Evaluation

* Synovial fluid analysis—only definitive method of diagnosing gouty arthritis is joint aspiration and demonstration of characteristic needle-shaped negatively birefringent MSU crystals by polarizing microscopy. Gram stain and culture should be performed on all fluid to rule out infection.
* Serum uric acid—normal levels do not rule out gout.
* Urine uric acid—excretion of >800 mg/d on regular diet in the absence of drugs suggests overproduction.
* Screening for risk factors—renal insufficiency, hyperlipidemia, diabetes.
* If overproduction is suspected, measurement of erythrocyte HGPRT and PRPP levels may be indicated.
* Joint x-rays—may demonstrate erosions late in disease.
* If renal stones suggested; abdominal flat plate (stones often radiolucent), possibly IVP.
* Chemical analysis of renal stones.

℞ TREATMENT

Asymptomatic Hyperuricemia As only about ~5% of hyperuricemic pts develop gout, treatment of asymptomatic hyperuricemia is not indicated. Exception is pts about to receive cytotoxic therapy for neoplasms.

Acute Gouty Arthritis Treatment is given for symptomatic relief only as attack is self-limited and will resolve spontaneously. Toxicity of therapy must be considered in each pt.

- Analgesia.
- NSAIDs—Rx of choice when not contraindicated.
- Colchicine—generally only effective within first 24 h of attack; overdose has potentially life-threatening side effects; use is contraindicated in pts with renal insufficiency, cytopenias, LFTs > 2× normal, sepsis. PO—0.6 mg qh until pt improves, has GI side effects, or maximal dose of 5 mg is reached. IV—dangerous and best avoided; if used, give no more than 2 mg over 24 h and no further drug for 7 days following; IV must never be given in a pt who has received PO colchicine.
- Intraarticular glucocorticoids—septic arthritis must be ruled out prior to injection.
- Systemic glucocorticoids—brief taper may be considered in pts with a polyarticular gouty attack for whom other modalities are contraindicated and where articular or systemic infection has been ruled out.

Uric Acid–Lowering Agents Indications for initiating uric acid–lowering therapy include recurrent frequent acute gouty arthritis, polyarticular gouty arthritis, tophaceous gout, renal stones, cytotoxic therapy prophylaxis. Should not start during an attack. Initiation can precipitate an acute flare; consider concomitant PO colchicine 0.6 mg qd until uric acid <5.0 mg/dL, then discontinue.

- Allopurinol: Decreases uric acid synthesis by inhibiting xanthine oxidase. Must be dose-reduced in renal insufficiency. Has significant side effects and drug interactions.
- Uricosuric drugs (probenecid, sulfinpyrazone): Increases uric acid excretion by inhibiting its tubular reabsorption; ineffective in renal insufficiency; should not be used in these settings: age >60, renal stones, tophi, increased urinary uric acid excretion, cytotoxic therapy prophylaxis.

PSEUDOGOUT
Definition and Pathogenesis

CPPD disease is characterized by acute and chronic inflammatory joint disease, usually affecting older individuals. The knee and other large joints most commonly affected. Calcium deposits in articular cartilage (chondrocalcinosis) may be seen radiographically; these are not always associated with symptoms.

CPPD may be hereditary; idiopathic, associated chiefly with aging; or occur secondary to hyperparathyroidism, hemochromatosis, hypophosphatasia, hypomagnesemia, hypothyroidism, gout, ochronosis, joint trauma, severe medical illness, or surgery.

Crystals are not thought to form in synovial fluid but probably are shed from articular cartilage into joint space where they are phagocytosed by neutrophils and incite an inflammatory response.

Clinical Manifestations

Acute "pseudogout"—occurs in ~25% of pts with CPPD disease; knee is most frequently involved, but other joints may be affected; involved joint is erythematous, swollen, warm, and painful; most pts have evidence of chondrocalcinosis. A minority will have involvement of multiple joints.

Degenerative CPPD disease—chronic arthropathy with progressive degenerative changes in multiple joints. Common sites include knee, wrist, MCP, hips, and shoulders. These pts may also have intermittent acute attacks.

Diagnosis

- Made by demonstration of calcium pyrophosphate dihydrate crystals (appearing as short blunt rods, rhomboids, and cuboids with weak positive birefringence) in synovial fluid.
- Radiographs may demonstrate chondrocalcinosis and degenerative changes (joint space narrowing, subchondral sclerosis/cysts).
- Secondary causes of CPPD should be considered in pts <50 years.

DIFFERENTIAL DIAGNOSIS   OA, RA, gout, septic arthritis.

 TREATMENT

- NSAIDs
- Intraarticular injection of glucocorticoids
- Colchicine is variably effective.

HYDROXYAPATITE ARTHROPATHY

Calcium hydroxyapatite (HA) deposition can cause a calcific bursitis or tendinitis and arthropathy primarily affecting the shoulder and knee. Abnormal HA accumulation can occur idiopathically or secondary to tissue damage, hypercalcemia, hyperparathyroidism, or chronic renal failure. HA is an important factor in *Milwaukee shoulder*, a destructive arthropathy of the elderly that occurs in the shoulders and knees. HA crystals are small; clumps may stain purplish on Wright's stain and bright red with alizarin red S. Definitive identification requires electron microscopy or x-ray diffraction studies. Radiographic appearance resembles CPPD disease. *Treatment*: NSAIDs, repeated aspiration, and rest of affected joint.

CALCIUM OXALATE DEPOSITION DISEASE

CaOx crystals may be deposited in joints in primary oxalosis (rare) or secondary oxalosis (a complication of end-stage renal disease). Clinical syndrome similar to gout and CPPD disease. *Treatment*: marginally effective.

For a more detailed discussion, see Wortmann RL: Disorders of Purine and Pyrimidine Metabolism, Chap. 347, p. 2268; and Reginato AJ: Gout and Other Crystal Arthropathies, Chap. 322, p. 1994, in HPIM-15.

164

PSORIATIC ARTHRITIS

Definition

Psoriatic arthritis is a chronic inflammatory arthritis that affects 5–42% of people with psoriasis. Some pts, especially those with spondylitis, will carry the HLA-B27 histocompatibility antigen. Onset of psoriasis usually precedes development of joint disease; approximately 15% of pts develop arthritis prior to onset of skin disease.

Patterns of Joint Involvement

- Asymmetric oligoarthritis: most common pattern affecting 16–70% (mean 47%); often involve DIP/PIP of hands and feet, knees, wrists, ankles; "sausage digits" may be present, reflecting tendon sheath inflammation.
- Symmetric polyarthritis (25%) resembles rheumatoid arthritis except rheumatoid factor is negative, absence of rheumatoid nodules.
- Predominantly distal interphalangeal joint involvement (10%): high frequency of association with psoriatic nail changes.
- "Arthritis mutilans" (3–5%): aggressive, destructive form of arthritis with severe joint deformities and bony dissolution.
- Spondylitis and/or sacroiliitis: axial involvement is present in 20–40% of pts with psoriatic arthritis; may occur in absence of peripheral arthritis.

Evaluation

- Negative tests for rheumatoid factor.
- Hypoproliferative anemia, elevated ESR.
- Hyperuricemia may be present.
- HIV should be suspected in fulminant disease.
- Inflammatory synovial fluid and biopsy without specific findings.
- Radiographic features include erosion at joint margin, bony ankylosis, tuft resorption of terminal phalanges, "pencil-in-cup" deformity (bone proliferation at base of distal phalanx with tapering of proximal phalanx), axial skeleton with asymmetric sacroiliitis, asymmetric nonmarginal syndesmophytes.

Diagnosis

Suggested by: pattern of arthritis and inflammatory nature, absence of rheumatoid factor, radiographic characteristics, presence of skin and nail changes of psoriasis (Fig. 161-1).

℞ TREATMENT

- Pt education, physical and occupational therapy.
- NSAIDs.
- Intraarticular steroid injections—useful in some settings. Systemic glucocorticoids should rarely be used as may induce rebound flare of skin disease upon tapering.
- Gold salts IM or PO—helpful in some pts, significant side-effect profile.
- Methotrexate (5–25 mg PO weekly)—in advanced cases, especially with severe skin involvement, significant side-effect profile.

For a more detailed discussion, see Schur PH: Psoriatic Arthritis and Arthritis Associated with Gastrointestinal Disease, Chap. 324, p. 2003, in HPIM-15.

165

REACTIVE ARTHRITIS AND REITER'S SYNDROME

Definition

Reiter's syndrome describes the triad of arthritis, conjunctivitis, and nongonococcal urethritis. This term is largely of historic interest and is now considered to be part of the spectrum of *reactive arthritis*, an acute nonpurulent arthritis complicating an infection elsewhere in the body (usually genitourinary or enteric) that may be accompanied by extraarticular features.

Pathogenesis

Up to 85% of pts possess the HLA-B27 alloantigen. It is thought that in individuals with appropriate genetic background, reactive arthritis may be triggered by an enteric infection with any of several *Shigella, Salmonella, Yersinia*, and *Campylobacter* species; by genitourinary infection with *Chlamydia trachomatis*; and possibly by other agents.

Clinical Manifestations

The sex ratio following enteric infection is 1:1, but genitourinary acquired reactive arthritis is predominantly seen in young males. In a majority of cases Hx will elicit Sx of genitourinary or enteric infection 1–4 weeks prior to onset of other features.

- Constitutional—fatigue, malaise, fever, weight loss.
- Arthritis—usually acute, asymmetric, oligoarticular, involving predominantly lower extremities; sacroiliitis may occur.
- Enthesitis—inflammation at insertion of tendons and ligaments into bone; "sausage digit," plantar fasciitis, and Achilles tendinitis common.
- Ocular features—conjunctivitis, usually minimal; uveitis, keratitis, and optic neuritis rarely present.
- Urethritis—discharge intermittent and may be asymptomatic.
- Other urogenital manifestations—prostatitis, cervicitis, salpingitis.
- Mucocutaneous lesions—painless lesions on glans penis (*circinate balanitis*) and oral mucosa in approximately a third of pts; *keratoderma blennorrhagica*: cutaneous vesicles that become hyperkerotic, most common on soles and palms.
- Uncommon manifestations—pleuropericarditis, aortic regurgitation, neurologic manifestations, secondary amyloidosis.
- Reiter's syndrome is associated with and may be the presenting Sx of HIV.

Evaluation

- Pursuit of *Chlamydia* infection by culture, DFA, or EIA of secretions from throat, urethra, cervix.

- Stool cultures may secure Dx of enteric pathogen.
- Rheumatoid factor and ANA negative.
- Mild anemia, leukocytosis, elevated ESR may be seen.
- HLA-B27 may be helpful in atypical cases.
- HIV screening should be performed in all pts.
- Synovial fluid analysis—often very inflammatory; negative for crystals or infection.
- Radiographs—erosions may be seen with new periosteal bone formation, ossification of entheses, sacroiliitis (often unilateral).

Differential Diagnosis

Includes septic arthritis (gram +/−), gonococcal arthritis, crystalline arthritis, psoriatic arthritis (Fig. 161 -1).

 TREATMENT

- Prolonged administration of antibiotics may benefit *Chlamydia*-induced disease.
- NSAIDs (e.g., indomethacin 25–50 mg PO tid) benefit most pts.
- Intraarticular glucocorticoids.
- Sulfasalazine up to 3 g/d in divided doses may help some pts with persistent arthritis.
- Cytotoxic therapy, such as azathioprine [1–2 (mg/kg)/d] or methotrexate (7.5–15 mg/week) may be considered for debilitating disease refractory to other modalities; contraindicated in HIV disease.
- Uveitis may require therapy with ocular or systemic glucocorticoids.

Outcome

Prognosis is variable; a third will have recurrent or sustained disease, with 15–25% developing permanent disability.

For a more detailed discussion, see Taurog JD, Lipsky PE: Ankylosing Spondylitis, Reactive Arthritis, and Undifferentiated Spondyloarthropathy, Chap. 315, p. 1949, in HPIM-15.

166

OTHER ARTHRITIDES

ENTEROPATHIC ARTHRITIS

Both peripheral and axial arthritis may be associated with ulcerative colitis or Crohn's disease. The arthritis can occur after or before the onset of intestinal symptoms. Peripheral arthritis is episodic, asymmetric, and most frequently affects knee and ankle. Attacks usually subside within several weeks and characteristically resolve completely without residual joint damage. Enthesitis (inflammation at insertion of tendons and ligaments into bone) can occur with manifestations of "sausage digit," Achilles tendinitis, plantar fasciitis. Axial involvement can manifest as spondylitis and/or sacroiliitis (often symmetric). Laboratory findings are nonspecific; rheumatoid factor (RF) absent; radiographs of peripheral joints usually normal; axial involvement is often indistinguishable from ankylosing spondylitis (Fig. 161-1).

 TREATMENT

Directed at underlying inflammatory bowel disease; NSAIDs may alleviate joint symptoms; sulfasalazine may benefit peripheral arthritis.

INTESTINAL BYPASS ARTHRITIS Some pts will develop arthritis-dermatitis following intestinal bypass surgery. Possibly related to bacterial overgrowth. Symptoms may be relieved by NSAIDs, suppression of bacterial overgrowth with tetracycline or other antibiotics, or surgical reanastomosis of bypassed segment.

WHIPPLE'S DISEASE Characterized by arthritis in up to 90% of pts that usually precedes appearance of intestinal symptoms. Usually polyarticular, symmetric, transient but may become chronic. GI and joint manifestations respond to antibiotic therapy.

NEUROPATHIC JOINT DISEASE

Also known as *Charcot's joint*, this is a severe destructive arthropathy that occurs in joints deprived of pain and position sense; may occur in diabetic neuropathy, tabes dorsalis, syringomyelia, amyloidosis, spinal cord or peripheral nerve injury. Usually begins in a single joint but may spread to involve other joints. Joint effusions are usually noninflammatory but can be hemorrhagic. Radiographs can reveal either bone resorption or new bone formation with bone dislocation and fragmentation.

 TREATMENT

Stabilization of joint; surgical fusion may improve function.

RELAPSING POLYCHONDRITIS

An idiopathic disorder characterized by recurrent inflammation of cartilaginous structures. Cardinal manifestations include ear and nose involvement with floppy ear and saddlenose deformities, inflammation and collapse of tracheal and bronchial cartilaginous rings, asymmetric episodic nondeforming polyarthritis. Other features can include scleritis, conjunctivitis, iritis, keratitis, aortic regurgitation, glomerulonephritis, and other features of systemic vasculitis. Onset is frequently abrupt, with the appearance of 1–2 sites of cartilaginous inflammation. Diagnosis is made clinically and may be confirmed by biopsy of affected cartilage. Diagnostic criteria have also been proposed.

 TREATMENT

Glucocorticoids (prednisone 40–60 mg/d with subsequent taper) may suppress acute features and reduce the severity/frequency of recurrences. Cytotoxic agents may be considered for unresponsive disease or for pts who require high glucocorticoid doses. Methotrexate has been found by some to be effective.

HYPERTROPHIC OSTEOARTHROPATHY

Syndrome consisting of periosteal new bone formation, digital clubbing, and arthritis. Most commonly seen in association with lung carcinoma but also occurs with chronic lung or liver disease; congenital heart, lung, or liver disease in children; and idiopathic and familial forms. Symptoms include burning and aching pain most pronounced in distal extremities. Radiographs show periosteal thickening with new bone formation of distal ends of long bones.

 TREATMENT

Identify and treat associated disorder; aspirin, NSAIDs, other analgesics, vagotomy or percutaneous nerve block may help to relieve symptoms.

FIBROMYALGIA

A common disorder characterized by pain, aching, stiffness of trunk and extremities, and presence of a number of specific tender points. More common in women than men. Frequently associated with sleep disorders. Diagnosis is made clinically; evaluation reveals soft tissue tender points but no objective joint abnormalities by exam, laboratory, or radiograph.

 TREATMENT

Benzodiazepines or tricyclics for sleep disorder, local measures (heat, massage, injection of tender points), NSAIDs.

REFLEX SYMPATHETIC DYSTROPHY SYNDROME (RSDS)

A syndrome of pain and tenderness, usually of a hand or foot, associated with vasomotor instability, trophic skin changes, and rapid development of bony demineralization. Frequently, development will follow a precipitating event (local trauma, myocardial infarction, stroke, or peripheral nerve injury). Early recognition and treatment can be effective in preventing disability.

 TREATMENT

Options include pain control, application of heat or cold, exercise, sympathetic nerve block, and short courses of high-dose prednisone in conjunction with physical therapy.

POLYMYALGIA RHEUMATICA (PMR)

Clinical syndrome characterized by aching and morning stiffness in the shoulder girdle, hip girdle, or neck for >1 month, elevated ESR, and rapid response to low-dose prednisone (15 mg qd). Rarely occurs before age 50. PMR can occur in association with giant cell (temporal) arteritis, which requires treatment with higher doses of prednisone. Evaluation should include a careful history to elicit Sx suggestive of giant cell arteritis (Chap. 160); ESR; labs to rule out other processes usually include RF, ANA, CBC, CPK, SPEP; and renal, hepatic, and thyroid function tests.

TREATMENT

Pts rapidly improve on prednisone, 10–20 mg qd, but may require treatment over months to years.

OSTEONECROSIS (AVASCULAR NECROSIS)

Caused by death of cellular elements of bone, believed to be due to impairment in blood supply. Frequent associations include glucocorticoid treatment, connective tissue disease, trauma, sickle cell disease, embolization, alcohol use. Commonly involved sites include femoral and humeral heads, femoral condyles, proximal tibia. Hip disease is bilateral in >50% of cases. Clinical presentation is usually the abrupt onset of articular pain. Early changes are not visible on plain radiograph and are best seen by MRI, later stages demonstrate bone collapse ("crescent sign"), flattening of articular surface with joint space loss.

 TREATMENT

Limited weight-bearing of unclear benefit; NSAIDs for Sx. Surgical procedures to enhance blood flow may be considered in early-stage disease but are of controversial efficacy; joint replacement may be necessary in late-stage disease for pain unresponsive to other measures.

PERIARTICULAR DISORDERS

BURSITIS Inflammation of the thin-walled bursal sac surrounding tendons and muscles over bony prominences. The subacromial and greater trochanteric bursae are most commonly involved.

 TREATMENT

Prevention of aggravating conditions, rest, NSAIDs, and local glucocorticoid injections.

TENDINITIS May involve virtually any tendon but frequently affects tendons of the rotator cuff around shoulder, especially the supraspinatus. Pain is dull and aching but becomes acute and sharp when tendon is squeezed below acromion.

 TREATMENT

NSAIDs, glucocorticoid injection, and physical therapy may be beneficial. The rotator cuff tendons or biceps tendon may rupture acutely, frequently requiring surgical repair.

CALCIFIC TENDINITIS Results from deposition of calcium salts in tendon, usually supraspinatus. The resulting pain may be sudden and severe.

ADHESIVE CAPSULITIS ("Frozen Shoulder") Results from conditions that enforce prolonged immobility of shoulder joint. Shoulder is painful and tender to palpation, and both active and passive range of motion is restricted.

 TREATMENT

Spontaneous improvement may occur; NSAIDs, local injections of glucocorticoids, and physical therapy may be helpful.

For a more detailed discussion, see Schur PH: Psoriatic Arthritis and Arthritis Associated with Gastrointestinal Diseases, Chap. 324, p. 2003; and

Gilliland BC: Relapsing Polychondritis and Other Arthritides, Chap. 325, p. 2005, in HPIM-15.

167

SARCOIDOSIS

Definition

A systemic granulomatous disease of unknown etiology. Affected organs are characterized by an accumulation of T lymphocytes and mononuclear phagocytes, noncaseating epithelioid granulomas, and derangements of normal tissue architecture.

Pathophysiology

Mononuclear cells, mostly T helper lymphocytes and mononuclear phagocytes, accumulate in affected organs followed by formation of granulomas. It does not appear that this process injures parenchyma by releasing mediators; rather, organ dysfunction results from the accumulated inflammatory cells distorting the architecture of the affected tissue. Severe damage of parenchyma can lead to irreversible fibrosis.

Clinical Manifestations

In 10–20% of cases, sarcoidosis may first be detected as asymptomatic hilar adenopathy. Sarcoid manifests clinically in organs where it affects function or where it is readily observed. Onset may be acute or insidious.

Acute sarcoid—20–40% of cases. Two acute syndromes: *Lofgren's syndrome*: hilar adenopathy, erythema nodosum, acute arthritis presenting in one or both ankles spreading to involve other joints; *Heerfordt-Waldenström syndrome*: parotid enlargement, fever, anterior uveitis, facial nerve palsy.

Insidious onset—40–70% of cases. Respiratory Sx most common presenting feature with constitutional or extrathoracic Sx less frequent.

Disease manifestations of sarcoid include:

- Constitutional symptoms—fever, weight loss, anorexia, fatigue.
- Lung—most commonly involved organ; 90% with sarcoidosis will have abnormal CXR some time during course. Features include: hilar adenopathy, alveolitis, interstitial pneumonitis; airways may be involved and cause obstruction to airflow; pleural disease and hemoptysis are uncommon.
- Lymph nodes—intrathoracic nodes enlarged in 75–90% of pts.
- Skin—25% will have skin involvement; lesions include erythema nodosum, plaques, maculopapular eruptions, subcutaneous nodules, and lupus pernio (indurated blue-purple shiny lesions on face, fingers, and knees).
- Eye—uveitis in ~25%; may progress to blindness.
- Upper respiratory tract—nasal mucosa involved in up to 20%, larynx 5%.
- Bone marrow and spleen—mild anemia and thrombocytopenia may occur.
- Liver—involved on biopsy in 60–90%; rarely important clinically.
- Kidney—parenchymal disease, nephrolithiasis secondary to abnormalities of calcium metabolism.

- Nervous system—cranial/peripheral neuropathy, chronic meningitis, pituitary involvement, space-occupying lesions, seizures.
- Heart— disturbances of rhythm and/or contractility, pericarditis.
- Musculoskeletal—dactylitis, chronic mono- or oligoarthritis of knee, ankle, PIP.
- Other organ systems affected: endocrine/reproductive, exocrine glands, GI.

Evaluation

- Hx and physical exam to rule out exposures and other causes of interstitial lung disease.
- CBC, Ca^{2+}, LFTs, ACE, PPD and control skin tests.
- CXR, ECG, PFTs.
- Biopsy of lung or other affected organ.
- Bronchoalveolar lavage and gallium scan of lungs may help decide when treatment is indicated and may help to follow therapy; however, these are not uniformly accepted.

Diagnosis

Made on basis of clinical, radiographic, and histologic findings. Biopsy of lung or other affected organ is mandatory to establish diagnosis before starting therapy. Transbronchial lung biopsy usually adequate to make diagnosis. No blood findings are diagnostic. Differential includes neoplasms, infections, HIV, other granulomatous processes.

℞ TREATMENT

Many cases remit spontaneously; therefore, deciding when treatment is necessary is difficult and controversial. Significant involvement of the eye, heart, or CNS or progressive lung disease is the main indication for treatment. Glucocorticoids are mainstay of therapy. Usual therapy is prednisone 1 (mg/kg)/d for 4–6 weeks followed by taper over 2—3 months. Anecdotal reports suggest that cyclosporine may be useful in extrathoracic sarcoid not responding to glucocorticoids.

Outcome

Most pts with acute disease are left with no significant sequelae. Overall, 50% of pts with sarcoid have some permanent organ dysfunction; in 15–20% disease remains active or recurrent; death directly due to disease occurs in 10% of cases. Respiratory tract abnormalities cause most of the morbidity and mortality related to sarcoid.

For a more detailed discussion, see Crystal RG: Sarcoidosis, Chap. 318, p. 1969, in HPIM-15.

168

AMYLOIDOSIS

Definition

A disease characterized by deposition of the fibrous protein amyloid in one or more sites of the body. Clinical manifestations depend on anatomic distribution and intensity of amyloid protein deposition and range from local deposition with little significance to involvement of virtually any organ system with consequent severe pathophysiologic changes.

Classification

Chemical characterization reveals several varieties of amyloid fibrils associated with different clinical situations (see Table 319-1, p. 1975, in HPIM-15):

- *Light chain amyloidosis* (AL): most common form of systemic amyloidosis seen in clinical practice; occurs in primary idiopathic amyloidosis and amyloid associated with multiple myeloma.
- *Amyloid A amyloidosis* (AA): occurs in secondary amyloidosis as a complication of chronic inflammatory disease and in familial Mediterranean fever (FMF).
- *Heredofamilial amyloidoses*
- *$A\beta_2M$*: Chronic hemodialysis-related amyloid; identical to β_2 microglobulin.
- *Localized or organ-limited amyloidoses*: includes $A\beta$: found in neuritic plaques and cerebrovascular walls of pts with Alzheimer's disease and Down's syndrome.

Clinical Manifestations

Clinical features are varied and depend entirely on biochemical nature of the fibril protein. Frequent sites of involvement:

- Kidney—seen with AA and AL; proteinuria, nephrosis, azotemia.
- Liver—occurs in AA, AL, and heredofamilial; hepatomegaly.
- Skin—characteristic of AL but can be seen in AA; raised waxy papules.
- Heart—common in AL and heredofamilial; CHF, cardiomegaly, arrhythmias.
- GI—common in all types; GI obstruction or ulceration, hemorrhage, protein loss, diarrhea, macroglossia, disordered esophageal motility.
- Joints—usually AL, frequently with myeloma; periarticular amyloid deposits, "shoulder pad sign": firm amyloid deposits in soft tissue around the shoulder, symmetric arthritis of shoulders, wrists, knees, hands.
- Nervous system—prominent in heredofamilial; peripheral neuropathy, postural hypotension, dementia. Carpal tunnel syndrome may occur in AL and $A\beta_2M$.
- Respiratory—lower airways can be affected in AL, localized amyloid can cause obstruction along upper airways.
- Hematologic—selective clotting factor deficiency.

Diagnosis

Requires demonstration of amyloid in a biopsy of affected tissue using appropriate stains (e.g., Congo red). Aspiration of abdominal fat pad or biopsy of rectal mucosa may demonstrate amyloid fibrils. Electrophoresis and immunoelectrophoresis of serum and urine may assist in detecting paraproteins.

Prognosis

Outcome is variable and depends on type of amyloidosis and organ involvement. Average survival of AL amyloid is ~12 months; prognosis is poor when associated with myeloma. Renal failure and heart disease are the major causes of death.

 TREATMENT

There is no specific therapy for any variety of amyloidosis. If present, an underlying disorder should be treated. Primary amyloidosis may respond to regimens incorporating prednisone and alkylating agents, presumably because of the effects of these agents on synthesis of the AL amyloid protein. Colchicine (1–2 mg/d) may prevent acute attacks in FMF and thus may block amyloid deposition. Renal transplantation may be effective in selected pts.

For a more detailed discussion, see Sipe JD, Cohen AS: Amyloidosis, Chap. 319, p. 1974, in HPIM-15.

169

DISORDERS OF THE ANTERIOR PITUITARY AND HYPOTHALAMUS

The anterior pituitary is often referred to as the "master gland" because, together with the hypothalamus, it orchestrates the complex regulatory functions of multiple other glands (Fig. 169-1). The anterior pituitary produces six major hormones: (1) prolactin (PRL), (2) growth hormone (GH), (3) adrenocorticotropin hormone (ACTH), (4) luteinizing hormone (LH), (5) follicle-stimulating hormone (FSH), and (6) thyroid-stimulating hormone (TSH). Pituitary hormones are secreted in a pulsatile manner, reflecting intermittent stimulation by specific hypothalamic releasing factors. Each of these pituitary hormones elicits specific responses in peripheral target glands. The hormonal products of these peripheral glands, in turn, exert feedback control at the level of the hypothalamus and pituitary to modulate pituitary function. Disorders of the pituitary include neoplasms that lead to mass effects and clinical syndromes due to excess or deficiency of one or more pituitary hormones.

PITUITARY TUMORS

Pituitary adenomas are benign monoclonal tumors that arise from one of the five anterior pituitary cell types and may cause clinical effects from either overproduction of a pituitary hormone or compressive effects on surrounding structures, including the hypothalamus, pituitary, or both. Tumors secreting prolactin are most common and have a greater prevalence in women than in men. GH- and ACTH-secreting tumors each account for about 10–15% of pituitary tumors. About one-third of all adenomas are clinically nonfunctioning and produce no distinct clinical hypersecretory syndrome. Adenomas are classified as microadenomas (<10 mm) or macroadenomas (≥ 10 mm). Other entities that can present as a sellar mass include craniopharyngiomas, Rathke's cleft cysts, sella chordomas, meningiomas, pituitary metastases, and gliomas.

Clinical Features Symptoms from mass effects include headache; visual loss through compression of the optic chiasm superiorly (classically a bitemporal hemianopia); and diplopia, ptosis, ophthalmoplegia, and decreased facial sensation from cranial nerve compression laterally. Pituitary stalk compression from the tumor may also result in mild hyperprolactinemia. Symptoms of hypopituitarism or hormonal excess may be present as well (see below).

Pituitary apoplexy is an endocrine emergency that typically presents with features that include severe headache, bilateral visual changes, ophthalmoplegia, and, in severe cases, cardiovascular collapse and loss of consciousness. It may result in hypotension, hypoglycemia, CNS hemorrhage, and death. Pts with no evident visual loss or impaired consciousness can usually be observed and managed conservatively with high-dose glucocorticoids; surgical decompression should be considered when these features are present.

Diagnosis Sagittal and coronal T1-weighted MRI images with specific pituitary cuts should be obtained before and after administration of gadolinium. In pts with lesions close to the optic chiasm, visual field assessment that uses perimetry techniques should be performed. Initial hormonal evaluation is listed in Table 169-1.

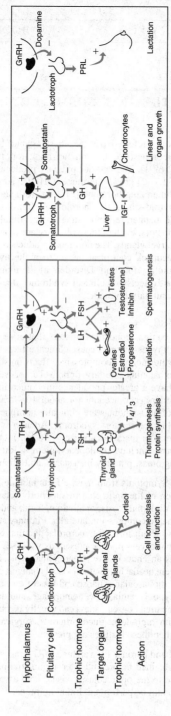

FIGURE 169-1 Diagram of pituitary axes. Hypothalamic hormones regulate anterior pituitary trophic hormones that, in turn, determine target gland secretion. Peripheral hormones feedback to regulate hypothalamic and pituitary hormones. For abbreviations, see text.

Table 169-1

Initial Hormonal Evaluation of Pituitary Adenomas

Pituitary Hormone	Test for Hyperfunction	Test for Deficiency
Prolactin	Prolactin	
Growth hormone	IGF-1	
ACTH	24-h urinary free cortisol or 1-mg overnight dexamethasone suppression test	8 **A.M.** serum cortisol
Gonadotropins	FSH, LH	Testosterone in men Menstrual history in women
TSH	TSH, free T_4	TSH, free T_4
Other	α-subunit	

   In pituitary apoplexy, CT or MRI of the pituitary may reveal signs of sellar hemorrhage, with deviation of the pituitary stalk and compression of pituitary tissue.

 TREATMENT

> Pituitary surgery is indicated for mass lesions that impinge on surrounding structures or to correct hormonal hypersecretion (see below). Transsphenoidal surgery, rather than transfrontal resection, is the desired surgical approach for most pts. The goal is selective resection of the pituitary mass lesion without damage to the normal pituitary tissue, to decrease the likelihood of hypopituitarism. Transient or permanent diabetes insipidus, hypopituitarism, CSF rhinorrhea, visual loss, and oculomotor palsy may occur postoperatively. Tumor invasion outside of the sella is rarely amenable to surgical cure, but debulking procedures may relieve tumor mass effects and reduce hormonal hypersecretion. Radiation may be used as an adjunct to surgery, but >50% of pts develop hormonal deficiencies within 10 years, usually due to hypothalamic damage. Prolactin-, GH-, ACTH-, and TSH-secreting tumors may also be amenable to medical therapy.

PITUITARY HORMONE HYPERSECRETION SYNDROMES
Hyperprolactinemia

Prolactin is unique among the pituitary hormones in that the predominant central control mechanism is inhibitory, reflecting dopamine-mediated suppression of prolactin release. Prolactin acts to induce and maintain lactation and decrease reproductive function and drive (via suppression of GnRH, gonadotropins, and gonadal steroidogenesis).

   Etiology Physiologic elevation of prolactin occurs in pregnancy and lactation. Otherwise, prolactin-secreting pituitary adenomas (prolactinomas) are the most common cause of prolactin levels >100 μg/L. Less pronounced hyperprolactinemia is commonly caused by medications (chlorpromazine, perphenazine, haloperidol, metoclopramide, opiates, H_2 antagonists, amitriptyline, SSRIs, calcium channel blockers, estrogens), pituitary stalk damage (tumors, lymphocytic hypophysitis, granulomas, trauma, irradiation), primary hypothyroidism, or renal failure. Nipple stimulation may also cause acute prolactin increases.

Clinical Features   In women, amenorrhea, galactorrhea, and infertility are the hallmarks of hyperprolactinemia. In men, symptoms of hypogonadism or mass effects are the usual presenting symptoms, and galactorrhea is uncommon.

Diagnosis   Fasting, morning prolactin levels should be measured; when clinical suspicion is high, measurement of levels on several different occasions may be required. If hyperprolactinemia is present, nonneoplastic causes should be excluded (e.g., pregnancy test, hypothyroidism, medications).

℞ TREATMENT

If pt is taking a medication that is known to cause hyperprolactinemia, the drug should be withdrawn, if possible. A pituitary MRI should be performed if the underlying cause of prolactin elevation is unknown. Resection of hypothalamic or sellar mass lesions can reverse hyperprolactinemia due to stalk compression. Medical therapy with a dopamine agonist is indicated in microprolactinomas for control of symptomatic galactorrhea, restoration of gonadal function, or when fertility is desired. Alternatively, estrogen replacement may be indicated if fertility is not desired. Dopamine agonist therapy for macroprolactinomas generally results in both adenoma shrinkage and reduction of prolactin levels. Cabergoline (initial dose 0.5 mg q week, usual dose 0.5–1 mg twice a week) or bromocriptine (initial dose 1.25 mg qhs, usual dose 2.5–5 mg po tid) are the two most frequently used dopamine agonists. These medications should initially be taken at bedtime with food, followed by gradual dose increases, to reduce the side effects of nausea and postural hypotension. Other side effects include constipation, nasal stuffiness, dry mouth, nightmares, insomnia, or vertigo; decreasing the dose usually alleviates these symptoms. Dopamine agonists may also precipitate or worsen underlying psychiatric conditions. Spontaneous remission of microadenomas, presumably caused by infarction, occurs in up to 30% of pts. Surgical debulking may be required for macroprolactinomas that do not respond to medical therapy.

Women with microprolactinomas who become pregnant should discontinue bromocriptine therapy, as the risk for significant tumor growth during pregnancy is low. In those with macroprolactinomas, visual field testing should be performed at each trimester. A pituitary MRI should be performed if severe headache and/or visual defects occur.

Acromegaly

Etiology   GH hypersecretion is usually the result of pituitary adenomas, but can rarely be due to extrapituitary production of GH or hypothalamic or peripheral GHRH secreting tumors.

Clinical Features   In children, GH hypersecretion prior to long bone epiphyseal closure results in gigantism. The presentation of acromegaly in adults is usually indolent. Pts may note a change in facial features, widened teeth spacing, deepening of the voice, snoring, increased shoe or glove size, ring tightening, hyperhidrosis, oily skin, arthropathy, and carpal tunnel syndrome. Frontal bossing, mandibular enlargement with prognathism, macroglossia, an enlarged thyroid, skin tags, thick heel pads, and hypertension may be present on examination. Associated conditions include cardiomyopathy, left ventricular hypertrophy, diastolic dysfunction, sleep apnea, diabetes mellitus, colon polyps, and colonic malignancy. Overall mortality is increased approximately threefold.

Diagnosis   Insulin-like growth factor (IGF) 1 levels are a useful screening measure, with elevation suggesting acromegaly. Due to the pulsatility of GH, measurement of a single random GH level is not useful for screening. The diagnosis of acromegaly is confirmed by demonstrating the failure of GH suppression to <1 μg/L within 1–2 h of a 75-g oral glucose load.

℞ TREATMENT

GH levels are not normalized by surgery alone in many pts with macroadenomas; somatostatin analogues provide adjunctive medical therapy that suppresses GH secretion with modest effects on tumor size. Octreotide (50 μg SC tid) is used for initial therapy. Once tolerance of side effects (nausea, abdominal discomfort, diarrhea, flatulence) is established, pts may be changed to long-acting depot formulations (20–30 mg IM q2–4 weeks). Pituitary irradiation may also be required as adjuvant therapy but has a high rate of late hypopituitarism.

Cushing's Disease

Etiology Pituitary adenomas account for 70% of pts with endogenous causes of Cushing's syndrome. Iatrogenic hypercortisolism, ectopic ACTH production by tumors, adrenal adenomas, carcinomas, and hyperplasia are other causes of hypercortisolism.

Clinical Features Typical features include thin, brittle skin, central obesity, hypertension, plethoric moon facies, purple striae, easy bruisability, glucose intolerance, osteoporosis, proximal muscle weakness, hypogonadism, acne, hirsutism, and psychological disturbances (depression, mania, and psychoses).

Diagnosis Elevated measurement of 24-h urine free cortisol and failure to suppress plasma cortisol after an overnight 1-mg dexamethasone suppression test can be used to screen pts for hypercortisolism. Measurement of an ACTH level, dynamic testing, and inferior petrosal sinus sampling may be used for localization (Table 328-13, p. 2049 in HPIM-15). Once biochemical localization confirms a pituitary source of Cushing's, pituitary MRI should be performed.

℞ TREATMENT

Transsphenoidal resection is the initial therapy for Cushing's disease and is successful in most pts with microadenomas. Repeat surgery or pituitary irradiation and steroidogenic inhibitors (ketoconazole, metyrapone, mitotane) may be required to suppress cortisol hypersecretion. Bilateral adrenalectomy may ultimately be required, though this necessitates permanent glucocorticoid and mineralocorticoid replacement and predisposes to Nelson's syndrome (pituitary adenoma enlargement).

Nonfunctioning and Gonadotropin-Producing Adenomas

These tumors usually present with symptoms of one or more hormonal deficiencies or mass effect. They typically produce small amounts of intact gonadotropins (usually FSH) as well as uncombined α and LHβ and FSHβ subunits. Surgery is indicated for mass effects or hypopituitarism; asymptomatic small adenomas may be followed with regular MRI and visual field testing. Diagnosis is based on immunohistochemical analysis of resected tumor tissue.

TSH-Secreting Adenomas

TSH-producing adenomas are rare but often large and locally invasive when they occur. Pts present with goiter and hyperthyroidism and/or sella mass effects. Diagnosis is based on elevated serum free T4 levels in the setting of inappropriately normal or high TSH secretion and MRI evidence of pituitary adenoma. Surgery is indicated and is usually followed by somatostatin therapy to treat residual tumor. Thyroid ablation or antithyroid drugs can be used to reduce thyroid hormone levels.

HYPOPITUITARISM

Etiology A variety of disorders may cause deficiencies of one or more pituitary hormones. These disorders may be congenital, traumatic (pituitary surgery, cranial irradiation, head injury), neoplastic (large pituitary adenoma, parasellar mass, craniopharyngioma, metastases, meningioma), infiltrative (hemochromatosis, lymphycytic hypophysitis, sarcoidosis, histiocytosis X), vascular (pituitary apoplexy, postpartum necrosis, sickle cell disease), or infectious (tuberculous, fungal, parasitic).

Clinical Features Hormonal abnormalities after cranial irradiation may occur 5 to 15 years later, with GH deficiency occurring first, followed sequentially by gonadotropin, TSH, and ACTH deficiency.

Each hormone deficiency is associated with specific findings:

- Prolactin: failure of lactation
- GH: growth disorders in children; increased intraabdominal fat, reduced lean body mass, hyperlipidemia, reduced bone mineral density, and social isolation in adults
- FSH/LH: menstrual disorders and infertility in women; hypogonadism in men
- ACTH: features of hypocortisolism without mineralocorticoid deficiency
- TSH: growth retardation in children, features of hypothyroidism in children and adults

Diagnosis Biochemical diagnosis of pituitary insufficiency is made by demonstrating low or inappropriately normal levels of pituitary hormones in the setting of low target hormone levels. Initial testing should include an 8 A.M. cortisol level, TSH and free T_4, IGF-1, testosterone in men, and assessment of menstrual cycles in women. Provocative tests may be required to assess pituitary reserve for individual hormones. Adult GH deficiency is diagnosed by demonstrating a subnormal GH response to a standard provocative test (insulin tolerance test, L-dopa, arginine, GHRH). Acute ACTH deficiency may be diagnosed by a subnormal response in an insulin tolerance test, metyrapone test, or CRH stimulation test. Standard ACTH (cosyntropin) stimulation tests may be normal in acute ACTH deficiency; with adrenal atrophy, the cortisol response to cosyntropin is blunted.

℞ **TREATMENT**

Hormonal replacement should aim to mimic physiologic hormone production. Effective dose schedules are outlined in Table 169-2. GH therapy, particularly when excessive, may be associated with fluid retention, joint pain, and carpal tunnel syndrome. Glucocorticoid replacement should always precede levothyroxine therapy to avoid precipitation of adrenal crisis. Pts requiring glucocorticoid replacement should wear a medical alert bracelet and should be instructed to take additional doses during stressful events such as acute illness, dental procedures, trauma, and acute hospitalization.

Table 169-2

Hormone Replacement Therapy for Adult Hypopituitarism[a]

Trophic Hormone Deficit	Hormone Replacement
ACTH	Hydrocortisone (10–20 mg A.M.; 10 mg P.M.)
	Cortisone acetate (25 mg A.M.; 12.5 mg P.M.)
	Prednisone (5 mg A.M.; 2.5 mg P.M.)
TSH	L-Thyroxine (0.075–0.15 mg daily)
FSH/LH	Males
	Testosterone enanthate (200 mg IM every 2 weeks)
	Testosterone skin patch (5 mg/d)
	Females
	Conjugated estrogen (0.65–1.25 mg qd for 25 days)
	Progesterone (5–10 mg qd) on days 16–25
	Estradiol skin patch (0.5 mg, every other day)
	For fertility: Menopausal gonadotropins, human chrorionic gonadotropins
GH	Adults: Somatotropin (0.3–1.0 mg SC qd)
	Children: Somatotropin [0.02–0.05 (mg/kg/day)]
Vasopressin	Intranasal desmopressin (5–20 μg twice daily)
	Oral 300–600 μg qd

[a] All doses shown should be individualized for specific patients and should be reassessed during stress, surgery, or pregnancy. Male and female fertility requirements should be managed as discussed in Chap. 54, HPIM-15.

For a more detailed discussion, see Melmed S: Disorders of the Anterior Pituitary and Hypothalamus, Chap. 328, p. 2029, in HPIM-15.

170

DISORDERS OF THE POSTERIOR PITUITARY

The neurohypophysis, or posterior pituitary gland, is formed by axons that project from the supraoptic and paraventricular nuclei of the hypothalamus. The posterior pituitary gland produces two hormones: (1) arginine vasopressin (AVP), also known as antidiuretic hormone (ADH), and (2) oxytocin. AVP acts on the renal tubules to induce water retention, leading to concentration of the urine. Oxytocin stimulates postpartum milk letdown in response to suckling. Clinical syndromes may result from deficiency or excess of AVP. There are no known clinical disorders associated with oxytocin deficiency or excess.

DIABETES INSIPIDUS

Etiology   Diabetes insipidus (DI) results from abnormalities of AVP production from the hypothalamus or action in the kidney (Table 170-1). AVP

Table 170-1

Causes of Diabetes Insipidus

Pituitary diabetes insipidus
Acquired
  Head trauma (closed and
    penetrating)
  Neoplasms
    Primary
      Craniopharyngioma
      Pituitary adenoma
        (suprasellar)
      Dysgerminoma
      Meningioma
    Metastatic (lung, breast)
    Hematologic (lymphoma,
      leukemia)
  Granulomas
    Neurosarcoid
    Histiocytosis
    Xanthoma disseminatum
  Infectious
    Chronic meningitis
    Viral encephalitis
    Toxoplasmosis
  Inflammatory
    Lymphocytic
      infundibuloneuro-
      hypophysitis
    Wegener's granulomatosis
    Lupus erythematosus
    Scleroderma
  Chemical toxins
    Tetrodotoxin
    Snake venom
  Vascular
    Sheehan's syndrome
    Aneurysm (internal carotid)
    Aortocoronary bypass
    Hypoxic encephalopathy
  Pregnancy (vasopressinase)
  Idiopathic
Congenital malformations
  Septooptic dysplasia
  Midline craniofacial defects
  Holoprosencephaly
  Hypogensis, ectopia of pituitary
Genetic
  Autosomal dominant (AVP-
    neurophysin gene)
  Autosomal recessive (AVP-
    neurophysin gene)
  Autosomal recessive-Wolfram-
    (4p − WFS 1 gene)
  X-linked recessive (Xq28)
  Deletion chromosome 7q

Nephrogenic diabetes insipidus
Acquired
  Drugs
    Lithium
    Demeclocycline
    Methoxyflurane
    Amphotericin B
    Aminoglycosides
    Cisplatin
    Rifampin
    Foscarnet
  Metabolic
    Hypercalcemia, hypercalciuria
    Hypokalemia
  Obstruction (ureter or urethra)
  Vascular
    Sickle cell disease and trait
    Ischemia (acute tubular
      necrosis)
  Granulomas
    Neurosarcoid
  Neoplasms
    Sarcoma
  Infiltration
    Amyloidosis
  Pregnancy
  Idiopathic
Genetic
  X-linked recessive (AVP
    receptor-2 gene)
  Autosomal recessive (aquaporin-2
    gene)
  Autosomal dominant (aquaporin-2
    gene)
Primary polydipsia
Acquired
  Psychogenic
    Schizophrenia
    Obsessive-compulsive
      disorder
  Dipsogenic (abnormal thirst)
    Granulomas
      Neurosarcoid
    Infectious
      Tuberculous meningitis
    Head trauma (closed and penetrating)
    Demyelination
      Multiple sclerosis
    Drugs
      Lithium
      Carbamazepine
    Idiopathic
  Iatrogenic

deficiency is characterized by production of large amounts of dilute urine. In *central DI*, insufficient AVP is released in response to physiologic stimuli. Causes include congenital, acquired, or genetic disorders, but almost half the time it is idiopathic. In gestational DI, increased metabolism of plasma AVP by an aminopeptidase produced by the placenta leads to a deficiency of AVP during pregnancy. *Primary polydipsia* results in secondary insufficiencies of AVP due to inhibition of AVP secretion by excessive fluid intake. *Nephrogenic DI* can be genetic or acquired from drug exposure or renal damage.

Clinical Features Symptoms include polyuria, excessive thirst, and polydipsia, with a 24-h urine output of >50(mL/kg)/day and a urine osmolality that is less than that of serum (<300 mosmol/kg; specific gravity <1.010). Clinical or laboratory signs of dehydration, including hypernatremia, occur only if the pt simultaneously has a thirst defect or does not have access to water. Other etiologies of hypernatremia are described in Chap. 26.

Diagnosis DI must be differentiated from other etiologies of polyuria (Chap. 25). Unless an inappropriately dilute urine is present in the setting of serum hyperosmolality, a fluid deprivation test is used to make the diagnosis of DI. This test should be started in the morning, and body weight, plasma osmolality, sodium concentration, and urine volume and osmolality should be measured hourly. The test should be stopped when body weight decreases by 5% or plasma osmolality/sodium exceed the upper limit of normal. If the urine osmolality is <300 mosmol/kg with serum hyperosmolality, desmopressin (0.03 µg/kg SC) should be administered with repeat measurement of urine osmolality 1–2 h later. An increase of >50% indicates severe pituitary DI, whereas a smaller or absent response suggests nephrogenic DI. Measurement of AVP levels before and after fluid deprivation may be required to diagnose partial DI. Occasionally, hypertonic saline infusion may be required if fluid deprivation does not achieve the requisite level of hypertonic dehydration.

℞ TREATMENT

Pituitary DI can be treated with desmopressin (DDAVP) subcutaneously (1–2 µg qd-bid), via nasal spray (10–20 µg bid-tid), or orally (100–400 µg bid-tid), with recommendations to drink to thirst. Chlorpropamide has also been used, though caution must be used to avoid hypoglycemia and a disulfuram-like reaction to ethanol. Symptoms of nephrogenic DI may be ameliorated by treatment with a thiazide diuretic and/or amiloride in conjunction with a low-sodium diet, or with prostaglandin synthesis inhibitors (e.g., indomethacin).

SYNDROME OF INAPPROPRIATE ANTIDIURETIC HORMONE (SIADH)

Etiology Excessive or inappropriate production of AVP predisposes to hyponatremia, reflecting water retention. The evaluation of hyponatremia is described in Chap. 26. Etiologies of SIADH include neoplasms (lung, GI, pancreas, thymoma), lung infections, CNS disorders, and drugs (desmopressin, chlorpropamide, vincristine, carbamazepine, phenothiazines, cyclophosphamide, narcotics, tricyclic antidepressants, SSRIs) (Table 170-2).

Clinical Features If the hyponatremia develops gradually, it may be asymptomatic. However, if it develops acutely, symptoms of water intoxication may include mild headache, confusion, anorexia, nausea, vomiting, coma, and convulsions. Laboratory findings include low BUN, creatinine, uric acid, and

Table 170-2

Causes of Syndrome of Inappropriate Antidiuretic Hormone (SIADH)

Neoplasms	Neurologic
Carcinomas	Guillain-Barré syndrome
Lung	Multiple sclerosis
Duodenum	Delerium tremens
Pancreas	Amytrophic lateral sclerosis
Ovary	Hydrocephalus
Bladder, ureter	Psychosis
Other neoplasms	Peripheral neuropathy
Thymoma	Congenital malformations
Mesothelioma	Agenesis corpus callosum
Bronchial adenoma	Cleft lip/palate
Carcinoid	Other midline defects
Gangliocytoma	Metabolic
Ewing's sarcoma	Acute intermittent porphyria
Head trauma (closed and penetrating)	Pulmonary
Infections	Asthma
Pneumonia, bacterial or viral	Pneumothorax
Abscess, lung or brain	Positive-pressure respiration
Cavitation (aspergillosis)	Drugs
Tuberculosis, lung or brain	Vasopressin or DDAVP
Meningitis, bacterial or viral	Chlorpropamide
Encephalitis	Oxytocin, high dose
AIDS	Vincristine
Vascular	Carbamazepine
Cerebrovascular occlusions, hemorrhage	Nicotine
Cavernous sinus thrombosis	Phenothiazines
	Cyclophosphamide
	Tricyclic antidepressants
	Monoamine oxidase inhibitors
	Serotonin reuptake inhibitors

albumin; serum Na <130 mmol/L and plasma osmolality <270 mmol/kg; urine is almost always hypertonic to plasma, and urinary Na+ is usually >20 mmol/L.

 TREATMENT

Fluid intake should be restricted to 500 mL less than urinary output. In patients with severe symptoms or signs, hypertonic (3%) saline can be infused at ≤0.05 mL/kg body weight IV per minute, with hourly sodium levels measured until Na increases by 12 mmol/L or to 130 mmol/L, whichever occurs first. However, if the hyponatremia has been present for more than 24–48 h and is corrected too rapidly, saline infusion has the potential to produce central pontine myelinolysis. Demeclocycline (150–300 mg PO tid-qid) or fludrocortisone (0.05–0.2 mg PO bid) may be required to manage chronic SIADH.

For a more detailed discussion, see Robertson, GL: Disorders of the Neurohypophysis, Chap. 329, p. 2052, in HPIM-15.

171

DISORDERS OF THE THYROID

Disorders of the thyroid gland result primarily from autoimmune processes that stimulate the overproduction of thyroid hormones (*thyrotoxicosis*) or cause glandular destruction and underproduction of thyroid hormones (*hypothyroidism*). *Neoplastic processes* in the thyroid gland can lead to benign nodules or thyroid cancer.

The hypothalamus releases thyrotropin-releasing hormone (TRH), which stimulates release of thyroid-stimulating hormone (TSH) from the anterior pituitary. TSH is secreted into the circulation and binds to receptors in the thyroid gland, where it controls production and release of thyroxine (T_4) and triiodothyronine (T_3), which in turn inhibit further release of TSH from the pituitary. Some T_3 is secreted by the thyroid, but most is produced by deiodination of T_4 in peripheral tissues. Both T_4 and T_3 are bound to carrier proteins [thyroid-binding globulin (TBG), transthyretin, and albumin] in the circulation. Increased levels of total T_4 and T_3 with normal free levels are seen in states of increased carrier proteins (pregnancy, estrogens, cirrhosis, hepatitis, and inherited disorders). Conversely, decreased total T_4 and T_3 levels with normal free levels are seen in severe systemic illness, chronic liver disease, and nephrosis.

HYPOTHYROIDISM

Etiology Deficient thyroid hormone secretion can be due to thyroid failure (primary hypothyroidism) or pituitary or hypothalamic disease (secondary hypothyroidism) (Table 171-1). Transient hypothyroidism may occur in silent or subacute thyroiditis. *Subclinical hypothyroidism* is a state of normal thyroid hormone levels and mild elevation of TSH; despite the name, some pts may have minor symptoms. With higher TSH levels and low free T_4 levels, symptoms become more readily apparent in *clinical* (or *overt*) *hypothyroidism*. In areas of iodine sufficiency, autoimmune disease and iatrogenic causes are most common.

Clinical Features Symptoms of hypothyroidism include lethargy, dry hair and skin, cold intolerance, hair loss, difficulty concentrating, poor memory, constipation, mild weight gain with poor appetite, dyspnea, hoarse voice, muscle cramping, and menorrhagia. Cardinal features on examination include bradycardia, mild diastolic hypertension, prolongation of the relaxation phase of deep tendon reflexes, and cool peripheral extremities. Carpal tunnel syndrome may be present. Cardiomegaly may be present due to pericardial effusion. The most extreme presentation is a dull, expressionless face, sparse hair, periorbital puffiness, large tongue, and pale, doughy, cool skin. The condition may progress into a hypothermic, stuporous state (*myxedema coma*) with respiratory depression. Factors that predispose to myxedema coma include cold exposure, trauma, infection, and administration of narcotics.

Diagnosis Decreased serum T_4 is common to all varieties of hypothyroidism. An elevated TSH is a sensitive marker of primary hypothyroidism. A summary of the investigations used to determine the existence and cause of hypothyroidism is provided in Figure 171-1. Thyroid peroxidase (TPO) antibodies are increased in 90–95% of patients with autoimmune-mediated hypothyroidism. Serum cholesterol, creatine phosphokinase, and lactic dehydrogenase may be elevated, and bradycardia, low-amplitude QRS complexes, and flattened or inverted T waves may be present on ECG.

Table 171-1

Causes of Hypothyroidism

Primary
    Autoimmune hypothyroidism: Hashimoto's thyroiditis, atrophic thyroiditis
    Iatrogenic: ^{131}I treatment, subtotal or total thyroidectomy, external irradiation
       of neck for lymphoma or cancer
    Drugs: iodine excess (including iodine-containing contrast media and amio-
       darone), lithium, antithyroid drugs, p-aminosalicyclic acid, interferon-α and
       other cytokines, aminoglutethimide
    Congenital hypothyroidism: absent or ectopic thyroid gland, dyshormono-
       genesis, TSH-R mutation
    Iodine deficiency
    Infiltrative disorders: amyloidosis, sarcoidosis, hemochromatosis, sclero-
       derma, cystinosis, Riedel's thyroiditis
Transient
    Silent thyroiditis, including postpartum thyroiditis
    Subacute thyroiditis
    Withdrawal of thyroxine treatment in individuals with an intact thyroid
    After ^{131}I treatment or subtotal thyroidectomy for Graves' disease
Secondary
    Hypopituitarism: tumors, pituitary surgery or irradiation, infiltrative disor-
       ders, Sheehan's syndrome, trauma, genetic forms of combined pituitary hor-
       mone deficiencies
    Isolated TSH deficiency or inactivity
    Bexarotene treatment
    Hypothalamic disease: tumors, trauma, infiltrative disorders, idiopathic

NOTE: TSH, thyroid-stimulating hormone; TSH-R, TSH receptor.

 TREATMENT

Adult pts <60 years without evidence of heart disease may be started on 50–
100 μg of levothyroxine (T_4) daily. In the elderly or in pts with known coronary artery disease, the starting dose of levothyroxine is 12.5–25 $\mu g/d$. The
dose should be adjusted in 12.5-to-25 μg increments at 6–8 week intervals
on the basis of TSH levels, until a normal TSH level is achieved. The usual
daily replacement dose is 1.5($\mu g/kg$)/d. Women on levothyroxine replacement
who become pregnant should have a TSH level checked at each trimester, as
dose increases are frequently required during pregnancy. Failure to recognize
and treat maternal hypothyroidism may adversely affect fetal neural development. Therapy for myxedema coma should include levothyroxine (200 μg)
and liothyroinine (25 μg) as a single IV bolus followed by daily treatment
with levothyroxine (50–100 $\mu g/d$) and liothyronine (10 μg q8h), along with
hydrocortisone (50 mg q6h) for impaired adrenal reserve, ventilatory support,
space blankets, and therapy of precipitating factors.

THYROTOXICOSIS

   Etiology   Causes of thyroid hormone excess include primary hyperthyroidism (Graves' disease, toxic multinodular goiter, toxic adenoma, iodine excess);
thyroid destruction (subacute thyroiditis, silent thyroiditis, amiodarone, radiation); extrathyroidal sources of thyroid hormone (thyrotoxicosis factitia, struma
ovarii, functioning follicular carcinoma); and secondary hyperthyroidism (TSH-
secreting pituitary adenoma, thyroid hormone resistance syndrome, hCG-se-
creting tumors, gestational thyrotoxicosis).

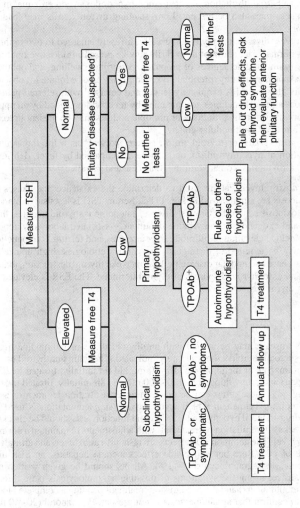

FIGURE 171-1 Evaluation of hypothyroidism. TPOAb⁺, thyroid peroxidase antibodies present; TPOAb⁻, thyroid peroxidase antibodies not present.

Clinical Features   Symptoms include nervousness, irritability, heat intolerance, excessive sweating, palpitations, fatigue and weakness, weight loss with increased appetite, frequent bowel movements, and oligomenorrhea. Pts are anxious, restless and fidgety. Skin is warm and moist, and fingernails may separate from the nail bed (Plummer's nails). Eyelid retraction and lid lag may be present. Cardiovascular findings include tachycardia, systolic hypertension, systolic murmur, and atrial fibrillation. A fine tremor, hyperreflexia, and proximal muscle weakness may also be present. Long-standing thyrotoxicosis may lead to osteopenia.

In Graves' disease, the thyroid is usually diffusely enlarged to two to three times its normal size, and a bruit or thrill may be present. Infiltrative ophthalmopathy (with variable degrees of proptosis, periorbital swelling, and ophthalmoplegia) and dermopathy (pretibial myxedema) may also be found. In subacute thyroiditis, the thyroid is exquisitely tender and enlarged with referred pain to the jaw or ear, and sometimes accompanied by fever and preceded by an upper respiratory tract infection. Solitary or multiple nodules may be present in toxic adenoma or toxic multinodular goiter.

Thyrotoxic crisis, or thyroid storm, is rare, presents as a life-threatening exacerbation of hyperthyroidism, and can be accompanied by fever, delirium, seizures, arrhythmias, coma, vomiting, diarrhea, and jaundice.

Diagnosis   Investigations used to determine the existence and causes of thyrotoxicosis are summarized in Fig. 171-2. Serum TSH is a sensitive marker of thyrotoxicosis caused by Graves' disease, autonomous thyroid nodules, thyroiditis, and exogenous levothyroxine treatment. Associated laboratory abnormalities include elevation of bilirubin, liver enzymes, and ferritin. Radionuclide uptake may be required to distinguish the various etiologies: high uptake in Graves' disease and nodular disease vs. low uptake in thyroid destruction, iodine excess, and extrathyroidal sources of thyroid hormone. The ESR is elevated in subacute thyroiditis.

℞ TREATMENT

Graves' disease may be treated with antithyroid drugs or radioiodine treatment; subtotal thyroidectomy is rarely indicated. The main antithyroid drugs are carbimazole or methimazole (10–20 mg bid-tid initially, titrated to 2.5–10 mg qd) and propylthiouracil (100–200 mg q6–8h initially, titrated to 50–100 mg qd). These drugs can be given in either a titration regimen or as a block-replace regimen in which levothyroxine supplementation is used to avoid drug-induced hypothyroidism. Thyroid function tests should be checked 3–4 weeks after initiation of treatment, with adjustments to maintain a normal free T_4 level. The common side effects are rash, urticaria, fever, and arthralgia (1–5% of pts). Rare but major side effects include hepatitis, an SLE-like syndrome, and agranulocytosis (<1%). All pts should be given written instructions regarding the symptoms of possible agranulocytosis (sore throat, fever, mouth ulcers) and the need to stop treatment pending a complete blood count to confirm that agranulocytosis is not present. Propranolol (20–40 mg q6h) or longer acting beta blockers such as atenolol (50 mg qd) may be useful to control adrenergic symptoms. Anticoagulation with warfarin should be considered in all pts with atrial fibrillation. Radioiodine can also be used as initial treatment or in pts who do not undergo remission after a 1–2 year trial of antithyroid drugs. Antecedent treatment with antithyroid drugs should be considered in elderly pts and those with cardiac problems, with cessation of antithyroid drugs 3–5 days prior to radioiodine administration. Radioiodine treatment is contraindicated in pregnancy; instead, symptoms should be con-

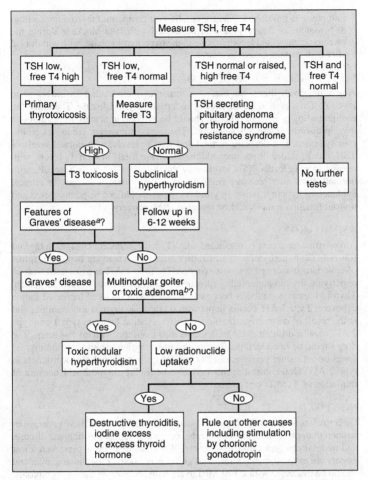

FIGURE 171-2 Evaluation of thyrotoxicosis. [a]Diffuse goiter, positive TPO antibodies, ophthalmopathy, dermopathy; [b]can be confirmed by radionuclide scan.

trolled with the lowest effective dose of propylthiouracil (PTU). Corneal drying may be relieved with artificial tears and taping the eyelids shut during sleep. Progressive exophthalmos with chemosis, ophthalmoplegia, or vision loss is treated with large doses of prednisone (60–80 mg qd) and ophthalmologic referral; orbital decompression may be required.

In thyroid storm, large doses of PTU (600-mg loading dose) should be administered orally, per nasogastric tube, or per rectum, followed 1 h later by ipodate or iopanoic acid (0.5 mg PO q12 h) or other available oral contrast agents. PTU (200–300 mg q6h) should be continued, along with propranolol (40–60 mg PO q4h or 2 mg IV q4h) and dexamethasone (2 mg q6h). Any underlying precipitating cause should be identified and treated.

Radioiodine is the treatment of choice for toxic nodular goiter. Subacute thyroiditis should be treated with NSAIDs and beta blockade to control symptoms, with monitoring of the TSH and free T_4 levels every 4 weeks. Transient levothyroxine replacement (50–100 μg qd) may be required if the hypothyroid phase is prolonged. Silent thyroiditis (or postpartum thyroiditis if within 3–6 months of delivery) should be treated with beta blockade during the thyrotoxic phase and levothyroxine in the hypothyroid phase, with withdrawal after 6–9 months to assess recovery.

SICK EUTHYROID SYNDROME

Any acute, severe illness can cause abnormalities of circulating thyroid hormone levels or TSH, even in the absence of underlying thyroid disease. Therefore, the routine testing of thyroid function should be avoided in acutely ill pts unless a thyroid disorder is strongly suspected. The most common pattern in sick euthyroid syndrome is a decrease in total and free T_3 levels, with normal levels of TSH and T_4. More ill pts may additionally have a fall in total T_4 levels, with normal free T_4 levels. TSH levels may range from <0.1 to >20 mU/L, with normalization after recovery from illness. Unless there is historic or clinical evidence of hypothyroidism, thyroid hormone should not be administered and thyroid function tests should be repeated after recovery.

AMIODARONE

Amiodarone treatment is associated with (1) acute, transient changes in thyroid function, (2) hypothyroidism, or (3) thyrotoxicosis. There are two major forms of amiodarone-induced thyrotoxicosis (AIT). Type 1 AIT is associated with an underlying thyroid abnormality (preclinical Graves' disease or nodular goiter). Thyroid hormone synthesis becomes excessive as a result of increased iodine exposure. Type 2 AIT occurs in pts with no intrinsic thyroid abnormalities and is the result of destructive thyroiditis. Differentiation between type 1 and type 2 AIT may be difficult as the high iodine load interferes with thyroid scans. The drug should be stopped, if possible, with administration of high-dose antithyroid drugs or potassium perchlorate (200 mg q6h) in type 1 and glucocorticoids in type 2 AIT. Oral contrast agents may also be useful in type 2 AIT because of inhibition of T_4 to T_3 conversion.

NONTOXIC GOITER

Goiter refers to an enlarged thyroid gland (>20–25 g) and is more common in women than men. Biosynthetic defects, iodine deficiency, autoimmune disease, and nodular diseases can lead to goiter. If thyroid function is preserved, most goiters are asymptomatic. Substernal goiter may obstruct the thoracic inlet and should be evaluated with CT or MRI in pts with obstructive signs or symptoms. Thyroid function tests should be performed in all pts with goiter to exclude thyrotoxicosis or hypothyroidism. Ultrasound is not generally indicated in the evaluation of diffuse goiter, unless a nodule is palpable on physical exam.

Iodine or thyroid hormone replacement induces variable regression of goiter in iodine deficiency. For other causes of nontoxic diffuse goiter, levothyroxine can be used in an attempt to reduce goiter size. Significant regression is usually seen within 3 to 6 months of treatment; after this time it is unlikely to occur. Because underlying autonomy may be present, suppression should be instituted gradually. In younger pts, the dose can be started at 100 μg/d and adjusted to suppress the TSH into the low-normal but detectable range. Treatment of elderly pts should be initiated at 50 μg/d. Surgery is rarely indicated for diffuse goiter; radioiodine reduces goiter size by about 50% in the majority of pts.

TOXIC MULTINODULAR GOITER AND TOXIC ADENOMA

TOXIC MULTINODULAR GOITER (MNG) In addition to features of goiter, the clinical presentation of toxic MNG includes subclinical hyperthyroidism or mild thyrotoxicosis. The pt is usually elderly and may present with atrial fibrillation or palpitations, tachycardia, nervousness, tremor, or weight loss. Recent exposure to iodine, from contrast dyes or other sources, may precipitate or exacerbate thyrotoxicosis. The TSH level is low. T_4 may be normal or minimally increased; T_3 is often elevated to a greater degree than T_4. Thyroid scan shows heterogeneous uptake with multiple regions of increased and decreased uptake; 24-h uptake of radioiodine may not be increased. Antithyroid drugs, often in combination with beta blockers, can normalize thyroid function and improve clinical features of thyrotoxicosis but may stimulate goiter growth. A trial of radioiodine should be considered before subjecting pts, many of whom are elderly, to surgery.

TOXIC ADENOMA   A solitary, autonomously functioning thyroid nodule is referred to as *toxic adenoma*. Most pts with solitary hyperfunctioning nodules have acquired somatic, activating mutations in the TSH receptor. A thyroid scan provides a definitive diagnostic test, demonstrating focal uptake in the hyperfunctioning nodule and diminished uptake in the remainder of the gland, as activity of the normal thyroid is suppressed. Radioiodine ablation (e.g., 10–29.9 mCi ^{131}I) is usually the treatment of choice.

THYROID NEOPLASMS

Etiology   Thyroid neoplasms may be benign (adenomas) or malignant (carcinomas). Benign neoplasms include macrofollicular (colloid) and normofollicular adenomas. Microfollicular, trabecular, and Hurthle cell variants raise greater concern. Carcinomas of the follicular epithelium include papillary, follicular, and anaplastic thyroid cancer. Papillary thyroid cancer is the most common type of thyroid cancer. It tends to be multifocal and to invade locally. Follicular thyroid cancer is difficult to diagnose via fine-needle aspiration because the distinction between benign and malignant follicular neoplasms rests largely on evidence of invasion into vessels, nerves, or adjacent structures. It tends to spread hematogenously, leading to bone, lung, and CNS metastases. Anaplastic carcinoma is rare, highly malignant, and rapidly fatal. Thyroid lymphoma often arises in the background of Hashimoto's thyroiditis and occurs in the setting of a rapidly expanding thyroid mass. Medullary thyroid carcinoma arises from parafollicular (C) cells and may occur sporadically or as a familial disorder, sometimes in association with multiple endocrine neoplasia type 2.

Clinical Features   It is important to distinguish between a solitary nodule or a prominent nodule in the context of a multinodular goiter, as the incidence of malignancy is greater in solitary nodules. Features suggesting carcinoma include recent or rapid growth of a nodule or mass, history of neck irradiation, lymph node involvement, and fixation to surrounding tissues. Glandular enlargement may result in compression and displacement of the trachea or esophagus and obstructive symptoms.

Diagnosis   An approach to the evaluation of a solitary nodule is outlined in Fig. 171-3.

℞ TREATMENT

Benign nodules should be monitored via serial examination, with consideration of TSH suppression with levothyroxine to prevent further growth. Surgical resection or radioiodine ablation may be required in multinodular goiters with compressive effects.

Near-total thyroidectomy with lymph node dissection is required for papillary and follicular carcinoma and should be performed by a surgeon who is highly experienced in the procedure. If risk factors and pathologic features

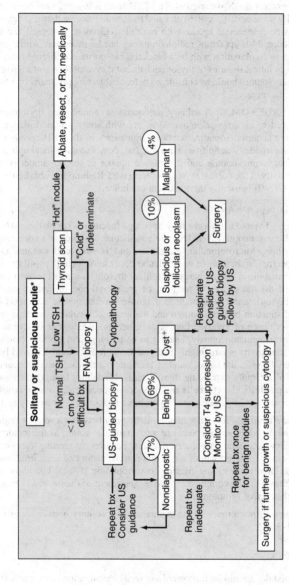

FIGURE 171-3 Approach to the patient with a thyroid nodule. *There are many exceptions to the suggested options. See text and references for detail. †About one-third of nodules are cystic or mixed solid-cystic. US, ultrasound.

indicate the need for radioiodine treatment, the pt should be treated for several weeks postoperatively with liothyronine (25 μg bid-tid), followed by withdrawal for an additional 2 weeks, in preparation for postsurgical radioablation of remnant tissue. A scanning dose of ^{131}I is administered when the TSH level is >50 IU/L, followed by a therapeutic dose. Subsequent levothyroxine suppression of TSH to a low, but detectable, level should be attempted in pts with a high risk of recurrence, and to 0.1–0.5 IU/L in those with a low risk of recurrence. Follow-up scans and thyroglobulin levels should be performed at regular intervals after either thyroid hormone withdrawal or administration of recombinant human TSH.

The management of medullary thyroid carcinoma is surgical, as these tumors do not take up radioiodine. Testing for the *RET* mutation should be considered. Elevated serum calcitonin provides a marker of residual or recurrent disease.

For a more detailed discussion, see Jameson JL and Weetman AP: Diseases of the Thyroid, Chap. 330, p. 2060, in HPIM-15.

172

DISORDERS OF THE ADRENAL GLAND

The adrenal cortex produces three major classes of steroids: (1) glucocorticoids, (2) mineralocorticoids, and (3) adrenal androgens. Clinical syndromes may result from deficiencies or excesses of these hormones. The adrenal medulla produces catecholamines, with excess leading to pheochromocytoma (Chap. 124).

HYPERFUNCTION OF THE ADRENAL GLAND

CUSHING'S SYNDROME *Etiology* Cushing's syndrome results from production of excess cortisol (and other steroid hormones) by the adrenal cortex. The major cause is bilateral adrenal hyperplasia secondary to hypersecretion of adrenocorticotropic hormone (ACTH) by the pituitary (Cushing's disease) or from ectopic sources such as small cell carcinoma of the lung, medullary carcinoma of the thyroid, or tumors of the thymus, pancreas, or ovary. Adenomas or carcinoma of the adrenal gland account for about 25% of Cushing's syndrome cases. Administration of glucocorticoids for therapeutic reasons may result in iatrogenic Cushing's syndrome.

Clinical Features Some common manifestations (central obesity, hypertension, osteoporosis, emotional lability, acne, amenorrhea, and diabetes mellitus) are relatively nonspecific. More specific findings include easy bruising, purple striae, proximal myopathy, fat deposition in the face and interscapular areas (moon facies and buffalo hump), and virilization. Hypokalemia and metabolic alkalosis are prominent, particularly with ectopic production of ACTH.

Diagnosis The diagnosis of Cushing's syndrome requires demonstration of increased cortisol production and abnormal cortisol suppression in response to dexamethasone (Fig. 172-1). For initial screening, the 1-mg overnight dexamethasone test (8 A.M. plasma cortisol <5 μg/dL) or measurement of 24-h urinary free cortisol is appropriate. Definitive diagnosis is established by inadequate suppression of urinary (<30 μg/d) or plasma cortisol (<5 μg/dL) after 0.5 mg dexamethasone q6h for 48 h. Once the diagnosis of Cushing's syndrome is established, further biochemical testing is required to localize the source. Low levels of plasma ACTH levels suggest an adrenal adenoma or carcinoma; inappropriately normal or high plasma ACTH levels suggest a pituitary or ectopic source. In 95% of ACTH-producing pituitary microadenomas, cortisol production is suppressed by high-dose dexamethasone (2 mg q6h for 48 h), and MRI of the pituitary should be obtained. However, because up to 10% of ectopic sources of ACTH may also suppress after high-dose dexamethasone testing, inferior petrosal sinus sampling may be required to distinguish pituitary from peripheral sources of ACTH. Imaging of the chest and abdomen is required to localize the source of ectopic ACTH production. Pts with chronic alcoholism and depression may have false-positive results in testing for Cushing's syndrome. Similarly, pts with acute illness may have abnormal laboratory test results, since major stress disrupts the normal regulation of ACTH secretion.

℞ TREATMENT

Therapy of adrenal adenoma or carcinoma requires surgical excision; stress doses of glucocorticoids must be given pre- and postoperatively. Metastatic and unresectable adrenal carcinomas are treated with mitotane in doses gradually increased to 6 g/d in three or four divided doses. Transsphenoidal surgery can be curative for pituitary microadenomas that secrete ACTH (see Chap. 169). On occasion, debulking of lung carcinoma or resection of carcinoid tumors can result in remission of ectopic Cushing's syndrome. If the source of ACTH cannot be resected, bilateral total adrenalectomy or medical management with ketoconazole (600–1200 mg/d), metyrapone (2–3 g/d), or mitotane (2–3 mg/d) may relieve manifestations of cortisol excess.

ALDOSTERONISM *Etiology* Aldosteronism is caused by hypersecretion of the adrenal mineralocorticoid aldosterone. Primary aldosteronism refers to an adrenal cause and can be due to either an adrenal adenoma or bilateral adrenal hyperplasia. The term *secondary aldosteronism* is used when an extraadrenal stimulus is present, as in renal artery stenosis or diuretic therapy.

Clinical Features Most pts with primary hyperaldosteronism have headaches and diastolic hypertension. Edema is characteristically absent, unless congestive heart failure or renal disease is present. Hypokalemia, caused by urinary potassium losses, may cause muscle weakness and fatigue, though potassium levels may be normal in mild primary aldosteronism. Hypernatremia and metabolic alkalosis may also occur.

Diagnosis The diagnosis is suggested by hypertension that is associated with persistent hypokalemia in a nonedematous pt who is not receiving potassium-wasting diuretics. In pts receiving potassium-wasting diuretics, the diuretic should be discontinued and potassium supplements should be administered for 1–2 weeks. If hypokalemia persists after supplementation, screening using a serum aldosterone and plasma renin activity should be performed. A ratio of serum aldosterone (in ng/dL) to plasma renin activity (in ng/mL per hour) >30 and an absolute level of aldosterone >15 ng/dL suggest primary aldosteronism.

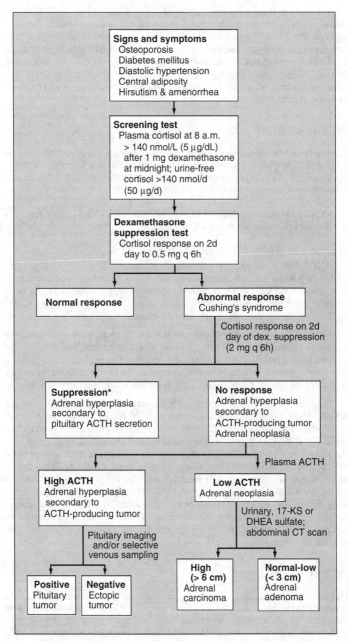

FIGURE 172-1 Diagnostic flowchart for evaluating patients suspected of having Cushing's syndrome. *This group probably includes some patients with pituitary-hypothalmic dysfunction and some with pituitary microadenomas. In some instances, a microadenoma may be visualized by pituitary MRI scanning. 17-KS, 17-ketosteroids; DHEA, dehydroepiandrosterone.

Failure to suppress plasma aldosterone (to <5 ng/dL after 500 mL/h of normal saline × 4 h) or urinary aldosterone after saline or sodium loading (to < 10 μg/d on day 3 of 200 mmol Na PO qd + fludrocortisone 0.2 mg bid × 3 days) confirms primary hyperaldosteronism. Localization should then be undertaken with a high-resolution CT scan of the adrenal glands. If the CT scan is negative, bilateral adrenal vein sampling may be required to diagnose a unilateral aldosterone-producing adenoma. Secondary hyperaldosteronism is associated with elevated plasma renin activity.

 TREATMENT

Surgery can be curative in pts with adrenal adenoma but is not effective for adrenal hyperplasia, which is managed with sodium restriction and spironolactone (25–100 mg tid) or amiloride. Secondary aldosteronism is treated with salt restriction and correction of the underlying cause.

SYNDROMES OF ADRENAL ANDROGEN EXCESS See Chap. 174 for discussion of hirsutism and virilization.

HYPOFUNCTION OF THE ADRENAL GLAND

ADDISON'S DISEASE *Etiology* Addison's disease occurs when >90% of adrenal tissue is destroyed surgically, by granulomatous disease (tuberculosis, histoplasmosis, coccidioidomycosis, cryptococcosis), or via autoimmune mechanisms. Bilateral tumor metastases, bilateral hemorrhage, CMV, HIV, amyloidosis, and sarcoidosis are rare causes.

Clinical Features Manifestations include fatigue, weakness, anorexia, nausea and vomiting, weight loss, abdominal pain, cutaneous and mucosal pigmentation, salt craving, hypotension, and occasionally, hypoglycemia. Routine laboratory parameters may be normal, or serum Na can be reduced and serum K is often increased. Extracellular fluid depletion accentuates hypotension.

Diagnosis The best screening test is the cortisol response 60 min after 250 μg ACTH (cosyntropin) IV or IM. Cortisol levels should normally be > 18 μg/dL 30–60 min after the ACTH. If the response is abnormal, then primary and secondary deficiency may be distinguished by measurement of aldosterone from the same blood samples. In secondary, but not primary, adrenal insufficiency, the aldosterone increment from baseline will be normal (≥ 5 ng/dL). Furthermore, in primary adrenal insufficiency, plasma ACTH is elevated, whereas in secondary adrenal insufficiency, plasma ACTH values are low or inappropriately normal. Pts with recent onset or partial pituitary insufficiency may have a normal response to the rapid ACTH stimulation test. In these pts, alternative testing (metyrapone test, insulin tolerance testing, or the 1-μg ACTH test) may be used for diagnosis.

 TREATMENT

Hydrocortisone, at 20–30 mg/d divided into 2/3 in the morning and 1/3 in the afternoon, is the mainstay of glucocorticoid replacement. Some pts benefit from doses administered three times daily, and other glucocorticoids may be given at equivalent doses. Mineralocorticoid supplementation is usually needed for primary adrenal insufficiency, with administration of 0.05–0.1 mg fludrocortisone PO qd and maintenance of adequate Na intake. Doses should be titrated to normalize Na and K levels and to maintain normal bp without postural changes. Measurement of plasma renin levels may also be useful in titrating the dose. All pts with adrenal insufficiency should be instructed in the parenteral self-administration of steroids and should be registered with a medical alert system. During periods of intercurrent illness, the dose of hydrocortisone should be doubled. During adrenal crisis, effective treatment of hypotension additionally requires repletion of Na and water deficits with normal saline.

HYPOALDOSTERONISM   Isolated aldosterone deficiency accompanied by normal cortisol production occurs with hyporeninism, as an inherited biosynthetic defect, postoperatively following removal of aldosterone-secreting adenomas, and during protracted heparin therapy. Hyporeninemic hypoaldosteronism is seen most commonly in adults with mild renal failure and diabetes mellitus in association with disproportionate hyperkalemia. Oral fludrocortisone (0.05–0.15 mg PO qd) restores electrolyte balance if salt intake is adequate. In pts with hypertension, mild renal insufficiency, or congestive heart failure, an alternative approach is to reduce salt intake and to administer furosemide.

INCIDENTAL ADRENAL MASSES

Adrenal masses are common findings on abdominal CT or MRI scans. More than 90% of such "incidentalomas" are nonfunctional, and the probability of an adrenal carcinoma is low (<0.01%). The first step in evaluation is to determine the functional status by measuring 24-h urinary catecholamines and metabolites, obtaining a serum potassium, and performing an overnight dexamethasone-suppression test. Surgery should be considered for nonfunctional masses >4 cm and for all functional masses. If surgery is not performed, a follow-up CT scan should be obtained in 3–6 months. In a pt with a known extraadrenal malignancy, there is a 30–50% chance that the incidentaloma is a metastasis.

CLINICAL USES OF GLUCOCORTICOIDS

Glucocorticoids are pharmacologic agents used for a variety of disorders such as asthma, rheumatoid arthritis, and psoriasis. The almost certain development of complications (weight gain, hypertension, Cushingoid facies, diabetes mellitus, osteoporosis, myopathy, increased intraocular pressure, ischemic bone necrosis, infection, and hypercholesterolemia) must be weighed against the potential therapeutic benefits of glucocorticoid therapy. These side effects can be minimized by a careful choice of steroid preparations (Table 172-1), alternate-

Table 172-1

Glucocorticoid Preparations

Generic Name	Relative Potency		Dose equivalent
	Glucocorticoid	Mineral-ocorticoid	
Short-acting			
Hydrocortisone	1.0	1.0	20.0
Cortisone	0.8	0.8	25.0
Intermediate-acting			
Prednisone	4.0	0.25	5.0
Methylprednisolone	5.0	0	4.0
Triamcinolone	5.0	0	4.0
Long-acting			
Dexamethasone	25.0	0	0.75
Betamethasone	25.0	0	0.6

Table 172-2

A Checklist for Use Prior to the Administration of Glucocorticoids in Pharmacologic Doses

Presence of tuberculosis or other chronic infection (chest x-ray, tuberculin test)
Evidence of glucose intolerance or history of gestational diabetes mellitus
Evidence of preexisting osteoporosis (bone density assessment in organ transplant recipients or postmenopausal patients)
History of peptic ulcer, gastritis, or esophagitis (stool guaiac test)
Evidence of hypertension or cardiovascular disease
History of psychological disorders

---

day or interrupted therapy; the use of topical steroids, i.e., inhaled, intranasal, or dermal whenever possible; and the judicious use of non-steroid therapies. Pts should be evaluated for the risk of complications before the initiation of glucocorticoid therapy (Table 172-2). Higher doses of glucocorticoids may be required during periods of stress, since the adrenal gland may atrophy in the setting of exogenous glucocorticoids. In addition, following long-term use, glucocorticoids should be tapered with the dual goals of allowing the pituitary-adrenal axis to recover and the avoidance of underlying disease flare.

For a more detailed discussion, see Williams GH, Dluhy RG: Diseases of the Adrenal Cortex, Chap. 331, p. 2084, in HPIM-15.

173

DIABETES MELLITUS

ETIOLOGY   Diabetes mellitus (DM) comprises a group of metabolic disorders that share the common phenotype of hyperglycemia. DM is currently classified on the basis of the pathogenic process that leads to hyperglycemia. Under this classification, the terms type 1 and type 2 DM have replaced insulin-dependent diabetes mellitus (IDDM) and noninsulin-dependent diabetes mellitus (NIDDM), respectively. Type 1 DM is characterized by insulin deficiency and a tendency to develop ketosis, whereas type 2 DM is a heterogeneous group of disorders characterized by variable degrees of insulin resistance, impaired insulin secretion, and increased glucose production. Other specific types include DM caused by genetic defects [maturity-onset diabetes of the young (MODY)], diseases of the exocrine pancreas (chronic pancreatitis, cystic fibrosis, hemochromatosis), endocrinopathies (acromegaly, Cushing's syndrome, glucagonoma, pheochromocytoma, hyperthyroidism), drugs (nicotinic acid, glucocorticoids, thiazides, protease inhibitors), and pregnancy (gestational diabetes mellitus).

DIAGNOSIS   Criteria for the diagnosis of DM include (1) fasting plasma glucose ≥ 7.0 mmol/L ($\geq$ 126 mg/dL), (2) symptoms of diabetes plus a random blood glucose concentration ≥ 11.1 mmol/L ($\geq$ 200 mg/dL), or (3) 2-h plasma glucose $\geq$ 11.1 mmol/L ($\geq$ 200 mg/dL during a 75-g oral glucose tolerance test. These criteria should be confirmed by repeat testing on a different day, unless unequivocal hyperglycemia with acute metabolic decompensation is present. Two intermediate categories have also been designated: impaired fasting glucose (IFG) for a fasting plasma glucose between 6.1 and 7.0 mmol/L (110 and 126 mg/dL) and impaired glucose tolerance (IGT) for plasma glucose levels between 7.8 and 11.1 mmol/L (140 and 200 mg/dL) 2 h after a 75-g oral glucose load. Individuals with IFG or IGT do not have DM but are at substantial risk for developing type 2 DM and cardiovascular disease in the future. The hemoglobin A_{1c} level is useful for monitoring responses to therapy but is not recommended for screening or diagnosis of DM.

Screening with a fasting plasma glucose level is recommended every 3 years for individuals over the age of 45, as well as for younger individuals with additional risk factors (Table 173-1).

CLINICAL FEATURES   Common presenting symptoms of DM include polyuria, polydipsia, weight loss, fatigue, weakness, blurred vision, frequent superficial infections, and poor wound healing. Acute complications of diabetes that may be seen on presentation include diabetic ketoacidosis (DKA) and non-ketotic hyperosmolar state (Chap. 40).

The chronic complications of DM are listed below:

- Ophthalmologic: nonproliferative or proliferative diabetic retinopathy
- Renal: proteinuria, end-stage renal disease (ESRD), type IV renal tubular acidosis
- Neurologic: distal symmetric polyneuropathy, polyradiculopathy, mononeuropathy, autonomic neuropathy
- Gastrointestinal: gastroparesis, diarrhea, constipation
- Genitourinary: cystopathy, erectile dysfunction, female sexual dysfunction
- Cardiovascular: coronary artery disease, congestive heart failure, peripheral vascular disease, stroke

Table 173-1

Risk Factors for Type 2 Diabetes Mellitus

- Family history of diabetes (i.e., parent or sibling with type 2 diabetes)
- Obesity (i.e., $\geq 20\%$ desired body weight or BMI $\geq$ 27 kg/m^2)
- Age ≥ 45 years
- Race/ethnicity (e.g., African American, Hispanic American, Native American, Asian American, Pacific Islander)
- Previously identified IFG or IGT
- History of GDM or delivery of baby over 9 lbs
- Hypertension (blood pressure $\geq$ 140/90 mm Hg)
- HDL cholesterol level ≤ 0.90 mmol/L (35 mg/dL) and/or a triglyceride level ≥ 2.82 mmol/L (250 mg/dL)
- Polycystic ovary syndrome

NOTE: BMI, body mass index; IFG, impaired fasting glucose; IGT, impaired glucose tolerance; GDM, gestational diabetes mellitus; HDL, high-density lipoprotein.
SOURCE: Adapted from American Diabetes Association, 2000.

- Lower extremity: foot deformity (hammer toe, claw toe, Charcot foot), ulceration, amputation

 TREATMENT

Optimal treatment of diabetes requires more than plasma glucose management. Comprehensive diabetes care should also detect and manage DM-specific complications and modify risk factors for DM-associated diseases. The pt with type 1 or type 2 DM should receive education about nutrition, exercise, care of diabetes during illness, and medications to lower the plasma glucose. In general, the target HbA_{1c} level should be <7.0%, though individual considerations (age, ability to implement a complex treatment regimen, and presence of other medical conditions) should also be taken into account. Intensive therapy reduces long-term complications but is associated with more frequent and more severe hypoglycemic episodes.

In general, pts with type 1 DM require 0.5–1.0 U/kg per day of insulin divided into multiple doses. Combinations of insulin preparations with different times of onset and duration of action should be used (Table 173-2). Commonly used regimens include twice-daily injections of an intermediate insulin combined with a short-acting insulin before the morning and evening meal, twice-daily injections of an intermediate insulin and preprandial lispro insulin, and continuous subcutaneous insulin using an infusion device.

Pts with type 2 DM may be managed with diet and exercise alone or in conjunction with oral glucose-lowering agents, insulin, or a combination of oral agents and insulin. The classes of oral glucose-lowering agents and dosing regimens are listed in Table 173-3. A reasonable treatment algorithm for initial therapy proposes either a sulfonlyurea or metformin as initial therapy

Table 173-2

Pharmacokinetics of Insulin Preparations

Preparation	Onset, h	Peak, h	Effective Duration, h	Maximum Duration, h
		Time of Action		
Short-acting				
Lispro	<0.25	0.5–1.5	3–4	4–6
Regular	0.5–1.0	2–3	3–6	6–8
Intermediate-acting				
NPH	2–4	6–10	10–16	14–18
Lente	3–4	6–12	12–18	16–20
Long-acting				
Ultralente	6–10	10–16	18–20	20–24
Glargine	4	—[a]	24	>24
Combinations				
75/25–75% NPH, 25% regular	0.5–1	Dual	10–16	14–18
70/30–70% NPH, 30% regular	0.5–1	Dual	10–16	14–18
50/50–50% NPH, 50% regular	0.5–1	Dual	10–16	14–18

[a] Glargine has minimal peak activity.
SOURCE: Adapted from JS Skyler, in *Therapy for Diabetes Mellitus and Related Disorders*, 1998

Table 173-3

Oral Glucose-Lowering Agents

Agent	Daily Dose, mg	Doses/d	Contraindications
Sulfonylureas			Renal/liver disease
Chlorpropamide	100–500	1–2	
Tolazamide	100–1000	1–2	
Tolbutamide	500–3000	2–3	
Glimepiride	1–8	1	
Glipizide	2.5–40	1–2	
Glipizide (ext. release)	5–10	1	
Glyburide	1.25–20	1–2	
Glyburide (micronized)	0.75–12	1–2	
Meglitinide			Liver disease
Repaglinide	0.5–16	1–3	
Biguanide			Cr>133 μmol/L (1.5 mg/dL) (men); >124 μmol/L (1.4 mg/dL) (women)
Metformin	500–2500	1–3	
α-Glucosidase inhibitor			IBD, liver disease, or Cr> 177 μmol/L (2.0 mg/dL)
Acarbose	25–300	1–3	
Miglitol	25–300	1–3	
Thiazolidinedione			Liver disease, CHF
Rosiglitazone	2–8	1–2	
Pioglitazone	15–45	1	

because of their efficacy, (1–2% decrease in HbA$_{1c}$), known side-effect profile, and relatively low cost (Fig. 173-1). Metformin has the advantage that it promotes mild weight loss, lowers insulin levels, improves the lipid profile slightly, and does not cause hypoglycemia when used as monotherapy, though it is contraindicated in renal insufficiency, congestive heart failure, any form of acidosis, liver disease, or severe hypoxia, and should be temporarily discontinued in pts who are seriously ill or receiving radiographic contrast material. Combinations of two oral agents may be used with additive effects, with stepwise addition of bedtime insulin or a third oral agent if adequate control is not achieved. As endogenous insulin production falls, multiple injections of intermediate-acting and short-acting insulin may be required, as in type 1 DM. Individuals who require >1 U/kg per day of intermediate-acting insulin should be considered for combination therapy with an insulin-sensitizing agent such as metformin or a thiazolidinedione.

The morbidity and mortality of DM-related complications can be greatly reduced by timely and consistent surveillance procedures (Table 173-4). A routine urinalysis may be performed as an initial screen for diabetic nephropathy. If it is positive for protein, quantification of protein on a 24-h urine collection should be performed. If the urinalysis is negative for protein, a spot or timed collection for microalbuminuria should be performed (present if 30–300 μg/mg creatinine on spot collection or 30–300 mg/d on timed collection on two of three tests within a 3–6 month period). Conditions that transiently increase albumin excretion must be excluded to avoid a false diagnosis. If the urinalysis has been negative for protein in the past, testing for the presence

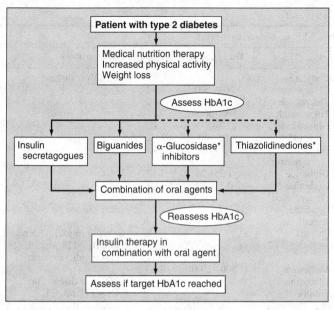

FIGURE 173-1   Glycemic management of type 2 diabetes. See text for discussion. *See text about use as monotherapy. The broken line indicates that biguanides or insulin secretagogues, but not α glucosidase inhibitors or thiazolidinediones, are preferred for initial therapy.

of microalbumin should be performed on an annual basis. A resting ECG should be performed in adults, with more extensive cardiac testing for high-risk pts. Therapeutic goals to prevent complications of DM include management of proteinuria with ACE inhibitor therapy, bp control (<130/85 mmHg if no proteinuria, <120/80 if proteinuria), and dyslipidemia management [LDL <2.6 mmol/L (<100 mg/dL) HDL >0.9 mmol/L (>35 mg/dL), triglycerides <2.6 mmol/L (<200 mg/dL)].

Management of the Hospitalized Patient   The goals of diabetes management during hospitalization are avoidance of hypoglycemia, optimization of glycemic control, and transition back to the outpatient diabetes treatment regimen. Individuals with type 1 DM undergoing general anesthesia and surgery, or with serious illness, should receive continuous insulin, either through an IV insulin infusion or by SC administration of a reduced dose of a long-

Table 173-4

Guidelines for Ongoing Medical Care for Patients with Diabetes

- Self-monitoring of blood glucose (individualized frequency)
- HbA1c testing (2–4 times/year)
- Patient education in diabetes management (annual)
- Medical nutrition therapy and education (annual)
- Eye examination (annual)
- Foot examination (1–2 times/year by physician; daily by patient)
- Screening for diabetic nephropathy (annual urine microalbumin)
- Blood pressure measurement (quarterly)
- Lipid profile (annual)

acting insulin. Short-acting insulin alone is insufficient to prevent the onset of diabetic ketoacidosis. Oral hypoglycemic agents may need to be discontinued in individuals with type 2 DM at the time of hospitalization. A low dose of intermediate-acting insulin can be used to keep glucose levels to <13.9 mmol/L (<250 mg/dL). An insulin infusion or a reduced dose (by 30–50%) of long- or intermediate-acting insulin and short-acting insulin (held, or reduced by 30–50%), with infusion of a solution of 5% dextrose, should be administered when pts are NPO for a procedure. Those with DM undergoing radiographic procedures with contrast dye should be well hydrated before and after dye exposure, and the serum creatinine should be monitored after the procedure.

For a more detailed discussion, see Powers AC: Diabetes Mellitus, Chap. 333, p. 2109, in HPIM-15.

174

DISORDERS OF THE MALE REPRODUCTIVE SYSTEM

The testes produce sperm and the steroid hormones that regulate male sexual development and function. Inadequate production of sperm can occur as an isolated defect, whereas inadequate formation of testosterone by the Leydig cells reduces virilization and libido and often impairs spermatogenesis secondarily. Classification of testicular function in adults is found in Table 174-1.

ANDROGEN DEFICIENCY

Etiology   Androgen deficiency can be due to either testicular failure (*primary hypogonadism*) or hypothalamic-pituitary defects (*secondary hypogonadism*).

Primary hypogonadism is diagnosed when testosterone levels are low and gonadotropin levels are high. Klinefelter's syndrome is the most common cause and is due to the presence of one or more extra X chromosomes, usually a 47, XXY karyotype. Acquired primary testicular failure usually results from viral orchitis, but may be due to trauma, radiation damage, or systemic diseases such as amyloidosis, Hodgkin's disease, sickle cell disease, or granulomatous diseases. Testicular failure can occur as a part of a polyglandular autoimmune failure syndrome in which multiple primary endocrine deficiencies coexist. Malnutrition, AIDS, renal failure, liver disease, myotonic dystrophy, paraplegia, and toxins such as alcohol, marijuana, heroin, methadone, lead, and antineoplastic and chemotherapeutic agents can also lead to testicular failure. Testosterone synthesis may be blocked by ketoconazole, or testosterone action may be diminished by competition at the androgen receptor by spironolactone and cimetidine.

Secondary hypogonadism is diagnosed when levels of both testosterone and gonadotropins are low (*hypogonadotropic hypogonadism*). Kallmann's syn-

Table 174-1

Abnormalities of Adult Testicular Function

Infertility with Underandrogenization	Infertility with Normal Virilization
HYPOTHALAMIC-PITUITARY	
Panhypopituitarism	
Isolated gonadotropin deficiency	Isolated FSH deficiency
Adrenal hypoplasia congenita	Congenital adrenal hyperplasia
Cushing's syndrome	Hyperprolactinemia
Hyperprolactinemia	Androgen use
Hemochromatosis	
TESTICULAR	
Developmental and structural defects	
Klinefelter's syndrome[a]	AZF mutations of the Y chromosome
XX male	Germinal cell aplasia
	Cryptorchidism
	Varicocele
	Immotile cilia syndrome
Acquired defects	
Viral orchitis*	*Mycoplasma* infection
Trauma	
Radiation	Radiation
Drugs (spironolactone, alcohol, keto-conazole, cyclophosphamide)	Drugs (cyclophosphamide)
Environmental toxins	Environmental toxins
Autoimmunity	Autoimmunity
Granulomatous disease	
Associated with systemic diseases	
Liver disease	Febrile illness
Renal failure	Celiac disease
Sickle cell disease	
Immune disease (AIDS, rheumatoid arthritis)	
Neurologic disease (myotonic dystrophy, spinobulbar muscular atrophy, and paraplegia)	Neurologic disease (paraplegia)
Androgen resistance	Androgen resistance
SPERM TRANSPORT	
	Obstruction of the epididymis or vas deferens (cystic fibrosis, diethylstilbesterol exposure, congenital absence)

[a] The common testicular causes of underandrogenization and infertility in adults—Klinefelter's syndrome and viral orchitis—are associated with small testes.

drome is due to impairment of the synthesis and/or release of gonadotropin-releasing hormone (GnRH) and is characterized by low levels of luteinizing hormone (LH) and follicle-stimulating hormone (FSH), and anosmia. Other individuals present with idiopathic congenital GnRH deficiency without anosmia.

Critical illness, Cushing's syndrome, congenital adrenal hyperplasia, hemochromatosis, and hyperprolactinemia (due to pituitary adenomas or drugs such as phenothiazines) are other causes of isolated hypogonadotropic hypogonadism. Destruction of the pituitary gland by tumors, infection, trauma, or metastatic disease causes hypogonadism in conjunction with disturbances in the production of other pituitary hormones.

Clinical Features If insufficient androgens are present before the onset of puberty, failure of sexual maturation (*eunuchoidism*) is evidenced by an infantile amount and distribution of body hair, poor development of skeletal muscles, and delayed closure of the epiphyses. In Klinefelter's syndrome, the testes are small and firm, gynecomastia is common, and azoospermia is usually present. Testosterone levels are low, and the gonadotropins are increased (FSH > LH). Variable features include eunuchoid habitus, mild mental deficiency, and diabetes mellitus.

Men who present with hypogonadism that occurred after puberty may report diminished libido, sexual function, general strength, and energy level. A decreased rate of beard growth may signify decreased virilization. On physical exam, gynecomastia and small or soft testes may be present.

Males without androgen deficiency may have isolated testosterone levels that are below the normal range during the day, particularly in the afternoon, so that repeat or pooled samples may be required to document testosterone deficiency. Levels of LH and FSH can be used to differentiate between primary (increased gonadotropins) and secondary hypogonadism (decreased gonadotropins).

℞ TREATMENT

Treatment of hypogonadal men with androgens restores normal male secondary sexual characteristics (beard, body hair, external genitalia), male sexual drive, and masculine somatic development (hemoglobin, muscle mass). Administration of gradually increasing doses of testosterone is recommended for disorders in which hypogonadism occurred prior to puberty. Testosterone levels in the normal range may be achieved through parenteral administration of a long-acting testosterone ester (100–200 mg testosterone enanthate at 1- to 3-week intervals) or daily application of transdermal testosterone patches or gel.

MALE INFERTILITY

Etiology Male infertility plays a role in one-third of infertile couples (couples who fail to conceive after 1 year of unprotected intercourse). Secondary impairment of spermatogenesis by androgen deficiency may occur, as described above. Isolated spermatogenic tubule dysfunction is usually idiopathic. However, known causes include Y chromosome microdeletions and substitutions, alterations of temperature of the testes as in varicocele, cryptorchidism, or immotile cilia syndrome. Ejaculatory obstruction can be a congenital (cystic fibrosis, in utero DES exposure, or idiopathic) or acquired (tuberculosis, leprosy, or gonorrhea) etiology of male infertility. Defects of the androgen receptor and disorders of sperm transport may also cause infertility. Radiation, chemotherapeutic agents, and environmental toxins have all been associated with isolated impaired spermatogenesis. Androgen abuse by male athletes can lead to testicular atrophy and a low sperm count.

Table 174-2

Some Organic Causes of Erectile Dysfunction in Men

I. Endocrine causes
   A. Testicular failure (primary or secondary)
   B. Hyperprolactinemia
II. Drugs
   A. Antiandrogens
      1. Spironolactone
      2. Ketoconazole
      3. H_2 blockers (e.g., cimetidine)
      4. Finasteride
   B. Antihypertensives
      1. Central-acting sympatholytics (e.g., clonidine and methyldopa)
      2. Peripheral acting sympatholytics (e.g., guanadrel)
      3. Beta blockers
      4. Thiazides
   C. Anticholinergics
   D. Antidepressants
   E. Antipsychotics
   F. Central nervous system depressants
      1. Sedatives (e.g., barbiturates)
      2. Antianxiety drugs (e.g., diazepam)
   G. Drugs of habituation or addiction
      1. Alcohol
      2. Heroin and methadone
      3. Tobacco
III. Penile diseases
   A. Peyronie's disease
   B. Previous priapism
   C. Penile trauma
IV. Neurologic diseases
   A. Anterior temporal lobe lesions
   B. Diseases of the spinal cord
   C. Pelvic surgery
   D. Diabetic autonomic neuropathy and various polyneuropathies
V. Vascular disease
   A. Aortic occlusion (Leriche syndrome)
   B. Atherosclerotic occlusion or stenosis of the pudendal and/or cavernosal arteries
   C. Venous leak
   D. Disease of the sinusoidal spaces
   E. Arterial damage from pelvic radiation

SOURCE: JD McConnell, JD Wilson: HPIM-14, p. 287.

Clinical Features Evidence of hypogonadism may be present. Testicular size and consistency may be abnormal, and a varicocele may be apparent on palpation. When the seminiferous tubules are damaged prior to puberty, the testes are small (usually <12 mL) and firm, whereas postpubertal damage causes the testes to be soft (the capsule, once enlarged, does not contract to its previous size). The key diagnostic test is a *semen analysis.* Sperm counts of <20 million/mL, with a motility of <40%, are associated with infertility. Testosterone levels should be measured if the sperm count is low on repeated exam or if there is clinical evidence of hypogonadism.

℞ TREATMENT

Men with primary hypogonadism occasionally respond to androgen therapy if there is minimal damage to the seminiferous tubules, whereas those with secondary hypogonadism require gonadotropin therapy to achieve fertility. Fertility occurs in about half of men with varicocele who undergo surgical repair. In vitro fertilization is an option for men with mild to moderate defects in sperm quality; intracytoplasmic sperm injection (ICSI) has been a major advance for men with severe defects in sperm quality.

ERECTILE DYSFUNCTION

Etiology   Erectile dysfunction (ED) is the failure to achieve erection, ejaculation, or both. It affects 10–25% of middle-aged and elderly men. Sexual dysfunction can be psychogenic but often has an organic component related to a systemic disease, urogenital disorders, or endocrinopathy. Some organic causes of ED are listed in Table 174-2.

Clinical Features   Men with sexual dysfunction may complain of loss of libido, inability to initiate or maintain an erection, ejaculatory failure, premature ejaculation, or inability to achieve orgasm. Evaluation includes a detailed general as well as genital physical exam. Penile abnormalities (Peyronie's disease), testicular size, and gynecomastia should be noted. Peripheral pulses should be palpated, and bruits should be sought. Neurologic exam should assess anal sphincter tone, perineal sensation, and bulbocavernosus reflex. Serum testosterone and prolactin should be measured. Penile artiography, electromyography, or penile Doppler ultrasound is occasionally performed.

℞ TREATMENT

An approach to the evaluation and treatment of ED is summarized in Fig. 174-1. Correction of the underlying disorders or discontinuation of respon-

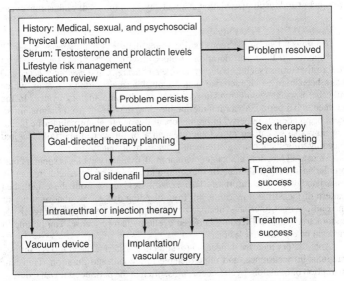

FIGURE 174-1   Algorithm for the evaluation and management of patients with ED.

sible medications should be attempted. Oral sildenafil enhances erections after sexual stimulation, with an onset of approximately 60–90 min. It is contraindicated in men receiving any form of nitrate therapy and should be avoided in those with congestive heart failure. Injection of alprostadil into the corpora cavernosa or urethra or vacuum constriction devices may also be effective. The insertion of penile prosthesis is rarely indicated.

For a more detailed discussion, see Griffin JE, Wilson JD: Disorders of the Testes, Chap. 335, p. 2143; Hall JE: Infertility and Fertility Control, Chap. 54, p. 301; McVary KT: Erectile Dysfunction, Chap. 51, p. 291, in HPIM-15.

175

DISORDERS OF THE FEMALE REPRODUCTIVE SYSTEM

The ovary is the source of ova for reproduction and produces estrogens and progestins, the hormones that induce secondary sexual characteristics in women and control the menstrual cycle. The pituitary hormones, luteinizing hormone (LH) and follicle-stimulating hormone (FSH) stimulate ovarian follicular development and result in ovulation at about day 14 of the 28-day menstrual cycle.

ABNORMAL UTERINE BLEEDING

Etiology During the reproductive years, the menstrual cycle averages 28 ± 3 days, and the mean duration of blood flow is 4 ± 2 days. A variety of descriptive terms (such as *menorrhagia, metrorrhagia,* and *menometrorrhagia*) have been used to characterize patterns of abnormal uterine bleeding, which may be associated with ovulatory cycles or with anovulatory cycles. In the premenarchal period, abnormal uterine bleeding may result from trauma, infection, or precocious puberty. In premenopausal women, abnormal uterine bleeding may also be caused by ectopic pregnancy or threatened abortion. Vaginal bleeding after menopause is frequently due to malignancy.

Menstrual bleeding associated with normal, ovulatory cycles is spontaneous, regular in onset, predictable in duration and amount of flow, and frequently associated with discomfort (*dysmenorrhea*). Deviations from the established pattern of menstrual flow can result from bleeding dyscrasias, abnormalities of the outflow tract (uterine synechiae or scarring), leiomyomas, adenomyosis, or endometrial polyps. Bleeding between cyclic ovulatory menses can be due to cervical or endometrial lesions.

Anovulatory menstrual bleeding (dysfunctional uterine bleeding) is painless, irregular in occurrence, and unpredictable in amount and duration. Transient disruption of ovulatory cycles occurs most often in the peripubertal years, during the perimenopausal period, or as the consequence of a variety of stresses and intercurrent illnesses. Persistent dysfunctional uterine bleeding in reproductive years is usually due to continuous estrogen effects on the uterus uninterrupted by cyclic fluctuations in progesterone associated with ovulation, and is most commonly due to polycystic ovarian syndrome.

Diagnosis The approach to a pt with dysfunctional uterine bleeding begins with a careful history of menstrual patterns and prior hormonal therapy. Since not all urogenital tract bleeding is from the uterus, rectal, bladder, vaginal, and cervical sources must be excluded by physical exam. If the bleeding is from the uterus, a pregnancy-related disorder such as abortion or ectopic pregnancy must be ruled out.

℞ TREATMENT

During a first episode of dysfunctional bleeding the pt can be observed, provided the bleeding is not copious and there is no evidence of a bleeding dyscrasia. If bleeding is more severe, control can be achieved with relatively high-dose estrogen oral contraceptives for 3 weeks. Hospitalization, bed rest, and IM injections of estradiol valerate (10 mg) and hydroxyprogesterone caproate (500 mg) or IV or IM conjugated estrogens (25 mg) usually control severe bleeding. Uterine biopsy should be performed in women approaching the age of menopause, or those who are massively obese, to evaluate for endometrial cancer. After initial treatment, iron replacement should be instituted along with either cyclic oral contraceptives or medroxyprogesterone acetate 10 mg PO qd for 10 days every 2–3 months. Additional evaluation (endometrial biopsy, hysteroscopy, or dilatation and curettage) may be required for diagnosis and therapy.

AMENORRHEA

Etiology Pregnancy should be excluded in women of childbearing age with amenorrhea, even when history and physical exam are not suggestive.

Primary amenorrhea is defined as failure of menarche by age 15, regardless of the presence or absence of secondary sexual characteristics; *secondary amenorrhea* is failure of menstruation for 6 months in a woman with previous periodic menses. The causes of primary and secondary amenorrhea overlap, and it is generally more useful to classify the disorder according to the source of dysfunction: (1) anatomic defects, (2) ovarian failure, or (3) chronic anovulation with or without estrogen present (Fig. 175-1).

Anatomic defects of the outflow tract that prevent vaginal bleeding include absence of vagina or uterus, imperforate hymen, transverse vaginal septae, and cervical stenosis. Ovarian failure may be due to Turner's syndrome, pure gonadal dygenesis, premature ovarian failure, the resistant-ovary syndrome, and chemotherapy or radiation therapy for malignancy. The diagnosis of premature ovarian failure is applied to women who cease menstruating before age 40. Chronic anovulation with estrogen present is usually due to polycystic ovarian syndrome (PCOS) and is characterized by amenorrhea or oligomenorrhea, infertility, and evidence of androgen excess (hirsutism, acne, male pattern balding). Features of PCOS are worsened by coexistent obesity. Additional disorders with a similar presentation include excess androgen production from adrenal or ovarian tumors, adult-onset adrenal hyperplasia due to partial 21-hydroxylase deficiency, and thyroid disorders. Women with chronic anovulation with absent estrogen usually have hypogonadotropic hypogonadism due to disease of either the hypothalamus or the pituitary. Hypothalamic causes include Kallmann's syndrome or Sheehan's syndrome, hypothalamic lesions (craniopharyngiomas and other tumors, tuberculosis, sarcoidosis, metastatic tumors), hypothalamic

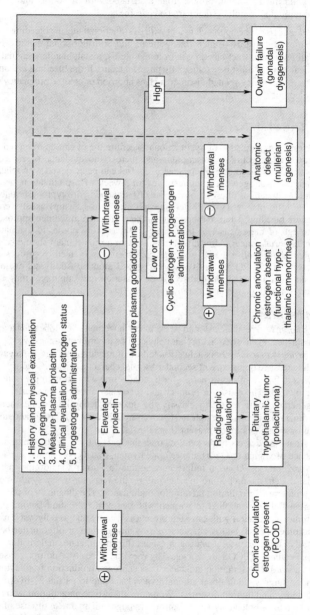

FIGURE 175-1 Flow diagram for the evaluation of women with amenorrhea. The most common diagnosis for each category is shown in parentheses. The dotted lines indicate that in some instances a correct diagnosis can be reached on the basis of history and physical exam alone. (*Reproduced from Carr BR, Bradshaw KD: HPIM-15, p. 2165.*)

trauma or irradiation, rigorous exercise, eating disorders, stressful events, and chronic debilitating diseases (end-stage renal disease, malignancy, malabsorption). Disorders of the pituitary can lead to amenorrhea by two mechanisms: direct interference with gonadotropin secretion or inhibition of gonadotropin secretion via excess prolactin (Chap. 169).

Diagnosis The initial evaluation involves careful physical exam, serum or urine human chorionic gonadotropin (hCG), serum prolactin assay, and evaluation of estrogen status (Fig. 175-1). To determine estrogen status, medroxyprogesterone acetate (10 mg po qd-bid × 5 days) or 100 mg of progesterone in oil IM should be administered. If estrogen levels are adequate and the outflow tract is intact, menstrual bleeding should occur within 1 week of ending progestin treatment. Ovarian failure is associated with a lack of withdrawal menses to progestin challenge and elevated plasma gonadotropin levels. Anatomic defects are usually diagnosed by physical exam and failure to induce menses, though hysterosalpingography or direct visual examination by hysteroscopy may be required. Chromosomal analysis should be performed when gonadal dysgenesis is suspected. The diagnosis of PCOS is based on the coexistence of chronic anovulation and androgen excess, after ruling out other etiologies for these features. The evaluation of hyperprolactinemia is described in Chap. 169. In the absence of a known etiology for hypogonadotropic hypogonadism, MRI of the pituitary-hypothalamic region should be performed when gonadotropins are low or inappropriately normal.

 TREATMENT

Disorders of the outflow tract are managed surgically. Decreased estrogen production, whether from ovarian failure or hypothalamic/pituitary disease, should be treated with cyclic estrogens, either in the form of oral contraceptives or conjugated estrogens (0.625–1.25 mg PO qd) and medroxyprogesterone acetate (2.5 mg PO qd or 5–10 mg during the last 5 days of the month). PCOS may be treated by oral contraceptive agents and weight reduction, along with treatment of hirsutism (see below). Individuals with PCOS should be screened for diabetes mellitus. Fertility may be enhanced by using insulin-sensitizing agents such as metformin.

PELVIC PAIN

Etiology Pelvic pain may be associated with normal or abnormal menstrual cycles and may originate in the pelvis or be referred from another region of the body. A high index of suspicion must be entertained for extrapelvic disorders that refer to the pelvis, such as appendicitis, diverticulitis, cholecystitis, intestinal obstruction, and urinary tract infections. Severe or incapacitating cramping with ovulatory menses in the absence of demonstrable disorders of the pelvis is termed *primary dysmenorrhea*. Pelvic pain due to organic causes may be classified as uterine (leiomyomas, adenomyosis, cervical stenosis, infections, cancer), adnexal (salpingo-oophoritis, cysts, neoplasms, torsion, endometriosis), vulvar or vaginal (*Monilia, Trichomonas, Gardnerella*, herpes, condyloma acuminatum, cysts or abscesses of Bartholin's glands), and pregnancy-associated (threatened or incomplete abortion, ectopic pregnancy). Many women experience lower abdominal discomfort with ovulation (*mittelschmerz*), characterized as a dull, aching pain at midcycle that lasts minutes to hours. In addition, ovulatory women may experience somatic symptoms during the few days prior to menses, including edema, breast engorgement, and abdominal bloating and discomfort. A symptom complex of cyclic irritability, depression, and lethargy is known as *premenstrual syndrome* (PMS).

Diagnosis Evaluation includes a history, pelvic exam, hCG measurement, pelvic ultrasound. Laparoscopy or laparotomy is indicated in some cases of pelvic pain of undetermined cause.

 TREATMENT

Primary dysmenorrhea is best treated with NSAIDs or oral contraceptive agents. Infections should be treated with the appropriate antibiotics. Symptoms from PMS may improve with SSRI therapy. Surgery may be required for structural abnormalities.

HIRSUTISM

Etiology Hirsutism, defined as excessive male-pattern hair growth, affects approximately 10% of women of reproductive age. It may be familial or caused by PCOS, ovarian or adrenal neoplasms, congenital adrenal hyperplasia, Cushing's syndrome, hyperprolactinemia, acromegaly, pregnancy, and drugs (androgens, oral contraceptives containing androgenic progestins). Other drugs, such as minoxidil, phenytoin, diazoxide, and cyclosporine, can cause excessive growth of non-androgen-dependent vellus hair, leading to hypertrichosis.

Clinical Features An objective clinical assessment of hair distribution and quantity is central to the evaluation. A commonly used method to grade hair growth is the Ferriman-Gallwey score (see Fig. 53-1 p. 299 in HPIM-15). Associated manifestations of androgen excess include acne and male-pattern balding (androgenic alopecia). Virilization, on the other hand, refers to the state in which androgen levels are sufficiently high to cause deepening of the voice, breast atrophy, increased muscle bulk, clitoromegaly, and increased libido. Historic elements include menstrual history and the age of onset, rate of progression, and distribution of hair growth. Sudden development of hirsutism, rapid progression, and virilization suggest an ovarian or adrenal neoplasm.

Diagnosis An approach to testing for androgen excess is depicted in Fig. 175-2. The dexamethasone androgen-suppression test (0.5 mg PO q6h × 4 days, with free testosterone levels obtained before and after administration of dexamethasone) may distinguish ovarian from adrenal overproduction. PCOS is a relatively common cause of hirsutism. Incomplete suppression suggests ovarian androgen excess. Congenital adrenal hyperplasia due to 21-hydroxylase deficiency can be excluded by a 17-hydroxyprogesterone level (either in the morning during the follicular phase or 1 h after administration of 250 μg of cosyntropin) that is <6 nmol/L (<2 μg/L). CT may localize an adrenal mass, and ultrasound will identify an ovarian mass, if evaluation suggests these possibilities.

 TREATMENT

Nonpharmacologic treatments include (1) bleaching; (2) depilatory such as shaving and chemical treatments; and (3) epilatory such as plucking, waxing, electrolysis, and laser therapy. Pharmacologic therapy includes oral contraceptives with a low androgenic progestin and spironolactone (100–200 mg PO qd), often in combination. Glucocorticoids (dexamethasone 0.25–0.5 mg qhs or prednisone 5–10 mg qhs) are the mainstay of treatment in pts with congenital adrenal hyperplasia. Attenuation of hair growth with pharmacologic therapy is typically not evident until 4–6 months after initiation of medical treatment and therefore should be used in conjunction with nonpharmacologic treatments.

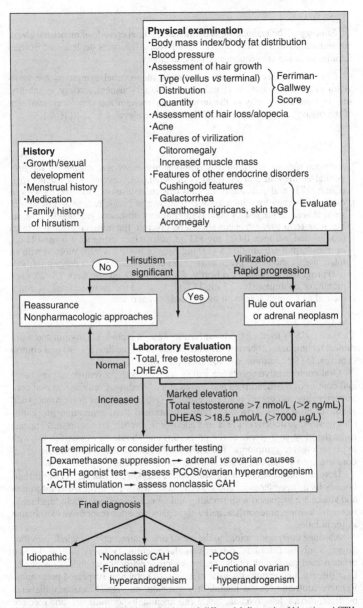

FIGURE 175-2 Algorithm for the evaluation and differential diagnosis of hirsutism. ACTH, adrenocorticotropic hormone; CAH, congenital adrenal hyperplasia; DHEAS, sulfated form of dehydroepiandrosterone; GnRH, gonadotropin-releasing hormone; PCOS, polycystic ovarian syndrome.

MENOPAUSE

Etiology The *menopause* is defined as the final episode of menstrual bleeding and occurs at a median age of 50–51 years. It reflects depletion of ovarian follicles or is the consequence of oophorectomy.

Clinical Features The most common menopausal symptoms are vasomotor instability (hot flashes), mood changes (nervousness, anxiety, irritability, and depression), atrophy of the urogenital epithelium and skin, decreased size of the breasts, and osteoporosis. FSH levels are elevated to $\geq$40 IU/L.

 TREATMENT

Estrogen therapy ameliorates vasomotor instability and atrophy of the urogenital epithelium and skin and is of benefit in prevention of osteoporosis (Chap. 177) and potentially of cardiovascular disease. However, low-dose estrogen therapy may increase the incidence of breast cancer and hypertension, as well as the risk of venous thromboembolism and gallbladder disease. For long-term use, estrogens should be given in the minimal effective doses (conjugated estrogen 0.625 mg PO qd, micronized estradiol 1.0 mg PO qd, or transdermal estradiol 0.05–1.0 mg once or twice a week). Women with an intact uterus should be given estrogen in combination with a progestin (medroxyprogesterone either cyclically, 5–10 mg PO qd for days 15–25 each month, or continuously, 2.5 mg PO qd) to avoid the increased risk of endometrial carcinoma seen with unopposed estrogen use.

CONTRACEPTION

The most widely used methods for fertility control include (1) rhythm and withdrawal techniques, (2) barrier methods, (3) intrauterine devices, (4) oral contraceptives, (5) sterilization, and (6) abortion.

Oral contraceptive agents are widely used for both prevention of pregnancy and control of dysmenorrhea and anovulatory bleeding. Combination oral contraceptive agents contain synthetic estrogen (ethinyl estradiol or mestranol) and synthetic progestins. Low-dose norgestimate and third-generation progestins (desogestrel, gestodene) have a less androgenic profile; levonorgestrel appears to be the most androgenic of the progestins and should be avoided in pts with hyperandrogenic symptoms. The three major formulation types include fixed-dose estrogen-progestin, phasic estrogen-progestin, and progestin only.

Despite overall safety, oral contraceptive users are at risk for venous thromboembolism, hypertension, and cholelithiasis. Risks for myocardial infarction and stroke are increased with smoking and aging. Side effects, including breakthrough bleeding, amenorrhea, and weight gain, are often responsive to a change in formulation.

Absolute contraindications to the use of oral contraceptives include previous thromboembolic disorders, cerebrovascular or coronary artery disease, known or suspected carcinoma of the breasts or other estrogen-dependent neoplasia, liver disease, undiagnosed genital bleeding, or known or suspected pregnancy. Relative contraindications include hypertension, migraine headaches, diabetes mellitus, uterine leiomyomas, sickle cell anemia, hyperlipidemia, and elective surgery.

Emergency contraceptive pills, containing progestin only or estrogen and progestin, can be used within 72 h of unprotected intercourse for prevention of pregnancy. Both Plan B and Preven are emergency contraceptive kits specifically designed for postcoital contraception. In addition, certain oral contraceptive pills may be dosed for emergency contraception. Progestin-only pills have a lower risk of nausea and vomiting than combination estrogen-progestin agents.

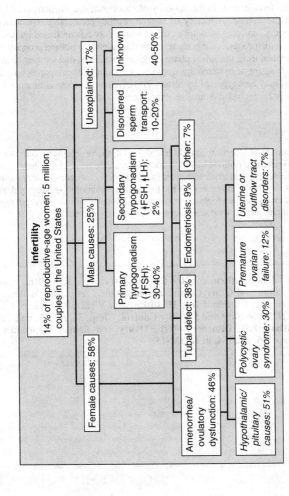

FIGURE 175-3 Causes of infertility. FSH, follicle-stimulating hormone; LH, luteinizing hormone.

INFERTILITY

Etiology Infertility is defined as the inability to conceive after 12 months of unprotected sexual intercourse. The causes of infertility are outlined in Fig. 175-3. Male infertility is discussed in Chap. 174.

Clinical Features The initial evaluation includes discussion of the appropriate timing of intercourse, semen analysis in the male, confirmation of ovulation in the female, and, in the majority of situations, documentation of tubal patency in the female. A history of regular, cyclic, predictable, spontaneous menses usually indicates ovulatory cycles, which may be confirmed by urinary ovulation predictor kits, basal body temperature graphs, or plasma progesterone measurements during the luteal phase of the cycle. Tubal disease can be evaluated by obtaining a hysterosalpingogram or by diagnostic laparoscopy. Endometriosis may be suggested by history and exam but is often clinically silent and can only be excluded definitively by laparoscopy.

℞ TREATMENT

The treatment of infertility should be tailored to the problems unique to each couple. Treatment options include expectant management, clomiphene citrate with or without intrauterine insemination (IUI), gonadotropins with or without IUI, and in vitro fertilization (IVF). In specific situations, surgery, pulsatile GnRH therapy, intracytoplasmic sperm injection (ICSI), or assisted reproductive technologies with donor egg or sperm may be required.

For a more detailed discussion, see Carr BR, Bradshaw KD: Disturbances of Menstruation and Other Common Gynecologic Complaints in Women, Chap. 52, p. 295; Ehrmann DA: Hirsutism and Virilization, Chap. 53, p. 297; Hall JE: Infertility and Fertility Control, Chap. 54, p. 301; and Carr BR, Bradshaw KD: Disorders of the Ovary and Female Reproductive Tract, Chap 336, p. 2154, in HPIM-15.

176

HYPERCALCEMIC AND HYPOCALCEMIC DISORDERS

HYPERCALCEMIA

Hypercalcemia from any cause can result in fatigue, depression, mental confusion, anorexia, nausea, constipation, renal tubular defects, polyuria, a short QT interval, and arrhythmias. CNS and GI symptoms can occur at levels of serum calcium >2.9 mmol/L (>11.5 mg/dL), and nephrocalcinosis and impairment of renal function occur when serum calcium is 3.2 mmol/L (>13 mg/dL). Severe hypercalcemia, usually defined as 3.7 mmol/L (>15 mg/dL), can be a medical emergency, leading to coma and cardiac arrest.

Etiology The causes of hypercalcemia are listed in Table 176-1. Hyperparathyroidism and malignancy account for 90% of cases.

Primary hyperparathyroidism is a generalized disorder of bone metabolism due to increased secretion of parathyroid hormone (PTH) by an adenoma (81%) or carcinoma (4%) in a single gland, or by parathyroid hyperplasia (15%). Familial hyperparathyroidism may be part of multiple endocrine neoplasia type 1 (MEN 1), which also includes pituitary and pancreatic islet tumors, or of MEN 2a, in which hyperparathyroidism occurs with pheochromocytoma and medullary carcinoma of the thyroid.

Hypercalcemia associated with malignancy is often severe and difficult to manage. Mechanisms for this include release of PTH-related protein (PTHrP) in lung, kidney, and squamous cell carcinoma; local bone destruction in myeloma and breast carcinoma; activation of lymphocytes leading to release of interleukin 1 (IL-1) and tumor necrosis factor (TNF) in myeloma and lymphoma; or an increased synthesis of $1,25(OH)_2D$ in lymphoma.

Several other conditions have been associated with hypercalcemia. These include: sarcoidosis and other granulomatous diseases, which lead to increased synthesis of $1,25(OH)_2D$; vitamin D intoxication from chronic ingestion of large vitamin doses ($50-100\times$ physiologic requirements); lithium therapy, which results in hyperfunctioning of the parathyroid glands; and familial hypocalciuric hypercalcemia (FHH) due to autosomal dominant inheritance of a mutation in the calcium-sensing receptor, which results in inappropriate secretion of PTH and enhanced renal calcium resorption. Severe secondary hyperparathyroidism may also complicate end-stage renal disease. Progression to tertiary hyperthyroidism occurs when PTH hypersecretion becomes autonomous and is no longer responsive to medical therapy.

Table 176-1

Classification of Causes of Hypercalcemia

I. Parathyroid-related
   A. Primary hyperparathyroidism
      1. Solitary adenomas
      2. Multiple endocrine neoplasia
   B. Lithium therapy
   C. Familial hypocalciuric hypercalcemia
II. Malignancy-related
   A. Solid tumor with humoral mediation of hypercalcemia (lung, kidney)
   B. Solid tumor with metastases (breast)
   C. Hematologic malignancies (multiple myeloma, lymphoma, leukemia)
III. Vitamin D–related
   A. Vitamin D intoxication
   B. ↑ $1,25(OH)_2D$; sarcoidosis and other granulomatous diseases
   C. Idiopathic hypercalcemia of infancy
IV. Associated with high bone turnover
   A. Hyperthyroidism
   B. Immobilization
   C. Thiazides
   D. Vitamin A intoxication
V. Associated with renal failure
   A. Severe secondary hyperparathyroidism
   B. Aluminum intoxication
   C. Milk-alkali syndrome

SOURCE: Potts JT Jr: HPIM-15, p. 2209.

Clinical Features Most pts with hyperparathyroidism are asymptomatic, even when the disease involves the kidneys and the skeletal system. Pts frequently have hypercalciuria and polyuria, and calcium can be deposited in the renal parenchyma or form calcium oxalate stones. The characteristic skeletal lesion is osteopenia or, rarely, the more severe disorder osteitis fibrosa cystica. Resorption of the phalangeal tufts, subperiosteal resorption of bone in the digits, and tiny "punched out" lesions in the skull may also be present. Increased bone resorption primarily involves cortical rather than trabecular bone. Hypercalcemia may be intermittent or sustained, and serum phosphate is usually low but may be normal.

Diagnosis Primary hyperparathyroidism is confirmed by demonstration of an inappropriately high PTH level for the degree of hypercalcemia. Hypercalciuria helps to distinguish this disorder from FHH, in which PTH levels are usually in the normal range and the urine calcium level is low. Levels of PTH are low in hypercalcemia of malignancy (Table 176-2).

℞ TREATMENT

The type of treatment is based on the severity of the hypercalcemia and the nature of the associated symptoms. Table 176-3 shows general recommendations that apply to therapy of acute hypercalcemia from any cause.

In pts with severe primary hyperparathyroidism, surgical parathyroidectomy should be performed promptly. Asymptomatic disease may not require surgery; usual surgical indications include age <50, nephrolithiasis, urine Ca >400 mg/d, reduced creatinine clearance, reduction in bone mass <2 SD below normal, or serum calcium >0.25 mmol/L (>1 mg/dL above the normal range). If neck exploration does not reveal an abnormal gland, sestamibi scans, ultrasound, CT, or intraarterial digital angiography may help localize the abnormal tissue. Postoperative management requires close monitoring of calcium and phosphorus. Calcium supplementation is given for symptomatic hypocalcemia.

No therapy is recommended for FHH. Secondary hyperparathyroidism should be treated with phosphate restriction, the use of nonabsorbable antacids, and calcitriol. Tertiary hyperparathyroidism requires parathyroidectomy.

Table 176-2

Differential Diagnosis of Hypercalcemia: Laboratory Criteria

	Blood[a]			
	Ca	P_i	$1,25(OH)_2D$	iPTH
Primary hyperparathyroidism	↑	↓	↑,↔	↑(↔)
Malignancy-associated hypercalcemia:				
Humoral hypercalcemia	↑↑	↓	↓,↔	
Local destruction (osteolytic metastases)	↑	↔	↓,↔	

[a] Symbols in parentheses refer to values rarely seen in the particular disease.
NOTE: P_i, inorganic phosphate; iPTH, immunoreactive parathyroid hormone.
SOURCE: JT Potts Jr: HPIM-12, p. 1911.

Table 176-3

Therapies for Severe Hypercalcemia

Treatment	Onset of Action	Duration of Action	Advantages	Disadvantages
Hydration with saline (6 L/d)	Hours	During infusion	Rehydrates Rapid action	Volume overload Electrolyte disturbance
Forced diuresis (furosemide q4–12h along with aggressive hydration)	Hours	During treatment	Rapid action	Monitoring required to avoid dehydration
Bisphosphonates (Pamidronate 30–90 mg IV over 4h)	1–2 days	10–14 days	High potency Prolonged action	Fever in 20% Hypophosphatemia Hypocalcemia Hypomagnesemia
Calcitonin (2–8 U/kg IV/IM/SQ 6–12 h)	Hours	2–3 days	Rapid onset	Limited effect Tachyphylaxis
Glucocorticoids (prednisone 10–25 mg PO qid)	Days	Days–weeks	Useful in myeloma, lymphoma, breast CA, sarcoid, vitamin D intox	Effects limited to certain disorders Glucocorticoid side effects
Dialysis	Hours	During use–2 days	Useful in renal failure Immediate effect	Complex procedure

HYPOCALCEMIA

Chronic hypocalcemia is less common than hypercalemia but is usually symptomatic and requires treatment. Symptoms include peripheral and perioral paresthesia, muscle spasms, carpopedal spasm, laryngeal spasm, seizure, and respiratory arrest. Increased intracranial pressure and papilledema may occur with longstanding hypocalcemia, and other manifestations may include irritability, depression, psychosis, intestinal cramps, and chronic malabsorption. Chvostek's and Trousseau's signs are frequently positive, and the QT interval is prolonged. Both hypomagnesemia and alkalosis lower the threshold for tetany.

Etiology   Transient hypocalcemia often occurs in critically ill pts with burns, sepsis, and acute renal failure; following transfusion with citrated blood; or with medications such as protamine and heparin. Hypoalbuminemia can reduce serum calcium below normal, although ionized calcium levels remain normal. A simplified correction is sometimes used to assess whether the serum calcium concentration is abnormal when serum proteins are low. The correction is to add 0.25 mmol/L (1 mg/dL) to the serum calcium level for every 10 g/L (1 g/dL) by which the serum albumin level is below 40 g/L (4.0 g/dL). Alkalosis increases calcium binding to proteins, and in this setting direct measurements of ionized calcium should be used.

The causes of hypocalcemia can be divided into those in which PTH is absent (hereditary or acquired hypoparathyroidism, hypomagnesemia), PTH is ineffective (chronic renal failure, vitamin D deficiency, intestinal malabsorption, pseudohypoparathyroidism), or PTH is overwhelmed (severe, acute hyperphosphatemia in tumor lysis, acute renal failure, or rhabdomyolysis; hungry bone syndrome postparathyroidectomy). The cause of hypocalcemia associated with acute pancreatitis is unclear.

 TREATMENT

Symptomatic hypocalcemia may be treated with intravenous calcium gluconate (1 mg/mL in D_5W infused 30–100 mL/h). Management of chronic hypocalcemia requires an oral calcium preparation, usually along with a vitamin D preparation (Chap. 177). Hypoparathyroidism requires administration of calcium (1–3 g/d) and vitamin D or calcitriol (0.25–1 μg/d), adjusted according to serum calcium levels and urinary excretion. Restoration of magnesium stores may be required to reverse hypocalcemia in the setting of severe hypomagnesemia (<1.0 mg/dL).

HYPOPHOSPHATEMIA

Mild hypophosphatemia is not usually associated with clinical symptoms. In severe hypophosphatemia (≤1.0 mg/dL), pts may have muscle weakness, numbness, and paresthesia. Rhabdomyolysis is common in chronic alcoholism or can be precipitated during treatment of diabetic ketoacidosis or by hyperalimentation or refeeding in a malnourished pt. Respiratory insufficiency can result from diaphragm muscle weakness.

Etiology   The causes of hypophosphatemia include: decreased intestinal absorption (vitamin D deficiency, phosphorus-binding antacids, malabsorption, vitamin D–dependent rickets); urinary losses (hyperparathyroidism, vitamin D deficiency, vitamin D–dependent rickets, hyperglycemic states, oncogenic osteomalacia, alcoholism); and shifts of phosphorus from extracellular to intracellular compartments (administration of insulin or consumption of nutrients that stimulate insulin release).

TREATMENT

Mild hypophosphatemia can be replaced orally with milk, carbonated beverages, or Neutraphos or K-phos (up to 3 g/d in 4–6 divided doses/d). For severe hypophosphatemia, >3 g/d of phosphorus may be required over several days. Intravenous phosphorus (1g in 1L fluid over 8–12 h) can be administered with caution: a serum calcium × phosphorus product of >70 markedly increases the risk of soft tissue calcification and nephrocalcinosis.

HYPERPHOSPHATEMIA

In adults, hyperphosphatemia is defined as a level ≥1.6 mmol/L (>5 mg/dL). The most common causes are acute and chronic renal failure, but it may also be seen in hypoparathyroidism, vitamin D intoxication, acidosis, rhabdomyolysis, and hemolysis. In addition to treating the underlying disorder, dietary phosphorus intake should be limited. For control of chronic hyperphosphatemia, oral calcium or aluminum phosphate binders may be used.

HYPOMAGNESEMIA

Muscle weakness, prolonged PR and QT intervals, and cardiac arrhythmias are the most common manifestations of hypomagnesemia. Magnesium is important for effective PTH secretion as well as the renal and skeletal responsiveness to PTH. Therefore, hypomagnesemia is often associated with hypocalcemia.

Etiology   Hypomagnesemia generally results from a derangement in renal or intestinal handling of magnesium and is classified as primary (hereditary) or secondary (acquired). Secondary causes are much more common, with renal losses being due to volume expansion, hypercalcemia, osmotic diuresis, loop diuretics, alcohol, aminoglycosides, cisplatin, cyclosporine, and amphotericin B, and gastrointestinal losses most commonly resulting from vomiting and diarrhea.

 TREATMENT

For mild deficiency, oral replacement is effective, though diarrhea may result. Parenteral magnesium administration (2 g of magnesium sulfate IV, with a cumulative dose of 6 g over 24 h) is usually needed for serum levels <1.2 mg/dL (1.0 meq/L). Patients with associated seizures or acute arrhythmias can be given 1–2 g of magnesium sulfate IV over 5–10 min.

HYPERMAGNESEMIA

Hypermagnesemia is rare but can be seen in renal failure when pts are taking magnesium-containing antacids, laxatives, enemas, or infusions, or in acute rhabdomyolysis. The most readily detectable clinical sign of hypermagnesemia is the disappearance of deep tendon reflexes, but paralysis of respiratory muscles, complete heart block, and cardiac arrest can occur. Treatment includes stopping the preparation, dialysis against a low magnesium bath, or, if associated with life-threatening complications, 100–200 mg of elemental calcium IV over 5–10 minutes.

For a more detailed discussion, see Holick MF, Krane SM: Introduction to Bone and Mineral Metabolism, Chap. 340, p. 2192; and Potts JT Jr: Dis-

eases of the Parathyroid Gland and Other Hyper- and Hypocalcemic Disorders, Chap. 341, p. 2205, in HPIM-15.

177

OSTEOPOROSIS AND OSTEOMALACIA

OSTEOPOROSIS

Osteoporosis is defined as a reduction in bone mass (or density) or the presence of fragility fracture. It is defined operationally as a bone density that falls 2.5 SD below the mean for a young normal individual (a T-score of <-2.5). Those with a T-score of <1.0 have low bone density and are at increased risk for osteoporosis. The most common sites for osteoporosis-related fractures are the vertebrae, hip, and distal radius.

Etiology   Low bone density may result from low peak bone mass or increased bone loss. Risk factors for an osteoporotic fracture are listed in Table 177-1, and diseases associated with osteoporosis are listed in Table 177-2. Certain drugs, primarily glucocorticoids, cyclosporine, cytotoxic drugs, anticonvulsants, aluminum, and heparin, also have detrimental effects on the skeleton.

Clinical Features   Pts with multiple vertebral crush fractures may have height loss, kyphosis, and secondary pain from altered biomechanics of the back. Thoracic fractures can be associated with restrictive lung disease, whereas lumbar fractures are sometimes associated with abdominal symptoms. Dual-energy x-ray absorptiometry has become the standard for measuring bone density in most centers. Criteria approved for Medicare reimbursement of bone mass measurement are summarized in Table 177-3. A general laboratory evaluation includes complete blood count, serum calcium, and urine calcium. Further testing is based on clinical suspicion and may include thyroid-stimulating hormone (TSH), urinary free cortisol, parathyroid hormone (PTH), serum and

Table 177-1

Risk Factors for Osteoporosis Fracture

Nonmodifiable	Estrogen deficiency
Personal history of fracture as	Early menopause (<45 year) or
an adult	bilateral ovariectomy
History of fracture in first-	Prolonged premenstrual amen-
degree relative	orrhea (>1 year)
Femal sex	Low calcium intake
Advanced age	Alcoholism
Caucasian race	Impaired eyesight despite ade-
Dementia	quate correction
Potentially modifiable	Recurrent falls
Current cigarette smoking	Inadequate physical activity
Low body weight [<58 kg	Poor health/frailty
(127 lb)]	

Table 177-2

Diseases Associated with an Increased Risk of Generalized Osteoporosis in Adults

---

Hypogonadal states
  Turner syndrome
  Klinefelter syndrome
  Anorexia nervosa
  Hypothalamic amenorrhea
  Hyperprolactinemia
  Other primary or secondary
    hypogonadal states
Endocrine disorders
  Cushing's syndrome
  Hyperparathyroidism
  Thyrotoxicosis
  Insulin-dependent diabetes
    mellitus
  Acromegaly
  Adrenal insufficiency
Nutritional and gastrointestinal
  disorders
  Malnutrition
  Parenteral nutrition
  Malabsorption syndromes
  Gastrectomy
  Severe liver disease,
    especially biliary
    cirrhosis
  Pernicious anemia
Rheumatologic disorders
  Rheumatoid arthritis
  Ankylosing spondylitis

Hematologic disorders/malignancy
  Multiple myeloma
  Lymphoma and leukemia
  Malignancy-associated
    parathyroid hormone–related
    (PTHrP) production
  Mastocytosis
  Hemophilia
  Thalassemia
Selected inherited disorders
  Osteogenesis imperfecta
  Marfan syndrome
  Hemochromatosis
  Hypophosphatasia
  Glycogen storage diseases
  Homocystinuria
  Ehlers-Danlos syndrome
  Porphyria
  Menkes' syndrome
  Epidermolysis bullosa
Other disorders
  Immobilization
  Chronic obstructive pulmonary
    disease
  Pregnancy and lactation
  Scoliosis
  Multiple sclerosis
  Sarcoidosis
  Amyloidosis

---

urine electrophoresis, and testosterone levels (in men). Markers of bone resorption (e.g., urine cross-linked N-telopeptide) may be helpful in detecting an early response to antiresorptive therapy if measured prior to and 4 to 6 months after initiating therapy.

Table 177-3

FDA-Approved Indications for BMD Tests[a]

Estrogen-deficient women at clinical risk of osteoporosis
Vertebral abnormalities on x-ray suggestive of osteoporosis (osteopenia, vertebral fracture)
Glucocorticoid treatment equivalent to ≥7.5 mg of prednisone, or duration of therapy >3 months
Primary hyperparathyroidism
Monitoring response to an FDA-approved medication for osteoporosis
Repeat BMD evaluations at >23-month intervals, or more frequently, if medically justified

---

[a] Criteria adapted from the 1998 Bone Mass Measurement Act.
NOTE: FDA, U.S. Food and Drug Administration; BMD, bone mineral density.

TREATMENT

Treatment involves the management of acute fractures, modifying risk factors, and treating any underlying disorders that lead to reduced bone mass. Treatment decisions are based on an individual's risk factors, but active treatment is generally recommended if the T-score is < -2.5. Oral calcium (1–1.5 g/d of elemental calcium in divided doses), vitamin D (400–800 IU qd), exercise, and smoking cessation should be initiated in all patients with osteoporosis. Estrogen (0.625 mg/d for conjugated estrogens) in postmenopausal women decreases the rate of bone reabsorption and should be given with a progestin in women with an intact uterus. Bisphosphonates (alendronate 10 mg PO qAM, risedronate 5 mg PO qAM) augment bone density and decrease fracture rates. Alendronate can also be administered as a single weekly 70- mg dose. Bisphosphonates are poorly absorbed and should be taken in the morning on an empty stomach with 0.25 L (8 oz) of tap water. Raloxifene (60 mg PO qd), a selective estrogen receptor modulator, increases bone density and decreases total and LDL cholesterol without stimulating endometrial hyperplasia, though it may precipitate hot flashes.

OSTEOMALACIA

Etiology Defective mineralization of the organic matrix of bone results in osteomalacia. Osteomalacia is caused by inadequate intake or malabsorption of vitamin D (chronic pancreatic insufficiency, gastrectomy, malabsorption), acquired or inherited disorders of vitamin D metabolism (anticonvulsant therapy, chronic renal failure), chronic acidosis (renal tubular acidosis, acetazolamide ingestion), renal tubular defects that produce hypophosphatemia (Fanconi's syndrome), and chronic administration of aluminum-containing antacids.

Clinical Features Skeletal deformities may be overlooked until fractures occur after minimal trauma. Symptoms include diffuse skeletal pain and bony tenderness and may be subtle. Pain in the hips may result in an altered gait. Proximal muscle weakness may mimic primary muscle disorders. A decrease in bone density is usually associated with loss of trabeculae and thinning of the cortices. Characteristic x-ray findings are radiolucent bands (Looser's zones or pseudofractures) ranging from a few millimeters to several centimeters in length, usually perpendicular to the surface of the femur, pelvis, scapula, upper fibula, or metatarsals. Changes in serum calcium, phosphorus, 25(OH)D, and 1,25(OH)$_2$D levels vary depending on the cause. However, modest vitamin D deficiency leads to compensatory secondary hyperparathyroidism characterized by increased levels of PTH and alkaline phosphatase and lower levels of ionized calcium. 1,25 dihydroxyvitamin D levels may be preserved, reflecting upregulation of 1α hydroxylase activity.

 TREATMENT

In osteomalacia due to vitamin D deficiency, vitamin D$_2$ (ergocalciferol) or D$_3$ (cholecalciferol) is given orally in doses of 800–4000 IU daily for 6–12 weeks, followed by daily supplements of 200–600 IU. Elderly persons may require 50,000 IU weekly for 8 weeks to treat vitamin D deficiency. Osteomalacia due to malabsorption requires still larger doses of vitamin D (up to 100,000 IU/d) and calcium (calcium carbonate 4 g/d). In pts taking anticonvulsants, concurrent vitamin D should be administered in doses that maintain the serum calcium and 25(OH)D levels in the normal range. Calcitriol (0.25– 1 μg PO qd or 1.0–2.5 μg IV thrice weekly) is effective in treating hypocalcemia or osteodystrophy caused by chronic renal failure.

For a more detailed discussion, see Holick MF, Krane SM: Introduction to
Bone and Mineral Metabolism, Chap. 340, p. 2192; and Lindsay R, Cosman
F: Osteoporosis, Chap. 342, p. 2226, in HPIM-15.

178

DISORDERS OF LIPID METABOLISM

More than half of the coronary artery disease (CAD) in the U.S. is attributable
to abnormalities in the levels and metabolism of plasma lipids and lipoproteins.
Hyperlipoproteinemia may be characterized by hypercholesterolemia, isolated
hypertriglyceridemia, or both (Table 178-1). Diabetes mellitus, ethanol consumption, oral contraceptives, renal disease, hepatic disease, and hypothyroidism can cause secondary hyperlipoproteinemias or worsen underlying hyperli-
poproteinemic states.

Standard lipoprotein analysis assesses total cholesterol, HDL, and triglycerides with a calculation of LDL levels using the equation: LDL = total cholesterol − HDL − triglycerides/5. The LDL cholesterol concentration can be
estimated using this method only if triglycerides are <4.5 mmol/L (< 400 mg/
dL). Both LDL and HDL cholesterol levels are temporarily decreased for several
weeks after myocardial infarction or acute inflammatory states but can be accurately measured if blood is obtained within 8 h of the event.

ISOLATED HYPERCHOLESTEROLEMIA

Elevated levels of fasting plasma total cholesterol [>5.2 mmol/L (>200 mg/
dL)] in the presence of normal levels of triglycerides are almost always associated with increased concentrations of plasma LDL cholesterol. A rare individual with markedly elevated HDL cholesterol may also have increased plasma
total cholesterol levels. Elevations of LDL cholesterol can result from single-
gene defects, polygenic disorders, or from the secondary effects of other disease
states.

FAMILIAL HYPERCHOLESTEROLEMIA (FH)   FH is a codominant
genetic disorder that is due to mutations in the gene for the LDL receptor.
Plasma LDL levels are elevated at birth and remain so throughout life. In untreated heterozygous adults, total cholesterol levels range from 7.1–12.9 mmol/
L (275–500 mg/dL). Plasma triglyceride levels are typically normal, and HDL
cholesterol levels are normal or reduced. Heterozygotes, especially men, are
prone to accelerated atherosclerosis and premature CAD. *Tendon xanthomas*
(most commonly of the Achilles tendons and the extensor tendons of the knuckles), *tuberous xanthomas* (softer, painless nodules on the ankles and buttocks),
and *xanthelasmas* (deposits on the eyelids) are common.

FAMILIAL DEFECTIVE APO B   This autosomal dominant disorder impairs the synthesis and/or function of apo B100, thereby reducing the affinity
for the LDL receptor, slowing LDL catabolism, and causing a phenocopy of
FH.

Table 178-1

Characteristics of Common Hyperlipidemias

Lipid Phenotype	Plasma Lipid Levels, mmol/L (mg/dL)
ISOLATED HYPERCHOLESTEROLEMIA	
Familial hypercholesterolemia	Heterozygotes: total chol = 7–13 (275–500)
	Homozygotes: total chol > 13 (>500)
Familial defective apo B100	Heterozygotes: total chol = 7–13 (275–500)
Polygenic hypercholesterolemia	Total chol = 6.5–9.0 (250–350)
ISOLATED HYPERTRIGLYCERIDEMIA	
Familial hypertriglyceridemia	TG = 2.8–8.5 (250–750) (plasma may be cloudy)
Familial lipoprotein lipase deficiency	TG > 8.5 (>750) (plasma may be milky)
Familial apo CII deficiency	TG > 8.5 (>750) (plasma may be milky)
HYPERTRIGLYCERIDEMIA AND HYPERCHOLESTEROLEMIA	
Combined hyperlipidemia	TG = 2.8–8.5 (250–750) Total chol = 6.5–13.0 (250–500)
Dysbetalipoproteinemia	TG = 2.8–5.6 (250–500) Total chol = 6.5–13.0 (250–500)

NOTE: Total chol, the sum of free and esterified cholesterol; LDL, low-density lipoprotein; TG, triglycerides; VLDL, very low density lipoproteins; IDL, intermediate-density lipoprotein.
SOURCE: From HN Ginsberg, IJ Goldberg: HPIM-15, p. 2250.

POLYGENIC HYPERCHOLESTEROLEMIA Most moderate hypercholesterolemia [<9.1 mmol/L (<350 mg/dL)] arises from an interaction of multiple genetic defects and environmental factors such as diet, age, and exercise. Plasma HDL and triglyceride levels are normal, and xanthomas are not present.

 TREATMENT

An algorithm for the evaluation and treatment of hypercholesterolemia is displayed in Fig. 178-1. Therapy for all of these disorders includes restriction of dietary cholesterol, HMG-CoA reductase inhibitors, and bile acid–binding resins (Table 178-2).

ISOLATED HYPERTRIGLYCERIDEMIA

The diagnosis of hypertriglyceridemia is made by measuring plasma lipid levels after an overnight fast. Hypertriglyceridemia in adults is defined as a triglyceride

Lipoproteins		
Elevated	Phenotype	Clinical Signs
LDL	IIa	Usually develop xanthomas in adulthood and vascular disease at 30–50 years
LDL	IIa	Usually develop xanthomas and vascular disease in childhood
LDL	IIa	
LDL	IIa	Usually asymptomatic until vascular disease develops; no xanthomas
VLDL	IV	Asymptomatic; may be associated with increased risk of vascular disease
Chylomicrons	I, V	May be asymptomatic; may be associated with pancreatitis, abdominal pain, hepatosplenomegaly
Chylomicrons	I, V	As above
VLDL, LDL	IIb	Usually asymptomatic until vascular disease develops; familial form may also present as isolated high TG or an isolated high LDL cholesterol
VLDL, IDL; LDL normal	III	Usually asymptomatic until vascular disease develops; may have palmar or tuboeruptive xanthomas

level >2.3 mmol/L (>200 mg/dL). An isolated increase in plasma triglycerides indicates that chylomicrons and/or very low density lipoprotein (VLDL) are increased. Plasma is usually clear when triglyceride levels are <4.5 mmol/L (<400 mg/dL) and cloudy when levels are higher due to VLDL (and/or chylomicron) particles becoming large enough to scatter light. When chylomicrons are present, a creamy layer floats to the top of plasma after refrigeration for several hours. Tendon xanthomas and xanthelasmas do not occur with isolated hypertriglyceridemia, but *eruptive xanthomas* (small orange-red papules) can appear on the trunk and extremities and *lipemia retinalis* (orange-yellow retinal vessels) may be seen when the triglyceride levels are >11.3 mmol/L (>1000 mg/dL). Pancreatitis is associated with these high concentrations.

FAMILIAL HYPERTRIGLYCERIDEMIA   In this autosomal dominant disorder, increased plasma VLDL causes plasma triglyceride concentrations to range from 2.3–5.6 mmol/L (200–500 mg/dL). Obesity, hyperglycemia, and hyperinsulinemia are characteristic, and diabetes mellitus, ethanol consumption, oral contraceptives, and hypothyroidism may exacerbate the condition. Because atherosclerosis is accelerated, vigorous attempts should be made to control all exacerbating factors, and intake of saturated fat should be severely restricted.

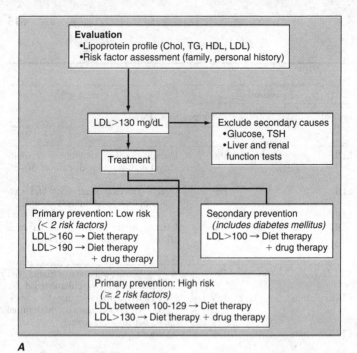

A

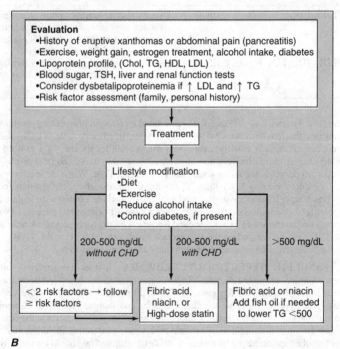

B

FIGURE 178-1 Algorithms for the evaluation and treatment of hypercholesterolemia (*A*) and hypertriglyceridemia (*B*). Statin, HMG-CoA reductase inhibitor; Chol, cholesterol; HDL, high-density lipoprotein; LDL, low-density lipoprotein; TG, triglyceride; TSH, thyroid-stimulating hormone; CHD, coronary heart disease.

Table 178-2

Hypolipidemic Drugs

Drugs	Lipoprotein Class Affected	Common Side Effects	Contraindications
HMG-CoA reductase inhibitors Lovastatin (Mevacor) 10–80 mg/d Pravastatin (Pravachol) 10–40 mg/d Simvastatin (Zocor) 5–40 mg/d Fluvastatin (Lescol) 20–40 mg/d Atorvastatin (Lipitor) 10–80 mg/d Cerivastatin (Baycol) 0.3–0.4 mg/d	↓ LDL 25–55% ↓ VLDL, ↓ TG 10–20% ↑ HDL 5–10%	Hepatic dysfunction <2%, severe myositis <1%, ↑ CPK, len opacities may occur	Risk of myositis increased by impaired renal function and in combination with gemfibrozil or nicotinic acid
Nicotinic acid Niacin 50–100 mg tid initially, then increase to 1.0–2.5 g tid Niaspan 1–2 g/d	↓ TG 25–35% ↓ VLDL 25–35% ↓ LDL 15–25% ↑ HDL 15–30%	Flushing (may be relieved by aspirin), hepatic dysfunction, tachycardia, atrial arrhythmias, pruritus, dry skin, nausea, diarrhea, glucose intolerance, hyperuricemia	Peptic ulcer disease, cardiac arrhythmias, hepatic disease, gout, diabetes mellitus
Bile acid–binding resins Cholestyramine (Questran) 8–12 g bid or tid Cholestipol (Cholestid) 10–15 g bid or tid	↓ LDL 20–30% ↑ HDL 5% ↑ TG 10%	Constipation, gastric discomfort, nausea, hemorrhoidal bleeding, theoretical ↑ lithogenicity of bile	Biliary tract obstruction, gastric outlet obstruction
Fibric acid derivatives Clofibrate (Atromid) 1000 mg bid Gemfibrozil (Lopid) 600 mg bid Fenofibrate (Tricor) 200 mg qd	↓ TG 25–40% ↑ or ↓ LDL ↑ HDL 5–15%	↑ Lithogenicity of bile, gallstones, nausea, hepatic dysfunction, myositis <1%, cardiac arrhythmias	Hepatic or biliary disease, renal insufficiency associated with ↑ risk of myositis
Probucol Probucol (Lorelco) 500 mg bid	↓ LDL 10–15% ↓ HDL 20–25%	Diarrhea, nausea, abdominal pain, cardiac arrhythmias	Prolonged QT interval, primary biliary cirrhosis

NOTE: LDL, low-density lipoprotein; VLDL, very low density lipoprotein; TG, triglycerides; HDL, high-density lipoprotein; LPL, lipoprotein lipase; CPK, creative phosphokinase.

FAMILIAL LIPOPROTEIN LIPASE DEFICIENCY This rare autosomal recessive disorder results from the absence or deficiency of lipoprotein lipase, which in turn retards the metabolism of chylomicrons. Accumulation of chylomicrons in plasma causes recurrent bouts of pancreatitis, usually beginning in childhood. Eruptive xanthomas occur on buttocks, trunk, and extremities. The plasma is milky or creamy (lipemic). Accelerated atherosclerosis is not a feature.

FAMILIAL APO CII DEFICIENCY This rare autosomal recessive disorder is due to the absence of apo CII, an essential cofactor for lipoprotein lipase. As a result, chylomicrons and triglycerides accumulate and cause manifestations similar to those in lipoprotein lipase deficiency. Diagnosis is made by protein electrophoresis, which reveals the absence of apo CII.

 TREATMENT

An algorithm for the evaluation and treatment of hypertriglyceridemia is displayed in Fig. 178-1. All pts with hypertriglyceridemia should be placed on a fat-free diet. In those with familial hypertriglyceridemia, fibric acid derivatives should be administered if dietary measures fail.

HYPERCHOLESTEROLEMIA AND HYPERTRIGLYCERIDEMIA

Elevations of both triglycerides and cholesterol are caused by elevations in both VLDL and LDL or in VLDL remnant particles.

FAMILIAL COMBINED HYPERLIPIDEMIA (FCHL) This inherited disorder can cause different lipoprotein abnormalities in affected individuals, including hypercholesterolemia, hypertriglyceridemia, or both. Atherosclerosis is accelerated. All pts should restrict dietary cholesterol and fat and avoid alcohol and oral contraceptives. Elevated triglycerides may respond to fibric acid derivatives. An HMG-CoA reductase inhibitor plus a bile acid–binding resin may be used when cholesterol is elevated. Combinations of reductase inhibitors and niacin or fibric acid derivatives is associated with a 2–3% risk of myositis.

DYSBETALIPOPROTEINEMIA This rare disorder is associated with homozygosity for apo E2, but the development of disease requires additional environmental and/or genetic factors. Plasma cholesterol and triglycerides are increased due to accumulation of VLDL and chylomicron remnant particles. Severe atherosclerosis involves the coronary arteries, internal carotids, and the abdominal aorta and causes premature MI, intermittant claudication, and gangrene. Cutaneous xanthomas are distinctive, in the form of *xanthoma striata palmaris* and tuberous or *tuberoeruptive xanthomas*. Triglycerides and cholesterol are both elevated. Diagnosis is established by finding a broad beta band on lipoprotein electrophoresis. If present, hypothyroidism and diabetes mellitus should be treated, and fibric acid derivatives may be necessary.

PREVENTION OF THE COMPLICATIONS OF ATHEROSCLEROSIS

The National Cholesterol Education Program guidelines (Fig. 178-1) are based on plasma LDL levels and estimations of other risk factors. The goal in pts with the highest risk (secondary prevention after MI, primary treatment of known atherosclerotic heart disease, and diabetes mellitus) is to lower LDL cholesterol to <2.6 mmol/L (<100 mg/dL). The goal is an LDL cholesterol <3.4 mmol/L (<130 mg/dL) in pts with two or more risk factors for atherosclerotic heart disease. Risk factors include (1) men >age 45, women > age 55 or after menopause; (2) family history of early CAD (< 55 years in a male parent or sibling and <65 years in a female parent or sibling); (3) hypertension (even if it is controlled with medications); (4) cigarette smoking (>10 cigarettes/day); (5) diabetes mellitus; or (6) HDL cholesterol <0.9 mmol/L (<35 mg/dL). Note that one risk factor may be subtracted if HDL cholesterol >1.6 mmol/L (>60 mg/dL). Therapy begins with a low-fat diet, but pharmacologic intervention is often required (Table 178-2).

For a more detailed discussion, see Ginsberg HN, Goldberg IJ: Disorders of Lipoprotein Metabolism, Chap. 344, p. 2245, in HPIM-15.

179

HEMOCHROMATOSIS, PORPHYRIAS, AND WILSON'S DISEASE

HEMOCHROMATOSIS

Hemochromatosis is a disorder of iron storage that results in increased intestinal iron absorption with Fe deposition and damage to many tissues, including the liver, heart, pancreas, joints, and pituitary. Two major causes of hemochromatosis exist: hereditary (due to inheritance of mutant *HFE* genes) and secondary iron overload (usually the result of disordered erythropoiesis or excessive Fe ingestion). Alcoholic liver disease and chronic excessive iron ingestion may also be associated with a moderate increase in hepatic Fe and elevated body Fe stores.

Clinical Features Early symptoms include weakness, lassitude, weight loss, a bronze pigmentation or darkening of skin, abdominal pain, and loss of libido. Hepatomegaly occurs in 95% of pts, sometimes in the presence of normal LFTs. Other signs include spider angiomas, splenomegaly, arthropathy, ascites, cardiac arrythmias, CHF, loss of body hair, palmar erythema, gynecomastia, and testicular atrophy. Diabetes mellitus occurs in about 65%, usually in pts with family history of diabetes. Adrenal insufficiency, hypothyroidism, and hypoparathyroidism rarely occur.

Diagnosis Serum Fe, percent transferrin saturation, and serum ferritin levels are increased (Table 179-1). If either the percent transferrin saturation or the serum ferritin level is abnormal, genetic testing for hemochromatosis should be performed. All first-degree relatives of pts with hemochromatosis should be tested for the C282Y and H63D mutations. Liver biopsy may be required in affected individuals to evaluate possible cirrhosis or to quantify tissue iron. An algorithm for evaluating pts with possible hemochromatosis is shown in Fig. 179-1. Death in untreated pts results from cardiac failure (30%), cirrhosis (25%), and hepatocellular carcinoma (30%); the latter may develop despite adequate Fe removal.

Table 179-1

Representative Iron Values in Normal Subjects, Patients with Hemochromatosis, and Patients with Alcoholic Liver Disease

Determination	Normal	Symptomatic Hemochromatosis	Homozygotes with Early, Asymptomatic Hemochromatosis	Heterozygotes	Alcoholic Liver Disease
Plasma iron, μmol/L (μg/dL)	9–27 (50–150)	32–54 (180–300)	Usually elevated 36–54 (200–300)	Elevated or normal	Often elevated 45–66 (250–370)
Total iron-binding capacity, μmol/L (μg/dL)	45–66 (250–370)	36–54 (200–300)	36–54 (200–300)	Elevated or normal	45–66 (250–370)
Transferrin saturation, percent	22–46	50–100	50–100	Normal or elevated	27–60
Serum ferritin, μg/L	10–200	900–6000	200–500	Usually <500	10–500
Urinary iron,[a] mg/24 h	0–2	9–23	2–5	2–5	Usually <5
Liver iron, μg/g dry wt	300–1400	6000–18,000	2000–4000	300–3000	300–2000
Hepatic iron index $\dfrac{(\mu g/g\ \text{dry wt})}{56 \times \text{age}}$	<1.0	>2	Usually >2	<2	<2

[a] After intramuscular administration of 0.5 g deferoxamine.

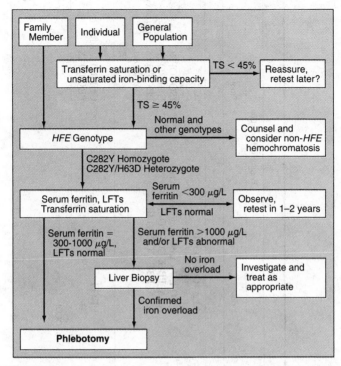

FIGURE 179-1 Algorithm for screening for *HFE*-associated hemochromatosis. LFT, liver function tests; TS, transferrin saturation. (*With permission from The Canadian Journal of Gastroenterology.*)

TREATMENT

Involves removal of excess body Fe, usually by intermittent phlebotomy. Since 1 unit of blood contains ~250 mg Fe, and since ≥25 g of Fe must be removed, phlebotomy is performed weekly for 1–2 years. Less frequent phlebotomy is then used to maintain serum Fe at <27 μmol/L (<150 μg/dL). Chelating agents such as deferoxamine (infused SC using a portable pump) remove 10–20 mg iron per day, a fraction of that mobilized by weekly phlebotomy. Chelation therapy is indicated, however, when phlebotomy is inappropriate.

PORPHYRIAS

The porphyrias are inherited or acquired disturbances in heme biosynthesis. Each disorder causes a unique pattern of overproduction, accumulation, and excretion of intermediates of heme synthesis (Table 179-2). Manifestations include intermittent nervous system dysfunction and/or sensitivity of skin to sunlight.

ACUTE INTERMITTENT PORPHYRIA This is an autosomal dominant disorder with variable expressivity. Manifestations include colicky abdominal pain, vomiting, constipation, port-wine colored urine, and neurologic and psychiatric disturbances. Acute attacks rarely occur before puberty and may last from days to months. Photosensitivity does not occur. Clinical and biochemical

Table 179-2

The Major Metabolites Accumulated in the Human Porphyrias

Type/Porphyria	Increased Erythrocyte Porphyrins	Porphyrin Excretion	
		Urine	Stool
HEPATIC PORPHYRIAS			
ALA dehydratase deficiency (ADP)	PROTO	ALA, COPRO III	—
Acute intermittent porphyria (AIP)	—	ALA, PBG	—
Porphyria cutanea tarda (PCT)	—	URO I, 7-carboxylate porphyrin	ISOCOPRO
Hereditary coproporphyria (HCP)	—	ALA, PBG, COPRO III	COPRO III
Variegate porphyria (VP)	—	ALA, PBG COPRO III	PROTO IX, 5-carboxylate porphyrin
ERYTHROPOIETIC PORPHYRIAS			
X-linked sideroblastic anemia (XLSA)	—	—	—
Congenital erythropoietic porphyria (CEP)	URO I	URO I	COPRO I, URO I
Erythropoietic protoporphyria (EPP)	PROTO IX	—	PROTO IX

NOTE: ALA, δ-aminolevulinic acid; PBG, porphobilinogen; COPRO I, coproporphyrinogen; ISOCOPRO, isocoproporphyrin; URO, uroporphyrinogen; PROTO, protoporphyrinogen.

manifestations may be precipitated by barbiturates, anticonvulsants, estrogens, oral contraceptives, alcohol, or low-calorie diets. Diagnosis is established by demonstrating elevation of urinary porphobilinogen (PBG) and γ-aminolevulinic acid (ALA) during an acute attack. Fresh urine may darken on standing because PBGs polymerize spontaneously to uroporphyrin and porphobilin.

 TREATMENT

As soon as possible after the onset of an attack, 3–4 mg of heme, in the form of heme arginate, heme albumin, or hematin, should be infused daily for 4 days. Administration of IV glucose at rates up to 20 g/h or parenteral nutrition, if oral feeding is not possible for long periods, can be effective in acute attacks. Narcotic analgesics may be required during acute attacks for abdominal pain, and phenothiazines are useful for nausea, vomiting, anxiety, and restlessness. Treatment between attacks involves adequate nutritional intake, avoidance of drugs known to exacerbate the disease, and prompt treatment of other intercurrent diseases or infections.

PORPHYRIA CUTANEA TARDA This is the most common porphyria and is characterized by chronic skin lesions and, usually, hepatic disease. It is due to deficiency (inherited or acquired) of uroporphyrinogen decarboxylase. Photosensitivity causes facial pigmentation, increased fragility of skin, erythema, and vesicular and ulcerative lesions, typically involving face, forehead, and forearms. Neurologic manifestations are not observed. Contributing factors include excess alcohol, iron, and estrogens. Pts with liver disease are at risk for hepatocellular carcinoma. Urine uroporphyrin and coproporphyrin are increased.

 TREATMENT

Avoidance of precipitating factors, including abstinence from alcohol, estrogens, iron supplements, and other exacerbating drugs, is the first line of therapy. A complete response can almost always be achieved by repeated phlebotomy (every 1–2 weeks) until hepatic iron is reduced. Chloroquine or hydroxychloroquine may be used in low doses (e.g., 125 mg chloroquine phosphate twice weekly) to promote porphyrin excretion in pts unable to undergo or unresponsive to phlebotomy.

ERYTHROPOIETIC PORPHYRIAS In the erythropoietic porphyrias, porphyrins from bone marrow erythrocytes and plasma are deposited in the skin and lead to cutaneous photosensitivity. The disorders include X-linked sideroblastic anemia, congenital erythropoietic porphyria, and erythropoietic protoporphyria. Diagnosis and treatment vary depending on the type of porphyria but often require transfusions to suppress erythropoiesis and avoidance of exposure to sunlight.

WILSON'S DISEASE

Wilson's disease is an inherited disorder of copper metabolism, resulting in the toxic accumulation of copper in the liver, brain, and other organs. Individuals with Wilson's disease have mutations in the *ATP7B* gene.

Clinical Features In about half of pts, one of four types of hepatic disease herald the clinical onset: acute hepatitis, parenchymal liver disease, cirrhosis, or fulminant hepatitis. In most other pts, neurologic or psychiatric disturbances are the first clinical sign and are always accompanied by Kayser-Fleischer rings (corneal deposits of copper). In about 5% of pts, the first manifestation may be primary or secondary amenorrhea or repeated spontaneous abortions.

Diagnosis The diagnosis is confirmed by a serum ceruloplasmin level <200 μg/L (< 20 mg/dL) and either (1) Kayser-Fleischer rings or (2) an elevated copper level on liver biopsy.

 TREATMENT

Penicillamine is administered in an initial dose of 1 g PO qd on an empty stomach, along with 25 mg of pyridoxine. Penicillamine should be discontinued if rash, fever, leukopenia, thrombocytopenia, lymphadenopathy, proteinuria, or neurologic features worsen. It can be replaced with trientine, 250 mg PO qid, given on an empty stomach.

For a more detailed discussion, see Powell LW, Isselbacher KI: Hemochromatosis, Chap. 345, p. 2257; Desnick RJ: The Porphyrias, Chap. 346, p. 2261; Scheinberg IH: Wilson's Disease, Chap. 348, p. 2274, in HPIM-15.

THE NEUROLOGIC EXAMINATION

MENTAL STATUS EXAM

The goal of the mental status exam is to evaluate attention, orientation, memory, insight, judgment, and grasp of general information. Attention is tested by asking the pt to respond every time a specific item recurs in a list. Orientation is evaluated by asking about the day, date, and location. Memory can be tested by asking the pt to immediately recall a sequence of numbers and by testing recall of a series of objects after defined times (e.g., 5 and 15 min). More remote memory is evaluated by assessing pt's ability to provide a cogent chronologic history of his or her illness or personal life events. Recall of major historic events or dates of major current events can be used to assess knowledge. Evaluation of language function should include assessment of spontaneous speech, naming, repetition, reading, writing, and comprehension. Additional tests such as ability to draw and copy, perform calculations, interpret proverbs or logic problems, identify right vs. left, name and identify body parts, etc. are also important.

CRANIAL NERVE (CN) EXAM

CN I   Occlude each nostril sequentially and ask pt to gently sniff and correctly identify a mild test stimulus, such as soap, toothpaste, coffee, or lemon oil.

CN II   Check visual acuity with and without correction using a Snellen chart (distance) and Jaeger's test type (near). Map visual fields (VFs) by confrontation testing in each quadrant of visual field for each eye individually. The best method is to sit facing pt (2–3 ft apart), have pt cover one eye gently, and fix uncovered eye on examiner's nose. A small white object (e.g., a cotton-tipped applicator) is then moved slowly from periphery of field toward center until seen. Pt's VF should be mapped against examiner's for comparison. Formal perimetry and tangent screen exam are essential to identify and delineate small defects. Optic fundi should be examined with an ophthalmoscope, and the color, size, and degree of swelling or elevation of the optic disc recorded. The retinal vessels should be checked for size, regularity, AV nicking at crossing points, hemorrhage, exudates, aneurysms. The retina, including the macula, should be examined for abnormal pigmentation and other lesions.

CNS III, IV, VI   Describe size, regularity, and shape of pupils, reaction (direct and consensual) to light and convergence (pt follows an object as it moves closer). Check for lid drooping, lag, or retraction. Ask pt to follow your finger as you move it horizontally to left and right and vertically with each eye first fully adducted then fully abducted. Check for failure to move fully in particular directions and for presence of regular, rhythmic, involuntary oscillations of eyes (nystagmus). Test quick voluntary eye movements (saccades) as well as pursuit (e.g., follow the finger).

CN V   Feel the masseter and temporalis muscles as pt bites down and test jaw opening, protrusion, and lateral motion against resistance. Examine sensation over entire face as well as response to touching each cornea lightly with a small wisp of cotton.

Table 180-1

Muscles That Move Joints

	Muscle	Nerve	Segmental Innervation
Shoulder	Supraspinatus	Suprascapular n.	C5,6
	Deltoid	Axillary n.	C5,6
Forearm	Biceps	Musculocutaneous n.	C5,6
	Brachioradialis	Radial n.	C5,6
	Triceps	Radial n.	C6,7,8
	Ext. carpi radialis	Radial n.	C5,6
	Ext. carpi ulnaris	P. interosseous n.	C7,8
	Ext. digitorum	P. interosseous n.	C7,8
	Supinator	P. interosseous n.	C6,7
	Flex. carpi radialis	Median n.	C6,7
	Flex. carpi ulnaris	Ulnar n.	C7,8,T1
	Pronator teres	Median n.	C6,7
Wrist	Ext. carpi ulnaris	Ulnar n.	C7,8,T1
	Flex. carpi radialis	Median n.	C6,7
Hand	Lumbricals	Median + ulnar n.	C8,T1
	Interossei	Ulnar n.	C8,T1
	Flex. Digitorum	Median + A. interosseous n.	C7,C8,T1
Thumb	Opponens pollicis	Median n.	C8,T1
	Ext. pollicis	P. interosseous n.	C7,8
	Add. Pollicis	Median n.	C8,T1
	Abd. Pollicis	Ulnar n.	C8,T1
	Flex. Pollicis br.	Ulnar n.	C8,T1
Thigh	Iliopsoas	Femoral n.	L1,2,3
	Glutei	Sup. + inf. gluteal n.	L4,L5,S1,S2
	Quadriceps	Femoral n.	L2,3,4
	Adductors	Obturator n.	L2,3,4
	Hamstrings	Sciatic n.	L5,S1,S2
Foot	Gastrocnemius	Tibial n.	S1,S2
	Tibialis ant.	Deep peroneal n.	L4,5
	Peronei	Deep peroneal n.	L5,S1
	Tibialis post.	Tibial n.	L4,5
Toes	Ext. hallucis l.	Deep peroneal n.	L5,S1

CN VII Look for asymmetry of face at rest and with spontaneous as well as emotion-induced (e.g., laughing) movements. Test eyebrow elevation, forehead wrinkling, eye closure, smiling, frowning; check puff, whistle, lip pursing, and chin muscle contraction. Observe for differences in strength of lower and upper facial muscles. Taste on the anterior two-thirds of tongue can be affected by lesions of the seventh CN proximal to the chorda tympani. Test taste for sweet (sugar), salt, sour (lemon), and bitter (quinine) using a cotton-tipped applicator moistened in appropriate solution and placed on lateral margin of protruded tongue halfway back from tip.

CN VIII Check ability to hear tuning fork, finger rub, watch tick, and whispered voice at specified distances with each ear. Check for air vs. mastoid bone conduction (Rinne) and lateralization of a tuning fork placed on center of forehead (Weber). Accurate, quantitative testing of hearing requires formal audiometry. Remember to examine tympanic membranes.

CNS IX, X Check for symmetric elevation of palate-uvula with phonation ("ahh"), as well as position of uvula and palatal arch at rest. Sensation in region

Function

Abduction of upper arm
Abduction of upper arm
Flexion of the supinated forearm
Forearm flexion with arm between pronation and supination
Extension of forearm
Extension and abduction of hand at the wrist
Extension and adduction of hand at the wrist
Extension of fingers at the MCP joints
Supination of the extended forearm
Flexion and abduction of hand at the wrist
Flexion and adduction of hand at the wrist
Pronation of the forearm
Extension/adduction at the wrist
Flexion/abduction at the wrist
Extension of fingers at PIP joint with the MCP joint extended and fixed
Abduction/adduction of the fingers
Flexion of the fingers
Touching the base of the 5th finger with thumb
Extension of the thumb
Adduction of the thumb
Abduction of the thumb
Flexion of the thumb
Flexion of the thigh
Abduction, extension, and internal rotation of the leg
Extension of the leg at the knee
Adduction of the leg
Flexion of the leg at the knee
Plantar flexion of the foot
Dorsiflexion of the foot
Eversion of the foot
Inversion of the foot
Dorsiflexion of the great toe

of tonsils, posterior pharynx, and tongue may also require testing. Pharyngeal ("gag") reflex is evaluated by stimulating posterior pharyngeal wall on each side with a blunt object (e.g., tongue blade). Direct examination of vocal cords by laryngoscopy is necessary in some situations.

   CN XI   Check shoulder shrug (trapezius muscle) and head rotation to each side (sternocleidomastoid muscle) against resistance.

   CN XII   Examine bulk and power of tongue. Look for atrophy, deviation from midline with protrusion, tremor, and small flickering or twitching movements (fibrillations, fasciculations).

MOTOR EXAM
Power should be systematically tested for major movements at each joint (Table 180-1). Strength should be recorded using a reproducible scale (e.g., 0 = no movement, 1 = flicker or trace of contraction with no associated movement at a joint, 2 = movement present but cannot be sustained against gravity, 3 =

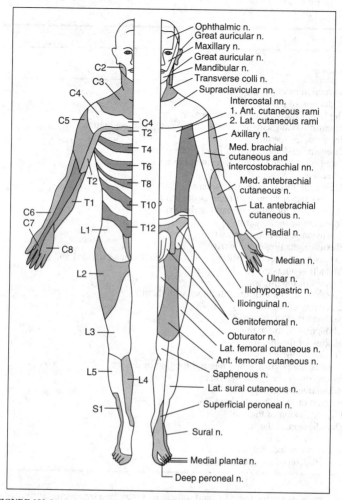

FIGURE 180-1   Anterior view of dermatomes (*left*) and cutaneous areas supplied by individual peripheral nerves (*right*). (*From HPIM-15, p. 130.*)

movement against gravity but not against applied resistance, 4 = movement against some degree of resistance, and 5 = full power; values can be supplemented with the addition of + and − signs to provide additional gradations). The speed of movement, the ability to promptly relax contractions, and fatigue with repetition should all be noted. Loss in bulk and size of muscle (atrophy) should be noted, as well as the presence of irregular involuntary contraction (twitching) of groups of muscle fibers (fasciculations). Any involuntary movements should be noted at rest, during maintained posture, and with voluntary action (Chap. 11).

REFLEXES

Important muscle-stretch reflexes to test routinely and the spinal cord segments involved in their reflex arcs include biceps (**C5**, 6); brachioradialis (C5, **6**);

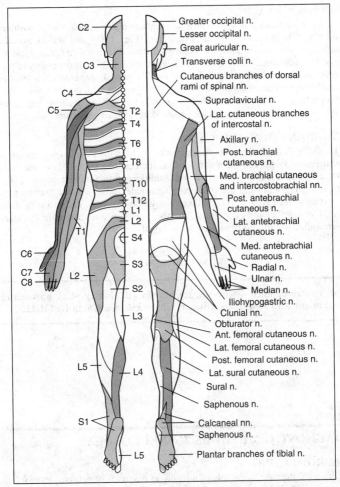

FIGURE 180-2 Posterior view of dermatomes (*left*) and cutaneous areas supplied by individual nerves (*right*). *(From HPIM-15, p. 131.)*

triceps (**C7**, 8); patellar (**L3**, 4); and Achilles (**S1**, 2). A common grading scale is 0 = absent, 1 = present but diminished, 2 = normal, 3 = hyperactive, and 4 = hyperactive with clonus (repetitive rhythmic contractions with maintained stretch). The plantar reflex should be tested by using a blunt-ended object such as the point of a key to stroke the outer border of the sole of the foot from the heel toward the base of the great toe. An abnormal response (Babinski sign) is extension (dorsiflexion) of the great toe at the metatarsophalangeal joint. In some cases this may be associated with abduction (fanning) of other toes and variable degrees of flexion at ankle, knee, and hip. Normal response is plantar flexion of the toes. Abdominal, anal, and sphincteric reflexes are important in certain situations, as are additional muscle-stretch reflexes.

SENSORY EXAM

For most purposes it is sufficient to test sensation to pinprick, touch, position, and vibration in each of the four extremities (Figs. 180-1 and 180-2). Specific problems often require more thorough evaluation. Patients with cerebral lesions may have abnormalities in "discriminative sensation" such as the ability to perceive double simultaneous stimuli, to localize stimuli accurately, to identify closely approximated stimuli as separate (two-point discrimination), to identify objects by touch alone (stereognosis), or to judge weights, evaluate texture, or identify letters or numbers written on the skin surface (graphesthesia).

COORDINATION AND GAIT

The ability to move the index finger accurately from the nose to the examiner's outstretched finger and the ability to slide the heel of each foot from the knee down the shin are tests of coordination. Additional tests (drawing objects in the air, following a moving finger, tapping with index finger against thumb or alternately against each individual finger) may also be useful. The ability to stand with feet together and eyes closed (Romberg test), to walk a straight line (tandem walk), and to turn should all be observed.

For a more detailed discussion, see Martin JB, Hauser SL: Approach to the Patient with Neurologic Disease, Chap. 356, p. 2326, in HPIM-15.

181

DIAGNOSTIC METHODS IN NEUROLOGY

NEUROIMAGING

A dramatic increase in the role of imaging in diagnosis of neurologic disorders occurred with the development of computed tomography (CT) in the early 1970s and of magnetic resonance imaging (MRI) in the 1980s. In general, MRI is more sensitive than CT for the evaluation of most lesions affecting the CNS, particularly those in the spinal cord, cranial nerves, and posterior fossa. CT is more sensitive than MRI for visualizing fine osseous detail, such as temporal bone anatomy and fractures. Recent developments, such as helical CT, CT angiography, MR angiography, positron emission tomography, Doppler ultrasound, and interventional angiography, have continued to advance diagnosis and guide therapy. Conventional angiography is reserved for cases in which small-vessel detail is essential for diagnosis (Table 181-1).

ELECTROENCEPHALOGRAPHY

An EEG records the electrical activity of the brain from multiple electrodes placed on the scalp. It is used primarily in the investigation and management of epilepsy. It is also useful in the evaluation of altered mental status, coma, sleep disorders, and brain death.

Table 181-1

Guidelines for the Use of CT, Ultrasound, and MRI

Condition	Recommended Technique
Hemorrhage	
Acute parenchymal	CT > MRI
Subacute/chronic	MRI
Subarachnoid hemorrhage	CT, lumbar puncture → angiography
Aneurysm	Angiography > ?MRA
Ischemic infarction	
Hemorrhagic infarction	CT or MRI
Bland infarction	MRI > CT
Carotid or vertebral dissection	MRI/MRA
Vertebral basilar insufficiency	MRI/MRA
Carotid stenosis	Doppler ultrasound, MRA, CTA
Suspected mass lesions	
Neoplasm, primary or metastatic	MRI + contrast
Infection/abscess	MRI + contrast
Immunosuppression with focal findings	MRI + contrast
Vascular malformations	MRI ± angiography
White matter disorders	MRI
Demyelinating disease	MRI ± contrast
Dementia	MRI or CT
Trauma	
Acute trauma	CT (noncontrast)
Shear injury/chronic hemorrhage	MRI
Headache/migraine	CT (noncontrast) or MRI
Seizure	
First time, no focal neurologic deficits	MRI > CT as screen
Partial complex/refractory	MRI + coronal T2W imaging
Cranial neuropathy	MRI + contrast
Meningeal disease	MRI + contrast
SPINE	
Low back pain	
No neurologic deficits	Conservative therapy, consider MRI or CT after 4 weeks
With focal deficits	MRI > CT
Spinal stenosis	MRI or CT
Cervical spondylosis	MRI or CT myelography
Infection	MRI + contrast > CT
Myelopathy	MRI + contrast, consider myelography if MRI negative
Arteriovenous malformations	MRI, myelography/angiography

NOTE: MRA, MR angiography; CTA, CT angiography; T2W, T2-weighted.

NORMAL EEG RHYTHMS IN ADULTS   In an awake pt lying quietly with eyes closed, an 8- to 12-Hz alpha rhythm should be present over the posterior head regions and attenuate with eye opening. There may be beta activity (>13 Hz) as well, which is more pronounced with drowsiness and certain drugs. Theta (4–7 Hz) activity is present predominantly over the temporal regions with drowsiness and light sleep. Normal sleep activity includes delta activity (<4 Hz), sleep spindles, and vertex waves.

ABNORMAL EEG RHYTHMS IN ADULTS   The EEG in a patient with epilepsy may show ictal, interictal, or normal activity. An electrographic seizure consists of abnormal, repetitive, rhythmic activity having abrupt onset and termination. Interictal epileptiform activity in correlation with an appropriate history strongly suggests epilepsy and includes bursts of abnormal spike and sharp wave discharges. Generalized 3-Hz spike-and-wave activity is present in absence seizures. Focal interictal activity makes partial complex seizures more likely. A normal EEG does not exclude the diagnosis of epilepsy. Continuous inpatient or portable monitoring increases the likelihood of capturing a spell in difficult cases.

In pts with altered mental status, there may be generalized or focal slowing; triphasic waves suggest a metabolic cause. Reactivity of the record correlates with a better prognosis. Loss of reactivity or a burst-suppression pattern is present with severe coma. Electrocerebral silence in the absence of drug overdose or hypothermia implies that useful cognitive recovery will not occur. Periodic lateralized epileptiform discharges (PLEDs) can be seen with herpes simplex encephalitis. Generalized periodic complexes in the presence of a dementing disorder are consistent with Creutzfeld-Jakob disease. The EEG does not reliably distinguish between dementia and pseudodementia.

EVOKED POTENTIALS

Evoked potentials (EPs) are averaged time-locked cortical potentials following stimulation of visual, auditory, or somatosensory afferents. Prolongation of the latency of these potentials reflects a lesion in the specific pathway being tested but is nonspecific. They are most often used in the evaluation of possible multiple sclerosis (MS).

VISUAL EVOKED POTENTIALS (VEPS)   Elicited by monocular stimulation with a reversing checkerboard pattern and recorded from the occipital region of the scalp. A P100 response is recorded at a latency of approximately 100 ms. Latency, amplitude, and symmetry of the response are measured. VEPs are most commonly abnormal with optic neuritis (active or residual) but can be abnormal with other lesions of the optic nerve such as compression or with glaucoma.

BRAINSTEM AUDITORY EVOKED POTENTIALS   Using earphones, clicks presented to one ear produce seven wave forms (I–VII) recorded from the scalp, representing successive activation of the auditory nerve and brainstem auditory pathways. Applications include screening for acoustic neuroma, localization of level of the lesion in coma (usually normal in toxic/metabolic coma or bihemispheric disease and abnormal with brainstem pathology), and hearing evaluation of infants.

SOMATOSENSORY EVOKED POTENTIALS (SEPS)   Generated by delivering multiple small electrical stimuli to large sensory nerve fibers of the limbs to produce afferent volleys recorded at many levels along the somatosensory pathway (proximal peripheral nerve trunks, spinal cord dorsal columns, and primary sensory cortex). The SEP may be abnormal in multiple disorders, including MS when there is a lesion in the cord, vitamin B_{12} deficiency, AIDS, cervical stenosis, or Lyme disease. The presence or absence of SEPs may have prognostic significance with coma and spinal cord injury. They can also be used intraoperatively during spine surgery or carotid endarterectomy to indicate possible iatrogenic injury to the cord or parietal cortex.

ELECTROMYOGRAPHY (EMG)/NERVE CONDUCTION STUDIES (NCS)

The EMG/NCS primarily assesses the peripheral nervous system (motor neuron, dorsal root ganglion, peripheral nerve, neuromuscular junction, and muscle). EMG/NCS can be used to localize or exclude a lesion in the peripheral nervous system and to identify characteristics of these lesions that help with diagnosis, treatment, and/or prognosis. For example, neuropathies can be categorized as focal, multifocal, or generalized; sensory or motor; axonal or demyelinating. EMG/NCS is useful to localize and characterize focal neuropathies (location along nerve, axonal or conduction block, complete or partial). The presence and type of spontaneous activity in a myopathy can direct diagnosis and treatment. Some CNS disorders can also be evaluated by EMG (tremor, ataxia, asterixis, myoclonus, and dystonia).

NERVE CONDUCTION STUDIES NCS involve electrical stimulation of large myelinated motor and sensory nerves, recording a response over the muscle and distal sensory nerves, respectively. Distal latency, duration, and conduction velocity of the response usually reflect the integrity of myelin. The amplitude reflects the integrity of axons. Late responses include F and H waves, which provide information about the proximal conduction in motor (F waves) or motor and sensory (H waves) nerves. F waves can be particularly important in the early diagnosis of inflammatory neuropathies such as Guillain-Barré syndrome. Blink reflexes evaluate the conduction in branches of the trigeminal and facial nerves.

REPETITIVE STIMULATION Repetitive stimulation of motor nerves can identify and characterize disorders of the neuromuscular junction. A train of supramaximal stimuli is delivered to a motor nerve, recording over the muscle at rest and after exercise. A decrement of the compound muscle action potential amplitudes is seen in myasthenia gravis and congenital myasthenia. An increment is seen with Lambert-Eaton myasthenic syndrome and botulism.

ELECTROMYOGRAPHY EMG involves placing a needle in skeletal muscle and recording the electrical activity of the muscle at rest (spontaneous activity) and with activation (motor unit action potentials, or MUAPs). Resting muscle does not show activity except at the motor endplate. Abnormal spontaneous activity, such as fibrillation potentials and positive waves, is seen with denervation and certain types of myopathy. MUAPs are of a characteristic duration and morphology in each muscle. Short-duration MUAPs suggest a myopathic process or disorder of the neuromuscular junction. Long-duration MUAPs are present with axonal neuropathies and motor neuron disease. The pattern of activation (reduced or rapid recruitment) reflects a neurogenic or myopathic process, respectively.

Single-Fiber EMG Single-fiber EMG is a sensitive but not specific technique for disorders of the neuromuscular junction. The firing of a pair of muscle fibers from the same motor unit is recorded in the muscle. The variation of the time interval between the two fibers is called *jitter*, and disappearance of the second muscle fiber action potential is called *blocking*. An increase in jitter and/or blocking is seen in disorders of the neuromuscular junction.

AUTONOMIC TESTING

Autonomic studies include determination of heart rate variation with respiration, Valsalva ratio, heart rate response to standing/tilting, blood pressure response to sustained hand grip, and a measure of sympathetic skin response. These tests can provide objective evidence of autonomic insufficiency (central or peripheral) and provide a measure of function for small unmyelinated peripheral axons.

LUMBAR PUNCTURE

INDICATIONS Lumbar puncture is used to obtain pressure measurements and secure a sample of CSF for cellular, chemical, immunologic, and bacteriologic examination in the evaluation of infections of the CNS, meningeal cancer, inflammatory neuropathies, acute demyelinating disorders, benign intracranial hypertension, and other unexplained neurologic disorders (see Chap. 203 for normal values). It is also used for adminstration of spinal anesthesia, antibiotics, or antitumor agents and to inject contrast agents for myelography.

CONTRAINDICATIONS These include thrombocytopenia or other disorders of blood coagulation, the presence of local skin or soft tissue infection along the needle tract, and increased intracranial pressure. If increased intracranial pressure is suspected, a head CT or MRI should be performed prior to the study to exclude a mass lesion. CSF should always be obtained with suspected meningitis. A fine-bore needle should be used. If the pressure is >400 mmHg, the minimal amount of fluid should be removed with administration of mannitol or dexamethasone if needed to prevent herniation.

COMPLICATIONS The most common complication is a positional headache due to persistent leakage of CSF. Treatment is discussed in Chap. 4. Seeding of the subarachnoid space with bacteria is rare.

For a more detailed discussion, see Martin JB, Hauser SL: Approach to the Patient with Neurologic Disease, Chap. 356, p. 2326; Aminoff MJ: Electrophysiologic Studies of the Central and Peripheral Nervous Systems, Chap. 357, p. 2331; Dillon WP: Neuroimaging in Neurologic Disorders, Chap. 358, p. 2337; and Engstrom JW, Martin JB: Disorders of the Autonomic Nervous System, Chap. 366, p. 2416, in HPIM-15.

182

SEIZURES AND EPILEPSY

A seizure is a paroxysmal event due to abnormal, excessive, hypersynchronous discharges from an aggregate of CNS neurons. Epilepsy is diagnosed when there are recurrent seizures due to a chronic, underlying process.

Seizure Classification

Proper seizure classification is essential for diagnosis, therapy, and prognosis. *Partial* (or *focal*) *seizures* originate in localized area of cortex; *generalized seizures* involve diffuse regions of the brain in a bilaterally symmetric fashion. *Simple-partial seizures* do not affect consciousness and may have motor, sensory, autonomic, or psychic symptoms. *Complex-partial seizures* include alteration in consciousness coupled with automatisms (e.g., lip smacking, chewing, aimless walking, or other complex motor activities).

Generalized seizures may occur as a primary disorder or result from secondary generalization of a partial seizure. *Tonic-clonic seizures* (grand mal) cause sudden loss of consciousness, loss of postural control, tonic muscular contraction producing teeth-clenching and rigidity in extension (tonic phase), followed by rhythmic muscular jerking (clonic phase). Tongue-biting and incontinence may occur during the seizure. Recovery of consciousness is typically gradual over many minutes to hours. Headache and confusion are common postictal phenomena. In *absence seizures* (petit mal) there is sudden, brief impairment of consciousness without loss of postural control. Events rarely last longer than 5–10 s but can recur many times per day. Minor motor symptoms

Table 182-1

The Causes of Seizures

Neonates (<1 month)	Perinatal hypoxia and ischemia
	Intracranial hemorrhage and trauma
	Acute CNS infection
	Metabolic disturbances (hypoglycemia, hypocalcemia, hypomagnesemia, pyridoxine deficiency)
	Drug withdrawal
	Developmental disorders
	Genetic disorders
Infants and children (>1 mo and <12 years)	Febrile seizures
	Genetic disorders (metabolic, degenerative, primary epilepsy syndromes)
	CNS infection
	Developmental disorders
	Trauma
	Idiopathic
Adolescents (12–18 years)	Trauma
	Genetic disorders
	Infection
	Brain tumor
	Illicit drug use
	Idiopathic
Young adults (18–35 years)	Trauma
	Alcohol withdrawal
	Illicit drug use
	Brain tumor
	Idiopathic
Older adults (>35 years)	Cerebrovascular disease
	Brain tumor
	Alcohol withdrawal
	Metabolic disorders (uremia, hepatic failure, electrolyte abnormalities, hypoglycemia)
	Alzheimer's disease and other degenerative CNS diseases
	Idiopathic

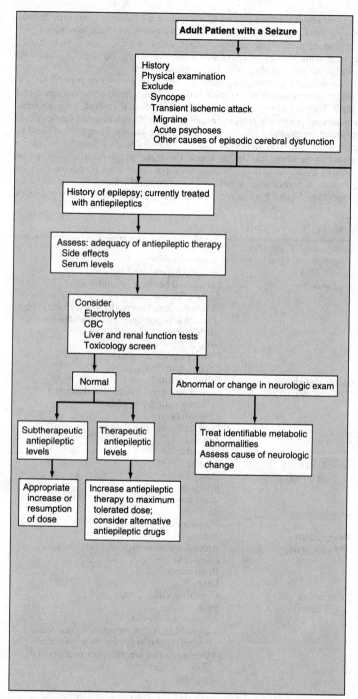

FIGURE 182-1 Evaluation of the adult patient with a seizure.

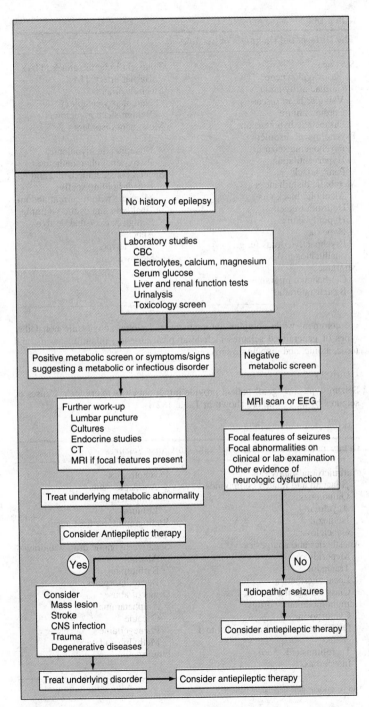

FIGURE 182-1 *(continued)*

Table 182-2

The Differential Diagnosis of Seizures

Syncope	Transient ischemic attack (TIA)
Vasovagal syncope	Basilar artery TIA
Cardiac arrhythmia	Sleep disorders
Valvular heart disease	Narcolepsy/cataplexy
Cardiac failure	Benign sleep myoclonus
Orthostatic hypotension	Movement disorders
Psychological disorders	Tics
Psychogenic seizure	Nonepileptic myoclonus
Hyperventilation	Paroxysmal choreoathetosis
Panic attack	Special considerations in children
Metabolic disturbances	Breath-holding spells
Alcoholic blackouts	Migraine with recurrent abdom-
Delirium tremens	inal pain and cyclic vomiting
Hypoglycemia	Benign paroxysmal vertigo
Hypoxia	Apnea
Psychoactive drugs (e. g.,	Night terrors
hallucinogens)	Sleepwalking
Migraine	
Confusional migraine	
Basilar migraine	

are common, while complex automatisms and clonic activity are not. Other types of generalized seizures include atypical absence, infantile spasms, and tonic, atonic, and myoclonic seizures.

Etiology

Seizure type and age of patient provide important clues to etiology. Causes of seizures by age group are shown in Table 182-1.

Table 182-3

Drugs and Other Substances That Can Cause Seizures

Antimicrobials/antivirals	Psychotropics
β-lactam and related compounds	Antidepressants
Quinolones	Antipsychotics
Acyclovir	Lithium
Isoniazid	Radiographic contrast agents
Ganciclovir	Theophylline
Anesthetics and analgesics	Sedative-hypnotic drug withdrawal
Meperidine	Alcohol
Tramadol	Barbiturates
Local anesthetics	Benzodiazepines
Class 1B agents	Drugs of abuse
Immunomodulatory drugs	Amphetamine
Cyclosporine	Cocaine
OKT3 (monoclonal antibodies to T	Phencyclidine
cells)	Methylphenidate
Tacrolimus (FK-506)	Flumazenil[a]
Interferons	

[a] In benzodiazepine-dependent patients.

Clinical Evaluation

Careful history is essential since diagnosis of seizures and epilepsy is often based solely on clinical grounds. Differential diagnosis (Table 182-2) includes syncope or psychogenic seizures (pseudoseizures). General exam includes search for infection, trauma, toxins, systemic illness, neurocutaneous abnormalities, and vascular disease. A number of drugs lower the seizure threshold (Table 182-3). Asymmetries in neurologic exam suggest brain tumor, stroke, trauma, or other focal lesions. An algorithmic approach to the pt with a seizure is illustrated in Fig. 182-1.

℞ TREATMENT

Acutely, the pt should be placed in semiprone position with head to the side to avoid aspiration. Tongue blades or other objects should not be forced between clenched teeth. Oxygen should be given via face mask. Reversible metabolic disorders (e. g. , hypoglycemia, hyponatremia, hypocalcemia, drug or alcohol withdrawal) should be promptly corrected. Treatment of status epilepticus is discussed in Chap. 38.

Longer-term therapy includes treatment of underlying conditions, avoidance of precipitating factors, prophylactic therapy with antiepileptic medications or surgery, and addressing various psychological and social issues. Choice of antiepileptic drug therapy depends on a variety of factors including seizure type, dosing schedule, and potential side effects (Tables 182-4 and 182-5). Therapeutic goal is complete cessation of seizures without side effects using a single drug (monotherapy). If ineffective, medication should be increased to maximal tolerated dose based primarily on clinical response rather than serum levels. If unsuccessful, a second drug should be added, and when control is obtained, the first drug can be slowly tapered. Approximately one-third of pts will require polytherapy with two or more drugs. Pts with certain epilepsy syndromes (e. g. , temporal lobe epilepsy) are often refractory to medical therapy and benefit from surgical excision of the seizure focus.

Table 182-4

Antiepileptic Drugs of Choice

	Primary Generalized Tonic-Clonic	Partial[a]	Absence	Atypical Absence, Myoclonic, Atonic
First-line	Valproic acid Lamotrigine	Carbamazepine Phenytoin Valproic acid Lamotrigine	Ethosuximide Valproic acid	Valproic acid
Alternatives	Phenytoin Carbamazepine Topiramate Primidone Phenobarbital Felbamate	Gabapentin[b] Topiramate[b] Tiagabine[b] Primidone Phenobarbital	Lamotrigine Clonazepam	Lamotrigine Topiramate[b] Clonazepam Felbamate

[a] Includes simple partial, complex partial, and secondarily generalized seizures.
[b] As adjunctive therapy.

Table 182-5

First-Line Antiepileptic Drugs

Generic Name	Trade Name	Principal Uses	Typical Dosage and Dosing Intervals	Half-Life
Phenytoin (di-phenyl-hydan-toin	Dilantin	Tonic-clonic (grand mal) Focal-onset	300–400 mg/d (3–6 mg/kg, adult; 4–8 mg/kg, child) qd-bid	24 h (wide variation, dose-dependent)
Carbamazepine	Tegretol Carbatrol	Tonic-clonic Focal-onset	600–1800 mg/d (15–35 mg/kg, child) bid-qid	10–17 h
Valproic acid	Depakene Depakote	Tonic-clonic Absence Atypical absence Myoclonic Focal-onset	750–2000 mg/d (20–60 mg/kg) bid-qid	15 h
Lamotrigine	Lamictal	Focal-onset Tonic-clonic Atypical absence Myoclonic Lennox-Gastaut syndrome	150–500 mg/d bid	25 h 14 h (with enzyme-inducers) 59 h (with valproic acid)
Ethosuximide	Zarontin	Absence (petit mal)	750–1250 mg/d (20–40 mg/kg) qd-bid	60 h, adult 30 h, child

[a] Phenytoin, carbamazepine, phenobarbital

| Therapeutic Range | Adverse Effects | | Drug Interactions |
	Neurologic	Systemic	
10–20 μg/mL	Dizziness Diplopia Ataxia Incoordination Confusion	Gum hyperplasia Lymphadenopathy Hirsutism Osteomalacia Facial coarsening Skin rash	Level increased by isoniazid, sulfonamides Level decreased by enzyme-inducing drugs[a] Altered folate metabolism
6–12 μg/mL	Ataxia Dizziness Diplopia Vertigo	Aplastic anemia Leukopenia Gastrointestinal irritation Hepatotoxicity Hyponatremia	Level decreased by enzyme-inducing drugs[a] Level increased by erythromycin, propoxyphene, isoniazid, cimetidine
50–150 μg/mL	Ataxia Sedation Tremor	Hepatotoxicity Thrombocytopenia Gastrointestinal irritation Weight gain Transient alopecia Hyperammonemia	Level decreased by enzyme-inducing drugs[a]
Not established	Dizziness Diplopia Sedation Ataxia Headache	Skin rash Stevens-Johnson syndrome	Level decreased by enzyme-inducing drugs[a] Level increased by valproic acid
40–100 μg/mL	Ataxia Lethargy Headache	Gastrointestinal irritation Skin rash Bone marrow suppression	

For a more detailed discussion, see Lowenstein DH: Seizures and Epilepsy, Chap. 360, p. 2354, in HPIM-15.

183

TUMORS OF THE NERVOUS SYSTEM

Brain tumors present with: (1) progressive focal neurologic deficits, (2) seizures, or (3) "nonfocal" neurologic disorders (headache, dementia, personality change, gait disorder). Systemic symptoms (malaise, anorexia, weight loss, fever) suggest metastatic rather than primary brain tumor.

- *Focal neurologic deficits*—due to compression of neurons or white matter by tumor, or edema
- *Seizures*—caused by stimulation of excitatory or loss of inhibitory cortical circuits
- *Nonfocal neurologic disorders*—due to increased intracranial pressure (ICP), hydrocephalus, or diffuse tumor spread
- *Headache*—caused by focal irritation/displacement of pain-sensitive structures or increased ICP. Elevated ICP suggested by papilledema, impaired lateral gaze, headache that intensifies with recumbency
- *Strokelike onset*—may reflect hemorrhage into tumor

Brain tumors may be large at presentation if located in clinically silent region (i.e., prefrontal) or slow-growing; diencephalic, frontal, or temporal lobe tumors may present as psychiatric disorder.

Laboratory Evaluation

Primary brain tumors have no systemic features of malignancy, unlike metastases. CSF exam is limited to diagnosis of possible meningitis or meningeal metastases but may cause brain herniation in setting of a large brain mass or obstructive hydrocephalus. Neuroimaging reveals mass effect (volume of neoplasm and surrounding edema) and contrast enhancement (breakdown of blood-brain barrier permitting leakage of contrast into brain parenchyma).

 TREATMENT

> **Symptomatic Treatment** Glucocorticoids (dexamethasone 12–20 mg/d in divided doses) to temporarily reduce edema; prophylaxis with anticonvulsants (phenytoin, carbamazepine, or valproic acid) for tumors involving cortex or hippocampus. Low-dose subcutaneous heparin for immobile patients.

Intracranial Tumors

The only known risk factor is ionizing radiation. Adverse effects of primary brain tumors are caused by local growth. Biopsy is essential for tissue diagnosis.

Astrocytomas Most common primary intracranial neoplasm. Prognosis poor if age >65 years, poor baseline functional status, high-grade tumor. Difficult to treat; infiltration along white matter pathways prevents total resection. Imaging studies fail to indicate full tumor extent. Surgery for pathologic diagnosis and to control mass effect. Survival ranges from an average of 93 months for low-grade tumors to 12 months for high-grade tumors. Radiation therapy (RT) prolongs survival and improves quality of life. Systemic chemotherapy with nitrosoureas is only marginally effective, often employed as adjunct to RT for high-grade gliomas. Role of stereotaxic radiosurgery (single dose, highly focused radiation—gamma knife) unclear; most useful for tumors <3 cm in diameter. Interstitial brachytherapy (stereotaxic implantation of radioactive beads) reserved for tumor recurrence; associated with necrosis of normal brain tissue. For low-grade astrocytoma, optimal management is uncertain.

Oligodendrogliomas Supratentorial; mixture of astrocytic and oligodendroglial cells. As oligodendroglial component increases, so does long-term survival; 5-year survival >50%. Total surgical resection often possible; may respond dramatically to chemotherapy if deletions of chromosomes 1p and 19q are found.

Ependymomas Derived from ependymal cells; highly cellular. Location—spinal canal in adults. If histologically aggressive (cellular atypia, frequent mitotic figures), recurrence is certain. If total excision, 5-year disease-free survival >80%. Radiosensitive.

Germinomas Tumors of midline brain structures; onset in second decade. Neuroimaging—uniformly enhancing mass. Treatment—complete surgical excision; 5-year survival >85%. Radiosensitive and chemosensitive.

Primitive Neuro-Ectodermal Tumors (PNET) Half in posterior fossa; highly cellular; derived from neural precursor cells. Treatment—surgery, chemotherapy, and RT.

Primary CNS Lymphomas B cell malignancy; most occur in immunosuppressed pts (organ transplantation, AIDS). May present as a single mass lesion (immunocompetent pts), multiple mass lesions, or meningeal disease (immunosuppressed pts). Prognosis generally poor. Dramatic, transient responses occur with glucocorticoids. In immunocompetent pts, RT and combination chemotherapy may increase survival to ≥18 months; AIDS-related cases survive ≤3 months.

Meningiomas Extraaxial mass attached to dura; dense and uniform contrast enhancement is diagnostic. Total surgical resection of benign meningiomas is curative. With subtotal resection, local RT reduces recurrence to <10%. Small, asymptomatic meningiomas may be followed radiologically. Rare aggressive meningiomas—treat with excision and RT.

Schwannomas Vestibular schwannomas present as progressive, unexplained unilateral hearing loss. MRI reveals dense, uniformly enhancing tumor at the cerebellopontine angle. Surgical excision may preserve hearing.

Tumors Metastatic to Brain Disseminate to brain by hematogenous spread. Skull metastases rarely invade CNS; may compress adjacent brain or cranial nerves or obstruct intracranial venous sinuses. Primary tumors that metastasize to the nervous system are listed in Table 183-1. Brain metastases are well demarcated by MRI and enhance with gadolinium; triple-dose contrast is

Table 183-1

Frequency of Primary Tumors That Metastasize to the Nervous System

Site of Primary Tumor	Brain Metastases, %	Leptomeningeal Metastases, %	Spinal Cord Compression, %
Lung	40	24	18
Breast	19	41	24
Melanoma	10	12	4
Gastrointestinal tract	7	13	6
Genitourinary tract	7		18
Other	17	10	30

most sensitive for detection; ring enhancement is nonspecific. Differential diagnosis includes brain abscess, radiation necrosis, toxoplasmosis, granulomas, demyelinating lesions, primary brain tumors, CNS lymphoma, stroke, hemorrhage, and trauma. CSF cytology is unnecessary—intraparenchymal metastases rarely shed cells into CSF. One-third of pts presenting with brain metastasis have unknown primary (ultimately small cell lung cancer, melanoma most frequent); primary tumor never identified in 30%. CXR is best screening test for occult cancer; if negative, obtain chest CT. If chest CT negative, obtain CT scan of abdomen and pelvis. Further imaging studies unhelpful if above studies negative. Biopsy of primary tumor or accessible brain metastasis is needed to plan treatment. Treatment is palliative—glucocorticoids, anticonvulsants, or RT may improve quality of life. Whole-brain RT is given, because multiple microscopic tumor deposits are likely throughout the brain. A single metastasis is often surgically excised followed by whole-brain RT. Systemic chemotherapy may produce dramatic responses in isolated cases.

Leptomeningeal Metastases Presents as multifocal cranial nerve or polyradicular involvement in setting of known malignancy. Diagnosis by CSF cytology, MRI (nodular meningeal tumor deposits or diffuse meningeal enhancement), or meningeal biopsy. Associated with hydrocephalus due to CSF pathway obstruction; detected by complete neuraxis MRI. Aggressive treatment (intrathecal chemotherapy, focal external beam RT) produces sustained response (~6 months) in 20% of pts.

Spinal Cord Compression from Metastases (See Chap. 194) Expansion of vertebral body metastasis posteriorly (usually lung, breast, or prostate primary) into epidural space compresses cord. Back pain (>90%) usually precedes development of weakness, sensory level, or incontinence. Medical emergency; early recognition of impending spinal cord compression is essential to avoid permanent devastating sequelae. Diagnosis is by spine MRI. Progression may be slowed by administration of glucocorticoids while awaiting surgery or RT.

Complications of Radiation Therapy

Three patterns of radiation injury after CNS RT:

1. Acute—headache, sleepiness, worse neurologic deficits during or immediately after RT. Self-limited and glucocorticoid-responsive.
2. Early delayed—somnolence (children), Lhermitte's sign; within 4 months of RT. Increased T2 signal on MRI. Also self-limited and improves with glucocorticoids.
3. Late delayed—dementia or other progressive neurologic deficits; typically >1 year after RT. White matter abnormalities on MRI; ring-enhancing mass due to radiation necrosis. Positron emission tomography (PET) distinguishes delayed necrosis from tumor recurrence. Progressive radiation necrosis is best treated palliatively with surgical resection. Endocrine dysfunction due to hypothalamus or pituitary gland injury can be due to delayed effects of RT.

For a more detailed discussion, see Sagar SM, Israel MA: Primary and Metastic Tumors of the Nervous System, Chap. 370, p. 2442, in HPIM-15.

184

BACTERIAL INFECTIONS OF THE CENTRAL NERVOUS SYSTEM

ACUTE BACTERIAL MENINGITIS

The pathogens most frequently involved in bacterial meningitis in immunocompetent adults are *Streptococcus pneumoniae* ("pneumococcus") and *Neisseria meningitidis* ("meningococcus"). Predisposing factors for pneumococcal meningitis include distant foci of infection (otitis, sinusitis, pneumonia, endocarditis), asplenia, sickle cell disease, hypogammaglobulinemia, multiple myeloma, alcoholism, cirrhosis, and recent head trauma with CSF leak. Pts with deficiency of terminal complement components, or properdin, are at increased risk of meningococcal infection, which may also occur in epidemics. Although vaccination has dramatically reduced the incidence of *Haemophilus influenzae* meningitis, this organism is still an important cause of meningitis in unvaccinated children (age 3 mos to 18 yrs) and in adults with predisposing risk factors (e.g., otitis, sinusitis, epiglottitis, pneumonia, alcoholism, diabetes, immunocompromise, asplenia). Pts with impaired cell-mediated immunity, neonates, the elderly, diabetics, and alcoholics are at increased risk of infection caused by *Listeria monocytogenes* and a variety of gram-negative organisms. Recent head trauma, neurosurgery, or ventricular shunts are risk factors for both gram-negative and staphylococcal infections.

Clinical Manifestations Presentation is either as an acute fulminant illness that progresses over a few hours or as a subacute infection that progressively worsens over several days. 85% of adults have headache, fever, and meningismus (stiff neck). Additional signs can include altered mental status (75%), nausea and vomiting, cranial nerve palsies, seizures (40%), myalgias, sweating, and photophobia. Signs of meningismus include resistance to neck flexion, Kernig's sign (patient in supine position, hip and knee flexed; pain induced by attempt to extend leg), and Brudzinski's sign (passive flexion of neck results in spontaneous flexion of hip and knees). Meningismus and fever may be absent in neonates and the elderly. The rash of meningococcemia begins as a diffuse maculopapular rash resembling a viral exanthem but rapidly becomes petechial on trunk and lower extremities, mucous membranes and conjunctiva, and occasionally on palms and soles. Rash may also occur with other organisms.

Laboratory Findings Lumbar puncture (LP) is critical to the diagnosis of bacterial meningitis (Table 184-1). Key CSF findings include a CSF leukocytosis with neutrophilic predominance, an elevated protein, hypoglycorrhachia (decreased glucose), and elevated opening pressure. Mononuclear cells may predominate as infection continues. CSF white counts >50,000/μL should suggest the possibility of intraventricular rupture of brain abscess. Gram stain reveals organisms in 75% of untreated pts, and cultures are positive in 70–80%. Latex agglutination test may be helpful, especially in partially treated meningitis. Blood cultures should always be obtained and are positive in 50% of pts. Petechial skin lesions should also be biopsied if the etiology is in doubt. In pts with focal neurologic findings or papilledema, LP may be deferred pending emergency CT or MRI; however, treatment must not be delayed in such cases but should be started empirically after obtaining blood cultures.

Differential Diagnosis Includes viral meningoencephalitis, especially herpes simplex virus encephalitis (distinctive neuroimaging and EEG features;

Table 184-1

Cerebrospinal Fluid Abnormalities in Bacterial Meningitis

Opening pressure	>180 mmH$_2$O
White blood cells	>10/μL to <10,000/μL; neutrophils predominate
Red blood cells	Absent, unless traumatic tap
Glucose	<2.2 mmol/L (<40 mg/dL)
CSF: serum glucose ratio	<0.40
Protein	>0.45 g/L (>45 mg/dL)
Gram's stain	Positive in 70–90% of untreated cases
Culture	Positive in 80% of cases
Latex agglutination	Specific for antigens of *S. pneumoniae*, *N. meningitidis*, *E. coli*, *H. influenzae*, type b, and group B streptococcus
Limulus amebocyte lysate assay	Positive in gram-negative meningitis
PCR for bacterial DNA	Specificity and sensitivity unknown

NOTE: PCR, polymerase chain reaction.

Chap. 185); rickettsial diseases such as Rocky Mountain spotted fever (immunoflourescent staining of skin lesions); focal suppurative CNS infections including subdural empyema and brain abcess (see below); subarachnoid hemorrhage (diagnostic neuroimaging and CSF features; Chap. 35); and the demyelinating disease acute disseminated encephalomyelitis.

 TREATMENT

Recommendations for empirical therapy, shown in Table 184-2, are based on the pt's age, immunologic status, presence or absence of recent head trauma or neurosurgery, and CSF Gram's stain results. Therapy is then modified based on results of CSF culture (Table 184-3). In general, the treatment course is 7 days for meningococcus, 14 days for pneumococcus, 21 days for gram-negative meningitis, and at least 21 days for *L. monocytogenes*. Children (≥2 mos) should receive adjunctive IV dexamethasone (0.15 mg/kg q6h for 2 d), with the initial dexamethasone dose given 20 min before or with the first antibiotic dose. Data concerning the efficacy in adults is less conclusive; one trial demonstrated reduced mortality in pneumococcal meningitis with use of dexamethasone treatment (0.15 mg/kg q6h for 2–4 d). Dexamethasone may reduce penetration of vancomycin into the CSF.

In cases of meningococcal meningitis, all close contacts should receive chemoprophylaxis with rifampin [600 mg in adults (10 mg/kg in children > 1 year)] q12h for 2 d; rifampin is not recommended in pregnant women. Alternatively, adults can be treated with one dose of ciprofloxacin (750 mg), one dose of azithromycin (500 mg), or one IM dose of ceftriaxone (250 mg).

Complications Include increased intracranial pressure (ICP), infarction, cerebral sinus or venous thrombosis, seizures, obstructive hydrocephalus, subdural effusion (children), and hearing loss. Moderate or severe neurologic sequelae occur in ~25% of survivors, although the exact incidence varies with the infecting organism.

BRAIN ABSCESS

A focal suppurative infection involving brain parenchyma. Common etiologic agents include mixed flora, aerobic or microaerophilic streptococci, *Staphylo-*

Table 184-2

Antibiotics Used in Empirical Therapy of Bacterial Meningitis and Focal CNS Infections

Indication	Antibiotic
Preterm infants to infants <1 month	Ampicillin + cefotaxime
Infants 1–3 months	Ampicillin + (cefotaxime or ceftriaxone) (consider adjunctive dexamethasone)
Immunocompetent children >3 months, adults <50	(Cefotaxime or ceftriaxone) + vancomycin
Adults >50, individuals with alcoholism or other debilitating illnesses	Ampicillin + vancomycin + (cefotaxime or ceftriaxone)
Hospital-acquired meningitis, meningitis after head trauma or neurosurgery, neutropenic patients	Ceftazidime + vancomycin
Impaired cell-mediated immunity (at any age)	Ceftazidime (in place of cefotaxime or ceftriaxone) + ampicillin

	Total Daily Dose and Dosing Interval	
Antimicrobial Agent	Child (> 1 month)	Adult
Ampicillin	200–300 (mg/kg)/d, q4h	12 g/d, q4h
Cefotaxime	300 (mg/kg)/d, q6h	12 g/d, q4h
Ceftriaxone	100–200 (mg/kg)/d, q12h	4 g/d, q12h
Ceftazidime	150 (mg/kg)/d, q8h	6 g/d, q8h
Metronidazole	30 (mg/kg)/d, q6h	2000 mg/d, q6h
Nafcillin	100–200 (mg/kg)/d, q6h	9–12 g/day, q4h
Vancomycin	60 (mg/kg)/d, q6h	2 g/d, q6h

coccus aureus, aerobic gram-negative bacilli, and anaerobes. Risk factors include sinusitis, otitis, dental infections, head trauma, neurosurgery, and distant foci of infection.

Clinical Features Solitary abscesses involve frontal > temporal > parietal > cerebellar > occipital lobes of the brain, in decreasing order of frequency. Hematogenous spread of infection to brain frequently results in multiple abscesses. Specific clinical features are shown in Table 184-4.

Diagnosis CT and MRI are the most useful diagnostic tools and serve to identify the location and number of abscesses and the presence of associated parameningeal or sinus infection. Typical CT appearance is of a hypodense lesion with a uniformly enhancing ring surrounded by an outer zone of hypodense-appearing edema. Typical features may be absent in early lesions and in pts receiving glucocorticoids. Neoplasms, granulomas, resolving hematomas, and infarcts may resemble abscesses on CT and MRI. LP is contraindicated in pts with suspected or known brain abscess as it rarely adds useful diagnostic information and may precipitate herniation.

℞ TREATMENT

Optimal therapy of encapsulated abscesses includes surgical drainage (aspiration or total excision) and antibiotics. Unencapsulated abscesses ("cerebri-

Table 184-3

Antimicrobial Therapy of CNS Bacterial Infections Based on Pathogen[a]

Organism	Antibiotic	Total Daily Adult Dose and Dosing Interval
Neisseria meningitidis		
Penicillin-sensitive	Penicillin G	20–24 million U/d, q4h
	or	
	Ampicillin	12 g/d, q4h
Penicillin-resistant	Ceftriaxone	4 g/d, q12h
	or	
	Cefotaxime	12 g/d, q4h
Streptococcus pneumoniae		
Penicillin-sensitive	Penicillin G	20–24 million U/d, q4h
Relatively penicillin-resistant	Ceftriaxone	4 g/d, q12h
	or	
	Cefotaxime	12 g/d, q4h
Penicillin-resistant	Vancomycin	2 g/d, q6h
	plus	
	Ceftriaxone	4 g/d, q12h
	or	
	Cefotaxime	12 g/d, q4h
	±	
	Intraventricular vancomycin	20 mg/d
Gram-negative bacilli (except *P. aeruginosa*)	Ceftriaxone	4 g/d, q12h
	or	
	Cefotaxime	12 g/d, q4h
Pseudomonas aeruginosa	Ceftazidime	6 g/d, q8h
Staphylococci		
Methicillin-sensitive	Nafcillin	9–12 g/d, q4h
Methicillin-resistant	Vancomycin	2 g/d, q6h
Listeria monocytogenes	Ampicillin	12 g/d, q4h
Haemophilus influenzae	Ceftriaxone	4 g/d, q12h
	or	
	Cefotaxime	12 g/d, q4h
Streptococcus agalactiae	Ampicillin	12 g/d, q4h
	or	
	Penicillin G	20–24 million U/d, q4h
Bacteroides fragilis	Metronidazole	2000 mg/d, q6h
Fusobacterium spp.	Metronidazole	2000 mg/d, q6h

[a] All antibiotics are administered intravenously; doses indicated are for patients with normal renal function.

tis") may respond to antimicrobial therapy alone. Empirical antibiotic therapy should be modified based on the results of abscess cultures. Typical regimens for empirical therapy are shown in Table 184-5; all pts should receive a minimum of 6–8 weeks of parenteral antibiotics. Prophylactic anticonvulsant therapy is also recommended for ≥3 months. Short-term glucocorticoid therapy should be used only in pts with proven or suspected elevation in ICP.

SUBDURAL EMPYEMA

A collection of pus between the dural and arachnoid membranes. Major pathogens include aerobic and anaerobic streptococci, staphylococci, and aerobic

Table 184-4

Clinical Manifestations of Brain Abscess

Symptoms or Sign	Percent
Headache	50–75
Triad of fever, headache, focal deficit	<50
Fever	40–50
Focal neurologic deficit	~50
Seizures	25–40
Nausea/vomiting	22–50
Nuchal rigidity	~25
Papilledema	~25

NOTE: Other symptoms and signs are dependent on location.

gram-negative bacilli. Infection may spread to the subdural space through thrombophlebitis of the cranial veins or by contiguous spread of cranial osteomyelitis. Paranasal sinusitis is a major predisposing factor. Other risk factors include otitis, mastoiditis, cranial trauma, neurosurgery, and distant foci of infection.

Clinical Manifestations Empyema can present as a rapidly progressive life-threatening condition. Signs and symptoms reflect the antecedent infection (e.g., sinusitis), meningeal irritation, the presence of a focal CNS lesion, and increased ICP. These can include fever, headache, nausea and vomiting, declining mental status, focal or generalized seizures, and hemiparesis or hemiplegia.

Diagnosis CT with contrast enhancement and MRI are diagnostic. Typical CT appearance is an area of crescentic hypodensity beneath the cranium, with a fine line of contrast enhancement between the empyema margin and the subjacent cortex. CT and MRI also help delineate associated otitis or sinusitis. LP rarely adds useful information and is contraindicated because of the risk of herniation.

Table 184-5

Empirical Therapy of Brain Abscess Based on Source of Infection

Source	Antimicrobial Therapy
Paranasal sinusitis	Penicillin or a third-generation cephalosporin (cefotaxime or ceftriaxone) + metronidazole
Otitis media	Penicillin + metronidazole + ceftazidime
Dental infection	Penicillin + metronidazole
Endocarditis	Nafcillin or vancomycin + metronidazole + third-generation cephalosporin
Lung abscess, urinary sepsis, intra-abdominal source	Ceftazidime + metronidazole + penicillin
Head trauma	Nafcillin or vancomycin + third-generation cephalosporin
Neurosurgical procedure	Vancomycin + ceftazidime
Cyanotic congenital heart disease	Penicillin or third-generation cephalosporin + metronidazole

TREATMENT

Subdural empyema is a surgical emergency. Treatment consists of emergent surgical drainage combined with antibiotic treatment. Typical empirical antibiotic regimens include vancomycin plus metronidazole plus ceftriaxone or cefotaxime (Tables 184-3 and 184-5). Treatment should be continued for a minimum of 4 weeks, with final duration of therapy determined by the pt's clinical condition and the resolution of infection on neuroimaging studies.

For a more detailed discussion, see Roos KL, Tyler KL: Bacterial Meningitis and Other Suppurative Infections, Chap. 372, p. 2462, in HPIM-15.

185

ASEPTIC MENINGITIS, VIRAL ENCEPHALITIS, AND PRION DISEASES

VIRAL MENINGITIS

The syndrome of viral meningitis consists of fever, headache, and meningeal irritation associated with a CSF lymphocytic pleocytosis, slightly elevated protein, and normal glucose. Associated symptoms can include malaise, anorexia, nausea and vomiting, abdominal pain, and diarrhea. The presence of significant impairment in consciousness, seizures, or focal neurologic findings suggests parenchymal involvement and is not typical of uncomplicated viral meningitis.

ETIOLOGY (See Tables 185-1, 185-2) Most cases of viral meningitis are due to enteroviruses (coxsackie-, polio-, echo-, enterovirus), including the majority of culture-negative cases. Other common causes of viral meningitis include herpes simplex virus (HSV) type 2, arboviruses, and HIV. The incidence of enteroviral and arboviral infections is greatly increased during the summer.

Table 185-1

Viruses Causing Aseptic Meningitis

Common	Less Common	Rare
Enteroviruses	HSV-1	Adenoviruses
Arboviruses	LCMV	CMV
HIV	Mumps	EBV
HSV-2		Influenza A, B; measles; parainfluenza; rubella; VZV

NOTE: CMV, cytomegalovirus; EBV, Epstein-Barr virus; HSV, herpes simplex virus; LCMV, lymphocytic choriomeningitis virus; VZV, varicella-zoster virus.

Table 185-2

Seasonal Prevalence of Viruses Commonly Causing Meningitis

Summer–Early Fall	Fall and Winter	Winter and Spring	Nonseasonal
Arboviruses	LCMV	Mumps	HIV
Enteroviruses			HSV

NOTE: For abbreviations, see Table 185-1.

DIAGNOSIS CSF polymerase chain reaction (PCR) tests have greatly facilitated diagnosis of viral meningitis and encephalitis. PCR testing is the procedure of choice for rapid, sensitive, and specific identification of viral infections caused by enteroviruses, HSV, EBV, varicella zoster virus (VZV), and CMV. Attempts should also be made to culture virus from CSF and other sites and body fluids including blood, throat swabs, feces, and urine. Serologic studies, including those utilizing paired CSF and serum specimens, may be helpful for retrospective diagnosis.

DIFFERENTIAL DIAGNOSIS Consider bacterial, fungal, tuberculous, spirochetal, and other infectious causes of meningitis; parameningeal infections; partially treated bacterial meningitis; neoplastic meningitis; noninfectious inflammatory diseases including sarcoid and Behçet's disease.

 TREATMENT

For the majority of cases of viral meningitis, supportive or symptomatic therapy is sufficient and hospitalization is not generally required. Neonates, the elderly, and immunocompromised pts should be hospitalized, as should individuals in whom the diagnosis is uncertain or when bacterial or other nonviral causes of meningitis cannot be excluded. The course and severity of meningitis due to HSV, EBV, and VZV may be shortened or ameliorated by antiviral treatment, specifically IV acyclovir (10 mg/kg q8h for 7 d); in mildly affected pts, a 1-week course of oral acyclovir (800 mg five times daily), famciclovir (500 mg q8h) or valacyclovir (1000 mg q8h) may be adequate. HIV meningitis should be treated with highly active antiretroviral therapy. Additional supportive or symptomatic therapy can include analgesics and antipyretics. In adults, the prognosis for full recovery from viral meningitis is excellent.

VIRAL ENCEPHALITIS

Viral encephalitis is an infection of the brain parenchyma commonly associated with meningitis ("meningoencephalitis"). Clinical features are those of viral meningitis plus symptoms and signs indicative of brain tissue involvement. These commonly include altered consciousness, seizures, and focal neurologic findings such as aphasia, hemiparesis, involuntary movements, and cranial nerve deficits.

ETIOLOGY (See Table 185-3) The most common cause of acute sporadic encephalitis is HSV type 1. Arboviruses are responsible for both sporadic and epidemic cases of encephalitis (Table 185-4). Other common viral causes of encephalitis include enteroviruses, mumps, EBV, and VZV.

DIAGNOSIS (See Fig. 185-1) CSF should be examined in all cases of suspected viral encephalitis. The typical CSF profile is similar to that for viral meningitis. The use of CSF PCR tests has dramatically improved the diagnosis

Table 185-3

Viruses Causing Encephalitis

Common	Less Common	Rare
Arboviruses, enteroviruses, HSV-1, mumps	CMV, EBV, HIV, measles, VZV	Adenoviruses, CTFV, influenza A, LCMV, parainfluenza, rabies, rubella

NOTE: For abbreviations, see Table 185-1; also, CTFV, Colorado tick fever virus.

of viral encephalitis; it allows for rapid and reliable diagnosis of infections due to HSV, EBV, VZV, CMV, and enteroviruses. CSF should be sent for culture, although this is often negative. Cultures of blood, throat swab, feces, urine, and skin lesions should also be obtained. Serologic studies, including paired CSF and serum samples, are useful for retrospective diagnosis. MRI is the neuroimaging procedure of choice and will frequently show areas of increased T2 signal. Bitemporal and orbitofrontal areas of increased signal are seen in HSV encephalitis but are not diagnostic. Multiple areas of increased T2 signal associated with decreased T1 signal and gadolinium enhancement suggest postinfectious immune-mediated demyelination. The EEG may suggest seizures and may show temporally predominant periodic spikes on a slow, low-amplitude background suggestive of HSV encephalitis.

DIFFERENTIAL DIAGNOSIS Includes both infectious and noninfectious causes of encephalitis, including vascular diseases; abscess and empyema; fungal (*Cryptococcus* and *Mucor*), spirochetal (*Leptospira*), rickettsial, bacterial (*Listeria*), tuberculous, and mycoplasma infections; tumors; Reye's syndrome; toxic encephalopathy; SLE; and acute disseminated encephalomyelitis.

 TREATMENT

All pts with suspected HSV encephalitis should be treated with IV acyclovir (10 mg/kg q8h). Pts with a PCR-confirmed diagnosis of HSV encephalitis should receive a 14-day course of therapy. CSF PCR testing for HSV, performed by an experienced and reliable laboratory, is sufficiently sensitive that with rare exceptions a negative result excludes the diagnosis of HSV encephalitis and allows acyclovir therapy to be discontinued. Acyclovir treatment may also benefit pts with encephalitis due to EBV and VZV, although clinical studies are limited. No specific therapy is currently available for enteroviral encephalitis or encephalitis caused by mumps or measles. Intravenous ribovarin [15–25 (mg/kg)/d given in 3 divided doses] has been reported to be of benefit in isolated cases of severe arbovirus encephalitis due to California encephalitis (LaCrosse) virus. Encephalitis due to HIV infection should be treated with appropriate antiretroviral therapy. CMV encephalitis, which occurs almost exclusively in immunocompromised pts, should be treated with ganciclovir, foscarnet, or a combination of the two drugs; cidofovir may provide an alternative for nonresponders. Additional treatment should be directed at reducing or controlling fever, elevations in intracranial pressure, and seizures. Appropriate measures should be taken to reduce the risk of aspiration pneumonia, decubitus ulcers, thrombophlebitis, pulmonary emboli, and gastritis.

PROGNOSIS There is considerable variation in the incidence of sequelae following infection with different agents. In patients with HSV encephalitis

Table 185-4

Features of Selected Arbovirus Encephalitides

Feature	WEE	EEE	VEE	SLE	CE
Region	West, midwest	Atlantic and Gulf	South	All	East and north-central
Age	Infants, adults >50 years	Children	Adults	Adults >50 years	Children
Deaths	5–15%	50–75%	1%	2–20%	<1%
Sequelae	Low to moderate	80%	Rare	20%	Rare
Vector	Mosquito	Mosquito	Mosquito	Mosquito	Mosquito
Animal host	Birds	Birds	Horses, small mammals	Birds	Rodents

NOTE: CE, California encephalitis virus; EEE, Eastern equine encephalitis virus; SLE, St. Louis encephalitis virus; VEE, Venezuelan equine encephalitis virus; WEE, Western equine encephalitis virus.
SOURCE: After RJ Whitley N Engl J Med 323:242, 1990.

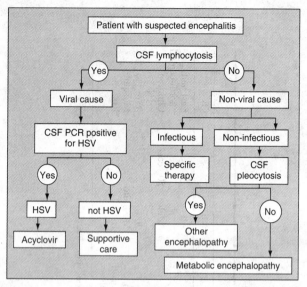

FIGURE 185-1 Approach to the patient with suspected encephalitis. HSV, herpes simplex virus.

treated with acyclovir, data indicates 81% survival; neurologic sequelae were mild or absent in 46%, moderate in 12%, and severe in 42%.

HERPES ZOSTER (SHINGLES)

Paresthesia or dysesthesia in a dermatomal distribution, followed by a localized cutaneous eruption of clear vesicles on an erythematous base, most commonly involving the lower thoracic (T5-10) dermatomes.

℞ TREATMENT

Oral acyclovir (800 mg 5 times a day), famciclovir (500 mg tid), or valacyclovir (1 g tid) for 7 days if instituted within 72 h of rash onset will diminish the duration and severity of viral shedding, new lesion formation, and acute pain. These effects are modest, and supportive therapy alone is sufficient for immunocompetent pts <50 years of age whose lesions do not involve the trigeminal dermatome. A role for antiviral drugs in reducing the incidence of postherpetic neuralgia (PHN), defined as pain persisting for >4–6 weeks after zoster rash, has been suggested but not established. PHN rarely occurs in patients <50 years of age. Treatment of PHN can include nonnarcotic analgesics, tricyclic antidepressants (amitriptyline), anticonvulsants (carbamazepine, gabapentin, phenytoin, sodium valproate), and topical capsaicin ointment. Additional complications of VZV infection can include meningoencephalitis, cerebellitis, myelitis, and granulomatous arteritis.

NEUROLOGIC COMPLICATIONS OF HIV INFECTION

Direct neurologic manifestations of HIV infection are myriad. They can involve any part of the nervous system and can occur at any stage of HIV infection (Fig. 185-2). Aseptic meningitis may occur at the time of initial infection with

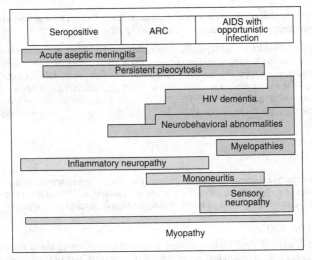

FIGURE 185-2   Relative frequency and timing of major neurologic complications of direct HIV infection. Diseases that affect the CNS are given light shading; those that affect the peripheral nervous system are shown with darker shading. Height of the boxes is a relative indicator of the frequency of each type of disease.

HIV. HIV dementia typically occurs late in illness. Pts present with psychomotor slowing, apathy, difficulty with memory and concentration, and gait abnormalities. Vacuolar myelopathy also occurs in advanced HIV infection and may mimic the myelopathy of vitamin B_{12} deficiency. Peripheral neuropathies can occur at any stage of illness and may be either axonal or demyelinating, with predominant sensory or sensorimotor involvement.

   Secondary neurologic complications of HIV infection result from opportunistic infections and neoplasia and typically occur in immunocompromised patients. Common causes of CNS lesions include toxoplasmosis, progressive multifocal leukoencephalopathy (PML), and primary CNS lymphoma (PCNSL). Infection with CMV can result in retinitis, meningoencephalitis, myelitis, or radiculopathy. VZV infection can produce shingles, disseminated zoster, meningoencephalitis, CNS vasculitis, or myelitis.

℞ TREATMENT

Direct neurologic complications of HIV infection may stabilize or improve with optimization of antiretroviral therapy. The incidence of opportunistic infections appears to be lower in pts in whom antiretroviral therapy results in improvement of immunologic function. Specific therapy is available for toxoplasmosis, CMV, and VZV. No therapy is currently available for PML. Radiation plus chemotherapy may produce modest increases in survival of PCNSL.

PROGRESSIVE MULTIFOCAL LEUKOENCEPHALOPATHY (PML)

A progressive multifocal demyelinating disease of the CNS resulting from infection of oligodendrocytes by JC virus. Clinical manifestations reflect the location, extent, and number of lesions and can include mental status impairment, visual field abnormalities, and focal weakness. Almost all pts have an underlying immunosuppressive disorder, most commonly HIV infection.

DIAGNOSIS MRI typically shows multifocal white matter lesions that do not enhance with contrast and are without mass effect. The CSF cell counts and chemistries are typically normal. Amplification of JC virus DNA from CSF using PCR techniques, in association with the typical clinical and neuroimaging findings, is diagnostic. A negative CSF PCR decreases the likelihood but does not exclude the diagnosis of PML. Definitive diagnosis may require brain biopsy.

 TREATMENT

No effective therapy for PML is currently available. Improvement of immune status (e.g., by optimization of antiretroviral therapy in HIV-infected individuals) has been reported to result in stabilization or remission of disease.

PRION DISEASES

Prion diseases of the CNS may present as sporadic, rapidly progressive dementia associated with myoclonus (Creutzfeldt-Jakob disease, CJD), or less commonly as familial forms of rapidly progressive dementia (familial CJD); cerebellar degeneration (Gerstmann-Straussler-Scheinker disease, GSS); or complex syndromes of insomnia, hallucinations, motor abnormalities, and autonomic and endocrine disturbances (fatal familial insomnia, FFI). Iatrogenic prion diseases can result from use of contaminated corneal or dura grafts, neurosurgical instruments, or cadaveric-derived pituitary hormones. Approximately 70 cases of an atypical form of CJD (*new variant CJD*) characterized by early age of onset and prominent initial neuropsychiatric and behavioral abnormalities followed by ataxia and progressive dementia have been reported, initially from England and France. It has been suggested, but not definitively established, that these cases may be the result of human exposure to food or other products derived from cattle infected with bovine spongiform encephalopathy ("mad cow disease").

DIAGNOSIS CT and MRI are often normal but may show rapidly progressive atrophy or increased T2 signal in the basal ganglia (MRI). CSF cell counts and chemistries are normal. Both CSF and neuroimaging studies may help exclude other diagnoses. It has been reported that the presence in CSF of a specific protein (14-3-3) is suggestive but not diagnostic of CJD. EEG may show periodic sharp wave complexes in CJD, but these are absent or occur only rarely in GSS, FFI, and new variant CJD. Definitive diagnosis of sporadic forms of prion disease requires brain biopsy; findings include neuronal loss, astrogliosis, spongiform changes, absence of inflammatory response, and the presence, in GSS and new variant CJD, of typical plaques containing protease-resistant prion protein. The detection of protease-resistant prion proteins by immunoblotting or immunocytochemistry establishes the diagnosis. If the pt has a family history suggestive of inherited CJD, sequencing the prion protein gene may facilitate the diagnosis.

 TREATMENT

CNS prion diseases are all inexorably progressive and invariably fatal. No effective treatment is currently available.

For a more detailed discussion, see Tyler KL: Viral Meningitis and Encephalitis, Chap. 373, p. 2471, in HPIM-15; Prusiner SB, Bosque P: Prion
Diseases, Chap. 375, p. 2486 in HPIM-15; and HPIM-15 chapters covering
specific organisms or infections.

186

CHRONIC MENINGITIS

Chronic inflammation of the meninges (pia, arachnoid, and dura) can produce
profound neurologic disability and may be fatal if not successfully treated. The
causes are varied. Five categories of disease account for most cases of chronic
meningitis: (1) meningeal infections, (2) malignancy, (3) noninfectious inflammatory disorders, (4) chemical meningitis, and (5) parameningeal infections.
Neurologic manifestations consist of persistent headache with or without stiff
neck and hydrocephalus, cranial neuropathies, radiculopathies, and cognitive or
personality changes (Table 186-1). On occasion the diagnosis is made when a
neuroimaging study shows contrast enhancement of the meninges. Once chronic
meningitis is confirmed by CSF examination, effort is focused on identifying
the cause (Tables 186-2 and 186-3) by (1) further analysis of the CSF, (2)
diagnosis of an underlying systemic infection or noninfectious inflammatory
condition, or (3) pathologic examination of meningeal biopsy specimens.

Table 186-1

Symptoms and Signs of Chronic Meningitis

Symptoms	Signs
Chronic headache	+/− Papilledema
Neck or back pain	Brudzinski's or Kernig's sign of meningeal irritation
Change in personality	Altered mental status—drowsiness, inatten-tion, disorientation, memory loss, frontal release signs (grasp, suck, snout), perservera-tion
Facial weakness	Peripheral seventh CN palsy
Double vision	Palsy of CNs III, IV, VI
Visual loss	Papilledema, optic atrophy
Hearing loss	Eighth CN palsy
Arm or leg weakness	Myelopathy or radiculopathy
Numbness in arms or legs	Myelopathy or radiculopathy
Sphincter dysfunction	Myelopathy or radiculopathy Frontal lobe dysfunction
Clumsiness	Ataxia

NOTE: CN, cranial nerve.

Table 186-2

Infectious Causes of Chronic Meningitis

COMMON BACTERIAL CAUSES

Partially treated suppurative meningitis
Parameningeal infection
Mycobacterium tuberculosis
Lyme disease (Bannwarth's syndrome): *Borrelia burgdorferi*
Syphilis (secondary, tertiary): *Treponema pallidum*

UNCOMMON BACTERIAL CAUSES

Actinomyces
Nocardia
Brucella
Whipple's disease: *Tropherema whippelii*

RARE BACTERIAL CAUSES

Leptospirosis; *Pseudoallescheria boydii*

FUNGAL CAUSES

Cryptococcus neoformans
Coccidioides immitis
Candida sp.
Histoplasma capsulatum
Blastomyces dermatitidis
Aspergillus sp.
Sporothrix schenckii

RARE FUNGAL CAUSES

Cladophialophora bantiana; *Mucor*

PROTOZOAL CAUSES

Toxoplasma gondii
Trypanosomiasis *Trypanosoma gambiense*, *Trypanosoma rhodesiense*

RARE PROTOZOAL CAUSES

Acanthamoeba sp.

HELMINTHIC CAUSES

Cysticercosis (infection with cysts of *Taenia solium*)
Gnathostoma spinigerum
Angiostrongylus cantonensis
Baylisascaris procyonis (raccoon ascarid)

RARE HELMINTHIC CAUSES

Trichinella spiralis (trichinosis); *Echinococcus* cysts; *Schistosoma* sp.

VIRAL CAUSES

Mumps
Lymphocytic choriomeningitis
Echovirus
HIV (acute retroviral syndrome)
Herpes simplex (HSV)

Table 186-3

Noninfectious Causes of Chronic Meningitis

Malignancy
Chemical compounds (may cause recurrent meningitis)
Primary inflammation
    CNS sarcoidosis
    Vogt-Koyanagi-Harada syndrome (recurrent meningitis)
    Isolated granulomatous angiitis of the nervous system
    Systemic lupus erythematosus
    Behçet's syndrome (recurrent meningitis)
    Chronic benign lymphocytic meningitis
    Mollaret's recurrent meningitis
    Drug hypersensitivity
    Wegener's granulomatosis
Other: multiple sclerosis, Sjögren's syndrome, and rarer forms of vasculitis
    (e.g., Cogan's syndrome)

_____ *Approach to the Patient* _____

Proper analysis of the CSF is essential; if the possibility of raised intracranial
pressure (ICP) exists, a brain imaging study should be performed before LP. In
pts with communicating hydrocephalus caused by impaired resorption of CSF,
LP is safe and may lead to temporary improvement. However, if ICP is elevated
because of a mass lesion, *brain swelling*, or a block in ventricular CSF outflow
(obstructive hydrocephalus), then LP carries the potential risk of brain herniation. Obstructive hydrocephalus usually requires direct ventricular drainage of
CSF.

Contrast-enhanced MRI or CT studies of the brain and spinal cord can identify meningeal enhancement, parameningeal infections (including brain abscess), encasement of the spinal cord (malignancy or inflammation and infection), or nodular deposits on the meninges or nerve roots (malignancy or
sarcoidosis). Imaging studies are also useful to localize areas of meningeal disease prior to meningeal biopsy. Cerebral angiography may identify arteritis.

A meningeal biopsy should be considered in pts who are disabled, who need
chronic ventricular decompression, or whose illness is progressing rapidly. The
diagnostic yield of meningeal biopsy can be increased by targeting regions that
enhance with contrast on MRI or CT. In a series from the Mayo Clinic, biopsy
of an enhancing region was diagnostic in 80% of cases; biopsy of nonenhancing
regions was diagnostic in only 9%; sarcoid (31%) and metastatic adenocarcinoma (25%) were the most common conditions identified.

In approximately one-third of cases, the diagnosis is not known despite
careful evaluation. A number of the organisms that cause chronic meningitis
may take weeks to be identified by cultures. It is prudent to wait until cultures
are finalized if symptoms are mild and not progressive. In many cases progressive neurologic deterioration occurs, and rapid treatment is required. In general,
empirical therapy in the U.S. consists of antimycobacterial agents, amphotericin
for fungal infection, or glucocorticoids for noninfectious inflammatory causes.
It is important to direct empirical therapy of lymphocytic meningitis at tuberculosis, particularly if the condition is associated with hypoglycorrhachia and
sixth and other cranial nerve palsies, since untreated disease is fatal in 4–8
weeks. Carcinomatous or lymphomatous meningitis may be difficult to diagnose
initially, but the diagnosis becomes evident with time. Important causes of

chronic meningitis in AIDS include infection with *Toxoplasma, Cryptococcus, Nocardia, Candida*, or other fungi; syphilis; and lymphoma.

For a more detailed discussion, see Koroshetz WJ and Swartz MN: Chronic and Recurrent Meningitis, Chap. 374, p. 2481, in HPIM-15.

187

MULTIPLE SCLEROSIS (MS)

Characterized by chronic inflammation and selective destruction of CNS myelin; peripheral nervous system is spared. Pathologically, the multifocal scarred lesions of MS are termed *plaques*. Etiology is thought to be autoimmune, with susceptibility determined by genetic and environmental factors. MS affects 350,000 Americans; onset is most often in early to middle adulthood, and women are affected approximately twice as often as men.

Clinical Manifestations

Onset may be dramatic or insidious. Most common are recurrent attacks of focal neurologic dysfunction, typically lasting weeks or months, and followed by variable recovery; some pts initially present with slowly progressive neurologic deterioration. Symptoms often transiently worsen with fatigue, stress, exercise, or heat. The manifestations of MS are protean (Table 187-1) but commonly include weakness and/or sensory symptoms involving a limb, visual difficulties, abnormalities of gait and coordination, urinary urgency or frequency, and abnormal fatigue. Motor involvement can present as a heavy, stiff, weak, or clumsy limb. Localized tingling, "pins and needles," and "dead" sensations are common. Optic neuritis can result in blurring or misting of vision, especially in the central visual field, often with associated retroorbital pain accentuated by eye movement. Involvement of the brainstem may result in diplopia, nystagmus, vertigo, or facial symptoms of pain, numbness, weakness, hemispasm, or myokymia (rippling muscular contractions). Ataxia, tremor, and dysarthria may reflect disease of cerebellar pathways. Lhermitte's symptom, a momentary electric shock-like sensation evoked by neck flexion, indicates disease in the cervical spinal cord. Diagnostic criteria are listed in Table 187-2.

Physical Examination

Abnormal signs usually more widespread than expected from the history. Check for abnormalities in visual fields, loss of visual acuity, disturbed color perception, optic pallor or papillitis, abnormalities in pupillary reflexes, nystagmus, internuclear ophthalmoplegia (slowness or loss of adduction in one eye with nystagmus in the abducting eye on lateral gaze), facial numbness or weakness,

Table 187-1

Initial Symptoms of MS	
Symptom	Percent of Cases
Sensory loss	37
Optic neuritis	36
Weakness	35
Paresthesia	24
Diplopia	15
Ataxia	11
Vertigo	6
Paroxysmal attacks	4
Bladder	4
Lhermitte	3
Pain	3
Dementia	2
Visual loss	2
Facial palsy	1
Impotence	1
Myokymia	1
Epilepsy	1
Falling	1

SOURCE: From SL Hauser, DE Goodkin: HPIM-15, p.2454.

dysarthria, incoordination, ataxia, weakness and spasticity, hyperreflexia, loss of abdominal reflexes, ankle clonus, upgoing toes, sensory abnormalities.

Disease Course

Four general categories:

- *Relapsing-remitting MS* is characterized by recurrent attacks of neurologic dysfunction with or without recovery; between attacks, no progression of neurologic impairment is noted.
- *Secondary progressive MS* initially presents with a relapsing-remitting pattern but evolves to be gradually progressive.
- *Primary progressive MS* is characterized by gradual progression of disability from onset.
- *Progressive-relapsing MS* is a rare form that begins with a primary progressive course, but superimposed relapses occur.

MS is a chronic illness; 15 years after diagnosis, 20% of pts have no functional limitation, 70% are limited or unable to perform major activities of daily living, and 75% are not employed.

Laboratory Findings

MRI reveals multifocal bright areas on T2-weighted sequences in > 90% of pts; gadolinium DPTA results in enhancement of active lesions due to disruption of blood-brain barrier. MRI also useful to exclude disorders that mimic MS. CSF findings include mild lymphocytic pleocytosis (5–75 cells in 25%), oligoclonal bands (75–90%), elevated IgG (80%), and normal total protein level. Visual, auditory, and somatosensory evoked response tests can identify lesions that are clinically silent; one or more evoked response tests abnormal in > 80% of patients. Urodynamic studies aid in management of bladder symptoms.

Table 187-2

Diagnostic Criteria for MS

1. Examination must reveal objective abnormalities of the CNS.
2. Involvement must reflect predominantly disease of white matter long tracts, usually including (a) pyramidal pathways, (b) cerebellar pathways, (c) medial longitudinal fasciculus, (d) optic nerve, and (e) posterior columns.
3. Examination or history must implicate involvement of two or more areas of the CNS.
   a. MRI may be used to document a second lesion when only one site of abnormality has been demonstrable on examination. A confirmatory MRI must have either four lesions involving the white matter or three lesions if one is periventricular in location. Acceptable lesions must be >3 mm in diameter. For pts >50 years, two of the following criteria must also be met: (a) lesion size >5 mm; (b) lesions abut the bodies of the lateral ventricles; or, (c) lesion(s) present in the posterior fossa.
   b. Evoked response testing may be used to document a second lesion not evident on clinical examination.
4. The clinical pattern must consist of (a) two or more separate episodes of worsening involving different sites of the CNS, each lasting at least 24 h and occurring at least 1 month apart, or (b) gradual or stepwise progression over at least 6 months if accompanied by increased CSF IgG synthesis or two or more oligoclonal bands.
5. Age of onset between 15 and 60 years of age.
6. The pt's neurologic condition could not be better attributed to another disease. Laboratory testing that may be advisable in certain cases includes (a) CSF analysis, (b) MRI of the head or spine, (c) serum B12 level, (d) human T cell lymphotropic virus type I (HTLV-I) titer, (e) ESR (f) rheumatoid factor, antinuclear, anti-DNA antibodies (SLE), (g) serum VDRL, (h) angiotensin-converting enzyme (sarcoidosis), (i) *Borrelia* serology (Lyme disease), (j) very long chain fatty acids (adrenoleukodystrophy), and (k) serum or CSF lactate, muscle biopsy, or mitochondrial DNA analysis (mitochondrial disorders).

DIAGNOSTIC CATEGORIES

1. *Definite MS*: All six criteria fulfilled.
2. *Probable MS*: All six criteria fulfilled except (a) only one objective abnormality despite two symptomatic episodes or (b) one symptomatic episode despite two or more objective abnormalities.
3. *At risk for MS*: All six criteria fulfilled except one symptomatic episode and one objective abnormality.

SOURCE: From SL Hauser, DE Goodkin: HPIM-15, p. 2455.

℞ **TREATMENT** (Fig. 187-1 and Table 187-3)

Prophylaxis Against Relapses Three treatments are available: Interferon (IFN) β1b (Betaseron), IFN-β1a (Avonex), and copolymer 1 (Copaxone). Each of these therapies reduces annual exacerbation rates by approximately one-third; IFN-β1a most convincingly delays the time to onset of sustained progression. Injection site reactions are common in IFN-β1b and copolymer 1 recipients. Approximately 15% of copolymer 1 recipients experience transient flushing, chest tightness, dyspnea, and palpitations. Approximately 40% of IFN-β1b and 5–25% of IFN-β1a recipients develop neutralizing antibodies within 12 months of initiating therapy, and these pts appear to lose the benefit of therapy.

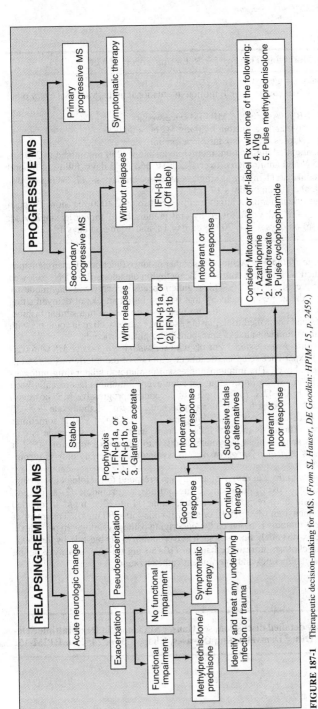

FIGURE 187-1 Therapeutic decision-making for MS. (*From SL Hauser, DE Goodkin: HPIM-15, p. 2459.*)

Table 187-3

Disease-Modifying Therapy for Relapsing Forms of MS

1. Prophylaxis against relapses
   a. IFN-β1b (Betaseron): 8 million international units (MIU) SC every other day
   b. IFN-β1a (Avonex): 6 MIU IM once weekly
   c. Copolymer 1 (Copaxone): 20 mg SC once daily
2. Acute relapses: methylprednisolone-prednisone
   a. Inpatient administration: methylprednisolone, 250 mg, mixed in 250 mL D5W and administered over 1–2 h IV q6h for 3 days, followed by oral prednisone (1 mg/kg as single A.M. dose) on days 4–17, 20 mg on day 18, and 10 mg on days 19–21
   b. Outpatient administration: methylprednisolone, 1000 mg slow IV push daily for 3 days, followed by oral prednisone (1 mg/kg as single A.M. dose) on days 4–17, 20 mg on day 18, and 10 mg on days 19–21

Acute Relapses Acute relapses that produce functional impairment may be treated with a short course of IV methylprednisolone (MePDN) followed by oral prednisone (PDN). This regimen speeds recovery and may modestly improve the degree of recovery that occurs. Initial attacks of demyelinating disease—such as optic neuritis or myelitis—are treated in a similar fashion. In one small controlled trial, plasma exchange was effective in some pts with unusually fulminant attacks unresponsive to glucocorticoids.

Chronic Progression For pts with *secondary progressive MS* who continue to experience relapses, treatment with one of the interferons is reasonable (see above). The immunosuppressant/immunomodulator drug mitoxantrone (12 mg/m^2 by intravenous infusion every 3 months) has recently been approved in the U.S. for treatment of secondary progressive MS; however, dose-related cardiac toxicity is an important concern. Methotrexate (7.5–20 mg po once each week) or azathioprine [2–3 (mg/kg)/d PO] is sometimes tried, but efficacy is modest. Pulse therapy with cyclophosphamide is employed in some centers for young adults with aggressive forms of MS. For patients with *primary progressive MS*, symptomatic therapy only is recommended.

Symptomatic Therapy Spasticity may respond to baclofen (15–80 mg/d in divided doses), diazepam (2 mg bid-tid), or tizanidine (2–8 mg tid). Dysesthesia may respond to carbamazepine (100–1200 mg/d in divided doses), phenytoin (300 mg/d), or amitriptyline (50–200 mg/d). Treatment of bladder symptoms is based on the underlying pathophysiology: hyperreflexia is treated with anticholinergics such as oxybutinin (5 mg bid-tid), hyporeflexia with the cholinergic drug bethanecol (10–50 mg tid-qid), and dyssynergia with anticholinergics and intermittent catheterization.

For a more detailed discussion, see Hauser SL, Goodkin DE: **Multiple Sclerosis and Other Demyelinating Diseases, Chap. 371, p. 2452, in HPIM-15.**

188

ALZHEIMER'S DISEASE AND OTHER DEMENTIAS

DEMENTIA

Dementia is a deterioration in cognitive ability. Memory loss is most common, but other mental faculties affected may include attention, judgment, comprehension, orientation, learning, calculation, problem solving, mood, and behavior. Agitation or withdrawal, hallucinations, delusions, insomnia, and loss of inhibitions are also common. Dementia is chronic, whereas delirium is an acute condition associated with fluctuating altered consciousness (agitation or lethargy); often accompanied by fever, tachycardia, or tremor.

DIAGNOSIS The mini-mental status examination is a useful screening test for dementia (Table 188-1). A score of <24 points (out of 30) indicates a need for more detailed cognitive and physical assessment.

DIFFERENTIAL DIAGNOSIS Dementia has many causes (Table 188-2); it is essential to exclude treatable etiologies. Pseudodementia (depression) can be difficult to distinguish from dementia, but memory is usually intact on careful testing. Prior bouts of depression suggest pseudodementia. Some clinical clues suggest a treatable disorder—early, prominent gait disturbance; urinary incontinence (normal-pressure hydrocephalus); resting tremor, bradykinesia (Parkinson's disease); neuropathy (vitamin B_{12} deficiency); bradycardia; delayed relaxation of stretch reflexes (hypothyroidism); early-onset seizures (neoplasm); insomnia, anxiety, psychiatric disturbance, seizures (drug intoxication

Table 188-1

The Mini-Mental Status Examination

	Points
Orientation	
Name: season/date/day/month/year	5 (1 for each name)
Name: hospital/floor/town/state/country	5 (1 for each name)
Registration	
Identify three objects by name and ask patient to repeat	3 (1 for each object)
Attention and calculation	
Serial 7s; subtract from 100 (e.g., $93 - 86 - 79 - 72 - 65$)	5 (1 for each subtraction)
Recall	
Recall the three objects presented earlier	3 (1 for each object)
Language	
Name pencil and watch	2 (1 for each object)
Repeat "No ifs, ands, or buts"	1
Follow a 3-step command (e.g., "Take this paper, fold it in half, and place it on the table")	3 (1 for each command)
Write "close your eyes" and ask pt to obey written command	1
Ask pt to write a sentence	1
Ask pt to copy a design (e.g., intersecting pentagons)	<u>1</u>
TOTAL	30

SOURCE: Bird TD: HPIM-15.

Table 188-2

Differential Diagnosis of Dementia

MOST COMMON CAUSES OF DEMENTIA

Alzheimer's disease
Alcoholism[a]
Vascular dementia[a]
  Multi-infarct
  Diffuse white matter disease
  (Binswanger's)

Parkinson's disease
Drug/medication intoxication[a]

LESS COMMON CAUSES OF DEMENTIA

Vitamin deficiencies
  Thiamine (B_1): Wernicke's
  encephalopathy[a]
  B12 (Pernicious anemia)[a]
  Nicotinic acid (pellagra)[a]
Endocrine and other organ failure
  Hypothyroidism[a]
  Adrenal insufficiency and
  Cushing's syndrome[a]
  Hypo- and hyperparathyroidism[a]
  Renal failure[a]
  Liver failure[a]
  Pulmonary failure[a]
Chronic infections
  HIV
  Neurosyphilis[a]
  Papovavirus (progressive multi-
  focal leukoencephalopathy)
  Prion (Creutzfeldt-Jakob and
  Gerstmann-Sträussler-Scheinker
  disease)
  Tuberculosis, fungal, and proto-
  zoal[a]
  Sarcoidosis[a]
  Whipple's disease[a]
Toxic disorders
  Drug, medication, and narcotic
  poisoning[a]
  Heavy metal intoxication[a]
  Dialysis dementia (aluminum)
  Organic toxins
Psychiatric
  Depression (peudodementia)[a]
  Schizophrenia[a]
  Conversion reaction[a]
Degenerative disorders
  Huntington's disease
  Pick's disease
  Diffuse Lewy body disease
  Progressive supranuclear palsy
  (Steel-Richardson syndrome)

Multisystem degeneration
  (Shy-Drager syndrome)
Hereditary ataxias (some forms)
Motor neuron disease
  [amyotrophic lateral sclerosis
  (ALS); some forms]
Frontal lobe dementia
Cortical basal degeneration
Multiple sclerosis
Head trauma and diffuse brain
damage
  Dementia pugilistica
  Chronic subdural hematoma[a]
  Postanoxia
  Postencephalitis
  Normal-pressure hydrocephalus[a]
Neoplastic
  Primary brain tumor[a]
  Metastatic brain tumor[a]
  Paraneoplastic limbic encephalitis
  Adult Down's syndrome with
  Alzheimer's
  ALS-Parkinson's-Dementia
  complex of Guam
Miscellaneous
  Vasculitis[a]
  Acute intermittent porphyria[a]
  Recurrent nonconvulsive seizures[a]
Additional conditions in children or
adolescents
  Hallervorden-Spatz disease
  Subacute sclerosing panence-
  phalitis
  Metabolic disorders (e.g.,
  Wilson's[a] and Leigh's diseases,
  leukodystrophies, lipid storage
  diseases, mitochondrial
  mutations)

[a] Potentially treatable dementia.

or withdrawal); rapid progression with ataxia, rigidity, myoclonus (Creutzfeldt-Jakob disease); fever, meningismus (chronic infection); confusion, ophthalmoparesis, ataxia, followed by severe anterograde and retrograde amnesia (Wernicke-Korsakoff syndrome).

_____ *Approach to the Patient* _____

An approach to the workup of dementia is outlined in Table 188-3. Brain MRI or CT identifies multi-infarct dementia, brain tumors, subdural hematoma, and normal-pressure hydrocephalus. Several laboratory tests (thyroid function, vitamin B_{12}, CBC, electrolytes, VDRL) indicated in all pts; additional tests (e.g., HIV, liver and renal function, LP, toxic screen, angiogram, or brain biopsy) determined by the clinical situation. EEG indicated if seizures or Creutzfeldt-Jakob disease suspected; EEG is normal in pseudodementia.

ALZHEIMER'S DISEASE (AD)

Most common cause of dementia; affects 3–4 million persons in the U.S. Cost >\$50 billion dollars/year.

CLINICAL MANIFESTATIONS Pts present with subtle recent memory loss then develop slowly progressive dementia. Memory loss is often not recognized initially—in part due to preservation of social graces until later phases; impaired activities of daily living (keeping track of finances, appointments) draw attention of friends/family. Disorientation, poor judgment, poor concentration, aphasia, apraxia, and alexia increasingly occur as the disease progresses. Pts may be frustrated or unaware of deficit. Death from malnutrition or secondary infection. Typical duration 8–10 years.

PATHOGENESIS Risk factors for AD are old age, positive family history. Pathology: neuritic plaques composed of Aβ amyloid and other proteins; neurofibrillary tangles composed of abnormally phosphorylated tau protein. The apolipoprotein E (apo E) gene (chromosome 21) has a role in pathogenesis; the ε4 allele appears to modify age of onset of AD and is associated with sporadic and late-onset familial cases of AD. Apo E testing is not indicated as a predictive test at this time. Rare genetic causes of AD are Down's syndrome (trisomy 21), amyloid precursor protein (APP) gene mutations (chromosome 21), mutations in presenilin I (chromosome 14) and presenilin II (chromosome 1) genes.

℞ **TREATMENT**

There is no definitive treatment for AD; management of behavioral/neurologic problems in conjunction with family and caregivers is essential. Depression is common in early stages and may respond to antidepressants (SSRIs, tricyclics). Mild sedation may help insomnia. Agitation controlled with low-dose haloperidol (0.5–2 mg). Notebooks and posted daily reminders can function as memory aids in early stages. Kitchens, bathrooms, and bedrooms need evaluation for safety. Pts must eventually stop driving. Caregiver burnout is common; nursing home placement may be necessary. Local and national support groups (Alzheimer's Disease and Related Disorders Association) are valuable resources.

Drug therapy is limited. Centrally acting cholinesterase inhibitors approved for mild-moderate AD presumably function by increasing cerebral levels of acetylcholine. Donepezil (Aricept), 5–10 mg/d PO, has the advantages of few side effects and is given in a single daily dosage. Clinical trials show improved caregiver ratings of pt function and a decreased rate in decline

Table 188-3

Evaluation of the Demented Patient

Routine Evaluation	Optional Focused Tests
History	HIV
Physical examination	Chest x-ray
Laboratory tests	Lumbar puncture
Thyroid function (TSH)	Liver function
Vitamin B_{12}	Renal function
Complete blood count	Urine toxin screen
Electrolytes	Psychometric testing
VDRL	Apolipoprotein E
CT/MRI	

Occasionally Helpful Tests	
EEG	Sedimentation rate
Parathyroid function	Angiogram
Adrenal function	Brain biopsy
Urine heavy metals	

DIAGNOSTIC CATEGORIES

Treatable Causes	Untreatable/Degenerative Dementias
Examples	Examples
Hypothyroidism	Alzheimer's
Thiamine deficiency	Pick's
Vitamin B_{12} deficiency	Huntington's
Normal-pressure hydrocephalus	Diffuse Lewy body disease
Chronic infection	Multi-infarct
Brain tumor	Leukoencephalopathies
Drug intoxication	Parkinson's

Associated Treatable Conditions	Psychiatric Disorders
Depression	Depression
Seizure	Schizophrenia
Insomnia	Conversion reaction
Agitation	
Caregiver "burnout"	
Drug side effects	

of cognitive test scores. Estrogen may be helpful as a preventive measure in postmenopausal women. The value of vitamin E is uncertain.

OTHER CAUSES OF DEMENTIA

VASCULAR DEMENTIA Typically follows multiple strokelike episodes (multi-infarct dementia) or rarely develops in a slow progressive fashion (diffuse white matter or Binswanger's disease). Unlike AD, focal neurologic signs (e.g., hemiparesis) are usually present at presentation.

FRONTOTEMPORAL DEMENTIA Responsible for 10% of all cases of dementia. Patients often irritable, disinhibited; better performance than AD on tests of construction, copying, and calculation. May be sporadic or inherited; some familial cases due to intronic mutations of tau gene on chromosome 17.

DIFFUSE LEWY BODY DISEASE Dementia with rigidity and other parkinsonian features. Lewy bodies are intraneuronal cytoplasmic inclusions.

NORMAL-PRESSURE HYDROCEPHALUS (NPH) Presents as a gait disorder (ataxic or apractic), dementia, and urinary incontinence; gait improves in 30–50% of pts following ventricular shunting; dementia and incontinence do not improve.

HUNTINGTON'S DISEASE Presents as chorea and altered behavior. Typical onset fourth to fifth decade but can present at almost any age. Autosomal dominant inheritance; the abnormal gene has expanded trinucleotide repeat resulting in a protein (huntingtin) with an expanded polyglutamine tract; function of huntingtin is unknown. Diagnosis confirmed with genetic testing coupled with genetic counseling. Symptomatic treatment of movements and behaviors; SSRIs may help depression.

For a more detailed discussion, see Bird TD: Memory Loss and Dementia, Chap. 26, p. 148; and Alzheimer's Disease and Other Primary Dementias, Chap. 362, p. 2391, HPIM-15.

189

PARKINSON'S DISEASE

Clinical Features

Parkinsonism consists of tremor, rigidity, bradykinesia, and characteristic abnormalities of gait and posture; may occur with many disorders. Parkinson's disease (PD) is idiopathic parkinsonism without evidence of more widespread neurologic involvement. Onset between 40 and 70 years with insidious progression. Tremor ("pill rolling" of hands) at rest (4–6 Hz); worsens with stress. A faster (7–8 Hz) "action tremor" may also occur when the hands are held against gravity. Presentation with tremor confined to one limb or side of body is common. Other findings: rigidity ("cogwheeling"—increased ratchet-like resistance to passive limb movements), bradykinesia (slowness of voluntary movements), fixed expressionless face (facial masking) with reduced frequency of blinking, hypophonic voice, drooling, impaired rapid alternating movements, micrographia (small handwriting), reduced arm swing while walking, flexed "stooped" posture with walking, shuffling gait, difficulty initiating or stopping walking, en-bloc turning (multiple small steps required to turn), retropulsion (tendency to fall backwards). In advanced PD—intellectual deterioration, aspiration pneumonia, and bedsores (due to immobility) common. Normal muscular strength, deep tendon reflexes, and sensory exam. Diagnosis based upon history and examination; neuroimaging, EEG, and CSF studies usually normal for age.

Etiology

Degeneration of pigmented pars compacta neurons of the substantia nigra in the midbrain resulting in lack of dopaminergic input to striatum; accumulation of eosinophilic intraneural inclusion granules (Lewy bodies). Cause of cell death is unknown, but it may result from generation of free radicals and oxidative stress, perhaps by oxidation of dopamine itself. Rare forms of parkinsonism are due to mutations in α-synuclein or parkin genes.

Differential Diagnosis

Features of parkinsonism may occur with: depression (paucity of vocal inflection and facial movement); essential tremor (high-frequency tremor with limbs held against gravity; head tremor common; improves with alcohol intake); normal-pressure hydrocephalus (apraxic gait, urinary incontinence, dementia); Wilson's disease (early age of onset, Kayser-Fleischer rings, low serum copper, low ceruloplasmin); Huntington's disease (positive family history, chorea, dementia); multiple system atrophy (parkinsonism, impaired autonomic function, or pyramidal or cerebellar or lower motor neuron signs); other neurodegenerative diseases (progressive supranuclear palsy, olivopontocerebellar atrophy, cortical-basal ganglionic degeneration, striatonigral degeneration, diffuse Lewy body disease, Creutzfeldt-Jakob disease, Alzheimer's disease).

℞ TREATMENT

It is not always possible to exclude other causes of parkinsonism prior to initiating treatment for PD. Primary goal of treatment is to restore function (i.e., reduce disabling tremor). A summary of commonly used drugs for PD is listed in Table 189-1; an algorithmic approach to overall management is shown in Fig. 189-1. Amantadine is useful for mild symptoms and acts by potentiating release of endogenous dopamine. Tremor responds best to anticholinergic drugs (trihexyphenidyl, benztropine). Early use of dopamine agonist drugs alone (bromocriptine, pergolide, pramipexole) may delay the emergence of late side effects associated with chronic Sinemet use.

Sinemet is most helpful for bradykinesia. Sinemet consists of levodopa, the metabolic precurser of dopamine, combined with an extracerebral inhibitor of dopa decarboxylase. The combination maximizes entry of levodopa into the brain. A common initial dose is 25/100 PO tid. Late complications: (1) end-dose phenomenon—deterioration shortly before next dose; and (2) on-off phenomenon—abrupt, transient fluctuations in function without warning or obvious relationship to dosing. On-off may be partially controlled by reducing dosing intervals, restricting dietary protein, and administering levodopa 1 h prior to meals. Response fluctuations to oral levodopa may be reduced by frequent dosing, continuous gastric infusion, or parenteral administration. Controlled-release Sinemet may reduce dosing frequency. Pramipexole may be used with Sinemet to reduce Sinemet dose and drug-response fluctuations. Selegiline, an inhibitor of monoamine oxidase B, may reduce oxidative damage and slow disease progression; the usual dose is 5 mg twice daily. Selective inhibitors of catechol-O-methyltransferase (COMT) such as tolcapone (100 mg tid) or entacapone (200 mg with each Sinemet dose) may enhance the benefits of levodopa therapy.

In refractory cases, unilateral pallidotomy may be effective in relieving signs of PD on the contralateral side. Long-term efficacy is still being defined. Deep brain stimulation of the globus pallidus or subthalamic nucleus has a lower morbidity than pallidotomy and appears to improve clinical status. Adrenal medullary transplants may benefit individuals < 50 years. Transplantation of fetal midbrain cells remains experimental.

Table 189-1

Drugs Used in Parkinson's Disease

Drug	Trade Name	Dose	Side Effects
Trihexyphenidyl	Artane	2–5 mg tid	Dry mouth, blurred vision, confusion
Benztropine	Cogentin	0.5–2 mg tid	Dry mouth, confusion
Carbidopa/levodopa	Sinemet	10/100–25/250 mg; increase slowly to tid or qid	Orthostatic hypotension, GI complaints, hallucinations, confusion, chorea, dyskinesias
Amantadine	Symmetrel	100 mg bid	Depression, postural hypotension, psychosis, urinary retention
Bromocriptine	Parlodel	7.5–30 mg qd in divided doses	Postural hypotension, nausea and vomiting, hallucinations, psychosis, dyskinesias
Pergolide	Permax	0.05–3 mg qd in divided doses	Nausea, dizziness, hallucinations, confusion, constipation, postural hypotension, dyskinesias
Pramipexole	Mirapex	0.5–1.5 mg tid	Dizziness, confusion, nausea, peripheral edema, altered sleep

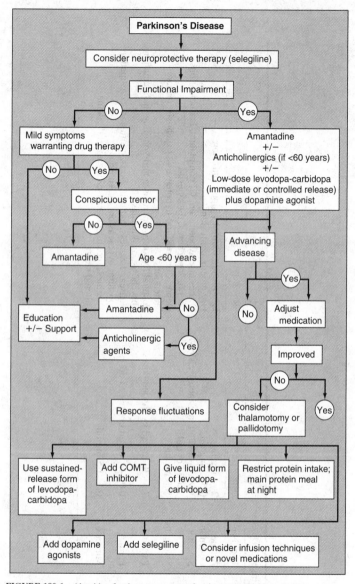

FIGURE 189-1 Algorithm for the management of patients with Parkinson's disease.

For a more detailed discussion, see Aminoff MJ: Parkinson's Disease and Other Extrapyramidal Disorders, Chap. 363, p. 2399, in HPIM-15.

190

ATAXIC DISORDERS

Clinical Presentation

Symptoms and signs of ataxia may include gait instability, nystagmus, dysarthria (scanning speech), impaired limb coordination, intention tremor (i.e., with movement), hypotonia. *Differential diagnosis:* Unsteady gait associated with vertigo can resemble gait instability of cerebellar disease but produces a sensation of head movement, dizziness, or light-headedness. Bilateral proximal leg weakness or sensory ataxia, in particular with neuropathies (e.g., Fisher variant of Guillain-Barré syndrome), can also simulate cerebellar ataxia.

—————— Approach to the Patient ——————

Causes are best grouped by determining whether ataxia is symmetric or asymmetric and by the time course (Table 190-1). It is also important to distinguish whether ataxia is present in isolation or is part of a multisystem neurologic disorder. Acute symmetric ataxia is usually due to medications, toxins, viral infection, or a postinfectious syndrome (especially varicella). Subacute or chronic symmetric ataxia can result from hypothyroidism, vitamin deficiencies, infections, alcohol, and other toxins. Progressive nonfamilial cerebellar ataxia

Table 190-1

Etiology of Cerebellar Ataxia

Acute (Hours to Days)	Subacute (Days to Weeks)	Chronic (Months to Years)
SYMMETRIC SIGNS		
Alcohol, lithium, phenytoin, barbiturates, mercury (positive history and toxicology screen)	Intoxication: mercury, solvents, gasoline, glue; cytotoxic chemotherapeutic drugs	Paraneoplastic syndrome
		Hypothyroidism
		Inherited diseases
Acute viral cerebellitis (CSF supportive of acute viral infection)	Alcoholic-nutritional (vitamin E, B_1 or B_{12} deficiency)	Tabes dorsalis (tertiary syphilis)
Postinfection syndrome	Lyme disease	
ASYMMETRIC SIGNS		
Vascular: cerebellar infarction, hemorrhage, or subdural hematoma	Neoplastic: cerebellar glioma or metastatic tumor (positive for neoplasm on MRI/CT)	Stable gliosis secondary to vascular lesion or demyelinating plaque (stable lesion on MRI/CT older than several months)
Infectious: cerebellar abscess (positive mass lesion on MRI/CT, positive history in support of lesion)	Demyelinating: Multiple sclerosis (history, CSF and MRI are consistent) AIDS-related progressive multifocal leukoencephalopathy (positive HIV test and CD4+ cell count for AIDS)	Congenital lesion: Dandy-Walker or Arnold-Chiari malformations (malformation noted on MRI/CT)

SOURCE: Modified from RN Rosenberg: HPIM-15, p. 2407.

after age 45 suggests a paraneoplastic syndrome, either subacute cortical cerebellar degeneration (ovarian, breast, small cell lung, Hodgkin's) or opsoclonus-myoclonus (neuroblastoma, breast).

Unilateral ataxia suggests a focal lesion in the ipsilateral cerebellar hemisphere or its connections. An important cause of acute unilateral ataxia is stroke. Mass effect from cerebellar hemorrhage or swelling from ischemic cerebellar infarction can compress brainstem structures, producing altered consciousness and ipsilateral pontine signs (small pupil, lateral gaze or sixth nerve paresis, facial weakness); limb ataxia may not be prominent. Other diseases resulting in subacute-to-chronic unilateral or asymmetric ataxia include tumors, multiple sclerosis, progressive multifocal leukoencephalopathy (immunodeficiency states) or congenital malformations.

Inherited Ataxias

May be autosomal dominant, autosomal recessive, or mitochondrial (maternal inheritance); 24 different disorders recognized (Table 364-2, HPIM-15). Friedreich's ataxia is most common; autosomal recessive; ataxia with areflexia, upgoing toes, vibration and position sensation deficits, cardiomyopathy, hammer toes, scoliosis; linked to expanded trinucleotide repeat in the intron of "frataxin" gene; a second genetic form of Friedreich's is associated with vitamin E deficiency. Common dominantly inherited ataxias are spinocerebellar ataxia (SCA) 1 (olivopontocerebellar degeneration; "ataxin-1" gene) and SCA 3 (Machado-Joseph disease); both present with ataxia and brainstem and extrapyramidal signs; SCA 3 may also have dystonia and amyotrophy; genes for each disorder contain unstable trinucleotide repeats in coding region.

Evaluation

The differential diagnosis is driven by the symmetry and time course of the ataxia (Table 190-1). For symmetric ataxias, drug and toxicology screens; vitamin B_1, B_{12}, and E levels; thyroid function tests; antibody tests for syphilis and Lyme infection; paraneoplastic autoantibodies (anti-Yo, anti-Ri, anti-Hu); and CSF studies often indicated. Genetic testing is available for many inherited ataxias but should be carried out only with genetic counseling. For unilateral or asymmetric ataxias, brain MRI or CT scan is the initial test of choice.

Hypothyroidism, vitamin deficiency, infectious and parainfectious causes of ataxia are treatable. With paraneoplastic ataxias, identification of underlying cancer is important for the pt, but as a rule ataxia does not improve following treatment of tumor. Cerebellar hemorrhage and other mass lesions of the posterior fossa may require surgical treatment to prevent fatal brainstem compression.

For a more detailed discussion, see Rosenberg RN: Ataxic Disorders, Chap. 364, p. 2406, in HPIM-15.

191

ALS AND OTHER MOTOR NEURON DISEASES

Etiology

Amyotrophic lateral sclerosis (ALS) is the most important of the motor neuron diseases (Table 191-1). ALS is caused by degeneration of motor neurons at all levels of the CNS, including anterior horns of the spinal cord, brainstem motor nuclei, and motor cortex. Familial ALS (FALS) represents 5–10% of the total and is inherited as an autosomal dominant disorder. Syndromes clinically indistinguishable from classic ALS may result rarely from intoxication with mercury, lead, or aluminum and in hyperparathyroidism, thyrotoxicosis, immunologic or paraneoplastic mechanisms, and hereditary biochemical disorders. Tumors near the foramen magnum, high spinal cord tumors, cervical spondylosis, chronic polyradiculopathies, polymyositis, spinal muscle atrophies, and diabetic, syphilitic, and postpolio amyotrophies can all produce signs and symptoms similar to those seen in ALS and should be carefully considered in differential diagnosis (Table 191-2).

Clinical History

Onset is usually midlife, with most cases progressing to death in 3–5 years. Common initial symptoms are weakness, muscle wasting, stiffness and cramping, and twitching in muscles of hands and arms. Legs are less severely involved than arms, with complaints of leg stiffness, cramping, and weakness common. Symptoms of brainstem involvement include dysarthria and dysphagia.

Physical Examination

Lower motor neuron disease results in weakness and wasting that often first involves intrinsic hand muscles but later becomes generalized. Fasciculations occur in involved muscles, and fibrillations may be seen in the tongue. Hyper-

Table 191-1

Sporadic Motor Neuron Diseases

CHRONIC

Upper and lower motor neurons
  Amyotrophic lateral sclerosis
Predominantly upper motor neurons
  Primary lateral sclerosis
Predominantly lower motor neurons
  Multifocal motor neuropathy with conduction block
  Motor neuropathy with paraproteinemia or cancer
  Motor-predominant peripheral neuropathies
Other
  Associated with other degenerative disorders
  Secondary motor neuron disorders (see Table 191-2)

ACUTE

Poliomyelitis
Herpes zoster
Coxsackie virus

SOURCE: RH Brown, Jr: HPIM-15, p. 2412.

Table 191-2

Etiology and Investigation of Motor Neuron Disorders

Diagnostic Categories	Investigations

Structural lesions
  Parasagittal or foramen magnum tumors
  Cervical spondylosis
  Chiari malformation or syrinx
  Spinal cord arteriovenous malformation
	MRI scan of head (including foramen magnum), cervical spine[a]

Infections
  Bacterial—tetanus, Lyme
  Viral—poliomyelitis, herpes zoster
  Retroviral myelopathy
	CSF exam, culture[a]
	Lyme antibody titer[a]
	Antiviral antibody titers (e.g., enteroviruses)
	HTLV-1, HTLV-2 titers

Intoxications, physical agents
  Toxins—lead, aluminum, other metals
  Drugs—strychnine, phenytoin
  Electric shock, x-irradiation
	24-h urine for heavy metals[a]
	Serum and urine for lead, aluminum

Immunologic mechanisms
  Plasma cell dyscrasias
  Autoimmune polyradiculoneuropathy
  Motor neuropathy with conduction block
	Complete blood count[a]
	Sedimentation rate[a]
	Immunoprotein electrophoresis[a]
	Anti-G_{M1} antibodies[a]

Paraneoplastic	Anti-Hu antibody
Paracarcinomatous/lymphoma	MRI scan, bone marrow biopsy
Metabolic Hypoglycemia	Fasting blood sugar (FBS), routine chemistries including calcium[a]
Hyperparathyroidism	PTH, calcium, phosphate
Hyperthyroidism	Thyroid functions[a]
Deficiency of vitamins B_{12}, E, and folate	Vitamin B_{12}, vitamin E, folate levels[a]
Malabsorption	24-h stool fat, carotene, prothrombin time
Mitochondrial dysfunction	Fasting lactate, pyruvate, ammonia Consider mtDNA analysis
Hereditary biochemical disorders Superoxide dismutase 1 mutation	White blood cell DNA analysis
Androgen receptor defect (Kennedy's disease)	Abnormal CAG insert in androgen receptor gene
Hexosaminidase deficiency	Lysosomal enzyme screen
Infantile (α-glucosidase deficiency (Pompe's disease)	
Hyperlipidemia	Lipid electrophoresis
Hyperglycinuria	Urine and serum amino acids
Methylcrotonylglycinuria	CSF amino acids

[a] Denotes studies that should be obtained in all cases.
NOTE: HTLV, human T cell leukemia virus.
SOURCE: From RH Brown, Jr: HPIM-15, p. 2414.

reflexia, spasticity, and upgoing toes in weak, atrophic limbs provide evidence of upper motor neuron disease. Brainstem disease produces wasting of the tongue, difficulty in articulation, phonation, and deglutition, and pseudobulbar palsy (e.g., involuntary laughter, crying). Important additional features that characterize ALS are preservation of intellect, lack of sensory abnormalities, and absence of bowel or bladder dysfunction.

Laboratory Findings

EMG provides objective evidence of muscle denervation as well as of involvement of muscles innervated by different peripheral nerves and nerve roots. Myelography, CT, or MRI may be useful to exclude compressive lesions. CSF is usually normal. Muscle enzymes (e.g., CK) may be elevated. Pulmonary function studies may aid in management of ventilation. Useful tests to exclude other diseases can include urine and serum screens for heavy metals, thyroid functions, serum immunoelectrophoresis, lysosomal enzyme screens, anti-GM_1 antibodies, vitamin B_{12} levels, VDRL, CBC, ESR, and serum chemistries. In FALS, one subset has mutations in the gene encoding the cytosolic enzyme superoxide dismutase 1 (SOD1).

Complications

Weakness of ventilatory muscles leads to respiratory insufficiency; dysphagia may result in aspiration pneumonia and compromised energy intake.

 TREATMENT

There is no treatment capable of arresting ALS. The drug riluzole produces modest lengthening of survival; in one trial the survival rate at 18 months with riluzole (100 mg/d) was similar to placebo at 15 months. It may act by diminishing glutamate release and thereby decreasing excitotoxic neuronal cell death. Side effects of riluzole include nausea, dizziness, weight loss, and elevation of liver enzymes. In a single study, insulin-like growth factor (IGF-1) was found to slow ALS progression modestly, but the effect was not confirmed in a second trial; IGF-1 is not routinely available as an ALS treatment at this time. Clinical trials of several other agents are in progress, including brain-derived neurotrophic factor, glial-derived neurotrophic factor, the anti-glutamate compound topiramate, and creatine. In a single study from France, vitamin E was beneficial in sporadic ALS. Several types of secondary motor neuron disorders that resemble ALS are treatable (Table 191-2). All pts should have a careful search for these disorders. Supportive care can include home care ventilation and pulmonary support; speech therapy; nonverbal, electronic, or mechanical communication systems for anarthric pts; and dietary management to ensure adequate energy intake. Attention to use of rehabilitative devices (braces, splints, canes, walkers, mechanized wheelchairs) is essential to improve care.

For a more detailed discussion, see **Brown RH Jr: Amyotrophic Lateral Sclerosis and Other Motor Neuron Diseases, Chap. 365, p. 2412, in HPIM-15.**

192

CRANIAL NERVE DISORDERS

Disorders of vision and ocular movement are discussed in Chaps. 10 and 48; dizziness and vertigo in Chap. 9; and disorders of hearing in Chap. 49;

OLFACTORY NERVE (I)

The sense of smell may be impaired by (1) interference with access of odorant to olfactory neuroepithelium (*transport loss*), e.g., by swollen nasal mucous membrane in URI, allergic rhinitis, or structural changes in nasal cavity such as with a deviated septum, nasal polyps, or neoplasm; (2) injury to receptor region (*sensory loss*), e.g., destruction of olfactory neuroepithelium by viral infections, neoplasms, inhalation of toxic chemicals, or radiation to head; and (3) damage to central olfactory pathways (*neural loss*), e.g., by head trauma with or without fractures of cribriform plate, neoplasms of anterior cranial fossa, neurosurgical procedures, neurotoxic drugs, or congenital disorders such as Kallmann's syndrome.

TRIGEMINAL NERVE (V)   (See Fig. 192-1)

Trigeminal Neuralgia (Tic Douloureux) Frequent, excruciating paroxysms of pain in lips, gums, cheek, or chin (rarely in ophthalmic division of fifth nerve) lasting seconds to minutes. Appears in middle or old age. Pain is often stimulated at trigger points. Sensory deficit cannot be demonstrated. Must be distinguished from other forms of facial pain arising from diseases of jaw, teeth, or sinuses. Tic is rarely caused by herpes zoster or a tumor. Onset in young adulthood raises the possibility of multiple sclerosis.

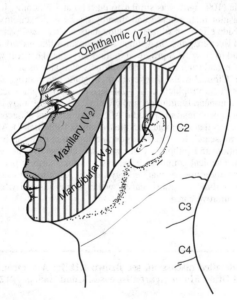

FIGURE 192-1 The three major sensory divisions of the trigeminal nerve consist of the ophthalmic, maxillary, and mandibular nerves.

℞ TREATMENT

Carbamazepine is effective in 75% of cases. Begin at 100 mg single daily dose taken with food and advance by 100 mg every 1–2 days until substantial (50%) pain relief occurs. Most pts require 200 mg qid; doses >1200 mg daily usually provide no additional benefit. Follow CBC for rare complication of aplastic anemia. For nonresponders, phenytoin (300–400 mg qd) or baclofen (5–20 mg tid-qid) can be tried. When medications fail, surgical gangliolysis or suboccipital craniectomy for decompression of trigeminal nerve are options; in some centers, microvascular decompression is recommended if a tortuous or redundant blood vessel is found in the posterior fossa near the trigeminal nerve.

Trigeminal Neuropathy Usually presents as facial sensory loss or weakness of jaw muscles. Causes are varied (Table 192-1) including tumors of middle cranial fossa or trigeminal nerve, metastases to base of skull, or lesions in cavernous sinus (affecting first and second divisions of fifth nerve) or superior orbital fissure (affecting first division of fifth nerve).

FACIAL NERVE (VII)

Lesions of the seventh nerve or nucleus produce hemifacial weakness that includes muscles of forehead and orbicularis oculi; if lesion is in middle ear portion, taste is lost over the anterior two-thirds of tongue and there may be hyperacusis; if lesion is at internal auditory meatus, there may be involvement of auditory and vestibular nerves, whereas pontine lesions usually affect abducens nerve and often corticospinal tract as well. Peripheral nerve lesions with incomplete recovery may result in diffuse continuous contraction of affected facial muscles +/− associated movements (synkinesis) of other facial muscle groups and facial spasms.

Bell's Palsy Most common form of idiopathic facial paralysis, found in 23/100,000 annually, or 1 in 60–70 persons over a lifetime. Pathogenesis un-

Table 192-1

Trigeminal Nerve Disorders

Nuclear (brainstem) lesions	Peripheral nerve lesions
Multiple sclerosis	Nasopharyngeal carcinoma
Stroke	Trauma
Syringobulbia	Guillain-Barré syndrome
Glioma	Sjögren's syndrome
Lymphoma	Collagen-vascular diseases
Preganglionic lesions	Sarcoidosis
Acoustic neuroma	Leprosy
Meningioma	Drugs (stilbamidine, trichloroethylene)
Metastasis	Idiopathic trigeminal neuropathy
Chronic meningitis	
Cavernous carotid aneurysm	
Gasserian ganglion lesions	
Trigeminal neuroma	
Herpes zoster	
Infection (spread from otitis	
media or mastoiditis)	

SOURCE: From MF Beal, SL Hauser: HPIM-15, p. 2422.

certain, but an association with herpes simplex virus type 1 has been documented. Weakness evolves over 12–48 h, sometimes preceded by retroaural pain. Fully 80% recover within several weeks or months.

 TREATMENT

Involves protection of eye with paper tape to depress the upper eyelid during sleep. Prednisone (60–80 mg qd over 5 d, tapered off over the next 5 d) when started early appears to shorten the recovery period and modestly improve functional outcome. In one study, treatment within 3 days of onset with both prednisone and acyclovir (400 mg five times daily for 10 d) improved outcome.

Other Facial Nerve Disorders *Ramsay Hunt Syndrome* is caused by herpes zoster infection of geniculate ganglion; distinguished from Bell's palsy by a vesicular eruption in pharynx, external auditory canal, and other parts of the cranial integument. *Acoustic neuromas* often compress the seventh nerve. *Pontine tumors* or *infarcts* may cause a lower motor neuron facial weakness. *Bilateral facial diplegia* may appear in Guillain-Barré syndrome, sarcoidosis, Lyme disease, and leprosy. *Hemifacial spasm* may result from Bell's palsy, irritative lesions (e.g., acoustic neuroma, basilar artery aneurysm, or aberrant vessel compressing the nerve) or as an idiopathic disorder. *Blepharospasm* consists of involuntary recurrent spasms of both eyelids, usually occurring in the elderly and sometimes with associated facial spasm. May subside spontaneously. Severe cases of hemifacial spasm or blepharospasm can be treated by local injection of botulinus toxin into the orbicularis oculi; spasms are relieved for 3–4 months, and injections can be repeated.

GLOSSOPHARYNGEAL NERVE (IX)

Glossopharyngeal Neuralgia Paroxysmal, intense pain in tonsillar fossa of throat that may be precipitated by swallowing. There is no demonstrable sensory or motor deficit. Other diseases affecting this nerve include herpes zoster or compressive neuropathy due to tumor or aneurysm in region of jugular foramen (when associated with vagus and accessory nerve palsies).

 TREATMENT

Carbamazepine or phenytoin is often effective, but surgical division of the ninth nerve near the medulla is sometimes necessary.

VAGUS NERVE (X)

Lesions of vagus nerve cause symptoms of dysphagia and dysphonia. Unilateral lesions produce drooping of soft palate, loss of gag reflex, and "curtain movement" of lateral wall of pharynx with hoarse, nasal voice. Diseases that may involve the vagus include diphtheria (toxin), neoplastic and infectious processes of the meninges, tumors and vascular lesions in the medulla, or compression of the recurrent laryngeal nerve by intrathoracic processes.

HYPOGLOSSAL NERVE (XII)

The twelfth cranial nerve supplies the ipsilateral muscles of the tongue. Atrophy and fasciculations of the tongue develop weeks to months after interruption of the nerve. Lesions affecting the motor nucleus may occur in the brainstem (tu-

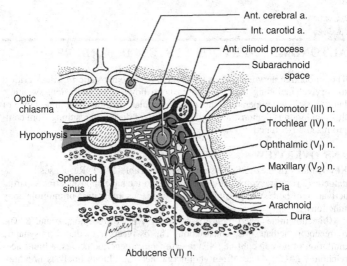

FIGURE 192-2 Anatomy of the cavernous sinus in coronal section, illustrating the location of the cranial nerves in relation to the vascular sinus, internal carotid artery (which loops anteriorly to the section), and surrounding structures.

mor, poliomyelitis, or motor neuron disease), during the course of the nerve in the posterior fossa (platybasia, Paget's disease), or in the hypoglossal canal.

MULTIPLE CRANIAL NERVE PALSIES

The main clinical problem is to determine whether the process is within the brainstem or outside it. Lesions that lie on the surface of the brainstem tend to involve adjacent cranial nerves in succession with only late and slight involvement of long sensory and motor pathways within the brainstem. The opposite is true of processes within the brainstem. Involvement of multiple cranial nerves outside of the brainstem may be due to diabetes, trauma, infectious and noninfectious causes of meningitis; granulomatous diseases including sarcoidosis, tuberculosis, and Wegener's granulomatosis; tumors; and enlarging saccular aneurysms. A purely motor disorder raises a question of myasthenia gravis. *Facial diplegia* is common in Guillain-Barré syndrome. *Ophthalmoplegia* may occur with Guillain-Barré syndrome (Fisher variant) or Wernicke's disease. Involvement of the *cavernous sinus* (Fig. 192-2) may be due to infection, aneurysm, a carotid-cavernous fistula, nasopharyngeal carcinoma, or a granulomatous disease. Finally, an *idiopathic multiple cranial nerve disorder* may occur, consisting of boring unilateral or bilateral facial pain followed by paralysis of motor cranial nerves; inflammation of the dura mater may be visualized by MRI, and treatment is with glucocorticoids.

For a more detailed discussion, see Beal MF, Hauser SL: Common Disorders of the Cranial Nerves, Chap. 367, p. 2421, in HPIM-15.

193

AUTONOMIC NERVOUS SYSTEM DISORDERS

The autonomic nervous system (ANS) regulates homeostatic functions critical to survival including blood pressure, blood flow, tissue perfusion, sweating, hunger, satiety, temperature, thirst, and circadian rhythms. The importance of this regulation is demonstrated by the severity of disability resulting from compromised ANS function.

ANS OVERVIEW

Key features of the ANS are summarized in Table 193-1. Responses to sympathetic (S) or parasympathetic (P) activation often have opposite effects; partial activation of both systems allows for simultaneous integration of multiple body functions.

Catecholamines exert their effects on two types of receptors, α and β. The α_1 receptor mediates vasoconstriction. The α_2 receptor mediates presynaptic inhibition of norepinephrine (NE) release from adrenergic nerves, inhibits acetylcholine (ACh) release from cholinergic nerves, inhibits lipolysis in adipocytes, inhibits insulin secretion, and stimulates platelet aggregation. The β_1 receptor responds to both NE and epinephrine (E) and mediates cardiac stimulation and lipolysis. The β_2 receptor is more responsive to E than NE and mediates vasodilatation and bronchodilation.

DISORDERS OF THE ANS

The CNS, peripheral nervous system, or both may be affected; disorders may be generalized (with or without CNS signs) or focal (Table 193-2). Clinical signs and symptoms are due to interruption of the afferent limb, CNS processing centers, or efferent limb of the reflex arc controlling the autonomic responses. Clinical manifestations are influenced by the organ involved, normal balance of sympathetic-parasympathetic innervation, nature of the underlying illness, and severity/stage of disease. Orthostatic hypotension (OH) is defined as a postural decrease in BP from the supine to standing position of at least 20 mmHg systolic or 10 mmHg diastolic BP sustained for at least 2 min. OH is often disabling. Syncope or near syncope results when the drop in BP impairs cerebral perfusion. Presyncopal symptoms that may appear on standing include light-headedness, dimming of vision, nausea, diminished hearing, hyperhidrosis, hypohidrosis, pallor, and weakness.

Table 193-1

ANS Overview

	Sympathetic NS	Parasympathetic NS
CNS location of preganglionic neurons	C8-L1 cord segments	Brainstem and sacral spinal cord
Neurotransmitter		
Preganglionic	Acetylcholine (ACh)	ACh
Postganglionic	Norepinephrine (NE)[a]	ACh
Mechanism of inactivation	Reuptake	Synaptic cleft metabolism

[a] ACh for sweat glands and adrenal medulla.

Table 193-2

Classification of ANS Disorders

GENERALIZED ANS DISORDERS

With CNS signs
Multiple system atrophy
Spinal cord disorders (MS, tabes dorsalis, trauma, syrinx, hereditary degeneration)
Parkinson's and Huntington's disease
Tumors
Multiple cerebral infarcts
Hypothalamic disorders
Wernicke's encephalopathy
Without CNS signs
Diabetes mellitus
Pure autonomic failure
Guillain-Barré syndrome
Chronic idiopathic anhidrosis
Acute pandysautonomia
Paraneoplastic (sensory neuropathy, enteric neuropathy)
Tangier's and Fabry's disease
Postural orthostatic tachycardia syndrome (POTS)
Raynaud's syndrome
Familial dysautonomia—Riley-Day syndrome
Neuromuscular junction disorders (botulism, LEMS)
Other neuropathies (alcoholism, porphyria, uremia, collagen vascular disease, leprosy, Chagas' disease, HIV, vitamin B_{12} deficiency, etc.)

FOCAL ANS DISORDERS

Reflex sympathetic dystrophy (CRPS I)
Causalgia (CRPS II)
Adie's syndrome
Horner's syndrome
Radiculopathy
Reinnervation anomalies ("Crocodile" tears)

MISCELLANEOUS

Prolonged bed rest or space flight
Advanced age
Dopamine β-hydroxylase deficiency
Monoamine oxidase deficiency

Approach to the Patient

The evaluation of symptomatic OH begins with the exclusion of treatable causes. Most causes of OH are not due to nervous system disease (Table 193-3). In nonneurogenic OH, the drop in blood pressure with standing is usually associated with an appropriate, compensatory rise in heart rate, in contrast to neurogenic OH in which a compensatory rise in heart rate does not occur. History should include a review of medications (e.g., diuretics) and medical problems (e.g., diabetes). Exaggerated medication responses may be the first sign of underlying autonomic disorder. The relationship of symptoms to meals (splanchnic shunting of blood) and awakening in the morning (relative intravascular volume depletion) should be sought. Examination of mental status

Table 193-3

Nonneurogenic Causes of Orthostatic Hypotension

Cardiac pump failure
  Myocardial infarction
  Myocarditis
  Constructive pericarditis
  Aortic stenosis
  Tachyarrhythmias
  Bradyarrhythmias
  Salt-losing nephropathy
  Adrenal insufficiency
  Diabetes insipidus
  Venous obstruction
Reduced intravascular volume
  Straining of heavy lifting, uri-
    nation, defecation
  Dehydration
  Diarrhea, emesis
  Hemorrhage
  Burns
Metabolic
  Adrenocortical insufficiency
  Hypoaldosteronism
  Pheochromocytoma
  Severe potassium depletion

Venous pooling
  Alcohol
  Postprandial dilation of
    splanchnic vessel beds
  Vigorous exercise with dilation
    of skeletal vessel beds
  Heat: hot environment, hot
    showers and baths, fever
  Prolonged recumbancy or
    standing
  Sepsis
Medications
  Antihypertensives
  Diuretics
  Vasodilators: nitrates, hydrala-
    zine
  Alpha- and beta-blocking
    agents
  CNS sedatives: barbiturates,
    opiates
  Tricylic antidepressants
  Phenothiazines

(e.g., neurodegenerative disorders), cranial nerves (e.g., impaired downgaze with progressive supranuclear palsy), motor function (e.g., parkinsonian syndromes), and sensory function (e.g., polyneuropathy) is necessary. Disorders of autonomic function need to be considered in the differential diagnosis of pts with impotence, bladder dysfunction (urinary frequency, hesitancy, or incontinence), diarrhea, constipation, or altered sweating (hyperhidrosis or hypohidrosis).

Autonomic Testing

The most commonly used autonomic tests assess cardiovascular function; they are noninvasive, easy to administer, and provide quantitative information; normative data from healthy controls is essential. Heart rate variation with deep breathing is a measure of vagal function. The Valsalva maneuver measures changes in heart rate and blood pressure while a constant expiratory pressure of 40 mmHg for 15 s is maintained. The Valsalva ratio is calculated as the maximum heart rate during the maneuver divided by the minimum heart rate following the maneuver. The ratio reflects the integrity of the entire baroreceptor reflex arc and sympathetic efferents to blood vessels (Chap. 366, HPIM-15). Tilt-table beat-to-beat BP measurements in the supine, 80° tilt, and tilt-back positions can be used to evaluate orthostatic failure in BP control in pts with unexplained syncope.

    Other tests of autonomic function include the quantitative sudomotor axon reflex test (QSART), the thermoregulatory sweat test (TST), and the cold pressor test. The QSART provides a quantitative, regional measure of sweating in response to iontophoresis of ACh. The TST provides a qualitative measure of regional sweating over the entire anterior surface of the body in response to a standardized elevation of body temperature. The cold pressor test is used to assess sympathetic efferent function. For a more complete discussion of autonomic function tests, see Chap. 366, HPIM-15.

SPECIFIC SYNDROMES OF ANS DYSFUNCTION   Diseases of the CNS may cause ANS dysfunction at the level of the hypothalamus, brainstem, or spinal cord (Table 193-1). *Multiple system atrophy* (MSA) refers to several overlapping CNS syndromes with a variable combination of symptoms and signs including postural hypotension, impotence, bladder and bowel dysfunction, defective sweating, rigidity, tremor, loss of associative movements, upper motor neuron signs, cerebellar signs, or abnormal eye movements. Pts may present with only one symptom or sign and later develop the full clinical spectrum of MSA.

Spinal cord injury may be accompanied by autonomic hyperreflexia affecting bowel, bladder, sexual, temperature regulation, or cardiovascular functions. Dangerous increases or decreases in body temperature may result from the inability to experience the sensory accompaniments of heat or cold exposure below the level of the injury. Markedly increased autonomic discharge (autonomic dysreflexia) can be elicited by bladder pressure or stimulation of the skin or muscles. Bladder distention from palpation, catheter insertion, catheter obstruction, or urinary infection are common and correctable causes of autonomic dysreflexia.

Peripheral neuropathies are the most common cause of *chronic autonomic insufficiency* (Chap. 366, HPIM-15). Autonomic involvement in *diabetes mellitus* may begin at any stage in the disease. Diabetic enteric neuropathy may result in gastroparesis, nausea and vomiting, malnutrition, and bowel incontinence. Impotence, urinary incontinence, pupillary abnormalities, and postural hypotension may occur as well. Prolongation of the QT interval may occur and enhances the risk of sudden death. Autonomic neuropathy occurs in both sporadic and familial forms of *amyloidosis*. Pts may present with distal, painful polyneuropathy. Cardiac or renal disease is the usual cause of death. *Alcoholic polyneuropathy* produces clinical symptoms of autonomic failure only when the signs of peripheral neuropathy are severe. BP fluctuation and cardiac arrhythmias can be severe in *Guillain-Barré syndrome*. Attacks of *acute intermittent porphyria* (AIP) are associated with tachycardia, sweating, urinary retention, and hypertension. *Botulism* is associated with blurred vision, dry mouth, nausea, unreactive pupils, urinary retention, and constipation. *Postural orthostatic tachycardia syndrome* (POTS) consists of symptoms of orthostatic intolerance—including shortness of breath, light-headedness, and exercise intolerance—accompanied by an increase in heart rate but no drop in BP. The importance of postprandial hypotension in healthy elderly persons and hypertensive pts taking BP medications with meals is drawing increasing attention. *Primary hyperhidrosis* affects 0.6–1.0% of the population; the usual symptoms are excessive sweating of the palms and soles. Onset is in adolescence, and symptoms tend to improve with age. Although not dangerous, this condition is socially embarrassing.

REFLEX SYMPATHETIC DYSTROPHY (RSD) AND CAUSALGIA
The role of the ANS in RSD and causalgia is controversial, and there is no generally accepted pathogenic mechanism to explain these disorders. The terms *complex regional pain syndrome* (CRPS) type I and CRPS type II have been proposed as substitutes for the terms *RSD* and *causalgia*, respectively.

In causalgia, spontaneous pain develops within the territory of an injured nerve and may spread outside, but contiguous to, the distribution of the affected nerve. *Allodynia* (the perception of a nonpainful stimulus as painful) and *hyperpathia* (an exaggerated pain response to a mildly painful stimulus) are common. RSD is a regional pain syndrome that develops after trauma. Unlike causalgia, limb symptoms are not confined to the distribution of a single peripheral nerve. Although pain is the primary feature of both causalgia and RSD, vasomotor, sudomotor, or edematous changes must be present to satisfy criteria for diagnosis. Treatment of both disorders is a difficult therapeutic challenge (Chap. 366 in HPIM-15).

℞ **TREATMENT**

Management of autonomic failure is limited typically to alleviating disability caused by symptoms. A review of medications, relationship of symptoms to meals, medical illnesses, and other symptoms of possible autonomic origin is mandatory. Orthostatic hypotension requires treatment only if it causes symptoms. In early stages, pts can maintain normal function by using simple measures. Alcohol use and exposure to elevated temperature should be avoided because vaosdilatation can suddenly lower BP. Drugs that affect BP should be used with great caution. Salt intake should be increased to the maximum tolerated. Sleeping in reverse Trendelenburg position (head-up tilt) minimizes supine hypertension. Frequent, small meals may improve postprandial hypotension. Most pts require drug therapy for the management of neurogenic OH. Fludrocortisone (0.1 mg/d–0.3 mg bid PO) is the initial drug of choice; potassium supplementation is necessary with chronic administration. Midodrine (5 mg tid–10 mg q4h PO) is an α_1 agonist approved by the FDA for treatment of neurogenic OH. Other drugs may be effective for postprandial OH (indomethacin, caffeine), OH associated with diarrhea (clonidine), and OH associated with anemia (erythropoietin). Many agents can be used to elevate BP, but supine hypertension or a lack of symptomatic improvement often limits their value. Management during anesthesia poses unique problems since pts may have abnormal baroreceptor reflexes, sympathetic innervation of peripheral arterioles, abnormal fluid balance, and adrenal medullary insufficiency.

For a more detailed discussion, see Engstrom JW, Martin JB: Disorders of the Autonomic Nervous System, Chap. 366, p. 2416, in HPIM-15.

194

SPINAL CORD DISEASES

Diseases of the spinal cord can be devastating, but many are treatable if recognized early (Table 194-1). A working knowledge of relevant spinal cord anatomy is often the key to correct diagnosis (Fig. 194-1).

Table 194-1

Some Treatable Spinal Cord Disorders

Compressive
  Epidural, intradural, or intramedullary neoplasm
  Epidural abscess
  Epidural hemorrhage
  Cervical spondylosis
  Herniated disc
  Posttraumatic compression by fractured or displaced vertebra or hemorrhage
Vascular
  Arteriovenous malformation
Inflammatory
  Transverse myelitis
  Multiple sclerosis
Infectious
  Viral: Herpes simplex type 2
  Bacterial: Syphilis, tuberculosis, listeria, other
  Parasitic: Schistosomiasis, toxoplasmosis
Developmental
  Syringomyelia
Metabolic
  Subacute combined degeneration

Symptoms and Signs

Principal signs are loss of sensation below a horizontal meridian on the trunk ("sensory level"), accompanied by weakness and spasticity.

Sensory Symptoms Often paresthesia; may begin in one or both feet and ascend. Sensory level to pin sensation or vibration often correlates well with location of transverse lesions. May have isolated pain/temperature sensation loss over the shoulders ("cape" or "syringomyelic" pattern) or loss of sensation to vibration/position on one side of the body and pain/temperature loss on the other (Brown-Séquard hemicord syndrome).

Motor Impairment Disruption of corticospinal tracts causes quadriplegia or paraplegia with increased muscle tone, hyperactive deep tendon reflexes, and extensor plantar responses. With acute severe lesions there may be initial flaccidity and areflexia (spinal shock).

Segmental Signs These are approximate indicators of level of lesion, e.g., band of hyperalgesia/hyperpathia, isolated flaccidity, atrophy, or single lost tendon reflex.

Autonomic Dysfunction Primarily urinary retention; should raise suspicion of spinal cord disease when associated with back or neck pain, weakness, and/or a sensory level.

Pain Midline back pain is of localizing value; interscapular pain may be first sign of midthoracic cord compression; radicular pain may mark site of more laterally placed spinal lesion; pain from lower cord (conus medullaris) lesion may be referred to low back.

Specific Signs by Spinal Cord Level

Lesions Near the Foramen Magnum Weakness of the ipsilateral shoulder and arm, followed by weakness of ipsilateral leg, then contralateral leg, then contralateral arm, with respiratory paralysis.

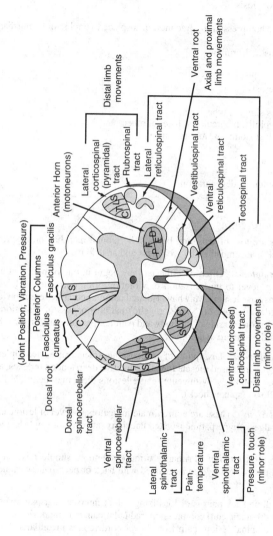

FIGURE 194-1 Transverse section through the spinal cord, composite representation, illustrating the principal ascending (*left*) and descending (*right*) pathways. The lateral and ventral spinothalamic tracts (*dark blue*) ascend contralateral to the side of the body that is innervated. C, cervical; T, thoracic; L, lumbar; S, sacral; P, proximal; D, distal; F, flexors; E, extensors.

Posterior Columns
(Joint Position, Vibration, Pressure)

Fasciculus cuneatus

Fasciculus gracilis

Anterior Horn (motoneurons)

Lateral corticospinal (pyramidal) tract

Rubrospinal tract

Lateral reticulospinal tract

Distal limb movements

Vestibulospinal tract

Ventral reticulospinal tract

Ventral root

Axial and proximal limb movements

Tectospinal tract

Dorsal root

Dorsal spinocerebellar tract

Ventral spinocerebellar tract

Lateral spinothalamic tract

Pain, temperature

Ventral spinothalamic tract

Pressure, touch (minor role)

Ventral (uncrossed) corticospinal tract

Distal limb movements (minor role)

888

Cervical Cord   Best localized by noting pattern of motor weakness and areflexia; shoulder (C5), biceps (C5-6), brachioradialis (C6), triceps/finger and wrist extensors (C7), finger flexors (C8).

Thoracic Cord   Localized by identification of a sensory level on the trunk.

Lumbar Cord   Upper lumbar cord lesions paralyze hip flexion and knee extension, whereas lower lumbar lesions affect foot and ankle movements, knee flexion, and thigh extension.

Sacral Cord (Conus Medullaris)   Saddle anesthesia and early bladder/bowel/sexual dysfunction.

Cauda Equina   Lesions below spinal cord termination at the L1 vertebral level produce a flaccid, areflexic, asymmetric paraparesis with bladder/bowel dysfunction and sensory loss below L1; pain is common and projected to perineum or thighs.

Intramedullary and Extramedullary Syndromes

Spinal cord disorders may be intramedullary (arising from within the substance of the cord) or extramedullary (compressing the cord or its blood supply). Extramedullary lesions often produce radicular pain, early corticospinal signs, and sacral sensory loss. Intramedullary lesions produce poorly localized burning pain, less prominent corticospinal signs, and often spare perineal/sacral sensation.

Acute and Subacute Spinal Cord Diseases

Commonly due to spinal cord compression (by tumor, infection, spondylosis, or trauma), infarction or hemorrhage, inflammation, or infection. Evaluation consists of MRI scans that provide excellent resolution of the spinal cord and identify most compressive lesions. Plain x-rays or CT of spine may be useful to assess presence of fractures and alignment of vertebral column. CSF analysis useful for infectious and inflammatory processes.

1. *Tumors of spinal cord*: May be metastatic or primary, epidural or intradural; most are epidural metastases from adjacent vertebra. Malignancies commonly responsible: breast, lung, prostate, lymphoma, and plasma cell dyscrasias. Initial symptom is commonly back pain, worse when recumbent, with local tenderness preceding other symptoms by many weeks. Spinal cord compression due to metastases is a medical emergency; in general, therapy will not reverse paralysis of >48 h duration. Treatment consists of glucocorticoids (dexamethasone 40 mg daily) to reduce interstitial edema, local radiotherapy initiated as early as possible to the symptomatic lesion, and specific therapy for the underlying tumor type. Intradural tumors are generally benign—meningiomas or neurofibromas; treatment is surgical resection.

2. *Spinal epidural abscess*: Triad of fever, localized spinal pain, and myelopathy (progressive weakness and bladder symptoms); once neurologic signs appear, cord compression rapidly progresses. Treatment is emergency decompressive laminectomy with debridement combined with long-term antibiotic therapy.

3. *Spinal epidural hemorrhage and hematomyelia*: Presents as acute transverse myelopathy evolving over minutes or hours with severe pain. Causes: minor trauma, LP, anticoagulation, hematologic disorder, AV malformation, hemorrhage into tumor—most are idiopathic. Treatment is surgical evacuation and correction of any underlying bleeding disorder.

4. *Acute disk protrusion*: Cervical and thoracic disk herniations are less common than lumbar.

5.   *Acute trauma with spinal fracture/dislocation*: May not produce myelopathy until mechanical stress further displaces destabilized spinal column.

6.   *Inflammatory myelopathies*: Acute transverse myelitis presents as sensory and motor symptoms, often with bladder involvement, evolving over hours to days. May follow infection, vaccination, or be the first sign of multiple sclerosis. Glucocorticoids, consisting of IV methylprednisolone followed by oral prednisone (Chap. 187), are indicated for moderate to severe symptoms. Rarely, a rapidly ascending necrotic myelopathy may occur as a paraneoplastic syndrome.

7.   *Infectious myelopathies*: Herpes zoster is the most common viral agent; schistosomiasis is an important cause worldwide.

8.   *Spinal cord infarction*: Anterior spinal artery infarction produces paraplegia or quadriplegia, dissociated sensory loss affecting pain/temperature and sparing vibration/position sensations (supplied by posterior spinal arteries), and loss of sphincter control. Associated conditions: aortic atherosclerosis, dissecting aortic aneurysm, hypotension. Treatment is symptomatic.

Chronic Myelopathies

1.   *Spondylitic myelopathies*: Presents as neck and shoulder pain, radicular arm pain, and progressive spastic paraparesis with paresthesia and loss of vibration sense; in advanced cases, urinary incontinence may occur. Results from combinations of disk bulging, osteophytic spur formation, partial subluxation, and hypertrophy of the dorsal spinal ligament. Treatment is surgical (Chap. 5).

2.   *Vascular malformations*: An important treatable cause of progressive myelopathy. May occur at any level; diagnosis is made by contrast-enhanced MRI, confirmed by selective spinal angiography. Treatment is embolization with occlusion of the major feeding vessels.

3.   *Retrovirus-associated myelopathies*: Infection with HTLV-I or HTLV-II may produce a slowly progressive spastic paraparesis with variable pain, sensory loss, and bladder disturbance; diagnosis is made by demonstration of specific serum antibody. Treatment is symptomatic. A progressive vacuolar myelopathy may also occur in AIDS.

4.   *Syringomyelia*: Cavitary expansion of the spinal cord resulting in progressive myelopathy; may be an isolated finding or associated with protrusion of cerebellar tonsils into cervical spinal canal (Chiari type 1) or with incomplete closure of spinal canal (Chiari type 2). Classic presentation is loss of pain/temperature sensation in the neck, shoulders, forearms, or hands with areflexic weakness in the upper limbs and progressive spastic paraparesis; cough headache, facial numbness, or thoracic kyphoscoliosis may occur. Diagnosis is made by MRI; treatment is surgical.

5.   *Multiple sclerosis*: See Chap. 187.

6.   *Subacute combined degeneration (vitamin B_{12} deficiency)*: Paresthesia in hands and feet, early loss of vibration/position sense, progressive spastic/ataxic weakness, and areflexia due to associated peripheral neuropathy; mental changes ("megaloblastic madness") may be present. Diagnosis is confirmed by a low serum B_{12} level and a positive Schilling test. Treatment is vitamin replacement.

7.   *Tabes dorsalis*: May present as lancinating pains, gait ataxia, bladder disturbances, and visceral crises. Cardinal signs are areflexia in the legs, impaired vibration/position sense, Romberg's sign, and Argyll Robertson pupils, which fail to constrict to light but react to accommodation.

8.   *Familial spastic paraplegia*: Progressive spasticity and weakness in the legs occurring on a familial basis; may be autosomal dominant, recessive, or X-linked.

Complications

Damage to urinary tract due to urinary retention with bladder distention and injury to detrusor muscle; UTI; paroxysmal hypertension or hypotension with volume changes; ileus and gastritis; in high cervical cord lesions, mechanical respiratory failure; severe hypertension and bradycardia in response to noxious stimuli or bladder or bowel distention; pressure sores; venous thrombosis and pulmonary embolism.

For a more detailed discussion, see Hauser SL: Diseases of the Spinal Cord, Chap. 368, p. 2425, in HPIM-15.

195

PERIPHERAL NEUROPATHIES INCLUDING GUILLAIN-BARRÉ SYNDROME

Peripheral neuropathy (PN) refers to a peripheral nerve disorder of any cause. Nerve involvement may be single (mononeuropathy) or multiple (polyneuropathy); pathology may be axonal or demyelinating. An approach to pts with suspected neuropathy appears in Fig. 195-1.

POLYNEUROPATHY

CLINICAL FEATURES The typical axonal polyneuropathy begins with sensory symptoms (tingling or burning) distally in the toes or feet. Symptoms spread proximally to the ankles, then involve the calves. Ankle reflexes are lost. Once sensory loss reaches the knees, proximal spread extends into the thighs and numbness of fingers appears. This pattern results in a "stocking-glove" distribution of sensory and motor findings. Further progression results in loss of knee reflexes. Light touch may be perceived as uncomfortable (allodynia) or pinprick as excessively painful (hyperpathia). Weakness and atrophy evolve from distal to proximal—initial toe dorsiflexion weakness may progress to bilateral foot drop, intrinsic hand muscle weakness, or (in extreme cases) impairment of muscles needed for ventilation and sphincter function. A family history for neuropathy should be sought, since adult-onset hereditary motor and sensory neuropathy (HMSN II) is not uncommon. In contrast to axonal neuropathy, demyelinating neuropathy does not produce stocking-glove deficits; diffuse loss of reflexes and strength is usual, and nerves are often palpably enlarged.

DIAGNOSTIC EVALUATION Diagnosis is aided by classification into axonal or demyelinating pathology (Table 195-1) and consideration of the time course of the neuropathy (Table 195-2). EMG is particularly helpful when history and examination do not clarify the diagnosis. EMG can distinguish axonal from demyelinating neuropathy, neuropathy from myopathy, nerve root or plexus disorders from distal nerve involvement, generalized polyneuropathy

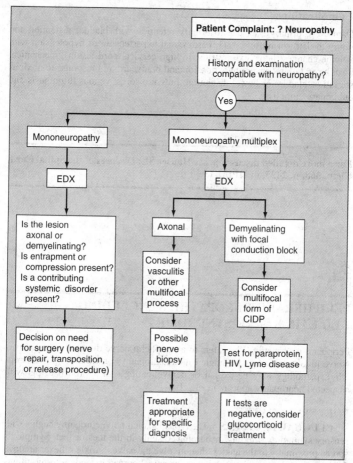

FIGURE 195-1 Approach to the evaluation of peripheral neuropathies, CIDP, chronic inflammatory demyelinating polyradiculoneuropathy; EDX, electrodiagnostic studies; GBS, Guillain-Barré syndrome; IVIg, intravenous immunoglobulin. (*After AK Asbury, in Harrison's Textbook of Internal Medicine, Update IV, New York, McGraw-Hill, 1983.*)

from mononeuropathy multiplex, and central weakness from peripheral nerve weakness. Sural nerve biopsy is helpful when vasculitis, multifocal demyelination, amyloidosis, leprosy, or sarcoidosis are considerations; biopsy results in lateral foot sensory loss, and rarely a painful neuroma may form at the biopsy site. Screening laboratory studies in a distal, symmetric axonal polyneuropathy are Hb A_{1C}, ESR, serum protein/immunoelectrophoresis, and vitamin B_{12}, BUN, and creatinine levels. Other studies are suggested by the differential diagnosis; it is important to recall that many systemic diseases, drugs, and toxins can produce neuropathy.

SPECIFIC POLYNEUROPATHIES

1. *Acute inflammatory demyelinating polyneuropathy (AIDP) or Guillain-Barré syndrome (GBS)*: an ascending, usually demyelinating, motor > sensory

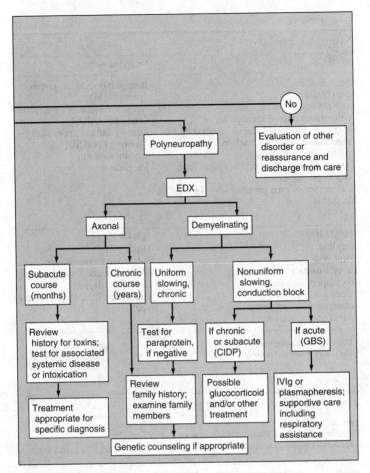

FIGURE 195-1 *(continued)*

Table 195-1

Polyneuropathies (PN)*a*

Axonal	Demyelinative
ACQUIRED	
Diabetes	Diabetes
Uremia	Carcinoma
B_{12} deficiency	HIV infection
Critical illness	Lymphoma
HIV infection	Multiple myeloma

(continued)

Table 195-1 *(Continued)*

Polyneuropathies (PN)[a]

Axonal	Demyelinative
Lyme disease	Benign monoclonal gammo-pathy (IgM)
Lymphoma	
Multiple myeloma	Acute inflammatory demyelin-ating PN (AIDP)
Acute motor axonal neuropathy	
Drugs: cisplatin, hydralazine, isoniazid, metronidazole, nitrofurantoin, phenytoin, pyridoxine, vincristine	Chronic inflammatory demye-linating PN (CIDP)
Toxins: arsenic, thallium, inorganic lead, organophosphates	Diphtheria toxin
Benign monoclonal gammopathy (IgA, IgG)	Idiopathic
Idiopathic	

HEREDITARY

HMSN II[b]	HMSN I
Amyloid	HMSN III
Porphyria	Adrenomyeloneuropathy
Fabry's disease	Metachromatic leukodystrophy
Abetalipoproteinemia	Refsum's disease
Friedreich's ataxia	Hereditary liability to pressure palsies
Adrenomyeloneuropathy	
Ataxia telangiectasia	

[a] Does not include rare causes.
[b] Hereditary motor and sensory neuropathy

Table 195-2

Diagnostic Considerations in Polyneuropathy

Type of Polyneuropathy	Time Course	Causes
AXONAL		
Acute	Days to weeks	Massive intoxications (arsenic; inhalants); porphyria; Guillain-Barré syndrome
Subacute	Weeks to months	Usually toxic or metabolic; eliminate toxins and treat underlying systemic disorder
Chronic	Months to years	<5 years, consider toxic or metabolic; >5 years, hereditary, diabetic, dysproteinemic causes
DEMYELINATIVE		
Acute	Days to weeks	Guillain-Barré syndrome; rarely diptheria or buckthorn berry intoxication
Subacute	Weeks to months	CIDP; rarely toxins listed above plus auro-thioglucose or taxol
Chronic	Months to years	Many possibilities including hereditary; inflammatory; dysproteinemias; other metabolic or toxic causes

NOTE: CIDP, chronic inflammatory demyelinating polyneuropathy.

Table 195-3

Common Mononeuropathies—Findings and Treatment

	Median	Ulnar	Common Peroneal
Site	Wrist—carpal tunnel	Elbow—cubital tunnel or condylar groove	Knee—fibular head
Sensory loss	Lateral palm: 1st–3rd finger ± 4th finger	Medial palm: 5th ± 4th finger	Dorsal foot Lateral calf
Motor weakness	Thumb abduction Thumb opposition	Index finger abduction 5th finger abduction	Foot dorsiflexion Foot aversion
Conservative Rx	Wrist splint, NSAIDs	Elbow pad Avoid elbow trauma	Avoid direct compression
Surgical Rx	Transverse carpal ligament section	Cubital tunnel release; ulnar nerve transposition	—

polyneuropathy accompanied by areflexia, motor paralysis, and elevated CSF total protein without pleocytosis. Over two-thirds are preceded by infection with EBV or other herpesviruses, *Campylobacter jejuni* gastroenteritis, HIV, other viruses, or *Mycoplasma*. Maximum weakness is usually reached within 2 weeks; demyelination by EMG. Most pts are hospitalized; one-third require ventilatory assistance. 85% make a complete or near-complete recovery with supportive care. Intravenous immune globulin (IVIg) (2 g/kg given over 5 d) or plasma-pheresis (40–50 mL/kg daily for 4–5 d) significantly shorten the course. Glucocorticoids are ineffective. Variants of GBS include Fisher syndrome (ophthalmoparesis, facial diplegia, ataxia, areflexia; associated with antibodies to ganglioside GQ1b) and acute motor axonal neuropathy (more severe course than demyelinating GBS; antibodies to GM_1 in some cases).

2. *Chronic inflammatory demyelinating polyneuropathy (CIDP)*: a slowly progressive or relapsing polyneuropathy characterized by diffuse hyporeflexia or areflexia, diffuse weakness, elevated CSF protein without pleocytosis, and demyelination by EMG. Begin treatment when progression is rapid or walking is compromised. Initial treatment is usually IVIg; most pts require periodic retreatment at 6-week intervals. Other treatment options include plasmapheresis or glucocorticoids; immunosuppressants (azothiaprine, methotrexate, cyclophosphamide) used in refractory cases.

3. *Diabetic neuropathy*: typically a distal symmetric, sensorimotor, axonal polyneuropathy, but many variations occur. A mixture of demyelination and axonal loss is frequent. Isolated sixth or third cranial nerve palsies, asymmetric proximal motor neuropathy in the legs, truncal neuropathy, autonomic neuropathy, and an increased frequency of entrapment neuropathy at common sites of nerve compression all occur.

4. *Mononeuropathy multiplex (MM)*: defined as involvement of multiple noncontiguous nerves. One-third of adults with MM have an acquired demyelinating disorder that is treatable. The remainder have an axonal disorder; 50% of these have vasculitis—usually due to a connective tissue disorder. In this latter group, immunosuppressive treatment of the underlying disease is indicated.

MONONEUROPATHY

CLINICAL FEATURES Mononeuropathies are usually caused by trauma, compression, or entrapment. Sensory and motor symptoms are in the distribution of a single nerve—most commonly ulnar or median nerves in the arms or peroneal nerve in the leg. Clinical features favoring conservative management of median neuropathy at the wrist (carpal tunnel syndrome) or ulnar neuropathy at the elbow include sudden onset, no motor deficit, few or no sensory findings (pain or paresthesia may be present), and no evidence of axonal loss by EMG. Factors favoring surgical decompression include chronic course (lack of response to conservative treatment), motor deficit, and electrodiagnostic evidence of axonal loss. Patterns of weakness, sensory loss, and conservative/surgical treatment options are listed in Table 195-3.

For a more detailed discussion, see Asbury AK: Approach to the Patient With Peripheral Neuropathy, Chap. 377, p. 2498; and Asbury AK, Hauser SL: Guillain-Barré Syndrome and Other Immune-Mediated Neuropathies, Chap. 378, p. 2507, in HPIM-15.

196

MYASTHENIA GRAVIS (MG)

An autoimmune neuromuscular disorder resulting in weakness and fatiguability of skeletal muscles, due to autoantibodies directed against acetylcholine receptors (AChRs) at neuromuscular junctions (NMJs).

Clinical Features

May present at any age. Symptoms fluctuate throughout the day and are provoked by exertion. Characteristic distribution: cranial muscles (lids, extraocular muscles, facial weakness, "nasal" or slurred speech, dysphagia); in 85%, limb muscles (often proximal and asymmetric) become involved. Reflexes and sensation normal. May be limited to extraocular muscles only—particularly in elderly. Complications: aspiration pneumonia (weak bulbar muscles), respiratory failure (weak chest wall muscles), exacerbation of myasthenia due to administration of drugs with neuromuscular junction blocking effects (tetracycline, aminoglycosides, procainamide, propranolol, phenothiazines, lithium).

Pathophysiology

Specific anti-AChR antibodies reduce the number of AChRs at the NMJ. Postsynaptic folds are flattened or "simplified," with resulting inefficient neuromuscular transmission. During repeated or sustained muscle contraction, decrease in amount of ACh released per nerve impulse, combined with decrease in postsynaptic AChRs, results in pathologic fatigue. Thymus is abnormal in 75% of pts (65% hyperplasia, 10% thymoma). Other autoimmune diseases in 10%; thyroiditis, Graves' disease, rheumatoid arthritis, lupus erythematosus, red cell aplasia.

Differential Diagnosis

1. Lambert-Eaton syndrome (autoantibodies to calcium channels in presynaptic motor nerve terminals)—reduced ACh release; associated with malignancy or idiopathic
2. Neurasthenia—weakness/fatigue without underlying organic disorder
3. Penicillamine may cause MG; resolves weeks to months after discontinuing drug
4. Hyperthyroidism
5. Botulism—toxin inhibits presynaptic ACh release
6. Intracranial mass lesion—compression of nerves to extraocular muscles
7. Progressive external ophthalmoplegia—seen in mitochondrial disorders

Laboratory Evaluation

- AChR antibodies—no correlation with disease severity; 80% of all MG patients positive; 50% with ocular findings only are positive; positive antibodies are diagnostic.
- Tensilon (edrophonium) test—a short-acting anticholinesterase—look for rapid and transient improvement of strength; false-positive (placebo response, motor neuron disease) and false-negative tests occur.
- EMG—low frequency (2–4 Hz) repetitive stimulation produces decrement in amplitude of evoked motor responses.
- Chest CT/MRI—search for thymoma.

- Consider thyroid and other studies (e.g., ANA) for associated autoimmune disease.

 TREATMENT

(See Fig. 196-1) The anticholinesterase drug pyridostigmine (Mestinon) titrated to assist pt with functional activities (chewing, swallowing, strength during exertion); usual initial dose of 60 mg 3–5 times daily; long-acting tablets help at night. Muscarinic side effects (diarrhea, abdominal cramps,

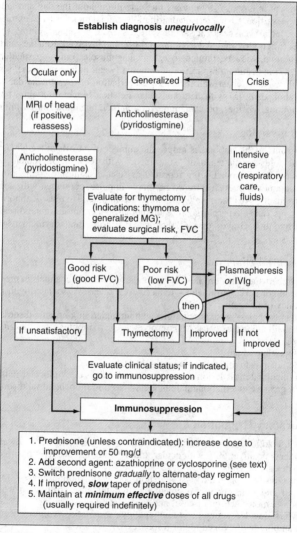

FIGURE 196-1 Algorithm for the management of myasthenia gravis. FVC, forced vital capacity. *(From DM Drachman: HPIM-15, p. 2518)*

salivation, nausea) blocked with propantheline if required. Plasmapheresis and IV immune globulin [IVIg; 400 (mg/kg)/d × 5 d] provide temporary boost for seriously ill pts; used to improve condition prior to surgery or during myasthenic crisis (severe exacerbation of weakness). Thymectomy improves likelihood of long-term remission in adult (less consistently in elderly) pts. Glucocorticoids are a mainstay of treatment; begin prednisone at low dose (15–25 mg/d), increase by 5 mg/d q2–3 d until marked clinical improvement or dose of 50 mg/d is reached. Maintain high dose for 1–3 months, then decrease to alternate-day regimen. Long-term treatment with low-dose prednisone usual. Immunosuppressive drugs (azathioprine, cyclosporine, mycophenolate mofetil, cyclophosphamide) may spare dose of prednisone required to control symptoms; azathioprine [2–3 (mg/kg)/d] most often used. Myasthenic crisis is defined as an exacerbation of weakness, usually with respiratory failure, sufficient to endanger life; expert management in an intensive care setting essential.

For a more detailed discussion, see Drachman DB: Myasthenia Gravis and Other Diseases of the Neuromuscular Junction, Chap. 380, p. 2515, in HPIM-15.

197

MUSCLE DISEASES

Muscle diseases usually present as intermittent or persistent weakness. These disorders are usually painless; however, *myalgias*, or muscle pains, may occur. Myalgias must be distinguished from *muscle cramps*, i.e., painful muscle contractions, usually due to neurogenic disorders. A *muscle contracture* due to an inability to relax after an active muscle contraction is associated with energy failure in glycolytic disorders. *Myotonia* is a condition of prolonged muscle contraction followed by slow muscle relaxation. It is important to distinguish between true muscle weakness and a complaint of fatigue; fatigue without abnormal clinical or laboratory findings almost never indicates a true muscle disorder. An approach to pts with muscle weakness is summarized in Figs. 197-1 and 197-2.

MUSCULAR DYSTROPHIES

A group of inherited, progressive degenerations of muscle that vary widely in their clinical and pathologic features and mode of inheritance.

Duchenne Dystrophy

X-linked recessive mutation of the dystrophin gene that affects males almost exclusively. Onset is by age 5; symmetric and progressive weakness in hip and shoulder girdle muscles leading to difficulty in climbing, running, jumping, hopping, etc. By age 8–10, most children require leg braces; by age 12, the

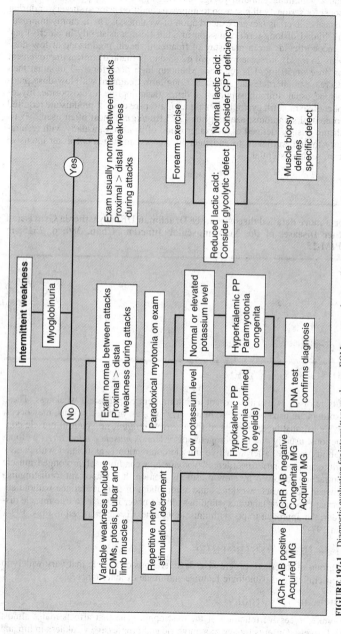

FIGURE 197-1 Diagnostic evaluation for intermittent weakness. EOMs, extraocular muscles; AChR AB, acetylcholine receptor antibody; PP, periodic paralysis; CPT, carnitine palmityl transferase; MG, myasthenia gravis.

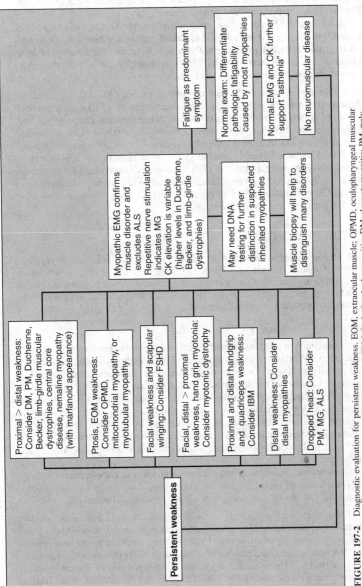

FIGURE 197-2 Diagnostic evaluation for persistent weakness. EOM, extraocular muscle; OPMD, oculopharyngeal muscular dystrophy; FSHD, facioscapulohumeral muscular dystrophy; IBM, inclusion body myositis; DM, dermatomyositis; PM, polymyositis; MG, myasthenia gravis, ALS, amyotrophic lateral sclerosis; CK, creatine kinase.

majority are nonambulatory. Survival beyond age 25 is rare. Becker dystrophy is a less severe form, with a slower course and later age of onset (5–15) but similar clinical, laboratory, and genetic features.

Associated problems include tendon and muscle contractures (e.g., heel cords), progressive kyphoscoliosis, impaired pulmonary function, cardiomyopathy, and intellectual impairment. Palpable enlargement and firmness of some muscles (e.g., calves) results initially from hypertrophy and later from replacement of muscle by fat and connective tissue.

Laboratory Findings   Include massive elevations (20–100 × normal) of muscle enzymes (CK, aldolase), a myopathic pattern on EMG testing, and evidence of groups of necrotic muscle fibers with regeneration, phagocytosis, and fatty replacement of muscle on biopsy. Diagnosis is established by determination of dystrophin in muscle tissue by western blot and/or immunochemical staining. Mutations in the dystrophin gene can be identified in approximately two-thirds of pts using a battery of cDNA probes. ECG abnormalities (increased net RS in V_1, deep Q in precordial leads) reflect the presence of cardiomyopathy. Serum CK is elevated in 50% of female carriers. Testing is now available for detecting carriers and prenatal diagnosis.

 TREATMENT

Glucocorticoids [prednisone, 0.75 (mg/kg)/d] may significantly alter progression of disease for up to 3 years, but complications of chronic use often outweigh the benefits. Passive stretching of muscles, tenotomy, bracing, physiotherapy, mechanical assistance devices, and avoidance of prolonged immobility provide symptomatic benefit.

Myotonic Dystrophy

The most common adult muscular dystrophy. Autosomal dominant with genetic anticipation. Weakness typically becomes obvious in the second to third decade and initially involves the muscles of the face, neck, and distal extremities. This results in a distinctive facial appearance ("hatchet face") characterized by ptosis, temporal wasting, drooping of the lower lip, and sagging of the jaw. Myotonia manifests as a peculiar inability to relax muscles rapidly following a strong exertion (e.g., after tight hand grip), as well as by sustained contraction of muscles following percussion (e.g., of tongue or thenar eminence).

Associated problems can include frontal baldness, posterior subcapsular cataracts, gonadal atrophy, respiratory and cardiac problems, endocrine abnormalities, intellectual impairment, and hypersomnia. Cardiac complications, including complete heart block, may be life-threatening. Respiratory function should be carefully followed, as chronic hypoxia may lead to cor pulmonale.

Laboratory Studies   Normal or mildly elevated CK, characteristic myotonia and myopathic features on EMG, and a typical pattern of muscle fiber injury on biopsy, including selective type I fiber atrophy. Pts have an unstable region of DNA with an increased number of trinucleotide CTG repeats at chromosome location 19q13.3. The expanded repeat may alter expression of a nearby protein kinase gene. Genetic testing for early detection and prenatal diagnosis is possible.

 TREATMENT

Phenytoin, procainamide, and quinine may help myotonia, but they must be used carefully in pts with heart disease as they may worsen cardiac conduction. Pacemaker insertion may be required for syncope or heart block. Orthoses may control foot drop, stabilize the ankle, and decrease falling.

Facioscapulohumeral Dystrophy

An autosomal dominant, slowly progressive disorder with onset in the third to fourth decade. Weakness involves facial, shoulder girdle, and proximal arm muscles and can result in atrophy of biceps, triceps, scapular winging, and slope shoulders. Facial weakness results in inability to whistle and loss of facial expressivity. Foot drop and leg weakness may cause falls and progressive difficulty with ambulation.

Laboratory Studies Normal or slightly elevated CK and mixed myopathic-neuropathic features on EMG and muscle biopsy. Pts have deletions at chromosome 4q35. A genetic probe can be used in carrier detection and prenatal diagnosis. Orthoses and other stabilization procedures may be of benefit for selected pts.

Limb-Girdle Dystrophy

A constellation of diseases with proximal muscle weakness involving the arms and legs as the core symptom. Age of onset, rate of progression, severity of manifestations, inheritance pattern (autosomal dominant or autosomal recessive) and associated complications (e.g., cardiac, respiratory) vary with the specific subtype of disease. Laboratory findings include elevated CK and myopathic features on EMG and muscle biopsy. At least eight autosomal recessive forms have been identified by molecular genetic analysis.

Oculopharyngeal Dystrophy (Progressive External Ophthalmoplegia)

Onset in the fifth to sixth decade of ptosis, limitation of extraocular movements, and facial and cricopharyngeal weakness. Most patients are Hispanic or of French-Canadian descent.

INFLAMMATORY MYOPATHIES

The most common group of acquired and potentially treatable skeletal muscle disorders. Three major forms: polymyositis (PM), dermatomyositis (DM), and inclusion body myositis (IBM). Usually present as progressive and symmetric muscle weakness; extraocular muscles spared but pharyngeal weakness and neck drop common. IBM is characterized by early involvement of quadriceps and distal muscles. Progression is over weeks or months in PM and DM, but typically over years in IBM. Skin involvement in DM may consist of a heliotrope rash (blue-purple discoloration) on the upper eyelids with edema, a flat red rash on the face and upper trunk, or erythema over knuckles. A variety of cancers, including ovarian, breast, melanoma, and colon cancer, are associated with DM. Diagnostic criteria are summarized in Table 197-1.

℞ **TREATMENT**

Often effective for PM and DM but not for IBM. Step 1: Glucocorticoids [prednisone, 1 (mg/kg)/d for 3–4 weeks, then tapered very gradually]; step 2: Azathioprine [up to 3 (mg/kg)/d] or methotrexate (7.5 mg/week gradually increasing to 25 mg/week); step 3: Intravenous immunoglobulin (2 g/kg divided over 2–5 d); step 4: Cyclosporine, chlorambucil, cyclophosphamide, or mycophenolate mofetil. IBM is generally resistant to immunosuppressive

Table 197-1

Criteria for Definite Diagnosis of Inflammatory Myopathies

Criterion	Polymyositis	Dermatomyositis	Inclusion Body Myositis
Muscle strength	Myopathic muscle weakness[a]	Myopathic muscle weakness[a,b]	Myopathic muscle weakness with early involvement of distal muscles[a]
Electromyographic findings	Myopathic	Myopathic	Myopathic with mixed potentials
Muscle enzymes	Elevated (up to 50-fold)	Elevated (up to 50-fold) or normal	Elevated (up to 10-fold) or normal
Muscle biopsy findings[c]	Diagnostic[d,e]	Diagnostic or nonspecific	Diagnostic[d,f]
Rash or calcinosis	Absent	Present and diagnostic[d,g]	Absent

[a] Myopathic muscle weakness, affecting proximal muscles more than distal ones and sparing eye and facial muscles, is characterized by a subacute onset (weeks to months) and rapid progression in patients who have no family history of neuromuscular disease, no endocrinopathy, no exposure to myotoxic drugs or toxins, and no biochemical muscle disease (excluded on the basis of muscle-biopsy findings).

[b] In some cases with the typical rash, the muscle strength is seemingly normal (*dermatomyositis sine myositis*); these patients often have new onset of easy fatigue and reduced endurance. Careful muscle testing may reveal mild muscle weakness.

[c] See HPIM 15, Chap. 382, for details.

[d] An adequate trial of prednisone or other immunosuppressive drugs is warranted in probable cases. If, in retrospect, the disease is unresponsive to therapy, another muscle biopsy should be considered to exclude other diseases or possible evolution in inclusion body myositis.

[e] Probable polymyositis is present if muscle biopsy shows nonspecific myopathy without inflammation.

[f] Probable inclusion body myositis is present if muscle biopsy shows chronic nonspecific myopathy with inflammation but no vacuoles.

[g] If rash is absent but muscle biopsy findings are characteristic of dermatomyositis, diagnosis is definite.

therapies; many experts recommend a short trial of glucocorticoids together with azathioprine or methotrexate.

METABOLIC MYOPATHIES

These disorders result from abnormalities in utilization by muscle of glucose or fatty acids as sources of energy. Pts present with either an acute syndrome of myalgia, myolysis, and myoglobinuria or chronic progressive muscle weakness. Definitive diagnosis requires biochemical-enzymatic studies of biopsied muscle. However, muscle enzymes, EMG, and muscle biopsy are all typically abnormal and may suggest specific disorders.

Glycogen storage disorders can mimic muscular dystrophy or polymyositis. In some types the presentation is one of episodic muscle cramps and fatigue provoked by exercise. The ischemic forearm lactate test is helpful as normal postexercise rise in serum lactic acid does not occur. In adults, progressive muscle weakness beginning in the third or fourth decade can be due to the adult form of *acid maltase deficiency*, or *debranching enzyme deficiency*. Exercise intolerance with recurrent myoglobinuria may be due to *myophosphorylase deficiency* (McArdle's disease) or *phosphofructokinase deficiency*. Disorders of fatty acid metabolism present with similar clinical picture. In adults, the most common cause is *carnitine palmitoyltransferase deficiency*. Exercise-induced cramps, myolysis, and myoglobinuria are common; the picture can resemble polymyositis or muscular dystrophy. Some pts benefit from special diets (medium-chain triglyceride-enriched), oral carnitine supplements, or glucocorticoids.

MITOCHONDRIAL MYOPATHIES

More accurately referred to as *mitochondrial cytopathies* because multiple tissues are usually affected, these disorders result from defects in mitochondrial DNA. The clinical presentations vary enormously: muscle symptoms may include weakness, ophthalmoparesis, pain, stiffness, or may even be absent; age of onset ranges from infancy to adulthood; associated clinical presentations include ataxia, encephalopathy, seizures, strokelike episodes, and recurrent vomiting. The characteristic finding on muscle biopsy is "ragged red fibers," which are muscle fibers with accumulations of abnormal mitochondria. Genetics show a maternal pattern of inheritance because mitochondrial genes are inherited almost exclusively from the oocyte.

PERIODIC PARALYSES

Characterized by muscle stiffness due to electrical irritability of the muscle membrane (*myotonia*), usually without significant muscle weakness until late in the course. Onset is usually in childhood or adolescence. Episodes typically

Table 197-2

Toxic Myopathies

Distribution	Clinical Features	Compound
Generalized	Myotonia	Propranolol, cyclosporine, iodides, clofibrate
	Inflamation	Cimetidine, penicillamine, procainamide
	Weakness, myalgias, rhabdomyolysis, myoglobinuria, high serum CK	Chloroquine, clofibrate, gemfibrozil, lovastatin, simvastatin, pravastatin, niacin, colchicine, cyclosporine, emetine, ε-aminocaproic acid, glucocorticoids, labetalol, perhexilline, propranolol, vincristine, zidovudine, alcohol, amphetamine, barbiturates, cocaine, heroin, phencyclidine
	Malignant hyperthermia	Ethyl chloride, ethylene, diethyl ether, gallamine, halothane, lidocaine, mepivacaine, methoxylflurane, trichloroethylene, succinylcholine
Focal	Possible focal weakness, myalgia	Pentazocine, meperidine, heroin

occur after rest or sleep, often following earlier exercise. May be due to genetic disorders of calcium (hypokalemic periodic paralysis), sodium (hyperkalemic period paralysis), or chloride channels. Acute attacks of hypokalemic periodic paralysis are treated with potassium chloride, and prophylaxis with acetazolamide (125–1000 mg/d in divided doses) or dichorphenamide (50–200 mg/d) is usually effective.

MISCELLANEOUS DISORDERS

Myopathies may be associated with endocrine disorders, especially those involving hypo- or hyperfunction of the thyroid, parathyroid, pituitary, and adrenal glands. Drugs (esp. glucocorticoids) and certain toxins (e.g., alcohol) are commonly associated with myopathies (Table 197-2), as are deficiencies of vitamins D and E. In most cases weakness is symmetric and involves proximal limb girdle muscles. Weakness, myalgia, and cramps are common symptoms. Diagnosis often depends on resolution of signs and symptoms with correction of underlying disorder or removal of offending agent.

For a more detailed discussion, see Mendell JR: Approach to the Patient with Muscle Disease, Chap. 381, p. 2520; Dalakas MC: Polymyositis, Dermatomyositis, and Inclusion Body Myositis, Chap. 382, p. 2524; Brown RH Jr., Mendell JR: Muscular Dystrophies and Other Muscle Diseases, Chap. 383, p. 2529, in HPIM-15.

198

APPROACH TO THE PATIENT WITH PSYCHIATRIC SYMPTOMS

Disorders of mood, thinking and behavior may be due to a primary psychiatric diagnosis (DSM-IV* Axis I major psychiatric disorders) or a personality disorder (DSM-IV Axis II disorders) or may be secondary to metabolic abnormalities, drug toxicities, focal cerebral lesions, seizure disorders, or degenerative neurologic disease. Any pt presenting with new onset of psychiatric symptoms must be evaluated for underlying psychoactive substance abuse and/or medical or neurologic illness. Specific psychiatric medications are discussed in Chap. 199. The DSM-IV-PC (Primary Care) Manual provides a synopsis of mental disorders commonly seen in medical practice.

MAJOR PSYCHIATRIC DISORDERS (AXIS I DIAGNOSES)
Mood Disorders (Major Affective Disorders)

MAJOR DEPRESSION *Clinical Features* Affects 15% of the general population at some point in life and extracts high disability and societal cost. Diagnosis is made when a depressed/irritable mood or a lack of normal interest/pleasure exists for at least 2 weeks, in combination with four or more of the following symptoms: (1) change in appetite plus change in weight; (2) insomnia or hypersomnia; (3) fatigue or loss of energy; (4) motor agitation or retardation; (5) feelings of worthlessness, self-reproach, or guilt; (6) decreased ability to concentrate and make decisions; (7) recurrent thoughts of death or suicide. A small number of pts with major depression will have psychotic symptoms—hallucinations and delusions—with their depressed mood; many present with a "masked depression," unable to describe their psychological distress but with multiple diffuse somatic complaints.

Onset of a first depressive episode is typically in the thirties or forties, although major depression is found in children and adolescents as well as geriatric pts. Untreated episodes generally resolve spontaneously in 5–9 months; however, a sizeable number of pts suffer from chronic, unremitting depression or from partial treatment response. Half of all pts experiencing a first depressive episode will go on to a recurrent course, with a second episode occurring within 2 years. Untreated or partially treated episodes put the pt at risk for future problems with mood disorder. A family history of mood disorder is common and tends to predict a recurrent course. Major depression can also be the initial presentation of bipolar disorder (manic depressive illness).

Suicide Most suicides occur in pts with a mood disorder, and many pts seek contact with a physician prior to their suicide attempt. Physicians must always inquire about suicide when evaluating a pt with depression. Features that place a pt at high risk for suicidal behavior include: (1) a formulated plan and a method, as well as an intent; (2) prior attempts; (3) concomitant alcohol

---

*Diagnostic and Statistical Manual, Fourth Edition, American Psychiatric Association

or other psychoactive substance use; (4) psychotic symptoms; (5) older age; (6) male gender; (7) Caucasian; (8) social isolation; (9) serious medical illness; (10) recent loss and/or profound hopelessness.

 TREATMENT

Pts with suicidal ideation require treatment by a psychiatrist and may require hospitalization. Most other pts with an uncomplicated unipolar major depression (a major depression that is not part of a cyclical mood disorder, such as a bipolar disorder) can be successfully treated by a nonpsychiatric physician. Vigorous intervention and successful treatment appear to decrease the risk of future relapse. Pts who do not respond fully to standard treatment should be referred to a psychiatrist.

Antidepressant medication is the mainstay of treatment; symptoms are ameliorated after 2–6 weeks at a therapeutic dose. Antidepressants should be continued for 9–12 months, then tapered slowly. Pts must be monitored carefully after termination of treatment since relapse is common. The combination of pharmacotherapy with psychotherapy [usually cognitive-behavioral therapy (CBT) or interpersonal therapy (IPT)] produces better and longer-lasting results than drug therapy alone. Electroconvulsive therapy is generally reserved for pts with life-threatening depression unresponsive to medication or for pts in whom the use of antidepressants is medically contraindicated.

BIPOLAR DISORDER (MANIC DEPRESSIVE ILLNESS) *Clinical Features* A cyclical mood disorder in which episodes of major depression are interspersed with episodes of mania or hypomania; 1–2% of the population is affected. Most pts initially present with a manic episode in adolescence or young adulthood, but 20% present with a major depression. Antidepressant therapy is usually contraindicated in pts with a cyclical mood disorder because it may provoke a manic episode or make the cycles between mania and depression more frequent and more intense ("rapid cycling"). Pts with a major depressive episode and a prior history of "highs" (mania or hypomania—which can be pleasant/euphoric or irritable/impulsive) and/or a family history of bipolar disorder should not be treated with antidepressants but must be referred promptly to a psychiatrist.

With mania, an elevated, expansive mood, irritability, angry outbursts, and impulsivity are characteristic. Specific symptoms include: (1) increased motor activity and restlessness; (2) unusual talkativeness; (3) flight of ideas and racing thoughts; (4) inflated self-esteem that can become delusional; (5) decreased need for sleep (often the first feature of an incipient manic episode); (6) decreased appetite; (7) distractability; (8) excessive involvement in risky activities (buying sprees, sexual indiscretions). Pts with full-blown mania can become psychotic. Hypomania is characterized by attenuated manic symptoms and is greatly underdiagnosed, especially in nonpsychiatric settings. "Mixed episodes," where both depressive and manic or hypomanic symptoms co-exist simultaneously, are also underrecognized and misdiagnosed.

Untreated, a manic or depressive episode typically lasts for 1–3 months, with cycles of 1–2 episodes per year. Risk for manic episodes increases in the spring and fall. Variants of bipolar disorder include rapid and ultrarapid cycling (manic and depressed episodes occurring at cycles of weeks, days, or hours). In many pts, especially females, antidepressants trigger rapid cycling and worsen the course of illness. Pts with bipolar disorder are at risk for psychoactive substance use, especially alcohol abuse, and for medical consequences of risky sexual behavior (STDs).

Bipolar disorder has a strong genetic component. Pts with bipolar disorder are vulnerable to sleep deprivation, to changes in the photoperiod, and to the effects of jet lag.

 TREATMENT

Bipolar disorder is a serious, chronic illness that requires lifelong monitoring by a psychiatrist. Acutely manic pts often require hospitalization to reduce environmental stimulation and to protect themselves and others from the consequences of their reckless behavior. Mood stabilizers (lithium, carbamazepine, valproic acid, gabapentin, lamotrigine, topiramate) are effective treatment and are used for the resolution of acute episodes and for prophylaxis of future episodes. Antipsychotic medication, benzodiazepines, and antidepressants such as buproprion may be part of the treatment regimen. As in unipolar depression, rapid therapeutic intervention may decrease the risk of future relapse.

Schizophrenia and Other Psychotic Disorders

SCHIZOPHRENIA   *Clinical Features*   Occurs in 1% of the population worldwide; 30–40% of the homeless are affected. Characterized by a waxing and waning vulnerability to psychosis, i.e., an impaired ability to monitor reality, resulting in altered mood, thinking, language, perceptions, behavior, and interpersonal interactions. Pts usually present between late adolescence and the third decade, often after an insidious premorbid course of subtle psychosocial difficulties. Core psychotic features last ≥6 months and include: (1) delusions, which can be paranoid, jealous, somatic, grandiose, religious, nihilistic, or simply bizarre; (2) hallucinations, often auditory hallucinations of a voice or voices maintaining a running commentary; (3) disorders of language and thinking: incoherence, loosening of associations, tangentiality, illogical thinking; (4) inappropriate affect and bizarre, catatonic, or grossly disorganized behavior.

Many pts stabilize after the first 5 years of illness. 30–40% show a deteriorating course, but at least 25% do well, especially with early intervention. Females tend to have a later age of onset and a more benign course than males. Comorbid substance abuse is common, especially of nicotine, alcohol, and stimulants.

 TREATMENT

Hospitalization is required for acutely psychotic pts, especially those with violent command hallucinations, who may be dangerous to themselves or others. Conventional antipsychotic medications are effective against hallucinations, agitation, and thought disorder (the so-called positive symptoms) in 60% of pts but are often less useful for apathy, blunted affect, social isolation, and anhedonia (negative symptoms). The novel antipsychotic medications— clozapine, risperidone, olanzapine, quetiapine, and others—have become the mainstay of treatment as they are helpful in pts unresponsive to conventional neuroleptics and may also be useful for negative and cognitive symptoms. Long-acting injectable forms of haloperidol and fluphenazine are ideal for noncompliant pts. Psychosocial intervention, rehabilitation, and family support are also essential.

OTHER PSYCHOTIC DISORDERS   These include schizoaffective disorder (where symptoms of chronic psychosis are interspersed with major mood episodes) and delusional disorders (in which a fixed, unshakable delusional belief is held in the absence of the other stigmata of schizophrenia). Pts with somatic delusions can be especially difficult to diagnose; they may become violent towards the physician if they feel misunderstood or thwarted and they almost always resist referral to a psychiatrist.

Anxiety Disorders

Characterized by severe, persistent anxiety or sense of dread in the absence of psychosis or a severe change in mood. Most prevalent psychiatric illness seen in the community; present in 15–20% of medical clinic patients.

PANIC DISORDER   Occurs in 1–2% of the population; female:male ratio of 2:1. Familial aggregation may occur. Onset in second or third decade. Initial presentation is almost always to a nonpsychiatric physician, frequently in the ER, as a possible heart attack or serious respiratory problem. The disorder is often initially unrecognized or misdiagnosed. Prompt diagnosis and treatment can greatly reduce morbidity.

Clinical Features   Characterized by panic attacks, which are sudden, unexpected, overwhelming paroxysms of terror and apprehension with multiple associated somatic symptoms. Attacks usually last 10–20 min, then slowly resolve spontaneously. Diagnostic criteria for panic disorder require four or more panic attacks within 4 weeks occurring in nonthreatening or nonexertional settings, and attacks must be accompanied by at least four of the following: dyspnea, palpitations, chest pain or discomfort, choking/smothering feelings, dizziness/vertigo/unsteady feelings, feelings of unreality, paresthesia, hot and cold flashes, sweating, faintness, trembling, and fear of dying, going crazy, or doing something uncontrolled during an attack. Panic disorder is often associated with a concomitant major depression.

When the disorder goes unrecognized and untreated, pts often experience significant morbidity: they become afraid of leaving home and may develop anticipatory anxiety, agoraphobia, and other spreading phobias; many turn to self-medication with alcohol or benzodiazepines.

Panic disorder must be differentiated from cardiovascular and respiratory disorders. Conditions that may mimic or worsen panic attacks include hyper- and hypothyroidism, pheochromocytoma, complex partial seizures, hypoglycemia, drug ingestions (amphetamines, cocaine, caffeine, sympathomimetic nasal decongestants), and drug withdrawal (alcohol, barbiturates, opiates, minor tranquilizers).

 TREATMENT

Cognitive-behavioral psychotherapy (identifying and aborting panic attacks through relaxation and breathing techniques)—either alone or combined with medication—is highly effective. Selective serotonin reuptake inhibitors (SSRIs), tricyclic antidepressants, and monoamine oxidase inhibitors all treat the disorder and prevent spontaneous attacks. Clonazepam, lorazepam, or other benzodiazepines may be used in the short term while waiting for antidepressants to take effect (2–3 weeks).

GENERALIZED ANXIETY DISORDER (GAD)   Characterized by persistent, chronic anxiety but without the specific symptoms of phobic, panic, or obsessive-compulsive disorders; occurs in 2–3% of the population.

Clinical Features   Pts experience persistent motor hyperactivity (shakiness, trembling, restlessness, easy startle), autonomic hyperactivity, apprehensive expectation (anxiety, fear, rumination, anticipation of misfortune, etc.), and vigilance (distractability, poor concentration, insomnia, impatience, and irritability). These symptoms are chronic and pervasive, rather than situational. Secondary depression is common.

 TREATMENT

Benzodiazepines are the initial agents of choice when generalized anxiety is severe and acute enough to warrant drug therapy. A trial of an SSRI antidepressant should then be started as many pts will experience significant relief with this class of medications. Physicians must be alert to psychological and physical dependence on benzodiazepines. A subgroup of pts respond to buspirone, a nonbenzodiazepine anxiolytic. Psychotherapy and relaxation training can be useful.

OBSESSIVE-COMPULSIVE DISORDER (OCD) A severe disorder present in 4–6% of the population and characterized by recurrent obsessions (persistent intrusive thoughts) and compulsions (repetitive behaviors) that the pt experiences as involuntary, senseless, or repugnant. Pts are often ashamed of their symptoms and only seek help after they have become debilitated.

Clinical Features Common obsessions include thoughts of violence (such as killing a loved one), obsessive slowness for fear of making a mistake, fears of germs or contamination, and excessive doubt or uncertainty. Examples of compulsions include repeated checking to be assured that something was done properly, hand washing, extreme neatness and ordering behavior, and counting rituals, such as numbering one's steps while walking.

Onset is usually in adolescence, with 65% of cases manifest before age 25. It is more common in males and in first-born children. In families of OCD patients, an increased incidence of both OCD and Tourette's syndrome is found. The course of OCD is usually episodic with periods of incomplete remission. Pts with severe disease may become completely housebound. Major depression, substance abuse, and social impairment are common.

 TREATMENT

Clomipramine and the SSRIs are highly effective. A combination of drug therapy and CBT is most effective for the majority of pts. Education and referral to a national support organization is also useful.

POSTTRAUMATIC STRESS DISORDER (PTSD) Occurs in a subgroup of individuals exposed to a severe life-threatening trauma. Predisposing factors include a prior history of traumatization and/or a diathesis toward anxiety responses. Early psychological intervention following a traumatic event may reduce the risk for chronic PTSD.

Clinical Features Three core sets of symptoms: (1) *reexperiencing*, where the pt unwillingly reexperiences the trauma through recurrent intrusive recollections, recurrent dreams, or by suddenly feeling as if the traumatic event is recurring; (2) *avoidance and numbing*, where the pt experiences reduced responsiveness to, and involvement with, the external world, a sense of a foreshortened future, and avoidance of activities that arouse recollection of the traumatic event; (3) *arousal*, characterized by hypervigilance, hyperalertness, an exaggerated startle response, sleep disturbance, guilt about having survived when others have not or about behavior required for survival, memory impairment or trouble concentrating, and intensification of symptoms by exposure to events that symbolize or resemble the traumatic event. Comorbid substance abuse and other mood and anxiety disorders are common. This disorder is extremely debilitating, particularly as it becomes chronic and affects psychosocial functioning. Most pts require referral to a psychiatrist for ongoing care.

 TREATMENT

Medications used with varying success include a combination of an SSRI and trazodone, 50–200 mg qhs for sleep; tricyclic antidepressants; and mood stabilizers. Group psychotherapy (with other trauma survivors), alone or with individual psychotherapy, is useful.

PHOBIC DISORDERS *Clinical Features* Recurring, irrational fears of specific objects, activities, or situations, with subsequent avoidance behavior of the phobic stimulus. Diagnosis is made only when the avoidance behavior is a significant source of distress or interferes with social or occupational functioning.

1. *Agoraphobia:* Fear of being in public places. May occur in absence of panic disorder, but is almost invariably preceded by that condition.
2. *Social phobia:* Persistent irrational fear of, and need to avoid, any situation where there is risk of scrutiny by others, with potential for embarrassment or humiliation. Common examples include excessive fear of public speaking and excessive fear of social engagements.
3. *Simple phobias:* Persistent irrational fears and avoidance of specific objects. Common examples include fear of heights (acrophobia), closed spaces (claustrophobia), and animals.

 TREATMENT

Agoraphobia is treated as for panic disorder. SSRIs are very helpful in treating social phobias. Social and simple phobias respond well to CBT and relaxation techniques and to systematic desensitization and exposure treatment.

SOMATOFORM DISORDERS *Clinical Features* Pts with multiple somatic complaints that cannot be explained by a known medical condition or by the effects of substances; seen commonly in primary care practice (prevalence of 5%). In somatization disorder, the pt presents with multiple physical complaints referable to different organ systems. Onset is before age 30, and the disorder is persistent; pts with somatization disorder can be impulsive and demanding. In *conversion disorder*, the symptoms involve voluntary motor or sensory function. In *hypochondriasis*, the pt believes there is a serious medical illness, despite reassurance and appropriate medical evaluation. As with somatization disorder, these pts have a history of poor relationships with physicians due to their sense that they have not received adequate evaluation. Hypochondriasis can be disabling and show a waxing and waning course. In *factitious illnesses*, the pt consciously and voluntarily produces physical symptoms; the sick role is gratifying. *Munchausen's syndrome* refers to individuals with dramatic, chronic, or severe factitious illness. A variety of signs, symptoms, and diseases have been simulated in factitious illnesses; most common are chronic diarrhea, fever of unknown origin, intestinal bleeding, hematuria, seizures, hypoglycemia. In *malingering*, the fabrication of illness derives from a desire for an external gain (narcotics, disability).

℞ TREATMENT

Pts with somatoform disorders are usually subjected to multiple diagnostic tests and exploratory surgeries in an attempt to find their "real" illness. This approach is doomed to failure. Successful treatment is achieved through behavior modification, in which access to the physician is adjusted to provide a consistent, sustained, and predictable level of support that is not contingent on the pt's level of presenting symptoms or distress. Visits are brief, supportive, and structured and are not associated with a need for diagnostic or treatment action. Pts often benefit from antidepressant treatment. Consultation with a psychiatrist is essential.

PERSONALITY DISORDERS (AXIS II DIAGNOSES)

Defined as an inappropriate, stereotyped, maladaptive use of a certain set of psychological characteristics; affects 5–15% of the general population. The pattern of behavior is enduring and affects the person's relationships and ability to function satisfactorily in life.

Comorbid Axis I diagnosis is common, as is a psychoactive substance use disorder. In medical and surgical settings, pts with personality disorders often become engaged in hostile, manipulative, or unproductive relationships with their physicians. Long-term psychotherapy is beneficial for pts who are motivated to change. Antidepressants and antipsychotic medications can be helpful, particularly for episodes of decompensation, but should be prescribed in consultation with a psychiatrist as misdiagnosis is common.

DSM-IV describes three major categories of personality disorders; pts usually present with a combination of features.

Cluster A Personality Disorders

Affected pts are often characterized as "wild" or "mad." The *paranoid* personality is suspicious, hypersensitive, guarded, hostile, and can occasionally become threatening or dangerous. The *schizoid* personality is interpersonally isolated, cold, and indifferent, while the *schizotypal* personality is eccentric and superstitious, with magical thinking and unusual beliefs resembling schizophrenia.

Cluster B Personality Disorders

Patients with these disorders are often "wild" or "bad." The *borderline* personality is impulsive and manipulative, with unpredictable and fluctuating intense moods and unstable relationships, a fear of abandonment, and occasional rageful micropsychotic episodes. The *histrionic* pt is dramatic, engaging, seductive, and attention-seeking. The *narcissistic* pt is self-centered and has an inflated sense of self-importance combined with a tendency to devalue or demean others, while pts with *antisocial* personality disorder use other people to achieve their own ends and engage in exploitative and manipulative behavior with no sense of remorse. Some aspects of the Cluster B personality disorders appear related to mood disorders.

Cluster C Personality Disorders

Patients with these disorders are often "whiny" or "sad." The *dependent* pt fears separation, tries to engage others to assume responsibility, and often has a help-rejecting style. Pts with *compulsive* personality disorder are meticulous and perfectionistic but also inflexible and indecisive, while those who are *passive-aggressive* request help, appear compliant on the surface, but undo or resist all efforts aimed at change. *Avoidant* pts are anxious about social contact and have difficulty assuming responsibility for their isolation. The personality disorders share some features with the anxiety disorders

---

For a more detailed discussion, see Reus VI: Mental Disorders, Chap. 385, p. 2542, in HPIM-15.

199

PSYCHIATRIC MEDICATIONS

Four major classes of psychiatric medications are commonly used in adults: (1) antidepressants, (2) anxiolytics, (3) antipsychotics, and (4) mood stabilizing agents. Nonpsychiatric physicians should become familiar with one or two drugs in each of the first three classes so that the indications, dose range, efficacy, potential side effects, and interactions with other medications are well known.

GENERAL PRINCIPLES OF USE

1. Most treatment failures are due to undermedication and impatience. For a proper medication trial to take place, an effective dose must be taken for an adequate amount of time. For antidepressants, antipsychotics, and mood stabilizers, full effects may take weeks or months to occur.
2. History of a positive response to a medication usually indicates that a response to the same drug will occur again. A family history of a positive response to a specific medication is also useful.
3. Pts who fail to respond to one drug will often respond to another in the same class; one should attempt another trial with a drug that has a different mechanism of action or a different chemical structure. Treatment failures should be referred to a psychiatrist, as should all pts with psychotic symptoms or who require mood stabilizers.
4. Avoid polypharmacy; a pt who is not responding to standard monotherapy requires referral to a psychiatrist.
5. Pharmacokinetics may be altered in the elderly, with smaller volumes of distribution, reduced renal and hepatic clearance, longer biologic half-lives, and greater potential for CNS toxicity. The rule with elderly pts is to "start low and go slow."
6. Never stop treatment abruptly; especially true for antidepressants and anxiolytics. In general, medications should be slowly tapered and discontinued over 2–4 weeks.
7. Review possible side effects each time a drug is prescribed; educate pts and family members about side effects and need for patience in awaiting a response.

Antidepressants

Useful to group according to known actions on CNS monoaminergic systems (Table 199-1). The selective serotonin reuptake inhibitors (SSRIs) have predominant effects on serotonergic neurotransmission, also reflected in side effect profile. The TCAs, or tricyclic antidepressants (ADs), affect noradrenergic and, to a lesser extent, serotonergic neurotransmission but also have anticholinergic and antihistaminic effects. Venlafaxine and mirtazapine have relatively "pure" noradrenergic and serotonergic effects. Bupropion has dopamine reuptake inhibitor properties. Trazodone and nefazodone have mixed effects on serotonin receptors and on other neurotransmitter systems. The MAOIs inhibit monoamine oxidase, the primary enzyme responsible for the degradation of monoamines in the synaptic cleft.

ADs are effective against major depression, particularly when neurovegetative symptoms and signs are present. In very severe depression with many endogenous features, TCAs or MAOIs are more efficacious than SSRIs. ADs are also useful in treatment of panic disorder, posttraumatic stress disorder, chronic pain syndromes, and generalized anxiety disorder. The SSRIs and the TCA clomipramine successfully treat obsessive-compulsive disorder.

All ADs require at least 2 weeks at a therapeutic dose before clinical improvement is observed. All ADs also have the potential to trigger a manic episode or rapid cycling when given to a pt with bipolar disorder. The MAOIs must not be prescribed concurrently with other ADs or with narcotics, as potentially fatal reactions may occur. "Withdrawal syndromes" usually consisting of malaise can occur when ADs are stopped abruptly.

ANXIOLYTICS

Antianxiety agents include the benzodiazepines and the nonbenzodiazepine buspirone.

Benzodiazepines bind to stereospecific sites on the γ-aminobutyric acid receptor and are cross-tolerant with alcohol and with barbiturates. Four clinical properties: (1) sedative, (2) anxiolytic, (3) skeletal muscle relaxant, and (4) antiepileptic. Individual drugs differ in terms of potency, onset of action, duration of action (related to half-life and presence of active metabolites), and metabolism (Table 199-2). Benzodiazepines have additive effects with alcohol; like alcohol, they can produce tolerance and physiologic dependence, with serious withdrawal syndromes (tremors, seizures, delirium, and autonomic hyperactivity) if discontinued too quickly, especially for those with short half-lives.

Buspirone is an anxiolytic that is nonsedating, is not cross-tolerant with alcohol, and does not induce tolerance or dependence. It acts via serotonergic pathways and requires at least 2 weeks at therapeutic doses to achieve full effects.

ANTIPSYCHOTIC MEDICATIONS

These include the typical (or conventional) neuroleptics, which act by blocking dopamine D_2 receptors, and the atypical (or novel) neuroleptics, which act on dopamine, serotonin, and other neuroreceptor systems. Some antipsychotic effect may occur within hours or days of initiating treatment, but full effects usually require 6 weeks to several months of daily, therapeutic dosing.

CONVENTIONAL ANTIPSYCHOTICS Useful to group into high-, mid-, and low-potency neuroleptics (Table 199-3). High-potency neuroleptics are least sedating, have almost no anticholinergic side effects, and have a strong tendency to induce extrapyramidal side effects (EPSEs) secondary to dopamine receptor blockade. The EPSEs occur within several hours to several weeks of beginning treatment and include acute dystonias, akathisia, and pseudo-parkinsonism. They are treated by judicious dose reduction and by use of anticholin-

Table 199-1

Antidepressants

Name	Usual Daily Dose, mg
SSRIs	
Fluoxetine (Prozac)	10–80
Sertraline (Zoloft)	50–200
Paroxetine (Paxil)	20–60
Fluvoxamine (Luvox)	100–300
Citalopram (Celexa)	20–60
TCAs	
Amitriptyline (Elavil)	150–300
Nortriptyline (Pamelor)	50–200
Imipramine (Tofranil)	150–300
Desipramine (Norpramin)	150–300
Doxepin (Sinequan)	150–300
Clomipramine (Anafranil)	150–300
Dopamine Reuptake Inhibitor	
Bupropion (Wellbutrin)	250–450
Mixed Norepinephrine/Serotonin Reuptake Inhibitors	
Venlafaxine (Effexor)	75–375
Mirtazapine (Remeron)	15–45
Mixed Action	
Trazodone (Desyrel)	200–600
Nefazodone (Serzone)	300–600
MAOIs	
Phenelzine (Nardil)	45–90
Tranylcypromine (Parnate)	20–50

NOTE: ADD, attention deficit disorder; MAOI, monoamine oxidase inhibitor; REM, rapid eye movement; SSRI, selective serotonin reuptake inhibitor; TCA, tricyclic antidepressant.

ergic and dopamine agonist medications. Low-potency neuroleptics are very sedating, may cause orthostasis, are anticholinergic, and therefore tend not to induce EPSEs. Mid-potency agents are best tolerated by the average pt.

10–20% of pts treated with conventional antipsychotic agents for >1 year develop tardive dyskinesia (probably due to dopamine receptor supersensitivity), an abnormal involuntary movement disorder most often observed in the face and distal extremities. Treatment includes gradual withdrawal of the neuroleptic, with possible switch to a novel neuroleptic; anticholinergic agents can worsen the disorder.

Side Effects	Comments
Headache; nausea and other GI effects; jitteriness; insomnia; sexual dysfunction; can affect plasma levels of other meds (except sertraline, citalopram); akathisia (rare)	Once-daily dosings, usually in A.M.; fluoxetine has very long half-life; must not be combined with MAOIs
Anticholinergic (dry mouth, tachycardia, constipation, urinary retention, blurred vision); sweating; tremor; postural hypotension; cardiac conduction delay; sedation; weight gain	Once-daily dosing, usually qhs; blood levels of most TCAs available; can be lethal in O.D. (lethal dose = 2 g); nortriptyline best tolerated, especially by elderly
Jitteriness; flushing; seizures in at-risk pts; anorexia; tachycardia; psychosis	Fewer sexual side effects than SSRIs or TCAs; may be useful for adult ADD; used for nicotine cessation; may be better tolerated by bipolar pts than other ADs
Nausea; dizziness; dry mouth; headaches; increased blood pressure; anxiety and insomnia	Lower potential for drug-drug interactions than SSRIs; contraindicated with MAOIs
Somnolence; weight gain; neutropenia (rare)	Once-daily dosing
Sedation; dry mouth; ventricular irritability; postural hypotension; priapism (rare)	Useful in low doses for sleep because of sedating effects with no anticholinergic side effects
Sedation; headache; dry mouth; nausea; constipation	Once-daily dosing; no effect on REM sleep, unlike other antidepressants
Insomnia; hypotension; anorgasmia; weight gain; hypertensive crisis; tyramine cheese reaction; lethal reactions with SSRIs and narcotics	May be more effective in pts with atypical features or treatment-refractory depressions

1–2% of pts exposed to neuroleptics develop neuroleptic malignant syndrome (NMS), a life-threatening complication with a mortality rate as high as 25%; hyperpyrexia, autonomic hyperactivity, muscle rigidity, obtundation, and agitation are characteristic, associated with increased WBC, increased CPK, and myoglobinuria. Treatment involves immediate discontinuation of neuroleptics, supportive care, and use of dantrolene and bromocriptine.

NOVEL ANTIPSYCHOTICS   A new class of agents that has become the first line of treatment (Table 199-3); efficacious in treatment-resistant pts, tend not to induce EPSEs or tardive dyskinesia, and appear to have uniquely beneficial properties on negative symptoms and cognitive dysfunction. Main prob-

Table 199-2

Anxiolytics

Name	Equivalent PO dose, mg	Onset of Action	Half-life, h	Comments
Benzodiazepines				
Diazepam (Valium)	5	Fast	20–70	Active metabolites; quite sedating
Flurazepam (Dalmane)	15	Fast	30–100	Flurazepam is a pro-drug; metabolites are active; quite sedating
Triazolam (Halcion)	0.25	Intermediate	1.5–5	No active metabolites; can induce confusion and delirium, especially in elderly
Lorazepam (Ativan)	1	Intermediate	10–20	No active metabolites; direct hepatic glucuronide conjugation; quite sedating
Alprazolam (Xanax)	0.5	Intermediate	12–15	Active metabolites; not too sedating; may have specific antidepressant and antipanic activity; tolerance and dependence develop easily
Chlordiazepoxide (Librium)	10	Intermediate	5–30	Active metabolites; moderately sedating
Oxazepam (Serax)	15	Slow	5–15	No active metabolites; direct glucuronide conjugation; not too sedating
Temazepam (Restoril)	15	Slow	9–12	No active metabolites; moderately sedating
Clonazepam (Klonopin)	0.5	Slow	18–50	No active metabolites; moderately sedating
Nonbenzodiazepines				
Buspirone (BuSpar)	7.5	2 weeks	2–3	Active metabolites; tid dosing—usual daily dose 10–20 mg tid; nonsedating; no additive effects with alcohol; useful for agitation in demented or brain-injured pts

Table 199-3

Antipsychotic Agents

Name	Usual PO Daily Dose, mg	Side Effects	Sedation	Comments
Conventional antipsychotics				
Low-potency				
Chlorpromazine (Thorazine)	100–1000	Anticholinergic effects; orthostasis; photosensitivity; cholestasis	+++	EPSEs usually not prominent; can cause anticholinergic delirium in elderly pts
Thioridazine (Mellaril)	100–800		++	Well tolerated by most pts
Mid-potency				
Trifluoperatine (Stelazine)	2–15	Fewer anticholinergic side effects; fewer EPSEs than with higher potency agents		
Perphenazine (Trilafon)	4–32			
High-potency				
Haloperidol (Haldol)	0.5–10	No anticholinergic side effects; EPSEs often prominent	0/+	Often prescribed in doses that are too high; long-acting injectable forms of haloperidol and fluphenazine available
Fluphenazine (Prolixin)	1–10			
Thiothixene (Navane)	2–20			
Novel antipsychotics				
Clozapine (Clozaril)	200–600	Agranulocytosis (1%); weight gain; seizures; drooling; hyperthermia	++	Requires weekly WBC initially, then q 2 weeks
Risperidone (Risperdal)	2–6	Orthostasis	+	Requires slow titration; EPSEs observed with doses >6 mg qd
Olanzapine (Zyprexa)	10–20	Weight gain	++	Rapid weight gain; hyperglycemia/insulin resistance; can cause confusion
Seroquel (Quietapine)	300–400	Sedation; weight gain; anxiety	+++	Bid dosing

NOTE: EPSEs, extrapyramidal side effects.

Table 199-4

Mood-stabilizing Agents

Name	Usual Daily Dose, mg	Side Effects	Comments
Lithium	600–2400	Tremor, nausea, ataxia, polyuria–diabetes insipidus, acne, psoriasis, hypothyroidism, weight gain, edema, benign leukocytosis	Dose adjusted to serum concentration 0.8–1.2 mEq/L; contraindicated during pregnancy; diuretics and prostaglandin-synthetase inhibitors can increase lithium to toxic levels; severe toxicity can lead to coma and death
Carbamazepine (Tegretol)	400–1600	Agranulocytosis and aplastic anemia (rare); dizziness; ataxia; sedation; pruritus; Stevens-Johnson syndrome (rare)	Plasma levels of 8–12 μg/mL needed to treat manic episodes; monitor hepatic, hematologic, and cardiac status; multiple drug interactions, including decrease of blood concentrations of oral contraceptives
Valproic acid	500–1500	Nausea, vomiting, sedation, headache; (tolerance to these side effects usually develops); pancreatitis (rare), hepatitis (rare)	Avoid in hepatic and renal disease; monitor LFTs; plasma levels of 50–100 μg/mL therapeutic
Gabapentin	1200–3000	Usually very well tolerated; can cause sedation; dizziness; weight gain	Useful for pain, anxiety, insomnia
Lamotrigine	100–250	Highly antigenic—possibility of serious rash; headache, sedation, tremor, nausea	Start low and go slowly; valproic acid increases levels; useful for treatment-resistant depression and rapid cycling
Topiramate	25–150	Sedation, cognitive dysfunction, weight loss	Useful as an adjunct when there has been adverse wt gain on other meds

lem is side effect of weight gain (most prominent in clozapine and in olanzapine; can induce onset of diabetes mellitus).

MOOD-STABILIZING AGENTS

Three mood stabilizers in common use: lithium, carbamazepine, and valproic acid or divalproex sodium. Three additional mood stabilizers being increasingly used: gabapentin, lamotrigine, topiramate (Table 199-4). Lithium is the "gold standard" and the best studied, and along with carbamazepine and valproic acid, is used for treatment of acute manic episodes; 1–2 weeks to reach full effect. As prophylaxis, the mood stabilizers reduce frequency and severity of both manic and depressed episodes in cyclical mood disorders. Believed to work at various sites of gaba-ergic and glutamenergic neurotransmission and second-messenger signal transduction systems in the CNS. In refractory bipolar disorder, combinations of mood stabilizers are often beneficial.

For a more detailed discussion, see Reus VI: Mental Disorders, Chap. 385, p. 2542, in HPIM-15.

200

ALCOHOLISM

Alcoholism and alcohol abuse are defined by the regular and excessive use of alcohol with concomitant social, occupational, and/or physical problems; alcohol is associated with half of all traffic fatalities and half of all homicides. In *alcohol dependence*, the regular use of alcohol has resulted in a state of physiologic tolerance and dependence. A pt may never suffer from withdrawal symptoms and still meet criteria for *alcohol abuse*.

Alcoholism is a multifactorial disorder in which genetic, biologic, and sociocultural factors interact. Typically, the first major life problem from excessive alcohol use appears in early adulthood, followed by periods of exacerbation and remission; the lifespan of the alcoholic is shortened by an average of 15 years due to increased risk of death from heart disease, cancer, accidents, or suicide.

Clinical Features

One out of five of the average physician's pts will suffer from alcoholism. Routine medical care requires attention to potential alcohol-related illness and to alcoholism itself:

1. Neurologic—blackouts, seizures, delirium tremens, cerebellar degeneration, neuropathy, myopathy
2. Gastrointestinal—esophagitis, gastritis, pancreatitis, hepatitis, cirrhosis, GI hemorrhage
3. Cardiovascular—hypertension, cardiomyopathy
4. Hematologic—macrocytosis, folate deficiency, thrombocytopenia, leukopenia

5. Endocrine—gynecomastia, testicular atrophy, amenorrhea, infertility
6. Skeletal—fractures, osteonecrosis
7. Cancer—breast cancer, oral and esophageal cancers, rectal cancers.

Most alcoholic pts do not have dramatic physical symptoms but instead present with psychosocial difficulties. Most common are marital difficulties, job problems (tardiness, absenteeism), and legal problems resulting from driving while intoxicated. A positive answer to any of the "CAGE questions" indicates a high probability of alcoholism: Are you . . . *C*utting down, or feel the need to? *A*nnoyed when people criticize your drinking? *G*uilty about your drinking? *E*ye-opening with a drink in the morning? Typically, pts will describe a host of difficulties but will then deny that they have a problem with alcohol abuse. Denial is a characteristic, if not the core, symptom of alcoholism.

Alcohol is a CNS depressant that acts on receptors for γ-aminobutyric acid (GABA), the major inhibitory neurotransmitter in the nervous system. Behavioral, cognitive, and psychomotor changes can occur at blood alcohol levels as low as 4–7 mmol/L (20–30 mg/dL), a level achieved after the ingestion of one or two typical drinks. Mild to moderate intoxication occurs at 17–43 mmol/L (80–200 mg/dL). Incoordination, tremor, ataxia, confusion, stupor, coma, and even death occur at progressively higher blood alcohol levels.

Chronic alcohol use produces CNS dependence. In such individuals, the earliest sign of alcohol withdrawal is tremulousness ("shakes" or "jitters"), which usually occurs 8–24 h after the last drink. This may be followed by generalized seizures ("rum fits") in the first 24–48 h; these do not require initiation of anti-seizure medications. With severe withdrawal, autonomic hyperactivity ensues (sweating, hypertension, tachycardia, tachypnea, fever), accompanied by insomnia, nightmares, anxiety, and GI symptoms.

Delirium tremens (DTs), which may begin 3–5 days after the last drink, is a very severe withdrawal syndrome characterized by profound autonomic hyperactivity, extreme confusion, agitation, vivid delusions, and hallucinations (often visual and tactile); mortality is 5–15%. Wernicke's encephalopathy is an alcohol-related syndrome characterized by ataxia, ophthalmoplegia, and confusion, often with associated nystagmus, peripheral neuropathy, cerebellar signs, and hypotension; there is impaired short-term memory, inattention, and emotional lability. Korsakoff's syndrome follows as the encephalopathy and ocular findings resolve; it is characterized by anterograde and retrograde amnesia and confabulation. Wernicke-Korsakoff's syndrome is caused by chronic thiamine deficiency, resulting in damage to thalamic nuclei, mamillary bodies, and brainstem and cerebellar structures.

Laboratory Findings

Clues to alcoholism include mild anemia with macrocytosis, folate deficiency, thrombocytopenia, granulocytopenia, abnormal LFTs, hyperuricemia, and elevated triglycerides. Decreases in serum K, Mg, Zn, and PO_4 levels are common. Diagnostic studies such as GI radiology or endoscopy, abdominal ultrasound or CT, liver-spleen scan, liver biopsy, ECG, echocardiogram, brain CT or MRI, EEG, and nerve conduction studies may show evidence of alcohol-related organ dysfunction.

℞ TREATMENT

Acute Withdrawal Acute alcohol withdrawal is treated with thiamine (50–100 mg IV or 100 mg PO daily for 5 d) to replenish depleted stores; if Wernicke-Korsakoff's syndrome is suspected, the IV route must be used, since intestinal absorption is unreliable in alcoholics. CNS depressant drugs that enhance GABA-mediated inhibition are used when seizures or autonomic hyperactivity are present. These drugs halt the rapid state of withdrawal in the CNS and allow for a slower, more controlled reduction of the substance. Low-potency benzodiazepines with long half-lives are the medication of choice (e.g., diazepam, chlordiazepoxide), because they produce fairly steady blood levels of drug and there is a wide dose range within which to work. These benefits must be weighed against the risk of overmedication and over-sedation, which occur less commonly with shorter-acting agents (e.g. oxa-zepam, lorazepam). Typical doses are diazepam 5–10 mg or chlordiazepoxide 25–50 mg PO every 1–4 h prn objective signs of alcohol withdrawal (such as pulse < 90). Extremely high doses are sometimes required for the chronic alcoholic.

In severe withdrawal or DTs, the physician must also look for evidence of trauma or infection that may be masked by prominent withdrawal symp-toms or that contribute to the pt's debilitated state. Fluid and electrolyte status and blood glucose levels should be closely followed as well. Cardiovascular and hemodynamic monitoring are crucial, as hemodynamic collapse and car-diac arrhythmia are not uncommon.

Recovery and Sobriety The definitive treatment of alcoholism requires a successful confrontation of the pt's denial, followed by the pt's motivation to change. It may take multiple encounters between physician and pt over a period of years for a pt to achieve this level of motivation. Once pts commit to treatment, an initial stage of recovery (early abstinence) is followed by ongoing sobriety. The physician should counsel the pt about the need for continued abstinence as a primary treatment goal and about the usefulness of regular participation in self-help resources such as AA (and Alanon for family members).

Once sobriety has been achieved, pts should be evaluated for the presence of any other underlying psychiatric disorder (such as major depression) and vigorously treated. The physician should also recognize the relapsing/remit-ting nature of alcoholism, and be prepared to help pts reenter treatment pe-riodically.

Disulfiram (Antabuse), a drug that inhibits aldehyde dehydrogenase and results in toxic symptoms (nausea, vomiting, diarrhea, tremor) if the pt con-sumes alcohol, is used in some centers but is not an effective therapy in the absence of psychosocial intervention. Preliminary studies show that naltrex-one and acamprosate may reduce recidivism in abstinent alcoholics.

For a more detailed discussion, see Schuckit MA: Alcohol and Alcoholism, Chap. 387, p. 2561, in HPIM-15.

201

NARCOTIC ABUSE

Narcotics, or opiates, bind to specific opioid receptors in the CNS and elsewhere in the body. These receptors mediate the opiate effects of analgesia, euphoria, respiratory depression, and constipation. Endogenous opiate peptides (enkephalins and endorphins) are natural ligands for the opioid receptors and play a role in analgesia, memory, learning, reward, mood regulation, and stress tolerance.

The prototypic opiates, morphine and codeine, are derived from the juice of the opium poppy, *Papaver somniferum*. The semisynthetic drugs produced from morphine include hydromorphone (Dilaudid), diacetylmorphine (heroin), and oxycodone. Purely synthetic agents are meperidine (Demerol), propoxyphene (Darvon), and methadone. All of these substances produce analgesia and euphoria as well as physical dependence when taken in high enough doses for prolonged periods of time.

1% of the U.S. population meets criteria for narcotic abuse or dependence at some time in their lives. 70% of narcotic-addicted individuals have another psychiatric disorder (usually major depression, alcoholism, or a personality disorder). Three groups of abusers can be identified: (1) "medical" abusers—pts with chronic pain syndromes who misuse their prescribed analgesics; (2) physicians, nurses, dentists, and pharmacists with easy access to narcotics; and (3) "street" abusers. The street abuser is typically a higher functioning individual who began by using tobacco, alcohol, and marijuana and then moved on to opiates.

Clinical Features

Acutely, all opiates have the following CNS effects: sedation, euphoria, decreased pain perception, decreased respiratory drive, and vomiting. In larger doses, markedly decreased respirations, bradycardia, pupillary miosis, stupor, and coma ensue. Additionally, the adulterants used to "cut" street drugs (quinine, phenacetin, strychnine, antipyrine, caffeine, powdered milk) can produce permanent neurologic damage, including peripheral neuropathy, amblyopia, and myelopathy. The shared use of contaminated needles is a major cause of brain abscesses, acute endocarditis, hepatitis B, AIDS, septic arthritis, and soft tissue infections. At least 25% of street abusers die within 10–20 years of starting active opiate abuse.

Chronic use of opiates will result in tolerance (requiring higher doses to achieve psychotropic effects) and physical dependence. With shorter-acting opiates such as heroin, morphine, or oxycodone, withdrawal signs begin 8–12 h after the last dose, peak at 2–3 days, and subside over 7–10 days. With longer-acting opiates such as methadone, withdrawal begins 2–4 days after the last dose, peaks at 3–4 days, and lasts several weeks.

Withdrawal produces diarrhea, coughing, lacrimation, rhinorrhea, diaphoresis, twitching muscles, piloerection, fever, tachypnea, hypertension, diffuse body pain, insomnia, and yawning. Relief of these exceedingly unpleasant symptoms by narcotic administration leads to more frequent narcotic use. Eventually, all of the person's efforts are consumed by drug-seeking behavior.

℞ TREATMENT

Overdose   High doses of opiates, whether taken in a suicide attempt or accidentally when the potency is misjudged, are frequently lethal. Toxicity occurs immediately after IV administration and with a variable delay after oral ingestion. Symptoms include miosis, shallow respirations, bradycardia, hypothermia, stupor or coma, and pulmonary edema. Treatment requires cardiorespiratory support and administration of the opiate antagonist naloxone (0.4 mg IV repeated in 3–10 min if no or only partial response). Because the effects of naloxone diminish in 2–3 h compared with longer-lasting effects of heroin (up to 24 h) or methadone (up to 72 h), pts must be observed for at least 1–3 days for reappearance of the toxic state.

Withdrawal or Abstinence Syndromes   Clonidine is effective in decreasing the sympathetic nervous system hyperactivity observed in opiate withdrawal. Doses of 0.3–0.5 mg/d are used for the 2–3 weeks of the withdrawal period. Although it is highly unpleasant, opiate withdrawal is not physically dangerous or life-threatening per se in adults (unlike alcohol withdrawal). However, withdrawal syndromes in newborns of street abusers are fatal in 3–30% of cases.

Methadone maintenance (to avoid withdrawal or abstinence syndromes) is a widely used treatment strategy in the management of opiate addiction. Long-acting oral methadone is most convenient: 1 mg methadone is equivalent to 3 mg morphine, 1 mg heroin, or 20 mg meperidine. Most patients receive 10–25 mg methadone bid, with higher doses given if withdrawal symptoms break through. Although methadone has mood-elevating effects in some individuals, maintenance nevertheless leads to reduced opiate and non-opiate drug use, reduced criminal behavior, and decreased symptoms of depression.

L-Alpha-acetylmethadol (LAAM) is a long-acting synthetic narcotic that may be given only 3 times a week; however, some pts experience nervousness and stimulation on LAAM. Buprenorphine is a partial receptor agonist that blocks some of the subjective effects of narcotics and may be as effective as low-dose methadone in maintenance treatment.

To help prevent relapses in the abstinent pt, the oral antagonist naltrexone is used in doses of 50–150 mg/d. It blocks the euphoric and analgesic effects of the opiate when a pt relapses and uses narcotics.

Chronic Pain Syndromes   Physicians should avoid encouraging narcotic addiction in pts with established chronic pain syndromes (this is to be distinguished from prescribing adequate analgesia in pts with acute pain). Once tolerance and physical dependence are established in the pt with a chronic pain syndrome, withdrawal and abstinence syndromes will intensify the pt's pain and confuse the management of an already difficult problem. Pts should be educated that medications will be used to minimize the effects of pain on their physical function but that they will not abolish the pain entirely. Nonpharmacologic approaches to pain management should also be part of the treatment plan.

Identification of the Chronic Narcotic User   Blood and urine screens for opiates, or the naloxone challenge test, can be used to identify chronic narcotic users. In the naloxone challenge test, 0.4 mg is given slowly IV over 5 min, and the pt is observed for 1–2 h for signs of withdrawal.

Realistic expectations for rehabilitation are possible only when the pt is motivated to make a long-term commitment to a drug-free lifestyle. Specialized counseling and peer programs, including Narcotics Anonymous, are a mainstay of treatment. In many cases, adjunctive pharmacologic management is helpful, either to block the euphoric effects of opiates or to impede withdrawal/abstinence syndromes (discussed above). Any co-morbid psychiatric diagnoses (the "dual diagnosis" pt) must be evaluated and treated vigorously.

Special issues exist for medical staff. Physicians should never prescribe opiates for themselves or members of their families. Medical organizations need to be prepared to identify and rehabilitate substance-impaired physicians as quickly as possible.

For a more detailed discussion, see Shuckit MA, Segal DS: Opioid Drug Abuse and Dependence, Chap. 388, p. 2567, in HPIM-15.

202

ADVERSE DRUG REACTIONS

Adverse drug reactions are among the most frequent problems encountered clinically and represent a common cause for hospitalization. They occur most frequent in pts receiving multiple drugs and are caused by

1. Errors in self-administration of prescribed drugs (quite common in the elderly).
2. Exaggeration of intended pharmacologic effect (e.g., hypotension in a pt given antihypertensive drugs).
3. Concomitant administration of drugs with synergistic effects (e.g., aspirin and warfarin).
4. Cytotoxic reactions (e.g., hepatic necrosis due to acetaminophen).
5. Immunologic mechanisms (e.g., quinidine-induced thrombocytopenia, hydralazine-induced SLE).
6. Genetically determined enzymatic defects (e.g., primaquine-induced hemolytic anemia in G6PD deficiency).
7. Idiosyncratic reactions (e.g., chloramphenicol-induced aplastic anemia).

RECOGNITION History is of prime importance. Consider (1) nonprescription drugs and topical agents as potential offenders; (2) previous reaction to identical drugs; (3) temporal association between drug administration and development of clinical manifestations; (4) subsidence of manifestations when the agent is discontinued or reduced in dose; (5) recurrence of manifestations with cautious readministration (for less hazardous reactions); (6) *rare:* (a) biochemical abnormalities, e.g., red cell G6PD deficiency as cause of drug-induced hemolytic anemia, (b) abnormal serum antibody in pts with agranulocytosis, thrombocytopenia, hemolytic anemia.

Table 202-1 lists a number of clinical manifestations of adverse effects of drugs. It is not designed to be complete or exhaustive.

Table 202-1

Clinical Manifestations of Adverse Reactions to Drugs

MULTISYSTEM MANIFESTATIONS

Anaphylaxis	**Angioedema**
Cephalosporins	ACE inhibitors
Dextran	**Drug-induced lupus**
Insulin	**erythematosus**
Iodinated drugs or contrast	Cephalosporins
media	Hydralazine
Lidocaine	Iodides
Penicillins	Isoniazid
Procaine	Methyldopa

(continued)

Table 202-1 *(Continued)*

Clinical Manifestations of Adverse Reactions to Drugs

MULTISYSTEM MANIFESTATIONS *(Continued)*

Phenytoin
Procainamide
Quinidine
Sulfonamides
Thiouracil
Fever
  Aminosalicylic acid
  Amphotericin B
  Antihistamines
  Penicillins

Hyperpyrexia
  Antipsychotics
Serum sickness
  Aspirin
  Penicillins
  Propylthiouracil
  Sulfonamides

ENDOCRINE MANIFESTATIONS

Addisonian-like syndrome
  Busulfan
  Ketoconazole
Galactorrhea (may also cause
  amenorrhea)
  Methyldopa
  Phenothiazines
  Tricyclic antidepressants
Gynecomastia
  Calcium channel antagonists
  Digitalis
  Estrogens
  Griseofulvin
  Isoniazid
  Methyldopa
  Phenytoin
  Spironolactone
  Testosterone
Sexual dysfunction
  Beta blockers
  Clonidine
  Diuretics

  Guanethidine
  Lithium
  Major tranquilizers
  Methyldopa
  Oral contraceptives
  Sedatives
**Thyroid function tests, disorders
of**
  Acetazolamide
  Amiodarone
  Chlorpropamide
  Clofibrate
  Colestipol and nicotinic acid
  Gold salts
  Iodides
  Lithium
  Oral contraceptives
  Phenothiazines
  Phenylbutazone
  Phenytoin
  Sulfonamides
  Tolbutamide

METABOLIC MANIFESTATIONS

Hyperbilirubinemia
  Rifampin
Hypercalcemia
  Antacids with absorbable alkali
  Thiazides
  Vitamin D
Hyperglycemia
  Chlorthalidone
  Diazoxide
  Encainide
  Ethacrynic acid
  Furosemide
  Glucocorticoids
  Growth hormone

  Oral contraceptives
  Thiazides
Hypoglycemia
  Insulin
  Oral hypoglycemics
  Quinine
Hyperkalemia
  ACE inhibitors
  Amiloride
  Cytotoxics
  Digitalis overdose
  Heparin
  Lithium

(continued)

METABOLIC MANIFESTATIONS *(Continued)*

Potassium preparations includ-
  ing salt substitute
Potassium salts of drugs
Spironolactone
Succinylcholine
Triamterene
Hypokalemia
Alkali-induced alkalosis
Amphotericin B
Diuretics
Gentamicin
Insulin
Laxative abuse
Mineralocorticoids, some
  glucocorticoids
Osmotic diuretics
Sympathomimetics
Tetracycline
Theophylline
Vitamin B_{12}
Hyperuricemia
Aspirin
Cytotoxics

Ethacrynic acid
Furosemide
Hyperalimentation
Thiazides
Hyponatremia
1. Dilutional
  Carbamazepine
  Chlorpropamide
  Cyclophosphamide
  Diuretics
  Vincristine
2. Salt wasting
  Diuretics
  Enemas
  Mannitol
Metabolic acidosis
Acetazolamide
Paraldehyde
Salicylates
Spironolactone

DERMATOLOGIC MANIFESTATIONS

Acne
Anabolic and androgenic
  steroids
Bromides
Glucocorticoids
Iodides
Isoniazid
Oral contraceptives
Alopecia
Cytotoxics
Ethionamide
Heparin
Oral contraceptives (with-
  drawal)
Eczema
Captopril
Cream and lotion perservatives
Lanolin
Topical antihistamines
Topical antimicrobials
Topical local anesthetics
**Erythema multiforme or Steven-
Johnson syndrome**
Barbiturates
Chlorpropamide
Codeine
Penicillins
Phenylbutazone

Phenytoin
Salicylates
Sulfonamides
Sulfones
Tetracyclines
Thiazides
Erythema nodosum
Oral contraceptives
Penicillins
Sulfonamides
Exfoliative dermatitis
Barbiturates
Gold salts
Penicillins
Phenylbutazone
Phenytoin
Quinidine
Sulfonamides
Fixed drug eruptions
Barbiturates
Captopril
Phenylbutazone
Quinine
Salicylates
Sulfonamides
Hyperpigmentation
Bleomycin
Busulfan

(continued)

Table 202-1 *(Continued)*

Clinical Manifestations of Adverse Reactions to Drugs

DERMATOLOGIC MANIFESTATIONS *(Continued)*

Chloroquine and other
  antimalarials
Corticotropin
Cyclophosphamide
Gold salts
Hypervitaminosis A
Oral contraceptives
Phenothiazines
Lichenoid eruptions
Aminosalicylic acid
Antimalarials
Chlorpropamide
Gold salts
Methyldopa
Phenothiazines
Photodermatitis
Captopril
Chlordiazepoxide
Furosemide
Griseofulvin
Nalidixic acid
Oral contraceptives
Phenothiazines
Sulfonamides
Sulfonylureas
Tetracyclines, particularly
  demeclocycline
Thiazides
Purpura (see also thrombocyto-
penia)
Allopurinol
Ampicillin

Aspirin
Glucocorticoids
Rashes (nonspecific)
Allopurinol
Ampicillin
Barbiturates
Indapamide
Methyldopa
Phenytoin
Skin necrosis
Warfarin
Toxic epidermal necrolysis
(bullous)
Allopurinol
Barbiturates
Bromides
Iodides
Nalidixic acid
Penicillins
Phenylbutazone
Phenytoin
Sulfonamides
Urticaria
Aspirin
Barbiturates
Captopril
Enalapril
Penicillins
Sulfonamides

HEMATOLOGIC MANIFESTATIONS

Agranulocytosis (see also
Pancytopenia)
Captopril
Carbimazole
Chloramphenicol
Cytotoxics
Gold salts
Indomethacin
Methimazole
Oxyphenbutazone
Phenothiazines
Phenylbutazone
Propylthiouracil
Sulfonamides
Tolbutamide
Tricyclic antidepressants

**Clotting abnormalities/hypo-
thrombinemia**
Cefamandole
Cefoperazone
Moxalactam
Eosinophilia
Aminosalicylic acid
Chlorpropamide
Erythromycin estolate
Imipramine
L-Tryptophan
Methotrexate
Nitrofurantoin
Procarbazine
Sulfonamides

(continued)

HEMATOLOGIC MANIFESTATIONS *(Continued)*

Hemolytic anemia
Aminosalicylic acid
Cephalosporins
Chlorpromazine
Dapsone
Insulin
Isoniazid
Levodopa
Mefenamic acid
Melphalan
Methyldopa
Penicillins
Phenacetin
Procainamide
Quinidine
Rifampin
Sulfonamides
Hemolytic anemias in G6PD deficiency
See Table 58-3
Leukocytosis
Glucocorticoids
Lithium
Lymphadenopathy
Phenytoin
Primidone
Megaloblastic anemia
Folate antagonists
Nitrous oxide
Oral contraceptives
Phenobarbital
Phenytoin
Primidone
Triamterene
Trimethroprim
Pancytopenia (aplastic anemia)
Carbamazepine
Chloramphenicol

Cytotoxics
Gold salts
Mephenytoin
Phenylbutazone
Phenytoin
Quinacrine
Sulfonamides
Trimethadione
Zidovudine (AZT)
Pure red cell aplasia
Azathioprine
Chlorpropamide
Isoniazid
Phenytoin
Thrombocytopenia (see also Pancytopenia)
Acetazolamine
Aspirin
Carbamazepine
Carbenicillin
Chlorpropamide
Chlorthalidone
Furosemide
Gold salts
Heparin
Indomethacin
Isoniazid
Methyldopa
Moxalactam
Phenylbutazone
Phenytoin and other hydantoins
Quinidine
Quinine
Thiazides
Ticarcillin

CARDIOVASCULAR MANIFESTATIONS

Angina exacerbation
Alpha blockers
Beta blocker withdrawal
Ergotamine
Excessive thyroxine
Hydralazine
Methysergide
Minoxidil
Nifedipine
Oxytocin
Vasopressin

Arrhythmias
Adriamycin
Antiarrhythmic drugs
Atropine
Anticholinesterases
Beta blockers
Digitalis
Emetine
Lithium
Phenothiazines
Sympathomimetics

(continued)

Table 202-1 *(Continued)*

Clinical Manifestations of Adverse Reactions to Drugs

CARDIOVASCULAR MANIFESTATIONS *(Continued)*

Thyroid hormone
Tricyclic antidepressants
Verapamil
AV block
 Clonidine
 Methyldopa
 Verapamil
Cardiomyopathy
 Adriamycin
 Daunorubicin
 Emetine
 Lithium
 Phenothiazines
 Sulfonamides
 Sympathomimetics
Fluid retention or congestive heart failure
 Beta blockers
 Calcium antagonists
 Estrogens
 Indomethacin
 Mannitol
 Minoxidil
 Phenylbutazone
 Steroids
Hypotension
 Calcium antagonists
 Citrated blood

Diuretics
Levodopa
Morphine
Nitroglycerin
Phenothiazines
Protamine
Quinidine
Hypertension
 Clonidine withdrawal
 Corticotropin
 Cyclosporine
 Glucocorticoids
 Monoamine oxidase inhibitors with sympathomimetics
 NSAIDs
 Oral contraceptives
 Sympathomimetics
 Tricyclic antidepressants with sympathomimetics
Pericarditis
 Emetine
 Hydralazine
 Methysergide
 Procainamide
Thromboembolism
 Oral contraceptives

RESPIRATORY MANIFESTATIONS

Airway obstruction
 Beta blockers
 Cephalosporins
 Cholinergic drugs
 NSAIDs
 Penicillins
 Pentazocine
 Streptomycin
 Tartrazine (drugs with yellow dye)
Cough
 ACE inhibitors
Pulmonary edema
 Contrast media
 Heroin
 Methadone
 Propoxyphene

Pulmonary infiltrates
 Acyclovir
 Amiodarone
 Azathioprine
 Bleomycin
 Busulfan
 Carmustine (BCNU)
 Chlorambucil
 Cyclophosphamide
 Melphalan
 Methotrexate
 Methysergide
 Mitomycin C
 Nitrofurantoin
 Procarbazine
 Sulfonamides

(continued)

GASTROINTESTINAL MANIFESTATIONS

Cholestatic jaundice
  Anabolic steroids
  Androgens
  Chlorpropamide
  Erythromycin estolate
  Gold salts
  Methimazole
  Nitrofurantoin
  Oral contraceptives
  Phenothiazines
Constipation or ileus
  Aluminum hydroxide
  Barium sulfate
  Calcium carbonate
  Ferrous sulfate
  Ion exchange resins
  Opiates
  Phenothiazines
  Tricyclic antidepressants
  Verapamil
Diarrhea or colitis
  Antibiotics (broad-spectrum)
  Colchicine
  Digitalis
  Magnesium in antacids
  Methyldopa
Diffuse hepatocellular damage
  Acetaminophen (paracetamol)
  Allopurinol
  Aminosalicylic acid
  Dapsone
  Erythromycin estolate
  Ethionamide
  Glyburide
  Halothane
  Isoniazid
  Ketoconazole
  Methimazole
  Methotrexate
  Methoxyflurane
  Methyldopa
  Monoamine oxidase inhibitors
  Niacin
  Nifedipine
  Nitrofurantoin
  Phenytoin
  Propoxyphene
  Propylthiouracil
  Pyridium
  Rifampin
  Salicylates

  Sodium valproate
  Sulfonamides
  Tetracyclines
  Verapamil
  Zidovudine (AZT)
Intestinal ulceration
  Solid KCl preparations
Malabsorption
  Aminosalicylic acid
  Antibiotics (broad-spectrum)
  Cholestyramine
  Colchicine
  Colestipol
  Cytotoxics
  Neomycin
  Phenobarbital
  Phenytoin
Nausea or vomiting
  Digitalis
  Estrogens
  Ferrous sulfate
  Levodopa
  Opiates
  Potassium chloride
  Tetracyclines
  Theophylline
Oral conditions
  1. Gingival hyperplasia
     Calcium antagonists
     Cyclosporine
     Phenytoin
  2. Salivary gland swelling
     Bretylium
     Clonidine
     Guanethidine
     Iodides
     Phenylbutazone
  3. Taste disturbances
     Biguanides
     Captopril
     Griseofulvin
     Lithium
     Metronidazole
     Penicillamine
     Rifampin
  4. Ulceration
     Aspirin
     Cytotoxics
     Gentian violet
     Isoproterenol (sublingual)
     Pancreatin

(continued)

Table 202-1 *(Continued)*

Clinical Manifestations of Adverse Reactions to Drugs

GASTROINTESTINAL MANIFESTATIONS *(Continued)*

Pancreatitis
  Azathioprine
  Ethacrynic acid
  Furosemide
  Glucocorticoids
  Opiates
  Oral contraceptives

  Sulfonamides
  Thiazides
Peptic ulceration or hemorrhage
  Aspirin
  Ethacrynic acid
  Glucocoricoids
  NSAIDs

RENAL/URINARY MANIFESTATIONS

Bladder dysfunction
  Anticholinergics
  Disopyramide
  Monoamine oxidase inhibitors
  Tricyclic antidepressants
Calculi
  Acetazolamide
  Vitamin D
**Concentrating defect with poly-
uria (or nephrogenic diabetes
insipidus)**
  Demeclocycline
  Lithium
  Methoxyflurane
  Vitamin D
Hemorrhagic cystitis
  Cyclophosphamide
Interstitial nephritis
  Allopurinol
  Furosemide
  Penicillins, esp. methicillin
  Phenindione
  Sulfonamides
  Thiazides
Nephropathies
  Due to analgesics (e.g.,
    phenacetin)

Nephrotic syndrome
  Captopril
  Gold salts
  Penicillamine
  Phenindione
  Probenecid
Obstructive uropathy
  Extrarenal: methysergide
  Intrarenal: cytotoxics
Renal dysfunction
  Cyclosporine
  NSAIDS
  Triamterene
Renal tubular acidosis
  Acetazolamide
  Amphotericin B
  Degraded tetracycline
Tubular necrosis
  Aminoglycosides
  Amphotericin B
  Colistin
  Cyclosporine
  Methoxyflurane
  Polymyxins
  Radioiodinated contrast me-
    dium
  Sulfonamides
  Tetracyclines

NEUROLOGIC MANIFESTATIONS

Exacerbation of myasthenia
  Aminoglycosides
  Polymyxins
Extrapyramidal effects
  Butyrophenones, e.g.,
    haloperidol
  Levodopa
  Methyldopa
  Metoclopramide
  Oral contraceptives
  Phenothiazines
  Tricyclic antidepressants

Headache
  Ergotamine (withdrawal)
  Glyceryl trinitrate
  Hydralazine
  Indomethacin
Peripheral neuropathy
  Amiodarone
  Chloramphenicol
  Chloroquine
  Chlorpropamide
  Clofibrate
  Demeclocycline

(continued)

NEUROLOGIC MANIFESTATIONS *(Continued)*

Disopyramide
Ethambutol
Ethionamide
Glutethimide
Hydralazine
Isoniazid
Methysergide
Metronidazole
Nalidixic acid
Nitrofurantoin
Phenytoin
Polymyxin, colistin
Procarbazine
Streptomycin
Tolbutamide
Tricyclic antidepressants
Vincristine
Pseudotumor cerebri (or intra-cranial hypertension)
Amiodarone
Glucocorticoids, mineralocorticoids

Hypervitaminosis A
Oral contraceptives
Tetracyclines
Seizures
Amphetamines
Analeptics
Isoniazid
Lidocaine
Lithium
Nalidixic acid
Penicillins
Phenothiazines
Physostigmine
Theophylline
Tricyclic antidepressants
Vincristine
Stroke
Oral contraceptives

OCULAR MANIFESTATIONS

Cataracts
Busulfan
Chlorambucil
Glucocorticoids
Phenothiazines
Color vision alteration
Barbiturates
Digitalis
Methaqualone
Streptomycin
Thiazides
Corneal edema
Oral contraceptives
Corneal opacities
Chloroquine
Indomethacin
Vitamin D

Glaucoma
Mydriatics
Sympathomimetics
Optic neuritis
Aminosalicylic acid
Chloramphenicol
Ethambutol
Isoniazid
Penicillamine
Phenothiazines
Phenylbutazone
Quinine
Streptomycin
Retinopathy
Chloroquine
Phenothiazines

EAR MANIFESTATIONS

Deafness
Aminoglycosides
Aspirin
Bleomycin
Chloroquine
Erythromycin
Ethacrynic acid

Furosemide
Nortriptyline
Quinine
Vestibular disorders
Aminoglycosides
Quinine

MUSCULOSKELETAL MANIFESTATIONS

Bone disorders
1. Osteoporosis
   Glucocorticoids
   Heparin

2. Osteomalacia
   Aluminum hydroxide
   Anticonvulsants
   Glutethimide

(continued)

Table 202-1 *(Continued)*

Clinical Manifestations of Adverse Reactions to Drugs

MUSCULOSKELETAL MANIFESTATIONS *(Continued)*

Myopathy or myalgia
  Amphotericin B
  Chloroquine
  Clofibrate
  Glucocorticoids
  Oral contraceptives

Myositis
  Gemfibrozil
  Lovastatin

PSYCHIATRIC MANIFESTATIONS

Delirious or confusional states
  Amantadine
  Aminophylline
  Anticholinergics
  Antidepressants
  Cimetidine
  Digitalis
  Glucocorticoids
  Isoniazid
  Levodopa
  Methyldopa
  Penicillins
  Phenothiazines
  Sedatives and hypnotics
Depression
  Amphetamine withdrawal
  Beta blockers
  Centrally acting antihypertensives (reserpine, methyldopa, clonidine)
  Glucocorticoids
  Levodopa
Drowsiness
  Antihistamines
  Anxiolytic drugs
  Clonidine
  Major tranquilizers
  Methyldopa
  Tricyclic antidepressants

Hallucinatory states
  Amantadine
  Beta blockers
  Levodopa
  Meperidine
  Narcotics
  Pentazocine
  Tricyclic antidepressants
Hypomania, mania, or excited reactions
  Glucocorticoids
  Levodopa
  Monoamine oxidase inhibitors
  Sympathomimetics
  Tricyclic antidepressants
Schizophrenic-like or paranoid reactions
  Amphetamines
  Bromides
  Glucocorticoids
  Levodopa
  Lysergic acid
  Monoamine oxidase inhibitors
  Tricyclic antidepressants
Sleep disturbances
  Anorexiants
  Levodopa
  Monoamine oxidase inhibitors
  Sympathomimetics

SOURCE: Adapted from AJJ Wood: HPIM-15, pp. 432–436.

For a more detailed discussion, see Wood AJJ: Adverse Reactions to Drugs, Chap. 71, p. 430, in HPIM-15.

203

LABORATORY VALUES OF CLINICAL IMPORTANCE

INTRODUCTORY COMMENTS

All laboratory appendices should be interpreted with caution since normal values differ widely among clinical laboratories. The values given in this Appendix are meant primarily for use with this text. In preparing the Appendix, the editors have taken into account the fact that the system of international units (SI, système international d'unités) is now used in most countries and in most medical and scientific journals.[1] However, clinical laboratories in many countries continue to report values in traditional units. Values in SI units appear first and traditional units appear in parentheses after the SI units. Conversions from one system to another can be made as follows:

$$\text{mmol/L} = \frac{\text{mg/dL} \times 10}{\text{atomic weight}}$$

$$\text{mg/dL} = \frac{\text{mmol/L} \times \text{atomic weight}}{10}$$

For a more complete list of laboratory values, consult the Appendix of HPIM-15e.

Table 203-1

Body Fluids and Other Mass Data	
	Reference Range: SI Units
Body fluid, total volume (lean) of body weight	50% (in obese) to 70%
Intracellular	0.3–0.4 of body weight
Extracellular	0.2–0.3 of body weight
Blood	
Total volume	
Males	69 mL per kg body weight
Females	65 mL per kg body weight
Plasma volume	
Males	39 mL per kg body weight
Females	40 mL per kg body weight

---

[1]Young DS: Implementation of SI units for clinical laboratory data. Ann Intern Med 106:114, 1987

Table 203-2

CEREBROSPINAL FLUID[a]

	Reference Range	
Constituent	SI Units	Conventional Units
pH	7.31–7.34	
Glucose	2.2–3.9 mmol/L	40–70 mg/dL
Total protein	0.2–0.5 g/L	20–50 mg/dL
Albumin	0.066–0.442 g/L	6.6–44.2 mg/dL
IgG	0.009–0.057 g/L	0.9–5.7 mg/dL
IgG index[b]	0.29–0.59	
Oligoclonal bands (OGB)	<2 bands not present in matched serum sample	
Myelin basic protein	<4 μg/L	
CSF pressure		50–180 mmH$_2$O
Leukocytes		
Total	<5 per μL	
Differential		
Lymphocytes	60–70%	
Monocytes	30–50%	
Neutrophils	None	

[a] Since cerebrospinal fluid concentrations are equilibrium values, measurements of the same parameters in blood plasma obtained at the same time are recommended. However, there is a time lag in attainment of equilibrium, and cerebrospinal levels of plasma constituents that can fluctuate rapidly (such as plasma glucose) may not achieve stable values until after a significant lag phase.

[b] $\text{IgG index} = \dfrac{\text{CSF IgG(mg/dL)} \times \text{serum albumin(g/dL)}}{\text{Serum IgG(g/dL)} \times \text{CSF albumin(mg/dL)}}$

Table 203-3

Chemical Constituents of Blood

	Reference Range	
Constituent	SI Units	Conventional Units
Albumin	35–55 g/L	3.5–5.5 g/dL
Aldolase	0–100 nkat/L	0–6 U/L
Aminotransferases		
Aspartate (AST, SGOT)	0–0.58 μkat/L	0–35 U/L
Alanine (ALT, SGPT)	0–0.58 μkat/L	0–35 U/L
Ammonia, as NH$_3$	6–47 μmol/L	10–80 μg/dL
Amylase	0.8–3.2 μkat/L	60–180 U/L
Angiotensin-converting enzyme (ACE)	<670 nkat/L	<40 U/L
Arterial blood gases		
[HCO$_3^-$]	21–28 mmol/L	21–30 meq/L
P$_{CO_2}$	4.7–5.9 kPa	35–45 mmHg
pH	7.38–7.44	
P$_{O_2}$	11–13 kPa	80–100 mmHg

(continued)

Table 203-3 *(Continued)*

Chemical Constituents of Blood

Constituent	Reference Range	
	SI Units	Conventional Units
Bilirubin, total	5.1–17 μmol/L	0.3–1.0 mg/dL
Direct	1.7–5.1 μmol/L	0.1–0.3 mg/dL
Indirect	3.4–12 μmol/L	0.2–0.7 mg/dL
Calcium, ionized	1.1–1.4 mmol/L	4.5–5.6 mg/dL
Calcium	2.2–2.6 mmol/L	9–10.5 mg/L
Carbon dioxide tension (P_{CO_2})	4.7–5.9 kPa	35–45 mmHg
Carbon monoxide content	Symptoms with 20% saturation of hemo-globin	
Chloride	98–106 mmol/L	98–106 meq/L
Cholesterol: see Table 203-10		
Creatine kinase		
Females	0.17–1.17 μkat/L	10–70 U/L
Males	0.42–1.50 μkat/L	25–90 U/L
Creatine kinase-MB	0–7 μg/L	
Creatinine	<133 μmol/L	<1.5 mg/dL
Ferritin		
Women	10–200 μg/L	10–200 ng/mL
Men	15–400 μg/L	15–400 ng/mL
Glucose (fasting)		
Normal	4.2–6.4 mmol/L	75–115 mg/dL
Diabetes mellitus	>7.8 mmol/L	>140 mg/dL
Glucose, 2 h postpran-dial		
Normal	<7.8 mmol/L	<140 mg/dL
Impaired glucose tolerance	7.8–11.1 mmol/L	140–200 mg/dL
Diabetes mellitus	>11.1 mmol/L	>200 mg/dL
Hemoglobin		
Male	140–180 g/L	14–18 g/dL
Female	120–160 g/L	12–16 g/dL
Hemoglobin A_{1c} up to 6% of total hemoglobin		
Iron	9–27 μmol/L	50–150 μg/dL
Iron-binding capacity	45–66 μmol/L	250–370 μg/dL
Saturation	0.2–0.45	20–45%
Lactate dehydrogenase	1.7–3.2 μkat/L	100–190 U/L
Lactate	0.6–1.7 mmol/L	5–15 mg/dL
Lipase	0–2.66 μkat/L	0–160 U/L
Magnesium	0.8–1.2 mmol/L	1.8–3 mg/dL
Myoglobin		
Male	19–92 μg/L	
Female	12–76 μg/L	
Osmolality	285–295 mmol/kg serum water	285–295 mosmol/kg serum water

(continued)

Table 203-3 *(Continued)*

Chemical Constituents of Blood

Constituent	Reference Range	
	SI Units	Conventional Units
Oxygen percent saturation (sea level)	0.97 mol/mol	97%
	0.60–0.85 mol/mol	60–85%
Oxygen tension (P_{O_2})	11–13 kPa	80–100 mmHg
pH	7.38–7.44	
Phosphatase, acid	0.90 nkat/L	0–5.5 U/L
Phosphatase, alkaline	0.5–2.0 nkat/L	30–120 U/L
Phosphorus, inorganic	1.0–1.4 mmol/L	3–4.5 mg/dL
Potassium	3.5–5.0 mmol/L	3.5–5.0 meq/L
Prostate-specific antigen (PSA)		
Female	<0.5 µg/L	<0.5 ng/mL
Male: <40 years	0.0–2.0 µg/L	0.0–2.0 ng/mL
≥40 years	0.0–4.0 µg/L	0.0–4.0 ng/mL
PSA, free, in males 45–75 years, with PSA values between 4 and 20 µg/mL	>0.25 associated with benign prostatic hyperplasia	>25% associated with benign prostatic hyperplasia
Protein, total	55–80 g/L	5.5–8.0 g/dL
Protein fractions		
Albumin	35–55 g/L	3.5–5.5 g/dL (50–60%)
Globulin	20–35 g/L	2.0–3.5 g/dL (40–50%)
Alpha$_1$	2–4 g/L	0.2–0.4 g/dL (4.2–7.2%)
Alpha$_2$	5–9 g/L	0.5–0.9 g/dL (6.8–12%)
Beta	6–11 g/L	0.6–1.1 g/dL (9.3–15%)
Gamma	7–17 g/L	0.7–1.7 g/dL (13–23%)
Sodium	136–145 mmol/L	136–145 meq/L
Transferrin	2.3–3.9 g/L	230–390 mg/dL
Triglycerides	<1.8 mmol/L	<160 mg/dL
Troponin I	0–0.4 µg/L	0–0.4 ng/mL
Troponin T	0–0.1 µg/L	0–0.1 ng/mL
Urea nitrogen	3.6–7.1 mmol/L	10–20 mg/dL
Uric acid:		
Men	150–480 µmol/L	2.5–8.0 mg/dL
Women	90–360 µmol/L	1.5–6.0 mg/dL

Table 203-4

Drug Levels

Drug	Therapeutic Range	
	Conventional Units	SI Units
Acetaminophen	10–30 μg/mL	66–199 μmol/L
Amikacin		
Peak	25–35 μg/mL	43–60 μmol/L
Trough	4–8 μg/mL	6.8–13.7 μmol/L
Carbamazepine	6–12 μg/mL	26–51 μmol/L
Clozapine	200–350 ng/mL	0.6–1 μmol/L
Digoxin	0.8–2.0 ng/mL	1.0–2.6 nmol/L
Ethanol		
Behavioral changes	>20 mg/dL	>4.3 mmol/L
Legal intoxication	>80 mg/dL	>17 mmol/L
Gentamicin		
Peak	8–10 μg/mL	16.7–20.9 μmol/L
Trough	<2–4 μg/mL	<4.2–8.4 μmol/L
Lithium	0.6–1.2 meq/L	0.6–1.2 nmol/L
Methadone	100–400 ng/mL	0.32–1.29 μmol/L
Phenytoin	10–20 μg/mL	40–79 μmol/L
Procainamide	4–10 μg/mL	17–42 μmol/L
Quinidine	2–5 μg/mL	6–15 μmol/L
Salicylates	150–300 μg/mL	1086–2172 μmol/L
Theophylline	8–20 μg/mL	44–111 μmol/L
Thiocyanate		
After nitroprusside infusion	6–29 μg/mL	103–499 μmol/L
Nonsmoker	1–4 μg/mL	17–69 μmol/L
Smoker	3–12 μg/mL	52–206 μmol/L
Tobramycin		
Peak	8–10 μg/mL	17–21 μmol/L
Trough	<4 μg/mL	<9 μmol/L
Valproic acid	50–150 μg/mL	347–1040 μmol/L
Vancomycin		
Peak	18–26 μg/mL	12–18 μmol/L
Trough	5–10 μg/mL	3–7 μmol/L

Table 203-5

Circulatory Function Tests

Test	Results: Reference Range	
	SI Units (Range)	Conventional Units (Range)
Arteriovenous oxygen difference	30–50 mL/L	30–50 mL/L
Cardiac output (Fick)	2.5–3.6 L/m^2 of body surface area per min	2.5–3.6 L/m^2 of body surface area per min
Ejection fraction: stroke volume/end-diastolic volume (SV/EDV)	0.67 (0.55–0.78)	0.67 (0.55–0.78)
End-diastolic volume	75 mL/m^2 (60–88 mL/m^2)	75 mL/m^2 (60–88 mL/m^2)
End-systolic volume	25 mL/m^2 (20–33 mL/m^2)	25 mL/m^2 (20–33 mL/m^2)
Pulmonary vascular resistance	2–12 (kPa·s)/L	20–120 (dyn·s)/cm^5
Systemic vascular resistance	77–150 (kPa·s)/L	770–1500 (dyn·s)/cm^5

Table 203-6

Urine Analysis

	Reference Range	
	SI Units	Conventional Units
Amylase/creatinine clearance ratio $[(Cl_{am}/Cl_{cr}) \times 100]$	1–5	1–5
Calcium (10 meq/d or 200-mg/d dietary calcium)	<7.5 mmol/d	<300 mg/d
Creatinine	8.8–14 mmol/d	1.0–1.6 g/d
Protein	<0.15 g/d	<150 mg/d
Potassium (varies with intake)	25–100 mmol/d	25–100 meq/d
Sodium (varies with intake)	100–260 mmol/d	100–260 meq/d

Table 203-7

Renal Function Tests

	Reference Range	
	SI Units	Conventional Units
Clearances (corrected to 1.72 m^2 body surface area):		
Endogenous creatinine clearance	1.5–2.2 mL/s	91–130 mL/min
Protein excretion, urine	<0.15 g/d	<150 mg/d
Males	0–0.06 g/d	0–60 mg/d
Females	0–0.09 g/d	0–90 mg/d
Specific gravity, maximal range	1.002–1.028	1.002–1.028
Tubular reabsorption, phosphorus	0.79–0.94 of filtered load	79–94% of filtered load

Table 203-8

Summary of Values Useful in Pulmonary Physiology

		Typical Values	
	Symbol	Man Aged 40, 75 kg, 175 cm Tall	Woman Aged 40, 60 kg, 160 cm Tall
PULMONARY MECHANICS			
Spirometry—volume-time curves			
Forced vital capacity	FVC	4.8 L	3.3 L
Forced expiratory volume in 1 s	FEV$_1$	3.8 L	2.8 L
FEV$_1$/FVC	FEV$_1$%	76%	77%
Maximal midexpiratory flow	MMF (FEF 25–27)	4.8 L/s	3.6 L/s
Maximal expiratory flow rate	MEFR (FEF 200–1200)	9.4 L/s	6.1 L/s
Spirometry—flow-volume curves			
Maximal expiratory flow at 50% of expired vital capacity	V$_{max}$ 50 (FEF 50%)	6.1 L/s	4.6 L/s
Maximal expiratory flow at 75% of expired vital capacity	V$_{max}$ 75 (FEF 75%)	3.1 L/s	2.5 L/s
LUNG VOLUMES			
Total lung capacity	TLC	6.4 L	4.9 L
Functional residual capacity	FRC	2.2 L	2.6 L
Residual volume	RV	1.5 L	1.2 L
Inspiratory capacity	IC	4.8 L	3.7 L
Expiratory reserve volume	ERV	3.2 L	2.3 L
Vital capacity	VC	1.7 L	1.4 L

(continued)

943

Table 203-8 (Continued)

Summary of Values Useful in Pulmonary Physiology

	Symbol	Typical Values
GAS EXCHANGE (SEA LEVEL)		
Arterial O_2 tension	Pa_{O_2}	12.7 ± 0.7 kPa (95 ± 5 mmHg)
Arterial CO_2 tension	Pa_{CO_2}	5.3 ± 0.3 kPa (40 ± 2 mmHg)
Arterial blood pH		7.40 ± 0.02
Arterial bicarbonate	HCO_3^-	$24 + 2$ meq/L
Diffusing capacity for CO (single breath)	DL_{CO}	0.42 mL CO/s/mmHg (25 mL CO/min/mmHg)
Dead space volume	V_D	2 mL/kg body wt
Alveolar-arterial difference for O_2	$P(A-a)_{O_2}$	≤ 2.7 kPa ≤ 20 kPa (≤ 20 mmHg)

944

Table 203-9

Classification of Total Cholesterol, LDL-Cholesterol, and HDL-Cholesterol Values

	Total Plasma Cholesterol		LDL-Cholesterol		HDL-Cholesterol	
	SI, mmol/L	C, mg/dL	SI, mmol/L	C, mg/dL	SI, mmol/L	C, mg/dL
Desirable	<5.2	<200	<3.36	<130	>1.55	>60
Borderline	5.20–6.18	200–239	3.36–4.11	130–159	0.9–1.55	35–60
Undesirable	≥6.21	≥240	≥4.14	≥160	<0.9	<35

NOTE: LDL, low-density lipoprotein; HDL, high-density lipoprotein; SI, SI units; C, conventional units
SOURCE: Modified from the report of the Expert Panel on Detection, Evaluation, and Treatment of High Blood Cholesterol in Adults: Second Report of the National Cholesterol Education Program (NCEP) expert panel on detection, evaluation, and treatment of high blood cholesterol (Adult Treatment Panel II). Circulation 89:1329, 1994.

Table 203-10

Metabolic and Endocrine Tests

Substance	Specimen	Reference Range	
		SI Units	Conventional Units
Adrenocorticotropin (ACTH), 8 A.M.	P	1.3–16.7 pmol/L	6.0–76.0 pg/mL
Aldosterone, 8 A.M., (patient supine, 100 mmol/L Na and 60–100 mmol/L K intake)	P	<220 pmol/L	<8 ng/dL
Aldosterone	U	14–53 nmol/d	5–19 μg/d
Androstenedione	P		
Women		3.5–7.0 nmol/L	1–2 ng/mL
Men		3.0–5.0 nmol/L	0.8–1.3 ng/mL
Catecholamines			
Epinephrine	U	<275 nmol/d	<50 μg/d
Free	U	<590 nmol/d	<100 μg/d
Metanephrine	U	<7 μmol/d	<1.3 mg/d
Norepinephrine	U	89–473 nmol/d	15–80 μg/d
Vanillylmandelic acid (VMA)	U	<40 μmol/d	<8 mg/d
Cortisol			
Free	U	25–140 nmol/d	10–50 μg/d
8 A.M.	P	140–690 nmol/L	5–25 μg/dL
4 P.M.	P	80–330 nmol/L	3–12 μg/dL
Estradiol	P		
Women (higher at ovulation)		70–220 pmol/L	20–60 pg/mL
Men		<180 pmol/L	<50 pg/mL
Gonadotropins			
Follicle-stimulating hormone (FSH)	P		
Women			
Mature, premenopausal, except at ovulation		1.4–9.6 IU/L	1.4–9.6 mIU/mL
Ovulatory surge		2.3–21 IU/L	2.3–21 mIU/mL
Postmenopausal		34–96 IU/L	34–96 mIU/mL
Men		0.9–15 IU/L	0.9–15 mIU/mL
Luteinizing hormone (LH)	P		
Children, prepubertal		1.0–5.9 IU/L	1.0–5.9 mIU/mL
Women			
Mature, premenopausal, except at ovulation		0.8–26 IU/L	0.8–26 mIU/mL
Ovulatory surge		25–57 IU/L	25–57 mIU/mL
Postmenopausal		40–104 IU/L	40–104 mIU/mL
Men		1.3–13 IU/L	1.3–13 mIU/mL

(continued)

Table 203-10 *(Continued)*

Metabolic and Endocrine Tests

Substance	Specimen	Reference Range	
		SI Units	Conventional Units
Hemoglobin A$_{1c}$	WB	0.038–0.064	3.8–6.4%
5-Hydroxyindoleacetic acid (5-HIAA)	U	≤31.4 μmol/d	≤6 mg/d
17-Ketosteroids	U		
Women		20–59 μmol/d	6–17 mg/d
Men		20–69 μmol/d	6–20 mg/d
Parathyroid hormone	S	10–60 ng/L	10–60 pg/mL
Prolactin	S	2–15 μg/L	2–15 ng/mL
Radioactive iodine uptake, 24 h (range varies in different areas due to variations in iodine intake)			5–30%
Renin (adult, normal-Na diet)	P		
Supine		0.08–0.83 ng/(L·s)	0.3–3.0 ng/(mL·h)
Upright		0.28–2.5 ng/(L·s)	1.0–9.0 ng/(mL·h)
Resin triiodothyronine (T$_3$)		0.25–0.35	25–35%
Reverse T$_3$(rT$_3$)	P	0.15–0.61 nmol/L	10–40 ng/dL
T$_3$	P	1.1–2.9 nmol/L	70–190 ng/dL
Testosterone	P		
Women		<3.5 nmol/L	<1 ng/mL
Men		10–35 nmol/L	3–10 ng/mL
Prepubertal boys and girls		0.17–0.7 nmol/L	0.05–0.2 ng/mL
Thyroglobulin	S	0–60 μg/L	0–60 ng/mL
Thyroid stimulating hormone (TSH)		0.4–5.0 mU/L	0.4–5.0 μU/mL
Thyroxine (T$_4$)	SR	64–154 nmol/L	5–12 μg/dL

NOTE: P, plasma; S, serum; SR, serum radioimmunoassay; U, urine; WB, whole blood.

Table 203-11

Hematologic Evaluations. See also "Chemical Constituents of Blood"

	Reference Range	
	SI Units	Conventional Units
Erythrocyte		
Count	$4.15-4.90 \times 10^{12}$/L	$4.15-4.90 \times 10^6$/mm^3
Mean corpuscular hemoglobin (MCH)	28–33 pg/cell	28–33 pg/cell
Mean corpuscular hemoglobin concentration (MCHC)	320–360 g/L	32–36 g/dL
Mean corpuscular volume (MCV)	86–98 fl	86–98 μm^3
Haptoglobin (serum)	0.5–2.2 g/L	50–220 mg/dL
Hematocrit		
Males	0.42–0.52	42–52%
Females	0.37–0.48	37–48%
Hemoglobin		
Plasma	0.01–0.05 g/L	1–5 mg/dL
Whole blood		
Males	8.1–11.2 mmol/L	13–18 g/dL
Females	7.4–9.9 mmol/L	12–16 g/dL
Leukocytes		
Count	$4.3-10.8 \times 10^9$/L	$4.3-10.8 \times 10^3$/mm^3
Differential		
Neutrophils	0.45–0.74	45–74%
Bands	0–0.04	0–4%
Lymphocytes	0.16–0.45	16–45%
Monocytes	0.04–0.10	4–10%
Eosinophils	0–0.07	0–7%
Basophils	0–0.02	0–2%
T cells: see Chap. 309		
Protein C (antigenic assay)		58–148%
Protein S (antigenic assay)		58–148%
Partial thromboplastin time (activated PTT) comparable to control		
Prothrombin time (quick one-stage) control ± 1 s		
Platelets	$130-400 \times 10^9$/L	130,000–400,000/mm^3
von Willebrand's antigen		60–150%
Sedimentation rate		
Westergren, <50 years of age		
Males		0–15 mm/h
Females		0–20 mm/h
Westergren, >50 years of age		
Males		0–20 mm/h
Females		0–30 mm/h

INDEX

Numbers in bold refer to whole sections; t and f refer to table and figure, respectively.